Prepare, Apply, Assess and Develop Employability Skills with MyLab Economics

83%

of students said it helped them earn higher grades on homework, exams, or the course

*Source: 2016 Student Survey, n 10,263

MyLab™ Economics is an online homework, tutorial, and assessment program constructed to work with this text to engage students and improve results. It was designed to help students develop and assess the skills and applicable knowledge that they will need to succeed in their courses and their future careers.

See what students had to say about MyLab Economics:

"Usually when I do homework myself and don't get it I am stuck, but [MyLab Economics] provided the tools necessary to help me learn how to work my way through the trickiest problems."

— Zainul Lughmani,
Binghamton University

Digital Interactives

Economic principles are not static ideas, and learning them shouldn't be either! Digital Interactives are dynamic and engaging assessment activities that promote **critical thinking** and **application** of key economic principles.

Question Help

MyLab Economics homework and practice questions are correlated to the textbook, and many generate algorithmically to give students unlimited opportunity for mastery of concepts. If students get stuck, Learning Aids including Help Me Solve This and eText Pages walk them through the problem and identify helpful information in the text, giving them assistance when they need it most.

"[MyLab Economics] provides ample practice and explanation of the concepts at hand."

— Heather Burkett, University of Nebraska at Omaha

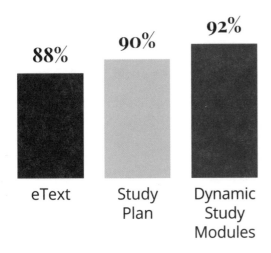

% of students who found learning tool helpful

Dynamic Study Modules help students study chapter topics effectively on their own by continuously assessing their **knowledge application** and performance in real time. These are available as prebuilt Prepare assignments, and are accessible on smartphones, tablets, and computers.

Pearson eText enhances student learning—both in and outside the classroom. Worked examples, videos, and interactive tutorials bring learning to life, while algorithmic practice and self-assessment opportunities test students' understanding of the material. Accessible anytime, anywhere via MyLab or the app.

The **MyLab Gradebook** offers an easy way for students and instructors to view course performance. Item Analysis allows instructors to quickly see trends by analyzing details like the number of students who answered correctly/incorrectly, time on task, and median time spend on a question by question basis. And because it's correlated with the AACSB Standards, instructors can track students' progress toward outcomes that the organization has deemed important in preparing students to be **leaders.**

87%

of students would tell their instructor to keep using MyLab Economics

For additional details visit: www.pearson.com/mylab/economics

Macroeconomics

Seventh Edition

R. Glenn Hubbard
Columbia University

Anthony Patrick O'Brien
Lehigh University

 Pearson

New York, NY

Vice President, Business, Economics, and UK Courseware: Donna Battista
Director of Portfolio Management: Adrienne D'Ambrosio
Specialist Portfolio Manager: David Alexander
Development Editor: Lena Buonanno
Editorial Assistant: Nicole Nedwidek
Vice President, Product Marketing: Roxanne McCarley
Senior Product Marketer: Tricia Murphy
Product Marketing Assistant: Marianela Silvestri
Manager of Field Marketing, Business Publishing: Adam Goldstein
Senior Field Marketing Manager: Carlie Marvel
Vice President, Production and Digital Studio, Arts and Business: Etain O'Dea
Director of Production, Business: Jeff Holcomb
Managing Producer, Business: Alison Kalil
Content Producer: Christine Donovan
Operations Specialist: Carol Melville
Design Lead: Kathryn Foot

Manager, Learning Tools: Brian Surette
Content Developer, Learning Tools: Sarah Peterson
Managing Producer, Digital Studio and GLP, Media Production and Development: Ashley Santora
Managing Producer, Digital Studio: Diane Lombardo
Digital Studio Producer: Melissa Honig
Digital Studio Producer: Alana Coles
Digital Content Team Lead: Noel Lotz
Digital Content Project Lead: Courtney Kamauf
Project Manager: Heidi Allgair, Cenveo® Publisher Services
Interior Design: Cenveo® Publisher Services
Cover Design: Studio Montage
Cover Photos: Phant/Shutterstock; Mariyana M/Shutterstock
Printer/Binder: LSC Communications, Inc./Kendallville
Cover Printer: Phoenix Color/Hagerstown

Microsoft and/or its respective suppliers make no representations about the suitability of the information contained in the documents and related graphics published as part of the services for any purpose. All such documents and related graphics are provided "as is" without warranty of any kind. Microsoft and/or its respective suppliers hereby disclaim all warranties and conditions with regard to this information, including all warranties and conditions of merchantability, whether express, implied or statutory, fitness for a particular purpose, title and non-infringement. In no event shall Microsoft and/or its respective suppliers be liable for any special, indirect or consequential damages or any damages whatsoever resulting from loss of use, data or profits, whether in an action of contract, negligence or other tortious action, arising out of or in connection with the use or performance of information available from the services.

The documents and related graphics contained herein could include technical inaccuracies or typographical errors. Changes are periodically added to the information herein. Microsoft and/or its respective suppliers may make improvements and/or changes in the product(s) and/or the program(s) described herein at any time. Partial screen shots may be viewed in full within the software version specified.

Microsoft® and Windows® are registered trademarks of the Microsoft Corporation in the U.S.A. and other countries. This book is not sponsored or endorsed by or affiliated with the Microsoft Corporation.

Library of Congress Cataloging-in-Publication Data.

Names: Hubbard, R. Glenn, author. | O'Brien, Anthony Patrick, author.
Title: Macroeconomics / R. Glenn Hubbard, Columbia University, Anthony
    Patrick O'Brien, Lehigh University.
Description: Seventh Edition. | New York : Pearson, [2018] | Revised edition
    of the authors' Macroeconomics, [2017] | Includes index.
Identifiers: LCCN 2017050532| ISBN 9780134738314 | ISBN 0134738314
Subjects: LCSH: Macroeconomics.
Classification: LCC HB172.5 .H86 2018 | DDC 339—dc23
LC record available at https://lccn.loc.gov/2017050532

2 18

Pearson

ISBN 10: 0-13-473831-4
ISBN 13: 978-0-13-473831-4

For Constance, Raph, and Will
—R. Glenn Hubbard

For Cindy, Matthew, Andrew, and Daniel
—Anthony Patrick O'Brien

ABOUT THE **AUTHORS**

Glenn Hubbard, policymaker, professor, and researcher. R. Glenn Hubbard is the dean and Russell L. Carson Professor of Finance and Economics in the Graduate School of Business at Columbia University and professor of economics in Columbia's Faculty of Arts and Sciences. He is also a research associate of the National Bureau of Economic Research and a director of Automatic Data Processing, Black Rock Closed-End Funds, and MetLife. He received a PhD in economics from Harvard University in 1983. From 2001 to 2003, he served as chair of the White House Council of Economic Advisers and chair of the OECD Economic Policy Committee, and from 1991 to 1993, he was deputy assistant secretary of the U.S. Treasury Department. He currently serves as co-chair of the nonpartisan Committee on Capital Markets Regulation. Hubbard's fields of specialization are public economics, financial markets and institutions, corporate finance, macroeconomics, industrial organization, and public policy. He is the author of more than 100 articles in leading journals, including *American Economic Review, Brookings Papers on Economic Activity, Journal of Finance, Journal of Financial Economics, Journal of Money, Credit, and Banking, Journal of Political Economy, Journal of Public Economics, Quarterly Journal of Economics, RAND Journal of Economics*, and *Review of Economics and Statistics*. His research has been supported by grants from the National Science Foundation, the National Bureau of Economic Research, and numerous private foundations.

Tony O'Brien, award-winning professor and researcher. Anthony Patrick O'Brien is a professor of economics at Lehigh University. He received a PhD from the University of California, Berkeley, in 1987. He has taught principles of economics for more than 20 years, in both large sections and small honors classes. He received the Lehigh University Award for Distinguished Teaching. He was formerly the director of the Diamond Center for Economic Education and was named a Dana Foundation Faculty Fellow and Lehigh Class of 1961 Professor of Economics. He has been a visiting professor at the University of California, Santa Barbara, and the Graduate School of Industrial Administration at Carnegie Mellon University. O'Brien's research has dealt with issues such as the evolution of the U.S. automobile industry, the sources of U.S. economic competitiveness, the development of U.S. trade policy, the causes of the Great Depression, and the causes of black–white income differences. His research has been published in leading journals, including *American Economic Review, Quarterly Journal of Economics, Journal of Money, Credit, and Banking, Industrial Relations, Journal of Economic History*, and *Explorations in Economic History*. His research has been supported by grants from government agencies and private foundations.

BRIEF **CONTENTS**

CONTENTS

* These end-of-chapter resource materials repeat in all chapters. Select chapters also include Real-Time Data Exercises. Students can complete all questions, problems, and exercises in **MyLab Economics**.

FLEXIBILITY **CHART**

The following chart helps you organize your syllabus based on your teaching preferences and objectives:

Core	Optional	Policy
Chapter 1: Economics: Foundations and Models	**Chapter 1 Appendix:** Using Graphs and Formulas	
Chapter 2: Trade-offs, Comparative Advantage, and the Market System		
Chapter 3: Where Prices Come From: The Interaction of Demand and Supply		
	Chapter 4 Appendix: Quantitative Demand and Supply Analysis	**Chapter 4:** Economic Efficiency, Government Price Setting, and Taxes
		Chapter 5: The Economics of Health Care
	Chapter 6: Firms, the Stock Market, and Corporate Governance	
	Chapter 6 Appendix: Tools to Analyze Firms' Financial Information	
Chapter 7: Comparative Advantage and the Gains from International Trade		
Chapter 8: GDP: Measuring Total Production and Income		
Chapter 9: Unemployment and Inflation		
Chapter 10: Economic Growth, the Financial System, and Business Cycles		
Chapter 11: Long-Run Economic Growth: Sources and Policies		

PREFACE

Our approach in this new edition remains what it was in the first edition, published nearly 15 years ago: to provide students and instructors an economics text that delivers complete economics coverage with many real-world business examples. Our goal has been to teach economics in a "widget-free" way by using real-world business and policy examples. We are gratified by the enthusiastic response from students and instructors who have used the first six editions of this book and who have made it a best-selling economics textbook.

Much has happened in the U.S. and world economies since we prepared the previous edition, including the election of a U.S. president with a distinctive approach to economic policy. We have incorporated many of these developments in the new real-world examples and policy discussions in this edition and also in the digital resources.

New to This Edition

We are grateful to the many instructors and students who made suggestions for improvements in the previous edition. We have done our best to incorporate as many of those suggestions as possible. Here is an overview of the revisions, followed by a more detailed description.

Overview of Changes

- All the chapter openers feature either new companies or have updated information. Students can visit MyLab Economics to watch a brief video that summarizes the key points of each chapter opener.
- Chapters 1–4, include new *An Inside Look* features to help students apply economic thinking to current events and policy debates as they are presented in news articles. Additional news articles and analyses appear weekly on MyLab Economics.
- There are 12 new *Apply the Concept* features (formerly titled *Making the Connection*) to help students tie economic concepts to current events and policy issues. The *Apply the Concept* features that were retained from the previous edition are updated. Students can visit MyLab Economics to watch more than 60 videos in which we summarize the key points in each feature. Related assessment accompanies each video, so students can test their understanding before moving on to a new section of the chapter.
- There are 2 new *Solved Problems* and 10 heavily revised *Solved Problems*. This feature helps students break down and answer economic problems step by step. There are additional Interactive *Solved Problems* on MyLab Economics, where students can receive feedback and tutorial help.
- There is a new category of end-of-chapter material titled *Critical Thinking Exercises*. We were motivated to add this new category of exercises because many instructors have told us that students need help building skills in the following areas: (1) analyzing and interpreting information; (2) applying reasoning and logic to new or unfamiliar ideas and situations; (3) examining ideas and concepts from multiple perspectives; and (4) clearly communicating their findings in a brief paper or class presentation. Students can complete these exercises on MyLab Economics and receive feedback and tutorial help.
- All the figures and tables are updated with the latest data available. Video animations of all the numbered figures and select tables are located on MyLab Economics. Graded practice exercises are included with these animations.

- We have replaced or updated many of the end-of-chapter *Problems and Applications*. In most chapters, one or two problems include graphs or tables for students to analyze. Select chapters have a category titled *Real-Time Data Exercises*, and we updated some of these exercises. Students can complete these exercises on MyLab Economics and receive feedback and tutorial help.

New Content and Features by Chapter

Here is a description of key changes by chapter.

Chapter 1, "Economics: Foundations and Models," opens with a new discussion of why Ford Motor Company manufactures cars in both the United States and Mexico. *An Inside Look* at the end of the chapter presents a news article and analysis of how likely it is that significant numbers of manufacturing jobs will return to the United States from overseas. New *Solved Problem 1.1* analyzes the marginal benefit and marginal cost of speed limits on highways. A new *Apply the Concept* examines why countries trade with each other and how economic concepts can help us evaluate policy debates about tariffs on imports. Taking a principles of economics class requires students to learn different terms, models, and a new way of analyzing real-world events. It can be challenging for students, especially non-majors, to appreciate how this course can help them in a career in business or government or in a nonprofit organization. We therefore decided to add to Chapter 1 a new section that describes economics as a career and highlights the key skills students of any major can gain from studying economics.

Chapter 2, "Trade-offs, Comparative Advantage, and the Market System," opens with an updated discussion of the resource allocation decisions managers at Tesla Motors face. *An Inside Look* at the end of the chapter discusses Tesla's decision to build a factory in Nevada to mass produce lithium-ion batteries for its electric cars. A new *Apply the Concept* illustrates how managers at the nonprofit organization Feeding America use the market mechanism to more efficiently allocate food based on the needs of food programs around the country.

Chapter 3, "Where Prices Come From: The Interaction of Demand and Supply," opens with a new discussion of how Coca-Cola and Pepsi-Cola responded to a fall in demand for sodas by introducing premium bottled water, sometimes called smart water. We use the market for premium bottled water to develop the demand and supply model. *An Inside Look* at the end of the chapter examines how McDonald's responded to shifts in consumer demand by serving breakfast all day and offering online ordering and home delivery. There are three new *Apply the Concepts*: "Virtual Reality Headsets: Will a Substitute Fail for a Lack of Complements?"; "Millennials Shake Up the Markets for Soda, Groceries, Big Macs, and Running Shoes"; and "Forecasting the Demand for Premium Bottled Water."

Chapter 4, "Economic Efficiency, Government Price Setting, and Taxes," opens with a new discussion about the economic link between food riots in Venezuela and the rise in popularity of Uber in the United States. At the end of the chapter, *An Inside Look* examines problems Uber has encountered in attempting to expand its services in the United Kingdom. There are two new *Apply the Concepts*: "The Consumer Surplus from Uber" and "Price Controls Lead to Economic Decline in Venezuela."

Chapter 5, "The Economics of Health Care," opens with a new discussion of how insurance companies are dealing with the effects of the Patient Protection and Affordable Care Act of 2010. There is also a discussion of the 2017 debate in Congress over whether that act should be extensively revised.

Chapter 6, "Firms, the Stock Market, and Corporate Governance," opens with a new comparison of the initial public offerings of Snap, Twitter, and Facebook. A new *Apply the Concept* explores why investors are concerned about potential corporate governance issues at Snap and other social media firms.

Chapter 7, "Comparative Advantage and the Gains from International Trade," opens with the decision by Mondelez to move production of Oreo cookies to Mexico to provide context for a new discussion of recent debates about the North American Free Trade Agreement (NAFTA) and the Trans-Pacific Partnership (TPP). A new *Apply the Concept* analyzes who gains and who loses from U.S. trade with China.

Chapter 8, "GDP: Measuring Total Production and Income," opens with an updated discussion of how Ford and other car companies deal with the business cycle. A new *Apply the Concept* discusses an innovative Web site created by Steve Ballmer, former CEO of Microsoft, that uses the preamble to the U.S. Constitution as a framework for reorganizing macroeconomic data.

Chapter 9, "Unemployment and Inflation," opens with a new discussion of Boeing's decision in 2017 to lay off workers, despite a growing U.S. economy. The chapter includes an updated analysis of the reasons for the decline in labor force participation among prime-aged males. A new *Apply the Concept* discusses how to characterize the unemployment resulting from Boeing's layoffs.

Chapter 10, "Economic Growth, the Financial System, and Business Cycles," opens with a new discussion of whether peak oil demand threatens the long-run growth of Chevron Corporation.

Chapter 11, "Long-Run Economic Growth: Sources and Policies," begins with a new opener that uses Wisconsin-based Rexnord Corporation's decision to relocate some production to Mexico to frame the discussion of whether that country is capable of increasing its growth rate.

Chapter 12, "Aggregate Expenditure and Output in the Short Run," contains thoroughly updated graphs and tables.

Chapter 13, "Aggregate Demand and Aggregate Supply Analysis," opens with a new discussion of the effect of the business cycle on KB Home and other home builders.

Chapter 14, "Money, Banks, and the Federal Reserve System," opens with a new discussion of why many people in India are using Paytm, an app that allows users to make payments at retail stores or online. A new *Apply the Concept* continues the analysis of this topic by discussing why some businesses in the United States and Europe no longer accept cash.

Chapter 15, "Monetary Policy," opens with an updated account of why interest rates on some mortgages in Europe are negative. An important new section describes the policy tools the Federal Reserve uses to manage its target for the federal funds rate, now that banks hold $2 trillion in excess reserves.

Chapter 16, "Fiscal Policy," opens with a new discussion of the effects of federal government infrastructure spending on Vulcan Materials and other construction firms, as well as on the wider economy. A centerpiece of President Trump's economic plan is using changes to the federal tax code, as well as other policies, to increase the annual growth rate of real GDP to 3 percent. We discuss what would be required to achieve this goal in a new section, "Explaining Long-Run Increases in Real GDP," and in a new *Apply the Concept*. New Table 16.4 summarizes how the Congressional Budget Office forecast real GDP growth for 2017–2027.

Chapter 17, "Inflation, Unemployment, and Federal Reserve Policy," opens with a new discussion of how the Fed's attempts to bring the economy in for a soft landing will affect General Motors, Toll Brothers, and other firms.

Chapter 18, "Macroeconomics in an Open Economy," opens with a new discussion of the effect of fluctuations in exchange rates on Amazon's profit. New *Solved Problem 18.2* analyzes how fluctuations in the value of the yen affect Toyota, and an updated *Apply the Concept* considers how the Trump administration has reacted to fluctuations in the value of the dollar.

Chapter 19, "The International Financial System," contains updated coverage of the struggles of the euro and the pressure the Trump administration has faced to label China a currency manipulator.

To make room for the new content described earlier, we have cut approximately 13 *Apply the Concepts* and 2 *Solved Problems* from the previous edition and transferred some of them to the book's *Instructor's Manual*, where they are available for instructors who wish to continue using them.

Solving Teaching and Learning Challenges

Many students who take a principles of economics course have difficulty seeing the relevance of the key concepts of opportunity cost, trade-offs, scarcity, and demand and supply to their lives and their careers. This reduces the willingness of some students to prepare for class and to be engaged during class. We address this challenge with contextual learning, a modern organization of content, and an extensive selection of digital assets available on MyLab Economics.

The Foundation:

Contextual Learning and Modern Organization

We believe a course is successful if students can apply what they have learned to both their personal lives and their careers, and if they have developed the analytical skills to understand what they read in the media. That's why we explain economic concepts by using many real-world business examples and applications in the chapter openers, graphs, *Apply the Concept* features, *An Inside Look* features, and end-of-chapter problems. This approach helps majors from all disciplines become educated consumers, voters, and citizens. In addition to our widget-free approach, we have a modern organization and place interesting policy topics early in the book to pique student interest.

Students come to study macroeconomics with a strong interest in understanding events and developments in the economy. We capture that interest and develop students' economic intuition and understanding by presenting macroeconomics in a way that is modern and based in the real world of business and economic policy. And we believe we achieve this presentation without making the analysis more difficult. We avoid the recent trend of using simplified versions of intermediate models, which are often more detailed and complex than what students need to understand the basic macroeconomic issues. Instead, we use a more realistic version of the familiar aggregate demand

and aggregate supply model to analyze short-run fluctuations and monetary and fiscal policy. We also avoid the "dueling schools of thought" approach often used to teach macroeconomics at the principles level. We emphasize the many areas of macroeconomics where most economists agree. And we present throughout real business and policy situations to develop students' intuition. Here are a few highlights of our approach to macroeconomics:

- **A careful discussion of macro statistics.** Many students pay some attention to the financial news and know that the release of statistics by federal agencies can cause movements in stock and bond prices. A background in macroeconomic statistics helps clarify some of the policy issues encountered in later chapters. In Chapter 8, "GDP: Measuring Total Production and Income," and Chapter 9, "Unemployment and Inflation," we provide students with an understanding of the uses and potential shortcomings of the key macroeconomic statistics, without getting bogged down in the minutiae of how the statistics are constructed. So, for instance, we discuss the important differences between the payroll survey and the household survey for understanding conditions in the labor market. We explain why financial markets react more strongly to news from the payroll survey. We provide a discussion of the employment–population ratio, which is not covered in some other texts but which many economists regard as a key measure of labor market performance.

- **Early coverage of long-run topics.** We place key macroeconomic issues in their long-run context in Chapter 10, "Economic Growth, the Financial System, and Business Cycles," and Chapter 11, "Long-Run Economic Growth: Sources and Policies." Chapter 10 puts the business cycle in the context of underlying long-run growth and discusses what actually happens during the phases of the business cycle. We believe this material is important if students are to have the understanding of business cycles they will need to interpret economic events; this material is often discussed only briefly or omitted entirely in other books. We know that many instructors prefer to have a short-run orientation to their macro courses, with a strong emphasis on policy. Accordingly, we have structured Chapter 10 so that its discussion of long-run growth is sufficient for instructors who want to move quickly to short-run analysis. Chapter 11 uses a simple neoclassical growth model to explain important growth issues. We apply the model to topics such as the decline of the Soviet economy, the long-run prospects for growth in China, the implications of the slowdown in productivity growth for the U.S. economy, and the failure of many developing countries to sustain high growth rates. *And* we challenge students with the discussion "Why Isn't the Whole World Rich?"

- **A dynamic model of aggregate demand and aggregate supply.** We take a fresh approach to the standard aggregate demand and aggregate supply (*AD–AS*) model. We realize there is no good, simple alternative to using the *AD–AS* model when explaining movements in the price level and in real GDP. But we know that more instructors are dissatisfied with the *AD–AS* model than with any other aspect of the macro principles course. The key problem, of course, is that *AD–AS* is a static model that attempts to account for dynamic changes in real GDP and the price level. Our approach retains the basics of the *AD–AS* model but makes it more accurate and useful by making it more dynamic. We emphasize two points: (1) Changes in the position of the short-run (upward-sloping) aggregate supply curve depend mainly on the state of expectations of the inflation rate; and (2) the existence of growth in the economy means that the long-run (vertical) aggregate supply curve shifts to the right every year. This "dynamic" *AD–AS* model provides students with a more accurate understanding of the causes and consequences of fluctuations in real GDP and the price level. Chapter 13, "Aggregate Demand and Aggregate Supply Analysis," includes a three-layer, full-color acetate for the key introductory dynamic *AD–AS* graph (Figure 13.8, "A Dynamic Aggregate Demand and Aggregate Supply Model," on page 460 and reproduced on the next page). We created this acetate to help students see how the graph builds step by step and to

The first acetate overlay adds the shifts in the long- and short-run aggregate supply curves.

The second acetate overlay adds the shifts in the aggregate demand curve to complete the dynamic model.

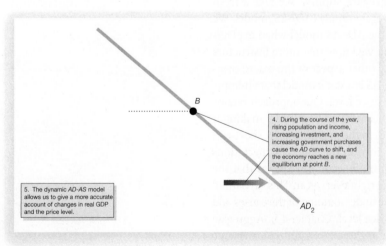

help make the graph easier for instructors to present. The acetate will help instructors who want to use dynamic *AD–AS* in class but believe the model needs to be developed carefully. We introduce this model in Chapter 13 and use it to discuss monetary policy in Chapter 15, "Monetary Policy," and fiscal policy in Chapter 16, "Fiscal Policy." The material on dynamic *AD–AS* is presented in self-contained sections in Chapters 13, 15, and 16, so instructors may safely omit the sections on the dynamic *AD–AS* model without any loss in continuity to the discussion of macroeconomic theory and policy.

- **Extensive coverage of monetary policy.** Because of the central role monetary policy plays in the economy and in students' curiosity about business and financial news, we devote two chapters—Chapter 15, "Monetary Policy," and Chapter 17, "Inflation, Unemployment, and Federal Reserve Policy"—to the topic. We emphasize the issues involved in the Fed's choice of monetary policy targets, and we include coverage of the Taylor rule. We also cover the new Fed's new policy tools and the debate over whether the Fed's policies during and after the 2007–2009 financial crisis were consistent with its mandate under the Federal Reserve Act.

- **Coverage of both the demand-side and supply-side effects of fiscal policy.** Our discussion of fiscal policy in Chapter 16, "Fiscal Policy," carefully distinguishes between automatic stabilizers and discretionary fiscal policy. We also provide significant coverage of the supply-side effects of fiscal policy. A new section discusses the requirements for the Trump administration to hit its goal of restoring the long-run annual growth rate of real GDP to 3 percent.

- **A self-contained but thorough discussion of the Keynesian income–expenditure approach.** The Keynesian income–expenditure approach (the "45°-line diagram," or "Keynesian cross") is useful for introducing students to the short-run relationship between spending and production. Many instructors, however, prefer to omit this material. Therefore, we use the 45°-line diagram only in Chapter 12, "Aggregate Expenditure and Output in the Short Run." The discussions of monetary and fiscal policy in Chapter 15, "Monetary Policy," and Chapter 16, "Fiscal Policy," respectively, use only the *AD–AS* model, making it possible to omit Chapter 12.

- **Extensive international coverage.** We include three chapters devoted to international topics: Chapter 7, "Comparative Advantage and the Gains from International Trade," Chapter 18, "Macroeconomics in an Open Economy," and Chapter 19, "The International Financial System." Having a good understanding of the international trading and financial systems is essential to understanding the macroeconomy and to satisfying students' curiosity about the economic world around them. In addition to the material in our three international chapters, we weave international comparisons into the narratives of several other chapters, including our discussion of labor market policies in Chapter 17, "Inflation, Unemployment, and Federal Reserve Policy," and central banking in Chapter 14, "Money, Banks, and the Federal Reserve System."

- **Flexible chapter organization.**   Because we realize that there are a variety of approaches to teaching principles of macroeconomics, we have structured our chapters for maximum flexibility. For example, our discussion of long-run economic growth in Chapter 10, "Economic Growth, the Financial System, and Business Cycles," makes it possible for instructors to omit the more thorough discussion of these issues in Chapter 11, "Long-Run Economic Growth: Sources and Policies." Our discussion of the Keynesian 45°-line diagram is confined to Chapter 12, "Aggregate Expenditure and Output in the Short Run," so that instructors who do not use this approach can proceed directly to aggregate demand and aggregate supply analysis in Chapter 13, "Aggregate Demand and Aggregate Supply Analysis." While we devote two chapters to monetary policy, the first of these—Chapter 15, "Monetary Policy"—is a self-contained discussion, so instructors may safely omit the material in Chapter 17, "Inflation, Unemployment, and Federal Reserve Policy," if they choose to. Finally, instructors may choose to omit all three of the international chapters (Chapter 7, "Comparative Advantage and the Gains from International Trade," Chapter 18, "Macroeconomics in an Open Economy," and Chapter 19, "The International Financial System"), cover just Chapter 7 on international trade, cover just Chapter 18, or cover Chapters 18 and 19 while omitting Chapter 7. Please refer to the flexibility chart shown earlier on pages xviii–xix to help select the chapters and order best suited to your classroom needs.

MyLab Economics

OVERVIEW

Reach every student by pairing this text with MyLab Economics

MyLab is the teaching and learning platform that empowers you to reach *every* student. By combining trusted author content with digital tools and a flexible platform, MyLab personalizes the learning experience and improves results for each student. Learn more about MyLab Economics at www.pearson.com/mylab/economics.

Deliver trusted content

You deserve teaching materials that meet your own high standards for your course. That's why we partner with highly respected authors to develop interactive content and course-specific resources that you can trust—and that keep your students engaged.

Empower each learner

Each student learns at a different pace. Personalized learning pinpoints the precise areas where each student needs practice, giving all students the support they need—when and where they need it—to be successful.

Teach your course your way

Your course is unique. So whether you'd like to build your own assignments, teach multiple sections, or set prerequisites, MyLab gives you the flexibility to easily create *your* course to fit *your* needs.

Improve student results

When you teach with MyLab, student performance improves. That's why instructors have chosen MyLab for over 15 years, touching the lives of over 50 million students.

FEATURES IN THE BOOK AND SUPPORTING RESOURCES ON MYLAB ECONOMICS

Students and instructors will find the following features in the seventh edition and supporting online resources on MyLab Economics.

Business Cases and An Inside Look *News Articles*

Each chapter-opening case provides a real-world context for learning, sparks students' interest in economics, and helps unify the chapter. The case describes an actual company facing a real situation. The company is integrated in the narrative, graphs, and pedagogical features of the chapter. Some of the chapter openers focus on the role of entrepreneurs in developing new products and bringing them to market. For example, Chapter 2 features Elon Musk of Tesla Motors; Chapter 13 features KB Home founders Donald Kaufman and Eli Broad; Chapter 14 features Paytm founder Vijay Shekhar Sharma; and Chapter 18 features Jeff Bezos of Amazon.

Students can visit MyLab Economics to watch a brief video we developed and filmed to summarize the key points of each chapter opener.

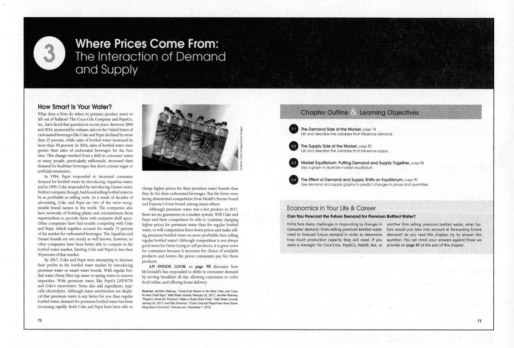

An Inside Look is a two-page feature that shows students how to apply the concepts from the chapter to the analysis of a news article. The feature appears at the end of Chapters 1–4. *An Inside Look* presents an excerpt from an article, analysis of the article, a graph(s), and critical thinking questions. Additional articles that are continuously updated are located on MyLab Economics.

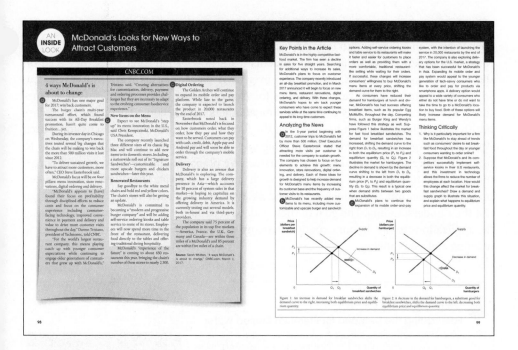

Solved Problems

Many students have great difficulty handling applied economics problems. We help students overcome this hurdle by including in each chapter two or three worked-out problems that analyze real-world economic issues they hear and read about in the news. Our goals are to keep students focused on the main ideas of each chapter and give them a model of how to solve an economic problem by breaking it down step by step. We tie additional exercises in the end-of-chapter *Problems and Applications* section to every *Solved Problem*. Additional *Solved Problems* appear in the *Instructor's Manuals*. In addition, the Test Banks include problems tied to the *Solved Problems* in the main book. Each of the 32 *Solved Problems* in the printed text is accompanied by a similar Interactive *Solved Problem* on MyLab Economics, so students can have more practice and build their problem-solving skills. These interactive tutorials help students learn to think like economists and apply basic problem-solving skills to homework, quizzes, and exams. Each *Solved Problem* on MyLab Economics and in the digital eText also includes at least one additional graded practice exercise for students.

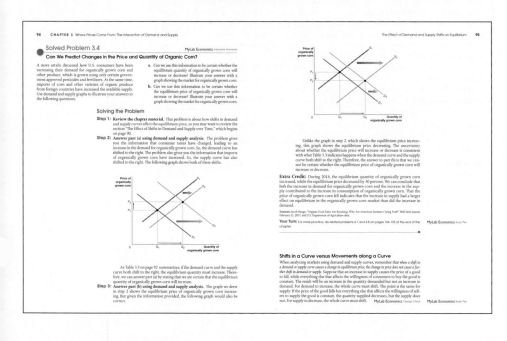

Apply the Concept

Each chapter includes two to four *Apply the Concept* features that provide real-world reinforcement of key concepts and help students learn how to interpret what they read on the Web and in newspapers. Most of the over 60 *Apply the Concept* features use relevant, stimulating, and provocative news stories focused on businesses and policy issues. One-third of them are new to this edition, and most others have been updated. Several discuss health care and trade, which have been at the forefront of recent policy discussions. Each *Apply the Concept* has at least one supporting end-of-chapter problem to allow students to test their understanding of the topic discussed. We prepared and filmed a two- or three-minute video to explain the key point of each *Apply the Concept*. These videos are located on MyLab Economics. We include related assessment with each video, so students can test their understanding. The goal of these videos is to summarize key content and bring the applications to life. In our experience, many students benefit from this type of online learning and assessment.

Apply the Concept   MyLab Economics Video

Forecasting the Demand for Premium Bottled Water

It's important for managers to forecast the demand for their products accurately because doing so helps them determine how much of a good to produce. Firms typically set manufacturing schedules at least a month ahead of time. Premium bottled water is a rapidly growing market, and firms need to carefully plan increases in productive capacity. Firms that fail to produce a large enough quantity to keep pace with increasing demand can lose out to competitors. But will the demand for premium bottled water continue to grow at such a rapid pace?

Sara Stathas/Alamy Stock Photo

How will changes in demographics, income, and tastes shape the market for premium bottled water?

Richard Tedlow of the Harvard Business School has developed a theory of the "three phases of marketing" that can provide some insight into how the markets for many consumer products develop over time. The first phase often has a very large number of firms, each producing a relatively small volume of goods and charging high prices. This phase corresponds to the carbonated soft drink industry in the late nineteenth century, the automobile industry in the early twentieth century, and the personal computer industry in the late 1970s. In the second phase, the market consolidates, with one or a few brands attaining high market shares by selling a large number of units at lower prices. This phase corresponds to the soft drink industry during the middle of the twentieth century, the automobile industry during the 1920s, and the personal computer industry during the 1980s.

Managers at beverage firms will have to take into account a number of factors when estimating the future demand for premium bottled water. Factors that will tend to lead to higher demand for premium bottled water include the popularity of the product with millennials, the trend toward healthier eating habits that has led to declining consumption of carbonated beverages, the taxes on soda that cities have been imposing to both fight obesity and raise tax revenue, and the possibility of attracting consumers who now prefer energy drinks such as Red Bull and sports drinks such as Gatorade. But an obstacle to the rapid growth of demand for premium bottled water comes from doubts raised by some analysts about the benefits from the electrolytes and other ingredients it contains that are not in regular bottled water. If consumers come to believe that these ingredients serve no useful purpose, they may prefer to buy regular bottled water, which typically has a lower price.

As we saw in Chapter 1, economists can use formal models to forecast future values of economic variables. In this case, an economist forecasting the demand for premium bottled water would want to include the factors mentioned in the previous paragraphs as well as other data, including changes over time in demographics and projected income growth.

Sources: Jennifer Maloney, "PepsiCo Gives Its 'Premium' Water a Super Bowl Push," *Wall Street Journal*, January 24, 2017; Quentin Fottrell, "Bottled Water Overtakes Soda as America's No. 1 Drink—Why You Should Avoid Both," marketwatch.com, March 12, 2017; and Richard Tedlow, *New and Improved: The Story of Mass Marketing in America*, Cambridge, MA: Harvard Business School Press, 1996.

Your Turn: Test your understanding by doing related problem 1.17 on page 102 at the end of this chapter.

Don't Let This Happen to You

We know from many years of teaching which concepts students find most difficult. We include in each chapter a box feature called *Don't Let This Happen to You* that alerts students to the most common pitfalls in that chapter's material. We follow up with a related question in the end-of-chapter *Problems and Applications* section. The questions are also available on MyLab Economics, where students can receive instant feedback and tutorial help.

Concept Checks

Each section of each learning objective concludes with a Concept Check on MyLab Economics that contains one or two multiple-choice, true/false, or fill-in questions. These checks act as "speed bumps" that encourage students to stop and check their understanding of fundamental terms and concepts before moving on to the next section. The goal of this digital resource is to help students assess their progress on a section-by-section basis so they can be better prepared for homework, quizzes, and exams.

Don't Let This Happen to You

Remember: A Change in a Good's Price Does *Not* Cause the Demand or Supply Curve to Shift

Suppose a student is asked to draw a demand and supply graph to illustrate how an increase in the price of oranges would affect the market for apples, with other variables being constant. He draws the graph on the left and explains it as follows: "Because apples and oranges are substitutes, an increase in the price of oranges will cause an initial shift to the right in the demand curve for apples, from D_1 to D_2. However, because this initial shift in the demand curve for apples results in a higher price for apples, P_2, consumers will find apples less desirable, and the demand curve will shift to the left, from D_2 to D_3, resulting in a final equilibrium price of P_3." Do you agree or disagree with the student's analysis?

You should disagree. The student has correctly understood that an increase in the price of oranges will cause the demand curve for apples to shift to the right. But, the second demand curve shift the student describes, from D_2 to

D_3, will not take place. Changes in the price of a product do not result in shifts in the product's demand curve. Changes in the price of a product result only in movements along a demand curve.

The graph on the right shows the correct analysis. The increase in the price of oranges causes the demand curve for apples to increase from D_1 to D_2. At the original price, P_1, the increase in demand initially results in a shortage of apples equal to $Q_3 - Q_1$. But, as we have seen, a shortage causes the price to increase until the shortage is eliminated. In this case, the price will rise to P_2, where both the quantity demanded and the quantity supplied are equal to Q_2. Notice that the increase in price causes a decrease in the *quantity demanded*, from Q_3 to Q_2, but does *not* cause a decrease in demand.

MyLab Economics Study Plan

Your Turn: Test your understanding by doing related problems 4.13 and 4.14 on page 105 at the end of this chapter.

Graphs and Summary Tables

Graphs are an indispensable part of a principles of economics course but are a major stumbling block for many students. Every chapter except Chapter 1 includes end-of-chapter problems that require students to draw, read, and interpret graphs. Interactive graphing exercises appear on the book's supporting Web site. We use four devices to help students read and interpret graphs:

1. Detailed captions
2. Boxed notes
3. Color-coded curves
4. Summary tables with graphs (see pages 80, 85, and 444 for examples)

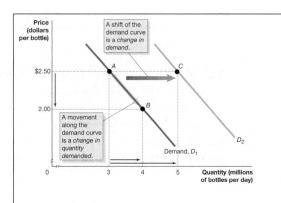

MyLab Economics Animation

Figure 3.3

A Change in Demand versus a Change in Quantity Demanded

If the price of premium bottled water falls from $2.50 to $2.00, the result will be a movement along the demand curve from point A to point B—an increase in quantity demanded from 3 million bottles to 4 million. If consumers' incomes increase, or if another factor changes that makes consumers want more of the product at every price, the demand curve will shift to the right—an increase in demand. In this case, the increase in demand from D_1 to D_2 causes the quantity of premium bottled water demanded at a price of $2.50 to increase from 3 million bottles at point A to 5 million at point C.

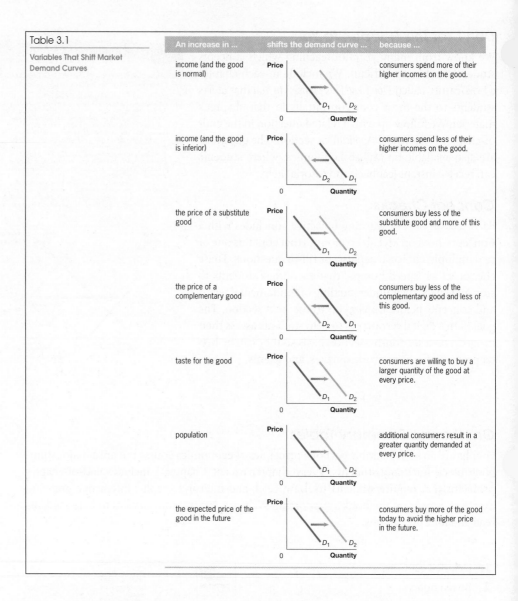

Table 3.1

Variables That Shift Market
Demand Curves

An increase in ...	shifts the demand curve ...	because ...
income (and the good is normal)		consumers spend more of their higher incomes on the good.
income (and the good is inferior)		consumers spend less of their higher incomes on the good.
the price of a substitute good		consumers buy less of the substitute good and more of this good.
the price of a complementary good		consumers buy less of the complementary good and less of this good.
taste for the good		consumers are willing to buy a larger quantity of the good at every price.
population		additional consumers result in a greater quantity demanded at every price.
the expected price of the good in the future		consumers buy more of the good today to avoid the higher price in the future.

Each of the 156 numbered figures in the text has a supporting animated version on MyLab Economics. The goal of this digital resource is to help students understand shifts in curves, movements along curves, and changes in equilibrium values. Having an animated version of a graph helps students who have difficulty interpreting the static version in the printed text. We include graded practice exercises with the animations. In our experience, many students benefit from this type of online learning.

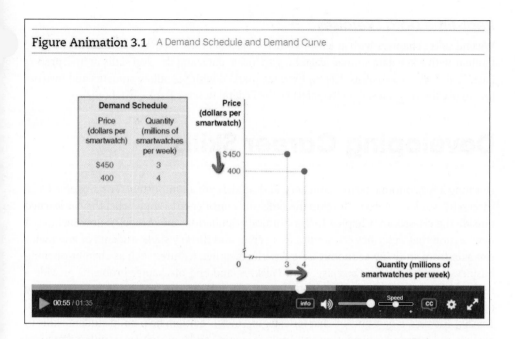

Figure Animation 3.1 A Demand Schedule and Demand Curve

Approximately 35 graphs are continuously updated online with the latest available data from FRED (Federal Reserve Economic Data), which is a comprehensive, up-to-date data set maintained by the Federal Reserve Bank of St. Louis. Students can display a pop-up graph that shows new data. The goal of this digital feature is to help students understand how to work with data and understand how including new data affects graphs.

Review Questions and *Problems and Applications*—Grouped by Learning Objective to Improve Assessment

We group the main end-of-chapter material—*Summary*, *Review Questions*, and *Problems and Applications*—under learning objectives. The goals of this organization are to make it easier for instructors to assign problems based on learning objectives, both in the book and on MyLab Economics, and to help students efficiently review material that they find difficult. If students have difficulty with a particular learning objective, an instructor can easily identify which end-of-chapter questions and problems support that objective and assign them as homework or discuss them in class. Every exercise in a chapter's *Problems and Applications* section is available on MyLab Economics. Using MyLab Economics, students can complete these and many other exercises online, get tutorial help, and receive instant feedback and assistance on exercises they answer incorrectly. Also, student learning will be enhanced by having the summary material and problems grouped together by learning objective, which allows them to focus on the parts of the chapter they find most challenging. Each major section of the chapter, paired with a learning objective, has at least two review questions and three problems.

As in the previous editions, we include one or more end-of-chapter problems that test students' understanding of the content presented in the *Solved Problem*, *Apply the Concept*, and *Don't Let This Happen to You* special features in the chapter. Instructors can cover a feature in class and assign the corresponding problem(s) for homework. The Test Bank Files also include test questions that pertain to these special features.

Real-Time Data Exercises

We end select chapters with at least two *Real-Time Data Exercises* that help students become familiar with a key data source, learn how to locate data, and develop skills in interpreting data. *Real-Time Data Analysis (RTDA) Exercises*, marked with ⊕, allow students and instructors to use the very latest data from FRED, the Federal Reserve Bank of St. Louis.

Developing Career Skills

Learning key economic terms, concepts, and models are all important. For a course to be successful, students need to develop the skills and confidence to apply what they've learned outside the classroom. Chapter 1, "Economics: Foundations and Models," now includes a new section that describes economics as a career and the key skills students of any major can gain from studying economics. As described earlier, features such as chapter-opening business cases, *Apply the Concepts, Solved Problems*, and end-of-chapter problems provide a real-world context for learning that exposes students to economics as applied in a variety of large and small businesses, government agencies, and nonprofit organizations. *Critical Thinking Exercises*, a new end-of-chapter category in this edition, help build student skills to analyze and interpret information and apply reasoning and logic to new or unfamiliar ideas and situations.

Economics in Your Life & Career

After the chapter-opening real-world business case, we have a feature titled *Economics in Your Life & Career* that adds a personal dimension to the chapter opener by asking students to consider how economics affects their lives and careers. The feature piques the interest of students and emphasizes the connection between the material they are learning and their personal and career decisions

---

Economics in Your Life & Career

Can You Forecast the Future Demand for Premium Bottled Water?

Firms face many challenges in responding to changes in consumer demand. Firms selling premium bottled water need to forecast future demand in order to determine how much production capacity they will need. If you were a manager for Coca-Cola, PepsiCo, Nestlé, Bai, or another firm selling premium bottled water, what factors would you take into account in forecasting future demand? As you read this chapter, try to answer this question. You can check your answers against those we provide on **page 97** at the end of this chapter.

At the end of the chapter, we use the chapter concepts to answer the questions asked at the beginning of the chapter.

Economics in Your Life & Career

Can You Forecast the Future Demand for Premium Bottled Water?

At the beginning of this chapter, we asked what variables you would take into account in forecasting future demand if you were a manager for a firm selling premium bottled water. In Section 3.1, we discussed the factors that affect the demand for a product and provided a list of the most important variables. In the *Apply the Concept* on page 81, we discussed how economists often use formal models to forecast future demand for a product.

In forecasting demand for premium bottled water, you should take into account factors such as changing demographics, as millennials become a larger fraction of prime-age consumers, and the likelihood that the demand for competing goods, such as carbonated sodas, will decline as consumers turn toward buying healthier products and as more cities impose soda taxes. You may also need to consider whether increased advertising of premium bottled water by large firms such as Coca-Cola and PepsiCo will raise consumer awareness of the product and increase demand for the premium bottled water being sold by other firms as well.

The factors discussed in this chapter provide you with the basic information needed to forecast demand for premium bottled water, although arriving at numerical forecasts requires using statistical analysis that you can learn in more advanced courses.

Instructor Teaching Resources

The authors and Pearson Education have worked together to integrate the text, print, and media resources to make teaching and learning easier.

Supplements Available to Instructors for Download at www.pearsonhighered.com	Features of the Supplement
Instructor's Manual Authored by Edward Scahill of the University of Scranton	• Chapter-by-chapter summaries organized by learning objectives • Extended examples and class exercises • Teaching outlines incorporating key terms and definitions, teaching tips, topics for class discussion • New *Solved Problems* • New *Apply the Concept* features • Solutions to all review questions, problems, and real-time data exercises in the book
Test Bank Authored by Randy Methenitis of Richland College	• 4,000 multiple-choice, true/false, short-answer, and graphing questions. • Test questions are annotated with the following categories: **Difficulty**—1 for straight recall; 2 for some analysis; and 3 for complex analysis **Type**—multiple-choice, true/false, short-answer, essay **Topic**—the term or concept the question supports **Learning outcome** **Page number** in the main book **Special feature** in the main book **The Association to Advance Collegiate Schools of Business** (AACSB) **Guidelines** (see description on the next page)
Computerized TestGen	• Allows instructors to customize, save, and generate classroom tests. • Instructors can edit, add, or delete questions from the Test Banks; analyze test results; and organize a database of tests and student results. • Many options are available for organizing and displaying tests, along with search and sort features. • The software and the Test Banks can be downloaded from www.pearsonhighered.com.
Three Sets of PowerPoint Lecture Presentations Authored by Paul Holmes of Ashland University	• A comprehensive set of PowerPoint slides can be used by instructors for class presentations or by students for lecture preview or review. These slides include all the graphs, tables, and equations in the textbook. Two versions are available— step-by-step mode, in which you can build graphs as you would on a blackboard, and automated mode, in which you use a single click per slide. • A comprehensive set of PowerPoint slides have Classroom Response Systems (CRS) questions built in so that instructors can incorporate CRS "clickers" into their classroom lectures. • Student versions of the PowerPoint slides are available as .pdf files. This version allows students to print the slides and bring them to class for note taking.

What Is the AACSB?

The Association to Advance Collegiate Schools of Business (AACSB) is a not-for-profit corporation of educational institutions, corporations, and other organizations devoted to the promotion and improvement of higher education in business administration and accounting. A collegiate institution offering degrees in business administration or accounting may volunteer for AACSB accreditation review. The AACSB expects a curriculum to include learning experiences in the following categories of Assurance of Learning Standards: Written and Oral Communication; Ethical Understanding and Reasoning; Analytical Thinking; Information Technology; Interpersonal Relations and Teamwork, Diverse and Multicultural Work; Reflective Thinking; and Application of Knowledge. Test Bank questions that test skills relevant to these standards are tagged with the appropriate standard. For example, a question testing the moral questions associated with externalities would receive the Ethical Understanding and Reasoning tag.

Acknowledgements

The guidance and recommendations of the following instructors helped us develop the revision plans for the seventh edition and the supplements package. While we could not incorporate every suggestion from every consultant board member, reviewer, or accuracy checker, we do thank each and every one of you and acknowledge that your feedback was indispensable in developing this text. We greatly appreciate your assistance in making this the best text it could be; you have helped a whole new generation of students learn about the exciting world of economics.

Consultant Board

Shawn Abbott, College of the Siskiyous
Gbenga Ajilore, The University of Toledo
Kalok Chu, Loyola University-Chicago
Eva Dziadula, University of Notre Dame
Robert Gillette, University of Kentucky
William L. Goffe, Pennsylvania State University
Randy Methenitis, Richland College
Christian Raschke, Sam Houston State University
Michael J. Ryan, Western Michigan University
Edward Scahill, University of Scranton

Accuracy Review Board

Our accuracy checkers did a particularly painstaking and thorough job of helping us proof the graphs, equations, and features of the text and supplements. We are grateful for their time and commitment:

Fatma Abdel-Raouf, Goldey-Beacom College
Gbenga Ajilore, The University of Toledo
Harry Ellis, University of North Texas
Robert Gillette, University of Kentucky
Anthony Gyapong, Pennsylvania State University–Abington
Randy Methenitis, Richland College
Brian Rosario, University of California–Davis
Edward Scahill, University of Scranton

Reviewers

The guidance and thoughtful recommendations of many instructors helped us develop and implement a revision plan that improved the book's content, enhanced the figures, and strengthened the assessment features. We extend special thanks to Edward Scahill of the University of Scranton for helping us revise the chapter openers and the solutions to the end-of-chapter questions and problems, to Randy Methenitis of Richland College for helping us revise the *An Inside Look* feature in Chapters 1–4, and to Fernando Quijano for creating all the figures in the book and supplements. We are grateful for the comments and many helpful suggestions received from the following reviewers:

Mark Abajian, University of San Diego
Anna Antus, North Hennepin Community College
Ali Arshad, Central New Mexico Community College
David Barrus, Brigham Young University–Idaho
Leon Battista, Quinnipiac University
Susan Bell, Seminole State College of Florida
Bruce Bellner, The Ohio State University
Jennis Biser, Austin Peay State University
Kelly Blanchard, Purdue University
Michaël Bonnal, University of Tennessee at Chattanooga
Walter Boyle, Fayetteville Technical Community College
Dave Brown, Pennsylvania State University
Regina Cassady, Valencia College
Basanta Chaudhuri, Rutgers University
Mark Cullivan, University of San Diego
Hong Duong, Salisbury University
Edward Durkin, Cuyahoga Community College
Maria Edlin, Middle Tennessee State University
Fatma El-Hamidi, Dietrich School of Arts and Sciences
Irene Foster, The George Washington University
Mark Gius, Quinnipiac University
Brian Goegan, Arizona State University
Timothy Hamilton, Columbia College
Wayne Hickenbottom, University of Texas at Austin
Mike Hilmer, San Diego State University
Mark Isaac, Florida State University
Rus Janis, University of Massachusetts–Amherst
Sarah Jenyk, Youngstown State University
Stephanie Brewer Jozefowicz, Indiana University of Pennsylvania
Shawna Koger, Arlington Public Schools/Metro Community College
Susan Laury, Georgia State University
Jim Lee, Texas A&M University–Corpus Christi
An Li, University of Massachusetts–Amherst
Yan Li, University of Wisconsin–Eau Claire
Svitlana Maksymenko, University of Pittsburgh
David McClough, Ohio Northern University

Scott McGann, Grossmont College

Merve Meral, University of Massachusetts–Dartmouth

Robert Mohr, University of New Hampshire

Mike Munoz, Northwest Vista College

John Nader, Davenport University

John Neri, University of Maryland

Charles Newton, Houston Community College

Eric Nielsen, St. Louis Community College–Meramec

Dan Norgard, Normandale Community College

Nitin Paranjpe, Wayne State University, Oakland University

Azucena Peralta, El Paso Community College

Claudiney Pereira, Arizona State University

Dennis Petruska, Youngstown State University

Ryan Phelps, Stephen F. Austin State University

Cristina Reiser, University of New Mexico

Giacomo Rondina, University of Colorado Boulder

Eric Rothenburg, Kingsborough Community College

Rolando Sanchez, Northwest Vista College

Jonathan Silberman, Oakland University

Richard Slotkin, Pasadena City College

Arjun Sondhi, Wayne State University

Derek Stimel, University of California, Davis

Bedassa Tadesse, University of Minnesota–Duluth

Regina Trevino, University of San Diego

Roger Wehr, University of Texas–Arlington

Elizabeth Wheaton, Southern Methodist University

Daniel Wolman, Nassau Community College

Sourushe Zandvakili, University of Cincinnati

Previous Edition Class Testers, Accuracy Reviewers, and Consultants

The guidance and recommendations of the following instructors helped us shape the previous editions.

Class Testers

We are grateful to both the instructors who class-tested manuscript of the first edition and their students for providing useful recommendations on how to make chapters more interesting, relevant, and accurate:

Charles A. Bennett, Gannon University

Anne E. Bresnock, University of California, Los Angeles, and California State Polytechnic University–Pomona

Linda Childs-Leatherbury, Lincoln University, Pennsylvania

John Eastwood, Northern Arizona University

David Eaton, Murray State University

Paul Elgatian, St. Ambrose University

Patricia A. Freeman, Jackson State University

Robert Godby, University of Wyoming

Frank Gunter, Lehigh University

Ahmed Ispahani, University of La Verne

Brendan Kennelly, Lehigh University and National University of Ireland–Galway

Ernest Massie, Franklin University

Carol McDonough, University of Massachusetts–Lowell

Shah Mehrabi, Montgomery College

Sharon Ryan, University of Missouri–Columbia

Bruce G. Webb, Gordon College

Madelyn Young, Converse College

Susan Zumas, Lehigh University

Accuracy Review Boards

We are grateful to the following accuracy checkers of the previous editions for their hard work on the book and supplements:

Fatma Abdel-Raouf, Goldey-Beacom College

Anne Alexander, University of Wyoming

Clare Battista, California Polytechnic State University

Mohammad Bajwa, Northampton Community College

Cynthia Bansak, St. Lawrence University

Hamid Bastin, Shippensburg University

Doris Bennett, Jacksonville State University

Kelly Hunt Blanchard, Purdue University

Don Bumpass, Sam Houston State University

Charles Callahan III, State University of New York–Brockport

Mark S. Chester, Reading Area Community College

Kenny Christianson, Binghamton University

Ishita Edwards, Oxnard College

Harold Elder, University of Alabama

Harry Ellis, University of North Texas

Can Erbil, Brandeis University

Marc Fusaro, Arkansas Tech University

Sarah Ghosh, University of Scranton

Robert Gillette, University of Kentucky

Maria Giuili, Diablo Valley College

Mark Gius, Quinnipiac University

Robert Godby, University of Wyoming

William L. Goffe, Pennsylvania State University

Edward T. Gullason, formerly, Dowling College

Anthony Gyapong, Pennsylvania State University—Abington

Travis Hayes, University of Tennessee–Chattanooga

Carol Hogan, University of Michigan–Dearborn

Anisul M. Islam, University of Houston–Downtown

Aaron Jackson, Bentley College

Nancy Jianakoplos, Colorado State University

Thomas C. Kinnaman, Bucknell University

Mary K. Knudson, University of Iowa

Faik A. Koray, Louisiana State University

Stephan Kroll, California State University–Sacramento

Tony Lima, California State University–East Bay

Randy Methenitis, Richland College

Normal C. Miller, Miami University

David Mitch, University of Maryland–Baltimore County

James A. Moreno, Blinn College

Michael Potepan, San Francisco State University

Mary L. Pranzo, California State University–Fresno

Fernando Quijano, Dickinson State University

Matthew Rafferty, Quinnipiac University

Ratha Ramoo, Diablo Valley College
Jeff Reynolds, Northern Illinois University
Brian Rosario, University of California, Davis
Joseph M. Santos, South Dakota State University
Edward Scahill, University of Scranton
Mark V. Siegler, California State University–Sacramento
Rachel Small, University of Colorado–Boulder
Stephen Smith, Bakersfield College
Rajeev Sooreea, Pennsylvania State University–Altoona
Rebecca Stein, University of Pennsylvania
Ed Steinberg, New York University
Michael Stone, Quinnipiac University
Arlena Sullivan, Jones County Junior College
Wendine Thompson–Dawson, University of Utah
Julianne Treme, University of North Carolina–Wilmington
Robert Whaples, Wake Forest University

Consultant Boards

We received guidance from a dedicated consultant board during the development of the previous editions at several critical junctures. We relied on the board for input on content, figure treatment, and design:

Kate Antonovics, University of California, San Diego
Robert Beekman, University of Tampa
Valerie Bencivenga, University of Texas–Austin
Kelly Blanchard, Purdue University
Susan Dadres, Southern Methodist University
Harry Ellis, Jr., University of North Texas
Sherman T. Folland, Oakland University
Robert Gillette, University of Kentucky
Robert Godby, University of Wyoming
William L. Goffe, Pennsylvania State University
Jane S. Himarios, University of Texas–Arlington
Donn M. Johnson, Quinnipiac University
Mark Karscig, Central Missouri State University
Jenny Minier, University of Kentucky
David Mitch, University of Maryland–Baltimore County
Nicholas Noble, Miami University
Michael Potepan, San Francisco State University
Matthew Rafferty, Quinnipiac University
Helen Roberts, University of Illinois–Chicago
Robert Rosenman, Washington State University
Joseph M. Santos, South Dakota State University
Stephen Snyder, University of Pittsburgh
Martin C. Spechler, Indiana University–Purdue University Indianapolis
Robert Whaples, Wake Forest University
Jonathan B. Wight, University of Richmond

Reviewers

ALABAMA

William P. Aldridge, University of Alabama
Doris Bennett, Jacksonville State University
Harold W. Elder, University of Alabama–Tuscaloosa
Wanda Hudson, Alabama Southern Community College
Keith D. Malone, University of North Alabama
Edward Merkel, Troy University
James L. Swofford, University of Southern Alabama
Christopher Westley, Jacksonville State University

ARIZONA

Doug Conway, Mesa Community College
John Eastwood, Northern Arizona University
Price Fishback, University of Arizona
Mehul Rangwala, University of Phoenix
Anne Williams, Gateway Community College

ARKANSAS

Jerry Crawford, Arkansas State University
Marc Fusaro, Arkansas Tech University
Randall Kesselring, Arkansas State University
Dan Marburger, Arkansas State University

CALIFORNIA

Shawn Abbott, College of the Siskiyous
Renatte Adler, San Diego State University
Ercument Aksoy, Los Angeles Valley College
Maneeza Aminy, Golden Gate University
Kate Antonovics, University of California, San Diego
Becca Arnold, Mesa College
Asatar Bair, City College of San Francisco
Diana Bajrami, College of Alameda
Robert Bise, Orange Coast Community College
Victor Brajer, California State University–Fullerton
Anne E. Bresnock, University of California, Los Angeles, and California State Polytechnic University–Pomona
David Brownstone, University of California, Irvine
Maureen Burton, California State Polytechnic University–Pomona
Annette Chamberlin, National College
Anoshua Chaudhuri, San Francisco State University
James G. Devine, Loyola Marymount University
Jose Esteban, Palomar College
Roger Frantz, San Diego State University
Craig Gallet, California State University–Sacramento
Andrew Gill, California State University–Fullerton
Maria Giuili, Diablo Valley College
Julie Gonzalez, University of California–Santa Cruz
Lisa Grobar, California State University–Long Beach
Steve Hamilton, California State University–Fullerton
Dewey Heinsma, Mt. San Jacinto Community College
Jessica Howell, California State University–Sacramento
Greg Hunter, California State University–Pomona
John Ifcher, Santa Clara University
Ahmed Ispahani, University of LaVerne
George A. Jouganatos, California State University–Sacramento
Jonathan Kaplan, California State University–Sacramento
Leland Kempe, California State University–Fresno

Philip King, San Francisco State University

Lori Kletzer, University of California, Santa Cruz

Stephan Kroll, California State University–Sacramento

David Lang, California State University–Sacramento

Carsten Lange, California State Polytechnic University–Pomona

Don Leet, California State University–Fresno

Rose LeMont, Modesto Junior College

Tony Lima, California State University–East Bay

Solina Lindahl, California Polytechnic State University–San Luis Obispo

Roger Mack, DeAnza College

Michael Marlow, California Polytechnic State University

Scott McGann, Grossmont College

Kristen Monaco, California State University–Long Beach

W. Douglas Morgan, University of California, Santa Barbara

Nivedita Mukherji, Oakland University

Solomon Namala, Cerritos College

Andrew Narwold, University of San Diego

Fola Odebunmi, Cypress College

Hanna Paulson, West Los Angeles College

Joseph M. Pogodzinksi, San Jose State University

Michael J. Potepan, San Francisco State University

Mary L. Pranzo, California State University–Fresno

Sasha Radisich, Glendale Community College

Ratha Ramoo, Diablo Valley College

Scott J. Sambucci, California State University–East Bay

Ariane Schauer, Marymount College

Frederica Shockley, California State University–Chico

Mark Siegler, California State University–Sacramento

Jonathan Silberman, Oakland University

Lisa Simon, California Polytechnic State University–San Louis Obispo

Richard Lee Slotkin, Pasadena City College

Stephen Smith, Bakersfield College

Rodney B. Swanson, University of California–Los Angeles

Martha Stuffler, Irvine Valley College

Lea Templer, College of the Canyons

Kristin A. Van Gaasbeck, California State University–Sacramento

Va Nee Van Vleck, California State University–Fresno

Michael Visser, Sonoma State University

Steven Yamarik, California State University–Long Beach

Guy Yamashiro, California State University–Long Beach

Kevin Young, Diablo Valley College

Anthony Zambelli, Cuyamaca College

COLORADO

Mohammed Akacem, Metropolitan State College of Denver

Rhonda Corman, University of Northern Colorado

Dale DeBoer, University of Colorado–Colorado Springs

Debbie Evercloud, University of Colorado–Denver

Karen Gebhardt, Colorado State University

Scott Houser, Colorado School of Mines

Murat Iyigun, University of Colorado at Boulder

Nancy Jianakoplos, Colorado State University

Jay Kaplan, University of Colorado–Boulder

William G. Mertens, University of Colorado–Boulder

Rachael Small, University of Colorado–Boulder

Stephen Weiler, Colorado State University

CONNECTICUT

Christopher P. Ball, Quinnipiac University

Mark Gius, Quinnipiac University

Mark Jablonowski, University of Hartford

Donn M. Johnson, Quinnipiac University

Robert Martel, University of Connecticut

Charles Meyrick, Housatonic Community College

Judith Mills, Southern Connecticut State University

Matthew Rafferty, Quinnipiac University

Christian Zimmermann, University of Connecticut

DELAWARE

Fatma Abdel-Raouf, Goldey-Beacom College

Ali Ataiifar, Delaware County Community College

Andrew T. Hill, University of Delaware

FLORIDA

Frank Albritton, Seminole State College

Herman Baine, Broward Community College

Robert L. Beekman, University of Tampa

William Browning, Florida Gulf Coast University

Eric P. Chiang, Florida Atlantic University

Martine Duchatelet, Barry University

Hadley Hartman, Santa Fe Community College

Richard Hawkins, University of West Florida

Brad Kamp, University of South Florida

Brian Kench, University of Tampa

Carrie B. Kerekes, Florida Gulf Coast University

Thomas McCaleb, Florida State University

Barbara A. Moore, University of Central Florida

Augustine Nelson, University of Miami

Jamie Ortiz, Florida Atlantic University

Deborah Paige, Santa Fe Community College

Robert Pennington, University of Central Florida

Bob Potter, University of Central Florida

Jerry Schwartz, Broward Community College–North

William Stronge, Florida Atlantic University

Nora Underwood, University of Central Florida

Zhiguang Wang, Florida International University

Joan Wiggenhorn, Barry University

GEORGIA

Greg Brock, Georgia Southern University

Donna Fisher, Georgia Southern University

Shelby Frost, Georgia State University

John King, Georgia Southern University

Constantin Ogloblin, Georgia Southern University

Dr. Greg Okoro, Georgia Perimeter College–Clarkston

Michael Reksulak, Georgia Southern University

Bill Yang, Georgia Southern University

IDAHO

Cynthia Hill, Idaho State University
Don Holley, Boise State University
Tesa Stegner, Idaho State University

ILLINOIS

Teshome Abebe, Eastern Illinois University
Ali Akarca, University of Illinois–Chicago
Zsolt Becsi, Southern Illinois University–Carbondale
James Bruehler, Eastern Illinois University
Louis Cain, Loyola University and Northwestern University
Rosa Lea Danielson, College of DuPage
Kevin Dunagan, Oakton Community College
Scott Gilbert, Southern Illinois University
Rajeev K. Goel, Illinois State University
David Gordon, Illinois Valley Community College
Alan Grant, Eastern Illinois University
Rik Hafer, Southern Illinois University–Edwardsville
Alice Melkumian, Western Illinois University
Christopher Mushrush, Illinois State University
Jeff Reynolds, Northern Illinois University
Helen Roberts, University of Illinois–Chicago
Thomas R. Sadler, Western Illinois University
Eric Schulz, Northwestern University
Dennis Shannon, Southwestern Illinois College
Charles Sicotte, Rock Valley Community College
Neil T. Skaggs, Illinois State University
Kevin Sylwester, Southern Illinois University–Carbondale
Wendine Thompson-Dawson, Monmouth College
Tara Westerhold, Western Illinois University
Mark Witte, Northwestern University
Laurie Wolff, Southern Illinois University–Carbondale
Paula Worthington, Northwestern University

INDIANA

Kelly Blanchard, Purdue University
Cecil Bohanon, Ball State University
Kirk Doran, University of Notre Dame
Eva Dziadula, University of Notre Dame
Mary Flannery, University of Notre Dame
Thomas Gresik, University of Notre Dame
Robert B. Harris, Indiana University–Purdue University Indianapolis
Fred Herschede, Indiana University–South Bend
Tom Lehman, Indiana Wesleyan University
Abraham Mathew, Indiana University–Purdue University Indianapolis
John Pomery, Purdue University
Curtis Price, University of Southern Indiana
Rob Rude, Ivy Tech Community College
James K. Self, Indiana University–Bloomington
Esther-Mirjam Sent, University of Notre Dame
Virginia Shingleton, Valparaiso University
Martin C. Spechler, Indiana University–Purdue University Indianapolis

Arun K. Srinivasan, Indiana University–Southeast Campus
Geetha Suresh, Purdue University

IOWA

Terry Alexander, Iowa State University
Paul Elgatian, St. Ambrose University
Jennifer Fuhrman, University of Iowa
Ken McCormick, University of Northern Iowa
Andy Schuchart, Iowa Central Community College
John Solow, University of Iowa
Jonathan Warner, Dordt College

KANSAS

Guatam Bhattacharya, University of Kansas
Amanda Freeman, Kansas State University
Dipak Ghosh, Emporia State University
Alan Grant, Baker University
Wayne Oberle, St. Ambrose University
Jodi Messer Pelkowski, Wichita State University
Martin Perline, Wichita State University
Joel Potter, Kansas State University
Joshua Rosenbloom, University of Kansas
Shane Sanders, Kansas State University
Dosse Toulaboe, Fort Hays State University
Bhavneet Walia, Kansas State University

KENTUCKY

Tom Cate, Northern Kentucky University
Nan-Ting Chou, University of Louisville
David Eaton, Murray State University
Ann Eike, University of Kentucky
Robert Gillette, University of Kentucky
Barry Haworth, University of Louisville
Gail Hoyt, University of Kentucky
Donna Ingram, Eastern Kentucky University
Waithaka Iraki, Kentucky State University
Hak Youn Kim, Western Kentucky University
Martin Milkman, Murray State University
Jenny Minier, University of Kentucky
David Shideler, Murray State University
John Vahaly, University of Louisville

LOUISIANA

Lara Gardner, Southeastern Louisiana University
Jay Johnson, Southeastern Louisiana University
Faik Koray, Louisiana State University
Paul Nelson, University of Louisiana–Monroe
Sung Chul No, Southern University and A&M College
Tammy Parker, University of Louisiana–Monroe
Wesley A. Payne, Delgado Community College
Nancy Rumore, University of Louisiana at Lafayette

MARYLAND

Carey Borkoski, Anne Arundel Community College
Kathleen A. Carroll, University of Maryland–Baltimore County
Jill Caviglia-Harris, Salisbury University
Dustin Chambers, Salisbury University
Karl Einolf, Mount Saint Mary's University
Marsha Goldfarb, University of Maryland–Baltimore City

Bruce Madariaga, Montgomery College
Shah Mehrabi, Montgomery College
Gretchen Mester, Anne Arundel Community College
David Mitch, University of Maryland–Baltimore County
John Neri, University of Maryland
Henry Terrell, University of Maryland

MASSACHUSETTS

William L. Casey, Jr., Babson College
Arthur Schiller Casimir, Western New England College
Michael Enz, Western New England College
Can Erbil, Brandeis University
Lou Foglia, Suffolk University
Gerald Friedman, University of Massachusetts
Todd Idson, Boston University
Aaron Jackson, Bentley College
Russell A. Janis, University of Massachusetts–Amherst
Anthony Laramie, Merrimack College
Carol McDonough, University of Massachusetts–Lowell
William O'Brien, Worcester State College
Ahmad Saranjam, Bridgewater State College
Howard Shore, Bentley College
Janet Thomas, Bentley College
John Tommasi, University of Massachusetts–Lowell
Gregory H. Wassall, Northeastern University
Bruce G. Webb, Gordon College
Gilbert Wolpe, Newbury College
Jay Zagorsky, Boston University

MICHIGAN

Eric Beckman, Delta College
Jared Boyd, Henry Ford Community College
Victor Claar, Hope College
Dr. Sonia Dalmia, Grand Valley State University
Daniel Giedeman, Grand Valley State University
Allen C. Goodman, Wayne State University
Steven Hayworth, Eastern Michigan University
Gregg Heidebrink, Washtenaw Community College
Carol Hogan, University of Michigan–Dearborn
Marek Kolar, Delta College
Susan J. Linz, Michigan State University
James Luke, Lansing Community College
Ilir Miteza, University of Michigan–Dearborn
John Nader, Grand Valley State University
Norman P. Obst, Michigan State University
Laudo M. Ogura, Grand Valley State University
Robert J. Rossana, Wayne State University
Michael J. Ryan, Western Michigan University
Charles A. Stull, Kalamazoo College
Michael J. Twomey, University of Michigan–Dearborn
Mark Wheeler, Western Michigan University
Wendy Wysocki, Monroe County Community College

MINNESOTA

Mary Edwards, Saint Cloud State University
Phillip J. Grossman, Saint Cloud State University
Monica Hartman, University of St. Thomas
Matthew Hyle, Winona State University

David J. O'Hara, Metropolitan State University–Minneapolis
Kwang Woo (Ken) Park, Minnesota State University–Mankato
Artatrana Ratha, Saint Cloud State University
Ken Rebeck, Saint Cloud State University
Katherine Schmeiser, University of Minnesota

MISSISSIPPI

Becky Campbell, Mississippi State University
Randall Campbell, Mississippi State University
Patricia A. Freeman, Jackson State University
Arlena Sullivan, Jones County Junior College

MISSOURI

Chris Azevedo, University of Central Missouri
Ariel Belasen, Saint Louis University
Catherine Chambers, University of Central Missouri
Paul Chambers, University of Central Missouri
Kermit Clay, Ozarks Technical Community College
Ben Collier, Northwest Missouri State University
John R. Crooker, University of Central Missouri
Jo Durr, Southwest Missouri State University
Julie H. Gallaway, Southwest Missouri State University
Terrel Gallaway, Southwest Missouri State University
Mark Karscig, Central Missouri State University
Nicholas D. Peppes, Saint Louis Community College–Forest Park
Steven T. Petty, College of the Ozarks
Sharon Ryan, University of Missouri–Columbia
Ben Young, University of Missouri–Kansas City

MONTANA

Agnieszka Bielinska-Kwapisz, Montana State University–Bozeman
Jeff Bookwalter, University of Montana–Missoula

NEBRASKA

John Dogbey, University of Nebraska–Omaha
Ward Hooker, Central Community College
Allan Jenkins, University of Nebraska–Kearney
James Knudsen, Creighton University
Craig MacPhee, University of Nebraska–Lincoln
Kim Sosin, University of Nebraska–Omaha
Mark E. Wohar, University of Nebraska–Omaha

NEVADA

Michael H. Lampert, Truckee Meadows Community College
Bernard Malamud, University of Nevada–Las Vegas
Sheri Perez, College of Southern Nevada
Bill Robinson, University of Nevada–Las Vegas

NEW HAMPSHIRE

Evelyn Gick, Dartmouth College
Neil Niman, University of New Hampshire

NEW JERSEY

Len Anyanwu, Union County College
Maharuk Bhiladwalla, Rutgers University–New Brunswick
Giuliana Campanelli-Andreopoulos, William Paterson University

Gary Gigliotti, Rutgers University–New Brunswick
John Graham, Rutgers University–Newark
Berch Haroian, William Paterson University
Paul Harris, Camden County College
Jeff Rubin, Rutgers University
Henry Ryder, Gloucester County College
Laura Storino, Rowan University
Donna Thompson, Brookdale Community College

NEW MEXICO

Donald Coes, University of New Mexico
Kate Krause, University of New Mexico
Curt Shepherd, University of New Mexico

NEW YORK

Seemi Ahmad, Dutchess Community College
Chris Annala, State University of New York–Geneseo
Erol Balkan, Hamilton College
John Bockino, Suffolk County Community College–Ammerman
Charles Callahan III, State University of New York–Brockport
Michael Carew, Baruch College
Sean Corcoran, New York University
Ranjit S. Dighe, City University of New York–Bronx Community College
Debra Dwyer, Stony Brook University
Glenn Gerstner, Saint John's University–Queens
Susan Glanz, Saint John's University–Queens
Wayne A. Grove, LeMoyne College
Nancy Howe, Hudson Valley Community College
Christopher Inya, Monroe Community College
Ghassan Karam, Pace University
Clifford Kern, State University of New York–Binghamton
Mary Lesser, Iona College
Anna Musatti, Columbia University
Theodore Muzio, St. John's University, New York
Emre Ozsoz, Fashion Institute of Technology
Howard Ross, Baruch College
Ed Steinberg, New York University
Leonie Stone, State University of New York–Geneseo
Ganti Subrahmanyam, University of Buffalo
Jogindar S. Uppal, State University of New York–Albany
Susan Wolcott, Binghamton University

NORTH CAROLINA

Rita Balaban, University of North Carolina
Otilia Boldea, North Carolina State University
Robert Burrus, University of North Carolina–Wilmington
Lee A. Craig, North Carolina State University
Alexander Deshkovski, North Carolina Central University
Kathleen Dorsainvil, Winston–Salem State University
Lydia Gan, School of Business, University of North Carolina–Pembroke
Michael Goode, Central Piedmont Community College
Salih Hakeem, North Carolina Central University

Melissa Hendrickson, North Carolina State University
Haiyong Liu, East Carolina University
Kosmas Marinakis, North Carolina State University
Todd McFall, Wake Forest University
Shahriar Mostashari, Campbell University
Jonathan Phillips, North Carolina State University
Bobby Puryear, North Carolina State University
Jeff Sarbaum, University of North Carolina–Greensboro
Peter Schuhmann, University of North Carolina–Wilmington
Robert Shoffner, Central Piedmont Community College
Catherine Skura, Sandhills Community College
Carol Stivender, University of North Carolina–Charlotte
Vera Tabakova, East Carolina University
Eric Taylor, Central Piedmont Community College
Julianne Treme, University of North Carolina–Wilmington
Hui-Kuan Tseng, University of North Carolina at Charlotte
Robert Whaples, Wake Forest University
John Whitehead, Appalachian State University
Gary W. Zinn, East Carolina University
Rick Zuber, University of North Carolina at Charlotte

OHIO

Olugbenga Ajilore, The University of Toledo
Benjamin Blair, Columbus State University
John P. Blair, Wright State University
Bolong Cao, Ohio University–Athens
Kyongwook Choi, Ohio University
James D'Angelo, University of Cincinnati
Darlene DeVera, Miami University
Rudy Fichtenbaum, Wright State University
Tim Fuerst, Bowling Green University
Harley Gill, Ohio State University
Leroy Gill, Ohio State University
Steven Heubeck, Ohio State University
Daniel Horton, Cleveland State University
Michael Jones, University of Cincinnati
Kristen Keith, University of Toledo
Janice Kinghorn, Miami University
Jean Kujawa, Lourdes College
Ernest Massie, Franklin University
Ida A. Mirzaie, Ohio State University
Jay Mutter, University of Akron
Mike Nelson, University of Akron
Nicholas Noble, Miami University
Dennis C. O'Neill, University of Cincinnati
Joseph Palardy, Youngstown State University
Charles Reichheld, Cuyahoga Community College
Teresa Riley, Youngstown State University
Rochelle Ruffer, Youngstown State University
Kate Sheppard, University of Akron
Richard Stratton, University of Akron
Albert Sumell, Youngstown State University
Steve Szheghi, Wilmington College
Melissa Thomasson, Miami University

Yaqin Wang, Youngstown State University
Bert Wheeler, Cedarville University
Kathryn Wilson, Kent State University
Sourushe Zandvakili, University of Cincinnati

OKLAHOMA

David Hudgins, University of Oklahoma
Bill McLean, Oklahoma State University
Denny Myers, Oklahoma City Community College
Ed Price, Oklahoma State University
Abdulhamid Sukar, Cameron University
Zhen Zhu, University of Central Oklahoma

OREGON

Bill Burrows, Lane Community College
Tom Carroll, Central Oregon Community College
Tim Duy, University of Oregon
Alan S. Fudge, Linn-Benton Community College
B. Starr McMullen, Oregon State University
Ted Scheinman, Mount Hood Community College
Larry Singell, University of Oregon
Ayca Tekin-Koru, Oregon State University

PENNSYLVANIA

Bradley Andrew, Juniata College
Mohammad Bajwa, Northampton Community College
Gustavo Barboza, Mercyhurst College
Charles A. Bennett, Gannon University
Cynthia Benzing, West Chester University
Howard Bodenhorn, Lafayette College
Milica Bookman, St. Joseph's University
Robert Brooker, Gannon University
Eric Brucker, Widener University
Shirley Cassing, University of Pittsburgh
Linda Childs-Leatherbury, Lincoln University
Scott J. Dressler, Villanova University
Satyajit Ghosh, University of Scranton
William L. Goffe, Pennsylvania State University
Anthony Gyapong, Pennsylvania State University–Abington
Mehdi Haririan, Bloomsburg University
Andrew Hill, Federal Reserve Bank of Philadelphia
Steven Husted, University of Pittsburgh
James Jozefowicz, Indiana University of Pennsylvania
Stephanie Jozefowicz, Indiana University of Pennsylvania
Nicholas Karatjas, Indiana University of Pennsylvania
Mary Kelly, Villanova University
Brendan Kennelly, Lehigh University
Thomas C. Kinnaman, Bucknell University
Christopher Magee, Bucknell University
Svitlana Maksymenko, University of Pittsburgh
Katherine McCann, Penn State
Judy McDonald, Lehigh University
Ranganath Murthy, Bucknell University
Hong V. Nguyen, University of Scranton
Cristian Pardo, Saint Joseph's University
Iordanis Petsas, University of Scranton
Denis Raihall, West Chester University

Adam Renhoff, Drexel University
Nicole L. Sadowski, York College of Pennsylvania
Edward Scahill, University of Scranton
Ken Slaysman, York College of Pennsylvania
Rajeev Sooreea, Pennsylvania State University–Altoona
Rebecca Stein, University of Pennsylvania
Sandra Trejos, Clarion University
Peter Zaleski, Villanova University
Ann Zech, Saint Joseph's University
Lei Zhu, West Chester University
Susan Zumas, Lehigh University

RHODE ISLAND

Jongsung Kim, Bryant University
Leonard Lardaro, University of Rhode Island
Nazma Latif-Zaman, Providence College

SOUTH CAROLINA

Calvin Blackwell, College of Charleston
Ward Hooker, Orangeburg–Calhoun Technical College
Woodrow W. Hughes, Jr., Converse College
John McArthur, Wofford College
Victoria Willis-Miller, Piedmont Technical College
Chad Turner, Clemson University
Madelyn Young, Converse College

SOUTH DAKOTA

Joseph M. Santos, South Dakota State University
Jason Zimmerman, South Dakota State University

TENNESSEE

Sindy Abadie, Southwest Tennessee Community College
Charles Baum, Middle Tennessee State University
John Brassel, Southwest Tennessee Community College
Bichaka Fayissa, Middle Tennessee State University
Michael J. Gootzeit, University of Memphis
Travis Hayes, University of Tennessee–Chattanooga
Christopher C. Klein, Middle Tennessee State University
Leila Pratt, University of Tennessee at Chattanooga
Millicent Sites, Carson-Newman College

TEXAS

Carlos Aguilar, El Paso Community College
Rashid Al-Hmoud, Texas Tech University
William Beaty, Tarleton State University
Klaus Becker, Texas Tech University
Alex Brown, Texas A&M University
Jack A. Bucco, Austin Community College–Northridge and Saint Edward's University
Don Bumpass, Sam Houston State University
Marilyn M. Butler, Sam Houston State University
Mike Cohick, Collin County Community College
Cesar Corredor, Texas A&M University
Steven Craig, University of Houston
Patrick Crowley, Texas A&M University–Corpus Christi
Richard Croxdale, Austin Community College
Susan Dadres, Southern Methodist University
David Davenport, McLennan Community College
Harry Ellis, Jr., University of North Texas

Paul Emberton, Texas State University

Diego Escobari, Texas A&M University

Christi Esquivel, Navarro College

Nicholas Feltovich, University of Houston–Main

Charles Harold Fifield, Baylor University

Jamal G. Husein, Angelo State University

Mark Frank, Sam Houston State University

Alejandro Gelves, Midwestern State University

Edgar Ghossoub, University of Texas–San Antonio

Richard Gosselin, Houston Community College–Central

Sheila Amin Gutierrez de Pineres, University of Texas–Dallas

Tina J. Harvell, Blinn College–Bryan Campus

James W. Henderson, Baylor University

Jane S. Himarios, University of Texas–Arlington

James Holcomb, University of Texas–El Paso

Jamal Husein, Angelo State University

Ansul Islam, University of Houston–Downtown

Karen Johnson, Baylor University

Kathy Kelly, University of Texas–Arlington

Thomas Kemp, Tarrant County College–Northwest

Jim Lee, Texas A&M University–Corpus Christi

Ronnie W. Liggett, University of Texas–Arlington

Akbar Marvasti, University of Houston–Downtown

James Mbata, Houston Community College

Kimberly Mencken, Baylor University

Randy Methenitis, Richland College

Carl Montano, Lamar University

James Moreno, Blinn College

Camille Nelson, Texas A&M University

Michael Nelson, Texas A&M University

Charles Newton, Houston Community College–Southwest College

John Pisciotta, Baylor University

Shofiqur Rahman, University of Texas–El Paso

Sara Saderion, Houston Community College–Southwest College

George E. Samuels, Sam Houston State University

David Schutte, Mountain View College

Ivan Tasic, Texas A&M University

David Torres, University of Texas–El Paso

Ross vanWassenhove, University of Houston

Roger Wehr, University of Texas–Arlington

Jim Wollscheid, Texas A&M University–Kingsville

J. Christopher Wreh, North Central Texas College

David W. Yoskowitz, Texas A&M University–Corpus Christi

Inske Zandvliet, Brookhaven College

UTAH

Chris Fawson, Utah State University

Lowell Glenn, Utah Valley State College

Aric Krause, Westminster College

Arden Pope, Brigham Young University

VERMONT

Nancy Brooks, University of Vermont

VIRGINIA

Lee Badgett, Virginia Military Institute

Lee A. Coppock, University of Virginia

Erik Craft, University of Richmond

Janelle Davenport, Hampton University

Philip Heap, James Madison University

George E. Hoffer, Virginia Commonwealth University

Oleg Korenok, Virginia Commonwealth University

Larry Landrum, Virginia Western Community College

Frances Lea, Germanna Community College

Carrie Meyer, George Mason University

John Min, Northern Virginia Community College

Eugene Bempong Nyantakyi, West Virginia University

James Roberts, Tidewater Community College–Virginia Beach

Robert Rycroft, University of Mary Washington

Araine A. Schauer, Mary Mount College

Sarah Stafford, The College of William & Mary

Bob Subrick, James Madison University

Susanne Toney, Hampton University

Michelle Vachris, Christopher Newport University

James Wetzel, Virginia Commonwealth University

George Zestos, Christopher Newport University

WASHINGTON

Genevieve Briand, Washington State University

Lisa Citron, Cascadia College

Andrew Ewing, University of Washington

Stacey Jones, Seattle University

Dean Peterson, Seattle University

Robert Rosenman, Washington State University

WEST VIRGINIA

Jacqueline Agesa, Marshall University

Richard Agesa, Marshall University

Robin S. McCutcheon, Marshall University College of Business

WISCONSIN

Peng Huang, Ripon College

Marina Karabelas, Milwaukee Area Technical College

Elizabeth Sawyer Kelly, University of Wisconsin–Madison

Pascal Ngoboka, University of Wisconsin–River Falls

Kevin Quinn, St. Norbert College

John R. Stoll, University of Wisconsin–Green Bay

WYOMING

Robert Godby, University of Wyoming

DISTRICT OF COLUMBIA

Leon Battista, American Enterprise Institute

Robert Berman, American University

Michael Bradley, George Washington University

Colleen M. Callahan, American University

Eliane P. Catilina, Graduate School USA

Robert Feinberg, American University

Walter Park, American University

Ralph Sonenshine, American University

INTERNATIONAL

Minh Quang Dao, Carleton University–Ottawa, Canada

A Word of Thanks

Once again, we benefited greatly from the dedication and professionalism of the Pearson Economics team. Portfolio Manager David Alexander's energy and support were indispensable. David helped mold the presentation and provided words of encouragement whenever our energy flagged. Content Editor Lena Buonanno worked tirelessly to ensure that this text was as good as it could be and to coordinate the many moving parts involved in a project of this magnitude. This new edition posed particular challenges, and we remain astonished at the amount of time, energy, and unfailing good humor she brings to this project. As we worked on the first edition, former Director of Key Markets David Theisen provided invaluable insight into how best to structure a principles text. His advice helped shape nearly every chapter. We extend our thanks to Tricia Murphy, our Product Marketing Manager, and Carlie Marvel, our Field Marketer, for their energy and creativity in presenting our book and digital products to both professors and students.

Christine Donovan managed the entire production process and the extensive supplement package that accompanies the book. Editorial Assistant Nicole Nedwidek assisted the team in completing several tasks, including review surveys and summaries, to help produce both the book and media resources.

We received excellent research assistance on previous editions from Dante DeAntonio, Ed Timmons, Matthew Saboe, David Van Der Goes, and Jason Hockenberry. We thank Elena Zeller, Jennifer Brailsford, Ellen Vandevort Wolf, Emily Webster, Mollie Sweet, Jayme Wagner, and Rebecca Barney for their careful proofreading of first- and second-round page proofs. Over all editions of our books, we received helpful feedback and recommendations from Lehigh University faculty colleagues Frank R. Gunter, Thomas J. Hyclak, and Robert J. Thornton.

As instructors, we recognize how important it is for students to view graphs that are clear and accessible. We are fortunate to have Fernando Quijano render all the figures in our books and also our supplements. Market feedback on the figures continues to be positive. We extend our thanks to Fernando not only for collaborating with us and creating the best figures possible but also for his patience with our demanding schedule.

This seventh edition has several media components, which required skilled and patient creators and developers. We extend special thanks to Andy Taylor of Hodja Media for preparing the video clips and to Paul Graf of the University of Indiana–Bloomington for preparing the graph animations. These videos and animations are an important part of our revision.

A good part of the burden of an undertaking on this scale is borne by our families. We appreciate the patience, support, and encouragement of our wives and children.

Economics:
Foundations and Models

Why Does Ford Assemble Cars in Both the United States and Mexico?

Until recently, did most U.S. firms operate only within the United States? Although some people believe so, in fact, many U.S. firms have been producing goods abroad for decades. For example, Henry Ford founded the Ford Motor Company in Dearborn, Michigan, in 1903. By the next year, Ford was assembling cars in Ontario, Canada. Ford began assembling cars in Manchester, England, in 1911, and in Mexico in 1925. Clearly, for many decades, Ford has been a multinational corporation, manufacturing and selling its cars around the world. In 2017, though, Ford's non-U.S. operations, particularly those in Mexico, were the subject of political controversy.

Some of the cars Ford assembles in Mexico are sold there, but Ford also exports cars from Mexico to the United States and other countries. In 2017, in an attempt to increase manufacturing employment in the United States, President Donald Trump considered imposing a 35 percent tariff—in effect, a tax—on cars that Ford and other U.S. companies assembled in Mexico for sale in the United States. If the tariff were enacted, U.S. car companies would have to pay the U.S. government an amount equal to 35 percent of the price of these cars at the border. The tariff would increase the prices consumers would pay for these cars and, therefore, reduce their sales. President Trump argued that the tariffs would give U.S. car companies an *economic incentive* to assemble more cars in the United States, which would increase employment in U.S. manufacturing.

U.S. car companies were assembling some cars in Mexico because in a *market system*, firms respond to economic incentives. In this case, the lower wages the companies can pay Mexican workers and the lower prices for auto parts in Mexico reduced Ford's costs by more than $1,000 per car. Typically, technological progress creates economic incentives for firms to change how they produce goods and services. For example, robotics can lead automobile manufacturers to automate some jobs, reducing

Jonathan Ernst/Reuters/Alamy Stock Photo

employment in the industry. Firms also respond to changes in consumer tastes, as when more people become interested in buying electric cars. But sometimes firms respond to incentives from changes in government policy. For instance, in 1994, the governments of Canada, Mexico, and the United States agreed to the North American Free Trade Agreement (NAFTA), which made it easier for U.S. firms like Ford to ship products from Mexico to the United States. In 2017, some policymakers in Washington believed that a tariff on imports to the United States from Mexico was needed to reverse the economic incentives in NAFTA.

In this chapter and the remainder of this book, we will see how economics provides us with the tools to analyze how firms, consumers, and workers respond to economic incentives and how government policymakers can attempt to reach their objectives by changing those incentives.

AN INSIDE LOOK on **page 20** discusses how likely it is that significant numbers of manufacturing jobs will return to the United States from overseas.

Sources: Dee-Ann Durbin, "Made in Mexico, Popular on U.S. Highways," Associated Press, February 8, 2017; David Welch and David Merrill, "Why Trump Tariffs on Mexican Cars Probably Won't Stop Job Flight," bloomberg.com, January 4, 2017; and Allan Nevins and Frank Ernest Hill, *Ford: Expansion and Challenge, 1915–1933*, New York: Charles Scribner's Sons, 1957, Ch. 14.

Chapter Outline & Learning Objectives

Economics in Your Life & Career

Should You Consider a Career in Manufacturing?

In the late 1940s and early 1950s, a third of workers in the United States were employed in manufacturing. Traditionally, many high school graduates viewed working on a manufacturing assembly line as a way to earn a middle-class income. Many college graduates in engineering, accounting, management, and other fields have also found employment in manufacturing. But will manufacturing be a good source of careers in the future? In December 2016, total employment in U.S. manufacturing was 12.3 million. But the U.S. Bureau of Labor Statistics forecasts that by 2024, this number will decline to 11.4 million. What is the basis for this forecast, and how reliable is it? As you read this chapter, try to answer this question. You can check your answer against the one we provide on **page 19** at the end of this chapter.

In this book, we use economics to answer questions such as the following:

- What determines the prices of goods and services from bottled water to smartphones to automobiles?
- Why have health care costs risen so rapidly?
- Why do firms engage in international trade, and how do government policies, such as tariffs, affect international trade?
- Why does the government control the prices of some goods and services, and what are the effects of those controls?

Economists do not always agree on the answer to every question, and there are lively debates on some issues. Because new economic questions are constantly arising, economists are always developing new methods to analyze them.

All the topics we discuss in this book illustrate a basic fact of life: To attain our goals, we must make choices. We must make choices because we live in a world of **scarcity**, which means that although our wants are *unlimited*, the resources available to fulfill those wants are *limited*. You might want to own a BMW and spend each summer vacationing at five-star European hotels, but unless Bill Gates is a close and generous relative, you probably lack the funds to fulfill these wants. Every day, you make choices as you spend your limited income on the many goods and services available. The finite amount of time you have also limits your ability to attain your goals. If you spend an hour studying for your economics midterm, you have one hour less to study for your history midterm. Firms and the government are in the same situation as you: They must also attain their goals with limited resources. **Economics** is the study of the choices consumers, business managers, and government officials make to attain their goals, given their scarce resources.

We begin this chapter by discussing three important economic ideas that we will return to many times in the following chapters: *People are rational, people respond to economic incentives,* and *optimal decisions are made at the margin.* Then, we consider the three fundamental questions that any economy must answer: *What* goods and services will be produced? *How* will the goods and services be produced? and *Who* will receive the goods and services produced? Next, we consider the role of *economic models* in analyzing economic issues. **Economic models** are simplified versions of reality used to analyze real-world economic situations. We will explore why economists use models and how they construct them. Finally, we will discuss the difference between microeconomics and macroeconomics, and we will preview some important economic terms.

Scarcity A situation in which unlimited wants exceed the limited resources available to fulfill those wants.

Economics The study of the choices people make to attain their goals, given their scarce resources.

Economic model A simplified version of reality used to analyze real-world economic situations.

 ## 1.1 Three Key Economic Ideas

LEARNING OBJECTIVE: Explain these three key economic ideas: People are rational, people respond to economic incentives, and optimal decisions are made at the margin.

Whether your goal is to buy a smartphone or find a part-time job, you will interact with other people in *markets*. A **market** is a group of buyers and sellers of a good or service and the institution or arrangement by which they come together to trade. Examples of markets are the markets for smartphones, houses, haircuts, stocks and bonds, and labor. Most of economics involves analyzing how people make choices and interact in markets. Here are the three important ideas about markets that we'll return to frequently:

Market A group of buyers and sellers of a good or service and the institution or arrangement by which they come together to trade.

1. People are rational.
2. People respond to economic incentives.
3. Optimal decisions are made at the margin.

People Are Rational

Economists generally assume that people are rational. This assumption does *not* mean that economists believe everyone knows everything or always makes the "best" decision. It means that economists assume that consumers and firms use all available information as they act to achieve their goals. Rational individuals weigh the benefits and costs of each action, and they choose an action only if the benefits outweigh the costs. For example, if Apple charges a price of $649 for its new iPhone, economists assume that the managers at Apple have estimated that this price will earn the company the most profit. Even though the managers may be wrong—maybe a price of $625 or $675 would be more profitable—economists assume that the managers at Apple have acted rationally, on the basis of the information available to them, in choosing the price of $649. Although not everyone behaves rationally all the time, the assumption of rational behavior is very useful in explaining most of the choices that people make.   **MyLab Economics** Concept Check

People Respond to Economic Incentives

People act from a variety of motives, including envy, compassion, and religious belief. While not ignoring other motives, economists emphasize that consumers and firms consistently respond to *economic incentives*. This point may seem obvious, but it is often overlooked. For example, according to an article in the *Wall Street Journal*, the FBI couldn't understand why banks were not taking steps to improve security in the face of an increase in robberies: "FBI officials suggest that banks place uniformed, armed guards outside their doors and install bullet-resistant plastic, known as a 'bandit barrier,' in front of teller windows." FBI officials were surprised that few banks took their advice. But the article also reported that installing bullet-resistant plastic costs $10,000 to $20,000, and a well-trained security guard receives $50,000 per year in salary and benefits. The average loss in a bank robbery is only about $1,200. The economic incentive to banks is clear: It is less costly to put up with bank robberies than to take additional security measures. FBI agents may be surprised by how banks respond to the threat of robberies—but economists are not.

In each chapter, the *Apply the Concept* feature discusses a news story or another application related to the chapter material. Read this *Apply the Concept* for a discussion of whether people respond to economic incentives even when deciding how much to eat and how much to exercise.   **MyLab Economics** Concept Check

 ## Apply the Concept   **MyLab Economics** Video

Does Health Insurance Give People an Incentive to Become Obese?

Obesity is a factor in a variety of diseases, including heart disease, stroke, diabetes, and hypertension, making it a significant health problem in the United States. Body mass index (BMI) is a measurement of a person's weight relative to the person's height. According to the U.S. Centers for Disease Control and Prevention (CDC), an adult with a body mass index (BMI) of 30 or greater is considered *obese*. For example, a 5'6" adult with a BMI of 30 is 40 pounds overweight.

The following two maps show the dramatic increase in obesity between 1994 and 2015. In 1994, in a majority of states, only between 10 percent and 14 percent of the adult population was obese, and in no state was more than 20 percent of the adult population obese. By 2015, in every state, at least 20 percent of the adult population was obese, and in 44 states, at least 25 percent of the adult population was obese.

Many people who suffer from obesity have underlying medical conditions. For these people, obesity is a medical problem that they cannot control. The fact that obesity has increased, though, indicates that for some people, obesity is the result of diet and lifestyle choices. Potential explanations for the increase in obesity include greater intake of high-calorie fast foods, insufficient exercise, and a decline in the physical

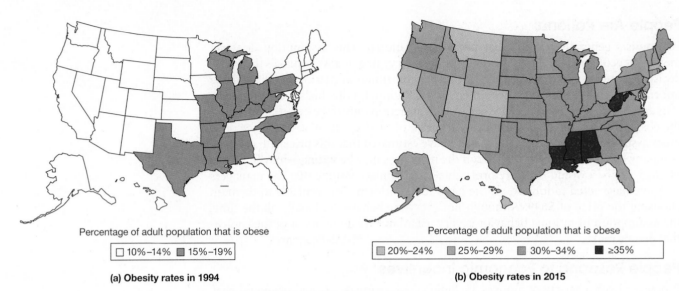

Percentage of adult population that is obese

□ 10%–14%	■ 15%–19%

(a) Obesity rates in 1994

Percentage of adult population that is obese

20%–24%	25%–29%	30%–34%	≥35%

(b) Obesity rates in 2015

Source: Centers for Disease Control and Prevention, "Prevalence of Self-Reported Obesity among U.S. Adults."

activity associated with many jobs. The CDC recommends that teenagers get a minimum of 60 minutes of aerobic exercise per day, a standard that only 15 percent of high school students meet. In 1960, 50 percent of jobs in the United States required at least moderate physical activity. Today, only 20 percent of jobs do. As a result, a typical worker today who may work at a computer is burning off about 130 *fewer* calories per workday than a worker in the 1960s who was more likely to have worked in a manufacturing plant.

In addition to eating too much and not exercising enough, could having health insurance be a cause of obesity? Obese people tend to suffer more medical problems and so incur higher medical costs. Obese people with health insurance that will reimburse them for only part of their medical bills, or who have no health insurance, must pay some or all of these higher medical bills themselves. People with health insurance that covers most of their medical bills will not suffer as large a monetary cost from being obese. In other words, by reducing some of the costs of obesity, health insurance may give people an economic incentive to gain weight.

At first glance, this argument may seem implausible. Some people suffer from medical conditions that can make physical activity difficult or that can cause weight gain even with moderate eating, so they may become obese, regardless of which type of health insurance they have. The people who are obese because of poor eating habits or lack of exercise probably don't consider health insurance when deciding whether to have a slice of chocolate cake or to watch Netflix instead of going to the gym. But if economists are correct about the importance of economic incentives, then we would expect that if we hold all other personal characteristics—such as age, gender, and income—constant, people with health insurance will be more likely to be overweight than people without health insurance.

Jay Bhattacharya and Kate Bundorf of Stanford University, Noemi Pace of the University of Venice, and Neeraj Sood of the University of Southern California, have analyzed the effects of health insurance on weight. Using a sample that followed nearly 80,000 people from 1989 to 2004, they found that after controlling for factors including age, gender, income, education, and race, people with health insurance were significantly more likely to be overweight than people without health insurance. Having private health insurance increased BMI by 1.3 points. Having public health insurance, such as Medicaid, which is a program under which the government provides health care to low-income people, increased BMI by 2.3 points. These findings do not mean that health insurance is the sole cause, or even the most important cause, of obesity. The findings do suggest that people respond to economic incentives even when making decisions about what they eat and how much they exercise. In Section 1.3, we will see that economists modify conclusions as they collect additional data.

Note: The exact formula for the body mass index is BMI = (Weight in pounds/Height in inches^2) $\times$ 703.

Sources: Centers for Disease Control and Prevention, "Prevalence of Self-Reported Obesity among U.S. Adults," www.cdc. gov; Katherine M. Flegal, Margaret D. Carroll, Cynthia L. Ogden, and Lester R. Curtin, "Prevalence and Trends in Obesity among U.S. Adults, 1999–2008," *Journal of the American Medical Association*, Vol. 303, No. 3, January 20, 2010, pp. 235–241; Jay Bhattacharya, Kate Bundorf, Noemi Pace, and Neeraj Sood, "Does Health Insurance Make You Fat?" in Michael Grossman and Naci H. Mocan, eds., *Economic Aspects of Obesity*, Chicago: University of Chicago Press, 2011; and Tara Parker-Pope, "Less Active at Work, Americans Have Packed on Pounds," *New York Times*, May 25, 2011.

Your Turn: Test your understanding by doing related problems 1.7 and 1.8 on page 23 at the end of this chapter.

MyLab Economics Study Plan

Optimal Decisions Are Made at the Margin

Some decisions are "all or nothing." For instance, when an entrepreneur decides whether to open a new restaurant, she starts the new restaurant or she doesn't. When you decide whether to attend graduate school, you either enroll in graduate school or you don't. But rather than being all or nothing, most decisions in life involve doing a little more or a little less. If you are trying to decrease your spending and increase your saving, the decision is not really between saving all the money you earn or spending it all. Rather, many small choices are involved, such as whether to buy a caffè mocha at Starbucks every day or just once a week.

Economists use the word *marginal* to mean "extra" or "additional." Should you watch another hour of television or spend that hour studying? The *marginal benefit* (MB) of watching more television is the additional enjoyment you receive. The *marginal cost* (MC) is the reduction in your test score from having studied a little less. Should Apple produce an additional 300,000 iPhones? Firms receive *revenue* from selling goods. Apple's marginal benefit is the additional revenue it receives from selling 300,000 more iPhones. Apple's marginal cost is the additional cost—for wages, parts, and so forth—of producing 300,000 more iPhones. *Economists reason that the optimal decision is to continue any activity up to the point where the marginal benefit equals the marginal cost—that is, to the point where* MB = MC. Often we apply this rule without consciously thinking about it. Usually you will know whether the additional enjoyment from watching a television program is worth the additional cost you pay by not spending that hour studying without giving the decision a lot of thought. In business situations, however, firms often have to make careful calculations to determine, for example, whether the additional revenue received from increasing production is greater or less than the additional cost of the production. Economists refer to analysis that involves comparing marginal benefits and marginal costs as **marginal analysis**.

Marginal analysis Analysis that involves comparing marginal benefits and marginal costs.

In each chapter, you will see the feature *Solved Problem*. This feature will increase your understanding of the material by leading you through the steps of solving an applied economic problem. After reading the problem, test your understanding by doing the related problems that appear at the end of the chapter. You can also complete Solved Problems on www.pearson.com/mylab/economics and receive tutorial help.

MyLab Economics Concept Check

Solved Problem 1.1

MyLab Economics Interactive Animation

The Marginal Benefit and Marginal Cost of Speed Limits

In an opinion column in the *New York Times*, economists Sendhil Mullainathan of Harvard University and Richard Thaler of the University of Chicago noted, "We do not post 10-mile-per-hour speed limits on all highways, even though that would be safer." Why is a 10-mile-per-hour speed limit unlikely to be optimal? How could a state highway department use marginal analysis to decide whether to increase the speed limit on a highway from 55 to 65 miles per hour?

Solving the Problem

Step 1: **Review the chapter material.** This problem is about making decisions, so you may want to review the section "Optimal Decisions Are Made at the Margin," which appears on this page.

Step 2: **Discuss how we can decide what the optimal speed limit is and why it is unlikely to be 10 miles per hour.** The faster people drive, the more likely they are to have accidents because the less time they have to react to problems on the highway. In addition, the faster a car or truck is traveling, the more likely it is that an accident will cause damage to the vehicles involved and injuries to the vehicles' occupants. These are the main costs of increasing the speed limit. These costs will increase with each additional mile per hour the speed limit is increased. In other words, the marginal cost from increasing the speed limit is positive.

Increasing the speed limit has benefits as well. The higher the speed limit, the faster people and freight will reach their destinations. These benefits will increase with each additional mile per hour the speed limit is increased, so the marginal benefit from increasing the speed limit is positive. The optimal speed limit will be the one where the marginal cost of decreased safety equals the marginal benefit of faster travel. We know that we have reached the optimal speed limit when increasing the limit further would result in marginal cost being greater than marginal benefit.

A 10-mile-per-hour speed limit would result in very long travel times. So, we can reasonably conclude that a 10-mile-per-hour speed limit isn't optimal because the marginal benefit from increasing it is likely to be much greater than the marginal cost.

Step 3: **Explain how a state highway department could use marginal analysis to decide whether to increase the speed limit on a highway from 55 to 65 miles per hour.** Increasing the speed limit by 10 miles per hour will reduce travel times for people and freight—so there will be a marginal benefit—but will likely also increase the number of accidents and the damage from those accidents. The state highway department should try to estimate the dollar values of the marginal cost and marginal benefit of making the change. If the marginal benefit is greater than the marginal cost, the speed limit should be increased. Although it can be difficult to assign dollar values to the marginal benefit and marginal cost of an action, marginal analysis captures the steps you can follow to make optimal decisions in many situations.

Extra Credit: Suppose that the highway department calculates that increasing the speed limit will result in reduced travel time valued at $100 million. This information would not be enough to decide that the speed limit should be raised because it represents only the marginal benefit from the higher speed limit. If the dollar value of more severe accidents from greater speed turns out to be $125 million, then the marginal cost of increasing the speed limit would be greater than the marginal benefit, and the speed limit should not be raised. Marginal benefit and marginal cost both have to be considered in arriving at an optimal decision.

Source: Sendhil Mullainathan and Richard Thaler, "Waiting in Line for the Illusion of Security," *New York Times,* May 27, 2016.

MyLab Economics Study Plan   **Your Turn:** For more practice, do related problems 1.9 and 1.10 on page 23 at the end of this chapter.

1.2 The Economic Problem That Every Society Must Solve

LEARNING OBJECTIVE: Discuss how an economy answers these questions: What goods and services will be produced? How will the goods and services be produced? Who will receive the goods and services produced?

Because we live in a world of scarcity, any society faces the *economic problem* that it has only a limited amount of economic resources—such as workers, machines, and raw materials—and so can produce only a limited amount of goods and services. Therefore, every society faces **trade-offs**: Producing more of one good or service means producing less of another good or service. The best measure of the cost of producing a good or service is the value of what has to be given up to produce it. The **opportunity cost** of any activity—such as producing a good or service—is the highest-valued alternative that must be given up to engage in that activity. The concept of opportunity cost is very important in economics and applies to individuals, firms, and society as a whole. For instance, suppose that you earn a salary of $100,000 per year working as a manager for Ford. You decide to leave your job and open your own management consulting firm. In this case, the opportunity cost of the labor you supply to your own firm is the $100,000 you give up by not working for Ford, *even if you do not explicitly pay yourself a salary.* As in this example, opportunity costs often do not involve actual payments of money.

Trade-offs force society to make choices when answering three fundamental questions:

1. *What* goods and services will be produced?
2. *How* will the goods and services be produced?
3. *Who* will receive the goods and services produced?

Throughout this book, we will return to these questions many times. For now, we briefly introduce each question.

What Goods and Services Will Be Produced?

How will society decide whether to produce more economics textbooks or more smartphones? More daycare facilities or more football stadiums? Of course, "society" doesn't make decisions; only individuals make decisions. The answer to the question of what will be produced is determined by the choices that consumers and people working for firms or the government make. Every day, you help decide which goods and services firms will produce when you choose to buy an iPhone instead of a Samsung Galaxy or a caffè mocha rather than a chai tea. Similarly, managers at Apple must choose whether to devote the company's scarce resources to making more iPhones or more smartwatches. Members of Congress and the president must choose whether to spend more of the federal government's limited budget on breast cancer research or on repairing highways. In each case, consumers, managers of firms, and government policymakers face the problem of scarcity by trading off one good or service for another. And each choice made comes with an opportunity cost, measured by the value of the best alternative given up.   **MyLab Economics** Concept Check

How Will the Goods and Services Be Produced?

Firms choose how to produce the goods and services they sell. In many cases, firms face a trade-off between using more workers and using more machines. For example, a local service station has to choose whether to provide car repair services using more diagnostic computers and fewer auto mechanics or fewer diagnostic computers and more auto mechanics. Similarly, movie studios have to choose whether to produce animated films using highly skilled animators to draw them by hand or fewer animators and more computers. In deciding whether to move production offshore to China, firms may need to choose between a production method in the United States that uses fewer workers and more machines and a production method in China that uses more workers and fewer machines.   **MyLab Economics** Concept Check

Who Will Receive the Goods and Services Produced?

In the United States, who receives the goods and services produced depends largely on how income is distributed. The higher a person's income, the more goods and services he or she can buy. Often, people are willing to give up some of their income—and, therefore, some of their ability to purchase goods and services—by donating to charities to increase the incomes of poorer people. Americans donate more than $370 billion per year to charity, or an average donation of about $2,900 for each household in the country. An important policy question, however, is whether the

Trade-off The idea that, because of scarcity, producing more of one good or service means producing less of another good or service.

Opportunity cost The highest-valued alternative that must be given up to engage in an activity.

government should intervene to make the distribution of income more equal. Such intervention already occurs in the United States because people with higher incomes pay a larger fraction of their incomes in taxes and because the government makes payments to people with low incomes. There is disagreement over whether the current attempts to redistribute income are sufficient or whether there should be more or less redistribution. MyLab Economics Concept Check

Centrally Planned Economies versus Market Economies

Centrally planned economy An economy in which the government decides how economic resources will be allocated.

Market economy An economy in which the decisions of households and firms interacting in markets allocate economic resources.

To answer the three questions—what, how, and who—societies organize their economies in two main ways. A society can have a **centrally planned economy** in which the government decides how economic resources will be allocated. Or a society can have a **market economy** in which the decisions of households and firms interacting in markets allocate economic resources.

From 1917 to 1991, the most important centrally planned economy in the world was that of the Soviet Union, which was established when Vladimir Lenin and the Communist Party staged a revolution and took control of the Russian Empire. In the Soviet Union, the government decided what goods to produce, how the goods would be produced, and who would receive the goods. Government employees managed factories and stores. The objective of these managers was to follow the government's orders rather than to satisfy the wants of consumers. Centrally planned economies like that of the Soviet Union have not been successful in producing low-cost, high-quality goods and services. As a result, the standard of living of the average person in a centrally planned economy tends to be low. All centrally planned economies have also been political dictatorships. Dissatisfaction with low living standards and political repression finally led to the collapse of the Soviet Union in 1991. Today, only North Korea still has a completely centrally planned economy.

All high-income democracies, including the United States, Canada, Japan, and the countries of Western Europe, have market economies. Market economies rely primarily on privately owned firms to produce goods and services and to decide how to produce them. Markets, rather than the government, determine who receives the goods and services produced. In a market economy, firms must produce goods and services that meet the wants of consumers, or the firms will go out of business. In that sense, it is ultimately consumers who decide what goods and services will be produced. Because firms in a market economy compete to offer the highest-quality products at the lowest price, they are under pressure to use the lowest-cost methods of production. For example, as we saw in the chapter opener, Ford moved some production to Mexico to lower its production costs in the face of competition from both foreign and domestic car firms.

In a market economy, the income of an individual is determined by the payments he receives for what he or she has to sell. If you become a civil engineer, and firms are willing to pay a salary of $85,000 per year for someone with your training and skills, you will have this amount of income to purchase goods and services. If you also buy a house that you rent out, your income will be even higher. One of the attractive features of markets is that they reward hard work. Generally, the more extensive the training you have received and the longer the hours you work, the higher your income will be. Of course, luck—both good and bad—also plays a role here. Someone might have a high income because she won the state lottery, while someone else might have a low income because he has severe medical problems. We can conclude that market economies respond to the question "Who receives the goods and services produced?" with the answer "Those who are most willing and able to buy them." MyLab Economics Concept Check

The Modern "Mixed" Economy

In the 1800s and early 1900s, the U.S. government engaged in relatively little regulation of markets for goods and services. Beginning in the mid-1900s, government intervention in the economy dramatically increased in the United States and other market economies. This increase was primarily caused by the high rates of unemployment and business bankruptcies during the Great Depression of the 1930s. Some government intervention was also intended to raise the incomes of the elderly, the sick, and people with limited skills. For example, in the 1930s, Congress established the *Social Security system*, which provides government payments to retired and disabled workers, and enacted *minimum wage* legislation, which sets a floor on the wages employers can pay workers in many occupations. In more recent years, government intervention in the economy has also expanded to meet goals such as protecting the environment, promoting civil rights, and providing medical care to low-income and elderly people.

Some economists argue that the extent of government intervention makes it no longer accurate to refer to the economies of the United States, Canada, Japan, and Western Europe as pure market economies. Instead, they should be called *mixed economies*. A **mixed economy** is still primarily a market economy because most economic decisions result from the interaction of buyers and sellers in markets. However, the government plays a significant role in the allocation of resources. As we will see in later chapters, economists continue to debate the role government should play in a market economy.

Mixed economy An economy in which most economic decisions result from the interaction of buyers and sellers in markets but in which the government plays a significant role in the allocation of resources.

One of the most important developments in the international economy in recent years has been the movement of China from being a centrally planned economy to being a mixed economy. The Chinese economy suffered decades of economic stagnation following the takeover of the government in 1949 by Mao Zedong and the Communist Party. Although China remains a political dictatorship, the production of most goods and services is now determined in the market rather than by the government. The result has been rapid economic growth that has lifted more than a billion people in China out of poverty.   MyLab Economics Concept Check

Efficiency and Equity

Market economies tend to be more efficient than centrally planned economies. There are two types of efficiency. **Productive efficiency** occurs when a good or service is produced at the lowest possible cost. **Allocative efficiency** occurs when production is in accordance with consumer preferences. Markets tend to be efficient because they promote competition and facilitate voluntary exchange. With **voluntary exchange**, both the buyer and the seller of a product are made better off by the transaction. We know that they are both made better off because, otherwise, the buyer would not have agreed to buy the product or the seller would not have agreed to sell it. Productive efficiency is achieved when competition among firms forces them to produce goods and services at the lowest cost. Allocative efficiency is achieved when the combination of competition among firms and voluntary exchange between firms and consumers results in firms producing the mix of goods and services that consumers prefer the most. Competition will result in firms continuing to produce and sell goods and services as long as the additional benefit to consumers is greater than the additional cost of production. In this way, the mix of goods and services produced will match consumer preferences.

Productive efficiency A situation in which a good or service is produced at the lowest possible cost.

Allocative efficiency A state of the economy in which production is in accordance with consumer preferences; in particular, every good or service is produced up to the point where the last unit provides a marginal benefit to society equal to the marginal cost of producing it.

Voluntary exchange A situation that occurs in markets when both the buyer and the seller of a product are made better off by the transaction.

Although markets promote efficiency, they don't guarantee it. Inefficiency can arise from various sources. For instance, it may take some time for firms to learn how to efficiently produce a good or service. When smartphones were introduced, firms did not instantly achieve productive efficiency because it took time to discover the lowest-cost method of producing this good. As we will discuss in later chapters, inefficiency can also arise if governments interfere with voluntary exchange in markets. For example, many governments limit the imports of some goods from foreign countries. This limitation reduces efficiency by keeping goods from being produced at the lowest cost, a point we discuss further in the *Apply the Concept* on page 15. The production of some goods damages the environment. In this case, government intervention can increase efficiency because without such intervention, firms may ignore the costs of environmental damage and thereby fail to produce the goods at the lowest possible cost.

Equity The fair distribution of economic benefits.

Not everyone will consider a particular outcome to be desirable, even if the outcome is economically efficient. Many people prefer economic outcomes that they consider fair or equitable, even if those outcomes are less efficient. **Equity** is harder to define than efficiency because there isn't an agreed-upon definition of fairness. For some people, equity means a more equal distribution of economic benefits than would result from an emphasis on efficiency alone. For example, some people support raising taxes on people with higher incomes to provide the funds for programs that aid the poor. Although governments may increase equity by reducing the incomes of high-income people and increasing the incomes of the poor, these policies may reduce efficiency. People have less incentive to open new businesses, work hard, and save if the government takes a significant amount of the income they earn from working or saving. The result is that fewer goods and services are produced, and less saving takes place. As this example illustrates, *there is often a trade-off between efficiency and equity.* Government policymakers frequently confront this trade-off.

MyLab Economics Study Plan

MyLab Economics Concept Check

1.3 Economic Models

LEARNING OBJECTIVE: Explain how economists use models to analyze economic events and government policies.

As mentioned at the start of the chapter, economic models are simplified versions of reality. Many professions rely on models: An engineer may use a computer model of a bridge to help test whether it will withstand high winds, or a biologist may make a physical model of a nucleic acid to better understand its properties. Economists rely on economic models, or theories, to analyze real-world issues ranging from the effects of tariffs on the prices of imported goods to the most efficient policies for reducing pollution. (This book uses the words *model* and *theory* interchangeably.) One purpose of economic models is to make economic ideas sufficiently explicit and concrete so that individuals, firms, or the government can use them to make decisions. For example, we will see in Chapter 3 that the model of demand and supply is a simplified version of how the prices of products are determined by the interactions among buyers and sellers in markets.

Economists use economic models to answer questions such as "How many people will be employed in manufacturing in 2024?" Economists at the U.S. Bureau of Labor Statistics (BLS) build models that allow them to forecast future employment in different occupations. The BLS models provide estimates of future demand for U.S. manufacturing production and estimates of how many employees manufacturing firms will require to produce that level of output. As mentioned at the beginning of the chapter, the BLS forecasts that employment in manufacturing will decline significantly by 2024.

Sometimes economists use an existing model to analyze a real-world problem or issue, but in other cases, they have to develop a new model. To develop a model, economists generally follow these steps:

1. Decide on the assumptions to use.
2. Formulate a testable hypothesis.
3. Use economic data to test the hypothesis.
4. Revise the model if it fails to explain the economic data well.
5. Retain the revised model to help answer similar economic questions in the future.

The Role of Assumptions in Economic Models

Any model is based on assumptions because models have to be simplified to be useful. Economic models make *behavioral assumptions* about the motives of consumers and firms. Economists assume that consumers will buy the goods and services that will maximize their well-being or their satisfaction. Similarly, economists assume that firms act to maximize their profits. These assumptions are simplifications because they do not describe the motives of every consumer and every firm. How can we know whether the assumptions in a model are too simplified or too limiting? We can determine the usefulness of assumptions by forming hypotheses based on the assumptions and then testing the hypotheses using real-world information.

MyLab Economics Concept Check

Forming and Testing Hypotheses in Economic Models

An **economic variable** is something measurable that can have different values, such as the number of people employed in manufacturing. In an economic model, a hypothesis is a statement about an economic variable that may be either correct or incorrect. An example of a hypothesis in an economic model is the statement that increased use of industrial robots and information technology in U.S. factories has resulted in a decline in manufacturing employment. The hypothesis may be correct if the main effect of industrial robots has been to replace assembly line workers, thereby reducing employment. Or the hypothesis may be incorrect if the use of robots and other information technology has increased firms' demand for software programmers and other technology workers, thereby increasing employment. An economic hypothesis is usually about a *causal relationship*; in this case, the hypothesis states that increased use of robots and information technology causes, or leads to, lower employment in manufacturing.

Before we can accept a hypothesis, we have to test it by analyzing statistics on the relevant economic variables. In our example, we would gather statistics on how the use of industrial robots and information technology in manufacturing has changed over time, on employment in manufacturing, and perhaps on other variables. Testing a hypothesis can be tricky. For example, showing that employment in manufacturing declined at the same time that use of robots increased would not be enough to demonstrate that the increased use of robots *caused* the decline in employment. Just because two things are correlated—that is, they happen at the same time—does not mean that one caused the other. For example, suppose that at the same time that use of robots in U.S. manufacturing was increasing, U.S. manufacturing firms faced declining sales due to increased competition from foreign firms. In that case, the declining sales, rather than the increased use of robots, may explain the decrease in U.S. manufacturing employment. Over a period of time, many economic variables change, which complicates the testing of hypotheses. In fact, when economists disagree about a hypothesis, it is often because of disagreements over interpreting the statistical analysis used to test the hypothesis.

Note that hypotheses must be statements that could, in principle, turn out to be incorrect. Statements such as "Increasing employment in manufacturing is good" or "Increasing employment in manufacturing is bad" are value judgments rather than hypotheses because it is not possible to disprove them.

Economists accept and use an economic model if it leads to hypotheses that are confirmed by statistical analysis. In many cases, the acceptance is tentative, however, pending the gathering of new data or further statistical analysis. In fact, economists often refer to a hypothesis having been "not rejected" rather than having been "accepted" by statistical analysis. But what if statistical analysis clearly rejects a hypothesis? For example, what if a model leads to a hypothesis that increased use of industrial robots will cause a decline in manufacturing employment, but the data reject this hypothesis? In this case, the model should be reconsidered. It may be that an assumption used in the model was too simplified or too limiting. For example, perhaps the model ignored the fact that the mix of products being manufactured in the United States was changing. For example, perhaps the assembly of electric cars requires more workers than does the assembly of gasoline-powered cars. Or perhaps the model did not include the effect of tariffs on the demand for U.S. manufactured goods because such tariffs had typically been low. If tariffs sharply increase, the model may not be able to accurately estimate the relationship between changes in the use of industrial robots and changes in employment.

As we saw at the beginning of the chapter, the U.S. Bureau of Labor Statistics (BLS) has forecast that total employment in U.S. manufacturing will decline from 12.3 million in December 2016 to 11.4 million in 2024. The BLS periodically analyzes the accuracy of its projections. It has had difficulty accurately projecting manufacturing employment. For example, in 2000, the BLS projected that in 2010, 19,047,000 people would be employed in manufacturing. In fact, in 2010, only 11,529,000 people were employed in manufacturing. The BLS concluded that this large error was the result of its model

Economic variable Something measurable that can have different values, such as the number of people employed in manufacturing.

failing to account for the extent to which U.S. firms would move manufacturing operations overseas, how quickly firms would improve their ability to produce the same output with fewer works, and the lasting effects of the severe 2007–2009 recession. Analyzing its errors helps the BLS to improve its models and employment projections.

The process of developing models, testing hypotheses, and revising models occurs not just in economics but also in disciplines such as physics, chemistry, and biology. This process is often called the *scientific method*. Economics is a *social science* because it applies the scientific method to the study of the interactions among individuals.   MyLab Economics Concept Check

Positive and Normative Analysis

Positive analysis Analysis concerned with what is.

Normative analysis Analysis concerned with what ought to be.

Throughout this book, as we build economic models and use them to answer questions, bear in mind the following important distinction: **Positive analysis** is concerned with *what is*, and **normative analysis** is concerned with *what ought to be*. Economics is about positive analysis, which measures the costs and benefits of different courses of action.

We can use the federal government's minimum wage law to compare positive and normative analysis. In 2017, under this law, it was illegal for an employer to hire a worker at a wage less than $7.25 per hour. (Some states and cities had enacted higher minimum wages.) Without the minimum wage law, some firms and workers would voluntarily agree to a lower wage. Because of the minimum wage law, some workers have difficulty finding jobs, and some firms end up paying more for labor than they otherwise would have. A positive analysis of the federal minimum wage law uses an economic model to estimate how many workers have lost their jobs because of the law, its effect on the costs and profits of businesses, and the gains to workers receiving the minimum wage. After economists complete this positive analysis, the decision as to whether the minimum wage law is a good or a bad idea is a normative one and depends on how people evaluate the trade-off involved. Supporters of the law believe that the losses to employers and workers who are unemployed as a result of the law are more than offset by the gains to workers who receive higher wages than they would without the law. Opponents of the law believe the losses are greater than the gains. The assessment by any individual depends, in part, on that person's values and political views. The positive analysis an economist provides would play a role in the decision but can't by itself decide the issue one way or the other.

In each chapter, you will see a *Don't Let This Happen to You* box like the one below. These boxes alert you to common pitfalls in thinking about economic ideas. After reading this box, test your understanding by working the related problem or problems at the end of the chapter.   MyLab Economics Concept Check

Don't Let This Happen to You

Don't Confuse Positive Analysis with Normative Analysis

"Economic analysis has shown that the minimum wage law is a bad idea because it causes unemployment." Is this statement accurate? As of 2017, the federal minimum wage law prevents employers from hiring workers at a wage of less than $7.25 per hour. This wage is higher than some employers are willing to pay some workers. If there were no minimum wage law, some workers who currently cannot find any firm willing to hire them at $7.25 per hour would be able to find employment at a lower wage. Therefore, positive economic analysis indicates that the minimum wage law causes unemployment. (In Chapter 4, we'll explore why economists disagree about *how much* unemployment the minimum wage law causes.) But some workers who

have jobs benefit from the minimum wage law because they are paid a higher wage than they otherwise would be. In other words, the minimum wage law creates both losers—the workers who become unemployed and the firms that have to pay higher wages—and winners—the workers who receive higher wages.

Should we value the gains to the winners more than we value the losses to the losers? The answer involves normative analysis. Positive economic analysis can show the consequences of a particular policy, but it cannot tell us whether the policy is "good" or "bad." So, the statement at the beginning of this box is inaccurate.

MyLab Economics Study Plan

Your Turn: Test your understanding by doing related problems 3.6 and 3.7 on page 25 at the end of this chapter.

Economics as a Social Science

Because economics studies the actions of individuals, it is a social science. Economics is therefore similar to other social science disciplines, such as psychology, political science, and sociology. Economics differs from other social sciences because it puts more emphasis on how the decisions of individuals explain outcomes such as the prices firms charge or the policies governments enact. Economics considers individual decision making in every context, not just in the context of business. Economists have studied issues such as why people have difficulty losing weight or attaining other goals, why people sometimes ignore relevant information when making decisions, and how couples decide to divide up household chores. Government policymakers have also increasingly relied on economic analysis when evaluating laws or regulations. As we will see throughout this book, economists have played an important role in influencing government policies in areas such as the environment, health care, and efforts to reduce poverty.   MyLab Economics Concept Check

● Apply the Concept   MyLab Economics Video

What Can Economics Contribute to the Debate over Tariffs?

What effect would proposed tariffs on imports of goods from Mexico and other countries have on the U.S. economy? Governments typically impose tariffs to raise revenue or to discourage imports by raising the selling prices of imported goods. If imports of goods decline, production and employment at domestic firms that compete with imports may increase. For example, a tariff on imports of cars assembled in Mexico would raise their prices and lead U.S. consumers to buy more cars assembled in the United States. We can create a preliminary list of potential winners and losers in a country that imposes a tariff: The government gains from collecting the tariff revenue, and domestic firms and their workers gain from the higher prices of competing imported goods. Consumers lose because they pay higher prices for goods on which the tariff has been enacted. If some of the imported goods are used as inputs or are sold by domestic firms—for example, Walmart may sell imported tires on which Congress has enacted a tariff—those firms will also lose from the tariff.

Erika Skogg/National Geographic/Getty images

Because of its fertile soil and warm climate, Colombia has a comparative advantage in coffee bean production relative to the United States.

Economics can provide valuable information to policymakers and the general public as they consider actions such as implementing tariffs. As we will discuss further in Chapters 2 and 9, economic analysis shows that trade between countries occurs primarily on the basis of comparative advantage. A country has a comparative advantage if it can produce a good at a lower opportunity cost than competitors. For example, due to the climate and soil in Colombia, coffee can be grown there without requiring the transfer of significant resources from producing other goods and services—so the opportunity cost of producing coffee in Colombia is low. The United States is not well suited for producing coffee, so the opportunity cost of producing coffee in the United States is very high. We can conclude that Colombia has a comparative advantage relative to the United States in producing coffee. Imposing a tariff on imports to the United States of Colombian coffee would reduce economic efficiency by shifting production of coffee from Colombia, where it can be grown at a low cost, to the United States, where it can only be grown at a high cost.

Economists can use models to estimate the dollar amounts gained by the winners from the imposition of a tariff, the amount lost by the losers, and the size of the loss of economic efficiency. Economic analysis of tariffs typically shows that the dollar losses from the government imposing a tariff are larger than the dollar gains, so the tariff causes a net loss for the country as a whole.

Although economic analysis can contribute to the debate over policy proposals by measuring their likely effects, it cannot by itself decide whether a proposal should be enacted. Policymakers and a majority of the general public may decide to enact a tariff because they place a higher value on the gains to some groups—workers and firms struggling to compete against imported goods—than on the losses to other groups—consumers as a whole. In other words, policymakers and the general public would be making a normative judgment in favor of tariffs. Ultimately policymakers and the general public are responsible for weighing trade-offs and deciding whether a proposal should be enacted.

Sources: John D. Stoll, "Donald Trump, GM, Ford and the Made-in-Mexico Car," *Wall Street Journal*, January 3, 2017; Mary Anastasia O'Grady, "Texas and the Real Forgotten Man," *Wall Street Journal*, February 12, 2017; and David Welch and David Merrill, "Why Trump Tariffs on Mexican Cars Probably Won't Stop Job Flight," bloomberg.com, January 4, 2017.

MyLab Economics Study Plan

Your Turn: Test your understanding by doing related problem 3.8 on page 25 at the end of this chapter.

Microeconomics and Macroeconomics

1.4

LEARNING OBJECTIVE: Distinguish between microeconomics and macroeconomics.

Microeconomics The study of how households and firms make choices, how they interact in markets, and how the government attempts to influence their choices.

Macroeconomics The study of the economy as a whole, including topics such as inflation, unemployment, and economic growth.

Economic models can be used to analyze decision making in many areas. We group some of these areas together as *microeconomics* and others as *macroeconomics*. **Microeconomics** is the study of how households and firms make choices, how they interact in markets, and how the government attempts to influence their choices. **Macroeconomics** is the study of the economy as a whole, including topics such as inflation, unemployment, and economic growth. Table 1.1 gives examples of microeconomic and macroeconomic issues.

The division between microeconomics and macroeconomics is not a bright line. Many economic situations have *both* a microeconomic aspect and a macroeconomic aspect. For example, the level of total investment by firms in new machinery and equipment helps to determine how rapidly the economy grows—which is a macroeconomic issue. But to understand how much new machinery and equipment firms decide to purchase, we have to analyze the incentives individual firms face—which is a microeconomic issue.

MyLab Economics Study Plan

MyLab Economics Concept Check

Table 1.1

Issues in Microeconomics and Macroeconomics

Examples of Microeconomic Issues	Examples of Macroeconomic Issues
• How consumers react to changes in product prices • How firms decide what prices to charge for the products they sell • Which government policy would most efficiently reduce obesity • The costs and benefits of approving the sale of a new prescription drug • The most efficient way to reduce air pollution	• Why economies experience periods of recession and increasing unemployment • Why, over the long run, some economies have grown much faster than others • What determines the inflation rate • What determines the value of the U.S. dollar in exchange for other currencies • Whether government intervention can reduce the severity of recessions

Economic Skills and Economics as a Career

1.5

LEARNING OBJECTIVE: Describe economics as a career and the key skills you can gain from studying economics.

How do economists do what they do? The following analogy may be helpful: When people are thinking of buying a house, they may hire a structural engineer as a consultant to examine the house and prepare a report. The engineer's report is likely to both *describe* any problems with the house—like cracks in the foundation—and *advise* the potential buyer how to fix the problems and the likely cost.

You have seen that economics is about making choices. Economists spend much of their time describing how individuals, businesses, and governments make choices and analyzing the results of the choices. Then, like a structural engineer advising a homeowner how to fix a leaky basement, economists advise on how better decisions can be made.

In this book, we will explore economic principles that you will find very useful in understanding what is happening in the world of economics and business and in your everyday life. Individuals can use economic principles to improve how they make important decisions, such as what career to pursue, what financial investment to make, or whether to lease or buy a car. Managers in businesses can also use economic principles to improve how they make important decisions, such as what prices to charge for their products, whether to begin selling their products in a foreign market, or whether to invest in new software. Government policymakers use economic principles to make decisions, such as whether to raise taxes on cigarettes to discourage teenage smoking, whether to raise interest rates to reduce the threat of inflation, or whether to allocate additional funds to research on cancer or to research on heart disease.

Many businesses, government agencies, and nonprofit organizations—including hospitals, museums, and charities—hire economists. Colleges and universities also hire economists to teach and to carry out academic research on business, the economy, and economic policy.

The Bureau of Labor Statistics (www.bls.gov/ooh/Life-Physical-and-Social-Science/Economists.htm#tab-2) lists activities economists often perform while pursuing careers in these organizations:

- An economist working for Ford Motor Company may forecast the demand for electric cars over the next 10 years.
- An economist working for Goldman Sachs, a Wall Street investment firm, may use economic models to forecast future values of interest rates.
- An economist working for McDonald's may assess whether the firm should open additional restaurants in China.
- An economist working for the U.S. Federal Trade Commission may gather and analyze data relevant to deciding whether two firms should be allowed to reduce competition in a market by merging to form a combined firm, as when chemical companies Dow Chemical and DuPont proposed merging in 2017.
- An economist working for one of the regional Federal Reserve Banks may forecast trends in employment and production in that region.
- A journalist who majored in economics and is working for the *Wall Street Journal* may report on the Federal Reserve, interpreting monetary policy for the paper's readers.
- An economist working for the World Bank, an international economic organization with the mission of reducing poverty and increasing economic growth, might write a report analyzing the effectiveness of a development program in a low-income country.

A first step for many students in deciding whether to pursue a career in economics is to seek a summer internship with a firm or an agency that employs economists.

Many of the choices we discuss in this book will be those that business firms make. Economics has developed a set of tools designed specifically to help business firms make better decisions. It is not too surprising that more chief executive officers of Fortune 500 firms majored in economics than in any other subject. But many students who do not pursue a career in economics can still benefit from the skills they learn by taking economics classes.   **MyLab Economics** Concept Check   **MyLab Economics** Study Plan

1.6   A Preview of Important Economic Terms

LEARNING OBJECTIVE: Define important economic terms.

In the following chapters, you will encounter certain important terms again and again. Becoming familiar with these terms is a necessary step in learning economics. Here we provide a brief introduction to some of these terms. We will discuss them all in greater depth in later chapters:

- ***Firm, company, or business.*** A *firm* is an organization that produces a good or service. Most firms produce goods or services to earn a profit, but there are also nonprofit firms, such as universities and some hospitals. Economists use the terms *firm*, *company*, and *business* interchangeably.

- **Entrepreneur.** An *entrepreneur* is someone who operates a business. In a market system, entrepreneurs decide what goods and services to produce and how to produce them. An entrepreneur starting a new business puts his or her own funds at risk. If an entrepreneur is wrong about what consumers want or about the best way to produce goods and services, his or her funds can be lost. Losing money in a failed business is not unusual: In the United States, about half of new businesses fail within four years. Without entrepreneurs willing to assume the risk of starting and operating businesses, economic progress would be impossible in a market system.

- **Innovation.** There is a distinction between an *invention* and an *innovation*. An *invention* is a new good or a new process for making a good. An *innovation* is the practical application of an invention. (*Innovation* may also be used more broadly to refer to any significant improvement in a good or in the means of producing a good.) Much time often passes between the appearance of a new idea and its development for widespread use. For example, the Wright brothers first achieved self-propelled flight at Kitty Hawk, North Carolina, in 1903, but the Wright brothers' plane was very crude, and it wasn't until the introduction of the DC-3 by Douglas Aircraft in 1936 that regularly scheduled intercity airline flights became common in the United States. Similarly, the first digital electronic computer—the ENIAC—was developed in 1945, but the first IBM personal computer was not introduced until 1981, and widespread use of computers did not have a significant effect on the productivity of U.S. businesses until the 1990s.

- **Technology.** A firm's *technology* is the processes it uses to produce goods and services. In the economic sense, a firm's technology depends on many factors, such as the skill of its managers, the training of its workers, and the speed and efficiency of its machinery and equipment.

- **Goods.** *Goods* are tangible merchandise, such as books, computers, or Blu-ray players.

- **Services.** *Services* are activities performed for others, such as providing haircuts or investment advice.

- **Revenue.** A firm's *revenue* is the total amount received for selling a good or service. We calculate it by multiplying the price per unit by the number of units sold.

- **Profit.** A firm's *profit* is the difference between its revenue and its costs. Economists distinguish between *accounting profit* and *economic profit*. In calculating accounting profit, we exclude the costs of some economic resources that the firm does not pay for explicitly. In calculating economic profit, we include the opportunity costs of all resources used by the firm. When we refer to *profit* in this book, we mean economic profit. It is important not to confuse *profit* with *revenue*.

- **Household.** A *household* consists of all persons occupying a home. Households are suppliers of factors of production—particularly labor—used by firms to make goods and services. Households also demand goods and services produced by firms and governments.

- **Factors of production, economic resources, or inputs.** Firms use *factors of production* to produce goods and services. The main factors of production are labor, capital, natural resources—including land—and entrepreneurial ability. Households earn income by supplying the factors of production to firms. Economists use the terms *factors of production*, *economic resources*, and *inputs* interchangeably.

- **Capital.** In everyday speech, the word *capital* can refer to *financial capital* or to *physical capital*. Financial capital includes stocks and bonds issued by firms, bank accounts, and holdings of money. In economics, though, *capital* refers to physical capital, which includes manufactured goods that are used to produce other goods and services. Examples of physical capital are computers, factory buildings, machine tools, warehouses, and trucks. The total amount of physical capital available in a country is called its *capital stock*.

- **Human capital.** *Human capital* refers to the accumulated training and skills that workers possess. For example, college-educated workers generally have more skills and are more productive than workers who have only high school degrees; therefore, college-educated workers have more human capital.   **MyLab Economics** Concept Check   **MyLab Economics** Study Plan

Continued from page 3

Economics in Your Life & Career

Should You Consider a Career in Manufacturing?

At the beginning of this chapter, we posed the question "What is the basis for the BLS's forecast that manufacturing employment will decline by 2024, and how reliable is this forecast?" As we saw in this chapter, the BLS uses economic models to forecast future employment in U.S. manufacturing. In recent years, the BLS has had difficulty accurately forecasting manufacturing employment. For example, in 2000, the BLS forecast that manufacturing employment would increase over the following 10 years, when in fact it declined substantially. The BLS analyzes errors like these in attempting to improve its forecasts. So, it is likely that the BLS's forecasts will become more accurate over time, but it would be a mistake to expect the forecasts to be exact.

Conclusion

Economics is a group of useful ideas about how individuals make choices given their scarce resources. Economists have put these ideas into practice by developing economic models. Consumers, business managers, and government policymakers use these models every day to help make choices. In this book, we explore many key economic models and give examples of how to apply them in the real world.

Reading the news is an important part of understanding the current business climate and learning how to apply economic concepts to a variety of real-world events. At the end of each of the first four chapters, you will see a two-page feature titled *An Inside Look*. This feature consists of an excerpt from an article that relates to the company or economic issue introduced at the start of the chapter and also to the concepts discussed in the chapter. A summary and an analysis with a supporting table or graph highlight the key economic points of the article. Read the following *An Inside Look* for a discussion of how likely it is that significant numbers of manufacturing jobs will return to the United States from overseas. Test your understanding by answering the *Thinking Critically* questions.

Is Manufacturing Returning to the United States?

24/7 WALL ST.

Manufacturers Bringing the Most Jobs Back to America

The loss of American manufacturing jobs to foreign labor has been a central theme of several presidential candidates' campaigns. However, the trend of offshoring may be slowing, according to one organization.

According to non-profit advocacy group the Reshoring Initiative, offshoring resulted in a net loss of approximately 220,000 manufacturing jobs from 2000 to 2003. However, according to the group, the country added roughly as many jobs due to foreign investment and reshoring as it lost to offshoring last year. Some of the largest U.S.-based companies, likely for both public relations and practical reasons, have begun building factories domestically for operations that would likely have gone overseas a few years ago.

Offshoring, or shifting production from U.S. plants to foreign facilities, is a relatively recent phenomenon that has taken a considerable toll on the U.S. economy. In an interview with 24/7 Wall St., Harry Moser, founder and president of the Reshoring Initiative, explained that recent developments have made the prospect of manufacturing domestically much more feasible. Moser cited economic troubles and rising wages in China as one of the primary drivers of this recent trend.

Indeed, lower labor costs and fewer regulations in countries such as China have created an incentive for U.S. companies to relocate production there. Consequently, U.S. manufacturing has taken a major hit.

A study by the Economic Policy Institute found that the U.S. lost roughly 2.4 million manufacturing jobs to China alone from 2001 to 2013.

However, the same market forces that have pushed American jobs overseas are now bringing some of those jobs back. Recently, labor costs in places such as China have been rising, and when paired with high international shipping costs, offshore production presents less of a discount than it once did. Recently, General Electric shifted production of a water heater from China to a plant in Louisville, Kentucky. The move brought hundreds of manufacturing and engineering jobs back to the U.S.

While the reshoring phenomenon is primarily a byproduct of expensive labor abroad and high shipping costs, bringing manufacturing jobs back to the United States is often beneficial to a company's image. For example, Walmart contracted General Electric to manufacture high efficiency light bulbs in its plants in Ohio and Illinois as a part of Walmart's brand-boosting Made in USA initiative. Similarly, Farouk Systems, Inc. cites image as a primary reason for reshoring jobs. Along with Walmart and General Electric, Farouk Systems ranks among the companies bringing the most jobs back from overseas.

A variety of other logistical factors are also making reshoring more practical for businesses. In the era of Amazon, in which consumers expect quick turnaround on products, it can be more practical for companies to manufacture products in-country to have the product ready for customers faster and avoid shipping expenses. Moser further explained that reshoring can often improve the quality of the manufacturing product. "Many have done it because of the consumer preference for made in America products," Moser added.

The extent to which these factory openings are truly a sign of an American manufacturing renaissance or merely a pause from the ongoing departure of the industry from U.S. shores is still unclear. One certainty is that it will take more than a few thousand jobs to reverse the trend of decades of offshoring and heavy reliance on foreign imports. . . . It is perhaps much easier to make the argument that the service sector is experiencing a true revival. While several years ago it was common practice for American companies to offshore customer support call center jobs, many American companies and customer service contractors are adding or plan to add jobs in the U.S. As of last year, there were roughly five million Americans employed in some 66,000 call centers across the country. . . .

Key Points in the Article

Over the past few decades, many U.S. manufacturing companies relocated production overseas, a practice known as offshoring. The firms were responding to economic incentives such as lower labor costs and limited government regulations. Recently, however, some of these manufacturing jobs have been returning to the United States, a practice known as reshoring. Again, firms have been responding to economic incentives, including rising foreign wages, high international shipping costs, improved product quality in U.S. plants, and faster delivery times. According to the advocacy group the Reshoring Initiative, the United States added about as many jobs due to reshoring and foreign investment as it lost to offshoring in 2015, and some of the largest U.S.-based companies are now building domestic manufacturing facilities that would have likely been built in foreign countries only a few years ago.

Analyzing the News

Ⓐ The table below lists the eight U.S. companies that returned the most manufacturing jobs to the United States through reshoring from 2011 to 2016. These companies have shifted production from foreign factories to new or expanded factories in the United States for a variety of reasons,

including rising foreign labor costs. One key economic idea is that people are rational, and economists assume that consumers and firms use all available information as they act to achieve their goals. Economists would therefore conclude that managers at these reshoring companies are acting rationally in using all available information in making the decision to move manufacturing back to the United States.

Ⓑ Another key economic idea is that people respond to economic incentives. The Economic Policy Institute conducted a study that showed that approximately 2.4 million U.S. manufacturing jobs were offshored to China from 2001 to 2013, primarily due to lower wages and fewer regulations in that country. These factors created economic incentives for managers at U.S. manufacturing companies to move production to China in order to produce goods at a lower cost than would be possible in the United States. Recently, however, labor costs in China and some other countries have been rising, as has the cost to ship internationally. These cost increases have reduced the economic incentive to produce goods overseas and resulted in some manufacturing jobs returning to the United States.

Ⓒ Other reasons some manufacturing jobs are returning to the United States include a growing expectation by consumers that their orders will be delivered

quickly and an increasing preference by U.S. consumers for products made in the United States. These reasons also reflect the key economic ideas that people are rational and that they respond to economic incentives. When interacting in markets, sellers want to supply the goods that buyers desire. If buyers have increased their preference for domestically produced goods and want their orders to be delivered quickly, firms are acting rationally when they reshore manufacturing jobs to the United States.

Thinking Critically

1. During the 2016 presidential campaign, President Trump proposed enacting a 45 percent tariff on imports from China. How might a tariff of this magnitude provide an economic incentive for companies like General Electric to return additional manufacturing jobs from China to the United States through reshoring?

2. Evaluate the following statement in terms of positive analysis and normative analysis: "The table shows that General Motors brought back more than 2,300 manufacturing jobs to the United States through reshoring from Canada and Mexico from 2011 to 2016. Reshoring is a good idea because it increases employment in the United States."

Manufacturers Bringing the Most Jobs Back to the United States, 2011–2016

Company	Total Jobs Reshored (estimate)	Countries from Which Jobs Were Reshored	Industry
Ford	3,200	Mexico, Spain	Transportation equipment
Boeing	2,700	Not available	Transportation equipment
General Electric	2,656	China, Mexico	Electrical equipment and appliances
General Motors	2,345	Mexico, Canada	Transportation equipment
Caterpillar	2,100	Japan, Mexico	Machinery
Flextronics (Apple)	1,700	Not available	Computers
Farouk Systems	1,200	China	Electronic appliances
Mars	1,000	Not available	Food

Source: The Reshoring Initiative

Key Terms

1.1 Three Key Economic Ideas, pages 4–8

LEARNING OBJECTIVE: Explain these three key economic ideas: People are rational, people respond to economic incentives, and optimal decisions are made at the margin.

MyLab Economics Visit www.pearson.com/mylab/economics to complete these exercises online and get instant feedback.

Summary

Economics is the study of the choices consumers, business managers, and government officials make to attain their goals, given their scarce resources. We must make choices because of **scarcity**, which means that although our wants are unlimited, the resources available to fulfill those wants are limited. A **market** is a group of buyers and sellers who trade a good or service. Economists assume that people are rational in the sense that consumers and firms use all available information as they take actions intended to achieve their goals. Rational individuals weigh the benefits and costs of each action and choose an action only if the benefits outweigh the costs. Although people act from a variety of motives, ample evidence indicates that they respond to economic incentives. Economists use the word **marginal** to mean extra or additional. The optimal decision is to continue any activity up to the point where the marginal benefit equals the marginal cost.

Review Questions

1.1 Briefly discuss the meaning of each of the following economic ideas: People are rational, people respond to economic incentives, and optimal decisions are made at the margin.

1.2 What is scarcity? Why is scarcity central to the study of economics?

Problems and Applications

1.3 Discuss whether you agree with the following statement: "The problem with economics is that it assumes that consumers and firms always make the correct decisions. But we know that everyone makes mistakes."

1.4 According to the FBI Bank Crime Statistics, there were more than 4,000 bank robberies in the United States in 2015, an increase of 3.9 percent over 2014. The FBI claims that banks have made themselves easy targets by refusing to install clear acrylic partitions, called *bandit barriers*, that separate bank tellers from the public. According to a special agent with the FBI, "Bandit barriers are a great deterrent. We've talked to guys who rob banks, and as soon as they see a bandit barrier, they go find another bank." Despite this finding, many banks have been reluctant to install these barriers. Wouldn't banks have a strong incentive to install bandit barriers to deter robberies? Why, then, do so many banks not install them?

Sources: U.S. Department of Justice, Federal Bureau of Investigation, "Bank Crime Statistics 2015," and "Bank Crime Statistics 2014"; and Richard Cowen, "FBI Says Banks Are to Blame for Rise in Robberies," NorthJersey.com, March 10, 2009.

1.5 The grading system plays an important role in student learning. In their book *Effective Grading: A Tool for Learning and Assessment in College*, Barbara Walvoord and Virginia Anderson stated that "grading infuses everything that happens in the classroom." They also argued that grading "needs to be acknowledged and managed from the first moment that an instructor begins planning a class."

  a. How could the grading system a teacher uses affect the incentives of students to learn the course material?

  b. If teachers put too little weight in the grading scale on a certain part of the course, such as readings outside the textbook, how might students respond?

  c. Teachers often wish that students came to class prepared, having read the upcoming material. How could a teacher design the grading system to motivate students to come to class prepared?

Source: Barbara E. Walvoord and Virginia Johnson Anderson, *Effective Grading: A Tool for Learning and Assessment in College*, 2nd ed., San Francisco: Jossey-Bass, 2010, p. 1.

1.6 The federal government subsidizes some loans to college students. Typically, the more students who participate in these programs and the more they borrow, the higher the cost to the federal government. In 2011, President Barack Obama convinced Congress to pass these changes to the federal student loan programs: (1) Payments were capped at 10 percent of a borrower's discretionary income; (2) any unpaid balances for people working for government or in the nonprofit sector were forgiven after making 120 monthly payments (10 years' worth of payments); and (3) people working in the private sector had their loans forgiven after making 240 monthly payments (20 years of payments).

a. As a result of these changes in the federal student loan program, would you predict that the total amount that students borrowed under these programs increased or decreased? Briefly explain.

b. As part of his 2016 federal budget proposal, President Obama recommended significant changes to the federal student loan programs. Given your answer to part (a), do you think President Obama was likely to have recommended changes that would increase or changes that would decrease the payments that borrowers would have to make? Briefly explain.

c. How might President Obama and his advisers have failed to correctly forecast the effects of the 2011 changes to the loan programs?

Sources: Allesandra Lanza, "What Obama's 2016 Budget Proposal Means for Student Borrowers," usnews.com, February 11, 2015; and Josh Mitchell, "Student-Debt Forgiveness Plans Skyrocket, Raising Fears over Costs, Higher Tuition," *Wall Street Journal*, April 22, 2014.

1.7 **(Related to the Apply the Concept on page 5)** Many universities and corporations offer a health and wellness program that helps their employees improve or maintain their health and get paid (a relatively small amount) for doing so. The programs vary but typically consist of employees completing a health assessment, receiving a program for healthy living, and monitoring their monthly health activities.

a. Why would universities and corporations pay employees to improve or maintain their health?

b. How does health insurance affect the incentive of employees to improve or maintain their health?

c. Would a wellness program increase or decrease the health insurance premiums that an insurance company would charge the university or corporation to provide insurance coverage? Briefly explain.

1.8 **(Related to the Apply the Concept on page 5)** Jay Bhattacharya and Kate Bundorf of Stanford University have found evidence that people who are obese and who work for firms that provide health insurance receive lower wages than workers at those firms who are not obese. At firms that do not provide health insurance, obese workers do not receive lower wages than workers who are not obese.

a. Why might firms that provide workers with health insurance pay a lower wage to obese workers than to workers who are not obese?

b. Is Bhattacharya and Bundorf's finding relevant to the question of whether health insurance provides people with an incentive to become obese? Briefly explain.

Source: Jay Bhattacharya and M. Kate Bundorf, "The Incidence of the Health Care Costs of Obesity," *Journal of Health Economics*, Vol. 28, No. 3, May 2009, pp. 649–658.

1.9 **(Related to Solved Problem 1.1 on page 7)** For many years, McDonald's used frozen beef patties to make its hamburgers. It recently began market testing how consumers in the United States would respond to hamburgers made of fresh beef that had never been frozen. In early 2017, McDonald's expanded the market test from only 55 restaurants to more than 300. The switch to fresh, never-frozen beef patties would be a huge undertaking involving "how [the beef] is transported to the restaurants, how it is stored when it arrives and how much it affects employees' process of making burgers." If you were a manager at McDonald's, how would you go about analyzing whether to switch to fresh, never-frozen beef patties? In your answer, consider whether your decision would have to be all or nothing—all fresh, never-frozen beef patties in all McDonald's hamburgers—and whether you would have to switch in all McDonald's locations around the world (in 119 countries) or just in certain countries.

Sources: Samantha Bomkamp, "McDonald's Expands Fresh Beef Test Again," chicago.tribune.com, March 17, 2017.

1.10 **(Related to Solved Problem 1.1 on page 7)** Late in the semester, a friend tells you, "I was going to drop my psychology course so I could concentrate on my other courses, but I had already put so much time into the course that I decided not to drop it." What do you think of your friend's reasoning? Would it make a difference to your answer if your friend has to pass the psychology course at some point to graduate? Briefly explain.

1.11 In a paper written by Bentley College economists Patricia M. Flynn and Michael A. Quinn, the authors state:

> We find evidence that Economics is a good choice of major for those aspiring to become a CEO [chief executive officer]. When adjusting for the size of the pool of graduates, those with undergraduate degrees in Economics are shown to have had a greater likelihood of becoming an S&P 500 CEO than any other major.

A list of famous economics majors published by Marietta College includes business leaders Elon Musk, Warren Buffett, Steve Ballmer, David Rockefeller, Arnold Schwarzenegger, Bill Belichick, Diane von Furstenberg, and Sam Walton, as well as Presidents George H.W. Bush, Gerald Ford, Ronald Reagan, and Donald Trump, and Supreme Court Justice Sandra Day O'Connor. Why might studying economics be particularly good preparation for being the top manager of a corporation or a leader in government?

Sources: Patricia M. Flynn and Michael A. Quinn, "Economics: A Good Choice of Major for Future CEOs," *Social Science Research Network*, November 28, 2006; and *Famous Economics Majors*, Marietta College, Marietta, Ohio, November 21, 2014.

The Economic Problem That Every Society Must Solve, pages 8–12

LEARNING OBJECTIVE: Discuss how an economy answers these questions: What goods and services will be produced? How will the goods and services be produced? Who will receive the goods and services produced?

Summary

Society faces **trade-offs**: Producing more of one good or service means producing less of another good or service. The **opportunity cost** of any activity—such as producing a good or service—is the highest-valued alternative that must be given up to engage in that activity. The choices of consumers, firms, and governments determine what goods and services will be produced. Firms choose how to produce the goods and services they sell. In the United States, who receives the goods and services produced depends largely on how income is distributed in the marketplace. In a **centrally planned economy**, most economic decisions are made by the government. In a **market economy**, most economic decisions are made by consumers and firms. Most economies, including that of the United States, are **mixed economies** in which most economic decisions are made by consumers and firms but in which the government also plays a significant role. There are two types of efficiency: (1) **Productive efficiency**, which occurs when a good or service is produced at the lowest possible cost, and (2) **allocative efficiency**, which occurs when production corresponds with consumer preferences. **Voluntary exchange** is a situation that occurs in markets when both the buyer and the seller of a product are made better off by the transaction. **Equity** usually involves a fair distribution of economic benefits. Government policymakers often face a trade-off between equity and efficiency.

Review Questions

2.1 Why does scarcity imply that every society and every individual face trade-offs?

2.2 What are the three economic questions that every society must answer? Briefly discuss the differences in the way centrally planned, market, and mixed economies answer these questions.

2.3 What is the difference between productive efficiency and allocative efficiency?

2.4 What is the difference between efficiency and equity? Why do government policymakers often face a trade-off between efficiency and equity?

Problems and Applications

2.5 According to *Forbes* magazine, in 2017, Bill Gates was the world's richest person, with wealth of $86 billion. Does Bill Gates face scarcity? Does everyone? Are there any exceptions?

Source: "The World's Billionaires," forbes.com, March 20, 2017.

2.6 Consider an organization that exists to help the poor. The members of the organization are discussing alternative methods of aiding the poor, when a proponent of one particular method asserts, "If even one poor person is helped

with this method, then all our time and money would have been worth it." If you were a member of the organization, how would you reply to this assertion?

2.7 College football attendance, especially student attendance, has been on the decline. In 2016, home attendance at major college football games declined for the sixth consecutive year and was the lowest since 2000. The opportunity cost of engaging in an activity is the value of the best alternative that must be given up to engage in that activity. How does your opportunity cost of attending a game compare with the opportunity cost facing a college student 15 years ago? Can this change account for the decline in college football attendance? Briefly explain.

Source: Jon Solomon, "College Football Attendance in 2016: Crowds Decline for Sixth Straight Year," cbssports.com, December 16, 2016.

2.8 In a market economy, why does a firm have a strong incentive to be productively efficient and allocatively efficient? What does the firm earn if it is productively and allocatively efficient, and what happens if it is not?

2.9 Alberto Chong of Georgia State University and several colleagues conducted an experiment to test the efficiency of government postal services around the world. They mailed letters to nonexistent businesses in 159 countries and kept track of how many of the letters were returned. Was this test most relevant to evaluating the productive efficiency or the allocative efficiency of these postal services? Briefly explain.

Source: Alberto Chong, Rafael La Porta, Florencio Lopez-de-Silanes, and Andrei Shleifer, "Letter Grading Government Efficiency," *Journal of the European Economic Association*, Vol. 12, No. 2, April 2014, pp. 277–299.

2.10 The Food and Drug Administration (FDA) is part of the federal government's Department of Health and Human Services. Among its other functions, the FDA evaluates the safety and effectiveness of drugs and medical devices. FDA approval had to be granted before OraSure was allowed to market its home HIV test. In a centrally planned economy, the government decides how resources will be allocated. In a market economy, the decisions of households and firms interacting in markets allocate resources. Briefly explain which statement is more accurate: (a) The regulation of the production and sale of drugs and medical devices in the United States is an example of how resources are allocated in a centrally planned economy, or (b) the regulation of the production and sale of drugs and medical devices in the United States is an example of how resources are allocated in a market economy.

2.11 Would you expect a centrally planned economy to be better at productive efficiency or allocative efficiency? Be sure to define *productive efficiency* and *allocative efficiency* in your answer.

2.12 Leonard Fleck, a philosophy professor at Michigan State University, has written:

When it comes to health care in America, we have limited resources for unlimited health care needs. We want everything contemporary medical technology can offer that will improve the length or quality of our lives as we age. But as presently healthy taxpayers, we want costs controlled.

Why is it necessary for all economic systems to limit services such as health care? How does a market system prevent people from getting as many goods and services as they want?

Source: Leonard Fleck, *Just Caring: Health Care Rationing and Democratic Deliberation*, New York: Oxford University Press, 2009.

2.13 Suppose that your college decides to give away 1,000 tickets to the football game against your school's biggest rival. The athletic department elects to distribute the tickets by giving them away to the first 1,000 students who show up at the department's office at 10 A.M. the following Monday.

    a. Which groups of students will be most likely to try to get the tickets? Think of specific examples and then generalize.

    b. What is the opportunity cost to students of distributing the tickets this way?

    c. Productive efficiency occurs when a good or service (such as the distribution of tickets) is produced at the lowest possible cost. Is this an efficient way to distribute the tickets? If possible, think of a more efficient method of distributing the tickets.

    d. Is this an equitable way to distribute the tickets? Briefly explain.

Economic Models, pages 12–16

LEARNING OBJECTIVE: Explain how economists use models to analyze economic events and government policies.

MyLab Economics   Visit **www.pearson.com/mylab/economics** to complete these exercises online and get instant feedback.

Summary

An **economic variable** is something measurable that can have different values, such as the number of people employed in manufacturing. Economists rely on economic models when they apply economic ideas to real-world problems. **Economic models** are simplified versions of reality used to analyze real-world economic situations. Economists accept and use an economic model if it leads to hypotheses that are confirmed by statistical analysis. In many cases, the acceptance is tentative, however, pending the gathering of new data or further statistical analysis. Economics is a *social science* because it applies the scientific method to the study of the interactions among individuals. Economics is concerned with positive analysis rather than normative analysis. **Positive analysis** is concerned with what is. **Normative analysis** is concerned with what ought to be. As a social science, economics considers human behavior in every context of decision making, not just in business.

Review Questions

3.1 Why do economists use models? How are economic data used to test models?

3.2 Describe the five steps economists follow to arrive at a useful economic model.

3.3 What is the difference between normative analysis and positive analysis? Is economics concerned mainly with normative analysis or positive analysis? Briefly explain.

Problems and Applications

3.4 Suppose an economist develops an economic model and finds that it works great in theory but fails in practice. What should the economist do next?

3.5 Dr. Strangelove's theory is that the price of mushrooms is determined by the activity of subatomic particles that exist in another universe parallel to ours. When the subatomic particles are emitted in profusion, the price of mushrooms is high. When subatomic particle emissions are low, the price of mushrooms is also low. How would you go about testing Dr. Strangelove's theory? Discuss whether this theory is useful.

3.6 (Related to the Don't Let This Happen to You on page 14) Briefly explain which of the following statements represent positive analysis and which represent normative analysis.

    a. A 50-cent-per-pack tax on cigarettes will lead to a 12 percent reduction in smoking by teenagers.

    b. The federal government should spend more on AIDS research.

    c. Rising wheat prices will increase bread prices.

    d. The price of coffee at Starbucks is too high.

3.7 (Related to the Don't Let This Happen to You on page 14) Warren Buffett is the chief executive officer of the investment firm Berkshire Hathaway and one of the wealthiest people in the world. In an editorial in the *Wall Street Journal*, Buffett argued that economic policies in the United States should be designed so that people who are willing to work receive enough income to live a "decent lifestyle." He argued that an expansion of the Earned Income Tax Credit (EITC) would be superior to an increase in the minimum wage as a means to reach this goal. The EITC is a program under which the federal government makes payments to low-income workers. Is Buffett correct that it is the role of the federal government to make sure people who work will have enough income to live a "decent lifestyle"?

Source: Warren Buffett, "Better Than Raising the Minimum Wage," *Wall Street Journal*, May 21, 2015.

3.8 (Related to the Apply the Concept on page 15) The *Apply the Concept* feature explains that there are both positive and normative aspects to the debate over whether the federal government should enact tariffs on imports of cars from Mexico. What economic statistics would be most useful in evaluating the positive elements in this debate? Assuming that these statistics are available or could be gathered, are they likely to resolve the normative issues in this debate?

3.9 (Related to the Chapter Opener on page 2) According to an article on reuters.com, Fiat Chrysler Automobiles, the firm that sells Dodge and Chrysler cars and trucks in the

United States, decided to invest $1 billion to modernize two of its U.S. production plants. The article described the possible effect of President Trump's trade policies on Fiat Chrysler's decision.

    a. What trade policies was the article referring to? How would those policies affect Fiat Chrysler's decision about whether to expand production in the United States?

    b. The article also implied that Fiat Chrysler's decision might have been affected by the possibility that the Trump administration will relax environmental regulations, such as a rule requiring companies to increase their cars' miles per gallon, and attempt to reduce the taxes corporations pay on their profits. Why would these two factors affect Fiat Chrysler's decision?

    c. Which groups are likely to gain, and which groups are likely to lose as a result of Fiat Chrysler's decision to produce more cars in U.S. plants rather than in overseas plants?

    Source: Bernie Woodall and David Sheparhson, "Fiat Chrysler to Add U.S. Jobs as Trump Puts Spotlight on Industry," reuters.com, January 9, 2017.

3.10 Suppose you are building an economic model to forecast the number of people employed in U.S. manufacturing in 2024. Should your model take into account possible changes in economic policy enacted by the president and Congress? Briefly explain.

3.11 To receive a medical license in the United States, a doctor must complete a residency program at a hospital. Hospitals are not free to expand their residency programs in a particular medical specialty without approval from a residency review committee (RRC), which is made up of physicians in that specialty. A hospital that does not abide by the rulings of the RRC runs the risk of losing its accreditation from the Accreditation Council for Graduate Medical Education (ACGME). The RRCs and ACGME argue that this system ensures that residency programs do not expand to the point where they are not providing residents with high-quality training.

    a. How does this system help protect consumers?

    b. Is it possible that this system protects the financial interests of doctors more than the well-being of consumers? Briefly explain.

    c. Discuss whether you consider this system to be good or bad. Is your conclusion an example of normative economics or of positive economics? Briefly explain.

    Sources: Brian Palmer, "We Need More Doctors, Stat!" *Slate*, June 27, 2011; and Sean Nicholson, "Barriers to Entering Medical Specialties," Wharton School, September 2003.

1.4   Microeconomics and Macroeconomics, page 16

LEARNING OBJECTIVE: Distinguish between microeconomics and macroeconomics.

MyLab Economics   Visit **www.pearson.com/mylab/economics** to complete these exercises online and get instant feedback.

Summary

Microeconomics is the study of how households and firms make choices, how they interact in markets, and how the government attempts to influence their choices. **Macroeconomics** is the study of the economy as a whole, including topics such as inflation, unemployment, and economic growth.

Review Question

4.1 Briefly discuss the difference between microeconomics and macroeconomics.

4.2 Is every economic issue either strictly microeconomic or strictly macroeconomic? Briefly explain.

Problems and Applications

4.3 Briefly explain whether each of the following is primarily a microeconomic issue or a macroeconomic issue.

    a. The effect of higher cigarette taxes on the quantity of cigarettes sold

    b. The effect of higher income taxes on the total amount of consumer spending

    c. The reasons the economies of East Asian countries grow faster than the economies of sub-Saharan African countries

    d. The reasons for low rates of profit in the airline industry

4.4 Briefly explain whether you agree with the following assertion:

Microeconomics is concerned with things that happen in one particular place, such as the unemployment rate in one city. In contrast, macroeconomics is concerned with things that affect the country as a whole, such as how the rate of teenage smoking in the United States would be affected by an increase in the tax on cigarettes.

Critical Thinking Exercises

CT1.1 For this exercise, your instructor may assign you to a group. As you saw in this chapter, an economy must answer three key questions: what to produce, how to produce it, and who receives the goods and services produced. High-income countries like the United States, have capitalist economic systems, which economists call *market economies*. This exercise focuses on the ideas about capitalism that you and other students bring to this class so we can connect what you already know with how economists think about the economic system (and they think a lot about it!). Using the concepts in this chapter, explain common complaints you have about capitalism or that you have heard from others. Be sure to use the following terms or concepts in your analysis: *market, market economy, equity, allocative efficiency, centrally planned economy, normative analysis,* and *positive analysis*. Each member of the group should describe at least one complaint about capitalism and use at least one of the terms or concepts listed above. Each group should then produce a one-page paper for this analysis to either turn in or to discuss in class.

CT1.2 Suppose that you're very athletic. For example, you may like to run, swim, play volleyball, or bike. You would like to perform better at your next competition. Perhaps you want to run a 5-kilometer race 1 minute faster or perhaps you want your team to advance further in a team sports competition, like volleyball. What concept can you use from this chapter to design your training program? *Hint:* This question is not about using concepts like markets, positive or normative analysis, or assuming that people act rationally, but there is one concept introduced in this chapter that is applicable to improving your athletic performance.

Appendix

Using Graphs and Formulas

Graphs are used to illustrate key economic ideas. Graphs appear not just in economics textbooks but also on Web sites and in newspaper and magazine articles that discuss events in business and economics. Graphs serve two useful purposes: (1) They simplify economic ideas, and (2) they make the ideas more concrete so they can be applied to real-world problems. Economic, business, and policy issues can be complicated, but a graph can help cut through complications and highlight the key relationships needed to understand the issue. In that sense, a graph can be like a street map.

Suppose you take a bus to New York City to see the Empire State Building. After arriving at the Port Authority Bus Terminal, you will probably use Google Maps or a similar app to find your way to the Empire State Building.

Maps are simplified versions of reality. The following map shows the streets in this part of New York City and some of the most important buildings. The map does not show most stores, most buildings, or the names, addresses, and telephone numbers of the people who live and work in the area. In fact, the map shows almost nothing about the messy reality of life in this section of New York City, except how the streets are laid out, which is the essential information you need to get from the Port Authority Bus Terminal to the Empire State Building.

Maps are simplified versions of reality. This map shows only the streets and most important buildings in this area of New York City.

Think about someone who says, "I know how to get around in the city, but I just can't figure out how to read a map." It certainly is possible to find your destination in a city without a map, but it's a lot easier with one. The same is true of using graphs in economics. It is possible to arrive at a solution to a real-world problem in economics and business without using graphs, but it is usually a lot easier if you use them.

With practice, you will become familiar with the graphs and formulas in this text, and you will know how to use them to analyze problems that would otherwise seem very difficult. What follows is a brief review of how graphs and formulas are used.

Graphs of One Variable

Figure 1A.1 displays values for *market shares* in the U.S. automobile market, using two common types of graphs. Market shares show the percentage of industry sales accounted for by different firms. In this case, the information is for firms grouped by where the firm is headquartered: U.S.-based firms,[1] Japanese-based firms, European-based firms, and Korean-based firms. Panel (a) displays the information about market shares as a *bar graph*, with the market share of each group of firms represented by the height of its bar. Panel (b) displays the same information as a *pie chart*, with the market share of each group of firms represented by the size of its slice of the pie.

Information about an economic variable is also often displayed in a *time-series graph*, like Figure 1A.2, which shows on a coordinate grid how the values of a variable change over time. In a coordinate grid, we can measure the value of one variable along the vertical axis (or *y*-axis) and the value of another variable along the horizontal axis (or *x*-axis). The point where the vertical axis intersects the horizontal axis is called the *origin*. At the origin, the value of both variables is zero. The points on a coordinate grid represent values of the two variables.

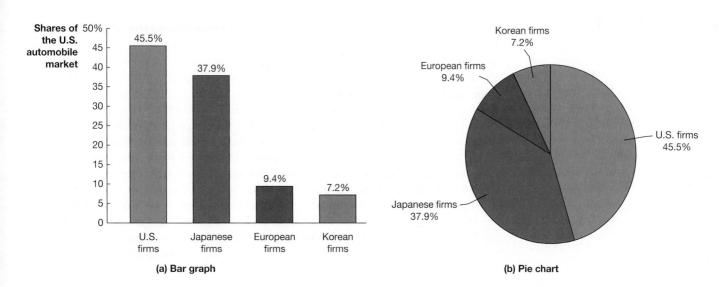

(a) Bar graph

(b) Pie chart

MyLab Economics Animation

Figure 1A.1 **Bar Graph and Pie Chart**

Values for an economic variable are often displayed as a bar graph or a pie chart. In this case, panel (a) shows market share data for the U.S. automobile industry as a bar graph, with the market share of each group of firms represented by the height of its bar. Panel (b) displays the same information

as a pie chart, with the market share of each group of firms represented by the size of its slice of the pie.

Source: "Auto Sales," *Wall Street Journal*, February 1, 2017.

---

[1] In this case, the category "U.S.-based firms" includes Chrysler, which while a member of the traditional U.S. "Big Three" automobile firms and producing most of its vehicles in North America, has been owned by the Italian-based Fiat Chrysler Automobiles NV since 2009.

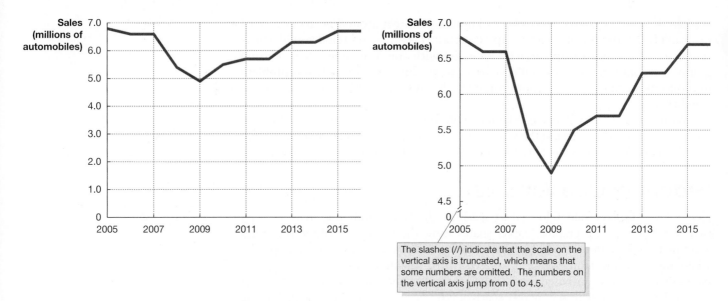

(a) Time-series graph where the scale is not truncated

(b) Time-series graph with truncated scale

The slashes (//) indicate that the scale on the vertical axis is truncated, which means that some numbers are omitted. The numbers on the vertical axis jump from 0 to 4.5.

MyLab Economics Animation

Figure 1A.2   **Time-Series Graphs**

Both panels present time-series graphs of Ford Motor Company's worldwide sales during each year from 2005 to 2016. In panel (a), the vertical axis starts at 0, and the distance between each pair of values shown is the same. In panel (b), the scale on the vertical axis is truncated, so although it starts

at 0, it then jumps to 4.5 million. As a result, the fluctuations in Ford's sales appear smaller in panel (a) than in panel (b).

Source: Ford Motor Company, *Annual Report*, various years.

In Figure 1A.2, we measure the number of automobiles and trucks sold worldwide by Ford Motor Company on the vertical axis, and we measure time on the horizontal axis. In time-series graphs, the height of the line at each date shows the value of the variable measured on the vertical axis. Both panels of Figure 1A.2 show Ford's worldwide sales during each year from 2005 to 2016. The difference between panel (a) and panel (b) illustrates the importance of the scale used in a time-series graph. In panel (a), the vertical axis starts at 0, and the distance between each pair of values shown is the same. In this panel, the decline in Ford's sales during 2008 and 2009 appears relatively small. In panel (b), the scale on the vertical axis is truncated, which means that although it starts at zero, it jumps to 4.5 million. As a result, the distance on the vertical axis from 0 to 4.5 million is much smaller than the distance from 4.5 million to 5.0 million. The slashes (//) near the bottom of the axis indicate that the scale is truncated. In panel (b), the decline in Ford's sales during 2008 and 2009 appears much larger than in panel (a). (Technically, the horizontal axis in both panels is also truncated because we start with 2005, not 0.)   **MyLab Economics** Concept Check

Graphs of Two Variables

We often use graphs to show the relationship between two variables. Suppose you are interested in the relationship between the price of a cheese pizza and the quantity of pizzas sold per week in the town of Statesboro, Georgia. A graph showing the relationship between the price of a good and the quantity of the good demanded at each price is called a *demand curve*. (As we will discuss later, in drawing a demand curve for a good, we have to hold constant any variables other than price that might affect the willingness of consumers to buy the good.) Figure 1A.3 shows the data collected on price and quantity. The figure shows a two-dimensional grid on which we measure the price of

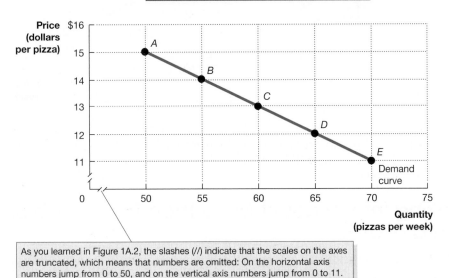

Price (dollars per pizza)	Quantity (pizzas per week)	Point
$15	50	A
14	55	B
13	60	C
12	65	D
11	70	E

As you learned in Figure 1A.2, the slashes (//) indicate that the scales on the axes are truncated, which means that numbers are omitted: On the horizontal axis numbers jump from 0 to 50, and on the vertical axis numbers jump from 0 to 11.

MyLab Economics Animation

Figure 1A.3

Plotting Price and Quantity Points in a Graph

The figure shows a two-dimensional grid on which we measure the price of pizza along the vertical axis (or *y*-axis) and the quantity of pizza sold per week along the horizontal axis (or *x*-axis). Each point on the grid represents one of the price and quantity combinations listed in the table. By connecting the points with a line, we can better illustrate the relationship between the two variables.

pizza along the *y*-axis and the quantity of pizza sold per week along the *x*-axis. Each point on the grid represents one of the price and quantity combinations listed in the table. We can connect the points to form the demand curve for pizza in Statesboro, Georgia. Notice that the scales on both axes in the graph are truncated. In this case, truncating the axes allows the graph to illustrate more clearly the relationship between price and quantity by excluding low prices and quantities.

Slopes of Lines

Once you have plotted the data in Figure 1A.3, you may be interested in how much the quantity of pizza sold increases as the price decreases. The *slope* of a line tells us how much the variable we are measuring on the *y*-axis changes as the variable we are measuring on the *x*-axis changes. We can use the Greek letter delta (Δ) to stand for the change in a variable. The slope is sometimes called the rise over the run. So, we have several ways of expressing slope:

$$\text{Slope} = \frac{\text{Change in value on the vertical axis}}{\text{Change in value on the horizontal axis}} = \frac{\Delta y}{\Delta x} = \frac{\text{Rise}}{\text{Run}}.$$

Figure 1A.4 reproduces the graph from Figure 1A.3. Because the slope of a straight line is the same at any point, we can use any two points in the figure to calculate the slope of the line. For example, when the price of pizza decreases from $14 to $12, the quantity of pizza sold increases from 55 per week to 65 per week. Therefore, the slope is:

$$\text{Slope} = \frac{\Delta \text{Price of pizza}}{\Delta \text{Quantity of pizza}} = \frac{(\$12 - \$14)}{(65 - 55)} = \frac{-2}{10} = -0.2.$$

The slope of this line shows us how responsive consumers in Statesboro, Georgia, are to changes in the price of pizza. The larger the value of the slope (ignoring the negative sign), the steeper the line will be, which indicates that not

MyLab Economics Animation

Figure 1A.4

Calculating the Slope of a Line

We can calculate the slope of a line as the change in the value of the variable on the *y*-axis divided by the change in the value of the variable on the *x*-axis. Because the slope of a straight line is constant, we can use any two points in the figure to calculate the slope of the line. For example, when the price of pizza decreases from $14 to $12, the quantity of pizza demanded increases from 55 per week to 65 per week. So, the slope of this line equals −2 divided by 10, or −0.2.

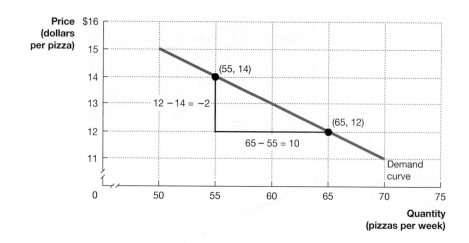

many additional pizzas are sold when the price falls. The smaller the value of the slope, the flatter the line will be, which indicates a greater increase in pizzas sold when the price falls.

MyLab Economics Concept Check

Taking into Account More Than Two Variables on a Graph

The demand curve in Figure 1A.4 shows the relationship between the price of pizza and the quantity of pizza demanded, but we know that the quantity of any good demanded depends on more than just the price of the good. For example, the quantity of pizza demanded in a given week in Statesboro, Georgia, can be affected by other variables—the price of hamburgers, whether an advertising campaign by local pizza parlors has begun that week, and so on. Allowing the values of any other variables to change will cause the position of the demand curve in the graph to change.

Suppose that the demand curve in Figure 1A.4 was drawn holding the price of hamburgers constant, at $1.50. If the price of hamburgers rises to $2.00, some consumers will switch from buying hamburgers to buying pizza, and more pizzas will be demanded at every price. The result on the graph will be to shift the line representing the demand curve to the right. Similarly, if the price of hamburgers falls from $1.50 to $1.00, some consumers will switch from buying pizza to buying hamburgers, and fewer pizzas will be demanded at every price. The result on the graph will be to shift the line representing the demand curve to the left.

The table in Figure 1A.5 shows the effect of a change in the price of hamburgers on the quantity of pizza demanded. On the graph, suppose that at first we are on the line labeled Demand curve$_1$. If the price of pizza is $14 (point *A*), an increase in the price of hamburgers from $1.50 to $2.00 increases the quantity of pizzas demanded from 55 to 60 per week (point *B*) and shifting the demand curve to the right to Demand curve$_2$. Or, if we start on Demand curve$_1$ and the price of pizza is $12 (point *C*), a decrease in the price of hamburgers from $1.50 to $1.00 decreases the quantity of pizzas demanded from 65 to 60 per week (point *D*) and shifts the demand curve to the left to Demand curve$_3$. By shifting the demand curve, we have taken into account the effect of changes in the value of a third variable—the price of hamburgers. We will use this technique of shifting curves to allow for the effects of additional variables many times in this book.

MyLab Economics Concept Check

Positive and Negative Relationships

We can use graphs to show the relationships between any two variables. Sometimes the relationship between the variables is *negative*, meaning that as one variable increases in value, the other variable decreases in value. This was the case with the price of pizza and the quantity of pizzas demanded. The relationship between two variables can also be *positive*, meaning that the values of both variables increase or

Quantity (pizzas per week)			
Price (dollars per pizza)	When the Price of Hamburgers = $1.00	When the Price of Hamburgers = $1.50	When the Price of Hamburgers = $2.00
$15	45	50	55
14	50	55	60
13	55	60	65
12	60	65	70
11	65	70	75

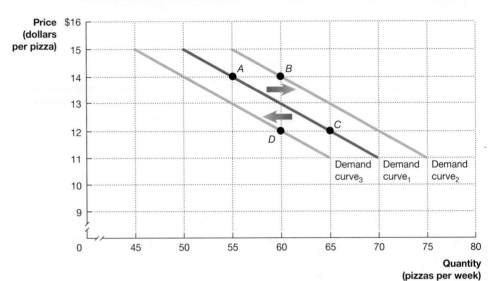

MyLab Economics Animation

Figure 1A.5

Showing Three Variables on a Graph

The demand curve for pizza shows the relationship between the price of pizzas and the quantity of pizzas demanded, *holding constant other factors that might affect the willingness of consumers to buy pizza.* If the price of pizza is $14 (point A), an increase in the price of hamburgers from $1.50 to $2.00 increases the quantity of pizzas demanded from 55 to 60 per week (point B) and shifts the demand curve to Demand curve$_2$. Or, if we start on Demand curve$_1$ and the price of pizza is $12 (point C), a decrease in the price of hamburgers from $1.50 to $1.00 decreases the quantity of pizza demanded from 65 to 60 per week (point D) and shifts the demand curve to Demand curve$_3$.

decrease together. For example, when the level of total income—or *disposable personal income*—received by households in the United States increases, the level of total *consumption spending,* which is spending by households on goods and services, also increases. The table in Figure 1A.6 shows the values (in billions of dollars) for income and consumption spending for 2013–2016. The graph plots the data from the table,

Year	Disposable Personal Income (billions of dollars)	Consumption Spending (billions of dollars)
2013	$12,396	$11,361
2014	13,023	11,863
2015	13,520	12,284
2016	14,046	12,753

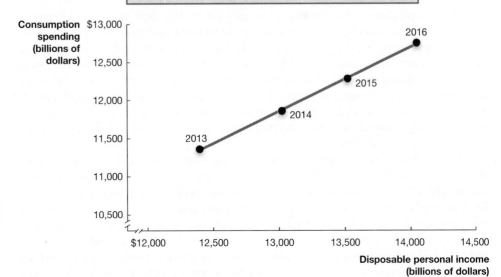

MyLab Economics Animation

Figure 1A.6

Graphing the Positive Relationship between Income and Consumption

In a positive relationship between two economic variables, as one variable increases, the other variable also increases. This figure shows the positive relationship between disposable personal income and consumption spending. As disposable personal income in the United States has increased, so has consumption spending.

Source: U.S. Department of Commerce, Bureau of Economic Analysis.

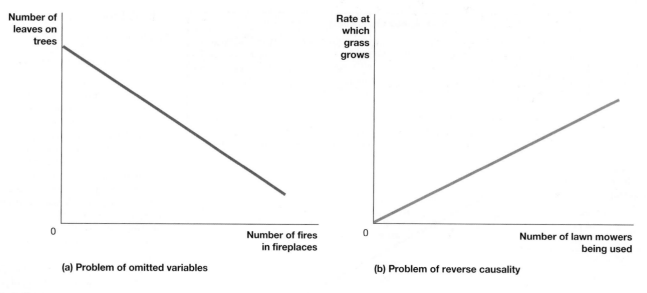

(a) Problem of omitted variables

(b) Problem of reverse causality

MyLab Economics Animation

Figure 1A.7 **Determining Cause and Effect**

Using graphs to draw conclusions about cause and effect can be hazardous. In panel (a), we see that there are fewer leaves on the trees in a neighborhood when many homes have fires burning in their fireplaces. We cannot draw the conclusion that using fireplaces causes the leaves to fall because we have an *omitted variable*—the season of the year.

In panel (b), we see that more lawn mowers are used in a neighborhood during times when the grass grows rapidly and fewer lawn mowers are used when the grass grows slowly. Concluding that using lawn mowers *causes* the grass to grow faster would be making the error of *reverse causality*.

with disposable personal income measured along the horizontal axis and consumption spending measured along the vertical axis. **MyLab Economics** Concept Check

Determining Cause and Effect

When we graph the relationship between two variables, we usually want to draw conclusions about whether changes in one variable are causing changes in the other variable. Doing so can, however, lead to mistakes. Suppose that over the course of a year, you graph the number of homes in a neighborhood that have a fire burning in the fireplace and the number of leaves on trees in the neighborhood and you get a relationship like that shown in panel (a) of Figure 1A.7: The more fireplaces in use in the neighborhood, the fewer leaves the trees have. Can we draw the conclusion from this graph that using a fireplace causes trees to lose their leaves? We know, of course, that such a conclusion is incorrect. In spring and summer, there are relatively few fireplaces being used, and the trees are full of leaves. In the fall, as trees begin to lose their leaves, fireplaces are used more frequently. And in winter, many fireplaces are being used and many trees have lost all their leaves. The reason that the graph in Figure 1A.7 is misleading in terms of cause and effect is that there is obviously an *omitted variable* in the analysis—the season of the year. An omitted variable is one that affects the other variables in the analysis, and its omission can lead to false conclusions about cause and effect.

Although in our example the omitted variable is obvious, there are many debates about cause and effect where the existence of an omitted variable has not been clear. For instance, it has been known for many years that people who smoke cigarettes suffer from higher rates of lung cancer than do nonsmokers. For some time, tobacco companies and some scientists argued that there was an omitted variable—perhaps failure to exercise or poor diet—that made some people both more likely to smoke and more likely to develop lung cancer. If this omitted variable existed, then the finding that smokers were more likely to develop lung cancer would not have been evidence that smoking *caused* lung cancer. In this case, however, nearly all scientists eventually concluded that the omitted variable did not exist and that, in fact, smoking does cause lung cancer.

A related problem in determining cause and effect is known as *reverse causality*. The error of reverse causality occurs when we conclude that changes in variable X cause changes in variable Y when, in fact, it is actually changes in variable Y that cause changes in variable X. For example, panel (b) of Figure 1A.7 plots the number of lawn mowers being used in a neighborhood against the rate at which grass on lawns in the neighborhood is growing. We could conclude from this graph that using lawn mowers *causes* the grass to grow faster. We know, however, that in reality, the causality is in the other direction: Rapidly growing grass during the spring and summer causes the increased use of lawn mowers, and slowly growing grass in the fall or winter or during periods of low rainfall causes the decreased use of lawn mowers.

Once again, in our example, the potential error of reverse causality is obvious. In many economic debates, however, cause and effect can be more difficult to determine. For example, changes in the money supply, or the total amount of money in the economy, tend to occur at the same time as changes in the total amount of income people in the economy earn. A famous debate in economics was about whether the changes in the money supply caused the changes in total income or whether the changes in total income caused the changes in the money supply. Each side in the debate accused the other side of committing the error of reverse causality. **MyLab Economics** Concept Check

Are Graphs of Economic Relationships Always Straight Lines?

The graphs of relationships between two economic variables that we have drawn so far have been straight lines. The relationship between two variables is *linear* when it can be represented by a straight line. Few economic relationships are actually linear. For example, if we carefully plot data on the price of a product and the quantity demanded at each price, holding constant other variables that affect the quantity demanded, we will usually find a curved—or *nonlinear*—relationship rather than a linear relationship. In practice, however, it is often useful to approximate a nonlinear relationship with a linear relationship. If the relationship is reasonably close to being linear, the analysis is not significantly affected. In addition, it is easier to calculate the slope of a straight line, and it is also easier to calculate the area under a straight line. So, in this text book, we often assume that the relationship between two economic variables is linear, even when we know that this assumption is not precisely correct. **MyLab Economics** Concept Check

Slopes of Nonlinear Curves

In some situations, we need to take into account the nonlinear nature of an economic relationship. For example, panel (a) of Figure 1A.8 shows the hypothetical relationship between Apple's total cost of producing iPhones and the quantity of iPhones produced. The relationship is curved rather than linear. In this case, the cost of production is increasing at an increasing rate, which often happens in manufacturing. In other words, as we move up the curve, its slope becomes larger. (Remember that with a straight line, the slope is always constant.) To see why, first remember that we calculate the slope of a curve by dividing the change in the variable on the y-axis by the change in the variable on the x-axis. As we move from point A to point B, the quantity produced increases by 1 million iPhones, while the total cost of production increases by $50 million. Farther up the curve, as we move from point C to point D, the change in quantity is the same—1 million iPhones—but the change in the total cost of production is now much larger—$250 million. Because the change in the y variable has increased, while the change in the x variable has remained the same, we know that the slope has increased.

To measure the slope of a nonlinear curve at a particular point, we measure the slope of the line that is tangent to that curve at that point. This tangent line will touch the curve only at that point. We can measure the slope of the tangent line just as we

(a) The slope of a nonlinear curve is not constant

(b) The slope of a nonlinear curve is measured by the slope of the tangent line

MyLab Economics Animation

Figure 1A.8   **The Slope of a Nonlinear Curve**

The relationship between the quantity of Apple iPhones produced and the total cost of production is curved rather than linear. In panel (a), when we move from point A to point B, the quantity produced increases by 1 million iPhones, while the total cost of production increases by $50 million. Farther up the curve, as we move from point C to point D, the change in quantity is the same—1 million iPhones—but the change in the total cost of production is now much larger—$250 million.

Because the change in the y variable has increased, while the change in the x variable has remained the same, we know that the slope has increased. In panel (b), we measure the slope of the curve at a particular point by calculating the slope of the tangent line at that point. The slope of the tangent line at point B is 75, and the slope of the tangent line at point C is 150.

would measure the slope of any other straight line. In panel (b), the tangent line at point B has a slope equal to:

$$\frac{\Delta \text{Cost}}{\Delta \text{Quantity}} = \frac{75}{1} = 75.$$

The tangent line at point C has a slope equal to:

$$\frac{\Delta \text{Cost}}{\Delta \text{Quantity}} = \frac{150}{1} = 150.$$

Once again, we see that the slope of the curve is larger at point C than at point B.

MyLab Economics Concept Check

Formulas

We have just seen that graphs are an important economic tool. In this section, we will review several useful formulas and show how to use them to summarize data and calculate important relationships.

Formula for a Percentage Change

The *percentage change* is the change in some economic variable, usually from one period to the next, expressed as a percentage. A key macroeconomic measure is the real gross domestic product (GDP). GDP is the value of all the final goods and services produced in a country during a year. "Real" GDP is corrected for the effects of inflation. When economists say that the U.S. economy grew 1.6 percent during 2016, they mean that real GDP was 1.6 percent higher in 2016 than it was in 2015. The formula for making this calculation is:

$$\left(\frac{GDP_{2016} - GDP_{2015}}{GDP_{2015}} \right) \times 100$$

or, more generally, for any two periods:

$$\text{Percentage change} = \left(\frac{\text{Value in the second period } - \text{ Value in the first period}}{\text{Value in the first period}} \right) \times 100.$$

In this case, real GDP was \$16,397 billion in 2015 and \$16,660 billion in 2016. So, the growth rate of the U.S. economy during 2016 was:

$$\left(\frac{\$16,660 - \$16,397}{\$16,397} \right) \times 100 = 1.6\%.$$

Notice that it doesn't matter that in using the formula, we ignored the fact that GDP is measured in billions of dollars. In fact, when calculating percentage changes, *the units don't matter*. The percentage increase from \$16,397 billion to \$16,660 billion is exactly the same as the percentage increase from \$16,397 to \$16,660.　**MyLab Economics** Concept Check

Formulas for the Areas of a Rectangle and a Triangle

Areas that form rectangles and triangles on graphs can have important economic meaning. For example, Figure 1A.9 shows the demand curve for Pepsi. Suppose that the price is currently \$2.00 and that 125,000 bottles of Pepsi are sold at that price. A firm's *total revenue* is equal to the amount it receives from selling its product, or the quantity sold multiplied by the price. In this case, total revenue will equal 125,000 bottles times \$2.00 per bottle, or \$250,000.

The formula for the area of a rectangle is:

$$\text{Area of a rectangle} = \text{Base} \times \text{Height.}$$

In Figure 1A.9, the shaded rectangle also represents the firm's total revenue because its area is given by the base of 125,000 bottles multiplied by the price of \$2.00 per bottle.

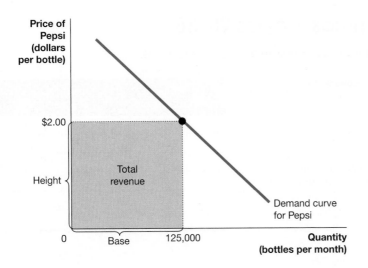

MyLab Economics Animation

Figure 1A.9

Showing a Firm's Total Revenue on a Graph

The area of a rectangle is equal to its base multiplied by its height. Total revenue is equal to quantity multiplied by price. Here, total revenue is equal to the quantity of 125,000 bottles times the price of \$2.00 per bottle, or \$250,000. The area of the shaded rectangle shows the firm's total revenue.

MyLab Economics Animation

Figure 1A.10

The Area of a Triangle

The area of a triangle is equal to 1/2 multiplied by its base multiplied by its height. The area of the shaded triangle has a base equal to 150,000 − 125,000, or 25,000, and a height equal to $2.00 − $1.50, or $0.50. Therefore, its area is equal to 1/2 × 25,000 × $0.50, or $6,250.

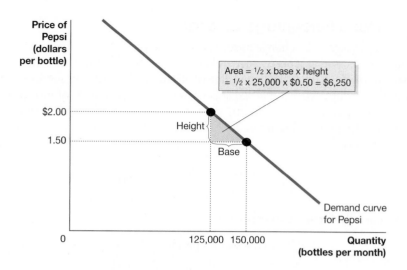

We will see in later chapters that areas that are triangles can also have economic significance. The formula for the area of a triangle is:

$$\text{Area of a triangle} = \frac{1}{2} \times \text{Base} \times \text{Height}.$$

The shaded area in Figure 1A.10 is a triangle. The base equals 150,000 − 125,000, or 25,000. Its height equals $2.00 − $1.50, or $0.50. Therefore, its area equals 1/2 × 25,000 × $0.50, or $6,250. Notice that the shaded area is a triangle only if the demand curve is a straight line, or linear. Not all demand curves are linear. However, the formula for the area of a triangle will usually still give a good approximation, even if the demand curve is not linear.

MyLab Economics Study Plan

MyLab Economics Concept Check

Summary of Using Formulas

You will encounter several other formulas in this book. Whenever you use a formula, you should follow these steps:

1. Make sure you understand the economic concept the formula represents.
2. Make sure you are using the correct formula for the problem you are solving.
3. Make sure the number you calculate using the formula is economically reasonable. For example, if you are using a formula to calculate a firm's revenue and your answer is a negative number, you know you made a mistake somewhere.

MyLab Economics Study Plan

MyLab Economics Concept Check

1A Using Graphs and Formulas, pages 28–38

LEARNING OBJECTIVE: Use graphs and formulas to analyze economic situations.

MyLab Economics   Visit www.pearson.com/mylab/economics to complete these exercises online and get instant feedback.

Problems and Applications

1A.1 The table on the right shows the relationship between the price of custard pies and the number of pies Jacob buys per week:

Price (dollars per pie)	Quantity of Pies	Week
$3.00	6	July 2
2.00	7	July 9
5.00	4	July 16
6.00	3	July 23
1.00	8	July 30
4.00	5	August 6

a. Is the relationship between the price of pies and the number of pies Jacob buys a positive relationship or a negative relationship?

b. Plot the data from the table on a graph similar to Figure 1A.3 on page 31. Draw a straight line that best fits the points.

c. Calculate the slope of the line.

1A.2 The following table gives information about the quantity of glasses of lemonade demanded on sunny and overcast days:

Price (dollars per glass)	Quantity (glasses of lemonade per day)	Weather
$0.80	30	Sunny
0.80	10	Overcast
0.70	40	Sunny
0.70	20	Overcast
0.60	50	Sunny
0.60	30	Overcast
0.50	60	Sunny
0.50	40	Overcast

Plot the data from the table on a graph similar to Figure 1A.5 on page 33. Draw two straight lines representing the two demand curves—one for sunny days and one for overcast days.

1A.3 Using the information in Figure 1A.2 on page 30, calculate the percentage change in Ford's auto sales from one year to the next. During which year did sales fall at the highest rate?

1A.4 Real GDP in 2014 was $15,982 billion. Real GDP in 2015 was $16,397 billion. What was the percentage change in real GDP from 2014 to 2015? What do economists call the percentage change in real GDP from one year to the next?

1A.5 Assume that the demand curve for Pepsi passes through the following two points:

Price per bottle of Pepsi (in dollars)	Quantity (bottles)
$2.50	100,000
1.25	200,000

a. Draw a graph with a linear demand curve that passes through these two points.

b. Show on the graph the areas representing total revenue at each price. Give the value for total revenue at each price.

1A.6 What is the area of the triangle shown in the following figure?

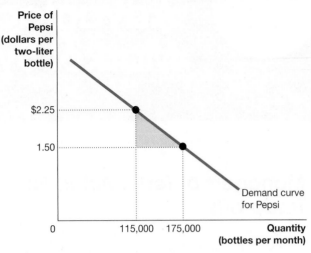

1A.7 Calculate the slope of the total cost curve at point A and at point B in the following figure.

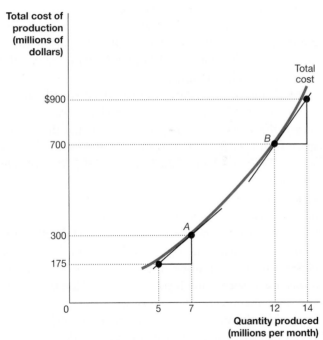

Managers at Tesla Motors Face Trade-offs

Are electric cars the wave of the future? If you're like most drivers, you probably like the idea of skipping the gas station in favor of powering up your car by plugging it into an electric outlet. Electric cars, though, have struggled to succeed in the marketplace for two key reasons: (1) The lithium batteries that power electric cars are costly, forcing up the prices of the cars, and (2) the batteries available today need to be recharged every 100 to 300 miles, making the cars impractical for long trips.

Tesla Motors is an American-based automobile manufacturer founded in 2003 by billionaire Elon Musk, who also started the online payment system PayPal and the private space firm SpaceX. Although in 2017, the firm held only a tiny 0.3 percent share of the U.S. car market, its goal is to become the first firm to sell large numbers of electric cars. Tesla is building a nationwide network of fast-charging stations to make it easier for drivers to make longer trips. Tesla's early models were priced at over $60,000. In 2017, the company introduced its new Model 3, with a lower price of $35,000, aimed at luring customers away from gasoline-powered cars such as the Toyota Camry and Honda Accord.

Tesla manufactures its cars in a single factory in Fremont, California. To compete in the automobile market, Tesla's managers must make many strategic decisions. For example, during the first half of 2017, Tesla sold a total of about 50,000 Model S sedans, with a base price of $68,000, and Model Xs, a sport utility vehicle (SUV), with a base price of $85,500. With a limited capacity to manufacture cars in its Fremont plant, Tesla had to decide whether it would be more profitable to produce more units of its Model S and Model X or to use that capacity to produce the Model 3. Ultimately, Tesla's plan to gain a significant share of the automobile market led its managers to decide to allocate resources to producing the Model 3, even though doing so meant it would be able to produce fewer units of its other models.

Tesla's managers must also decide how to sell and service its cars. Tesla has had difficulty opening company-owned

Joe White/Retuers

dealerships to sell its cars because some states have laws that require car manufacturers to sell through independent dealerships, which Tesla is unwilling to do. In those states, Tesla sells its cars only online and relies on company-owned service centers to provide maintenance and repair services. Some economists have questioned whether Tesla will be able to meet its future sales goals without selling cars through independent dealerships as most other car companies do.

Tesla's managers also face other key decisions. For instance, they intend to eventually manufacture 1 million vehicles annually. Doing so will likely require building at least one additional factory in which to assemble the cars, as well as additional factories to manufacture the battery cells that power the cars. Like other decisions managers make, this one involves a trade-off: Devoting more resources to building additional factories would leave fewer resources available for expanding production in its two existing car and battery factories.

AN INSIDE LOOK on **page 64** discusses the reasons Tesla decided to build a large battery plant in Nevada.

Sources: Dana Hull, "Tesla Keeping Model 3 Steady as Musk to Lose CFO, Seek Cash," bloomberg.com, February 22, 2017; and Tim Higgins, "Tesla Narrowly Misses 80,000-Vehicle Sales Goal in 2016," *Wall Street Journal*, January 3, 2017.

Chapter Outline & Learning Objectives

2.1 Production Possibilities Frontiers and Opportunity Costs, page 42
Use a production possibilities frontier to analyze opportunity costs and trade-offs.

2.2 Comparative Advantage and Trade, page 48
Describe comparative advantage and explain how it serves as the basis for trade.

2.3 The Market System, page 54
Explain the basics of how a market system works.

Economics in Your Life & Career

The Trade-offs When You Buy a Car

Although electric cars are much in the news and are increasing in popularity, most people still buy conventional gasoline-powered cars. When you buy a gasoline-powered car, you probably consider factors such as safety and fuel efficiency. To increase fuel efficiency, automobile manufacturers make some cars that are small and light. Large cars absorb more of the impact of an accident than do small cars, so people are usually safer driving large cars. What do these facts tell us about the relationship between safety and fuel efficiency? If you were a manager at an automobile company, how might you evaluate the relationship between safety and fuel efficiency when designing cars? As you read the chapter, try to answer these questions. You can check your answers against those provided on **page 63** at the end of this chapter.

Scarcity A situation in which unlimited wants exceed the limited resources available to fulfill those wants.

In a market system, managers are continually making decisions like those made by Tesla's managers. These decisions reflect a key fact of economic life: *Scarcity requires trade-offs.* **Scarcity** exists because we have unlimited wants but only limited resources available to fulfill those wants. Goods and services are scarce. So, too, are the economic resources, or *factors of production*—workers, capital, natural resources, and entrepreneurial ability—used to make goods and services. Your time is scarce, which means you face trade-offs: If you spend an hour studying for an economics exam, you have one less hour to spend studying for a psychology exam or going to the movies. If your university decides to use some of its scarce budget to buy new computers for the computer labs, those funds will not be available to buy new books for the library or to resurface the student parking lots. If Tesla decides to devote some of the scarce workers and machinery in its Fremont assembly plant to producing more Model 3s, those resources will not be available to produce more Model Ss.

Households and firms make many of their decisions in markets. Trade is a key activity that takes place in markets. Trade results from the decisions of millions of households and firms around the world. By engaging in trade, people can raise their incomes. In this chapter, we provide an overview of how the market system coordinates the independent decisions of these millions of households and firms. We begin our analysis of the economic consequences of scarcity and how a market system works by introducing an important economic model: the *production possibilities frontier.*

2.1 Production Possibilities Frontiers and Opportunity Costs

LEARNING OBJECTIVE: Use a production possibilities frontier to analyze opportunity costs and trade-offs.

As we saw in the chapter opener, Tesla operates an automobile factory in Fremont, California, where it assembles three vehicle models: Model S and Model 3 sedans, and Model X SUVs. Because the firm's resources—workers, machinery, materials, and entrepreneurial ability—are limited, Tesla faces a trade-off: Resources devoted to producing one model are not available for producing the other models. Chapter 1 explained that economic models can be useful in analyzing many questions. We can use a simple model called the *production possibilities frontier* to analyze the trade-offs Tesla faces in its Fremont plant. A **production possibilities frontier (PPF)** is a curve showing the maximum attainable combinations of two goods that can be produced with available resources and current technology. In Tesla's case, the company produces three vehicle models at its Fremont plant, using workers, materials, robots, and other machinery.

Production possibilities frontier (PPF) A curve showing the maximum attainable combinations of two goods that can be produced with available resources and current technology.

Graphing the Production Possibilities Frontier

Figure 2.1 uses a production possibilities frontier to illustrate that the key trade-off Tesla faced in 2017 was allocating resources between its two original models (Model S and Model X) and its new Model 3. The numbers from the table are plotted in the graph. The line in the graph represents Tesla's production possibilities frontier. If Tesla uses all its resources to produce its original models, it can produce 80 per day—point *A* at one end of the production possibilities frontier. If Tesla uses all its resources to produce its new Model 3, it can produce 80 per day—point *E* at the other end of the production possibilities frontier. If Tesla devotes resources to producing both its orginal models and the Model 3, it could be at a point like *B*, where it produces 60 of its original models and 20 Model 3s.

All the combinations either on the frontier—like points *A*, *B*, *C*, *D*, and *E*—or inside the frontier—like point *F*—are *attainable* with the resources available. Combinations on the frontier are *efficient* because all available resources are being fully utilized, and the

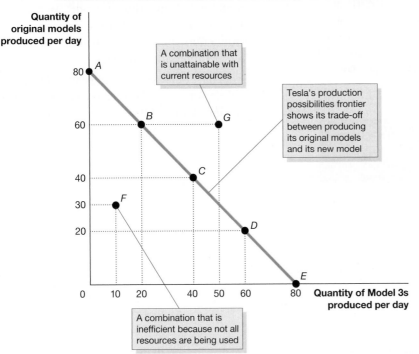

Tesla's Production Choices at Its Fremont Plant		
Choice	Quantity of Original Models Produced per Day	Quantity of Model 3s Produced per Day
A	80	0
B	60	20
C	40	40
D	20	60
E	0	80

MyLab Economics Animation

Figure 2.1

Tesla's Production Possibilities Frontier

Tesla faces a trade-off: To build one more of its original Model S and Model X cars, it must build one fewer of its new Model 3. The production possibilities frontier illustrates the trade-off Tesla faces. Combinations on the production possibilities frontier—like points A, B, C, D, and E—are *efficient* because the maximum output is being obtained from the available resources. Combinations inside the frontier—like point F—are *inefficient* because some resources are not being used. Combinations outside the frontier—like point G—are *unattainable* with current resources.

fewest possible resources are being used to produce a given amount of output. Combinations inside the frontier—like point F—are *inefficient* because maximum output is not being obtained from the available resources—perhaps because the assembly line is not operating at its capacity. Tesla might like to be beyond the frontier—at a point like G, where it would be producing 60 of its original models and 50 of its Model 3s per day—but points beyond the production possibilities frontier are *unattainable*, given the firm's current resources. To produce the combination at G, Tesla would need more machines and more workers.

Notice that if Tesla is producing efficiently and is on the production possibilities frontier, the only way to produce one more Model 3 is to produce one less of its original models. Recall from Chapter 1 that the **opportunity cost** of any activity is the highest-valued alternative that must be given up to engage in that activity. For Tesla, the opportunity cost of producing one more Model 3 is the number of original models the company will not be able to produce because it has shifted those resources to producing the additional Model 3. For example, if Tesla moves from point B to point C, the opportunity cost of producing 20 more Model 3s per day is the 20 fewer original models that it can produce.

What point on the production possibilities frontier is best? We can't tell without further information. If consumer demand for Model 3s is greater than the demand for the original models (as Tesla expected), the company is likely to choose a point closer to E. If demand for the original models is greater than the demand for Model 3s, the company is likely to choose a point closer to A. **MyLab Economics** Concept Check

Opportunity cost The highest-valued alternative that must be given up to engage in an activity.

Solved Problem 2.1

Drawing a Production Possibilities Frontier for Tesla Motors

Suppose, for simplicity, that during any given week, the machinery and number of workers at Tesla Motors's Fremont plant cannot be increased. So the number of original models or Model 3s the company can produce during the week depends on how many hours are devoted to assembling each of the different models. Assume that Model 3s are more difficult to assemble, so if Tesla devotes an hour to assembling its original Model S or Model X, it will produce 15 vehicles, but if Tesla devotes an hour to producing Model 3s, it will produce only 10 vehicles. Assume that the plant can run for 8 hours per day.

a. Use the information given to fill in the missing cells in the following table:

Choice	Hours Spent Making Original Models	Hours Spent Making Model 3s	Quantity Produced per Day Original Models	Quantity Produced per Day Model 3s
A	8	0		
B	7	1		
C	6	2		
D	5	3		
E	4	4		
F	3	5		
G	2	6		
H	1	7		
I	0	8		

b. Use the data in the table to draw a production possibilities frontier graph illustrating Tesla's trade-off between assembling original models and assembling Model 3s. Label the vertical axis "Quantity of original models produced per day." Label the horizontal axis "Quantity of Model 3s produced per day." Make sure to label the values where Tesla's production possibilities frontier intersects the vertical and horizontal axes.

c. Label the points representing choice D and choice E. If Tesla is at choice D, what is its opportunity cost of making 10 more Model 3s?

Solving the Problem

Step 1: Review the chapter material. This problem is about using production possibilities frontiers to analyze trade-offs, so you may want to review the section "Graphing the Production Possibilities Frontier," which begins on page 42.

Step 2: Answer part (a) by filling in the table. If Tesla can assemble 15 original models in 1 hour, then with choice A, it can assemble 120 original models and 0 Model 3s. Because Tesla can assemble 10 Model 3s in 1 hour, with choice B, it will produce 105 original models and 10 Model 3s. Using similar reasoning, you can fill in the remaining cells in the table as follows:

Choice	Hours Spent Making Original Models	Hours Spent Making Model 3s	Quantity Produced per Day Original Models	Quantity Produced per Day Model 3s
A	8	0	120	0
B	7	1	105	10
C	6	2	90	20
D	5	3	75	30
E	4	4	60	40
F	3	5	45	50
G	2	6	30	60
H	1	7	15	70
I	0	8	0	80

Step 3: **Answer part (b) by drawing the production possibilities frontier graph.** Using the data from the table in step 2, you should draw a graph that looks like this:

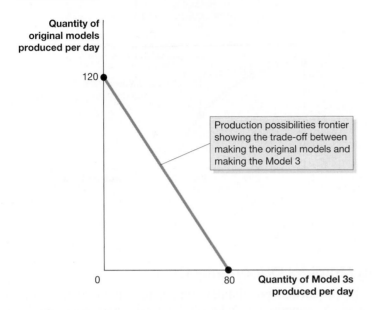

If Tesla devotes all 8 hours to assembling original models, it will produce 120 of them. Therefore, Tesla's production possibilities frontier will intersect the vertical axis at 120 original models produced. If Tesla devotes all 8 hours to assembling Model 3s, it will produce 80 of them. Therefore, Tesla's production possibilities frontier will intersect the horizontal axis at 80 Model 3s produced.

Step 4: **Answer part (c) by labeling choices D and E on your graph.** The points for choices *D* and *E* can be plotted using the information from the table:

Moving from choice *D* to choice *E* increases Tesla's production of Model 3s by 10 but lowers its production of original models by 15. Therefore, Tesla's opportunity cost of producing 10 more Model 3s is producing 15 fewer original models.

Your Turn: For more practice, do related problem 1.10 on page 67 at the end of this chapter.

Figure 2.2

Increasing Marginal Opportunity Costs

As the economy moves down the production possibilities frontier, it experiences *increasing marginal opportunity costs* because increasing automobile production by a given quantity requires larger and larger decreases in tank production. For example, to increase automobile production from 0 to 200—moving from point *A* to point *B*—the economy has to give up only 50 tanks. But to increase automobile production by another 200 vehicles—moving from point *B* to point *C*—the economy has to give up 150 tanks.

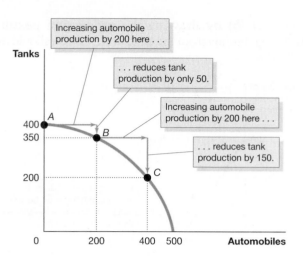

Increasing Marginal Opportunity Costs

We can use the production possibilities frontier to explore issues concerning the economy as a whole. Suppose we divide all the goods and services produced in the economy into just two types: military goods and civilian goods. In Figure 2.2, tanks represent military goods and automobiles represent civilian goods. If all the country's resources are devoted to producing military goods, 400 tanks can be produced in one year. If all resources are devoted to producing civilian goods, 500 automobiles can be produced in one year. Devoting resources to producing both goods results in the economy being at other points along the production possibilities frontier.

Notice that this production possibilities frontier is bowed outward rather than being a straight line. Because the curve is bowed out, the opportunity cost of automobiles in terms of tanks depends on where the economy currently is on the production possibilities frontier. For example, to increase automobile production from 0 to 200—moving from point *A* to point *B*—the economy has to give up only 50 tanks. But to increase automobile production by another 200 vehicles—moving from point *B* to point *C*—the economy has to give up 150 tanks.

As the economy moves down the production possibilities frontier, it experiences *increasing marginal opportunity costs* because increasing automobile production by a given quantity requires larger and larger decreases in tank production. Increasing marginal opportunity costs occur because some workers, machines, and other resources are better suited to one use than to another. At point *A*, some resources that are well suited to producing automobiles—such as workers who have years of experience on automobile assembly lines—are now producing tanks. Shifting these resources into producing automobiles by moving from point *A* to point *B* allows a substantial increase in automobile production without much loss of tank production. But as the economy moves down the production possibilities frontier, more and more resources that are better suited to tank production are switched to automobile production. As a result, the increases in automobile production become increasingly smaller, while the decreases in tank production become increasingly larger. We would expect in most situations that production possibilities frontiers will be bowed outward rather than linear, as we assumed in the Tesla example discussed earlier.

The idea of increasing marginal opportunity costs illustrates an important economic concept: *The more resources already devoted to an activity, the smaller the payoff to devoting additional resources to that activity.* For example:

- The more hours you have already spent studying economics, the smaller the increase in your test grade from each additional hour you spend—and the greater the opportunity cost of using the hour in that way.

- The more funds a firm has devoted to research and development during a given year, the smaller the amount of useful knowledge it receives from each additional dollar spent—and the greater the opportunity cost of using the funds in that way.
- The more funds the federal government spends cleaning up toxic waste dumps during a given year, the smaller the reduction in pollution from each additional dollar spent—and, once again, the greater the opportunity cost of using the funds in that way. **MyLab Economics** Concept Check

Economic Growth

At any given time, the total resources available to any economy are fixed. For example, if the United States produces more automobiles, it must produce less of something else—tanks in our example. The capital stock is the amount of machinery and other physical capital available in an economy. Over time, the resources available to an economy may increase because both the labor force and the capital stock increase. When the amount of resources increases, the economy's production possibilities frontier shifts outward, making it possible to produce both more automobiles and more tanks. Panel (a) of Figure 2.3 shows that over time, the economy can move from point *A* to point *B*, producing more tanks and more automobiles.

Similarly, technological change makes it possible to produce more goods with the same number of workers and the same amount of machinery, which also shifts the production possibilities frontier outward. Technological change need not affect all sectors equally. Panel (b) of Figure 2.3 shows the results of technological change in the automobile industry that increases the quantity of automobiles workers can produce per year while leaving unchanged the quantity of tanks they can produce.

Outward shifts in the production possibilities frontier represent **economic growth** because they allow the economy to increase the production of goods and services, which ultimately raises the standard of living. In the United States and other high-income countries, the market system has aided the process of economic growth, which over the past 200 years has greatly increased the well-being of the average person. **MyLab Economics** Concept Check

Economic growth The ability of the economy to increase the production of goods and services.

MyLab Economics Study Plan

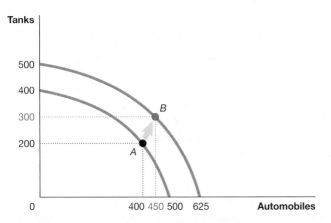

(a) Shifting out the production possibilities frontier

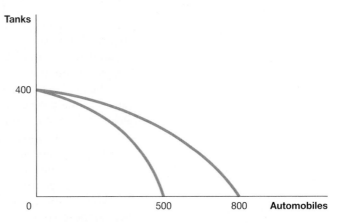

(b) Technological change in the automobile industry

MyLab Economics Animation

Figure 2.3   **Economic Growth**

Panel (a) shows that as more economic resources become available and technological change occurs, the economy can move from point *A* to point *B*, producing more tanks and more automobiles. Panel (b) shows the results of technological change in the automobile industry that increases the quantity of vehicles workers can produce per year while leaving unchanged the maximum quantity of tanks they can produce. Outward shifts in the production possibilities frontier represent *economic growth*.

Comparative Advantage and Trade

LEARNING OBJECTIVE: Describe comparative advantage and explain how it serves as the basis for trade.

Trade The act of buying and selling.

We can use the concepts of the production possibilities frontier and opportunity cost to understand the basic economic activity of *trade*. Markets are fundamentally about **trade**, which is the act of buying and selling. Sometimes we trade directly, as when children trade one baseball card for another baseball card. But often we trade indirectly: We sell our labor services as, say, an accountant, a salesperson, or a nurse for money, and then we use the money earned to buy goods and services. Although in these cases trade takes place indirectly, ultimately the accountant, salesperson, or nurse is trading his or her services for food, clothing, and other goods and services. One of the great benefits of trade is that it makes it possible for people to become better off by increasing both their production and their consumption.

Specialization and Gains from Trade

Consider the following situation: You and your neighbor both have fruit trees on your properties. Initially, suppose you have only apple trees and your neighbor has only cherry trees. In this situation, if you both like apples and cherries, there is an obvious opportunity for both of you to gain from trade: You trade some of your apples for some of your neighbor's cherries, making you both better off. But what if there are apple and cherry trees growing on both of your properties? In that case, there can still be gains from trade. For example, your neighbor might be very good at picking apples, and you might be very good at picking cherries. It would make sense for your neighbor to concentrate on picking apples and for you to concentrate on picking cherries. You can then trade some of the cherries you pick for some of the apples your neighbor picks. But what if your neighbor is actually better at picking both apples and cherries than you are?

We can use production possibilities frontiers (*PPFs*) to show how your neighbor can benefit from trading with you *even though she is better than you are at picking both apples and cherries*. (For simplicity, and because it will not have any effect on the conclusions we draw, we will assume that the *PPFs* in this example are straight lines.) The table in Figure 2.4 shows how many apples and how many cherries you and your neighbor can pick in one week. We can use the data in the table to construct *PPFs* for you and your neighbor. Panel (a) shows your *PPF*. If you devote all your time to picking apples, you can pick 20 pounds of apples per week. If you devote all your time to picking cherries, you can pick 20 pounds per week. Panel (b) shows that if your neighbor devotes all her time to picking apples, she can pick 30 pounds. If she devotes all her time to picking cherries, she can pick 60 pounds.

The *PPFs* in Figure 2.4 show how many apples and cherries you and your neighbor can consume *without trade*. Suppose that when you don't trade with your neighbor, you pick and consume 8 pounds of apples and 12 pounds of cherries per week. This combination of apples and cherries is represented by point *A* in panel (a) of Figure 2.5. When your neighbor doesn't trade with you, she picks and consumes 9 pounds of apples and 42 pounds of cherries per week. This combination of apples and cherries is represented by point *C* in panel (b).

After years in which you each pick and consume your own apples and cherries, suppose your neighbor makes the following proposal: Next week she will trade you 15 pounds of her cherries for 10 pounds of your apples. Should you accept this proposal? As we can see in Figure 2.5, you should accept because you will end up with more apples and more cherries to consume. To take advantage of her proposal, you should specialize in picking only apples rather than splitting your time between picking apples and picking cherries. We know specializing will allow you to pick 20 pounds of apples. You can trade 10 pounds of apples to your neighbor for 15 pounds of her cherries. The result is that you will be able to consume 10 pounds of apples and 15 pounds of cherries (point *B* in panel (a) of Figure 2.5). You are clearly

	You		Your Neighbor	
	Apples	Cherries	Apples	Cherries
Devote all time to picking apples	20 pounds	0 pounds	30 pounds	0 pounds
Devote all time to picking cherries	0 pounds	20 pounds	0 pounds	60 pounds

(a) Your production possibilities frontier

(b) Your neighbor's production possibilities frontier

MyLab Economics Animation

Figure 2.4 **Production Possibilities for You and Your Neighbor, without Trade**

The table shows how many pounds of apples and how many pounds of cherries you and your neighbor can each pick in one week. We can use the data from the table to construct PPFs for you and your neighbor. Panel (a) shows your PPF. If you devote all your time to picking apples and none to picking cherries, you can pick 20 pounds. If you devote all your time to picking cherries, you can pick 20 pounds. Panel (b) shows that if your neighbor devotes all her time to picking apples, she can pick 30 pounds. If she devotes all her time to picking cherries, she can pick 60 pounds.

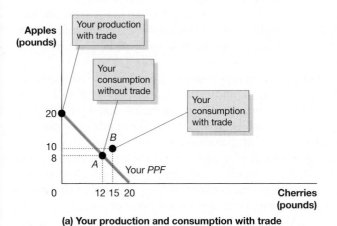

(a) Your production and consumption with trade

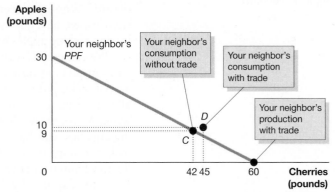

(b) Your neighbor's production and consumption with trade

MyLab Economics Animation

Figure 2.5 **Gains from Trade**

When you don't trade with your neighbor, you pick and consume 8 pounds of apples and 12 pounds of cherries per week—point A in panel (a). When your neighbor doesn't trade with you, she picks and consumes 9 pounds of apples and 42 pounds of cherries per week—point C in panel (b). If you specialize in picking apples, you can pick 20 pounds. If your neighbor specializes in picking cherries, she can pick 60 pounds. If you trade 10 pounds of your apples for 15 pounds of your neighbor's cherries, you will be able to consume 10 pounds of apples and 15 pounds of cherries—point B in panel (a). Your neighbor can now consume 10 pounds of apples and 45 pounds of cherries—point D in panel (b). You and your neighbor are both better off as a result of the trade.

MyLab Economics Animation

Table 2.1

A Summary of the Gains
from Trade

	You		Your Neighbor	
	Apples (in pounds)	Cherries (in pounds)	Apples (in pounds)	Cherries (in pounds)
Production *and* consumption *without* trade	8	12	9	42
Production *with* trade	20	0	0	60
Consumption *with* trade	10	15	10	45
Gains from trade (increased consumption)	2	3	1	3

better off as a result of trading with your neighbor: You can now consume 2 more pounds of apples and 3 more pounds of cherries than you were consuming without trading. You have moved beyond your *PPF*!

Your neighbor has also benefited from the trade. By specializing in picking only cherries, she can pick 60 pounds. She trades 15 pounds of cherries to you for 10 pounds of apples. She can then consume 10 pounds of apples and 45 pounds of cherries (point *D* in panel (b) of Figure 2.5). This combination is 1 more pound of apples and 3 more pounds of cherries than she was consuming before trading with you. She also has moved beyond her *PPF*. Table 2.1 summarizes the changes in production and consumption that result from your trade with your neighbor. (In this example, we chose one specific rate of trading cherries for apples—15 pounds of cherries for 10 pounds of apples. There are, however, many other rates of trading cherries for apples that would also make you and your neighbor better off.)   **MyLab Economics** Concept Check

Absolute Advantage versus Comparative Advantage

Perhaps the most remarkable aspect of the preceding example is that your neighbor benefits from trading with you even though she is better than you at picking both apples and cherries. **Absolute advantage** is the ability of an individual, a firm, or a country to produce more of a good or service than competitors, using the same amount of resources. Your neighbor has an absolute advantage over you in picking both apples and cherries because she can pick more of each fruit than you can in the same amount of time. Although it seems that your neighbor should pick her own apples *and* her own cherries, we have just seen that she is better off specializing in picking cherries and leaving picking apples to you.

We can consider further why both you and your neighbor benefit from specializing in picking only one fruit. First, think about the opportunity cost to each of you of picking the two fruits. We saw from the *PPF* in Figure 2.4 that if you devoted all your time to picking apples, you would be able to pick 20 pounds of apples per week. As you move down your *PPF* and shift time away from picking apples to picking cherries, you have to give up 1 pound of apples for each pound of cherries you pick (the slope of your *PPF* is −1). (For a review of calculating slopes, see the appendix to Chapter 1.) Therefore, your opportunity cost of picking 1 pound of cherries is 1 pound of apples. By the same reasoning, your opportunity cost of picking 1 pound of apples is 1 pound of cherries. Your neighbor's *PPF* has a different slope, so she faces a different trade-off: As she shifts time from picking apples to picking cherries, she has to give up 0.5 pound of apples for every 1 pound of cherries she picks (the slope of your neighbor's *PPF* is −0.5). As she shifts time from picking cherries to picking apples, she gives up 2 pounds of cherries for every 1 pound of apples she picks. Therefore, her opportunity cost of picking 1 pound of apples is 2 pounds of cherries, and her opportunity cost of picking 1 pound of cherries is 0.5 pound of apples.

Absolute advantage The ability of an individual, a firm, or a country to produce more of a good or service than competitors, using the same amount of resources.

	Opportunity Cost of Picking 1 Pound of Apples	Opportunity Cost of Picking 1 Pound of Cherries
You	1 pound of cherries	1 pound of apples
Your neighbor	2 pounds of cherries	0.5 pound of apples

Table 2.2

Opportunity Costs of Picking Apples and Cherries

Table 2.2 summarizes the opportunity costs for you and your neighbor of picking apples and cherries. Note that even though your neighbor can pick more apples in a week than you can, the *opportunity cost* of picking apples is higher for her than for you because when she picks apples, she gives up more cherries than you do. So, even though she has an absolute advantage over you in picking apples, it is more costly for her to pick apples than it is for you. The table also shows that her opportunity cost of picking cherries is lower than yours. **Comparative advantage** is the ability of an individual, a firm, or a country to produce a good or service at a lower opportunity cost than competitors. In picking apples, your neighbor has an *absolute advantage* over you, while you have a *comparative advantage* over her. Your neighbor has both an absolute advantage and a comparative advantage over you in picking cherries. As we have seen, you are better off specializing in picking apples, and your neighbor is better off specializing in picking cherries.   MyLab Economics Concept Check

Comparative advantage The ability of an individual, a firm, or a country to produce a good or service at a lower opportunity cost than competitors.

Comparative Advantage and the Gains from Trade

We have just arrived at an important economic principle: *The basis for trade is comparative advantage, not absolute advantage.* The fastest apple pickers do not necessarily do much apple picking. If the fastest apple pickers have a comparative advantage in some other activity—picking cherries, playing Major League Baseball, or being industrial engineers—they are better off specializing in that activity. Individuals, firms, and countries are better off if they specialize in producing goods and services for which they have a comparative advantage and obtain the other goods and services they need by trading. We will return to the important concept of comparative advantage in Chapter 9, which is devoted to the subject of international trade.   MyLab Economics Concept Check

MyLab Economics Study Plan

Don't Let This Happen to You

Don't Confuse Absolute Advantage and Comparative Advantage

First, make sure you know the definitions:

- **Absolute advantage.** The ability of an individual, a firm, or a country to produce more of a good or service than competitors, using the same amount of resources. In our example, your neighbor has an absolute advantage over you in both picking apples and picking cherries.

- **Comparative advantage.** The ability of an individual, a firm, or a country to produce a good or service at a lower opportunity cost than competitors. In our example, your neighbor has a comparative advantage in picking

cherries, but you have a comparative advantage in picking apples.

Keep these two key points in mind:

1. It is possible to have an absolute advantage in producing a good or service without having a comparative advantage. This is the case with your neighbor picking apples.

2. It is possible to have a comparative advantage in producing a good or service without having an absolute advantage. This is the case with your picking apples.

MyLab Economics Study Plan

Your Turn: Test your understanding by doing related problem 2.5 on page 69 at the end of this chapter.

Solved Problem 2.2

Comparative Advantage and the Gains from Trade

Suppose that Canada and the United States both produce maple syrup and honey, which are sold for the same price in both countries. These are the combinations of the two goods that each country can produce in one day, using the same amounts of capital and labor:

Canada		United States	
Honey (in tons)	Maple Syrup (in tons)	Honey (in tons)	Maple Syrup (in tons)
0	60	0	50
10	45	10	40
20	30	20	30
30	15	30	20
40	0	40	10
		50	0

a. Which country has a comparative advantage in producing maple syrup? Which country has a comparative advantage in producing honey?

b. Suppose that Canada is currently producing 30 tons of honey and 15 tons of maple syrup, and the United States is currently producing 10 tons of honey and 40 tons of maple syrup. Demonstrate that Canada and the United States can both be better off if they specialize in producing only one good and trade for the other.

c. Illustrate your answer to part (b) by drawing a *PPF* for Canada and a *PPF* for the United States. Show on your *PPFs* the combinations of honey and maple syrup produced and consumed in each country before and after trade.

Solving the Problem

Step 1: **Review the chapter material.** This problem is about comparative advantage, so you may want to review the section "Absolute Advantage versus Comparative Advantage," which begins on page 50.

Step 2: **Answer part (a) by calculating which country has a comparative advantage in each activity.** Remember that a country has a comparative advantage in producing a good if it can produce the good at the lowest opportunity cost. When Canada produces 1 more ton of honey, it produces 1.5 tons less of maple syrup. When the United States produces 1 more ton of honey, it produces 1 ton less of maple syrup. Therefore, for the United States, the opportunity cost of producing honey—1 ton of maple syrup—is lower than for Canada—1.5 tons of maple syrup. When Canada produces 1 more ton of maple syrup, it produces 0.67 ton less of honey. When the United States produces 1 more ton of maple syrup, it produces 1 ton less of honey. Therefore, Canada's opportunity cost of producing maple syrup—0.67 ton of honey—is lower than that of the United States—1 ton of honey. We can conclude that the United States has a comparative advantage in the production of honey and Canada has a comparative advantage in the production of maple syrup.

Step 3: **Answer part (b) by showing that specialization makes Canada and the United States better off.** We know that Canada and the United States should each specialize where it has a comparative advantage. If both countries specialize, Canada will produce 60 tons of maple syrup and 0 tons of honey, and the United States will produce 0 tons of maple syrup and 50 tons of honey. After both countries specialize, the United States could then trade 30 tons of honey to Canada for 40 tons of maple syrup. (Other mutually beneficial trades are possible as well.) We can summarize the results in a table:

	Before Trade		After Trade	
	Honey (in tons)	Maple Syrup (in tons)	Honey (in tons)	Maple Syrup (in tons)
Canada	30	15	30	20
United States	10	40	20	40

The United States is better off after trade because it can consume the same amount of maple syrup and 10 more tons of honey. Canada is better off after trade because it can consume the same amount of honey and 5 more tons of maple syrup.

Step 4: Answer part (c) by drawing the PPFs.

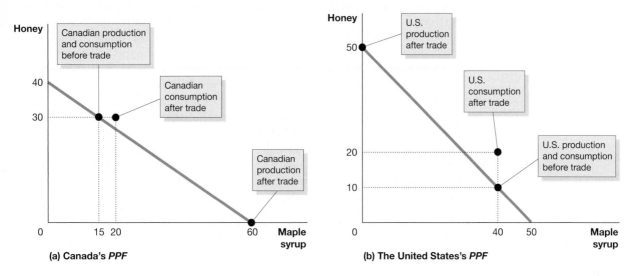

(a) Canada's *PPF*

(b) The United States's *PPF*

Your Turn: For more practice, do related problems 2.6 and 2.7 on page 69 at the end of this chapter.

MyLab Economics Study Plan

Apply the Concept   MyLab Economics Video

Comparative Advantage, Opportunity Cost, and Housework

Among roommates, married couples, and other people living together, dividing up the household chores can be a source of stress. Traditionally with married couples, women did most of the housework, such as preparing meals, cleaning, and doing laundry. In 1965, married women with children averaged about 32 hours of housework per week, while married men averaged only 4 hours. Today, women average about 15.5 hours of housework, while men average about 10 hours.

Housework doesn't seem to be part of buying, selling, and the usual topics of business and economics. In fact, we can use basic economic concepts to analyze housework. Consider first the most efficient way to divide up household chores. Suppose Jack and Jill need to decide how they will get the cooking and laundry done. Assume that Jack has an absolute advantage over Jill in both chores, but he has a big advantage over Jill in cooking—he takes much less time to prepare very tasty meals—but is only a little faster than Jill in doing laundry. In other words, assuming that they have the same amount of time available to do housework, Jack has a comparative advantage in cooking, while Jill has a comparative advantage in doing laundry. So rather than Jack and Jill both doing some of the cooking and some of the laundry, they would be better off if Jack follows his comparative advantage and does all the cooking, while Jill follows her comparative advantage and does all the laundry.

Economics can also provide some insight into the decline in the number of hours spent on housework since the 1960s. Combined, men and women now spend more than 30 percent fewer hours on housework. This decline has been partly driven by technology, particularly improvements in household appliances, such as dishwashers and microwave ovens. The decline in the number of hours women devote to housework also reflects the greater job opportunities available to women today than in the 1960s. The opportunity cost to a woman of spending time on housework and childcare is the wage she gives up by not spending that time in paid work. If a woman could work for an hour at a wage of $20 but spends that hour doing household chores, the opportunity cost of the time spent on chores is $20. As job opportunities for women and the wages those jobs pay have increased, so has the opportunity cost of doing housework. So in

What's the most efficient way to divide up household chores?

Rolf Bruderer/Flirt/Glow Images

addition to taking advantage of improved appliances, many families have found that the cost of hiring specialists in household chores, such as cleaning services and lawn care services, is lower than the cost of the wife (or husband) performing those chores.

As women's wages have risen relative to men's wages, the opportunity cost to women of doing housework has increased more than has the opportunity cost to men. So we would expect that in addition to women devoting fewer hours to housework, the gap between the hours women and men devote would narrow. In fact, while in 1965, women devoted 28 more hours per week to housework than did men, in 2016, they devoted only 6 more hours. The average number of hours women devoted to paid work increased from 8 hours per week to 20 hours.

Of course, changes in social attitudes also help explain changes in how men and women allocate their time. But we have seen that the basic economic concepts of comparative advantage and opportunity cost provide important insights into the not-so-wonderful world of household chores.

Sources: U.S. Bureau of Labor Statistics, "American Time Use Survey—2016," June 27, 2017; Kim Parker and Wendy Wang, "Modern Parenthood: Roles of Moms and Dads Converge as They Balance Work and Family," pewsocialtrends.org, March 14, 2013; Emily Oster, "You're Dividing the Chores Wrong," *Slate*, November 21, 2012; and Ellen Byron, "A Truce in the Chore Wars," *New York Times*, December 4, 2012.

MyLab Economics Study Plan

Your Turn: Test your understanding by doing related problems 2.14 and 2.15 on pages 69–70 at the end of this chapter.

2.3 The Market System

LEARNING OBJECTIVE: Explain the basics of how a market system works.

We have seen that households, firms, and the government face trade-offs and incur opportunity costs because resources are scarce. We have also seen that trade allows people to specialize according to their comparative advantage. By engaging in trade, people can raise their incomes and their standard of living. Of course, trade in the modern world is much more complex than the examples we have considered so far. Trade today involves the decisions of millions of people around the world. How are all of these decisions coordinated? In the United States and most other countries, trade is carried out in markets. Markets also determine the answers to the three fundamental questions discussed in Chapter 1:

1. What goods and services will be produced?
2. How will the goods and services be produced?
3. Who will receive the goods and services produced?

Market A group of buyers and sellers of a good or service and the institution or arrangement by which they come together to trade.

Recall that a **market** is a group of buyers and sellers of a good or service and the institution or arrangement by which they come together to trade. Markets take many forms: They can be physical places, such as the pizza parlors in your city or the New York Stock Exchange, or virtual places, such as eBay. In a market, the buyers are demanders of goods or services, and the sellers are suppliers of goods or services. Households and firms interact in two types of markets: product markets and factor markets. **Product markets** are markets for goods—such as smartphones—and services—such as medical treatment. In product markets, households are demanders and firms are suppliers. **Factor markets** are markets for the *factors of production*. **Factors of production** are the inputs used to make goods and services. Factors of production are divided into four broad categories:

Product market A market for goods—such as computers—or services—such as medical treatment.

Factor market A market for the factors of production, such as labor, capital, natural resources, and entrepreneurial ability.

Factors of production Labor, capital, natural resources, and other inputs used to make goods and services.

1. *Labor* includes all types of work, from the part-time labor of teenagers working at McDonald's to the work of senior managers in large corporations.
2. *Capital* refers to physical capital, such as computers, office buildings, and machine tools, used to produce other goods.
3. *Natural resources* include land, water, oil, iron ore, and other raw materials (or "gifts of nature") that are used in producing goods.

4. An *entrepreneur* is someone who operates a business. *Entrepreneurial ability* is the ability to bring together the other factors of production to successfully produce and sell goods and services.

The Circular Flow of Income

Two key groups participate in markets:

1. *Households* are all the individuals in a home. A household may consist of one person or several persons. Households are suppliers of factors of production—particularly labor—employed by firms to make goods and services. Households use the income they receive from selling the factors of production to purchase the goods and services supplied by firms. We are familiar with households as suppliers of labor because most people earn most of their income by going to work, meaning they are selling their labor services to firms in the labor market. But households own the other factors of production as well, either directly or indirectly, by owning the firms that own these resources. All firms are owned by households. Small firms, like a neighborhood restaurant, might be owned by one person. Large firms, like Apple, are owned by millions of households that buy shares of stock in them. When firms pay profits to the people who own them, the firms are paying for using the capital and natural resources that are supplied to them by those owners. So, we can generalize by saying that in factor markets, households are suppliers and firms are demanders.

2. *Firms* are suppliers of goods and services. Firms use the funds they receive from selling goods and services to buy or hire the factors of production needed to make the goods and services.

We can use a simple economic model called the **circular-flow diagram** to see how participants in markets are linked. Figure 2.6 shows that in factor markets, households supply labor and other factors of production in exchange for wages and other

Circular-flow diagram A model that illustrates how participants in markets are linked.

MyLab Economics Animation

Figure 2.6

The Circular-Flow Diagram

Households and firms are linked together in a circular flow of production, income, and spending. The blue arrows show the flow of the factors of production. In factor markets, households supply labor, entrepreneurial ability, and other factors of production to firms. Firms use these factors of production to make goods and services that they supply to households in product markets. The red arrows show the flow of goods and services from firms to households. The green arrows show the flow of funds. In factor markets, households receive wages and other payments from firms in exchange for supplying the factors of production. Households use these wages and other payments to purchase goods and services from firms in product markets. Firms sell goods and services to households in product markets, and they use the funds to purchase the factors of production from households in factor markets.

top: Ariel Skelley/Digital Vision/Getty images; left: Elena Elisseeva/Shutterstock; right: Stockbroker/MBI/Alamy Stock Photo; bottom: Mikael Damkier/Shutterstock payments from firms. In product markets, households use the payments they earn in factor markets to purchase the goods and services supplied by firms. Firms produce these goods and services using the factors of production supplied by households. In the figure, the blue arrows show the flow of factors of production from households through factor markets to firms. The red arrows show the flow of goods and services from firms through product markets to households. The green arrows show the flow of funds from firms through factor markets to households and the flow of spending from households through product markets to firms.

Like all economic models, the circular-flow diagram is a simplified version of reality. Figure 2.6 leaves out (1) the important role of government in buying goods from firms and in making payments, such as Social Security or unemployment insurance payments, to households; (2) the roles played by banks, the stock and bond markets, and other parts of the *financial system* in aiding the flow of funds from lenders to borrowers; and (3) the fact that some goods and services purchased by domestic households are produced in foreign countries and some goods and services produced by domestic firms are sold to foreign households. (We explore the government, the financial system, and the international sector in later chapters.) Despite these simplifications, the circular-flow diagram in Figure 2.6 helps us see how product markets, factor markets, and their participants are linked together. One of the great wonders of the market system is that it manages to successfully coordinate the independent activities of so many households and firms. **MyLab Economics** Concept Check

The Gains from Free Markets

Free market A market with few government restrictions on how a good or service can be produced or sold or on how a factor of production can be employed.

A **free market** exists when the government places few restrictions on how goods and services can be produced or sold or on how factors of production can be employed. Governments in all modern economies intervene more than is consistent with a fully free market. In that sense, we can think of the free market as being a benchmark against which we can judge actual economies. There are relatively few government restrictions on economic activities in the United States, Canada, Western Europe, Hong Kong, Singapore, and Estonia. So these countries come close to the free market benchmark. In countries such as Cuba and North Korea, the free market system has been rejected in favor of centrally planned economies with extensive government control over product and factor markets. Countries that come closest to the free market benchmark have been more successful than countries with centrally planned economies in providing their people with rising living standards.

The Scottish philosopher Adam Smith is considered the father of modern economics because his book, *An Inquiry into the Nature and Causes of the Wealth of Nations*, published in 1776, was an early and very influential argument for the free market system. Smith was writing at a time when extensive government restrictions on markets were common. In many parts of Europe, the *guild system* prevailed. Under this system, governments would give guilds, or organizations of producers, the authority to control the production of a good. For example, the shoemakers' guild controlled who was allowed to produce shoes, how many shoes they could produce, and what price they could charge. In France, the cloth makers' guild even dictated the number of threads in the weave of the cloth.

Smith argued that such restrictions reduced the income and wealth of a country and its people by restricting the quantity of goods produced. Some people at the time supported the restrictions of the guild system because it was in their financial interest to do so. If you were a member of a guild, the restrictions served to reduce the competition you faced. But other people believed that the alternative to the guild system was economic disorder. Smith argued that these people were wrong and that a country could enjoy a smoothly functioning economic system if firms were freed from restrictions placed on their operations either by guilds or directly by governments. **MyLab Economics** Concept Check

The Market Mechanism

In Smith's day, defenders of restrictions on how firms operate argued that if, for example, the shoemakers' guild did not control shoe production, either too many or too few shoes would be produced. In contrast, Smith maintained that prices would do a better job of coordinating the activities of buyers and sellers than the guilds could. A key to understanding Smith's argument is the assumption that *individuals usually act in a rational, self-interested way*. In particular, individuals take the actions that are most likely to make themselves better off financially. This assumption of rational, self-interested behavior underlies nearly all economic analysis. In fact, economics can be distinguished from other disciplines that study human behavior—such as sociology and psychology—by its emphasis on the assumption of self-interested behavior. Adam Smith understood— as economists today understand—that people's motives can be complex. But when we analyze people in the act of buying and selling, the motivation of financial reward usually provides the best explanation for the actions people take.

For example, suppose that a significant number of consumers switch from buying conventional gasoline-powered cars to buying either gasoline/electric-powered hybrid cars, such as the Toyota Prius, or all-electric cars, such as the Tesla Model 3. Firms will find that they can charge relatively higher prices for hybrid cars and electric cars than they can for gasoline-powered cars. The self-interest of these firms will lead them to respond to consumers' wishes by producing more hybrid and electric cars and fewer gasoline-powered cars. Or suppose that consumers decide that they want to eat less bread, pasta, and other foods that contain gluten. Then the prices firms can charge for gluten-free bread and pasta will increase. The self-interest of firms will lead them to produce more gluten-free bread and pasta and less regular bread and pasta, which, in fact, is what has happened over the past 10 years.

Note that for the market mechanism to work in response to changes in consumers' wants, *prices must be flexible*. The *relative price* is the price of one good or service relative to the prices of other goods or services. Changes in relative prices provide information, or a signal, to both consumers and firms. For example, consumers worldwide have increased their demand for cattle and poultry. Because corn is fed to cattle and poultry, prices for corn have increased relative to prices for other crops. Many farmers in the United States received this price signal and responded by increasing the amount of corn they planted and decreasing the amount of soybeans and wheat. One Kansas farmer was quoted as saying, "It seemed to me there was $100 to $150 per acre more money in the corn than there was in the beans. That's the kind of math that a lot of guys were using." In recent years, the United States has experienced record corn crops. Similarly, falling prices for DVDs and music CDs were a signal to movie studios and record companies to devote fewer resources to these products and more resources to making movies and music available to stream online.

In the United States today, governments at the federal, state, and local levels set or regulate the prices of only about 10 to 20 percent of goods and services. The prices of other goods and services are free to change as consumer preferences change and as costs of production change.

In the case where consumers want more of a product, and in the case where they want less of a product, the market system responds without a guild or the government giving orders about how much to produce or what price to charge. Economists have used Adam Smith's metaphor of the *invisible hand* to describe how the market leads firms to provide consumers with the goods they want. Firms respond *individually* to changes in prices by making decisions that *collectively* end up satisfying the preferences of consumers.   **MyLab Economics** Concept Check

Apply the Concept   **MyLab Economics** Video

A Story of the Market System in Action: How Do You Make an iPad?

Apple produces the iPad. Because Apple's headquarters is in Cupertino, California, it seems reasonable to assume that iPads are also manufactured in that state. A poll by the *New York Times* showed that, in fact, a majority of people interviewed believed that iPads are manufactured in the United States, if not specifically in California. Although engineers at Apple designed the iPad, the company produces none of the components

Qilai Shen/Bloomberg/Getty Images

The market coordinates the activities of many people spread around the world who contribute to making an iPad.

of the iPad, and it doesn't assemble the components into finished products. Far from being produced entirely by one company in one country, the iPad requires the coordinated activities of thousands of workers and dozens of firms spread around the world.

Foxconn, which is based in Taiwan, assembles most iPads in factories in China and Brazil and ships them to Apple for sale in the United States. Pegatron, another Taiwanese firm with factories in China, also assembles some iPads. Although Foxconn and Pegatron do final assembly, they don't make any of the components and, in fact, charge Apple only about $6 for assembling each iPad.

Multiple firms can supply a particular component for an iPad model. The following table lists just some of the firms that have supplied Apple with iPad components.

Firm	Location of the Firm	iPad Component Supplied
AKM	Japan	Motion sensor
AU Optronics	Taiwan	Display
Avago Technologies	United States (Pennsylvania)	Wireless technology
Bosch Sensortec	Germany	Accelerometer
Broadcom	United States (California)	Touchscreen controller and wireless chip
Cirrus Logic	United States (Texas)	Audio chip
Corning	United States (New York)	Glass screen cover
Dialog Semiconductor	Germany	Power management chip
Elpida	United States (Idaho)	System memory
Infineon Technologies	Germany	Semiconductors
LG Electronics	South Korea	Display
Quicomm	United Kingdom	Wireless section
Samsung	South Korea	Display, flash memory, and applications processor
Sharp	Japan	Display
SK Hynix	South Korea	Flash memory
Skyworks Solutions	United States (Massachusetts)	Wireless technology
STMicroelectronics	France/Italy	Motion sensors
Texas Instruments	United States (Texas)	Touchscreen controller
Toshiba	Japan	Flash memory
TriQuint Semiconductor	United States (Oregon)	Wireless technology

Each of these suppliers in turn relies on its own suppliers. For example, Broadcom designs the touchscreen controller for the iPad and supplies it to Apple, but it does not manufacture the components of the controller or assemble them. To manufacture the components, Broadcom relies on SilTerra, based in Malaysia; SMIC, based in mainland China; and Taiwan Semiconductor Manufacturing Corporation (TSMC) and UMC, based in Taiwan. TSMC's factories are for the most part not in Taiwan but in mainland China and Eastern Europe. To assemble the components, Broadcom uses several companies, including Amkor Technology, based in Chandler, Arizona, and STATS ChipPAC, based in Singapore.

All told, an iPad contains hundreds of parts that are designed, manufactured, and assembled by firms around the world. Many of these firms are not even aware of which other firms are also producing components for the iPad. Few of the managers of these firms have met managers of the other firms or shared knowledge of how their particular components are produced. In fact, no one person—from Tim Cook, the chief executive officer of Apple, on down—possesses the knowledge of how to produce all the components that are assembled into an iPad. Instead, the invisible hand of the market has led these firms to contribute their knowledge and resources to the process that ultimately results in an iPad available for sale in a store in the United States. Apple has so efficiently organized the process of producing the iPad that you can order a custom iPad with a personal engraving and have it delivered from an assembly plant in China or Brazil to your doorstep in the United States in as little as three days.

Sources: Don Reisinger, "iPad Air 2 Models Cost Apple $275 to $358, Teardowns Reveal," cnet.com, October 29, 2014; Marjorie Connelly, "Poll Finds Consumer Confusion on Where Apple Devices Are Made," *New York Times,* January 25, 2012; Andrew Rassweiler, "Still Air: Apple iPad Air 2 Largely Holds the Line on Features and Costs, IHS Teardown Reveals," technology.ihs.com, October 28, 2014; and Eva Dou and Tripp Mickle, "Apple Supplier Foxconn Plans Expansion in U.S.," *Wall Street Journal,* December 7, 2016.

Your Turn: Test your understanding by doing related problems 3.8 and 3.9 on page 70 at the end of this chapter.

MyLab Economics Study Plan

The Role of the Entrepreneur in the Market System

Entrepreneurs are central to a market system. An **entrepreneur** is someone who operates a business. Entrepreneurs first determine what goods and services they believe consumers want and then decide how to produce those goods and services most profitably, using the available factors of production—labor, capital, and natural resources. Successful entrepreneurs are able to search out opportunities to provide new goods and services. Frequently these opportunities are created by new technology. Consumers and existing businesses often do not at first realize that the new technology makes new products feasible. For example, even after the development of the internal combustion engine had made automobiles practicable, Henry Ford remarked: "If I had asked my customers what they wanted, they would have said a faster horse." Because consumers often cannot evaluate a new product before it exists, some of the most successful entrepreneurs, such as the late Steve Jobs of Apple, rarely use *focus groups,* or meetings with consumers in which the consumers are asked what new products they would like to see. Instead, entrepreneurs think of products that consumers may not even realize they need, such as, in Jobs's case, an MP3 player—the iPod—or a tablet computer—the iPad. Entrepreneurs are important to the economy because they are often responsible for making new products widely available to consumers, as Henry Ford did with the automobile and Steve Jobs did with the iPod.

The firms that entrepreneurs found are typically small at first, as Apple and Ford were. Table 2.3 on the next page lists some of the important products entrepreneurs at small firms introduced during the twentieth century.

Entrepreneurs put their own funds at risk when they start businesses. If they are wrong about what consumers want or about the best way to produce goods and services, they can lose those funds. In fact, it is not unusual for entrepreneurs who eventually achieve great success to fail at first. For instance, early in their careers, both Henry Ford and Sakichi Toyoda, who eventually founded the Toyota Motor Corporation, started companies that quickly failed. Research by Richard Freeman of Harvard University has shown that a typical entrepreneur earns less than an employee at a large firm who has the same education and other characteristics. Few entrepreneurs make the fortunes earned by Mark Zuckerberg (Facebook), Steve Jobs (Apple), or Bill Gates (Microsoft).

Entrepreneurs make vital contributions to economic growth through their roles in responding to consumer wants and introducing new products. Government policies that encourage entrepreneurship are also likely to increase economic growth and raise the standard of living. In the next section, we consider the legal framework required for a successful market in which entrepreneurs can succeed.   MyLab Economics Concept Check

Entrepreneur Someone who operates a business, bringing together the factors of production—labor, capital, and natural resources—to produce goods and services.

The Legal Basis of a Successful Market System

In a free market, government does not restrict how firms produce and sell goods and services or how they employ factors of production. But the absence of such government restrictions is not enough for the market system to succeed in providing people

Table 2.3

Important Products Introduced by Entrepreneurs at Small Firms

Biotechnology	Inventor
Biomagnetic imaging	Raymond Damadian
Biosynthetic insulin	Herbert Boyer
DNA fingerprinting	Alec Jeffries
High-resolution CAT scanner	Robert Ledley
Communication	**Inventor**
FM radio	Edwin Howard Armstrong
Consumer Goods	**Inventor**
Air conditioning	William Haviland Carrier
Disposable diaper	Marion Donovan
Oral contraceptives	Carl Djerassi
Quick-frozen foods	Clarence Birdseye
Safety razor	King Gillette
Soft contact lens	Kevin Tuohy
Zipper	Gideon Sundback
Information Technology	**Inventor**
Integrated circuit	Jack Kilby
Microprocessor	Ted Hoff
Optical scanner	Everett Franklin Lindquist
Personal computer	Steve Jobs and Steve Wozniak
Supercomputer	Seymour Cray
Vacuum tube (television)	Philo Farnsworth
Transportation	**Inventor**
Airplane	Orville and Wilbur Wright
Automobile, mass produced	Henry Ford
Automobile windshield wiper	Mary Anderson
Helicopter	Igor Sikorsky
Hydraulic brake	Malcolm Lockheed
Overnight delivery service	Fred Smith

Sources: William J. Baumol, *The Microtheory of Innovative Entrepreneurship*, Princeton, NJ: Princeton University Press, 2010; Lemelson-MIT Program; and various other sources. Note that historians sometimes dispute the identity of the person who first commercially developed a particular product.

with a high standard of living. Government has to take active steps to provide a *legal environment* that will allow markets to operate efficiently.

Protection of Private Property For the market system to work well, individuals must be willing to take risks. Someone with $250,000 can be cautious and keep it safely in a bank—or even in cash, if the person doesn't trust banks. But the market system won't work unless a significant number of people are willing to risk their funds by investing them in businesses. Investing in businesses is risky in any country. Many businesses fail every year in the United States and other high-income countries. But in high-income countries, someone who starts a new business or invests in an existing business doesn't have to worry that the government, the military, or criminal gangs might decide to seize the business or demand payments for not destroying it. Unfortunately, in many low-income countries, business owners are not well protected from having their businesses seized by the government or from having their profits taken by criminals. Where these problems exist, opening a business can be extremely risky. Cash can be concealed easily, but a business is difficult to conceal or move.

Property rights are the rights individuals or firms have to the exclusive use of their property, including the right to buy or sell it. Property can be physical property, such as a store or factory. Property can also be intangible, such as the right to an idea. Two amendments to the U.S. Constitution guarantee property rights: The Fifth Amendment states that the federal government shall not deprive any person "of life, liberty, or property, without due process of law." The Fourteenth Amendment extends this guarantee to the actions of state governments: "No state . . . shall deprive any person of life, liberty, or property, without due process of law." Similar guarantees exist in every high-income country. Unfortunately, in many developing countries, such guarantees do not exist or are poorly enforced.

In any modern economy, *intellectual property rights* are very important. Intellectual property includes books, films, software, and ideas for new products or new ways of producing products. To protect intellectual property, the federal government grants a *patent* that gives an inventor—often a firm—the exclusive right to produce and sell a new product for a period of 20 years from the date the patent was filed. For instance, because Apple has a patent on its Siri voice-recognition software for smartphones and other devices, other firms cannot sell their own versions of Siri. The government grants patents to encourage firms to spend money on the research and development necessary to create new products. If other companies could freely copy Siri, Apple would not have spent the funds necessary to develop it. Just as a new product or a new method of making a product receives patent protection, new books, films, and software receive *copyright* protection. Under U.S. law, the creator of a book, film, or piece of music has the exclusive right to use the creation during the creator's lifetime. The creator's heirs retain this exclusive right for 70 years after the death of the creator.

In providing copyright protection for only a limited time, Congress provides economic incentives to creators while eventually—after the period of copyright has ended—allowing the creators' works to be freely available to others. The longer the period of copyright, the longer the creator (or the creators' family) can restrict others from using the work.

Enforcement of Contracts and Property Rights

Business activity often involves someone agreeing to carry out some action in the future. For example, you may borrow $20,000 to buy a car and promise the bank—by signing a loan contract—that you will pay back the money over the next five years. Or Facebook may sign a licensing agreement with a small technology company, agreeing to use that company's technology for a period of several years in return for a fee. Usually these agreements take the form of legal contracts. For the market system to work, businesses and individuals have to rely on these contracts being carried out. If one party to a legal contract does not fulfill its obligations—perhaps the small company had promised Facebook exclusive use of its technology but then begins licensing it to other companies—the other party can go to court to have the agreement enforced. Similarly, if you believe that the federal or state government has violated your property rights under the Fifth or Fourteenth Amendments, you can go to court to have your rights enforced.

But going to court to enforce a contract or property rights will be successful only if the court system is independent and judges are able to make impartial decisions on the basis of the law. In the United States and other high-income countries, the court systems have enough independence from other parts of the government and enough protection from intimidation by outside forces—such as criminal gangs—that they are able to make their decisions based on the law. In many developing countries, the court systems lack this independence and will not provide a remedy if the government violates property rights, or if a person with powerful political connections decides to violate a business contract.

If property rights are not well enforced, fewer goods and services will be produced. This reduces economic efficiency, leaving the economy inside its production possibilities frontier.

MyLab Economics Concept Check

Property rights The rights individuals or firms have to the exclusive use of their property, including the right to buy or sell it.

MyLab Economics Study Plan

Apply the Concept

Managers at Feeding America Use the Market Mechanism to Reduce Hunger

Jim West/Alamy Stock Photo

Feeding America uses the market mechanism to improve its allocation of food donations.

Charitable giving doesn't seem to have much to do with markets. When donors give money, clothing, or food to a charity, they typically don't expect anything in exchange—beyond a possible tax deduction. In 1979, retired businessman John van Hengel started Feeding America. This charity collects donations of food from farmers, supermarkets, food processing plants, and governments and distributes the food to thousands of food pantries and food programs operated by churches, schools, and community centers around the country. These programs give the donated food away free or at a very low price to low-income families.

By 2004, Feeding America was providing 1.8 billion pounds of food per year to millions of low-income people, but the organization's managers realized that they could serve even more people if they could operate more efficiently. In particular, the managers were concerned that food was sometimes not allocated in ways that were consistent with the needs of local food programs. For example, potatoes might be shipped to food programs in Idaho—the country's leading potato growing state—or milk might be shipped to food programs that lacked the refrigeration capacity to keep it fresh long enough to distribute. In 2005, Feeding America asked Canice Prendergast, Don Eisenstein, and Harry Davis, professors at the University of Chicago's Booth School of Business, to design a more efficient way of allocating food to local food programs.

Feeding America had been allocating food by calculating how many low-income people lived in an area and then shipping a target number of pounds of food to food programs in the area. All food, whether fruit, bread, milk, or pasta, that weighed the same was treated the same in making allocations to local food programs. The food programs were not allowed to choose which foods they wanted to receive. Because Feeding America provided on average only about 20 percent of the total food donations local food programs received, it might ship food—for example, bread and breakfast cereal—the local program already had, while failing to ship food, such as fruits and vegetables, that the program needed.

The business professors advising Feeding American proposed changing the food allocation system to one that resembled a market. Each food program was given a number of "shares" that they could use in bidding against other food programs for the types of food that best met the needs of the low-income people using their program. In addition, any local program that had surplus food was allowed to sell it to other local programs in exchange for shares. Although this new system does not involve money, it operates like a market—in which consumers determine prices by competing against each other in buying goods. Goods for which consumers have a greater preference tend to have higher prices than goods for which consumers have a lesser preference; for instance, in supermarkets, organic produce often sells for a higher price than non-organic produce. Similarly, food programs turned out to have a stronger preference for fresh fruits and vegetables than for pasta. Under the previous system, a pound of fresh fruit would have been treated the same as a pound of pasta in calculating how much food Feeding America would allocate to a local program. But when under the new system local food banks were allowed to bid for food with shares, the price of a pound of fruit or vegetables was 116 times higher than the price of a pound of pasta.

Because under the new system food is allocated in a way that more closely fits the needs of local food programs, Feeding America is able to provide food to thousands more low-income people than was possible under the old system. In addition, because less food is wasted, people and organizations have been willing to donate more food to the program. Finally, Feeding America's managers have used the knowledge of which types of foods local food programs prefer to guide the types of food they ask companies to donate. For instance, in addition to fruits and vegetables, programs are willing to pay more shares for peanut butter and frozen chicken because these foods are easy to store. Even many critics of using a market mechanism to allocate food donations eventually embraced the system, including the director of one Michigan food program whose initial reaction was: "I am a socialist. That's why I run a food bank. I don't believe in markets."

The success of Feeding America's revised procedures for allocating food donations shows how powerfully market mechanisms can increase efficiency and raise living standards.

Sources: Sendhil Mullainathan, "Sending Potatoes to Idaho? How the Free Market Can Fight Poverty," *New York Times*, October 7, 2016; Canice Prendergast, "The Allocation of Food to Food Banks," Working Paper, University of Chicago, Booth School of Business, October 11, 2016; Ray Fisman and Tim Sullivan, "The Invisible Helping Hand," slate.com, June 7, 2016; and feedingamerica.org.

Your Turn: Test your understanding by doing related problem 3.16 on page 71 at the end of this chapter.

MyLab Economics Study Plan

Continued from page 41

Economics in Your Life & Career

The Trade-offs When You Buy a Car

At the beginning of the chapter, we asked you to think about two questions: What is the relationship between safety and fuel efficiency for gasoline-powered cars? and If you were a manager at an automobile company, how might you evaluate the relationship between safety and fuel efficiency when designing cars?

To answer the first question, you have to recognize that there is a trade-off between safety and fuel efficiency. With the technology available at any particular time, an automobile manufacturer can increase fuel efficiency by making a car smaller and lighter. But driving a lighter car increases your chances of being injured if you have an accident. The trade-off between safety and fuel efficiency would look much like the relationship in Figure 2.1 on page 43. To answer the second question, to increase both safety and fuel efficiency, automobile makers would have to discover new technologies that allow them to make cars lighter and safer at the same time. Such new technologies would make points like *G* in Figure 2.1 attainable. As a manager at an automobile company, you would need to take into account federal regulations that require certain levels of safety and fuel efficiency. Assuming that you had met those regulatory requirements, consumer preferences would determine how you would trade off safety versus fuel efficiency in designing cars.

Conclusion

We have seen that by trading in markets, people are able to specialize and pursue their comparative advantage. Trading on the basis of comparative advantage makes the participants better off. The key role of markets is to facilitate trade. In fact, the market system is a very effective means of coordinating the decisions of millions of consumers, workers, and firms. At the center of the market system is the consumer. To be successful, firms must respond to the preferences of consumers. These preferences are communicated to firms through prices. We continue to explore how markets work in Chapter 3, when we develop the model of demand and supply.

Before moving on to Chapter 3, read *An Inside Look* on the next page for a discussion of Tesla's Gigafactory in Nevada.

Tesla Bets Big on Nevada Battery Plant

ZACKS.COM

So, What Actually Is Tesla's Gigafactory?

Since 2014, electric car maker **Tesla Inc.** has been constructing what they call a Gigafactory. But what, exactly, does that mean? What makes it different from a regular manufacturing plant?

According to Tesla, one of its goals as a company is to expedite the process of transitioning to global sustainable transportation. In order to do this, enough vehicles must be produced to sway change in the automobile industry as a whole. Tesla plans to have a production rate of 500,000 electric cars every year by the second half of this decade, which will require a huge supply of lithium-ion batteries, a type of rechargeable battery.

Thus, the Gigafactory was born.

The name "Gigafactory" is a term that comes from Tesla's planned battery production amount per year of 35 gigawatt-hours (GWh). In quantifiable terms, "giga" is a measurement unit that stands for "billions"; one GWh is the same as generating one billion watts for one hour, or one million times more than that one kilowatt-hour (kWh).

The Tax Deal

ⓐ Tesla's Gigafactory is located outside the city of Sparks, Nevada, but the state had to go through a somewhat arduous process to win the factory deal. Three additional states were in the running: Arizona, Texas, and New Mexico.

According to The Verge, Nevada won the deal after the state controversially "offered an incentives package that was the largest in Nevada history, and became one of the 15 largest nationally. Over the next 20 years, Tesla could take in nearly $1.3 billion in tax benefits for building its Gigafactory in Nevada … [a]ssuming Tesla meets its obligations under the deal, it will spend 20 years free from sales tax, and 10 years free from property tax, while it receives millions of dollars more in tax credits…."

Production Plan

ⓑ Since the idea of the Gigafactory was conceived out of the necessity to increase the supply of lithium-ion batteries, it makes sense that the factory would utilize renewable production methods. The entire plant will be powered by renewable energy sources in order to achieve net zero energy. Most notably, the majority of the manufacturing processes will be under one roof, a choice that could potentially reduce cost, waste, and enhance innovation.

Tesla began lithium-ion battery cell production this past January, and the cells will be used in the company's Powerwall energy storage products. By 2018, Tesla expects the cost of its batteries to decline by over one-third thanks to large-scale production at the Gigafactory. Tesla also anticipates annual lithium-ion battery production of the factory to reach near its original goal of 35 gigawatt-hours by

the same year, which equals the total global production from 2014. Tesla hopes to reach full capacity by 2020.

The company also announced plans to invest $350 million in the Gigafactory for the production of electric motors and gearbox components for its Model 3 sedan, its highly-anticipated mass-market vehicle. The investment will create about 500 jobs.

Future of the Gigafactory

ⓒ Last January, electronics company Panasonic agreed to invest up to $1.6 billion in Tesla's Gigafactory. Kazuhiro Tsuga, President of Panasonic, said that "We are sort of waiting on the demand from Tesla. If Tesla succeeds and the electric vehicle becomes mainstream, the world will be changed and we will have lots of opportunity to grow."

Tesla is even considering building more Gigafactories. CEO Elon Musk has referred to the Nevada plant as "Gigafactory 1" in the past, and during the company's fiscal 2016 earnings release back in February, the electric car maker informed its shareholders [about] plans of two or three more potential Gigafactory plants.

"Later this year, we expect to finalize locations for Gigafactories 3, 4, and 5 (Gigafactory 2 is the Tesla solar plant in New York)," said the company in its earnings report….

Source: Madeleine Johnson, "So, What Actually Is Tesla's Gigafactory?" zacks.com, June 6, 2017.

Key Points in the Article

Tesla opened a large factory near Sparks, Nevada, to mass produce lithium-ion batteries. Tesla will use the batteries in its electric cars and in energy storage products the firm will sell to consumers and to other firms. Known as the Gigafactory, the multi-billion-dollar manufacturing facility will greatly increase the world's productive capacity for lithium-ion batteries. These batteries are a critical component of Tesla's cars, and the company hopes that by building such a large facility, it will be able to produce batteries at a lower cost per unit. Tesla will also be manufacturing batteries for its Powerwall energy storage products at its new facility as the company expands beyond the production of electric automobiles.

Analyzing the News

a Increasing battery production is vital to Tesla's success, so the strategic decisions of where, when, and how large to build a battery factory were important. When ultimately deciding to build the Gigafactory near Sparks, Nevada, managers at Tesla were choosing how to allocate resources. The investment in the factory represents a trade-off because it took resources away from other potential projects. Managers believed the best use of

Tesla's scarce resources was to build the battery plant because doing so allowed them to produce enough batteries to meet their production goals for cars and energy storage products.

b At its Nevada plant, Tesla is producing batteries for its automobiles as well as for home and commercial use, so it must choose how many of each product to produce. Like all other companies, Tesla faces trade-offs in choosing which goods to produce. Suppose Tesla must choose between producing batteries for its Model 3 sedan and batteries for its Powerwall energy storage product, and it has the capacity to produce 600,000 batteries in 2018. This capacity is represented by PPF_{2018} in the figure below. This curve shows that Tesla would have to sacrifice production (and therefore sales) of one type of battery to produce more of the other. If the market grows for both its Model 3 sedan and its Powerwall home batteries, Tesla will need to produce a larger number of total batteries, which is represented by PPF_{2022} in the figure.

c Future production was also a consideration for Tesla managers as they decided how to allocate resources. The company needed to look at the longer term when considering the trade-offs in allocating resources to the construction of the Nevada plant and also possible addi-

tional Gigafactories. Tesla partnered with Panasonic, the world's leading battery cell manufacturer, which agreed to invest up to $1.6 billion in the Nevada factory. These longer-term considerations play an integral part in Tesla's goal of gaining a comparative advantage in battery manufacturing and in successfully expanding its clean-energy business.

Thinking Critically

1. Suppose that from 2018 to 2022, the resources Tesla uses to produce its batteries remain constant, while improvements in technology allow Tesla to produce a larger quantity of Powerwall batteries but no additional batteries for the Model 3 sedan. Draw a graph that illustrates this technology change. Be sure to show both the 2018 PPF and the new 2022 PPF. What is the opportunity cost to Tesla of producing one Model 3 sedan battery in 2018? Is the opportunity cost higher or lower in 2022?

2. Assume that the figure below accurately represents Tesla's PPFs for 2018 and 2022. Now suppose that in 2022, Tesla receives orders for 750,000 Model 3 sedan batteries and 350,000 Powerwall batteries. Explain whether Tesla can fill all these orders.

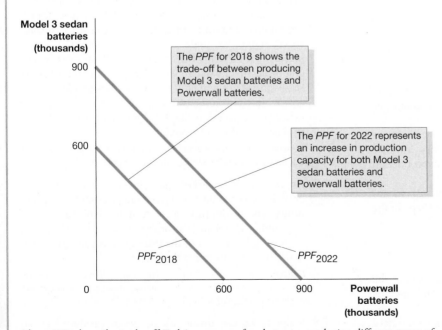

These *PPFs* show the trade-off Tesla's managers face between producing different types of batteries and how that trade-off may change over time.

Key Terms

Absolute advantage, p. 50

Circular-flow diagram, p. 55

Comparative advantage, p. 51

Economic growth, p. 47

Entrepreneur, p. 59

Factor market, p. 54

Factors of production, p. 54

Free market, p. 56

Market, p. 54

Opportunity cost, p. 43

Product market, p. 54

Production possibilities
frontier (*PPF*), p. 42

Property rights, p. 61

Scarcity, p. 42

Trade, p. 48

2.1 Production Possibilities Frontiers and Opportunity Costs, pages 42–47

LEARNING OBJECTIVE: Use a production possibilities frontier to analyze opportunity costs and trade-offs.

MyLab Economics   Visit **www.pearson.com/mylab/economics** to complete these exercises online and get instant feedback.

Summary

The **production possibilities frontier** (**PPF**) is a curve that shows the maximum attainable combinations of two goods that can be produced with available resources. The *PPF* is used to illustrate the trade-offs that arise from **scarcity**. Points on the *PPF* are technically efficient. Points inside the *PPF* are inefficient, and points outside the *PPF* are unattainable. The **opportunity cost** of any activity is the highest-valued alternative that must be given up to engage in that activity. Because of increasing marginal opportunity costs, *PPF*s are usually bowed out rather than straight lines. This illustrates the important economic concept that the more resources that are already devoted to any activity, the smaller the payoff from devoting additional resources to that activity is likely to be. **Economic growth** is illustrated by an outward shift in the *PPF*.

Review Questions

1.1 What do economists mean by *scarcity*? Can you think of anything that is not scarce according to the economic definition?

1.2 What is a production possibilities frontier? How can we show efficiency on a production possibilities frontier? How can we show inefficiency? What causes a production possibilities frontier to shift outward?

1.3 What does increasing marginal opportunity costs mean? What are the implications of this idea for the shape of the production possibilities frontier?

Problems and Applications

1.4 Draw a production possibilities frontier that shows the trade-off between the production of cotton and the production of soybeans.

   a. Show the effect that a prolonged drought would have on the initial production possibilities frontier.

   b. Suppose that genetic modification makes soybeans resistant to insects, allowing yields to double. Show the effect of this technological change on the initial production possibilities frontier.

1.5 (Related to the Chapter Opener on page 40) One of the trade-offs Tesla faces is between safety and the maximum range someone can drive an electric car before having to recharge it. For example, adding steel to a car makes it safer but also heavier, which results in fewer miles between recharges. Draw a hypothetical production possibilities frontier that Tesla engineers face that shows this trade-off.

1.6 According to an article in the *Wall Street Journal*, Staples Inc., an office supply store, "has found a new use for some of its roomy office-supply stores: make parts of them into offices." Because many businesses now store their records digitally and many consumers shop online rather than in stores, Staples no longer needs as much floor space for filing cabinets and some other products. To use the surplus space, Staples has undertaken a partnership with Workbar, an office-sharing firm, to offer small business owners and professionals shared workspaces inside select Staples retail stores. In these circumstances, does Staples incur a cost from using some of the space in its retail stores for office workspaces? If Staples does incur a cost, briefly explain what the cost would be.

Source: Drew FitzGerald and Suzanne Kapner, "Staples Finds New Use for Its Stores: Office Space," *Wall Street Journal*, April 4, 2016.

1.7 An economist remarked that "the cost of consuming a book is the combination of the retail price and the opportunity cost of the time spent reading." Isn't the cost of consuming a book just the price you pay to buy the book? Why include the cost of the time spent reading the book in the cost of consuming the book?

Source: Craig L. Garthwaite, "Demand Spillovers, Combative Advertising, and Celebrity Endorsements," *American Economic Journal: Applied Economics*, Vol. 6, No. 2, April 2014, p. 78.

1.8 Suppose we can divide all the goods produced by an economy into two types: consumption goods and capital goods. Capital goods, such as machinery, equipment, and computers, are goods used to produce other goods.

  a. Use a production possibilities frontier graph to illustrate the trade-off to an economy between producing consumption goods and producing capital goods. Is it likely that the production possibilities frontier in this situation will be a straight line (as in Figure 2.1 on page 43) or bowed out (as in Figure 2.2 on page 46)? Briefly explain.

  b. Suppose a technological change occurs and has a favorable effect on the production of capital goods but not consumption goods. Show the effect on the production possibilities frontier.

  c. Suppose that Lichtenstein and Luxembourg currently have identical production possibilities frontiers but that Lichtenstein devotes only 5 percent of its resources to producing capital goods over each of the next 10 years, while Luxembourg devotes 30 percent. Which country is likely to experience more rapid economic growth in the future? Illustrate using a production possibilities frontier graph. Your graph should include production possibilities frontiers for Lichtenstein and Luxembourg today and in 10 years.

1.9 Use the following production possibilities frontier for a country to answer the questions.

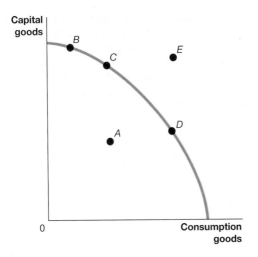

  a. Which point or points are unattainable? Briefly explain why.

  b. Which point or points are efficient? Briefly explain why.

  c. Which point or points are inefficient? Briefly explain why.

  d. At which point is the country's future growth rate likely to be the highest? Briefly explain why.

1.10 **(Related to Solved Problem 2.1 on page 44)** You have exams in economics and chemistry coming up, and you have 5 hours available for studying. The following table shows the trade-offs you face in allocating the time you will spend studying each subject:

	Hours Spent Studying		Midterm Score	
Choice	Economics	Chemistry	Economics	Chemistry
A	5	0	95	70
B	4	1	93	78
C	3	2	90	84
D	2	3	86	88
E	1	4	81	90
F	0	5	75	91

  a. Use the data in the table to draw a production possibilities frontier graph. Label the vertical axis "Score on economics exam" and label the horizontal axis "Score on chemistry exam." Make sure to label the values where your production possibilities frontier intersects the vertical and horizontal axes. (Note that the origin in your graph will not occur at the values 0,0.)

  b. Label the points representing choice C and choice D. If you are at choice C, what is your opportunity cost of increasing your chemistry score by 4 points?

  c. Under what circumstances would choice A be sensible?

1.11 Suppose the U.S. president is attempting to decide whether the federal government should spend more on research to find a cure for heart disease. Imagine that you are the president's economic advisor and need to prepare a report discussing the relevant factors the president should consider. Use the concepts of opportunity cost and trade-offs to discuss some of the main issues you would deal with in your report.

1.12 State government Medicaid programs provide medical insurance to poor and disabled people. A news article described a new prescription drug that costs as much as "$94,000 for one 12-week treatment regimen" to treat hepatitis C, a liver disease. Several states restricted access to the new drug under their Medicaid programs to patients who are most acutely ill (stage 3 or stage 4) with hepatitis C. State Medicaid programs are paid for, in part, out of state budgets. What trade-offs do state governments face when new prescription drugs are introduced with much higher prices than existing drugs? Do you agree with states providing expensive new drugs only to the patients who are most ill from a disease? Briefly explain.

Sources: Lisa Schencker, "State Switches Stance on Hepatitis C Drugs, Expands Access, but Not All Medicaid Patients Qualify," chicagotribune.com, September 12, 2016.

1.13 Lawrence Summers served as secretary of the Treasury in the Clinton administration and as director of the National Economic Council in the Obama administration. He has been quoted as giving the following defense of the economic approach to policy issues:

> There is nothing morally unattractive about saying: We need to analyze which way of spending money on health care will produce more benefit and which less, and using our money as efficiently as we can. I don't think there is anything immoral about seeking to achieve environmental benefits at the lowest possible costs.

Would it be more ethical to reduce pollution without worrying about the cost or by taking the cost into account? Briefly explain.

Source: David Wessel, "Precepts from Professor Summers," *Wall Street Journal*, October 17, 2002.

1.14 In *The Wonderful Wizard of Oz* and his other books about the Land of Oz, L. Frank Baum observed that if people's wants were limited enough, most goods would not be scarce. According to Baum, this was the case in Oz:

> There were no poor people in the Land of Oz, because there was no such thing as money.... Each person was given freely by his neighbors whatever he required for his use, which is as much as anyone may reasonably desire. Some tilled the lands and raised great crops of grain, which was divided equally among the whole population, so that all had enough. There were many tailors and dressmakers and shoemakers and the like, who made things that any who desired them might

wear. Likewise there were jewelers who made ornaments for the person, which pleased and beautified the people, and these ornaments also were free to those who asked for them. Each man and woman, no matter what he or she produced for the good of the community, was supplied by the neighbors with food and clothing and a house and furniture and ornaments and games. If by chance the supply ever ran short, more was taken from the great storehouses of the Ruler, which were afterward filled up again when there was more of any article than people needed....

> You will know, by what I have told you here, that the Land of Oz was a remarkable country. I do not suppose such an arrangement would be practical with us.

Briefly explain whether you agree with Baum that the economic system in Oz wouldn't work in the contemporary United States.

Source: L. Frank Baum, *The Emerald City of Oz*, 1910, pp. 30–31.

2.2 Comparative Advantage and Trade, pages 48–54

LEARNING OBJECTIVE: Describe comparative advantage and explain how it serves as the basis for trade.

MyLab Economics   Visit **www.pearson.com/mylab/economics** to complete these exercises online and get instant feedback.

Summary

Fundamentally, markets are about **trade**, which is the act of buying and selling. People trade on the basis of comparative advantage. An individual, a firm, or a country has a **comparative advantage** in producing a good or service if it can produce the good or service at the lowest opportunity cost. People are usually better off specializing in the activity for which they have a comparative advantage and trading for the other goods and services they need. It is important not to confuse comparative advantage with absolute advantage. An individual, a firm, or a country has an **absolute advantage** in producing a good or service if it can produce more of that good or service using the same amount of resources. It is possible to have an absolute advantage in producing a good or service without having a comparative advantage.

Review Questions

2.1 What is absolute advantage? What is comparative advantage? Is it possible for a country to have a comparative advantage in producing a good without also having an absolute advantage? Briefly explain.

2.2 What is the basis for trade: absolute advantage or comparative advantage? How can an individual or a country gain from specialization and trade?

Problems and Applications

2.3 Look again at the information in Figure 2.4 on page 49. Choose a rate of trading cherries for apples different from the rate used in the text (15 pounds of cherries for 10

pounds of apples) that will allow you and your neighbor to benefit from trading. Prepare a table like Table 2.1 on page 50 to illustrate your answer.

2.4 Using the same amount of resources, the United States and Canada can both produce lumberjack shirts and lumberjack boots, as shown in the following production possibilities frontiers:

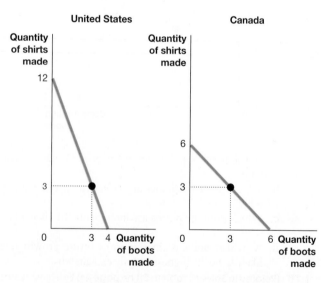

a. Which country has a comparative advantage in producing lumberjack boots? Which country has a comparative advantage in producing lumberjack shirts? Briefly explain.

b. Does either country have an absolute advantage in producing both goods? Briefly explain.

c. Suppose that both countries are currently producing three pairs of boots and three shirts. Show that both can be better off if they each specialize in producing one good and then trade for the other.

2.5 **(Related to the Don't Let This Happen to You on page 51)** A columnist for *Forbes* argues, "Even if China is always better than Spain at producing textiles, if the best thing that Spain could be doing is textiles, then that's what Spain should be doing."

   a. What does the columnist mean by "China is always better than Spain" in producing textiles (which include clothing, sheets, and similar products)? Was the columnist arguing that China has an absolute advantage over Spain in producing textiles, a comparative advantage, or both? Briefly explain.

   b. The columnist noted that, in fact, Spain exports significant quantities of textiles. If his description of the situation in China and Spain is accurate, briefly explain how Spanish firms are able to export textiles in competition with Chinese firms.

   Source: Tim Worstall, "Inditex's Zara and the Power of Comparative Advantage," forbes.com, July 7, 2015.

2.6 **(Related to Solved Problem 2.2 on page 52)** Suppose the United Kingdom and Norway both produce oil and fish oil, which are sold for the same prices in both countries. The following table shows the combinations of both goods that each country can produce in a day, measured in thousands of barrels, using the same amounts of capital and labor:

United Kingdom		Norway	
Oil	Fish oil	Oil	Fish Oil
0	8	0	4
2	6	1	3
4	4	2	2
6	2	3	1
8	0	4	0

   a. Which country has a comparative advantage in producing oil? Briefly explian.

   b. Can these two countries gain from trading oil and fish oil with each other? Briefly explain.

2.7 **(Related to Solved Problem 2.2 on page 52)** Suppose that France and Germany both produce schnitzel and wine. The following table shows combinations of the goods that each country can produce in a day:

France		Germany	
Wine (bottles)	Schnitzel (pounds)	Wine (bottles)	Schnitzel (pounds)
0	8	0	15
1	6	1	12
2	4	2	9
3	2	3	6
4	0	4	3
		5	0

   a. Which country has a comparative advantage in producing wine? Which country has a comparative advantage in producing schnitzel?

   b. Suppose that France is currently producing 1 bottle of wine and 6 pounds of schnitzel, and Germany is currently producing 3 bottles of wine and 6 pounds of schnitzel. Demonstrate that France and Germany can both be better off if they specialize in producing only one good and then trade for the other.

2.8 Can an individual or a country produce beyond its production possibilities frontier? Can an individual or a country consume beyond its production possibilities frontier? Briefly explain.

2.9 If Nicaragua can produce with the same amount of resources twice as much coffee as Colombia, explain how Colombia could have a comparative advantage in producing coffee.

2.10 Imagine that the next time the New England Patriots play the Miami Dolphins at Gillette Stadium in Foxborough, Massachusetts, Patriots star quarterback Tom Brady has a temporary lack of judgment and plans to sell Patriots memorabilia during the game because he realizes that he can sell five times more Patriots products than anyone in the stadium sports gear store. Likewise, imagine that you are a creative and effective manager at work and that you tell your employees that during the next six months, you plan to clean the offices because you can clean five times better than the cleaning staff. What error in judgment are both you and Tom making? Why shouldn't you and Tom do what you are better than anyone else at doing?

2.11 After Russia seized what had formerly been the Ukrainian territory of Crimea in February 2014, the United States and many other countries imposed economic sanctions that reduced the ability of Russia to engage in international trade. A columnist writing in the *New York Times* noted, "If sanctions push Russia onto a path of greater self-reliance, its manufacturing and service industries will surely grow faster." If the columnist is correct about the effect of the sanctions, are the sanctions likely to improve the economic well-being of the average Russian in the long run? Briefly explain.

   Source: Anatole Kaletsky, "Reasons to Welcome a Ukraine Deal," *New York Times*, September 18, 2014.

2.12 In colonial America, the population was spread thinly over a large area, and transportation costs were very high because it was difficult to ship products by road for more than short distances. As a result, most of the free population lived on small farms, where people not only grew their own food but also usually made their own clothes and very rarely bought or sold anything for money. Explain why the incomes of these farmers were likely to rise as transportation costs fell. Use the concept of comparative advantage in your answer.

2.13 During the 1928 U.S. presidential election campaign, Herbert Hoover, the Republican candidate, argued that the United States should import only products that could not be produced here. Briefly explain whether this policy would be likely to raise average income in the United States.

2.14 **(Related to the Apply the Concept on page 53)** In discussing dividing up household chores, Emily Oster, an economist at the University of Chicago, advised, "No, you shouldn't always unload the dishwasher because you're better at it." If you are better at unloading the dishwasher, why shouldn't you be the one to unload it?

Source: Emily Oster, "You're Dividing the Chores Wrong," *Slate*, November 21, 2012.

2.15 **(Related to the Apply the Concept on page 53)** The chapter mentions that in 1965, married women with children did an average of 32 hours of housework per week, while men did an average of only 4 hours of housework—a total

of 36 hours of housework. In 2016, the estimated average weekly hours of housework for women declined to 15.7, while the hours worked by men increased to about 9.7—a total of 25.4 hours of housework. Does the decrease in the total number of hours of housework—from 36 to 25.4—mean that families are willing to live in messier homes? Briefly explain.

Source: U.S. Bureau of Labor Statistics, "American Time Use—2016," June 27, 2017.

The Market System, pages 54–63

LEARNING OBJECTIVE: Explain the basics of how a market system works.

MyLab Economics   Visit **www.pearson.com/mylab/economics** to complete these exercises online and get instant feedback.

Summary

A **market** is a group of buyers and sellers of a good or service and the institution or arrangement by which they come together to trade. **Product markets** are markets for goods and services, such as computers and medical treatment. **Factor markets** are markets for the **factors of production**, such as labor, capital, natural resources, and entrepreneurial ability. A **circular-flow diagram** shows how participants in product markets and factor markets are linked. Adam Smith argued in his 1776 book *The Wealth of Nations* that in a **free market**, in which the government does not control the production of goods and services, changes in prices lead firms to produce the goods and services most desired by consumers. If consumers demand more of a good, its price will rise. Firms respond to rising prices by increasing production. If consumers demand less of a good, its price will fall. Firms respond to falling prices by producing less of a good. An **entrepreneur** is someone who operates a business. In the market system, entrepreneurs are responsible for organizing the production of goods and services. The market system will work well only if there is protection for **property rights**, which are the rights of individuals and firms to use their property.

Review Questions

3.1 What is a circular-flow diagram, and what does it demonstrate?

3.2 What are the two main categories of participants in markets? Which participants are of greatest importance in determining what goods and services are produced?

3.3 What is a free market? In what ways does a free market economy differ from a centrally planned economy?

3.4 What is an entrepreneur? Why do entrepreneurs play a key role in a market system?

3.5 Under what circumstances are firms likely to produce more of a good or service? Under what circumstances are firms likely to produce less of a good or service?

3.6 What are property rights? What role do they play in the working of a market system? Why are independent courts important for a well-functioning economy?

Problems and Applications

3.7 Identify whether each of the following transactions will take place in the factor market or in the product market

and whether households or firms are supplying the good or service or demanding the good or service.
   a. Tariq buys a Tesla Model 3.
   b. Tesla increases employment at its Fremont plant.
   c. Tariq works 20 hours per week at McDonald's.
   d. Tariq sells the land he owns to McDonald's so that it can build a new restaurant.

3.8 **(Related to the Apply the Concept on page 57)** The late Nobel Prize–winning economist Kenneth Arrow of Stanford University once wrote that the argument that the outcomes in a market system "may be very different from, and even opposed to, intentions is surely the most important intellectual contribution that economic thought has made." Briefly explain how it is possible for the outcomes in a market system to be different from what firms and consumers intended them to be. Why is this idea such an important intellectual contribution?

Sources: Kenneth J. Arrow, "Economic Equilibrium," *Encyclopedia of the Social Sciences*, 1968; and Encyclopedia.com.

3.9 **(Related to the Apply the Concept on page 57)** In a famous essay on the market system, the economist Leonard Read discussed how a pencil sold by the U.S. firm Eberhard Faber Pencil Company (now owned by Paper Mate) was made. He noted that logging companies in California and Oregon grew the cedar wood used in the pencil. The wood was milled into pencil-width slats at a factory in San Leandro, California. The graphite for the pencil was mined in Sri Lanka and mixed with clay purchased from a firm in Mississippi and wax from a firm in Mexico. The rubber was purchased from a firm in Indonesia. Was it necessary for the managers of all these firms to know how the components they produced were assembled into a pencil? Was it necessary for the chief executive officer of the Eberhard Faber Company to know this information? Briefly explain.

Source: Leonard E. Read, *I, Pencil: My Family Tree as Told to Leonard E. Read*, Irvington-on-Hudson, NY: The Foundation for Economic Education, Inc., December 1958.

3.10 Evaluate the following argument: "Adam Smith's analysis of the market system is based on a fundamental flaw: He assumes that people are motivated by self-interest. But this isn't true. I'm not selfish, and most people I know aren't selfish."

3.11 Writing in the *New York Times*, Michael Lewis argued that "a market economy is premised on a system of incentives designed to encourage an ignoble human trait: self-interest." Do you agree that self-interest is an "ignoble human trait"? What incentives does a market system provide to encourage self-interest?

Source: Michael Lewis, "In Defense of the Boom," *New York Times*, October 27, 2002.

3.12 Some economists have been puzzled that although entrepreneurs take on the risk of losing money by starting new businesses, on average their incomes are lower than those of people with similar characteristics who go to work at large firms. The late William Baumol believed part of the explanation for this puzzle may be that entrepreneurs are like people who buy lottery tickets. On average, people who don't buy lottery tickets are left with more money than people who buy tickets because lotteries take in more money than they give out. Baumol argued that "the masses of purchasers who grab up the [lottery] tickets are not irrational if they receive an adequate payment in another currency: psychic rewards."
  a. What are "psychic rewards"?
  b. What psychic rewards might an entrepreneur receive?
  c. Do you agree with Baumol that an entrepreneur is like someone buying a lottery ticket? Briefly explain.

Source: William J. Baumol, *The Microtheory of Innovative Entrepreneurship*, Princeton, NJ: Princeton University Press, 2010.

3.13 In the foreword to a report on property rights around the world, Peruvian economist Hernando De Soto noted, "Countries that have weak property rights also struggle to develop strong, innovative economic markets."
  a. What did De Soto mean by "strong, innovative economic markets"?
  b. Why would such markets be important for a country that is hoping to raise the standard of living of its residents? What do property rights have to do with developing such markets?

Source: Hernando De Soto, "Foreword," *International Property Rights Index*, 2016, internationalpropertyrightsindex.org.

3.14 According to an article on Phillyburbs.com, some farmers in rural Pennsylvania caused a "stink" by using pig manure for fertilizer. The farmers purchased the pig manure, which is an organic fertilizer, from a nearby pork processing plant and spread it across the fields where they grow corn and soybeans. The article asserted that the farmers switched to pig manure because of the skyrocketing price of chemical fertilizers. Some of the residents of the town of Milford complained about the smell, but the article said that the farmers were "likely protected under Pennsylvania's Right to Farm Act, which allows farmers to engage in practices that are common to agriculture."
  a. What price signal did the farmers respond to in their switch to the organic pig manure fertilizer?
  b. According to the Pennsylvania Right to Farm Act, do the farmers or the townspeople have the property right to the smell of the air around the farms? (Some of the residents did ask the township to urge the farmers to plow under the manure to reduce its stench.)

Source: Amanda Cregan, "Milford Farmers Switch to Pig Manure Causing a Stink for Neighbors," Phillyburbs.com, March 6, 2013.

3.15 The British historian Thomas Macaulay once remarked that copyrights are "a tax on readers." In what sense are copyrights a tax on readers? If copyrights are a tax on readers, why do governments enact them?

3.16 **(Related to the Apply the Concept on page 62)** The *Apply the Concept* feature explains that the Feeding American charity asked three professors at the University of Chicago's Booth School of Business to design a more efficient way of allocating food to local food programs and that the professors proposed changing the food allocation system to one that resembled a market.
  a. Under the new system, the "shares" each food program receives would be the equivalent to what economic variable that consumers use in the marketplace to bid for goods and services?
  b. The number of shares a food program needs to receive certain types of food would be equivalent to what economic variable in the marketplace for goods and services?
  c. One of the University of Chicago professors advising Feeding America noted, "Much of the food that is distributed through food banks often originates with donors—large manufacturers or distributors—far from [local food bank's] needy clients." Why might this fact make it more likely that a market mechanism would improve the well-being of people receiving food from local food banks?

Source: Canice Prendergast, "The Allocation of Food to Food Banks," Working Paper, University of Chicago, Booth School of Business, October 11, 2016.

Critical Thinking Exercises

CT2.1 For this exercise, your instructor may assign you to a group. Can you think of a good or service that is produced entirely by one company without the purchase of *any* raw materials or other goods or services from another company? First, each member of the group should propose at least one company that might meet this criterion by writing it down on a piece of paper and not showing it to other group members. Second, after each group member has written down a response, the members should then reveal their responses, and the group should discuss whether each company does indeed produce a good or service without any raw materials or goods and services from another company. If you cannot think of many such companies, which concepts from this chapter do you think this conclusion might illustrate?

CT2.2 On YouTube, watch one or two of the short videos on the "Primitive Technology" channel, www.youtube.com/channel/UCAL3JXZSzSm8AlZyD3nQdBA. You'll likely find it quite impressive how this single man can make so many different products, such as a hammer, a sling, and a hut, using only raw materials found in a forest and his Internet research. But how might an economist evaluate the efficiency of one person alone producing so many different products with no help from anyone else?

Note: See https://primitivetechnology.wordpress.com/about/ for more information on these videos.

3

Where Prices Come From:
The Interaction of Demand and Supply

How Smart Is Your Water?

What does a firm do when its primary product starts to fall out of fashion? The Coca-Cola Company and PepsiCo, Inc., have faced that question in recent years. Between 2004 and 2016, measured by volume, sales in the United States of carbonated beverages like Coke and Pepsi declined by more than 25 percent, while sales of bottled water increased by more than 50 percent. In 2016, sales of bottled water were greater than sales of carbonated beverages for the first time. This change resulted from a shift in consumer tastes as many people, particularly millennials, increased their demand for healthier beverages that don't contain sugar or artificial sweeteners.

In 1994, Pepsi responded to increased consumer demand for bottled water by introducing Aquafina water, and in 1999, Coke responded by introducing Dasani water. Neither company, though, had found selling bottled water to be as profitable as selling soda. As a result of decades of advertising, Coke and Pepsi are two of the most recognizable brand names in the world. The companies also have networks of bottling plants and commitments from supermarkets to provide them with extensive shelf space. Other companies have had trouble competing with Coke and Pepsi, which together account for nearly 75 percent of the market for carbonated beverages. The Aquafina and Dasani brands are not nearly as well known, however, so other companies have been better able to compete in the bottled water market, limiting Coke and Pepsi to less than 20 percent of that market.

By 2017, Coke and Pepsi were attempting to increase their profits in the bottled water market by introducing premium water or smart water brands. With regular bottled water, firms filter tap water or spring water to remove impurities. With premium water, like Pepsi's LIFEWTR and Coke's smartwater, firms also add ingredients, typically electrolytes. Although many nutritionists are skeptical that premium water is any better for you than regular bottled water, demand for premium bottled water has been increasing rapidly. Both Coke and Pepsi have been able to

Andrew Toth/Stringer/Getty Images

charge higher prices for their premium water brands than they do for their carbonated beverages. But the firms were facing determined competition from Nestlé's Perrier brand and Danone's Evian brand, among many others.

Although premium water was a hot product in 2017, there are no guarantees in a market system. Will Coke and Pepsi and their competitors be able to continue charging higher prices for premium water than for regular bottled water, or will competition force down prices and make selling premium bottled water no more profitable than selling regular bottled water? Although competition is not always good news for firms trying to sell products, it is great news for consumers because it increases the choice of available products and lowers the prices consumers pay for those products.

AN INSIDE LOOK on **page 98** discusses how McDonald's has responded to shifts in consumer demand by serving breakfast all day, allowing customers to order food online, and offering home delivery.

Sources: Jennifer Maloney, "Coca-Cola Needs to Be More Than Just Coke, Its Next Chief Says," *Wall Street Journal*, February 23, 2017; Jennifer Maloney, "PepsiCo Gives Its 'Premium' Water a Super Bowl Push," *Wall Street Journal*, January 24, 2017; and Feliz Solomon, "Coca-Cola and Pepsi Now Have Something Else in Common," fortune.com, December 7, 2016.

Chapter Outline & Learning Objectives

Economics in Your Life & Career

Can You Forecast the Future Demand for Premium Bottled Water?

Firms face many challenges in responding to changes in consumer demand. Firms selling premium bottled water need to forecast future demand in order to determine how much production capacity they will need. If you were a manager for Coca-Cola, PepsiCo, Nestlé, Bai, or another firm selling premium bottled water, what factors would you take into account in forecasting future demand? As you read this chapter, try to answer this question. You can check your answers against those we provide on **page 97** at the end of this chapter.

I n Chapter 1, we explored how economists use models to predict human behavior. In Chapter 2, we used the production possibilities frontiers (*PPF*) model to analyze scarcity and trade-offs. In this chapter and the next, we explore the model of demand and supply, which is the most powerful tool in economics, and use the model to explain how prices are determined.

Economic models are simplified versions of reality that are based on assumptions. In some cases, the assumptions of a model may not describe exactly the economic situation we are analyzing. For example, the model of demand and supply assumes that we are analyzing a **perfectly competitive market**, which is a market where there are many buyers and sellers, all the products sold are identical, and there are no barriers to new firms entering the market. These assumptions are very restrictive and apply exactly to only a few markets, such as the markets for wheat and other agricultural products. However, the model of demand and supply has proven to be very useful in analyzing markets where competition among sellers is intense, even if there are relatively few sellers and the products being sold are not identical. In recent studies, the model of demand and supply has been successful in analyzing markets with as few as four buyers and four sellers. As we will see in this chapter, this model is often successful in predicting changes in quantities and prices in many markets.

We begin studying the model of demand and supply by discussing consumers and the demand side of the market, and then we turn to firms and the supply side. Throughout this text, we will apply this model to understand business, the economy, and economic policy.

Perfectly competitive market A market that meets the conditions of having (1) many buyers and sellers, (2) all firms selling identical products, and (3) no barriers to new firms entering the market.

3.1 The Demand Side of the Market
LEARNING OBJECTIVE: List and describe the variables that influence demand.

We saw in Chapter 2 that in a market system, consumers ultimately determine which goods and services will be produced. The most successful businesses are the ones that respond best to consumer demand. But what determines consumer demand for a product? Certainly, many factors influence the willingness of consumers to buy a particular product. For example, consumers who are considering buying premium bottled water, such as Bai's Antiwater or Coca-Cola's smartwater, will make their decisions based on, among other factors, the income they have available to spend and the effectiveness of the advertising campaigns of the companies that sell premium bottled water. For most consumers, the primary factor in their buying decision is the price of the product. So, we focus on this factor first. As we discuss demand, keep in mind that we are considering not what a consumer *wants* to buy but what the consumer is both willing and *able* to buy.

Demand Schedules and Demand Curves
Tables that show the relationship between the price of a product and the quantity of the product demanded are called **demand schedules**. The table in Figure 3.1 shows the quantity of premium bottled water consumers would be willing and able to buy per day at five different prices. The amount of a good or service that a consumer is willing and able to purchase at a given price is called the **quantity demanded**. The graph in Figure 3.1 plots the numbers from the table as a **demand curve**, which shows the relationship between the price of a product and the quantity of the product demanded. (Note that, for convenience, we made the demand curve in Figure 3.1 a straight line, or linear. There is no reason that all demand curves need to be straight lines.) The demand curve in Figure 3.1 shows the **market demand**, which is the demand by all the consumers of a given good or service. The market for a product, such as restaurant meals, that is sold locally would include all the consumers in a city or a relatively small area. The market for a product, such as premium bottled water, that is sold internationally would include all the consumers in the world.

Demand schedule A table that shows the relationship between the price of a product and the quantity of the product demanded.

Quantity demanded The amount of a good or service that a consumer is willing and able to purchase at a given price.

Demand curve A curve that shows the relationship between the price of a product and the quantity of the product demanded.

Market demand The demand by all the consumers of a given good or service.

MyLab Economics Animation

Figure 3.1

A Demand Schedule and Demand Curve

As the price of premium bottled water changes, consumers change the quantity they are willing and able to buy. We can show this as a *demand schedule* in a table or as a *demand curve* on a graph. The table and graph both show that as the price of premium bottled water falls, the quantity demanded increases. When the price of water is $2.50 per bottle, consumers buy 3 million bottles per day. When the price falls to $2.00, consumers buy 4 million bottles. Therefore, the demand curve for premium bottled water is downward sloping.

The demand curve in Figure 3.1 slopes downward because consumers will buy more premium bottled water as the price falls. When the price of a bottle of water is $2.50, consumers buy 3 million bottles per day. When the price falls to $2.00, consumers buy 4 million. Buyers demand a larger quantity of a product as the price falls because the product becomes less expensive relative to other products and because they can afford to buy more at a lower price.   **MyLab Economics** Concept Check

The Law of Demand

The inverse relationship between the price of a product and the quantity of the product demanded is called the **law of demand**: Holding everything else constant, when the price of a product falls, the quantity demanded of the product will increase, and when the price of a product rises, the quantity demanded of the product will decrease. The law of demand holds for any market demand curve. Economists have found only a very few exceptions to this law.   **MyLab Economics** Concept Check

Law of demand A rule that states that, holding everything else constant, when the price of a product falls, the quantity demanded of the product will increase, and when the price of a product rises, the quantity demanded of the product will decrease.

What Explains the Law of Demand?

It makes sense that consumers will buy more of a good when its price falls and less of a good when its price rises, but let's look more closely at why this result holds. When the price of a product falls, consumers buy a larger quantity because of two effects:

1. The **substitution effect** refers to the change in the quantity demanded of a good that results because a change in price makes the good more or less expensive *relative* to other goods that are *substitutes*. When the price of premium bottled water falls, people will substitute buying premium bottled water for other goods, such as regular bottled water or carbonated soft drinks, like Coke and Pepsi.

2. The **income effect** of a price change refers to the change in the quantity demanded of a good that results because a change in the good's price increases or decreases consumers' purchasing power. *Purchasing power* is the quantity of goods a consumer can buy with a fixed amount of income. When the price of a good falls, the increased purchasing power of consumers' incomes will usually lead them to purchase a larger quantity of the good. When the price of a good rises, the decreased purchasing power of consumers' incomes will usually lead them to purchase a smaller quantity of the good.

Substitution effect The change in the quantity demanded of a good that results from a change in price, making the good more or less expensive relative to other goods that are substitutes.

Income effect The change in the quantity demanded of a good that results from the effect of a change in the good's price on consumers' purchasing power.

 Although we can analyze them separately, the substitution effect and the income effect occur simultaneously whenever a price changes. So, a fall in the price of premium bottled water leads consumers to buy more bottles both because the bottles are now less expensive relative to substitute products and because the purchasing power of consumers' incomes has increased.   **MyLab Economics** Concept Check

Holding Everything Else Constant: The *Ceteris Paribus* Condition

Notice that the definition of the law of demand contains the phrase *holding everything else constant*. In constructing the market demand curve for premium bottled water, we focused only on the effect that changes in the price of premium bottled water would have on the quantity consumers would be willing and able to buy. We were holding constant other variables that might affect the willingness of consumers to buy premium bottled water. Economists refer to the necessity of holding all variables other than price constant in constructing a demand curve as the **ceteris paribus condition**. *Ceteris paribus* means "all else equal" in Latin.

What would happen if we allowed a change in a variable—other than price—that might affect the willingness of consumers to buy premium bottled water? Consumers would then change the quantity they demanded at each price. We can illustrate this effect by shifting the market demand curve. A shift of a demand curve is *an increase or a decrease in demand*. A movement along a demand curve is *an increase or a decrease in the quantity demanded*. As Figure 3.2 shows, the demand curve shifts to the right if consumers decide to buy more premium bottled water at each price, and the demand curve shifts to the left if consumers decide to buy less at each price. **MyLab Economics** Concept Check

Variables That Shift Market Demand

Many variables other than price can influence market demand. These five are the most important:

- Income
- Prices of related goods
- Tastes
- Population and demographics
- Expected future prices

We next discuss how changes in each of these variables affect the market demand curve.

Income The income that consumers have available to spend affects their willingness and ability to buy a good. Suppose that the market demand curve in Figure 3.1 on page 75 represents the willingness of consumers to buy premium bottled water when average household income is $56,000. If average household income rises to $58,000, the demand for premium bottled water will increase, shifting the demand curve to the right. A good is a **normal good** when the demand for the good increases following a rise in income and decreases following a fall in income. Most goods are

---

Ceteris paribus **("all else equal") condition** The requirement that when analyzing the relationship between two variables—such as price and quantity demanded—other variables must be held constant.

Normal good A good for which the demand increases as income rises and decreases as income falls.

MyLab Economics Animation

Figure 3.2

Shifting the Demand Curve

When consumers increase the quantity of a product they want to buy at a given price, the demand curve shifts to the right, from D_1 to D_2. When consumers decrease the quantity of a product they want to buy at a given price, the demand curve shifts to the left, from D_1 to D_3.

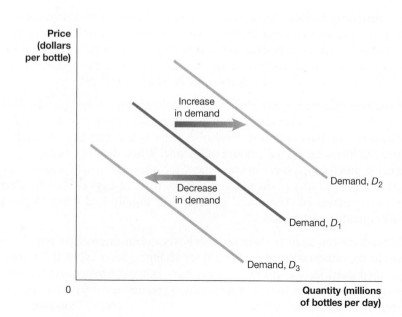

normal goods, but some goods are *inferior goods*. A good is an **inferior good** when the demand for it decreases following a rise in income and increases following a fall in income. For instance, as your income rises, you might buy fewer cans of tuna or packages of instant noodles and buy more salmon or whole grain pasta. So, for you, canned tuna and instant noodles would be examples of inferior goods—not because they are of low quality but because you buy less of them as your income increases.

Prices of Related Goods The prices of other goods can also affect consumers' demand for a product. Consumers who buy premium bottled water could buy regular bottled water instead. Goods and services that can be used for the same purpose are called **substitutes**. When two goods are substitutes, the more you buy of one, the less you will buy of the other. A decrease in the price of a substitute causes the demand curve for a good to shift to the left. An increase in the price of a substitute causes the demand curve for a good to shift to the right.

Suppose that the market demand curve in Figure 3.1 on page 75 represents the willingness and ability of consumers to buy premium bottled water during a day when the average price of regular bottled water is $0.75. If the average price of regular bottled water falls to $0.65, consumers will demand fewer bottles of premium water at every price, which shifts the demand curve for premium bottled water to the left.

Inferior good A good for which the demand increases as income falls and decreases as income rises.

Substitutes Goods and services that can be used for the same purpose.

Apply the Concept

MyLab Economics Video

Virtual Reality Headsets: Will a Substitute Fail for a Lack of Complements?

Firms can increase their profits if they successfully introduce a product that better serves a known consumer need than do existing products. Coke and Pepsi have used this strategy in trying to convince consumers that premium bottled water is superior to regular bottled water. Similarly, when firms such as Sony, Facebook, and HTC began selling virtual reality headsets, they hoped that consumers would consider them a superior alternative to existing game consoles, such as the Sony PlayStation and the Microsoft Xbox.

But to be an effective substitute for game consoles, virtual reality headsets were dependent on important complementary products—games that could be played using the headsets. Existing games that are playable on game consoles can't be played on virtual reality headsets. So, makers of these headsets were dependent on firms that develop and sell games and other software to release titles that could be used with the headsets. In early 2017, not many game developers were doing so. Although Sony had heavily advertised its PlayStation VR goggles during the 2016 holiday season, it had sold fewer than 1 million units. Some game developers considered those sales to be too low to take the risk of spending the funds needed to develop virtual reality games.

Bloomberg/Getty images

Is the success of virtual reality headsets being held back by a lack of complements?

Sony and the other firms selling virtual reality headsets had difficulty selling enough headsets to convince game developers they would be able to make a profit selling games for the headsets. But a key reason that sales of headsets lagged was that many consumers didn't believe there were enough games and other software available to justify buying headsets rather than game consoles. The firms making headsets hoped the problem could gradually be overcome as the number of games increased and as consumers became more familiar with the product. As one industry analyst put it, "This is going to be a long slog, as the technology continues to improve, more content becomes available and awareness increases."

Until then, the success of virtual reality headsets as a substitute for game consoles was being held back by the limited availability of a complementary good: games and other software that could be used with the headsets.

Sources: Takashi Mochizuki, "Sony's Virtual-Reality Headset Confronts Actual Reality of Modest Sales," *Wall Street Journal,* February 27, 2017; Joshua Brustein, "Will VR Ever Matter?" bloomberg.com, October 20, 2016; and Nick Wingfield, "Sticker Shock, and Maybe Nausea, Hamper Sales of Virtual Reality Gear," *New York Times,* January 8, 2017.

MyLab Economics Study Plan

Your Turn: Test your understanding by doing related problem 1.12 on page 101 at the end of this chapter.

Complements Goods and services that are used together.

Goods and services that are used together—such as hot dogs and hot dog buns—are called **complements**. When two goods are complements, the more consumers buy of one, the more they will buy of the other. A decrease in the price of a complement causes the demand curve for a good to shift to the right. An increase in the price of a complement causes the demand curve for a good to shift to the left.

When working out at the gym, many people drink a premium water such as Water Joe, Pepsi's LIFEWTR, or Fiji Water. So, for many people, premium bottled water and a gym membership are complements. Suppose that the market demand curve in Figure 3.1 on page 75 represents the willingness of consumers to buy premium bottled water at a time when the average price of a gym membership is $40 per month. If the price of gym memberships drops to $30 per month, consumers will buy more gym memberships *and* more premium bottled water, so the demand curve for premium bottled water will shift to the right.

Tastes An advertising campaign for a product can influence consumer demand. For example, PepsiCo paid millions of dollars to advertise LIFEWTR during the 2017 Super Bowl. If other firms making premium bottled water begin to advertise heavily, consumers are likely to buy more of it at every price, and the demand curve will shift to the right. An economist would say that the advertising campaign has affected consumers' *taste* for premium bottled water. Taste is a catchall category that refers to the many subjective elements that can enter into a consumer's decision to buy a product. Sometimes trends play a substantial role. For example, the popularity of low-carbohydrate diets caused a decline in demand for some goods, such as bread and donuts, and an increase in demand for fish. In general, when consumers' taste for a product increases, the demand curve will shift to the right, and when consumers' taste decreases, the demand curve will shift to the left.

Population and Demographics As the population of a country increases, the number of consumers will increase, as will the demand for most products. The **demographics** of a population refers to its characteristics, with respect to age, race, and gender. As the demographics of a country or region change, the demand for particular goods will increase or decrease because different categories of people tend to have different preferences for those goods. For instance, the U.S. Census Bureau forecasts that Hispanics will increase from 18 percent of the U.S. population in 2016 to 29 percent in 2060. This increase will expand demand for Spanish-language books, Web sites, and cable television channels, among other goods and services.

Demographics The characteristics of a population with respect to age, race, and gender.

Millennials have a greater demand for bottled water and smaller demand for soda than do older generations.

Apply the Concept

MyLab Economics Video

Millennials Shake Up the Markets for Soda, Groceries, Big Macs, and Running Shoes

Changing demographics can affect the demand for products. The usefulness of some products varies with age. For example, when birth rates are high, the demand for baby products such as formula and diapers increases. Similarly, when there are more older people, the demand for nursing homes increases. Many retail analysts believe that *tastes* for products may also differ across generations, so that some products that are popular with older generations may be much less popular with younger generations. There are no exact definitions of generations, but the following chart shows common labels.

Years Born	Generation Label	Age Range in 2017	Number of People in the Generation in 2017
1946–1964	Baby boom generation	53–71	79 million
1965–1984	Generation X	33–52	83 million
1985–2004	Millennials, or generation Y	13–32	87 million

The millennials outnumber the two generations that preceded them, but the size of each generation doesn't tell the whole story for retailers. Market research indicates that consumers between the ages of 18 and 49 account for a large fraction of all retail sales. This fact helps explain why firms are willing to pay high prices to run commercials on television programs, such as AMC's *The Walking Dead*, that this "prime demographic" watches. Note that the whole of the baby boom generation is now older than this demographic. Members of generation X are also beginning to age out of this group, and over time millennials will begin to make up the bulk of this demographic.

Because of their importance as consumers, firms become concerned if millennials don't have a strong demand for their products. For instance, according to the *Wall Street Journal*, only 20 percent of millennials have ever eaten a Big Mac, McDonald's most important menu item. Millennials are more likely to visit "fast-casual" restaurants, such as Panera Bread, than they are fast-food restaurants, such as McDonald's or Burger King. Millennials are also less likely to play golf or to enter marathons or other races or even to run noncompetitively. Many millennials prefer to attend fitness classes or to work out on their own. As fewer young people play golf, sales of golf equipment, rounds of golf at golf courses, and ratings of golf tournaments on television have all declined. Sales of running shoes and other running gear have also declined. The reduced demand for these products from millennials helped push retail chains Sports Authority, Bob's Stores, and Eastern Mountain Sports into bankruptcy and forced Dick's Sporting Goods to close some of its stores.

Millennials are also less likely to shop at grocery stores, preferring online retailers like Amazon Fresh or using smartphone apps like Seamless and Grubhub to order from restaurants. Spending at grocery stores by people aged 25 to 34 dropped by more than 25 percent between 1990 and 2016, after adjusting for inflation. As we saw in the chapter opener, in 2016, for the first time U.S. consumers purchased more bottled water than carbonated beverages. As a result, many traditional beverage companies like Coca-Cola and PepsiCo have begun to increase their production of bottled water. In particular, by 2017, these companies were heavily promoting premium bottled water brands, such as smartwater and LIFEWTR. As one of PepsiCo's top managers put it, "What we see developing is a premium water segment of the water category, driven heavily by millennials." But these companies faced the challenge of convincing millennials and other consumers that the electrolytes and other ingredients added to premium bottled water were enough to justify paying a significantly higher price than for regular bottled water. As one skeptical appraisal said, "To put it simply, in most situations plain old water will suffice. Unless you're running a marathon or partaking in an intense hike."

Regardless of whether the demand for premium water continues to expand rapidly, as firms make plans for the long run, they have to take into account how changing demographics may affect demand for their products.

Sources: Julie Jargon, "McDonald's Knows It's Losing the Burger Battle—Can It Come Back?" *Wall Street Journal*, October 6, 2016; Sara Germano, "Dick's Drops Brands as It Expands In-house Labels," *Wall Street Journal*, March 7, 2017; Heather Haddon, "Grocers Feel Chill from Millennials," *Wall Street Journal*, October 27, 2016; John Kell, "PepsiCo to Launch Premium Water Brand LIFEWTR," fortune.com, December 9, 2016; and Hayley Sugg, "Pepsi's New Enhanced Water Brand Follows Trend," cookinglight.com, February 8, 2017.

Your Turn: Test your understanding by doing related problems 1.13 and 1.14 on page 101 at the end of this chapter.

MyLab Economics Study Plan

Expected Future Prices

Consumers choose not only which products to buy but also when to buy them. For instance, if enough consumers become convinced that houses will be selling for lower prices in three months, the demand for houses will decrease now, as some consumers postpone their purchases to wait for the expected price decrease. Alternatively, if enough consumers become convinced that the price of houses will be higher in three months, the demand for houses will increase now, as some consumers try to beat the expected price increase.

Table 3.1 summarizes the most important variables that cause market demand curves to shift. Note that the table shows the shift in the demand curve that results from an *increase* in each of the variables. A *decrease* in these variables would cause the demand curve to shift in the opposite direction.   **MyLab Economics** Concept Check

Table 3.1

Variables That Shift Market Demand Curves

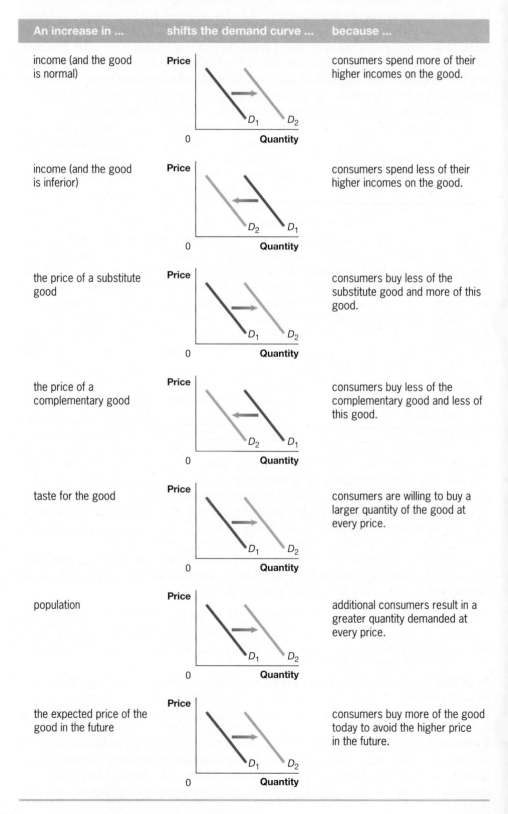

An increase in ...	shifts the demand curve ...	because ...
income (and the good is normal)		consumers spend more of their higher incomes on the good.
income (and the good is inferior)		consumers spend less of their higher incomes on the good.
the price of a substitute good		consumers buy less of the substitute good and more of this good.
the price of a complementary good		consumers buy less of the complementary good and less of this good.
taste for the good		consumers are willing to buy a larger quantity of the good at every price.
population		additional consumers result in a greater quantity demanded at every price.
the expected price of the good in the future		consumers buy more of the good today to avoid the higher price in the future.

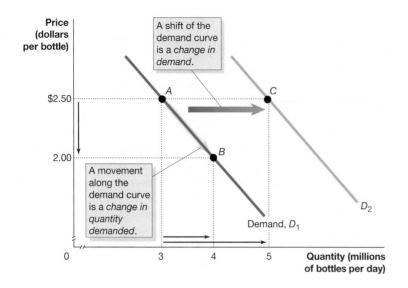

MyLab Economics Animation

Figure 3.3

A Change in Demand versus a Change in Quantity Demanded

If the price of premium bottled water falls from $2.50 to $2.00, the result will be a movement along the demand curve from point A to point B—an increase in quantity demanded from 3 million bottles to 4 million. If consumers' incomes increase, or if another factor changes that makes consumers want more of the product at every price, the demand curve will shift to the right—an increase in demand. In this case, the increase in demand from D_1 to D_2 causes the quantity of premium bottled water demanded at a price of $2.50 to increase from 3 million bottles at point A to 5 million at point C.

A Change in Demand versus a Change in Quantity Demanded

It is important to understand the difference between a *change in demand* and a *change in quantity demanded*. A change in demand refers to a shift of the demand curve. A shift occurs if there is a change in one of the variables—*other than the price of the product*—that affects the willingness of consumers to buy the product. A change in quantity demanded refers to a movement along the demand curve as a result of a change in the product's price. Figure 3.3 illustrates this important distinction. If the price of premium bottled water falls from $2.50 to $2.00, the result will be a movement along the demand curve from point A to point B—an increase in quantity demanded from 3 million bottles to 4 million. If consumers' incomes increase, or if another factor changes that makes consumers want more of the product at every price, the demand curve will shift to the right—an increase in demand. In this case, the increase in demand from D_1 to D_2 causes the quantity of premium bottled water demanded at a price of $2.50 to increase from 3 million bottles at point A to 5 million at point C.   **MyLab Economics** Concept Check

Apply the Concept   MyLab Economics Video

Forecasting the Demand for Premium Bottled Water

It's important for managers to forecast the demand for their products accurately because doing so helps them determine how much of a good to produce. Firms typically set manufacturing schedules at least a month ahead of time. Premium bottled water is a rapidly growing market, and firms need to carefully plan increases in productive capacity. Firms that fail to produce a large enough quantity to keep pace with increasing demand can lose out to competitors. But will the demand for premium bottled water continue to grow at such a rapid pace?

Richard Tedlow of the Harvard Business School has developed a theory of the "three phases of marketing" that can provide some insight into how the markets for many consumer products develop over time. The first phase often has a very large number of firms, each producing a relatively small volume of goods and charging high prices. This phase corresponds to the carbonated soft drink industry in the late nineteenth century, the automobile industry in the early twentieth century, and the personal computer industry in the late 1970s. In the second phase, the market consolidates, with one or a few brands attaining high market shares by selling a large number of units at lower prices. This phase corresponds to the soft drink industry during the middle of the twentieth century, the automobile industry during the 1920s, and the personal computer industry during the 1980s.

Sara Stathas/Alamy Stock Photo

How will changes in demographics, income, and tastes shape the market for premium bottled water?

The third phase of marketing involves a rapid multiplication of products introduced by the dominant firms. Carbonated soft drinks, automobiles, and personal computers are all currently in this phase. For instance, Coca-Cola and Pepsi are the dominant firms in the carbonated soft drink industry, but they offer an incredible variety of products, from basic Coke and Pepsi to caffeine-free, Diet Cherry Coke, and Black Cherry French Vanilla Diet Pepsi Jazz.

The premium bottled water industry is probably in the second phase of marketing, with Coca-Cola, PepsiCo, Danone, and Nestlé each having market shares of at least 10 percent, and dozens of smaller firms making up the remainder of the market. Whether these smaller firms will be able to thrive or whether the industry will face rapid consolidation and move quickly into the third phase of marketing is crucial to managers planning the future at these firms.

Managers at beverage firms will have to take into account a number of factors when estimating the future demand for premium bottled water. Factors that will tend to lead to higher demand for premium bottled water include the popularity of the product with millennials, the trend toward healthier eating habits that has led to declining consumption of carbonated beverages, the taxes on soda that cities have been imposing to both fight obesity and raise tax revenue, and the possibility of attracting consumers who now prefer energy drinks such as Red Bull and sports drinks such as Gatorade. But an obstacle to the rapid growth of demand for premium bottled water comes from doubts raised by some analysts about the benefits from the electrolytes and other ingredients it contains that are not in regular bottled water. If consumers come to believe that these ingredients serve no useful purpose, they may prefer to buy regular bottled water, which typically has a lower price.

As we saw in Chapter 1, economists can use formal models to forecast future values of economic variables. In this case, an economist forecasting the demand for premium bottled water would want to include the factors mentioned in the previous paragraphs as well as other data, including changes over time in demographics and projected income growth.

Sources: Jennifer Maloney, "PepsiCo Gives Its 'Premium' Water a Super Bowl Push," *Wall Street Journal*, January 24, 2017; Quentin Fottrell, "Bottled Water Overtakes Soda as America's No. 1 Drink—Why You Should Avoid Both," marketwatch. com, March 12, 2017; and Richard Tedlow, *New and Improved: The Story of Mass Marketing in America*, Cambridge, MA: Harvard Business School Press, 1996.

MyLab Economics Study Plan

Your Turn: Test your understanding by doing related problem 1.17 on page 102 at the end of this chapter.

3.2 The Supply Side of the Market

LEARNING OBJECTIVE: List and describe the variables that influence supply.

Just as many variables influence the willingness and ability of consumers to buy a particular good or service, many variables influence the willingness and ability of firms to supply a good or service. The most important of these variables is price. The amount of a good or service that a firm is willing and able to supply at a given price is the **quantity supplied**. Holding other variables constant, when the price of a good rises, producing the good is more profitable, and the quantity supplied will increase. When the price of a good falls, selling the good is less profitable, and the quantity supplied will decrease. In addition, as we saw in Chapter 2, devoting more and more resources to the production of a good results in increasing marginal costs. For example, if Coca-Cola, PepsiCo, Fiji, Bai, and other firms increase production of premium bottled water during a given time period, they are likely to find that the cost of producing additional bottles increases as they run existing factories for longer hours and pay higher prices for electrolytes and other ingredients and higher wages for workers. With higher marginal costs, firms will supply a larger quantity only if the price is higher.

Quantity supplied The amount of a good or service that a firm is willing and able to supply at a given price.

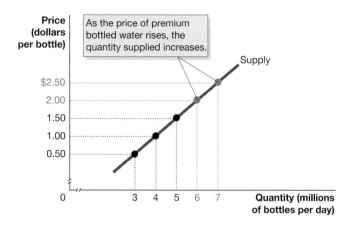

Supply Schedule	
Price (dollars per bottle)	Quantity (millions of bottles per day)
$2.50	7
2.00	6
1.50	5
1.00	4
0.50	3

As the price of premium bottled water rises, the quantity supplied increases.

MyLab Economics Animation

Figure 3.4

A Supply Schedule and Supply Curve

As the price of producing premium bottled water changes, Coca-Cola, PepsiCo, Fiji, Bai, and other firms change the quantity they are willing to supply. We can show this as a *supply schedule* in a table or as a *supply curve* on a graph. The supply schedule and supply curve both show that as the price of premium bottled water rises, firms will increase the quantity they supply. At a price of $2.00 per bottle, firms will supply 6 million bottles per day. At a price of $2.50, firms will supply 7 million.

Supply schedule A table that shows the relationship between the price of a product and the quantity of the product supplied.

Supply curve A curve that shows the relationship between the price of a product and the quantity of the product supplied.

Supply Schedules and Supply Curves

A **supply schedule** is a table that shows the relationship between the price of a product and the quantity of the product supplied. The table in Figure 3.4 is a supply schedule showing the quantity of premium bottled water that firms would be willing to supply per month at different prices. The graph in Figure 3.4 plots the numbers from the table as a **supply curve**, which shows the relationship between the price of a product and the quantity of the product supplied. The supply schedule and supply curve both show that as the price of premium bottled water rises, firms will increase the quantity they supply. At a price of $2.00 per bottle, firms will supply 6 million bottles per day. At a higher price of $2.50, firms will supply 7 million. (Once again, we are assuming for convenience that the supply curve is a straight line, even though not all supply curves are actually straight lines.)   **MyLab Economics** Concept Check

The Law of Supply

The *market supply curve* in Figure 3.4 is upward sloping. We expect most supply curves to be upward sloping, according to the **law of supply**, which states that, holding everything else constant, increases in price cause increases in the quantity supplied, and decreases in price cause decreases in the quantity supplied. Notice that the definition of the law of supply—like the definition of the law of demand—contains the phrase *holding everything else constant*. If only the price of the product changes, there is a movement along the supply curve, which is *an increase or a decrease in the quantity supplied*. As Figure 3.5 shows, if any other variable that affects the willingness of firms to supply a good changes, the supply curve will shift, which is *an increase or a decrease in supply*. When firms increase the quantity of a product they want to sell at a given price, the supply curve shifts to the right. The shift from S_1 to S_3 represents *an increase in supply*. When firms decrease the quantity of a product they want to sell at a given price, the supply curve shifts to the left. The shift from S_1 to S_2 represents *a decrease in supply*.   **MyLab Economics** Concept Check

Law of supply A rule that states that, holding everything else constant, increases in price cause increases in the quantity supplied, and decreases in price cause decreases in the quantity supplied.

Variables That Shift Market Supply

Many variables other than price can affect market supply. These five are the most important:

- Prices of inputs
- Technological change
- Prices of related goods in production
- Number of firms in the market
- Expected future prices

We next discuss how changes in each of these variables affect the market supply curve.

Prices of Inputs The factor most likely to cause the supply curve for a product to shift is a change in the price of an input. An *input* is anything used in the production of a good or service. For instance, if the price of electrolytes used in many premium

MyLab Economics Animation

Figure 3.5

Shifting the Supply Curve

When firms increase the quantity of a product they want to sell at a given price, the supply curve shifts to the right. The shift from S_1 to S_3 represents an *increase in supply*. When firms decrease the quantity of a product they want to sell at a given price, the supply curve shifts to the left. The shift from S_1 to S_2 represents a *decrease in supply*.

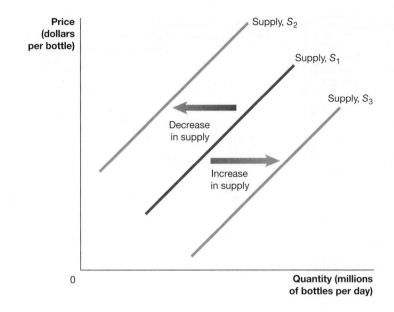

Technological change A positive or negative change in the ability of a firm to produce a given level of output with a given quantity of inputs.

bottled waters or the price of plastic bottles rises, the cost of producing premium bottled water will increase, making it less profitable at every price. The supply of premium bottled water will decline, and the market supply curve will shift to the left. Similarly, if the price of an input falls, the supply of premium bottled water will increase, and the market supply curve will shift to the right.

Technological Change A second factor that causes a change in supply is **technological change**, which is a positive or negative change in the ability of a firm to produce a given level of output with a given quantity of inputs. Positive technological change occurs whenever a firm is able to produce more output using the same amount of inputs. In other words, the *productivity* of the firm's workers or machines has increased. For example, suppose that PepsiCo develops a better way to lay out the plants where LIFEWTR is bottled so that it can produce more bottles per day, using the same number of workers and amount of machinery. If a firm can produce more output with the same amount of inputs, its costs will be lower, and the good will be more profitable to produce at any given price. As a result, when positive technological change occurs, the firm will increase the quantity supplied at every price, and its supply curve will shift to the right.

Negative technological change is relatively rare, although it could result from an earthquake or another natural disaster or from a war that reduces the ability of firms to supply as much output with a given amount of inputs. Negative technological change will raise firms' costs, and firms will earn lower profits from producing the good. Therefore, negative technological change will cause the market supply curve to shift to the left.

Prices of Related Goods in Production Firms often choose which good or service they will produce. Alternative goods that a firm could produce are called *substitutes in production*. Many of the firms that produce premium bottled water also produce other beverages, such as regular bottled water, juices, or carbonated soft drinks. For example, PepsiCo produces Aquafina bottled water, Tropicana orange juice, and Pepsi-Cola, among other beverages. If the price of carbonated soft drinks decreases relative to the price of premium bottled water, soft drinks will become less profitable, and Coca-Cola, PepsiCo, and other firms will shift some of their productive capacity away from soft drinks and toward premium bottled water. The firms will offer more bottles of premium water for sale at every price, so the supply curve for premium bottled water will shift to the right.

Goods that are produced together are called *complements in production*. For example, the same geological formations that contain oil usually also contain natural gas. If the price of oil rises, oil companies that begin pumping more oil from these formations will also produce more natural gas. As a result, an increase in the price of oil will cause the supply curve for natural gas—a complement in production—to shift to the right.

Number of Firms in the Market A change in the number of firms in the market will change supply. When new firms *enter* a market, the supply curve shifts to the right, and when existing firms leave, or *exit*, a market, the supply curve shifts to the left. In early 2017, for instance, PepsiCo entered the market for premium bottled water when it introduced LIFEWTR, which shifted the market supply curve to the right.

Expected Future Prices If a firm expects that the price of its product will be higher in the future, it has an incentive to decrease supply now and increase it in the future. For instance, if Coca-Cola believes that prices for premium bottled water are temporarily low—perhaps because of a recession—it may store some of its production of smartwater today to sell later on, when it expects prices to be higher.

Table 3.2 summarizes the most important variables that cause market supply curves to shift. Note that the table shows the shift in the supply curve that results from an *increase* in each of the variables. A *decrease* in these variables would cause the supply curve to shift in the opposite direction.   **MyLab Economics** Concept Check

Table 3.2

Variables That Shift Market Supply Curves

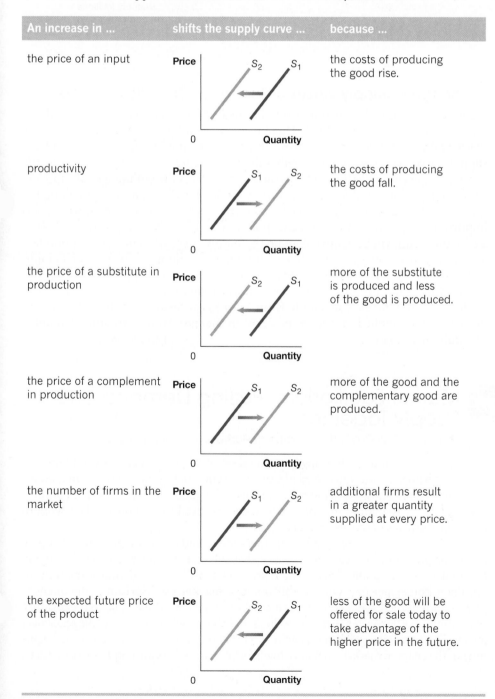

An increase in ...	shifts the supply curve ...	because ...
the price of an input		the costs of producing the good rise.
productivity		the costs of producing the good fall.
the price of a substitute in production		more of the substitute is produced and less of the good is produced.
the price of a complement in production		more of the good and the complementary good are produced.
the number of firms in the market		additional firms result in a greater quantity supplied at every price.
the expected future price of the product		less of the good will be offered for sale today to take advantage of the higher price in the future.

MyLab Economics Animation

Figure 3.6

A Change in Supply versus a Change in Quantity Supplied

If the price of premium bottled water rises from $2.00 to $2.50, the result will be a movement up the supply curve from point *A* to point *B*—an increase in the quantity supplied by Coca-Cola, PepsiCo, Bai, and other firms from 6 million bottles to 7 million. If the price of an input decreases, or if another factor changes that causes sellers to supply more of the product at every price, the supply curve will shift to the right—an increase in supply. In this case, the increase in supply from S_1 to S_2 causes the quantity of premium bottled water supplied at a price of $2.50 to increase from 7 million at point *B* to 9 million at point *C*.

MyLab Economics Study Plan

A Change in Supply versus a Change in Quantity Supplied

We noted in Section 3.1 the important difference between a change in demand and a change in quantity demanded. There is a similar difference between a *change in supply* and a *change in quantity supplied*. A change in supply refers to a shift of the supply curve. The supply curve will shift when there is a change in one of the variables—*other than the price of the product*—that affects the willingness of suppliers to sell the product. A change in quantity supplied refers to a movement along the supply curve as a result of a change in the product's price. Figure 3.6 illustrates this important distinction. If the price of premium bottled water rises from $2.00 to $2.50, the result will be a movement up the supply curve from point *A* to point *B*—an increase in quantity supplied from 6 million to 7 million. If the price of an input decreases, or if another factor changes that causes sellers to supply more of a product at every price, the supply curve will shift to the right—an increase in supply. In this case, the increase in supply from S_1 to S_2 causes the quantity of premium bottled water supplied at a price of $2.50 to increase from 7 million at point *B* to 9 million at point *C*.

MyLab Economics Concept Check

Market equilibrium A situation in which quantity demanded equals quantity supplied.

3.3 Market Equilibrium: Putting Demand and Supply Together

LEARNING OBJECTIVE: Use a graph to illustrate market equilibrium.

The purpose of markets is to bring buyers and sellers together. As we saw in Chapter 2, instead of being chaotic and disorderly, the interaction of buyers and sellers in markets ultimately results in firms being led to produce the goods and services that consumers want most. To understand this process, we first need to see how markets work to reconcile the plans of buyers and sellers.

In Figure 3.7, we bring together the market demand curve and the market supply curve for premium bottled water. Notice that the demand curve crosses the supply curve at only one point. This point represents a price of $1.50 and a quantity of 5 million bottles per day. Only at this point of **market equilibrium** is the quantity of premium bottled water consumers are willing and able to buy equal to the quantity of premium bottled water firms are willing and able to sell. In this case, the *equilibrium price* is $1.50, and the *equilibrium quantity* is 5 million bottles. As we noted at the beginning of the chapter, markets that have many buyers and sellers are competitive markets,

MyLab Economics Animation

Figure 3.7

Market Equilibrium

Where the demand curve crosses the supply curve determines market equilibrium. In this case, the demand curve for premium bottled water crosses the supply curve at a price of $1.50 and a quantity of 5 million bottles. Only at this point is the quantity of premium bottled water consumers are willing to buy equal to the quantity that Coca-Cola, PepsiCo, Bai, and other firms are willing to sell: The quantity demanded is equal to the quantity supplied.

and equilibrium in these markets is a **competitive market equilibrium**. In the market for premium bottled water, there are many buyers but only about 45 firms. Whether 45 firms are enough for our model of demand and supply to apply to this market is a matter of judgment. In this chapter, we are assuming that the market for premium bottled water has enough sellers to be competitive.

Competitive market equilibrium A market equilibrium with many buyers and sellers.

How Markets Eliminate Surpluses and Shortages

A market that is not in equilibrium moves toward equilibrium. Once a market is in equilibrium, it remains in equilibrium. To see why, consider what happens if a market is not in equilibrium. Suppose that the price in the market for premium bottled water was $2.00 rather than the equilibrium price of $1.50. As Figure 3.8 shows, at a price of $2.00, the quantity of bottles supplied would be 6 million, and the quantity of bottles demanded would be 4 million. When the quantity supplied is greater than

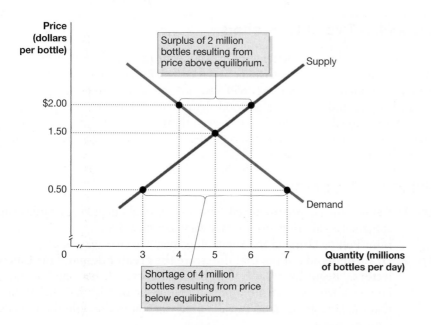

MyLab Economics Animation

Figure 3.8

The Effect of Surpluses and Shortages on the Market Price

When the market price is above equilibrium, there will be a *surplus*. A price of $2.00 for premium bottled water results in 6 million bottles being supplied but only 4 million being demanded, or a surplus of 2 million. As Coca-Cola, PepsiCo, Bai, and other firms cut the price to dispose of the surplus, the price will fall to the equilibrium price of $1.50. When the market price is below equilibrium, there will be a *shortage*. A price of $0.50 results in 7 million bottles being demanded but only 3 million being supplied, or a shortage of 4 million. As firms find that consumers who are unable to find premium bottled water available for sale are willing to pay higher prices to get it, the price will rise to the equilibrium price of $1.50.

Surplus A situation in which the quantity supplied is greater than the quantity demanded.

the quantity demanded, there is a **surplus** in the market. In this case, the surplus is equal to 2 million bottles (6 million − 4 million = 2 million). When there is a surplus, firms will have unsold goods piling up, which gives them an incentive to increase their sales by cutting the price. Cutting the price will simultaneously increase the quantity demanded and decrease the quantity supplied. This adjustment will reduce the surplus, but as long as the price is above $1.50, there will be a surplus, and downward pressure on the price will continue. Only when the price falls to $1.50 will the market be in equilibrium.

If, however, the price were $0.50, the quantity demanded would be 7 million bottles, and the quantity supplied would be 3 million, as shown in Figure 3.8. When the quantity demanded is greater than the quantity supplied, there is a **shortage** in the market. In this case, the shortage is equal to 4 million bottles (7 million − 3 million = 4 million). When a shortage occurs, some consumers will be unable to buy premium bottled water at the current price. In this situation, firms will realize that they can raise the price without losing sales. A higher price will simultaneously increase the quantity supplied and decrease the quantity demanded. This adjustment will reduce the shortage, but as long as the price is below $1.50, there will be a shortage, and upward pressure on the price will continue. Only when the price rises to $1.50 will the market be in equilibrium.

Shortage A situation in which the quantity demanded is greater than the quantity supplied.

At a competitive market equilibrium, all consumers willing to pay the market price will be able to buy as much of the product as they want, and all firms willing to accept the market price will be able to sell as much of the product as they want. As a result, there will be no reason for the price to change unless either the demand curve or the supply curve shifts. **MyLab Economics** Concept Check

Demand and Supply Both Count

Keep in mind that the interaction of demand and supply determines the equilibrium price. Neither consumers nor firms can dictate what the equilibrium price will be. No firm can sell anything at any price unless it can find a willing buyer, and no consumer can buy anything at any price without finding a willing seller. **MyLab Economics** Concept Check

Solved Problem 3.3

MyLab Economics Interactive Animation

Demand and Supply Both Count: A Tale of Two Letters

Which letter is likely to be worth more: one written by Abraham Lincoln or one written by his assassin, John Wilkes Booth? Lincoln is one of the greatest presidents, and many people collect anything he wrote. The demand for letters written by Lincoln surely would seem to be much greater than the demand for letters written by Booth. Yet, when R.M. Smythe and Co. auctioned off on the same day a letter written by Lincoln and a letter written by Booth, the Booth letter sold for $31,050, and the Lincoln letter sold for only $21,850. Use a demand and supply graph to explain how the Booth letter has a higher market price than the Lincoln letter, even though the demand for letters written by Lincoln is greater than the demand for letters written by Booth.

Solving the Problem

Step 1: **Review the chapter material.** This problem is about prices being determined at market equilibrium, so you may want to review the section "Market Equilibrium: Putting Demand and Supply Together," which begins on page 86.

Step 2: **Draw demand curves that illustrate the greater demand for Lincoln's letters.** Begin by drawing two demand curves. Label one "Demand for Lincoln's letters" and the other "Demand for Booth's letters." Make sure that the Lincoln demand curve is much farther to the right than the Booth demand curve.

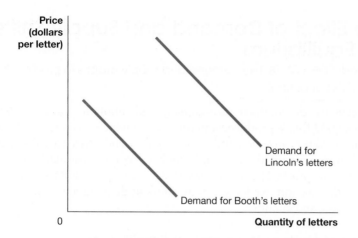

Step 3: **Draw supply curves that illustrate the equilibrium price of Booth's letters being higher than the equilibrium price of Lincoln's letters.** Based on the demand curves you have just drawn, think about how it might be possible for the market price of Lincoln's letters to be lower than the market price of Booth's letters. This outcome can occur only if the supply of Lincoln's letters is much greater than the supply of Booth's letters. Draw on your graph a supply curve for Lincoln's letters and a supply curve for Booth's letters that will result in an equilibrium price of Booth's letters of $31,050 and an equilibrium price of Lincoln's letters of $21,850. You have now solved the problem.

Extra Credit: The explanation for this puzzle is that both demand and supply count when determining market price. The demand for Lincoln's letters is much greater than the demand for Booth's letters, but the supply of Booth's letters is very small. Historians believe that only eight letters written by Booth exist today. (Note that the supply curves for letters written by Booth and by Lincoln are upward sloping, even though only a fixed number of each of these letters is available and, obviously, no more can be produced. The upward slope of the supply curves occurs because the higher the price, the larger the quantity of letters that will be offered for sale by people who currently own them.)

Your Turn: For more practice, do related problems 3.5, 3.6, and 3.7 on pages 103–104 at the end of this chapter.

3.4 The Effect of Demand and Supply Shifts on Equilibrium

LEARNING OBJECTIVE: Use demand and supply graphs to predict changes in prices and quantities.

We have seen that the interaction of demand and supply in markets determines the quantity of a good that is produced and the price at which it is sold. We have also seen that several variables cause demand curves to shift and other variables cause supply curves to shift. As a result, demand and supply curves in most markets are constantly shifting, and the prices and quantities that represent equilibrium are constantly changing. In this section, we look at how shifts in demand and supply curves affect equilibrium price and quantity.

The Effect of Shifts in Demand on Equilibrium

Because premium bottled water is a normal good, when incomes increase, the market demand curve shifts to the right. Figure 3.9 shows the effect of a demand curve shifting to the right, from D_1 to D_2. This shift causes a shortage at the original equilibrium price, P_1. To eliminate the shortage, the equilibrium price rises to P_2, and the equilibrium quantity rises from Q_1 to Q_2. In contrast, if the price of a substitute good, such as regular bottled water, were to fall, the demand for premium bottled water would decrease, shifting the demand curve to the left. When the demand curve shifts to the left, both the equilibrium price and quantity will decrease.   **MyLab Economics** Concept Check

The Effect of Shifts in Supply on Equilibrium

When PepsiCo entered the market by selling LIFEWTR, the market supply curve for premium bottled water shifted to the right. Figure 3.10 shows the supply curve shifting from S_1 to S_2. When the supply curve shifts to the right, there will be a surplus at the original equilibrium price, P_1. The surplus is eliminated as the equilibrium price falls to P_2 and the equilibrium quantity rises from Q_1 to Q_2. If an existing firm exits the market, the supply curve will shift to the left, causing the equilibrium price to rise and the equilibrium quantity to fall.   **MyLab Economics** Concept Check

The Effect of Shifts in Demand and Supply over Time

Whenever only demand or only supply shifts, we can easily predict the effect on equilibrium price and quantity. But, what happens if *both* curves shift? For

---

MyLab Economics Animation

Figure 3.9

The Effect of an Increase in Demand on Equilibrium

Increases in income will cause the equilibrium price and quantity to rise:
1. Because premium bottled water is a normal good, as income increases, the quantity demanded increases at every price, and the market demand curve shifts to the right, from D_1 to D_2, which causes a shortage at the original price, P_1.
2. The equilibrium price rises from P_1 to P_2.
3. The equilibrium quantity rises from Q_1 to Q_2.

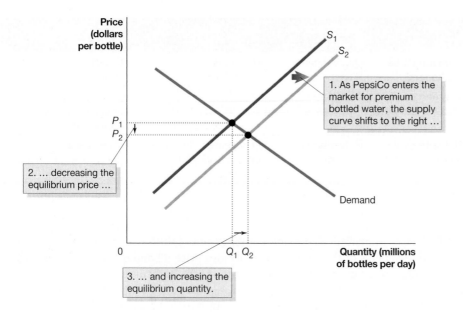

MyLab Economics Animation

Figure 3.10

The Effect of an Increase in Supply on Equilibrium

If a firm enters a market, as PepsiCo entered the market for premium bottled water, the equilibrium price will fall, and the equilibrium quantity will rise:

1. As PepsiCo enters the market, a larger quantity of premium bottled water will be supplied at every price, so the market supply curve shifts to the right, from S_1 to S_2, which causes a surplus at the original price, P_1.
2. The equilibrium price falls from P_1 to P_2.
3. The equilibrium quantity rises from Q_1 to Q_2.

instance, in many markets, the demand curve shifts to the right over time as population and income increase. The supply curve also often shifts to the right as new firms enter the market and positive technological change occurs. Whether the equilibrium price in a market rises or falls over time depends on whether demand shifts to the right more than does supply. Panel (a) of Figure 3.11 shows that when demand shifts to the right more than supply, the equilibrium price rises, while panel (b) shows that when supply shifts to the right more than demand, the equilibrium price falls.

(a) Demand shifting more than supply

(b) Supply shifting more than demand

MyLab Economics Animation

Figure 3.11 Shifts in Demand and Supply over Time

Whether the price of a product rises or falls over time depends on whether demand shifts to the right more than supply.

In panel (a):
1. Demand shifts to the right more than supply.
2. The equilibrium price rises from P_1 to P_2.

In panel (b):
1. Supply shifts to the right more than demand.
2. The equilibrium price falls from P_1 to P_2.

Table 3.3

How Shifts in Demand and Supply Affect Equilibrium Price (P) and Quantity (Q)

The entry in red shows that if the demand curve shifts to the right and the supply curve also shifts to the right, the equilibrium quantity will increase, while the equilibrium price may increase, decrease, or remain unchanged.

	Supply Curve Unchanged	Supply Curve Shifts to the Right	Supply Curve Shifts to the Left
Demand curve unchanged	Q unchanged P unchanged	Q increases P decreases	Q decreases P increases
Demand curve shifts to the right	Q increases P increases	Q increases P increases, decreases, or is unchanged	Q increases, decreases, or is unchanged P increases
Demand curve shifts to the left	Q decreases P decreases	Q increases, decreases, or is unchanged P decreases	Q decreases P increases, decreases, or is unchanged

Table 3.3 summarizes all possible combinations of shifts in demand and supply over time and the effects of the shifts on equilibrium price (P) and quantity (Q). For example, the entry in red in the table shows that if the demand curve shifts to the right and the supply curve also shifts to the right, the equilibrium quantity will increase, while the equilibrium price may increase, decrease, or remain unchanged. To make sure you understand each entry in the table, draw demand and supply graphs to check whether you can reproduce the predicted changes in equilibrium price and quantity. If the entry in Table 3.3 indicates that the equilibrium price or quantity can increase, decrease, or remain unchanged, draw three graphs similar to panels (a) or (b) of Figure 3.11—one showing the equilibrium price or quantity increasing, one showing it decreasing, and one showing it unchanged. **MyLab Economics** Concept Check

Apply the Concept

MyLab Economics Video

Lower Demand for Orange Juice—But Higher Prices?

Joe Raedle/Getty Images News/ Getty Images

Citrus greening disease in Brazil and the United States decreased the supply of oranges.

For many years, Florida orange growers used the advertising slogan "A morning without orange juice is like a day without sunshine." And many Americans agreed, regularly drinking a glass of orange juice with their breakfast. In recent years, though, many consumers have replaced orange juice in their diets with bottled water, tea, coffee, smoothies, or energy drinks. Although assessments of the nutritional value of orange juice vary, some consumers have decided to switch to beverages with fewer calories and less sugar. Between 2011 and 2016, sales of orange juice in the United States declined by more than 15 percent. A 2017 *Wall Street Journal* article quoted an analyst at Deutsche Bank as saying, "People are shifting to low-calorie, natural products."

Ordinarily, when demand for a product is falling, consumers who continue to buy it will pay a lower price. This outcome results from the demand curve shifting to the left, which causes a lower equilibrium price—provided that the supply curve doesn't shift. In fact, though, in recent years the supply curve for orange juice has shifted to the left, largely because of problems in growing oranges in Brazil and the United States, the two leading orange growing countries. Orange groves in both Brazil and Florida had been suffering from an incurable disease called citrus greening, which causes oranges to shrivel and to produce bitter fruit. During the 2016–2017 growing season, Florida produced fewer oranges than in any year since the 1960s.

The following figure shows the market for orange juice. Because of a change in consumer tastes, the demand curve has shifted to the left. Because of citrus greening reducing the orange crops in Brazil and Florida, the supply curve has also shifted to the left. In early 2017, a 64-ounce bottle of orange juice was selling for about $4.00, up from about $3.25 two years earlier. At the same time, total U.S. consumption of orange juice had fallen from the equivalent of 371 million bottles in 2015 to 338 million bottles in 2017.

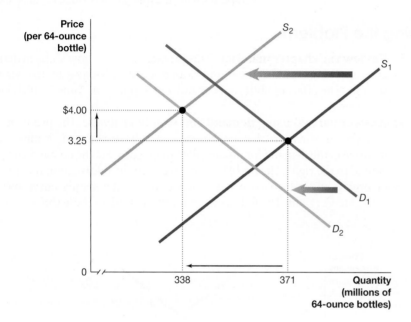

In recent years, the orange juice market has experienced decreases in both demand and supply. If the decrease in demand had been larger than the decrease in supply, we would have seen the price of orange juice decline. Because the price of orange juice has actually increased, we know the decrease in supply must have been larger than the decrease in demand. (To convince yourself of this last point, try drawing another version of the figure in which the demand and supply curves both shift to the left, but the equilibrium price decreases.)

Sources: Ellen Byron, "Last on the Shelf: How Products Dwindle Out of Favor," *Wall Street Journal*, January 10, 2017; Hayley Peterson, "Orange Juice Is Being Called a Massive Scam—And Now It's Disappearing from Breakfast in America," businessinsider.com, October 13, 2016; Fabiana Batista, "Too Much Water Is Diluting Juice from World's No. 1 Orange Crop," bloomberg.com, February 13, 2017; Arian Campo-Flores, "Florida Orange Production Forecast Lowered to 70 Million Boxes," *Wall Street Journal*, February 10, 2017; and data from the U.S. Department of Agriculture.

Your Turn: Test your understanding by doing related problem 4.6 on page 104 at the end of this chapter.

MyLab Economics Study Plan

Solved Problem 3.4

Can We Predict Changes in the Price and Quantity of Organic Corn?

A news article discussed how U.S. consumers have been increasing their demand for organically grown corn and other produce, which is grown using only certain government-approved pesticides and fertilizers. At the same time, imports of corn and other varieties of organic produce from foreign countries have increased the available supply. Use demand and supply graphs to illustrate your answers to the following questions.

a. Can we use this information to be certain whether the equilibrium quantity of organically grown corn will increase or decrease? Illustrate your answer with a graph showing the market for organically grown corn.

b. Can we use this information to be certain whether the equilibrium price of organically grown corn will increase or decrease? Illustrate your answer with a graph showing the market for organically grown corn.

Solving the Problem

Step 1: **Review the chapter material.** This problem is about how shifts in demand and supply curves affect the equilibrium price, so you may want to review the section "The Effect of Shifts in Demand and Supply over Time," which begins on page 90.

Step 2: **Answer part (a) using demand and supply analysis.** The problem gives you the information that consumer tastes have changed, leading to an increase in the demand for organically grown corn. So, the demand curve has shifted to the right. The problem also gives you the information that imports of organically grown corn have increased. So, the supply curve has also shifted to the right. The following graph shows both of these shifts.

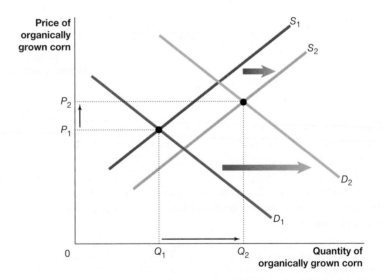

As Table 3.3 on page 92 summarizes, if the demand curve and the supply curve both shift to the right, the equilibrium quantity must increase. Therefore, we can answer part (a) by stating that we are certain that the equilibrium quantity of organically grown corn will increase.

Step 3: **Answer part (b) using demand and supply analysis.** The graph we drew in step 2 shows the equilibrium price of organically grown corn increasing. But given the information provided, the following graph would also be correct.

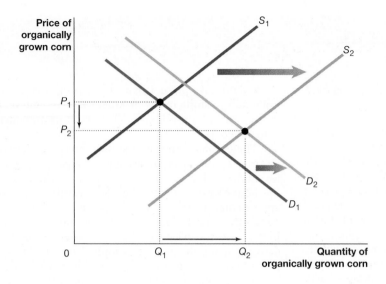

Unlike the graph in step 2, which shows the equilibrium price increasing, this graph shows the equilibrium price decreasing. The uncertainty about whether the equilibrium price will increase or decrease is consistent with what Table 3.3 indicates happens when the demand curve and the supply curve both shift to the right. Therefore, the answer to part (b) is that we cannot be certain whether the equilibrium price of organically grown corn will increase or decrease.

Extra Credit: During 2016, the equilibrium quantity of organically grown corn increased, while the equilibrium price decreased by 30 percent. We can conclude that *both* the increase in demand for organically grown corn and the increase in the supply contributed to the increase in consumption of organically grown corn. That the price of organically grown corn fell indicates that the increase in supply had a larger effect on equilibrium in the organically grown corn market than did the increase in demand.

Sources: Jacob Bunge, "Organic Food Sales Are Booming; Why Are American Farmers Crying Foul?" *Wall Street Journal*, February 21, 2017; and U.S. Department of Agriculture data.

Your Turn: For more practice, do related problems 4.7 and 4.8 on pages 104–105 at the end of this chapter.

MyLab Economics Study Plan

Shifts in a Curve versus Movements along a Curve

When analyzing markets using demand and supply curves, remember that *when a shift in a demand or supply curve causes a change in equilibrium price, the change in price does not cause a further shift in demand or supply.* Suppose that an increase in supply causes the price of a good to fall, while everything else that affects the willingness of consumers to buy the good is constant. The result will be an increase in the quantity demanded but not an increase in demand. For demand to increase, the whole curve must shift. The point is the same for supply: If the price of the good falls but everything else that affects the willingness of sellers to supply the good is constant, the quantity supplied decreases, but the supply does not. For supply to decrease, the whole curve must shift.   MyLab Economics Concept Check   MyLab Economics Study Plan

Don't Let This Happen to You

Remember: A Change in a Good's Price Does *Not* Cause the Demand or Supply Curve to Shift

Suppose a student is asked to draw a demand and supply graph to illustrate how an increase in the price of oranges would affect the market for apples, with other variables being constant. He draws the graph on the left and explains it as follows: "Because apples and oranges are substitutes, an increase in the price of oranges will cause an initial shift to the right in the demand curve for apples, from D_1 to D_2. However, because this initial shift in the demand curve for apples results in a higher price for apples, P_2, consumers will find apples less desirable, and the demand curve will shift to the left, from D_2 to D_3, resulting in a final equilibrium price of P_3." Do you agree or disagree with the student's analysis?

You should disagree. The student has correctly understood that an increase in the price of oranges will cause the demand curve for apples to shift to the right. But, the second demand curve shift the student describes, from D_2 to D_3, will not take place. Changes in the price of a product do not result in shifts in the product's demand curve. Changes in the price of a product result only in movements along a demand curve.

The graph on the right shows the correct analysis. The increase in the price of oranges causes the demand curve for apples to increase from D_1 to D_2. At the original price, P_1, the increase in demand initially results in a shortage of apples equal to $Q_3 - Q_1$. But, as we have seen, a shortage causes the price to increase until the shortage is eliminated. In this case, the price will rise to P_2, where both the quantity demanded and the quantity supplied are equal to Q_2. Notice that the increase in price causes a decrease in the *quantity demanded*, from Q_3 to Q_2, but does *not* cause a decrease in demand.

MyLab Economics Study Plan

Your Turn: Test your understanding by doing related problems 4.13 and 4.14 on page 105 at the end of this chapter.

Continued from page 73

Economics in Your Life & Career

Can You Forecast the Future Demand for Premium Bottled Water?

At the beginning of this chapter, we asked what variables you would take into account in forecasting future demand if you were a manager for a firm selling premium bottled water. In Section 3.1, we discussed the factors that affect the demand for a product and provided a list of the most important variables. In the *Apply the Concept* on page 81, we discussed how economists often use formal models to forecast future demand for a product.

In forecasting demand for premium bottled water, you should take into account factors such as changing demographics, as millennials become a larger fraction of prime-age consumers, and the likelihood that the demand for competing goods, such as carbonated sodas, will decline as consumers turn toward buying healthier products and as more cities impose soda taxes. You may also need to consider whether increased advertising of premium bottled water by large firms such as Coca-Cola and PepsiCo will raise consumer awareness of the product and increase demand for the premium bottled water being sold by other firms as well.

The factors discussed in this chapter provide you with the basic information needed to forecast demand for premium bottled water, although arriving at numerical forecasts requires using statistical analysis that you can learn in more advanced courses.

Conclusion

The interaction of demand and supply determines market equilibrium. The model of demand and supply is a powerful tool for predicting how changes in the actions of consumers and firms will cause changes in equilibrium prices and quantities. As we have seen in this chapter, we can use the model to analyze markets that do not meet all the requirements for being perfectly competitive. As long as there is intense competition among sellers, the model of demand and supply can often successfully predict changes in prices and quantities. We will use this model in the next chapter to analyze economic efficiency and the results of government-imposed price floors and price ceilings.

Before moving on to Chapter 4, read *An Inside Look* on the next page for a discussion of strategies McDonald's is using to reverse a trend of declining sales.

McDonald's Looks for New Ways to Attract Customers

CNBC.COM

4 ways McDonald's is about to change

McDonald's has one major goal for 2017: win back customers.

The burger chain's multi-year turnaround effort, which found success with its All-Day Breakfast promotion, hasn't quite come to fruition…yet.

During its investor day in Chicago on Wednesday, the company's executives touted several big changes that the chain will be making to win back the more than 500 million visits it lost since 2012.

"To deliver sustained growth, we have to attract more customers, more often," CEO Steve Easterbrook said.

McDonald's focus will be on four pillars: menu innovation, store renovations, digital ordering and delivery.

"McDonald's appears to [have] found their focus on profitability through disciplined efforts to reduce costs and focus on the consumer experience including consumer-facing technology, improved convenience in payment and delivery and value to drive more customer visits throughout the day," Darren Tristano, president of Technomic, told CNBC.

"For the world's largest restaurant company, this means playing catch up with younger consumer expectations while continuing to engage older generations of consumers that grew up with McDonald's,"

Tristano said. "Creating alternatives for customization, delivery, payment and ordering processes provides challenges but they are necessary to adapt to the evolving consumer foodservice experience."

New Items on the Menu

Expect to see McDonald's "step up" its menu innovation in the U.S., said Chris Kempczinski, McDonald's USA President.

The company recently launched three different sizes of its classic Big Mac and will continue to add new items to its domestic stores. Including, a nationwide roll out of its "Signature Sandwiches"—customizable and more upscale burgers and chicken sandwiches—later this year.

Renovated Restaurants

Say goodbye to the white metal chairs and bold red and yellow colors. The chain's stores will also be getting an update.

McDonald's is committed to becoming a "modern and progressive burger company" and will be adding self-service ordering kiosks and table service to some of its stores. Employees will now spend more time in the front of the restaurant, delivering food directly to the tables and offering traditional dining hospitality.

McDonald's "experience of the future" is coming to about 650 restaurants this year, bringing the chain's number of these stores to nearly 2,500.

Digital Ordering

The Golden Arches will continue to expand its mobile order and pay platform. While late to the game, the company is expected to launch the product in 20,000 restaurants by the end of 2017.

Easterbrook noted back in November that McDonald's is focused on how customers order, what they order, how they pay and how they want to be served. Customers can pay with cash, credit, debit, Apple pay and Android pay and will soon be able to order through the company's mobile service.

Delivery

Delivery is also an avenue that McDonald's is exploring. The company, which has a large delivery presence in Asia—which accounts for 10 percent of system sales in that market—is hoping to capitalize on the growing industry demand by offering delivery in America. It is currently testing out several models, both in-house and via third-party providers.

The company said 75 percent of the population in its top five markets —America, France, the U.K., Germany and Canada—are within three miles of a McDonald's and 85 percent are within five miles of a chain.

Source: Sarah Whitten, "4 ways McDonald's is about to change," CNBC.com, March 1, 2017.

Key Points in the Article

McDonald's is in the highly competitive fast-food market. The firm has seen a decline in sales for five straight years. Searching for additional ways to increase its sales, McDonald's plans to focus on customer experience. The company recently introduced an all-day breakfast promotion, and in March 2017 announced it will begin to focus on new menu items, restaurant renovations, digital ordering, and delivery. With these changes, McDonald's hopes to win back younger consumers who have come to expect these services while at the same time continuing to appeal to its long-time customers.

Analyzing the News

(a) In the 5-year period beginning with 2012, customer trips to McDonald's fell by more than 500 million. Chief Executive Officer Steve Easterbrook stated that attracting more visits per customer is needed for the company to sustain growth. The company has chosen to focus on four elements to achieve this growth: menu innovation, store renovations, digital ordering, and delivery. Each of these ideas for growth is designed to help increase demand for McDonald's menu items by increasing its customer base and the frequency of customer visits to its restaurants.

(b) McDonald's has recently added new items to its menu, including more customizable and upscale burger and sandwich options. Adding self-service ordering kiosks and table service to its restaurants will make it faster and easier for customers to place orders as well as providing them with a more comfortable, traditional restaurant-like setting while waiting for their orders. If successful, these changes will increase consumers' willingness to buy McDonald's menu items at every price, shifting the demand curve for them to the right.

As consumers have reduced their demand for hamburgers at lunch and dinner, McDonald's has had success offering breakfast items, such as its popular Egg McMuffin, throughout the day. Competing firms, such as Burger King and Wendy's have followed this strategy as well. Suppose Figure 1 below illustrates the market for fast food breakfast sandwiches. The demand for breakfast sandwiches has increased, shifting the demand curve to the right from D_1 to D_2, resulting in an increase in both the equilibrium price (P_1 to P_2) and equilibrium quantity (Q_1 to Q_2). Figure 2 illustrates the market for hamburgers. The decline in demand is shown by the demand curve shifting to the left from D_1 to D_2, resulting in a decrease in both the equilibrium price (P_1 to P_2) and equilibrium quantity (Q_1 to Q_2). This result is a typical one when demand shifts between two goods that are substitutes.

(c) McDonald's plans to continue the expansion of its mobile order-and-pay system, with the intention of launching the service in 20,000 restaurants by the end of 2017. The company is also exploring delivery options for the U.S. market, a strategy that has been successful for McDonald's in Asia. Expanding its mobile order and pay system would appeal to the younger generation of tech-savvy consumers who like to order and pay for products via smartphone apps. A delivery option would appeal to a wide variety of consumers who either do not have time or do not want to take the time to go to a McDonald's location to buy food. Both of these options will likely increase demand for McDonald's menu items.

Thinking Critically

1. Why is it particularly important for a firm like McDonald's to stay ahead of trends such as consumers' desire to eat breakfast food throughout the day or younger consumers wanting to order online?

2. Suppose that McDonald's and its competitors successfully implement self-service kiosks in their U.S restaurants, and this investment in technology allows the firms to reduce the number of employees at each location. How would this change affect the market for breakfast sandwiches? Draw a demand and supply graph to illustrate this situation, and explain what happens to equilibrium price and equilibrium quantity.

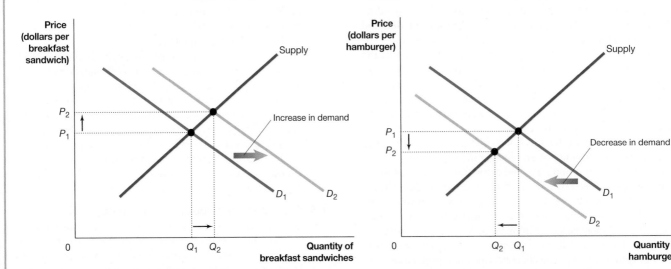

Figure 1: An increase in demand for breakfast sandwiches shifts the demand curve to the right, increasing both equilibrium price and equilibrium quantity.

Figure 2: A decrease in the demand for hamburgers, a substitute good for breakfast sandwiches, shifts the demand curve to the left, decreasing both equilibrium price and equilibrium quantity.

CHAPTER SUMMARY AND PROBLEMS

Key Terms

Ceteris paribus ("all else equal") condition, p. 76

Competitive market equilibrium, p. 87

Complements, p. 78

Demand curve, p. 74

Demand schedule, p. 74

Demographics, p. 78

Income effect, p. 75

Inferior good, p. 77

Law of demand, p. 75

Law of supply, p. 83

Market demand, p. 74

Market equilibrium, p. 86

Normal good, p. 76

Perfectly competitive market, p. 74

Quantity demanded, p. 74

Quantity supplied, p. 82

Shortage, p. 88

Substitutes, p. 77

Substitution effect, p. 75

Supply curve, p. 83

Supply schedule, p. 83

Surplus, p. 88

Technological change, p. 84

 3.1

The Demand Side of the Market, pages 74–82

LEARNING OBJECTIVE: List and describe the variables that influence demand.

MyLab Economics Visit www.pearson.com/mylab/economics to complete these exercises online and get instant feedback.

Summary

The model of demand and supply is the most powerful tool in economics. The model applies exactly only to **perfectly competitive markets**, where there are many buyers and sellers, all the products sold are identical, and there are no barriers to new sellers entering the market. But the model can also be useful in analyzing markets that don't meet all these requirements.

The **quantity demanded** is the amount of a good or service that a consumer is willing and able to purchase at a given price. A **demand schedule** is a table that shows the relationship between the price of a product and the quantity of the product demanded. A **demand curve** is a graph that shows the relationship between the price of a product and the quantity of the product demanded. **Market demand** is the demand by all consumers of a given good or service. The **law of demand** states that *ceteris paribus*—holding everything else constant—the quantity of a product demanded increases when the price falls and decreases when the price rises. Demand curves slope downward because of the **substitution effect**, which is the change in quantity demanded that results from a price change making one good more or less expensive relative to another good, and the **income effect**, which is the change in quantity demanded of a good that results from the effect of a change in the good's price on consumer purchasing power. Changes in income, the prices of related goods, tastes, population and demographics, and expected future prices all cause the demand curve to shift. **Substitutes** are goods that can be used for the same purpose. **Complements** are goods that are used together. A **normal good** is a good for which demand increases as income increases. An **inferior good** is a good for which demand decreases as income increases. **Demographics** refers to the characteristics of a population with respect to age, race, and gender. A change in demand refers to a shift of the demand curve. A change in quantity demanded refers to a movement along the demand curve as a result of a change in the product's price.

Review Questions

1.1 What is a demand schedule? What is a demand curve?

1.2 What do economists mean when they use the Latin expression *ceteris paribus*?

1.3 What is the difference between a change in demand and a change in quantity demanded?

1.4 What is the law of demand? Use the substitution effect and the income effect to explain why an increase in the price of a product causes a decrease in the quantity demanded.

1.5 What are the main variables that will cause the demand curve to shift? Give an example of each.

Problems and Applications

1.6 For each of the following pairs of products, briefly explain which are complements, which are substitutes, and which are unrelated.
  a. New cars and used cars
  b. Houses and washing machines
  c. UGG boots and Pepsi's LIFEWTR
  d. Pepsi's LIFEWTR and Diet Coke

1.7 The Toyota Prius is a gasoline/electric hybrid car that gets 54 miles to the gallon. An article in the *Wall Street Journal* noted that sales of the Prius had been hurt by low gasoline prices and that "Americans are now more likely to trade in a hybrid or an electric vehicle for an SUV." Does the article indicate that gasoline-powered cars and gasoline are substitutes or complements? Does it indicate that gasoline-powered cars and hybrids are substitutes or complements? Briefly explain.
  Source: Sean McClain, "Toyota's Prius Pays Price for Cheap Gasoline," *Wall Street Journal*, September 6, 2016.

1.8 **[Related to the Chapter Opener on page 72]** In recent years, a number of cities have passed taxes on carbonated sodas to help reduce obesity and raise tax revenues. An article in the *New York Times* observed, "With that public momentum, a soda tax may be coming to a city near you." If this forecast is correct, what will be the effect on the demand for premium bottled water? Briefly explain.
  Source: Anahad O'Connor and Margot Sanger-Katz, "As Soda Taxes Gain Wider Acceptance, Your Bottle May Be Next," *New York Times*, November 26, 2016.

1.9 State whether each of the following events will result in a movement along the demand curve for McDonald's Quarter Pounder hamburgers or whether it will cause the curve to shift. If the demand curve shifts, indicate whether it will shift to the left or to the right and draw a graph to illustrate the shift.

a. The price of Burger King's Whopper hamburger declines.

b. McDonald's distributes coupons for $1.00 off the purchase of a Quarter Pounder.

c. Because of a shortage of potatoes, the price of French fries increases.

d. McDonald's switches to using fresh, never-frozen beef patties in its Quarter Pounders.

e. The U.S. economy enters a period of rapid growth in incomes.

1.10 Suppose that the following table shows the quantity demanded of UGG boots at five different prices in 2018 and 2019.

	Quantity Demanded (thousands of pairs of boots)	
Price	**2018**	**2019**
$160	5,000	4,000
170	4,500	3,500
180	4,000	3,000
190	3,500	2,500
200	3,000	2,000

Name two different variables that, if their values were to change, would cause the quantity demanded of UGG boots to change from 2018 to 2019, as indicated in the table.

1.11 Suppose that the curves in the following graph represent two demand curves for traditional chicken wings (basket of six) at Buffalo Wild Wings. What would cause a movement from point *A* to point *B* on D_1? Name two variables that, if their values were to change, would cause a movement from point *A* to point *C*.

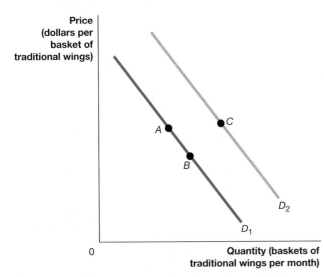

1.12 [**Related to the Apply the Concept on page 77**] A news article about virtual reality headsets observed, "For any hardware platform, it is critical to attract outside developers and build a virtuous cycle in which popular software titles drive hardware sales, which in turn brings in more software developers." The article referred to two types of software: games, such as *Final Fantasy*, that were already available for video game consoles, and software intended only for use with virtual reality headsets. As both these types of software become available, are they likely to make virtual reality headsets closer or less close substitutes for video game consoles? Briefly explain.

Source: Takashi Mochizuki, "Sony's Virtual-Reality Headset Confronts Actual Reality of Modest Sales," *Wall Street Journal*, February 27, 2017.

1.13 [**Related to the Apply the Concept on page 78**] From 1979 to 2015, China had a policy that allowed couples to have only one child. (Since 2016, couples have been allowed to have two children.) The one-child policy caused a change in the demographics of China. Between 1980 and 2015, the share of the population aged 14 and under decreased from 36 percent to 17 percent. And, as parents attempted to ensure that the lone child was a son, the number of male children relative to female children increased. Choose three goods and explain how the demand for them has been affected by China's one-child policy.

Sources: World Bank, *World Development Indicators*, April 2016; and "China New 'Two Child' Policy Increases Births by 7.9 Percent, Government Says," cbsnews.com, January 23, 2017.

1.14 [**Related to the Apply the Concept on page 78**] Would you pay $12 for a cup of coffee? Starbucks is betting enough people will say "yes," as it launches a chain of luxury coffee shops called Starbucks Reserve. Which generation(s) do you expect Starbucks Reserve to attract: baby boomers (ages 53 and over), generation X (ages 33 to 52), or millennials (ages 13 to 32)? Briefly explain. To be successful as a luxury coffee bar, how does Starbucks need to distinguish Starbucks Reserve coffee shops from its standard Starbucks coffee shops?

Source: Julie Jargon, "Middle-Market Woes Inspire Starbucks's Bet on Luxury Coffee," *Wall Street Journal*, December 5, 2016.

1.15 Suppose the following table shows the price of a base model Toyota Prius hybrid and the quantity of Priuses sold for three years. Do these data indicate that the demand curve for Priuses is upward sloping? Briefly explain.

Year	Price	Quantity
2016	$31,880	35,265
2017	30,550	33,250
2018	33,250	36,466

1.16 Consider the following two uses of the word *demand* in news articles:

a. An article in the *Wall Street Journal* noted that an "increase in the price of oil quickly reduces demand for oil."

b. A different article in the *Wall Street Journal* noted, "Electric cars are poised to reduce U.S. gasoline demand by 5% over the next two decades."

Do you agree with how these two articles use the word *demand*? Briefly explain.

Sources: Josh Zumbrun, "Oil's Plunge Could Help Send Its Price Back Up," *Wall Street Journal*, February 22, 2015; and Lynn Cook and Alison Sider, "U.S. Gasoline Demand Is Likely to Slide," *Wall Street Journal*, June 20, 2016.

1.17 **Related to the Apply the Concept on page 81]** An article on marketwatch.com stated, "While the fizzy soda drinks companies have experienced an annual volume sales decline since 2003, bottled water grew every year over the last two decades, except 2009 during the depths of the Great Recession."

a. What factors have caused a decline in sales of carbonated ("fizzy") beverages? Is it likely that those factors will lead to further declines in demand in the future? Briefly explain.

b. Why might sales of bottled water be likely to decline during a recession, when employment and household incomes fall? Would sales of premium bottled water be likely to decline by more or by less during a recession than sales of regular bottled water? Briefly explain.

Source: Quentin Fottrell, "Bottled Water Overtakes Soda as America's No. 1 Drink—Why You Should Avoid Both," marketwatch.com, March 12, 2017.

3.2 The Supply Side of the Market, pages 82–86

LEARNING OBJECTIVE: List and describe the variables that influence supply.

MyLab Economics Visit **www.pearson.com/mylab/economics** to complete these exercises online and get instant feedback.

Summary

The **quantity supplied** is the amount of a good that a firm is willing and able to supply at a given price. A **supply schedule** is a table that shows the relationship between the price of a product and the quantity of the product supplied. A **supply curve** is a curve that shows the relationship between the price of a product and the quantity of the product supplied. When the price of a product rises, producing the product is more profitable, and a greater amount will be supplied. The **law of supply** states that, holding everything else constant, the quantity of a product supplied increases when the price rises and decreases when the price falls. Changes in the prices of inputs, technology, prices of related goods in production, the number of firms in a market, and expected future prices all cause the supply curve to shift. **Technological change** is a positive or negative change in the ability of a firm to produce a given level of output with a given quantity of inputs. A change in supply refers to a shift of the supply curve. A change in quantity supplied refers to a movement along the supply curve as a result of a change in the product's price.

Review Questions

2.1 What is a supply schedule? What is a supply curve?

2.2 What is the difference between a change in supply and a change in quantity supplied?

2.3 What is the law of supply? What are the main variables that cause a supply curve to shift? Give an example of each.

Problems and Applications

2.4 Briefly explain whether each of the following statements describes a change in supply or a change in quantity supplied.

a. To take advantage of high prices for snow shovels during a snowy winter, Alexander Shovels, Inc., decides to increase output.

b. The success of Pepsi's LIFEWTR and Coke's smartwater leads more firms to begin producing premium bottled water.

c. In the six months following the Japanese earthquake and tsunami in 2011, production of automobiles in Japan declined by 20 percent.

2.5 According to a news story about the International Energy Agency, the agency forecast that "the current slide in [oil] prices won't [reduce] global supply." Would a decline in oil prices ever cause a reduction in the supply of oil? Briefly explain.

Source: Sarah Kent, "Plunging Oil Prices Won't Dent Supply in Short Term," *Wall Street Journal*, December 12, 2014.

2.6 Suppose that the curves in the following graph represent two supply curves for traditional chicken wings (basket of six) at Buffalo Wild Wings. What would cause a movement from point *A* to point *B* on S_1? Name two variables that, if their values were to change, would cause a movement from point *A* to point *C*.

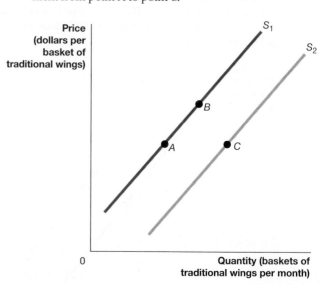

2.7 Suppose that the following table shows the quantity supplied of UGG boots at five different prices in 2018 and 2019.

	Quantity Supplied (thousands of pairs of boots)	
Price	2018	2019
$160	3,000	2,000
170	3,500	2,500
180	4,000	3,000
190	4,500	3,500
200	5,000	4,500

Name two different variables that, if their values were to change, would cause the quantity supplied of UGG boots to change from 2018 to 2019, as indicated in the table.

2.8 In most cities, firms that own office buildings can renovate them for use as residential apartments. According to a news story, in many cities "residential rents are surpassing office rents." Predict the effect of this trend on the supply of office space in these cities. Use a graph to illustrate your answer.

Source: Eliot Brown, "Developers Turn Former Office Buildings into High-End Apartments," *Wall Street Journal*, May 7, 2014.

2.9 Oil prices plummeted from over $100 per barrel in mid-2014 to under $30 in early 2016. According to a Reuters article, oil traders in 2015 and 2016 put massive amounts of oil in storage (even on tankers at sea), anticipating higher prices in the future. The article noted that in early 2017, "traders are turning the spigots to drain the priciest storage tanks holding U.S. crude stockpiles as strengthening markets make it unprofitable to store for future sale." What effect would the strategy of stockpiling crude oil have had for the supply of oil in 2015 and 2016? Use a graph to illustrate your answer.

Source: Catherine Ngai and Liz Hampton, "Traders Drain Pricey U.S. Oil Storage as OPEC Deal Bites," reuters.com, February 24, 2017.

(3.3) Market Equilibrium: Putting Demand and Supply Together, pages 86–89

LEARNING OBJECTIVE: Use a graph to illustrate market equilibrium.

MyLab Economics Visit **www.pearson.com/mylab/economics** to complete these exercises online and get instant feedback.

Summary

Market equilibrium occurs where the demand curve intersects the supply curve. A **competitive market equilibrium** has a market equilibrium with many buyers and sellers. Only at this point is the quantity demanded equal to the quantity supplied. Prices above equilibrium result in **surpluses**, with the quantity supplied being greater than the quantity demanded. Surpluses cause the market price to fall. Prices below equilibrium result in **shortages**, with the quantity demanded being greater than the quantity supplied. Shortages cause the market price to rise.

Review Questions

3.1 What do economists mean by *market equilibrium*?

3.2 What do economists mean by *shortage*? By *surplus*?

3.3 What happens in a market if the current price is above the equilibrium price? What happens if the current price is below the equilibrium price?

Problems and Applications

3.4 Briefly explain whether you agree with the following statement: "When there is a shortage of a good, consumers eventually give up trying to buy it, so the demand for the good declines, and the price falls until the market is finally in equilibrium."

3.5 [**Related to Solved Problem 3.3 on page 88**] In *The Wealth of Nations*, Adam Smith discussed what has come to be known as the "diamond and water paradox":

> Nothing is more useful than water: but it will purchase scarce anything; scarce anything can be had in exchange for it. A diamond, on the contrary, has scarce any value in use; but a very great quantity of other goods may frequently be had in exchange for it.

Graph the market for diamonds and the market for water. Show how it is possible for the price of water to be much lower than the price of diamonds, even though the demand for water is much greater than the demand for diamonds.

Source: Adam Smith, *An Inquiry into the Nature and Causes of the Wealth of Nations*, Vol. I, Oxford, UK: Oxford University Press, 1976; original edition, 1776.

3.6 [**Related to Solved Problem 3.3 on page 88**] An article discusses the market for autographs by Mickey Mantle, the superstar center fielder for the New York Yankees during the 1950s and 1960s, "At card shows, golf outings, charity dinners, Mr. Mantle signed his name over and over." One expert on sports autographs was quoted as saying, "He was a real good signer…. He is not rare." Yet the article quoted another expert as saying, "Mr. Mantle's autograph ranks No. 3 of most-popular autographs, behind Babe Ruth and Muhammad Ali." A baseball signed by Mantle is likely to sell for the relatively high price of $250 to $400. By contrast, baseballs signed by Whitey Ford, a teammate of Mantle's on the Yankees, typically sell for less than $150. Use one graph to show both the demand and supply for autographs by Whitey Ford and the demand and supply for autographs by Mickey Mantle. Show how it is possible for the price of Mantle's autographs to be higher than the price of Ford's autographs, even though the supply of Mantle autographs is larger than the supply of Ford autographs.

Source: Beth DeCarbo, "Mantle Autographs Not Rare, but Collectors Don't Care," *Wall Street Journal*, August 4, 2008.

3.7 [**Related to Solved Problem 3.3 on page 88**] Comic book fans eagerly compete to buy copies of *Amazing Fantasy* No. 15, which contains the first appearance of the superhero Spider-Man. At the same time the publisher printed copies of the comic for the U.S. market, with the price printed on the cover in cents, it printed copies for the U.K. market, with the price printed on the cover in British pence. About 10 times as many U.S. copies of *Amazing Fantasy* No. 15 have survived as U.K. copies. Yet in auctions that occurred at about the same time, a U.S. copy sold for $29,000, while a U.K. copy in the same condition sold for only $10,755. Use a demand and supply graph to explain how the U.S. version of the comic has a higher price than the U.K. version, even though the supply of the U.S. version is so much greater than the supply of the U.K. version.

Source: Auction price data from *GPA Analysis for CGC Comics*, www.comics.gpanalysis.com.

3.8 If a market is in equilibrium, is it necessarily true that all buyers and sellers are satisfied with the market price? Briefly explain.

3.9 A news story from 2017 about the oil market stated, "crude oil prices fell … in part [due to] renewed concerns about the global supply glut."

   a. What does the article mean by a "glut"? What does a glut imply about the quantity demanded of oil relative to the quantity supplied?

   b. What would be the effect of the glut on oil prices?

   c. Briefly explain what would make the glut start to shrink.

Source: Paul Ebeling, "Crude Oil Prices Falling, Traders Worry About Global Supply Glut," livetradingnews.com, March 27, 2017.

3.4 The Effect of Demand and Supply Shifts on Equilibrium, pages 90–97

LEARNING OBJECTIVE: Use demand and supply graphs to predict changes in prices and quantities.

MyLab Economics Visit **www.pearson.com/mylab/economics** to complete these exercises online and get instant feedback.

Summary

In most markets, demand and supply curves shift frequently, causing changes in equilibrium prices and quantities. Over time, if demand increases more than supply, equilibrium price will rise. If supply increases more than demand, equilibrium price will fall.

Review Questions

4.1 Draw a demand and supply graph to show the effect on the equilibrium price in a market in the following situations.

   a. The demand curve shifts to the right.

   b. The supply curve shifts to the left.

4.2 If, over time, the demand curve for a product shifts to the right more than the supply curve does, what will happen to the equilibrium price? What will happen to the equilibrium price if the supply curve shifts to the right more than the demand curve? For each case, draw a demand and supply graph to illustrate your answer.

Problems and Applications

4.3 **[Related to the Chapter Opener on page 72]** Suppose the demand for premium bottled water increases rapidly during 2018. At the same time, six more firms begin producing premium bottled water. A student remarks that, because of these events, we can't know for certain whether the price of premium bottled water will rise or fall. Briefly explain whether you agree. Be sure to include a demand and supply graph of the market for premium bottled water to illustrate your answer.

4.4 According to an article in the *Wall Street Journal*, in early 2017, President Donald Trump was considering whether to reverse a requirement by the Environmental Protection Agency that oil refiners increase the amount of ethanol they blend with gasoline. If the requirement were to remain, the result would be an increase in demand for ethanol, which is made from corn. Many U.S. farmers can use the same acreage to grow either corn or soybeans. Use a demand and supply graph to analyze the effect on the

equilibrium price of soybeans resulting from an increase in the demand for corn.

Source: Siobhan Hughes, Natalie Andrews, and Kristina Peterson, "Senate Looks to Move Fast on Trump Administration Hearings, Health Law," *Wall Street Journal*, January 8, 2017.

4.5 According to a news article on bloomberg.com, the demand for coffee is increasing as "millennials' seemingly unquenchable thirst for coffee is helping to push global demand to a record." At the same time, coffee crops in Brazil and Asia have been hampered by dry weather and droughts. The article noted that "consumption is rising as supplies are getting tighter."

   a. Use a demand and supply graph of the coffee market to illustrate how the equilibrium quantity of coffee can increase as a result of these events. Be sure that all curves on your graphs are properly labeled, that you show any shifts in those curves, and that you indicate the initial and final equilibrium points.

   b. The article contains a chart showing changes in worldwide sales of coffee from 2006 through 2016. The chart is labeled "World demand has expanded in the past decade." Are data on the quantity of coffee sold and data on the demand for coffee the same thing? Can the quantity of coffee sold increase if the demand for coffee hasn't increased? Briefly explain.

Source: Marvin G. Perez, "Coffee-Loving Millennials Push Demand to a Record," bloomberg.com, October 30, 2016.

4.6 **[Related to the Apply the Concept on page 92]** Suppose that many cities begin to pass taxes on carbonated sodas, while at the same time scientists discover a cure for citrus greening, which is reducing orange crops in Florida and Brazil. Use a demand and supply graph to illustrate your answers to the following questions.

   a. Can we use this information to be certain whether the equilibrium price of orange juice will increase or decrease?

   b. Can we use this information to be certain whether the equilibrium quantity of orange juice will increase or decrease?

4.7 **[Related to Solved Problem 3.4 on page 94]** The demand for watermelons is highest during summer and lowest during winter. Yet watermelon prices are normally lower in summer than in winter. Use a demand and supply graph to demonstrate how this is possible. Be sure to carefully label the curves in your graph and to clearly indicate the equilibrium summer price and the equilibrium winter price.

4.8 [**Related to Solved Problem 3.4 on page 94**] According to one observer of the lobster market: "After Labor Day, when the vacationers have gone home, the lobstermen usually have a month or more of good fishing conditions, except for the occasional hurricane." Use a demand and supply graph to explain whether lobster prices are likely to be higher or lower during the fall than during the summer.

Source: Jay Harlow, "Lobster: An Affordable Luxury," www.Sallybernstein.com.

4.9 Years ago, an apple producer argued that the United States should enact a tariff, or a tax, on imports of bananas. His reasoning was that "the enormous imports of cheap bananas into the United States tend to curtail the domestic consumption of fresh fruits produced in the United States."

    a. Was the apple producer assuming that apples and bananas are substitutes or complements? Briefly explain.

    b. If a tariff on bananas acts as an increase in the cost of supplying bananas in the United States, use two demand and supply graphs to show the effects of the apple producer's proposal. One graph should show the effect on the banana market in the United States, and the other graph should show the effect on the apple market in the United States. Be sure to label the change in equilibrium price and quantity in each market and any shifts in the demand and supply curves.

Source: Douglas A. Irwin, *Peddling Protectionism: Smoot-Hawley and the Great Depression*, Princeton, NJ: Princeton University Press, 2011, p. 22.

4.10 In early 2017, an article in the *Financial Times* about the oil market quoted the chief economist of oil company BP as saying, "Pricing pressure is likely to come from the supply side, because of strong growth in US shale oil (crude oil found within shale formations), and the demand side as the rise of renewable energy, including electric vehicles, gradually slows growth in oil consumption." After reading this article, a student argues: "From this information, we would expect that the price of oil will fall, but we don't know whether the equilibrium quantity of oil will increase or decrease." Is the student's analysis correct? Illustrate your answer with a demand and supply graph.

Source: Andrew Ward, "BP Warns of Price Pressures from Long-Term Oil Glut," *Financial Times*, January 25, 2017.

4.11 Historically, the production of many perishable foods, such as dairy products, was highly seasonal. As the supply of those products fluctuated, prices tended to fluctuate tremendously—typically by 25 to 50 percent or more—over the course of the year. One effect of mechanical refrigeration, which was commercialized on a large scale in the last decade of the nineteenth century, was that suppliers could store perishable foods from one season to the next. Economists have estimated that as a result of refrigerated storage, wholesale prices rose by roughly 10 percent during peak supply periods, while they fell by almost the same amount during the off season. Use a demand and supply graph for each season to illustrate how refrigeration affected the market for perishable food.

Source: Lee A. Craig, Barry Goodwin, and Thomas Grennes, "The Effect of Mechanical Refrigeration on Nutrition in the U.S.," *Social Science History*, Vol. 28, No. 2, Summer 2004, pp. 327–328.

4.12 If the equilibrium price and quantity of a product were $100 and 1,000 units per month in 2017 and $150 and 800 units per month in 2018, did this product experience a larger shift in its demand curve or in its supply curve from 2017 to 2018? Briefly explain.

4.13 [**Related to the Don't Let This Happen to You on page 96**] A student writes the following: "Increased production leads to a lower price, which in turn increases demand." Do you agree with his reasoning? Briefly explain.

4.14 [**Related to the Don't Let This Happen to You on page 96**] A student was asked to draw a demand and supply graph to illustrate the effect on the market for premium bottled water of a fall in the price of electrolytes used in some brands of premium bottled water, holding everything else constant. She drew the following graph and explained it as follows:

> Electrolytes are an input to some brands of premium bottled water, so a fall in the price of electrolytes will cause the supply curve for premium bottled water to shift to the right (from S_1 to S_2). Because this shift in the supply curve results in a lower price (P_2), consumers will want to buy more premium bottled water, and the demand curve will shift to the right (from D_1 to D_2). We know that more premium bottled water will be sold, but we can't be sure whether the price of premium bottled water will rise or fall. That depends on whether the supply curve or the demand curve has shifted farther to the right. I assume that the effect on supply is greater than the effect on demand, so I show the final equilibrium price (P_3) as being lower than the initial equilibrium price (P_1).

Explain whether you agree with the student's analysis. Be careful to explain exactly what—if anything—you find wrong with her analysis.

4.15 The following four graphs represent four market scenarios, each of which would cause either a movement along the supply curve for premium bottled water or a shift of the supply curve. Match each scenario with the appropriate graph.

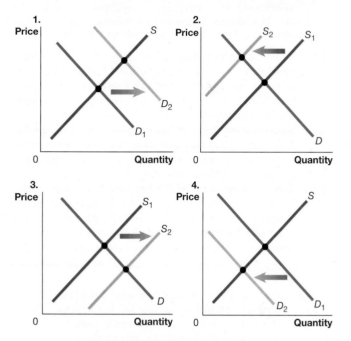

a. A decrease in the supply of sports drinks
b. A drop in the average household income in the United States from $56,000 to $52,000
c. An improvement in the bottling technology for premium bottled water
d. An increase in the prices of electrolytes used in premium bottled water

4.16 Proposals have been made to increase government regulation of firms providing childcare services by, for instance, setting education requirements for childcare workers. Suppose that these regulations increase the quality of childcare and cause the demand for childcare services to increase. At the same time, assume that complying with the new government regulations increases the costs of firms providing childcare services. Draw a demand and supply graph to illustrate the effects of these changes in the market for childcare services. Briefly explain whether the total quantity of childcare services purchased will increase or decrease as a result of the regulations.

4.17 Which of the following graphs best represents what happens in the market for hotel rooms at a ski resort during the winter? Briefly explain. From the graph you picked, what would be the result during the winter if hotel rates stayed at their summer level?

4.18 The following graphs show the supply and demand curves for two markets. One of the markets is for electric automobiles, and the other is for a cancer-fighting drug, without which lung cancer patients will die. Briefly explain which graph most likely represents each market.

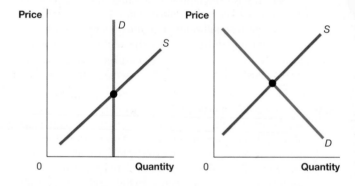

Critical Thinking Exercises

CT3.1 For this exercise, your instructor may assign you to a group. Which curve did you find more difficult to understand: the demand curve or the supply curve? What specific difficulties did you have in understanding that curve? Working together, explain your thinking in a one-paragraph report you will either submit to your instructor or discuss with the rest of the class.

CT3.2 Graphs simplify economic ideas and make them more concrete. Consider the data available on these two Web sites:
- www.eia.gov/dnav/pet/pet_pri_gnd_a_epmr_pte_dpgal_w.htm provides data on the retail price of gasoline (what we pay at the pump) for both the United States overall and for different regions and states.
- www.eia.gov/dnav/pet/PET_CONS_REFMG_D_NUS_VTR_MGALPD_M.htm provides data on gasoline sales for the United States.

If you were to use a graph to explain changes in these data over time, would you use a graph of the demand curve, a graph of the supply curve, or a graph of a market? Write a paragraph to explain your thinking.

CT3.3 Review Figure 3.9 on page 90 and its analysis of the market for premium bottled water. The figure shows several different changes occurring: (a) a shift in a curve, (b) some event external to the market that affects the market, (c) and a new equilibrium. What is the order in which these three different changes occur? In the analysis of other markets that you will carry out later in the course, must the order of these three changes stay the same as in this example, or can the order be different?

Economic Efficiency, Government Price Setting, and Taxes

What Do Food Riots in Venezuela and the Rise of Uber in the United States Have in Common?

In 2016 and 2017, news stories described riots in Venezuela as crowds stormed supermarkets and street gangs fought over food. Food deliveries to stores were made under armed guard, and in some cities the government had to send in troops to protect stores from looting. As one news story put it: "Venezuela is convulsing from hunger."

In many cities in the United States, you can't legally operate a taxi unless you have a permit from the city government. For example, New York City requires taxi drivers to purchase a medallion. The number of medallions issued is limited, and until recently, the price of a medallion could exceed $1 *million*. By 2017, though, people could hail a ride using a mobile app from firms such as Uber or Lyft. Drivers who want to work for these firms sign up, agree to meet certain requirements, and use their own vehicles to pick up riders. Hundreds of thousands of riders in New York City began using these services, which drove the price of a taxi medallion to as little as $250,000.

What's the connection between food riots in Venezuela and the rise of Uber in the United States? Both cases were ultimately the result of governments intervening to change equilibrium prices determined by the market. As we saw in Chapter 3, in a competitive market equilibrium, all consumers willing to pay the market price will be able to buy as much of the product as they want, and all firms willing to accept the market price will be able to sell as much of the product as they want. But this observation doesn't mean that all consumers and firms will be *happy* with the market price. Consumers would typically prefer to pay a lower price, and firms would prefer to receive a higher price. In some cases, either buyers or sellers can convince the government to enact *price controls*, which are legally binding maximum or minimum prices. In Venezuela, the government's attempts to expand control over private businesses led to disruptions in the supply of many

Bloomberg/Getty images

goods, including food. As market prices rose as a result of the reductions in supply, the government imposed rules that kept prices from rising to their new equilibrium levels. The result was food shortages that led to riots.

In New York and other cities, government limits on the supply of taxis pushed the price of a ride well above the competitive market level. High prices provided Travis Kalanick, the founder of Uber, and other entrepreneurs the opportunity to earn a profit using mobile technology to offer ride-hailing services at a lower price than taxis were charging.

As we'll see in this chapter, when governments interfere with the prices determined by markets, they create both winners and losers, and they typically reduce economic efficiency.

AN INSIDE LOOK on **page 132** explores problems Uber has encountered in attempting to expand its services in the United Kingdom.

Sources: Nicholas Casey, "Venezuelans Ransack Stores as Hunger Grips the Nation," *New York Times*, June 19, 2016; Maria Ramirez and Kejal Vyas, "Venezuela Deploys Troops after Weekend Riots," *Wall Street Journal*, December 19, 2016; Elena Holodny, "Uber and Lyft Are Demolishing New York City Taxi Drivers," businnessinsider.com, October 12, 2016; and Emma G. Fitzsimmons and Winnie Hu, "The Downside of Ride-Hailing: More New York City Gridlock," *New York Times*, March 6, 2017.

Economics in Your Life & Career

As a Member of the City Council, Should You Support Rent Control?

Suppose you have been elected to your city council. A group of renters have become concerned that rising rents are making it difficult for them to find affordable apartments. They propose that the city council enact a rent control law that will keep rents in the future from rising above their current levels. If you and the other city council members vote to enact this law, is it likely that in the future it will be easier for renters to find an affordable apartment in your city? Who in your city would benefit, and who would lose from this law? As you read the chapter, try to answer these questions. You can check your answers against the ones we provide on **page 131** at the end of this chapter.

In a competitive market, the price adjusts to ensure that the quantity demanded equals the quantity supplied. As a result, in equilibrium, every consumer willing to pay the market price is able to buy as much of the product as the consumer wants, and every firm willing to accept the market price can sell as much as it wants. Consumers would naturally prefer to pay a lower price, and sellers would prefer to receive a higher price. Normally, consumers and firms have no choice but to accept the equilibrium price if they wish to participate in the market.

Occasionally, however, consumers or firms persuade the government to intervene to try to lower or raise the market price of a good or service:

Price ceiling A legally determined maximum price that sellers may charge.

- Consumers sometimes succeed in having the government impose a **price ceiling**, which is a legally determined maximum price that sellers may charge. Rent control, which puts a legal limit on the rent that landlords can charge for an apartment, is an example of a price ceiling.

Price floor A legally determined minimum price that sellers may receive.

- Firms sometimes succeed in having the government impose a **price floor**, which is a legally determined minimum price that sellers may receive. In markets for farm products such as milk, the federal government has been setting price floors above the equilibrium market price since the 1930s.

Another way the government intervenes in markets is by imposing taxes. The government relies on the revenue raised from taxes to finance its operations. But taxes also affect the decisions that consumers and firms make.

Each of these government interventions has predictable negative consequences for economic efficiency. Economists have developed the concepts of *consumer surplus, producer surplus,* and *deadweight loss* to help policymakers and voters analyze the economic effects of price ceilings, price floors, and taxes.

4.1 Consumer Surplus and Producer Surplus

LEARNING OBJECTIVE: Distinguish between the concepts of consumer surplus and producer surplus.

Consumer surplus measures the dollar benefit consumers receive from buying goods or services in a particular market. Producer surplus measures the dollar benefit firms receive from selling goods or services in a particular market. Economic surplus in a market is the sum of consumer surplus and producer surplus. As we will see, *when the government imposes a price ceiling or a price floor, the amount of economic surplus in a market is reduced.* In other words, price ceilings and price floors reduce the total benefit to consumers and firms from buying and selling in a market. To understand why this is true, we need to understand how consumer surplus and producer surplus are determined.

Consumer Surplus

Consumer surplus The difference between the highest price a consumer is willing to pay for a good or service and the actual price the consumer pays.

Consumer surplus is the difference between the highest price a consumer is willing to pay for a good or service and the actual price the consumer pays. Suppose you want to stream the movie *Wonder Woman*. Before you check the price to rent it on iTunes or Amazon, you decide that $5.99 is the highest price you would be willing to pay. On iTunes, you find that the rental price is actually $3.99, so you rent the movie. Your consumer surplus in this example is $2: the difference between the $5.99 you were willing to pay and the $3.99 you actually paid.

We can use the demand curve to measure the total consumer surplus in a market. Demand curves show the willingness of consumers to purchase a product at different prices. Consumers are willing to purchase a product up to the point where the marginal benefit of consuming a product is equal to its price. The **marginal benefit** is the additional benefit to a consumer from consuming one more unit of a good or service. As a simple example, suppose there are only four consumers in the market for chai tea: Theresa, Tom, Terri, and Tim. Because these four consumers have different tastes for tea and different incomes, the marginal benefit each of them receives from consuming

Marginal benefit The additional benefit to a consumer from consuming one more unit of a good or service.

Consumer	Highest Price Willing to Pay
Theresa	$6
Tom	5
Terri	4
Tim	3

MyLab Economics Animation

Figure 4.1

Deriving the Demand Curve for Chai Tea

With four consumers in the market for chai tea, the demand curve is determined by the highest price each consumer is willing to pay. At prices above $6, no tea is sold because $6 is the highest price any consumer is willing to pay. At prices of $3 and below, each of the four consumers is willing to buy one cup of tea.

a cup of tea will be different. Therefore, the highest price each is willing to pay for a cup of tea is also different. In Figure 4.1, the information from the table is used to construct a demand curve for chai tea. At prices above $6 per cup, no tea is sold because $6 is the highest price any of the consumers is willing to pay. At a price of $5, both Theresa and Tom are willing to buy tea, so two cups are sold. At prices of $3 and below, all four consumers are willing to buy tea, and four cups are sold.

Suppose the market price of tea is $3.50 per cup. As Figure 4.2 shows, the demand curve allows us to calculate the total consumer surplus in this market. Panel (a) shows

(a) Consumer surplus with a market price of $3.50

(b) Consumer surplus with a market price of $3.00

MyLab Economics Animation

Figure 4.2   Measuring Consumer Surplus

Panel (a) shows the consumer surplus for Theresa, Tom, and Terri when the price of tea is $3.50 per cup. Theresa's consumer surplus is equal to the area of rectangle A and is the difference between the highest price she would pay—which is $6—and the market price of $3.50. Tom's consumer surplus is equal to the area of rectangle B, and Terri's consumer surplus is equal to the area of rectangle C. Total consumer surplus in this market is equal to the sum of the areas of rectangles A, B, and C, or the total area below the demand curve and above the market price. In panel (b), consumer surplus increases by the dark blue area as the market price declines from $3.50 to $3.00.

MyLab Economics Animation

Figure 4.3

Total Consumer Surplus in the Market for Chai Tea

The demand curve shows that most buyers of chai tea would have been willing to pay more than the market price of $2.00. For each buyer, consumer surplus is equal to the difference between the highest price he or she is willing to pay and the market price actually paid. Therefore, the total amount of consumer surplus in the market for chai tea is equal to the area below the demand curve and above the market price. Consumer surplus represents the benefit to consumers in excess of the price they paid to purchase a product.

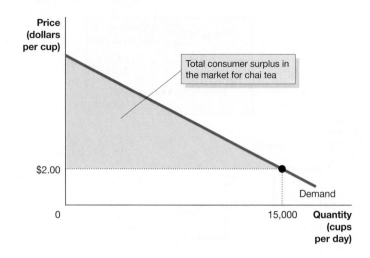

that the highest price Theresa is willing to pay is $6, but because she pays only $3.50, her consumer surplus is $2.50 (shown by the area of rectangle A). Similarly, Tom's consumer surplus is $1.50 (rectangle B), and Terri's consumer surplus is $0.50 (rectangle C). Tim is unwilling to buy a cup of tea at a price of $3.50, so he doesn't participate in this market and receives no consumer surplus. In this simple example, the total consumer surplus is equal to $2.50 + $1.50 + $0.50 = $4.50 (or the sum of the areas of rectangles A, B, and C). Panel (b) shows that a lower price will increase consumer surplus. If the price of tea falls from $3.50 per cup to $3.00, Theresa, Tom, and Terri each receive $0.50 more in consumer surplus (shown by the dark blue areas), so the total consumer surplus in the market rises to $6.00. Tim now buys a cup of tea but doesn't receive any consumer surplus because the price is equal to the highest price he is willing to pay. In fact, Tim is indifferent between buying the cup or not; his well-being is the same either way.

The market demand curves shown in Figures 4.1 and 4.2 do not look like the typical smooth demand curve because in this case we have only a small number of consumers, each consuming a single cup of tea. With many consumers, the market demand curve for chai tea will have the normal smooth shape shown in Figure 4.3. In this figure, the quantity demanded at a price of $2.00 is 15,000 cups per day. We can calculate total consumer surplus in Figure 4.3 the same way we did in Figures 4.1 and 4.2—by adding up the consumer surplus received on each unit purchased. Once again, we can draw an important conclusion: *The total amount of consumer surplus in a market is equal to the area below the demand curve and above the market price.* Consumer surplus is shown as the shaded area in Figure 4.3 and represents the benefit to consumers in excess of the price they paid to purchase a product—in this case, chai tea.　　　**MyLab Economics** Concept Check

Apply the Concept

MyLab Economics Video

The Consumer Surplus from Uber

Consumer surplus allows us to measure the benefit consumers receive in excess of the price they pay to purchase a product. As we noted in the chapter opener, in many cities, local governments have artificially reduced the quantity of taxi services supplied by legally restricting the number of taxis allowed to operate. The government restrictions on taxis generally do not apply to Uber, Lyft, and other ride-hailing services that use mobile apps. As a result, the services have become very popular among both drivers and riders. In 2017, in New York City alone, more than 50,000 people had signed up as drivers with the services, and hundreds of thousands of consumers were using the services each day.

The enthusiastic response by consumers to the ride-hailing services indicates that they have resulted in a substantial increase in consumer surplus. Peter Cohen and Jonathan Hall, economists who work for Uber, along with Robert Hahn of the University of Oxford and Steven Levitt and Robert Metcalfe of the University of Chicago, have estimated the consumer surplus attributed to Uber. Uber practices "surge pricing," which means that the firm varies the prices its drivers charge depending on the weather, the time of day, the availability of drivers in the area, and whether an event such as a football game or a New Year's Eve celebration is occurring. The firm has particularly good data available for economists to use in estimating its demand curve because it has so many riders and because it has information both on the quantity of rides accepted at a particular price and the quantity of rides not accepted because a potential rider decides that a surge price is higher than he or she wishes to pay.

The economists analyzed data on millions of instances of riders using the app to get pricing information for a potential trip—including both sessions where the rider went ahead, summoned a driver, and paid for a trip and sessions where the rider decided against making the trip. The data were for Uber's basic UberX service in its four largest markets: New York, San Francisco, Chicago, and Los Angeles. To carry out the analysis, the economists estimated the demand curve for Uber's service and then computed the shaded area shown in the following graph.

The economists analyzed a six-month period in 2015, during which consumers took about 111 million trips using Uber in these four cities. The demand curve shows the marginal benefit consumers receive from using Uber rather than making the trip some other way or not making the trip at all. The shaded area below the demand curve and above the $13.30 base price that Uber charges represents the difference between the price consumers would have paid rather than do without Uber's service and the $13.30 they did pay. The shaded area in the graph represents the total consumer surplus in the market for Uber's service. Cohen and his colleagues estimate that the value of this area is $2.88 billion per year. Extrapolating this result to the country as a whole, they estimate that the total consumer surplus from Uber during 2015 was $6.76 billion. This value is one year's benefit to the consumers who used Uber's ride-hailing service.

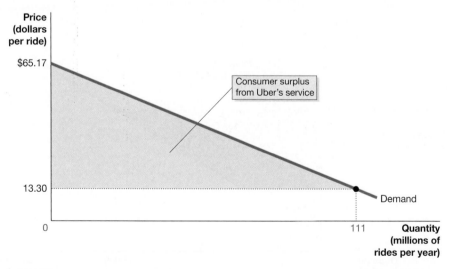

Note: This figure illustrates the approach of Cohen and his colleagues but doesn't reproduce it exactly. Among other simplifications, the figure assumes that the demand curve for Uber's service is linear.

Sources: Peter Cohen et al., "Using Big Data to Estimate Consumer Surplus: The Case of Uber," National Bureau of Economic Research, Working Paper No. 22627, September 2016; Adam Creighton, "Uber's Pricing Formula Has Allowed Economists to Map Out a Real Demand Curve," *Wall Street Journal*, September 19, 2016; and Jayson Derrick, "What Would Be the Social Cost if Uber Vanishes?" finance.yahoo.com, September 8, 2016.

Your Turn: For more practice do related problem 1.13 on page 135 at the end of this chapter.   MyLab Economics Study Plan

Producer Surplus

Just as demand curves show the willingness of consumers to buy a product at different prices, supply curves show the willingness of firms to supply a product at different prices. The willingness to supply a product depends on the cost of producing it. Firms will supply an additional unit of a product only if they receive a price equal to the additional cost of producing that unit. **Marginal cost** is the additional cost to a firm of producing one more unit of a good or service. Consider the marginal cost to the firm Heavenly Tea of producing one more cup of tea: In this case, the marginal cost includes the ingredients to make the tea and the wages paid to the worker preparing the tea. Often, the marginal cost of producing a good increases as more of the good is produced during a given period of time. Increasing marginal cost is the key reason that supply curves are upward sloping.

Panel (a) of Figure 4.4 shows Heavenly Tea's producer surplus. For simplicity, we show Heavenly producing only a small quantity of tea. The figure shows that Heavenly's marginal cost of producing the first cup of tea is $1.25, its marginal cost of producing the second cup is $1.50, and so on. The marginal cost of each cup of tea is the lowest price Heavenly is willing to accept to supply that cup. The supply is therefore also a marginal cost curve. Suppose the market price of tea is $2.00 per cup. On the first cup of tea, the price is $0.75 higher than the lowest price that Heavenly is willing to accept. **Producer surplus** is the difference between the lowest price a firm would be willing to accept for a good or service and the price it actually receives. Therefore, Heavenly's producer surplus on the first cup is $0.75 (shown by the area of rectangle A), its producer surplus on the second cup is $0.50 (rectangle B), and its producer surplus on the third cup is $0.25 (rectangle C). Heavenly will not be willing to supply the fourth cup because the marginal cost of producing it is greater than the market price. Heavenly's total producer surplus is equal to $0.75 + $0.50 + $0.25 = $1.50 (or the sum of the areas of rectangles A, B, and C). A higher price will increase producer surplus. For example, if the market price of chai tea rises from $2.00 to $2.25, Heavenly's producer surplus will increase from $1.50 to $2.25. (Make sure you understand how the new level of producer surplus was calculated.)

Marginal cost The additional cost to a firm of producing one more unit of a good or service.

Producer surplus The difference between the lowest price a firm would be willing to accept for a good or service and the price it actually receives.

(a) Producer surplus for Heavenly Tea

(b) Total producer surplus in the market for chai tea

MyLab Economics Animation

Figure 4.4 **Measuring Producer Surplus**

Panel (a) shows Heavenly Tea's producer surplus. The lowest price Heavenly Tea is willing to accept to supply a cup of tea is equal to its marginal cost of producing that cup. When the market price of tea is $2.00, Heavenly receives producer surplus of $0.75 on the first cup (the area of rectangle A), $0.50 on the second cup (rectangle B), and $0.25 on the third cup (rectangle C). In panel (b), the total amount of producer surplus tea sellers receive from selling chai tea can be calculated by adding up for the entire market the producer surplus received on each cup sold. In the figure, total producer surplus is equal to the shaded area above the supply curve and below the market price.

The supply curve shown in panel (a) of Figure 4.4 does not look like the typical smooth supply curve because we are looking at a single firm producing only a small quantity of tea. With many firms, the market supply curve for chai tea will have the normal smooth shape shown in panel (b) of Figure 4.4. In panel (b), the quantity supplied at a price of $2.00 is 15,000 cups per day. We can calculate total producer surplus in panel (b) the same way we did in panel (a): by adding up the producer surplus received on each cup sold. Therefore, *the total amount of producer surplus in a market is equal to the area above the market supply curve and below the market price.* The total producer surplus tea sellers receive from selling chai tea is shown as the shaded area in panel (b) of Figure 4.4.
MyLab Economics Concept Check

What Consumer Surplus and Producer Surplus Measure

We have seen that consumer surplus measures the benefit to consumers from participating in a market, and producer surplus measures the benefit to producers from participating in a market. It is important to be clear about what these concepts are measuring:

- Consumer surplus measures the *net* benefit to consumers from participating in a market rather than the *total* benefit. That is, if the price of a product were zero, the consumer surplus in a market would be all of the area under the demand curve. When the price is not zero, consumer surplus is the area below the demand curve and above the market price. So, consumer surplus in a market is equal to the total benefit consumers receive minus the total amount they must pay to buy the good or service.
- Producer surplus measures the *net* benefit received by producers from participating in a market. If producers could supply a good or service at zero cost, the producer surplus in a market would be all of the area below the market price. When cost is not zero, producer surplus is the area below the market price and above the supply curve. So, producer surplus in a market is equal to the total dollar amount firms receive from consumers minus the cost of producing the good or service.
MyLab Economics Concept Check   MyLab Economics Study Plan

4.2 The Efficiency of Competitive Markets

LEARNING OBJECTIVE: Explain the concept of economic efficiency.

Recall that a *competitive market* is a market with many buyers and many sellers. An important advantage of the market system is that it results in efficient economic outcomes. But what does *economic efficiency* mean? The concepts we have developed so far in this chapter give us two ways to think about the economic efficiency of competitive markets. We can think in terms of marginal benefit and marginal cost. We can also think in terms of consumer surplus and producer surplus. As we will see, these two approaches lead to the same outcome, but using both can increase our understanding of economic efficiency.

Marginal Benefit Equals Marginal Cost in Competitive Equilibrium

Figure 4.5 again shows the market for chai tea. Recall that the demand curve shows the marginal benefit received by consumers, and the supply curve shows the marginal cost of production. For this market to achieve economic efficiency, the marginal benefit from the last unit sold should equal the marginal cost of production. In the figure, this equality occurs at competitive equilibrium where 15,000 cups per day are produced and marginal benefit and marginal cost are both equal to $2.00. This outcome is economically efficient because every cup of chai tea has been produced where the marginal benefit to buyers is greater than or equal to the marginal cost to producers.

To further understand why the level of output at competitive equilibrium is efficient, consider what the situation would be if output were at a different level. Suppose that output of chai tea is 14,000 cups per day. Figure 4.5 shows that at this level

Figure 4.5

Marginal Benefit Equals Marginal Cost Only at Competitive Equilibrium

In a competitive market, equilibrium occurs at a quantity of 15,000 cups and a price of $2.00 per cup, where marginal benefit equals marginal cost. This level of output is economically efficient because every cup has been produced for which the marginal benefit to buyers is greater than or equal to the marginal cost to producers.

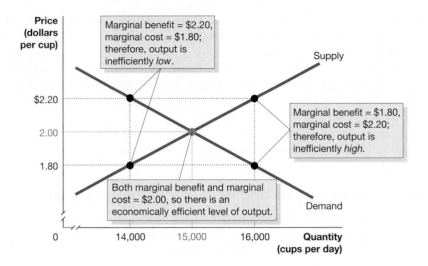

of output, the marginal benefit from the last cup sold is $2.20, while the marginal cost is only $1.80. This level of output is not efficient because 1,000 more cups could be produced for which the additional benefit to consumers would be greater than the additional cost of production. Consumers would willingly purchase those cups, and tea sellers would willingly supply them, making both consumers and sellers better off. Similarly, if the output of chai tea is 16,000 cups per day, the marginal cost of the 16,000th cup is $2.20, while the marginal benefit is only $1.80. Tea sellers would only be willing to supply this cup at a price of $2.20, which is $0.40 higher than consumers would be willing to pay. In fact, consumers would not be willing to pay the price tea sellers would need to receive for any cup beyond the 15,000th.

To summarize: *Equilibrium in a competitive market results in the economically efficient level of output, at which marginal benefit equals marginal cost.*   **MyLab Economics** Concept Check

Economic Surplus

Economic surplus The sum of consumer surplus and producer surplus.

Economic surplus in a market is the sum of consumer surplus and producer surplus. In a competitive market, with many buyers and sellers and no government restrictions, economic surplus is at a maximum when the market is in equilibrium. To see this point, let's look at the market for chai tea shown again in Figure 4.6. The consumer surplus in this market is the blue area below the demand curve and above the line indicating the equilibrium price of $2.00. The producer surplus is the red area above the supply curve and below the price line.   **MyLab Economics** Concept Check

Figure 4.6

Economic Surplus Equals the Sum of Consumer Surplus and Producer Surplus

The economic surplus in a market is the sum of the blue area, representing consumer surplus, and the red area, representing producer surplus.

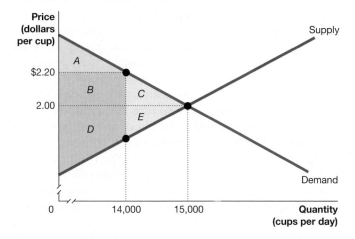

	At Competitive Equilibrium	At a Price of $2.20
Consumer surplus	A + B + C	A
Producer surplus	D + E	B + D
Deadweight loss	None	C + E

MyLab Economics Animation

Figure 4.7

When a Market Is Not in Equilibrium, There Is a Deadweight Loss

Economic surplus is maximized when a market is in competitive equilibrium. When a market is not in equilibrium, there is a deadweight loss. For example, when the price of chai tea is $2.20 instead of $2.00, consumer surplus declines from an amount equal to the sum of areas A, B, and C to just area A. Producer surplus increases from the sum of areas D and E to the sum of areas B and D. At competitive equilibrium, there is no deadweight loss. At a price of $2.20, there is a deadweight loss equal to the sum of triangles C and E.

Deadweight Loss

To show that economic surplus is maximized at equilibrium, consider a situation in which the price of chai tea is *above* the equilibrium price, as shown in Figure 4.7. At a price of $2.20 per cup, the number of cups consumers are willing to buy per day falls from 15,000 to 14,000. At competitive equilibrium, consumer surplus is equal to the sum of areas A, B, and C. At a price of $2.20, fewer cups are sold at a higher price, so consumer surplus declines to just the area of A. At competitive equilibrium, producer surplus is equal to the sum of areas D and E. At the higher price of $2.20, producer surplus changes to be equal to the sum of areas B and D. The sum of consumer and producer surplus—economic surplus—has been reduced to the sum of areas A, B, and D. Notice that this sum is less than the original economic surplus by an amount equal to the sum of triangles C and E. Economic surplus has declined because at a price of $2.20, all the cups between the 14,000th and the 15,000th, which would have been produced in competitive equilibrium, are not being produced. These "missing" cups are not providing any consumer or producer surplus, so economic surplus has declined. The reduction in economic surplus resulting from a market not being in competitive equilibrium is called the **deadweight loss**. In the figure, deadweight loss is equal to the sum of the triangles C and E.   **MyLab Economics** Concept Check

Deadweight loss The reduction in economic surplus resulting from a market not being in competitive equilibrium.

Economic Surplus and Economic Efficiency

Consumer surplus measures the benefit to consumers from buying a particular product, such as chai tea. Producer surplus measures the benefit to firms from selling a particular product. Therefore, economic surplus—which is the sum of the benefit to firms plus the benefit to consumers—is the best measure we have of the benefit to society from the production of a particular good or service. Economic surplus gives us a second way of characterizing the economic efficiency of a competitive market: *Equilibrium in a competitive market results in the greatest amount of economic surplus, or total net benefit to society, from the production of a good or service.* Anything that causes the market for a good or service not to be in competitive equilibrium reduces the total benefit to society from the production of that good or service.

Now we can give a more general definition of *economic efficiency* in terms of our two approaches: **Economic efficiency** is a market outcome in which the marginal benefit to consumers of the last unit produced is equal to its marginal cost of production and in which the sum of consumer surplus and producer surplus is at a maximum.   **MyLab Economics** Concept Check

Economic efficiency A market outcome in which the marginal benefit to consumers of the last unit produced is equal to its marginal cost of production and in which the sum of consumer surplus and producer surplus is at a maximum.

MyLab Economics Study Plan

Government Intervention in the Market: Price Floors and Price Ceilings

4.3

LEARNING OBJECTIVE: Explain the economic effect of government-imposed price floors and price ceilings.

Notice that we have *not* concluded that every *individual* is better off if a market is at competitive equilibrium. We have concluded only that economic surplus, or the *total* net benefit to society, is greatest at competitive equilibrium. Any individual producer would rather receive a higher price, and any individual consumer would rather pay a lower price, but usually producers can sell and consumers can buy only at the competitive equilibrium price.

Producers or consumers who are dissatisfied with the competitive equilibrium price can lobby the government to legally require that producers charge a different price. In the United States, the government only occasionally overrides the market outcome by setting prices. When the government does intervene, it can attempt to aid either sellers by requiring that a price be above equilibrium—a price floor—or aid buyers by requiring that a price be below equilibrium—a price ceiling. To affect the market outcome, the government must set a legal price floor that is above the equilibrium price or set a legal price ceiling that is below the equilibrium price. Otherwise, the price ceiling or price floor will not be *binding* on buyers and sellers. We can use the concepts of consumer surplus, producer surplus, and deadweight loss to understand more clearly why price floors and price ceilings reduce economic efficiency.

Price Floors: Government Policy in Agricultural Markets

The Great Depression of the 1930s was the worst economic disaster in U.S. history, affecting every sector of the economy. Many farmers could sell their products only at very low prices, so they convinced the federal government to set price floors for many agricultural products, such as wheat and corn. Government intervention in agriculture—often called the *farm program*—has continued ever since. To understand how a price floor in an agricultural market works, suppose that the equilibrium price in the wheat market is $6.50 per bushel, but the government decides to set a price floor of $8.00 per bushel. As Figure 4.8 shows, the price of wheat rises from $6.50 to $8.00, and the quantity of wheat sold falls from 2.0 billion bushels per year to 1.8 billion. Initially, suppose that production of wheat also falls to 1.8 billion bushels.

MyLab Economics Animation

Figure 4.8

The Economic Effect of a Price Floor in the Wheat Market

If wheat farmers convince the government to impose a price floor of $8.00 per bushel, the amount of wheat sold will fall from 2.0 billion bushels per year to 1.8 billion. If we assume that farmers produce 1.8 billion bushels, producer surplus then increases by rectangle A—which is transferred from consumer surplus—and falls by triangle C. Consumer surplus declines by rectangle A plus triangle B. There is a deadweight loss equal to triangles B and C, representing the decline in economic efficiency due to the price floor. In reality, a price floor of $8.00 per bushel will cause farmers to expand their production from 2.0 billion to 2.2 billion bushels, resulting in a surplus of wheat.

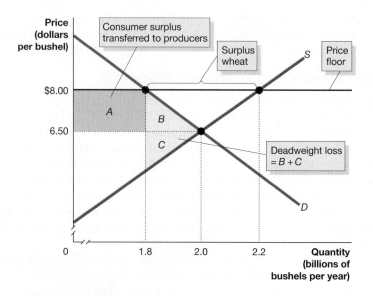

The producer surplus received by wheat farmers increases by an amount equal to the area of rectangle *A* and decreases by an amount equal to the area of triangle *C*. (This is the same result we saw in the market for chai tea in Figure 4.7.) The area of rectangle *A* represents a transfer from consumer surplus to producer surplus. The total fall in consumer surplus is equal to the sum of the areas of rectangle *A* and triangle *B*. Wheat farmers benefit from this program, but consumers lose. There is also a deadweight loss equal to the areas of triangles *B* and *C* because economic efficiency declines as the price floor reduces the amount of economic surplus in the market for wheat. In other words, the price floor has caused the marginal benefit of the last bushel of wheat to be greater than the marginal cost of producing it. We can conclude that a price floor reduces economic efficiency.

We assumed initially that farmers reduce their production of wheat to the amount consumers are willing to buy. In fact, as Figure 4.8 shows, a price floor will cause the quantity of wheat that farmers want to supply to increase from 2.0 billion to 2.2 billion bushels. Because the higher price also reduces the amount of wheat consumers want to buy, the result is a surplus of 0.4 billion bushels of wheat (the 2.2 billion bushels supplied minus the 1.8 billion demanded).

The federal government's farm programs have often resulted in large surpluses of wheat and other agricultural products. In response, the government has usually either bought the surplus food or paid farmers to restrict supply by taking some land out of cultivation. Because both of these options are expensive, Congress passed the Freedom to Farm Act of 1996. The intent of the act was to phase out price floors and government purchases of surpluses and return to a free market in agriculture. To allow farmers time to adjust, the federal government began paying farmers *subsidies*, or cash payments based on the number of acres planted. Although the subsidies were originally scheduled to be phased out, Congress has passed additional farm bills that have resulted in the continuation of subsidies requiring substantial federal government spending. In 2017, the Congressional Budget Office estimated that the farm program would result in federal spending of more than $66.5 billion over the following 10 years.   **MyLab Economics** Concept Check

Apply the Concept   **MyLab Economics** Video

Price Floors in Labor Markets: The Debate over Minimum Wage Policy

The minimum wage may be the most controversial "price floor." Supporters see the minimum wage as a way of raising the incomes of low-skilled workers. Opponents argue that it results in fewer jobs and imposes large costs on small businesses.

Since 2009, the national minimum wage as set by Congress has been $7.25 per hour for most occupations. It is illegal for an employer to pay less than this wage in these occupations. Although only about 4 percent of workers in the United States earn the minimum wage or less, many people are concerned that workers who receive the minimum wage or a wage a little above the minimum are not earning a "living wage" that would allow them to escape from poverty. Some members of Congress have introduced legislation to raise the minimum wage in several steps to $12 per hour. In recent years, protests in a number of cities brought pressure on fast-food restaurants and other employers to voluntarily raise the minimum wage they paid to $15 per hour. Several cities and states are increasing their minimum wage, typically in a series of steps phased in over several years. Currently, only a few cities and states plan to eventually raise their minimum wage as high as $15 per hour. In 2017, President Donald Trump and a majority of Congress seemed unlikely to support raising the federal minimum wage.

For many workers, the legal minimum wage is irrelevant because it is well below the wage employers are voluntarily willing to pay them. But for some low-skilled workers— such as restaurant workers—the minimum wage is above the wage they would otherwise receive. The following figure shows the effect of the minimum wage on employment in the market for low-skilled labor.

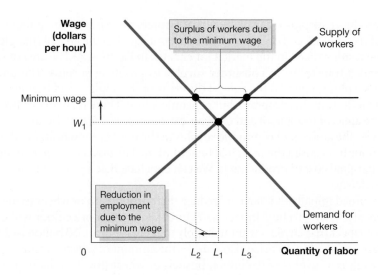

Without a minimum wage, the equilibrium wage would be W_1 and the number of workers hired would be L_1. With a minimum wage set above the equilibrium wage, the number of workers employers demand declines from L_1 to L_2, and the quantity of labor supplied increases to L_3, leading to a surplus of workers unable to find jobs equal to $L_3 - L_2$. The quantity of labor supplied increases because the higher wage attracts more people to work. For instance, some teenagers may decide that working after school is worthwhile at the minimum wage of $7.25 per hour but would not be worthwhile at a lower wage.

This analysis is very similar to our analysis of the wheat market in Figure 4.8. Just as a price floor in the wheat market leads to less wheat being consumed, a price floor in the labor market should lead to fewer workers being hired. Views differ sharply among economists, however, concerning how large a reduction in employment the minimum wage causes. The U.S. Congressional Budget Office (CBO) estimates that raising the minimum wage to $10.10 per hour, as President Barack Obama had proposed in 2015, would result in a decline in employment of 500,000 workers. Some economists believe that the effects of the minimum wage on employment are far smaller, however. For instance, David Card of the University of California, Berkeley, and Alan Krueger of Princeton University conducted a study of fast-food restaurants in New Jersey and Pennsylvania. Their study indicated that the effect of past minimum wage increases on employment has been very small. This study has been controversial, and other economists have examined similar data and come to the different conclusion that the minimum wage leads to a significant decrease in employment.

Whatever the extent of employment losses from the minimum wage, because it is a price floor, it will cause a deadweight loss, just as a price floor in the wheat market does. Therefore, many economists favor alternative policies for attaining the goal of raising the incomes of low-skilled workers. One policy many economists support is the *earned income tax credit*, which reduces the amount of tax that low-income wage earners pay to the federal government. Workers with very low incomes who do not owe any tax receive a payment from the government. Unlike with the minimum wage, the earned income tax credit can increase the incomes of low-skilled workers without reducing employment. The earned income tax credit also places a lesser burden on the small businesses that employ many low-skilled workers and may cause a smaller loss of economic efficiency.

Sources: Steven Greenhouse, "How the $15 Minimum Wage Went from Laughable to Viable," *New York Times*, April 1, 2016; U.S. Bureau of Labor Statistics, "Characteristics of Minimum Wage Workers, 2015," BLS Reports 1061, April 2016; U.S. Congressional Budget Office, "The Effects of a Minimum-Wage Increase on Employment and Family Income," February 2014; David Card and Alan B. Krueger, *Myth and Measurement: The New Economics of the Minimum Wage*, Princeton, NJ: Princeton University Press, 1995; and David Neumark and William Wascher, "Minimum Wages and Employment: A Case Study of the Fast-Food Industry in New Jersey and Pennsylvania: Comment," *American Economic Review*, Vol. 90, No. 5, December 2000, pp. 1362–1396.

MyLab Economics Study Plan   **Your Turn:** Test your understanding by doing related problem 3.9 on page 137 at the end of this chapter.

Price Ceilings: Government Rent Control Policy in Housing Markets

Support for governments setting price floors typically comes from sellers, and support for governments setting price ceilings typically comes from consumers. For example, when there is a sharp increase in gasoline prices, some policymakers and consumer groups will propose that the government impose a price ceiling on the market for gasoline. A number of cities impose rent control, which puts a ceiling on the maximum rent that landlords can charge for an apartment.

Figure 4.9 shows the market for apartments in a city that has rent control. Without rent control, the equilibrium rent would be $2,500 per month, and 2,000,000 apartments would be rented. With a maximum legal rent of $1,500 per month, landlords reduce the quantity of apartments supplied to 1,900,000. The fall in the quantity of apartments supplied can be the result of landlords converting some apartment buildings into offices, selling apartments off as condominiums, or converting multi-unit buildings into single-family homes. During World War II, governments imposing rent controls resulted in the largest increase in home ownership in U.S. history because many landlords sold off rental housing that was no longer profitable to rent to tenants. Over time, landlords may even abandon some rental housing. At one time in New York City, rent control resulted in landlords abandoning whole city blocks of apartment houses because they were unable to cover their costs with the rents the government allowed them to charge. In London, when rent controls were applied to rooms and apartments located in a landlord's own home, the quantity of these apartments supplied decreased by 75 percent.

In Figure 4.9, with the rent ceiling of $1,500 per month, the quantity of apartments demanded rises to 2,100,000, resulting in a shortage of 200,000 apartments. Consumer surplus increases by rectangle A and falls by triangle B. Rectangle A would have been part of producer surplus if rent control were not in place. With rent control, it is part of consumer surplus. Rent control causes the producer surplus that landlords receive to fall by rectangle A plus triangle C. Triangles B and C represent the deadweight loss, which results from rent control reducing the amount of economic surplus in the market for apartments. Rent control has caused the marginal benefit of the last apartment rented to be greater than the marginal cost of supplying it. We can conclude that a price ceiling, such as rent control, reduces economic efficiency. The appendix to this chapter shows how we can make quantitative estimates of the deadweight loss and provides an example of the changes in consumer surplus and producer surplus that can result from rent control.

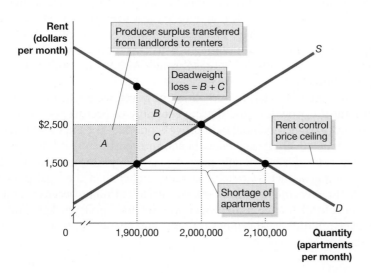

MyLab Economics Animation

Figure 4.9

The Economic Effect of a Rent Ceiling

Without rent control, the equilibrium rent is $2,500 per month. At that price, 2,000,000 apartments would be rented. If the government imposes a rent ceiling of $1,500 per month, the quantity of apartments supplied decreases to 1,900,000, and the quantity of apartments demanded increases to 2,100,000, resulting in a shortage of 200,000 apartments. Producer surplus equal to the area of rectangle A is transferred from landlords to renters, and there is a deadweight loss equal to the areas of triangles B and C.

Don't Let This Happen to You

Don't Confuse "Scarcity" with "Shortage"

At first glance, the following statement seems correct: "There is a shortage of every good that is scarce." In everyday conversation, we describe a good as "scarce" if we have trouble finding it. For instance, if you are looking for a gift for a child, you might call the latest hot toy "scarce" if you are willing to buy it at its listed price but can't find it online or in any store. But recall that economists have a broader definition of *scarce*. In the economic sense, almost everything—except undesirable things like garbage—is scarce. A shortage of a good occurs only if the quantity demanded is greater than the quantity supplied at the current price. Therefore, the preceding statement—"There is a shortage of every good that is scarce"—is incorrect. In fact, there is no shortage of most scarce goods.

MyLab Economics Study Plan

Your Turn: Test your understanding by doing related problem 3.12 on page 138 at the end of this chapter.

Renters as a group benefit from rent controls—total consumer surplus is larger—but landlords lose. Because of the deadweight loss, the total loss to landlords is greater than the gain to renters. Notice also that although renters as a group benefit, the number of renters is reduced, so some renters are made worse off by rent controls because they are unable to find an apartment at the legal rent.   **MyLab Economics** Concept Check

Black Markets and Peer-to-Peer Sites

When governments regulate prices by enacting price ceilings or price floors, buyers and sellers often find a way around the regulations. As a result, renters may be worse off and landlords may be better off than Figure 4.9 makes it seem. We have assumed that renters and landlords actually abide by the price ceiling, but sometimes they don't. Because rent control leads to a shortage of apartments, renters who would otherwise not be able to find apartments have an incentive to offer landlords rents *above* the legal maximum. The result is a **black market** in which buying and selling take place at prices that violate government price regulations.

Black market A market in which buying and selling take place at prices that violate government price regulations.

Online peer-to-peer rental sites like Airbnb have provided landlords and tenants another way to avoid rent controls. Landlords can use these sites to convert a regular yearly rental into a series of short-term rentals for which they can charge above the legal maximum rent. Tenants can also use the sites to make a profit from rent controls. In San Francisco in recent years, some tenants have moved out of the city but kept their rent-controlled apartments and rented them using peer-to-peer rental sites. Both San Francisco and New York have taken actions against peer-to-peer rental sites because some government officials believe the sites undermine rent control. Both cities have laws that prohibit landlords from renting apartments for less than 30 days. San Francisco also requires anyone renting rooms through Airbnb and similar sites to pay the city's 14 percent hotel tax.

Some government officials in both cities, however, were reluctant to take actions that might limit the growth of the sharing economy of peer-to-peer rental sites. The sharing economy has the potential to improve economic efficiency and make available to consumers goods, such as cars, bikes, boats, and apartments, at lower prices. When cities have rent control laws, though, peer-to-peer sites perform a somewhat different function, making apartments available at rents higher than the legal price ceiling—apartments that renters might otherwise have difficulty finding because of the shortage caused by rent control. It remains to be seen whether local policymakers can resolve the conflict between putting legal ceilings on rents and encouraging peer-to-peer sites to operate in their cities.

Solved Problem 4.3

What's the Economic Effect of a Black Market in Renting Apartments?

In many cities that have rent controls, such as New York and San Francisco, the actual rents paid can be much higher than the legal maximum. Because rent controls cause a shortage of apartments, desperate tenants are often willing to pay landlords rents that are higher than the law allows, perhaps by writing a check for the legally allowed rent and paying an additional amount in cash. Look again at Figure 4.9 on page 121. Suppose that competition among tenants results in the black market rent rising to $3,500 per month. At this rent, tenants demand 1,900,000 apartments. Draw a graph showing the market for apartments and compare this situation with the one shown in Figure 4.9. Be sure to note any differences in consumer surplus, producer surplus, and deadweight loss.

Solving the Problem

Step 1: **Review the chapter material.** This problem is about price controls in the market for apartments, so you may want to review the section "Price Ceilings: Government Rent Control Policy in Housing Markets," which begins on page 121.

Step 2: **Draw a graph similar to Figure 4.9, with the addition of the black market price.**

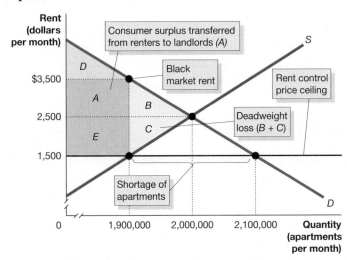

Step 3: **Analyze the changes from Figure 4.9.** The black market rent is now $3,500 per month—even higher than the original competitive equilibrium rent shown in Figure 4.9. So, consumer surplus declines by an amount equal to the sum of the areas of rectangle A and rectangle E. The remaining consumer surplus is triangle D. Note that rectangle A, which would have been part of consumer surplus without rent control, represents a transfer from renters to landlords. Compared with the situation shown in Figure 4.9, producer surplus has increased by an amount equal to the sum of the areas of rectangles A and E, and consumer surplus has declined by the same amount. Deadweight loss is equal to the sum of the areas of triangles B and C, the same as in Figure 4.9.

Extra Credit: This analysis leads to a surprising result: With an active black market in apartments, rent control may leave renters as a group worse off—with less consumer surplus—than if there were no rent control. There is one more possibility to consider, however. If enough landlords become convinced that they can get away with charging rents above the legal ceiling, the quantity of apartments supplied will increase. Eventually, the market could even end up at the competitive equilibrium, with an equilibrium rent of $2,500 and equilibrium quantity of 2,000,000 apartments. In that case, the rent control price ceiling becomes nonbinding—not because it was set below the equilibrium price but because the government didn't effectively enforce it.

Your Turn: For more practice, do related problem 3.13 on page 138 at the end of this chapter.

Rent controls can also lead to an increase in racial and other types of illegal discrimination. With rent controls, more renters are looking for apartments than there are apartments to rent. Landlords are more likely to indulge their prejudices by refusing to rent to people from groups they don't like, even if doing so is illegal. In cities without rent controls, landlords face more competition, which makes it more difficult to reject tenants on the basis of irrelevant characteristics, such as race.   **MyLab Economics** Concept Check

The Results of Government Price Controls: Winners, Losers, and Inefficiency

When the government imposes price floors or price ceilings, three important results occur:

1. **Some people win.** The winners from rent control are the people who are paying less for rent because they live in rent-controlled apartments. Landlords may also gain if they break the law by charging rents above the legal maximum for their rent-controlled apartments, provided that those illegal rents are higher than the competitive equilibrium rents would be.
2. **Some people lose.** The losers from rent control are the landlords of rent-controlled apartments who abide by the law and renters who are unable to find apartments to rent at the controlled price.
3. **There is a loss of economic efficiency.** Rent control reduces economic efficiency because fewer apartments are rented than would be rented in a competitive market (refer again to Figure 4.9 on page 121). The resulting deadweight loss measures the decrease in economic efficiency.   **MyLab Economics** Concept Check

Apply the Concept   **MyLab Economics** Video

Price Controls Lead to Economic Decline in Venezuela

In 2017, the Venezuelan economy was in a shambles. Although the government was no longer publishing accurate statistics, economists estimate that by the end of 2017 real GDP—the value of goods and services produced in Venezuela, corrected for inflation—would be 25 percent lower than in 2015. That decline was comparable to the worst years of the Great Depression of the 1930s in the United States. Venezuela's inflation rate, a measure of how quickly prices are rising, was above 500 percent—easily the highest in the world. The unemployment rate was above 10 percent, and Caracas, the country's capital, had the highest murder rate of any capital city in the world. As we saw in the chapter opener, some desperate people in Venezuela engaged in food riots at supermarkets.

Many economists believe the problems with the Venezuelan economy are due to the policies of Hugo Chavez, who was elected president in 1999, and Nicolas Maduro, who became president following Chavez's death in 2013. Under Chavez, the government seized control of thousands of private firms, including firms in the oil industry—the source of most of Venezuela's exports. The government seized large farms and redistributed the land to low-income Venezuelans, many of whom had no experience in farming, lacked access to loans needed to finance purchases of seeds, fertilizers, and pesticides, and were not connected to distribution networks to sell their crops. One farmer was quoted as saying, "They encouraged me to seize this land from its previous owner, but now I can't get loans, and the state agricultural store doesn't have seeds, fertilizers or insecticides. How can I plant crops with nothing?"

Disruptions to Venezuela's agricultural sector led to a sharp reduction in food production. For several years, the Venezuelan government was able to ensure that sufficient food would be available in supermarkets by using its oil revenues to buy imported food. But a large decline in oil prices beginning in 2014 meant the government could no longer pay for food imports. The falling supply of food would ordinarily have resulted in price increases that would have increased the quantity of food grown domestically. But the Venezuelan government imposed price controls that kept prices well below their new equilibrium levels. In an interview, Nicholas Casey, a reporter for the *New York Times*, described the resulting shortages:

> [You] go outside as early as 5 a.m, sometimes 4:30, you see people lining up in front of stores to try to see what's going to be there when they open their doors. And sometimes even these stores—after you're waiting through a line that might be 500, 1,000 people sometimes … you get to the front of the line, and you find that they've only got cooking oil. They don't have flour. They don't have any of the basic things that you need there.

The price controls resulted in a thriving black market in many goods run by what Venezuelans call *bachaqueros*. These small-scale entrepreneurs buy up food and other groceries at the below-market controlled prices and resell them to consumers who would otherwise be unable to buy these goods. Consider the case of cornmeal, which is used to make arepa, a corn pancake that is an important part of most Venezuelans' diet. In late 2016, the government price ceiling for a 2-pound bag of cornmeal was 190 bolivars, the Venezuelan currency (its symbol is Bs). The equilibrium market price of cornmeal was about 975 bolivars, but few supermarkets had any for sale. Many Venezuelans had to buy cornmeal on the black market at a price of 3,500 bolivars. The figure below, which is similar to Figure 4.9, illustrates the situation.

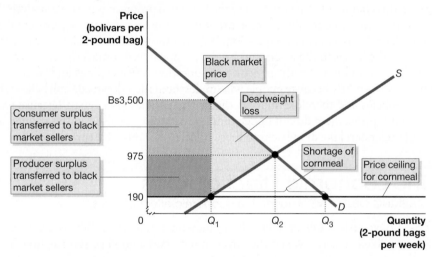

The figure shows that most consumers are worse off because of the price controls. Less cornmeal is available for sale (Q_1 rather than the market equilibrium quantity Q_2), and at the price ceiling, there is a shortage of cornmeal equal to $Q_3 - Q_1$. Although a few consumers may be able to buy cornmeal at the low price ceiling price of 190 bolivars, most supermarkets have no cornmeal available on their shelves, forcing many consumers to pay the black market price of 3,500 bolivars. Note that the situation for Venezuelan consumers may be worse than the figure indicates. Although the high black market price might provide an incentive for some farmers to expand their production of cornmeal, news reports indicate that domestic production has increased very little. Instead, some black market sellers, particularly those living along the border with Colombia, are buying cornmeal at controlled prices and smuggling it out of Venezuela, were it can be sold in Colombia at the market equilibrium price. Although this price is below the black market price, people selling on the black market in Venezuela risk being arrested by the government. So, the actual amount of cornmeal available to Venezuelan consumers might be less than Q_1 shown in the figure.

Tragically, news reports indicate that hunger is widespread in Venezuela, and economists estimate that more than 80 percent of the population is living in poverty.

Sources: Nicholas Casey, "No Food, No Medicine, No Respite: A Starving Boy's Death in Venezuela, *New York Times*, December 25, 2016; Patrick Gillespie and Osmary Hernandez, "Venezuela's Food Prices Skyrocket as People Go Hungry," cnn.com, October 21, 2016; "Venezuela's Leaders Ignore Reality," *Economist*, January 26, 2017; Terry Gross, "Bust Times in Oil-Rich Venezuela: 'The Banks Don't Have Money to Give Out,'" Fresh Air interview with Nicholas Casey, npr.org, June 8, 2016; Peter Wilson, "Venezuelan Food Shortages Bode Ill for Chavez's Re-election," usatoday.com,

August 13, 2012; and Mery Mogollon, "Packs of Black-Market Foot Soldiers Raid Venezuela Markets," latimes.com, April 1, 2015.

MyLab Economics Study Plan   **Your Turn:** Test your understanding by doing related problems 3.14 and 3.15 on page 138 at the end of this chapter.

Positive and Normative Analysis of Price Ceilings and Price Floors

Are rent controls, government farm programs, and other price ceilings and price floors bad? As we saw in Chapter 1, questions of this type do not have right or wrong answers. Economists are generally skeptical of government attempts to interfere with competitive market equilibrium. Economists know the role competitive markets have played in raising the average person's standard of living. They also know that too much government intervention has the potential to reduce the ability of the market system to produce similar increases in living standards in the future. The situation in Venezuela today appears to fit this description.

But recall the difference between positive and normative analysis. Positive analysis is concerned with *what is*, and normative analysis is concerned with *what should be*. Our analysis in this chapter of rent control and the U.S. farm program is positive analysis. We discussed the economic results of these programs. Whether these programs are desirable or undesirable is a normative question. Whether the gains to the winners more than make up for the losses to the losers and for the decline in economic efficiency is a matter of judgment and not strictly an economic question. Price ceilings and price floors continue to exist partly because people who understand their downside still believe they are good policies and therefore support them. The policies also persist because many people who support them do not understand the economic analysis in this chapter and

MyLab Economics Study Plan   so do not understand the drawbacks to these policies.   MyLab Economics Concept Check

4.4 The Economic Effect of Taxes

LEARNING OBJECTIVE: Analyze the economic effect of taxes.

Supreme Court Justice Oliver Wendell Holmes once remarked, "Taxes are what we pay for a civilized society." When the government taxes a good or service, however, it affects the market equilibrium for that good or service. Just as with a price ceiling or price floor, one result of a tax is a decline in economic efficiency. Analyzing taxes is an important part of the field of economics known as *public finance*. In this section, we will use the model of demand and supply and the concepts of consumer surplus, producer surplus, and deadweight loss to analyze the economic effect of taxes.

The Effect of Taxes on Economic Efficiency

Whenever a government taxes a good or service, less of that good or service will be produced and consumed. For example, a tax on cigarettes will raise the cost of smoking and reduce the amount of smoking that takes place. We can use a demand and supply graph to illustrate this point. Figure 4.10 shows the market for cigarettes.

Without the tax, the equilibrium price of cigarettes would be $5.00 per pack, and 4 billion packs of cigarettes would be sold per year (point *A*). If the federal government requires sellers of cigarettes to pay a $1.00-per-pack tax, then their cost of selling cigarettes will increase by $1.00 per pack. This increase in cost causes the supply curve for cigarettes to shift up by $1.00 because sellers will now require a price that is $1.00 greater to supply the same quantity of cigarettes. In Figure 4.10, the supply curve shifts up by $1.00 to show the effect of the tax, and there is a new equilibrium price of $5.90 and a new equilibrium quantity of 3.7 billion packs (point *B*).

The federal government will collect tax revenue equal to the tax per pack multiplied by the number of packs sold, or $3.7 billion. The area shaded in green in Figure 4.10 represents the government's tax revenue. Consumers will pay a higher price

MyLab Economics Animation

Figure 4.10

The Effect of a Tax on the Market for Cigarettes

Without the tax, market equilibrium occurs at point *A*. The equilibrium price of cigarettes is $5.00 per pack, and 4 billion packs of cigarettes are sold per year. A $1.00-per-pack tax on cigarettes will cause the supply curve for cigarettes to shift up by $1.00, from S_1 to S_2. The new equilibrium occurs at point *B*. The price of cigarettes will increase by $0.90, to $5.90 per pack, and the quantity sold will fall to 3.7 billion packs. The tax on cigarettes will increase the price paid by consumers from $5.00 to $5.90 per pack. Producers will receive a price of $5.90 per pack (point *B*), but after paying the $1.00 tax, they will be left with $4.90 (point *C*). The government will receive tax revenue equal to the green-shaded box. Some consumer surplus and some producer surplus will become tax revenue for the government, and some will become deadweight loss, shown by the yellow-shaded area.

of $5.90 per pack. Although sellers appear to be receiving a higher price per pack, once they have paid the tax, the price they receive falls from $5.00 per pack to $4.90 per pack. There is a loss of consumer surplus because consumers are paying a higher price. The price producers receive falls, so there is also a loss of producer surplus. Therefore, the tax on cigarettes has reduced *both* consumer surplus and producer surplus. Some of the reduction in consumer and producer surplus becomes tax revenue for the government. The rest of the reduction in consumer and producer surplus is equal to the deadweight loss from the tax, shown by the yellow-shaded triangle in the figure.

We can conclude that the true burden of a tax is not just the amount consumers and producers pay the government but also includes the deadweight loss. The deadweight loss from a tax is called the *excess burden* of the tax. *A tax is efficient if it imposes a small excess burden relative to the tax revenue it raises.* One contribution economists make to government tax policy is to advise policymakers on which taxes are most efficient. **MyLab Economics** Concept Check

Tax Incidence: Who Actually Pays a Tax?

The answer to the question "Who pays a tax?" seems obvious: Whoever is legally required to send a tax payment to the government pays the tax. But there can be an important difference between who is legally required to pay the tax and who actually *bears the burden* of the tax. Economists call the actual division of the burden of a tax between buyers and sellers **tax incidence**. For example, as of April 2017, the federal government levied an excise tax of 18.4 cents per gallon of gasoline sold. Gas station owners collect this tax and forward it to the federal government, but who actually bears the burden of the tax?

Tax incidence The actual division of the burden of a tax between buyers and sellers in a market.

Determining Tax Incidence on a Demand and Supply Graph

Suppose that currently the federal government does not impose a tax on gasoline. In Figure 4.11, equilibrium in the retail market for gasoline occurs at the intersection of the demand curve and supply curve, S_1. The equilibrium price is $2.50 per gallon, and the equilibrium quantity is 144 billion gallons per year. Now suppose that the federal government imposes a 10-cents-per-gallon tax. As a result of the tax, the supply curve for gasoline will shift up by 10 cents per gallon. At the new equilibrium, where the demand curve intersects the supply curve, S_2, the price has risen by 8 cents per gallon, from $2.50 to $2.58. Notice that only in the extremely unlikely case that demand is a vertical line will the market price rise by the full amount of the tax. Consumers are paying 8 cents more per gallon. Sellers of gasoline receive a new higher price of $2.58 per gallon, but after paying the 10-cents-per-gallon tax, they are left with $2.48 per gallon, or 2 cents less than they were receiving in the old equilibrium.

Although the sellers of gasoline are responsible for collecting the tax and sending the tax receipts to the government, they do not bear most of the burden of the tax.

MyLab Economics Animation

Figure 4.11

The Incidence of a Tax on Gasoline

With no tax on gasoline, the price would be $2.50 per gallon, and 144 billion gallons of gasoline would be sold each year. A 10-cents-per-gallon excise tax shifts the supply curve up, from S_1 to S_2, raises the price consumers pay from $2.50 to $2.58, and lowers the price sellers receive from $2.50 to $2.48. Therefore, consumers pay 8 cents of the 10-cents-per-gallon tax on gasoline, and sellers pay 2 cents.

In this case, consumers pay 8 cents of the tax because the market price has risen by 8 cents, and sellers pay 2 cents of the tax because after sending the tax to the government, they are receiving 2 cents less per gallon of gasoline sold. Expressed in percentage terms, consumers pay 80 percent of the tax, and sellers pay 20 percent of the tax.

Solved Problem 4.4

MyLab Economics Interactive Animation

When Do Consumers Pay All of a Sales Tax Increase?

A student makes the following statement: "If the federal government raises the sales tax on gasoline by $0.25, then the price of gasoline will rise by $0.25. Consumers can't get by without gasoline, so they have to pay the whole amount of any increase in the sales tax." Under what circumstances will the student's statement be true? Use a graph of the market for gasoline to illustrate your answer.

Solving the Problem

Step 1: **Review the chapter material.** This problem is about tax incidence, so you may want to review the section "Tax Incidence: Who Actually Pays a Tax?" which begins on page 127.

Step 2: **Draw a graph like Figure 4.11 to illustrate the circumstances when consumers will pay all of an increase in a sales tax.**

Step 3: **Use the graph to evaluate the statement.** The graph shows that consumers will pay all of an increase in a sales tax only if the demand curve is a vertical line. It is very unlikely that the demand for gasoline would look like this because we expect that for every good, an increase in price will cause a decrease in the quantity demanded. Because the demand curve for gasoline is not a vertical line, the statement is incorrect.

Your Turn: For more practice, do related problem 4.8 on page 140 at the end of the chapter.

MyLab Economics Study Plan

●

Does It Make a Difference Whether the Government Collects a Tax from Buyers or Sellers?

We have already seen the important distinction between who is legally required to pay a tax and who actually bears the burden of a tax. We can reinforce this point by noting explicitly that the incidence of a tax does *not* depend on whether the government collects a tax from the buyers of a good or from the sellers. Figure 4.12 illustrates this point by showing the effect on equilibrium in the market for gasoline if a 10-cents-per-gallon tax is imposed on buyers rather than on sellers. That is, we are now assuming that instead of sellers having to collect the 10-cents-per-gallon tax at the pump, buyers are responsible for keeping track of how many gallons of gasoline they purchase and sending the tax to the government. (Of course, it would be very difficult for buyers to keep track of their purchases or for the government to check whether they were paying all of the taxes they owe. That is why the government collects the tax on gasoline from sellers.)

Figure 4.12 is similar to Figure 4.11 except that it shows the gasoline tax being imposed on buyers rather than on sellers. In Figure 4.12, the supply curve does not shift because nothing has happened to change the quantity of gasoline sellers are willing to supply at any given price. The demand curve has shifted, however, because consumers now have to pay a 10-cent tax on every gallon of gasoline they buy. Therefore, at every quantity, they are willing to pay a price 10 cents lower than they would have paid without the tax. In the figure, we indicate the effect of the tax by shifting the demand curve down by 10 cents, from D_1 to D_2. Once the tax has been imposed and the demand curve has shifted down, the new equilibrium quantity of gasoline is 140 billion gallons, which is exactly the same as in Figure 4.11.

The new equilibrium price after the tax is imposed appears to be different in Figure 4.12 than in Figure 4.11, but if we include the tax, buyers will pay the same price, and sellers will receive the same price in both figures. To see this point, notice that in Figure 4.11, buyers pay sellers a price of $2.58 per gallon. In Figure 4.12, they pay sellers only $2.48, but they must also pay the government a tax of 10 cents per gallon. So, the total price buyers pay remains $2.58 per gallon. In Figure 4.11, sellers receive $2.58 per gallon from buyers, but after they pay the tax of 10 cents per gallon, they are left with $2.48, which is the same amount they receive in Figure 4.12.   **MyLab Economics** Concept Check

MyLab Economics Animation

Figure 4.12

The Incidence of a Tax on Gasoline Paid by Buyers

With no tax on gasoline, the demand curve is D_1. If a 10-cents-per-gallon tax is imposed that consumers are responsible for paying, the demand curve shifts down by the amount of the tax, from D_1 to D_2. In the new equilibrium, consumers pay a price of $2.58 per gallon, including the tax. Producers receive $2.48 per gallon. The result is the same as when producers were responsible for paying the tax.

Apply the Concept

Is the Burden of the Social Security Tax Really Shared Equally between Workers and Firms?

Most people who receive paychecks have several different taxes withheld by their employers, who forward the taxes directly to the government. In fact, after getting their first job, many people are shocked when they discover the gap between their gross pay and their net pay after taxes have been deducted. The largest tax many people of low or moderate income pay is FICA, which stands for the Federal Insurance Contributions Act. FICA funds the Social Security and Medicare programs, which provide income and health care to elderly and disabled people. FICA is sometimes called the *payroll tax*. When Congress passed the act, it wanted employers and workers to equally share the burden of the tax. In 2017, FICA was 15.3 percent of wages, with workers paying 7.65 percent, which is withheld from their paychecks, and employers paying the other 7.65 percent.

But does requiring workers and employers to each pay half the tax mean that the burden of the tax is also shared equally? Our discussion in this chapter shows that the answer is "no." In the labor market, employers are buyers, and workers are sellers. As we saw in the example of the federal tax on gasoline, whether the tax is collected from buyers or from sellers does not affect the incidence of the tax. Most economists believe, in fact, that the burden of FICA falls almost entirely on workers. The following figure, which shows the market for labor, illustrates why.

In the market for labor, the demand curve represents the quantity of labor demanded by employers at various wages, and the supply curve represents the quantity of labor supplied by workers at various wages. The intersection of the demand curve and the supply curve determines the equilibrium wage. In both panels, the equilibrium wage without a Social Security payroll tax is $10 per hour. For simplicity, let's assume that the payroll tax equals $1 per hour of work. In panel (a), we assume that employers must pay the tax. The tax causes the demand for labor curve to shift down by $1 at every quantity of labor because firms must now pay a $1 tax for every hour of labor they hire. We have drawn the supply curve for labor as being very steep because most economists believe the quantity of labor supplied by workers does not change much as the wage rate changes. In panel (a), after the tax is imposed, the equilibrium wage declines from $10 per hour to $9.05 per hour. Firms are now paying a total of $10.05 for every hour of work they hire: $9.05 in wages to workers and $1 in tax to the government. In other words, workers have paid $0.95 of the $1 tax, and firms have paid only $0.05.

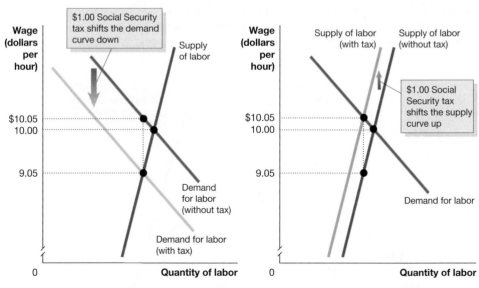

(a) The Social Security tax paid by employers   **(b) The Social Security tax paid by workers**

Panel (b) shows that this result is exactly the same when the tax is imposed on workers rather than on firms. In this case, the tax causes the supply curve for labor to shift up by $1 at every quantity of labor because workers must now pay a tax of $1 for every hour they work. After the tax is imposed, the equilibrium wage increases to $10.05 per hour. But workers receive only $9.05 after they have paid the $1.00 tax. Once again, workers have paid $0.95 of the $1 tax, and firms have paid only $0.05.

Although the figure presents a simplified analysis, it reflects the conclusion of most economists who have studied the incidence of FICA: Even though Congress requires employers to pay half the tax and workers to pay the other half, in fact, the burden of the tax falls almost entirely on workers. This conclusion would not be changed even if Congress revised the law to require either employers or workers to pay all of the tax. The forces of demand and supply working in the labor market, and not Congress, determine the incidence of the tax.

Your Turn: Test your understanding by doing related problems 4.9 and 4.10 on page 140 at the end of this chapter.

MyLab Economics Study Plan

Continued from page 109

Economics in Your Life & Career

As a Member of the City Council, Should You Support Rent Control?

At the beginning of the chapter, we posed the following questions: If you and the other city council members vote to enact a rent control law, is it likely that in the future it will be easier for renters to find an affordable apartment in your city? Who in your city would benefit, and who would lose from the law?

This chapter has shown that although rent control can keep rents lower than they might otherwise be, it can also lead to a permanent shortage of apartments. Renters may have to search for a long time to find a suitable apartment, and landlords may even ask renters to make additional payments, in violation of the rent control law, which would make the actual rent paid higher than the controlled rent. Finding an apartment in a city after enactment of rent control will typically be more difficult. People who are able to find an apartment at the controlled rent will benefit if the city council enacts the law, while landlords and renters who are unable to find an apartment at the controlled rent will lose. As the chapter also notes, whether rent control should be enacted is a normative question—one that you and the rest of the city council will have to answer.

Conclusion

Our discussion of the model of demand and supply shows that markets free from government intervention eliminate surpluses and shortages and do a good job of responding to the wants of consumers. We have seen that both consumers and firms sometimes try to use the government to change market outcomes in their favor. The concepts of consumer surplus, producer surplus, and deadweight loss allow us to measure the benefits consumers and producers receive from competitive market equilibrium. These concepts also allow us to measure the effects of government price floors and price ceilings and the economic effect of taxes.

Read *An Inside Look* on the next page for a discussion of problems Uber has encountered in attempting to expand its services in the United Kingdom.

CNBC.COM

Meet the Lawyer Trying to Make US Tech Giants Pay More Taxes. His First Target: Uber

Lawyer Jolyon Maugham took an Uber on Monday in London, but it was no normal ride. He was on his way to deliver a letter to the ride-hailing service's headquarters that could kick off legal proceedings potentially costing the U.S. start-up millions of dollars.

Maugham's case revolves around how much tax Uber pays in the U.K. and, if successful, could have wide-reaching implications across Europe. Britain has something called value-added tax (VAT), which is paid when you buy goods or services. The current rate is 20 percent.

Uber pays no VAT in the U.K. because the ride-hailing app does not class its drivers as employees. Instead it says it is connecting riders to drivers.

"Uber says that it is a business-to-business service. It says that it is supplying the taxi drivers with an introduction service but that proposition suffers from two deficiencies. The first is that it doesn't really accord with what you and I would think of as reality because we think that Uber is a consumer facing brand, it's not a business facing brand. So it doesn't look like reality looks like," Maugham told CNBC by phone on Friday.

"In an employment tribunal case last year, they found that Uber was engaging its drivers as workers and it also went on to say, and this is the necessary logical consequence of the first proposition, that Uber is supplying transportation services and it is making a VAT-able supply."

The lawyer is referring to a landmark U.K. case last year in which judges ruled that Uber drivers are not self-employed and should get all the benefits of full workers' rights such as holiday pay and pensions. Uber has appealed the decision and it is still ongoing. The company also said that its drivers, not the company, pay VAT. If you are self-employed, you can be liable to pay VAT if your turnover for a 12-month period is over £83,000 ($103,552). But it is unlikely an Uber driver would make this in a year.

"Drivers who use the Uber app are subject to the same VAT laws as any other transportation provider in the U.K.," an Uber spokesperson told CNBC by email.

Maugham said that he hopes this will go to the High Court in London to be heard next month. What's at stake here for Uber is large sums of money as well as implications that could span across other jurisdictions. If Uber loses, it will have to increase fares by 20 percent to accommodate for VAT, and could be liable to pay tax on previous revenues it earned. The company has not released its financials in the U.K. for 2016, but Maugham believes it could be liable to pay £200 million ($249 million) in VAT for last year. If Uber loses any potential case, its VAT payments could be assessed across the entire European Union (EU).

A rise in fares is not something that will please most Uber users given they use the service for the cheaper prices and convenience. The lawyer said he was not worried about any backlash from the public.

"I think there will be a much larger constituency that believes that nobody is above the law, and everybody has to pay taxes that parliament demand. Unless these big powerful corporations pay their taxes, society cannot operate. There will be people who will be irritated they have to pay more for their Uber taxi, but [I] think they will be in the minority," Maugham told CNBC.

The affairs of U.S. technology firms in Europe have been in focus over the past few years. Last year, the European Commission, the European Union's executive arm, said Ireland must recover 13 billion euros ($14 billion) in "illegal tax benefits" it granted to Apple. The iPhone maker has appealed the decision. And Google agreed to pay the U.K. £130 million in back taxes last year, in a move that was criticized at the time as a "sweetheart deal." Google at the time said it was going to be paying more tax in the U.K. moving forward.

Maugham said he is going after Uber because the public sees such stories which leads to distrust in the government. He wants to put pressure on the government "to take this behavior more seriously." …

Source: Arjun Kharpal, "Meet the Lawyer Trying to Make US Tech Giants Pay More Taxes. His First Target: Uber," cnbc.com, March 24, 2017.

Key Points in the Article

British lawyer Joylon Maugham has brought a lawsuit against Uber to require the ride-hailing company to pay the United Kingdom's value-added tax (VAT), which is similar to the U.S. sales tax. Uber argues that its drivers are already subject to the same VAT laws that apply to other transportation providers. Uber classifies its drivers as self-employed, and requires the self-employed to pay VAT only if yearly earnings are over £83,000 (approximately $103,000), which is more than most Uber drivers earn. In a 2016 case, however, judges in the United Kingdom ruled that Uber drivers are not self-employed, which would mean that the company, and not its drivers, is subject to the VAT. Uber has appealed this decision, but if unsuccessful, Uber will have to raise fares to cover the 20 percent VAT and could be ordered to pay the tax on past earnings as well.

Uber is not the only U.S. company operating in Europe to be confronted about taxes in recent years. In 2016, the European Union told Ireland that it must recover €13 billion in tax benefits granted to Apple, and Google agreed to pay back taxes to the United Kingdom and also to pay more taxes in the future.

Analyzing the News

(a) Like many other European countries, the United Kingdom charges a value-added tax (VAT) on the purchase of goods and services. The current VAT is 20 percent. Uber has not been paying the VAT, arguing that the company doesn't employ its drivers but instead acts only as an intermediary that connects drivers and passengers. A lawyer has challenged Uber's claim that the company is not required to pay the tax, and, if successful, the result could cost Uber millions of dollars as well as set a precedent for other European countries in which Uber operates.

(b) A court ruled in 2016 that Uber drivers are not self-employed, a decision that Uber has appealed. If Uber loses the appeal, it will have to increase fares as its costs rise because of the VAT. The figure below shows a hypothetical example of the effect of this tax on the market for ride-hailing services like those offered by Uber and Lyft. Without the tax, the equilibrium price is £30 per ride, with a quantity of 12,000 rides being provided each day. With a 20 percent tax (£6), the supply curve shifts up by £6, increasing the price the consumer pays to £33, decreasing the price ride-hailing firms receive to £27, and decreasing the quantity of rides being provided to 8,500. The tax revenue is equal to £51,000 per day (£6 per ride × 8,500 rides). The imposition of the 20 percent tax on Uber rides will generate revenue for the government, but it will also reduce economic efficiency by reducing consumer and producer surplus. Consumers will pay a higher price for rides, which reduces consumer surplus, and firms will receive a lower price per ride, which reduces producer surplus. Some of the reduction in consumer and producer surplus will become tax revenue, but the rest is deadweight loss from the tax, a result of the decrease in the number of rides due to the imposition of the tax. Economic efficiency could also be reduced across Europe if Uber and other ride-hailing services are required to pay a VAT in additional countries.

(c) Uber is just one of several U.S. companies facing increased taxes in Europe. In 2016, the European Commission cited both Apple and Google as companies not paying their fair share of taxes. As with Uber, tax increases for these companies will result in higher prices as less of their goods and services will be produced and consumed; the tax increases will also reduce economic efficiency.

Thinking Critically

1. The figure shows the market for rides before and after the imposition of a 20 percent tax. How can we use the figure to measure the effect the tax has on economic efficiency? Redraw the graph and show the area representing the excess burden created by the implementation of the tax.

2. Uber and other ride-hailing firms may be required to start paying the U.K.'s VAT. The figure shows a hypothetical example of the effects of this tax on the market for rides in the United Kingdom. Redraw the graph to show what would happen if riders, instead of ride-hailing firms, were responsible for directly paying the tax to the government. Explain any differences in price, quantity, and tax incidence.

The British government's imposing a 20 percent VAT shifts the supply curve up by £6 in the market for rides arranged using ride-hailing apps, increasing the price paid by the consumer from £30 to £33 and decreasing the price received by ride-hailing firms from £30 to £27.

Key Terms

Black market, p. 122

Consumer surplus, p. 110

Deadweight loss, p. 117

Economic efficiency, p. 117

Economic surplus, p. 116

Marginal benefit, p. 110

Marginal cost, p. 114

Price ceiling, p. 110

Price floor, p. 110

Producer surplus, p. 114

Tax incidence, p. 127

4.1 Consumer Surplus and Producer Surplus, pages 110–115

LEARNING OBJECTIVE: Distinguish between the concepts of consumer surplus and producer surplus.

MyLab Economics   Visit www.pearson.com/mylab/economics to complete these exercises online and get instant feedback.

Summary

Although most prices are determined by demand and supply in markets, the government sometimes imposes *price ceilings* and *price floors*. A **price ceiling** is a legally determined maximum price that sellers may charge. A **price floor** is a legally determined minimum price that sellers may receive. Economists analyze the effects of price ceilings and price floors by using the concepts of *consumer surplus, producer surplus,* and *deadweight loss*. **Marginal benefit** is the additional benefit to a consumer from consuming one more unit of a good or service. The demand curve is also a marginal benefit curve. **Consumer surplus** is the difference between the highest price a consumer is willing to pay for a good or service and the actual price the consumer pays. The total amount of consumer surplus in a market is equal to the area below the demand curve and above the market price. **Marginal cost** is the additional cost to a firm of producing one more unit of a good or service. The supply curve is also a marginal cost curve. **Producer surplus** is the difference between the lowest price a firm is willing to accept for a good or service and the price it actually receives. The total amount of producer surplus in a market is equal to the area above the supply curve and below the market price.

Review Questions

1.1 What is marginal benefit? Why is the demand curve referred to as a marginal benefit curve?

1.2 What is marginal cost? Why is the supply curve referred to as a marginal cost curve?

1.3 What is consumer surplus? How does consumer surplus change as the equilibrium price of a good rises or falls?

1.4 What is producer surplus? How does producer surplus change as the equilibrium price of a good rises or falls?

Problems and Applications

1.5 On a shopping trip, Melanie decided to buy a light blue coat that had a price tag of $79.95. When she brought the coat to the store's sales clerk, Melanie was told that the coat was on sale, and she would pay 20 percent less than the price on the tag. After the discount was applied, Melanie paid $63.96, $15.99 less than the original price.

Was the value of Melanie's consumer surplus from this purchase $79.95? $63.96? $15.99? Or some other amount? Briefly explain.

1.6 (Related to the Chapter Opener on page 108) Uber is an app people use to arrange transportation with drivers who use their own cars for this purpose. Customers pay for their rides with the Uber smartphone app. Uber's prices fluctuate with the demand for the service. This "surge pricing" can result in different prices for the same distance traveled at different times of day or days of the week. Annie Lowrey, a writer for the *New York Times*, explained that she paid $13 for a 10 P.M. 2-mile trip in downtown Washington, DC, on New Year's Eve. Three hours later she paid $47 for the return trip to her home. Did she receive negative consumer surplus on her return trip? Briefly explain.

Source: Annie Lowrey, "Is Uber's Surge-Pricing an Example of High Tech Gouging?" *New York Times*, January 10, 2014.

1.7 Consider the information given in the following table on four consumers in the market for premium bottled water.

Consumer	Highest Price Willing to Pay
Jill	$4
Jose	3
Josh	2
Jordan	1

a. If the price of a bottle of premium bottled water is $1.50, what is the total consumer surplus received by these consumers? Illustrate your answer with a graph.

b. Suppose the price of premium bottled water rises to $2.50. Now what is the consumer surplus received by these consumers? Illustrate your answer by using the graph you prepared in part (a).

1.8 Suppose that a frost in Florida reduces the size of the orange crop, which causes the supply curve for oranges to shift to the left. Briefly explain whether consumer surplus will increase or decrease and whether producer surplus will increase or decrease. Use a demand and supply graph to illustrate your answers.

1.9 An article in the *Wall Street Journal* discussed research at Ohio State University that may lead to producing carbon black—an important input in automobile tire making—out of eggshells, tomato skins, and other food waste. According to the article, this research could lead to a reduction in the cost of producing tires.

a. Assuming that the research is successful, use a demand and supply graph to show the effect of these falling costs on consumer surplus in the market for tires.

b. Can we be certain whether these falling costs will increase producer surplus? Briefly explain.

Source: Daniel Akst, "Making Tire Filler from Eggshells" *Wall Street Journal*, March 9, 2017.

1.10 A student makes the following argument: "When a market is in equilibrium, there is no consumer surplus. We know this because in equilibrium, the market price is equal to the price consumers are willing to pay for the good." Briefly explain whether you agree with the student's argument.

1.11 In the following graph, is the consumer surplus larger with demand curve D_1 or demand curve D_2? Briefly explain. Compare the producer surplus with demand curve D_1 and with demand curve D_2.

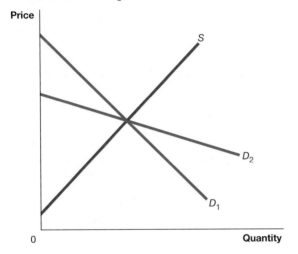

1.12 Assume that the following graph illustrates the market for a breast cancer–fighting drug, without which breast cancer patients cannot survive. What is the consumer surplus in this market? How does it differ from the consumer surplus in the markets you have studied up to this point?

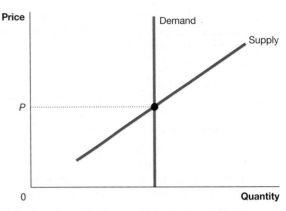

1.13 (Related to the Apply the Concept on page 112) The *Apply the Concept* states that the value of the area representing consumer surplus from Uber's service was $2.88 billion per year for the four cities involved in the study. Use the information from the graph in the *Apply the Concept* to show how this value was calculated. (For a review of how to calculate the area of a triangle, see the appendix to Chapter 1.)

1.14 The following graph shows the market for tickets to a concert that will be held in a local arena that seats 15,000 people. What is the producer surplus in this market? How does it differ from the producer surplus in the markets you have studied up to this point?

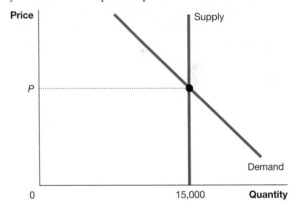

The Efficiency of Competitive Markets, pages 115–117

4.2

LEARNING OBJECTIVE: Explain the concept of economic efficiency.

MyLab Economics   Visit www.pearson.com/mylab/economics to complete these exercises online and get instant feedback.

Summary

Equilibrium in a competitive market is economically efficient. **Economic surplus** is the sum of consumer surplus and producer surplus. **Economic efficiency** is a market outcome in which the marginal benefit to consumers from the last unit produced is equal to the marginal cost of production and in which the sum of consumer surplus and producer surplus is at a maximum. When the market price is above or below the equilibrium price, there is a reduction in economic surplus. The reduction in economic surplus resulting from a market not being in competitive equilibrium is called the **deadweight loss**.

Review Questions

2.1 Define *economic surplus* and *deadweight loss*.

2.2 What is economic efficiency? Why do economists define efficiency in this way?

Problems and Applications

2.3 An article about record high avocado prices discussed how avocado crops had suffered from hot weather, droughts, and an invasive beetle that kills avocado trees. Use a demand and supply graph of the avocado market to illustrate the effect of the hot weather, droughts, and invasive beetle. How are producer surplus and consumer surplus affected? Briefly explain.

Source: Rafi Letzter, "Avocado Prices Just Hit a Record High, and Show No Signs of Coming Down. Here's Why," businessinsider.com, November 3, 2016.

2.4 Briefly explain whether you agree with the following statement: "A lower price in a market always increases economic efficiency in that market."

2.5 Briefly explain whether you agree with the following statement: "If at the current quantity, marginal benefit is greater than marginal cost, there will be a deadweight loss in the market. However, there is no deadweight loss when marginal cost is greater than marginal benefit."

2.6 According to an article in the *Wall Street Journal*, restaurant chains, including Subway, McDonald's, and Chick-fil-A, have begun serving only chickens that were raised without being fed antibiotics. Using this method of raising chickens increases their cost. Suppose that consumers react to the news of restaurants selling antibiotic-free chicken sandwiches by increasing their demand for the sandwiches. Can you tell whether economic surplus will increase in the market for chicken sandwiches? Use a graph of the market for chicken sandwiches to illustrate your answer.

Source: Jacob Bunge, "Perdue Farms Eliminated Antibiotics from Chicken Supply," *Wall Street Journal*, October 6, 2016.

2.7 Briefly explain whether you agree with the following statement: "If consumer surplus in a market increases, producer surplus must decrease."

2.8 Using the following graph, show the effects on consumer surplus and producer surplus of an increase in supply from S_1 to S_2. By how much does economic surplus increase?

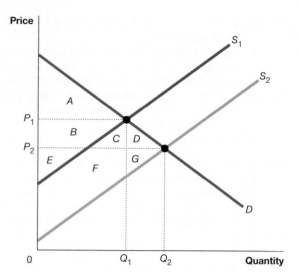

2.9 A student argues: "Economic surplus is greatest at the level of output where the difference between marginal benefit and marginal cost is largest." Do you agree? Briefly explain.

2.10 Using the following graph, explain why economic surplus would be smaller if Q_1 or Q_3 were the quantity produced than if Q_2 is the quantity produced.

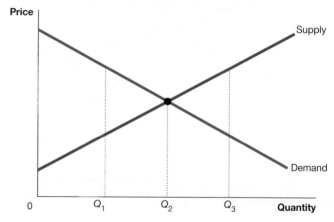

4.3 Government Intervention in the Market: Price Floors and Price Ceilings, pages 118–126

LEARNING OBJECTIVE: Explain the economic effect of government-imposed price floors and price ceilings.

MyLab Economics   Visit www.pearson.com/mylab/economics to complete these exercises online and get instant feedback.

Summary

Producers or consumers who are dissatisfied with the equilibrium in a market can attempt to convince the government to impose a price floor or a price ceiling. Price floors usually increase producer surplus, decrease consumer surplus, and cause a deadweight loss. Price ceilings usually increase consumer surplus, reduce producer surplus, and cause a deadweight loss. The results of the government imposing price ceilings and price floors are that some people win, some people lose, and a loss of economic efficiency occurs. Price ceilings and price floors can lead to a **black market**, in which buying and selling take place at prices that violate government price regulations. Positive analysis is concerned with *what is*, and normative analysis is concerned with *what should be*. Positive analysis shows that price ceilings and price floors cause deadweight losses. Whether these policies are desirable or undesirable, though, is a normative question.

Review Questions

3.1 Why do some consumers tend to favor price controls while others tend to oppose them?

3.2 Do producers tend to favor price floors or price ceilings? Briefly explain.

3.3 What is a black market? Under what circumstances do black markets arise?

3.4 Can economic analysis provide a final answer to the question of whether the government should intervene in markets by imposing price ceilings and price floors? Briefly explain.

Problems and Applications

3.5 The following graph shows the market for apples. Assume that the government has imposed a price floor of $10 per crate.

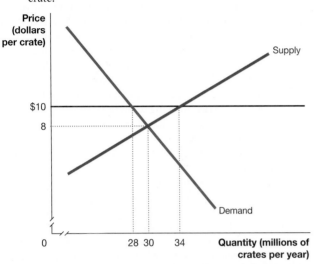

a. How many crates of apples will be sold to consumers after the price floor has been imposed?

b. Will there be a shortage or a surplus of apples? If there is a shortage or a surplus, how large will it be?

c. Will apple producers benefit from the price floor? If so, explain how they will benefit.

3.6 Use the information on the kumquat market in the table to answer the following questions.

Price (per crate)	Quantity Demanded (millions of crates per year)	Quantity Supplied (millions of crates per year)
$10	120	20
15	110	60
20	100	100
25	90	140
30	80	180
35	70	220

a. What are the equilibrium price and quantity? How much revenue do kumquat producers receive when the market is in equilibrium? Draw a graph showing the market equilibrium and the area representing the revenue kumquat producers receive.

b. Suppose the federal government decides to impose a price floor of $30 per crate. Now how many crates of kumquats will consumers purchase? How much revenue will kumquat producers receive? Assume that the government does not purchase any surplus kumquats. On your graph from part (a), show the price floor, the change in the quantity of kumquats purchased, and the revenue kumquat producers receive after the price floor is imposed.

c. Suppose the government imposes a price floor of $30 per crate and purchases any surplus kumquats from producers. Now how much revenue will kumquat producers receive? How much will the government spend on purchasing surplus kumquats? On your graph from part (a), show the area representing the amount the government spends to purchase the surplus kumquats.

3.7 Suppose that the government sets a price floor for milk that is above the competitive equilibrium price and that the government does not purchase any surplus milk.

a. Draw a graph showing this situation. Be sure your graph shows the competitive equilibrium price, the price floor, the quantity that would be sold in competitive equilibrium, and the quantity that would be sold with the price floor.

b. Compare the economic surplus in this market when there is a price floor and when there is not.

3.8 In Allentown, Pennsylvania, in the summer of 2014, the average price of a gallon of gasoline was $3.68—a 22-cent increase from the year before. Many consumers were upset by the increase. One consumer was quoted in a local newspaper as saying, "It's crazy. The government should step in." Suppose the government had stepped in and imposed a price ceiling equal to the old price of $3.46 per gallon.

a. Draw a graph showing the effect of the price ceiling on the market for gasoline. Be sure that your graph shows:
   i. The price and quantity of gasoline before and after the price ceiling is imposed
   ii. The areas representing consumer surplus and producer surplus before and after the price ceiling is imposed
   iii. The area of deadweight loss

b. Will the consumer who was complaining about the increase in the price of gasoline definitely be made better off by the price ceiling? Briefly explain.

Source: Sam Kennedy, "Valley Feeling Pain at the Pump," (Allentown, PA) *Morning Call*, June 21, 2014.

3.9 **(Related to the Apply the Concept on page 119)** An article in the *Wall Street Journal* noted that a study by the U.S. Congressional Budget Office "estimated raising the minimum wage to $10.10 an hour would reduce U.S. employment by 500,000 but lift 900,000 Americans out of poverty." Why might raising the minimum wage reduce employment? How would it raise some people out of poverty? What effect might these estimates have on a *normative* analysis of the minimum wage?

Source: Julie Jargon and Eric Morath, "As Wage Debate Rages, Some Have Made the Shift," *Wall Street Journal*, April 8, 2014.

3.10 If San Francisco were to repeal its rent control law, would the prices for short-term rentals in the city listed on Airbnb and other peer-to-peer sites be likely to rise or fall? Briefly explain.

3.11 The competitive equilibrium rent in the city of Lowell is currently $1,000 per month. The government decides to enact rent control and establish a price ceiling of $750 per month for apartments. Briefly explain whether rent control is likely to make each of the following people better or worse off.

a. Someone currently renting an apartment in Lowell

b. Someone who will be moving to Lowell next year and who intends to rent an apartment

c. A landlord who intends to abide by the rent control law

d. A landlord who intends to ignore the law and illegally charge the highest rent possible for his apartments

3.12 **(Related to the Don't Let This Happen to You on page 122)** Briefly explain whether you agree with the following statement: "If there is a shortage of a good, it must be scarce, but there is not a shortage of every scarce good."

3.13 **(Related to Solved Problem 4.3 on page 123)** Use the information on the market for apartments in Bay City in the table to answer the following questions.

Rent	Quantity Demanded	Quantity Supplied
$500	375,000	225,000
600	350,000	250,000
700	325,000	275,000
800	300,000	300,000
900	275,000	325,000
1,000	250,000	350,000

a. In the absence of rent control, what is the equilibrium rent, and what is the equilibrium quantity of apartments rented? Draw a demand and supply graph of the market for apartments to illustrate your answer. In equilibrium, will there be any renters who are unable to find an apartment to rent or any landlords who are unable to find a renter for an apartment?

b. Suppose the government sets a ceiling of $600 per month on rents. What is the quantity of apartments demanded, and what is the quantity of apartments supplied?

c. Assume that all landlords abide by the law in part (b). Use a demand and supply graph to illustrate the effect of this price ceiling on the market for apartments. Be sure to indicate on your graph each of the following: (i) the area representing consumer surplus after the price ceiling has been imposed, (ii) the area representing producer surplus after the price ceiling has been imposed, and (iii) the area representing the deadweight loss after the price ceiling has been imposed.

d. Assume that the quantity of apartments supplied is the same as you determined in (b), but now assume that landlords ignore the law and rent this quantity of apartments for the highest rent they can get. Briefly explain what this rent will be.

3.14 **(Related to the Apply the Concept on page 124)** According to an article in the *New York Times*, the Venezuelan government "imposes strict price controls that are intended to make a range of foods and other goods more affordable for the poor. They are often the very products that are the hardest to find."

a. Why would imposing price controls on goods make the goods hard to find?

b. One of the goods subject to price controls was toothpaste. Draw a graph to illustrate this situation. On your graph, be sure to indicate the areas representing consumer surplus, producer surplus, and deadweight loss.

Source: William Neuman, "With Venezuelan Cupboards Bare, Some Blame Price Controls," *New York Times*, April 20, 2012.

3.15 **(Related to the Apply the Concept on page 124)** According to a news story, in late 2016, a recent college graduate

in Caracas, Venezuela, hadn't eaten meat in a month. He was quoted as saying it was "not because we can't find meat, but because it's very expensive." Meat, like other food in Venezuela, was subject to a price ceiling. Why then was it very expensive? Illustrate your answer with a graph.

Source: Patrick Gillespie and Osmary Hernandez, "Venezuela's Food Prices Skyrocket as People Go Hungry," cnn.com, October 21, 2016.

3.16 A student makes the following argument: "A price floor reduces the amount of a product that consumers buy because it keeps the price above the competitive market equilibrium. A price ceiling, though, increases the amount of a product that consumers buy because it keeps the price below the competitive market equilibrium." Do you agree with the student's reasoning? Use a demand and supply graph to illustrate your answer.

3.17 University towns with major football programs experience an increase in demand for hotel rooms during home football weekends. Hotels respond to the increase in demand by increasing the prices they charge for rooms. Periodically, there is an outcry against the higher prices, accompanied by accusations of "price gouging."

a. Draw a demand and supply graph of the market for hotel rooms in Boostertown for weekends with home football games and another graph for weekends without home football games. If the Boostertown city council passes a law stating that prices for rooms are not allowed to rise, what would happen to the market for hotel rooms during home football game weekends? Show your answer on your graph.

b. If the prices of hotel rooms are not allowed to increase, what will be the effect on out-of-town football fans?

c. How might the city council's law affect the supply of hotel rooms over time? Briefly explain.

d. University towns are not the only places that face peak and nonpeak "seasons." Can you think of other locations that face a large increase in demand for hotel rooms during particular times of the year? Why do we typically not see laws limiting the prices hotels can charge during peak seasons?

3.18 Suppose that initially the gasoline market is in equilibrium, at a price of $2.50 per gallon and a quantity of 45 million gallons per month. Then a war in the Middle East disrupts imports of oil into the United States, shifting the supply curve for gasoline from S_1 to S_2. The price of gasoline begins to rise, and consumers protest. The federal government responds by setting a price ceiling of $2.50 per gallon. Use the graph to answer the following questions.

a. If there were no price ceiling, what would be the equilibrium price of gasoline, the quantity of gasoline demanded, and the quantity of gasoline supplied? Now assume that the price ceiling is imposed and that there is no black market in gasoline. What are the price of gasoline, the quantity of gasoline demanded, and the quantity of gasoline supplied? How large is the shortage of gasoline?

b. Assume that the price ceiling is imposed, and there is no black market in gasoline. Show on the graph the areas representing consumer surplus, producer surplus, and deadweight loss.

c. Now assume that there is a black market, and the price of gasoline rises to the maximum that consumers are willing to pay for the amount supplied by producers, at $2.50 per gallon. Show on the graph the areas representing producer surplus, consumer surplus, and deadweight loss.

d. Are consumers made better off with the price ceiling than without it? Briefly explain.

3.19 An editorial in the *Economist* magazine discusses the fact that in most countries—including the United States—it is illegal for individuals to buy or sell body parts, such as kidneys.

a. Draw a demand and supply graph for the market for kidneys. Show on your graph the legal maximum price of zero and indicate the quantity of kidneys supplied at this price. (*Hint:* Because we know that some kidneys are donated, the quantity supplied will not be zero.)

b. The editorial argues that buying and selling kidneys should be legalized:

> With proper regulation, a kidney market would be a big improvement over the current sorry state of affairs. Sellers could be checked for disease and drug use, and cared for after operations. ... Buyers would get better kidneys, faster. Both sellers and buyers would do better than in the illegal market, where much of the money goes to middlemen.

Do you agree with this argument? Should the government treat kidneys like other goods and allow the market to determine the price?

Source: "Psst, Wanna Buy a Kidney?" *Economist*, November 18, 2006.

The Economic Effect of Taxes, pages 126–131

4.4

LEARNING OBJECTIVE: Analyze the economic effect of taxes.

MyLab Economics   Visit www.pearson.com/mylab/economics to complete these exercises online and get instant feedback.

Summary

Most taxes result in a loss of consumer surplus, a loss of producer surplus, and a deadweight loss. The true burden of a tax is not just the amount consumers and producers pay to the government but also includes the deadweight loss. The deadweight loss from a tax is called the excess burden of the tax. **Tax incidence** is the actual division of the burden of a tax. In most cases, consumers and firms share the burden of a tax levied on a good or service.

Review Questions

4.1 What is meant by *tax incidence*?

4.2 What do economists mean by an *efficient tax*?

4.3 Does who is legally responsible for paying a tax—buyers or sellers—make a difference in the amount of tax each pays? Briefly explain.

4.4 As explained in the chapter, economic efficiency is a market outcome in which the marginal benefit to consumers of the last unit produced is equal to its marginal cost of production. Using this explanation of economic efficiency, explain why a tax creates a deadweight loss.

Problems and Applications

4.5 Suppose that the current equilibrium price of a quarter-pound hamburger is $5, and 10 million quarter-pound hamburgers are sold per month. After the federal government imposes a tax of $0.50 per hamburger, the equilibrium price of hamburgers rises to $5.20, and the equilibrium quantity falls to 9 million. Illustrate this situation with a demand and supply graph. Be sure your graph shows the equilibrium price before and after the tax; the equilibrium quantity before and after the tax; and the areas representing consumer surplus after the tax, producer surplus after the tax, tax revenue collected by the government, and deadweight loss.

4.6 The following graph shows the effect of a tax imposed on soft drinks. Use this graph to answer the questions.

a. Which areas in the graph represent the excess burden (deadweight loss) of the tax?

b. Which areas represent the revenues collected by the government from the tax?

c. Would economists consider this tax to be efficient? Briefly explain.

4.7 Use the following graph of the market for cigarettes to answer the questions.

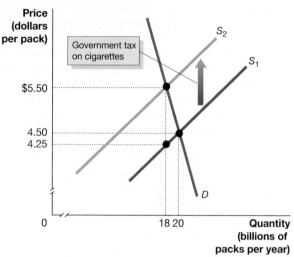

a. According to the graph, how much is the government tax on cigarettes?
b. What price do producers receive after paying the tax?
c. How much tax revenue does the government collect?
d. How would the graph be different if the tax were collected from the buyers of cigarettes?
e. If the tax were collected from buyers, what would be the new equilibrium price that buyers pay producers of cigarettes?
f. Including the tax, what would be the total amount that cigarette buyers pay per pack?

4.8 **(Related to Solved Problem 4.4 on page 128)** Suppose the federal government decides to impose a sales tax of $1.00 per pizza. Briefly explain whether you agree with the following statement, made by a representative of the pizza industry:

> The pizza industry is very competitive. As a result, pizza sellers will have to pay the whole tax because they are unable to pass any of it on to consumers in the form of higher prices. Therefore, a sales tax of $1.00 per pizza will result in pizza sellers receiving $1.00 less on each pizza sold, after paying the tax.

Illustrate your answer with a graph.

4.9 **(Related to the Apply the Concept on page 130)** According to a news story, Pennsylvania's liquor tax is "paid by the seller—the restaurant or bar owner—when the seller buys liquor from state-run wine and spirit stores." Briefly explain the effect of how liquor taxes in Pennsylvania are collected has on the price of a glass of wine a consumer purchases in a restaurant in the state.

Source: Matt Assad, "How Booze Brings Heady Development," (Allentown, PA) *Morning Call*, February 22, 2015.

4.10 **(Related to the Apply the Concept on page 130)** Suppose the government imposes a payroll tax of $1 per hour of work and collects the tax from employers. Use a graph for the market for labor to show the effect of the payroll tax, assuming the special case of a vertical supply curve of labor. By how much does the new equilibrium wage that employers pay workers fall?

Critical Thinking Exercises

CT4.1 For this exercise, your instructor may assign you to a group. The chapter describes how a market can be economically efficient. Before you took this class, you might have heard someone say that "markets are efficient." Compare the description of efficiency in this chapter with what you thought about efficiency prior to taking this class. Write up your thoughts in a paragraph (that you may be asked to turn in or to discuss in class). In your group, each member should make the comparison. Then, as a group, prepare a one-paragraph summary of what you discussed and be prepared to turn in the summary or discuss it with the class.

CT4.2 Suppose that the mayor of New York abolishes rent control. A friend of yours who lives in New York complains about the higher apartment rents that result. This friend has never taken an economics class. Explain to your friend why the apartment market is now more efficient because rent control has been abolished. Your explanation should be two paragraphs long and contain a visual, such as a graph or table, that illustrates your argument. Include in your answer whether you think it's likely that your friend will change her opinion of rent control on the basis of your analysis.

CT4.3 In 1948, the United States experienced a potato surplus. Watch the video clip "Farm Journalist Potato Surplus" located in the MyLab course available for this text. For there to be a surplus, what must be happening in this market? Explain your reasoning in a paragraph and be sure to use an appropriate graph.

Appendix

Quantitative Demand and Supply Analysis

Graphs help us understand economic change *qualitatively*. For instance, a demand and supply graph can tell us that if household incomes rise, the demand curve for a normal good will shift to the right, and the price of the good will rise. Often, though, economists, business managers, and policymakers want to know more than the qualitative direction of change; they want a *quantitative estimate* of the size of the change.

In this chapter, we carried out a qualitative analysis of rent controls. We saw that imposing rent controls involves a trade-off: Renters as a group gain, but landlords lose, and the market for apartments becomes less efficient, as shown by the deadweight loss. To better evaluate rent controls, we need to know more than just that these gains and losses exist; we need to know how large they are. A quantitative analysis of rent controls will tell us how large the gains and losses are.

Demand and Supply Equations

The first step in a quantitative analysis is to supplement our use of demand and supply curves with demand and supply *equations*. Economists use data on prices, quantities, and other economic variables to statistically estimate equations for demand and supply curves. For example, suppose that economists have estimated that the demand for apartments in New York City is:

$$Q^D = 4{,}750{,}000 - 1{,}000P,$$

and the supply of apartments is:

$$Q^S = -1{,}000{,}000 + 1{,}300P.$$

We have used Q^D for the quantity of apartments demanded per month, Q^S for the quantity of apartments supplied per month, and P for the apartment rent, in dollars per month. In reality, both the quantity of apartments demanded and the quantity of apartments supplied will depend on more than just the rental price of apartments in New York City. The demand for apartments in New York City will also depend, for instance, on the average incomes of families in the New York area and on the rents of apartments in the surrounding cities. For simplicity, we will ignore these other factors.

With no government intervention, we know that at competitive market equilibrium, the quantity demanded must equal the quantity supplied, or:

$$Q^D = Q^S.$$

We can use this equation, which is called an *equilibrium condition*, to solve for the equilibrium monthly apartment rent by setting the quantity demanded from the demand equation equal to the quantity supplied from the supply equation:

$$4{,}750{,}000 - 1{,}000P = -1{,}000{,}000 + 1{,}300P$$

$$5{,}750{,}000 = 2{,}300P$$

$$P = \frac{5{,}750{,}000}{2{,}300} = \$2{,}500.$$

We can then substitute this price back into either the supply equation or the demand equation to find the equilibrium quantity of apartments rented:

MyLab Economics Animation

Figure 4A.1

Graphing Demand and Supply Equations

After statistically estimating demand and supply equations, we can use the equations to draw demand and supply curves. In this case, the equilibrium rent for apartments is $2,500 per month, and the equilibrium quantity of apartments rented is 2,250,000. The demand equation tells us that at a rent of $4,750, the quantity of apartments demanded will be zero. The supply equation tells us that at a rent of $769, the quantity of apartments supplied will be zero. The areas representing consumer surplus and producer surplus are also indicated on the graph.

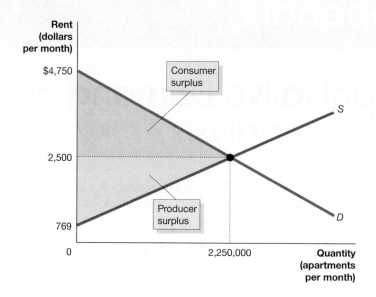

$$Q^D = 4{,}750{,}000 - 1{,}000P = 4{,}750{,}000 - 1{,}000(2{,}500) = 2{,}250{,}000,$$

or:

$$Q^S = -1{,}000{,}000 + 1{,}300P = -1{,}000{,}000 + 1{,}300(2{,}500) = 2{,}250{,}000.$$

Figure 4A.1 illustrates the information from these equations in a graph. The figure shows the values for rent when both the quantity supplied and the quantity demanded are zero. These values can be calculated from the demand and supply equations by setting Q^D and Q^S equal to zero and solving for price:

$$Q^D = 0 = 4{,}750{,}000 - 1{,}000P$$

$$P = \frac{4{,}750{,}000}{1{,}000} = \$4{,}750$$

and:

$$Q^S = 0 = -1{,}000{,}000 + 1{,}300P$$

$$P = \frac{-1{,}000{,}000}{-1{,}300} = \$769.23.$$

MyLab Economics Concept Check

Calculating Consumer Surplus and Producer Surplus

Figure 4A.1 shows consumer surplus and producer surplus in this market.

Recall that the sum of consumer surplus and producer surplus equals the net benefit that renters and landlords receive from participating in the market for apartments. We can use the values from the demand and supply equations to calculate the value of consumer surplus and producer surplus. Remember that consumer surplus is the area below the demand curve and above the line representing market price. Notice that this area forms a right triangle because the demand curve is a straight line—it is *linear*. As we noted in the appendix to Chapter 1, the area of a triangle is equal to ½ × Base × Height. In this case, the area is:

$$\frac{1}{2} \times (2{,}250{,}000) \times (4{,}750 - 2{,}500) = \$2{,}531{,}250{,}000.$$

So, this calculation tells us that the consumer surplus in the market for rental apartments in New York City is about $2.5 billion per month.

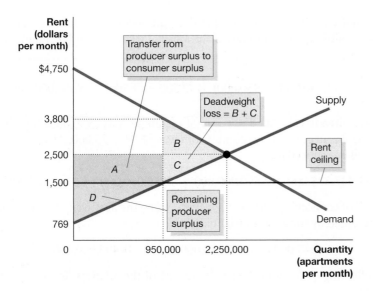

MyLab Economics Animation

Figure 4A.2

Calculating the Economic Effect of Rent Controls

Once we have estimated equations for the demand and supply of rental housing, a graph can guide our numerical estimates of the economic effects of rent control. Consumer surplus falls by an amount equal to the area of triangle B and increases by an amount equal to the area of rectangle A. Producer surplus falls by an amount equal to the sum of the areas of rectangle A and triangle C. The remaining producer surplus is equal to the area of triangle D. Deadweight loss is equal to the sum of the areas of triangles B and C.

We can calculate producer surplus in a similar way. Remember that producer surplus is the area above the supply curve and below the line representing market price. Because the supply curve is also a straight line, producer surplus in the figure is equal to the area of the triangle:

$$\frac{1}{2} \times 2,250,000 \times (2,500 - 769) = \$1,947,375,000.$$

This calculation tells us that the producer surplus in the market for rental apartments in New York City is about $1.9 billion per month.

We can use the same type of analysis to measure the effect of rent control on consumer surplus, producer surplus, and economic efficiency. For instance, suppose the city imposes a rent ceiling of $1,500 per month. Figure 4A.2 can help guide us as we measure the effect.

First, we can calculate the quantity of apartments that will actually be rented by substituting the rent ceiling of $1,500 into the supply equation:

$$Q^S = -1,000,000 + (1,300 \times 1,500) = 950,000.$$

We also need to know the price on the demand curve when the quantity of apartments is 950,000. We can do this by substituting 950,000 for quantity in the demand equation and solving for price:

$$950,000 = 4,750,000 - 1,000P$$

$$P = \frac{-3,8000,000}{-1,000} = \$3,800.$$

Compared with its value in competitive equilibrium, consumer surplus has been reduced by a value equal to the area of triangle B but increased by a value equal to the area of rectangle A. The area of triangle B is:

$$\frac{1}{2} \times (2,250,000 - 950,000) \times (3,800 - 2,500) = \$845,000,000,$$

and the area of rectangle A is Base × Height, or:

$$(\$2,500 - \$1,500) \times (950,000) = \$950,000,000.$$

The value of consumer surplus in competitive equilibrium was $2,531,250,000. As a result of the rent ceiling, it will be increased to:

$$(\$2,531,250,000 + 950,000,000) - \$845,000,000 = \$2,636,250,000.$$

Compared with its value in competitive equilibrium, producer surplus has been reduced by a value equal to the sum of the areas of triangle C and rectangle A. The area of triangle C is:

$$\frac{1}{2} \times (2{,}250{,}000 - 950{,}000) \times (2{,}500 - 1{,}500) = \$650{,}000{,}000.$$

We have already calculated the area of rectangle A as \$950,000,000. The value of producer surplus in competitive equilibrium was \$1,947,375,000. As a result of the rent ceiling, it will be reduced to:

$$\$1{,}947{,}375{,}000 - \$650{,}000{,}000 - \$950{,}000{,}000 = \$347{,}375{,}000.$$

The loss of economic efficiency, as measured by the deadweight loss, is equal to the value represented by the areas of triangles B and C, or:

$$\$845{,}000{,}000 + \$650{,}000{,}000 = \$1{,}495{,}000{,}000.$$

The following table summarizes the results of the analysis (the values are in millions of dollars):

Consumer Surplus		Producer Surplus		Deadweight Loss	
Competitive Equilibrium	Rent Control	Competitive Equilibrium	Rent Control	Competitive Equilibrium	Rent Control
\$2,531	\$2,636	\$1,947	\$347	\$0	\$1,495

Qualitatively, we know that imposing rent control will make consumers better off, make landlords worse off, and decrease economic efficiency. The advantage of the analysis we have just gone through is that it puts dollar values on the qualitative results. We can now see how much consumers have gained, how much landlords have lost, and how great the decline in economic efficiency has been. Sometimes the quantitative results can be surprising. Notice, for instance, that after the imposition of rent control, the deadweight loss is actually much greater than the remaining producer surplus. Of course, these results are dependent on the numbers we chose for the demand and supply curve equations. Choosing different numbers would have changed the results.

Economists often study issues where the qualitative results of actions are apparent, even to non-economists. You don't have to be an economist to understand who wins and who loses from rent control or that if a company cuts the price of its product, its sales will increase. Business managers, policymakers, and the general public do, however, need economists to measure quantitatively the effects of different actions—including policies such as rent control—so that they can better assess the results of these actions.

MyLab Economics Study Plan

MyLab Economics Concept Check

Quantitative Demand and Supply Analysis, pages 141–144

LEARNING OBJECTIVE: Use quantitative demand and supply analysis.

MyLab Economics   Visit **www.pearson.com/mylab/economics** to complete these exercises online and get instant feedback.

Review Questions

4A.1 In a linear demand equation, what economic information is conveyed by the intercept on the price axis? Similarly, what economic information is conveyed by the intercept on the price axis in a linear supply equation?

4A.2 Suppose you were assigned the task of choosing a price that maximizes economic surplus in a market. What price would you choose? Why?

4A.3 Consumer surplus is used as a measure of a consumer's net benefit from purchasing a good or service. Explain why consumer surplus is a measure of net benefit.

4A.4 Why would economists use the term *deadweight loss* to describe the effect on consumer surplus and producer surplus from a price control?

Problems and Applications

4A.5 Suppose that you have been hired to analyze the effect on employment from the imposition of a minimum wage in the labor market. Further suppose that you estimate the demand and supply functions for labor, where L stands for the quantity of labor (measured in thousands of workers) and W stands for the wage rate (measured in dollars per hour):

$$\text{Demand: } L^D = 100 - 4W$$

$$\text{Supply: } L^S = 6W$$

First, calculate the free market equilibrium wage and quantity of labor. Now suppose the proposed minimum wage is $12. How large will the surplus of labor in this market be?

4A.6 The following graphs illustrate the markets for two different types of labor. Suppose that an identical minimum wage is imposed in both markets. In which market will the minimum wage have the largest impact on employment? Why?

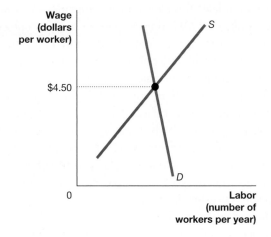

4A.7 Suppose that you are the vice president of operations of a manufacturing firm that sells an industrial lubricant in a competitive market. Further suppose that your economist gives you the following demand and supply functions:

$$\text{Demand: } Q^D = 45 - 2P$$

$$\text{Supply: } Q^S = -15 + P$$

What is the consumer surplus in this market? What is the producer surplus?

4A.8 The following graph shows a market in which a price floor of $3.00 per unit has been imposed. Calculate the values of each of the following.

a. The deadweight loss
b. The transfer of producer surplus to consumers or the transfer of consumer surplus to producers
c. Producer surplus after the price floor is imposed
d. Consumer surplus after the price floor is imposed

4A.9 Construct a table like the one in this appendix on page 144 but assume that the rent ceiling is $2,000 rather than $1,500.

5

The Economics of Health Care

Where Will You Find Health Insurance?

When Donald Trump took office as president in January 2017, he pledged to "repeal and replace" the Patient Protection and Affordable Care Act (ACA). The ACA was enacted by President Barack Obama and Congress in 2010 and is often referred to as "Obamacare." During 2017, two bills to revise the ACA failed in Congress, reflecting the lack of political consensus about the role of the federal government in the health care system. One controversial feature of the ACA was the fine imposed on individuals who do not have health insurance. In 2017, if you did not have health insurance, you were fined $695 or 2.5 percent of your income, whichever amount was higher. Many young, healthy individuals chose to pay the fine, which was typically lower than the premiums they would have to pay to buy health insurance.

This outcome was bad news for companies like Humana that sell insurance policies on the health insurance marketplaces established by the ACA. Under the ACA, insurance companies were not allowed to charge higher premiums for older people or people with chronic medical problems ("preexisting conditions"). Insurance companies were also required to include in every policy coverage for contraceptives, physical examinations, tests to screen for diseases, and certain other services without any additional charge to the policyholder. If you did not expect to use those services, you might prefer to buy a policy with more limited coverage. Insurance companies would be able to charge lower premiums for such policies, but weren't allowed to offer them under the ACA.

As more younger and healthier people did not buy individual health insurance policies, the remaining consumers on the health insurance marketplaces became, on average, older and less healthy—and more likely to file claims with the insurance companies. If Humana and other insurance companies responded by raising their premiums, they ran the risk of even fewer young and healthy people buying policies, which would require further premium increases, and so on. Humana and some other companies responded by leaving the insurance marketplaces. In 2016, 85 percent of people enrolled in the health insurance marketplaces had

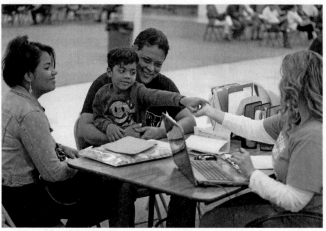

e Raedle/Getty Images

a choice of at least three insurance companies from which to buy a policy; in 2017, only 57 percent had that choice. In more than 1,000 counties nationwide, only one insurance company was left offering policies on the marketplaces.

Some people participate in their employers' health insurance plan rather than buy an individual policy on the health insurance marketplaces. But as the costs of medical services continue to rise, employers are increasing the amounts they deduct from worker paychecks to pay for the insurance, and they are offering plans with higher deductibles, which means workers are paying more before insurance begins covering their medical expenses.

The increasing health care costs individuals and businesses face are reflected in trends in health care spending in the overall economy, which increased from about 5 percent of gross domestic product (GDP) in 1960 to more than 18 percent in 2017. In this chapter, we will discuss the role economic analysis can play in the debate over health care policy in the United States.

Sources: Anna Wilde Mathews and Stephanie Armour, "Humana's Decision to Pull Out of Health Exchanges Pressures Republicans," *Wall Street Journal*, February 15, 2017; Zachary Tracer, "Trump Points to Humana Exit from Obamacare as Sign of Failure," bloomberg.com, February 14, 2017; Cynthia Cox et al., "2017 Premium Changes and Insurer Participation in the Affordable Care Act's Health Insurance Marketplaces," kff.org, November 1, 2016; and U.S. Centers for Medicare & Medicaid Studies, "National Health Expenditure Data," www.cms.gov.

Chapter Outline & Learning Objectives

5.1 The Improving Health of People in the United States,
Use data to discuss trends in U.S. health over time.

5.2 Health Care around the World,
Compare the health care systems and health care outcomes in the United States and other countries.

5.3 Information Problems and Externalities in the Market for Health Care,
Define information problems and externalities and explain how they affect the market for health care.

5.4 The Debate over Health Care Policy in the United States,
Explain the major issues involved in the debate over health care policy in the United States.

Economics in Your Life & Career

Is Your Take-Home Pay Affected by What Your Employer Spends on Your Health Insurance?

If you work for a firm that offers health insurance, the firm will withhold some amount from each of your paychecks to pay for the insurance. Typically, firms pay the majority of the cost of health insurance for their employees. In 2016, on average, employees paid only 18 percent of the cost of coverage for themselves or 29 percent of the cost of coverage for their family. Your paycheck probably doesn't show the amount your employer pays on your behalf for health insurance, but does that amount affect your take-home pay? As you read this chapter, try to answer this question. You can check your answer against the one we provide on **page 173** at the end of this chapter.

Source: The Kaiser Family Foundation and Health Research and Educational Trust, *Employer Health Benefits, 2016 Annual Survey*, September 14, 2016.

Health care Goods and services, such as prescription drugs, consultations with a doctor, and surgeries, that are intended to maintain or improve a person's health.

Health care refers to goods and services, such as prescription drugs, consultations with a doctor, and surgeries, that are intended to maintain or improve a person's health. Health care makes up more than one-sixth of the U.S. economy—about the size of the entire economy of France. Improvements in health care are an important part of the tremendous increase in living standards people in the United States and other high-income countries have experienced over the past 100 years. Health care has seen rapid technological change, with new products, such as MRI units and other diagnostic equipment; prescription drugs to treat cancer, high blood pressure, diabetes, and AIDS; vaccinations for meningitis and other illnesses; and new surgical techniques, such as cardiac catheterizations for treatment of heart disease.

Health care is provided through markets, just as are most other goods and services, such as smartphones and haircuts. So, we can apply to health care the tools of economic analysis we used in previous chapters. But the government plays a larger role in the market for health care than it does in other markets. In the United States, doctors and hospitals that supply most health care are primarily private firms, but the government provides some health care services directly through the Veterans Health Administration, which is part of the U.S. Department of Veterans Affairs, and indirectly through the Medicare and Medicaid programs. In addition, under the Affordable Care Act (ACA), the government regulates the health insurance policies that insurance companies offer.

In addition to having a large role for government, the market for health care differs from most markets in other ways. Most importantly, a typical consumer of health care doesn't pay the full price for that care. Most people have private health insurance, either provided through their employers or purchased on the government-run health insurance marketplaces, or they are enrolled in the Medicare or Medicaid programs. Consumers who have insurance make different decisions about the quantity of health care they wish to consume than they would if they were paying the full cost of the services. So, to analyze the market for health care, we need to use economic tools beyond those introduced in previous chapters. We begin our analysis of health care with an overview of health care around the world.

5.1 The Improving Health of People in the United States

LEARNING OBJECTIVE: Use data to discuss trends in U.S. health over time.

Two hundred years ago, the whole world was very poor by modern standards. Today, an average person in a high-income country has a standard of living well beyond what even the richest people in the past could have imagined. One aspect of this higher standard of living is the improved health the average person enjoys. For example, in the late 1700s, England had the highest level of income per person of any large country. But the average person in England had a short life span, and many people suffered from diseases—such as cholera, yellow fever, dysentery, and smallpox—that have disappeared from high-income countries today. The average life expectancy at birth was only 38 years, and 30 percent of the population died before reaching age 30. Even people who survived to age 20 could expect to live only an average of 34 more years. Today, the average life expectancy at birth in the United Kingdom and other high-income countries is around 80 years. People in eighteenth-century England were also short by modern standards. The average height of an adult male was 5 feet, 5 inches compared with 5 feet, 9 inches today.

In this section, we discuss the health of people in the United States. In Section 5.2, we compare the health care systems in the United States and other countries.

Variable	1850	2016
Life expectancy at birth	38.3 years	78.8 years
Average height (adult males)	5'7"	5'9.3"
Infant mortality (death of a child under 1 year of age)	228.9 per 1,000 live births	5.8 per 1,000 live births

Note: The data on height for 1850 include only native-born white and black male citizens. The data on height for 2016 were gathered in 2007–2010 and represent the median height of adult males 20 years and older.

Sources: Susan B. Carter et al., eds., *Historical Statistics of the United States: Millennium Edition*; U.S. National Center for Health Statistics, *Anthropometric Reference Data for Children and Adults: United States, 2007–2010*, October 2012; and Centers for Disease Control and Prevention, *National Vital Statistics Reports*, various issues.

Changes over Time in U.S. Health

When economists measure changes over time in the standard of living in a country, they usually look first at increases in income per person. However, changes in health are also important because health is an essential part of a person's well-being and, therefore, of his or her standard of living. The health of the average person in the United States improved significantly during the 1800s and 1900s, and by and large, it continues to improve today.

Table 5.1 compares three indicators of health in the United States in 1850 and 2016. Individuals in the United States today are taller, live much longer, and are much less likely to die in the first months of life than was true 165 years ago. Economists often use height as a measure of long-run changes in the average well-being of a population. A person's height depends partly on genetics—that is, tall parents tend to have tall children—but also on a person's *net nutritional status*. Net nutritional status depends on a person's food intake relative to the work the person has to perform, whether the person is able to remain warm in cold weather, and the diseases to which the person is exposed. Over time, people in the United States and other high-income countries have, on average, become taller, which is an indication that their nutritional status has improved.   **MyLab Economics** Concept Check

Reasons for Long-Run Improvements in U.S. Health

For most of the country's history, the health of people in the United States has steadily improved, with life expectancies increasing and death rates decreasing. Panel (a) of Figure 5.1 shows for the years 1900–2016 the increase in life expectancy and the decline in the mortality rate, or death rate, measured as deaths per 100,000 people. Note that the mortality rate is "age adjusted," which means that it is not affected by changes in the number of people in each age group. Life expectancy at birth in the United States increased from 47.3 years in 1900 to 78.8 years in 2016. Panel (b) shows for recent years the change in the overall mortality rate of the U.S. population, measured as deaths per 100,000 people, and the age-adjusted mortality rates for several diseases. In the panel, the mortality rates in 1981 are set equal to 100, and the rates for 2015 are measured relative to their 1981 levels. The overall mortality rate decreased by more than 25 percent between 1981 and 2015. Over this same period, deaths from cancer and from cardiovascular disease, such as heart attacks and strokes, declined significantly. Cancer deaths were 23 percent lower in 2015 than they were in 1981, while deaths from cardiovascular disease declined by 60 percent. Deaths from diabetes and kidney disease both increased during this period, largely due to the effects of increasing obesity. The overall decline in death rates in the United States since 1981 has been due to changes in lifestyle, particularly a decline in smoking, and advances in new diagnostic equipment, prescription drugs, and surgical techniques.

What explains increases in life expectancy and declines in death rates over the longer time span since 1850? Improvements in sanitation and in the distribution of food during the late 1800s and early 1900s led to better health during that period. More generally, the late Nobel Laureate Robert Fogel of the University of Chicago and Roderick Floud of Gresham College, along with coauthors, described a process by which better health makes it possible for people to work harder as they become taller, stronger, and

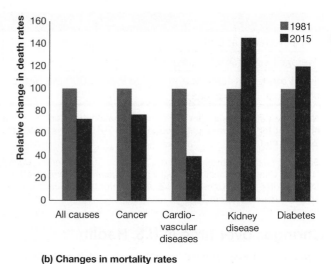

(a) Life expectancy at birth and the death rate per 100,000 people in the United States

(b) Changes in mortality rates

MyLab Economics Animation

Figure 5.1 **The Improving Health of the U.S. Population**

Panel (a) shows that since 1900, life expectancy has increased and mortality rates have decreased in the United States. Panel (b) shows that since 1981, there have been significant decreases in rates of death due to cardiovascular diseases and cancer. Rates of death due to kidney disease and diabetes have increased, primarily because of an increase in obesity. Note that in panel (a), the increase in mortality and decrease in life expectancy in 1918 are due to the severe influenza epidemic of that year.

Sources: For panel (a): Susan B. Carter et al., eds., *Historical Statistics of the United States: Millennium Edition*, Series Ab644; and Centers for Disease Control and Prevention, *National Vital Statistics Reports*, various issues; for panel (b): Centers for Disease Control and Prevention, *National Vital Statistics Reports*, various issues; and Jiaquan Xu, et al., "National Center for Health Statistics, Data Brief 267: Mortality in the United States, 2015," December 2016.

more resistant to disease. Working harder raises a country's total income, making it possible for the country to afford better sanitation, more food, and a better system for distributing the food. In effect, improving health shifts out a country's production possibilities frontier. Higher incomes also allow the country to devote more resources to research and development, including medical research. The United States has been a pioneer in the development of medical technology, new surgical techniques, and new pharmaceuticals, which have played important roles in lengthening life spans and reducing the death toll from diseases.

MyLab Economics Study Plan

MyLab Economics Concept Check

5.2 Health Care around the World

LEARNING OBJECTIVE: Compare the health care systems and health care outcomes in the United States and other countries.

In the United States, private firms provide most health care, through either doctors' practices or hospitals. The main exception is the care the government provides through the network of hospitals operated by the federal government's Veterans Health Administration, although some cities also own and operate hospitals. Governments in most countries outside the United States have a more substantial direct role in paying for or providing health care. Policymakers and economists debate the effects of greater government involvement in the health care system on health outcomes such as life expectancy, infant mortality, and successful treatment of diseases.

The U.S. Health Care System

One important difference among health care systems in different countries is the way people pay for their health care. Most people in the United States have *health insurance* that helps them pay their medical bills. **Health insurance** is a contract under which a buyer agrees to make payments, or *premiums*, in exchange for the provider's agreeing to pay some or all of the buyer's medical bills. Figure 5.2 shows the sources of health insurance in the United States in 2016. About 49 percent of people received health insurance through their employer, and about 7 percent directly purchased an individual or

Health insurance A contract under which a buyer agrees to make payments, or *premiums*, in exchange for the provider's agreeing to pay some or all of the buyer's medical bills.

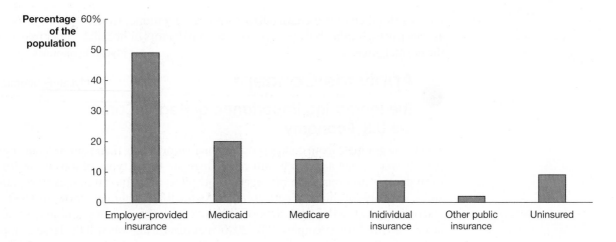

MyLab Economics Animation

Figure 5.2   **Sources of Health Insurance in the United States, 2016**

In 2016, about 49 percent of people received health insurance through their employer and about 7 percent directly purchased an individual or family health insurance policy from an insurance company. About 35 percent of people received health insurance through a government program, including Medicaid, Medicare, and other public insurance (including the program run by the Department of Veterans Affairs). About 9 percent of people were uninsured.

Note: Because some people have more than one type of health insurance, the sum of the values for each category shown is greater than 100 percent.

Source: Kaiser Family Foundation estimates based on data in U.S. Census Bureau, *Current Population Survey*, March 2017.

family health insurance policy from an insurance company, often using the state health insurance marketplaces Congress established under the Affordable Care Act. About 35 percent of people received health insurance through a government program including Medicaid, Medicare, and the program run by the Department of Veterans Affairs.

Most people who have private health insurance receive it through their employer. According to a survey of employers by the Kaiser Family Foundation, in 2016, 98 percent of firms employing more than 200 workers and 55 percent of firms employing between 3 and 199 workers offered health insurance as a fringe benefit (that is, a type of non-wage compensation) to their employees. Private health insurance companies can be either not-for-profit firms, such as some of the Blue Cross and Blue Shield organizations, or for-profit firms, such as Humana, Aetna, and John Hancock, which typically also sell other types of insurance. Private health insurance companies sell *group plans* to employers to cover all of their employees and individual plans directly to the public. Some health insurance plans reimburse doctors and hospitals on a **fee-for-service** basis, which means that doctors and hospitals receive a payment for each service they provide. Other health insurance plans are organized as *health maintenance organizations* (HMOs), which typically reimburse doctors mainly by paying a flat fee per patient rather than paying a fee for each individual office visit or other service provided.

Fee-for-service A system under which doctors and hospitals receive a payment for each service they provide.

About 9 percent of people were not covered by health insurance in 2016. This percentage was lower than in previous years, partly as a result of Congress passing the Affordable Care Act, but still represented more than 28 million uninsured people. Many people lack health insurance because their incomes are low, and they believe they cannot afford to buy private health insurance, even with government subsidies. Some low-income people either do not qualify for Medicaid or choose not to participate in that program. More than 70 percent of uninsured people live in families in which at least one member has a job. These individuals either were not offered health insurance through their employers or chose not to purchase it. Some young people opt out of employer-provided health insurance because they are healthy and do not believe that the cost of the premium their employer charges for the insurance is worth the benefit of having the insurance. More than half the uninsured were younger than age 35. Although most large firms offer their employees health insurance, fewer than two-thirds accept it. The remaining employees are covered by a spouse's policy, are not eligible for coverage, or have decided to go uninsured because they do not want to pay the premium for the insurance. The uninsured must pay for their own medical bills *out of pocket*, with money from their own income, just as they pay their other bills, or receive care from doctors or hospitals either free or below the normal price.   **MyLab Economics** Concept Check

Apply the Concept

MyLab Economics Video

The Increasing Importance of Health Care in the U.S. Economy

When you graduate from college, you are much more likely than your parents or grandparents were to get a job in health care. There are many types of jobs in health care, from doctors and nurses to managers at hospitals and nursing homes to researchers and salespeople at pharmaceutical firms. As the following maps show, in 1990, manufacturing was the largest source of employment in most states, and in no state was health care the largest employer. By 2000, manufacturing was still the largest employer in 27 states, but health care had become the largest employer in two states. The results for 2016 are strikingly different, with manufacturing the largest employer in only 7 states and health care the largest employer in 35 states.

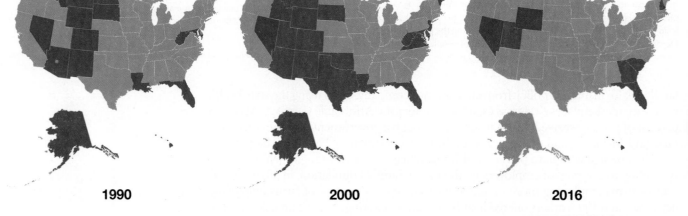

| 1990 | 2000 | 2016 |

■ Manufacturing   ■ Retail trade   ■ Accommodation and food services   ■ Health care and social assistance

In 1990, almost twice as many people in the United States worked in manufacturing as worked in health care. Today, employment in health care has doubled, while employment in manufacturing has declined by more than 30 percent. And these trends are likely to continue. The U.S. Bureau of Labor Statistics forecasts that 13 of the 20 fastest-growing occupations over the next 10 years will be in health care.

What explains these trends? We discuss explanations for rising health care spending in the United States in Section 5.4. For now, note that the growth of employment in health care is similar to that in other service industries, such as retail stores and restaurants, and that the growth of employment in the health care and service industries is much faster than that in goods-producing industries, such as manufacturing. In addition, there is evidence that as people's incomes grow, their demand for health care grows faster than their demand for most other goods and services. The average age of the U.S. population is also increasing, and older people have a greater demand for health care. Finally, the Affordable Care Act has increased the demand for health care among low-income people in two ways: by providing subsidies to buy health insurance for people whose incomes fall below a certain level and by expanding the Medicaid system.

Whatever changes Congress may make to the Affordable Care Act, it seems likely that health care will continue to be a booming sector of the economy and an important source of new jobs in the coming decades.

Sources: U.S. Bureau of Labor Statistics; U.S. Census Bureau; Rani Molla, "How America's Top Industries Have Changed," *Wall Street Journal*, July 28, 2014; and "Why Nurses Are the New Auto Workers," *Economist*, July 25, 2014.

MyLab Economics Study Plan   **Your Turn:** Test your understanding by doing related problem 2.9 on page 175 at the end of this chapter.

The Health Care Systems of Canada, Japan, and the United Kingdom

In many countries, such as Canada, Japan, and the United Kingdom, the government either supplies health care directly by operating hospitals and employing doctors and nurses or pays for most health care expenses, even if hospitals are not government owned and doctors are not government employees. In this section, we look briefly at the health care systems in these three countries.

Canada Canada has a **single-payer health care system**, in which the government provides *national health insurance* to all Canadian residents. Each of the 10 Canadian provinces has its own system, although each system must meet the federal government's requirement of covering 100 percent of the cost of all medically necessary procedures. Individuals pay nothing for doctor's visits or hospital stays; instead, they pay for medical care indirectly through the taxes they pay to the provincial and federal governments. As in the United States, most doctors and hospitals are private businesses, but unlike in the United States, doctors and hospitals are required to accept the fees that are set by the government. Also as in the United States, doctors and hospitals are typically reimbursed on a fee-for-service basis.

Japan Japan has a system of *universal health insurance* under which every resident of the country is required to enroll either in one of the many nonprofit health insurance societies that are organized by industries or professions or in the health insurance program provided by the national government. The system is funded by a combination of premiums paid by employees and firms and a payroll tax similar to the tax that funds the Medicare program in the United States. Unlike the Canadian system, the Japanese system requires substantial *copayments*, under which patients pay as much as 30 percent of their medical bills, while health insurance pays for the rest. Japanese health insurance does not pay for most preventive care, such as annual physical exams, or for medical expenses connected with pregnancies, unless complications result. Health insurance in the United States and Canada typically does cover these expenses. As in the United States, most doctors in Japan do not work for the government, and there are many privately owned hospitals. The number of government-run hospitals, though, is greater than in the United States.

The United Kingdom In the United Kingdom, the government, through the National Health Service (NHS), owns nearly all hospitals and directly employs nearly all doctors. (Note that England, Scotland, Wales, and Northern Ireland run their health care systems independently, although their main features are the same.) This system contrasts with those in the United States, Canada, and Japan, where the government employs relatively few doctors and owns relatively few hospitals. Because there are few private insurance plans and private hospitals in the United Kingdom, its health care system is often called **socialized medicine**. With 1.4 million employees, the NHS is the largest government-run health care system in the world. Apart from a small copayment for prescriptions, the NHS supplies health care services without charge to patients and receives its funding from income taxes. The NHS concentrates on preventive care and care for acute conditions. Nonemergency care, also called *elective care*—such as hip replacements, knee surgery following a sports injury, or reconstructive surgery following a mastectomy—is a low priority. The NHS's goals result in waiting lists for elective care that can be very long, with patients sometimes waiting a year or more for a procedure that would be available in a few weeks or less in the United States. To avoid the waiting lists, more than 10 percent of the population also has private health insurance, frequently provided by employers, which the insured use to pay for elective care. The NHS essentially trades off broader coverage for longer waiting times and performing fewer procedures, particularly nonemergency surgeries.   **MyLab Economics** Concept Check

Single-payer health care system A system, such as the one in Canada, in which the government provides health insurance to all of the country's residents.

Socialized medicine A health care system under which the government owns most of the hospitals and employs most of the doctors.

MyLab Economics Animation

Figure 5.3

Levels of Income per Person and Spending per Person on Health Care

The United States is well above the line showing the average relationship between income per person and health care spending per person, which indicates that the United States spends more on health care per person than do other countries, even taking into account the relatively high levels of income in the United States.

Note: Income per person is measured as real GDP per person.

Source: Organization for Economic Co-operation and Development, *OECD Health Data 2016,* November 2016.

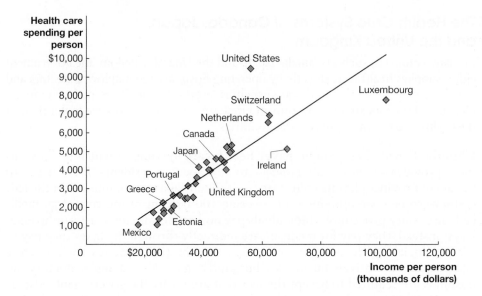

Comparing Health Care Outcomes around the World

We have seen that the way health care systems are organized varies significantly across countries. Health care outcomes and the amounts countries spend on health care are also quite different. In Figure 5.3, each green diamond represents a combination of health care spending per person and income per person for 35 high-income countries. The figure shows that, typically, the higher the level of income per person in a country, the higher the level of spending per person on health care. This result is not surprising because health care is a *normal good.* We know that as income increases, so does spending on normal goods (see Chapter 3, Section 3.1). The line in the figure shows the average relationship between income per person and health care spending per person. The diamonds for most countries are fairly close to the line, but note that the diamond representing the United States is significantly above the line. Being well above the line indicates that health care spending per person in the United States is higher than in other countries, even taking into account the relatively high income levels in the United States. In Section 5.4, we will discuss explanations for the high level of health care spending in the United States.

Has the high level of health care spending in the United States resulted in better health outcomes? Are people in the United States healthier, and do they have their medical problems addressed more rapidly than do people in other countries? Table 5.2 compares several health outcomes for the countries that are members of the Organization for Economic Co-operation and Development (OECD), a group of 35 high-income countries. The table shows that the United States does relatively poorly with respect to infant mortality, while it does somewhat below average with respect to life expectancy at birth but about average with respect to life expectancy at age 65. People in the United States are significantly more likely to be obese than are people in other high-income countries, which can lead to developing diabetes and other health problems.

The United States rates well in the availability of medical equipment that can be used in diagnosing and treating illness. Table 5.2 shows that the United States has more than twice as many MRI units per person and over 50 percent more CT scanners per person than the average of high-income countries, although the United States has relatively fewer of these machines than does Japan. The United States also appears to do well in cancer treatment, with a lower rate of cancer deaths, particularly given that people in the United States are more likely to develop cancer, and a relatively low mortality ratio from cancer. The mortality ratio measures the rate at which people die from cancer relative to the rate at which they are diagnosed with cancer. A low cancer mortality ratio indicates that the U.S. health care system does a relatively good job of reducing the death rate among people diagnosed with cancer. **MyLab Economics** Concept Check

Table 5.2

Health Outcomes in High-Income Countries

Health Care Outcome	United States	Canada	Japan	United Kingdom	OECD Average
Life Expectancy					
Life expectancy at birth	78.8 years	81.0 years	83.7 years	81.4 years	80.6 years
Male life expectancy at age 65	18.0 years	18.8 years	19.3 years	18.8 years	17.9 years
Female life expectancy at age 65	20.5 years	21.7 years	24.2 years	21.3 years	21.3 years
Infant mortality (deaths per 1,000 live births)	6.0	4.9	2.1	3.9	4.0
Health Problems					
Obesity (percentage of the population with BMI > 30)	38.2%	28.0%	3.9%	25.6%	22.3%
Diagnostic Equipment					
MRI units per 1,000,000 population	38.1	8.9	51.7	6.1	15.7
CT scanners per 1,000,000 population	41.0	14.7	107.1	8.0	26.4
Cancer					
Cancer per 100,000 population	318.0	295.7	217.1	272.9	269.8
Deaths from cancer per 100,000 population	189.5	207.5	179.0	221.9	202.1
Risk of dying of cancer before age 75	11.2%	10.8%	9.3%	11.3%	11.5%
Mortality ratio for cancer	33.3%	34.9%	43.2%	40.3%	40.4%

Sources: Organization for Economic Co-operation and Development, *OECD Health Statistics, 2016*, most recent data available, typically 2014, but 2012 for the data in the last two rows on cancer; and World Health Organization, Agency for Research on Cancer, "Globocan 2012: Estimated Cancer Incidence, Mortality, and Prevalence Worldwide in 2012." For cancer data, the final column uses the average for European Union countries rather than for OECD countries. Data on death from cancers are standardized for age differences across countries.

How Useful Are Cross-Country Comparisons of Health Outcomes?

Health economists and other researchers disagree strongly about the usefulness of cross-country comparisons of health outcomes in measuring the effectiveness of different health care systems. Here are some factors that make cross-country comparisons in health outcomes difficult:

- **Data problems.** Countries do not always collect data on diseases and other health problems in the same way. So, there are not enough consistent data available to compare health outcomes for more than a few diseases.
- **Problems with measuring health care delivery.** The easiest outcomes to measure are deaths because a specific event has occurred. So, measures of life expectancy, infant mortality, and mortality rates from some diseases, such as cancer, are available across countries. But much of health care involves treatment for injuries, simple surgeries, writing of pharmaceutical prescriptions, and other activities for which outcomes are difficult to measure. For example, although the United Kingdom does well in many of the measures shown in Table 5.2, patients often have long waiting times for elective surgeries, such as joint replacements, that can be arranged much more quickly in some other countries, including the United States. Economists have difficulty measuring the cost to patients of these waiting times.
- **Problems with distinguishing health care effectiveness from lifestyle choices.** Health outcomes depend partly on the effectiveness of doctors and hospitals in delivering medical services. But they also depend on the choices of individuals. For example, in the United States, the high rates of obesity and hospitalizations for

diabetes—which can be a complication of obesity—may be caused more by the decisions individuals make about diet and exercise than by the effectiveness of the U.S. health care system.

- **Problems with determining consumer preferences.** In most markets, we can assume that the quantities and prices we observe reflect the interactions of the preferences of consumers (demand) with the costs to firms of producing goods and services (supply). Given their incomes and preferences, consumers compare the prices of different goods and services when making their buying decisions. The prices firms charge represent the costs of providing the good or service. In the market for health care, however, the government plays the dominant role in supplying the service in most countries other than the United States, so the cost of the service is not fully represented in its price, which in some countries is zero. Even in countries where consumers must pay for medical services, the prices they pay usually do not represent the cost of providing the service. In the United States, for instance, consumers with private health insurance typically pay only 10 to 20 percent of the price as a copayment. For these reasons, it is difficult to determine whether some countries do a better job than others in providing health care services whose cost and effectiveness are consistent with consumer preferences.

MyLab Economics Study Plan   **MyLab Economics** Concept Check

5.3 Information Problems and Externalities in the Market for Health Care

LEARNING OBJECTIVE: Define information problems and externalities and explain how they affect the market for health care.

Asymmetric information A situation in which one party to an economic transaction has less information than the other party.

The market for health care is significantly affected by the problem of **asymmetric information**, which occurs when one party to an economic transaction has less information than the other party. Understanding the concept of asymmetric information can help us analyze the actions of buyers and sellers of health care and health insurance and the actions of the government in the health care market. The consequences of asymmetric information may be easier to understand if we first consider its effect on the market for used automobiles, which is the market in which economists first began to carefully study this problem.

Adverse Selection and the Market for "Lemons"

Nobel Laureate George Akerlof of Georgetown University pointed out that the seller of a used car will always have more information on the true condition of the car than will potential buyers. For example, a car that has not had its oil changed regularly can have damage that even a trained mechanic may have difficulty detecting.

If potential buyers of used cars know that they will have difficulty distinguishing good used cars from bad used cars, or "lemons," they will take this fact into account in the prices they are willing to pay. Consider the following simple example: Suppose that half of the 2015 Honda Civics offered for sale have been well maintained and are good, reliable used cars. The other half have been poorly maintained and are lemons that will be unreliable. Suppose that potential buyers of 2015 Civics would be willing to pay $10,000 for a reliable one but only $5,000 for an unreliable one. The sellers know how well they have maintained their cars and whether they are reliable, but the buyers do not have this information and so have no way of distinguishing the reliable used cars from the unreliable ones.

In this situation, buyers will generally offer a price somewhere between the price they would be willing to pay for a good car and the price they would be willing to pay for a lemon. With a 50–50 chance of buying a good car or a lemon, buyers might offer $7,500, which is halfway between the price they would pay if they knew for certain the car was a good one and the price they would pay if they knew it was a lemon.

Unfortunately for used car buyers, a major glitch arises at this point. From the buyers' perspective, given that they don't know whether any particular car offered for sale is a good car or a lemon, an offer of $7,500 seems reasonable. But the sellers do know whether the cars they are offering are good cars or lemons. To a seller of a good car, an offer of $7,500 is $2,500 below the true value of the car, and the seller will be reluctant to sell. But to a seller of a lemon, an offer of $7,500 is $2,500 above the true value of the car, and the seller will be quite happy to sell. As sellers of lemons take advantage of knowing more about the cars they are selling than buyers do, buyers in the used car market will fall victim to **adverse selection**: Most used cars offered for sale will be lemons. In other words, because of asymmetric information, the market has selected adversely the cars that will be offered for sale. Notice as well that the problem of adverse selection reduces the total quantity of used cars bought and sold in the market because few good cars are offered for sale.　　　　　MyLab Economics Concept Check

Adverse selection The situation in which one party to a transaction takes advantage of knowing more than the other party to the transaction.

Asymmetric Information in the Market for Health Insurance

Asymmetric information problems are particularly severe in the markets for all types of insurance, including health insurance. To understand this point, first consider how insurance works. Insurance companies provide the service of *risk pooling* when they sell policies to households. For example, if you own a $150,000 house but do not have a fire insurance policy, a fire that destroys your house can be a financial catastrophe. But an insurance company can pool the financial risk of your house burning down by selling fire insurance policies to you and thousands of other homeowners. Homeowners are willing to accept the certain cost represented by the premium they pay for insurance in return for eliminating the uncertain—but potentially very large—cost should their house burn down.

Notice that for the insurance company to cover all of its costs, the total amount it receives in premiums must be greater than the amount it pays out in claims to policyholders. To survive, insurance companies have to predict accurately the amount they are likely to pay out to policyholders. For instance, if an insurance company predicts that the houses of only 2 percent of policyholders will burn down during a year when 5 percent of houses actually burn down, the company will suffer losses. However, if the company predicts that 8 percent of houses will burn down when only 5 percent actually do, the company will have charged premiums that are too high. A company that charges premiums that are too high will lose customers to other companies and may eventually be driven out of business.

Adverse Selection in the Market for Health Insurance Health insurance companies face a key obstacle to accurately predicting the number of claims policyholders will make: Buyers of health insurance policies always know more about the state of their health—and, therefore, how likely they are to submit medical bills for payment—than do the insurance companies. In other words, insurance companies face an adverse selection problem because sick people are more likely to want health insurance than are healthy people. If insurance companies have trouble determining who is healthy and who is sick, they are likely to sell policies to more sick people than they had expected, with the result that the premiums they charge will be too low to cover their costs.

An insurance company faces a financial problem if the premiums it is charging are too low to cover the costs of the claims being submitted. The company might try to increase the premiums it charges, but this may make the adverse selection problem worse. If premiums rise, then younger, healthier people who rarely visit the doctor may respond to the increase in premiums by dropping their insurance. The higher premiums make the adverse selection problem worse for the insurance company because it will have fewer healthy policyholders than it had before the premium increase. The situation is similar to that facing a used car buyer who knows that adverse selection is a problem in the used car market and decides to compensate for it by lowering the price he is willing to pay for a car. The lower price will reduce the number of sellers of good cars willing to sell to him, making his adverse selection problem worse.

One way to deal with the problem of adverse selection is for the government to require every person to buy insurance. Doing so would increase the ability of insurance companies to engage in risk pooling. Most states require all drivers to buy automobile insurance so that both high-risk and low-risk drivers will carry insurance. The Patient Protection and Affordable Care Act (ACA), passed in 2010, requires residents of the United States to buy health insurance or pay a fine. This provision of the law is known as the *individual mandate* and has been controversial. We discuss it further in Section 5.4.

Moral Hazard in the Market for Health Insurance The insurance market is subject to a second consequence of asymmetric information. **Moral hazard** refers to actions people take after they have entered into a transaction that make the other party to the transaction worse off. Moral hazard in the insurance market occurs when people change their behavior after becoming insured. For example, once a firm has taken out a fire insurance policy on a warehouse, its managers might be reluctant to install an expensive sprinkler system. Similarly, someone with health insurance may visit the doctor for treatment of a cold or other minor illness, which he would not do if he lacked insurance. Or someone with health insurance might engage in risky activities, such as riding a motorcycle, which she would not do if she lacked insurance.

One way to think about the basic moral hazard problem with insurance is to note that normally there are two parties to an economic transaction: the buyer and the seller. The insurance company becomes a third party to the purchase of medical services because the insurance company, rather than the patient, pays for some or all of the service. For this reason, economists refer to traditional health insurance as a *third-party payer* system. Because of this system, consumers of health care do not pay a price that reflects the full cost of providing the service. This lower price leads consumers to use more health care than they otherwise would.

> **Moral hazard** Actions people take after they have entered into a transaction that make the other party to the transaction worse off.

Don't Let This Happen to You

Don't Confuse Adverse Selection with Moral Hazard

The two key consequences of asymmetric information are adverse selection and moral hazard. It is easy to mix up these concepts. One way to keep the concepts straight is to remember that:

- Adverse selection refers to what happens at the time of entering into a transaction. An example would be an insurance company selling a life insurance policy to a terminally ill person because the company lacks full information on the person's health.

- Moral hazard refers to what happens after entering into a transaction, such as a nonsmoker buying a life insurance policy and then starting to smoke four packs of cigarettes a day.

It may help to remember that *a* comes before *m* alphabetically, just as *a*dverse selection comes before *m*oral hazard.

MyLab Economics Study Plan

Your Turn: Test your understanding by doing related problems 3.9 and 3.10 on page 176 at the end of this chapter.

Third-party payer health insurance can also lead to another consequence of moral hazard, known as the *principal–agent problem*, because some doctors may be led to take actions that are not necessarily in the best interests of their patients, such as increasing their incomes by prescribing unnecessary tests or other treatments for which the doctors receive payment. The **principal–agent problem** results from agents—in this case, doctors—pursuing their own interests rather than the interests of the principals—in this case, patients—who hired them. If patients had to pay the full price of lab tests, MRI scans, and other procedures, they would be more likely to question whether the procedures were really necessary. Because health insurance pays most of the bill for these procedures, patients are more likely to accept them. Note that the fee-for-service aspect of most health insurance in the United States can make the principal–agent problem worse because doctors and hospitals are paid for each service performed, whether or not the service was necessary or effective.

The number of medical procedures performed in the United States has been continually increasing. Many doctors argue that the increasing number of medical

> **Principal–agent problem** A problem caused by agents pursuing their own interests rather than the interests of the principals who hired them.

procedures is not the result of third-party payer health insurance. Instead, the increase is due to the improved effectiveness of the procedures in diagnosing illness and the tendency of some doctors to practice "defensive medicine" because they fear that if they fail to correctly diagnose an illness, a patient may file a *malpractice lawsuit* against them.

How Insurance Companies Deal with Adverse Selection and Moral Hazard Insurance companies can take steps to reduce adverse selection and moral hazard problems. For example, insurance companies can use deductibles and coinsurance (or copayments) to reduce moral hazard. A deductible requires the policyholder to pay a certain dollar amount before the insurance begins paying claims. With coinsurance, the insurance company pays only a percentage of any claim. Suppose you have a health insurance policy with a $200 deductible and 20 percent coinsurance, and you receive a medical bill for $1,000. You must pay the first $200 of the bill and 20 percent of the remaining $800. Deductibles and coinsurance make the policies less attractive to people who intend to file many claims, thereby reducing the adverse selection problem. Deductibles and coinsurance also provide policyholders with an incentive to avoid filing claims, thereby reducing the moral hazard problem. Deductibles have been increasing in many employer-provided health insurance plans. According to a survey by the Kaiser Family Foundation, in 2006 only 10 percent of workers were enrolled in plans with deductibles of $1,000 per year or more, but by 2016, 51 percent of workers were enrolled in such plans. Notice, though, that deductibles and coinsurance reduce, but do not eliminate, adverse selection and moral hazard. People who anticipate having large medical bills will still have a greater incentive than healthy people to buy insurance, and people with health insurance are still more likely to visit the doctor even for a minor illness than are people without health insurance.

Prior to the passage of the ACA in 2010, to reduce the problem of adverse selection, insurance companies typically limited coverage of *preexisting conditions*, which are medical problems, such as heart disease or cancer, that the buyer already has before purchasing insurance. Critics argue that by excluding coverage of preexisting conditions, insurance companies were forcing people with serious illnesses to pay the entire amount of what might be very large medical bills or to go without medical care. Some people with chronic or terminal illnesses found it impossible to buy an individual health insurance policy. The insurance companies argued that if they did not exclude coverage of preexisting conditions, they might have been unable to offer any health insurance policies or might have been forced to charge premiums that were so high as to cause relatively healthy people to not renew their policies, which would have made adverse selection problems worse. To some extent, the debate over coverage of preexisting conditions is a normative one. Ordinarily, in a market system, people who cannot afford a good or service must do without it. However, many people do not want others to be without health insurance because they cannot afford it. As we will discuss in the next section, Congress included significant restrictions on the ability of insurance companies to limit coverage of preexisting conditions when it passed the ACA.   **MyLab Economics** Concept Check

Externalities in the Market for Health Care

For most goods and services, we assume that the consumer receives all the benefits from consuming the good and that the firm producing the good bears all of the costs of production. Some goods or services, though, involve an *externality*, which is a benefit or cost that affects someone who is not directly involved in the production or consumption of a good or service. For example, if a utility burns coal to produce electricity, the result will be air pollution, which causes a *negative externality* because people with asthma or other breathing problems may bear a cost even though they were not involved in buying or selling the electricity that caused the pollution. College education may result in a *positive externality* because college-educated people are less likely to commit crimes and, by being better-informed voters, are more likely to contribute to better government policies. So, although you receive most of the benefits of your college education, other people also receive some of the benefits.

Externalities interfere with the economic efficiency of a market equilibrium. A competitive market achieves economic efficiency by maximizing the sum of consumer surplus and producer surplus (see Chapter 4, Section 4.1). But when there is a negative externality in production, as with air pollution, the market will produce more than the efficient quantity. When there is a positive externality in consumption, as with college educations, the market will produce less than the efficient quantity.

Many economists believe that several aspects of health care involve externalities. For example, anyone vaccinated against a communicable disease not only protects herself or himself but also reduces the chances that people who have not been vaccinated will contract the disease. The positive externality from vaccinations causes a difference between the *private benefit* from being vaccinated and the *social benefit*. The *private benefit* is the benefit you receive as a consumer of a good or service. The *social benefit* is the total benefit from consuming a good or service, and it is equal to the private benefit plus any external benefit, such as the benefit to others from a reduced chance of getting a disease for which you have been vaccinated. Because of the positive externality, the social benefit of vaccinations is greater than the private benefit.

Figure 5.4 shows the market for vaccinations. If people receiving vaccinations could capture all the benefits, the demand curve would be D_2, which represents the marginal social benefit. The actual demand curve is D_1, however, which represents only the marginal private benefit received by people getting vaccinations. The efficient equilibrium would occur at price $P_{Efficient}$ and quantity $Q_{Efficient}$. At this equilibrium, economic surplus is maximized. The market equilibrium, at price P_{Market} and quantity Q_{Market}, will not be efficient because the demand curve is above the supply curve for production of the vaccinations between Q_{Market} and $Q_{Efficient}$. That is, the marginal benefit—including the external benefit—for producing these vaccinations is greater than the marginal cost. As a result, there is a deadweight loss equal to the area of the yellow triangle. Because of the positive externality, economic efficiency would be improved if more people were vaccinated.

Figure 5.4 assumes that the market for vaccinations is like the market for goods such as hamburgers, with consumers paying the full price of the vaccinations. In practice, people with health insurance pay a reduced price for vaccinations, and the government often provides further subsidies to the firms that produce vaccines. One reason for the government subsidies is to overcome the effects of the positive externality.

Externalities are important in health care markets, though economists and policymakers continue to debate the extent to which they require significant government involvement in health care.   **MyLab Economics** Concept Check

MyLab Economics Animation

Figure 5.4

The Effect of a Positive Externality on the Market for Vaccinations

People who do not get vaccinated still benefit from other people being vaccinated. As a result, the marginal social benefit from vaccinations is greater than the marginal private benefit to people being vaccinated. Because only the marginal private benefit is represented in the market demand curve D_1, the quantity of vaccinations produced, Q_{Market}, is too low. If the market demand curve were D_2 instead of D_1, the level of vaccinations would be $Q_{Efficient}$, which is the efficient level. At the market equilibrium of Q_{Market}, there is a deadweight loss equal to the area of the yellow triangle.

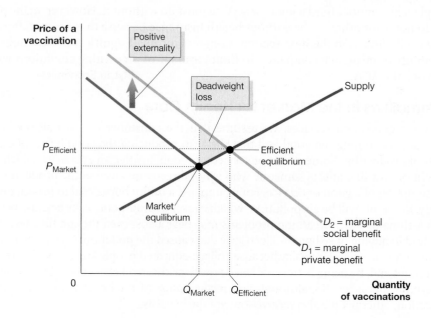

Should the Government Run the Health Care System?

Some members of Congress have proposed expanding the federal government's role in health care by adopting a system similar to the single-payer system used in Canada, under which the government would provide health care to all residents of the United States. What role the federal government should play in health care is a controversial public policy issue.

Is Health Care a Public Good? Economists categorize goods on the basis of whether they are *rival* and *excludable*. Rivalry occurs when one person consuming a unit of a good means no one else can consume it. If you consume a salad from Panera Bread, for example, no one else can consume it. Excludability means that anyone who does not pay for a good cannot consume it. If you don't pay for a salad, for example, Panera can exclude you from consuming it. A *public good* is both nonrival and non-excludable. Public goods are often, although not always, supplied by a government rather than by private firms. The classic example of a public good is national defense. Your consuming national defense does not interfere with your neighbor consuming it, so consumption is nonrival. You also cannot be excluded from consuming it, whether you pay for it or not. No private firm would be willing to supply national defense because everyone can consume national defense without paying for it.

Is health care a public good that government should supply—or, at least, pay for? Is it a private good, like furniture, clothing, or computers, that private firms should supply and consumers should pay for without government aid? Should private firms supply most health care, subject to some government regulation? Economists differ in their answers to these questions because the delivery of health care involves a number of complex issues, but we can consider briefly some of the most important points. Because public goods must be both nonrival and nonexcludable, health care does not qualify as a public good under the usual definition. More than one person cannot simultaneously "consume" the same surgical operation performed by a particular doctor in a particular hospital. And someone who will not pay for an operation can be excluded from consuming it. (Most states require hospitals to treat patients who are too poor to pay for treatment, and many doctors will treat poor people at a reduced price. But health care does not fit the definition of a public good because there is nothing about health care that keeps people who do not pay for it from being excluded from consuming it.)

Do Externalities in Health Care Justify More Government Intervention? Aspects of the delivery of health care have convinced some economists that government intervention is justified. For example, consuming certain types of health care generates positive externalities. Being vaccinated against a communicable disease, such as influenza or meningitis, reduces not only the chance that the person vaccinated will catch the disease but also the probability that an epidemic of the disease will occur. Therefore, the market may supply an inefficiently small quantity of vaccinations unless vaccinations receive a government subsidy.

Do Information Problems with Health Care Justify More Government Intervention? Information problems are also important in the market for private health insurance. Consumers who buy health insurance often know much more about the state of their health than do the companies selling health insurance. This information problem may raise costs to insurance companies when the pool of people being insured is small, making insurance companies less willing to offer health insurance to consumers the companies suspect may file too many claims. Economists debate how important information problems are in health care markets and whether government intervention is required to reduce them.

Or Should There Be Greater Reliance on Market-Based Policies? Many economists believe that market-based policies are the best approach to improving the health care system. As we saw in Table 5.2 on page 155, the United States has a mixed record on health outcomes. The United States is, however, a world leader in innovation in medical technology and prescription drugs. The market-oriented approach to reforming health care starts with the goal of improving health care outcomes while preserving incentives for U.S. firms to continue with innovations in medical screening equipment, surgical procedures, and prescription drugs. Presently, markets are delivering inaccurate signals to consumers because when buying health care, unlike when buying most other goods and services, consumers pay a price well below the true cost of providing the service. Under current tax laws, people do not pay taxes on health insurance benefits they receive from their employers, and this benefit encourages them to want generous coverage that reduces incentives to control costs. As we will discuss in Section 5.4, market-based approaches to health care reform attempt to address these issues.

It remains an open question whether the U.S. health care system will continue to move toward greater government intervention, which is the approach adopted in most other countries, or whether market-based reforms will be implemented. Because health care is so important to consumers and because health care is an increasingly large part of the U.S. economy, the role of the government in the health care system is likely to be the subject of intense debate for some time to come.

MyLab Economics Study Plan   **MyLab Economics** Concept Check

5.4 The Debate over Health Care Policy in the United States

LEARNING OBJECTIVE: Explain the major issues involved in the debate over health care policy in the United States.

Shortly after taking office in January 2009, President Barack Obama proposed far-reaching changes in the U.S. health care system. The result was the Patient Protection and Affordable Care Act (ACA), which Congress passed in March 2010. The act was controversial, with every Republican member of Congress and 34 Democratic members voting against it. Since passage of the ACA, economists have vigorously debated its effects on health care and the economy. During 2017, bills to significantly amend the ACA failed in Congress, although other proposals to amend the ACA appeared likely to follow.

Before discussing the details of the ACA and the debate over the legislation's effect, we explore the issue of rising health care costs, which played an important role in the health care debate.

The Rising Cost of Health Care

Figure 5.5 illustrates a key fact underlying the debate over health care policy in the United States: Health care's share of gross domestic product (GDP), which is the total value of output in the economy, is increasing. Panel (a) shows that spending on health care was less than 6 percent of GDP in 1965 but had risen to nearly 18 percent in 2017 and is projected to continue rising in future years. In other words, an increasing percentage of total production in the United States is being devoted to health care. Panel (b) shows increases in health care spending per person in the United States and 10 other high-income countries. Spending on health care has grown faster in the United States than in other countries.

Does it matter that spending on health care is an increasing share of total spending and output in the U.S. economy? The shares of different products in total spending change frequently. For instance, in the United States, the shares of spending on smartphones or streaming movies were much greater in 2017 than in 2010. Spending on food as a share of total spending has been declining for decades. Economists interpret these changes as reflecting in part consumers' preferences: Consumers choose to spend relatively more of their incomes on smartphones and relatively less on food. As we have seen, though, most people pay for health care by relying on third-party payers, such as employer-provided health insurance or government-provided Medicare or Medicaid. Out-of-pocket spending, spending on health care that consumers pay out of their own incomes rather than through health insurance, has been declining.

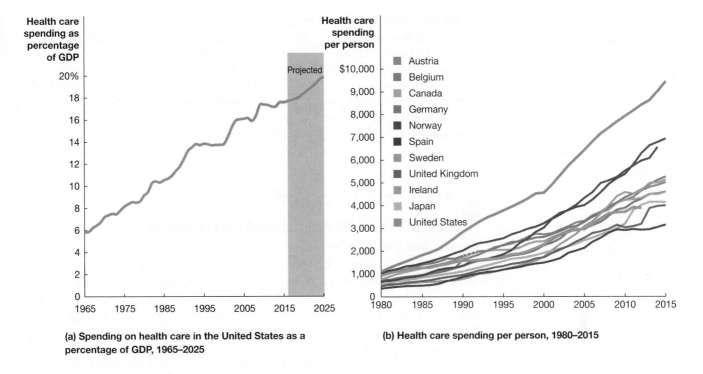

(a) Spending on health care in the United States as a percentage of GDP, 1965–2025

(b) Health care spending per person, 1980–2015

MyLab Economics Real-time Data

Figure 5.5   **Spending on Health Care around the World**

Panel (a) shows that health care spending has been a rising percentage of GDP in the United States. Health care spending rose from less than 6 percent of GDP in 1965 to nearly 18 percent in 2017 and it is projected to rise further in future years. (The projected increases are shown by the line in the shaded area.)

Panel (b) shows that health care spending per person has been growing faster in the United States than in other high-income countries.

Sources: For panel (a): U.S. Department of Health and Human Services, Centers for Medicare & Medicaid Services; for panel (b): Organization for Economic Co-operation and Development, *OECD Health Data 2016*, November 2016.

Figure 5.6 shows that out-of-pocket spending on health care as a percentage of all spending on health care has fallen steadily since 1960. In 1960, 48 percent of all health care spending was out of pocket, while today only about 10 percent is. As a result, in recent years, consumers of health care have been directly paying for only a small fraction of the true cost of providing health care, with third-party payers picking up the remainder. As average incomes rise, consumers might be expected to spend a rising share of the increase on health care. But because consumers do not pay the full cost of increases in health care spending, they may not be willing to buy as much health care as they currently receive if they had to pay the full price.

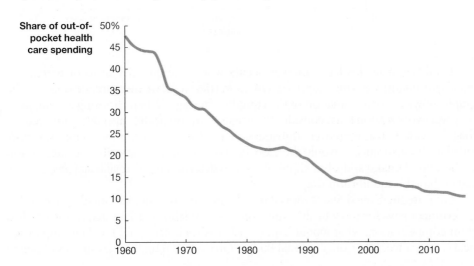

MyLab Economics Animation

Figure 5.6

The Declining Share of U.S. Out-of-Pocket Health Care Spending

Out-of-pocket spending on health care has declined sharply as a fraction of all health care spending, while the fraction of spending accounted for by third-party payers, such as firms or the government, has increased.

Source: U.S. Department of Health and Human Services, Centers for Medicare & Medicaid Services.

Because the federal and state governments in the United States pay for just over half of health care spending through Medicare, Medicaid, and other programs, increases in health care spending can cause problems for government budgets. The Medicare and Medicaid programs began in 1965. By 2017, spending on these programs had grown to 7 percent of GDP. That percentage is expected to double over the next 40 years unless health care costs begin to grow at a slower rate. Congress and the president have been struggling to find ways to pay for the projected increases in Medicare and Medicaid without severely cutting other federal spending or sharply raising taxes.   **MyLab Economics** Concept Check

Apply the Concept

MyLab Economics Video

Are U.S. Firms Handicapped by Paying for Their Employees' Health Insurance?

Some members of Congress and some business leaders argue that the high cost of health care in the United States handicaps U.S. firms in competition with foreign firms. In many countries, firms do not purchase health insurance for their workers, as most large firms do in the United States. Do foreign firms in fact have an advantage over U.S. firms because of high U.S. health care costs? We can analyze this assertion by using the demand and supply for labor.

The following figure illustrates the market for labor in a particular industry (for example, automobiles). The demand curve is downward sloping because the lower the wage, the larger the quantity of workers firms will demand. The supply curve is upward sloping because as the wage rises, more workers will want to work in this industry.

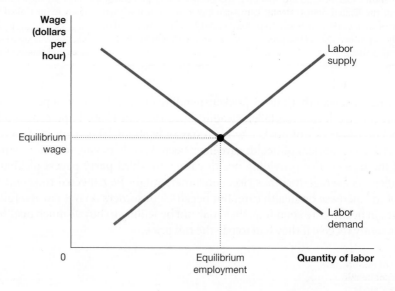

Equilibrium in this labor market occurs where the quantity of labor demanded equals the quantity of labor supplied. On the vertical axis, we measure the wage, so the graph shows the determination of the equilibrium wage. When choosing among jobs, however, workers don't just consider the wages firms offer; they also take into account *fringe benefits,* such as employer contributions to retirement accounts or employer-provided health insurance. It would therefore be more accurate to describe the intersection of the labor demand and labor supply curves as determining *the equilibrium compensation* rather than the equilibrium wage.

Suppose the United States moved to a health care system like Canada's, where the government pays for most health care from taxes. If labor markets determine equilibrium compensation, what would happen if firms no longer paid for their employees' health insurance? The Congressional Budget Office (CBO) undertakes studies of policy issues for Congress. In an overview of proposals for reforming health insurance in the United States, the CBO addressed this question:

> Some observers have asserted that domestic producers that provide health insurance to their workers face higher costs for compensation than competitors based in countries where insurance is not employment based and that fundamental changes to the health insurance system could reduce or eliminate that disadvantage. However, such a cost reduction is unlikely to occur. . . . The equilibrium level of overall compensation in the economy is determined by the supply of and the demand for labor. Fringe benefits (such as health insurance) are just part of that compensation. Consequently, the costs of fringe benefits are borne by workers largely in the form of lower cash wages than they would receive if no such benefits were provided by their employer. Replacing employment-based health care with a government-run system could reduce employers' payments for their workers' insurance, but the amount that they would have to pay in overall compensation would remain essentially unchanged.

To give an example, suppose a firm was paying its workers $50,000 in wages and paying $10,000 per worker for health insurance, thereby providing total compensation of $60,000. If the government began paying all health care expenses, it might appear that the firm's labor costs would drop by $10,000 per worker. But if the firm offered its employees only $50,000 in wages as their total compensation, many would leave to work for other firms. The firm would have to pay its employees an additional $10,000 in wages so that the total compensation it offered would be at the equilibrium level of $60,000 for the industry. In other words, basic demand and supply analysis indicates that having firms rather than the government provide health insurance to workers changes the *composition* of the compensation that firms pay workers but does not change the *amount* of compensation that firms pay.

Source: Congressional Budget Office, "Key Issues in Analyzing Major Health Insurance Proposals," December 2008, p. 167.

Your Turn: Test your understanding by doing related problem 4.10 on page 178 at the end of this chapter.   MyLab Economics Study Plan

Explaining Increases in Health Care Spending

In this section, we briefly discuss some explanations for why health care's share of the U.S. economy has been continually increasing. We start by reviewing explanations that policymakers and journalists sometimes offer but that are unlikely to account for most of the increases in health care costs.

Factors That Do *Not* Explain Sustained Increases in Health Care Spending The two panels of Figure 5.5 on page 163 show that spending on health care has been growing faster than the economy as a whole for at least the past several decades. Explaining the rapid growth of health care spending requires identifying factors that have more than a one-time effect. For example, because the U.S. health care system relies on many independent hospitals, medical practices, and insurance companies, some observers argue that it generates more paperwork, duplication, and waste than systems in other countries. Even if this observation is correct, it cannot account for health care's rising share of GDP unless paperwork and waste are *increasing* year after year, which seems unlikely.

Unlike in most other countries, it is relatively easy in the United States for patients who have been injured by medical errors to sue doctors and hospitals for damages. The Congressional Budget Office (CBO) estimates, though, that the payments to settle malpractice lawsuits plus the premiums doctors pay for malpractice insurance amount to less than 1 percent of health care costs. Other economists believe that the CBO estimate is too low and that the costs of malpractice lawsuits, including the costs of unnecessary tests and procedures doctors order to avoid being sued, are as much as 7 percent of total health care costs. Still, these costs have not been significantly increasing over time.

Somewhere between 1 and 4 percent of health care costs are due to uninsured patients receiving treatments at hospital emergency rooms that could have been provided less expensively in doctors' offices. But once again, prior to the implementation of the ACA, this cost was not increasing rapidly enough to account for much of the increase in health care costs as a percentage of GDP, and as the implementation of the ACA has led to a decrease in the number of uninsured people, this cost has declined.

In the next sections, we discuss three factors that many economists believe help explain the sustained increases in health care spending.

"Cost Disease" in the Health Care Sector Some economists argue that health care suffers from a problem often encountered in service industries. In the sectors of the economy that produce goods, such as the manufacturing sector, *productivity*, or the amount of output each worker can produce in a given period, increases steadily. These increases in productivity occur because over time firms provide workers with more machinery and equipment, including computers and software, with which to work, and because technological progress results in improvements in machinery and equipment and in other parts of the production process. As workers produce more goods, firms are able to pay them higher wages. By contrast, in service-producing industries, increasing output per worker is more difficult. In medicine, MRI units, CT scanners, and other medical technology have improved diagnosis and treatment, but most medicine still requires a face-to-face meeting between a doctor or medical technologist and a patient. As wages rise in industries in which productivity is increasing rapidly, service industries in which productivity is increasing less rapidly must match these wage increases or lose workers. Because increases in wages are not offset by increases in productivity in service industries, the cost to firms of supplying services increases.

William Baumol of New York University has labeled the tendency for low productivity in service industries to lead to higher costs in those industries as "the cost disease of the service sector." Health care probably suffers from this cost disease because growth in labor productivity in the health care sector has been less than half as fast as labor productivity growth in the economy as a whole. This slow growth in productivity can help explain why the cost of health care has been rising rapidly, thereby increasing health care's share of total spending and output.

The Aging of the Population and Advances in Medical Technology As people age, they increase their spending on health care. Firms continue to develop new prescription drugs and medical equipment that typically have higher costs than the drugs and equipment they replace. The aging of the U.S. population and the introduction of higher-cost drugs and medical equipment interact to drive up spending on the federal government's Medicare program and on health care generally. People over age 65 disproportionately use many newly introduced drugs and diagnostic tools. Partly as a result, health care spending on people over age 65 is six times greater than spending on people aged 18 to 24 and four times greater than on people aged 25 to 44. In 2017, about 58 million people were enrolled in Medicare, and that number is expected to grow to 74 million by 2025. As we have seen, even in the absence of the development of new drugs and other medical technology, low rates of productivity in the health care sector could be expected to drive up costs. In fact, as Figure 5.7 illustrates, the CBO estimates that more of the increase in federal spending on Medicare and Medicaid benefits will be due to increases in the cost of providing health care rather than to the aging of the population. In the figure, "effect of excess cost growth" refers to the extent to which health care costs per person grow faster than GDP per person. An aging population and increases in the cost of providing health care are key reasons health care spending is an increasing percentage of GDP.

Distorted Economic Incentives As we noted earlier, some part of the increase in health care spending over the years results from consumers' choosing to allocate more of their incomes to health care as their incomes rise. But as we have also seen,

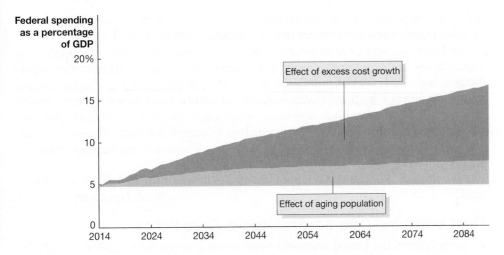

MyLab Economics Animation

Figure 5.7

Reasons for Rising Federal Spending on Medicare and Medicaid

Although the aging of the U.S. population will increase federal government spending on the Medicare and Medicaid programs, increases in the cost of providing health care will have a larger effect on government spending on these programs.

Note: In addition to spending on the Medicare and Medicaid programs, the figure includes federal spending on the Children's Health Insurance Program (CHIP) and federal spending on subsidies to the health insurance marketplaces established under the ACA.

Source: U.S. Congressional Budget Office.

consumers usually pay less than the true cost of medical treatment because a third party—typically an insurance company or the government—often pays most of the bill. For example, once they have satisfied their insurance plan's deductible, consumers who have health insurance provided by their employers usually pay only a small amount—perhaps $20—for a visit to a doctor's office, when the true cost of the visit might be $80 or $90. The result is that consumers demand a larger quantity of health care services than they would if they paid a price that better represented the cost of providing the services.

Figure 5.8 illustrates this situation. If consumers paid the full price of medical services, their demand would be D_1. The marginal benefit to consumers from medical services would equal the marginal cost of producing the services, and the equilibrium quantity would be at the efficient level $Q_{Efficient}$. However, because consumers pay only a fraction of the true cost of medical services, their demand increases to D_2. In this equilibrium, the quantity of medical services produced increases to Q_{Market}, which is beyond the efficient level. The marginal cost of producing these additional units is greater than the marginal benefit consumers receive from them. As a result, there is a deadweight loss equal to the area of the yellow triangle. Doctors and other suppliers of medical services receive a price, P_{Market}, that is well above the price, P, paid by consumers. Note that the effect of a third-party payer is common to nearly all health care systems, whether

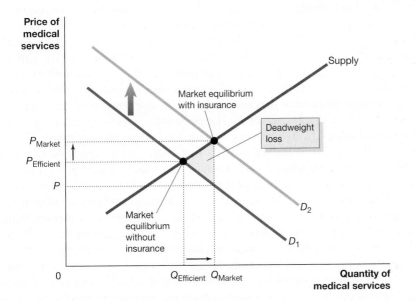

MyLab Economics Animation

Figure 5.8

The Effect of the Third-Party Payer System on the Demand for Medical Services

If consumers paid the full price of medical services, their demand would be D_1, and the equilibrium quantity would be at the efficient level $Q_{Efficient}$. Because consumers pay only a fraction of the true cost of medical services, their demand is D_2, and the equilibrium quantity of medical services produced increases to Q_{Market}, which is beyond the efficient level. There is a deadweight loss equal to the yellow triangle. Doctors and other suppliers of medical services receive a price, P_{Market}, that is well above the price, P, paid by consumers.

the government provides health care directly, as is done in the United Kingdom, or whether many people have private health insurance, as in the United States.

In important ways, health insurance is different from other types of insurance. As we discussed earlier, the basic idea of insurance is that the financial risk of an unpredictable, high-cost event—a house fire or a serious car accident—is pooled among the many consumers who buy insurance. Health insurance, though, also typically covers many planned expenses, such as routine health checkups, annual physicals, and contraceptives, and other low-cost events, such as treatment for minor illnesses. By disguising the true cost of these routine expenses, health insurance encourages overuse of health care services.

We discuss the role of economic incentives in health care further in the next section. **MyLab Economics** Concept Check

The Continuing Debate over Health Care Policy

As we have seen, the United States has been unusual among high-income countries in relying on private health insurance, usually purchased through employers or the health insurance marketplaces, to provide health care coverage to the majority of the population. Most other high-income countries either provide health care directly, as the United Kingdom does, through government-owned hospitals and government-employed doctors, or provide health insurance to all residents, as Canada does, without directly employing doctors or owning hospitals. There have been several attempts to reorganize the U.S. health care system to make it more like the systems in other countries. In 1945, President Harry Truman proposed a plan for *national health insurance*, under which anyone could purchase health insurance from the federal government. The health insurance would have covered treatment received from doctors and hospitals that agreed to enroll in the system. Congress declined to enact the plan. In 1993, President Bill Clinton proposed a health care plan intended to provide universal insurance coverage. While somewhat complex, the plan was based on requiring most businesses to provide health insurance to their employees and new government-sponsored health alliances that would ensure coverage for anyone who otherwise would not have health insurance. After a prolonged political debate, Congress chose not to enact President Clinton's plan.

The Patient Protection and Affordable Care Act In 2009, President Barack Obama proposed health care legislation that after much debate and significant changes was signed into law as the **Patient Protection and Affordable Care Act (ACA)** in March 2010. The act was long and complex at more than 20,000 pages and touched nearly every aspect of health care in the United States. Here is a summary of only the main provisions of the act:

Patient Protection and Affordable Care Act (ACA) Health care reform legislation passed by Congress and signed by President Barack Obama in 2010.

- **Individual mandate.** The act requires that, with limited exceptions, every resident of the United States have health insurance that meets certain basic requirements. Individuals who do not acquire health insurance are subject to a fine. In 2017 the fine was $695 or 2.5 percent of income, whichever was greater. (The fine will rise with inflation in future years.) For example, in 2017 an adult with an income of $40,000 per year paid a fine of $1,000 if he or she did not have health insurance.
- **State health insurance marketplaces.** Each state must establish a marketplace called an Affordable Insurance Exchange. Separate marketplaces were established for individuals and small businesses with fewer than 50 employees. The marketplaces offer health insurance policies that meet certain specified requirements. Although the marketplaces were intended to be run by a state government agency or a nonprofit firm, a majority of states decided to allow the federal government to run their marketplaces. Private insurance companies compete by offering policies on the marketplaces to individuals and small businesses. Low-income individuals and small businesses with 25 or fewer employees are eligible for tax credits to offset the costs of buying health insurance. The purpose of the marketplaces is to allow greater risk pooling and lower administrative costs than existed in the market for health insurance policies sold to individuals or small businesses. If successful, greater risk pooling and lower administrative costs make it possible for individuals

and small businesses to buy polices with lower premiums than were formerly available. In 2017, about 11 million people purchased health insurance policies through the marketplace. As we saw in the chapter opener, though, some insurance firms, including Humana, Aetna, and UnitedHealth, had pulled out of the marketplaces in at least some states. These firms found that adverse selection problems—with the proportion of older, sicker patients turning out to be higher than expected—and higher administrative costs resulted in their suffering losses on the policies they offered in the marketplaces.

- **Employer mandate.** Every firm with more than 200 full-time employees must offer health insurance to its employees and must automatically enroll them in the plan. In 2017, firms with 50 or more full-time employees must offer health insurance that meets certain requirements or pay a fee of up to $3,390 to the federal government for every employee who receives a tax credit from the federal government for obtaining health insurance through a health insurance marketplace. A worker is a full-time employee if he or she works at least 30 hours per week.

- **Regulation of health insurance.** Insurance companies are required to participate in a high-risk pool that will insure individuals with preexisting medical conditions who have been unable to buy health insurance for at least six months. All individual and group policies must provide coverage for dependent children up to age 26. Lifetime dollar maximums on coverage are prohibited. Limits are also placed on the size of deductibles and on the waiting period before coverage becomes effective.

- **Changes to Medicare and Medicaid.** Eligibility for Medicaid was originally expanded to persons with incomes up to 138 percent of the federal poverty line, although a 2012 Supreme Court decision resulted in the states being allowed to opt out of this requirement. In an attempt to control increases in health care costs, the Independent Payment Advisory Board (IPAB) was established and given the power to reduce Medicare payments for prescription drugs and the use of diagnostic equipment and other technology if Medicare spending exceeds certain levels. Some Medicare reimbursements to hospitals and doctors were reduced.

- **Taxes.** Several new taxes help fund the program. Workers earning more than $200,000 pay higher Medicare payroll taxes, and people who earn more than $200,000 pay a new 3.8 percent tax on their investment income. Beginning in 2018, a tax is scheduled to be imposed on employer-provided health insurance plans that have a value above $10,200 for an individual or $27,500 for a family—so-called *Cadillac plans*. In 2017, Congress was considering proposals to repeal this tax. Pharmaceutical firms, health insurance firms, and firms producing medical devices also pay new taxes.

Solved Problem 5.4

MyLab Economics Interactive Animation

Recent Trends in U.S. Health Care

An article in the *New York Times* on the effects of the Patient Protection and Affordable Care Act (ACA) and other developments in the U.S. health care system through the end of 2016 mentioned these three trends:

1. Deductibles increased in many employer-provided health care plans, as well as in the policies offered on the ACA health insurance marketplaces.
2. There was an increase in the number of surgeries and other medical procedures performed in doctor's offices or clinics rather than in higher-cost hospital settings.

3. There was a decline in patients being readmitted to hospitals after the ACA imposed penalties on hospitals that readmit too many patients.

   a. Use a graph of the market for medical services to show the effect of these trends, holding constant other factors affecting the market for medical services. Be sure to explain any shifts in the demand curve or supply curve.
   b. Assuming that these are the only changes happening in the market for medical services, can we be certain whether they will result in an increase or decrease in the equilibrium price of medical services? In the equilibrium quantity of medical services? Briefly explain.

Solving the Problem

Step 1: **Review the chapter material.** This problem is about explaining changes in health care spending, so you may want to review the section "Explaining Increases in Health Care Spending," which begins on page 165.

Step 2: **Answer part (a) by drawing a graph of the market for medical services that shows the effect of the three trends and by explaining shifts in the curves.** The first trend—higher deductibles—reduces moral hazard and adverse selection problems by increasing the quantity of medical services that employees and people who receive insurance on the ACA health insurance exchanges purchase out-of-pocket. Employees are likely to visit doctors less frequently for minor illnesses such as colds. So, the demand curve for medical services will shift to the left. The second trend—the increase in the number of surgeries and other medical procedures performed outside hospitals—reduces the cost of providing these types of medical services, which will shift the supply curve for medical services to the right. The third trend—a decline in the number of patients being readmitted to hospitals—should reduce the cost of hospitalizations because more patients are being successfully treated in a single stay. This trend will also cause the supply curve for medical services to shift to the right.

Your graph should look like the one below.

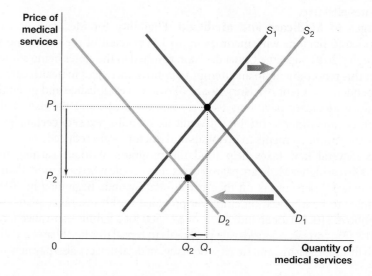

Step 3: **Answer part (b) by explaining whether these trends will increase or decrease the equilibrium price and quantity of medical services.** The graph in part (a) shows both the equilibrium price and the equilibrium quantity declining. We can be certain that the equilibrium price will decline because the shift of the demand curve to the left and the shift of the supply curve to the right both cause the equilibrium price to decline. However, we can't be certain that the equilibrium quantity will decline because the effect of the supply curve shifting to the right is to make the equilibrium quantity *increase*. Whether the equilibrium quantity declines depends on whether the demand curve shifts more or less than the supply curve shifts. Although two of the trends listed affect supply and only one affects demand, we do not know the size of the shift that results from any of the trends, so we can't tell with certainty what the effect will be on the equilibrium quantity.

Extra Credit: The cost of medical care has continued to increase. In 2017, however, economists were analyzing the reasons for a slowdown in the *rate* of that increase. The trends mentioned in this problem were among the likely factors. The quantity of medical services continued to increase, at least partly as a result of the effects of the Affordable Care Act. The act provides subsidies to buy health insurance for people whose incomes fall below a certain level and has expanded the Medicaid system, thereby increasing the demand for health care among low-income people.

Source: Margot Sanger-Katz, "Grading Obamacare: Successes, Failures and 'Incompletes,'" *New York Times*, February 5, 2017.

Your Turn: For more practice, do related problem 4.12 on page 178 at the end of this chapter.

MyLab Economics Study Plan

The Debate over the ACA Since its passage, the ACA has remained the source of considerable debate among policymakers and economists. As mentioned in the chapter opener, President Trump took office in January 2017, vowing to "repeal and replace" the act. Changes to the act proposed by the Trump administration focused on incorporating market-based incentives intended to reduce the costs of providing health care and to improve economic incentives. Other critics of the act, including Vermont senator and 2016 Democratic presidential candidate Bernie Sanders, argued that the act should be amended (or replaced) to allow for an expanded role for the government in health care similar to the role played by governments in other high-income countries.

As we discussed in the previous section, some economists and policymakers believe that information problems and externalities in the market for health care are sufficiently large that the government should either provide health care directly through government-owned hospitals and government-employed doctors or pay for health care through national health insurance (that is, a single-payer system). Those in favor of moving toward greater government involvement in health care often raise three arguments:

1. A single-payer system would reduce the paperwork and waste caused by the current system.
2. The current Medicare system—which is essentially a single-payer system for people over age 65—has had lower administrative costs than have private health insurance companies.
3. The systems in most other high-income countries have lower levels of health care spending per person and lower rates of increase in total health care spending, while providing good health outcomes.

Some economists and policymakers support **market-based reforms**, which involve changing the market for health care so that it becomes more like the markets for other goods and services. With such reforms, the prices consumers pay and suppliers receive would do a better job of conveying information on consumer demand and supplier costs. The expectation is that increased competition among doctors, hospitals, pharmaceutical companies, and other providers of health care would reduce costs and increase economic efficiency. Economists who support market-based reforms as the best way to improve the health care system were disappointed that the ACA did not adopt this approach. Currently, markets are delivering inaccurate signals to consumers because when buying health care, unlike when buying most other goods and services, consumers pay a price well below the true cost of providing the service.   MyLab Economics Concept Check

Market-based reforms Changes in the market for health care that would make it more like the markets for other goods and services.

Apply the Concept
MyLab Economics Video

How Much Is That MRI Scan?

Magnetic resonance imaging (MRI) units play an important role in modern medicine. First introduced in the early 1980s, they allow doctors to see inside the body's soft tissues to identify medical problems such as tumors and torn muscles. As we noted in Section 5.2, MRI units are more widely available in the United States than in most other countries. We would normally expect that when a product is widely available, competition among firms will result in the price of the product being about the same everywhere. Customers would not buy a best-selling book from Amazon.com if the price were 50 percent higher than on BarnesandNoble.com.

Does competition equalize the prices of medical services? The evidence indicates that it doesn't. The data in the following table demonstrate that the prices of abdominal MRI scans vary widely. In most cities in the United States, the most expensive MRI scan has a price that is more than double the least expensive scan. And prices for MRI scans also vary widely across cities.

City	Highest Price	Lowest Price	Difference
San Francisco, California	$5,500	$725	$4,775
Chicago, Illinois	4,700	330	4,370
New York, New York	4,900	550	4,350
Houston, Texas	4,600	575	4,025
Atlanta, Georgia	4,400	825	3,575
Baton Rouge, Louisiana	4,200	700	3,500
Omaha, Nebraska	4,100	650	3,450
Lexington, Kentucky	4,000	675	3,325
Orlando, Florida	3,300	750	2,550
Charlotte, North Carolina	2,250	650	1,600

Two reporters looking at prices for shoulder MRI scans in Pensacola, Florida, found that Sacred Heart Hospital was charging $800 for a shoulder MRI scan, while Pensacola Open MRI & Imaging, a private firm located less than a mile away, was charging only $450 for the same scan. Pensacola Open MRI & Imaging was actually using newer MRI units that give higher-resolution images, so it was charging less for a better service. How can some providers of medical services charge hundreds or thousands of dollars more than competitors and remain in business? The answer is that most patients are not concerned about prices because they either do not pay them or they pay only a small fraction of them. Patients typically rely on doctors to refer them to a facility for an MRI scan or other procedure and make little or no effort to determine the price the facility charges. A goal of market-based reforms of the health care system is to give patients an incentive to pay more attention to the prices of medical services.

Sources: Caitlin Kenney, "Shopping for an MRI," www.npr.org, November 6, 2009; MRI prices from newchoicehealth. com, March 30, 2017.

MyLab Economics Study Plan   **Your Turn:** Test your understanding by doing related problem 4.13 on page 178 at the end of this chapter.

Supporters of market-based reforms note that employees have to pay federal income and payroll taxes on the wages their employers pay them, but in most circumstances they do not pay taxes on the value of the health insurance their employers provide them. This feature of the tax laws encourages employees to want generous health care coverage; in fact, if offered the choice between a $1,000 salary increase or increased health care coverage worth $1,000, many people would choose the increased health care coverage because it would be tax free (although someone who was young and healthy and did not expect to have medical bills would probably choose the increase in salary). The size of this tax break is quite substantial—more than $250 billion in 2015. But individuals typically get no tax break when buying an individual health insurance policy or when they spend money on health care out of pocket.[1]

Some economists have proposed making the tax treatment of employer-provided health insurance the same as the tax treatment of individually purchased health insurance and out-of-pocket health care spending. They argue that this change could, potentially, significantly reduce spending on health care without reducing the effectiveness of the health care received. Such tax law changes would make it more likely that employer-provided health insurance would focus on large medical bills—such as those resulting from hospitalizations—while consumers would pay prices closer to the

[1] Individuals receive a deduction on their federal income tax only if their medical expenses are greater than 10 percent of their income. Only a relatively small number of individuals have expenses high enough to use that deduction. Self-employed individuals can typically deduct the cost of health insurance from their income when paying their federal income tax.

costs of providing routine medical care. John Cogan of the Hoover Institution, Glenn Hubbard of Columbia University, and Daniel Kessler of Stanford University estimated that repealing the tax preference for employer-provided health insurance would reduce spending by people enrolled in these programs by 33 percent.

Currently, the U.S. health care system is a world leader in innovation in medical technology and prescription drugs. About two-thirds of pharmaceutical patents are issued to U.S. firms and about two-thirds of research on new medicines is carried out in the United States. One goal of market-based reforms would be to ensure that U.S. firms continue with innovations in medical screening equipment, surgical procedures, and prescription drugs. Executives of U.S. pharmaceutical firms have voiced concern over whether aspects of the ACA will affect their ability to profitably bring new prescription drugs to market. In particular, managers at these firms worry that the new Independent Payment Advisory Board (IPAB) might reduce the payments Medicare would make for new prescription drugs.

Both critics of the ACA who favor greater government involvement in health care and those who favor market reforms raise questions about the act's individual mandate, which requires every U.S. resident to have health insurance. The mandate was considered necessary because otherwise healthy people might avoid buying insurance until they become ill. Because insurance companies would not be allowed to deny coverage for preexisting conditions, they would end up paying large medical bills for people who had not been paying premiums to support the system while they were healthy. People who do not buy insurance are subject to fines under the act, but there were questions about how effective the fines would be in pushing people to buy insurance. In 2016, several million people paid the fine rather than buy insurance.   **MyLab Economics** Study Plan

Continued from page 147

Economics in Your Life & Career

Is Your Take-Home Pay Affected by What Your Employer Spends on Your Health Insurance?

At the beginning of this chapter, we asked you to think about this question: Your paycheck doesn't show the amount your employer pays on your behalf for health insurance, but does that amount affect your take-home pay? The *Apply the Concept* on page 164 shows that the equilibrium compensation that workers receive in labor markets is made up partly of wages and partly of fringe benefits such as health insurance. So, while the amount that a firm pays on your behalf for health insurance may not affect your total compensation, it will affect the amount of your take-home pay. For a given level of compensation, the more a firm pays for your health insurance, the less it will pay you in wages.

A related question is why a firm would buy health insurance for you rather than increase your wages by the same amount and let you buy your own insurance. We have seen that there are two important reasons so many people receive health insurance from their employers: (1) The wage an employer pays you is taxable income to you, but the money an employer spends to buy health insurance for you is not taxable; and (2) insurance companies are typically willing to charge lower premiums for group insurance, particularly to large employers, because risk pooling is improved and adverse selection and moral hazard problems are lower than with individual policies.

Conclusion

In this chapter, we have seen that economic analysis can provide important insights into the market for health care. As with many other policy issues, though, economic analysis can help inform the debate but cannot resolve it. Because health care is so important to consumers and health care services are such a large part of the U.S. economy, the role of the government in the health care system is likely to be the subject of intense debate for years to come.

Visit **MyLab Economics** for a news article and analysis related to the concepts in this chapter.

CHAPTER SUMMARY
AND PROBLEMS

Key Terms

5.1 The Improving Health of People in the United States, pages 148–150

LEARNING OBJECTIVE: Use data to discuss trends in U.S. health over time.

MyLab Economics Visit www.pearson.com/mylab/economics to complete these exercises online and get instant feedback.

Summary

Health care refers to goods and services, such as prescription drugs and consultations with a doctor, that are intended to maintain or improve health. Over time, the health of people in most countries has improved. In the United States, as a result of improving health, life expectancy has increased, death rates have decreased, infant mortality has decreased, and the average person has become taller.

Review Questions

1.1 Briefly discuss the most important differences between the market for health care and the markets for other goods and services.

1.2 Briefly describe changes over time in the health of the average person in the United States.

1.3 How can improvements in health increase a country's total income? How can increases in a country's total income improve health?

Problems and Applications

1.4 In what sense have improvements in the health of the average American caused the U.S. production possibilities frontier to shift out? Panel (a) in Figure 5.1 on page 150 indicates that life expectancy in the United States declined in 1918. What effect did this decline in life expectancy likely have on the U.S. production possibilities frontier? Briefly explain.

1.5 The widespread acceptance in the late 1800s of the idea that bacteria causes diseases helped lead to a public health movement. This movement eventually brought sewers, clean drinking water, and garbage removal to all U.S. cities. What effect did the public health movement in the United States in the late 1800s and early 1900s have on the country's production possibilities frontier?

1.6 Between 1830 and 1890, the height of the average adult male in the United States declined by about 2 inches at the same time that average incomes more than tripled. Did the standard of living in the United States increase during this period? What insight into the health and well-being of the U.S. population might the decline in height provide? Briefly explain.

5.2 Health Care around the World, pages 150–156

LEARNING OBJECTIVE: Compare the health care systems and health care outcomes in the United States and other countries.

MyLab Economics Visit www.pearson.com/mylab/economics to complete these exercises online and get instant feedback.

Summary

Health insurance is a contract under which a buyer agrees to make payments, or premiums, in exchange for the provider agreeing to pay some or all of the buyer's medical bills. A majority of people in the United States live in households that have private health insurance, which they typically obtain through an employer. Other people have health insurance through the Veteran's Administration or the Medicare and Medicaid programs. In 2016, about 9 percent of people in the United States lacked health insurance. Many health insurance plans operate on a **fee-for-service** basis, under which doctors and hospitals receive a payment for each service they provide. Most countries outside the United States have greater government involvement in their health care systems. Canada has a **single-payer health care system**, in which the government provides national health insurance to all Canadian residents. In the United Kingdom, the government owns most hospitals and employs most doctors, so the health care system is referred to as **socialized medicine**. The United States spends more per person on health care than do other high-income countries; has lower life expectancy, higher infant mortality, and a greater incidence of obesity than do other high-income countries; and has more medical technology per person and has lower mortality rates for people diagnosed with cancer than do other high-income countries. Data and other problems make it difficult to compare health care outcomes across countries.

Review Questions

2.1 Define the following terms:
  a. Health insurance
  b. Fee-for-service
  c. Single-payer health care system
  d. Socialized medicine

2.2 What are the main sources of health insurance in the United States?

2.3 Briefly compare the health care systems in Canada, Japan, and the United Kingdom with the health care system in the United States.

2.4 What is meant by the phrase "health outcome"? How do health outcomes in the United States compare with those of other high-income countries? What problems arise in attempting to compare health outcomes across countries?

Problems and Applications

2.5 An article in the *Economist* noted that the National Health Service (NHS) in the United Kingdom "provides health care free at the point of use."
  a. What does "free at the point of use" mean? Is health care actually free to residents of the United Kingdom? Briefly explain.
  b. The same article suggested that funding problems at the NHS could be alleviated by "reducing demand for unnecessary treatments" and noted that while two-thirds of the 35 countries in the Organization for Economic Co-operation and Development (OECD) charge patients for an appointment with a general practitioner, the NHS does not. Is there a possible connection between the NHS's funding problem and its failure to charge patients for doctor appointments? Briefly explain.
  Source: "Accident and Emergency," *Economist*, September 10, 2016.

2.6 In an opinion column about improving the performance of doctors in the United States, a health economist observed that "it's very hard to measure the things we really care about, like quality of life and improvements in functioning." Why is it difficult to measure outcomes like these? Does the economist's observation have relevance to comparisons in health outcomes across countries? Briefly explain.
  Source: Aaron E. Carroll, "The Problem with 'Pay for Performance' in Medicine," *New York Times*, July 28, 2014.

2.7 An article in the *Economist* on evaluating health outcomes is subtitled "To Improve Health Care, Governments Need to Use the Right Data." Among the data not currently being collected in most countries, the article mentioned "how soon after surgery patients get back to work." Why don't governments currently collect such data? Why might such data be important in evaluating the effectiveness of a country's health care system?
  Source: "Measuring Health Care," *Economist*, February 1, 2014.

2.8 An article in the *Wall Street Journal* discussed Aspire Health, a startup firm that believes that it can use software to "predict which patients are likely to die in the next year and reduce their medical bills substantially by offering them palliative care at home.... Palliative care focuses on easing symptoms such as pain and shortness of breath that are often overlooked amid aggressive efforts to save seriously ill patients."
  a. Should providing palliative care to very ill patients, who are typically elderly, be an important goal of a health care system? Are there other goals that should have a higher priority? (*Note:* This question is basically a normative one without a definitive correct or incorrect answer. You are being asked to consider what the goals of a health care system *should be*.)
  b. Would it be possible to measure how successful the health care systems of different countries are in providing palliative care? If so, how might it be done?
  Source: Melinda Beck, "Can a Death-Predicting Algorithm Improve Care?" *Wall Street Journal*, December 2, 2016.

2.9 **(Related to the Apply the Concept on page 152)** A report from the American Council on Competitiveness noted that "there has been some recent progress in the digital health sector, which aims to better integrate information and software technologies into all aspects of healthcare." The report also concluded that "the U.S. has rather poor health outcomes relative to other developed countries and stands out as having exceptionally low healthcare productivity when measuring outcomes against spending."
  a. Briefly discuss the evidence for and against U.S. health care performing poorly relative to other countries when comparing outcomes to spending.
  b. If the U.S. health care sector makes increasing use of information technology, will it be likely to employ more workers or fewer workers than if it fails to widely adopt this technology? Briefly explain.
  Source: Jonathan Rothwell, "No Recovery: An Analysis of Long-Term U.S. Productivity Decline," U.S. Council on Competitiveness, 2016, pp. 54 and 76.

5.3 ## Information Problems and Externalities in the Market for Health Care, pages 156–162

LEARNING OBJECTIVE: Define information problems and externalities and explain how they affect the market for health care.

MyLab Economics Visit **www.pearson.com/mylab/economics** to complete these exercises online and get instant feedback.

Summary

The market for health care is affected by the problem of **asymmetric information**, which occurs when one party to an economic transaction has less information than the other party. **Adverse selection**, the situation in which one party to a transaction takes advantage of knowing more than the other party to the transaction, is a problem for firms selling health insurance policies because it results in people who are less healthy being more likely to buy insurance than people who are healthier. **Moral hazard**, actions people take after they have entered into a transaction that make the other party to the transaction worse off, is also a problem for insurance companies because once people have health insurance, they are likely to make more visits to their doctors and in other ways increase their use of medical services. Moral hazard can also involve a **principal–agent problem**, in which doctors may order more lab tests, MRI scans, and other procedures than they would if their patients lacked health insurance. Insurance companies use deductibles and copayments to reduce the problems of adverse selection and moral hazard. There may be externalities involved with medicine and health care because, for example, people who are vaccinated against influenza or other diseases may not receive all of the benefits from having been vaccinated, and people who become obese may not bear all of the costs from their obesity.

Review Questions

3.1 Define the following terms:
 a. Asymmetric information
 b. Adverse selection
 c. Moral hazard
 d. Principal–agent problem

3.2 What are the asymmetric information problems in the market for health insurance?

3.3 How do health insurance companies deal with asymmetric information problems?

3.4 What is an externality? Are there externalities in the market for health care? Briefly explain.

Problems and Applications

3.5 Suppose you see a 2015 Honda Civic hatchback advertised in the campus newspaper for $9,000. If you could be sure that the car is reliable, you would be willing to pay $10,000 for it. If you could be sure that the car is unreliable, you would be willing to pay $5,000 for it. Under what circumstances should you buy the car?

3.6 What is the *lemons problem*? Is there a lemons problem in the market for health insurance? Briefly explain.

3.7 An article in the *Economist* referred to "the basic logic of the insurance industry—that it is impossible to predict who will be hit by what misfortune when, and that people should therefore pool their risks." In what sense does insurance involve pooling risks? How does the problem of adverse selection affect the ability of insurance to provide the benefit of pooling risk?

 Source: "Risk and Reward," *Economist*, May 12, 2015.

3.8 Under the Social Security retirement system, the federal government collects a tax on most people's wage income and makes payments to retired workers above a certain age who are covered by the system. (The age to receive full Social Security retirement benefits varies based on the year the worker was born.) The Social Security retirement system is sometimes called a program of social insurance. Is Social Security an insurance program in the same sense as a health insurance policy that a company provides to its workers? Briefly explain.

3.9 **(Related to the Don't Let This Happen to You on page 158)** Briefly explain whether you agree with the following statement: "The reluctance of healthy young adults to buy health insurance creates a moral hazard problem for insurance companies."

3.10 **(Related to the Don't Let This Happen to You on page 158)** While teaching the concepts of asymmetric information, a professor asked his students for examples of adverse selection or moral hazard in marriage. One of the students, who happened to be married, replied: "Your spouse doesn't bring you flowers anymore!" Would the student's reply be an example of adverse selection or moral hazard? Briefly explain.

3.11 A news article noted that some features of the U.S. health care system contribute "to the high cost of medical care by encouraging hospitals and doctors to perform tests and procedures regardless of the value to a patient." What features is the article referring to? Why would hospitals and doctors perform tests that may not be of any value to patients?

 Source: Reed Abelson, "Industry Group to Back Results-Focused Care," *New York Times*, January 28, 2015.

3.12 An opinion column in the *Wall Street Journal* observed about "defensive medicine" that "many physicians maintain that fear of lawsuits significantly affects the practice of medicine, and that reform of the malpractice system is crucial for containing costs." Is there another economic explanation—apart from fear of lawsuits—for why doctors may end up ordering unnecessary tests and other medical procedures? Briefly explain.

 Source: Amitabh Chandra, Anupam B. Jena, and Seth A. Seabury, "Defensive Medicine May Be Costlier Than It Seems," *Wall Street Journal*, February 7, 2013.

3.13 An article in the *Economist* argued that the real problem with health insurance is:

> The healthy people who decide not to buy insurance out of rational self-interest, and who turn out to be right. By not buying insurance, those (largely young) healthy people will be failing to subsidize the people insurance is meant for: the ones who end up getting sick.

 a. Why is it rational for healthy people not to buy health insurance?
 b. Do you agree that health insurance is meant for people who end up getting sick?
 c. Why is the situation described here a problem for a system of health insurance? If it is a problem, suggest possible solutions.

 Source: "Romney on Health Care: To Boldly Go Where He Had Already Been Before," *Economist*, May 13, 2011.

3.14 **(Related to the Chapter Opener on page 146)** An article on the usnews.com site about the Patient Protection and Afford Care Act (ACA) reported that "the participation (enrollment) of the prized 'young invincibles' . . . has been elusive." ("Young invincibles" refers to 18- to 34-year-olds who don't buy health insurance because they expect to remain healthy.) The article noted that the number of people with preexisting conditions enrolled in the health insurance marketplaces has risen relative to the number of young invincibles and asserted that this "imbalance has caused premiums to rise, which can also cause some healthier beneficiaries to avoid plans."

 a. Why is the participation of young invincibles important to the success of the ACA health insurance marketplaces?
 b. Why would an increase in the ratio of people with preexisting conditions to young invincibles result in

increases in premiums? What economic problem that occurs in the market for health care does this increase illustrate?

c. If the ratio of people with preexisting conditions to young invincibles continues to rise, what will be the consequences for the health insurance marketplaces?

Source: Kimberly Leonard, "'Young Invincibles' Remain Elusive for Obamacare," usnews.com, September 7, 2016.

3.15 Explain whether you agree with the following statement:

> Providing health care is obviously a public good. If one person becomes ill and doesn't receive treatment, that person may infect many other people. If many people become ill, then the output of the economy will be negatively affected. Therefore, providing health care is a public good that should be supplied by the government.

5.4   The Debate over Health Care Policy in the United States, pages 162–173

LEARNING OBJECTIVE: Explain the major issues involved in the debate over health care policy in the United States.

MyLab Economics   Visit **www.pearson.com/mylab/economics** to complete these exercises online and get instant feedback.

Summary

In 2010, Congress passed the **Patient Protection and Affordable Care Act (ACA)**, which significantly reorganized the U.S. health care system. Spending on health care in the United States has been growing rapidly as a percentage of GDP, and spending per person on health care has been growing more rapidly than in other high-income countries. Third-party payers, such as employer-provided health insurance and the Medicare and Medicaid programs, have financed an increasing fraction of health care spending, while out-of-pocket payments have sharply declined as a fraction of total health care spending. Several explanations have been offered for the rapid increase in health care spending in the United States: Slow rates of growth of labor productivity in health care may be driving up costs, the U.S. population is becoming older, medical technology and new prescription drugs have higher costs, and the tax system and the reliance on third-party payers have distorted the economic incentives of consumers and suppliers of health care. The ACA has several important provisions: (1) an individual mandate that requires every resident of the United States to obtain health insurance or be fined; (2) the establishment of health exchanges that will be run by the state or federal governments and provide a means for individuals and small businesses to purchase health insurance; (3) an employer mandate that requires every firm with more than 200 employees to offer health insurance to them; (4) increased regulation of health insurance companies; (5) expansion of eligibility for Medicaid and the establishment of the Independent Payment Advisory Board (IPAB), which has the power to reduce Medicare payments for prescription drugs and for the use of diagnostic equipment and other technology if Medicare spending exceeds certain levels; and (6) increased taxes on people with incomes above $200,000. Some critics of the ACA argue that it does not go far enough in increasing government involvement in the health care system, while other critics argue that health care reform should rely more heavily on **market-based reforms**, which involve changing the market for health care so that it becomes more like the markets for other goods and services.

Review Questions

4.1 What is the Patient Protection and Affordable Care Act (ACA)? Briefly list its major provisions.

4.2 In the United States, what has been the trend in health care spending as a percentage of GDP? Compare the increases in health care spending per person in the United States with the increases in health care spending per person in other high-income countries. What implications do current trends in health care spending have for the growth of federal government spending in the United States?

4.3 Briefly discuss how economists explain the rapid increases in health care spending.

4.4 What arguments do economists and policymakers who believe that the federal government should have a larger role in the health care system make in criticizing the ACA?

4.5 What arguments do economists and policymakers who believe that market-based reforms are the key to improving the health care system make in criticizing the ACA?

Problems and Applications

4.6 Figure 5.7 on page 167 shows that the Congressional Budget Office forecasts that less than half of future increases in spending on Medicare and Medicaid as a percentage of GDP will be due to the aging of the population. What factors explain most of the increase?

4.7 Improvements in technology usually result in lower costs of production or new and improved consumer goods and services. Assume that an improvement in medical technology results in an increase in life expectancy for people 65 years of age and older. How would this technological advance be likely to affect expenditures on health care?

4.8 Some economists and policymakers have argued that one way to control federal government spending on Medicare is to have a board of experts decide whether new medical technologies are worth their higher costs. If the board decided that they are *not* worth the costs, Medicare would not pay for them. Other economists and policymakers argue that the costs to beneficiaries should more closely represent the costs of providing medical services. This result might be attained by raising premiums, deductibles, and copayments or by "means testing," which would limit the Medicare benefits that high-income individuals receive. Political columnist David Brooks summarized these two ways to restrain the growth of spending on Medicare: "From the top, a body of experts can be empowered to make rationing decisions. . . . Alternatively, at the bottom, costs can be shifted to beneficiaries with premium supports to help them handle the burden."

a. What are "rationing decisions"? How would these decisions restrain the growth of Medicare spending?

b. How would shifting the costs of Medicare to beneficiaries restrain the growth of Medicare spending? What does Brooks mean by "premium supports"?

c. Should Congress and the president be concerned about the growth of Medicare spending? If so, which of these approaches should they adopt, or is there a third approach that might be better? (*Note:* This question is normative and has no definitive answer. It is intended to lead you to consider possible approaches to the Medicare program.)

Source: David Brooks, "The Missing Fifth," *New York Times*, May 9, 2011.

4.9 The late Nobel Laureate Robert Fogel of the University of Chicago argued, "Expenditures on health care are driven by demand, which is spurred by income and by advances in biotechnology that make health interventions increasingly effective."

a. If Fogel was correct, should policymakers be concerned by projected increases in health care spending as a percentage of GDP?

b. What objections do some economists raise to Fogel's analysis of what is driving increases in spending on health care?

Source: Robert Fogel, "Forecasting the Cost of U.S. Healthcare," *The American*, September 3, 2009.

4.10 (Related to the Apply the Concept on page 164) Employees in most circumstances do not pay taxes on the value of the health insurance provided by their employers. If employees were taxed on the value of the employer-provided health insurance, what would you expect to happen to the overall compensation employers pay employees? To the value of health insurance provided by employers? To the wages paid to employees? Briefly explain.

4.11 Suppose consumers pay less than the true cost of medical services because a third party, such as an insurance company or the government, pays most of the bill. In the following graph, D_1 represents the demand for medical services if consumers paid the full price of medical services; D_2 represents the demand for medical services when consumers pay only a fraction of the true cost of medical services; and S represents the supply of medical services. Use the graph to answer the following questions. Briefly explain your answers.

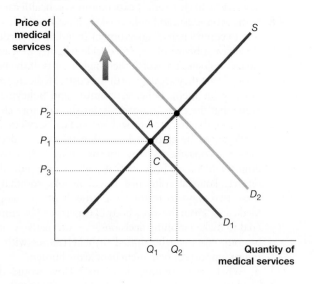

a. What is the equilibrium market price received by doctors and other suppliers of medical services?

b. What is the efficient quantity of medical services?

c. What is the price paid by consumers of medical services?

d. Which area represents the deadweight loss resulting from consumers not paying the full price of medical services?

4.12 (Related to Solved Problem 5.4 on page 169) In 2017, an article in the *Wall Street Journal* discussed trends in the health care sector. The article noted the "adoption of new health information technology," using "advanced algorithms and natural-language processing technologies to read and reformat" data on patients. Assuming that health information technology continues to advance, use a graph of the market for medical services to show the effect. Explain any shifts in the demand curve or supply curve and the effect on the equilibrium price and quantity of medical services.

Sources: Jonathan D. Rockoff and Peter Loftus, "Facing Criticism, Drug Makers Keep Lid on Price Increases," *Wall Street Journal*, February 26, 2017; and Sara Castellanos, "A New Tool to Analyze Medical Records," *Wall Street Journal*, January 25, 2017.

4.13 (Related to the Apply the Concept on page 171) A column in the *Wall Street Journal* observed, "Independent websites like Edmunds.com, AutoTrader.com and Kelley Blue Book publish detailed pricing information [on automobiles] for consumers and do so for free. Consumers want such information and businesses see opportunity in providing it, even for free, in order to attract eyeballs for advertising. . . . Such information doesn't exist in health care." Why aren't there Web sites that offer pricing data on health care and make a profit from selling advertisements?

Source: Holman W. Jenkins, Jr., "The Young Won't Buy ObamaCare," *Wall Street Journal*, June 18, 2013.

4.14 Some firms offer their employees a health care plan with high deductibles, sometimes as much as $4,500 per year. What effect do high-deductible plans have on how often employees visit doctors or otherwise use health care services? If the federal government were to require that employer health care plans have deductibles that were no greater than $200 per year, would the employees in these plans be better off? Would the employers offering these plans be worse off? Briefly explain.

Critical Thinking Exercises

CT5.1 After graduation, you accept a job with a new small startup. Your manager asks you to evaluate health insurance plans and identify which plan is most likely to help attract good employees. One idea she proposes is to offer health insurance to employees with no deductibles and no copays. What advice might you give your manager? After hearing your advice, she asks if offering more generous health insurance will increase the total employee compensation she will need to offer employees over the next 10 years. How would you answer her, using concepts from the chapter?

CT5.2 From your local paper, bloomberg.com, cnn.com, or another site, locate two articles that advocate specific changes in the U.S. health care system. Avoid news articles that only describe the debate over health care. Instead, try to locate articles that present arguments in favor of *specific changes*. How would you describe the differences between the proposals presented in the two articles? Would it be possible for Congress and the president to enact both proposals? Briefly explain.

Firms, the Stock Market, and Corporate Governance

Is Snapchat the Next Facebook . . . or the Next Twitter?

You probably can't imagine a world without Facebook, Twitter, and Snapchat. These social media applications ("apps") are all businesses that started small but grew rapidly. To finance that growth, they needed to raise funds. Some businesses raise funds by borrowing from banks. Once firms grow large enough, they can become *public firms* and sell stocks and bonds to investors in financial markets, such as the New York Stock Exchange. Firms that do not sell stock are called *private firms*. Facebook, Twitter, and Snapchat have all made the transition to being public firms.

Once a firm goes public, it has access to greater financing but also faces pressure from investors to earn a profit. During its first year as a public company, Facebook struggled to meet the expectations of its investors. From the time Mark Zuckerberg started Facebook in 2004 as a sophomore in college until the company went public with an *initial public offering (IPO)* of stock in 2012, he was the unquestioned leader of the company. But when the firm was losing money, investors questioned Zuckerberg's leadership. Advertising is the main source of revenue for social media apps. Eventually, Zuckerberg found a better way to target advertising on the Facebook app. By late 2017, the firm's stock price had increased from its initial price of $38 a share to over $170 a share.

But the situations at Twitter and Snapchat seemed less promising. When Twitter became a public company with an IPO in 2013, its stock sold for $45 per share. In early 2017, Twitter announced that its losses at the end of 2016 had doubled to $167 million as it struggled to increase its revenue from selling advertising. During that same period, Facebook had earned a profit of $3.57 *billion*. The price of Twitter's stock fell to less than $17 per share in late 2017.

As Stanford University undergraduates, Evan Spiegel and Bobby Murphy developed the Snapchat app, which allows photographs to automatically disappear shortly

after being sent. Snapchat's parent firm, Snap, became a public company with an IPO in March 2017. Investors wondered whether the company would become as successful as Facebook or struggle as Twitter has. Although Snapchat is especially popular among teenagers, popularity can be difficult to turn into revenue. Twitter and Snap both struggled to convince firms to advertise on their apps. Both companies tried to increase their appeal to advertisers by getting users to spend more time on their app: Twitter live streamed some NFL games, and Snap allowed users to search its popular Stories feature.

As we will see in this chapter, the ability of firms such as Facebook, Twitter, and Snap to raise funds in financial markets is crucial to the health of the economy. Financial markets are also an important source of investment opportunities to households as they accumulate savings to buy houses, pay for college, and prepare for retirement.

Sources: Deepa Seetharaman and Ezequiel Minaya, "Twitter Rethinks Ad Strategy in Effort to Translate User Growth into Additional Revenue," *Wall Street Journal*, February 9, 2017; Georgia Wells, "Snapchat Launches New Search Tool in Quest for More Engagement," *Wall Street Journal*, March 31, 2017; and Mike Shields, "Neither Trump Nor the NFL Delivered Big Rewards for Twitter," *Wall Street Journal*, February 9, 2017.

Chapter Outline & Learning Objectives

Economics in Your Life & Career

Would You Recommend That Snapchat or Twitter Start Charging Users?

You can use Facebook or Twitter for free—or can you? Social media apps don't charge you directly; instead, they earn their revenue primarily by displaying ads as you use the app. Most sites collect data about your Web searches and browsing habits and then display ads for products they think you might buy. But many people see these targeted ads as an invasion of their privacy.

Suppose you work as an economist for a social media company and you are asked to consider a proposal to begin charging app users in exchange for their not having to see advertisements. What factors would you need to take into account in evaluating this proposal? As you read this chapter, try to answer this question. You can check your answer against the one we provide on **page 199** at the end of this chapter.

I n this chapter, we look at firms: how they are organized, how they raise funds, and the information they provide to investors. As we have discussed in earlier chapters, firms in a market system are responsible for organizing the factors of production to produce goods and services. Entrepreneurs start firms to earn a profit by offering a good or service. To succeed, entrepreneurs must meet consumers' wants by producing new or better goods and services or by finding ways to produce existing goods and services at a lower cost so that they can be sold at a lower price than by competing firms. Entrepreneurs also need access to sufficient funds, and they must be able to efficiently organize production. As the typical firm in many industries has become larger over the past 100 years, the task of efficiently organizing production has become more difficult. In the final section of this chapter, we look at problems of *corporate governance* that are particularly likely to occur in large firms. We also look at the steps firms and the government have taken to overcome these problems.

6.1 Types of Firms

LEARNING OBJECTIVE: Categorize the major types of firms in the United States.

In studying a market economy, it is important to understand the basics of how firms operate. In the United States, there are three main categories of firms:

Sole proprietorship A firm owned by a single individual and not organized as a corporation.

Partnership A firm owned jointly by two or more persons and not organized as a corporation.

Corporation A legal form of business that provides owners with protection from losing more than their investment should the business fail.

1. A **sole proprietorship** is a firm owned by a single individual. Although most sole proprietorships are small, some employ many workers and earn large profits.
2. A **partnership** is a firm owned jointly by two or more—sometimes many—persons. Most law and accounting firms are partnerships. Some of them can be quite large. For instance, in 2017, the Baker McKenzie law firm based in Chicago had more than 1,500 partners.
3. A **corporation** is a legal form of business that provides owners with protection from losing more than their investment in the firm should the business fail. Most large firms are organized as corporations.

Who Is Liable? Limited and Unlimited Liability

A key distinction among the three types of firms is that the owners of sole proprietorships and partnerships have unlimited liability, which means there is no legal distinction between the personal assets of the owners of the firm and the assets of the firm. An **asset** is anything of value owned by a person or a firm. If a sole proprietorship or a partnership owes a lot of money to the firm's suppliers or employees, the suppliers and employees have a legal right to sue the firm for payment, even if it means the firm's owners have to sell some of their personal assets, such as stocks or bonds, to pay their debts. In other words, with sole proprietorships and partnerships, the owners are not legally distinct from the firms they own.

Asset Anything of value owned by a person or a firm.

It may seem fair that the owners of a firm should be responsible for the firm's debts. But in the early 1800s, many state legislatures in the United States realized that unlimited liability was a significant problem for any firm that was attempting to raise funds from large numbers of investors. An investor might be interested in making a relatively small investment in a firm but might be unwilling to become a partner in the firm for fear of placing at risk all of his or her personal assets if the firm were to fail. To get around this problem, state legislatures began to pass *general incorporation laws*, which allowed firms to more easily be organized as corporations. Under the corporate form of business, the owners of a firm have **limited liability**, which means that if the firm fails, the owners can never lose more than the amount they have invested in the firm. In other words, the owners of the firm do not risk losing their personal assets. In fact, in the eyes of the law, a corporation is a legal "person," separate from its owners. Limited liability has made it possible for corporations to raise funds by issuing shares of stock to large numbers of investors. For example, if you buy a share of Twitter stock, you

Limited liability A legal provision that shields owners of a corporation from losing more than they have invested in the firm.

Table 6.1

Differences among Business Organizations

	Sole Proprietorship	Partnership	Corporation
Advantages	• Control by owner • No layers of management	• Ability to share work • Ability to share risks	• Limited personal liability • Greater ability to raise funds
Disadvantages	• Unlimited personal liability • Limited ability to raise funds	• Unlimited personal liability • Limited ability to raise funds	• Costly to organize • Possible double taxation of income

are a part owner of the firm, but if Twitter were to go bankrupt, you would not be personally responsible for any of Twitter's debts. Therefore, you could not lose more than the amount you paid for the stock.

Organizing a firm as a corporation also has some disadvantages. In the United States, corporate profits are taxed twice—once at the corporate level and again when investors in the firm receive a share of the firm's profits. Corporations generally are larger than sole proprietorships and partnerships and are therefore more difficult to organize and run. Table 6.1 reviews the advantages and disadvantages of the three types of business organizations.   **MyLab Economics** Concept Check

Corporations Earn the Majority of Revenue and Profits

Figure 6.1 gives basic statistics on the three types of business organizations. Panel (a) shows that almost three-quarters of all firms are sole proprietorships. Panels (b) and (c) show that although only 18 percent of all firms are corporations, they account for a majority of the revenue and profit earned by all firms. *Profit* is the difference between revenue and the total cost to a firm of producing the goods and services it offers for sale.

There are nearly 5.9 million corporations in the United States, but only 37,000 have annual revenues of more than $50 million. We can think of these 37,000 firms—including Apple, McDonald's, and Snap—as representing "big business." These large firms earn more than 80 percent of the total profits of all corporations in the United States.   **MyLab Economics** Concept Check

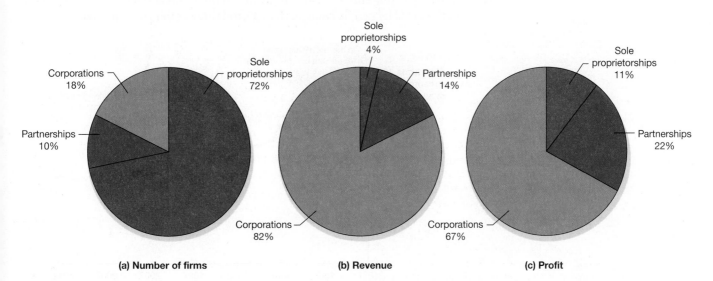

(a) Number of firms   (b) Revenue   (c) Profit

MyLab Economics Animation

Figure 6.1   Business Organizations: Sole Proprietorships, Partnerships, and Corporations

The three types of firms in the United States are sole proprietorships, partnerships, and corporations. Panel (a) shows that only 18 percent of all firms are corporations. Yet, as panels (b) and (c) show, corporations account for a majority of the revenue and profit earned by all firms.

Source: Internal Revenue Service, *Statistics of Income*, Fall 2016.

Apply the Concept

MyLab Economics Video

Why Are Fewer Young People Starting Businesses?

We have seen that although a large majority of all firms are sole proprietorships, they account for only a small fraction of the total revenue and profit earned by all firms. In fact, more than 70 percent of people work at firms that have 50 or more employees. Does this mean that small businesses are not important to the U.S. economy?

On the contrary, most economists would argue that small businesses are vital to the health of the economy. Starting a small firm provides an entrepreneur with a vehicle for bringing a new product or process to market. During the late nineteenth and early twentieth centuries, Thomas Edison, Henry Ford, and the Wright brothers introduced important products shortly after starting what were initially very small firms. In more recent years, Bill Gates, Steve Jobs, Michael Dell, and Mark Zuckerberg decided that the best way to develop their ideas was by founding Microsoft, Apple, Dell Computer, and Facebook rather than by working for large corporations.

In most years, more than 400,000 new firms open in the United States, and, of these, more than 95 percent employ fewer than 20 workers. In a typical year, new small firms create 3.3 million jobs, which is more than 40 percent of all new jobs. Looking only at newly started firms, more than 85 percent of jobs created are created by small firms.

Because of the importance of small firms, some economists and policymakers have been concerned by a slowdown in recent years in the number of firms started. As the following graph shows, in the late 1970s, about 16 percent of all firms were less than a year old. In recent years, only about 8 percent of firms were less than a year old. In absolute numbers, in recent years business startups have been running about 25 percent below the levels of just 10 years ago. The decline in starting new businesses is not concentrated in one industry or geographic area but has occurred across industries, including the information and high-tech sectors, and in most states and cities. In fact, one study of census data indicates that during the 2010–2014 period, more than half of new businesses were started in just five cities: New York, Miami, Los Angeles, Houston, and Dallas.

The decline in starting new firms has been particularly large among people under the age of 35. At first, this trend may seem surprising because of the publicity received by high-tech startups such as Twitter, Facebook, Snap, Uber, and Airbnb, all of which were started by young entrepreneurs. But while in the 1990s about one-third of all new firms were started by people younger than 35, today fewer than one-quarter are.

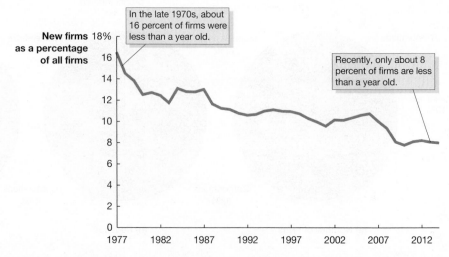

Source: U.S. Census Bureau, "Business Dynamics Statistics, Firm Characteristics Data Tables," September 2016.

Economists have not reached a consensus on the reasons for the decline in business startups. Some economists believe that despite the publicity received by innovative high-tech firms, the overall U.S. economy is experiencing a slowdown in technological progress. With fewer new technologies being introduced, there are fewer opportunities to start firms selling new goods and services. Some economists believe that an increase in government regulations has raised the costs of starting and running a small business. In particular, state and local governments have imposed licensing requirements on many occupations. According to a study by the Bureau of Labor Statistics, while in the 1950s only 5 percent of workers were in an occupation that required a license, today nearly 25 percent are. More than 1,100 occupations require a license in at least one state. In 2016, a study of New York City businesses by the city comptroller found that "nearly one third of . . . business owners report waiting six months or longer to complete the necessary approvals to open their business, and 13% take more than a year." In a rare example of agreement over policy, during the 2016 presidential campaign, Hillary Clinton and Donald Trump agreed that the federal government should reduce barriers to people wanting to open new businesses.

Many economists and policymakers worry that without an increase in young entrepreneurs starting new firms, the U.S. economy will become less dynamic and less able to sustain high rates of economic growth.

Sources: Janet Adamy, "The Five Megacities Where Business Startups Have Boomed," *Wall Street Journal*, February 1, 2017; Nicole Schubert and Jennifer Fermino, "Controller Scott Stringer Plans to Cut Red Tape Strangling Approvals for NYC Small Businesses," *New York Daily News*, March 28, 2016; Ian Hathaway and Robert E. Litan, "What's Driving the Decline in the Firm Formation Rate? A Partial Explanation," *Brookings Economic Studies*, November 20, 2014; Morris M. Kleiner and Alan B. Krueger, "Analyzing the Extent and Influence of Occupational Licensing on the Labor Market," *Journal of Labor Economics*, Vol. 31, No. S1 (Part 2), April 2013, pp. S173–S202; David Neumark, Brandon Wall, and Junfu Zhang, "Do Small Businesses Create More Jobs? New Evidence for the United States from the National Establishment Time Series," *Review of Economics and Statistics*, Vol. 93, No. 1, February 2011, pp. 16–29.

Your Turn: Test your understanding by doing related problems 1.8 and 1.9 on page 202 at the end of this chapter.

MyLab Economics Study Plan

MyLab Economics Study Plan

The Structure of Corporations and the Principal–Agent Problem

Large corporations account for a majority of revenue and profit in the economy, so it is important to know how they are managed. Most large corporations have a similar management structure. The way in which a corporation is structured and the effect that structure has on the corporation's behavior is referred to as **corporate governance**. Figure 6.2 shows the structure of the typical corporation.

Unlike the owners of family businesses, the top management of a large corporation does not generally own a large share of the firm's stock, so large corporations have a **separation of ownership from control**. Although the shareholders actually own the firm, the top management controls the firm's day-to-day operations. Because top managers own only a small percentage of the firm's stock, they may decrease the firm's profit by spending money to purchase private jets or schedule management

Corporate governance The way in which a corporation is structured and the effect that structure has on the corporation's behavior.

Separation of ownership from control A situation in a corporation in which the top management, rather than the shareholders, controls day-to-day operations.

MyLab Economics Animation

Figure 6.2   **The Structure of the Typical Corporation**

A corporation's shareholders elect a board of directors to represent their interests. The board of directors appoints a chief executive officer (CEO) to run the day-to-day operations of the corporation. Sometimes the board of directors also appoints other members of top management, such as the chief financial officer (CFO). At other times, the CEO appoints other members of top management. Members of top management—sometimes called C-suite executives—including the CEO and CFO, often serve on the board of directors. They are called inside directors. Members of the board of directors who do not have a direct management role in the firm are called outside directors. The outside directors are intended to act as a check on the decisions of top managers.

Principal–agent problem A problem caused by an agent pursuing the agent's own interests rather than the interests of the principal who hired the agent.

meetings at luxurious resorts. The conflict between the interests of shareholders and the interests of the top management is called the **principal–agent problem.**[1] This problem occurs when agents—in this case, a firm's top management—pursue their own interests rather than the interests of the principal who hired them—in this case, the shareholders of the corporation. Because the outside directors are not involved with the daily operations of the firm, they may have difficulty deciding whether the actions top managers take really are in the best interests of shareholders. To reduce the effects of the principal–agent problem, many boards of directors in the 1990s began to tie the salaries of top managers to the firm's profit or to the price of the firm's stock. They hoped this step would give top managers an incentive to make the firm as profitable as possible, thereby benefiting its shareholders. Sometimes, though, top managers act in ways that increase the profit of the firm in the short run—and the salaries and bonuses of the top managers—but actually reduce the profit of the firm in the long run.

MyLab Economics Study Plan

MyLab Economics Concept Check

 ## 6.2 How Firms Raise Funds

LEARNING OBJECTIVE: Explain how firms raise the funds they need to operate and expand.

Owners and managers of firms operate them to earn a profit. To succeed, a firm must raise funds to pay for its operations, including paying its employees and buying or renting computers and other machinery and equipment. In fact, a central challenge for anyone running a firm, whether that person is a sole proprietor or a top manager of a large corporation, is raising the funds needed to operate and expand the business. Suppose you develop a new social media app, and you decide to start a business using $100,000 you have saved in a bank. You use the $100,000 to rent an office, buy computers and other information technology, and pay other startup expenses. Your firm is a great success, and you decide to expand it by moving to a larger office and buying more information technology. As the owner of a small business, you can raise the funds for this expansion in three ways:

1. If you are making a profit, you could reinvest the profit back into your firm. Profits that are reinvested in a firm rather than taken out of the firm and paid to the firm's owners are called *retained earnings*.
2. You could raise funds by recruiting additional owners to invest in the firm. This arrangement would increase the firm's *financial capital*.
3. You could borrow the funds from relatives, friends, or a bank.

The managers of a large public firm have some additional ways to raise funds, as we will see in the next section.

Sources of External Funds

Unless firms rely on retained earnings, they have to raise the *external funds* they need from those who have funds available to invest. It is the role of an economy's *financial system* to transfer funds from savers to firms and other borrowers.

Indirect finance A flow of funds from savers to borrowers through financial intermediaries such as banks. Intermediaries raise funds from savers to lend to firms (and other borrowers).

Most firms raise external funds in two ways. The first way, called **indirect finance**, relies on financial intermediaries such as banks. If you put $1,000 in a checking account or in a certificate of deposit (CD), the bank will loan most of those funds to borrowers. The bank will combine your funds with those of other depositors and, for example, make a $100,000 loan to a local business. Small businesses rely heavily on bank loans as their primary source of external funds.

A second way for firms to acquire external funds is through *financial markets*. Raising funds in these markets, such as the New York Stock Exchange on Wall Street in

---

[1] In Chapter 5, we saw that the principal–agent problem arises from moral hazard that can occur because of asymmetric information. In this case, the asymmetric information involves top managers knowing more about how the firm is actually run than do the firm's shareholders.

New York City, is called **direct finance**. Direct finance usually takes the form of the borrower selling a *financial security* to the lender. A financial security is a document—often in electronic form—that states the terms under which the funds pass from the buyer of the security (who is lending funds) to the borrower. *Bonds* and *stocks* are the two main types of financial securities. Typically, only large corporations are able to sell bonds and stocks on financial markets. Investors are generally unwilling to buy securities issued by small and medium-sized firms because the investors lack sufficient information on the financial health of smaller firms.

Bonds **Bonds** are financial securities that represent promises to repay a fixed amount of funds. When Apple sells a bond to raise funds, it promises to pay the purchaser of the bond an interest payment each year for the term of the bond, as well as a payment of the loan amount, or the *principal*, at the end of the term. Apple may need to raise many millions of dollars to build new offices, but each individual bond has a principal, or *face value*, of $1,000, which is the amount each bond purchaser is lending Apple. So, Apple must sell many bonds to raise all the funds it needs. Suppose Apple promises it will pay interest of $40 per year to anyone who buys one of its bonds. The interest payments on a bond are called **coupon payments**. The **interest rate** is the cost of borrowing funds, usually expressed as a percentage of the amount borrowed. We can calculate the interest rate on the bond, called the *coupon rate*, by dividing the coupon by the face value of the bond. In this case, the coupon rate is:

$$\frac{\$40}{\$1,000} = 0.04, \text{ or } 4\%.$$

Many bonds that corporations issue have terms, or *maturities*, of 30 years. In this example, if you bought a bond from Apple, Apple would pay you $40 per year for 30 years, and at the end of the thirtieth year, Apple would repay the $1,000 principal to you.

The interest rate that a corporation selling a bond has to pay depends in part on how likely bond buyers—investors—think that the corporation is to default, or not make the promised coupon or principal payments. The higher the *default risk* on a bond, the higher the interest rate will be. For example, investors see the federal government as being very unlikely to default on its bonds, so federal government bonds pay a lower interest rate than do bonds of a firm such as Apple. In turn, Apple pays a lower interest rate on its bonds than does a corporation that investors believe is not as likely to make its bond payments. The interest rate on bonds also depends on how high investors expect the inflation rate to be. The higher the inflation rate, the fewer goods and services investors can buy with any given coupon payment, and the higher coupon payment investors will require before being willing to buy a bond. For example, suppose that Apple is able to sell bonds with a coupon of $40 when investors expect the inflation rate in future years will be 2 percent. If investors come to expect that the inflation rate will rise to 4 percent, they may be unwilling to buy Apple's bonds unless the firm raises the coupon rate to $60.

Direct finance A flow of funds from savers to firms through financial markets, such as the New York Stock Exchange.

Bond A financial security that represents a promise to repay a fixed amount of funds.

Coupon payment An interest payment on a bond.

Interest rate The cost of borrowing funds, usually expressed as a percentage of the amount borrowed.

Apply the Concept

MyLab Economics Video

The Rating Game: Are the Federal Government or State Governments Likely to Default on Their Bonds?

Federal regulations require that before they can sell bonds to investors, firms and governments must first have bonds rated by one of the credit-rating agencies. The three largest rating agencies are Moody's Investors Service, Standard & Poor's Corporation, and Fitch Ratings. These private firms rate bonds by giving them letter grades—AAA or Aaa being the highest—that reflect the likelihood that the firm or government will be able to make the payments on the bond. The following table shows the ratings:

	Moody's Investors Service	Standard & Poor's (S&P)	Fitch Ratings	Meaning of the Ratings
Investment-grade bonds	Aaa	AAA	AAA	Highest credit quality
	Aa	AA	AA	Very high credit quality
	A	A	A	High credit quality
	Baa	BBB	BBB	Good credit quality
Non-investment-grade bonds	Ba	BB	BB	Speculative
	B	B	B	Highly speculative
	Caa	CCC	CCC	Substantial default risk
	Ca	CC	CC	Very high levels of default risk
	C	C	C	Exceptionally high levels of default risk (for Moody's: "typically in default")
	—	D	D	Default

Note: The entries in the "Meaning of the Ratings" column are slightly modified from those that Fitch uses. The other two rating agencies have similar descriptions. For each rating from Aa to Caa, Moody's adds a numerical modifier of 1, 2, or 3. The rating Aa1 is higher than the rating Aa2, and the rating Aa2 is higher than the rating Aa3. Similarly, Standard & Poor's and Fitch Ratings add a plus (+) or minus (−) sign. The rating AA+ is higher than the rating AA, and the rating AA is higher than the rating AA−.

Source: *Money, Banking, and the Financial System*, 3rd ed., by R. Glenn Hubbard and Anthony Patrick O'Brien. Copyright © 2018 by Pearson Education, Inc. Reprinted and electronically reproduced by permission of Pearson Education, Inc., New York.

Investors can use the ratings in deciding how much risk they are willing to accept when buying a bond. Generally, the lower the rating, the higher the interest rate an investor will receive but also the higher the risk that the issuer of the bond will default.

The rating agencies charge firms and governments—rather than investors—for their services. This arrangement raises the question of whether rating agencies face a conflict of interest. Some economists and policymakers are concerned that because firms issuing bonds can choose which of the agencies to hire to rate their bonds, the agencies may have an incentive to give higher ratings than might be justified in order to keep the firms' business.

Some investors worry that the U.S. government might someday default on the bonds that it has sold. Over the past 15 years, the federal government has been spending more than it has been collecting in taxes. The result is a federal budget deficit, which forces the Treasury to sell bonds equal to the amount of the deficit. The budget deficit was particularly large during and immediately after the 2007–2009 recession, which resulted in sharp declines in tax receipts and increases in government spending. Forecasts from the U.S. Congressional Budget Office indicate that large budget deficits will continue indefinitely because spending on Social Security, Medicare, Medicaid, and other government programs is expected to increase faster than tax revenues.

In 2011, Standard & Poor's (S&P) decided that because of these continuing deficits, it would downgrade U.S. Treasury bonds from AAA to AA+. Never before had a rating agency given Treasury bonds less than an AAA rating. Is it likely that the U.S. Treasury will default on its bonds? S&P argued that while a default is still unlikely, the continuing large deficits increased the chance that someday the Treasury might not make the interest payments on its bonds. Most investors, though, appear confident that the Treasury will not default and are willing to buy Treasury bonds despite the historically low interest rates on the bonds.

Some investors worry that some U.S. state governments might default on their bonds. Many states have substantial obligations to make pension payments to retired teachers and other public employees. Making these payments may be difficult without large increases in taxes or cuts in other state spending. During 2016, S&P reduced the ratings on bonds issued by four states. As a result, interest rates on the bonds issued by these states rose. But even the state of Illinois, with a bond rating of just BBB, had the interest rate on its bonds rise only to 4 percent. Although this rate was about 1.5 percentage points higher than the rates on bonds issued by states with better credit ratings, it was still low enough to indicate that investors did not believe there was substantial risk that Illinois would fail to make the payments on its bonds.

Sources: Greg Ip, "Sovereign Default: It's Not Personal, Just Business," *Wall Street Journal*, May 25, 2016; Reuters, "S&P Cuts Illinois' Credit Rating on State's 'Weak' Management," cnbc.com, October 1, 2016; and Cyrus Sanati, "S.E.C. Urges Changes to Ratings-Agency Rules," *New York Times*, August 28, 2009.

Your Turn: Test your understanding by doing related problems 2.8 and 2.9 on page 203 at the end of this chapter.

MyLab Economics Study Plan

Stocks When you buy a newly issued bond from a firm, you are lending funds to that firm. When you buy **stock** issued by a firm, you are actually buying part owner-ship of that firm. A corporation selling stock is doing the same thing the owner of a small business does when he or she takes on a partner: The firm is increasing its financial capital by bringing additional owners into the firm. Any one shareholder usually owns only a small fraction of the total shares of stock issued by a corporation.

Many small investors buy shares of *mutual funds* rather than directly buying stocks issued by individual companies. Mutual funds, such as Fidelity Investment's Magellan Fund, sell shares to investors and use the funds to invest in a portfolio of financial assets, such as stocks and bonds. By buying shares in a mutual fund, small investors reduce the costs they would pay to buy many individual stocks and bonds. Small savers who have only enough money to buy a few individual stocks and bonds can use mutual funds to *diversify*, which lowers their investment risk because most mutual funds hold a large num-ber of stocks and bonds. If a firm issuing a stock or bond declares bankruptcy, causing the stock or bond to lose all of its value, the effect on a mutual fund's portfolio is likely to be small. The effect might be devastating, though, to a small investor who invested most of his or her savings in the stock or bond. Because mutual funds are willing to buy back their shares at any time, they also provide savers with easy access to their money.

Exchange-traded funds (ETFs) are similar to mutual funds in that when you buy shares in an ETF, you are buying a claim to a portfolio of stocks or bonds. But mutual funds can only be bought from or sold back to the firm that issues them. ETFs can be bought and sold to other investors in financial markets, just like individual stocks or bonds. And while mutual funds can only be sold at the end of the trading day (4:30 P.M. on the New Stock Exchange), ETFs can be bought and sold throughout the day.

A shareholder is entitled to a portion of the corporation's profits, if there are any. Corporations generally keep some of their profits as retained earnings to finance future expansion. The remaining profits are paid to shareholders as **dividends**. If a firm uses its retained earnings to grow and earn an economic profit, its share price rises, which provides a *capital gain* for investors. If a corporation is unable to make a profit, it usually does not pay a dividend. Under the law, corporations must make payments on any debt they have before making payments to their owners. That is, a corporation must make promised payments to bondholders before it can make any dividend payments to share-holders. Unlike bonds, stocks do not have a maturity date, so the firm is not obliged to return the investor's funds at any particular date.   **MyLab Economics** Concept Check

> **Stock** A financial security that represents partial ownership of a firm.

> **Dividends** Payments by a corporation to its shareholders.

Stock and Bond Markets Provide Capital—and Information

The original purchasers of stocks and bonds may resell them to other investors. In fact, most of the buying and selling of stocks and bonds that takes place each day involves investors reselling existing stocks and bonds to each other rather than corporations selling new stocks and bonds to investors. The buyers and sellers of stocks and bonds together make up the *stock and bond markets*. There is no single place where stocks and bonds are bought and sold. Some trading of stocks and bonds takes place in buildings known as *exchanges*, such as the New York Stock Exchange or the Tokyo Stock Exchange. In the United States, the stocks and bonds of the largest corporations are traded on the New York Stock Exchange. The development of computer technology has spread the trading of stocks and bonds outside exchanges to *securities dealers* linked by computers. These dealers comprise the *over-the-counter market*. The stocks of many high-technology firms—including Apple, Snap, Twitter, and Facebook—are traded in the most impor-tant of the over-the-counter markets, the *National Association of Securities Dealers Automated Quotations* system, which is referred to by its acronym, NASDAQ. Today, even stocks and bonds that are traded on exchanges like the New York Stock Exchange are typically traded electronically rather than face-to-face by dealers on the floor of the exchange.

Shares of stock represent claims on the profits of the firms that issue them. Therefore, as the fortunes of the firms change and they earn more or less profit, the prices of the stock the firms have issued should also change. Similarly, bonds represent claims to receive coupon payments and one final payment of the principal. Therefore, a particular bond that was issued in the past may have its price go up or down, depending on whether the coupon payments being offered on newly issued bonds are higher or lower than those on existing bonds. If you hold a bond with a coupon of $30 per year, and similar newly issued bonds have coupons of $40 per year, the price of your bond will fall because it is less attractive to investors. The price of a bond will also be affected by changes in *default risk*, which reflects investors' expectations of the issuing firm's ability to make the coupon payments. For example, if investors begin to believe that a firm may soon go out of business and stop making coupon payments to its bondholders, the price of the firm's bonds will fall to very low levels.

Changes in the value of a firm's stocks and bonds provide important information for a firm's managers, as well as for investors. An increase in the stock price means that investors are more optimistic about the firm's profit prospects, and the firm's managers might want to expand the firm's operations as a result. By contrast, a decrease in the firm's stock price indicates that investors are less optimistic about the firm's profit prospects, so management may want to shrink the firm's operations. Similarly, changes in the value of the firm's bonds imply changes in the cost of external funds to finance the firm's investment in research and development or in new factories. A higher bond price indicates a lower cost of new external funds, while a lower bond price indicates a higher cost of new external funds.   **MyLab Economics** Concept Check

The Fluctuating Stock Market

When economists, investors, and policymakers are interested in measuring the performance of the stock market, they don't do so by following the price of any one company—even a company as large and important as Apple, Walmart, or General Motors. Instead,

Don't Let This Happen to You

When Snap Shares Are Sold, Snap Doesn't Get the Money

Shares of Snap, the parent company of the social media app Snapchat, are a popular investment, with investors buying and selling shares often as their views about the value of the firm shift. That's great for Snap, right? Think of Snap collecting all that money as shares change hands and the stock price goes up. *Wrong*. Snap raises funds in a primary market, but its shares trade in a secondary market. Those trades don't put money into Snap's hands, but they do give important information to the firm's managers. Let's see why.

Primary markets are markets in which firms sell newly issued stocks and bonds to initial buyers. Businesses can raise funds in a primary financial market in two ways—by borrowing (selling bonds) or selling shares of stock—which result in different types of claims on the borrowing firm's future income. Although you may hear about stock market fluctuations every day in news updates, bonds actually account for more of the funds raised by borrowers. The total value of bonds in the United States is typically about twice the value of stocks.

In *secondary markets*, stocks and bonds that have already been issued are sold by one investor to another. When Snap sells shares to the public, it is turning to a primary market for new funds. (When a private company goes public by selling stock for the first time, the stock sale is called an *initial public offering* [*IPO*].) Once Snap's shares are issued, investors trade the shares in the secondary market. Snap does not receive any new funds when its shares are traded. The initial seller of a stock or bond raises funds from an investor only in the primary market. Secondary markets convey information to firms' managers and investors by determining the prices of stocks and bonds. For example, a major increase in Snap's stock price conveys the market's optimism about the firm, and Snap may decide to raise funds to expand. So, secondary markets are valuable sources of information for corporations that are considering raising funds.

Primary and secondary markets are both important, but they play different roles. As an investor, you principally trade stocks and bonds in a secondary market. If you become a corporate manager, you may help decide how to raise new funds to expand the firm where you work.

MyLab Economics Study Plan

Your Turn: Test your understanding by doing related problem 2.11 on page 203 at the end of this chapter.

they measure the overall performance of the stock market by using *stock market indexes,* which are averages of stock prices.

The most widely followed stock market indexes are the three that appear on the first page of the *Wall Street Journal*'s Web site: the Dow Jones Industrial Average, the S&P 500, and the NASDAQ Composite Index. Although the Dow is an average of the prices of the stocks of just 30 large firms, including Coca-Cola, Microsoft, and Walt Disney, it is the most familiar index to many individual investors. The S&P 500 index includes the 30 stocks that are in the Dow as well as stocks issued by 470 other large companies, each of which has a market capitalization of at least $5 billion. Because these firms are so large, the total value of their stocks represents about 80% of the value of all publicly traded U.S. firms. The NASDAQ Composite Index includes the more than 3,000 stocks that are traded in the NASDAQ over-the-counter market. Some firms in the NASDAQ Composite Index, such as Microsoft and Intel, are also included in the Dow and in the S&P 500, but the NASDAQ includes stocks issued by many smaller technology firms that are not included in the other indexes.

There are two key points about index numbers, like the stock market indexes, to keep in mind:

1. The numbers are not measured in dollars or any other units. Indexes are set equal to 100 in a particular year, called the *base year*. Because indexes are designed to show movements in a variable over time, the year chosen as the base year is not important.
2. The values of index numbers aren't meaningful by themselves; changes in their values are important. For instance, the value of the S&P 500 was 2095 in 2016. No one is particularly interested in that value by itself, but the fact that the S&P 500 increased from 2061 in 2015 to 2095 in 2016 is interesting because it tells us that this measure of stock prices increased by:

$$\left(\frac{2095 - 2061}{2061} \right) \times 100 = 1.6 \text{ percent.}$$

(For a review of how to calculate percentage increases, see the appendix to Chapter 1.) This increase is relatively small when compared to the long-run increase in stock prices, which has averaged about 10 percent per year.

Figure 6.3 shows movements from 1999 to 2017 in the three most widely followed stock indexes. (The shaded areas represent months in which the U.S. economy

(a) Dow Jones Industrial Average   (b) S&P 500   (c) NASDAQ Composite Index

Figure 6.3   **Movements in Stock Market Indexes, 1999 to 2017**

The performance of the U.S. stock market is often measured by market indexes, which are averages of stock prices. The three most important indexes are the Dow Jones Industrial Average, the S&P 500, and the NASDAQ Composite Index. During the period from 1999 to 2017, the three indexes followed similar patterns, rising when the U.S. economy was expanding and falling when the economy was in recession. Note that in all three panels, the vertical axis does not start at zero.

was in a business cycle recession, when the production and profits of many firms were falling.)

As we have seen, ownership of a firm's stock represents a claim on the firm's profits. So, the larger the firm's profits are, the higher its stock price will be. When the overall economy is expanding, incomes, employment, and spending will all increase, as will corporate profits. When the economy is in a recession, incomes, employment, and spending will fall, as will corporate profits. Therefore, we would expect that stock prices will rise when the economy is expanding and fall when the economy is in recession. We see this pattern reflected in the three stock market indexes shown in Figure 6.3. All three indexes follow a roughly similar pattern: increases in stock prices during the economic expansion of the late 1990s; declines after the "dot-com crash" of 2000 and the recession of 2001; increases from late 2001 to late 2007; declines as the U.S. economy entered a recession at the end of 2007; and then increases beginning in early 2009. In 2017, as recovery from the recession continued, all three indexes had reached their highest values ever.   **MyLab Economics** Concept Check

Apply the Concept   MyLab Economics Video

Why Are Many People Poor Stock Market Investors?

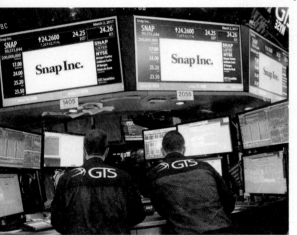

Monika Graff/UPI/Newscom

New information about Snap's future profitability would cause the price of its stock to change.

You've probably heard this standard advice about investing: "Buy low and sell high." That is, you should buy shares of stocks and other financial assets when their prices are low and sell them when their prices are high. Unfortunately, many people do the opposite. For instance, many people bought shares of Apple stock when it was selling for more than $130 per share in May 2015 and sold when it was below $94 per share in April 2016 . . . only to regret the sale when the price bounced back to $143 per share in April 2017.

Stock prices are difficult to predict, but many people convince themselves that a stock whose price has been rising will continue to rise and that a stock whose price has been falling will continue to fall. As a result, people end up buying high and selling low rather than the reverse. Studies have shown that individual investors consistently earn lower returns on their investments when they frequently buy and sell stock hoping to predict changes in stock prices.

But why are stock prices so difficult to predict? The key reason is that stock prices are based less on the *current* profitability of firms than on their *expected* future profitability. After all, few investors would be willing to pay a high price for a stock that was profitable today but was expected to suffer large losses tomorrow. Similarly, investors in the fall of 2017 were willing to pay $14 per share for Snap even though the firm was suffering losses because they expected it would earn profits in the future. If you look carefully at Figure 6.3, you can see that stock prices start to rise when investors begin to expect that an economic recovery will soon begin rather than after the recovery has already begun.

Many Wall Street investment professionals spend a lot of time and money gathering all possible information about the future profitability of firms, hoping to buy stock in the most profitable firms. As a result, all of the information about a firm that is available in newspapers, financial magazines, cable business shows, and online is reflected in the firm's stock price. For example, if at the end of a particular day, Snap is selling for $15 per share, that price reflects all the information available about Snap's future profitability. What might cause Snap's stock price to change? *Only new information about its future profitability.* For example, if Snap releases new data showing that its advertising sales on Snapchat have been lower than investors had expected, its stock price will fall.

Even highly paid professional investors cannot consistently predict stock prices. The managers of mutual funds and ETFs who try to earn high returns by frequently buying and selling stocks are rarely able to beat the stock market averages, such as the S&P 500. One study found that, in a typical year, only one-third of mutual fund managers were able to earn their investors a higher return than a small investor could earn by investing in an index mutual fund that buys only the stocks in the S&P 500. Only 10 percent of mutual fund managers earned a higher return than an index fund for two consecutive years.

Whichever way you—or Wall Street professionals—predict stock prices will move in the future, you are as likely to be wrong as you are to be right.

Sources: Morgan Housel, "Three Mistakes Investors Keep Making Again and Again," *Wall Street Journal*, September 12, 2014; Chris Dieterich, "Hedge Fund Short Bets Are Going the Wrong Way . . . Again," *Wall Street Journal*, February 7, 2017; Deepa Seetharaman, "A Rival's Shadow Looms Over Snapchat IPO," *Wall Street Journal*, February 5, 2017; and Howard Gold, "Almost No One Can Beat the Market," marketwatch.com, October 25, 2013.

Your Turn: Test your understanding by doing related problem 2.12 on page 203 at the end of this chapter.

MyLab Economics Study Plan

Solved Problem 6.2

MyLab Economics Interactive Animation

Why Does Warren Buffett Like Mutual Funds?

Warren Buffett is considered one of the greatest investors who has ever lived. His ability to predict which firms' stocks are likely to rise in price helped make him one of the richest people in the world. Yet Buffett advises that individual investors not try to pick individual stocks but instead use 90 percent of their savings to buy shares in mutual funds that charge low fees, such as those offered by the Vanguard Group. Is it likely that anyone investing mostly in mutual funds will become as wealthy as Buffett? Why would Buffett give this advice?

Solving the Problem

Step 1: Review the chapter material. This problem is about investing in the stock market, so you may want to review the section "The Fluctuating Stock Market," which begins on page 190, and the *Apply the Concept* "Why Are Many People Poor Stock Market Investors?" which begins on page 192.

Step 2: Answer the first question by explaining whether investing in low-cost mutual funds is a way to become as wealthy as Warren Buffett. Most investors who have become wealthy have done so by making large investments in just a few firms. Mutual funds typically hold large numbers of stocks and bonds, so even if one or two of the stocks do extremely well, the total investment return from the fund will be held back by the smaller increases (or losses) in the other stocks in the fund. By investing in mutual funds, you can accumulate significant amounts to pay for a house, a college education, or retirement. Many people who have earned only middle-class incomes have accumulated a million dollars or more by retirement age by investing in low-cost mutual funds. But no one is known to have become fabulously wealthy with this approach to saving.

Step 3: Answer the second question by explaining why Warren Buffett would advise most people to put their savings in mutual funds, even though they are unlikely to become wealthy by doing so. Mutual funds give individual investors a low-cost way to diversify. Although it's possible to earn a high return investing in the stocks of individual firms, it's also easy for a small investor to lose all of his or her money if those firms run into financial problems. As Buffett put it in one of his annual letters to investors in his company, Berkshire Hathaway: "Active investment management by professionals—in aggregate—[will] over a period of years underperform the returns achieved by rank amateurs who simply [sit] still . . . [by investing] in an unmanaged low-cost index fund."

Extra Credit: Warren Buffett may have become a billionaire by being better than other investors at predicting the future profits of the firms he invests in. Or he may have become a billionaire because he was lucky that the firms he invested in did particularly well—in which case he may not be better at forecasting the future profitability of firms than are other investors. Given that nearly all other equally intelligent and hard-working professional investors have been unable to consistently "beat the market" by earning higher returns than those earned by the typical low-cost, well-diversified mutual fund, it is impossible to know with certainty the true reasons for Buffett's success.

Source: Warren Buffett, *Letter to Berkshire Shareholders*, February 25, 2017, p. 21.

MyLab Economics Study Plan   **Your Turn:** For more practice, do related problem 2.13 on page 203 at the end of this chapter.

 ## Using Financial Statements to Evaluate a Corporation

LEARNING OBJECTIVE: Describe the information corporations include in their financial statements.

To raise funds, a firm's managers must persuade potential lenders or investors that the firm will be profitable. Before a firm can sell new issues of stocks or bonds, it must first provide investors and financial regulators with information about its finances. To borrow from a bank, a firm must also provide the bank with financial information.

The Securities and Exchange Commission (SEC) requires publicly owned firms to report their performance in financial statements prepared using standard accounting methods, often referred to as *generally accepted accounting principles*. Such disclosure reduces the cost to investors of gathering information about firms, but it doesn't eliminate these costs—for two reasons. First, some firms may be too young to have much information for potential investors to evaluate. Second, managers may try to present the required information in the most favorable way so that investors will overvalue their securities.

Private firms also collect information on business borrowers and sell the information to lenders and investors. If the information-gathering firms do a good job, lenders and investors purchasing the information will be better able to judge the quality of borrowing firms. Some firms—including Moody's Investors Service, Standard & Poor's Corporation, Value Line, and Dun & Bradstreet—collect information from businesses and sell it to subscribers. Buyers include individual investors, libraries, and financial intermediaries. You can find some of these publications in your college library or through online information services.

What kind of information do investors and firm managers need? A firm must answer three basic questions: What to produce? How to produce it? What price to charge? To answer these questions, a firm's managers need two pieces of information: The first is the firm's revenues and costs, and the second is the value of the property and other assets the firm owns and the firm's debts, or other **liabilities**, that it owes to households and other firms. Potential investors in the firm also need this information to decide whether to buy the firm's stocks or bonds. The information can be found in the firm's *financial statements*, principally its income statement and balance sheet, which we discuss next.

Liability Anything owed by a person or a firm.

The Income Statement

A firm's **income statement** shows its revenues, costs, and profit over a period of time. Corporations issue annual income statements, although the 12-month *fiscal year* covered may be different from the calendar year to better represent the seasonal pattern of the business. We explore income statements in greater detail in the appendix to this chapter.

Income statement A financial statement that shows a firm's revenues, costs, and profit over a period of time.

Accounting Profit An income statement shows a firm's revenue, costs, and profit for the firm's fiscal year. To determine profitability, the income statement starts with the firm's revenue and subtracts its operating expenses and taxes paid. The remainder, *net income*, is the **accounting profit** of the firm.

Economic Profit Accounting profit provides information on a firm's current net income, measured according to accepted accounting standards. Accounting profit is not, however, the ideal measure of a firm's profit because it doesn't include some of the firm's costs. *Economic profit* provides a better indication than accounting profit of how successful a firm is because economic profit is calculated using all of a firm's costs. Firms making an economic profit will remain in business and may even expand. Firms making an *economic loss* are unlikely to remain in business in the long run. To understand how economic profit is calculated, remember that economists always measure cost as *opportunity cost*. The **opportunity cost** of any activity is the highest-valued alternative that must be given up to engage in that activity. Costs are either *explicit* or *implicit*. When a firm spends money, an **explicit cost** results. If a firm incurs an opportunity cost but does not spend money, an **implicit cost** results. For example, firms incur an explicit labor cost when they pay wages to employees. Firms have many other explicit costs as well, such as the cost of the electricity used to light their buildings or the costs of advertising or insurance.

Some costs are implicit, however. The most important of these is the opportunity cost to investors of the funds they have invested in the firm. Economists use the term *normal rate of return* to refer to the minimum amount that investors must earn on the funds they invest in a firm, expressed as a percentage of the amount invested. If a firm fails to provide investors with at least a normal rate of return, it will not be able to remain in business over the long run because investors will not continue to invest their funds in the firm. For example, by 2013, once-popular teen clothing retailer Wet Seal was suffering from falling sales due to declining customer traffic in malls and competition from online sellers. Many investors expected the firm to eventually declare bankruptcy, and as a result, the price of its stock dropped from $5 per share to less than $1 per share. In 2017, the firm closed all its stores, and its remaining assets were sold off. The return (in dollars) that investors require to continue investing in a firm is a true cost to the firm and should be subtracted from the firm's revenues to calculate its profit.

The rate of return that investors require to continue investing in a firm varies from firm to firm. If the investment is risky—as would be the case with a biotechnology startup—investors may require a high rate of return to compensate them for the risk. Investors in firms in more established industries, such as electric utilities, may require lower rates of return. The exact rate of return investors require to invest in any particular firm is difficult to calculate, which also makes it difficult for an accountant to include the return as a cost on an income statement. Firms have other implicit costs, besides the return investors require, that can also be difficult to calculate. As a result, the rules of accounting generally require that only explicit costs be included in the firm's financial records. *Economic costs* include both explicit costs *and* implicit costs. **Economic profit** is equal to a firm's revenues minus its economic costs. Because accounting profit excludes some implicit costs, it is larger than economic profit.   MyLab Economics Concept Check

The Balance Sheet

A firm's **balance sheet** shows its financial position on a particular day, usually the end of a quarter or year. Recall that an asset is anything of value that a firm owns, and a liability is a debt or an obligation owed by a firm. Subtracting the value of a firm's liabilities from the value of its assets leaves its *net worth*. We can think of the net worth as what the firm's owners would be left with if the firm were closed, its assets were sold, and its liabilities were paid off. Investors can determine a firm's net worth by inspecting its balance sheet. We analyze balance sheets in more detail in the appendix to this chapter.   MyLab Economics Concept Check   MyLab Economics Study Plan

Accounting profit A firm's net income, measured as revenue minus operating expenses and taxes paid.

Opportunity cost The highest-valued alternative that must be given up to engage in an activity.

Explicit cost A cost that involves spending money.

Implicit cost A nonmonetary opportunity cost.

Economic profit A firm's revenues minus all of its implicit and explicit costs.

Balance sheet A financial statement that sums up a firm's financial position on a particular day, usually the end of a quarter or year.

6.4 Recent Issues in Corporate Governance Policy

LEARNING OBJECTIVE: Discuss the debate over corporate governance policy.

Accurate and easy-to-understand financial statements help a firm's managers make decisions and provide information to investors who are considering buying the firm's stock or bonds. In fact, the information in financial statements helps guide resource allocation in the economy.

Firms disclose financial statements in periodic filings to the federal government and in *annual reports* to shareholders. An investor is more likely to buy a firm's stock if the firm's income statement shows a large after-tax profit and if its balance sheet shows a large net worth. The top management of a firm has at least two reasons to attract investors and keep the firm's stock price high. First, a higher stock price increases the funds the firm can raise when it sells a given amount of stock. Second, to reduce the principal–agent problem, boards of directors often tie the salaries of top managers to the firm's stock price or to the profitability of the firm.

Top managers clearly have an incentive to maximize the profit reported on the income statement and the net worth reported on the balance sheet. If top managers make good decisions, the firm's profit will be high, and the firm's assets will be large relative to its liabilities. Problems that surfaced during the early 2000s, however, revealed that at some firms, top managers inflated profits and concealed liabilities that should have been listed on their balance sheets. At other firms, managers took on more risk than they disclosed to investors. We will explore problems with corporate governance and the government's reaction to these problems by discussing the accounting scandals of the early 2000s and problems that many financial firms encountered during the recession of 2007–2009.

The Accounting Scandals of the Early 2000s

In the early 2000s, the top managers of several well-known firms, including Enron, an energy trading firm, and WorldCom, a telecommunications firm, falsified their firms' financial statements in order to mislead investors about how profitable the firms actually were. Several top managers were sentenced to long prison terms, and some of the firms, including Enron, went out of business.

How was it possible for corporations such as Enron and WorldCom to falsify their financial statements? The federal government regulates how financial statements are prepared, but this regulation cannot by itself guarantee the accuracy of the statements. All firms that issue stock to the public have certified public accountants who work for outside firms *audit* their financial statements. Unfortunately, as the Enron and World-Com scandals revealed, top managers who are determined to deceive investors about the true financial condition of their firms can also deceive outside auditors.

To guard against future scandals, new federal legislation was enacted in 2002. The landmark *Sarbanes-Oxley Act* of 2002 requires that CEOs personally certify the accuracy of financial statements. The Sarbanes-Oxley Act also requires that financial analysts and auditors disclose whether any conflicts of interest might exist that would limit their independence in evaluating a firm's financial condition. On balance, most observers acknowledge that the Sarbanes-Oxley Act increased confidence in the U.S. corporate governance system. However, as we will discuss in the next section, problems during 2007–2009 at financial firms again raised questions about whether corporations were adequately disclosing information to investors.   **MyLab Economics** Concept Check

Corporate Governance and the Financial Crisis of 2007–2009

Beginning in 2007 and lasting into 2009, the U.S. economy suffered its worst financial crisis since the Great Depression of the 1930s. At the heart of the crisis was a problem in the market for home mortgages. When people buy houses, they typically borrow the money by taking out a mortgage loan from a bank or another financial institution. The house they are buying is pledged as collateral for the loan, meaning that the bank can take possession of the house and sell it if the borrower defaults by failing to make the payments on the loan. In a process called *securitization*, banks and other financial firms bundled many mortgages together into *mortgage-backed securities*, which are very similar to bonds in that the investor who buys one receives regular interest payments. In this case, owners of the securities would receive payments that came from the payments being made on the original mortgage loans.

By the early 2000s, banks and other financial institutions were loosening the standards for granting mortgages. Lenders began granting mortgages to *subprime borrowers*, whose credit histories included failing to pay all their bills on time, and *Alt-A borrowers*, who failed to document that their incomes were high enough to afford their mortgage payments. The ease of obtaining a mortgage increased demand for housing and caused prices to soar.

This *housing bubble* began to deflate in mid-2006, with prices in many cities beginning a sharp downturn. By 2007, many borrowers—particularly subprime and Alt-A borrowers—began to default on their mortgages. These defaults were bad news for anyone owning mortgage-backed securities because the value of these securities depended on steady payments being made on the underlying mortgages. As prices of these securities plunged, the result was a financial crisis as many financial institutions suffered heavy losses, and some of the largest of them remained in business only because they received aid from the federal government. Some economists argue that the firms did a poor job of correctly assessing the risk of the investments they made in these securities. This failure may be an indication of poor corporate governance if top managers were unable to effectively monitor the employees who were deciding to invest in risky securities.　　　　　　　　　　　　　　　　　　　　**MyLab Economics** Concept Check

Government Regulation in Response to the Financial Crisis

During the financial crisis, many investors complained that they weren't aware of the riskiness of some of the assets—particularly mortgage-backed securities—on the balance sheets of financial firms. Some observers believed that the managers of many financial firms had intentionally misled investors about the riskiness of these assets. Others argued that the managers themselves had not understood how risky the assets were. As the crisis passed, in July 2010, Congress overhauled the regulation of the financial system with the passage of the **Wall Street Reform and Consumer Protection Act**, referred to as the **Dodd-Frank Act**. Among its provisions, the act created the Consumer Financial Protection Bureau, housed in the Federal Reserve—the central bank of the United States—to write rules intended to protect consumers in their borrowing and investing activities. The act also established the Financial Stability Oversight Council, which includes representatives from all the major federal financial regulatory bodies, including the SEC and the Federal Reserve. The council is intended to identify and act on risks to the financial system. Economists are divided in their opinions about whether the Dodd-Frank Act will significantly reduce the risk of future financial crises. In 2017, President Donald Trump argued that Dodd-Frank was doing more harm than good to the financial system and that its provisions should be modified.　　　　　　　　　　　　　　　　　　　　**MyLab Economics** Concept Check

Wall Street Reform and Consumer Protection Act (Dodd-Frank Act) Legislation passed during 2010 that was intended to reform regulation of the financial system.

Did Principal–Agent Problems Help Cause the 2007–2009 Financial Crisis?

As we have seen, the process of securitizing mortgages played an important role in the financial crisis of 2007–2009. Beginning in the 1990s, private investment banks began to securitize mortgages. Unlike commercial banks, whose main activities are accepting deposits and making loans, investment banks had traditionally concentrated on providing advice to corporations on selling new stocks and bonds and on *underwriting* the issuance of stocks and bonds by guaranteeing a price to the firm selling them.

Why did investment banks take on so much risk by originating securities backed by mortgages granted to borrowers who had a significant likelihood of defaulting on the loans? Michael Lewis, a financial journalist and former Wall Street bond salesman, argued that a key reason was a change in how the investment banks were organized.

Traditionally, large Wall Street investment banks had been organized as partnerships, but by 2000, they had all converted to being publicly traded corporations. As we have seen, in a partnership, the funds of the relatively small group of owners are put directly at risk, and the principal–agent problem is reduced because there is little separation of ownership from control. With a publicly traded corporation, on the other hand, the principal–agent problem can be severe. Lewis argued:

> No investment bank owned by its employees would have . . . bought and held $50 billion in [exotic mortgage-backed securities] . . . or even allow [these securities] to be sold to its customers. The hoped-for short-term gain would not have justified the long-term hit.

Issues of corporate governance will clearly continue to be a concern for economists, policymakers, and investors. **MyLab Economics** Concept Check

Apply the Concept

MyLab Economics Video

Should Investors Worry about Corporate Governance at Snapchat?

We saw in the chapter opener that advertising is the main factor determining whether a social media app will be profitable. In 2017, Facebook had succeeded in attracting substantial advertising and was very profitable. Twitter, in contrast, struggled to attract advertising and was suffering losses. In March 2017, as Snap began selling stock in an *initial public offering* (IPO), many investors were uncertain whether the Snapchat app would earn enough advertising revenue to become profitable.

But some investors were concerned as well about potential corporate governance issues at Snap. Snap's IPO was unusual in that investors buying newly issued shares would not have the voting rights that shareholders typically have. Snap has three classes of stock:

Lucas Jackson/REUTERS/Alamy Stock Photo

Snap's co-founders, Evan Spiegel and Bobby Murphy, own 90 percent of the voting shares in the company, which worries some investors.

Class of Stock	Voting Rights	Relevance to Snap's IPO
Class A	No voting rights	The IPO consisted only of Class A shares, meaning that investors who bought them would have no votes in electing members of Snap's board of directors.
Class B	1 vote per share	Class B shares were sold to early investors who had provided funds to the firm prior to the IPO.
Class C	10 votes per share	Evan Spiegel and Bobby Murphy, Snap's cofounders, retained all of the Class C shares.

The result of this structure is that Spiegel and Murphy own 90 percent of the voting shares in the company, giving them much more control than top managers typically have at a public company. As a financial columnist for the *New York Times* put it, "The only way the two founders are ever really going to lose control of Snap is if both die."

Google and Facebook also have issued non-voting shares, but Snap became the first firm in the history of U.S. financial markets to have an IPO that consisted entirely of non-voting shares. Does Snap's governance structure matter? Many investors apparently don't think so because on the day of its IPO, March 2, 2017, Snap had no trouble selling 200 million Class A shares, which raised $3.4 billion for the firm. Other investors, though, particularly some pension funds and other institutional investors, were unwilling to invest in Snap because of the firm's governance structure. They worried that without the ability to elect outside directors, there would be no chance to bring in new top managers if Spiegel and Murphy failed to make the Snapchat app profitable.

Similarly, it wouldn't be possible for the directors to sell the firm to outside investors even if doing so would likely increase the value of the Class A shares. As one investor put it, Snap's governance structure "reduces the role of a board [of directors] member to that of an adviser who works at the behest or pleasure of the founder."

Spiegel and Murphy, and the founders of other technology firms, argue, though, that they have good reason to limit the voting rights of shareholders. They believe that shareholders with voting rights can push top management into making decisions that might help boost profit in the short run but that will be bad for the firm—and its shareholders—in the long term. As an article in the *Wall Street Journal* put it, "They wanted to decide what Snap should do and which products to create whether or not anyone else agreed." Academic studies have shown that the stock prices of companies that issue non-voting shares perform about as well as the stock prices of companies that do not issue non-voting shares.

In the end, many investors seemed to believe that Snap's future success would depend more on its ability to expand its advertising revenue by attracting users beyond its core audience of teenagers and young adults than on its corporate governance structure.

Sources: Maureen Farrell, "Tech Founders Want IPO Riches without Those Pesky Shareholders," *Wall Street Journal*, April 3, 2017; Steven Davidoff Solomon, "Snap's Plan Is Most Unfriendly to Outsiders," *New York Times*, February 3, 2017; Maureen Farrell, "In Snap IPO, New Investors to Get Zero Votes, while Founders Keep Control," *Wall Street Journal*, January 16, 2017; and Justin Fox, "Snap's Experiment in Totalitarian Capitalism," bloomberg.com, March 6, 2017.

Your Turn: Test your understanding by doing related problems 4.5 and 4.6 on page 204 at the end of this chapter.

MyLab Economics Study Plan

Continued from page 181

Economics in Your Life & Career

Would You Recommend That Snapchat or Twitter Start Charging Users?

At the beginning of the chapter, we asked what factors you, as an economist for a social media company, would consider in evaluating a proposal for the app to start charging users in exchange for their not having to view advertisements. One factor to consider is how much the app should charge users. A business columnist suggested that after five free tweets, Twitter should charge users 2 cents per tweet. To evaluate this strategy, you would need to gather information on how responsive users of the app would be to being charged for the service. In part, this responsiveness would depend on how annoyed the typical app user is by targeted ads. Some people actually find the information in targeted ads useful and would prefer to see the ads rather than pay any fee.

In practice, people have become increasingly reluctant to pay anything to download and use an app. Some free apps are downloaded millions of times, while very similar apps that charge a small fee have significantly fewer downloads. In a given year, only about one-third of smartphone or tablet owners will pay for any apps. App developers have mostly adopted the business model of allowing their apps to be downloaded and used for free while trying to still earn money from users. For instance, the popular games *Clash of Clans* and *Candy Crush Saga* can be downloaded and played for free. The developers earn a profit from people who pay to play the game faster, get extra turns, or otherwise receive benefits not available to those who play for free. The usefulness of social media apps increases as more people use them. If only a few people were on Facebook, Twitter, or Snapchat, these apps wouldn't be much fun. So, these apps can't afford the significant decline in users that would likely occur if they began to charge a fee. The remaining users who were paying would likely find the apps less fun because fewer people would be on them, and they might gradually stop using them.

So, as an economist working for one of these social media companies, you might advise them that charging app users is probably not a good way to increase revenue.

Conclusion

In a market system, firms make independent decisions about which goods and services to produce, how to produce them, and what prices to charge. In modern high-income countries, such as the United States, large corporations account for a majority of the sales and profits earned by firms. Generally, the managers of these corporations do a good job of representing the interests of stockholders while providing the goods and services demanded by consumers. As the business scandals of the early 2000s and the problems with financial firms in 2007–2009 showed, however, the principal–agent problem can sometimes become severe. Economists debate the costs and benefits of regulations proposed to address these problems.

Visit **MyLab Economics** for a news article and analysis related to the concepts in this chapter.

Key Terms

Accounting profit, p. 195

Asset, p. 182

Balance sheet, p. 195

Bond, p. 187

Corporate governance, p. 185

Corporation, p. 182

Coupon payment, p. 187

Direct finance, p. 187

Dividends, p. 189

Economic profit, p. 195

Explicit cost, p. 195

Implicit cost, p. 195

Income statement, p. 194

Indirect finance, p. 186

Interest rate, p. 187

Liability, p. 194

Limited liability, p. 182

Opportunity cost, p. 195

Partnership, p. 182

Principal–agent problem, p. 186

Separation of ownership from control, p. 185

Sole proprietorship, p. 182

Stock, p. 189

Wall Street Reform and Consumer Protection Act (Dodd-Frank Act), p. 197

6.1 Types of Firms, pages 182–186

LEARNING OBJECTIVE: Categorize the major types of firms in the United States.

MyLab Economics Visit www.pearson.com/mylab/economics to complete these exercises online and get instant feedback.

Summary

There are three types of firms: A **sole proprietorship** is a firm owned by a single individual and not organized as a corporation; a **partnership** is a firm owned jointly by two or more persons and not organized as a corporation; and a **corporation** is a legal form of business that provides its owners with limited liability. An **asset** is anything of value owned by a person or a firm. The owners of sole proprietorships and partnerships have unlimited liability, which means there is no legal distinction between the personal assets of the owners of the business and the assets of the business. The owners of corporations have **limited liability**, which means they can never lose more than their investment in the firm. Although only 18 percent of firms are corporations, they account for the majority of revenue and profits earned by all firms. **Corporate governance** refers to the way in which a corporation is structured and the effect the structure has on the firm's behavior. Most corporations have a similar management structure: The shareholders elect a board of directors that appoints the corporation's top managers, such as the chief executive officer (CEO). Because top managers often do not own a large fraction of the stock in the corporation, large corporations have a **separation of ownership from control**. When top managers have less incentive to increase the corporation's profits than to increase their own salaries and their own enjoyment, corporations can suffer from the **principal–agent problem**. The principal-agent problem exists when the principals—in this case, the shareholders of the corporation—have difficulty getting the agent—the corporation's top management—to carry out their wishes.

Review Questions

1.1 What are the three major types of firms in the United States? Briefly discuss the most important characteristics of each type.

1.2 What is limited liability? Why does the government grant limited liability to the owners of corporations? Why is limited liability more important for firms trying to raise funds from a large number of investors than for firms trying to raise funds from a small number of investors?

1.3 What does it mean to describe large corporations as having a separation of ownership from control? How is the separation of ownership from control related to the principal–agent problem?

Problems and Applications

1.4 Suppose that shortly after graduating from college, you decide to start your own business. Will you be likely to organize the business as a sole proprietorship, a partnership, or a corporation? Explain your reasoning.

1.5 An article discussing the reasons that the Connecticut state legislature passed a general incorporation law in 1837 observed that prior to the passage of the law, investors were afraid that large businesses "were not a safe bet for their money." Briefly explain the author's reasoning.

Source: Anne Rajotte, "Connecticut's General Incorporation Law Was the First of Its Kind," ctstatelibrary.org, June 10, 2014.

1.6 Evaluate the following argument:

> I would like to invest in the stock market, but I think that buying shares of stock in a corporation is too risky. Suppose I buy $10,000 of Twitter stock, and the company ends up going bankrupt. Because as a stockholder I'm part owner of the company, I might be responsible for paying hundreds of thousands of dollars of the company's debts.

1.7 According to an article in the *Economist*, historian David Faure argued that the Chinese economy failed to grow rapidly during the nineteenth century because "family-run companies . . . could not raise sufficient capital to exploit the large-scale opportunities tied to the rise of the steam engine, notably railways and (with limited exceptions) global shipping and automated manufacturing."

How did the United States solve the problem of firms raising enough funds to operate railroads and other large-scale businesses?

Source: "The PCCW Buy-out in Court," *Economist*, April 21, 2009.

1.8 **(Related to the Apply the Concept on page 184)** Two economists at the Brookings Institution argued that "new firms rather than existing ones have accounted for a disproportionate share of disruptive and thus highly productivity enhancing innovations in the past—the automobile, the airplane, the computer and personal computer, air conditioning, and Internet search, to name just a few."

a. Why might new firms be more likely than older firms to introduce "disruptive" innovations?

b. Assuming that these economists are correct about the most important source of productivity enhancing innovations, what are the implications for the future of the U.S. economy of recent trends in the formation of new businesses?

Source: Ian Hathaway and Robert E. Litan, "What's Driving the Decline in the Firm Formation Rate? A Partial Explanation," *Brookings Economic Studies*, November 20, 2014.

1.9 **(Related to the Apply the Concept on page 184)** While running for president, former Secretary of State Hillary Clinton published a position paper outlining how, if elected, she would make it easier to start a small business. One of her proposals was:

Any state and locality willing to make starting a business cheaper and easier and meaningfully streamline unnecessary licensing programs will receive federal funding to support innovative programs and offset forgone licensing revenue.

a. Why might this proposal be expected to increase the rate at which small businesses are formed?

b. Given your answer to part (a), why did state and local governments pass such licensing requirements in the first place?

Source: "Hillary Clinton Will Make Life Easier for Small Business at Every Step of the Way," hillaryclinton.com, August 23, 2016.

1.10 The principal–agent problem arises almost everywhere in the business world, and it also crops up even closer to home. Discuss the principal–agent problem that exists in the college classroom. Who is the principal? Who is the agent? What potential conflicts in objectives exist between this principal and this agent?

1.11 Salespeople, whether selling life insurance, automobiles, or pharmaceuticals, typically get paid on commission instead of a straight hourly wage. How does paying a commission help solve the principal–agent problem between the owners of a business and their salespeople?

1.12 Private equity firms, such as Blackstone and Kohlberg Kravis Roberts & Co., search for firms where the managers appear not to be maximizing profits. A private equity firm can buy stock in these firms and have its employees elected to the firms' boards of directors and may even acquire control of the targeted firm and replace the top management. Does the existence of private equity firms reduce any problems in corporate governance? Briefly explain.

6.2 How Firms Raise Funds, pages 186–194

LEARNING OBJECTIVE: Explain how firms raise the funds they need to operate and expand.

MyLab Economics Visit **www.pearson.com/mylab/economics** to complete these exercises online and get instant feedback.

Summary

Firms rely on retained earnings—which are profits kept by the firm and not paid out to the firm's owners—or on using the savings of households for the funds they need to operate and expand. With **direct finance**, the savings of households flow directly to businesses when investors buy **stocks** and **bonds** in financial markets. With **indirect finance**, savings flow indirectly to businesses when households deposit money in savings and checking accounts in banks and the banks lend these funds to businesses. Federal, state, and local governments also sell bonds in financial markets, and households also borrow funds from banks. When a firm sells a bond, it is borrowing money from the buyer of the bond. Firms make **coupon payments** to buyers of bonds. The **interest rate** is the cost of borrowing funds, usually expressed as a percentage of the amount borrowed. When a firm sells stock, it is selling part ownership of the firm to the buyer of the stock. **Dividends** are payments by a corporation to its shareholders. The original purchasers of stocks and bonds may resell them in stock and bond markets, such as the New York Stock Exchange. The performance of the U.S. stock market is often measured using stock market indexes. The three most widely followed stock indexes are the Dow Jones Industrial Average, the S&P 500, and the NASDAQ Composite Index.

Review Questions

2.1 What is the difference between direct finance and indirect finance? If you borrow money from a bank to buy a new car, are you using direct finance or indirect finance?

2.2 Why is a bond considered to be a loan but a share of stock is not? Why do corporations issue both bonds and shares of stock?

2.3 How do the stock and bond markets provide information to businesses? Why do stock and bond prices change over time?

Problems and Applications

2.4 Suppose that a firm in which you have invested is losing money. Would you rather own the firm's stock or the firm's bonds? Briefly explain.

2.5 Suppose you originally invested in a firm when it was small and unprofitable. Now the firm has grown to be large and profitable. Would you be better off if you had bought the firm's stock or the firm's bonds? Briefly explain.

2.6 If you deposit $20,000 in a savings account at a bank, you might earn 1 percent interest per year. Someone who borrows $20,000 from a bank to buy a new car might have to pay an interest rate of 6 percent per year on the loan. Knowing this, why don't you just lend your money directly to the car buyer and cut out the bank?

2.7 **(Related to the Chapter Opener on page 180)** Were the shares of stock issued as a result of Snap's initial public offering (IPO) sold in a primary market or a secondary market? Was the IPO an example of direct finance or indirect finance?

2.8 **(Related to the Apply the Concept on page 187)** According to an article by Reuters News Agency, in November 2016, Fitch Ratings cut its rating on McDonald's bonds from BBB+ to BBB.

    a. What is Fitch's top bond rating? Under what circumstances would Fitch, or the other bond rating agencies, be likely to cut the rating on a firm's bonds?

    b. What will be the likely result of this rating's cut for the interest rate McDonald's will have to pay when it sells new bonds? Briefly explain.

    Source: "Fitch Downgrades McDonald's IDR to 'BBB'; Outlook Stable," reuters.com, November 7, 2016.

2.9 **(Related to the Apply the Concept on page 187)** Investors use the bond ratings from Moody's, S&P, and Fitch to determine which bonds they will buy and the prices they are willing to pay for them. The rating services charge the firms and governments that issue bonds, rather than investors, for their services. Critics argue that the rating agencies may give higher ratings than are justified in order to continue to sell their services to bond issuing firms. To avoid this impression, why don't Moody's, S&P, and Fitch sell their services directly to investors?

2.10 What effect would the following events be likely to have on the price of Google's stock?

    a. A competitor launches a search engine that is better than Google's.

    b. The corporate income tax is abolished.

    c. Google's board of directors becomes dominated by close friends and relatives of its top management.

    d. The price of wireless Internet connections in developing countries unexpectedly drops, so more and more people worldwide use the Internet.

    e. Google announces a profit of $10 billion, but investors anticipated that Google would earn a profit of $11 billion.

2.11 **(Related to the Don't Let This Happen to You on page 190)** Briefly explain whether you agree with the following statement: "The total value of the shares of Microsoft stock traded on the NASDAQ last week was $500 million, so the firm actually received more revenue from stock sales than from selling software."

2.12 **(Related to the Apply the Concept on page 192)** A column in the *Wall Street Journal* listed "trying to forecast what stocks will do next" as one of the three mistakes investors make repeatedly. Briefly explain why trying to forecast stock prices would be a mistake for the average investor.

    Source: Morgan Housel, "Three Mistakes Investors Keep Making Again and Again," *Wall Street Journal*, September 12, 2014.

2.13 **(Related to Solved Problem 6.2 on page 193)** In a letter to his company's stockholders, Warren Buffett offered the following opinion: "Most investors, of course, have not made the study of business prospects a priority in their lives. . . . I have good news for these non-professionals: The typical investor doesn't need this skill." Briefly explain Buffett's reasoning.

    Source: Warren Buffett, *Letter to Berkshire Shareholders*, March 1, 2014, p. 20.

 6.3

Using Financial Statements to Evaluate a Corporation, pages 194–195

LEARNING OBJECTIVE: Describe the information corporations include in their financial statements.

MyLab Economics   Visit **www.pearson.com/mylab/economics** to complete these exercises online and get instant feedback.

Summary

A firm's **income statement** shows its revenues, costs, and profit over a period of time. A firm's **balance sheet** shows its financial position on a particular day, usually the end of a quarter or year. A balance sheet records a firm's assets and liabilities. A **liability** is anything owed by a person or a firm. Firms report their **accounting profit** on their income statements. Accounting profit does not always include all of a firm's **opportunity cost**. **Explicit cost** is a cost that involves spending money. **Implicit cost** is a nonmonetary opportunity cost. Because accounting profit excludes some implicit costs, it is larger than **economic profit**.

Review Questions

3.1 What is the difference between a firm's assets and its liabilities? Give an example of an asset and an example of a liability.

3.2 What is the difference between a firm's balance sheet and its income statement?

3.3 Distinguish between a firm's explicit costs and its implicit costs and between a firm's accounting profit and its economic profit.

3.4 Would a business be expected to survive in the long run if it earned a positive accounting profit but a negative economic profit? Briefly explain.

Problems and Applications

3.5 Paolo currently has $100,000 invested in bonds that earn him 4 percent interest per year. He wants to open a pizza restaurant and is considering either selling the bonds and using the $100,000 to start his restaurant or borrowing $100,000 from a bank, which would charge him an annual interest rate of 6 percent. He finally decides to sell the bonds and not take out the bank loan. He reasons: "Because I already have the $100,000 invested in the bonds, I don't have to pay anything to use the money. If I take out the bank loan, I have to pay interest, so my costs of producing pizza will be higher if I take out the loan than if I sell the bonds." Evaluate Paolo's reasoning.

3.6 Paolo and Alfredo are twins who both want to open pizza restaurants. Their parents have always liked Alfredo best, and they buy two pizza ovens and give both to him. Unfortunately, Paolo must buy his own pizza ovens.

Does Alfredo have a lower cost of producing pizza than Paolo does because Alfredo received his pizza ovens as a gift, while Paolo had to pay for his? Briefly explain.

3.7 Dane decides to give up a job earning $200,000 per year as a corporate lawyer and converts the duplex that he owns into a UFO museum. (He had been renting out the duplex for $20,000 a year.) His explicit costs are $75,000 per year paid to his assistants and $10,000 per year for utilities. Fans flock to the museum to see his collection of extraterrestrial paraphernalia, which he could easily sell on eBay for $1,000,000. Over the course of the year, the museum brings in revenues of $200,000.
   a. How much is Dane's accounting profit for the year?
   b. Is Dane earning an economic profit? Explain.

3.8 Snap was founded in 2011, but it wasn't until 2017 that it filed its first annual report with the Securities and Exchange Commission (SEC). Briefly explain why.

3.9 Jay Ritter, a professor at the University of Florida, was quoted in the *Wall Street Journal* as saying about Facebook: "It's entirely possible for a company to have solid growth prospects while its stock is overvalued."
   a. What does it mean to describe a stock as "overvalued"?
   b. Why might a firm's stock be overvalued despite the firm having "solid growth prospects"?

Source: Mark Hulbert, "A Year after Its Debut, Facebook Still Looks Overpriced," *Wall Street Journal*, May 17, 2013.

6.4 Recent Issues in Corporate Governance Policy, pages 196–200

LEARNING OBJECTIVE: Discuss the debate over corporate governance policy.

Summary

Because their compensation often rises with the profitability of the corporation that employs them, top managers have an incentive to overstate the profits reported on their firm's income statements. During the early 2000s, it became clear that the top managers of several large corporations had done this, even though intentionally falsifying financial statements is illegal. The *Sarbanes-Oxley Act* of 2002 took several steps intended to increase the accuracy of financial statements and increase the penalties for falsifying them. The financial crisis of 2007–2009 revealed that many financial firms held assets that were far riskier than investors had realized. Congress passed the **Wall Street Reform and Consumer Protection Act (Dodd-Frank Act)** in July 2010 to address some of the issues raised by the financial crisis of 2007–2009.

Review Questions

4.1 What is the Sarbanes-Oxley Act? Why did Congress pass it?

4.2 What was the source of the problems encountered by many financial firms during the crisis of 2007–2009?

Problems and Applications

4.3 Tronc is a publishing firm that owns several newspapers, including the *Los Angeles Times* and the *Chicago Tribune*. In early 2017, one of Tronc's largest investors sent the corporation a letter stating that he was "troubled by the company's corporate governance, or lack thereof." In particular, he was unhappy with a limit of 25 percent on how many of the corporation's shares he could own and with an attempt to remove him from the board of directors.
   a. What is corporate governance? In whose interest should corporations be governed? Briefly explain.
   b. Is limiting the percentage of a firm's stock that one person can hold an example of good corporate

governance or bad corporate governance? Briefly explain.

Sources: Lukas I. Alpert, "Tronc's Second-Largest Shareholder Raises Corporate Governance Questions," *Wall Street Journal*, March 27, 2017.

4.4 According to an article in the *Wall Street Journal*: "There is infrequent turnover among directors at S&P 500 corporations, where the median director was 63 years old.... The research found that at 24% of the companies, a majority of the board had been in place for at least 10 years." Is having members of boards of directors serve for longer periods likely to be good news or bad news for corporate governance? Briefly explain.

Source: Joann S. Lublin, "Corporate Heavyweights Back Governance Practices," *Wall Street Journal*, July 21, 2016.

4.5 **(Related to the Apply the Concept on page 198)** An opinion columnist in the *New York Times* asserted that "Snap Inc. is aiming to adopt the most shareholder-unfriendly governance in an initial public offering, ever."
   a. What did the columnist mean by "governance"?
   b. Why would he consider Snap's governance to be "shareholder-unfriendly"? If Snap's governance is shareholder unfriendly, why would investors have bought Snap's stock when the company engaged in an IPO in March 2017?

Source: Steven Davidoff Solomon, "Snap's Plan Is Most Unfriendly to Outsiders," *New York Times*, February 3, 2017.

4.6 **(Related to the Apply the Concept on page 198)** An opinion columnist for bloomberg.com observed, "A lot of people seem to think that committed, long-term shareholders should get more say than those who can bail out at any moment."
   a. What does the columnist mean by a shareholder who can bail out at any moment?
   b. What is the argument in favor of long-term shareholders having more say in running a corporation than shareholders who can bail out at any moment? How did Snap attempt to achieve this goal?
   c. Is there a good argument against giving long-term shareholders more say in running a corporation? Briefly explain.

Source: Justin Fox, "Snap's Experiment in Totalitarian Capitalism," bloomberg.com, March 6, 2017.

Critical Thinking Exercises

CT6.1 For this exercise, your instructor may assign you to a group. What did you find surprising in this chapter, based on what you knew before you read it? Compare your answers with those of others in your group. Write a paragraph on each topic that at least two students in the group found surprising and explain why the members of the group were surprised.

CT6.2 This chapter described the concept of a firm's balance sheet. Individuals and households have balance sheets as well, and the broad categories in them are the same as those on a firm's balance sheet. That is, an asset is something that an individual owns, a liability is something that an individual owes, and net worth is the difference between the value of assets and the value of liabilities. Construct a balance sheet for yourself. You can make estimates about the type and value of assets, liabilities, and net worth. The focus of this exercise is on what counts as assets and liabilities for an individual.

CT6.3 Many news articles on firms describe recent changes in their finances. Locate and read one recent article on a firm's balance sheet or income statement from sources such as a local newspaper, cnn.com, or bloomberg.com. What significant changes does the article report about the firm's balance sheet or income statement?

Appendix

Tools to Analyze Firms' Financial Information

As we saw in the chapter, firms are not just "black boxes" transforming inputs into output. The majority of business revenue and profit are earned by large corporations. Unlike founder-dominated firms, the typical large corporation is run by managers who generally do not own a controlling interest in the firm. Large firms raise funds from outside investors, and outside investors seek information on firms and the assurance that the managers of firms will act in the interests of the investors.

This chapter shows how corporations raise funds by issuing stocks and bonds. This appendix provides more detail to support that discussion. We begin by analyzing *present value* as a key concept in determining the prices of financial securities. We then provide greater information on *financial statements* issued by corporations, using Twitter as an example.

Using Present Value to Make Investment Decisions

Firms raise funds by selling equity (stock) and debt (bonds and loans) to investors and lenders. If you own a share of stock or a bond, you will receive payments in the form of dividends or coupons over a number of years. Most people value funds they already have more highly than funds they will receive some time in the future. For example, you would probably not trade $1,000 you already have for $1,000 you will not receive for one year. The longer you have to wait to receive a payment, the less value it will have for you. One thousand dollars you will not receive for two years is worth less to you than $1,000 you will receive after one year. The value you give today to money you will receive in the future is called the future payment's **present value**. The present value of $1,000 you will receive in one year will be less than $1,000.

Present value The value in today's dollars of funds to be paid or received in the future.

Why is the $1,000 you will not receive for one year less valuable to you than the $1,000 you already have? The most important reason is that if you have $1,000 today, you can use that $1,000 today. You can buy goods and services with the money and receive enjoyment from them. The $1,000 you receive in one year does not have direct use to you now.

Also, prices will likely rise during the year you are waiting to receive your $1,000. So, when you finally do receive the $1,000 in one year, you will not be able to buy as much with it as you could with $1,000 today. Finally, there is some risk that you will not receive the $1,000 in one year. The risk may be very great if an unreliable friend borrows $1,000 from you and vaguely promises to pay you back in one year. The risk may be very small if you lend money to the federal government by buying a U.S. Treasury bond. In either case, though, there is at least some risk that you will not receive the funds promised.

When someone lends money, the lender expects to be paid back both the amount of the loan and some additional interest. Say you are willing to lend $1,000 today if you are paid back $1,100 one year from now. In this case, you are charging $100/$1,000 = 0.10, or 10 percent interest on the funds you have loaned. Economists would say that you value $1,000 today as equivalent to the $1,100 to be received one year in the future.

Notice that $1,100 can be written as $1,000 × (1 + 0.10). That is, the value of money received in the future is equal to the value of money in the present multiplied by 1 plus the interest rate, with the interest rate expressed as a decimal. Or:

$$\$1,100 = \$1,000 \times (1 + 0.10).$$

Notice, also, that if we divide both sides by (1 + 0.10), we can rewrite this formula as:

$$\$1,000 = \frac{\$1,100}{(1 + 0.10)}.$$

The rewritten formula states that the present value is equal to the future value to be received in one year divided by 1 plus the interest rate. This formula is important because you can use it to convert any amount to be received in one year into its present value. Writing the formula generally, we have:

$$\text{Present value} = \frac{\text{Future value}_1}{(1 + i)}.$$

The present value of funds to be received in one year—Future value$_1$—can be calculated by dividing the amount of those funds to be received by 1 plus the interest rate. With an interest rate of 10 percent, the present value of $1,000,000 to be received one year from now is:

$$\frac{\$1,000,000}{(1 + 0.10)} = \$909,090.91.$$

This formula allows us to calculate the value today of funds that will be received in one year. But financial securities such as stocks and bonds involve promises to pay funds over many years. Therefore, it would be useful if we could expand this formula to calculate the present value of funds to be received more than one year in the future.

Go back to the original example, where we assumed you were willing to loan out your $1,000 for one year, provided that you received 10 percent interest. Suppose you are asked to lend the funds for two years and that you are promised 10 percent interest per year for each year of the loan. That is, you are lending $1,000, which at 10 percent interest will grow to $1,100 after one year, and you are agreeing to loan that $1,100 for a second year at 10 percent interest. So, after two years, you will be paid back $1,100 × (1 + 0.10), or $1,210. Or:

$$\$1,210 = \$1,000 \times (1 + 0.10) \times (1 + 0.10),$$

or:

$$\$1,210 = \$1,000 \times (1 + 0.10)^2.$$

This equation can also be rewritten as:

$$\$1,000 = \frac{\$1.210}{(1 + 0.10)^2}.$$

To put this equation in words, the $1,210 you receive two years from now has a present value equal to $1,210 divided by the quantity 1 plus the interest rate squared. If you agree to lend out your $1,000 for three years at 10 percent interest, you will receive:

$$\$1,331 = \$1,000 \times (1 + 0.10)^3.$$

Notice, again, that:

$$\$1,000 = \frac{\$1,331}{(1 + 0.10)^3}.$$

You can probably see a pattern here. We can generalize the concept to say that the present value of funds to be received n years in the future—whether n is 1, 20, or 85 does not matter—equals the amount of the funds to be received divided by the quantity 1 plus the interest rate raised to the nth power. For instance, with an interest rate of 10 percent, the value of $1,000,000 to be received 25 years in the future is:

$$\text{Present value} = \frac{\$1,000,000}{(1 + 0.10)^{25}} = \$92,296.$$

Or, more generally:

$$\text{Present value} = \frac{\text{Future value}_n}{(1 + i)^n},$$

where Future value$_n$ represents funds that will be received in n years.

Solved Problem 6A.1

MyLab Economics Interactive Animation

How to Receive Your Contest Winnings

Suppose you win a contest and are given the choice of the following prizes:

Prize 1: $50,000 to be received right away, with four additional payments of $50,000 to be received each year for the next 4 years

Prize 2: $175,000 to be received right away

Explain which prize you would choose and the basis for your decision.

Solving the Problem

Step 1: **Review the material.** This problem involves applying the concept of present value, so you may want to review the section "Using Present Value to Make Investment Decisions," which begins on page 206.

Step 2: **Explain the basis for choosing the prize.** Unless you need cash immediately, you should choose the prize with the highest present value.

Step 3: **Calculate the present value of each prize.** Prize 2 consists of one payment of $175,000 received right away, so its present value is $175,000. Prize 1 consists of five payments spread out over time. To find the present value of the prize, we must find the present value of each of these payments and add them together. To calculate present value, we must use an interest rate.

Let's assume an interest rate of 10 percent. In that case, the present value of Prize 1 is:

$$\$50,000 + \frac{\$50,000}{(1 + 0.10)} + \frac{\$50,000}{(1 + 0.10)^2} + \frac{\$50,000}{(1 + 0.10)^3} + \frac{\$50,000}{(1 + 0.10)^4}$$

$$= \$50,000 + \$45,454.55 + \$41,322.31 + \$37,565.74 + \$34,150.67$$

$$= \$208,493.27$$

Step 4: **State your conclusion.** Prize 1 has the greater present value, so you should choose it rather than Prize 2.

Your Turn: For more practice, do related problems 6A.6, 6A.7, 6A.8, and 6A.9 on page 214 at the end of this appendix.

MyLab Economics Study Plan

Using Present Value to Calculate Bond Prices

Anyone who buys stocks or bonds is really buying a promise to receive certain payments—dividends in the case of stocks or coupons in the case of bonds. The price investors are willing to pay for a financial asset should be equal to the value of the payments they will receive as a result of owning the asset. Because most of the coupon or dividend payments will be received in the future, it is their present value that matters. We therefore have the following important idea: *The price of a financial asset should be equal to the present value of the payments to be received from owning that asset.*

Let's look at an example. Suppose that in 1990, General Electric issued a bond with an $80 coupon that will mature in 2020. It is now 2018, and that bond has been bought and sold by investors many times. You are considering buying it. If you buy the bond, you will receive two years of coupon payments plus a final payment of the bond's principal, or face value, of $1,000. Suppose, once again, that you need an interest rate of 10 percent to invest your funds. If the bond has a coupon of $80, the present value of the payments you receive from owning the bond—and, therefore, the present value of the bond—will be:

$$\text{Present value} = \frac{\$80}{(1 + 0.10)} + \frac{\$80}{(1 + 0.10)^2} + \frac{\$1,000}{(1 + 0.10)^2} = \$965.29.$$

That is, the present value of the bond will equal the present value of the three payments you will receive during the two years you own the bond. You should, therefore, be willing to pay $965.29 to own this bond and have the right to receive these payments from GE. This process of calculating present values of future payments is used to determine bond prices, with one qualification: The relevant interest rate used by investors in the bond market to calculate the present value and, therefore, the price of an existing bond is usually the coupon rate on comparable newly issued bonds. Therefore, the general formula for the price of a bond is:

$$\text{Bond price} = \frac{\text{Coupon}_1}{(1 + i)} + \frac{\text{Coupon}_2}{(1 + i)^2} + \cdots + \frac{\text{Coupon}_n}{(1 + i)^n} + \frac{\text{Face value}}{(1 + i)^n}.$$

where:

- Coupon$_1$ is the coupon payment to be received after one year.
- Coupon$_2$ is the coupon payment to be received after two years.
- Coupon$_n$ is the coupon payment received in the year the bond matures.
- The ellipsis takes the place of the coupon payments—if any—received between the second year and the year when the bond matures.
- Face value is the amount that will be received when the bond matures.
- i is the interest rate on comparable newly issued bonds.   **MyLab Economics** Concept Check

Using Present Value to Calculate Stock Prices

When you own a firm's stock, you are legally entitled to your share of the firm's profit. Remember that the payments a firms makes to its shareholders are called *dividends*. The price of a share of stock should equal the present value of the dividends investors expect to receive as a result of owning that stock. Therefore, the general formula for the price of a stock is:

$$\text{Stock price} = \frac{\text{Dividend}_1}{(1 + i)} + \frac{\text{Dividend}_2}{(1 + i)^2} + \ \ldots$$

Notice that this formula looks very similar to the one we used to calculate the price of a bond, with two important differences:

1. Unlike a bond, a share of stock has no maturity date, so we have to calculate the present value of an infinite number of dividend payments. It may seem that the stock's price must be infinite as well, but remember that dollars you don't receive for many years are worth very little today. For instance, a dividend payment of $10 that will be received 40 years in the future is worth only a little more than $0.20 today at a 10 percent interest rate.
2. You know with certainty the coupon payments you will receive from owning the bond because they are set when the bond is issued and cannot be changed (unless the firm that issued the bond declares bankruptcy). However, you don't know for sure what the dividend payments from owning a stock will be. How large a dividend payment you will receive depends on how profitable the company will be in the future.

Although it is possible to forecast the future profitability of a company, this cannot be done with perfect accuracy. To emphasize this point, some economists rewrite the basic stock price formula by adding a superscript e to each dividend term to emphasize that these are *expected* dividend payments. Because the future profitability of companies is often very difficult to forecast, it is not surprising that differences of opinion exist over what the price of a particular stock should be. Some investors will be optimistic about the future profitability of a company and will, therefore, believe that the company's stock should have a high price. Other investors might be pessimistic and believe that the company's stock should have a low price.   **MyLab Economics** Concept Check

A Simple Formula for Calculating Stock Prices

It is possible to simplify the formula for determining the price of a stock. If we assume that dividends will grow at a constant rate, we get the following equation:

$$\text{Stock price} = \frac{\text{Dividend}}{(i - \text{Growth rate})}.$$

In this equation, Dividend is the dividend expected to be received one year from now, and Growth rate is the rate at which those dividends are expected to grow. If a company pays a dividend of $1 per share to be received one year from now and Growth rate is 10 percent, the company is expected to pay a dividend of $1.10 the following year, $1.21 the year after that, and so on.

Now suppose that IBM will pay a dividend of $5 per share at the end of the year, the consensus of investors is that these dividends will increase at a rate of 5 percent per year for the indefinite future, and the interest rate is 10 percent. Then the price of IBM's stock should be:

$$\text{Stock price} = \frac{\$5.00}{(0.10 - 0.05)} = \$100.00.$$

In recent years, investors have debated whether the high prices of the stocks of many high-tech firms, including Twitter and Snap, were justified, given that many of these companies had not made any profit yet and so had not paid any dividends. Is there any way that a rational investor would pay a high price for the stock of a company that is currently not earning profits? The formula for determining stock prices shows that it is possible, provided that the investor's assumptions are optimistic enough! For example, suppose that a stock analyst predicts that Snap will soon be earning $1 per share of stock. That is, Snap's total earnings divided by the number of shares of its stock outstanding would be $1. Suppose Snap pays out that $1 in dividends and that the $1 will grow rapidly over the years, by, say, 7 percent per year. Then the formula indicates that the price of Snap's stock should be:

$$\text{Stock price} = \frac{\$1.00}{(0.10 - 0.07)} = \$33.33.$$

If you are sufficiently optimistic about the future prospects of a company, a high stock price can be justified even if the company is not currently earning a profit. But investors in stocks must be careful. Suppose investors decide that the growth rate of Snap's dividend is likely to be only 4 percent per year instead of 7 percent because they expect the firm to have trouble attracting older consumers to its Snapchat app, which would reduce the firm's profitability. Then our formula indicates that the price of Snap's stock should be:

$$\text{Stock price} = \frac{\$1.00}{(0.10 - 0.04)} = \$16.67.$$

This price is only half the price determined assuming a more optimistic growth rate. We can conclude that investors use information about a firm's profitability and growth prospects to determine what the firm is worth.   **MyLab Economics** Concept Check

Going Deeper into Financial Statements

Corporations disclose substantial information about their business operations and financial position to actual and potential investors. Some of this information meets the demands of participants in financial markets and of information-collection agencies, such as Moody's Investors Service, which develops credit ratings that help investors judge how risky corporate bonds are. Other information meets the legal reporting requirements of the U.S. Securities and Exchange Commission.

Key sources of information about a corporation's profitability and financial position are its principal financial statements—the *income statement* and the *balance sheet*. These important information sources were first introduced in the chapter. In the following section we go into more detail, using recent data for Twitter as an example.

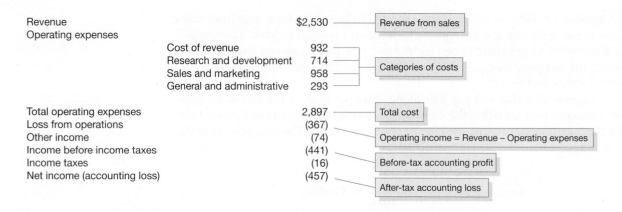

Revenue	$2,530	Revenue from sales
Operating expenses		
Cost of revenue	932	
Research and development	714	Categories of costs
Sales and marketing	958	
General and administrative	293	
Total operating expenses	2,897	Total cost
Loss from operations	(367)	
Other income	(74)	Operating income = Revenue – Operating expenses
Income before income taxes	(441)	
Income taxes	(16)	Before-tax accounting profit
Net income (accounting loss)	(457)	After-tax accounting loss

Note: All numbers are in millions of dollars.

MyLab Economics Animation

Figure 6A.1   **Twitter's Income Statement for 2016**

Twitter's income statement shows the company's revenue, costs, and profit for 2016. The difference between its revenue ($2,530 million) and its operating expenses ($2,897 million) is its operating income (a loss of $367 million). Most corporations also have interest expenses and income from investments, such as government and corporate bonds. In this case, Twitter paid more in interest than it earned on its investments, so its *income before* income taxes was a loss of $441 million. After paying taxes, Twitter had a net loss, or accounting loss, of $457 million for the year.

Note: Negative values in the figure are shown in parentheses.

Source: Twitter, *Annual Report, 2016.*

Analyzing Income Statements

As discussed in the chapter, a firm's income statement summarizes its revenues, costs, and profit over a period of time. Figure 6A.1 shows Twitter's income statement for 2016.

Twitter's income statement presents the results of the company's operations during the year. Listed first are the revenues it earned, largely from selling advertising on its app, from January 1, 2016, to December 31, 2016: $2,530 million. Listed next are Twitter's operating expenses, the most important of which is its *cost of revenue*—which is commonly known as *cost of sales* or *cost of goods sold*: $932 million. Cost of revenue is the direct cost of producing the products sold, including in this case the salaries of the computer programmers Twitter hires to write the software for its app. Twitter also has substantial costs for researching and developing its products ($714 million) and for sales and marketing them ($958 million). General and administrative expenses ($293 million) include costs such as the salaries of top managers.

The difference between a firm's revenue and its costs is its *profit*. Profit shows up in several forms on an income statement. A firm's *operating income* is the difference between its revenue and its operating expenses. Most corporations, including Twitter, also have interest expenses and income from investments, such as government and corporate bonds. In this case, Twitter paid more in interest than it earned on its investments. Because its costs were greater than its revenue, Twitter's *income before income taxes* was a loss of $441 million. (A loss in financial statements is indicated by the use of parentheses.) Twitter paid $16 million in taxes, so its *net income* after taxes was a loss of $457 million. The fact that Twitter could experience a loss while still having a high stock price is an indication that investors were expecting Twitter to earn significant profits in the future. The net income that firms report on their income statements is referred to as their after-tax *accounting profit*.   MyLab Economics Concept Check

Analyzing Balance Sheets

As discussed in the chapter, while a firm's income statement reports the firm's activities for a period of time, a firm's balance sheet summarizes its financial position on a particular day, usually the end of a quarter or year. To understand how a balance sheet

Assets		Liabilities and Stockholders' Equity	
Current assets	$4,747	Current liabilities	$ 584
Property and equipment	784	Long-term liabilities	1,681
Goodwill	1,185	Total liabilities	2,265
Other assets	154	Stockholders' equity	4,605
Total assets	$6,870	Total liabilities and stockholders' equity	$6,870

Note: All values are in millions of dollars.

MyLab Economics Animation

Figure 6A.2

Twitter's Balance Sheet as of December 31, 2016

Corporations list their assets on the left of their balance sheets and their liabilities on the right. The difference between the value of a firm's assets and the value of its liabilities equals the net worth of the firm, or stockholders' equity. Stockholders' equity is listed on the right side of the balance sheet. Therefore, the value of the left side of the balance sheet must always equal the value of the right side.

Source: Twitter, *Annual Report, 2016.*

Stockholders' equity The difference between the value of a corporation's assets and the value of its liabilities; also known as *net worth.*

is organized, first recall that an asset is anything of value that the firm owns, and a liability is a debt or an obligation that the firm owes. Subtracting the value of a firm's liabilities from the value of its assets leaves its *net worth.* Because a corporation's stockholders are its owners, net worth is often listed as **stockholders' equity** on a balance sheet. Using these definitions, we can state the balance sheet equation (also called the basic accounting equation) as follows:

$$\text{Assets} - \text{Liabilities} = \text{Stockholders Equity,}$$

or:

$$\text{Assets} = \text{Liabilities} + \text{Stockholders Equity.}$$

This equation tells us that the value of a firm's assets must equal the value of its liabilities plus the value of stockholders' equity. An important accounting convention dating back to the beginning of modern bookkeeping in fifteenth-century Italy holds that balance sheets should list assets on the left side and liabilities and net worth, or stockholders' equity, on the right side. Notice that this means that *the value of the left side of the balance sheet must always equal the value of the right side.* Figure 6A.2 shows Twitter's balance sheet as of December 31, 2016.

Two of the entries on the asset side of the balance sheet may be unfamiliar:

1. *Current assets* are assets that the firm could convert into cash quickly, such as the balance in its checking account or its accounts receivable, which is money currently owed to the firm for products that have been delivered but not yet paid for.
2. *Goodwill* represents the difference between the purchase price of a company and the market value of its assets. It represents the ability of a business to earn an economic profit from its assets. For example, if you buy a restaurant that is located on a busy intersection and you employ a chef with a reputation for preparing delicious food, you may pay more than the market value of the tables, chairs, ovens, and other assets. This additional amount you pay will be entered on the asset side of your balance sheet as goodwill.

We can note two entries on the liabilities side of the balance sheet:

1. *Current liabilities* are short-term debts such as accounts payable, which is money owed to suppliers for goods received but not yet paid for, or bank loans that will be paid back in less than one year.
2. *Long-term liabilities* are long-term bank loans, the value of outstanding corporate bonds, and other long-term debts.

MyLab Economics Concept Check   MyLab Economics Study Plan

Key Terms

Tools to Analyze Firms' Financial Information, pages 206–213

6A

LEARNING OBJECTIVE: Explain the concept of present value and describe the information contained on a firm's income statement and balance sheet.

Review Questions

6A.1 Why is money you receive at some future date worth less to you than money you receive today? If the interest rate rises, what effect does this have on the present value of payments you receive in the future?

6A.2 Give the formula for calculating the present value of a bond that will pay a coupon of $100 per year for 10 years and that has a face value of $1,000.

6A.3 Compare the formula for calculating the present value of the payments you will receive from owning a bond to the formula for calculating the present value of the payments you will receive from owning a stock. What are the key similarities? What are the key differences?

6A.4 How is operating income calculated? How does operating income differ from net income? How does net income differ from accounting profit?

6A.5 What is the key difference between a firm's income statement and its balance sheet? What is listed on the left side of a balance sheet? What is listed on the right side?

Problems and Applications

6A.6 **(Related to Solved Problem 6A.1 on page 208)** If the interest rate is 10 percent, what is the present value of a bond that matures in 2 years, pays $85 1 year from now, and pays $1,085 2 years from now?

6A.7 **(Related to Solved Problem 6A.1 on page 208)** Before the 2017 National Football League season, the New York Giants signed defensive lineman Jason Pierre-Paul to a contract that would pay him an immediate $5 million signing bonus and the following amounts: $2.5 million for the 2017 season, $17.5 million for the 2018 season, $19.5 million for the 2019 season, and $17.5 million for the 2020 season. Assume that Pierre-Paul receives each of his four seasonal salaries as a lump-sum payment at the end of the year.
   a. One newspaper article said that "Pierre-Paul's deal is worth $62 million." Do you agree that $62 million was the value of this contract? Briefly explain.
   b. What was the present value of Pierre-Paul's contract at the time he signed it, assuming an interest rate of 10 percent?
   c. If you use an interest rate of 5 percent, what was the present value of Pierre-Paul's contract?

   Sources: Bill Pennington, "Jason Pierre-Paul Agrees to Four-Year Contract with Giants," *New York Times*, March 17, 2017; the terms of the contract are from sportrac.com.

6A.8 **(Related to Solved Problem 6A.1 on page 208)** A winner of the Pennsylvania Lottery was given the choice of receiving $18 million at once or $1,440,000 per year for 25 years.
   a. If the winner had opted for the 25 annual payments, how much in total would she have received?

b. At an interest rate of 10 percent, what would be the present value of the 25 payments?

c. At an interest rate of 5 percent, what would be the present value of the 25 payments?

d. What interest rate would make the present value of the 25 payments equal to the one payment of $18 million? (This question is difficult and requires the use of a financial calculator or a spreadsheet. *Hint:* If you are familiar with the Excel spreadsheet program, use the RATE function. You can answer parts (b) and (c) by using the Excel PV [Present Value] function.)

6A.9 **(Related to Solved Problem 6A.1 on page 208)** Before the start of the 2000 baseball season, the New York Mets decided that they didn't want Bobby Bonilla playing for them any longer. But Bonilla had a contract with the Mets for the 2000 season that would have obliged the Mets to pay him $5.9 million. When the Mets released Bonilla, he agreed to take the following payments in lieu of the $5.9 million the Mets would have paid him in the year 2000: He would receive 25 equal payments of $1,193,248.20 each July 1 from 2011 to 2035. If you were Bobby Bonilla, which would you rather have had, the lump-sum $5.9 million in 2000 or the 25 payments beginning in 2011? Explain the basis for your decision.

   Source: Mike Sielski, "There's No Accounting for This," *Wall Street Journal*, July 1, 2010.

6A.10 Suppose that eLake, an online auction site, is paying a dividend of $2 per share. You expect this dividend to grow 2 percent per year, and the interest rate is 10 percent. What is the most you would be willing to pay for a share of stock in eLake? If the interest rate is 5 percent, what is the most you would be willing to pay? When interest rates in the economy decline, would you expect stock prices in general to rise or fall? Briefly explain.

6A.11 Suppose you buy the bond of a large corporation at a time when the inflation rate is very low. If the inflation rate increases during the time you hold the bond, what is likely to happen to the price of the bond?

6A.12 Use the information in the following table for calendar year 2016 to prepare an income statement for McDonald's Corporation. Be sure to include entries for operating income and net income.

Revenue from company restaurants	$15,295 million
Revenue from franchised restaurants	9,327 million
Cost of operating company-owned restaurants	12,699 million
Income taxes	2,180 million
Interest expense	885 million
General and administrative cost	2,460 million
Cost of restaurant leases	1,718 million

Source: McDonalds Corp., *Annual Report, 2016.*

6A.13 Use the information in the following table on the financial situation of Starbucks Corporation as of October 2, 2016 (the end of the firm's financial year), to prepare a balance sheet for the firm. Be sure to include an entry for stockholders' equity.

Current assets	$4,761 million
Current liabilities	4,547 million
Property and equipment	4,534 million
Long-term liabilities	3,892 million
Goodwill	1,720 million
Other assets	3,316 million

Source: Starbucks Corp., *Annual Report, 2016.*

6A.14 The *current ratio* is equal to a firm's current assets divided by its current liabilities. Use the information in Figure 6A.2 on page 213 to calculate Twitter's current ratio on December 31, 2016. Investors generally prefer that a firm's current ratio be greater than 1.5. What problems might a firm encounter if the value of its current assets is low relative to the value of its current liabilities?

Comparative Advantage and the Gains from International Trade

President Trump, Oreo Cookies, and Free Trade

Does it matter if the cookies you buy are made in the United States or in Mexico? In 2016, Mondelez International, Inc., a U.S. food company that makes Oreo cookies, announced that it would eliminate 600 jobs at its Chicago factory and begin producing Oreos in a plant in Mexico. Decisions like these played a major role in the 2016 presidential election. As a candidate, Donald Trump promised to renegotiate the North American Free Trade Agreement (NAFTA), a 1994 treaty that removed restrictions on trade and investment among the United States, Canada, and Mexico. Trump blamed NAFTA, which he called "the single worst trade deal ever approved in this country" for causing a loss of jobs in the United States as U.S. firms moved some of their operations to other countries.

President Trump pulled the United States out of negotiations on the Trans-Pacific Partnership (TPP), an agreement that had been intended to reduce trade barriers between the United States and 11 other countries, including Canada, Japan, Mexico, and Vietnam. Many economists, however, support trade agreements like NAFTA and the TPP, arguing that they benefit U.S. consumers by reducing the prices they pay for food, clothing, and many other goods. These economists maintain that the agreements improve economic efficiency because they result in goods being produced at the lowest opportunity cost. Some U.S. firms also support these trade agreements. In 2016, the value of the industrial equipment that U.S.-based Caterpillar Inc. exported to Mexico was worth $33 million more than the parts Caterpillar imported from Mexico. Trade analyst Chris Rogers noted the advantages to the company from having a "flexible, cross-border supply chain . . . to move parts and completed vehicles to where the optimal labor cost and skill sets are, without . . . tariff hurdles."

Kristoffer Tripplaar/Alamy Stock Photo

But those arguments in favor of free trade are unconvincing to workers who have lost their jobs. More than 2 million U.S. manufacturing jobs may have been lost to Chinese imports since 1999. Although trade with China has created other jobs throughout the United States, President Trump carried several Midwestern states during the 2016 election in part because of discontent over the loss of manufacturing jobs there.

Does eliminating government restrictions on international trade help or hurt workers and consumers in the United States? Few government policies are as hotly debated as those involving international trade. In this chapter, we will explore the economics of trade and the debate over trade policies.

Sources: Azam Ahmed and Elizabeth Malkin, "For Commerce Pick Wilbur Ross, 'Inherently Bad' Deals Paid Off," *New York Times*, February 25, 2017; Jacob M. Schlesinger, Andrew Tangel, and Valerie Bauerlein, "NAFTA's Net U.S. Impact Is Modest," *Wall Street Journal*, January 27, 2017; and "Trade, at What Price?" *Economist*, April 2, 2016.

Chapter Outline & Learning Objectives

Economics in Your Life & Career

Should a Member of Congress Support a Tariff on Running Shoes?

Suppose that you are an aide to a member of Congress who is considering whether to vote for a bill that would eliminate the U.S. tariff on running shoes. She asks you to prepare a memorandum recommending how she should vote, taking into account both the economic interests of the firms and workers in her district and the broader interests of the U.S. economy as a whole. What facts and conclusions from the economic analysis of international trade should you include in your memorandum? As you read this chapter, try to answer this question. You can check your answer against the one we provide on **page 242** at the end of this chapter.

*T*rade is simply the act of buying or selling. Is there a difference between trade that takes place within a country and international trade? Within the United States, domestic trade makes it possible for consumers in Ohio to eat salmon caught in Alaska and for consumers in Montana to drive cars built in Michigan or Kentucky. Similarly, international trade makes it possible for consumers in the United States to drink wine from France and use smartphones assembled in China. One significant difference between domestic trade and international trade is that international trade is more controversial. At one time, nearly all the televisions, shoes, clothing, and toys bought in the United States were also produced here. Today, firms in other countries produce most of these goods. This shift has benefited U.S. consumers because foreign-made goods have lower prices or higher quality than the U.S.-made goods they have replaced. At the same time, though, many U.S. firms that produced these goods have gone out of business, and their workers have had to find other jobs. Some cities in the industrial Midwest have been devastated as factories have closed down and few new firms have replaced them. Some families who had worked for several generations in the same factory have been faced with accepting major income declines or moving elsewhere to find jobs. Cities and towns in New England and in the Carolinas and Georgia have faced similar difficulties as shoe, clothing, textile, and furniture factories have closed in the face of foreign competition. Not surprisingly, opinion polls show that many Americans favor reducing international trade because they believe doing so will preserve jobs in the United States. But is this belief accurate?

We can use the tools of demand and supply to analyze markets for internationally traded goods and services. We have seen that trade in general—whether within a country or between countries—is based on the principle of comparative advantage (see Chapter 2, Section 2.2). In this chapter, we look more closely at the role of comparative advantage in international trade. We also use the concepts of consumer surplus, producer surplus, and deadweight loss (see Chapter 4, Section 4.2) to analyze government policies that interfere with trade. With this background, we can return to the political debate over whether the United States benefits from international trade. We begin by looking at the role international trade plays in the U.S. economy.

7.1 The United States in the International Economy

LEARNING OBJECTIVE: Discuss the role of international trade in the U.S. economy.

International trade has grown tremendously over the past 50 years, due primarily to three factors: the decreasing costs of shipping products around the world, the spread of inexpensive and reliable communications, and changes in government policies. Firms can use large container ships to send their products across oceans at low cost. Businesspeople today can travel to Europe or Asia, using fast, inexpensive, and reliable air transportation. The Internet, cellphones, and text messaging allow managers to communicate instantaneously and at a very low cost with customers and suppliers around the world. These and other improvements in transportation and communication have created an integrated global marketplace that earlier generations of businesspeople could only dream of.

Over the past 50 years, many governments have changed policies to facilitate international trade. For example, tariff rates have fallen. A **tariff** is a tax imposed by a government on *imports* into a country. **Imports** are goods and services purchased domestically that have been produced in other countries. In the 1930s, the United States charged an average tariff rate above 50 percent. Today, the rate is less than 1.5 percent. In North America, most tariffs between Canada, Mexico, and the United States were eliminated following the passage of the North American Free Trade Agreement (NAFTA) in 1994.

Tariff A tax imposed by a government on imports.

Imports Goods and services purchased domestically that are produced in other countries.

In Europe, 28 countries have formed the European Union, which has eliminated all tariffs among member countries, greatly increasing both imports and **exports**, which are goods and services produced domestically and sold in other countries. In 2017, though, the policy of reducing government restrictions on trade seemed newly in doubt. In Europe, the United Kingdom was withdrawing from the European Union and possibly facing new barriers to trading with the remaining members. And, as we saw in the chapter opener, the Trump administration had withdrawn from negotiations aimed at concluding the Trans-Pacific Partnership (TPP), which was to have been an agreement to increase trade between the United States and 11 other countries around the Pacific Ocean, including Canada, Japan, Mexico, and Vietnam. The Trump administration wished to renegotiate NAFTA, and doing so could result in greater barriers to trade among the United States, Mexico, and Canada.

Exports Goods and services produced domestically and sold in other countries.

The Importance of Trade to the U.S. Economy

U.S. consumers are buying increasing quantities of goods and services produced in other countries. At the same time, U.S. businesses are selling increasing quantities of goods and services to consumers in other countries. Figure 7.1 shows that since 1970, both exports and imports have tended to increase as a fraction of U.S. gross domestic product (GDP). GDP is the value of all the final goods and services produced in a country during a year. World trade declined sharply during the severe worldwide recession of 2007–2009 and has grown relatively slowly since that time. The slowdown in trade seems to have been caused by slower income growth in some countries, including China, Brazil, and many countries in Europe, combined with some firms deciding to produce fewer of their products in foreign countries. In the United States, imports and exports have been growing more slowly than GDP in the past few years. Despite this slowdown, exports and imports increased from being less than 6 percent of U.S. GDP in 1970 to being more than 12 percent in 2016.

Not all sectors of the U.S. economy are affected equally by international trade. For example, although it's difficult to import or export some services, such as haircuts and appendectomies, a large percentage of U.S. agricultural production is exported. Each year, the United States exports about 50 percent of its wheat and rice crops and 20 percent of its corn crop.

Many U.S. manufacturing industries also depend on trade. About 20 percent of U.S. manufacturing jobs depend directly or indirectly on exports. In some industries, such as pharmaceutical drugs, output is directly exported. In other industries, such as steel, output is used to make other products, such as bulldozers or machine tools, that are then exported. In all, about two-thirds of U.S. manufacturing industries depend on exports for at least 10 percent of jobs. **MyLab Economics** Concept Check

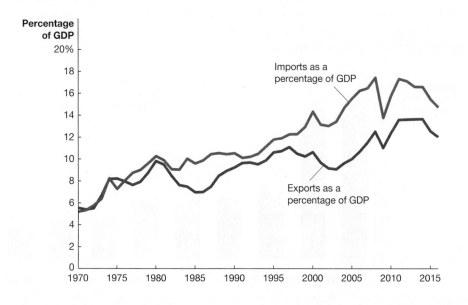

MyLab Economics Real-time data

Figure 7.1

The Increasing Importance of International Trade to the United States

Exports and imports of goods and services as a percentage of total production—measured by GDP—show the importance of international trade to an economy. In 2016, both imports and exports were much larger fractions of U.S. GDP than they were in 1970.

Source: U.S. Department of Commerce, Bureau of Economic Analysis.

MyLab Economics Animation

Figure 7.2

The Eight Leading Exporting Countries

China is the leading exporting country, accounting for 12.1 percent of total world exports. The United States is second, with a 10.3 percent share. The values are the shares of total world exports of merchandise and commercial services.

Source: World Trade Organization, *International Trade Statistics*, 2016.

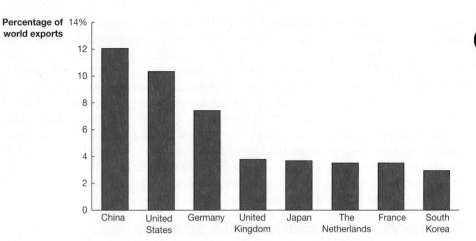

U.S. International Trade in a World Context

The United States is the second-largest exporter in the world, just behind China, as Figure 7.2 illustrates. Six of the other seven leading exporting countries are also high-income countries. Although China is still a relatively low-income country, the rapid growth of the Chinese economy over the past 35 years has resulted in its becoming the largest exporter. Three of the top exporting countries are in East Asia, four are in Western Europe, and one is in North America.

Figure 7.3 shows that international trade is less important to the United States than it is to many other countries, with imports and exports being lower percentages of GDP. In some smaller countries, such as Belgium and the Netherlands, imports and exports make up more than half of GDP. In the larger European economies, imports and exports make up one-quarter to one-half of GDP.   MyLab Economics Concept Check

MyLab Economics Study Plan

 ## 7.2 Comparative Advantage in International Trade

LEARNING OBJECTIVE: Explain the difference between comparative advantage and absolute advantage in international trade.

Why have businesses around the world increasingly looked for markets in other countries? Why have consumers increasingly purchased goods and services made in other countries? People trade for one reason: Trade makes them better off. Whenever a buyer and seller agree to a sale, they must both believe they are better off; otherwise, there would be no sale. This outcome must hold whether the buyer and seller live in the same city or in different countries. As we will see, governments are more likely to interfere with international trade than they are with domestic trade, but the reasons for the interference are more political than economic.

MyLab Economics Real-time data

Figure 7.3

International Trade as a Percentage of GDP

International trade is still less important to the United States than it is to most other countries.

Source: Organization for Economic Co-operation and Development, *Country Statistical Profiles*, April 2017.

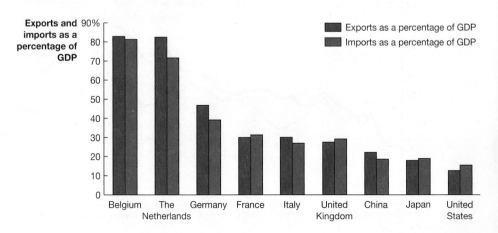

A Brief Review of Comparative Advantage

Recall that **comparative advantage** is the ability of an individual, a firm, or a country to produce a good or service at a lower opportunity cost than competitors. **Opportunity cost** is the highest-valued alternative that must be given up to engage in an activity. People, firms, and countries specialize in economic activities in which they have a comparative advantage. In trading, we benefit from the comparative advantage of other people (or firms or countries), and they benefit from our comparative advantage.

A good way to think of comparative advantage is to recall the example of you and your neighbor picking fruit (see Chapter 2, Section 2.2). Your neighbor is better at picking both apples and cherries than you are. Why, then, doesn't your neighbor pick both types of fruit? Because the opportunity cost to your neighbor of picking her own apples is very high: She is a particularly skilled cherry picker, and every hour spent picking apples is an hour taken away from picking cherries. You can pick apples at a much lower opportunity cost than your neighbor, so you have a comparative advantage in picking apples. Your neighbor can pick cherries at a much lower opportunity cost than you can, so she has a comparative advantage in picking cherries. Your neighbor is better off specializing in picking cherries, and you are better off specializing in picking apples. You can then trade some of your apples for some of your neighbor's cherries, and both of you will end up with more of each fruit. (If you have trouble following the point here, refer to Chapter 2, Tables 2.1 and 2.2.) **MyLab Economics** Concept Check

Comparative Advantage and Absolute Advantage

The principle of comparative advantage can explain why people pursue different occupations. It can also explain why countries produce different goods and services. International trade involves many countries importing and exporting many different goods and services. Countries are better off if they specialize in producing the goods for which they have a comparative advantage. They can then trade for the goods for which other countries have a comparative advantage.

We can illustrate why specializing on the basis of comparative advantage makes countries better off with a simple example involving just two countries and two products. Suppose the United States and China produce only smartphones and wheat. Assume that each country uses only labor to produce each good and that there are no differences between Chinese and U.S. smartphones or between Chinese and U.S. wheat. Table 7.1 shows how much each country can produce of each good with one hour of labor.

Notice that Chinese workers are more productive than U.S. workers in making both goods. In one hour, Chinese workers can produce six times as many smartphones and one and one-half times as many bushels of wheat as U.S. workers. China has an *absolute advantage* over the United States in producing both goods. **Absolute advantage** is the ability to produce more of a good or service than competitors when using the same amount of resources. In this case, China can produce more of both goods using the same amount of labor as the United States.

It might seem at first that China has nothing to gain from trading with the United States because it has an absolute advantage in producing both goods. However, China is better off specializing in producing only smartphones and obtaining the wheat it needs by exporting smartphones to the United States in exchange for wheat. The reason China benefits from trade is that although it has an *absolute advantage* in the production of both goods, it has a *comparative advantage* only in the production of smartphones. The United States has a comparative advantage in the production of wheat.

Comparative advantage The ability of an individual, a firm, or a country to produce a good or service at a lower opportunity cost than competitors.

Opportunity cost The highest-valued alternative that must be given up to engage in an activity.

Absolute advantage The ability to produce more of a good or service than competitors when using the same amount of resources.

	Output per Hour of Work	
	Smartphones	Wheat (bushels)
China	12	6
United States	2	4

Table 7.1

An Example of Chinese Workers Being More Productive Than U.S. Workers

Table 7.2

The Opportunity Costs of Producing Smartphones and Wheat

The table shows the opportunity cost each country faces in producing smartphones and wheat. For example, the first entry in the "Wheat" column shows that China must give up 2 smartphones for every bushel of wheat it produces.

	Opportunity Costs	
	Smartphones	Wheat (bushels)
China	0.5 bushel of wheat	2 smartphones
United States	2 bushels of wheat	0.5 smartphone

If it seems contrary to common sense that China should import wheat from the United States even though China can produce more wheat per hour of labor, think about the opportunity cost to each country of producing each good. If China wants to produce more wheat, it has to switch labor away from smartphone production. Every hour of labor switched from producing smartphones to producing wheat reduces smartphone production by 12 and increases wheat production by 6 bushels. China has to give up 12 smartphones for every 6 bushels of wheat it produces. Therefore, the opportunity cost to China of producing 1 more bushel of wheat is 12/6, or 2 smartphones.

If the United States switches one hour of labor from smartphones to wheat, production of smartphones falls by 2, and production of wheat rises by 4 bushels. Therefore, the opportunity cost to the United States of producing 1 more bushel of wheat is 2/4, or 0.5 smartphone. The United States has a lower opportunity cost of producing wheat and, therefore, has a comparative advantage in making this product. By similar reasoning, we can see that China has a comparative advantage in producing smartphones. Table 7.2 summarizes the opportunity cost each country faces in producing these goods.

MyLab Economics Study Plan

MyLab Economics Concept Check

 ## 7.3 How Countries Gain from International Trade

LEARNING OBJECTIVE: Explain how countries gain from international trade.

Can China really gain from producing only smartphones and trading with the United States for wheat? To see that it can, assume at first that China and the United States do not trade with each other. A situation in which a country does not trade with other countries is called **autarky**. Assume that in autarky, each country has 1,000 hours of labor available to produce the two goods, and each country produces the quantities of the two goods shown in Table 7.3. Because there is no trade, these quantities also represent consumption of the two goods in each country.

Autarky A situation in which a country does not trade with other countries.

Increasing Consumption through Trade

Suppose now that China and the United States begin to trade with each other. The **terms of trade** is the ratio at which a country can trade its exports for imports from other countries. For simplicity, let's assume that the terms of trade end up with China and the United States being willing to trade one smartphone for one bushel of wheat, even though we know that in reality the price of a smartphone is much higher than the price of a bushel of wheat.

Terms of trade The ratio at which a country can trade its exports for imports from other countries.

Once trade has begun, the United States and China can exchange wheat for smartphones or smartphones for wheat. For example, if China specializes by using all 1,000 available hours of labor to produce smartphones, it will be able to produce 12,000

Table 7.3

Production without Trade

	Production and Consumption	
	Smartphones	Wheat (bushels)
China	9,000	1,500
United States	1,500	1,000

MyLab Economics Animation

Table 7.4

Gains from Trade for China and the United States

Without Trade

Production and Consumption

	Smartphones	Wheat
China	9,000	1,500
United States	1,500	1,000

With Trade

	Production with Trade		Trade		Consumption with Trade	
	Smartphones	Wheat	Smartphones	Wheat	Smartphones	Wheat
China	12,000	0	Export 1,500	Import 1,500	10,500	1,500
United States	0	4,000	Import 1,500	Export 1,500	1,500	2,500

With trade, the United States and China specialize in the good they have a comparative advantage in producing . . .

. . . and export some of that good in exchange for the good the other country has a comparative advantage in producing.

Gains from Trade

Increased Consumption

China	1,500 Smartphones
United States	1,500 Bushels of wheat

The increased consumption made possible by trade represents the gains from trade.

smartphones. It could then export 1,500 smartphones to the United States in exchange for 1,500 bushels of wheat. (Remember that we are assuming the terms of trade are 1 smartphone for 1 bushel of wheat.) China ends up with 10,500 smartphones and 1,500 bushels of wheat. Compared with the situation before trade, China has the same number of bushels of wheat but 1,500 more smartphones. If the United States specializes in producing wheat, it will be able to produce 4,000 bushels of wheat. It could then export 1,500 bushels of wheat to China in exchange for 1,500 smartphones. The United States ends up with 2,500 bushels of wheat and 1,500 smartphones. Compared with the situation before trade, the United States has the same number of smartphones but 1,500 more bushels of wheat. Trade has allowed both countries to increase the quantities of goods consumed. Table 7.4 summarizes the gains from trade for the United States and China.

By trading, China and the United States are able to consume more than they could without trade. This outcome is possible because world production of both goods increases after trade. (In this example, our "world" consists of just the United States and China.)

Why does total production of smartphones and wheat increase when China specializes in producing smartphones and the United States specializes in producing wheat? A domestic analogy helps answer this question: If a company shifts production from an old factory to a more efficient modern factory, its output will increase. Similarly, if a farmer shifts from growing wheat on land that is suffering from soil exhaustion to land that is fertile, the farmer's wheat output will increase. The same thing happens in our example. Producing wheat in China and smartphones in the United States is inefficient. Shifting production to the more efficient country—the one with the comparative advantage—increases total production. The key point is: *Countries gain from specializing in producing goods in which they have a comparative advantage and trading for goods in which other countries have a comparative advantage.*

MyLab Economics Concept Check

Solved Problem 7.3

The Gains from Trade

The first discussion of comparative advantage appears in *On the Principles of Political Economy and Taxation*, a book written by the British economist David Ricardo in 1817. Ricardo provided a famous example of the gains from trade, using wine and cloth production in Portugal and England. The following table is adapted from Ricardo's example, with cloth measured in sheets and wine measured in kegs:

	Output per Year of Labor	
	Cloth	**Wine**
Portugal	100	150
England	90	60

a. Explain which country has an absolute advantage in the production of each good.

b. Explain which country has a comparative advantage in the production of each good.

c. Suppose that Portugal and England currently do not trade with each other. Each country has 1,000 workers, so each has 1,000 years of labor time to use in producing cloth and wine, and the countries are currently producing the amounts of each good shown in the following table:

	Cloth	**Wine**
Portugal	18,000	123,000
England	63,000	18,000

Show that Portugal and England can both gain from trade. Assume that the terms of trade are that one sheet of cloth can be traded for one keg of wine.

Solving the Problem

Step 1: Review the chapter material. This problem is about absolute and comparative advantage and the gains from trade, so you may want to review the sections "Comparative Advantage in International Trade," which begins on page 220, and "How Countries Gain from International Trade," which begins on page 222.

Step 2: Answer part (a) by determining which country has an absolute advantage. Remember that a country has an absolute advantage over another country when it can produce more of a good using the same resources. The first table in the problem shows that Portugal can produce more cloth *and* more wine with 1 year's worth of labor than can England. Therefore, Portugal has an absolute advantage in the production of both goods, and England does not have an absolute advantage in the production of either good.

Step 3: Answer part (b) by determining which country has a comparative advantage. A country has a comparative advantage when it can produce a good at a lower opportunity cost. To produce 100 sheets of cloth, Portugal must give up producing 150 kegs of wine. Therefore, Portugal's opportunity cost of producing 1 sheet of cloth is 150/100, or 1.5 kegs of wine. England has to give up producing 60 kegs of wine to produce 90 sheets of cloth, so its opportunity cost of producing 1 sheet of cloth is 60/90, or 0.67 keg of wine. The opportunity costs of producing wine can be calculated in the same way. The following table shows the opportunity cost to Portugal and England of producing each good.

	Opportunity Costs	
	Cloth	**Wine**
Portugal	1.5 kegs of wine	0.67 sheet of cloth
England	0.67 keg of wine	1.5 sheets of cloth

Portugal has a comparative advantage in wine because its opportunity cost is lower. England has a comparative advantage in cloth because its opportunity cost is lower.

Step 4: Answer part (c) by showing that both countries can benefit from trade. By now it should be clear that both countries will be better off if they specialize in producing the good for which they have a comparative advantage and trade for the other good. The following table is very similar to Table 7.4 and shows one example of trade making both countries better off. (To test your understanding, construct another example.)

Without Trade		
	Production and Consumption	
	Cloth	**Wine**
Portugal	18,000	123,000
England	63,000	18,000

With Trade						
	Production with Trade		**Trade**		**Consumption with Trade**	
	Cloth	**Wine**	**Cloth**	**Wine**	**Cloth**	**Wine**
Portugal	0	150,000	Import 18,000	Export 18,000	18,000	132,000
England	90,000	0	Export 18,000	Import 18,000	72,000	18,000

Gains from Trade	
	Increased Consumption
Portugal	9,000 wine
England	9,000 cloth

Your Turn: For more practice, do related problems 3.5 and 3.6 on page 245 at the end of this chapter.

MyLab Economics Study Plan

Why Don't We See Complete Specialization?

In our example of two countries producing only two products, each country specializes in producing one of the goods. In the real world, many goods and services are produced in more than one country. For example, the United States, Japan, Germany, China, Canada, Mexico, India, and other countries produce automobiles. We do not see complete specialization in the real world for three main reasons:

1. **Not all goods and services are traded internationally.** For example, even if Japan had a comparative advantage in the production of medical services, it would be difficult for it to specialize in producing medical services and then export them. There is no easy way for U.S. patients who need appendectomies to receive them from surgeons in Japan.
2. **Production of most goods involves increasing opportunity costs.** Recall that production of most goods involves increasing opportunity costs (see Chapter 2, Section 2.1). Although we didn't include this fact in our example, if the United States devotes more workers to producing wheat, the opportunity cost of producing more wheat will increase. At some point, the opportunity cost of producing wheat in the United States may rise to the level of the opportunity cost of producing wheat in China. When that happens, international trade will no longer push the United States further toward specialization. The same will be true of China: The increasing opportunity cost of producing smartphones will cause China to stop short of complete specialization.

3. **Tastes for products differ.** Most products are *differentiated*. Smartphones, laptops, cars, and televisions—to name just a few products—have a variety of features. When buying automobiles, some people look for reliability and fuel efficiency, others look for room to carry seven passengers, and still others want styling and high performance. So, some car buyers prefer Toyota Prius hybrids, and some prefer Chevy Suburbans, and others prefer BMWs. As a result, Japan, the United States, and Germany may each have a comparative advantage in producing different types of automobiles.   **MyLab Economics** Concept Check

Does Anyone Lose as a Result of International Trade?

In our smartphone and wheat example, consumption increases in both the United States and China as a result of trade. Everyone gains, and no one loses. Or do they? In our example, we referred repeatedly to "China" or the "United States" producing smartphones or wheat. But countries do not produce goods—firms do. In a world without trade, there would be smartphone firms and wheat farms in both China and the United States. In a world with trade, there would be only Chinese smartphone firms and U.S. wheat farms. Chinese wheat farms and U.S. smartphone firms would be competed out of business. Overall, total employment would not change, and production would increase as a result of trade. Nevertheless, the owners of Chinese wheat farms, the owners of U.S. smartphone firms, and the people who work for them are worse off as a result of trade. The losers from trade are likely to try to persuade the Chinese and U.S. governments to interfere with trade by barring imports of the competing products from the other country or by imposing high tariffs on them.   **MyLab Economics** Concept Check

Don't Let This Happen to You

Remember That Trade Creates Both Winners and Losers

The following statement is from a Federal Reserve publication: "Trade is a win–win situation for all countries that participate." People sometimes interpret statements like this to mean that there are no losers from international trade. But notice that the statement refers to *countries*, not individuals. When countries participate in trade, they make their consumers better off by increasing the quantity of goods and services available to them.

As we have seen, however, expanding trade eliminates the jobs of workers employed at companies that are less efficient than foreign companies. Trade also creates new jobs at companies that export products to foreign markets. But it may be difficult for workers who lose their jobs because of trade to easily

find others. That is why in the United States the federal government uses the *Trade Adjustment Assistance (TAA)* program to provide funds for workers who have lost their jobs due to international trade. Qualified unemployed workers can use these funds to pay for retraining, searching for new jobs, or relocating to areas where new jobs are available. This program—and similar programs in other countries—recognizes that there are losers from international trade as well as winners.

Source: Federal Reserve Bank of Dallas, "International Trade and the Economy," www.dallasfed.org/educate/everyday/ev7.html.

MyLab Economics Study Plan

Your Turn: Test your understanding by doing related problem 3.11 on page 246 at the end of this chapter.

Apply the Concept   **MyLab Economics** Video

Who Gains and Who Loses from U.S. Trade with China?

Early in his administration, President Donald Trump criticized what he saw as unbalanced trade between the United States and China and warned, "We can no longer have massive trade deficits . . . and job losses." From Mao Zedong's founding of the People's Republic of China in 1949 until the mid-1970s, China was a centrally planned economy that rejected free markets and had very little trade with the United States. Beginning in the 1970s, when Deng Xiaoping succeeded Mao as leader of China, the government adopted market-based reforms of the economy and began exporting significant quantities of goods to the United States and other countries. This process accelerated after China became a member of the World Trade Organization (WTO) in 2001, which gave it greater access to world markets.

The following figure shows the growth since 2000 in U.S. imports from China and U.S. exports to China. While U.S. exports of goods to China were more than four times higher in 2016 than in 2000, the dollar increase in U.S. imports of goods from China was much larger. As a result, the gap between U.S. imports of goods from China and exports to China (the U.S. trade deficit with China) had swelled to nearly $300 billion. Some economists and policymakers have labeled the surge in Chinese imports beginning in 2001 the *China shock*.

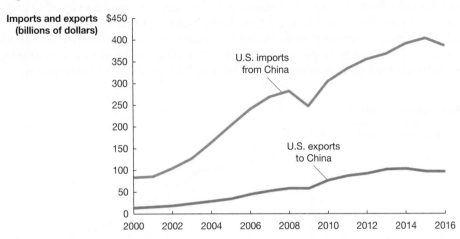

The following figure shows the distribution of U.S. imports of goods from China by broad product categories. Many of the products the United States currently imports from China were at one time manufactured in the United States. Chinese firms were able to win a large share of these markets typically by offering goods at lower prices than U.S. firms (or firms in other foreign countries that were also competing in the U.S. market). These lower prices have benefited U.S. consumers. Lower-income consumers in particular have benefitted from the low prices of textile products, such as clothing, sheets, and towels. Smartphones and other consumer electronics products would have much higher prices if they were assembled in the United States rather than in China and other foreign countries. (However, as we saw in the *Apply the Concept* in Chapter 2, page 57, U.S. firms have been able to produce some components of iPads and other consumer electronics.)

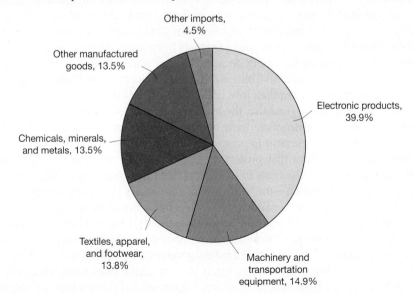

Because consumers pay lower prices for goods imported from China, they have more of their income available to spend on other goods and services produced in the United States. A family that buys low-price Chinese-made clothes at Walmart can more easily afford to dine out at the local Red Lobster restaurant or to buy fresh fruits and vegetables grown at local farms. In this sense, the losses suffered by U.S. firms (and their workers) that have been forced out of business by Chinese competitors have resulted in gains to other U.S. firms (and their workers).

But David Autor of the Massachusetts Institute of Technology and other economists studying the effects of the China shock on the U.S. economy point out that the firms most hurt by Chinese imports have been concentrated in certain states, particularly in the Midwest and Southeast. As noted in the chapter opener, some cities in these areas have been devastated as local manufacturing plants have closed and workers have had difficulty finding other jobs. Dissatisfaction among these workers played a significant role in the 2016 presidential election. As the following figure shows, the fraction of U.S. workers employed in manufacturing began declining long before the China shock began. In 1944, nearly 38 percent of U.S. workers were employed in manufacturing. At the start of the surge in imports from China in 2001, only about 12 percent were.

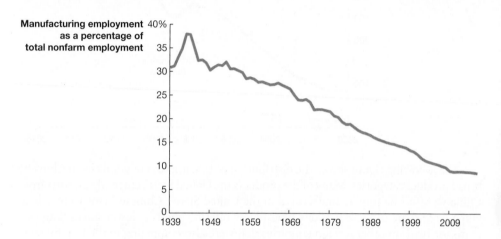

Autor, David Dorn of the University of Zurich, and Gordon Hanson of the University of California, San Diego estimate that between 1999 and 2011, the China shock resulted in the loss of 2.4 million jobs and may have accounted for 25 percent of the decline in manufacturing jobs during those years. Although total employment in the United States increased by substantially more than this amount over the same period, the job losses happened relatively quickly and were heavily concentrated in manufacturing industries that competed with Chinese imports. Firms and workers in these industries had more difficulty adjusting to the increase in imports from China than other firms and workers had to the somewhat slower increases in imports from Japan, Mexico, and other countries that had occurred during earlier decades. The fraction of the population employed declined in areas most exposed to Chinese imports and has recovered only slowly, which indicates that workers who lost their jobs have struggled to find new ones.

President Trump has argued that the best response to the difficulties caused by rising imports is either to renegotiate trade agreements with other countries in order to protect U.S. firms and workers or to impose tariffs on imports. Some policymakers and economists, though, believe that protecting U.S. firms will raise prices U.S. consumers pay and will also raise the costs to U.S. firms that buy inputs from foreign firms. In addition, because automation—the replacement of workers by robots, computers, and other capital—has increased in manufacturing, it is unlikely that increased production of manufactured goods in the United States would reverse the long-run decline in manufacturing employment. Some policymakers and economists support expanded use of Trade Adjustment Assistance (TAA), which is a federal government program that provides funds to workers who have lost their jobs as a result of competition from foreign imports. The funds can be used for job training, job searches, relocations to find new jobs, payments for health insurance, and replacement of lost wages. But studies by the Department of Labor, which administers the program, indicate that significant numbers of workers who lost their jobs as a result of the China shock had not found new jobs paying comparable wages by the time their TAA benefits had run out, which is typically two years.

The effects of the China surge have led policymakers and economists to reassess the balance between winners and losers from international trade and to consider whether current policies to help the losers are adequate.

Sources: Chun Han Wong, "China Digs in on Trade as Trump Warns of 'Very Difficult' Summit," *Wall Street Journal*, March 31, 2017; Bob Davis and Jon Hilsenrath, "How the China Shock, Deep and Swift, Fueled the Rise of Trump," *Wall Street Journal*, August 11, 2016; David H. Autor, David Dorn, and Gordon H. Hanson, "The China Shock: Learning from Labor-Market Adjustment to Large Changes in Trade," *Annual Review of Economics*, Vol. 8, 2016, pp. 205–240; David H. Autor, David Dorn, and Gordon H. Hanson, "The China Syndrome: Local Labor Market Effects of Import Competition in the United States," *American Economic Review*, Vol. 103, No. 6, October 2013, pp. 2121–2168; and data from the U.S. International Trade Commission and from the Federal Reserve Bank of St. Louis.

Your Turn: Test your understanding by doing related problems 3.12 and 3.13 on page 246 at the end of this chapter.

MyLab Economics Study Plan

Where Does Comparative Advantage Come From?

Among the main sources of comparative advantage are the following:

- **Climate and natural resources.** This source of comparative advantage is the most obvious. Because of geology, Saudi Arabia has a comparative advantage in the production of oil. Because of climate and soil conditions, Costa Rica has a comparative advantage in the production of bananas, and the United States has a comparative advantage in the production of wheat.

- **Relative abundance of labor and capital.** Some countries, such as the United States, have many highly skilled workers and a great deal of machinery. Other countries, such as China, have many unskilled workers and relatively little machinery. As a result, the United States has a comparative advantage in the production of goods that require highly skilled workers or sophisticated machinery, such as aircraft and computer software. China has a comparative advantage in the production of goods, such as furniture, clothing, and children's toys, that require unskilled workers and small amounts of simple machinery. In fact, many economists believe that the surge in Chinese imports to the United States and other countries following China's admittance to the World Trade Organization (WTO) was fueled by the low cost of producing manufactured goods using low-wage, unskilled workers. These workers had become available to manufacturing firms after economic reforms allowed large numbers of workers to leave unproductive collective farms and state-owned companies for higher-paid factory work.

- **Technology.** Broadly defined, *technology* is the processes firms use to turn inputs into goods and services. At any given time, firms in different countries do not all have access to the same technologies. In part, this difference is a result of past investments countries have made in higher education or in supporting research and development. Some countries are strong in *product technologies*, which involve the ability to develop new products. For example, firms in the United States have pioneered the development of such products as radios, televisions, digital computers, airliners, medical equipment, and many prescription drugs. Other countries are strong in *process technologies*, which involve the ability to improve the processes used to make existing products. For example, Japanese-based firms, such as Toyota and Honda, have succeeded by greatly improving the processes for designing and manufacturing automobiles.

- **External economies.** It is difficult to explain the location of some industries on the basis of climate, natural resources, the relative abundance of labor and capital, or technology. For example, why does southern California have a comparative advantage in making movies or Switzerland in making watches or New York in providing financial services? The answer is that once an industry becomes established in an area, firms located in that area gain advantages over firms located elsewhere. The advantages include the availability of skilled workers, the opportunity to interact with other firms in the same industry, and proximity to suppliers. These advantages result in lower costs to firms located in the area. Because these lower costs result from increases in the size of the industry in an area, economists refer to them as **external economies**.   MyLab Economics Concept Check

External economies Reductions in a firm's costs that result from an increase in the size of an industry.

MyLab Economics Study Plan

7.4 Government Policies That Restrict International Trade

LEARNING OBJECTIVE: Analyze the economic effects of government policies that restrict international trade.

Free trade Trade between countries that is without government restrictions.

Free trade, or trade between countries without government restrictions, makes consumers better off. We can expand on this idea by using the concepts of consumer surplus and producer surplus (see Chapter 4, Section 4.1). Figure 7.4 shows the market in the United States for the biofuel ethanol, which can be used as a substitute for gasoline. The figure shows the situation of autarky, where the United States does not trade with other countries. The equilibrium price of ethanol is $2.00 per gallon, and the equilibrium quantity is 6.0 billion gallons per year. The blue area represents consumer surplus, and the red area represents producer surplus.

Now suppose that the United States begins importing ethanol from Brazil and other countries that produce ethanol for $1.00 per gallon. Because the world market for ethanol is large, we will assume that the United States can buy as much ethanol as it wants without causing the *world price* of $1.00 per gallon to rise. Therefore, once imports of ethanol are allowed into the United States, U.S. firms will not be able to sell ethanol at prices higher than the world price of $1.00, and the U.S. price will become equal to the world price.

Figure 7.5 shows the result of allowing imports of ethanol into the United States. With the price lowered from $2.00 to $1.00, U.S. consumers increase their purchases from 6.0 billion gallons to 9.0 billion gallons. Equilibrium moves from point *F* to point *G*. In the new equilibrium, U.S. producers have reduced the quantity of ethanol they supply from 6.0 billion gallons to 3.0 billion gallons. Imports will equal 6.0 billion gallons, which is the difference between U.S. consumption and U.S. production.

Under autarky, consumer surplus would be area *A* in Figure 7.5. With imports, the reduction in price increases consumer surplus, so it is now equal to the sum of areas *A*, *B*, *C*, and *D*. Although the lower price increases consumer surplus, it reduces producer surplus. Under autarky, producer surplus was equal to the sum of areas *B* and *E*. With imports, it is equal to only area *E*. Recall that economic surplus equals the sum of consumer surplus and producer surplus. Moving from autarky to allowing imports increases economic surplus in the United States by an amount equal to the sum of areas *C* and *D*.

MyLab Economics Animation

Figure 7.4

The U.S. Market for Ethanol under Autarky

This figure shows the market for ethanol in the United States, assuming autarky, where the United States does not trade with other countries. The equilibrium price of ethanol is $2.00 per gallon, and the equilibrium quantity is 6.0 billion gallons per year. The blue area represents consumer surplus, and the red area represents producer surplus.

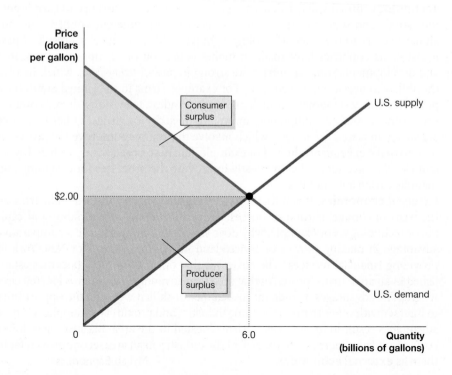

	Under Autarky	With Imports
Consumer Surplus	A	A + B + C + D
Producer Surplus	B + E	E
Economic Surplus	A + B + E	A + B + C + D + E

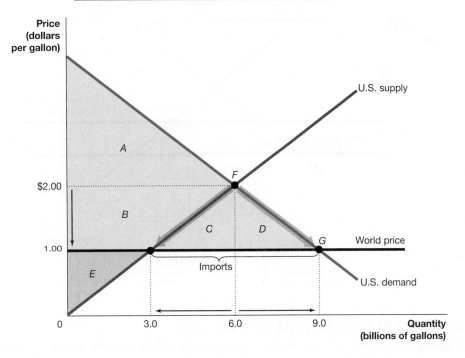

MyLab Economics Animation

Figure 7.5

The Effect of Imports on the U.S. Ethanol Market

When imports are allowed into the United States, the price of ethanol falls from $2.00 to $1.00. U.S. consumers increase their purchases from 6.0 billion gallons to 9.0 billion gallons. Equilibrium moves from point F to point G. U.S. producers reduce the quantity of ethanol they supply from 6.0 billion gallons to 3.0 billion gallons. Imports equal 6.0 billion gallons, which is the difference between U.S. consumption and U.S. production. Consumer surplus equals the sum of areas A, B, C, and D. Producer surplus equals the area E.

We can conclude that international trade helps consumers but hurts firms that are less efficient than foreign competitors. As a result, these firms and their workers are often strong supporters of government policies that restrict trade. These policies usually take one of two forms: (1) *tariffs* or (2) *quotas* and *voluntary export restraints*.

Tariffs

The most common interferences with trade are *tariffs*, which are taxes imposed by a government on goods imported into the country. Like any other tax, a tariff increases the cost of selling a good. Figure 7.6 shows the effect of a tariff of $0.50 per gallon on ethanol imports into the United States. The $0.50 tariff raises the price of ethanol in the United States from the world price of $1.00 per gallon to $1.50 per gallon. At this higher price, U.S. ethanol producers increase the quantity they supply from 3.0 billion gallons to 4.5 billion gallons. U.S. consumers, though, cut back their purchases of ethanol from 9.0 billion gallons to 7.5 billion gallons. Imports decline from 6.0 billion gallons (9.0 billion − 3.0 billion) to 3.0 billion gallons (7.5 billion − 4.5 billion). Equilibrium moves from point G to point H.

By raising the price of ethanol from $1.00 to $1.50, the tariff reduces consumer surplus by the sum of areas A, T, C, and D. Area A is the increase in producer surplus from the higher price. The government collects tariff revenue equal to the tariff of $0.50 per gallon multiplied by the 3.0 billion gallons imported. Area T represents the government's tariff revenue. Areas C and D represent losses to U.S. consumers that are not captured by anyone. These areas are deadweight loss and represent the decline in economic efficiency resulting from the ethanol tariff. Area C shows the effect of U.S. consumers being forced to buy from U.S. producers that are less efficient than foreign producers, and area D shows the effect of U.S. consumers buying less ethanol than they would have at the world price. As a result of the tariff, economic surplus has been reduced by the sum of areas C and D.

We can conclude that the tariff succeeds in helping U.S. ethanol producers but hurts U.S. consumers and the efficiency of the U.S. economy.   **MyLab Economics** Concept Check

Figure 7.6

The Effects of a Tariff on Ethanol

Without a tariff on ethanol, U.S. producers will sell 3.0 billion gallons of ethanol, U.S. consumers will purchase 9.0 billion gallons, and imports will be 6.0 billion gallons. The U.S. price will equal the world price of $1.00 per gallon. The $0.50-per-gallon tariff raises the price of ethanol in the United States to $1.50 per gallon, and U.S. producers increase the quantity they supply to 4.5 billion gallons. U.S. consumers reduce their purchases to 7.5 billion gallons. Equilibrium moves from point G to point H. The ethanol tariff causes a loss of consumer surplus equal to the area A + C + T + D. The area A is the increase in producer surplus due to the higher price. The area T is the government's tariff revenue. The areas C and D represent deadweight loss.

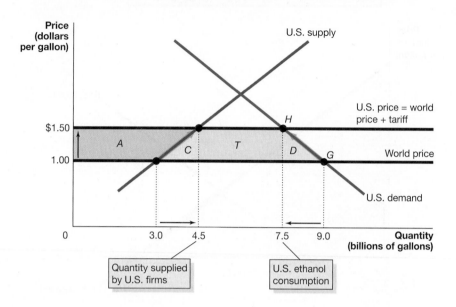

Loss of Consumer Surplus	=	Increase in Producer Surplus	+	Government Tariff Revenue	+	Deadweight Loss
A + C + T + D		A		T		C + D

Quota A numerical limit a government imposes on the quantity of a good that can be imported into the country.

Voluntary export restraint (VER) An agreement negotiated between two countries that places a numerical limit on the quantity of a good that can be imported by one country from the other country.

Quotas and Voluntary Export Restraints

A **quota** is a numerical limit on the quantity of a good that can be imported, and it has an effect similar to that of a tariff. A quota is imposed by the government of the importing country. A **voluntary export restraint (VER)** is an agreement negotiated between two countries that places a numerical limit on the quantity of a good that can be imported by one country from the other country. In the 1980s, the United States and Japan negotiated a VER that limited the quantity of automobiles the United States would import from Japan. The Japanese government agreed to the VER primarily because it was afraid that if it did not, the United States would impose a tariff or quota on imports of Japanese automobiles. Quotas and VERs have similar economic effects.

The main purpose of most tariffs and quotas is to reduce the foreign competition that domestic firms face. For many years, Congress has imposed a quota on sugar imports to protect U.S. sugar producers. Figure 7.7 shows the actual statistics for the U.S. sugar market in 2016. The effect of a quota is very similar to the effect of a tariff. By limiting imports, a quota forces the domestic price of a good above the world price. In this case, the sugar quota limits sugar imports to 6.7 billion pounds per year (shown by the bracket in Figure 7.7), forcing the U.S. price of sugar up to $0.28 per pound, or $0.10 higher than the world price of $0.18 per pound. The U.S. price is above the world price because the quota keeps foreign sugar producers from selling the additional sugar in the United States that would drive the U.S. price down to the world price. At a price of $0.28 per pound, U.S. producers increase the quantity of sugar they supply from the 9.6 billion pounds they would supply at the world price to 18.0 billion pounds, and U.S. consumers cut back their purchases of sugar from the 27.0 billion pounds they would purchase at the world price to the 24.7 billion pounds they are willing to purchase at the higher U.S. price. If there were no import quota, equilibrium would be at the world price (point E), but with the quota, equilibrium is at the U.S. price (point F).   **MyLab Economics** Concept Check

Measuring the Economic Effect of the Sugar Quota

We can use the concepts of consumer surplus, producer surplus, and deadweight loss to measure the economic impact of the sugar quota. Without a sugar quota, the world price of $0.18 per pound would also be the U.S. price. In Figure 7.7, without a sugar quota, consumer surplus would equal the area above the $0.18 price line and below

Loss of Consumer Surplus		Gain to U.S. Sugar Producers		Gain to Foreign Sugar Producers		Deadweight Loss
A + B + C + D	=	A	+	B	+	C + D
$2.59 billion	=	$1.38 billion	+	$0.67 billion	+	$0.54 billion

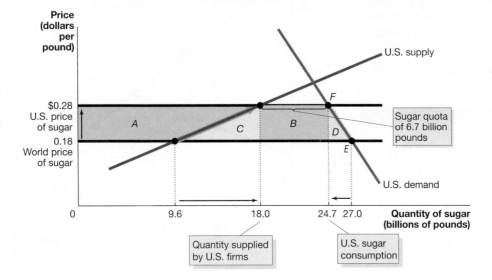

MyLab Economics Animation

Figure 7.7

The Economic Effect of the U.S. Sugar Quota

Without a sugar quota, U.S. sugar producers would have sold 9.6 billion pounds of sugar, U.S. consumers would have purchased 27.0 billion pounds of sugar, and imports would have been 17.4 billion pounds. The U.S. price would have equaled the world price of $0.18 per pound. Because the sugar quota limits imports to 6.7 billion pounds (the bracket in the graph), the price of sugar in the United States rises to $0.28 per pound, and U.S. producers supply 18.0 billion pounds. U.S. consumers purchase 24.7 billion pounds rather than the 27.0 billion pounds they would purchase at the world price. Without the import quota, equilibrium would be at point E; with the quota, equilibrium is at point F. The sugar quota causes a loss of consumer surplus equal to the area A + B + C + D. The area A is the gain to U.S. sugar producers. The area B is the gain to foreign sugar producers. The areas C and D represent deadweight loss. The total loss to U.S. consumers in 2016 was $2.59 billion.

Note: The quota amount shown in the figure includes some imports outside the quota, including imports from Mexico.

the demand curve. The sugar quota causes the U.S. price to rise to $0.28 and reduces consumer surplus by the area A + B + C + D. Without a sugar quota, producer surplus received by U.S. sugar producers would be equal to the area below the $0.18 price line and above the supply curve. The higher U.S. price resulting from the sugar quota increases the producer surplus of U.S. sugar producers by an amount equal to area A.

A foreign producer must have a license from the U.S. government to import sugar under the quota system. Therefore, a foreign sugar producer that is lucky enough to have an import license also benefits from the quota because it is able to sell sugar in the U.S. market at $0.28 per pound instead of $0.18 per pound. Area B is the gain to foreign sugar producers. Areas A and B represent transfers from U.S. consumers of sugar to U.S. and foreign producers of sugar. Areas C and D represent losses to U.S. consumers that are not captured by anyone. These areas are deadweight loss and represent the decline in economic efficiency resulting from the sugar quota. Area C shows the effect of U.S. consumers being forced to buy from U.S. producers that are less efficient than foreign producers, and area D shows the effect of U.S. consumers buying less sugar than they would have at the world price.

Figure 7.7 provides enough information to calculate the dollar value of each of the four areas. The table in the figure shows the results of these calculations. The total loss to consumers from the sugar quota was $2.59 billion in 2016. About 53 percent of the loss to consumers, or $1.38 billion, was gained by U.S. sugar producers as increased producer surplus. About 26 percent, or $0.67 billion, was gained by foreign sugar producers as increased producer surplus, and about 21 percent, or $0.54 billion, was a deadweight loss to the U.S. economy. The U.S. International Trade Commission estimates that eliminating the sugar quota would result in the loss of about 3,000 jobs in the U.S. sugar industry. The cost to U.S. consumers of saving these jobs is equal to $2.59 billion/3,000, or about $860,000 per job each year. In fact, this cost is an underestimate because eliminating the sugar quota would result in new jobs being created, particularly in the candy industry. Over the years, several U.S. candy companies—including the makers of Life Savers and Star Brite mints—have moved factories to other countries to escape the effects of the sugar quota. Partly as a result of the sugar quota, total employment in U.S. chocolate and candy firms that use sugar as an input declined by one-third between 1996 and 2016.   **MyLab Economics** Concept Check

Solved Problem 7.4

Measuring the Economic Effect of a Quota

Suppose that the United States currently both produces and imports apples. The U.S. government then decides to restrict international trade in apples by imposing a quota that allows imports of only 4 million boxes of apples into the United States each year. The figure shows the results of imposing the quota.

Fill in the following table, using the prices, quantities, and letters in the figure:

	Without Quota	With Quota
World price of apples		
U.S. price of apples		
Quantity supplied by U.S. firms		
Quantity demanded by U.S. consumers		
Quantity imported		
Area of consumer surplus		
Area of domestic producer surplus		
Area of deadweight loss		

Solving the Problem

Step 1: **Review the chapter material.** This problem is about measuring the economic effects of a quota, so you may want to review the sections "Quotas and Voluntary Export Restraints," and "Measuring the Economic Effect of the Sugar Quota," which both begin on page 232.

Step 2: **Fill in the table.** After studying Figure 7.7, you should be able to fill in the table. Remember that consumer surplus is the area below the demand curve and above the market price.

	Without Quota	With Quota
World price of apples	$10	$10
U.S. price of apples	$10	$12
Quantity supplied by U.S. firms	6 million boxes	10 million boxes
Quantity demanded by U.S. consumers	16 million boxes	14 million boxes
Quantity imported	10 million boxes	4 million boxes
Area of consumer surplus	A + B + C + D + E + F	A + B
Area of domestic producer surplus	G	G + C
Area of deadweight loss	No deadweight loss	D + F

Your Turn: For more practice, do related problem 4.11 on page 248 at the end of this chapter.

The High Cost of Preserving Jobs with Tariffs and Quotas

The sugar quota is not the only government policy that imposes a high cost on U.S. consumers to save jobs at U.S. firms. The tariff on shoe imports has been estimated to cost U.S. consumers $300,000 per year for each job saved just for women's shoes and rubber shoes. In 2009, the United States imposed a tariff on imports of Chinese tires. As a result, U.S. consumers spent about $1.1 billion more per year on tires. The tariff saved an estimated 1,200 jobs in the U.S. tire industry, at a cost of $900,000 per year per job saved.

Just as the sugar quota costs jobs in the candy industry, other tariffs and quotas cost jobs outside the industries immediately affected. For example, in 1991, the United States imposed tariffs on flat-panel displays used in laptop computers. The tariff was good news for U.S. producers of these displays but bad news for companies producing laptop computers. Toshiba, Sharp, and Apple all closed their U.S. laptop production facilities and moved production overseas. In fact, whenever one industry receives tariff or quota protection, other domestic industries lose jobs. The 2009 tariff on imports of Chinese tires may have cost more than 3,000 jobs in retail stores because the higher price of tires left consumers with less to spend on other goods and services.
MyLab Economics Concept Check

Apply the Concept
MyLab Economics Video

Smoot-Hawley, the Politics of Tariffs, and the Cost of Protecting a Vanishing Industry

In the 1920s, Congress and the president responded to the financial hardship U.S. farmers faced. As a result of that response, in 2017 many U.S. businesses that import foreign-made shoes into the United States paid tariffs of 35 percent or more on the value of the shoes. Sound illogical? The politics of tariffs can certainly seem to be.

Here is the connection between farmers in the 1920s and shoes today: The 1920s were a period of rapid economic progress in the United States, with the mass production of automobiles, the expansion of electricity use in homes and businesses, improvements in public health, a boom in housing construction, and the development of network radio and talking films. But the incomes of many farmers declined, partly because of increasing agricultural production from foreign competitors. During the 1928 presidential election, Herbert Hoover, the Republican Party candidate, promised that if elected, he would aid farmers by raising tariffs on agricultural goods imported into the United States.

i4images/Alamy Stock Photo

How does the Smoot-Hawley Tariff Act of 1930 affect what you pay for your shoes today?

After Hoover won the election, Congress in 1929 considered a new tariff bill. During congressional negotiations, the number of products on which tariffs would be raised quickly expanded beyond agricultural products, in a process known as *logrolling*. Logrolling refers to members of Congress promising to support each other's legislation. In this case, a member of Congress from a district with many dairy farms who wanted the tariff on milk increased would seek out a member of Congress from a district with shoe factories and negotiate along these lines: "If you vote to increase tariffs on milk, I'll vote to increase tariffs on shoes." The law Congress finally passed in 1930, the *Smoot-Hawley Tariff Act*, raised tariffs to the highest level in U.S. history. As a percentage of the value of imports covered by the law, tariffs reached nearly 60 percent.

The process of logrolling can lead to very detailed and complex tariffs as members of Congress attempt to protect specific firms in their districts from competition from foreign producers. For example, the 2017 tariff on shoes contains hundreds of entries, many aimed at very specific types of shoes. Here are *just a few* of those entries:

Type of Shoe	Tariff
Footwear designed to be worn over, or in lieu of, other footwear as a protection against water, oil, grease, or chemicals or cold or inclement weather	37.5%
Parts of footwear (including uppers whether or not attached to soles other than outer soles); removable insoles, heel cushions and similar articles; gaiters, leggings and similar articles, and parts thereof: Valued over $3/pair but not over $6.50	63 cents per pair plus 26.2%
Tennis shoes, basketball shoes, gym shoes, training shoes and the like, costing more than $12 per pair	20.0%
Footwear with open toes or open heels; footwear of the slip-on type, that is held to the foot without the use of laces or buckles or other fasteners, the foregoing except footwear of subheading 6402.99.20 and except footwear having a foxing or a foxing-like band wholly or almost wholly of rubber or plastics applied or molded at the sole and overlapping the upper: Having outer soles with textile materials having the greatest surface area in contact with the ground, but not taken into account under the terms of additional U.S. note 5 to this chapter	12.5%
House slippers valued not over $3 per pair having outer soles with textile materials having the greatest surface area in contact with the ground, but not taken into account under the terms of additional U.S. note 5 to this chapter	12.5%
Footwear with outer soles of rubber, plastics, leather or composition leather and uppers of textile materials: Having soles (or mid-soles, if any) of rubber or plastics which are affixed to the upper exclusively with an adhesive (any mid-soles also being affixed exclusively to one another and to the sole with an adhesive); the foregoing except footwear having uppers of vegetable fibers and having outer soles with textile materials having the greatest surface area in contact with the ground, but not taken into account under the terms of additional U.S. note 5 to this chapter	7.5%
Sandals and similar footwear of plastics, produced in one piece by molding	3.0%

Are you having trouble understanding the entries in the table? Imagine being the owner of a small business in 2017 who wants to import shoes. You will have a lot of difficulty determining what tariff to pay, given the complexity of the law.

Canada, the largest trading partner of the United States, reacted to passage of the Smoot-Hawley Tariff Act by enacting large increases in tariffs on U.S. imports. Other countries raised tariffs as well, resulting in a *trade war* that led to a sharp decrease in global trade and helped increase the severity of the Great Depression of the 1930s.

Since the end of World War II in 1945, the United States and most other countries have greatly reduced tariffs on most goods. But the United States continues to impose high tariffs on shoes 85 years after the passage of Smoot-Hawley. During that time, employment in the U.S. shoe industry has fallen from 275,000 workers to fewer than 15,000, as more than 98 percent of the shoes sold in the United States are imported. The total cost to U.S. consumers from higher shoe prices due to the tariff is more than $2 billion per year. The fact that high tariffs on shoes have survived despite few shoes being manufactured in the United States anymore demonstrates how difficult it can sometimes be to remove government protection for an industry once the protection has been enacted.

One way to avoid logrolling when passing tariff laws is for Congress to give the president *fast-track authority* when negotiating trade agreements with other countries. Under fast-track authority, once the president has finished negotiating an agreement with other countries, Congress can either pass or reject the agreement but cannot change any of its provisions. Fast-track authority would have prevented the vote trading that occurred during the Congressional deliberations over Smoot-Hawley. Some members of Congress have recently become skeptical about the merits of free trade, so it seems less likely that Congress will grant presidents fast-track authority in the future.

Sources: U.S. International Trade Commission, *Official Harmonized Tariff Schedule of the United States (2017)*, http://hts.usitc.gov; Carl Hulse and Gardiner Harris, "House Republicans and White House Try to Revive Trade Bill Stalled by Democrats," *New York Times*, June 15, 2015; and Blake W. Krueger, "A Shoe Tariff with a Big Footprint," *Wall Street Journal*, November 22, 2012.

MyLab Economics Study Plan   **Your Turn:** Test your understanding by doing related problems 4.13 and 4.14 on page 248 at the end of this chapter.

Gains from Unilateral Elimination of Tariffs and Quotas

It is easier for policymakers to gain political support for reducing or eliminating tariffs or quotas if it is done as part of an agreement with other countries that requires those countries to eliminate some of their tariffs or quotas. But as the example of the sugar quota shows, *the U.S. economy would experience a gain in economic surplus from the elimination of tariffs and quotas even if other countries did not reduce their tariffs and quotas.* **MyLab Economics** Concept Check

Other Barriers to Trade

In addition to tariffs and quotas, governments sometimes erect other barriers to trade. For example, all governments require that imports meet certain health and safety requirements. Sometimes, however, governments use these requirements to shield domestic firms from foreign competition. For example, a government may impose stricter health and safety requirements on imported goods than on goods produced by domestic firms.

Many governments also restrict imports of certain products on national security grounds. The argument is that in time of war, a country should not be dependent on imports of critical war materials. Once again, these restrictions are sometimes used more to protect domestic companies from competition than to protect national security. For years, the U.S. government would buy military uniforms only from U.S. manufacturers, even though uniforms are not a critical war material. The Defense Department gives each army recruit a voucher to purchase a pair of athletic shoes for training. New Balance has attempted to force the Defense Department to require the vouchers be used only to purchase U.S.-made shoes. Many officials in the Defense Department didn't see soldiers training in foreign-made running shoes as a threat to national security. **MyLab Economics** Concept Check

MyLab Economics Study Plan

7.5 The Debate over Trade Policies and Globalization

LEARNING OBJECTIVE: Evaluate the debate over trade policies and globalization.

The debate over whether the U.S. government should regulate international trade has continued since the founding of the country. One particularly controversial attempt to restrict trade took place during the Great Depression of the 1930s. At that time, the United States and other countries attempted to help domestic firms by raising tariffs on imports. The United States started the process by passing the Smoot-Hawley Tariff Act in 1930, which raised average tariff rates to nearly 60 percent. As other countries retaliated by raising their tariffs, international trade collapsed.

By the end of World War II in 1945, government officials in the United States and Europe were looking for a way to reduce tariffs and revive international trade. To help achieve this goal, they set up the General Agreement on Tariffs and Trade (GATT) in 1948. Countries that joined the GATT agreed not to impose new tariffs or import quotas. In addition, a series of *multilateral negotiations,* called *trade rounds,* took place, in which countries agreed to reduce tariffs from the very high levels of the 1930s.

In the 1940s, most international trade was in goods, and the GATT agreement covered only goods. In the following decades, trade in services and products incorporating *intellectual property,* such as software programs and movies, grew in importance. Many GATT members pressed for a new agreement that would cover services and intellectual property, as well as goods. A new agreement was negotiated, and in January 1995, the GATT was replaced by the **World Trade Organization (WTO)**, headquartered in Geneva, Switzerland. More than 150 countries are currently members of the WTO.

World Trade Organization (WTO) An international organization that oversees international trade agreements.

Why Do Some People Oppose the World Trade Organization?

During the years immediately after World War II, many low-income, or developing, countries enacted high tariffs and restricted investment by foreign companies. When these policies failed to produce much economic growth, many of these countries

Globalization The process of countries becoming more open to foreign trade and investment.

decided during the 1980s to become more open to foreign trade and investment. This process became known as **globalization**. Most developing countries joined the WTO and began to follow its policies.

During the 1990s, opposition to globalization began to increase. Over the years, protests, which have sometimes turned violent, have occurred in cities hosting WTO meetings. Why would attempts to reduce trade barriers with the objective of increasing income around the world cause such a furious reaction? The opposition to the WTO comes from three sources. First, some opponents are specifically against the globalization process that began in the 1980s and became widespread in the 1990s. Second, other opponents have the same motivation as the supporters of tariffs in the 1930s—to erect trade barriers to protect domestic firms from foreign competition. Third, some critics of the WTO support globalization in principle but believe that the WTO favors the interests of the high-income countries at the expense of the low-income countries. Let's look more closely at the sources of opposition to the WTO.

Anti-globalization Many of those who protest at WTO meetings distrust globalization. Some believe that free trade and foreign investment destroy the distinctive cultures of many countries. As developing countries began to open their economies to imports from the United States and other high-income countries, the imports of food, clothing, movies, and other goods began to replace the equivalent local products. So, a teenager in Thailand might be eating in a McDonald's restaurant, wearing Levi's jeans and a Ralph Lauren shirt, listening to a song by Lady Gaga on his iPhone, before downloading *Wonder Woman* to his iPad. Globalization has increased the variety of products available to consumers in developing countries, but some people argue that this is too high a price to pay for what they see as damage to local cultures.

Globalization has also allowed multinational corporations to relocate factories from high-income countries to low-income countries. These new factories in Indonesia, Malaysia, Pakistan, and other countries pay much lower wages than are paid in the United States, Europe, and Japan and often do not meet the environmental or safety regulations that are imposed in high-income countries. Some factories use child labor, which is illegal in high-income countries. Some people have argued that firms with factories in developing countries should pay workers wages as high as those paid in high-income countries. They also believe these firms should abide by the health, safety, and environmental regulations that exist in the high-income countries.

The governments of most developing countries have resisted these proposals. They argue that when the currently rich countries were poor, they also lacked environmental or safety standards, and their workers were paid low wages. They argue that it is easier for rich countries to afford high wages and environmental and safety regulations than it is for poor countries. They also point out that many jobs that seem to have very low wages based on the standards of high-income countries are often better than the alternatives available to workers in low-income countries.

Protectionism The use of trade barriers to shield domestic firms from foreign competition.

"Old-Fashioned" Protectionism The anti-globalization argument against free trade and the WTO is relatively new. Another argument against free trade, called *protectionism*, has been around for centuries. **Protectionism** is the use of trade barriers to shield domestic firms from foreign competition. Some of the recent opposition to free trade in the United States appears to be protectionist. For as long as international trade has existed, governments have attempted to restrict it to protect domestic firms. As we saw with the analysis of the sugar quota, protectionism causes losses to consumers and eliminates jobs in the domestic industries that buy the protected product. In addition, by reducing the ability of countries to produce according to comparative advantage, protectionism reduces incomes.

Why, then, does protectionism attract support, and why has support for protectionist policies increased recently among some policymakers in the United States? Protectionism is usually justified on the basis of one of the following arguments:

- **Saving jobs.** President Trump and other supporters of protectionist policies argue that free trade reduces employment by driving domestic firms out of business. It is true that when more-efficient foreign firms drive less-efficient domestic firms out of business, jobs are lost, but jobs are also lost when more-efficient domestic firms drive less-efficient domestic firms out of business. Economists have traditionally argued that these job losses are rarely permanent. In the U.S. economy, jobs are lost and new jobs are created continually. No economic study has ever found a long-term connection between the total number of jobs available in the United States as a whole and the level of tariff protection for domestic industries. But, as we discussed in the *Apply the Concept* on page 226, recent studies of the effects of the surge of imports from China that began in 2001 have shown that employment losses in areas most affected by imports have proven to be long-lasting. People living in some cities and towns that were home to firms that have closed because of competition from foreign imports have experienced significant hardships. Some of these areas have suffered from declining populations as workers have left to find jobs elsewhere, and the lower incomes of many people who remain have resulted in reduced sales by local businesses. The main streets in some of these towns have many boarded-up storefronts, and local governments have struggled to maintain services in the face of declining tax revenue. But, as we have also seen, trade restrictions destroy jobs in some industries at the same time that they preserve jobs in others. The U.S. sugar quota may have saved jobs in the U.S. sugar industry, but it has also destroyed jobs in the U.S. candy industry.
- **Protecting high wages.** Some people worry that firms in high-income countries will have to start paying much lower wages to compete with firms in developing countries. For the country as a whole, this fear is misplaced, however, because free trade actually raises living standards by increasing economic efficiency. When a country practices protectionism and produces goods and services it could obtain more inexpensively from other countries, it reduces its standard of living. The United States could ban imports of coffee and begin growing it domestically. But doing so would entail a very high opportunity cost because coffee could only be grown in the continental United States in greenhouses and would require large amounts of labor and equipment. The coffee would have to sell for a very high price to cover these costs. Suppose the United States did ban coffee imports. Eliminating the ban at some future time would cause U.S. coffee workers to lose their jobs, but the standard of living in the United States would rise as coffee prices declined and labor, machinery, and other resources were moved out of coffee production and into production of goods and services for which the United States has a comparative advantage. But again, recent experience indicates that while trade contributes to raising the standard of living of the country as a whole, it can lead to long-lived declines in income in areas that are most exposed to competition from imports. Such a decline appears to have taken place in areas of the Midwest and Southeast where firms were most exposed to competition from Chinese imports.
- **Protecting infant industries.** It is possible that firms in a country may have a comparative advantage in producing a good, but because the country begins production of the good later than other countries, its firms initially have higher costs. Producing some goods and services involves substantial "learning by doing." As workers and firms produce more of the good or service, they gain experience and become more productive. Over time, these firms will have lower costs and can charge lower prices. As the firms in the "infant industry" gain experience, they will be able to compete successfully with foreign producers. Under free trade, however, they may not get a chance. The established foreign producers can sell the product at a lower price and drive domestic producers out of business before they gain enough experience to compete. To economists, the infant industry argument is the most persuasive of the protectionist arguments. It has a significant drawback, however. Tariffs eliminate the need for firms in an infant industry to become

productive enough to compete with foreign firms. After World War II, the governments of many developing countries used the infant industry argument to justify high tariff rates. Unfortunately, most of their infant industries never grew up, and they continued for years as inefficient drains on their economies.

- **Protecting national security.** A country will typically not want to rely on other countries for goods that are critical to its military defense. For example, the United States would probably not want to import all its jet fighter engines from China. The definition of which goods are critical to military defense is a slippery one, however. In fact, it is rare for an industry to ask for protection without raising the issue of national security, even if its products have mainly nonmilitary uses.   **MyLab Economics** Concept Check

Apply the Concept   **MyLab Economics** Video

Protecting Consumer Health or Protecting U.S. Firms from Competition?

Lucenet Patrice/Oredia/Alamy Stock Photo

Are restrictions on catfish imports protecting the health of U.S. consumers or the interests of U.S. producers?

The World Trade Organization and other international agreements limit the use of tariffs and quotas. So to protect firms from foreign competition, governments sometimes regulate imports by claiming that they pose a threat to consumer health or safety.

Is imported catfish safe for U.S. consumers to eat, or does it contain bacteria and dangerous chemicals? The U.S. states that produce the most catfish are Alabama, Arkansas, Mississippi, and Texas. In 2008, members of Congress from those states pushed through legislation setting up a catfish inspection office in the U.S. Department of Agriculture (USDA). By 2014, the office had spent $20 million but had not actually inspected any imported catfish. The money had been spent on just setting up offices and paying administrators' salaries. That year, Congress set a deadline for the inspection program to begin. In the following years, the office has spent $14 million annually inspecting catfish.

Vietnam and other countries that export catfish to the United States have objected that the real purpose of the inspections is to erect a barrier to trade. Those governments argue that the inspections violate the commitments of the United States under the World Trade Organization not to erect barriers to trade. A study by the U.S. Government Accountability Office indicated that the health risk to U.S. consumers from imported catfish was very low, even without the proposed inspections. Some members of Congress from states that do not produce catfish also argue that new inspections of imported catfish were unnecessary and result in U.S. consumers paying higher prices. Despite these arguments, an attempt in Congress to eliminate the USDA's catfish inspection office failed in 2016.

Policymakers are often caught in a dilemma over imports. Firms want to reduce or eliminate sales lost to imports, but imposing trade barriers reduces economic efficiency, lowers incomes, and invites retaliation from foreign governments. Although some imported goods can, in fact, pose threats to the health and safety of U.S. consumers, some health and safety regulations are intended to protect the U.S. firms involved rather than U.S. consumers.

Sources: William R. Jones, "Waste and Duplication in the USDA Catfish Inspection Program," statement before the Subcommittee on Health, Committee on Energy and Commerce, U.S. House of Representatives, December 7, 2016; David Williams, "The Catfish (Inspection Program) that Survived Commonsense," thehill.com, December 7, 2016; Bruce Einhorn and Chau Mai, "The Catfish Wars Could Derail U.S.–Asia Trade," businessweek.com, June 30, 2014; and U.S. Government Accountability Office, *Seafood Safety: Responsibility for Inspecting Catfish Should Not Be Assigned to USDA*, GAO 12-411, May 2012.

MyLab Economics Study Plan   **Your Turn:** Test your understanding by doing related problems 5.9 and 5.10 on page 250 at the end of this chapter.

Dumping

In recent years, the United States has extended protection to some domestic industries by using a provision in the WTO agreement that allows governments to impose tariffs in the case of *dumping*. **Dumping** is selling a product for a price below its cost of production. Using tariffs to offset the effects of dumping is controversial, despite being allowed under the WTO agreement.

In practice, it is difficult to determine whether foreign companies are dumping goods because the true production costs of a good are not easy for governments to calculate. As a result, the WTO allows countries to determine that dumping has occurred if a product is exported for a lower price than it sells for on the home market. There is a problem with this approach, however. Often there are good business reasons for a firm to sell a product for different prices to different consumers. For example, the airlines charge business travelers higher ticket prices than leisure travelers. Firms also use "loss leaders"—products that are sold below cost, or even given away free—when introducing a new product or, in the case of retailing, to attract customers who will also buy full-price products. For example, during the holiday season, Walmart sometimes offers toys at prices below what it pays to buy them from manufacturers. It's unclear why these normal business practices should be unacceptable when used in international trade. **MyLab Economics** Concept Check

Dumping Selling a product for a price below its cost of production.

Positive versus Normative Analysis (Once Again)

Economists emphasize the burden on the economy imposed by tariffs, quotas, and other government restrictions on free trade. Does it follow that these interferences are bad? Remember that positive analysis concerns what *is*, while normative analysis concerns what *ought to be*. Measuring the effect of the sugar quota on the U.S. economy is an example of positive analysis. Asserting that the sugar quota is bad public policy and should be eliminated is normative analysis. The sugar quota—like all other interferences with trade—makes some people better off and some people worse off, and it reduces total income and consumption. Whether increasing the profits of U.S. sugar companies and the number of workers they employ justifies the costs imposed on consumers and the reduction in economic efficiency is a normative question.

Most economists do not support interferences with trade, such as the sugar quota, because they believe that markets should be as free as possible. But the opposite view is certainly intellectually respectable. It is possible for someone to understand the costs of tariffs and quotas but still believe that they are a good idea, perhaps because he or she believes unrestricted free trade would cause too much disruption to the economy.

The success of industries in getting the government to erect barriers to foreign competition depends partly on some members of the public knowing the costs of trade barriers but supporting them anyway. However, two other factors are also at work:

1. The costs that tariffs and quotas impose on consumers are large in total but relatively small per person. For example, the sugar quota imposes a total burden of $2.59 billion per year on consumers. Spread across 325 million Americans, the burden is only about $8 per person—too little for most people to worry about, even if they know the burden exists.
2. The jobs lost to foreign competition are easy to identify, but the jobs created by foreign trade are less easy to identify.

In other words, the industries that benefit from tariffs and quotas benefit a lot—for example, the sugar quota increases the profits of U.S. sugar producers by $1.38 billion per year—while each consumer loses relatively little. This concentration of benefits and widely spread burdens makes it easy to understand why members of Congress receive strong pressure from some industries to enact tariffs and quotas and relatively little pressure from the general public to reduce them. **MyLab Economics** Concept Check   **MyLab Economics** Study Plan

Continued from page 217

Economics in Your Life & Career

Should a Member of Congress Support a Tariff on Running Shoes?

At the beginning of the chapter, we asked you to suppose you are an aide to a member of Congress who is considering whether to vote for a bill that would eliminate the U.S. tariff on running shoes. We asked what facts and conclusions from the economic analysis of international trade you should include in your memorandum advising the member on her vote.

The *Apply the Concept* "Smoot-Hawley, the Politics of Tariffs, and the Cost of Protecting a Vanishing Industry" on page 235 notes that currently the federal government imposes a tariff of 35 percent on most imported running shoes. The cost to consumers from this tariff is estimated to be about $2 billion per year. So, one factor to include in your memo is that local businesses in the member's district that sell running shoes and local consumers who buy them would both benefit from removing the tariff. A possibly more important factor, though, influencing the member's vote will be whether there are any shoe factories in her district. If so, it may be difficult politically to vote to eliminate the tariff on running shoes, even though the gain to other local businesses and to local consumers is likely to be greater in dollar terms than the losses to the owners of the shoe factory and its workers. As the *Apply the Concept* also noted, logrolling during the writing of the 1930 Smoot-Hawley Tariff Act is a reason the shoe tariff was enacted and a key reason it survives to the present. Even if there is no shoe factory in the member's district, other members of Congress who do have shoe factories in their districts may offer to trade their votes on issues that concern your member in exchange for her vote to uphold the shoe tariff. Such is the mixture of positive and normative considerations that result in tariffs and other laws!

Conclusion

There are few issues economists agree upon more than the economic benefits of free trade. However, there are few political issues as controversial as government policy toward trade. Some people who would be reluctant to see the government interfere with domestic trade support interference with international trade. The damage high tariffs inflicted on the world economy during the 1930s shows what can happen when governments around the world abandon free trade. Whether future episodes of that type can be avoided is by no means certain.

Visit **MyLab Economics** for a news article and analysis related to the concepts in this chapter.

CHAPTER SUMMARY
AND PROBLEMS

Key Terms

Absolute advantage, p. 221

Autarky, p. 222

Comparative advantage, p. 221

Dumping, p. 241

Exports, p. 219

External economies, p. 229

Free trade, p. 230

Globalization, p. 238

Imports, p. 218

Opportunity cost, p. 221

Protectionism, p. 238

Quota, p. 232

Tariff, p. 218

Terms of trade, p. 222

Voluntary export restraint (VER), p. 232

World Trade Organization (WTO), p. 237

7.1 The United States in the International Economy, pages 218–220

LEARNING OBJECTIVE: Discuss the role of international trade in the U.S. economy.

MyLab Economics Visit **www.pearson.com/mylab/economics** to complete these exercises online and get instant feedback.

Summary

International trade has been increasing in recent decades, in part because of reductions in *tariffs* and other barriers to trade. A **tariff** is a tax imposed by a government on imports. The quantity of goods and services the United States imports and exports has been continually increasing. **Imports** are goods and services bought domestically but produced in other countries. **Exports** are goods and services produced domestically and sold to other countries. Today, the United States is the second-leading exporting country in the world behind China, and about 20 percent of U.S. manufacturing jobs depend on exports.

Review Questions

1.1 Briefly explain whether the value of U.S. exports is typically larger or smaller than the value of U.S. imports. Are imports and exports now a smaller or larger fraction of GDP than they were 40 years ago?

1.2 Briefly explain whether you agree with the following statement: "International trade is more important to the U.S. economy than it is to most other economies."

Problems and Applications

1.3 If the United States were to stop trading goods and services with other countries, which U.S. industries would be likely to see their sales decline the most? Briefly explain.

1.4 Briefly explain whether you agree with the following statement: "Japan has always been much more heavily involved in international trade than are most other nations. In fact, today Japan exports a larger fraction of its GDP than Germany, the United Kingdom, or the United States."

1.5 Why might a smaller country, such as the Netherlands, be more likely to import and export larger fractions of its GDP than would a larger country, such as China or the United States?

7.2 Comparative Advantage in International Trade, pages 220–222

LEARNING OBJECTIVE: Explain the difference between comparative advantage and absolute advantage in international trade.

MyLab Economics Visit **www.pearson.com/mylab/economics** to complete these exercises online and get instant feedback.

Summary

Comparative advantage is the ability of an individual, a firm, or a country to produce a good or service at the lowest **opportunity cost**. **Absolute advantage** is the ability to produce more of a good or service than competitors when using the same amount of resources. Countries trade on the basis of comparative advantage, not on the basis of absolute advantage.

Review Questions

2.1 What is the difference between absolute advantage and comparative advantage? If a country has an absolute advantage in producing a good, will it always be an exporter of that good? Briefly explain.

2.2 A World Trade Organization (WTO) publication called comparative advantage "arguably the single most powerful insight in economics." What is comparative advantage? What makes it such a powerful insight?

Source: World Trade Organization, "Understanding the WTO," www.wto.org/english/thewto_e/whatis_e/tif_e/fact3_e.htm.

Problems and Applications

2.3 A book on the Roman Empire made the following observation: "Romans bought their pots from professional potters, and bought their defence from professional soldiers. From both they got a quality product—much better than if they had had to do their soldiering and potting themselves." Briefly explain what economic concept the author is illustrating in this passage. How does he know that Romans got better pots and better defense by relying on this economic concept?

Source: Bryan Ward-Perkins, *The Fall of Rome and the End of Civilization*, Oxford: Oxford University Press, 2005, p. 49.

2.4 In the 2016 Summer Olympic Games, Ashton Eaton (from the United States) won a gold medal in the decathlon, which requires athletes to compete in 10 different track and field events. In one of these events Eaton ran a 100-meter race in 10.46 seconds. In a separate event, Usain Bolt (from Jamaica) won a gold medal by running 100 meters in 9.81 seconds.
 a. Which performance—Eaton's or Bolt's—is better explained by the concept of comparative advantage? Briefly explain.
 b. Based on their performance at the 2016 Olympic Games, can we say whether Eaton or Bolt was the better athlete? Briefly explain.

2.5 An article in the *New York Times* quoted an economist as arguing that "global free trade and the European single market . . . encourage countries to specialize in sectors where they enjoy comparative advantage. Germany's [comparative advantage] is in cars and machine tools." For the author's observation to be correct, must Germany be able to produce more cars and machine tools per hour worked than do France, Italy, Spain, and Germany's other trading partners? Briefly explain.

Source: Anatole Kaletsky, "In Disguise, a Budget That Britain Needs," *New York Times*, March 24, 2014.

2.6 Briefly explain whether you agree with the following argument: "Unfortunately, Bolivia does not have a comparative advantage with respect to the United States in the production of any good or service." (*Hint:* You do not need any specific information about the economies of Bolivia or the United States to be able to answer this question.)

2.7 The following table shows the hourly output per worker for Greece and Italy measured as quarts of olive oil and pounds of pasta.

	Output per Hour of Work	
	Olive Oil	Pasta
Greece	4	2
Italy	4	8

Calculate the opportunity cost of producing olive oil and pasta in both Greece and Italy.

2.8 Using the numbers in the following table, explain which country has a comparative advantage in producing smartphones.

	Output per Hour of Work	
	Smartphones	Fitness Bracelets
Switzerland	8	10
Canada	5	3

2.9 Patrick J. Buchanan, a political commentator and former presidential candidate, argued in his book on the global economy that there is a flaw in David Ricardo's theory of comparative advantage:

> Classical free trade theory fails the test of common sense. According to Ricardo's law of comparative advantage . . . if America makes better computers and textiles than China does, but our advantage in computers is greater than our advantage in textiles, we should (1) focus on computers, (2) let China make textiles, and (3) trade U.S. computers for Chinese textiles.... The doctrine begs a question. If Americans are more efficient than Chinese in making clothes … why surrender the more efficient American industry? Why shift to a reliance on a Chinese textile industry that will take years to catch up to where American factories are today?

Do you agree with Buchanan's argument? Briefly explain.

Source: Patrick J. Buchanan, *The Great Betrayal: How American Sovereignty and Social Justice Are Being Sacrificed to the Gods of the Global Economy*, Boston: Little, Brown & Company, 1998, p. 66.

7.3 How Countries Gain from International Trade, pages 222–229

LEARNING OBJECTIVE: Explain how countries gain from international trade.

MyLab Economics Visit **www.pearson.com/mylab/economics** to complete these exercises online and get instant feedback.

Summary

Autarky is a situation in which a country does not trade with other countries. The **terms of trade** is the ratio at which a country can trade its exports for imports from other countries. When a country specializes in producing goods for which it has a comparative advantage and trades for the other goods it needs, the country will have a higher level of income and consumption. We do not see complete specialization in production for three reasons: (1) Not all goods and services are traded internationally, (2) production of most goods involves increasing opportunity costs, and (3) tastes for products differ across countries. Although the population of a country as a whole benefits from trade, firms—and their workers—that are unable to compete with lower-cost foreign producers lose. Among the main sources of comparative advantage are climate and natural resources, relative abundance of labor and capital, technology, and external economies. **External economies**

are reductions in a firm's costs that result from an increase in the size of an industry.

Review Questions

3.1 Briefly explain how international trade increases a country's consumption.

3.2 What is meant by a country specializing in the production of a good? Is it typical for countries to be completely specialized? Briefly explain.

3.3 What are the main sources of comparative advantage?

3.4 Does everyone gain from international trade? If not, explain which groups lose.

Problems and Applications

3.5 (Related to Solved Problem 7.3 on page 224) The following table shows the hourly output per worker in two industries in Chile and Argentina.

	Output per Hour of Work	
	Hats	Beer (barrels)
Chile	8	6
Argentina	1	2

a. Explain which country has an absolute advantage in the production of hats and which country has an absolute advantage in the production of beer.

b. Explain which country has a comparative advantage in the production of hats and which country has a comparative advantage in the production of beer.

c. Suppose that Chile and Argentina currently do not trade with each other. Each has 1,000 hours of labor to use producing hats and beer, and the countries are currently producing the amounts of each good shown in the following table.

	Hats	Beer (barrels)
Chile	7,200	600
Argentina	600	800

Using this information, give a numerical example of how Chile and Argentina can both gain from trade. Assume that after trading begins, one hat can be exchanged for one barrel of beer.

3.6 (Related to Solved Problem 7.3 on page 224) A political commentator makes the following statement:

> The idea that international trade should be based on the comparative advantage of each country is fine for rich countries like the United States and Japan. Rich countries have educated workers and large quantities of machinery and equipment. These advantages allow them to produce every product more efficiently than poor countries can. Poor countries like Kenya and Uruguay have nothing to gain from international trade based on comparative advantage.

Do you agree with this argument? Briefly explain.

3.7 The following data summarize the trade between Canada and the United States in 2015 and 2016.

	Exports from the United States to Canada (billions of U.S. dollars)	Exports from Canada to the United States (billions of U.S. dollars)
2015	$ 280.6	$ 296.2
2016	266.8	278.1

In both years, the value of Canada's exports to the United States exceeded the value of U.S. exports to Canada. Can we conclude that foreign trade between the two countries benefited Canada more than it benefited the United States? Briefly explain.

Source: U.S. Department of Commerce, Census Bureau, Economic Indicators Division.

3.8 An article in the *New Yorker* stated, "The main burden of trade-related job losses and wage declines has fallen on middle- and lower-income Americans. But . . . the very people who suffer most from free trade are often, paradoxically, among its biggest beneficiaries." Explain how it is possible that middle- and lower-income Americans are both the biggest losers and at the same time the biggest winners from free trade.

Source: James Surowiecki, "The Free-Trade Paradox," *New Yorker*, May 26, 2008.

3.9 Hal Varian, chief economist at Google, made the following two observations about international trade:

1. Trade allows a country "to produce more with less."
2. "There is little doubt who wins [from trade] in the long run: consumers."

Briefly explain whether you agree with either or both of these observations.

Source: Hal R. Varian, "The Mixed Bag of Productivity," *New York Times*, October 23, 2003.

3.10 Suppose the following graph shows Tanzania's production possibilities frontier (*PPF*) for cashew nuts and mangoes. Assume that the output per hour of work is 8 bushels of cashew nuts or 2 bushels of mangoes and that Tanzania has 1,000 hours of labor. Without trade, Tanzania evenly splits its labor hours between cashews and mangoes and produces and consumes at point A.

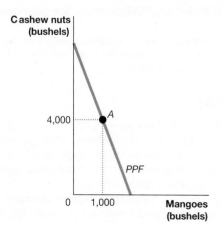

a. Suppose Tanzania opens trade with Kenya, and Kenya's output per hour of work is 1 bushel of cashew nuts or 1 bushel of mangoes. Having the comparative advantage, Tanzania completely specializes in cashew nuts. How many bushels of cashew nuts can Tanzania produce? Denote this point on the graph as point *B*.

b. Suppose Tanzania keeps 5,000 bushels of cashew nuts and exports the remaining 3,000 bushels. If the terms of trade are 1 bushel of mangoes for 2 bushels of cashew nuts, how many bushels of mangoes will Tanzania get in exchange? Denote on the graph the quantity of cashew nuts and mangoes that Tanzania consumes with trade and label this point as point *C*. How does point *C* with trade compare to point *A* without trade?

c. With trade, is Tanzania producing on its *PPF*? With trade, is Tanzania consuming on its *PPF*?

3.11 (Related to the Don't Let This Happen to You on page 226) Former President Barack Obama once described a trade agreement reached with the government of Colombia as a "'win–win' for both our countries." Is everyone in both countries likely to win from the agreement? Briefly explain.

Source: Kent Klein, "Obama: Free Trade Agreement a 'Win–Win' for US, Colombia," voanews.com.

3.12 (Related to the Apply the Concept on page 226) An article in the *Wall Street Journal* discussing the effect of Chinese imports on the U.S. economy made the following observation: "[China's] emergence as a trade powerhouse rattled the American economy more violently than economists and policy makers anticipated at the time. . . . The U.S. workforce adapted more slowly than expected."

a. What does the article mean that China's emergence as a trade powerhouse rattled the U.S. economy?

b. Why didn't economists and policymakers expect the economic effect of imports from China to be as great as it turned out to be?

c. In what sense has the U.S. workforce adapted more slowly than expected?

Source: Bob Davis and Jon Hilsenrath, "How the China Shock, Deep and Swift, Fueled the Rise of Trump," *Wall Street Journal*, August 11, 2016.

3.13 (Related to the Apply the Concept on page 226) An article in the *Economist* discussing the effects of Chinese imports on U.S. jobs referred to the "China-shock literature" and included a graph showing for the period from 1990 to 2016 the decrease in U.S. manufacturing employment as a percentage of the working-age population along with the increase in imports of goods from China as a percentage of GDP.

a. What does the article mean by the "China-shock literature?"

b. What has caused most of the decline in U.S. manufacturing employment since the 1940s?

c. The article noted that "places in America more exposed to these Chinese imports [were] typically those with lots of labor-intensive manufacturing." Why would places with lots of labor-intensive manufacturing be more exposed to Chinese imports?

Source: "Trade with China: Shock Horror," *Economist*, March 11, 2017

3.14 An article in the *New York Times* discussed the number of innovative food companies, particularly those selling natural foods, that have become established in Boulder, Colorado, in recent years. According to the article, Boulder has a large number of people with experience in managing food companies, lenders who know the industry, food distributors, and food processing plants. The article quoted one entrepreneur as asserting: "There's an ecosystem here that supports food entrepreneurs that you just don't find in other places. Everything you need, including a lot of experience and expertise, is right here." What advantages does being located in Boulder give to startup natural food firms? In what circumstances can natural food firms located elsewhere overcome these advantages? Are Boulder's advantages likely to persist over time?

Source: Stephanie Strom, "Foodies Know: Boulder Has Become a Hub for New Producers," *New York Times*, February 4, 2017.

 7.4 **Government Policies That Restrict International Trade, pages 230–237**

LEARNING OBJECTIVE: Analyze the economic effects of government policies that restrict international trade.

MyLab Economics Visit www.pearson.com/mylab/economics to complete these exercises online and get instant feedback.

Summary

Free trade is trade between countries without government restrictions. Government policies that interfere with trade usually take the form of *tariffs*, *quotas*, or *voluntary export restraints*. A **quota** is a numerical limit imposed by a government on the quantity of a good that can be imported into the country. A **voluntary export restraint (VER)** is an agreement negotiated between two countries that places a numerical limit on the quantity of a good that can be imported by one country from the other country. The federal government's sugar quota costs U.S. consumers $2.59 billion per year, or about $860,000 per year for each job saved in the sugar industry. Saving jobs by using tariffs and quotas is often very expensive.

Review Questions

4.1 What is a tariff? What is a quota? Give an example, other than a quota, of a nontariff barrier to trade.

4.2 Who gains and who loses when a country imposes a tariff or a quota on imports of a good?

Problems and Applications

4.3 Political commentator B. Bruce-Briggs once wrote the following in the *Wall Street Journal*: "This is not to say that the case for international free trade is invalid; it is just irrelevant. It is an 'if only everybody' . . . argument . . . . In the real world almost everybody sees benefits in economic nationalism." What do you think he means by "economic nationalism"? Do you agree that a country benefits from free trade only if every other country also practices free trade? Briefly explain.

Source: B. Bruce-Biggs, "The Coming Overthrow of Free Trade," *Wall Street Journal*, February 24, 1983.

4.4 **(Related to the Chapter Opener on page 216)** While running for the 2016 Democratic nomination for president, Vermont Senator Bernie Sanders opposed the Trans-Pacific Partnership in part because he believed that as a result of the agreement, "the U.S. will lose more than 130,000 jobs to Vietnam and Japan alone." Do you agree that reducing barriers to trade reduces the number of jobs available to workers in the United States? Briefly explain.

Source: Bernie Sanders, "Senator Bernie Sanders: The Trans-Pacific Trade (TPP) Agreement Must Be Defeated," www.sanders.senate.gov/download/the-trans-pacific-trade-tpp-agreement-must-be-defeated?inline=file.

4.5 The United States produces beef and also imports beef from other countries.
   a. Draw a graph showing the demand and supply of beef in the United States. Assume that the United States can import as much as it wants at the world price of beef without causing the world price of beef to increase. Be sure to indicate on your graph the quantity of beef imported. Assume that the world price of beef is lower than the U.S. price.
   b. Now show on your graph the effect of the United States imposing a tariff on beef. Be sure to indicate on your graph the quantity of beef sold by U.S. producers before and after the tariff is imposed, the quantity of beef imported before and after the tariff, and the price of beef in the United States before and after the tariff.
   c. Discuss who benefits and who loses when the United States imposes a tariff on beef.

4.6 A student makes the following argument:

> Tariffs on imports of foreign goods into the United States will cause the foreign companies to add the amount of the tariff to the prices they charge in the United States for those goods. Instead of putting a tariff on imported goods, we should ban importing them. Banning imported goods is better than putting tariffs on them because U.S. producers benefit from the reduced competition, and U.S. consumers don't have to pay the higher prices caused by tariffs.

Briefly explain whether you agree with the student's reasoning.

4.7 A columnist for bloomberg.com offered the following observation about economic legislation: "History shows that concentrated opposition beats diffuse support every time."

   a. Briefly explain what this columnist means.
   b. Does his observation apply to tariffs? Briefly explain.

Source: Peter Coy, "Show Us Your Tax Reforms," bloomberg.com, March 30, 2017.

4.8 The following graph shows the effect on consumer surplus, producer surplus, government tariff revenue, and economic surplus of a tariff of $1 per unit on imports of plastic combs into the United States. Use the areas denoted by letters in the graph to answer the following questions.

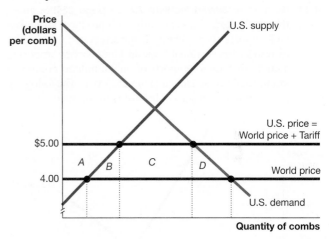

   a. Which area shows the losses to U.S. consumers of buying a smaller quantity of combs than they would have if they could have purchased them at the world price?
   b. Which area shows the losses to U.S. consumers of having to buy combs from U.S. producers who are less efficient than foreign producers?
   c. Which areas show the deadweight loss to the U.S. economy as a result of the tariff on combs?

4.9 The following graph shows the situation after the U.S. government removes a tariff on imports of canned tuna.

   a. Which areas show the gain in consumer surplus?
   b. Which area shows the loss in producer surplus?
   c. Which area shows the loss in government tariff revenue?
   d. Which areas show the gain in economic surplus?

4.10 According to an editorial in the *Washington Post*, "Sugar protectionism is a burden on consumers and a job-killer."
   a. In what sense does the United States practice "sugar protectionism"?
   b. In what way is sugar protectionism a burden on consumers? In what way is it a job-killer?
   c. If sugar protectionism has the bad effects stated in the editorial, why don't Congress and the president eliminate it?

   Source: "Sourball," *Washington Post*, March 22, 2010.

4.11 (Related to Solved Problem 7.4 on page 234) Suppose that the United States currently both produces kumquats and imports them. The U.S. government then decides to restrict international trade in kumquats by imposing a quota that allows imports of only 6 million pounds of kumquats into the United States each year. The following figure shows the results of imposing the quota.

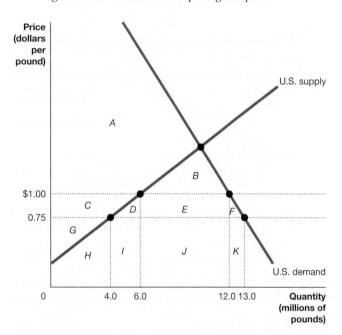

Fill in the table below using the letters in the figure.

	Without Quota	With Quota
World price of kumquats		
U.S. price of kumquats		
Quantity supplied by U.S. firms		
Quantity demanded		
Quantity imported		
Area of consumer surplus		
Area of domestic producer surplus		
Area of deadweight loss		

4.12 Suppose the government is considering imposing either a tariff or a quota on canned peaches. Assume that the proposed quota has the same effect on the U.S. price of canned peaches as the proposed tariff. Use the graph to answer the following questions.

   a. If the government imposes a tariff, which area shows the government tariff revenue?
   b. If the government imposes a quota, which area shows the gain to foreign producers of canned peaches?
   c. As a consumer of peaches, would you prefer that the government impose the tariff or the quota? Briefly explain.

4.13 (Related to the Apply the Concept on page 235) An economic analysis of a proposal to impose a quota on steel imports into the United States indicated that the quota would save 3,700 jobs in the steel industry but cost about 35,000 jobs in other U.S. industries. Why would a quota on steel imports cause employment to decline in other industries? Which other industries is a steel quota likely to affect?

   Source: Douglas A. Irwin, *Free Trade under Fire*, Princeton, NJ: Princeton University Press, 2002, p. 82.

4.14 (Related to the Apply the Concept on page 235) For several years, the United States imposed a tariff on tire imports. According to an analysis by economists Gary Clyde Hufbauer and Sean Lowry of the Peterson Institute, of the additional $1.1 billion consumers spent on tires as a result of the tariff on Chinese tires, the workers whose jobs were saved in the U.S. tire industry received only about $48 million in wages. Wouldn't it have been cheaper for the federal government to have raised taxes on U.S. consumers and given the money to tire workers rather than to have imposed a tariff? If so, why didn't the federal government adopt this alternative policy?

   Source: Gary Clyde Hufbauer and Sean Lowry, "US Tire Tariffs: Saving Few Jobs at High Cost," Peterson Institute for International Economics, Policy Brief Number PB12-9, April 2012.

The Debate over Trade Policies and Globalization, pages 237–242

7.5

LEARNING OBJECTIVE: Evaluate the debate over trade policies and globalization.

MyLab Economics Visit **www.pearson.com/mylab/economics** to complete these exercises online and get instant feedback.

Summary

The **World Trade Organization (WTO)** is an international organization that enforces trade agreements among members. The WTO has promoted **globalization**, the process of countries becoming more open to foreign trade and investment. Some critics of the WTO argue that globalization has damaged local cultures around the world. Other critics oppose the WTO because they believe in **protectionism**, which is the use of trade barriers to shield domestic firms from foreign competition. The WTO allows countries to use tariffs in cases of **dumping**, when an imported product is sold for a price below its cost of production.

Review Questions

5.1 What events led to the General Agreement on Tariffs and Trade (GATT)? Why did the WTO eventually replace the GATT?

5.2 What is globalization? Why are some people opposed to globalization? What is protectionism? Who benefits and who loses from protectionist policies? What are the main arguments people use to justify protectionism?

5.3 What is dumping? Who benefits and who loses from dumping? What problems arise when anti-dumping laws are implemented?

Problems and Applications

5.4 In 2017, shortly after President Trump took office, the U.S. Department of Commerce considered imposing tariffs on European steel companies it accused of dumping steel on the U.S. market. An article in the *Wall Street Journal* quoted Secretary of Commerce Wilbur Ross as asserting, "A healthy steel industry is critical to our economy and manufacturing base, yet our steel industry today is under assault from foreign producers that dump and subsidize their exports." What is dumping? If the United States imposes tariffs on imports of steel from Europe, briefly explain who is likely to gain and who is likely to lose.

Source: Andrea Thomas and Ulrike Dauer, "Germany Hits Back at U.S. Proposals of Anti-dumping Tariffs on Steel Imports," *Wall Street Journal*, March 31, 2017.

5.5 Steven Landsburg, an economist at the University of Rochester, wrote the following in an article in the *Wall Street Journal*:

> Free trade is not only about the right of American consumers to buy at the cheapest possible price; it's also about the right of foreign producers to earn a living. Steelworkers in West Virginia struggle hard to make ends meet. So do steelworkers in South Korea. To

protect one at the expense of the other, solely because of where they happened to be born, is a moral outrage.

How does the U.S. government protect steelworkers in West Virginia at the expense of steelworkers in South Korea? Is Landsburg making a positive statement or a normative statement? A few days later, Tom Redburn published an article disagreeing with Landsburg. Redburn argued that caring about the welfare of people in the United States more than about the welfare of people in other countries isn't "some evil character flaw." According to Redburn, "A society that ignores the consequences of economic disruption on those among its citizens who come out at the short end of the stick is not only heartless, it also undermines its own cohesion and adaptability."

Which of the two arguments do you find most convincing?

Sources: Steven E. Landsburg, "Who Cares if the Playing Field Is Level?" *Wall Street Journal*, June 13, 2001; and Tom Redburn, "Economic View: Of Politics, Free Markets, and Tending to Society," *New York Times*, June 17, 2001.

5.6 Suppose you are explaining the benefits of free trade and someone states, "I don't understand all the principles of comparative advantage and gains from trade. I just know that if I buy something produced in America, I create a job for an American, and if I buy something produced in Brazil, I create a job for a Brazilian." Do you agree with this statement? When the United States imports products for which it does not have a comparative advantage, does this mean there are fewer jobs in the United States? In the example in Section 7.3 with China and the United States producing and trading smartphones and wheat, when the United States imports smartphones from China, does the number of jobs in the United States decline? Briefly explain.

5.7 Every year, the Gallup Poll asks a sample of people in the United States whether they believe foreign trade provides "an opportunity for economic growth through increased U.S. exports" or whether they believe foreign trade represents "a threat to the economy from foreign imports." The following table shows the responses for 2 years.

	View of Foreign Trade		
Year	Favorable to Foreign Trade	Unfavorable	State of the U.S. Economy
2008	41%	52%	Deep economic recession
2017	72%	23%	Economic expansion

a. Do you believe that foreign trade helps or hurts the economy? (Be sure to define what you mean by "helps" or "hurts.")

b. Why might the general public's opinion of foreign trade be substantially different during an economic recession, when production and employment are falling, than during an economic expansion, when production and employment are increasing?

c. Typically polls show that people in the United States under 30 years of age have a more favorable opinion of foreign trade than do people age 65 and over. Why might younger people have a more favorable view of foreign trade than older people?

Source: Art Swift, "In US, Record-High 72% See Foreign Trade as Opportunity," gallup.com, February 16, 2017.

5.8 At one time, Eastman Kodak was the world's largest producer of photographic film, employing nearly 145,000 workers worldwide, including thousands at its headquarters in Rochester, New York. The firm eventually laid off most of those workers because its sales declined as it failed to adjust to digital photography as quickly as many of its foreign competitors. A member of Congress from Rochester described the many new firms that were now located in buildings that were formerly owned by Kodak. A *New York Times* columnist concluded, "which, of course, is precisely the way globalization is supposed to work." Briefly explain what the columnist meant. Do you agree with his conclusion?

Does the outcome in Rochester show that globalization is good? Briefly explain.

Source: Joe Nocera, "Don't Blame NAFTA," *New York Times*, January 23, 2015.

5.9 (Related to the Apply the Concept on page 240) According to an opinion column in the *New York Times*, because of attempts to make it more difficult to import catfish into the United States, many Vietnamese businesses that export catfish shifted from exporting to the United States to exporting to China. Briefly explain who gained and who lost as a result of this adjustment by Vietnamese businesses resulting from U.S. trade restrictions.

Source: Roger Cohen, "Of Catfish Wars and Shooting Wars," *New York Times*, March 26, 2015.

5.10 (Related to the Apply the Concept on page 240) In 2016, an editorial in the *Wall Street Journal* was in favor of, "repealing the notorious catfish program that has become a byword for Washington waste and protectionism? This should be an easy call." Why would a federal government program to inspect catfish be considered an example of protectionism? If repealing the program is "an easy call," as the editorial asserts, why was the program still in place in 2017, more than a year after the editorial was published?

Source: "A Chance of a Catfish Vote," *Wall Street Journal*, July 6, 2016.

Critical Thinking Exercises

CT7.1 As we saw in this chapter, comparative advantage is an important economic concept. We often use a table and some arithmetic to explain it, but how might you use words to explain comparative advantage to someone not taking this course, such as a roommate, a family member, or a friend? *Hint:* You might want to explain the concept using just two people or perhaps two businesses that trade goods and services with each other, where one is more efficient in the production of all goods and services and yet both benefit from trading with each other.

CT7.2 A key part of this chapter is the section "Where Does Comparative Advantage Come From?" starting on page 229. The section explains the main sources of comparative advantage among countries. Comparative advantage also applies to people. Describe some sources of comparative advantage between people; that is, why might one person have a comparative advantage in the production of a good or service relative to another person?

CT7.3 In Chapter 3, we used the demand and supply model to understand markets. Can we also use this model to understand comparative advantage?

The Ford Motor Company Meets Macroeconomics

Top managers at Ford Motor Company must answer many important questions that can determine whether the company succeeds: How much of their resources should they devote to producing electric cars? Should they develop self-driving cars? Should they relocate some factories from the United States to Mexico? The managers can control how they answer these questions, but they also face challenges that are beyond their control—challenges from the state of the economy.

Cars have high prices and are durable goods, so when the economy suffers a downturn, sales decline as unemployment increases, incomes fall, and many people decide to keep their current cars rather than buy new ones. It was no surprise that beginning in 2008, with the U.S. economy suffering from its worst downturn since the 1930s, the automobile industry was badly hurt, with sales of new vehicles tumbling from 16.1 million in 2007 to 10.4 million in 2009. In 2016, the economy was several years into its recovery from the downturn, and Ford's sales had risen by more than one-third since their low point in 2009. In early 2017, the U.S. economy experienced slow growth, and Ford's sales declined. These fluctuations in sales didn't have much to do with how Ford's managers were designing, manufacturing, and marketing their vehicles. Instead, Ford and the automobile industry as a whole were experiencing the effects of the *business cycle,* which refers to alternating periods of economic *expansion* and economic *recession.* Production and employment increase during expansions and decrease during recessions.

Whether the general level of economic activity is increasing is important not just to firms like Ford, but also

Luke Sharret/Bloomberg/Getty images

to workers wondering whether they will be able to keep their jobs and to college students wondering whether they will find jobs when they graduate. One study found that during the slow recovery from the 2007–2009 recession, only 56 percent of students who graduated from college in the spring of 2010 had found a job a year later. And salaries of graduates who did find jobs were typically lower than before the recession. By the time the class of 2016–2017 graduated, however, the job market was much stronger, and graduates were finding jobs at higher salaries. The overall state of the economy is clearly important!

Sources: Adrienne Roberts and Christina Rogers, "Ford's Profit Falls 35% on Recall Costs, Weaker U.S. Sales," *Wall Street Journal*, April 27, 2017; Kelsey Gee, "Salaries Soar for the Class of 2017," *Wall Street Journal*, May 12, 2017; Catherine Rampell, "Many with New College Degrees Find the Job Market Humbling," *New York Times*, May 18, 2011; and Lisa B. Kahn, "The Long-Term Labor Market Consequences of Graduating from College in a Bad Economy," *Labour Economics*, Vol. 17, No. 2, April 2010, pp. 303–316.

Chapter Outline & Learning Objectives

8.1 Gross Domestic Product Measures Total Production, page 255
Explain how total production is measured.

8.2 Does GDP Measure What We Want It to Measure? page 262
Discuss whether GDP is a good measure of well-being.

8.3 Real GDP versus Nominal GDP, page 265
Discuss the difference between real GDP and nominal GDP.

8.4 Other Measures of Total Production and Total Income, page 269
Describe other measures of total production and total income.

Economics in Your Life & Career

What's the Best Country for You to Work In?

Suppose that Ford offers you a job after you graduate in 2020. The firm has vacancies in Canada and China, and because you are fluent in both English and Mandarin, you get to choose the country where you will work and live. Gross domestic product (GDP) is a measure of an economy's total production of goods and services, so one factor in your decision is likely to be the growth rate of GDP in each country. The International Monetary Fund's forecasts for 2020 show GDP increasing by 1.8 percent in Canada and by 5.9 percent in China. What effect do these two very different growth rates have on your decision to work and live in one country or the other? Would China's much higher growth rate lead you to decide to work and live there? As you read this chapter, try to answer these questions. You can check your answers against those we provide on **page 271** at the end of this chapter.

Microeconomics The study of how households and firms make choices, how they interact in markets, and how the government attempts to influence their choices.

Macroeconomics The study of the economy as a whole, including topics such as inflation, unemployment, and economic growth.

Business cycle Alternating periods of economic expansion and economic recession.

Expansion The period of a business cycle during which total production and total employment are increasing.

Recession The period of a business cycle during which total production and total employment are decreasing.

Economic growth The ability of an economy to produce increasing quantities of goods and services.

Inflation rate The percentage increase in the price level from one year to the next.

As we saw in Chapter 1, we can divide economics into the subfields of micro-economics and macroeconomics. **Microeconomics** is the study of how households and firms make choices, how they interact in markets, and how the government attempts to influence their choices. Studying how Ford's managers determine whether to devote resources to developing self-driving cars is an example of microeconomic analysis.

Macroeconomics is the study of the economy as a whole, including topics such as inflation, unemployment, and economic growth. In microeconomic analysis, economists generally study individual markets, such as the market for smartphones. In macroeconomic analysis, economists study factors that affect many markets at the same time.

In the following chapters, we will deal with many key macroeconomic issues, including:

- The **business cycle**, which refers to the alternating periods of expansion and recession that the U.S. economy has experienced since at least the early nineteenth century. A business cycle **expansion** is a period during which total production and total employment are increasing. A business cycle **recession** is a period during which total production and total employment are decreasing. We will discuss the factors that influence the business cycle and policies the government may use to reduce its effects.

- **Economic growth**, which refers to the ability of an economy to produce increasing quantities of goods and services. Economic growth is important because an economy that grows too slowly fails to raise living standards. In some countries in Africa, little economic growth has occurred in the past 50 years, and many people remain in severe poverty. Macroeconomics analyzes both what determines a country's rate of economic growth and the reasons growth rates differ so greatly across countries.

- Fluctuations in the total level of employment in an economy. In the short run, the level of employment is significantly affected by the business cycle, but in the long run, the effects of the business cycle disappear, and other factors determine the level of employment. A related question is why some economies are more successful than others at maintaining high levels of employment over time.

- Fluctuations in the **inflation rate**, which is the percentage increase in the average level of prices from one year to the next. Like employment, inflation is affected both by the business cycle and by long-run factors.

- Linkages among economies in the form of international trade and international finance.

Macroeconomic analysis provides information that consumers and firms need in order to understand current economic conditions and to help predict future conditions. A family may be reluctant to buy a house if employment in the economy is declining because some family members may be at risk of losing their jobs. Similarly, firms may be willing to invest in building new factories or to undertake major new expenditures on information technology only if they expect future sales to be strong. For example, in 2017, Ford announced it would begin manufacturing electric cars in China. Ford was relying on macroeconomic forecasts indicating that the Chinese economy would continue to grow rapidly and that sales of electric cars and other electric vehicles in the country would increase from 500,000 in 2016 to more than 30 million in 2025. Macroeconomic analysis can also assist the federal government design policies that help the U.S. economy perform more efficiently.

In this and the following chapters, we begin our study of macroeconomics by considering how best to measure key macroeconomic variables. We start by considering measures of total production and total income in an economy.

8.1 Gross Domestic Product Measures Total Production

LEARNING OBJECTIVE: Explain how total production is measured.

"U.S. Second-Quarter GDP Rose 3.1%"

"Canada GDP Stalls in February"

"China Premier Says GDP Growth Target Is around 6.5% for 2017"

"German GDP Grows at Fastest Rate in Five Years"

"Indian GDP Growth Hurt by New Delhi's Cash Crackdown"

These headlines are from articles that appeared in the *Wall Street Journal* during 2017. Why is GDP so often the focus of news stories? In this section, we explore what GDP is and how it is measured. We also explore why understanding GDP is important to consumers, firms, and government policymakers.

Measuring Total Production: Gross Domestic Product

Economists use **gross domestic product (GDP)** to measure total production. GDP is the market *value* of all *final* goods and services produced in a country during a period of time, typically one year. In the United States, the Bureau of Economic Analysis (BEA) in the Department of Commerce compiles the data needed to calculate GDP. The BEA issues reports on the GDP every three months. GDP is a central concept in macroeconomics, so we need to consider its definition carefully.

Gross domestic product (GDP) The market value of all final goods and services produced in a country during a period of time, typically one year.

GDP Is Measured Using Market Values, Not Quantities
The word *value* is important in the definition of GDP. In microeconomics, we measure production in quantity terms: the number of cars Ford produces, the tons of wheat U.S. farmers grow, or the number of turkey sandwiches Panera Bread sells. When we measure total production in the economy, we can't just add together the quantities of every good and service because the result would be a meaningless jumble. Numbers of cars would be added to tons of wheat, gallons of milk, numbers of sandwiches, and so on. Instead, we measure production by taking the *value*, in dollar terms, of all the goods and services produced.

GDP Includes Only the Market Value of Final Goods
In measuring GDP, we include only the value of *final goods and services*. A **final good or service** is one that is purchased by its final user and is not included in the production of any other good or service. Examples of final goods are a hamburger purchased by a consumer and a computer purchased by a business. In contrast, **intermediate goods and services** become part of other goods and services. For example, Ford does not produce tires for its cars and trucks; it buys them from tire companies, such as Goodyear and Michelin. The tires are an *intermediate good,* while a Ford truck is a *final good.* In calculating GDP, we include the value of a Ford truck but not the value of a tire. If we included the value of the tire, we would be *double counting*: The value of the tire would be counted once when the tire company sold it to Ford and a second time when Ford sold the truck, with the tire installed, to a consumer.

Final good or service A good or service purchased by a final user.

Intermediate good or service A good or service that is an input into another good or service, such as a tire on a truck.

GDP Includes Only Current Production
GDP includes only production that takes place during the indicated time period. For example, GDP in 2018 includes only the goods and services produced during that year. In particular, GDP does *not* include the value of used goods. If you buy a Blu-ray of *The Avengers: Infinity War* from Amazon.com, the purchase is included in GDP. If six months later you resell the Blu-ray on eBay, that transaction is not included in GDP.   **MyLab Economics** Concept Check

Solved Problem 8.1

Calculating GDP

MyLab Economics Interactive Animation

Suppose that a very simple economy produces only four goods and services: eye examinations, pizzas, shoes, and cheese. Assume that all the cheese in this economy is used in the production of pizzas. Use the information in the following table to calculate GDP for the year 2019.

Production and Price Statistics for 2019		
Product	(1) Quantity	(2) Price per Unit
Eye examinations	100	$50.00
Pizzas	80	10.00
Shoes	20	100.00
Cheese	80	2.00

Solving the Problem

Step 1: Review the chapter material. This problem is about GDP, so you may want to review the section "Measuring Total Production: Gross Domestic Product," which begins on page 255.

Step 2: Determine which goods and services listed in the table should be included in the calculation of GDP. GDP is the market value of all final goods and services. Therefore, we need to calculate the value of the final goods and services listed in the table. Eye examinations, pizzas, and shoes are final goods. Cheese would also be a final good if, for instance, a consumer bought it to use in a meal. However, here we are assuming that restaurants buy all the cheese to use in making pizzas, so the cheese is an intermediate good, and its value is not included in GDP.

Step 3: Calculate the value of the three final goods and services listed in the table. Value is equal to the quantity produced multiplied by the price per unit, so we multiply the numbers in column (1) by the numbers in column (2) to calculate the numbers in column (3).

Product	(1) Quantity	(2) Price per Unit	(3) Value
Eye examinations	100	$50	$5,000
Pizzas	80	10	800
Shoes	20	100	2,000

Step 4: Add the value for each of the three final goods and services to find GDP. GDP = Value of eye examinations produced + Value of pizzas produced + Value of shoes produced = $5,000 + $800 + $2,000 = $7,800.

MyLab Economics Study Plan   **Your Turn:** For more practice, do related problem 1.11 on page 273 at the end of this chapter.

Production, Income, and the Circular-Flow Diagram

When we measure the value of total production in the economy by calculating GDP, we are at the same time measuring the value of total income. To see why the value of total production is equal to the value of total income, consider what happens to the money you spend on a single product. Suppose you buy a pair of New Balance running shoes for $149 at a Foot Locker store. *All* of that $149 must end up as someone's income. New Balance and Foot Locker will receive some of the $149 as profits, workers at New Balance will receive some as wages, the salesperson who sold you the shoes will receive some as salary, the firms that sell components to New Balance will receive some as profits, the workers for those firms will receive some as wages, and so on. So the amount that you spend on the shoes equals the amount of income received by the people who make and sell the shoes. Therefore, if we add up the values of every good and service sold in the economy, we must get a total that is exactly equal to the value of all the income in the economy.

Figure 8.1 is circular-flow diagram like the one we introduced in Chapter 2, Section 2.3 to illustrate the interaction of firms and households in markets. We use it here to illustrate the flow of spending and money in the economy. Firms sell goods and services to three groups: domestic households, foreign firms and households, and the government. Expenditures by foreign firms and households (shown as "Rest of the World" in the diagram) on domestically produced goods and services are called *exports*. For example, American Airlines sells many tickets to passengers in Europe and Asia.

Firms use the *factors of production*—labor, capital, natural resources, and entrepreneurial ability—to produce goods and services. Households supply the factors of

top: Ariel Skelley/Digital Vision/Getty images; left: Eric Gevaert/ Shutterstock; middle: Yoshio Tomii/Super Stock; right: Bill Aron/ Photo Edit, Inc.; bottom: Mikael Damkier/Shutterstock

MyLab Economics Animation

Figure 8.1   **The Circular Flow and the Measurement of GDP**

The circular-flow diagram illustrates the flow of spending and money in the economy. Firms sell goods and services to three groups: domestic households, foreign households, and the government. To produce goods and services, firms use factors of production: labor, capital, natural resources, and entrepreneurship. Households supply the factors of production to firms in exchange for income in the form of wages, interest, rent, and profit. The sum of wages, interest, rent, and profit is total income in the economy. The diagram also shows that households use their income to purchase goods and services, pay taxes, and save for the future. Firms and the government borrow the funds that flow from households into the financial system. We can measure GDP either by calculating the total value of expenditures on final goods and services or by calculating the value of total income.

Transfer payments Payments by the government to households for which the government does not receive a new good or service in return.

production to firms in exchange for income. We divide income into four categories: wages, interest, rent, and profit. Firms pay wages to households in exchange for labor services, interest for the use of capital, and rent for natural resources such as land. Profit is the income that remains after a firm has paid wages, interest, and rent. Profit is the return to entrepreneurs and other business owners for bearing the risk of producing and selling goods and services. As Figure 8.1 shows, federal, state, and local governments make payments of wages and interest to households in exchange for hiring workers and other factors of production. Governments also make *transfer payments* to households. **Transfer payments** include Social Security payments to retired and disabled people and unemployment insurance payments to unemployed workers. These payments are not included in GDP because they are not received in exchange for production of a new good or service. The sum of wages, interest, rent, and profit is total income in the economy. As noted at the top of Figure 8.1, we can measure GDP as the total income received by households.

The diagram also allows us to trace the four ways that households use their income: to purchase domestically produced goods and services; to purchase *imports*, which are foreign-produced goods and services; to pay taxes to the government (note that firms also pay taxes to the government); and to save by making deposits in checking or savings accounts in banks or by buying stocks or bonds. Banks and stock and bond markets make up the *financial system*. The flow of funds from households into the financial system makes it possible for the government and firms to borrow. As we will see beginning in Chapter 10, the health of the financial system is vital to an economy. Without the ability to borrow funds through the financial system, firms will have difficulty expanding and adopting new technologies. In fact, no country without a well-developed financial system has been able to sustain high levels of economic growth.

The circular-flow diagram shows that we can measure GDP either by calculating the total value of expenditures on final goods and services or by calculating the value of total income. We get the same dollar amount of GDP with either approach.   **MyLab Economics** Concept Check

Components of GDP

The BEA divides its statistics on GDP into four major categories of expenditures: consumption, investment, government purchases, and net exports. Economists use these categories to understand why GDP fluctuates and to forecast future GDP.

Consumption Spending by households on goods and services, not including spending on new houses.

Personal Consumption Expenditures, or "Consumption" Consumption expenditures are made by households and are divided into three categories:

1. Expenditures on *services*, such as medical care, education, and haircuts
2. Expenditures on *nondurable goods*, such as food and clothing
3. Expenditures on *durable goods*, such as automobiles and furniture

The spending by households on new houses is not included in consumption. Instead, spending on new houses is included in the investment category, which we discuss next.

Investment Spending by firms on new factories, office buildings, machinery, and additions to inventories, plus spending by households and firms on new houses.

Gross Private Domestic Investment, or "Investment" Spending on *gross private domestic investment*, or simply **investment**, is also divided into three categories:

1. *Business fixed investment* is spending by firms on new factories, office buildings, and machinery used to produce other goods. Since 2013, this category of investment has included business spending on research and development. The BEA had previously considered such spending to be an intermediate good.
2. *Residential investment* is spending by households and firms on new single-family and multi-unit houses.
3. *Changes in business inventories* are changes in the stocks of goods that have been produced but not yet sold. If Ford has $200 million worth of unsold cars at the beginning of the year and $350 million worth of unsold cars at the end of the year, then the firm has spent $150 million on inventory investment during the year.

Don't Let This Happen to You

Remember What Economists Mean by *Investment*

Notice that the definition of *investment* in this chapter is narrower than in everyday use. For example, people often say they are investing in the stock market or in rare coins. As we have seen, economists reserve the word *investment* for purchases of machinery, factories, and houses. Economists don't include purchases of shares of stock or rare coins or deposits in savings accounts in the definition of investment because these activities don't result in the production of new goods. For example, a share of Twitter's stock represents part ownership of that company. When you buy a share of Twitter's stock, nothing new is produced; there is just a transfer from the seller to you of that small piece of ownership of Twitter. Similarly, buying a rare coin or putting $1,000 into a savings account does not result in an increase in production. GDP is not affected by any of these activities, so they are not included in the economic definition of investment.

MyLab Economics Study Plan

Your Turn: Test your understanding by doing related problem 1.12 on page 273 at the end of this chapter.

Government Consumption and Gross Investment, or "Government Purchases" **Government purchases** are spending by federal, state, and local governments on goods and services, such as teachers' salaries, highways, and aircraft carriers. Again, government spending on transfer payments is not included in government purchases because the spending does not result in the production of new goods and services.

> **Government purchases** Spending by federal, state, and local governments on goods and services.

Net Exports of Goods and Services, or "Net Exports" **Net exports** are equal to *exports* minus *imports*. Exports are goods and services produced in the United States and purchased by foreign firms, households, and governments. We add exports to our other categories of expenditures because otherwise we would not be including all spending on new goods and services produced in the United States. For example, if a farmer in South Dakota sells wheat to China, the value of the wheat is included in GDP because it represents production in the United States. Imports are goods and services produced in foreign countries and purchased by U.S. firms, households, and governments. We subtract imports from total expenditures because otherwise we would be including spending that does not result in production of new goods and services in the United States. For example, if U.S. consumers buy $1 billion worth of furniture manufactured in China, that spending is included in consumption expenditures. But the value of those imports is subtracted from GDP because the imports do not represent production in the United States.   **MyLab Economics** Concept Check

> **Net exports** Exports minus imports.

An Equation for GDP and Some Actual Values

A simple equation sums up the components of GDP:

$$Y = C + I + G + NX.$$

The equation tells us that GDP (denoted as Y) equals consumption (C) plus investment (I) plus government purchases (G) plus net exports (NX). Figure 8.2 shows the values of the components of GDP for the year 2016. The graph in the figure highlights the fact that consumption is by far the largest component of GDP. The table provides a more detailed breakdown and shows several interesting points:

- Consumer spending on services is more than double the spending on durable and nondurable goods combined. There has been a continuing trend in the United States and other high-income countries away from the production of goods and toward the production of services. As the populations of these countries have become, on average, both older and wealthier, their demand for services such as medical care and financial advice has increased faster than their demand for goods.
- Business fixed investment is the largest component of investment. As we will see in later chapters, spending by firms on new factories, computers, and machinery can

COMPONENTS OF GDP (billions of dollars)		
Consumption		$12,758
Durable goods	$1,403	
Nondurable goods	2,696	
Services	8,660	
Investment		3,036
Business fixed investment	2,309	
Residential investment	706	
Change in business inventories	21	
Government purchases		3,277
Federal	1,245	
State and local	2,032	
Net Exports		–501
Exports	2,232	
Imports	2,734	
Total GDP		$18,569

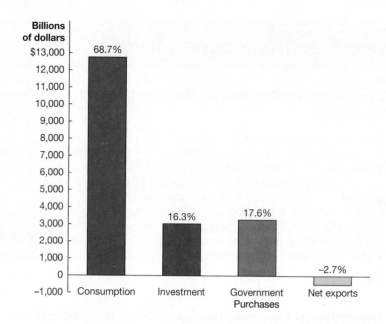

MyLab Economics Real-time data

Figure 8.2 **Components of GDP in 2016**

Consumption accounts for a much larger percentage of GDP than any of the other components. In recent years, net exports have typically been negative, which reduces GDP. Note that the subtotals may not sum to the totals for each category because of rounding.

Source: U.S. Bureau of Economic Analysis.

fluctuate. For example, a decline in business fixed investment contributed to the severity of the 2007–2009 recession.

- Purchases made by state and local governments are greater than purchases made by the federal government. This result shouldn't be surprising because basic government activities, such as education and law enforcement, occur largely at the state and local levels.

- Imports are greater than exports, so net exports are negative. We will discuss in Chapter 18, Section 18.4 why imports have typically been larger than exports for the U.S. economy.   MyLab Economics Concept Check

Apply the Concept

MyLab Economics Video

Microsoft's Steve Ballmer Uses the U.S. Constitution to Reorganize Government Data

Courtesy of www.usafacts.org

Has Steve Ballmer developed a better way to measure government spending at his Web site, http://usafacts.org/?

As CEO of Microsoft from 2000 to 2014, Steve Ballmer had considerable experience in analyzing businesses. Every public corporation is legally required to file with the federal Securities and Exchange Commission (SEC) a 10-K form with information on its operations and financial condition. Most corporations post a 10-K form to their Web sites each year. When Ballmer retired—with wealth of more than $20 billion—his wife suggested that they devote some of their time and money to philanthropy. Ballmer replied, "At the end of the day, the biggest philanthropy in the U.S. is the government. So as long as we pay our taxes, we're doing our part." But then he decided to check whether his assertion was accurate by studying federal government spending. Unfortunately, he discovered that there was no one place where the government's operations and finances were summarized in the way that a 10-K form does for a business.

So, Ballmer decided to spend $10 million to hire a team of researchers to bring together all government data in one place. In 2017, the results were made available on the Web site usafacts.org. The Bureau of Economic Analysis (BEA) operates a Web site, bea.gov, that presents data on GDP like that shown in Figure 8.2. What data are available on Ballmer's Web site that can't be found on bea.gov or other existing government Web sites? In fact, nearly all the data on usafacts.org are available elsewhere, but Ballmer has made the data more accessible by bringing them together in one place.

In addition, as shown in the following table, Ballmer took the unusual approach of organizing government spending data on the basis of four "missions" for government that he identified in the preamble to the U.S. Constitution:

Category, taken from the preamble to the U.S. Constitution	Examples of Government Spending in This Category	Percentage of Total Government Spending at All Levels (Federal, State, and Local)	Percentage of Spending in This Category Carried Out by State and Local Governments
1. Establish justice and ensure domestic tranquility	Police, firefighting, and prisons; the court system; and disaster relief	8%	89%
2. Provide for the common defense	National defense, payments to veterans, maintaining embassies in foreign countries, and securing the nation's borders	16	0
3. Promote the general welfare	Infrastructure, such as highways and bridges; public housing; public health; and government-owned businesses such as transit systems and public hospitals	23	66
4. Secure the blessings of liberty to ourselves and our posterity	Education, environmental protection, and the Social Security, Medicare, and Medicaid systems	54	41

The table uses data from usafacts.org to show the percentage of total local, state, and federal government spending that falls into each of these four categories and the percentage of spending in each category that is carried out by state and local governments rather than the federal government. (Note that because the site includes transfer payments and some other government spending that is not for purchases of final goods and services, its measures of government spending include more than the government purchases shown in the table in Figure 8.2.) The table reinforces the point made earlier that most of the basic activities of government are conducted at the state and local levels rather than at the federal level.

The BEA looks for ways to improve its presentation of data on bea.gov to make it more usable by businesses, policymakers, and the general public. It seems unlikely, though, that the federal government would go to the expense of organizing data using Steve Ballmer's approach on usafacts.org. (Ballmer expects to spend $5 million per year to maintain the site.) Also, users of the existing government sites are familiar with the way government spending data are currently categorized. In addition, policymakers, economists, and investors in financial markets are often interested in trends in spending data over long periods of time. Such long *time series* aren't available for all of the data categories on Ballmer's site.

Still, usafacts.org provides a user-friendly way to explore government spending in the United States.

Sources: Andrew Ross Sorkin, "Steve Ballmer Serves up a Fascinating Data Trove," *New York Times*, April 17, 2017; Dina Bass, "Steve Ballmer's Plan to Make America Great Involves Excel Spreadsheets," bloomberg.com, November 7, 2016; Adam Lashinsky, "Steve Ballmer Thinks U.S. Citizens Should Know More about Government Spending," fortune.com, April 19, 2017; and usafacts.org.

Your Turn: Test your understanding by doing related problem 1.13 on page 273 at the end of this chapter.

MyLab Economics Study Plan

Table 8.1

Calculating Value Added

Firm	Value of Product	Value Added	
Cotton farmer	Value of raw cotton = $1	Value added by cotton farmer	= $1
Textile mill	Value of raw cotton woven into cotton fabric = $3	Value added by textile mill = ($3 − $1)	= $2
Shirt company	Value of cotton fabric made into a shirt = $15	Value added by shirt company = ($15 − $3)	= $12
L.L.Bean	Value of shirt for sale on L.L.Bean's Web site = $35	Value added by L.L.Bean = ($35 − $15)	= $20
	Total Value Added		**= $35**

Value added The market value a firm adds to a product.

Measuring GDP Using the Value-Added Method

We have seen that GDP can be calculated by adding together all expenditures on final goods and services. An alternative way of calculating GDP is the *value-added method.* **Value added** refers to the additional market value a firm gives to a product and is equal to the difference between the price for which the firm sells a good and the price it paid other firms for intermediate goods. Table 8.1 gives a hypothetical example of the value added by each firm involved in the production of a shirt offered for sale on L.L.Bean's Web site.

Suppose a cotton farmer sells $1 of raw cotton to a textile mill. If, for simplicity, we ignore any inputs the farmer may have purchased from other firms—such as cottonseed or fertilizer—then the farmer's value added is $1. The textile mill then weaves the raw cotton into cotton fabric, which it sells to a shirt company for $3. The textile mill's value added ($2) is the difference between the price it paid for the raw cotton ($1) and the price for which it can sell the cotton fabric ($3). Similarly, the shirt company's value added is the difference between the price it paid for the cotton fabric ($3) and the price it receives for the shirt from L.L.Bean ($15). L.L.Bean's value added is the difference between the price it pays for the shirt ($15) and the price for which it can sell the shirt on its Web site ($35). Notice that *the price of the shirt on L.L.Bean's Web site is exactly equal to the sum of the value added by each firm involved in the production of the shirt.* We can calculate GDP by adding up the market value of every final good and service produced during a particular period. Or, we can arrive at the same value for GDP by adding up the value added by every firm involved in producing those final goods and services.

MyLab Economics Study Plan

MyLab Economics Concept Check

 8.2 Does GDP Measure What We Want It to Measure?

LEARNING OBJECTIVE: Discuss whether GDP is a good measure of well-being.

Economists use GDP to measure total production in the economy. For that purpose, we would like GDP to be as comprehensive as possible, not overlooking any significant production that takes place in the economy. Most economists believe that GDP does a good—but not flawless—job of measuring production. GDP is also sometimes used as a measure of well-being. Although it is generally true that the more goods and services people have, the better off they are, we will see that GDP provides only a rough measure of well-being.

Shortcomings in GDP as a Measure of Total Production

When the BEA calculates GDP, it does not include two types of production: production in the home and production in the underground economy.

Household Production With few exceptions, the BEA does not attempt to estimate the value of goods and services that are not bought and sold in markets. If a carpenter makes and sells bookcases, the value of those bookcases will be counted in GDP. If the carpenter makes a bookcase for personal use, it will not be counted in GDP. *Household production* refers to goods and services people produce for themselves. The most important type of household production is the services a homemaker provides to the homemaker's family. If a person has been caring for children, cleaning the house, and preparing the family meals, the value of such services is not included in GDP. If the person then decides to work outside the home, enrolls the children in day care, hires a cleaning service, and begins buying the family's meals in restaurants, the value of GDP will rise by the amount paid for day care, cleaning services, and restaurant meals, even though production of these services has not actually increased.

The Underground Economy Individuals and firms sometimes conceal the buying and selling of goods and services, in which case their production isn't counted in GDP. Individuals and firms conceal what they buy and sell for three main reasons: (1) They are dealing in illegal goods and services, such as drugs or prostitution; (2) they want to avoid paying taxes on the income they earn; or (3) they want to avoid government regulations. This concealed buying and selling is called the **underground economy**. Estimates of the size of the underground economy in the United States vary widely, but it is at most 10 percent of measured GDP, and probably less. The underground economy in some low-income countries, such as Zimbabwe or Peru, may be more than 50 percent of measured GDP. Recently, countries in Western Europe have decided to include estimates of spending on illegal drugs and prostitution in their measures of GDP. To this point, the BEA has decided not to follow this approach. If it did, estimates are that measured U.S. GDP would increase by about 3 percent.

> **Underground economy** Buying and selling of goods and services that is concealed from the government to avoid taxes or regulations or because the goods and services are illegal.

Is not counting household production or production in the underground economy a serious shortcoming of GDP? Most economists would answer "no" because the most important use of GDP is to measure changes in how the economy is performing over short periods of time, such as from one year to the next. For this purpose, omitting household production and production in the underground economy doesn't matter because there is not likely to be much change in these types of production from one year to the next.

We also use GDP to measure how production of goods and services grows over fairly long periods of a decade or more. For this purpose, omitting household production and production in the underground economy may be more important. For example, beginning in the 1970s, the number of women working outside the home increased dramatically. Some of the goods and services—such as childcare and restaurant meals—produced in the following years were not true additions to total production; rather, they were replacing what had been household production.   **MyLab Economics** Concept Check

Apply the Concept   **MyLab Economics** Video

Why Do Many Developing Countries Have Such Large Underground Economies?

Recent estimates put the size of the underground economy at 8 percent of measured GDP in the United States and 13 percent in Western Europe. The underground economy is much larger in many developing countries— perhaps 50 percent or more of measured GDP. According to one estimate, in 2016, as many as 2 billion people in developing countries worked in the underground economy. The underground economy is also called the *informal sector,* as opposed to the *formal sector,* in which output of goods and services is measured. Although it might not seem to matter whether production of goods and services is measured and included in GDP or unmeasured, a large informal sector can be a sign of government policies that are holding back economic growth.

Because firms in the informal sector are operating illegally, they tend to be smaller and have less capital than firms operating legally. The entrepreneurs who start firms in the informal sector may be afraid the government could someday close or confiscate their firms. Therefore, the entrepreneurs limit their investments in these firms. They also are reluctant to apply to banks for loans because they would have to provide information to the bank that might come to the attention of the government. As a consequence, workers in these firms have less machinery and equipment to work with and so can produce fewer goods and services and are paid low wages. Entrepreneurs in this sector also have to pay the costs of avoiding government authorities. For example, construction firms operating in the informal sector in Brazil have to employ

Mohamed Nureldin Abdallah/Reuters

In some developing countries, more than half the workers may be in the underground economy.

lookouts who can warn workers to hide when government inspectors come around. In many countries, firms in the informal sector have to pay substantial bribes to government officials to remain in business. This sector is large in some developing economies because taxes are high and government regulations are extensive. For example, firms in Brazil pay 85 percent of all taxes collected, compared with 40 percent in the United States. Not surprisingly, about half of all Brazilian workers are employed in the informal sector. According to one estimate, because they evade taxes, firms in this sector in Brazil can earn three times the profit of similar-sized firms in the formal sector. In Zimbabwe and Peru, the fraction of workers in the informal sector may be as high as 60 or 70 percent. One estimate puts the size of this sector in India at nearly 50 percent.

Many economists believe taxes in developing countries are so high because these countries are attempting to pay for government sectors that are as large relative to their economies as the government sectors of industrial economies. Including transfer payments, government spending in Brazil, for example, is 41 percent of measured GDP, compared to 36 percent in the United States. In the early twentieth century, when the United States was much poorer than it is today, government spending was only about 8 percent of GDP, so the tax burden on U.S. firms was much lower. In countries such as Brazil, bringing firms into the formal sector from the informal sector may require reductions in government spending and taxes. In most developing countries, however, voters are reluctant to see government services reduced.

Sources: "Bringing Light to the Gray Economy," *Economist*, October 15, 2016; Simon Constable, "What Is the Shadow Economy and Why Does It Matter?" *Wall Street Journal*, March 5, 2017; "The Price Is Wrong," *Economist*, September 28, 2013; "Dynamic but Dirty," *Economist*, December 2, 2010; Mary Anastasia O'Grady, "Why Brazil's Underground Economy Grows and Grows," *Wall Street Journal*, September 10, 2004; and the International Monetary Fund.

MyLab Economics Study Plan   **Your Turn:** Test your understanding by doing related problems 2.8 and 2.9 on page 274 at the end of this chapter.

Shortcomings of GDP as a Measure of Well-Being

The main purpose of GDP is to measure a country's total production. GDP is also frequently used, though, as a measure of well-being. For example, news stories often include tables that show for different countries the levels of GDP per person, which is usually called *GDP per capita*. GDP per capita is calculated by dividing the value of GDP for a country by the country's population. These articles imply that people in the countries with higher levels of GDP per capita are better off. Although increases in a country's GDP often do lead to increases in the well-being of the population, it's important to be aware that GDP is not a perfect measure of well-being for the following reasons.

The Value of Leisure Is Not Included in GDP If an economic consultant decides to retire, GDP will decline even though the consultant may value increased leisure more than the income she was earning from running a consulting firm. The consultant's well-being has increased, but GDP has decreased. In 1890, the typical American worked 60 hours per week. Today, the typical American works fewer than 40 hours per week. If Americans still worked 60-hour weeks, GDP would be much higher than it is now, but the well-being of a typical person would be lower because less time would be available for leisure activities.

GDP Is Not Adjusted for Pollution or Other Negative Effects of Production When a dry cleaner cleans and presses clothes, the value of this service is included in GDP. If the dry cleaner uses chemicals that pollute the air or water, GDP is not adjusted to compensate for the cost of the pollution. Similarly, the value of cigarettes produced is included in GDP, with no adjustment made for the cost of the lung cancer that some smokers develop.

We should note, though, that increasing GDP often leads countries to devote more resources to pollution reduction. For example, in the United States between 1970 and 2017, as GDP was steadily increasing, emissions of the six main air pollutants declined by more than 50 percent. Developing countries often have higher levels of pollution than high-income countries because the lower GDPs of the developing countries make them more reluctant to spend resources on pollution reduction. Levels of pollution in China are much higher than those in the United States, Japan, or the countries of Western Europe. According to the World Health Organization, 7 of the 10 most polluted cities in the world are in China, but as China's GDP continues to rise, the country is likely to devote more resources to reducing pollution.

GDP Is Not Adjusted for Changes in Crime and Other Social Problems An increase in crime reduces well-being but may actually increase GDP if it leads to greater spending on police, security guards, and alarm systems. GDP is also not adjusted for changes in divorce rates, drug addiction, or other factors that may affect people's well-being.

GDP Measures the Size of the Pie but Not How the Pie Is Divided When a country's GDP increases, the country has more goods and services, but those goods and services may be very unequally distributed. Therefore, GDP may not provide good information about the goods and services consumed by a typical person.

To summarize, we can say that a person's well-being depends on many factors that are not considered in calculating GDP. Because GDP is designed to measure total production, it should not be surprising that it does an imperfect job of measuring well-being.   **MyLab Economics** Concept Check   **MyLab Economics** Study Plan

8.3 Real GDP versus Nominal GDP

LEARNING OBJECTIVE: Discuss the difference between real GDP and nominal GDP.

Because GDP is measured in value terms, we have to be careful about interpreting changes over time. To see why, consider interpreting an increase in the total value of pickup truck production from $40 billion in 2018 to $44 billion in 2019. Because $44 billion is 10 percent greater than $40 billion, did the economy produce 10 percent more trucks in 2019 than in 2018? We can draw this conclusion only if the average price of trucks did not change between 2018 and 2019. In fact, when GDP increases from one year to the next, the increase is due partly to increases in production of goods and services and partly to increases in prices. Because we are mainly interested in GDP as a measure of production, we need a way of separating the price changes from the quantity changes.

Calculating Real GDP

The BEA separates price changes from quantity changes by calculating a measure of production called *real GDP*. **Nominal GDP** is calculated by summing the current values of final goods and services. **Real GDP** is calculated by designating a particular year as the *base year* and then using the prices of goods and services in the base year to calculate the value of goods and services in all other years. For instance, if the base year is 2009, real GDP for 2019 would be calculated by using prices of goods and services from 2009. By keeping prices constant, we know that changes in real GDP represent changes in the quantity of goods and services produced in the economy.

Nominal GDP The value of final goods and services evaluated at current-year prices.

Real GDP The value of final goods and services evaluated at base-year prices.

Solved Problem 8.3

MyLab Economics Interactive Animation

Calculating Real GDP

Suppose that a very simple economy produces only the following three final goods and services: eye examinations, pizzas, and shoes. Use the information in the table on the right to compute real GDP for the year 2019. Assume that the base year is 2009.

Product	2009 Quantity	2009 Price	2019 Quantity	2019 Price
Eye examinations	80	$40	100	$50
Pizzas	90	11	80	10
Shoes	15	90	20	100

Solving the Problem

Step 1: Review the chapter material. This problem is about calculating real GDP, so you may want to review the section, "Calculating Real GDP," which begins on this page.

Step 2: **Calculate the value of the three goods and services listed in the table, using the quantities for 2019 and the prices for 2009.** Real GDP is the value of all final goods and services, evaluated at base-year prices. In this case, the base year is 2009, and we have the price of each product in that year:

Product	2019 Quantity	2009 Price	Value
Eye examinations	100	$40	$4,000
Pizzas	80	11	880
Shoes	20	90	1,800

Step 3: **Add up the values of the three products to find real GDP.** Real GDP for 2019 equals the sum of:

Quantity of eye examinations in 2019 $\times$ Price of eye examinations in 2009 = $4,000
Quantity of pizzas produced in 2019 $\times$ Price of pizzas in 2009 = $880
Quantity of shoes produced in 2019 $\times$ Price of shoes in 2009 = $1,800
or, $6,680

Extra Credit: Notice that the quantities of each good produced in 2009 were irrelevant for calculating real GDP in 2019. Notice also that the value of $6,680 for real GDP in 2019 is lower than the value of $7,800 for nominal GDP in 2019 that we calculated in Solved Problem 8.1 on page 256.

MyLab Economics Study Plan

Your Turn: For more practice, do related problem 3.4 on page 275 at the end of this chapter.

One drawback to calculating real GDP using base-year prices is that, over time, prices may change relative to each other. For example, the price of smartphones may fall relative to the price of milk. Because this change is not reflected in the fixed prices from the base year, the estimate of real GDP is somewhat distorted. The further away the current year is from the base year, the worse the problem becomes. To make the calculation of real GDP more accurate, in 1996, the BEA switched to using *chain-weighted prices*, and it now publishes statistics on real GDP in "chained (2009) dollars."

The details of calculating real GDP using chain-weighted prices are more complicated than we need to discuss here, but the basic idea is straightforward: Starting with the base year, the BEA takes an average of prices in that year and prices in the following year. It then uses this average to calculate real GDP in the year following the base year (currently the year 2009). For the next year—in other words, the year that is two years after the base year—the BEA calculates real GDP by taking an average of prices in that year and the previous year. In this way, prices in each year are "chained" to prices from the previous year, and the distortion from changes in relative prices is minimized.

Holding prices constant means that the *purchasing power* of a dollar remains the same from one year to the next. Ordinarily, the purchasing power of the dollar falls every year as price increases reduce the amount of goods and services that a dollar can buy. **MyLab Economics** Concept Check

Comparing Real GDP and Nominal GDP

Real GDP holds prices constant, which makes it a better measure than nominal GDP of changes in the production of goods and services from one year to the next. In fact, growth in the economy is almost always measured as growth in real GDP. If a headline in the *Wall Street Journal* states "U.S. Economy Grew 2.3% Last Year," the article will report that real GDP increased by 2.3 percent during the previous year.

We describe real GDP as being measured in "base-year dollars." For example, nominal GDP in 2016 was $18,569 billion, and, with a base year of 2009, real GDP in 2016 was $16,662 billion in 2009 dollars. Because, on average, prices rise from one year to the next, real GDP is greater than nominal GDP in years before the base year and less than nominal GDP for years after the base year. In the base year, real GDP and nominal GDP are the same because both are calculated for the base year using the same prices and quantities. Figure 8.3 shows movements in nominal GDP and real GDP between 1995 and 2016. In the years before 2009, prices were, on average, lower than in 2009,

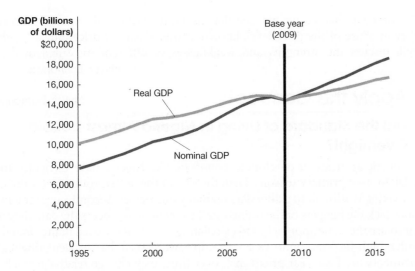

GDP (billions of dollars)

MyLab Economics Real-time data

Figure 8.3

Nominal GDP and Real GDP, 1995–2016

Currently, the base year for calculating GDP is 2009. In the years before 2009, prices were, on average, lower than in 2009, so nominal GDP was lower than real GDP. In 2009, nominal and real GDP were equal. Since 2009, prices have been, on average, higher than in 2009, so nominal GDP is higher than real GDP. **Source:** U.S. Bureau of Economic Analysis.

so nominal GDP was lower than real GDP. In 2009, nominal and real GDP were equal. Since 2009, prices have been, on average, higher than in 2009, so nominal GDP is higher than real GDP.   **MyLab Economics** Concept Check

The GDP Deflator

Economists and policymakers are interested not just in the level of total production, as measured by real GDP, but also in the *price level*. The **price level** measures the average prices of goods and services in the economy. One of the goals of economic policy is to maintain a stable price level. We can use values for nominal GDP and real GDP to compute a measure of the price level called the *GDP deflator*. We calculate the **GDP deflator** using this formula:

$$\text{GDP deflator} = \frac{\text{Nominal GDP}}{\text{Real GDP}} \times 100.$$

Price level A measure of the average prices of goods and services in the economy.

GDP deflator A measure of the price level, calculated by dividing nominal GDP by real GDP and multiplying by 100.

To see why the GDP deflator is a measure of the price level, think about what would happen if prices of goods and services rose while production remained the same. In that case, nominal GDP would increase, but real GDP would remain constant, so the GDP deflator would increase. In reality, both prices and production usually increase each year, but the more prices increase relative to the increase in production, the more nominal GDP increases relative to real GDP, and the higher the value for the GDP deflator. Increases in the GDP deflator allow economists and policymakers to track increases in the price level over time.

Remember that in the base year (currently 2009), nominal GDP is equal to real GDP, so the value of the GDP price deflator will always be 100 in the base year. The following table gives the values for nominal and real GDP for 2015 and 2016:

	2015	2016
Nominal GDP	$18,037 billion	$18,569 billion
Real GDP	$16,397 billion	$16,662 billion

We can use the information from this table to calculate values for the GDP price deflator for 2015 and 2016:

Formula	Applied to 2015	Applied to 2016
GDP deflator $= \left(\dfrac{\text{Nominal GDP}}{\text{Real GDP}}\right) \times 100$	$\left(\dfrac{\$18,037\text{ billion}}{\$16,397\text{ billion}}\right) \times 100 = 110.0$	$\left(\dfrac{\$18,569\text{ billion}}{\$16,662\text{ billion}}\right) \times 100 = 111.4$

From these values for the deflator, we can calculate that the price level increased by 1.3 percent between 2015 and 2016:

$$\left(\frac{111.4 - 110.0}{110.0}\right) \times 100 = 1.3\%.$$

In the next chapter, we will see that economists and policymakers also rely on another measure of the price level, known as the consumer price index. In addition, we will discuss the strengths and weaknesses of different measures of the price level.

MyLab Economics Study Plan

MyLab Economics Concept Check

Apply the Concept

MyLab Economics Video

Did the Standard of Living in Nigeria Almost Double Overnight?

Government agencies in developing countries like Nigeria have difficulty measuring GDP for two primary reasons: First, the size of the underground economy may be large, making it difficult to gather data on many businesses. Second, government agencies may lack the budgets or the trained staff to accurately process the data they do collect or to use the same approaches to calculating GDP that are used in the United States and other high-income countries. For example, we've seen that in calculating real GDP, governments use base-year prices that, over time, may change relative to each other, potentially distorting the measurement. To deal with this problem, the BEA changes the base year fairly frequently and uses chain-weighted prices. This approach, though, can be difficult for developing countries to implement because it can be expensive to have government employees collect large amounts of price data.

By 2010, the government of Nigeria knew that the data it was publishing on real GDP were inaccurate because it was still using 1990 as its base year, even though the economy had changed dramatically over the years. The Nigerian National Bureau of Statistics was given a larger budget and the task of both changing the real GDP base year to 2010 and gathering data on previously unrecorded output in the underground economy. As an article in the *Wall Street Journal* put it: "Nigerian number crunchers traversed the West African nation by motorcycle and speedboat, visiting Internet cafe owners, movie producers and other businesspeople to record previously uncaptured commercial activity." The number of businesses being surveyed for data increased from 85,000 to 850,000.

When the new data on GDP were released in 2014, the results were dramatic. The estimate for real GDP for 2013 was changed from $270 billion to $510 billion, an 89 percent increase. The increase was large enough for Nigeria to pass South Africa as the largest economy in Africa. As the figure below shows, the new data also gave a more accurate picture of the structure of the Nigerian economy. For instance, where previously the service sector was believed to make up less than one-third of the economy, it was shown to actually be more than half the economy. In addition, although not shown in the figure, the telecommunications sector actually makes up 9 percent of the economy, rather than the 1 percent in previous estimates, and the oil industry is only 14 percent of the economy rather than 33 percent.

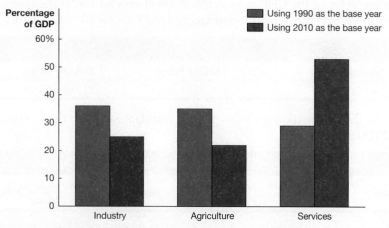

The government of Kenya also updated and expanded the data used to calculate base-year prices and found that its economy was 25 percent larger than it had previously estimated. After following a similar process, the government of Ghana announced that its economy was 60 percent larger than previously estimated. But had the standard of living of the typical person in these countries actually increased? Certainly, the new estimates made it appear so. For instance, estimated real GDP per person in Nigeria increased from $1,500 to $2,688. Of course, all that had really changed was how accurately the governments were measuring real GDP. The countries were producing no more goods and services on the day the new GDP data were announced than they had been the day before.

These experiences with measuring GDP demonstrate the problems governments have in accurately constructing these statistics and how misleading they can be as measures of a country's standard of living.

Sources: "Rewriting GDP History," *Economist*, May 2, 2016; Drew Hinshaw and Patrick McGroarty, "Nigeria's Economy Surpasses South Africa's in Size," *Wall Street Journal*, April 6, 2014; Javier Blas and William Wallis, "Nigeria Almost Doubles GDP in Recalculation," *Financial Times*, April 7, 2014; and "How Nigeria's Economy Grew by 89% Overnight," *Economist*, April 7, 2014.

Your Turn: Test your understanding by doing related problem 3.10 on page 275 at the end of this chapter.   MyLab Economics Study Plan

---

8.4 Other Measures of Total Production and Total Income

LEARNING OBJECTIVE: Describe other measures of total production and total income.

National income accounting refers to the methods the BEA uses to track total production and total income in the economy. The statistical tables containing this information are called the *National Income and Product Accounts (NIPA)* tables. Every quarter, the BEA releases NIPA tables containing data on several measures of total production and total income. We have already discussed GDP, which is the most important measure of total production and total income. In addition to computing GDP, the BEA computes the following four measures of production and income: gross national product, national income, personal income, and disposable personal income.

Gross National Product

We have seen that GDP is the value of final goods and services produced within the United States. *Gross national product (GNP)* is the value of final goods and services produced by residents of the United States, even if the production takes place *outside* the United States. U.S. firms have facilities in foreign countries, and foreign firms have facilities in the United States. Ford, for example, has assembly plants in the United Kingdom, and Toyota has assembly plants in the United States. GNP includes foreign production by U.S. firms but excludes U.S. production by foreign firms. For the United States, GNP is almost the same as GDP. For example, in 2016, GDP was $18,569 billion, and GNP was $18,776 billion, or only about 1.1 percent more than GDP.

For many years, GNP was the main measure of total production compiled by the federal government and used by economists and policymakers in the United States. However, in many countries other than the United States, a significant percentage of domestic production takes place in foreign-owned facilities. For those countries, GDP is much larger than GNP and is a more accurate measure of the level of production within the country's borders. As a result, many countries and international agencies had long preferred using GDP to using GNP. In 1991, the United States joined those countries in using GDP as its main measure of total production.   MyLab Economics Concept Check

National Income

In the production of goods and services, some machinery, equipment, and buildings wear out and have to be replaced. The value of this worn-out machinery, equipment, and buildings is called *depreciation*. In the NIPA tables, depreciation is called the *consumption of fixed capital*. If we subtract this value from GDP, we are left with *national income*.

In Section 8.1, we stressed that the value of total production is equal to the value of total income. This point is not strictly true if by "value of total production" we mean

GDP and by "value of total income" we mean national income because national income will always be smaller than GDP by an amount equal to depreciation. In practice, though, the difference between the value of GDP and the value of national income does not matter for most macroeconomic issues. MyLab Economics Concept Check

Personal Income

Personal income is income received by households. To calculate personal income, we subtract the earnings that corporations retain rather than pay to shareholders in the form of dividends. We also add the payments households receive from the government in the form of *transfer payments* or interest on government bonds. MyLab Economics Concept Check

Disposable Personal Income

Disposable personal income is equal to personal income minus personal tax payments, such as the federal personal income tax. It is the best measure of the income households actually have available to spend.

Figure 8.4 shows the values of these measures of total production and total income for 2016 in a table and a graph. MyLab Economics Concept Check

The Division of Income

Figure 8.1 on page 257 illustrates the important fact that we can measure GDP in terms of total expenditure or as the total income received by households. GDP calculated as the sum of income payments to households is sometimes called *gross domestic income*. Figure 8.5 shows the division of total income among wages, interest, rent, profit, and certain non-income items. The non-income items are included in gross domestic income because sales taxes, depreciation, and a few other items are included in the value of goods and services produced but are not directly received by households as income. *Wages* include all compensation received by employees, including fringe benefits such as health insurance. *Interest* is net interest received by households, or the difference between the interest received on savings accounts, government bonds, and other investments and the interest paid on car loans, home mortgages, and other debts. *Rent* is rent received by households. *Profit* includes the profits of sole proprietorships, which are usually small businesses, and the profits of

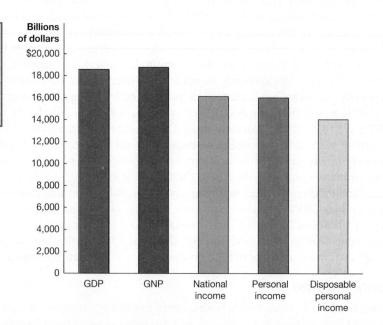

Measure	Billions of dollars
GDP	$18,569
GNP	18,776
National income	16,130
Personal income	16,012
Disposable personal income	14,046

MyLab Economics Real-time data

Figure 8.4 **Measures of Total Production and Total Income, 2016**

The most important measure of total production and total income is gross domestic product (GDP). As we will see in later chapters, for some purposes, the other measures of total production and total income shown in the figure turn out to be more useful than GDP.
Source: U.S. Bureau of Economic Analysis.

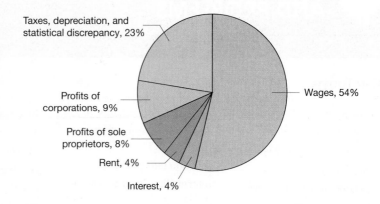

COMPONENTS OF GROSS DOMESTIC INCOME (billions of dollars)		
Wages		$10,114
Interest		676
Rent		705
Profit		3,093
Profits of sole proprietors	1,418	
Profits of corporations	1,676	
Taxes, depreciation, and statistical discrepancy		4,246

MyLab Economics Animation

Figure 8.5   **The Division of Income, 2016**

We can measure GDP in terms of total expenditure or as the total income received by households. The largest component of income received by households is wages, which are more than three times as large as the profits received by sole proprietors and the profits received by corporations combined.

Note: The components in the figure do not sum to 100 percent because of rounding.
Source: U.S. Bureau of Economic Analysis.

corporations. Figure 8.5 shows that the largest component of gross domestic income is wages, which are more than three times as large as profits.

Since 2008, labor's share of national income has declined by several percentage points in the United States and most European countries. Economists debate the reasons for this decline, with some believing it can be accounted for by measurement problems. David Autor, of the Massachusetts Institute of Technology, and colleagues argue that the decline may be due to the rise of "superstar firms," which account for an increasing fraction of sales in a number of industries. Because these firms have high levels of profit, they have relatively low shares of labor income relative to their revenue.

MyLab Economics Concept Check   **MyLab Economics** Study Plan

Continued from page 253

Economics in Your Life & Career

What's the Best Country for You to Work In?

At the beginning of the chapter, we posed two questions: What effect should Canada's and China's two very different growth rates have on your decision to work and live in one country or the other? Would China's much higher growth rate lead you to decide to work and live there?

This chapter has shown that although it is *generally* true that the more goods and services people have, the better off they are, GDP provides only a rough measure of well-being. GDP does not include the value of leisure, nor is it adjusted for pollution and other negative effects of production or crime and other social problems. So, in deciding where to live and work, you would need to balance China's much higher growth rate of GDP against these other considerations. You would also need to take into account that although China's *growth rate* is higher than Canada's, Canada's current *level* of real GDP is higher than China's.

Conclusion

In this chapter, we have begun the study of macroeconomics by examining an important concept: how a country's total production and income can be measured. Understanding GDP is important for understanding the business cycle and the process of long-run economic growth. In the next chapter, we discuss the issues involved in measuring two other key economic variables: the unemployment rate and the inflation rate.

Visit **MyLab Economics** for a news article and analysis related to the concepts in this chapter.

Key Terms

Business cycle, p. 254

Consumption, p. 258

Economic growth, p. 254

Expansion, p. 254

Final good or service, p. 255

GDP deflator, p. 267

Government purchases, p. 259

Gross domestic product (GDP), p. 255

Inflation rate, p. 254

Intermediate good or service, p. 255

Investment, p. 258

Macroeconomics, p. 254

Microeconomics, p. 254

Net exports, p. 259

Nominal GDP, p. 265

Price level, p. 267

Real GDP, p. 265

Recession, p. 254

Transfer payments, p. 258

Underground economy, p. 263

Value added, p. 262

8.1 Gross Domestic Product Measures Total Production, pages 255–262

LEARNING OBJECTIVE: Explain how total production is measured.

MyLab Economics Visit **www.pearson.com/mylab/economics** to complete these exercises online and get instant feedback.

Summary

Economics is divided into the subfields of **microeconomics**—which studies how households and firms make choices—and **macroeconomics**—which studies the economy as a whole. An important macroeconomic topic is the **business cycle**, which refers to alternating periods of economic expansion and economic recession. An **expansion** is a period during which production and employment are increasing. A **recession** is a period during which production and employment are decreasing. Another important macroeconomic topic is **economic growth**, which refers to the ability of the economy to produce increasing quantities of goods and services. Macroeconomics also studies the **inflation rate**, or the percentage increase in the price level from one year to the next. Economists measure total production by **gross domestic product (GDP)**, which is the value of all *final goods and services* produced in an economy during a period of time. A **final good or service** is purchased by a final user. An **intermediate good or service** is an input into another good or service and is not included in GDP. When we measure the value of total production in the economy by calculating GDP, we are simultaneously measuring the value of total income. GDP is divided into four major categories of expenditures: consumption, investment, government purchases, and net exports. **Consumption** is spending by households on goods and services, not including spending on new houses. **Investment** is spending by firms on new factories, office buildings, machinery, research and development, and additions to inventories, plus spending by households and firms on new houses. **Government purchases** is spending by federal, state, and local governments on goods and services. **Net exports** are equal to exports minus imports. Government **transfer payments** are not included in GDP because they are payments to individuals for which the government does not receive a good or service in return. We can also calculate GDP by adding up the **value added** by every firm involved in producing final goods and services.

Review Questions

1.1 Why in microeconomics do we measure production in terms of quantity, but in macroeconomics we measure production in terms of market value?

1.2 An article in the *Wall Street Journal* stated that "GDP figures are a measure of all the goods and services that are produced in an economy during a particular period." Briefly explain whether you agree with this definition of GDP.

Source: Jon Sindreu, "Why U.S. GDP Figures Might Be Better than They Look," *Wall Street Journal*, July 29, 2016.

1.3 In the circular flow of income, why must the value of total production in an economy equal the value of total income?

1.4 Describe the four major components of expenditures in GDP and write the equation that represents the relationship between GDP and the four expenditure components.

1.5 What is meant by a firm's "value added"?

Problems and Applications

1.6 A student remarks: "It doesn't make sense that intermediate goods are not counted in GDP. A computer chip is an intermediate good, and without it, a laptop won't work. So, why don't we count the computer chip in GDP?" Provide an answer to the student's question.

1.7 Briefly explain whether each of the following transactions represents the purchase of a final good.
   a. The purchase of flour by a bakery
   b. The purchase of an aircraft carrier by the federal government
   c. The purchase of French wine by a U.S. consumer
   d. The purchase of a new airliner by American Airlines

1.8 An article in the *Wall Street Journal* stated that a change in inventories "dragged down the overall growth in GDP by nearly a full percentage point" below what it otherwise would have been. For this result to have occurred, is it likely that inventories increased or decreased? Briefly explain.

Source: Josh Mitchell, "U.S. GDP Growth Slowed on Tepid Consumer," *Wall Street Journal*, April 28, 2017.

1.9 **(Related to the Chapter Opener on page 252)** Which component of GDP will be affected by each of the following transactions involving the Ford Motor Company? If you believe that a transaction will affect none of the components of GDP, briefly explain why.

a. You purchase a new Ford Escape hybrid from a Ford dealer.

b. You purchase a 2013 Ford Escape hybrid from a friend.

c. Ford purchases door handles for the Escape from an auto parts manufacturer in Indiana.

d. Ford produces 1,000 Escapes in a factory in Missouri and ships them to a car dealer in Shanghai, China.

e. Ford purchases new machine tools to use in its Missouri Escape factory.

f. The state of Missouri builds a new highway to help improve access to the Ford Escape plant.

1.10 Is the value of a house built in 2008 and resold in 2019 included in the GDP of 2019? Briefly explain. Would the services of the real estate agent who helped sell (or buy) the house in 2019 be counted in GDP for 2019? Briefly explain.

1.11 **(Related to Solved Problem 8.1 on page 256)** Suppose that a simple economy produces only four goods: shoes, hamburgers, shirts, and cotton. Assume that all the cotton is used in the production of shirts. Use the information in the following table to calculate nominal GDP for 2019.

Production and Price Statistics for 2019		
Product	Quantity	Price
Shoes	100	$60.00
Hamburgers	100	2.00
Shirts	50	25.00
Cotton	80	0.60

1.12 **(Related to the Don't Let This Happen to You on page 259)** Briefly explain whether you agree with the following statement: "In years when people buy many shares of stock, investment will be high and, therefore, so will GDP."

1.13 **(Related to the Apply the Concept on page 260)** During an interview with a reporter, former Microsoft CEO Steve Ballmer discussed the data compiled on the usafacts.org Web site. Ballmer asked if the reporter knew how many people the government employed and provided the answer: "Almost 24 million. Would you have guessed that?"

a. Is local, state, and federal governments spending on salaries and benefits for these employees considered production as measured by GDP? Briefly explain.

b. According to data on the usafacts.org site, in 2014 the federal government spent $57.3 billion on Social Security payments to retired and disabled people. Is this federal government spending considered production as measured by GDP? Briefly explain.

Source: Andrew Ross Sorkin, "Steve Ballmer Serves up a Fascinating Data Trove," *New York Times*, April 17, 2017.

1.14 An artist buys scrap metal from a local steel mill as a raw material for her metal sculptures. Last year, she bought $5,000 worth of the scrap metal. During the year, she produced 10 metal sculptures that she sold for $800 each to a local art store. The local art store sold all of the sculptures to local art collectors, at an average price of $1,000 each. For the 10 metal sculptures, what was the total value added by the artist, and what was the total value added by the local art store?

 8.2 Does GDP Measure What We Want It to Measure? pages 262–265

LEARNING OBJECTIVE: Discuss whether GDP is a good measure of well-being.

MyLab Economics   Visit www.pearson.com/mylab/economics to complete these exercises online and get instant feedback.

Summary

GDP does not include household production, which refers to goods and services people produce for themselves, nor does it include production in the **underground economy**, which consists of concealed buying and selling. The underground economy in some developing countries may be more than half of measured GDP. GDP is not a perfect measure of well-being because it does not include the value of leisure, it is not adjusted for pollution or other negative effects of production, and it is not adjusted for changes in crime and other social problems.

Review Questions

2.1 Why does the size of a country's GDP matter? How does it affect the quality of life of the country's people?

2.2 What is the underground economy? Why do some countries have larger underground economies than other countries?

2.3 Why is GDP an imperfect measure of economic well-being? What types of production does GDP not measure? If GDP included these types of production, would it still be an imperfect measure of economic well-being?

Problems and Applications

2.4 Which of the following are likely to increase measured GDP, and which are likely to reduce it?

a. The fraction of women working outside the home increases.

b. There is a sharp increase in the crime rate.

c. Higher tax rates cause some people to ask to be paid in cash so they can hide more of the income they earn.

2.5 Michael Burda of Humboldt University in Germany and Daniel Hamermesh of the University of Texas examined how workers in the United States who lost their jobs spent their time. They discovered that during the period when the workers were unemployed, the decline in the number of hours of paid work they did was almost the same as the increase in the number of hours they devoted to household production. Do Burda and Hamermesh's findings allow us to draw any conclusions about whether total production in the economy—whether that production is included in GDP or not—decreased when these workers became unemployed? Does your answer depend on whether the household production they carried out while unemployed were activities, such as childcare, that the workers had been paying other people to perform before they lost their jobs? Briefly explain.

Source: Michael Burda and Daniel S. Hamermesh, "Unemployment, Market Work, and Household Production," *Economic Letters*, Vol. 107, May 2010, pp. 131–133.

2.6 A typical U.S. worker today works fewer than 40 hours per week compared to 60 hours per week in 1890. Does this difference in the length of work weeks matter in comparing the economic well-being of U.S. workers today with that of 1890? Or can we use the difference between real GDP per capita today and in 1890 to measure differences in economic well-being while ignoring differences in the number of hours worked per week? Briefly explain.

2.7 An article in the *Economist* stated, "The appeal of GDP is that it offers, or seems to, a summary statistic of how well an economy is doing."
   a. In what sense does GDP offer a summary statistic of how well an economy is doing?
   b. Why qualify the statement about GDP as a summary statistic by including the phrase "or seems to"?

Source: "The Euro-Area Economy: Speeding Up," *Economist*, May 6, 2017.

2.8 **(Related to the Apply the Concept on page 263)** According to research by Rafael La Porta of Tuck School of Business at Dartmouth and Andrei Shleifer of Harvard University, in developing countries, the average firm in the informal sector, or underground economy, employs 4 workers as opposed to 126 workers employed by the average firm in the formal sector.
   a. What is the informal sector, or underground economy?
   b. Why would we expect firms in the informal sector to be so much smaller than firms in the formal sector?

Sources: Rafael La Porta and Andrei Shleifer, "Informality and Development," *Journal of Economic Perspectives*, Vol. 28, No. 3, Summer 2014, pp. 109–126.

2.9 **(Related to the Apply the Concept on page 263)** An article in the *Wall Street Journal* noted that many economists believe that GDP data for India are unreliable because "most enterprises are tiny and unregistered, and most workers are employed off the books. The government's infrequent surveys represent only a best guess of the value being added in back-alley workshops, outdoor markets and other cash-based corners of the economy."
   a. What does the article mean by working "off the books"? Why might it be difficult for the government to measure the production of small, cash-based firms?
   b. Why would the problems listed make it difficult for the Indian government to accurately measure GDP?
   c. What problems can be caused for a government or for businesses in a country if the government cannot accurately measure GDP?

Source: Raymond Zhong, "On Close Inspection, India's Sharp Growth Picture Gets Fuzzy," *Wall Street Journal*, May 1, 2016.

2.10 The following data for 2015 are from the Organization for Economic Co-operation and Development (OECD).

	Average Annual Hours Worked	Average Annual Wages
Germany	1,371	$44,925
United States	1,790	$58,714

The average German worker worked about 400 fewer hours per year and earned nearly $14,000 less than did the average worker in the United States. Can we conclude anything about the well-being of the average German worker versus the well-being of the average worker in the United States from these data? What other measures would you like to see in evaluating the well-being of workers in these two countries?

Source: stat.oecd.org.

8.3 Real GDP versus Nominal GDP, pages 265–269

LEARNING OBJECTIVE: Discuss the difference between real GDP and nominal GDP.

MyLab Economics   Visit **www.pearson.com/mylab/economics** to complete these exercises online and get instant feedback.

Summary

Nominal GDP is the value of final goods and services evaluated at current-year prices. **Real GDP** is the value of final goods and services evaluated at *base-year* prices. By keeping prices constant, we know that changes in real GDP represent changes in the quantity of goods and services produced in the economy. When the **price level**, the average prices of goods and services in the economy, is increasing, real GDP is greater than nominal GDP in years before the base year and less than nominal GDP for years after the base year. The **GDP deflator** is a measure of the price level and is calculated by dividing nominal GDP by real GDP and multiplying by 100.

Review Questions

3.1 Why does inflation make nominal GDP a poor measure of the increase in total production from one year to the next? How does the U.S. Bureau of Economic Analysis deal with this drawback?

3.2 What is the GDP deflator, and how is it calculated?

3.3 Assuming that inflation has occurred over time, what is the relationship between nominal GDP and real GDP in each of the following situations?
   a. In the years after the base year
   b. In the base year
   c. In the years before the base year

Problems and Applications

3.4 **(Related to Solved Problem 8.3 on page 265)** Suppose the information in the following table is for a simple economy that produces only four goods and services: shoes, hamburgers, shirts, and cotton. Assume that all the cotton is used in the production of shirts.

Product	2009		2018		2019	
	Quantity	Price	Quantity	Price	Quantity	Price
Shoes	90	$50.00	100	$60.00	100	$65.00
Hamburgers	75	2.00	100	2.00	120	2.25
Shirts	50	30.00	50	25.00	65	25.00
Cotton	100	0.80	800	0.60	120	0.70

a. Use the information in the table to calculate real GDP for 2018 and 2019, assuming that the base year is 2009.

b. What is the growth rate of real GDP during 2019?

3.5 For each of the following statements, briefly explain whether you agree.

a. "If nominal GDP is less than real GDP, then the price level must have fallen during the year."

b. "Whenever real GDP declines, nominal GDP must also decline."

c. "If a recession is so severe that the price level declines, then we know that both real GDP and nominal GDP must decline."

d. "Nominal GDP declined between 2008 and 2009; therefore, the GDP deflator must also have declined."

3.6 An article in the *Wall Street Journal* discussed the views of then Canadian Minister of Finance Joe Oliver on the effect of falling oil prices on the Canadian economy. According to the article, Oliver argued that "lower oil prices would have a broadly neutral impact on real … gross domestic product, but have a negative effect on nominal GDP." Given this view, can we tell what effect Oliver must have expected lower oil prices to have on the inflation rate? Briefly explain.

Source: Scott Haggett, "Canada Pushes Back Budget to April Due to Market Instability," *New York Times*, January 15, 2015.

3.7 The following table lists hypothetical values.

b. Fill in column (5) by calculating the annual percentage change in real GDP for each year, using the values from column (4), and fill in column (8) by calculating the annual percentage change in real GDP by using the values from column (7).

c. What effect does the change in the base year used to compute real GDP have on your calculations of the percentage changes in real GDP?

3.8 As of 2017, 19 countries in Europe had adopted the euro as their common currency. These countries are called the euro zone. According to an article in the *Economist*, "The euro zone's GDP grew at an annualized rate of around 2% in the first quarter." Is it likely that the article is referring to the growth in nominal GDP or the growth in real GDP? Briefly explain.

Source: "The World This Week," *Economist*, May 6, 2017.

3.9 Use the data in the following table to calculate the GDP deflator for each year (values are in billions of dollars).

Year	Nominal GDP	Real GDP
2012	$16,155	$15,355
2013	16,692	15,612
2014	17,393	15,982
2015	18,037	16,397
2016	18,569	16,662

Which year from 2013 to 2016 saw the largest percentage increase in the price level, as measured by changes in the GDP deflator? Briefly explain.

3.10 **(Related to the Apply the Concept on page 268)** An article in the *Economist* on the revisions to Nigeria's GDP commented: "The GDP revision is not mere trickery. It provides a truer picture of Nigeria's size by giving due weight to the bits of the economy, such as telecoms, banking and the Nollywood film industry, that have been growing fast in recent years."

a. What does the article mean by "giving due weight" to the sectors of the economy that have been growing quickly?

b. How did the Nigerian National Bureau of Statistics accomplish the task of giving these sectors their due weight?

c. Why does making this change in calculating GDP provide a truer picture of the size of Nigeria's economy?

Source: "Africa's New Number One," *Economist*, April 12, 2014.

(1) Year	(2) Nominal GDP	(3) GDP Deflator (base year = 2016)	(4) Real GDP (base year = 2016)	(5) Percentage Change in Real GDP	(6) GDP Deflator (base year = 2018)	(7) Real GDP (base year = 2018)	(8) Percentage Change in Real GDP
2014	$980	90		—	81.8		—
2015	1,020	92			83.6		
2016	1,050	100			90.9		
2017	1,200	105			95.5		
2018	1,400	110			100.0		

a. Fill in column (4) by calculating real GDP using the GDP deflator with a base year of 2016 from column (3). Fill in column (7) by calculating real GDP using the GDP deflator with a base year of 2018 from column (6).

8.4 Other Measures of Total Production and Total Income, pages 269–271

LEARNING OBJECTIVE: Describe other measures of total production and total income.

MyLab Economics Visit **www.pearson.com/mylab/economics** to complete these exercises online and get instant feedback.

Summary

The most important measure of total production and total income is gross domestic product (GDP). As we will see in later chapters, for some purposes, other measures of total production and total income are actually more useful than GDP. These measures are gross national product (GNP), national income, personal income, and disposable personal income.

Review Questions

4.1 What is the difference between GDP and GNP? Briefly explain whether the difference is important for the United States.

4.2 What are the differences between national income, personal income, and disposable personal income?

4.3 What is gross domestic income? Which component of gross domestic income is the largest?

Problems and Applications

4.4 Suppose Switzerland has many of its citizens temporarily working in other countries, and many of its firms have facilities in other countries. Furthermore, suppose relatively few citizens of foreign countries are working in Switzerland, and relatively few foreign firms have facilities in Switzerland. In these circumstances, which would you expect to be larger for Switzerland, GDP or GNP? Briefly explain.

4.5 Ireland is one of the few countries where GDP and GNP differ significantly. Using GDP per person, Ireland has the third-highest income per person in Europe. An article on the *Financial Times* website stated, "With GDP being about 20 percent larger than GNP, Irish people appear (when using GDP per person) to be richer than what they feel they are." Briefly explain the author's reasoning.

Source: Valentina Romei, "Ireland Is the Wealthiest Economy in Europe … or Not," ft.com, May 13, 2015.

4.6 Suppose the amount the federal government collects in personal income taxes increases, while the level of GDP remains the same. What will happen to the values of national income, personal income, and disposable personal income?

4.7 If you were attempting to forecast the level of consumption spending by households, which measure of total production or total income might be most helpful to you in making your forecast? Briefly explain.

4.8 Briefly discuss the accuracy of the following statement: "Corporate profits are much too high: Most corporations make profits equal to 50 percent of the price of the products they sell."

Real-Time Data Exercises

D8.1 **(Analyzing the components of personal consumption expenditures)** Go to the Web site of the Federal Reserve Bank of St. Louis (FRED) (fred.stlouisfed.org).

    a. Find the values for the most recent quarter for these four variables: (1) Personal Consumption Expenditures (PCEC); (2) Personal Consumption Expenditures: Durable Goods (PCDG); (3) Personal Consumption Expenditures: Nondurable Goods (PCND); and (4) Personal Consumption Expenditures: Services (PCESV).

    b. What percentage of total household expenditures is devoted to the consumption of goods (both durable and nondurable goods)?

D8.2 **(Analyzing the components of investment)** Go to the Web site of the Federal Reserve Bank of St. Louis (FRED) (fred.stlouisfed.org).

    a. Find the values for the most recent quarter for these three variables: (1) Gross Private Domestic Investment (GPDI); (2) Private Nonresidential Fixed Investment (PNFI); and (3) Private Residential Fixed Investment (PRFI).

    b. Use these values to calculate the difference between gross private domestic investment and residential and nonresidential private fixed investment. What component of GDP does the value calculated represent?

D8.3 **(Calculating net exports)** Go to the Web site of the Federal Reserve Bank of St. Louis (FRED) (fred.stlouisfed.org).

    a. Find the values for the most recent two years for Real Exports of Goods and Services (EXPGSCA) and Real Imports of Goods and Services (IMPGSCA).

    b. Compute the value of net exports for each of the two most recent years.

D8.4 **(Comparing GDP and GNP)** Go to the Web site of the Federal Reserve Bank of St. Louis (FRED) (fred.stlouisfed.org).

    a. Find the values for the most recent quarter for Gross Domestic Product (GDP) and Gross National Product (GNP).

    b. Given these values, explain whether foreign production by U.S. firms exceeded U.S. production by foreign firms.

D8.5 **(Analyzing the components of personal income)** Go to the Web site of the Federal Reserve Bank of St. Louis (FRED) (fred.stlouisfed.org).

    a. Find the values for the most recent quarter for these three variables: (1) Personal Income (PINCOME); (2) Disposable Personal Income (DPI); and (3) Personal Consumption Expenditures (PCEC).

    b. Use these values to calculate the difference between personal income and disposable personal income. What does this value represent?

D8.6 **(Calculating the GDP deflator and the inflation rate)** Go to the Web site of the Federal Reserve Bank of St. Louis (FRED) (fred.stlouisfed.org).

    a. Find the values for the most recent quarter and the values for the same quarter one year ago for nominal Gross Domestic Product (GDP) and Real Gross Domestic Product (GDPC1).

    b. Use these values to calculate the GDP price deflator for the most recent quarter and the GDP price deflator for the quarter one year ago.

    c. Using the two GDP price deflators, calculate the inflation rate during this year.

    d. Look again at Figure 8.3 on page 267. Briefly explain why the nominal and real GDP lines intersect at the base year. What is the value of the GDP deflator in the year when the nominal and real GDP lines intersect?

D8.7 **(Calculating real GDP and the real growth rate)** Go to the Web site of the Federal Reserve Bank of St. Louis (FRED) (fred.stlouisfed.org).

    a. Find the values for the most recent quarter and the same quarter one year ago for nominal Gross Domestic Product (GDP) and the GDP Implicit Price Deflator (GDPDEF)

    b. Use these values to calculate real GDP for the most recent quarter and for the quarter one year ago.

    c. Use the two real GDP values to calculate the real growth rate of the economy during this year.

Critical Thinking Exercises

CT8.1 For this exercise, your instructor may assign you to a group.

    a. Each person in the group should reread the portion of Section 8.1 on investment, including the *Don't Let This Happen to You* "Remember What Economists Mean by Investment."

    b. Each person should write down what he or she finds surprising about this definition and share it with the group.

    c. The group should prepare a brief report on how this definition is different from what most of the group members expected before reading the chapter.

CT8.2 Carefully explain what you found surprising about the definition of GDP. Does GDP include some components that you were not expecting? Are some components excluded that you expected to be included?

CT8.3 For this question, use the following table:

Type of GDP	GDP in Year 1	GDP in Year 2
Nominal GDP	$10 trillion	$11 trillion
Real GDP	$10 trillion	$10 trillion

What is most likely happening in the economy that would result in the data shown in the table? Consider the possibility that these data are the result of an expansion, a recession, inflation, deflation, or some combination of these economic situations.

9

Unemployment and Inflation

Why Would Boeing Cut Thousands of Jobs As the Economy Expands?

When we study macroeconomics, we are looking at the big picture: total production, total employment, and the price level. But the big picture is made up of millions of individual consumers, workers, and firms. During recessions, like the ones that occurred in 2001 and 2007–2009, many firms suffer declines in sales and workers lose their jobs. Firms that produce durable goods, such as automobiles, appliances, and machine tools are likely to be particularly hard hit because as incomes and profits fall, households and businesses postpone new durable goods.

Founded in 1916, Boeing Company, now headquartered in Chicago, is one of the world's largest manufacturers of commercial jetliners, military aircraft, satellites, missiles, and defense systems. During recessions, air travel declines and airlines cut back their orders for new planes. The recession of 2001 caused a decline of more than 50 percent in Boeing's deliveries of planes, and the firm laid off 30,000 workers. Production had not yet fully recovered when the recession of 2007–2009 started, deliveries again declined, and Boeing laid off 7,000 workers.

By 2015, Boeing's deliveries of planes had reached a new peak, before declining in 2016, despite continued expansion of the U.S. and world economies. In 2017, the company announced that it was cutting 1,800 jobs in addition to the 7,000 jobs it had cut the year before. Boeing faced three key challenges. First, to compete successfully with its main rivals, the European firm Airbus Group and the Canadian firm Bombardier, Boeing had to cut prices, which has led it to lower costs by reducing employment. Second, many airlines had considered Boeing's 737 jetliner to be the finest single-aisle jetliner available. But in recent years, Airbus has made improvements to its competing A320 model and has begun winning a majority of new

Travis Dove/Bloomberg/Getty Images

orders for this category of jetliners. Third, cuts to military spending during the administration of President Barack Obama had led to declining sales in Boeing's defense and space unit.

In contrast to the layoffs at Boeing, the national unemployment rate, which had remained stubbornly high for several years after the 2007–2009 recession ended, had reached more normal levels by 2017. Some economists, though, were concerned that the fraction of people who either had jobs or were actively looking for them had risen slowly even as the unemployment rate had fallen.

In this chapter, we will focus on measuring changes in unemployment as well as changes in the price level, or inflation. Because both unemployment and inflation are major macroeconomic problems, it is important to understand how these variables are measured.

Sources: Doug Cameron, "More Than 1,800 Boeing Employees Accept Voluntary Buyouts," *Wall Street Journal*, March 3, 2017; Julie Johnsson, "Boeing to Dismiss Hundreds of Engineers Amid Sales Slowdown," bloomberg.com, April 17, 2017; Jon Ostrower, "Jet Prices Take Center Stage in Boeing Job Cuts," *Wall Street Journal*, March 31, 2016; and Boeing Company, *Annual Reports*, various years.

Chapter Outline & Learning Objectives

Economics in Your Life & Career

Should You Change Your Career Plans if You Graduate during a Recession?

Suppose that you are a sophomore, majoring in either economics or finance. You plan to find a job in the banking industry after graduation. Unfortunately, though, the economy is now in a deep recession, and substantial layoffs have occurred in the banking industry. Should you change your major? Should you still consider a job in this industry? As you read this chapter, try to answer these questions. You can check your answers against those we provide on **page 306** at the end of this chapter.

For many people, the state of the economy can be summarized in just two measures: the unemployment rate and the inflation rate. In the 1960s, Arthur Okun, who was chairman of the Council of Economic Advisers during President Lyndon Johnson's administration, coined the term *misery index*, which adds together the unemployment rate and the inflation rate to give a rough measure of the state of the economy. As we will see in later chapters, although unemployment and inflation are important problems in the short run, the long-run success of an economy is best judged by its ability to generate high levels of real GDP per person. We devote this chapter to discussing how the government measures the unemployment and inflation rates. In particular, we will look closely at the related statistics the federal government issues each month.

9.1 Measuring the Unemployment Rate, the Labor Force Participation Rate, and the Employment–Population Ratio

LEARNING OBJECTIVE: Define the unemployment rate, the labor force participation rate, and the employment–population ratio and understand how they are computed.

At 8:30 A.M. on a Friday early in each month, the U.S. Department of Labor reports its estimate of the previous month's unemployment rate. If the unemployment rate is higher or lower than expected, investors are likely to change their views on the health of the economy. The result is seen an hour later, when trading begins on the New York Stock Exchange. Good news about unemployment usually causes stock prices to rise, and bad news causes stock prices to fall. The unemployment rate can also have important political implications. In most presidential elections, the incumbent president is reelected if the unemployment rate is falling early in the election year but is defeated if the unemployment rate is rising. This relationship held true in 2012, when the unemployment rate was lower during the first six months of 2012 than it had been during the last six months of 2011, and incumbent Barack Obama was reelected.

The unemployment rate is a key macroeconomic statistic. But how does the Department of Labor prepare its estimates of the unemployment rate, and how accurate are these estimates? We will explore the answers to these questions in this section.

The Household Survey

Each month, the U.S. Census Bureau conducts the *Current Population Survey* (often called the *household survey*) to collect data needed to compute the unemployment rate. The bureau interviews adults in a sample of 60,000 households, chosen to represent the U.S. population, about the employment status of everyone in the household 16 years of age and older. The Department of Labor's Bureau of Labor Statistics (BLS) uses these data to calculate the monthly unemployment rate. People are considered:

Employed In government statistics, someone who currently has a job or who is temporarily away from his or her job.

- **Employed** if they worked during the week before the survey or if they were temporarily away from their jobs because they were ill, on vacation, on strike, or for other reasons

Unemployed In government statistics, someone who is not currently at work but who is available for work and who has actively looked for work during the previous month.

- **Unemployed** if they did not work in the previous week but were available for work and had actively looked for work at some time during the previous four weeks

Labor force The sum of employed and unemployed workers in the economy.

The **labor force** is the sum of employed and unemployed workers. The **unemployment rate** is the percentage of the labor force that is unemployed.

Unemployment rate The percentage of the labor force that is unemployed.

The BLS classifies the following groups of people who do not have a job and who are not actively looking for a job as *not in the labor force*:

- Retirees, homemakers, full-time students, patients in hospitals, and those on active military service or in prison.

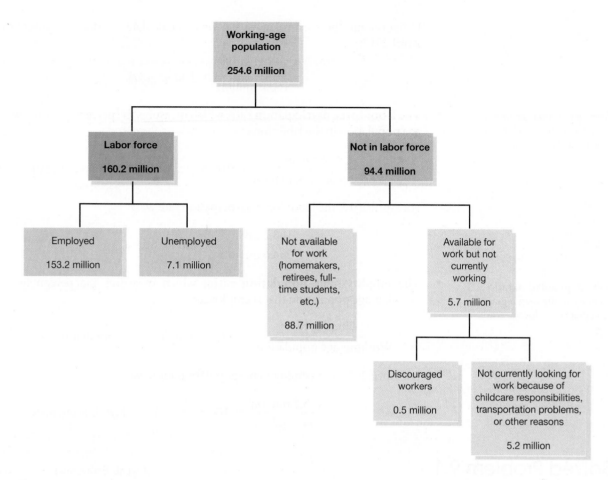

MyLab Economics Animation

Figure 9.1   **The Employment Status of the Civilian Working-Age Population, April 2017**

In April 2017, the working-age population of the United States was 254.6 million. The working-age population is divided into those in the labor force (160.2 million) and those not in the labor force (94.4 million). The labor force is divided into the employed (153.2 million) and the unemployed (7.1 million). Those not in the labor force are divided into those not available for work (88.7 million) and those available for work but not currently

working (5.7 million). Finally, those available for work but not in the labor force are divided into discouraged workers (0.5 million) and those not currently looking for work for other reasons (5.2 million).

Source: U.S. Department of Labor, Bureau of Labor Statistics, *The Employment Situation—April 2017*, May 5, 2017.

- People who are available for work and who have actively looked for a job at some point during the previous 12 months but have not looked during the previous 4 weeks. Some people are not actively looking for work for reasons such as childcare responsibilities or transportation difficulties.
- People who are available for work but have *not* actively looked for a job during the previous four weeks because they believe no jobs are available for them. These people are labeled **discouraged workers**.

Figure 9.1 shows the employment status of the civilian working-age population in April 2017.

We can use the information in the figure to calculate three important macroeconomic indicators:

- The unemployment rate, which measures the percentage of the labor force that is unemployed:

$$\frac{\text{Unemployed}}{\text{Labor force}} \times 100 = \text{Unemployment rate}.$$

Discouraged workers People who are available for work but have not looked for a job during the previous four weeks because they believe no jobs are available for them.

Using the numbers from Figure 9.1, we can calculate the unemployment rate for April 2017:

$$\frac{7.1 \text{ million}}{160.2 \text{ million}} \times 100 = 4.4\%.$$

Labor force participation rate
The percentage of the working-age population in the labor force.

- **The labor force participation rate**, which measures the percentage of the working-age population in the labor force:

$$\frac{\text{Labor force}}{\text{Working-age population}} \times 100 = \text{Labor force participation rate}.$$

For April 2017, the labor force participation rate was:

$$\frac{160.2 \text{ million}}{254.6 \text{ million}} \times 100 = 62.9\%.$$

Employment–population ratio
The percentage of the working-age population that is employed.

- **The employment–population ratio**, which measures the percentage of the working-age population that is employed:

$$\frac{\text{Employed}}{\text{Working-age population}} \times 100 = \text{Employment–population ratio}.$$

For April 2017, the employment–population ratio was:

$$\frac{153.2 \text{ million}}{254.6 \text{ million}} \times 100 = 60.2\%. \qquad \textbf{MyLab Economics} \text{ Concept Check}$$

Solved Problem 9.1

MyLab Economics Interactive Animation

What Happens if the BLS Includes the Military?

In the BLS household survey, people on active military service are not included in the totals for employment, the labor force, or the working-age population. Suppose the BLS included the military in these categories. How would the unemployment rate, the labor force participation rate, and the employment–population ratio change?

Solving the Problem

Step 1: **Review the chapter material.** This problem is about calculating the unemployment rate, the labor force participation rate, and the employment–population ratio, so you may want to review the section "Measuring the Unemployment Rate, the Labor Force Participation Rate, and the Employment–Population Ratio," which begins on page 280.

Step 2: **Show that including people in the military decreases the measured unemployment rate.** The unemployment rate is calculated as:

$$\frac{\text{Unemployed}}{\text{Labor force}} \times 100.$$

Including people in the military would increase the number of people counted as being in the labor force but would leave unchanged the number of people counted as unemployed. Therefore, the unemployment rate would decrease.

Step 3: **Show how including people in the military would affect the measured labor force participation rate and the measured employment–population ratio.** The labor force participation rate is calculated as:

$$\frac{\text{Labor force}}{\text{Working-age population}} \times 100,$$

and the employment–population ratio is calculated as:

$$\frac{\text{Employed}}{\text{Working-age population}} \times 100.$$

Including people in the military would increase the number of people in the labor force, the number of people employed, and the number of people in the working-age population, all by the same amount. The labor force participation rate and the employment–population ratio would both increase because adding the same number to both the numerator and the denominator of a fraction that is less than one increases the value of the fraction.

To help see this point, consider the following simple example. Suppose that 100,000,000 people are in the working-age population and 50,000,000 are in the labor force, not counting people in the military. Suppose that 1,000,000 people are in the military. Then, the labor force participation rate excluding the military is:

$$\frac{50,000,000}{100,000,000} \times 100 = 50\%,$$

and the labor force participation rate including the military is:

$$\frac{51,000,000}{101,000,000} \times 100 = 50.5.$$

A similar calculation shows that including the military would also increase the employment–population ratio.

Your Turn: For more practice, do related problem 1.8 on pages 307–308 at the end of this chapter.   MyLab Economics Study Plan

Problems with Measuring the Unemployment Rate

Although the BLS reports the unemployment rate measured to the tenth of a percentage point, it is not a perfect measure of the actual state of joblessness in the economy. One problem that the BLS confronts is distinguishing between people who are unemployed and people who are not in the labor force. During an economic recession, for example, an increase in discouraged workers usually occurs, as people who have had trouble finding a job stop actively looking. Because these workers are not counted as unemployed, the unemployment rate as measured by the BLS may understate the true degree of joblessness in the economy. The BLS also counts people as being employed if they hold part-time jobs but would prefer to hold full-time jobs. In a recession, counting as "employed" a part-time worker who wants to work full time makes the employment situation appear better than it is.

Not counting discouraged workers as unemployed and counting people as employed when they are working part time but would prefer to be working full time has a substantial effect on the measured unemployment rate. In Figure 9.2, the red line shows the official measure of the unemployment rate. The blue line shows what the unemployment rate would be if the BLS had counted as unemployed (1) all people who were available for work but not actively looking for jobs and (2) all people who were in part-time jobs but wanted full-time jobs. The difference between the two measures of the unemployment rate is substantial and was particularly large during the slow recovery following the 2007–2009 recession. In April 2017, using the broader definition of unemployment would have increased the measured unemployment rate from 4.4 percent to 8.6 percent.

There are other measurement problems, however, that cause the measured unemployment rate to *overstate* the true extent of joblessness. These problems arise because the BLS does not verify the responses of people included in the survey. Some people who claim to be unemployed and actively looking for work may not really be actively looking. A person might claim to be actively looking for a job in order to

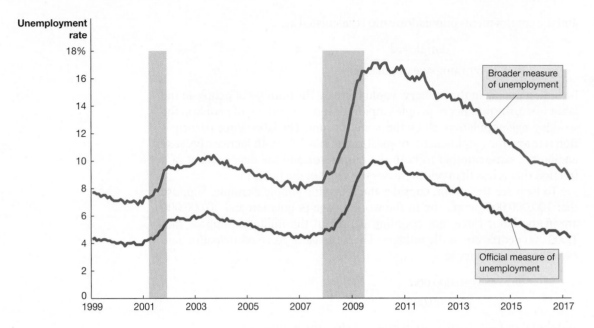

Figure 9.2   **The Official Unemployment Rate and a Broad Measure of the Unemployment Rate, 1999–2017**

The red line shows the official measure of the unemployment rate. The blue line shows what the unemployment rate would be if the BLS had counted as unemployed (1) all people who were available for work but not actively looking for jobs and (2) all people who were in part-time jobs but wanted full-time jobs. The difference between the measures was particularly large

during the 2007–2009 recession and the weak recovery that followed. Shaded areas indicate months during which the economy was in recession.

Note: The official measure (red line) is BLS series U-3, and the broader measure (blue line) is BLS series U-6.

Source: U.S. Bureau of Labor Statistics.

remain eligible for government payments to the unemployed. In this case, a person who is actually not in the labor force is counted as unemployed. Other people might be employed but engaged in illegal activity—such as drug dealing—or might want to conceal a legitimate job to avoid paying taxes. In these cases, individuals who are actually employed are counted as unemployed. These inaccurate responses to the survey bias the unemployment rate as measured by the BLS toward overstating the true extent of joblessness. We can conclude that, although the unemployment rate provides some useful information about the employment situation in the country, it is far from an exact measure of joblessness in the economy.   **MyLab Economics** Concept Check

Trends in Labor Force Participation

The labor force participation rate is important because it determines the amount of labor that will be available to the economy from a given population. The higher the labor force participation rate, the more labor that will be available and the higher a country's levels of GDP and GDP per person. Figure 9.3 highlights two important trends in the labor force participation rates of adults aged 16 years and over in the United States since 1948: the falling labor force participation rate of adult men and the rising labor force participation rate of adult women. (Note, though, that by 2016, the labor force participation rate of women had not yet returned to the level reached before the recession.)

The labor force participation rate of adult males fell from 87 percent in 1948 to 69 percent in 2016. Most of this decline was due to older men retiring earlier and younger men remaining in school longer. There has also been a decline in labor force participation among males who are not in school but who are too young to retire. Over the longer term, this decline in labor force participation among prime-age males appears to be partly due to Congress having made it easier for people to receive cash payments under the Social Security Disability Insurance program. In the shorter term, the decline may due to the lingering effects of the severe 2007–2009 recession.

The decline in the labor force participation rate of adult men has been more than offset by a sharp increase in the labor force participation rate of adult women, which

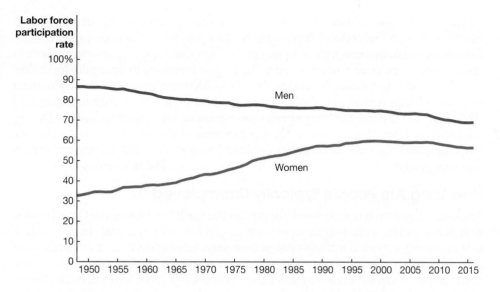

MyLab Economics Real-time data

Figure 9.3

Trends in the Labor Force: Participation Rates of Adult Men and Women since 1948

The labor force participation rate of adult men has declined gradually since 1948, while that of adult women has increased significantly, making the overall labor force participation rate higher today than it was in 1948.

Source: U.S. Bureau of Labor Statistics.

rose from 33 percent in 1948 to 57 percent in 2016. As a result, the overall labor force participation rate rose from 59 percent in 1948 to 63 percent in 2016. The increase in the labor force participation rate of women has several causes, including changing social attitudes due in part to the women's movement, federal legislation outlawing discrimination, increasing wages for women, the typical family having fewer children, and an increase in female-headed households.   **MyLab Economics** Concept Check

Unemployment Rates for Different Groups

Different groups in the population can have very different unemployment rates. Figure 9.4 shows unemployment rates in April 2017 for different ethnic groups and for groups with different levels of education. While the overall unemployment rate was 4.4 percent, Asians had an unemployment rate of 3.2 percent, and African Americans

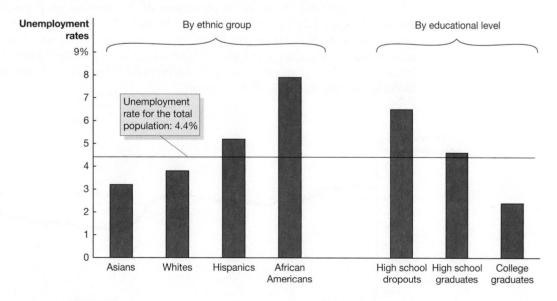

MyLab Economics Real-time data

Figure 9.4   **Unemployment Rates in the United States, April 2017**

The unemployment rate for African Americans is the highest of the four ethnic groups shown, while the unemployment rate for Asians is the lowest. High school dropouts have an unemployment rate that is more than double the unemployment rate for college graduates.

Notes: The unemployment rates for ethnic groups apply to people 16 years and older; the unemployment rates by educational attainment apply to people 25 years and older. People identified as Hispanic may be of any race.

Source: U.S. Department of Labor, Bureau of Labor Statistics, *The Employment Situation—April 2017*, May 5, 2017.

had an unemployment rate of 7.9 percent. The unemployment rate for people over age 25 without a high school degree was 6.5 percent, while the unemployment rate for college graduates was only 2.4 percent. Groups that have higher unemployment rates at any given time also experience the largest increases in unemployment during a recession. For example, during the 2007–2009 recession, the unemployment rates for African Americans, for Hispanics, and for high school dropouts increased more than did the unemployment rates for whites or for college graduates. During the recovery from that recession, the unemployment rates for African Americans, Hispanics, and high school dropouts declined by more than did the unemployment for other groups. **MyLab Economics** Concept Check

How Long Are People Typically Unemployed?

The longer a person is unemployed, the greater the hardship. During the Great Depression of the 1930s, some people were unemployed for years at a time. In the modern U.S. economy, a typical unemployed person stays unemployed for a relatively brief period of time, although that time lengthens significantly during a severe recession. For example, when the economy was expanding in early 2007, fewer than 20 percent of the unemployed had been jobless for more than six months. By the end of the 2007–2009 recession, though, half of the unemployed had been jobless for more than six months. The average period of unemployment had more than doubled from about 4 months to about 10 months. The severity of unemployment during and after the 2007–2009 recession was a sharp break with the normal U.S. experience, in which the typical person who loses a job will find another one or be recalled to a previous job within a few months. **MyLab Economics** Concept Check

 ## Apply the Concept   **MyLab Economics** Video

Eight Million Workers Are Missing!

Although the unemployment rate is the most widely followed measure of the state of the labor market, during the recovery from the 2007–2009 recession, many economists and policymakers became concerned about the employment–population ratio. As we saw earlier, this ratio measures the percentage of the working-age population that is employed. Figure 9.2 on page 284 shows that by mid-2017, the unemployment rate had fallen from its high of 10 percent in 2009 to 4.4 percent, or to levels consistent with most workers being able to find jobs without a long delay. But the red line in the figure below shows that the employment–population ratio did not recover completely from its decline during the 2007–2009 recession.

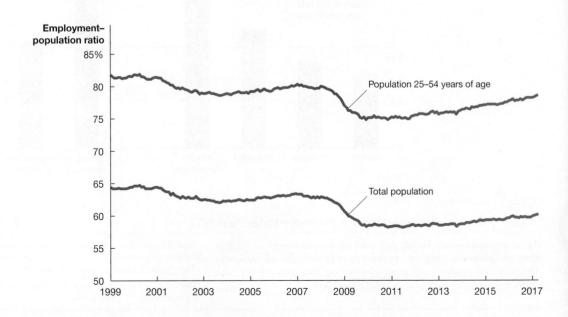

In 2006, before the start of the recession, the employment–population ratio was 63.4 percent. In April 2017, more than six years after the end of the recession, the ratio was still only 60.2 percent. If the employment–population ratio had regained its pre-recession level, an additional 8 million people would have been working in 2017 than actually were. With 8 million additional workers, GDP would have been significantly larger than it was.

Why hasn't the employment–population ratio returned to its pre-recession levels? Part of the explanation is that as the baby boom generation—people born between the years 1946 and 1964—has gotten older, the average age of the population has increased. Some people in their late 50s and older will have retired and so are less likely to have jobs than are younger people. This fact is illustrated by the blue line, which shows the employment–population ratio just for those in the prime working ages of 25 to 54. While the employment–population ratio for the whole working-age population declined by 3.2 percentage points between 2006 and 2017, the employment–population ratio for the prime-age population declined by 1.7 percentage points, or about half as much. Economists have not reached a consensus in explaining the remainder of the decline in the employment–population ratio, but here are several explanations they offer:

1. **"Labor market scarring."** The slow recovery from the 2007–2009 recession meant that some people were out of work for years. Often when people have not held a job for a long period, their skills deteriorate, and employers become more reluctant to hire them.
2. **An increased number of people receiving Social Security Disability Insurance.** Under this program, people with disabilities receive cash payments from the federal government and receive medical benefits under the Medicaid program. Some people who might otherwise be working are being supported by disability payments instead. Research by Alan Krueger of Princeton University indicates that about half of prime-age men who are not in labor force take pain medication, and most of them believe that their pain prevents from them taking full-time jobs. Interventions aimed at helping the disabled or those suffering from pain reenter the labor force may increase the employment–population ratio among the prime-age population.
3. **The Affordable Care Act.** Economists at the Congressional Budget Office (CBO) estimate that the Affordable Care Act, which provides subsidies to buy medical insurance and expands Medicaid coverage (see Chapter 5, Section 5.4), has resulted in a decline in employment. According to a CBO report, as a result of the act, "some people will decide not to work or to work fewer hours than would otherwise be the case—including some people who will choose to retire earlier than they would have otherwise, and some people who will work less themselves and rely more on a spouse's earnings."
4. **The minimum wage.** Economists Jeffrey Clemens and Michael Wither of the University of California, San Diego, analyzed the effects of the increase in the federal minimum wage from $5.15 an hour in 2007 to $7.25 an hour in 2009. They found that by making it more difficult for low-skilled workers to find jobs, the increase in the minimum wage reduced the employment–population ratio.
5. **Licensing requirements.** As we saw in Chapter 6, Section 6.1, new businesses are being started at lower rates than in past years, and barriers to entering certain occupations have increased as states have imposed additional licensing requirements. Difficulties in starting new businesses mean that some people who would otherwise be self-employed as small business owners may have left the labor force instead.
6. **Better videogames.** Mark Aguiar of Princeton University, and colleagues have noted that young men between the ages of 21 and 30 worked 12 percent fewer hours in 2015 than in 2000. This decline in employment was larger than for other groups. Aguiar and his colleagues argue that as much as 46 percent of the decline was due to improvements in videogames that led some young men to prefer leisure to working.

This hypothesis has proven controversial, with one official at the Federal Reserve noting that: "Japan has a lot of videogames, too, and they're not seeing the same effect that we are seeing here."

As we will see in later chapters, economic growth in the United States has slowed in recent years. Many economists believe that one key to increasing growth and living standards is for the government to develop policies that will help reverse the decline in the employment–population ratio.

Sources: Alan B. Krueger, "Where Have All the Workers Gone?" Federal Reserve Bank of Boston, 60th Economic Conference, October 14, 2016; Michael S. Derby, "Videogames Might Be Keeping Young Men Out of the Labor Force," *Wall Street Journal,* July 13, 2017; Doug Elmendorf, "Frequently Asked Questions about CBO's Estimates of the Labor Market Effects of the Affordable Care Act," cbo.gov, February 10, 2014; Jeffrey Clemens and Michael Wither, "The Minimum Wage and the Great Recession: Evidence of Effects on the Employment and Income Trajectories of Low-Skilled Workers," National Bureau of Economic Research 20724, December 2014; Janet L. Yellen, "Labor Market Dynamics and Monetary Policy," Speech at the Federal Reserve Bank of Kansas City Economic Symposium, Jackson Hole, Wyoming, August 22, 2014; Samuel Kapon and Joseph Tracy, "A Mis-Leading Labor Market Indicator," libertystreeteconomics.nyfed.org, February 3, 2014; and U.S. Bureau of Labor Statistics.

MyLab Economics Study Plan   **Your Turn:** Test your understanding by doing related problem 1.10 on page 308 at the end of this chapter.

The Establishment Survey: Another Measure of Employment

In addition to using the household survey, the BLS uses the *establishment survey,* sometimes called the *payroll survey,* to measure total employment in the economy. This monthly survey samples about 300,000 business establishments (such as factories, stores, and offices). A small company typically operates only one establishment, but a large company may operate many establishments. The establishment survey provides information on the total number of persons who are employed and *on a company payroll.* The establishment survey has four drawbacks:

1. The survey does not provide information on the number of self-employed persons because they are not on a company payroll.
2. The survey may fail to count some persons employed at newly opened firms that are not included in the survey.
3. The survey provides no information on unemployment.
4. The values for employment that the BLS initially announces can be significantly revised as data from additional establishments become available.

Despite these drawbacks, the establishment survey has the advantage of being determined by actual payrolls rather than by unverified answers, as is the case with the household survey. As a result, many economists rely more on establishment survey data than on household survey data in analyzing current labor market conditions. Some financial analysts who forecast the future state of the economy to help forecast stock prices also rely more on establishment survey data than on household survey data.

Table 9.1 shows household survey and establishment survey data for the months of March and April 2017. Notice that the household survey, because it includes the self-employed, gives a larger total for employment than does the establishment survey. The household survey provides information on the number of persons unemployed

Table 9.1   Household and Establishment Survey Data for March and April 2017   **MyLab Economics** Real-Time Data

	Household Survey			Establishment Survey		
	March	**April**	**Change**	**March**	**April**	**Change**
Employed	153,000,000	153,156,000	156,000	145,852,000	146,063,000	211,000
Unemployed	7,202,000	7,056,000	−146,000			
Labor force	160,201,000	160,213,000	12,000			
Unemployment rate	4.5%	4.4%	−0.1%			

Source: U.S. Department of Labor, Bureau of Labor Statistics, *The Employment Situation—April 2017,* May 5, 2017.

and on the number of persons in the labor force. This information is not available in the establishment survey. Between March and April 2017, employment rose by 211,000 in the establishment survey, but it rose by only 156,000 in the household survey. This discrepancy is due partly to the slightly different groups covered by the two surveys and partly to inaccuracies in the surveys.   **MyLab Economics** Concept Check

Revisions in the Establishment Survey Employment Data: How Bad Was the 2007–2009 Recession?

Economists and policymakers rely on government economic data, such as employment data from the establishment survey, to understand the current state of the economy. Given the size of the U.S. economy, though, government agencies, such as the Bureau of Economic Analysis, the Bureau of Labor Statistics, and the Census Bureau, need considerable time to gather complete and accurate data on GDP, employment, and other macroeconomic variables. To avoid long waits in supplying data to policymakers and the general public, government agencies typically issue preliminary estimates that they revise as additional information becomes available. As we noted earlier, the data on employment from the establishment survey can be subject to particularly large revisions over time.

Figure 9.5 shows for each month from December 2007 to December 2010 the difference between the value for the change in employment as initially reported in the establishment survey and the revised value available in April 2017. The green bars show months for which the BLS revised its preliminary estimates to show that fewer jobs were lost (or more jobs were created) than originally reported, and the red bars show months for which the BLS revised its preliminary estimates to show that more jobs were lost (or fewer jobs were created). For example, the BLS initially reported that employment declined by 159,000 jobs during September 2008. In fact, after additional data became available, the BLS revised its estimate to show that employment had declined by 450,000 jobs during the month—a difference of nearly 300,000 more jobs lost. As the recession deepened between April 2008 and April 2009, the BLS's initial reports underestimated the number of jobs lost by 2.3 million. In other words, the recession of 2007–2009 turned out to be much more severe than economists and policymakers realized at the time. In later chapters, we'll discuss how policymakers try to take into account the potential inaccuracy of the government's initial data releases when formulating economic policy.   **MyLab Economics** Concept Check

Job Creation and Job Destruction over Time

One important fact about employment is not very well known: The U.S. economy creates and destroys millions of jobs every year. (This process of the economy creating and destroying jobs is sometimes called *labor market churn*.) In 2016, for example, the economy

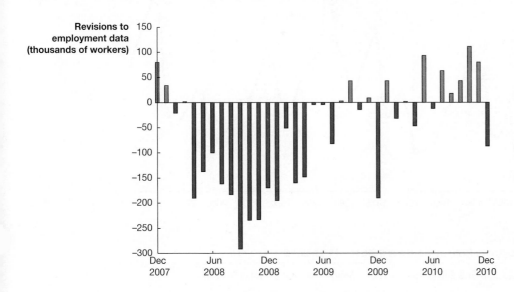

MyLab Economics Animation

Figure 9.5

Revisions to Employment Changes, as Reported in the Establishment Survey, 2007–2010

Over time, the BLS revises its preliminary estimates of changes in employment. During the 2007–2009 recession, many more jobs were lost than the preliminary estimates showed. The green bars show months for which the BLS revised its preliminary estimates to show that fewer jobs were lost (or that more jobs were created), and the red bars show months for which the BLS revised its preliminary estimates to show that more jobs were lost (or that fewer jobs were created).

Source: U.S. Bureau of Labor Statistics.

created about 29.6 million jobs and destroyed about 28.0 million jobs. This degree of job creation and destruction is not surprising in a vibrant market system where new firms are constantly being started, some existing firms are expanding, some existing firms are contracting, and some firms are going out of business. The creation and destruction of jobs results from changes in consumer tastes, technological progress, and the successes and failures of entrepreneurs in responding to the opportunities and challenges of shifting consumer tastes and technological change. The large volume of job creation and job destruction helps explain why during most years, the typical person who loses a job is unemployed for a relatively brief period of time.

When the BLS announces each month the increases or decreases in the number of persons employed and unemployed, these are net figures. That is, the change in the number of persons employed is equal to the total number of jobs created minus the number of jobs eliminated. Take, for example, the months from September to December 2016. During that period, the economy created 7,465,000 jobs and eliminated 7,089,000 jobs, for a net increase of 376,000 jobs. Because the net change is so much smaller than the total job increases and decreases, the net change doesn't fully represent how dynamic the U.S. job market really is.

MyLab Economics Study Plan   MyLab Economics Concept Check

 Types of Unemployment

LEARNING OBJECTIVE: Identify the three types of unemployment.

Figure 9.6 illustrates that the unemployment rate follows the business cycle, rising during recessions and falling during expansions. (The shaded areas in the figure represent years in which the U.S. economy was in a recession.) Notice, though, that the unemployment rate never falls to zero. To understand why, we need to discuss the three types of unemployment:

1. Frictional unemployment
2. Structural unemployment
3. Cyclical unemployment

Frictional Unemployment and Job Search

Workers have different skills, interests, and abilities, and jobs have different skill requirements, working conditions, and pay levels. As a result, a new worker entering

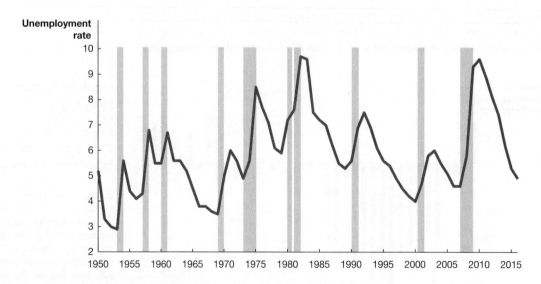

MyLab Economics Real-time data

Figure 9.6   **The Annual Unemployment Rate in the United States, 1950–2016**

The unemployment rate rises during recessions and falls during expansions. Shaded areas indicate recessions.

Source: U.S. Bureau of Labor Statistics.

the labor force or a worker who has lost a job probably will not find an acceptable job right away. Most workers spend at least some time in *job search*, just as most firms spend time searching for a new person to fill a job opening. **Frictional unemployment** is short-term unemployment that arises from the process of matching workers with jobs. Some frictional unemployment is unavoidable. As we have seen, the U.S. economy creates and destroys millions of jobs each year. The process of job search takes time, so there will always be some workers who are frictionally unemployed because they are between jobs and in the process of searching for new ones.

Seasonal unemployment refers to frictional unemployment due to factors such as weather or variations in tourism and other calendar-related events. For example, stores located in beach resort areas reduce their hiring during the winter, and ski resorts reduce their hiring during the summer. Department stores increase their hiring in November and December and reduce their hiring after New Year's Day. In agricultural areas, employment increases during harvest season and declines thereafter. Construction workers in many parts of the United States experience greater unemployment during the winter than during the summer. Because seasonal unemployment can make the unemployment rate seem artificially high during some months and artificially low during other months, the BLS reports two unemployment rates each month—one that is *seasonally adjusted* and one that is not seasonally adjusted. The seasonally adjusted data eliminate the effects of seasonal unemployment. Economists and policymakers rely on the seasonally adjusted data as a more accurate measure of the current state of the labor market.

Would eliminating all frictional unemployment be good for the economy? No, because some frictional unemployment actually increases economic efficiency. Frictional unemployment occurs because workers and firms take the time necessary to ensure a good match between the attributes of workers and the characteristics of jobs. By devoting time to job search, workers end up with jobs they find satisfying and in which they can be productive. Of course, having workers who are satisfied and productive is also in the best interest of firms. **MyLab Economics** Concept Check

> **Frictional unemployment** Short-term unemployment that arises from the process of matching workers with jobs.

Structural Unemployment

Computer-generated three-dimensional animation has replaced traditional hand-drawn two-dimensional animation in most films and television shows. As a result, many people who are highly skilled in hand-drawn animation lost their jobs. To become employed again, they had to either become skilled in computer-generated animation or find new occupations. In the meantime, they were unemployed. Economists consider people in situations like these animators faced *structurally unemployed*. **Structural unemployment** arises from a persistent mismatch between the job skills or attributes of workers and the requirements of jobs. While frictional unemployment is short term, structural unemployment can last for longer periods because workers need time to learn new skills. For example, employment by U.S. steel firms fell by more than half between the early 1980s and the early 2000s, and employment by U.S. furniture firms fell by more than 40 percent between 2000 and 2017. In both cases, the employment declines resulted from competition from foreign producers and technological change that substituted machines for workers. Many steelworkers and furniture workers found new jobs in other industries only after lengthy periods of retraining.

> **Structural unemployment** Unemployment that arises from a persistent mismatch between the skills or attributes of workers and the requirements of jobs.

Some workers lack even basic skills, such as literacy, or have addictions to alcohol or other drugs that make it difficult for them to perform adequately the duties of almost any job. These workers may remain structurally unemployed for long periods. **MyLab Economics** Concept Check

Cyclical Unemployment

When the economy moves into a recession, many firms find their sales falling and cut back on production. As production falls, firms start laying off workers. Workers who lose their jobs because of a recession are experiencing **cyclical unemployment**. For example, Ford Motor Company laid off workers during the recession of

> **Cyclical unemployment** Unemployment caused by a business cycle recession.

2007–2009. As the economy slowly recovered from the recession, Ford began rehiring those workers. The Ford workers who had been laid off from their jobs during the recession and then rehired during the following expansion had experienced cyclical unemployment.   **MyLab Economics** Concept Check

Full Employment

As the economy moves through the expansion phase of the business cycle, cyclical unemployment eventually drops to zero. The unemployment rate will not be zero, however, because of frictional and structural unemployment. As Figure 9.6 shows, the unemployment rate in the United States is rarely less than 4 percent. The fluctuations that we see in Figure 9.6 are mainly due to the changes in the level of cyclical unemployment. When the only remaining unemployment is structural and frictional unemployment, the economy is said to be at *full employment*.

Economists consider the sum of frictional and structural unemployment to be the normal underlying level of unemployment in the economy, or the **natural rate of unemployment**. Economists disagree on the exact value of the natural rate of unemployment, and there is good reason to believe that it doesn't remain constant over long periods of a decade or more. Currently, most economists estimate the natural rate to be between 4.0 percent and 5.0 percent. The natural rate of unemployment is also sometimes called the *full-employment rate of unemployment*.   **MyLab Economics** Concept Check

Natural rate of unemployment
The normal rate of unemployment, consisting of frictional unemployment and structural unemployment.

MyLab Economics Study Plan

Apply the Concept

MyLab Economics Video

How Should We Categorize the Unemployment Resulting from Boeing's Layoffs?

Travis Dove/Bloomberg/Getty Images

Which category of unemployment do the workers laid off at Boeing fit into?

We saw at the beginning of the chapter that Boeing announced in 2017 that it was laying off 1,800 workers in addition to the 7,000 workers it had cut the year before. Did these layoffs result in an increase in frictional unemployment, structural unemployment, or cyclical unemployment? In answering this question, we should acknowledge that dividing unemployment into these three categories is useful in understanding the sources of unemployment, but it can be difficult to apply these categories in a particular case. The BLS, for instance, provides estimates of total unemployment but does not classify it as frictional, structural, or cyclical.

Despite these difficulties, we can roughly categorize the unemployment resulting from the layoffs at Boeing. At the time of the layoffs in 2016 and 2017, the U.S. economy was expanding, and the U.S. unemployment rate had declined to less than 4.5 percent. The economies of the European and Asian countries to which Boeing sells jetliners were also expanding. So the layoffs at Boeing were not increasing cyclical unemployment, and the firm was unlikely to rehire the workers it was laying off, even if the economic recovery continued in future years.

In discussing Boeing's decision to lay off workers, an article in the *Wall Street Journal* noted that "Boeing in recent years has invested heavily in automated manufacturing equipment." Because other aerospace firms have been adopting similar technology, some of the laid-off Boeing workers were likely to need to retrain for other jobs before becoming employed again. So, these workers were structurally unemployed. Boeing was also laying off some workers because of declines in military spending by the federal government. In 2017, President Donald Trump was proposing increases in military spending including on Boeing's Super Hornet jet fighter, which is assembled in a factory in St. Louis, but it was uncertain whether Congress would approve the increases. Unless military spending increases, the workers Boeing laid off would be structurally unemployed because other defense contractors were facing similar cutbacks.

But Boeing was also laying off some workers because it was losing sales to Airbus and to Bombardier. Although Airbus is a European firm and Bombardier is a Canadian firm, both assemble some planes in the United States. If laid off Boeing workers eventually find jobs at these firms, then these workers would have been frictionally unemployed during the time they were out of work.

It therefore seems likely that some of the unemployment resulting from Boeing's layoffs was structural and some was frictional. Given the state of the economy, none of it was likely cyclical.

Sources: Julie Johnsson, "Boeing to Dismiss Hundreds of Engineers Amid Sales Slowdown," bloomberg.com, April 17, 2017; Doug Cameron, "More Than 1,800 Boeing Employees Accept Voluntary Buyouts," *Wall Street Journal*, March 3, 2017; Jon Ostrower, "Jet Prices Take Center Stage in Boeing Job Cuts," *Wall Street Journal*, March 31, 2016; and Doug Cameron, "Boeing to Cut Defense Jobs," *Wall Street Journal*, November 15, 2016.

Your Turn: Test your understanding by doing related problems 2.5, 2.6, and 2.7 on pages 308–309 at the end of this chapter.

MyLab Economics Study Plan

9.3 Explaining Unemployment

LEARNING OBJECTIVE: Explain what factors determine the unemployment rate.

In this section, we look at the factors that determine the levels of frictional and structural unemployment. In later chapters, we will explore the causes of the business cycle, which will help us understand cyclical unemployment.

Government Policies and the Unemployment Rate

Workers search for jobs by sending out résumés, registering with Internet job sites such as indeed.com, and getting job referrals from friends and relatives. Firms fill job openings by advertising in newspapers, listing openings online, participating in job fairs, and recruiting on college campuses. Here's how government policies can aid these private employment efforts:

- Governments can help reduce the level of frictional unemployment with policies that speed up matching unemployed workers with unfilled jobs. Government-sponsored job fairs are an example of this type of policy.
- Governments can help reduce structural unemployment by implementing policies that aid worker retraining. For example, the federal government's Trade Adjustment Assistance program offers training to workers who lose their jobs as a result of competition from foreign firms.

Some government policies, however, can add to the level of frictional and structural unemployment. These government policies increase the unemployment rate either by increasing the time workers devote to searching for jobs, by providing disincentives for firms to hire workers, or by keeping wages above their market level.

Unemployment Insurance and Other Payments to the Unemployed

Suppose you have been in the labor force for a few years but have just lost your job. You could probably find a low-wage job immediately if you needed to—perhaps at Walmart or McDonald's. But you might decide to search for a better, higher-paying job by sending out résumés and responding to want ads and Internet job postings. Remember that the *opportunity cost* of any activity is the highest-valued alternative that you must give up to engage in that activity. In this case, the opportunity cost of continuing to search for a job is the salary you are giving up at the job you could have taken. The longer you search, the greater your chances of finding a better, higher-paying job, but the longer you search, the more salary you have given up by not working, so the greater the opportunity cost.

In the United States and most other high-income countries, the unemployed are eligible for *unemployment insurance payments* from the government. In the United States, these payments vary by state but are generally equal to about half the average wage. The unemployed spend more time searching for jobs because they receive these payments. This additional time spent searching raises the unemployment rate. Can we conclude that the unemployment insurance program is a bad idea? Most economists would say "no." Before Congress established the unemployment insurance program at the end of the 1930s, unemployed workers suffered very large declines in their incomes, which led them to greatly reduce their spending. This reduced spending contributed to the severity of recessions. Unemployment insurance helps the unemployed maintain their income and spending, which lessens the personal hardship of being unemployed and also helps reduce the severity of recessions.

In the United States, unemployed workers are generally eligible to receive unemployment insurance payments for only six months, although this period is typically extended during recessions, as happened during and after the recession of 2007–2009. After that, the opportunity cost of continuing to search for a job rises. In many other high-income countries, such as Canada and most of the countries of Western Europe, workers are eligible to receive unemployment payments for a year or more, and the payments may equal as much as 70 percent of their previous wage. In addition, many of these countries have generous *social insurance programs* that allow unemployed adults to receive some government payments even after their eligibility for unemployment insurance has ended. In the United States, very few government programs make payments to healthy adults, with the exception of the Temporary Assistance for Needy Families program, which allows single parents to receive payments for up to five years. Although there are many reasons unemployment rates may differ across countries, most economists believe that because the opportunity cost of job search is lower in Canada and the countries of Western Europe, unemployed workers in those countries search longer for jobs and, therefore, the unemployment rates in those countries tend to be higher than in the United States. During the 2007–2009 recession, however, unemployment rates were lower in Canada and Germany than in the United States.

Minimum Wage Laws In 1938, the federal government enacted a national minimum wage law. At first, the lowest legal wage firms could pay workers was $0.25 per hour. Over the years, Congress has gradually raised the minimum wage; in 2017, it was $7.25 per hour. Some states and cities also have minimum wage laws. For example, in 2017, the minimum wage in California was $10.50 per hour, and the minimum wage in San Francisco was $14.00 per hour. If the minimum wage is set above the market wage determined by the demand and supply of labor, the quantity of labor supplied will be greater than the quantity of labor demanded. Some workers who would have been employed if there were no minimum wage will become unemployed. As a result, the unemployment rate will be higher than it would be without a minimum wage. Economists agree that the current minimum wage is above the market wage for some workers, but they disagree on the amount of unemployment that has resulted. Because teenagers generally have relatively few job-related skills, they are the group most likely to receive the minimum wage. Studies estimate that a 10 percent increase in the minimum wage reduces teenage employment by about 2 percent. Because teenagers and others receiving the minimum wage are less than 4 percent of the labor force, most economists believe that to this point the minimum wage has had a fairly small effect on the unemployment rate in the United States. **MyLab Economics** Concept Check

Labor Unions

Labor unions are organizations of workers that bargain with employers for higher wages and better working conditions for their members. In unionized industries, the wage is usually above what otherwise would be the market wage. This above-market wage results in employers in unionized industries hiring fewer workers, but does it also significantly increase the overall unemployment rate in the economy? Most economists would say the answer is "no" because in the United States only about 6.5 percent of workers outside the government sector are unionized. Although unions remain strong in a few industries, such as airlines, automobiles, steel, and telecommunications, most industries are not unionized. The result is that most workers who can't find jobs in unionized industries because the wage is above its market level can find jobs in other industries. **MyLab Economics** Concept Check

Efficiency Wages

Some firms pay above-market wages not because the government requires them to or because they are unionized but because they believe doing so will increase their profits. Because wages are the largest cost for many employers, paying higher wages seems like a good way for firms to *lower* profits rather than to increase them. The key to understanding this wage policy is that the level of wages can affect the level of workers' productivity. Many studies have shown that workers are motivated by higher wages to work harder. An **efficiency wage** is an above-market wage that a firm pays to motivate workers to be more productive. Can't firms ensure that workers work hard by supervising them? In some cases, they can. For example, a telemarketing firm can monitor workers electronically to ensure that they make the required number of phone calls per hour. In many business situations, however, it is much more difficult to monitor workers. Many firms must rely on workers being motivated enough to work hard. By paying an above-market wage, a firm raises the cost to workers of losing their jobs because many alternative jobs will pay only the market wage. The increase in productivity that results from paying the high wage can more than offset the extra cost of the wage, thereby lowering the firm's costs of production.

Efficiency wage An above-market wage that a firm pays to increase workers' productivity.

Because the efficiency wage is above the market wage, it results in the quantity of labor supplied being greater than the quantity of labor demanded, just as do minimum wage laws and labor unions. So, efficiency wages also contribute to economies experiencing some unemployment even when cyclical unemployment is zero.   **MyLab Economics** Concept Check

MyLab Economics Study Plan

9.4 | Measuring Inflation

LEARNING OBJECTIVE: Define the price level and the inflation rate and understand how they are computed.

One of the facts of economic life is that the prices of most goods and services rise over time. As a result, the cost of living continually rises. In 1914, Henry Ford began paying his workers a wage of $5 per day, which was more than twice as much as other automobile manufacturers were paying. Ford's $5-a-day wage provided his workers with a middle-class income because prices were so low. In 1914, Ford's Model T, the best-selling car in the country, sold for less than $600, the price of a man's suit was $15, the price of a ticket to a movie theater was $0.15, and the price of a box of Kellogg's Corn Flakes was $0.08. In 2017, with the cost of living being much higher than it was in 1914, the federal minimum wage law required firms to pay a wage of at least $7.25 per *hour*, more than Ford's highly paid workers earned in a day.

Knowing how the government compiles the employment and unemployment statistics is important in interpreting them. The same is true of the government's statistics on the cost of living. The **price level** measures the average prices of goods and services in the economy (see Chapter 8, Section 8.3). The **inflation rate** is the percentage increase in the price level from one year to the next. In the last chapter, we introduced the *GDP deflator* as a measure of the price level. The GDP deflator is the broadest measure we have of the price level because it includes the price of every final good and service. But for some purposes, it is too broad. For example, if we want to know how inflation affects a typical household, the GDP price deflator may be misleading because it includes the prices of products such as large electric generators and machine tools that are part of the investment component of GDP but are not purchased by households. In this chapter, we will focus on measuring the inflation rate by changes in the *consumer price index* because changes in this index come closest to measuring changes in the cost of living as experienced by a typical household. We will also briefly discuss a third measure of inflation: the *producer price index*.

Price level A measure of the average prices of goods and services in the economy.

Inflation rate The percentage increase in the price level from one year to the next.

The Consumer Price Index

To obtain prices of a representative group of goods and services, the BLS surveys 14,000 households nationwide on their spending habits. It uses the results of this survey to construct a *market basket* of 211 types of goods and services purchased by a typical

Figure 9.7

The CPI Market Basket, December 2016

The Bureau of Labor Statistics surveys 14,000 households on their spending habits. The results are used to construct a *market basket* of goods and services purchased by a typical urban family of four. The chart shows these goods and services, grouped into eight broad categories. The percentages represent the expenditure shares of the categories within the market basket. The categories housing, transportation, and food make up almost three-quarters of the market basket.

Source: U.S. Bureau of Labor Statistics.

- Other goods and services 3.2%
- Education and communication 7.0%
- Recreation 5.7%
- Medical care 8.5%
- Transportation 15.3%
- Apparel 3.0%
- Housing 42.6%
- Food and beverages 14.7%

Consumer price index (CPI) A measure of the average of the prices a typical urban family of four pays for the goods and services they purchase.

urban family of four. Figure 9.7 shows the goods and services in the market basket, grouped into eight broad categories. Almost three-quarters of the market basket falls into just three categories: housing, transportation, and food. Each month, hundreds of BLS employees visit 23,000 stores in 87 cities and record prices of the goods and services in the market basket. Each price in the consumer price index is given a weight equal to the fraction of a typical family's budget spent on that good or service.

The **consumer price index (CPI)** is a measure of the average of the prices a typical urban family of four pays for the goods and services they purchase. One year is chosen as the base year, and the value of the CPI is set equal to 100 for that year. In any year other than the base year, the CPI is equal to the ratio of the dollar amount necessary to buy the market basket of goods in that year divided by the dollar amount necessary to buy the market basket of goods in the base year, multiplied by 100. Because the CPI measures the cost to a typical family of buying a representative basket of goods and services, it is sometimes called the *cost-of-living index*.

A simple example can clarify how the CPI is constructed. For purposes of this example, we assume that the market basket has only three products: eye examinations, pizzas, and books:

Product	Base Year (2010)			2018		2019	
	Quantity	Price	Expenditures	Price	Expenditures (on base-year quantities)	Price	Expenditures (on base-year quantities)
Eye examinations	1	$50	$50	$100	$100	$85	$85
Pizzas	20	10	200	15	300	14.00	280
Books	20	25	500	25	500	27.50	550
TOTAL			$750		$900		$915

Suppose that during the base year, 2010, a survey determines that each month, a typical family purchases 1 eye examination, 20 pizzas, and 20 books. At 2010 prices, a family must spend $750 to purchase this market basket of goods and services. The CPI for every year after the base year is determined by dividing the amount necessary to purchase the market basket in that year by the amount required in the base year, then multiplying by 100. Notice that the quantities of the products purchased in 2018 and

2019 are irrelevant in calculating the CPI because *we are assuming that households buy the same market basket of products each month.* Using the numbers in the table, we can calculate the CPI for 2018 and 2019:

Formula	Applied to 2018	Applied to 2019
$CPI = \dfrac{\text{Expenditures in the current year}}{\text{Expenditures in the base year}} \times 100$	$\left(\dfrac{\$900}{\$750}\right) \times 100 = 120$	$\left(\dfrac{\$915}{\$750}\right) \times 100 = 122$

How do we interpret values such as 120 and 122? First, recognize that they are *index numbers*, which means they are not measured in dollars or any other units. *The CPI is intended to measure changes in the price level over time.* We can't use the CPI to tell us in an absolute sense how high the price level is—only how much it has changed over time. We measure the inflation rate as the percentage increase in the CPI from one year to the next. For our simple example, the inflation rate in 2019 would be the percentage change in the CPI from 2018 to 2019:

$$\left(\frac{122 - 120}{120}\right) \times 100 = 1.7\%.$$

Because the CPI is designed to measure the cost of living, we can also say that the cost of living increased by 1.7 percent during 2019. **MyLab Economics** Concept Check

Is the CPI Accurate?

The CPI is the most widely used measure of inflation. Policymakers use the CPI to track the state of the economy. Businesses use it to help set the prices of their products and the wages and salaries of their employees. Each year, the federal government increases the Social Security payments made to retired workers by an amount equal to the percentage increase in the CPI during the previous year. In setting alimony and child support payments in divorce cases, judges often order that the payments increase each year by the inflation rate, as measured by the CPI.

Don't Let This Happen to You

Don't Miscalculate the Inflation Rate

Suppose you are given the data in the following table and are asked to calculate the inflation rate for 2016:

Year	CPI
2015	237
2016	240

It is tempting to avoid any calculations and simply report that the inflation rate in 2016 was 140 percent because 240 is a 140 percent increase from 100. But 140 percent would be the wrong

answer. A value for the CPI of 240 in 2016 tells us that the price level in 2016 was 140 percent higher than in the *base year*, but the inflation rate is the percentage increase in the price level from the *previous year, not* the percentage increase from the base year. The correct calculation of the inflation rate for 2016 is:

$$\left(\frac{240 - 237}{237}\right) \times 100 = 1.3\%.$$

MyLab Economics Study Plan

Your Turn: Test your understanding by doing related problems 4.4 and 4.5 on page 310 at the end of this chapter.

It is important that the CPI be as accurate as possible, but four biases cause changes in the CPI to overstate the true inflation rate:

1. **Substitution bias.** In constructing the CPI, the BLS assumes that each month, consumers purchase the same amount of each product in the market basket. In fact, consumers are likely to buy fewer of the products that increase most in price

and more of the products that increase least in price (or fall the most in price). For instance, if apple prices rise rapidly during a particular month while orange prices fall, consumers will reduce their apple purchases and increase their orange purchases. Therefore, the prices of the market basket consumers actually buy will rise less than the prices of the market basket the BLS uses to compute the CPI.

2. **Increase in quality bias.** Over time, most products included in the CPI improve in quality: Automobiles get better gas mileage and side air bags become standard equipment, smartphones have better processors and more memory, dishwashers use less water while getting dishes cleaner, and so on. Increases in the prices of these products partly reflect their improved quality and partly are pure inflation. The BLS attempts to make adjustments so that only the pure inflation part of price increases is included in the CPI. These adjustments are difficult to make, however, so the recorded price increases overstate the pure inflation in some products.

3. **New product bias.** For many years, the BLS updated the market basket of goods used in computing the CPI only every 10 years. So, new products introduced between updates were not included in the market basket. For example, the 1987 update took place before cellphones were introduced. Although millions of U.S. households used cellphones by the mid-1990s, they were not included in the CPI until the 1997 update. The prices of many products, such as cellphones, Blu-ray players, and 4K televisions, decrease in the years immediately after they are introduced. If the market basket is not updated frequently, these price decreases are not included in the CPI.

4. **Outlet bias.** During the mid-1990s, many consumers began to increase their purchases from discount stores such as Sam's Club and Costco. By the late 1990s, the Internet began to account for a significant fraction of sales of some products. Because the BLS continued to collect price statistics from traditional full-price retail stores, the CPI did not reflect the prices some consumers actually paid.

Most economists believe these biases cause changes in the CPI to overstate the true inflation rate by 0.5 percentage point to 1 percentage point. That is, if the CPI indicates that the inflation rate is 2 percent, the actual inflation rate is probably between 1 percent and 1.5 percent. The BLS continues to take steps to reduce the size of the bias. For example, the BLS has reduced the size of the substitution and new product biases by updating the market basket every 2 years rather than every 10 years. The BLS has reduced the size of the outlet bias by conducting a point-of-purchase survey to track where consumers actually make their purchases. Finally, the BLS has used statistical methods to reduce the size of the quality bias. Prior to these changes, the size of the total bias in the CPI was probably greater than 1 percentage point.   **MyLab Economics** Concept Check

The Producer Price Index

Producer price index (PPI) An average of the prices received by producers of goods and services at all stages of the production process.

In addition to the GDP deflator and the CPI, the government also computes the **producer price index (PPI)**. Like the CPI, the PPI tracks the prices of a market basket of goods. But while the CPI tracks the prices of goods and services purchased by a typical household, the PPI tracks the prices firms receive for goods and services at all stages of production. The PPI includes the prices of intermediate goods, such as flour, yarn, steel, and lumber; and raw materials, such as raw cotton, coal, and crude petroleum. If the prices of these goods rise, the cost to firms of producing final goods and services will rise, which may lead firms to increase the prices of goods and services purchased by consumers. Changes in the PPI therefore can give an early warning of future movements in the CPI.   **MyLab Economics** Concept Check

MyLab Economics Study Plan

9.5 Using Price Indexes to Adjust for the Effects of Inflation

LEARNING OBJECTIVE: Use price indexes to adjust for the effects of inflation.

You are likely to receive a much higher salary after graduation than your parents did 25 or more years ago, but prices 25 years ago were, on average, much lower than prices today. In other words, the purchasing power of a dollar was much higher 25 years ago because the prices of most goods and services were much lower. Price indexes such as the CPI give us a way of adjusting for the effects of inflation so that we can compare dollar values from different years.

For example, suppose your mother received a salary of $25,000 in 1991. By using the CPI, we can calculate what $25,000 in 1991 was equivalent to in 2016. The CPI is 136 for 1991 and 240 for 2016. Because $240/136 = 1.8$, we know that, on average, prices were almost twice as high in 2016 as in 1991. We can use this result to inflate a salary of $25,000 received in 1991 to its value in terms of 2016 purchasing power:

$$\text{Value in 2016 dollars} = \text{Value in 1991 dollars} \times \left(\frac{\text{CPI in 2016}}{\text{CPI in 1991}}\right)$$

$$= \$25,000 \times \left(\frac{240}{136}\right) = \$44,118.$$

Our calculation shows that if you were paid a salary of $44,118 in 2016, you would be able to purchase roughly the same amount of goods and services that your mother could have purchased with a salary of $25,000 in 1991. Economic variables that are calculated in current-year prices are called *nominal variables*. The calculation we have just made uses a price index to adjust a nominal variable—your mother's salary—for the effects of inflation.

For some purposes, we are interested in tracking changes in an economic variable over time rather than in seeing what its value would be in today's dollars. In that case, to correct for the effects of inflation, we can divide the nominal variable by a price index and multiply by 100 to obtain a *real variable*. The real variable will be measured in dollars of the base year for the price index. Currently, the base year for the CPI is the average of prices in the years 1982 to 1984. **MyLab Economics** Concept Check   **MyLab Economics** Study Plan

Solved Problem 9.5

MyLab Economics Interactive Animation

What Has Been Happening to Real Wages in the United States?

In addition to data on employment, the BLS establishment survey gathers data on average hourly earnings of all employees working at private firms. Average hourly earnings are the wages or salaries earned by these employees per hour. Economists and policymakers closely follow changes in average hourly earnings because they are a broad measure of a typical employee's income. Note, though, that in order to measure changes in the purchasing power of these earnings, we have to convert the nominal values reported by the BLS to real values. Use the information in the following table to compute real average hourly earnings for each year. (Note that the CPI would increase slightly between 2014 and 2015 if we carry its

value out to one decimal point. We don't do so to simplify the calculation.) Compare the percentage change in nominal average hourly earnings between 2015 and 2016 with the percentage change in real average hourly earnings. Be sure to explain what the values you calculate for real average hourly earnings represent.

Year	Nominal Average Hourly Earnings	CPI (1982 – 1984 = 100)
2014	$24.46	237
2015	$25.01	237
2016	$25.67	240

Solving the Problem

Step 1: Review the chapter material. This problem is about using price indexes to correct for the effects of inflation, so you may want to review the section "Using Price Indexes to Adjust for the Effects of Inflation," which begins on page 298.

Step 2: Define real average hourly earnings, calculate the value of real average hourly earnings for each year, and explain what the values you calculated represent. Nominal average hourly earnings are the number of dollars a worker receives. To calculate real average hourly earnings, we have to divide the nominal average earnings by the CPI for that year and multiply by 100. For example, real average hourly earnings for 2014 equal:

$$\left(\frac{\$24.46}{237}\right) \times 100 = \$10.32.$$

The results for all three years are:

Year	Nominal Average Hourly Earnings	CPI (1982 – 1984 = 100)	Real Average Hourly Earnings (1982 – 1984 dollars)
2014	$24.46	237	$10.32
2015	$25.01	237	$10.55
2016	$25.67	240	$10.70

The base year for the CPI is the average of prices during the period 1982–1984. So, the values for the real average hourly earnings we calculated are in 1982–1984 dollars. In other words, these values for the real wage tell us that in 2015, $25.01 would buy what $10.55 would have bought in 1982–1984 and that in 2016, $25.67 would buy what $10.70 would have bought in 1982–1984.

Step 3: **Complete your answer by calculating the percentage change in nominal average hourly earnings and in real average hourly earnings between 2015 and 2016.** The percentage change in nominal average hourly earnings equals:

$$\left(\frac{\$25.67 - \$25.01}{\$25.01}\right) \times 100 = 2.6\%.$$

And the percentage change in real average hourly earnings equals:

$$\left(\frac{\$10.70 - \$10.55}{\$10.55}\right) \times 100 = 1.4\%.$$

We can conclude that real average hourly earnings increased by about 1 percentage point less than did nominal average hourly earnings.

Extra Credit: The values we computed for the real average hourly earnings are measured in 1982–1984 dollars. Because this period is more than 30 years ago, the values are somewhat difficult to interpret. We can convert the earnings to 2016 dollars by using the method we used on page 299 to calculate your mother's salary. But for purposes of calculating the *change* in the value of real average hourly earnings over time, converting the earnings to 2016 dollars doesn't matter. The change from 2015 to 2016 would still be 1.4 percent. You can check this point by using the "mother's salary" method to calculate the real average hourly earnings for 2015 and 2016 in 2016 dollars. Then calculate the percentage change. Unless you make an arithmetic error, you should find that the answer is still 1.4 percent. Finally, keep in mind that average hourly earnings do not include employee benefits, such as employer contributions to retirement programs or the value of employer-provided medical insurance. Because benefits have increased over the years relative to wages and salaries, changes in average hourly earnings can be a misleading measure of changes in the typical worker's standard of living.

MyLab Economics Study Plan   **Your Turn:** For more practice, do related problems 5.4, 5.5, 5.6, and 5.7 on pages 311–312 at the end of this chapter.

Nominal Interest Rates versus Real Interest Rates

9.6

LEARNING OBJECTIVE: Distinguish between the nominal interest rate and the real interest rate.

The difference between nominal and real values is important when money is being borrowed and lent. The *interest rate* is the cost of borrowing funds, expressed as a percentage of the amount borrowed (see Chapter 6, Section 6.2). If you lend someone $1,000 for one year and charge an interest rate of 4 percent, the borrower will pay back $1,040, or 4 percent more than the amount you lent. But is $1,040 received one year from now really 4 percent more than $1,000 today? If prices rise during the year, you will not be able to buy as much with $1,040 one year from now as you could with that amount today. Your true return from lending the $1,000 is equal to the percentage change in your purchasing power after taking into account the effects of inflation.

The stated interest rate on a loan is the **nominal interest rate**. The **real interest rate** corrects the nominal interest rate for the effect of inflation on purchasing power. As a simple example, suppose that the only good you purchase is DVDs, and at the beginning of the year the price of DVDs is $10.00. With $1,000, you can purchase 100 DVDs. If you lend the $1,000 out for one year at an interest rate of 4 percent, you will receive $1,040 at the end of the year. Suppose the inflation rate during the year is 2 percent, so that the price of DVDs has risen to $10.20 by the end of the year. How has your purchasing power increased as a result of making the loan? At the beginning of the year, your $1,000 could purchase 100 DVDs. At the end of the year, your $1,040 can purchase $1,040/$10.20 = 101.96 DVDs. In other words, you can purchase almost 2 percent more DVDs. So, in this case, the real interest rate you received from lending was a little less than 2 percent (actually, 1.96 percent). For low rates of inflation, a convenient approximation for the real interest rate is:

Real interest rate = Nominal interest rate − Inflation rate.

We can calculate the real interest rate in our example using this formula as:

4 percent − 2 percent = 2 percent,

which is close to the actual value of 1.96 percent. If the inflation rate during the year was 3 percent, the real interest rate would be only 1 percent. Holding the nominal interest rate constant, the higher the inflation rate, the lower the real interest rate. Notice that if the inflation rate turns out to be higher than expected, borrowers pay and lenders receive a lower real interest rate than either of them expected. For example, if both you and the person to whom you lent the $1,000 expected the inflation rate to be 2 percent, you both expected the real interest rate on the loan to be 2 percent. If the inflation rate turns out actually to be 3 percent, the real interest rate on the loan will be 1 percent: That's bad news for you but good news for your borrower.

For the economy as a whole, we can measure the nominal interest rate as the interest rate on three-month U.S. Treasury bills. U.S. Treasury bills are short-term loans investors make to the federal government and are the most important security in world financial markets. We can use the inflation rate as measured by changes in the CPI to calculate the real interest rate on Treasury bills. Figure 9.8 shows the nominal and real interest rates for the period from 1970 through the beginning of 2017. Notice that when the inflation rate is low, as it has been during most years since the early 1990s, the gap between the nominal and real interest rates is small. When the inflation rate is high, as it was during the mid- to late 1970s, the gap between the nominal and real interest rates becomes large. In fact, a particular nominal interest rate can be associated in different periods with very different real interest rates. For example, during late 1975, the nominal interest rate was about 5.5 percent, but because the inflation rate was 7 percent, the real interest rate was −1.5 percent. In early 1987, the nominal interest rate was also 5.5 percent, but because the inflation rate was only 2 percent, the real interest rate was 3.5 percent.

Nominal interest rate The stated interest rate on a loan.

Real interest rate The nominal interest rate minus the inflation rate.

Figure 9.8   **Nominal and Real Interest Rates, 1970–2017**

The real interest rate is equal to the nominal interest rate minus the inflation rate. The real interest rate provides a better measure of the true cost of borrowing and the true return to lending than does the nominal interest rate. The nominal interest rate in the figure is the interest rate on three-month U.S. Treasury bills. The inflation rate is measured by the percentage change in the CPI from the same quarter during the previous year.

Source: Federal Reserve Bank of St. Louis.

This example shows that it is impossible to know whether a particular nominal interest rate is "high" or "low." It all depends on the inflation rate. *The real interest rate provides a better measure of the true cost of borrowing and the true return from lending than does the nominal interest rate.* When firms are deciding whether to borrow the funds to buy an investment good, such as a new factory, they will look at the real interest rate because it measures the true cost to the firm of borrowing.

Is it possible for the nominal interest rate to be less than the real interest rate? Yes, but only when the inflation rate is negative. A negative inflation rate is referred to as **deflation** and occurs on the rare occasions when the price level falls. During the years shown in Figure 9.8, the inflation rate as measured by changes in the CPI was negative only during the first nine months of 2009 and the first three months of 2015.

Deflation A decline in the price level.

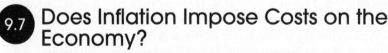

9.7 Does Inflation Impose Costs on the Economy?

LEARNING OBJECTIVE: Discuss the problems that inflation causes.

Imagine waking up tomorrow morning and finding that every price in the economy has doubled. The prices of food, gasoline, clothing, laptops, houses, and haircuts have all doubled. But suppose that all wages and salaries have also doubled. Will this doubling of prices and wages matter? Think about walking into McDonald's, expecting to find a Big Mac selling for $5.00. Instead, you find it selling for $10.00. Will you turn around and walk out? Probably not because your salary has also increased overnight, from $45,000 per year to $90,000 per year. So, the purchasing power of your salary has remained the same, and you are just as likely to buy the Big Mac today as you were yesterday.

This hypothetical situation makes an important point: Nominal incomes generally increase with inflation. Remember that we can think of the $5.00 price of a Big Mac as representing either the value of the product or the value of all the income generated in producing the product (see Chapter 8, Section 8.1). The two amounts are the same, whether the Big Mac sells for $4.50 or $9.00. When the price of the Big Mac rises from $5.00 to $10.00, that extra $5.00 ends up as income that goes to the workers at McDonald's, the firms selling supplies to McDonald's, or the stockholders of McDonald's, just as the first $5.00 did.

It's tempting to think that the problem with inflation is that, as prices rise, consumers can no longer afford to buy as many goods and services, but our example shows that this conclusion is a fallacy. An expected inflation rate of 10 percent will raise the average price of goods and services by 10 percent, but it will also raise average incomes by 10 percent. Goods and services will be as affordable to an average consumer as they would be if there were no inflation.

Inflation Affects the Distribution of Income

If inflation will not reduce the affordability of goods and services to an average consumer, why do people dislike inflation? One reason is that the argument in the previous section applies to the *average* person but not to every person. Some people will find their incomes rising faster than the rate of inflation, and so their purchasing power will rise. Other people will find their incomes rising more slowly than the rate of inflation—or not at all—and their purchasing power will fall. People on fixed incomes are particularly likely to be hurt by inflation. If a retired worker receives a pension fixed at $3,000 per month, over time, inflation will reduce the purchasing power of that payment. In that way, inflation can change the distribution of income in a manner that seems unfair to many people.

The extent to which inflation redistributes income depends in part on whether the inflation is *anticipated*—in which case consumers, workers, and firms can see it coming and can prepare for it—or *unanticipated*—in which case they do not see it coming and do not prepare for it.   **MyLab Economics** Concept Check

The Problem with Anticipated Inflation

Like many of life's problems, inflation is easier to manage if you see it coming. Suppose that everyone knows that the inflation rate for the next 10 years will be 10 percent per year. Workers know that unless their wages go up by at least 10 percent per year, the real purchasing power of their wages will fall. Businesses will be willing to increase workers' wages enough to compensate for inflation because they know that the prices of the products they sell will increase. Lenders will realize that the loans they make will be paid back with dollars that are losing 10 percent of their value each year, so they will charge higher interest rates to compensate. Borrowers will be willing to pay the higher interest rates because they also know they are paying back these loans with dollars that are losing value. So far, there don't seem to be costs to anticipated inflation.

Even when inflation is perfectly anticipated, however, some individuals and firms will experience a cost:

1. Inevitably, there will be a redistribution of income, as some people's incomes fall behind even an anticipated level of inflation.
2. Firms and consumers have to hold some paper money to facilitate their buying and selling. Anyone holding paper money will find its purchasing power decreasing each year by the rate of inflation. To avoid this cost, workers and firms will try to hold as little paper money as possible, but they will have to hold some.
3. Firms that print catalogs listing the prices of their products will have to update them more frequently. Supermarkets and other stores that mark prices on packages or on store shelves will have to devote more time and labor to changing the marked prices. The costs to firms of changing prices are called **menu costs**; the term refers to the fact that during times of significant inflation, restaurants have to reprint their menus more frequently. At moderate rates of anticipated inflation, menu costs are

Menu costs The costs to firms of changing prices.

relatively small, but at high rates of inflation, such as those experienced in some developing countries, menu costs can become substantial.

4. Taxes paid by investors will increase because investors are taxed on the nominal payments they receive from owning stocks and bonds or from making loans rather than on the real payments—the nominal payments corrected for inflation. Because investors are interested in the real, after-tax return they receive when investing in firms, the higher taxes that investors pay as a result of inflation mean that firms must pay more for the funds they need to expand.   **MyLab Economics** Concept Check

The Problem with Unanticipated Inflation

In any high-income economy—such as the United States—households, workers, and firms routinely enter into contracts that commit them to make or receive certain payments for years in the future. For example, when firms sign wage contracts with labor unions, they commit to paying a specified wage for the duration of the contract. When people buy homes, they usually borrow most of the amount they need from banks. These loans, called *mortgage loans*, commit a borrower to make a fixed monthly payment for the length of the loan. Most mortgage loans are for long periods, often as long as 30 years.

To make these long-term commitments, households, workers, and firms must forecast the rate of inflation. If Boeing believes the inflation rate over the next three years will be 3 percent per year, signing a three-year contract with one of its labor unions that grants wage increases of 5 percent per year may seem reasonable if Boeing expects to raise its prices by at least the rate of inflation each year and if it expects to be able to raise worker productivity. If over the next three years the inflation rate turns out to be only 1 percent per year rather than 3 percent, paying wage increases of 5 percent may significantly reduce Boeing's profit.

When people borrow money or a bank lends money, they must forecast the inflation rate so they can calculate the real rate of interest on a loan. In 1980, banks were charging interest rates of 18 percent or more on mortgage loans. This rate seems very high compared to the less than 5 percent charged on such loans in 2017, but the inflation rate in 1980 was more than 13 percent and was expected to remain high. In fact, the inflation rate *declined* unexpectedly, and by 1983, it was only about 3 percent. People who borrowed money for 30 years at the nominal interest rates of 1980 soon found that the real interest rate on their loans was much higher than they had expected.

When the actual inflation rate turns out to be very different from the expected inflation rate, some people gain, and other people lose. This outcome seems unfair to most people because they are either winning or losing only because something unanticipated has happened. This apparently unfair redistribution is a key reason people dislike unanticipated inflation.   **MyLab Economics** Concept Check

MyLab Economics Study Plan

● Apply the Concept   **MyLab Economics** Video

What's So Bad about Falling Prices?

We have just discussed how inflation being higher than expected can cause problems for consumers, workers, and firms. But what if an economy begins to experience falling prices—*deflation*, rather than inflation? A falling price level might seem like good news for the economy. After all, falling prices should encourage consumers to increase their spending as goods and services become less expensive. In fact, though, deflation tends to have the opposite effect on consumers. Episodes of deflation are relatively rare, but we can draw some lessons from two important deflationary episodes: the United States during the 1930s and Japan during the 1990s. In both cases, many consumers reduced their spending in the face of falling prices, apparently because they were waiting for prices to go even lower. Waiting for prices to fall even lower was also a problem for the U.S. housing market in the late 2000s. A large run-up in housing prices took place from 2002 to 2006. When prices began to decline, many potential buyers postponed purchases because they expected that prices would continue to fall.

The following figure shows changes in the CPI in the United States during the years between 1925 and 1940. (The shaded areas represent periods of recession, although economists generally consider the Great Depression to have lasted from 1929 to 1940.) The beginning of the Great Depression in 1929 caused the country to experience severe deflation.

The deflation of the 1930s hurt the U.S. economy not just because it may have led some consumers to postpone purchases but also because it increased the burden on borrowers. Suppose that in 1929 you had borrowed money for five years at a nominal interest rate of 5 percent. What real interest rate would you have paid during those years? We have seen that to calculate the real interest rate, we need to subtract the inflation rate from the nominal interest rate. With deflation, the change in the price level is negative, so to calculate the real interest rate, we are in effect *adding* the change in the price level to the nominal interest rate. The following table uses the actual deflation rate in each year to calculate the resulting real interest rates on your loan:

	1929	1930	1931	1932	1933
Nominal interest rate	5%	5%	5%	5%	5%
Change in the consumer price index	0	−2.3	−9.0	−9.9	−5.1
Real interest rate	5.0	7.3	14.0	14.9	10.1

The bottom row of the table shows that although the nominal interest rate on your loan is only 5 percent, in three of the five years the real interest rate you pay is greater than 10 percent. In fact, high real interest rates inflicted serious losses on both household and business borrowers during the early 1930s and contributed to the severity of the Great Depression.

During the 2001 and 2007–2009 recessions, some policymakers and economists feared that the U.S. economy would experience deflation. Fortunately, significant deflation did not occur. If it had, those recessions would likely have been more severe than they were.

Your Turn: Test your understanding by doing related problems 7.9 and 7.10 on page 314 at the end of this chapter.

MyLab Economics Study Plan

Continued from page 279

Economics in Your Life & Career

Should You Change Your Career Plans if You Graduate during a Recession?

At the beginning of this chapter, we asked whether layoffs in the banking industry should cause you to change your major and give up your plans to pursue a career in banking. We have seen in this chapter that unemployment rates are higher and layoffs are more common in a recession than in an economic expansion. Because you are a sophomore, you will graduate a few years later, when the recession will likely have ended and the unemployment rate will have declined. You might also want to investigate whether the layoffs in the banking industry represent a permanent contraction in the size of the industry or a temporary decline caused by the recession. If the reduction of banking jobs is more likely to be permanent, you might consider a career in another industry. If the layoffs appear to be related to the current recession, you probably do not need to change your career plans.

Conclusion

Inflation and unemployment are key macroeconomic problems. Presidential elections are often won and lost on the basis of which candidate is able to convince the public that he or she can best deal with these problems. Many economists, however, would argue that, in the long run, maintaining high rates of growth of real GDP per person is the most important macroeconomic concern. Only when real GDP per person is increasing will a country's standard of living increase. In the next chapter, we will look more closely at the important topic of economic growth.

Visit **MyLab Economics** for a news article and analysis related to the concepts in this chapter.

Key Terms

Consumer price index (CPI), p. 296

Cyclical unemployment, p. 291

Deflation, p. 302

Discouraged workers, p. 281

Efficiency wage, p. 295

Employed, p. 280

Employment–population ratio, p. 282

Frictional unemployment, p. 291

Inflation rate, p. 295

Labor force, p. 280

Labor force participation rate, p. 282

Menu costs, p. 303

Natural rate of unemployment, p. 292

Nominal interest rate, p. 301

Price level, p. 295

Producer price index (PPI), p. 298

Real interest rate, p. 301

Structural unemployment, p. 291

Unemployed, p. 280

Unemployment rate, p. 280

9.1 Measuring the Unemployment Rate, the Labor Force Participation Rate, and the Employment–Population Ratio, pages 280–290

LEARNING OBJECTIVE: Define the unemployment rate, the labor force participation rate, and the employment–population ratio and understand how they are computed.

MyLab Economics Visit www.pearson.com/mylab/economics to complete these exercises online and get instant feedback.

Summary

The U.S. Bureau of Labor Statistics uses the results of the monthly household survey to calculate the *unemployment rate,* the *labor force participation rate,* and the *employment–population ratio.* The **labor force** is the total number of people who have jobs (the **employed**) plus the number of people who do not have jobs but are actively looking for them (the **unemployed**). The **unemployment rate** is the percentage of the labor force that is unemployed. **Discouraged workers** are people who are available for work but who are not actively looking for a job because they believe no jobs are available for them. Discouraged workers are not counted as unemployed. The **labor force participation rate** is the percentage of the working-age population in the labor force. Since 1950, the labor force participation rate of women has been rising, while the labor force participation rate of men has been falling. The **employment–population ratio** measures the percentage of the working-age population that is employed. Asians, whites, and college graduates have below-average unemployment rates. African Americans, Hispanics, and high school dropouts have above-average unemployment rates. Except during severe recessions, a typical unemployed person finds a new job or returns to his or her previous job within a few months. Each year, millions of jobs are created in the United States, and millions of jobs are destroyed.

Review Questions

1.1 How is the unemployment rate measured? What are the three conditions someone needs to meet to be counted as unemployed?

1.2 What are the problems in measuring the unemployment rate? In what ways does the official BLS measure of the unemployment rate *understate* the true degree of unemployment? In what ways does the official BLS measure *overstate* the true degree of unemployment?

1.3 Which groups tend to have above-average unemployment rates, and which groups tend to have below-average unemployment rates?

1.4 What does the labor force participation rate measure? Since 1950, how have the labor force participation rates of men and women changed?

1.5 What does the employment–population ratio measure? How does an unemployed person dropping out of the labor force affect the unemployment rate? How does it affect the employment–population ratio?

1.6 What is the difference between the household survey and the establishment survey? Which survey do many economists prefer for measuring changes in employment? Why?

Problems and Applications

1.7 Fill in the missing values in the following table of data collected in the household survey for February 2017:

Working-Age Population	
Employment	152,528,000
Unemployment	
Unemployment rate	4.7%
Labor force	
Labor force participation rate	63.0%
Employment–population ratio	

Source: U.S. Department of Labor, Bureau of Labor Statistics, *The Employment Situation—February 2017,* March 10, 2017.

1.8 **(Related to Solved Problem 9.1 on page 282)** Homemakers are not included in the employment or labor force totals compiled in the BLS household survey. They are included in the working-age population totals. Suppose that homemakers were counted as employed and included in labor force statistics. How would that change affect the unemployment rate, the labor force participation rate, and the employment–population ratio?

1.9 The unemployment rate declined from 4.5 percent in March 2017 to 4.4 percent in April. The labor force participation rate also declined from March to April, from 63.0 percent to 62.9 percent. If the labor force participation rate had remained unchanged from March to April, would the unemployment rate for April have been lower than, higher than, or equal to 4.4 percent? Briefly explain.

1.10 (Related to the Apply the Concept on page 286) In discussing the labor market during the recovery from the 2007–2009 recession, Federal Reserve Chair Janet Yellen noted that "the employment-to-population ratio has increased far less over the past several years than the unemployment rate alone would indicate, based on past experience."

　a. During an economic expansion, why would we normally expect the employment–population ratio to increase as the unemployment rate falls?

　b. Why didn't the employment–population ratio increase as much as might have been expected during the recovery from the 2007–2009 recession?

Source: Janet L. Yellen, "Labor Market Dynamics and Monetary Policy," Speech at the Federal Reserve Bank of Kansas City Economic Symposium, Jackson Hole, Wyoming, August 22, 2014.

1.11 During the last three months of 2016, the employment–population ratio was unchanged, and the labor force participation rate was decreasing. Shouldn't both of these data series move in the same direction? Briefly explain how it is possible that they didn't.

1.12 An article in the *Wall Street Journal* contained the following observation: "Every month, millions of workers leave the job market because of retirement, to care for children or aging parents, to pursue more education, or out of discouragement. Millions of others jump in after graduating."

　a. Are the millions of workers leaving the job market for the reasons given counted as unemployed in the BLS data? Briefly explain.

　b. Will the BLS count people entering the job market after graduating from high school or college as part of the labor force even if they don't find a job right away? Briefly explain.

Source: Josh Zumbrun, "Labor-Market Dropouts Stay on the Sidelines," *Wall Street Journal*, December 28, 2014.

1.13 An article in the *Wall Street Journal* noted that over a four-month period in late 2014, employment in the state of Georgia "rose 1% even as the state's jobless rate climbed 1.2 percentage points." Briefly explain how the state's unemployment rate could have increased at the same time that employment in the state was increasing.

Source: Cameron McWhirter and Ben Leubsdorf, "Rising Jobless Rates Are a Southern Mystery," *Wall Street Journal*, October 5, 2014.

1.14 In his 2016 State of the Union address, President Barack Obama observed that in the previous 70 months, the U.S. economy had created "more than 14 million new jobs." Is it likely that the U.S. economy created only 14 million jobs during this time period? If not, what was President Obama referring to?

Source: Barack Obama, "Remarks of President Barack Obama— State of the Union Address As Delivered," obamawhitehouse.archives.gov, January 13, 2016.

9.2 Types of Unemployment, pages 290–293

LEARNING OBJECTIVE: Identify the three types of unemployment.

MyLab Economics Visit **www.pearson.com/mylab/economics** to complete these exercises online and get instant feedback.

Summary

There are three types of unemployment: frictional, structural, and cyclical. **Frictional unemployment** is short-term unemployment that arises from the process of matching workers with jobs. One type of frictional unemployment is *seasonal unemployment*, which refers to unemployment due to factors such as weather, variations in tourism, and other calendar-related events. **Structural unemployment** arises from a persistent mismatch between the job skills or attributes of workers and the requirements of jobs. **Cyclical unemployment** is caused by a business cycle recession. The **natural rate of unemployment** is the normal rate of unemployment, consisting of structural unemployment and frictional unemployment. The natural rate of unemployment is also sometimes called the *full-employment rate of unemployment*.

Review Questions

2.1 What are the three types of unemployment? Which type of unemployment do you consider most likely to result in the least hardship for people who are unemployed? Briefly explain.

2.2 What is the relationship between frictional unemployment and job search?

2.3 What is the natural rate of unemployment? What is the relationship between the natural rate of unemployment and full employment?

Problems and Applications

2.4 (Related to the Chapter Opener on page 278) Boeing Company employed fewer people in 2017 than it did in 1980. Is this decline in employment frictional, structural, cyclical, or some combination of these factors? What information would you need to arrive at a definite answer?

2.5 (Related to the Apply the Concept on page 292) What advice for finding a job would you give someone who is frictionally unemployed? What advice would you give someone who is structurally unemployed? What advice would you give someone who is cyclically unemployed?

2.6 (Related to the Apply the Concept on page 292) The BLS defines a *job quit* as a "voluntary separation initiated by an employee." The BLS estimated that there were 3.1 million job quits in March 2017.

    a. Economists distinguish three types of unemployment: frictional, structural, and cyclical. How would you classify unemployment caused by an increase in job quits?

    b. Would an increase in the number of job quits suggest that it was becoming easier or more difficult for people to find jobs? Briefly explain.

Source: Bureau of Labor Statistics, "Job Openings and Labor Turnover Survey—March 2017," May 9, 2017.

2.7 **(Related to the Apply the Concept on page 292)** The president of a manufacturing firm that makes precision tools in California's Silicon Valley was quoted in an article in the *Wall Street Journal* as saying that "production workers … are scarce" and that "many applicants lack even the most rudimentary skills." He added, "I would say in this valley, people looking for jobs are unemployed for a reason." Are these applicants likely to be cyclically, frictionally, or structurally unemployed, and what would be the reason that most of them are unemployed? Briefly explain.

Source: Jeffrey Sparshott, "Skilled Workers Are Scarce in Tight Labor Market," *Wall Street Journal*, February 2, 2017.

2.8 In May 2017, an article in the *New York Times* had the headline: "We're Getting Awfully Close to Full Employment." The article contained the following observation: "The so-called U-6 rate … fell to 8.6 percent in April from 8.9 percent [in March]."

    a. What is the U-6 unemployment rate? Why do economists and policymakers track changes in this measure of the unemployment rate?

    b. What is full employment? If the U.S. economy was close to full employment in May 2017, why was the U-6 measure of the unemployment rate still as high as 8.6?

Source: Neil Irwin, "We're Getting Awfully Close to Full Employment," *New York Times*, May 5, 2017.

Explaining Unemployment, pages 293–295

LEARNING OBJECTIVE: Explain what factors determine the unemployment rate.

MyLab Economics   Visit **www.pearson.com/mylab/economics** to complete these exercises online and get instant feedback.

Summary

Government policies can reduce the level of frictional and structural unemployment by aiding the search for jobs and the retraining of workers. Some government policies, however, can add to the level of frictional and structural unemployment. Unemployment insurance payments can raise the unemployment rate by extending the time that unemployed workers search for jobs. Government policies have caused the unemployment rates in most other high-income countries typically to be higher than in the United States. Wages above market levels can also increase unemployment. Wages may be above market levels because of the minimum wage, labor unions, and *efficiency wages*. An **efficiency wage** is a higher-than market wage that a firm pays to increase workers' productivity.

Review Questions

3.1 What effect does the payment of government unemployment insurance have on the unemployment rate? On the severity of recessions?

3.2 Discuss the effect of each of the following on the unemployment rate.

    a. The federal minimum wage law

    b. Labor unions

    c. Efficiency wages

3.3 Why has the unemployment rate in the United States typically been lower than the unemployment rates in Canada and the countries in Western Europe?

Problems and Applications

3.4 In an article in the *Wall Street Journal* about the effect of automation on jobs, Boston University economist James Bessen was quoted as saying that the problem is not "mass unemployment, it's transitioning people from one job to another."

    a. What does "transitioning people from one job to another" entail? During the transition period, what type(s) of unemployment would describe these people?

    b. The article noted that "other countries devote more resources than the U.S. to cushioning and retraining displaced workers." What type of policies do governments use to support displaced workers? What are the benefits and the costs to making the policies to cushion displaced workers more generous?

Source: Christopher Mims, "Automation Can Actually Create More Jobs," *Wall Street Journal*, December 11, 2016.

3.5 Jared Bernstein, an economist at the Center on Budget and Policy Priorities, stated, "I want to see receipt of unemployment insurance … go up in recessions." If government unemployment insurance payments didn't go up, he explains, it "would be a sign that something's very wrong." What would be very wrong about government unemployment insurance payments failing to rise during a recession? What would be the consequences for the unemployed and for the economy?

Source: Jared Bernstein, "Lessons of the Great Recession: How the Safety Net Performed," *New York Times*, June 24, 2013.

3.6 Discuss the likely effect of each of the following on the unemployment rate.

    a. The length of time workers are eligible to receive unemployment insurance payments doubles.

    b. The minimum wage is abolished.

    c. Most U.S. workers join labor unions.

    d. More companies make information about job openings easily available on Internet job sites.

3.7 In 1914, Henry Ford increased the wage he paid workers in his car factory in Dearborn, Michigan, to $5 per day. This wage was more than twice as much as other car manufacturers were paying. Ford was quoted as saying, "The payment of five dollars a day for an eight-hour day was one of the finest cost-cutting moves we ever made." How can paying an above-market wage result in a firm cutting its costs?

3.8 According to an article in the *New York Times*, in early 2015, Walmart received bad customer reviews: "They complained of dirty bathrooms, empty shelves, endless checkout lines and impossible-to-find employees." Shortly thereafter, Walmart announced that it was changing its

employment practice by, among other things, increasing wages. The article noted that a year and half later, "[Walmart store] managers describe a big shift in the kind of workers they can bring in by offering $10 an hour with a solid path to $15 an hour." Wouldn't raising wages from $10 per hour to $15 per hour reduce Walmart's profit? Why would the company have adopted such a policy?

Source: Neil Irwin, "How Did Walmart Get Cleaner Stores and Higher Sales? It Paid Its People More," *New York Times*, October 15, 2016.

9.4 Measuring Inflation, pages 295–298

LEARNING OBJECTIVE: Define the price level and the inflation rate and understand how they are computed.

MyLab Economics   Visit www.pearson.com/mylab/economics to complete these exercises online and get instant feedback.

Summary

The **price level** measures the average prices of goods and services. The **inflation rate** is equal to the percentage change in the price level from one year to the next. The federal government compiles statistics on three different measures of the price level: the consumer price index, the GDP price deflator, and the producer price index. The **consumer price index (CPI)** is a measure of the average change over time in the prices a typical urban family of four pays for the goods and services they purchase. Changes in the CPI are the best measure of changes in the cost of living as experienced by a typical household. Biases in the construction of the CPI cause changes in it to overstate the true inflation rate by 0.5 percentage point to 1 percentage point. The **producer price index (PPI)** is an average of prices received by producers of goods and services at all stages of production.

Review Questions

4.1 Briefly describe the three major measures of the price level.

4.2 Which price index does the government use to measure changes in the cost of living?

4.3 What potential biases exist in calculating the CPI? To have no substitution bias, what shape would the demand curve need to be for the products in the market basket? What steps has the Bureau of Labor Statistics taken to reduce the size of the biases?

Problems and Applications

4.4 (Related to the Don't Let This Happen to You on page 297) Briefly explain whether you agree with the following statement: "I don't believe the government price statistics. The CPI for 2016 was 240, but I know that the inflation rate couldn't have been as high as 140 percent in 2016."

4.5 (Related to the Don't Let This Happen to You on page 297) An article in the *Wall Street Journal* asked "How can inflation be low when everything is so expensive?" The article also noted that "the CPI shows that prices are the highest they've ever been." Is there a contradiction between a low inflation rate as measured by the CPI and the observations

that prices are "the highest they've ever been" and everything is "so expensive"? Briefly explain.

Source: Josh Zumbrun, "5 Things You Always Wanted to Know about Inflation Statistics," *Wall Street Journal*, May 15, 2014.

4.6 Consider a simple economy that produces only three products: haircuts, hamburgers, and streaming movies. Use the information in the following table to calculate the inflation rate for 2018, as measured by the CPI.

Product	Base Year (2010)		2017	2018
	Quantity	Price	Price	Price
Haircuts	2	$10.00	$13.00	$16.20
Hamburgers	10	2.00	2.45	2.40
Movies	6	20.00	13.00	12.00

4.7 The headline on an article in the *Wall Street Journal* was "Why Ice Cream Is More Important Than Bacon When Tracking Inflation." Considering how the CPI is constructed, why would ice cream be more important than bacon in calculating inflation?

Source: Sarah Chaney, "Why Ice Cream Is More Important Than Bacon When Tracking Inflation," *Wall Street Journal*, April 17, 2017.

4.8 The Standard & Poor's/Case-Shiller Home Price Index is one of the leading indicators of housing price trends in the United States. The base period for the index is January 2000. The following table lists index numbers for February 2016 and February 2017 for five cities.

City	February 2016	February 2017
New York	181.4	187.3
Miami	208.6	222.6
Phoenix	158.7	167.0
Dallas	160.2	172.1
San Francisco	224.2	238.3

a. In which of these five cities did housing prices increase the fastest from February 2016 to February 2017? In which did they increase the slowest? Briefly explain the basis for your answers.

b. In which of these five cities did housing prices increase the fastest since January 2000? In which did they increase the slowest? Briefly explain the basis for your answers.

c. Can you determine from these numbers which city had the highest house prices in February 2017? Briefly explain.

Source: Federal Reserve Bank of St. Louis.

4.9 Suppose the CPI of a country follows the path shown in the following figure.

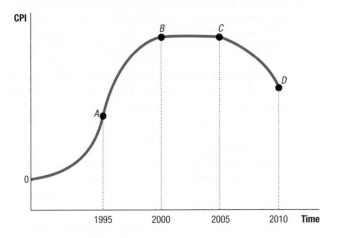

a. During which period did the country experience zero inflation?

b. During which period did the country experience deflation?

c. During which period did the country experience a slowdown in inflation, although the inflation rate remained positive? (This situation is called "disinflation.")

d. During which period did the country experience an increasing rate of inflation?

4.10 In the fall of 2017, Apple introduced two new models of its iPhone. The new models had faster processors and better cameras than the previous model and sold for higher prices. How did the introduction of the new models of the iPhone affect the CPI?

9.5 Using Price Indexes to Adjust for the Effects of Inflation, pages 298–300

LEARNING OBJECTIVE: Use price indexes to adjust for the effects of inflation.

MyLab Economics Visit www.pearson.com/mylab/economics to complete these exercises online and get instant feedback.

Summary

Price indexes are designed to measure changes in the price level over time, not the absolute level of prices. To correct for the effects of inflation, we can divide a *nominal variable* by a price index and multiply by 100 to obtain a *real variable*. The real variable will be measured in dollars of the base year for the price index.

Review Questions

5.1 What is the difference between a nominal variable and a real variable?

5.2 During a period of deflation, which is likely to increase faster: nominal average hourly earnings or real average hourly earnings? Briefly explain.

Problems and Applications

5.3 The Great Depression was the worst economic disaster in U.S. history in terms of declines in real GDP and increases in the unemployment rate. Use the data in the following table to calculate the percentage decline in real GDP between 1929 and 1933:

Year	Nominal GDP (billions of dollars)	GDP Price Deflator (2009 = 100)
1929	$104.6	9.9
1933	57.2	7.3

Source: U.S. Bureau of Economic Analysis.

5.4 (Related to Solved Problem 9.5 on page 299) In 1924, the famous novelist F. Scott Fitzgerald wrote an article for the *Saturday Evening Post* titled "How to Live on $36,000 a Year," in which he wondered how he and his wife had managed to spend all of that very high income without saving any of it. The CPI in 1924 was 17, and the CPI in 2016 was 240. What income would you have needed in 2016 to have had the same purchasing power that Fitzgerald's $36,000 had in 1924? Be sure to show your calculation.

Source: F. Scott Fitzgerald, "How to Live on $36,000 a Year," *Saturday Evening Post*, April 5, 1924.

5.5 (Related to Solved Problem 9.5 on page 299) Use the information in the following table to determine the percentage changes in the U.S. and French *real* minimum wages between 1957 and 2016. Does it matter for your answer that you have not been told the base year for the U.S. CPI or the French CPI? Was the percentage increase in the price level greater in the United States or in France during these years?

Year	United States		France	
	Minimum Wage (dollars per hour)	CPI	Minimum Wage (euros per hour)	CPI
1957	$1.00	27	€0.19	8
2016	7.25	240	9.76	106

Sources: For 1957: John M. Abowd, Francis Kramarz, Thomas Lemieux, and David N. Margolis, "Minimum Wages and Youth Employment in France and the United States," in D. Blanchflower and R. Freeman, eds., *Youth Employment and Joblessness in Advanced Countries*, Chicago: University of Chicago Press, 1999, pp. 427–472 (the value for the minimum wage is given in francs; it was converted to euros at a conversion rate of 1 euro = 6.55957 francs); For 2016: INSEE online data bank, www.insee.fr; U.S. Department of Labor; and U.S. Bureau of Labor Statistics.

5.6 **(Related to Solved Problem 9.5 on page 299)** In an article in the *Wall Street Journal*, a professor of financial planning noted the effect of rising prices on purchasing power: "Today, $2,000 a month seems reasonable [as an income for a retired person in addition to the person's Social Security payments], but 40 years from now that's going to be three cups of coffee and a donut." Suppose that in 2016 three cups of coffee and a donut can be purchased for $10. The CPI in 2016 was 240. What would the CPI have to be in 2056 for $2,000 to be able to purchase only three cups of coffee and a donut? Assume that the prices of coffee and donuts increase at the same rate as the CPI during these 40 years.

Source: Matthias Rieker, "Rising Use of Immediate Annuities Raises Some Concerns," *Wall Street Journal*, December 4, 2014.

5.7 **(Related to Solved Problem 9.5 on page 299)** The following table shows the top 10 films of all time through May 2017, measured by box office receipts in the United States, as well as several other notable films farther down the list.

The CPI in 2017 was 245. Use this information and the data in the table to calculate the box office receipts for each film in 2017 dollars. Assume that each film generated all of its box office receipts during the year it was released. Use your results to prepare a new list of the top 10 films, based on their earnings in 2017 dollars. (Some of the films, such as the first *Star Wars* film, *Gone with the Wind*, and *Snow White and the Seven Dwarfs*, were rereleased to theaters several times, so their receipts were actually earned during several different years, but we will ignore that complication.)

Sources: boxofficemojo.com; and U.S. Bureau of Labor Statistics.

Accompanies problem 5.7.

Rank	Film	Total Box Office Receipts	Year Released	CPI
1	Star Wars: The Force Awakens	$936,662,225	2015	237
2	Avatar	760,507,625	2009	215
3	Titanic	658,672,302	1997	161
4	Jurassic World	652,270,625	2015	237
5	Marvel's The Avengers	623,357,910	2012	230
6	The Dark Knight	534,858,444	2008	215
7	Rogue One: A Star Wars Story	532,177,324	2016	240
8	Beauty and the Beast (2017)	498,225,739	2017	245
9	Finding Dory	486,295,561	2016	240
10	Star Wars: Episode I—The Phantom Menace	474,544,677	1999	167
11	Star Wars	460,998,007	1977	61
15	ET: The Extra-Terrestrial	435,110,554	1982	97
94	Jaws	260,000,000	1975	54
182	Gone with the Wind	198,676,459	1939	14
206	Snow White and the Seven Dwarfs	184,925,486	1937	14
290	The Sound of Music	158,671,368	1965	32
340	101 Dalmatians	144,880,014	1961	30

5.8 An article in the *Economist* about Venezuela stated, "The economy is in such an appalling state, and inflation is so high, that Venezuelans greeted a rise of 60% in the minimum wage on May 1st with shrugs of 'so what?'" What would be two reasons the people of Venezuela would shrug off a rise in the minimum wage of 60 percent?

Source: "It's Up to the Army," *Economist*, May 6, 2017.

9.6 Nominal Interest Rates versus Real Interest Rates, pages 301–302

LEARNING OBJECTIVE: Distinguish between the nominal interest rate and the real interest rate.

MyLab Economics Visit www.pearson.com/mylab/economics to complete these exercises online and get instant feedback.

Summary

The stated interest rate on a loan is the **nominal interest rate**. The **real interest rate** is the nominal interest rate minus the inflation rate. Because it is corrected for the effects of inflation, the real interest rate provides a better measure of the true cost of borrowing and the true return from lending than does the nominal interest rate. The nominal interest rate is always greater than the real interest rate unless the economy experiences **deflation**, which is a decline in the price level.

Review Questions

6.1 What is the difference between the nominal interest rate and the real interest rate?

6.2 If inflation is expected to increase, what will happen to the nominal interest rate? Briefly explain.

6.3 The chapter states that it is impossible to know whether a particular nominal interest rate is "high" or "low." Briefly explain why.

6.4 If the economy is experiencing deflation, will the nominal interest rate be higher or lower than the real interest rate?

Problems and Applications

6.5 The following appeared in a news article: "Inflation in the Lehigh Valley during the first quarter of … [the year] was less than half the national rate. … So, unlike much of the nation, the fear here is deflation—when prices sink so low the CPI drops below zero." Do you agree with the reporter's definition of deflation? Briefly explain.

Source: Dan Shope, "Valley's Inflation Rate Slides," (Allentown, PA) *Morning Call*, July 9, 1996.

6.6 Suppose you were borrowing money to buy a car.
  a. Which of these situations would you prefer: The interest rate on your car loan is 20 percent and the inflation rate is 19 percent, or the interest rate on your car loan is 5 percent and the inflation rate is 2 percent? Briefly explain.
  b. Now suppose you are a manager at JPMorgan Chase, and you are making car loans. Which situation in part (a) would you now prefer? Briefly explain.

6.7 In April 2016, the nominal interest rate on a one-year Treasury bill was 0.54 percent. From April 2016 to April 2017, the consumer price index rose from 238.9 to 244.2. If you bought the one-year Treasury bill in April 2016, calculate the real interest rate you earned over the following 12-month period. Given the results of your calculation, why were investors willing to buy Treasury bills in April 2016?

6.8 Describing the economy in England in 1920, the historian Robert Skidelsky wrote the following: "Who would not borrow at 4 percent a year, with prices going up 4 percent a *month*?" What was the real interest rate paid by borrowers in this situation? (*Hint*: What is the annual inflation rate, if the monthly inflation rate is 4 percent?)

Source: Robert Skidelsky, *John Maynard Keynes: Volume 2, The Economist as Saviour 1920–1937*, New York: The Penguin Press, 1992, p. 39.

6.9 Suppose that the only good you purchase is premium bottled water and that at the beginning of the year, the price of a bottle is $2.00. Suppose you lend $1,000 for one year at an interest rate of 5 percent. At the end of the year, the price of premium bottled water has risen to $2.08. What is the real rate of interest you earned on your loan?

9.7 Does Inflation Impose Costs on the Economy? pages 302–306

LEARNING OBJECTIVE: Discuss the problems that inflation causes.

MyLab Economics Visit www.pearson.com/mylab/economics to complete these exercises online and get instant feedback.

Summary

Inflation does not reduce the affordability of goods and services to an average consumer, but it does impose costs on the economy. When inflation is anticipated, its main costs are that paper money loses some of its value and firms incur *menu costs*. **Menu costs** include the costs of changing prices on products and updating catalogs. When inflation is unanticipated, the actual inflation rate can turn out to be different from the expected inflation rate. As a result, income is redistributed as some people gain and some people lose.

Review Questions

7.1 Why do nominal incomes generally increase with inflation? If nominal incomes increase with inflation, does inflation reduce the purchasing power of an average consumer? Briefly explain.

7.2 How can inflation affect the distribution of income?

7.3 Which is a greater problem: anticipated inflation or unanticipated inflation? Briefly explain.

7.4 What are menu costs? What effect has the Internet had on menu costs?

7.5 What problems does deflation cause?

Problems and Applications

7.6 Suppose that the inflation rate turns out to be much higher than most people expected. In that case, would you rather have been a borrower or a lender? Briefly explain.

7.7 Suppose James and Frank both retire this year. For income during retirement, James will rely on a pension from his company that pays him a fixed $2,500 per month for as long as he lives. James hasn't saved anything for retirement. Frank has no pension but has saved a considerable amount, which he has invested in certificates of deposit (CDs) at his bank. Currently, Frank's CDs pay him interest of $2,300 per month.

   a. Ten years from now, is James or Frank likely to have a higher real income? In your answer, be sure to define *real income*.

   b. Now suppose that instead of being a constant amount, James's pension increases each year by the same percentage as the CPI. For example, if the CPI increases by 5 percent in the first year after James retires, then his pension in the second year equals $2,500 + ($2,500 × 0.05) = $2,625. In this case, 10 years from now, is James or Frank likely to have a higher real income?

7.8 Suppose that Apple and the investors buying the firm's bonds both expect a 2 percent inflation rate for the year. Given this expectation, suppose the nominal interest rate on the bonds is 6 percent and the real interest rate is 4 percent. Suppose that a year after the investors purchase the bonds, the inflation rate turns out to be 6 percent, rather than the 2 percent that had been expected. Who gains and who loses from the unexpectedly high inflation rate?

7.9 **(Related to the Apply the Concept on page 304)** During the spring of 2015, the United Kingdom experienced a brief period of deflation. According to an article in the *Wall Street Journal*, "The U.K.'s history of sticky and hard-to-control inflation suggests that a short period of falling prices will be taken as a reprieve for consumers, not as a signal to defer purchases." Why might consumers see deflation as a "signal to defer purchases"? Shouldn't lower prices cause consumers to buy more, not less? Briefly explain.

   Source: Richard Barley, "U.K. Deflation More Curiosity than Concern," *Wall Street Journal*, May 19, 2015.

7.10 **(Related to the Apply the Concept on page 304)** During the late nineteenth century in the United States, many farmers borrowed heavily to buy land. During most of the period between 1870 and the mid-1890s, the United States experienced mild deflation: The price level declined each year. Many farmers engaged in political protests during these years, and deflation was often a subject of their protests. Explain why farmers would have felt burdened by deflation.

Real-Time Data Exercises

D9.1 **(Using the CPI to measure inflation)** Go to the Web site of the Federal Reserve Bank of St. Louis (FRED) (fred.stlouisfed.org).

   a. Find values for the most recent month and for the same month one year earlier for the Consumer Price Index (CPIAUCSL).

   b. Use the values you found in part (a) to calculate the inflation rate for the past year.

D9.2 **(Using CPI data and Excel to calculate the inflation rate)** Go to the Web site of the Federal Reserve Bank of St. Louis (FRED) (fred.stlouisfed.org).

   a. Locate the data for the Consumer Price Index (CPIAUCSL). Click on the "Download" link on the top right of the page and choose Excel. Open the Excel file that you just downloaded. (*Note:* You can also use another compatible spreadsheet program, such as OpenOffice Calc.)

   b. Using Excel, calculate the percentage change in the CPI from a year earlier for each observation for the past six years. Consider the observation six years earlier than the most recent observation as the first observation. To calculate the inflation rate over the past 12 months, click on the blank cell next to the observation corresponding to the date one year after the first observation (which would be five years earlier than the most recent observation) and enter the following formula (note that in Excel, the symbol for multiplication is *):

$$\text{Percentage change} = \left(\frac{\text{CPI}_t - \text{CPI}_{t-1}}{\text{CPI}_{t-1}} \right) \times 100,$$

   where $t - 1$ is the first observation and t is the observation one year later. Repeat this process for the remaining observations to calculate the inflation rate over the previous 12 months for each observation. (To avoid having to retype the formula, click on the cell where you just calculated the inflation rate and then click on the right corner of the cell and drag it down through the remaining observations.)

   c. Using your calculations from part (b), create a graph of the inflation rate over the previous 12 months for each of the past six years.

   d. Use your calculations from part (b) to explain which period experienced the highest inflation rate. What was the inflation rate during that period?

D9.3 **(Using CPI data and Excel to calculate an alternative measure of the inflation rate)** In addition to calculating the CPI that includes all the prices of all products in the market basket, the BLS also calculates a CPI that does not include the prices of food and energy. Because the prices of food and energy tend to fluctuate more than other prices, some economists believe that omitting them provides a better measure of the long-run inflation rate. Go to the Web site of the Federal Reserve Bank of St. Louis (FRED) (fred.stlouisfed.org).

    a. Locate the data for the Consumer Price Index (CPIAUCSL). Click on the "Edit Graph" link in the top right of the page, choose "Add Line," enter Consumer Price Index less Food and Energy or CPILFESL, and click "Add data series." Click on the "Download" link on the top right of the page and choose Excel. Open the Excel file that you just downloaded. (*Note:* You can also use another compatible spreadsheet program, such as OpenOffice Calc.)

    b. Using Excel, calculate the percentage change in the CPI from a year ago for each of the observations, beginning with the observation 2009-07-01. To make this calculation, click on the blank cell next to the observation corresponding to 2009-07-01 and then enter the following formula (note that in Excel, the symbol for multiplication is *):

$$\text{Percentage change} = \left(\frac{\text{CPI}_t - \text{CPI}_{t-1}}{\text{CPI}_{t-1}} \right) \times 100$$

where $t - 1 = $ 2007-07-01 and $t = $ 2006-07-01. Repeat this process for the remaining observations. (To avoid having to retype the formula, click on the cell where you just calculated the inflation rate and then click on the right corner of the cell and drag it down through the remaining observations.)

    c. Using your calculations from part (b), create a graph of the inflation rates since July 2009 for both indexes. Make sure both data lines are on the same graph.

    d. Discuss differences between the two measures of the inflation rate. For instance, from your calculations, what was the inflation rate in the most recent month using the two CPI measures?

D9.4 **(Analyzing inflation in CPI categories)** Calculating inflation rates for categories of goods and services in the CPI market basket (see page 296) can provide insight into inflation in different sectors of the economy. Go to the Web site of the Federal Reserve Bank of St. Louis (FRED) (fred.stlouisfed.org).

    a. Find the most recent values and values from the same month in 2012 for the following four categories of the CPI: (1) Food and Beverages (CPIFABSL), (2) Apparel (CPIAPPSL), (3) Transportation (CPITRNSL), and (4) Medical Care (CPIMEDSL).

    b. Using the data from part (a), calculate the percentage change for the period from 2012 to the present for each of the four CPI categories.

    c. According to your calculations, which category experienced the least amount of inflation and which category experienced the most inflation?

D9.5 **(Analyzing the labor force and unemployment)** Go to the Web site of the Federal Reserve Bank of St. Louis (FRED) (fred.stlouisfed.org).

    a. Find the most recent values for these three variables: (1) Unemployment Level (UNEMPLOY), (2) Civilian Labor Force (CLF16OV), and (3) Employment Level – Part-Time for Economic Reasons, Slack Work or Business Conditions, All Industries (LNS12032195). Are these data reported annually, quarterly, or monthly? What units are these values reported in?

    b. Using the values you found in part (a), calculate the civilian unemployment rate and the civilian unemployment rate including persons who are underemployed (part-time for economic reasons).

D9.6 **(Calculating the unemployment rate for different groups)** Go to the Web site of the Federal Reserve Bank of St. Louis (FRED) (fred.stlouisfed.org).

    a. Find the most recent values for these four variables: (1) Unemployment Level – Men (LNS13000001), (2) Unemployment Level – Women (LNS13000002), (3) Civilian Labor Force Level – Men (LNS11000001), and (4) Civilian Labor Force Level – Women (LNS11000002). Are these data reported annually, quarterly, or monthly? What units are these values reported in?

    b. Using the values you found in part (a), calculate the unemployment rate for men and the unemployment rate for women.

D9.7 **(Calculating the employment–population ratio)** Go to the Web site of the Federal Reserve Bank of St. Louis (FRED) (fred.stlouisfed.org).

a. Find the most recent values for these three variables: (1) Unemployment Level (UNEMPLOY), (2) Civilian Employment Level (CE16OV), and (3) Not in Labor Force (LNS15000000).

b. Using the values you found in part (a), calculate the working-age population (in thousands) and the employment–population ratio.

c. Holding all other factors constant, what would you expect to happen to the employment–population ratio if the economy entered a recession? Briefly explain.

D9.8 **(Calculating the cyclical unemployment rate)** Go to the Web site of the Federal Reserve Bank of St. Louis (FRED) (fred.stlouisfed.org).

a. Find the value for the current quarter and for the same quarter two years ago for the Civilian Unemployment Rate (UNRATE) and the Natural Rate of Unemployment (NROU). To convert the civilian unemployment rate from a monthly frequency to a quarterly frequency, click the "Edit Graph" link in the top right of the page and change the "Modify frequency" pulldown to quarterly.

b. Using the values you found in part (a), calculate the cyclical rate of unemployment for the current quarter and for the same quarter two years ago.

c. Given the change in cyclical unemployment over this two-year period, what can you conclude about the state of the economy?

D9.9 **(The unemployment rate and the business cycle)** Go to the Web site of the Federal Reserve Bank of St. Louis (FRED) (fred.stlouisfed.org).

a. Find the most recent values for these four variables: (1) Unemployment Level (UNEMPLOY), (2) Civilian Employment Level (CE16OV), (3) Employment Level – Part-Time for Economic Reasons, All Industries (LNS12032194), and (4) Not in Labor Force, Searched for Work and Available (LNU05026642). The Not in Labor Force, Searched for Work and Available series counts persons not in the labor force who want and are available for work and have searched for a job sometime in the past 12 months but have not searched for work in the past four weeks.

b. Using the values you found in part (a), calculate the official unemployment rate.

c. Some economists argue that the official unemployment rate understates the degree of joblessness in the economy because it uses too narrow a definition of unemployment. The BLS also calculates a broader measure of the unemployment rate, which includes people who work part time for economic reasons and people who are available for work but not actively searching. Using the data you found in part (a), calculate this broader measure of the unemployment rate.

d. How would you expect the gap between the official rate of unemployment and the broader rate to change over the course of the business cycle?

D9.10 **(Calculating the real interest rate)** Go to the Web site of the Federal Reserve Bank of St. Louis (FRED) (fred.stlouisfed.org).

a. Find the most recent values for the 3-Month Treasury Bill: Secondary Market Rate (TB3MS) and the University of Michigan Inflation Expectation (MICH).

b. Using the data you found in part (a), calculate the expected real interest rate.

c. If the actual inflation rate is greater than the expected inflation rate, how are borrowers and lenders affected?

D9.11 **(Calculating the effect of inflation on real wages)** Go to the Web site of the Federal Reserve Bank of St. Louis (FRED) (fred.stlouisfed.org).

a. Find the values for the most recent month and for the month one year earlier for the Consumer Price Index for All Urban Consumers: All Items (CPIAUCNS) and Average Hourly Earnings of Production and Nonsupervisory Employees: Total Private (AHETPI).

b. Using the data you found in part (a), calculate the average hourly real wage for each year.

c. Calculate the percentage change in the average hourly nominal wage and the average hourly real wage during this year.

d. Given your calculation in part (c), explain whether an average worker was better or worse off than a year earlier.

Critical Thinking Exercises

CT9.1 Assume that the economy has just come out of a severe recession, and growth is booming. The labor force is growing because many unemployed people who thought they could not find a job during the recession now think they can and have started to look. But, these people do not find a job this month. What do you think will happen to the unemployment rate this month?

CT9.2 In Chapter 8, you learned how to compute one price index, the GDP deflator. In this chapter, you learned how to compute another price index, the CPI. In computing both indexes, something is held constant. In one paragraph, describe the construction of each index and explain what is held constant.

CT9.3 Visit "What are the interest rates for federal student loans?" at https://studentaid.ed.gov/sa/types/loans/interest-rates#rates and find the interest rate on Stafford Loans, the most common type of student loan. Suppose that you took out a loan at this rate. Note that this rate is constant for the life of the loan. Next, suppose that at your first job after graduation, there are two possibilities: (i) the inflation rate is 2%, and your wages rise by 4% or (ii) the inflation rate is 3%, and your wages rise by 5%. (No, you certainly do not get a choice of inflation rates, but pretend that you can for the sake of exploring this important concept.) Briefly explain whether you would prefer the first or the second situation.

Economic Growth, the Financial System, and Business Cycles

Economic Growth and the Business Cycle at Chevron Corporation

Whatever the state of the economy, people need to drive. And, over time, as population grows and people buy more cars, the demand for gasoline will always increase. What could be easier than selling gasoline? If you were to ask managers at Chevron Corporation, you would find that they face both short-run and long-run challenges to selling gasoline. Chevron began as the Pacific Coast Oil Company in 1879, before coming under the control of John D. Rockefeller's Standard Oil Company in 1900. The firm became independent in 1911 and later took the Chevron name. In its long history, Chevron has faced two key facts: (1) sales of gasoline rise and fall during the business cycle, and (2) technological change has played a major role in the long-run growth of the oil industry.

The recession of 2007–2009 was the worst economic downturn the United States has experienced since the Great Depression of the 1930s. As incomes fell and unemployment rose during and immediately after the recession, gasoline sales declined, and Chevron's profit from that portion of its business plunged by more than 80 percent. Over the long run, technological change at Chevron and other oil companies has continually reduced the cost of refining gasoline and other products made from crude oil. Because of technological change, oil companies were able to produce almost twice as much output from refineries in 2016 as in 1950 while using 60 percent fewer workers. Rapid increases in *labor productivity*, or output per worker, have occurred in many industries and have been a key to long-run economic growth in the United States.

But Chevron also faced long-run threats to the growth in demand for gasoline; technological change in the automobile industry has improved gasoline mileage for

Trong Nguyen/Shutterstock

conventional automobiles and the efficiency of hybrid and all-electric automobiles. Some industry analysts believe that *peak oil demand*, after which sales of gasoline and other oil-based products would begin to decline, might soon occur. Although the demand for oil more than tripled between 1965 and 2017, forecasters at the European oil firm Royal Dutch Shell predicted that peak oil demand could occur as early as 2025. Other analysts believed that peak demand would not occur until the mid-2040s, and economists at Chevron argued that it might not occur until even later. Whichever forecast turned out to be correct, economists and oil firm managers agreed that technological change was transforming the oil market.

In this chapter, we provide an overview of long-run growth and the business cycle and discuss their importance for firms, consumers, and the economy as a whole.

Sources: Lynn Cook and Elena Cherney, "Get Ready for Peak Oil Demand," *Wall Street Journal*, May 22, 2017; Tom Randall, "Here's How Electric Cars Will Cause the Next Oil Crisis," bloomberg.com, February 25, 2016; U.S. Energy Information Administration; and Chevron Corporation, *Annual Report*, various years.

Chapter Outline & Learning Objectives

Economics in Your Life & Career

Should Your Business Be Cautious at the Beginning of a Recession?

Suppose you and a partner own a sandwich shop. A recession is just beginning, and economic forecasts indicate that it may be severe. Your partner is very worried that your sales will fall off significantly and suggests that you cut costs by laying off two of your four employees and by dropping several items from your menu to save on the cost of ingredients. Do you agree with your partner's strategy for surviving the recession? As you read this chapter, try to answer this question. You can check your answer against the one we provide on **page 345** at the end of this chapter.

A successful economy is capable of increasing production of goods and services faster than the growth in population. Attaining this level of growth is the only way that the standard of living of the average person in a country can increase. Unfortunately, some economies around the world are not growing at all or are growing very slowly. Most people in those countries live on about the same levels of income as their ancestors did decades, or even centuries, ago. In the United States and other developed countries, however, incomes and living standards are much higher today than they were 50 years ago. An important macroeconomic topic is why some countries grow much faster than others.

As we will see, one determinant of economic growth is the ability of firms to expand their operations, buy additional equipment, train workers, and adopt new technologies. To carry out these activities, firms must acquire funds from households, either directly through financial markets—such as the stock and bond markets—or indirectly through financial intermediaries—such as banks. Financial markets and financial intermediaries together comprise the *financial system*. In this chapter, we present an overview of the financial system and look at how funds flow from households to firms through the *market for loanable funds*.

Since at least the early nineteenth century, the U.S. economy has experienced periods of expanding production and employment followed by periods of recession during which production and employment decline. These alternating periods of expansion and recession are called the **business cycle**. Business cycles are not uniform: Periods of expansion are not the same length, nor are periods of recession. But every period of expansion in U.S. history has been followed by a period of recession, and every period of recession has been followed by a period of expansion.

In this chapter, we begin to explore two key aspects of macroeconomics: the long-run growth that has steadily raised living standards in the United States and the short-run fluctuations of the business cycle.

Business cycle Alternating periods of economic expansion and economic recession.

10.1 Long-Run Economic Growth

LEARNING OBJECTIVE: Discuss the importance of long-run economic growth.

Most people in high-income countries such as the United States, Canada, Japan, and the countries in Western Europe expect that over time, their standard of living will improve. They expect that year after year, firms will introduce new and improved products, new prescription drugs and better surgical techniques will overcome more diseases, and their ability to afford these goods and services will increase. For most people, these are reasonable expectations.

In 1900, the United States was already enjoying the highest standard of living in the world. Yet in that year, only 3 percent of U.S. homes had electricity, only 15 percent had indoor flush toilets, and only 25 percent had running water. The lack of running water meant that before people could cook or bathe, they had to pump water from wells and haul it to their homes in buckets—on average about 10,000 gallons per year per family. Not surprisingly, water consumption averaged only about 5 gallons per person per day, compared with about 150 gallons today. The result was that people washed themselves and their clothing only infrequently. A majority of families living in cities had to use outdoor toilets, which they shared with other families. Diseases such as smallpox, typhus, dysentery, and cholera were still common. In 1900, 5,000 of the 45,000 children born in Chicago died before their first birthday. Life expectancy at birth was about 47 years, compared with 80 years in 2017. Few families had electric lights; they relied instead on candles or burning kerosene or coal oil in lamps. Many homes were heated in the winter by burning coal, which contributed to the severe pollution that fouled the air of most large cities. In 1900, there were no modern appliances, and housework was time-consuming and physically demanding. The typical American homemaker baked a half-ton of bread per year.

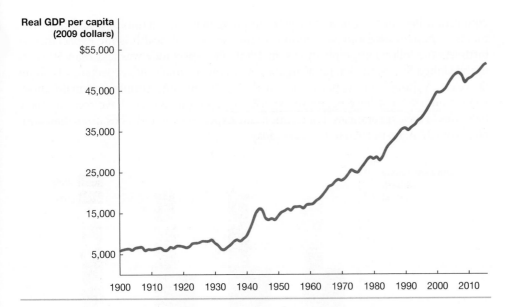

MyLab Economics Real-time data

Figure 10.1

The Growth in Real GDP per Capita, 1900–2016

Measured in 2009 dollars, real GDP per capita in the United States grew from about $6,000 in 1900 to about $51,500 in 2016. An average American in 2016 could buy more than eight times as many goods and services as an average American in 1900.

Sources: For 1900–1946: Louis Johnston and Samuel H. Williamson, "What Was the U.S. GDP Then?" MeasuringWorth, 2017; and for 1947–2016: U.S. Bureau of Economic Analysis.

The process of **long-run economic growth** brought the typical American from the standard of living of 1900 to the standard of living of today. The best measure of the standard of living is real GDP per person, which is usually called *real GDP per capita*. We measure long-run economic growth by increases in real GDP per capita over long periods of time, generally decades or more. We use real GDP rather than nominal GDP to adjust for changes in the price level over time. Figure 10.1 shows the growth in real GDP per capita in the United States from 1900 to 2016. The figure shows that the trend in real GDP per capita is strongly upward, although it fluctuates in the short run because of the business cycle. It is the upward trend in real GDP per capita that we focus on when discussing long-run economic growth.

The values in Figure 10.1 are measured in 2009 dollars, so they represent constant amounts of purchasing power. In 1900, real GDP per capita was about $6,000. More than a century later, in 2016, it had risen to about $51,500, which means that an average American in 2016 could purchase more than eight times as many goods and services as an average American in 1900. Large as it is, this increase in real GDP per capita actually understates the true increase in the standard of living of Americans in 2016 compared with 1900. Many of today's goods and services were not available in 1900. For example, if you lived in 1900 and became ill with a serious infection, you could not purchase antibiotics to treat your illness—no matter how high your income. You might have died from an illness for which even a very poor person in today's society could receive effective medical treatment. Nor would you have access to many of the products of modern life, including air conditioning, the Internet, and smartphones. Of course, the goods and services that a person can buy is not a perfect measure of how happy or contented that person may be. A person's happiness also depends on education, health, spiritual well-being, and many other factors ignored in calculating GDP. Nevertheless, economists rely heavily on comparisons of real GDP per capita because it is the best means of comparing the performance of one economy over time or the performance of different economies at any particular time.   **MyLab Economics** Concept Check

Long-run economic growth The process by which rising productivity increases the average standard of living.

Apply the Concept   **MyLab Economics** Video

The Connection between Economic Prosperity and Health

We can see the direct effect of economic growth on living standards by looking at improvements in health in high-income countries over the past 100 years. The research of the late Robert Fogel, winner of the Nobel Prize in Economics, highlights the close connection between economic growth, improvements in technology, and improvements in human physiology. One important measure of health is life expectancy at birth. As the following graph shows, in 1900, life expectancy was less than 50 years in the United States, the United Kingdom, and France. Today, life expectancy is about 80 years. Although life expectancies in the lowest-income countries remain short, some countries that have begun to experience economic growth have seen dramatic increases in life expectancies. For example, life expectancy in India has more than doubled from 27 years in 1900 to 69 years today.

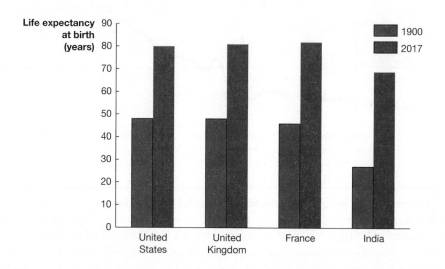

Many economists believe there is a link between health and economic growth. In the United States and Western Europe during the nineteenth century, improvements in agricultural technology and rising incomes led to dramatic improvements in the nutrition of the average person. The development of the germ theory of disease and technological progress in the purification of water in the late nineteenth century led to sharp declines in sickness due to waterborne diseases. As people became taller, stronger, and less susceptible to disease, they also became more productive. Evidence has also shown that, over time, people have become more intelligent, with scores on intelligence tests having increased about 30 percent over the past 100 years. These increases may be the result of rising incomes that both increase the health of children, allowing them to learn more in schools, and provide the means by which parents can afford to keep children in school longer. The greater learning will allow these children to be more productive as adults. Their higher productivity will allow them to earn higher incomes and have healthier children who will have greater opportunities for learning, and so on. Today, economists studying economic development have put increasing emphasis on the need for low-income countries to reduce disease and increase nutrition as important first steps toward increasing economic growth.

Many researchers believe that the state of human physiology will continue to improve as technology advances. In high-income countries, life expectancy at birth is expected to rise from about 80 years today to about 90 years by the middle of the twenty-first century. Technological advances will continue to reduce the average number of hours worked per day and the number of years an average person spends in the paid workforce. Individuals spend about 10 hours per day sleeping, eating, and bathing. Their remaining "discretionary hours" are divided between paid work and leisure. The following graph is based on estimates by Robert Fogel that contrast how individuals in the United States will divide their time in 2040 compared with 1880 and 1995. Not only will technology and economic growth allow people in the near future to live longer lives, but a much smaller fraction of those lives will need to be spent at paid work.

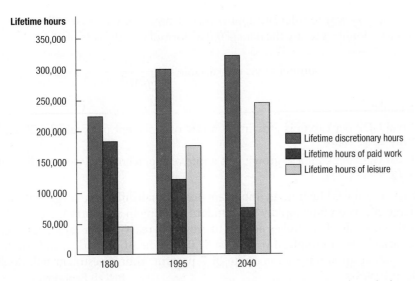

Sources: Robert William Fogel, *The Escape from Hunger and Premature Death, 1700–2100*, New York: Cambridge University Press, 2004; Alison Gopnik, "Smarter Every Year? Mystery of the Rising IQs," *Wall Street Journal*, May 27, 2015; and U.S. Central Intelligence Agency, *The 2017 World Factbook*, online version.

Your Turn: Test your understanding by doing related problem 1.6 on page 346 at the end of this chapter.

MyLab Economics Study Plan

Calculating Growth Rates and the Rule of 70

The growth rate of real GDP or real GDP per capita during a particular year is equal to the percentage change from the previous year. For example, measured in 2009 prices, real GDP equaled $16,397 billion in 2015 and rose to $16,662 billion in 2016. We calculate the growth of real GDP in 2016 as:

$$\left(\frac{\$16,\!662 \text{ billion} - \$16,\!397 \text{ billion}}{\$16.397 \text{ billion}} \right) \times 100 = 1.6\%.$$

For longer periods of time, we can use the *average annual growth rate*. For example, real GDP in the United States was $2,184 billion in 1950 and $16,662 billion in 2016. To find the average annual growth rate during this 66-year period, we compute the annual growth rate that would result in $2,184 billion increasing to $16,662 billion over 66 years. In this case, the growth rate is 3.1 percent. That is, if $2,184 billion grows at an average rate of 3.1 percent per year, after 66 years, it will have grown to $16,662 billion.

For shorter periods of time, we get approximately the same answer by averaging the growth rate for each year. For example, real GDP in the United States grew by 2.4 percent in 2014, 2.6 percent in 2015, and 1.6 percent in 2016. So, the average annual growth rate of real GDP for the period 2014–2016 was 2.2 percent, which is the average of the three annual growth rates:

$$\frac{2.4\% + 2.6\% + 1.6\%}{3} = 2.2\%.$$

Finally, when discussing long-run economic growth, we usually shorten "average annual growth rate" to "growth rate."

We can judge how rapidly an economic variable is growing by calculating the number of years it would take to double. For example, if real GDP per capita in a country doubles, say, every 20 years, most people in the country will experience significant increases in their standard of living over the course of their lives. If real GDP per capita doubles only every 100 years, increases in the standard of living will occur too slowly to notice. One easy way to calculate approximately how many years it will take real GDP per capita to double is to use the *rule of 70*. The formula for the rule of 70 is:

$$\text{Number of years to double} = \frac{70}{\text{Growth rate}}.$$

For example:

- If real GDP per capita is growing at a rate of 5 percent per year, it will double in 70/5 = 14 years.
- If real GDP per capita is growing at a rate of 2 percent per year, it will double in 70/2 = 35 years.

These examples illustrate an important point: Small differences in growth rates can have large effects on how rapidly the standard of living in a country increases. Finally, notice that the rule of 70 applies not just to growth in real GDP per capita but to growth in any variable. For example, if you invest $1,000 in the stock market, and your investment grows at an average annual rate of 7 percent, your investment will double to $2,000 in 10 years. **MyLab Economics** Concept Check

What Determines the Rate of Long-Run Growth?

A key point in explaining long-run growth is that *increases in real GDP per capita depend on increases in labor productivity*. **Labor productivity** is the quantity of goods and services that can be produced by one worker or by one hour of work. In analyzing long-run growth, economists usually measure labor productivity as output per hour of work to avoid the effects of fluctuations in the length of the workday and in the fraction of the population employed. If the quantity of goods and services consumed by the average person is to increase, the quantity of goods and services produced per hour of work must also increase. Why in 2016 was the average American able to consume more than eight times as many goods and services as the average American in 1900? Because the average American worker in 2016 was eight times as productive as the average American worker in 1900. As we saw in the chapter opener, Chevron and other oil companies have experienced large increases in labor productivity in refining oil. The ability of the U.S. economy to produce increasing amounts of gasoline and other oil-based products per worker is one of many reasons that the U.S. standard of living has increased substantially over time.

> **Labor productivity** The quantity of goods and services that can be produced by one worker or by one hour of work.

If increases in labor productivity are the key to long-run economic growth, what causes labor productivity to increase? Economists believe two key factors determine labor productivity:

1. The quantity of capital per hour worked
2. The level of technology

Therefore, economic growth occurs if the quantity of capital per hour worked increases and if there is technological change.

Increases in Capital per Hour Worked
Workers today in high-income countries such as the United States have more physical capital available than workers in low-income countries or workers in the high-income countries of 100 years ago. Recall that **capital** refers to manufactured goods that are used to produce other goods and services. Examples of capital are computers, factory buildings, machine tools, warehouses, and trucks. The total amount of physical capital available in a country is known as the country's *capital stock*.

> **Capital** Manufactured goods that are used to produce other goods and services.

As the amount of capital per hour worked increases, worker productivity increases. An accountant who records a firm's revenues and costs using Excel is more productive than an accountant who uses only pen and paper. A worker who uses a backhoe can excavate more earth than a worker who uses only a shovel.

In explaining economic growth, economists take into account not just *physical capital*, like computers and factories, but also *human capital*, which is the accumulated knowledge and skills workers acquire from education and training or from their life experiences. For example, workers with a college education generally have more skills and are more productive than workers who have only a high school degree. Increases in human capital are particularly important in stimulating economic growth.

Technological Change *Technology* refers to the processes a firm uses to turn inputs into outputs of goods and services. Economic growth depends more on *technological change* than on increases in capital per hour worked. Technological change is an increase in the quantity of output firms can produce, using a given quantity of inputs, and can come from many sources. For example, a firm's managers may rearrange a factory floor or the layout of a retail store to increase production and sales. Most technological change, however, is embodied in new machinery, equipment, or software. Technological change can improve labor productivity at existing firms, as has happened at Chevron with innovations in oil refining. But it can also disrupt existing firms by making possible new products or radical improvements in existing products, as when improvements in battery technology decreased the cost of electric cars and potentially undermined the long-term prospects of oil companies.

A key point is that just accumulating more inputs—such as labor, capital, and natural resources—will *not* ensure that an economy can generate an increasing standard of living for the average person unless technological change also occurs. For example, living standards in the Soviet Union stagnated, even though the country continued to increase the quantity of capital available per hour worked, because it experienced relatively little technological change.

Entrepreneurs are critical for implementing technological change. Recall that an entrepreneur is someone who operates a business, bringing together the factors of production—labor, capital, and natural resources—to produce goods and services (see Chapter 2, Section 2.3). In a market economy, entrepreneurs make the crucial decisions about whether to introduce new technology to produce better or lower-cost products. Entrepreneurs also decide whether to allocate a firm's resources to research and development that can result in new technologies. One of the difficulties centrally planned economies have in sustaining economic growth is that managers employed by the government are usually much slower to develop and adopt new technologies than are entrepreneurs in a market system.

Solved Problem 10.1

Where Does Productivity Come From?

One article in the *Wall Street Journal* argued that "productivity growth is a key ingredient to prosperity," while another article noted that "weak business spending on buildings and equipment … could be one factor behind tepid productivity gains."

a. What does the first article mean by "prosperity"? What is the connection between productivity growth and prosperity?

b. Why might weak business spending on buildings and equipment help explain slow increases in productivity?

Solving the Problem

Step 1: **Review the chapter material.** This problem is about what determines the rate of long-run growth, so you may want to review the section "What Determines the Rate of Long-Run Growth?" which begins on page 324.

Step 2: **Answer the first question in part (a) by explaining what the first article means by "prosperity" in this context.** By *prosperity*, most people mean a high standard of living. In the context of economic growth, the key measure of the standard of living is real GDP per capita.

Step 3: **Answer the second question in part (a) by explaining the connection between productivity growth and prosperity.** *Productivity* refers to the amount of goods and services produced per worker. As we have seen, per capita real GDP increases only if productivity increases. Therefore, increases in a country's standard of living—its prosperity—are tied to increases in productivity.

Step 4: **Answer part (b) by explaining the connection between business spending on buildings and equipment and productivity growth.** Buildings and equipment are part of capital. Most technological change is embodied in new capital. So, increased spending on buildings and equipment may increase productivity by facilitating technological change.

Sources: Jon Hilsenrath, "More Disturbing Findings Emerge on U.S. Productivity Path," *Wall Street Journal*, February 12, 2015; and Jeffrey Sparshott, "U.S. Productivity Fell in the First Quarter," *Wall Street Journal*, May 4, 2017.

MyLab Economics Study Plan **Your Turn:** For more practice, do related problems 1.9 and 1.10 on pages 346–347 at the end of this chapter.

Property Rights Finally, an additional requirement for economic growth is that the government must provide secure rights to private property. A market system cannot function unless rights to private property are secure (see Chapter 2, Section 2.3). The government can aid economic growth by establishing an independent court system that enforces contracts between private individuals. Many economists would also say that the government has a role in facilitating the development of an efficient financial system, as well as systems of education, transportation, and communication. Economist Richard Sylla of New York University has argued that every country that has experienced economic growth has first undergone a "financial revolution." For example, before the United States was able to begin significant economic growth in the early nineteenth century, the country's banking and monetary systems were reformed under the guidance of Alexander Hamilton, who was appointed the country's first secretary of the Treasury in 1789. Without supportive government policies, long-run economic growth is unlikely to occur. **MyLab Economics** Concept Check

Apply the Concept

MyLab Economics Video

Can India Sustain Its Rapid Growth?

When you have a computer problem and need technical support, the person who takes your call may well be in India. In recent years Indian firms have also made gains in the global markets for goods such as steel, oil, and automobiles.

To many people in the United States, the rapid economic rise of India has been unexpected. As the following figure shows, Indian real GDP per capita increased very slowly up to the time India became independent from England in 1947. As a result, in 1950, India was desperately poor. India's real GDP per capita in 1950 was less than $1,000 measured in 2017 dollars, or less than 7 percent of 1950 U.S. real GDP per capita. During the first 40 years of independence, India's growth rate increased but was still too slow to significantly reduce the country's poverty. Recent years tell a much different story, however. In 1991, the Indian government decided to scale back central planning, reduce regulations, and introduce market-based reforms. The result was that the growth rate doubled over the following decade. In the most recent period, growth has been even more rapid.

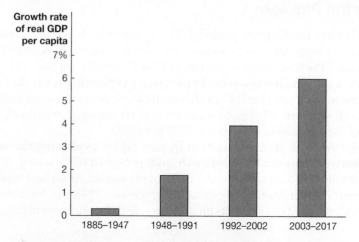

Still, India remains a very poor country. Nearly half of its population of 1.3 billion is employed in agriculture, and many can barely produce enough to feed themselves. Infant mortality rates are still at 10 times the levels in high-income countries, and nearly 40 percent of adult women and 20 percent of adult men are unable to read and write. The rapid economic growth that began in 1991 will have to continue in the coming decades if the average person in India is eventually to enjoy a standard of living equal to that in the United States and other high-income countries. But can India continue its rapid growth?

Some economists and policymakers worry that India's growth rates may begin to decline, leaving hundreds of millions of its people stuck in deep poverty. These economists point to several problems facing the Indian economy. The public education system has struggled to provide basic instruction, particularly in rural and poorer urban areas. India's expenditures on education rank 134th out of 173 countries and are far below the levels in most successful developing countries. As a result, many adults lack the basic skills needed for a productive workforce. Even many high school and college graduates lack the skills to work in firms that compete in global markets. High rates of infectious disease also reduce the productivity of the workforce. Only 60 percent of urban residents have access to modern sewage systems, and fewer than one-quarter of rural residents do. In general, India has struggled to meet its infrastructure needs, as highways, bridges, and its train system—which dates from the British colonial period—have deteriorated.

India also suffers from political problems with ethnic, religious, cultural, and geographic divisions—there are 15 official languages—often making it difficult for the government to successfully implement policy reforms. In 2016, the Indian parliament finally began the process of replacing a complex system of state and local taxes with a single federal tax. While a manager for the U.S.-based consulting firm KPMG described the change as "the mother of all economic reforms in India," the government was slow to implement the new tax system.

One estimate puts the size of the underground economy in India at more than 50 percent of GDP. In November 2016, the government attempted to reduce the size of the underground economy with a sudden announcement that it would withdraw the two largest currency denominations. Households and firms had until the end of the year to deposit the bills in banks or exchange them for newly printed bills. The government's intention was to force people who had accumulated cash in the underground economy to either account for how they had legally earned it or pay taxes on it. But with many household and firms—particularly in lower-income areas—conducting most transactions in cash, the government's new policy disrupted economic activity, at least in the short run.

Although Narendra Modi was elected prime minister in 2014 partly by promising new policies to spur economic growth, some economists and policymakers worry that the pace of market-oriented reforms has slowed over the years and that government corruption remains an obstacle to starting and expanding businesses. These economists and policymakers urge the government to allow greater foreign investment in the financial and retail sectors. Although foreign firms have been allowed to own retail stores in India since 2012, a requirement that at least 30 percent of the products sold be made in India has made it difficult for foreign firms like IKEA, the Swedish furniture store, to succeed. Greater foreign investment would allow India to gain access to new technology and to increase productivity.

The economic progress India has made in the past 25 years has already lifted hundreds of millions of people out of poverty. For that progress to continue, however, many economists believe that the Indian government will need to upgrade infrastructure, improve educational and health services, and renew its commitment to the rule of law and to market-based reforms.

Sources: Raymond Zhong, Niharika Mandhana, and Rajesh Roy, "Micromanager-in-Chief: Narendra Modi Upends How India Is Run," *Wall Street Journal*, March 9, 2017; "Ready, Steady, Go," *Economist*, April 18, 2015; Amartya Sen, "Why India Trails China," *New York Times*, June 19, 2013; "The Dire Consequences of India's Demonetisation Initiative," *Economist*, December 3, 2016; Preetika Rana, "IKEA's India Bet Runs into Thicket of Rules," *Wall Street Journal*, February 23, 2016;

data in graph are authors' calculations from the Maddison Project database, www.ggdc.net/maddison/maddison-project/home.htm and International Monetary Fund, *World Economic Outlook Database*.

MyLab Economics Study Plan

Your Turn: Test your understanding by doing related problems 1.12 and 1.13 on page 347 at the end of this chapter.

Potential GDP

Potential GDP The level of real GDP attained when all firms are producing at capacity.

Because economists take a long-run perspective in discussing economic growth, the concept of *potential GDP* is useful. **Potential GDP** is the level of real GDP attained when all firms are producing at *capacity*. The capacity of a firm is *not* the maximum output the firm is capable of producing. An automobile factory could operate 24 hours per day for 52 weeks per year and would be at its maximum production level. The factory's capacity, however, is measured by its production when operating on normal hours, using a normal workforce. If all firms in the economy were operating at capacity, the level of total production of final goods and services would equal potential GDP. Potential GDP increases over time as the labor force grows, new factories and office buildings are built, new machinery and equipment are installed, and technological change takes place.

From 1949 to 2017, potential GDP in the United States grew at an average annual rate of 3.2 percent. In other words, each year, on average, the capacity of the economy to produce final goods and services expanded by 3.2 percent. In any particular year, the *actual* level of real GDP increased by more or less than 3.2 percent as the economy moved through the business cycle. Figure 10.2 shows movements in actual and potential GDP for the years since 1989. The red line represents potential GDP, and the blue line represents actual real GDP. Notice that in each of the three recessions since 1989, actual real GDP has fallen below potential GDP. During the 2007–2009 recession, the gap between actual real GDP and potential GDP was particularly large, which indicates the severity of the recession.

MyLab Economics Study Plan

MyLab Economics Concept Check

MyLab Economics Real-time data

Figure 10.2 **Actual and Potential GDP**

Potential GDP increases every year as the labor force and the capital stock grow and technological change occurs. The red line represents potential GDP, and the blue line represents actual real GDP. During the three recessions since 1989, actual real GDP has been less than potential GDP.

Source: Federal Reserve Bank of St. Louis.

Saving, Investment, and the Financial System

0.2

LEARNING OBJECTIVE: Discuss the role of the financial system in facilitating long-run economic growth.

The process of economic growth depends on the ability of firms to expand their operations, buy additional equipment, train workers, and adopt new technologies. Firms can finance some of these activities from *retained earnings*, which are profits that are reinvested in the firm rather than paid to the firm's owners. For many firms, retained earnings are not sufficient to finance the rapid expansion required in economies experiencing high rates of economic growth. These firms can acquire funds from households, either directly through financial markets—such as the stock and bond markets—or indirectly through financial intermediaries—such as banks. Financial markets and financial intermediaries together comprise the **financial system**. Without a well-functioning financial system, economic growth is impossible because firms will be unable to expand and adopt new technologies. As we noted earlier, no country without a well-developed financial system has been able to sustain high levels of economic growth.

Financial system The system of financial markets and financial intermediaries through which firms acquire funds from households.

An Overview of the Financial System

The financial system channels funds from savers to borrowers and channels returns on the borrowed funds back to savers. In this section, we discuss the key components of the financial system and the services they provide to households and firms.

Financial Markets In **financial markets**, such as the stock market or the bond market, firms raise funds by selling financial securities directly to savers (see Chapter 6, Section 6.2). A *financial security* is a document—sometimes in electronic form—that states the terms under which funds pass from the buyer of the security—who is providing funds—to the seller. *Stocks* are financial securities that represent partial ownership of a firm. If you buy one share of stock in Chevron, you become one of millions of owners of that firm. *Bonds* are financial securities that represent promises to repay a fixed amount of funds. When Chevron sells a bond, the firm promises to pay the purchaser of the bond an interest payment each year for the term of the bond, as well as a final payment of the amount of the loan.

Financial markets Markets where financial securities, such as stocks and bonds, are bought and sold.

Financial Intermediaries **Financial intermediaries**, such as banks, mutual funds, pension funds, and insurance companies, act as go-betweens for borrowers and lenders. In effect, financial intermediaries borrow funds from savers and lend them to borrowers. When you deposit funds in your checking account, you are lending your funds to the bank. The bank may lend your funds (together with the funds of other savers) to an entrepreneur who wants to start a business. Suppose Lena wants to open a laundry. Rather than your lending money directly to Lena's Laundry, the bank acts as a go-between for you and Lena. Intermediaries pool the funds of many small savers to lend to many individual borrowers. The intermediaries pay interest to savers in exchange for the use of savers' funds and earn a profit by lending money to borrowers and charging them a higher rate of interest on the loans. For example, a bank might pay you as a depositor a 1 percent rate of interest, while it lends the money to Lena's Laundry at a 6 percent rate of interest.

Financial intermediaries Firms, such as banks, mutual funds, pension funds, and insurance companies, that borrow funds from savers and lend them to borrowers.

Banks, mutual funds, pension funds, and insurance companies also make investments in stocks and bonds on behalf of savers. For example, *mutual funds* sell shares to savers and then use the funds to buy a portfolio of stocks, bonds, mortgages, and other financial securities. Large mutual fund companies, such as Fidelity, Vanguard, and Dreyfus, offer many stock and bond funds. Some funds hold a wide range of stocks or bonds; others specialize in securities issued by a particular industry or sector, such as health care; and others invest as index funds in fixed market baskets of securities, such as shares of the Standard & Poor's 500 firms. Over the past 30 years, the role of mutual funds in the financial system has increased dramatically. Today, competition among hundreds of mutual fund firms gives investors thousands of funds from which to choose.

The Services the Financial System Provides: Risk Sharing, Liquidity, and Information In addition to matching households that have excess funds with firms that want to borrow funds, the financial system provides three key services for savers and borrowers:

1. **Risk sharing.** *Risk* is the chance that the value of a financial security will change relative to what you expect. For example, you may buy a share of stock in Chevron at a price of $90, only to have the price fall to $50. Most individual savers are not gamblers and seek a steady return on their savings rather than erratic swings between high and low earnings. The financial system provides *risk sharing* by allowing savers to spread their money among many financial investments. For example, you can divide your money among a bank certificate of deposit, individual bonds, and a stock mutual fund.

2. **Liquidity.** *Liquidity* is the ease with which a financial security can be exchanged for money. The financial system provides the service of liquidity by offering savers markets where they can sell their holdings of financial securities. For example, savers can easily sell their holdings of the stocks and bonds issued by large corporations on the major stock and bond markets.

3. **Information.** The financial system collects and communicates *information*, or facts about borrowers and expectations about returns on financial securities. For example, Lena's Laundry may want to borrow $10,000 from you. Finding out what Lena intends to do with the funds and how likely she is to pay you back may be costly and time-consuming. By depositing $10,000 in the bank, you are, in effect, allowing the bank to gather this information for you. Because banks specialize in gathering information about borrowers, they are able to do it faster and at a lower cost than can individual savers. The financial system plays an important role in communicating information. If you read a news story announcing that an automobile firm has invented a car with an engine that runs on water, how would you determine the effect of that discovery on the firm's profit? Financial markets do the job for you by incorporating information into the prices of stocks, bonds, and other financial securities. In this example, the expectation of higher future profit would boost the prices of the automobile firm's stock and bonds.   **MyLab Economics** Concept Check

The Macroeconomics of Saving and Investment

As we have seen, the funds available to firms through the financial system come from saving. When firms use funds to purchase machinery, factories, and office buildings, they are engaging in investment. In this section, we explore the macroeconomics of saving and investment. A key point we will develop is that *the total value of saving in the economy must equal the total value of investment*. *National income accounting* refers to the methods the Bureau of Economic Analysis uses to keep track of total production and total income in the economy (see Chapter 8, Section 8.4). We can use some relationships from national income accounting to understand why total saving must equal total investment.

We begin with the relationship between gross domestic product, GDP (Y), and its components, consumption (C), investment (I), government purchases (G), and net exports (NX):

$$Y = C + I + G + NX.$$

Remember that GDP is a measure of both total production in the economy and total income.

In an *open economy*, there is interaction with other economies in terms of both trading of goods and services and borrowing and lending. All economies today are open economies, although they vary significantly in the extent of their openness. In a *closed economy*, there is no trading or borrowing and lending with other economies. For simplicity, we will develop the relationship between saving and investment for a closed economy, which allows us to focus on the most important points in a simpler framework. (See Chapter 18, Section 18.3 for the case of an open economy.)

In a closed economy, net exports are zero, so we can rewrite the relationship between GDP and its components as:

$$Y = C + I + G.$$

The Saving Equals Investment Condition If we rearrange the equation showing the relationship between GDP and its components, we have an expression for investment in terms of the other variables:

$$I = Y - C - G.$$

This expression tells us that in a closed economy, investment spending is equal to total income minus consumption spending and minus government purchases.

We can also derive an expression for total saving. *Private saving* is equal to what households retain of their income after purchasing goods and services (C) and paying taxes (T). Households receive income for supplying the factors of production to firms. This portion of household income is equal to Y. Households also receive income from government in the form of *transfer payments* (TR), which include Social Security payments and unemployment insurance payments. We can write this expression for private saving ($S_{Private}$):

$$S_{Private} = Y + TR - C - T.$$

The government also engages in saving. *Public saving* (S_{Public}) equals the amount of tax revenue the government retains after paying for government purchases and making transfer payments to households:

$$S_{Public} = T - G - TR.$$

So, total saving in the economy (S) is equal to the sum of private saving and public saving:

$$S = S_{Private} + S_{Public},$$

or:

$$S = (Y + TR - C - T) + (T - G - TR),$$

or:

$$S = Y - C - G.$$

The right side of this expression is identical to the expression we derived earlier for investment spending. So, we can conclude that total saving must equal total investment:

$$S = I.$$

Budget Deficits and Budget Surpluses When the government spends the same amount that it collects in taxes, there is a *balanced budget*. When the government spends more than it collects in taxes, there is a *budget deficit*. In the case of a deficit, T is less than G + TR, which means that public saving is negative. Negative saving is also known as *dissaving*. How can public saving be negative? When the federal government runs a budget deficit, the U.S. Department of the Treasury sells Treasury bonds to borrow the money necessary to fund the gap between taxes and spending. In this case, rather than adding to the total amount of saving available to be borrowed for investment spending, the government is subtracting from it. (Notice that when households borrow more than they save, the total amount of saving also falls.) With less saving, investment must also be lower. We can conclude that, holding constant all other factors, there is a lower level of investment spending in the economy when there is a budget deficit than when there is a balanced budget.

When the government spends less than it collects in taxes, there is a *budget surplus*. A budget surplus increases public saving and the total level of saving in the economy.

A higher level of saving results in a higher level of investment spending. Therefore, holding constant all other factors, there is a higher level of investment spending in the economy when there is a budget surplus than when there is a balanced budget.

The U.S. federal government has experienced dramatic swings in the state of its budget over the past 20 years. A sharp decline in taxes and increase in government spending resulting from the recession of 2007–2009 led to a record budget deficit of $1.4 trillion in 2009. As the economy recovered, the budget deficit had declined to $587 billion by 2016. In 2017, the Trump administration proposed major changes to federal government spending and to the federal tax code. Whether Congress would enact these proposals and what their effects might be on the federal budget deficit remained to be seen. **MyLab Economics** Concept Check

The Market for Loanable Funds

We have seen that the value of total saving must equal the value of total investment, but we have not yet discussed how this equality is actually brought about in the financial system. We can think of the financial system as being composed of many markets through which funds flow from lenders to borrowers: the market for certificates of deposit at banks, the market for stocks, the market for bonds, the market for mutual fund shares, and so on. For simplicity, we can combine these markets into a single **market for loanable funds**. In the loanable funds model, the interaction of borrowers and lenders determines the market interest rate and the quantity of loanable funds exchanged. As we will discuss in a later chapter, firms can also borrow from savers in other countries (see Chapter 18, Section 18.3). For the remainder of this section, we will assume that there are no interactions between households and firms in the United States and those in other countries.

Demand and Supply in the Loanable Funds Market
The demand for loanable funds is determined by the willingness of firms to borrow to engage in new investment projects, such as building new factories or carrying out research and development of new products. In determining whether to borrow, firms compare the return they expect to make on an investment with the interest rate they must pay to borrow the necessary funds. For example, if Amazon is considering opening several new warehouses and expects to earn a return of 12 percent on its investment, the investment will be profitable if Amazon can borrow the funds at an interest rate of 8 percent but will not be profitable if the interest rate is 15 percent. In Figure 10.3, the demand for loanable funds is downward sloping because the lower the interest rate, the more investment projects firms can profitably undertake, and the greater the quantity of loanable funds they will demand.

The supply of loanable funds is determined by the willingness of households to save and by the extent of government saving or dissaving. When households save, they reduce

Market for loanable funds The interaction of borrowers and lenders that determines the market interest rate and the quantity of loanable funds exchanged.

MyLab Economics Animation

Figure 10.3

The Market for Loanable Funds

The demand for loanable funds is determined by the willingness of firms to borrow to engage in new investment projects. The supply of loanable funds is determined by the willingness of households to save and by the extent of government saving or dissaving. Equilibrium in the market for loanable funds determines the real interest rate and the quantity of loanable funds exchanged.

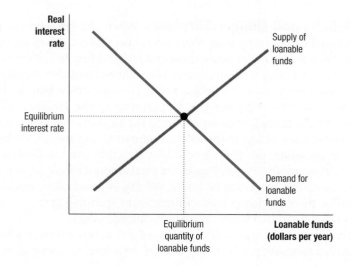

the amount of goods and services they can consume and enjoy today. The willingness of households to save rather than consume their incomes today will be determined in part by the interest rate they receive when they lend their savings. The higher the interest rate, the greater the reward for saving and the larger the amount of funds households will save. Therefore, the supply curve for loanable funds in Figure 10.3 is upward sloping because the higher the interest rate, the greater the quantity of saving supplied.

Recall the distinction between the *nominal interest rate* and the *real interest rate* (see Chapter 9, Section 9.6). The nominal interest rate is the stated interest rate on a loan. The real interest rate corrects the nominal interest rate for the effect of inflation and is equal to the nominal interest rate minus the inflation rate. Because both borrowers and lenders are concerned about the real interest rate they will receive or pay, equilibrium in the market for loanable funds determines the real interest rate rather than the nominal interest rate.

Apply the Concept

MyLab Economics Video

Ebenezer Scrooge: Accidental Promoter of Economic Growth?

Ebenezer Scrooge's name has become synonymous with miserliness. For most of Charles Dickens's *A Christmas Carol*, Scrooge is extraordinarily reluctant to spend money. Although he earns a substantial income, he lives in a cold, dark house that he refuses to heat or light adequately, and he eats a meager diet of gruel because he refuses to buy more expensive food. Dickens clearly disapproves of Scrooge's behavior. At the end of the book, when Scrooge has a change of heart and begins to spend lavishly on himself and others, Dickens clearly expects the reader to approve of Scrooge's new approach.

As economist Steven Landsburg of the University of Rochester points out, however, economically speaking, it may be the pre-reform Scrooge who is more worthy of praise:

> In this whole world, there is nobody more generous than the miser—the man who could deplete the world's resources but chooses not to. The only difference between miserliness and philanthropy is that the philanthropist serves a favored few while the miser spreads his largess far and wide.

Who was better for economic growth: Scrooge the saver or Scrooge the spender?

We can extend Landsburg's discussion to consider whether the actions of the pre-reform Scrooge or the actions of the post-reform Scrooge are more helpful to economic growth. Pre-reform Scrooge spends very little, investing most of his income in the financial markets. These funds became available for firms to borrow to build new factories and to carry out research and development. Post-reform Scrooge spends much more—and saves much less. Funds that he had previously saved are now spent on food for Bob Cratchit's family and on "making merry" at Christmas. In other words, the actions of post-reform Scrooge contribute to more consumption goods being produced and fewer investment goods. We can conclude that Scrooge's reform caused economic growth to slow down—if only by a little. The larger point is, of course, that savers provide the funds that are indispensable for the investment spending that economic growth requires, and the only way to save is to not consume.

Source: Steven Landsburg, "What I Like about Scrooge," *Slate*, December 9, 2004.

Your Turn: Test your understanding by doing related problems 2.14 and 2.15 on page 349 at the end of this chapter.

MyLab Economics Study Plan

Explaining Movements in Saving, Investment, and the Interest Rate
Equilibrium in the market for loanable funds determines the quantity of loanable funds that will flow from lenders to borrowers each period. Equilibrium also determines the real interest rate that lenders will receive and that borrowers must pay. We draw the demand curve for loanable funds by holding constant all factors, other than the interest rate, that affect the willingness of borrowers to demand funds.

MyLab Economics Animation

Figure 10.4

An Increase in the Demand for Loanable Funds

An increase in the demand for loanable funds increases the equilibrium interest rate from i_1 to i_2 and increases the equilibrium quantity of loanable funds from L_1 to L_2. As a result, saving and investment both increase.

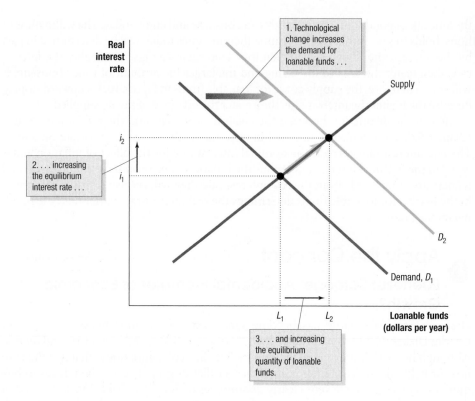

We draw the supply curve by holding constant all factors, other than the interest rate, that affect the willingness of lenders to supply funds. A shift in either the demand curve or the supply curve will change the equilibrium interest rate and the equilibrium quantity of loanable funds.

If, for example, the profitability of new investment increases due to technological change or because the government reduces corporate taxes, firms will increase their demand for loanable funds. Figure 10.4 shows the effect of an increase in demand in the market for loanable funds. As in the markets for goods and services, an increase in demand in the market for loanable funds shifts the demand curve to the right. In the new equilibrium, the interest rate increases from i_1 to i_2, and the equilibrium quantity of loanable funds increases from L_1 to L_2. Notice that an increase in the quantity of loanable funds means that both the quantity of saving by households and the quantity of investment by firms have increased. Increasing investment increases the capital stock and the quantity of capital per hour worked, helping to increase economic growth.

We can also use the market for loanable funds to examine the effect of a government budget deficit. Putting aside the effects of foreign saving, recall that if the government begins running a budget deficit, it reduces the total amount of saving in the economy. Suppose the government increases spending, which results in a budget deficit. We illustrate the effects of the budget deficit in Figure 10.5 by shifting the supply curve for loanable funds to the left. In the new equilibrium, the interest rate is higher, and the equilibrium quantity of loanable funds is lower. Running a deficit has reduced the level of total saving in the economy and, by increasing the interest rate, has also reduced the level of investment spending by firms. By borrowing to finance its budget deficit, the government will have *crowded out* some firms that would otherwise have been able to borrow to finance investment. **Crowding out** refers to a decline in private expenditures (in this case, investment spending) as a result of an increase in government purchases. In Figure 10.5, the decline in investment spending due to crowding out is shown by the movement from L_1 to L_2 on the demand for loanable funds curve. Lower investment spending decreases the capital stock and the quantity of capital per hour worked.

A government budget surplus has the opposite effect of a deficit: A budget surplus increases the total amount of saving in the economy, shifting the supply curve for

Crowding out A decline in private expenditures as a result of an increase in government purchases.

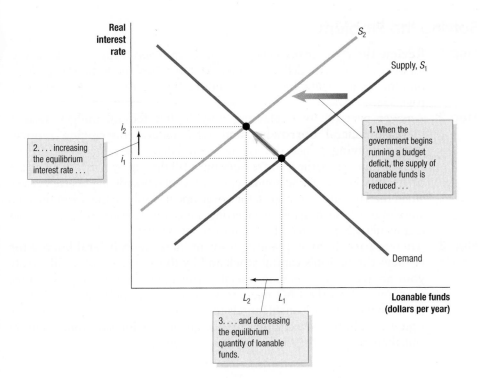

MyLab Economics Animation

Figure 10.5

The Effect of a Budget Deficit on the Market for Loanable Funds

When the government begins running a budget deficit, the supply curve for loanable funds shifts to the left. The equilibrium interest rate increases from i_1 to i_2, and the equilibrium quantity of loanable funds falls from L_1 to L_2. As a result, saving and investment both decline.

loanable funds to the right. In the new equilibrium, the interest rate will be lower, and the quantity of loanable funds will be higher. We can conclude that a budget surplus increases the level of saving and investment.

In practice, however, the effect of government budget deficits and surpluses on the equilibrium interest rate is relatively small. (This finding reflects in part the importance of global saving in determining the interest rate.) For example, one study found that increasing government borrowing by an amount equal to 1 percent of GDP would increase the equilibrium real interest rate by only about 0.003 percentage point. However, this small effect on interest rates does not imply that we can ignore the effect of deficits on economic growth. Paying off government debt in the future may require higher taxes, which can depress economic growth. In 2017, many economists and policymakers were concerned that the large deficits projected for future years might be an obstacle to growth.

In addition to budget deficits, other government policies can affect the supply of loanable funds. The federal government gives special tax incentives for saving. For example, individuals can delay paying taxes on income they put into 401(k) retirement accounts until they actually retire. The delay in paying taxes increases the after-tax return to saving, so this policy encourages individuals to save.

Solved Problem 10.2

MyLab Economics Interactive Animation

Are Future Budget Deficits a Threat to the Economy?

Congress gives the Congressional Budget Office (CBO) the responsibility of estimating the effects of federal spending and taxing policies on the economy. According to a forecast the CBO issued in 2017, "After declining for several years, federal budget deficits are on a path to rise during the next decade." The report also noted, "Because federal borrowing reduces national saving over time, the nation's capital stock ultimately would be smaller, and productivity and income would be lower than would be the case if the debt was smaller."

a. Why would higher federal budget deficits lead to higher federal borrowing? Why does federal borrowing reduce national saving?

b. Why would an increase in federal borrowing reduce the nation's capital stock? Illustrate your answer with a graph of the market for loanable funds.

c. Why would a smaller capital stock reduce productivity and income?

Solving the Problem

Step 1: **Review the chapter material.** This problem is about applying the market for loanable funds model, so you may want to review the section "Explaining Movements in Saving, Investment, and the Interest Rate," which begins on page 333.

Step 2: **Answer part (a) by explaining why higher federal budget deficits increase federal borrowing and why federal borrowing reduces national saving.** When the gap between federal tax receipts and federal spending increases, the U.S. Treasury must fill the gap by increasing its sales of Treasury bonds. These bonds represent federal borrowing. As we've seen, when the Treasury sells bonds, the government is subtracting from the total amount of saving available by diverting funds into Treasury bond purchases that would otherwise have flowed into private saving.

Step 3: **Answer part (b) by explaining how an increase in federal borrowing reduces the nation's capital stock and by drawing a graph to illustrate your answer.** An increase in federal borrowing reduces total saving in the economy (which the CBO refers to as "national saving"), thereby shifting the supply curve for loanable funds to the left. Your graph should look like Figure 10.5. In the new equilibrium, the quantity of loanable funds is lower and, therefore, so is the level of investment spending.

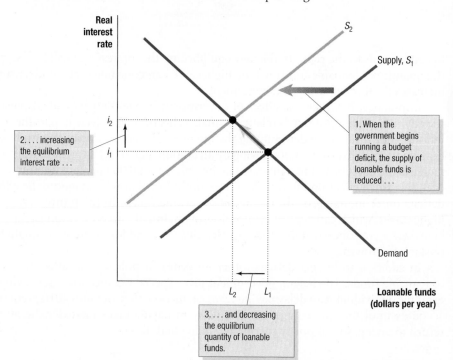

Step 4: **Answer part (c) by explaining why a smaller capital stock reduces productivity and income.** Investment spending is the means by which the capital stock increases, so less investment spending means that the capital stock will be lower than it would otherwise be. We've seen that increases in the capital stock increase labor productivity by increasing the amount of capital per hour worked and by providing a means for technological change to occur. Smaller increases in labor productivity will result in slower increases in real GDP per capita and, therefore, lower incomes than would otherwise have been attained.

Source: Congressional Budget Office, *The Budget and Economic Outlook: 2017 to 2027*, January 2017, p. 7.

Your Turn: For more practice, do related problem 2.17 on page 349 at the end of this chapter.

Table 10.1

Summary of Loanable
Funds Model

An increase in ...	will shift the ...	causing ...	Graph of the effect on equilibrium in the loanable funds market
the government's budget deficit	supply of loanable funds curve to the left	the real interest rate to increase and investment to decrease.	*graph: S_2 shifts left from S_1; axes r, L; D*
the desire of households to consume today	supply of loanable funds curve to the left	the real interest rate to increase and investment to decrease.	*graph: S_2 shifts left from S_1; axes r, L; D*
tax benefits for saving, such as 401(k) retirement accounts, which increase the incentive to save	supply of loanable funds curve to the right	the real interest rate to decrease and investment to increase.	*graph: S_1 shifts right to S_2; axes r, L; D*
expected future profits	demand for loanable funds curve to the right	the real interest rate and the level of investment to increase.	*graph: S; D_1 shifts right to D_2; axes r, L*
corporate taxes	demand for loanable funds curve to the left	the real interest rate and the level of investment to decrease.	*graph: S; D_1 shifts left to D_2; axes r, L*

Table 10.1 summarizes the key factors that cause shifts in the demand and supply curves for loanable funds.   **MyLab Economics** Concept Check   **MyLab Economics** Study Plan

The Business Cycle

LEARNING OBJECTIVE: Explain what happens during the business cycle.

Figure 10.1 on page 321 illustrates the tremendous increase during the past century in the standard of living of the average American. But close inspection of the figure reveals that real GDP per capita did not increase every year during this time. For example, during the first half of the 1930s, real GDP per capita *fell* for several years in a row. What accounts for these fluctuations in the long-run upward trend?

Some Basic Business Cycle Definitions

The fluctuations in real GDP *per capita* shown in Figure 10.1 reflect underlying fluctuations in real GDP. Since at least the early nineteenth century, the U.S. economy has experienced business cycles that consist of alternating periods of expanding and

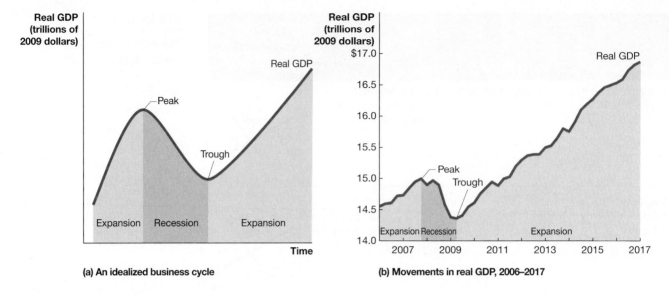

(a) An idealized business cycle

(b) Movements in real GDP, 2006–2017

MyLab Economics Real-time data

Figure 10.6   **The Business Cycle**

Panel (a) shows an idealized business cycle, with real GDP increasing smoothly in an expansion to a business cycle peak and then decreasing smoothly in a recession to a business cycle trough, which is followed by another expansion. The periods of expansion are shown in green, and the period of recession is shown in red. Panel (b) shows the actual movements in real GDP from 2006 to 2017. The recession that began following the business cycle peak in December 2007 was the longest and the most severe since the Great Depression of the 1930s.

contracting economic activity. Because real GDP is our best measure of economic activity, the business cycle is usually illustrated using movements in real GDP.

During the *expansion phase* of the business cycle, production, employment, and income are increasing. The period of expansion ends with a *business cycle peak*. Following the business cycle peak, production, employment, and income decline as the economy enters the *recession phase* of the cycle. The recession comes to an end with a *business cycle trough*, after which another period of expansion begins. Figure 10.6 illustrates the phases of the business cycle. Panel (a) shows an idealized business cycle, with real GDP increasing smoothly in an expansion to a business cycle peak and then decreasing smoothly in a recession to a business cycle trough, which is followed by another expansion. Panel (b) shows the somewhat messier reality of an actual business cycle by plotting fluctuations in real GDP during the period from 2006 to 2017. The figure shows that the expansion that began in 2001 continued until a business cycle peak was reached in December 2007. The following recession was the longest and the most severe since the Great Depression of the 1930s. The severity of the recession led some economists to refer to it as the "Great Recession." The economy reached a business cycle trough in June 2009, when the next expansion began. Although real GDP grew following the business cycle trough, the growth was slower than had been typical during previous business cycle expansions. **MyLab Economics** Concept Check

How Do We Know When the Economy Is in a Recession?

The federal government produces many statistics that make it possible to monitor the state of the economy. But the federal government does not officially decide when a recession begins or when it ends. Instead, most economists and policymakers accept the decisions of the Business Cycle Dating Committee of the National Bureau of Economic Research (NBER), a private research group located in Cambridge, Massachusetts. Although writers for newspapers, magazines, and online business news sites often define a recession as two consecutive quarters of declining real GDP, the NBER has a broader definition: "A recession is a significant decline in activity spread across the economy, lasting more than a few months, visible in industrial production, employment, real income, and wholesale–retail trade."

Table 10.2

The U.S. Business Cycle
since 1950

Peak	Trough	Length of Recession
July 1953	May 1954	10 months
August 1957	April 1958	8 months
April 1960	February 1961	10 months
December 1969	November 1970	11 months
November 1973	March 1975	16 months
January 1980	July 1980	6 months
July 1981	November 1982	16 months
July 1990	March 1991	8 months
March 2001	November 2001	8 months
December 2007	June 2009	18 months

Source: National Bureau of Economic Research.

The NBER is fairly slow in announcing business cycle dates because gathering and analyzing economic statistics takes time. Typically, the NBER will announce that the economy is in a recession only well after the recession has begun. For instance, it did not announce that a recession had begun in December 2007 until 11 months later, at the end of November 2008.

Table 10.2 lists the business cycle peaks and troughs that the NBER has identified for the years since 1950. The length of each recession is the number of months from each peak to the following trough. **MyLab Economics** Concept Check

What Happens during the Business Cycle?

Each business cycle is different. The lengths of the expansion and recession phases and the sectors of the economy that are most affected are rarely the same in any two cycles. But most business cycles share these characteristics:

1. As the economy nears the end of an expansion, interest rates are usually rising, and the wages of workers are usually increasing faster than prices. As a result of rising interest rates and wages, the profits of firms will be falling. Typically, toward the end of an expansion, both households and firms will have substantially increased their debts. These debts are the result of the borrowing that firms and households undertake to help finance their spending during the expansion. Rising debts can eventually lead households and firms to reduce their spending.
2. A recession will often begin with a decline in spending by firms on capital goods, such as machinery, equipment, new factories, and new office buildings, or by households on new houses and consumer durables, such as furniture and automobiles. As spending declines, firms that build houses and firms that sell capital goods and consumer durables will find their sales declining. As sales decline, firms cut back on production and begin to lay off workers. Rising unemployment and falling profits reduce income, which leads to further declines in spending.
3. As the recession continues, economic conditions eventually begin to improve. The declines in spending finally come to an end; households and firms begin to reduce their debts, thereby increasing their ability to spend; and interest rates decline, making it more likely that households and firms will borrow to finance new spending. Firms begin to increase their spending on capital goods as they anticipate the need for additional production during the next expansion. Increased spending by households on new houses and consumer durables and by businesses on capital goods will finally bring the recession to an end and begin the next expansion.

Chevron, Technology, and the Business Cycle We have seen that long-run economic growth depends on the development of new technologies. As we saw in the chapter opener, technology has been important for Chevron. Technological change from the nineteenth century through the present has enabled the firm to greatly increase labor productivity at its oil refineries. But technological change in the manufacture of electric cars threatens to undermine Chevron's sales of gasoline, which make up about half of the firm's sales of oil-based products. The business cycle also affects Chevron's sales of gasoline. During a recession, as incomes fall and unemployment increases, people cut back on the number of miles they drive. They also buy fewer cars. Cars are *durables*, which are goods that are expected to last for three or more years. Consumer durables also include furniture, laptops, and appliances. Producer durables include machine tools, electric generators, and commercial airplanes. *Nondurables* are goods that are expected to last for fewer than three years. Consumer nondurables include goods such as food, clothing, and gasoline. Durables are affected more by the business cycle than are nondurables. During a recession, workers reduce spending if they lose their jobs, fear losing their jobs, or suffer wage cuts. Because people can often continue using their existing automobiles, appliances, and smartphones, they are more likely to postpone spending on durables than spending on nondurables. Similarly, when firms experience declining sales and profits during a recession, they often cut back on purchases of producer durables.

Panel (a) of Figure 10.7 shows movements in real GDP for each quarter from the beginning of 1999 through the beginning of 2017. We can see both the upward trend in real GDP over time and the effects of the recessions of 2001 and 2007–2009. Panel (b) shows movements in the real value of automobile production and in retail sales of gasoline. To more easily graph data from both variables in the same panel, they have been converted to index numbers with their values for the first quarter of 1999 set equal to 100. Panel (b) shows that the business cycle strongly affects production of cars and trucks. During the 2007–2009 recession, real GDP declined by about 4 percent, while real motor vehicle production declined by 48 percent. This massive sales decline brought General Motors and Chrysler to the brink of bankruptcy. Only funds provided by the federal government enabled them to continue operating. The effect of the business cycle on gasoline sales is much milder. Gasoline sales declined by about 7 percent during the 2007–2009 recession, which was enough to cause Chevron's profit from that portion of its business to fall more than 80 percent, but the firm was never in danger of bankruptcy.

(a) Movements in real GDP

(b) Movements in the sales of motor vehicles and gasoline

MyLab Economics Real-time data

Figure 10.7   **The Effect of the Business Cycle on Chevron**

Panel (a) shows movements in real GDP for each quarter from the beginning of 1999 through the beginning of 2017. Panel (b) shows movements in the real value of automobile production and in gasoline sales for the same years. Both variables have been converted to index numbers with their values for the first

quarter of 1999 set equal to 100. Panel (b) shows the severe effect of the business cycle on sales of motor vehicles and the much milder effect on gasoline sales.

Sources: U.S. Bureau of Economic Analysis and U.S. Energy Information Administration; the data on retail gasoline sales were seasonally adjusted by the authors.

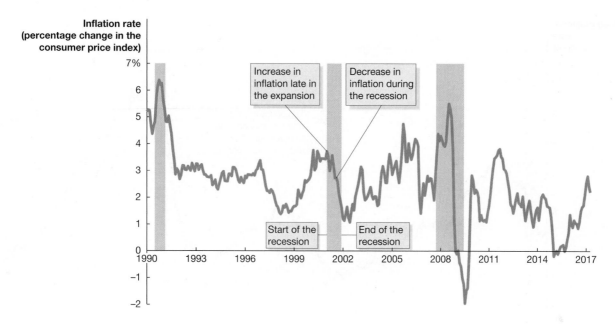

Figure 10.8   **The Effect of Recessions on the Inflation Rate**

Toward the end of a typical expansion, the inflation rate begins to rise. During recessions, marked by the shaded vertical bars, the inflation rate declines. By the end of a recession, the inflation rate is significantly below what it had been at the beginning of the recession.

Note: The points on the figure represent the annual inflation rate measured by the percentage change in the consumer price index from the same month during the previous year.

Source: U.S. Bureau of Labor Statistics.

The Effect of the Business Cycle on the Inflation Rate   The *price level* measures the average prices of goods and services in the economy, and the *inflation rate* is the percentage increase in the price level from one year to the next (see Chapter 9, Section 9.4). An important fact about the business cycle is that the inflation rate usually increases during economic expansions—particularly near the end of an expansion—and the inflation rate usually decreases during recessions. Figure 10.8 illustrates this pattern for the three recessions since 1990.

In every recession since 1950, the inflation rate has been lower during the 12 months after the recession ends than it was during the 12 months before the recession began. The average decline in the inflation rate has been about 2.5 percentage points. This result is not surprising. During a business cycle expansion, spending by businesses and households is strong, and producers of goods and services find it easier to raise prices. As spending declines during a recession, firms have a more difficult time selling their goods and services and are likely to increase prices less than they otherwise might have.

Don't Let This Happen to You

Don't Confuse the Price Level and the Inflation Rate

Do you agree with the following statement: "The consumer price index is a widely used measure of the inflation rate"? This statement may sound plausible, but it is incorrect. The consumer price index (CPI) tells us what a typical urban family of four pays for the goods and services they purchase relative to a base year, but values for the CPI do not directly measure the inflation rate (see Chapter 9, Section 9.4). We can measure the inflation rate as the

percentage change in the CPI from one year to the next. In macroeconomics, it is important not to confuse the level of a variable with the change in the variable. To give another example, real GDP does not measure economic growth. Economic growth is measured by the percentage change in real GDP from one year to the next.

MyLab Economics Study Plan

Your Turn: Test your understanding by doing related problem 3.7 on page 350 at the end of this chapter.

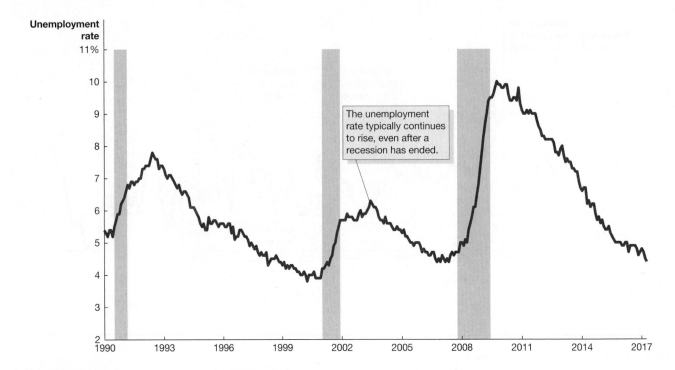

Figure 10.9 **How Recessions Affect the Unemployment Rate**

Unemployment rises during recessions and falls during expansions. The reluctance of firms to hire new employees during the early stages of a recovery usually causes the unemployment rate to continue to rise even after a recession has ended.

Source: U.S. Bureau of Labor Statistics.

The Effect of the Business Cycle on the Unemployment Rate Recessions cause the inflation rate to fall, but they cause the unemployment rate to rise. As firms see their sales decline, they begin to reduce production and lay off workers. Figure 10.9 illustrates this pattern for the three recessions since 1990. Notice in the figure that the unemployment rate continued to rise even after the recessions of 1990–1991, 2001, and 2007–2009 had ended. This lag before the unemployment rate begins to decline is typical and is due to two factors. First, even though employment begins to increase as a recession ends, it may be increasing more slowly than the increase in the labor force resulting from population growth as people graduate from school or otherwise look for jobs for the first time. If employment increases slowly enough relative to the growth in the labor force, it is possible for the unemployment rate to rise. Second, some firms continue to operate well below their capacity even after a recession has ended and sales have begun to increase. As a result, at first, firms may not hire back all the workers they have laid off and may even continue for a while to lay off more workers.

During the recessions since 1950, the unemployment rate has risen on average by about 1.2 percentage points during the 12 months after a recession has begun. So, on average, more than 1 million more workers have been unemployed during the 12 months after a recession has begun than during the previous 12 months.

Is the "Great Moderation" Over? Figure 10.10 shows the year-to-year percentage changes in real GDP since 1900. The figure illustrates that before 1950, real GDP went through much greater year-to-year fluctuations than it has since that time. Fluctuations since the mid-1980s have been particularly mild. By the early twenty-first century, some economists had begun referring to the absence of severe recessions in the United States as the *Great Moderation*. However, economists began questioning

Annual percentage change in real GDP

MyLab Economics Real-time data

Figure 10.10   **Fluctuations in Real GDP, 1900–2016**

Fluctuations in real GDP were greater before 1950 than they have been since 1950.

Sources: For 1900–1946: Louis Johnston and Samuel H. Williamson, "What Was the U.S. GDP Then? MeasuringWorth, 2017; and for 1947–2016: U.S. Bureau of Economic Analysis.

this view following the recession that began in December 2007. That recession was the longest and the most severe since the Great Depression of the 1930s and has been called the *Great Recession*. The percentage decline in real GDP during 2009 was the largest since 1932. Economists and policymakers remain unsure whether the steady increases in real GDP since 2009 represent a return of the stable growth seen during the Great Moderation.

The unusual severity of the 2007–2009 recession can be seen by comparing its length to the lengths of other recessions. Table 10.3 shows that in the late nineteenth century, the average length of recessions was equal to the average length of expansions. During the first half of the twentieth century, the average length of expansions decreased slightly, and the average length of recessions decreased significantly. As a result, expansions were about six months longer than recessions during those years. The most striking change came after 1950, when the length of expansions greatly increased and the length of recessions decreased. After 1950, expansions were more than five times as long as recessions. In other words, in the late nineteenth century, the U.S. economy spent as much time in recession as it did in expansion. After 1950, the U.S. economy experienced long expansions interrupted by relatively short recessions.

Table 10.3

Until 2007, the Business Cycle Had Become Milder

Period	Average Length of Expansions	Average Length of Recessions
1870–1900	26 months	26 months
1900–1950	25 months	19 months
1950–2009	61 months	11 months

The recession of 2007–2009 is an exception to this experience of relatively short, mild recessions. The recession lasted 18 months, the longest of the post-1950 period. Do the length and depth of the 2007–2009 recession indicate that the United States is returning to an era of severe fluctuations in real GDP? A full answer to this question will not be possible at least until we see how severe the next recession will turn out to be. But in the next section, we provide some perspective on the question by considering why the period from 1950 to 2007 was one of relative macroeconomic stability.   **MyLab Economics** Concept Check

Will the U.S. Economy Return to Stability?

Shorter recessions, longer expansions, and less severe fluctuations in real GDP have resulted in a significant improvement in the economic well-being of Americans. Economists have offered several explanations for why the U.S. economy experienced a period of relative stability from 1950 to 2007:

- **The increasing importance of services and the declining importance of goods.** As services such as medical care and investment advice have become a much larger fraction of GDP, there has been a corresponding relative decline in the production of goods. For example, at one time, manufacturing production accounted for about 40 percent of GDP, but in 2017, it accounted for less than 12 percent. Manufacturing production, particularly of durable goods such as automobiles, fluctuates more than the production of services because during a recession, households will cut back more on purchases of durables than they will on purchases of services. So, the increase in services as a percentage of GDP may have helped to stabilize the economy.

- **The establishment of unemployment insurance and other government transfer programs that provide funds to the unemployed.** Before the 1930s, programs such as unemployment insurance, which provides government payments to workers who lose their jobs, and Social Security, which provides government payments to retired and disabled workers, did not exist. These and other government programs make it possible for workers who lose their jobs during recessions to have higher incomes and, therefore, to spend more than they would otherwise. This additional spending may have helped to shorten recessions.

- **Active federal government policies to stabilize the economy.** Before the Great Depression of the 1930s, the federal government did not attempt to end recessions or prolong expansions. Because the Great Depression was so severe, with the unemployment rate rising to more than 20 percent of the labor force and real GDP declining by almost 30 percent, public opinion began favoring government attempts to stabilize the economy. In the years since World War II, the federal government has actively used macroeconomic policy measures to try to end recessions and prolong expansions. Many economists believe that these government policies have played a key role in stabilizing the economy. Other economists, however, argue that active government policy has had little effect. The debate over the role of macroeconomic policy became particularly intense during and after the 2007–2009 recession (see Chapters 15 and 16).

- **The increased stability of the financial system.** The severity of the Great Depression of the 1930s was caused in part by instability in the financial system. More than 5,000 banks failed between 1929 and 1933, reducing the savings of many households and making it difficult for households and firms to obtain the credit needed to maintain their spending. In addition, a decline of more than 80 percent in stock prices greatly reduced the wealth of many households and made it difficult for firms to raise funds by selling stock. Most economists believe that the return of financial instability during the 2007–2009 recession is a key reason the recession was so severe. If the United States is to return to macroeconomic stability, the financial system will have to avoid another episode of instability like that of 2007–2009.

MyLab Economics Concept Check

Continued from page 319

Economics in Your Life & Career

Should Your Business Be Cautious at the Beginning of a Recession?

At the beginning of this chapter, we asked you to suppose that you and a partner own a sandwich shop. With a recession beginning, your partner is worried that your sales will decline and suggests that you cut costs by laying off two of your four employees and cutting items from your menu. Should you agree with that strategy?

From what we've learned in the chapter, your partner is probably overreacting. During a recession, sales of durable goods like automobiles can decline significantly, particularly if the recession is as severe as the 2007–2009 recession. But you are selling food, and not a durable good, so it's likely that you will experience only a small decline in sales. Laying off two of your four workers and dropping items from your menu will cut your costs but will also make it harder to satisfy your customers by offering them speedy service and a varied menu. Of course, if the recession's effect in your area is likely to be particularly severe—say, a local factory is closing, resulting in you losing half of your lunchtime customers—then your partner's strategy may be correct. Otherwise, your partner's strategy is more likely to hurt your business than to help it.

Conclusion

The U.S. economy remains a remarkable engine for improving the well-being of Americans. The standard of living of Americans today is much higher than it was 100 years ago. But households and firms are still subject to the ups and downs of the business cycle. In the following chapters, we will continue our analysis of this basic fact of macroeconomics: Ever-increasing long-run prosperity is achieved in the context of short-run instability.

Visit **MyLab Economics** for a news article and analysis related to the concepts in this chapter.

CHAPTER SUMMARY AND PROBLEMS

Key Terms

Business cycle, p. 320

Capital, p. 324

Crowding out, p. 334

Financial intermediaries, p. 329

Financial markets, p. 329

Financial system, p. 329

Labor productivity, p. 324

Long-run economic growth, p. 321

Market for loanable funds, p. 332

Potential GDP, p. 328

10.1 Long-Run Economic Growth, pages 320–328

LEARNING OBJECTIVE: Discuss the importance of long-run economic growth.

MyLab Economics Visit www.pearson.com/mylab/economics to complete these exercises online and get instant feedback.

Summary

The U.S. economy has experienced both *long-run economic growth* and the *business cycle*. The **business cycle** refers to alternating periods of economic expansion and economic recession. **Long-run economic growth** is the process by which rising productivity increases the standard of living of the typical person. Because of economic growth, the typical American today can buy almost eight times as much as the typical American of 1900. Long-run growth is measured by increases in real GDP per capita. Increases in real GDP per capita depend on increases in labor productivity. **Labor productivity** is the quantity of goods and services that can be produced by one worker or by one hour of work. Economists believe two key factors determine labor productivity: the quantity of capital per hour worked and the level of technology. **Capital** refers to manufactured goods that are used to produce other goods and services. *Human capital* is the accumulated knowledge and skills workers acquire from education, training, or their life experiences. Economic growth occurs if the quantity of capital per hour worked increases and if technological change occurs. Economists often discuss economic growth in terms of growth in **potential GDP**, which is the level of GDP attained when all firms are producing at capacity.

Review Questions

1.1 By how much did real GDP per capita increase in the United States between 1900 and 2016? Discuss whether the increase in real GDP per capita is likely to have been greater or smaller than the true increase in living standards.

1.2 What is the rule of 70? If real GDP per capita grows at a rate of 5 percent per year, how many years will it take to double?

1.3 What two key factors cause labor productivity to increase over time?

1.4 What is potential GDP? Does potential GDP remain constant over time?

Problems and Applications

1.5 Briefly discuss whether you would rather live in the United States of 1900 with an income of $1 million per year or the United States of 2018 with an income of $50,000 per year. Assume that the incomes for both years are measured in 2018 dollars.

1.6 **(Related to the Apply the Concept on page 321)** Think about the relationship between economic prosperity and life expectancy. What implications does this relationship have for the size of an economy's health care sector? In particular, is this sector of the U.S. economy likely to expand or contract in coming years?

1.7 Use the following table to answer the questions.

Year	Real GDP (billions of 2009 dollars)
1990	$8,955
1991	8,948
1992	9,267
1993	9,521
1994	9,906

   a. Calculate the growth rate of real GDP for each year from 1991 to 1994.

   b. Calculate the average annual growth rate of real GDP for the period from 1991 to 1994.

1.8 As discussed in this chapter, real GDP per capita in the United States grew from about $6,000 in 1900 to about $51,500 in 2016, which represents an average annual growth rate of 1.9 percent. If the U.S. economy continues to grow at this rate, how many years will it take for real GDP per capita to double? If government economic policies meant to stimulate economic growth result in the annual growth rate increasing to 2.2 percent, how many years will it take for real GDP per capita to double?

1.9 **(Related to Solved Problem 10.1 on page 325)** In a column on bloomberg.com, Noah Smith noted that people who work at a computer have many ways to slack off or waste time—posting to Facebook, Twitter, or Instagram; watching YouTube videos; or playing video games—that weren't available to workers in previous decades. Smith calculated that "the average working American spends about 34.4 hours on the job. If we assume that's five days a week, it means that one hour of slacking per day means that true work hours are really only 85.5 percent of the official number."

 a. If Smith's estimates are correct, is the rate of growth of labor productivity as measured by government statistics overstated or understated? Briefly explain.

 b. What are the implications of your answer in part (a) for using increases in real GDP per capita, as calculated by the BEA, to measure increases in well-being?

 Source: Noah Smith, "Goofing off at Work Masks Rising Productivity," bloomberg.com, May 10, 2017.

1.10 (Related to Solved Problem 10.1 on page 325) An article in the *Wall Street Journal* noted that "raising productivity in the long run is the most effective way to elevate standards of living." Do you agree? Briefly explain.

 Source: Greg Ip, "Politicians Should Pay Heed to Productivity Problem," *Wall Street Journal*, July 22, 2015.

1.11 An article in the *Economist* noted that "for 60 years, from 1770 to 1830, growth in British wages, adjusted for inflation, was imperceptible because productivity growth was restricted to a few industries." Not until the late nineteenth century, when productivity "gains had spread across the whole economy," did a sustained increase in real wages begin. Why would you expect there to be a close relationship between productivity gains and increases in real wages?

 Source: "The Onrushing Wave," *Economist*, January 18, 2014.

1.12 (Related to the Apply the Concept on page 326) Nobel Laureate Amartya Sen, a professor of economics at Harvard University, argued, "For India to match China in its range of

manufacturing capacity … it needs a better-educated and healthier labor force at all levels of society." What role do education and health care play in economic growth? How has India been able to experience rapid economic growth since 1991, despite poor education and health care systems?

 Source: Amartya Sen, "Why India Trails China," *New York Times*, June 19, 2013.

1.13 (Related to the Apply the Concept on page 326) India's labor force has been gradually shifting out of the low-productivity agricultural sector into the higher-productivity service and industrial sectors.

 a. Briefly explain how this shift is affecting India's real GDP per capita.

 b. Is this shift likely to result in continuing increases in India's growth rate in coming decades? Briefly explain.

1.14 According to an article in the *Wall Street Journal*, Federal Reserve Chair Janet Yellen stated that unless obstacles to some women working in the paid labor force are removed, the United States will "incur a substantial loss to the productive capacity of our economy." Ms. Yellen also stated that more women in the labor force would "help overcome long-term challenges such as an aging population and slow productivity growth."

 a. What measure do economists use for the productive capacity of the economy?

 b. Why might an aging labor force and slow productivity growth pose long-term challenges to the U.S. economy? How might more women working in the paid labor force help overcome these challenges?

 Source: Harriet Torry, "Yellen Says Family-Friendly Work Policies Can Boost Economy," *Wall Street Journal*, May 5, 2017.

10.2 Saving, Investment, and the Financial System, pages 329–337

LEARNING OBJECTIVE: Discuss the role of the financial system in facilitating long-run economic growth.

MyLab Economics Visit www.pearson.com/mylab/economics to complete these exercises online and get instant feedback.

Summary

Financial markets and financial intermediaries together comprise the **financial system**. A well-functioning financial system is an important determinant of economic growth. Firms acquire funds from households, either directly through **financial markets**—such as the stock and bond markets—or indirectly through **financial intermediaries**—such as banks. The funds available to firms come from *saving*. There are two categories of saving in the economy: *private saving* by households and *public saving* by the government. The value of total saving in the economy is always equal to the value of total investment spending. In the model of the **market for loanable funds**, the interaction of borrowers and lenders determines the market interest rate and the quantity of loanable funds exchanged.

Review Questions

2.1 Why is a country's financial system important for long-run economic growth?

2.2 How does the financial system—both financial markets and financial intermediaries—provide risk sharing, liquidity, and information to savers and borrowers?

2.3 Briefly explain why the total value of saving in the economy must equal the total value of investment.

2.4 What are loanable funds? Why do businesses demand loanable funds? Why do households supply loanable funds?

Problems and Applications

2.5 Suppose you can receive an interest rate of 2 percent on a certificate of deposit at a bank that is charging borrowers 6 percent on new car loans. Why might you be unwilling to loan money directly to someone who wants to borrow from you to buy a new car, even if that person offers to pay you an interest rate higher than 2 percent?

2.6 An International Monetary Fund Factsheet made the following observation regarding sound financial systems: "A country's financial system … provide[s] a framework … [for] supporting economic growth." Do you agree with this observation? Briefly explain.

 Source: "Financial System Soundness," *International Monetary Fund Factsheet*, April 21, 2017.

2.7 Consider the following data for a closed economy:

$$Y = \$11 \text{ trillion}$$
$$C = \$8 \text{ trillion}$$
$$I = \$2 \text{ trillion}$$
$$TR = \$1 \text{ trillion}$$
$$T = \$3 \text{ trillion}$$

Use these data to calculate the following:
a. Private saving
b. Public saving
c. Government purchases
d. The government budget deficit or budget surplus

2.8 Consider the following data for a closed economy:

$$Y = \$12 \text{ trillion}$$
$$C = \$8 \text{ trillion}$$
$$G = \$2 \text{ trillion}$$
$$S_{\text{Public}} = -\$0.5 \text{ trillion}$$
$$T = \$2 \text{ trillion}$$

Use these data to calculate the following:
a. Private saving
b. Investment spending
c. Transfer payments
d. The government budget deficit or budget surplus

2.9 In problem 2.8, suppose that government purchases increase from $2 trillion to $2.5 trillion. If the values for Y and C are unchanged, what must happen to the values of S and I? Briefly explain.

2.10 Match each of the following scenarios with the appropriate graph of the market for loanable funds.

1.

2.

3.

4.

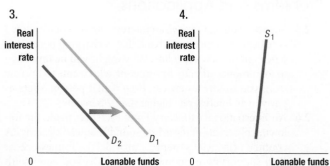

a. An increase in the real interest rate results in only a small increase in private saving by households.

b. A decrease in the real interest rate results in a substantial increase in spending on investment projects by businesses.
c. The federal government eliminates 401(k) retirement accounts.
d. The federal government reduces the tax on corporate profits. (Assume no change in the federal budget deficit or budget surplus.)

2.11 Use the following graph to answer the questions.

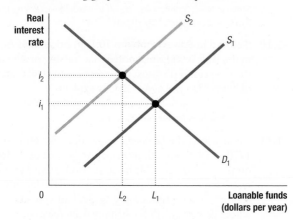

a. What might cause the supply curve for loanable funds to shift from S_1 to S_2?
b. With the shift in supply, what happens to the equilibrium quantity of loanable funds?
c. With the change in the equilibrium quantity of loanable funds, what happens to the quantity of saving? What happens to the quantity of investment?

2.12 Use the following graph to answer the questions.

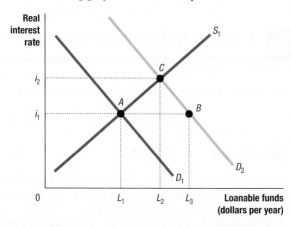

a. With the shift in the demand curve for loanable funds from D_1 to D_2, what happens to the equilibrium real interest rate and the equilibrium quantity of loanable funds?
b. How can the equilibrium quantity of loanable funds increase when the real interest rate increases? Doesn't the quantity of loanable funds demanded decrease when the interest rate increases?
c. How much would the quantity of loanable funds demanded have increased if the interest rate had remained at i_1?
d. How much does the quantity of loanable funds supplied increase with the increase in the interest rate from i_1 to i_2?

2.13 Firms care about their after-tax rate of return on investment projects. In the market for loanable funds, draw a graph and explain the effect of an increase in taxes on business profits. (For simplicity, assume no change in the federal budget deficit or budget surplus.) What happens to the equilibrium real interest rate and the quantity of loanable funds? What will be the effect on the level of investment by firms and the economy's capital stock in the future?

2.14 **(Related to the Apply the Concept on page 333)** A writer for the *Wall Street Journal* wrote a whimsical "Letter to Stingy American Consumers":

> Dear American Consumer:
>
> This is the *Wall Street Journal*. … The sun shined in April and you didn't spend much money. … You've been saving more too. … This saving is not like you. … Do you know the American economy is counting on you?

Economist Steven Landsburg praised Ebenezer Scrooge for choosing to save rather than spend his money, arguing that saving—not consumption—fuels economic growth. The *Wall Street Journal* letter pretends to chide the American consumer for saving rather than spending income, arguing that spending—not saving—fuels economic growth. Which argument is correct?

Source: Jon Hilsenrath, "Grand Central: A Letter to Stingy American Consumers," *Wall Street Journal*, June 2, 2015.

2.15 **(Related to the Apply the Concept on page 333)** The *Apply the Concept* claims that Ebenezer Scrooge promoted economic growth more when he was a miser and saved most of his income than when he reformed and began spending freely. Suppose, though, that after he reformed, he spent most of his income buying food for the Cratchits and other poor families. Many economists believe that there is a close connection between how much very poor people eat and how much they are able to work and how productive they are while working. Does this fact affect the conclusion about whether the pre-reform or post-reform Scrooge had a more positive impact on economic growth? Briefly explain.

2.16 An article in the *Wall Street Journal* on the use of artificial intelligence (AI) in the financial system stated that "similar to index-tracking funds, funds managed in part by artificial intelligence require less human intervention and therefore can often cost less to run." The article also noted that banks are using AI to decrease the costs and increase the accuracy of compliance with government regulations.
   a. What financial intermediary do "index-tracking funds" or "funds" refer to?
   b. How does the use of AI affect labor productivity in the financial system? Briefly explain.
   c. How would the financial system's use of AI affect the rate of long-run economic growth? Briefly explain using the loanable funds model.

Source: Kim S. Nash, "Artificial Intelligence Geared to Erase Capital Markets Jobs," *Wall Street Journal*, May 3, 2017.

2.17 **(Related to Solved Problem 10.2 on page 335)** The federal government in the United States has been running large budget deficits. Suppose that Congress and the president take actions that turn the budget deficits into budget surpluses.
   a. Use a market for loanable funds graph to illustrate the effect of the federal budget surpluses. What happens to the equilibrium real interest rate and the quantity of loanable funds? What happens to the level of saving and investment?
   b. Now suppose that households believe that surpluses will result in Congress and the president cutting taxes in the near future in order to move from budget surpluses to balanced budgets. As a result, households increase their consumption spending in anticipation of paying lower taxes. Briefly explain how your analysis in part (a) will be affected.

The Business Cycle, pages 337–345

LEARNING OBJECTIVE: Explain what happens during the business cycle.

MyLab Economics   Visit **www.pearson.com/mylab/economics** to complete these exercises online and get instant feedback.

Summary

During the expansion phase of the business cycle, production, employment, and income are increasing. The period of expansion ends with a business cycle peak. Following the business cycle peak, production, employment, and income decline during the recession phase of the cycle. The recession comes to an end with a business cycle trough, after which another period of expansion begins. The inflation rate usually rises near the end of a business cycle expansion and then falls during a recession. The unemployment rate declines during the latter part of an expansion and increases during a recession. The unemployment rate often continues to increase even after an expansion has begun. Until the severe recession of 2007–2009, recessions had been milder and the economy had been more stable in the period since 1950. Economists debate whether the economy will return to the stability it experienced during the period of the Great Moderation.

Review Questions

3.1 What are the names of the following events that occur during a business cycle?
   a. The high point of economic activity
   b. The low point of economic activity
   c. The period between the high point of economic activity and the following low point
   d. The period between the low point of economic activity and the following high point

3.2 Briefly describe the effect of the business cycle on the inflation rate and the unemployment rate. Why might the unemployment rate continue to rise during the early stages of an expansion?

3.3 Briefly compare the severity of recessions before and after 1950. What explanations have economists offered for the period of relative macroeconomic stability from 1950 to 2007?

Problems and Applications

3.4 **(Related to the Chapter Opener on page 318)** Briefly explain whether production of each of the following goods is likely to fluctuate more or less than real GDP does during the business cycle.
  a. Ford F-150 trucks
  b. McDonald's Big Macs
  c. Chevron's sales of advanced plastics to be used in automobile manufacturing
  d. Huggies diapers
  e. Boeing passenger aircraft

3.5 The National Bureau of Economic Research, a private group, is responsible for declaring when recessions begin and end in the United States. Can you think of reasons the Bureau of Economic Analysis, part of the federal government, might not want to take on this responsibility?

3.6 An article in the *Wall Street Journal* noted that "the total debt held by American households reached a record in early 2017, exceeding its 2008 peak." Does this information indicate that the U.S. economy was close to the end of an economic expansion in early 2017? Briefly explain.
  Source: Ben Leubsdorf, "U.S. Household Debt Hit Record in First Quarter," *Wall Street Journal*, May 17, 2017.

3.7 **(Related to the Don't Let This Happen to You on page 341)** Briefly explain whether you agree with this statement: "Real GDP in 2016 was $16.7 trillion. This value is a large number. Therefore, economic growth must have been high during 2016."

3.8 **(Related to the Chapter Opener on page 318)** From 2008 to 2009, the total revenue Chevron earned from all of its operations declined by more than 50 percent, while its expenditures on oil exploration remained unchanged. If the firm was suffering from declining sales of gasoline and other products during the recession, why would it maintain its spending on exploring for additional oil?
  Source: Chevron Corporation, *2009 4Q Earnings Release*, January 29, 2010.

3.9 Robert Samuelson, a columnist for the *Washington Post*, argued that the Great Moderation actually caused the Great Recession. During the Great Moderation, he wrote, "consumers could assume more debt—and lenders could lend more freely." Why might consumers have been willing to assume more debt and banks and other lenders have been willing to make loans more freely during the Great Moderation? Why might these actions have made the severe recession of 2007–2009 more likely?
  Source: Robert J. Samuelson, "Is the Economy Experiencing Another Great Moderation?" *Washington Post*, June 4, 2014.

Real-Time Data Exercises

D10.1 (Analyzing real GDP over the business cycle) Go to the Web site of the Federal Reserve Bank of St. Louis (FRED) (fred.stlouisfed.org).
  a. Find the values for the most recent quarter for the following three variables: (1) nominal gross domestic product (GDP), (2) real gross domestic product (GDPC1), and (3) real potential gross domestic product (GDPPOT).
  b. Using the data from part (a), calculate the GDP price deflator for the most recent quarter.
  c. Calculate for this quarter the percentage difference between real GDP and real potential GDP.
  d. Using Figure 10.2 on page 328, describe the relationship between real GDP and potential GDP over the past 10 years.

D10.2 (Analyzing saving and investment) Go to the Web site of the Federal Reserve Bank of St. Louis (FRED) (fred.stlouisfed.org).
  a. Find the most recent values and the values from the same quarter three years earlier for gross private saving (GPSAVE) and gross government saving (GGSAVE).
  b. Using the values found in part (a), calculate the value of total saving in the economy for these two periods.
  c. Draw a graph to show the loanable funds market in equilibrium. Explain which curve represents total saving.
  d. On the graph you drew in part (c), show the effect on the loanable funds market from the change you calculated in part (b) for total saving between the two periods.

D10.3 (Analyzing saving and investment) Go to the Web site of the Federal Reserve Bank of St. Louis (FRED) (fred.stlouisfed.org).
  a. Find the most recent value and the value from the same quarter four years earlier for gross government saving (GGSAVE).
  b. Total saving in the economy is composed of private saving and government saving. What does government saving represent?

c. Using the values found in part (a), explain whether the government budget in each of the two periods is balanced, in a surplus, or in a deficit. From the first period to the most recent period, has government saving increased, decreased, or remained constant?

d. Draw a graph showing the loanable funds market in equilibrium. Use the graph to show the effect of the change in government saving that you calculated in part (c) on the loanable funds market. (Assume that the level of private saving is unchanged.) Explain what will happen to the level of investment in the economy.

Critical Thinking Exercises

CT10.1 Figure 10.2 on page 328 shows that the growth of potential GDP slowed following the recession of 2007–2009. Use the data in the following table to discuss how movements in potential GDP can be explained by the analysis in this chapter.

Year	Investment as a Percentage of GDP	Annual Growth in Labor Productivity
2006	19.4%	0.9%
2007	18.3	1.6
2008	16.5	0.8
2009	13.0	3.2
2010	14.1	3.3
2011	14.4	0.1
2012	15.6	0.9
2013	16.2	0.3
2014	16.7	1.0
2015	17.1	1.2
2016	16.4	0.0

CT10.2 Which of the following three situations is least likely to occur at the same time as the other two situations?

- Real GDP is less than potential GDP.
- The economy has been in a strong expansion for 5 years.
- The unemployment rate is above the natural rate.

Carefully explain your selection.

Long-Run Economic Growth: Sources and Policies

What Explains Slow Growth in Mexico?

C. W. LeValley founded the firm that became Rexnord Corporation in Wisconsin in 1891 to manufacture metal chain belts for agricultural machinery. The company is one of many that over the decades provided high-wage manufacturing jobs in midwestern U.S. states. As we discussed in Chapter 7, in the past 15 years, many of these firms have faced intense competition from imports, particularly from Chinese firms. In response to this competition, some U.S. manufacturing firms have moved their operations to Mexico, where labor costs are much lower than in the United States. In 2016, Rexnord announced that it was closing a factory in Indianapolis, laying off 350 workers, and moving production of industrial ball bearings and valves to Mexico.

Rexnord's announcement received more attention than it might have otherwise because U.S. economic relations with Mexico were a key part of the 2016 U.S. presidential campaign. President Donald Trump vowed to renegotiate the North American Free Trade Agreement (NAFTA), the 1994 agreement among the governments of Canada, Mexico, and the United States that reduced barriers to trade in goods and services among the three countries. In particular, President Trump objected to the fact that NAFTA had made it easier for U.S. firms to ship products to the United States from factories in Mexico.

Even without pressure from the Trump administration, moving operations to Mexico could be risky for U.S. firms because of problems with organized crime and corruption. Coca-Cola, for example, suspended its operations in Chilpancingo because of attacks on its employees. Some local Mexican firms have been reluctant to expand because they fear attracting the attention of criminal gangs that might demand payments or government inspectors who might demand bribes. In 2017, an article in the *New York*

Rainer Unkel/Yario images/Alamy Stock Photo

Times described the business situation in Mexico as one of "unbridled corruption, weak economic growth, [and] soaring violence."

These problems indicate that the Mexican government has failed to fully establish the rule of law, which is critical for the long-term prospects of the Mexican economy. Without the rule of law, entrepreneurs cannot fulfill their role in the market system of bringing together the factors of production—labor, capital, and natural resources—to produce goods and services. Although Mexico has experienced some increases in real GDP per capita during the past 30 years, its record of economic growth has been disappointing, particularly in comparison with China and other rapidly growing countries in the developing world.

Sources: Kirk Semple, "A Mexican Governor's Race Carries Presidential Implications," *New York Times*, May 7, 2017; José de Córdoba, Brian Baskin, and Jacob M. Schlesinger, "Trump Moves Shake Deep U.S.–Mexico Relationship," *Wall Street Journal*, January 25, 2017; Andrew Tangel, "Indiana Firm Rexnord Signals Move to Mexico Despite Trump Criticism," *Wall Street Journal*, December 16, 2016; Andrew Tangel, "Companies Plow Ahead with Moves to Mexico, Despite Trump's Pressure," *Wall Street Journal*, February 8, 2017; and rexcon.com.

Chapter Outline & Learning Objectives

Economics in Your Life & Career

Would You Be Better Off without China?

For decades, China was a very poor country whose economy was growing very slowly. The government introduced economic reforms in 1978, which spurred rapid economic growth. Suppose that you could choose to live and work in a world with the Chinese economy growing very rapidly or in a world with the Chinese economy growing as slowly as it did before 1978. In which world would you choose to live? How does the current high-growth, high-export Chinese economy affect you as a consumer? How does it affect you as someone about to start a career? As you read the chapter, try to answer these questions. You can check your answers against those we provide on **page 383** at the end of this chapter.

Economic growth is not inevitable. For most of human history, no sustained increases in output per capita occurred, and, in the words of the philosopher Thomas Hobbes, the lives of most people were "poor, nasty, brutish, and short." Sustained economic growth first began with the Industrial Revolution in England in the late eighteenth century. From there, economic growth spread to the United States, Canada, and other countries in Western Europe. Following the end of World War II in 1945, rapid economic growth also began in Japan and, eventually, in several other Asian countries, but the economies of many other countries have stagnated, leaving their people trapped in poverty.

Real GDP per capita is the best measure of a country's standard of living because it represents the ability of the average person to buy goods and services. Economic growth occurs when real GDP per capita increases. In this chapter, we will develop a *model of economic growth* that will help us answer questions like these:

- Why have countries such as the United States and the United Kingdom, which had high standards of living at the beginning of the twentieth century, continued to grow rapidly?

- Why are some countries, such as Nicaragua or Zimbabwe, that were very poor at the beginning of the twentieth century still very poor?

- Why have some countries, such as South Korea and Japan, that once were very poor now become much richer?

- What explains China's recent very rapid growth rates?

11.1 Economic Growth over Time and around the World

LEARNING OBJECTIVE: Define economic growth, calculate economic growth rates, and describe global trends in economic growth.

You live in a world that is very different from the world as it was when your grandparents were young. You can listen to music on an iPhone that fits in your pocket; your grandparents played vinyl records on large stereo systems. You can send a text message to someone in another city, state, or country; your grandparents mailed letters that took days or weeks to arrive. More importantly, you have access to health care and medicines that have prolonged life and improved its quality. In many poorer countries, however, people endure grinding poverty and have only the bare necessities of life, just as their parents, grandparents, and great-grandparents did.

The difference between you and people in poor countries is that you live in a country that has experienced substantial economic growth. A growing economy produces both increasing quantities of goods and services and better goods and services. It is only through economic growth that living standards can increase, but through most of human history, no economic growth took place. Even today, billions of people are living in countries where economic growth is extremely slow.

Economic Growth from 1,000,000 B.C.E. to the Present

In 1,000,000 B.C.E., our ancestors survived by hunting animals and gathering edible plants. Farming was many years in the future, and production was limited to food, clothing, shelter, and simple tools. Bradford DeLong, an economist at the University of California, Berkeley, estimates that in those primitive circumstances, GDP per capita was about $150 per year in 2017 dollars, which was the minimum amount necessary to sustain life. DeLong estimates that real GDP per capita worldwide was still $150 in the year 1300. In other words, no sustained economic growth occurred between 1,000,000 B.C.E. and C.E. 1300. A peasant toiling on a farm in France in the year 1300 was no better off than his ancestors thousands of years before. In fact, for most of human existence, the typical person had only the bare minimum of food, clothing, and shelter necessary to sustain life. Economist Robert Allen of the University of Oxford has described the diet of the typical person in most countries around the year 1500: "Boiled grain or unleavened bread provide most of the calories, legumes [such as peas or beans] are a protein-rich complement, and butter or vegetable oil provides a little fat." Few people survived beyond age 40, and most people suffered from debilitating illnesses.

Sustained economic growth did not begin until the **Industrial Revolution**, which started in England around the year 1750. The production of cotton cloth in factories using machinery powered by steam engines marked the beginning of the Industrial Revolution. Before that time, production of goods had relied almost exclusively on human or animal power. The use of mechanical power spread to the production of many other goods, greatly increasing the quantity of goods each worker could produce. First England and then other countries, such as the United States, France, and Germany, experienced *long-run economic growth*, with sustained increases in real GDP per capita that eventually raised living standards in those countries to the high levels of today.

Industrial Revolution The application of mechanical power to the production of goods, beginning in England around 1750.

Apply the Concept

MyLab Economics Video

Why Did the Industrial Revolution Begin in England?

The Industrial Revolution was a key turning point in human history. Before the Industrial Revolution, economic growth was slow and halting. After the Industrial Revolution, economic growth became rapid and sustained in a number of countries. Although historians and economists agree on the importance of the Industrial Revolution, they have not reached a consensus on why it happened in the time and place that it did. Why the eighteenth century and not the sixteenth century or the twenty-first century? Why England and not China or India or Africa or Japan?

There is always a temptation to read history backward. We know when and where the Industrial Revolution occurred; therefore, it had to happen where it did and when it did. But what was so special about England in the eighteenth century? The late Nobel Laureate Douglass North of Washington University in St. Louis argued that institutions in England differed significantly from those in other countries in ways that greatly aided economic growth. North believed that the Glorious Revolution of 1688 was a key turning point. After that date, the British Parliament, rather than the king, controlled the government. In 1701, the British court system also became independent of the king. As a result, the British government was credible when it committed to upholding private property rights, protecting wealth, and eliminating arbitrary increases in taxes. These institutional changes gave entrepreneurs the confidence and the incentive to make the investments necessary to use the important technological developments of the second half of the eighteenth century—particularly the spinning jenny and the water frame, which were used in the production of cotton textiles, and the steam engine, which was used in mining and in the manufacture of textiles and other products. Without the institutional changes, entrepreneurs would have been reluctant to risk their property or their wealth by starting new businesses.

Although not all economists agree with North's specific argument about the origins of the Industrial Revolution, we will see that most economists accept the idea that economic growth is not likely to occur unless a country's government provides the type of institutional framework North describes.

Franck Iren/Invictus SARL/Alamy Stock Photo

The British government's guarantee of property rights set the stage for the Industrial Revolution.

Sources: Douglass C. North, *Understanding the Process of Economic Change*, Princeton, NJ: Princeton University Press, 2005; and Douglass C. North and Barry R. Weingast, "Constitutions and Commitment: The Evolution of Institutions Governing Public Choice in Seventeenth-Century England," *Journal of Economic History*, Vol. 49, No. 4, December 1989, pp. 803–832.

Your Turn: Test your understanding by doing related problem 1.3 on page 384 at the end of this chapter.

MyLab Economics Study Plan

Figure 11.1 shows how growth rates of real GDP per capita for the entire world have changed over long periods. Prior to c.e. 1300, there were no sustained increases in real

MyLab Economics Animation

Figure 11.1

Average Annual Growth Rates for the World Economy

World economic growth was essentially zero in the years before 1300, and it was very slow—an average of only 0.2 percent per year—between 1300 and 1800. The Industrial Revolution made possible the sustained increases in real GDP per capita that have allowed some countries to attain high standards of living. Growth accelerated during the twentieth century before slowing during the first years of the twenty-first century.

Sources: J. Bradford DeLong, "Estimates of World GDP, One Million B.C.–Present," working paper, University of California, Berkeley; and World Bank national accounts data.

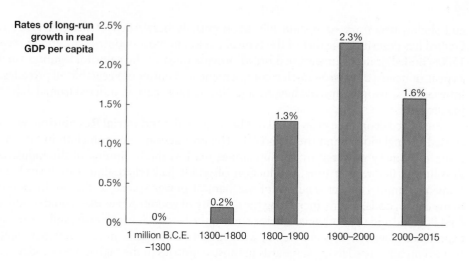

GDP per capita. Over the next 500 years, to 1800, there was very slow growth. Significant growth began in the nineteenth century, as a result of the Industrial Revolution. A further acceleration in growth occurred during the twentieth century, as the average growth rate increased from 1.3 percent per year to 2.3 percent per year. The first 15 years of the twenty-first century saw a deceleration of growth, with the average growth rate falling to 1.6 percent per year. That slow growth reflects the severity of the worldwide recession of 2007–2009 and the weak recovery that followed.   MyLab Economics Concept Check

Small Differences in Growth Rates Are Important

The difference between 1.3 percent and 2.3 percent may seem trivial, but over long periods, small differences in growth rates can have a large effect. Suppose you have $100 in a savings account earning an interest rate of 1.3 percent, which means you will receive an interest payment of $1.30 this year. If the interest rate on the account is 2.3 percent, you will earn $2.30. The difference of an extra $1.00 interest payment seems insignificant. But if you leave the interest as well as the original $100 in your account for another year, the difference becomes greater because now the higher interest rate is applied to a larger amount—$102.30—and the lower interest rate is applied to a smaller amount—$101.30. This process, known as *compounding*, magnifies even small differences in interest rates over long periods of time. Over a period of 50 years, your $100 would grow to $312 at an interest rate of 2.3 percent but to only $191 at an interest rate of 1.3 percent.

The principle of compounding applies to economic growth rates as well as to interest rates. For example, consider these three countries: Nigeria, Namibia, and Turkey. As the second column in Table 11.1 shows, in 1960, their levels of real GDP per capita measured in U.S. dollars at constant 2005 prices were similar. Over the following 56 years, their growth rates might seem to have been only slightly different. But as the last column in the table shows, these small differences in growth rates, compounded over several decades, have resulted in sharply different outcomes. Real GDP per capita in Turkey went from being only modestly higher than in the other countries to being nearly twice

Table 11.1

The Effects of Different Growth Rates on Living Standards

Country	Real GDP per Capita, 1960 (2005 U.S. dollars)	Growth in Real GDP per Capita, 1960–2016	Real GDP per Capita, 2016 (2005 U.S. dollars)
Nigeria	$3,970	0.5%	$5,266
Namibia	4,071	1.8	11,191
Turkey	4,628	2.7	20,431

Sources: Authors' calculation from data in Robert C. Feenstra, Robert Inklaar, and Marcel P. Timmer, "The Next Generation of the Penn World Table," *American Economic Review*, October 2015, Vol. 105, No. 10, pp. 3150–3182; and International Monetary Fund, *World Economic Outlook*.

as high as in Namibia and nearly four times as high as in Nigeria. Namibia's real GDP per capita went from being about the same as in Nigeria to being more than twice as high.

In other words, relatively small differences in the growth rates among these economies resulted in dramatic differences in the standard of living of a typical person living in them. Here is the key point to keep in mind: *In the long run, small differences in economic growth rates result in big differences in living standards.*   **MyLab Economics** Concept Check

Why Do Growth Rates Matter?

Why should anyone care about growth rates? Growth rates matter because an economy that grows too slowly fails to raise living standards. In some countries in Africa and Asia, very little economic growth has occurred in the past 50 years, and many people remain in severe poverty. In high-income countries, only 4 out of every 1,000 babies die before they are one year old. In the poorest countries, more than 100 out of every 1,000 babies die before they are one year old, and millions of children die annually from diseases that could be avoided by having access to clean water or that could be cured by using medicines that cost only a few dollars.

Although their problems are less dramatic, countries that experience slow growth have also missed opportunities to improve the lives of their citizens. For example, the failure of Nigeria to grow as rapidly as other countries that had similar levels of GDP per capita in 1960 has left many of its people in poverty. Life expectancy in Nigeria is 15 years less than in the United States and other high-income countries, and infant mortality is more than 10 times higher.   **MyLab Economics** Concept Check

Don't Let This Happen to You

Don't Confuse the Average Annual Percentage Change with the Total Percentage Change

When economists talk about growth rates over a period of more than one year, the numbers are always *average annual percentage changes* and *not* total percentage changes. For example, in the United States, real GDP per capita was $14,398 in 1950 and $51,523 in 2016. The percentage change in real GDP per capita between these two years is:

$$\left(\frac{\$51,523 - \$14,398}{\$14,398} \right) \times 100 = 258\%.$$

However, this is *not* the growth rate between the two years. The growth rate between these two years is the rate at which $14,398 in 1950 would have to grow on average *each year* to end up as $51,523 in 2016, which is 2.0 percent.

MyLab Economics Study Plan

Your Turn: Test your understanding by doing related problem 1.6 on page 385 at the end of this chapter.

"The Rich Get Richer and ... "

We can divide the world's economies into two groups:

1. The *high-income countries*, sometimes called the *industrial countries* or the *developed countries*, including Australia, Canada, Japan, New Zealand, the United States, and the countries of Western Europe
2. The lower-income countries, or *developing countries*, which include most of the countries of Africa, Asia, and Latin America

In the 1980s and 1990s, a small group of countries, mostly East Asian countries such as Singapore, South Korea, and Taiwan, began to experience high rates of growth and are sometimes called the *newly industrializing countries*.

Figure 11.2 shows the levels of GDP per capita around the world in 2016. GDP is measured in U.S. dollars, corrected for differences across countries in the cost of living. In 2016, GDP per capita ranged from a high of $129,700 in the Persian Gulf country

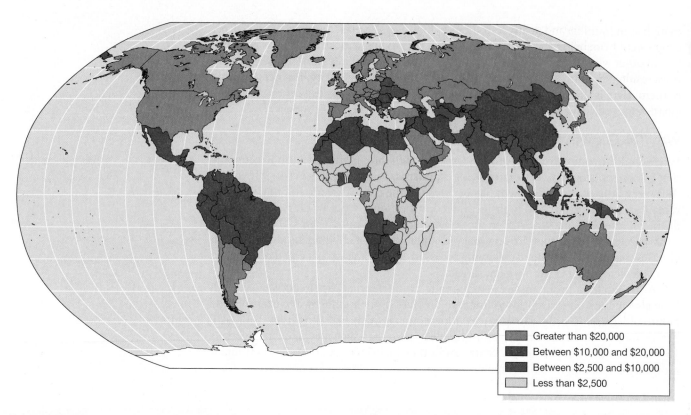

MyLab Economics Animation

Figure 11.2 **GDP per Capita, 2016**

GDP per capita is measured in U.S. dollars, corrected for differences across countries in the cost of living.

■	Greater than $20,000
■	Between $10,000 and $20,000
■	Between $2,500 and $10,000
□	Less than $2,500

MyLab Economics Study Plan

of Qatar to a low of $400 in the African country of Somalia. To understand why the gap between rich and poor countries exists, in the next section we look at what causes economies to grow.

MyLab Economics Concept Check

Apply the Concept

MyLab Economics Video

Is Income All That Matters?

The more income you have, the more goods and services you can buy. When people are surviving on very low incomes of $2 per day or less, their ability to buy even minimal amounts of food, clothing, and housing is limited. So, most economists argue that unless the incomes of the very poor increase significantly, they will be unable to attain a higher standard of living. In some countries—primarily those colored yellow in Figure 11.2—the growth in average income has been very slow, or even negative, over a period of decades. Most economists and policymakers have concluded that the standard of living in these countries has been largely unchanged for many years.

Some economists argue, though, that if we look beyond income to other measures of the standard of living, we can see that even the poorest countries have made significant progress in recent decades. Charles Kenny, an economist with the Center for Global Development, argues, "Those countries with the lowest quality of life are making the fastest progress in improving it—across a range of measures including health, education, and civil and political liberties." For example, since 1960, deaths among children have declined, often by more than 50 percent, in nearly all countries, including most of those with the lowest incomes. Even in sub-Saharan Africa, where growth in incomes

Joerg Boethling/Alamy Stock Photo

In sub-Saharan Africa and other parts of the world, increases in technology and knowledge are leading to improvements in health care and the standard of living.

has been very slow, the percentage of children dying before age five has decreased by more than 30 percent over the past 50 years. Similarly, the percentage of people able to read and write has more than doubled in sub-Saharan Africa since 1970. Many more people now live in democracies where basic civil rights are respected than at any other time in world history. Although some countries, such as Somalia, the Democratic Republic of the Congo, Syria, and Afghanistan, have suffered from civil wars, improved political stability in many countries has reduced the likelihood of dying from violence.

What explains these improvements in health, education, democracy, and political stability? William Easterly, an economist at New York University, has found that although, at any given time, countries that have a higher income also have a higher standard of living, over time, increases in income *within a particular country* are typically not the main cause of improvements in its standard of living in terms of health, education, individual rights, political stability, and similar factors. Kenny's argument and Easterly's finding are connected: Some increases in living standards do not require significant increases in income. The key factors in raising living standards in low-income countries have been increases in technology and knowledge—such as the development of inexpensive vaccines that reduce epidemics and the use of mosquito-resistant netting that reduces the prevalence of malaria—that are inexpensive enough to be widely available. Changes in attitudes, such as placing a greater value on education, particularly for girls, or increasing support for political freedoms, have also played a role in improving conditions in low-income countries.

There are limits, of course, to how much living standards can increase if incomes stagnate. Ultimately, much higher rates of economic growth will be necessary for low-income countries to significantly close the gap in living standards with high-income countries.

Sources: Charles Kenny, *Getting Better*, New York: Basic Books, 2011; Ursula Casabonne and Charles Kenny, "The Best Things in Life Are (Nearly) Free: Technology, Knowledge, and Global Health," *World Development*, Vol. 40, No. 1, January 2012, pp. 21–35; and William Easterly, "Life during Growth," *Journal of Economic Growth*, Vol. 4, No. 3, September 1999, pp. 239–276.

Your Turn: Test your understanding by doing related problems 1.7 and 1.8 on page 385 at the end of this chapter.

MyLab Economics Study Plan

11.2 What Determines How Fast Economies Grow?

LEARNING OBJECTIVE: Use the economic growth model to explain why growth rates differ across countries.

To explain changes in economic growth rates over time within countries and differences in growth rates among countries, we need to develop an *economic growth model*. An **economic growth model** explains growth rates in real GDP per capita over the long run. As we have seen, the average person can buy more goods and services only if the average worker produces more goods and services (see Chapter 10, Section 10.1). Recall that **labor productivity** is the quantity of goods and services that can be produced by one worker or by one hour of work. Because of the importance of labor productivity in explaining economic growth, the economic growth model focuses on the causes of long-run increases in labor productivity.

How can a country's workers become more productive? Economists believe two key factors determine labor productivity:

1. The quantity of capital available to workers
2. The level of technology

Therefore, to explain changes in real GDP per capita, the economic growth model focuses on technological change and changes over time in the quantity of capital available to workers. Recall that **technological change** is a change in the quantity of output firms can produce using a given quantity of inputs.

Economic growth model A model that explains growth rates in real GDP per capita over the long run.

Labor productivity The quantity of goods and services that can be produced by one worker or by one hour of work.

Technological change A change in the quantity of output a firm can produce using a given quantity of inputs.

There are three main sources of technological change:

1. **Better machinery and equipment.** Beginning with the steam engine during the Industrial Revolution, the invention of new machinery has been an important source of rising labor productivity. Today, continuing improvements in computers, factory machine tools, electric generators, and many other machines contribute to increases in labor productivity.

2. **Increases in human capital.** Capital refers to *physical capital*, including computers, factory buildings, machine tools, warehouses, and trucks. The more physical capital workers have available, the more output they can produce. **Human capital** is the accumulated knowledge and skills that workers acquire from education and training or from their life experiences. As workers increase their human capital through education or on-the-job training, their productivity also increases. The more educated workers are, the greater is their human capital.

3. **Better means of organizing and managing production.** Labor productivity increases if managers do a better job of organizing production. For example, the *just-in-time system*, first developed by Toyota Motor Corporation, involves assembling goods from parts that arrive at the factory at exactly the time workers need them. With this system, firms require fewer workers to store and keep track of parts in the factory, so the quantity of goods produced per hour worked increases.

Human capital The accumulated knowledge and skills that workers acquire from education and training or from their life experiences.

Note that technological change is *not* the same thing as more physical capital. New capital can *embody* technological change, as when a faster computer chip is embodied in a new computer. But simply adding more capital that is the same as existing capital is not technological change. To summarize: A country's standard of living will be higher the more capital workers have available on their jobs, the better the capital, the more human capital workers have, and the better the job managers do in organizing production.

The Per-Worker Production Function

Often when analyzing economic growth, we look at increases in real GDP *per hour worked* and increases in capital *per hour worked*. We use measures of GDP per hour and capital per hour rather than per person so that we can analyze changes in the underlying ability of an economy to produce more goods with a given amount of labor without having to worry about changes in the fraction of the population working or in the length of the workday. We can illustrate the economic growth model using the **per-worker production function**, which is the relationship between real GDP per hour worked and capital per hour worked, *holding the level of technology constant*. For simplicity, from now on we will shorten "per-worker production function" to just "production function." Figure 11.3 shows the production function as a graph. We measure capital per hour worked along the horizontal axis and real GDP per hour worked along the vertical axis. Letting K stand for capital, L stand for labor, and Y stand for real GDP, real GDP per hour worked is Y/L, and capital per hour worked is K/L. The curve represents the production function. Notice that we do not explicitly show technological change in the figure. We assume that as we move along the production function, the level of technology remains constant. As we will see, we can illustrate technological change using this graph by *shifting up* the curve representing the production function.

Per-worker production function The relationship between real GDP per hour worked and capital per hour worked, holding the level of technology constant.

The figure shows that increases in the quantity of capital per hour worked result in movements up along the production function, increasing the quantity of output each worker produces. When *we hold technology constant*, however, equal increases in the amount of capital per hour worked lead to *diminishing* increases in output per hour worked. For example, increasing capital per hour worked from $75 to $100 increases real GDP per hour worked from $48 to $53, an increase of $5. Another $25 increase in capital per hour worked, from $100 to $125, increases real GDP per hour worked from $53 to $57, an increase of only $4. Each additional $25 increase in capital per hour worked results in progressively smaller increases in real GDP per hour worked. In fact, at very high levels of capital per hour worked, further increases in capital per hour

MyLab Economics Animation

Figure 11.3

The Per-Worker Production Function

The per-worker production function shows the relationship between capital per hour worked and real GDP per hour worked, holding technology constant. Increases in capital per hour worked increase output per hour worked but at a diminishing rate. For example, an increase in capital per hour worked from $75 to $100 increases real GDP per hour worked from $48 to $53. An increase in capital per hour worked from $100 to $125 increases real GDP per hour worked by a smaller amount, from $53 to $57. Each additional $25 increase in capital per hour worked results in a progressively smaller increase in output per hour worked.

worked will not result in any increase in real GDP per hour worked. This effect results from the *law of diminishing returns*, which states that as we add more of one input—in this case, capital—to a fixed quantity of another input—in this case, labor—output increases by smaller additional amounts.

Why are there diminishing returns to capital? Consider a simple example in which you own a pizza restaurant. At first you have 10 employees but only 1 oven, so each of your workers is able to produce relatively few pizzas per day. When you buy and install a second oven, your employees will be able to produce more pizzas. Adding additional ovens will continue to increase your output—but by increasingly smaller amounts. For example, adding a twentieth oven to the 19 you already have will not increase the pizzas each worker is able to make by nearly as much as adding a second oven did. Eventually, adding additional ovens won't increase your output at all.   **MyLab Economics** Concept Check

Which Is More Important for Economic Growth: More Capital or Technological Change?

Technological change helps economies avoid diminishing returns to capital. Let's consider two simple examples of the effects of technological change. First, suppose you have 3 ovens in your restaurant. Each oven can produce 20 pizzas per hour. You don't believe that adding a fourth oven identical to the 3 you already have will significantly increase the number of pizzas your employees can produce in a day. Then you find out that a new oven has become available that cooks pizzas more quickly, making it possible to produce 30 pizzas per hour. If you replace your existing ovens with the new ovens, the productivity of your workers will increase. The replacement of existing capital with more productive capital is an example of technological change.

Or suppose you realize that the layout of your restaurant could be improved. Maybe the pizza dough is on shelves that are at the other end of the kitchen from the ovens, which requires your employees to spend time walking back and forth when preparing pizzas. By placing the pizza dough closer to the ovens, you can improve the productivity of your workers. Reorganizing how production takes place so as to increase output is also an example of technological change.   **MyLab Economics** Concept Check

Technological Change: The Key to Sustaining Economic Growth

Figure 11.4 shows that technological change shifts up the production function and allows an economy to produce more real GDP per hour worked with the same quantity of capital per hour worked. For example, if the current level of technology puts the

Figure 11.4

Technological Change Increases Output per Hour Worked

Technological change shifts up the production function and allows more output per hour worked with the same amount of capital per hour worked. For example, along Production function₁ with $150 in capital per hour worked, the economy can produce $60 in real GDP per hour worked. However, an increase in technology that shifts the economy to Production function₂ makes it possible to produce $65 in real GDP per hour worked with the same level of capital per hour worked.

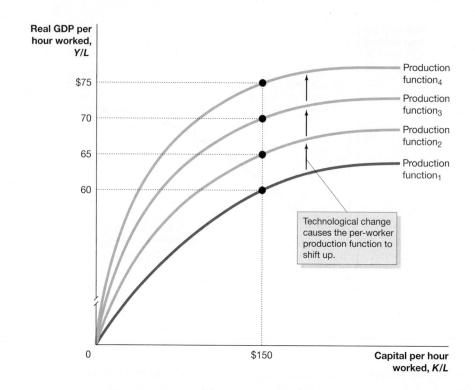

economy on Production function₁, when capital per hour worked is $150, real GDP per hour worked is $60. Technological change that shifts the economy to Production function₂ makes it possible to produce $65 in goods and services per hour worked with the same level of capital per hour worked. Further increases in technology that shift the economy to higher production functions result in further increases in real GDP per hour worked. Because of diminishing returns to capital, continuing increases in real GDP per hour worked can be sustained only if there is technological change. Remember that a country will experience increases in its standard of living only if it experiences increases in real GDP per hour worked. Therefore, we can draw the following important conclusion: *In the long run, a country will experience an increasing standard of living only if it experiences continuing technological change.* **MyLab Economics** Concept Check

● Apply the Concept

What Explains the Economic Failure of the Soviet Union?

The economic growth model can help explain one of the most striking events of the twentieth century: the economic collapse of the Soviet Union. The Soviet Union was formed from the old Russian Empire following the Russian Revolution of 1917. Under Communism, the Soviet Union was a centrally planned economy in which the government owned nearly every business and made all production and pricing decisions. In 1960, Nikita Khrushchev, the leader of the Soviet Union, addressed the United Nations in New York City. He declared to the United States and the other democracies: "We will bury you. Your grandchildren will live under Communism."

Many people at the time took Khrushchev's boast seriously. Capital per hour worked grew rapidly in the Soviet Union from 1950 through the 1980s. At first, these increases in capital per hour worked also produced rapid increases in real GDP per hour worked. Rapid increases in real GDP per hour worked during the 1950s caused some economists in the United States to predict incorrectly that the Soviet Union would someday surpass the United States economically. In 1960, leading U.S. economic textbooks predicted that the Soviet Union would overtake the United States in per capita real GDP

In the former Soviet Union, there were frequent shortages, and unhappy consumers often had to wait in long lines to shop for groceries and other goods.

Bettmann/Getty Images

by some time in the 1980s. In fact, by the time the Soviet Union dissolved in 1991, its per capita real GDP was *lower* relative to U.S. per capita real GDP than it had been in 1960. The problem facing the Soviet Union was that diminishing returns to capital meant that building additional factories resulted in smaller and smaller increases in real GDP per hour worked.

The Soviet Union did experience some technological change—but at a rate much slower than in the United States and other high-income countries. Why did the Soviet Union fail to implement new technologies that are crucial to sustained economic growth? The key reason is that in a centrally planned economy, the people managing most businesses are government employees and not entrepreneurs or independent businesspeople, as is the case in market economies. Soviet managers had little incentive to adopt new ways of producing goods and services. Their pay depended on producing the quantity of output specified in the government's economic plan, not on discovering new, better, and lower-cost ways to produce goods. In addition, these managers did not have to worry about competition from either domestic or foreign firms.

Entrepreneurs and managers of firms in the United States, by contrast, are under intense competitive pressure from other firms. They must constantly search for better ways of producing the goods and services they sell. Developing and using new technologies is an important way to gain a competitive edge and earn a higher profit. The drive for profit provides an incentive for technological change that centrally planned economies are unable to duplicate. In market economies, entrepreneurs and managers who have their own money on the line make decisions about which investments to make and which technologies to adopt. Nothing concentrates the mind like having your own funds at risk.

In hindsight, it is clear that a centrally planned economy, such as the Soviet Union's, could not, over the long run, grow faster than a market economy. The Soviet Union collapsed in 1991, and contemporary Russia now has a more market-oriented system, although the government continues to play a much larger role in the economy than does the government in the United States.

Note: For a discussion of the views of 1960s U.S. economics textbooks on Soviet growth, see David M. Levy and Sandra J. Peart, "Soviet Growth and American Textbooks: An Endogenous Past," *Journal of Economic Behavior and Organization,*" Vol. 78, No. 1–2, April 2011, pp. 110–125.

Your Turn: Test your understanding by doing related problems 2.6 and 2.7 on page 386 at the end of this chapter.

MyLab Economics Study Plan

Solved Problem 11.2

MyLab Economics Interactive Animation

Using the Economic Growth Model to Analyze the Failure of the Soviet Economy

Use the economic growth model and the information in the *Apply the Concept* on page 362 to analyze the economic problems the Soviet Union encountered.

Solving the Problem

Step 1: Review the chapter material. This problem is about using the economic growth model to explain the failure of the Soviet economy, so you may want to review the *Apply the Concept* that begins on page 362.

Step 2: Draw a graph like Figure 11.3 on page 361 to illustrate the economic problems of the Soviet Union. For simplicity, assume that the Soviet Union experienced no technological change.

The Soviet Union experienced rapid increases in capital per hour worked from 1950 through the 1980s, but its failure to implement new technology meant that output per hour worked grew at a slower and slower rate.

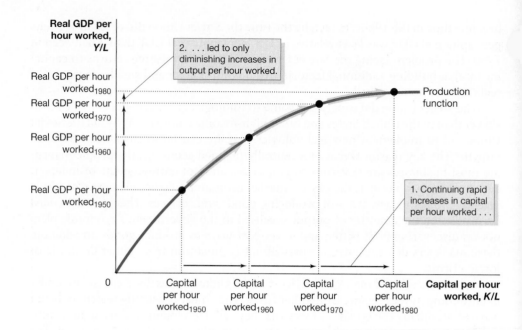

Extra Credit: The Soviet Union hoped to raise the standard of living of its citizens above that enjoyed in the United States and other high-income countries by making continuous increases in the quantity of capital available to its workers. The economic growth model helps us understand the flaws in this policy for achieving economic growth.

MyLab Economics Study Plan

Your Turn: For more practice, do related problems 2.8, 2.9, and 2.10 on pages 386–387 at the end of this chapter.

New Growth Theory

The economic growth model we have been using was first developed in the 1950s by Nobel Laureate Robert Solow of MIT. According to this model, productivity growth is the key factor in explaining long-run growth in real GDP per capita. Some economists believe that the model is incomplete because it does not explain the factors that determine productivity growth. Paul Romer, of New York University, developed the **new growth theory** to provide a more complete explanation of the sources of technological change that underlie productivity growth. Romer argues that how individuals and firms respond to economic incentives affects the rate of technological change. Earlier accounts of economic growth did not explain technological change or attributed it to factors such as chance scientific discoveries.

New growth theory A model of long-run economic growth which emphasizes that technological change is influenced by economic incentives and so is determined by the working of the market system.

Romer argues that the accumulation of *knowledge capital* is a key determinant of economic growth. Firms add to an economy's stock of knowledge capital when they engage in research and development or otherwise contribute to technological change. We have seen that accumulation of physical capital is subject to diminishing returns: Increases in capital per hour worked lead to increases in real GDP per hour worked but at a decreasing rate. Romer argues that the same is true of knowledge capital *at the firm level.* As firms add to their stock of knowledge capital, they increase their output but at a decreasing rate. At the level of the entire economy, however, Romer argues that knowledge capital is subject to *increasing returns.* Increasing returns can exist because knowledge, once discovered, becomes available to everyone. The use of physical capital, such as a computer or machine tool, is *rival* because if one firm uses it, other firms cannot, and it is *excludable* because the firm that owns the capital can keep other firms from using it. The use of knowledge capital, such as the chemical formula for a drug that cures cancer, is nonrival, however, because one firm's using that knowledge does not prevent another firm from using it. Knowledge capital is also nonexcludable because once something like a chemical formula becomes known, it becomes widely available for other firms to use (unless, as we discuss shortly, the government gives the firm that invents a new product the legal right to its exclusive use).

Because knowledge capital is nonrival and nonexcludable, firms can *free ride* on the research and development of other firms. Firms free ride when they benefit from the results of research and development they did not pay for. For example, transistor technology was first developed at Western Electric's Bell Laboratories in the 1950s and served as the basic technology of the information revolution. Bell Laboratories, however, received only a tiny fraction of the immense profits that were eventually made by all the firms that used this technology. Romer notes that firms are unlikely to invest in research and development up to the point where the marginal cost of the research equals the marginal return from the knowledge gained because *other* firms gain much of the marginal return. Therefore, there is likely to be an inefficiently small amount of research and development, slowing the accumulation of knowledge capital and economic growth.

Government policy can help increase the accumulation of knowledge capital in three ways:

1. **Protecting intellectual property with patents and copyrights.** Governments can increase the incentive to engage in research and development by giving firms the exclusive rights to their discoveries for a period of time. The U.S. government grants patents to companies that develop new products or new ways of making existing products. A **patent** gives a firm the exclusive legal right to a new product for a period of 20 years from the date the patent application is filed with the government. For example, a pharmaceutical firm that develops a drug that cures cancer can secure a patent on the drug, keeping other firms from manufacturing the drug without permission. The profit earned during the period the patent is in force provides firms with an incentive for undertaking research and development. The patent system has drawbacks, however. In filing for a patent, a firm must disclose information about the product or process. This information enters the public record and may help competing firms develop products or processes that are similar but that do not infringe on the patent. To avoid this problem, a firm may try to keep the results of its research a *trade secret*, without patenting it. (A famous example of a trade secret is the formula for Coca-Cola.) Tension also arises between the government's objectives of providing patent protection that gives firms the incentive to engage in research and development and making sure that the knowledge gained through the research is widely available, which increases the positive effect of the knowledge on the economy. Economists debate the features of an ideal patent system.

2. **Supporting research and development.** The government can help increase the quantity of research and development that takes place. In the United States, the federal government conducts some research directly. For example, the National Institutes of Health conducts medical research. The forerunner of the Internet— the Advanced Research Projects Agency Network (ARPANET)—was developed by the U.S. Department of Defense to improve communication among defense researchers around the country. The government also subsidizes research by providing grants and other payments to researchers in universities through the National Science Foundation and other agencies. Finally, the government provides tax benefits to firms that invest in research and development.

3. **Subsidizing education.** People with technical training carry out research and development. If firms are unable to capture all the profit from research and development, they will pay lower wages and salaries to technical workers. These lower wages and salaries reduce the incentive to workers to receive this training. If the government subsidizes education, it can increase the number of workers who have technical training. In the United States, the government subsidizes education by directly providing free education from grades kindergarten through 12 and by providing support for public colleges and universities. The government also provides student loans at reduced interest rates.

These government policies can bring the accumulation of knowledge capital closer to the optimal level. **MyLab Economics** Concept Check

Patent The exclusive right to produce a product for a period of 20 years from the date the patent application is filed with the government.

Joseph Schumpeter and Creative Destruction

The new growth theory has revived interest in the ideas of Joseph Schumpeter. Born in Austria in 1883, Schumpeter served briefly as that country's finance minister. In 1932, he became an economics professor at Harvard University. Schumpeter developed a model of growth that emphasized his view that new products unleash a "gale of creative destruction" that drives older products—and, often, the firms that produced them—out of the market. According to Schumpeter, the key to rising living standards is not small changes to existing products but, rather, new products that meet consumer wants in qualitatively better ways. For example, in the early twentieth century, the automobile displaced the horse-drawn carriage by meeting consumer demand for personal transportation in a way that was qualitatively better. In the early twenty-first century, the DVD and the DVD player displaced the VHS tape and the VCR by better meeting consumer demand for watching films at home. Downloading or streaming movies from the Internet are now displacing the DVD just as the DVD displaced the VHS tape.

To Schumpeter, the entrepreneur is central to economic growth: "The function of entrepreneurs is to reform or revolutionize the pattern of production by exploiting an invention or, more generally, an untried technological possibility for producing new commodities or producing an old one in a new way."

The profit an entrepreneur hopes to earn provides the incentive for bringing together the factors of production—labor, capital, and natural resources—to start new firms and introduce new goods and services. Successful entrepreneurs can use their profits to finance the development of new products and are better able to attract funds from investors.

MyLab Economics Study Plan

MyLab Economics Concept Check

11.3 Economic Growth in the United States

LEARNING OBJECTIVE: Discuss fluctuations in productivity growth in the United States.

The economic growth model can help us understand the record of growth in the United States. Figure 11.5 shows average annual growth rates in real GDP per hour worked since 1800. As the United States experienced the Industrial Revolution during the nineteenth century, U.S. firms increased the quantity of capital per hour worked. New technologies such as the steam engine, the railroad, and the telegraph also became available. Together, these factors resulted in an average annual growth rate of real GDP per worker of 1.3 percent from 1800 to 1900. Real GDP *per capita* grew at a slower rate of 1.1 percent during this period. At this growth rate, real GDP per capita would double about every 63 years, which means that living standards were growing steadily but relatively slowly.

By the twentieth century, technological change had been institutionalized. Many large corporations created research and development facilities to improve the quality of their products and the efficiency with which they produced them. Universities also began to conduct research that had business applications. After World War II, many corporations began to provide significant funds to universities to help pay for research. In 1950, the federal government created the National Science Foundation, whose main goal is to support university researchers. The accelerating rate of technological change led to more rapid growth rates.

Economic Growth in the United States since 1950

Continuing technological change allowed the U.S. economy to avoid the diminishing returns to capital that stifled growth in the Soviet economy. In fact, until the 1970s, the growth rate of the U.S. economy accelerated over time. As Figure 11.5 shows, growth in the first half of the twentieth century was faster than growth during the nineteenth century, and growth in the immediate post–World War II period from 1950 to 1973 was faster yet. Then the unexpected happened: For more than 20 years, from 1974 to 1995, the growth rate of real GDP per hour worked slowed. The growth rate during these years was more than 1 percentage point per year lower than during the 1950–1973 period. Beginning in the mid-1990s, the growth rate picked up again, and

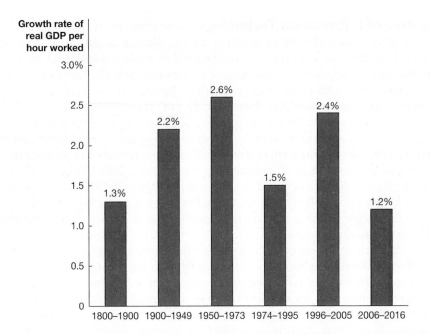

MyLab Economics Animation

Figure 11.5

Average Annual Growth Rates in Real GDP per Hour Worked in the United States, 1800–2016

The growth rate in the United States increased from 1800 through the mid-1970s. Then, for more than 20 years, growth slowed before increasing for a 10-year period beginning in the mid-1990s. During the past 10 years, growth has slowed again.

Note: The values for 1800–1900 are real GDP per worker. The values for 1900–2016 are real GDP per hour worked; for the period 1900–2016 they are the authors' calculations, based on the methods used in Neville Francis and Valerie A. Ramey, "The Source of Historical Economic Fluctuations: An Analysis Using Long-Run Restrictions," in Jeffrey Frankel, Richard Clarida, and Francesco Giavazzi, eds., *International Seminar in Macroeconomics*, Chicago: University of Chicago Press, 2005; the authors thank Neville Francis for kindly providing some of the data used.

many economists argued that the effects of the revolution in *information technology* (IT), including increased use of computers, software, cellphones, and related innovations, were causing a return to higher rates of long-run growth. But, then, beginning in 2006, growth again slowed.　　　　　　　　　　　　　　　**MyLab Economics** Concept Check

Is the United States Headed for a Long Period of Slow Growth?

Economists have not reached a consensus in explaining the swings in U.S. productivity growth since the mid-1970s. Broadly speaking, economists' views fall into two camps:

1. **The optimistic view.** Some economists argue that although productivity has become more difficult to measure, the United States is likely to experience high rates of productivity growth in the long run, which will significantly increase the standard of living of the average person in the decades ahead.
2. **The pessimistic view.** Other economists believe that productivity growth entered a long-run decline in the mid-1970s that was overcome for only a brief period of time by the initial effects of the revolution in information technology. These economists argue that future productivity growth rates are likely to remain low and, therefore, the standard of living of the average person in the United States will increase only slowly.

We can briefly discuss some of the key issues involved in this debate.

Measurement Issues　Some economists argue that recent productivity growth rates may appear worse than they are because of problems in measuring output. If growth in real GDP understates the true growth rate of output, then measured productivity growth will also understate the true growth rate of productivity. After 1970, services—such as haircuts and financial advice—became a larger fraction of GDP, and goods—such as automobiles and hamburgers—became a smaller fraction. It is more difficult to measure increases in the output of services than to measure increases in the output of goods. For example, before banks began using automated teller machines (ATMs) in the 1980s, you could withdraw money only by going to a bank before closing time—which was usually 3:00 P.M. Once ATMs became available, you could withdraw money at any time of the day or night at a variety of locations. This increased convenience from ATMs does not show up in GDP. Similarly, when people post to Facebook, Snapchat, or Twitter or search Google for information they pay a zero price yet receive substantial consumer surplus that is not captured in the GDP statistics.

The Role of Information Technology Some economists argue that the development of IT caused the higher productivity growth that began in the mid-1990s. As computers became less expensive and faster, they made it possible for people and organizations to communicate and process data more efficiently. Faster data processing has had a major effect on nearly every firm. Business record keeping, once done laboriously by hand, is now done more quickly and accurately by computers. During the 1990s, firms used the Internet to market and sell products. Smartphones, tablets, laptop computers, and wireless Internet access allow people to work at home and while traveling. These developments in IT have significantly increased labor productivity.

Despite the wonders of IT, productivity growth since 2006 has fallen to an even lower rate than during the period of slow growth from the mid-1970s to the mid-1990s. Is IT no longer a productivity booster, or are the data not capturing some of IT's benefits? What insight do the answers to these questions give us about how rapid growth will be in the coming decades?

As already noted, some economists believe that developments in IT have improved the delivery of services to both consumers and firms in ways that the GDP statistics fail to capture. In recent years, the widespread use of apps to arrange for car rides, make short-term room rentals, locate friends, post to social media, look up information, and stream movies and television shows have benefited consumers in ways that are either not measured or only partially measured by GDP. Similarly, a store manager can quickly check on available warehouse inventory using a dedicated smartphone or tablet app.

Economists who believe that IT is having large, but difficult-to-measure, effects on the economy are usually also optimistic about future growth rates. They believe that continuing advances in semiconductor technology—which underlie progress in IT—will result in substantial gains in labor productivity. The gains will come from higher productivity in the IT sector itself and in other sectors of the economy as a result of progress made possible by advances in IT. For example, ever more rapid and inexpensive computing lowers the cost and speeds the adoption of existing products, such as 3D printers, and helps innovators develop new products, which, in turn, raise productivity growth above its current levels. In addition, these economists argue that some firms have not adopted innovations arising from IT because of low rates of investment spending since the 2007–2009 recession. Larger firms, particularly those that operate globally, have generally experienced high rates of labor productivity growth, while smaller firms and those that sell primarily to the domestic market have experienced much slower—or no—productivity growth. As the economy continues to expand and investment spending increases, the effect of IT innovations will spread to more firms, and measured productivity may increase.

Other economists doubt that the unmeasured benefits of the IT revolution are any greater than the unmeasured benefits of earlier innovations. Robert J. Gordon of Northwestern University has argued that productivity increases from the IT revolution were in fact much smaller than increases resulting from earlier innovations, such as the railroad, electrification of homes and businesses, indoor plumbing, petroleum refining, and the automobile. Moreover, Gordon and some other economists argue that most of the productivity gains from the IT revolution occurred in the 1990s, as a result of the development of the World Wide Web, Windows 95, and computerized inventory control systems. These innovations raised labor productivity because they changed how businesses operated. By the early 2000s, the IT revolution was having a greater effect on consumer products, such as smartphones and tablets, than on labor productivity. Gordon identifies other factors, such as an aging population (productivity peaks for the typical worker in his or her 40s), declining educational achievement, and the consequences of increased regulations and higher taxes, that will lead to lower productivity growth rates. Gordon forecasts an extended period of productivity growth rates of 0.5 percent or less.

"Secular Stagnation … " In the late 1930s, toward the end of the Great Depression, Alvin Hansen of Harvard University predicted that the U.S. economy would experience an extended period of slow growth, or *secular stagnation*. The rapid growth rates the U.S. economy experienced beginning in 1950 indicate that Hansen's analysis was incorrect. Recently, however, Lawrence Summers also of Harvard University, along with some other economists, has revived the term in arguing that growth rates are likely to remain low in future years. These economists do not focus on potentially slow rates of technological progress. Instead, they believe that real GDP may grow slowly because of insufficient demand for investment spending.

In Chapter 10, Section 10.2, we saw that in the loanable funds model, the equilibrium level of saving and investment is determined at the level of the real interest rate where the quantity of loanable funds demanded equals the quantity of loanable funds supplied. Economists who forecast a future of secular stagnation believe that the demand for loanable funds may be low in coming years for three main reasons:

1. Slowing population growth in the United States will reduce the demand for housing.
2. Modern information technology firms, such as Twitter, Google, and Facebook, require much less capital than older industrial firms, such as General Motors or Whirlpool.
3. The price of capital, particularly information technology goods such as computers, has been falling relative to the prices of other goods. Accordingly, firms can meet their needs for capital with lower levels of expenditure.

As a result of these factors, the real interest rate that brings equality to the loanable funds market may be very low—possibly even negative. So, investment spending will be very low. With this component of GDP growing slowly, GDP will itself only grow slowly.

... or a Return to Faster Growth?

Critics of the secular stagnation view believe that low rates of investment in recent years have resulted from the severity of the recession of 2007–2009 and the relatively slow recovery from that recession. They argue that as the economic recovery continues, the demand for investment goods will increase. In addition, they argue that economic growth in other countries may increase the demand for U.S. goods, allowing exports to increase, thereby offsetting the effects on GDP of lower production of investment goods.

The debate over future growth rates is an important one. If the optimistic forecasts are correct, then in future decades, the U.S. standard of living will be much higher than if the pessimistic forecasts are correct. A large difference in the standard of living will have an enormous effect on nearly every aspect of life in the United States, including the extent of poverty, the ability of individuals and the government to finance increasing medical costs, and the ability of the country to deal with the effects of an aging population.   **MyLab Economics** Concept Check   **MyLab Economics** Study Plan

Why Isn't the Whole World Rich?

11.4

LEARNING OBJECTIVE: Explain economic catch-up and discuss why many poor countries have not experienced rapid economic growth.

The economic growth model tells us that economies grow when the quantity of capital per hour worked increases and when technological change occurs. This model seems to provide a good blueprint for developing countries to become rich:

1. Increase the quantity of capital per hour worked.
2. Use the best available technology.

There are economic incentives for both of these things to happen in poor countries. The profitability of using additional capital or better technology is generally greater in a developing country than in a high-income country. For example, replacing an existing computer with a new, faster computer will generally have a relatively small payoff for a firm in the United States. In contrast, installing a new computer in a Zambian firm where records have been kept by hand is likely to have an enormous payoff.

This observation leads to an important conclusion: *The economic growth model predicts that poor countries will grow faster than rich countries.* If this prediction is correct, we should observe poor countries catching up to rich countries in levels of GDP per capita (or income per capita). Has this **catch-up**—or *convergence*—actually occurred? Here we come to a paradox: If we look only at the group of countries that currently have high incomes, we see that the lower-income countries in this group have been catching up to the higher-income countries, but the developing countries as a group have not been catching up to the high-income countries as a group.

Catch-up The prediction that the level of GDP per capita (or income per capita) in poor countries will grow faster than in rich countries.

MyLab Economics Animation

Figure 11.6

The Catch-up Predicted by the Economic Growth Model

According to the economic growth model, countries that start with lower levels of real GDP per capita should grow faster (points near the upper-left section of the line) than countries that start with higher levels of real GDP per capita (points near the lower-right section of the line).

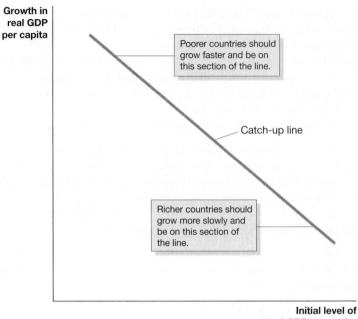

Catch-up: Sometimes but Not Always

We can construct a graph that makes it easier to see whether catch-up is happening. In Figure 11.6, the horizontal axis shows the initial level of real GDP per capita, and the vertical axis shows the rate at which real GDP per capita is growing. We can then plot points on the graph for rich and poor countries. Each point represents the combination of a country's initial level of real GDP per capita and its growth rate over the following years. The catch-up line in the figure shows the situation where the catch-up prediction holds exactly: Low-income countries should be on the upper-left section of the line because they would have low initial levels of real GDP per capita but fast growth rates. High-income countries should be in the lower-right section of the line because they would have high initial levels of real GDP per capita but slow growth rates. When we plot the actual observations for each country, the closer the points for each country are to the line, the more accurate the catch-up prediction.

Catch-up among the High-Income Countries If we look at only the countries that currently have high incomes, we can see the catch-up predicted by the economic growth model. Figure 11.7 shows that the high-income countries that had the lowest incomes in 1960, such as Korea, Singapore, Taiwan, and Hong Kong, grew the fastest between 1960 and 2014 (which is the most recent year for which comprehensive data are available). Countries that had the highest incomes in 1960, such as Switzerland, New Zealand, and the United States, grew the slowest.

Are the Developing Countries Catching up to the High-Income Countries? If we expand our analysis to include every country for which statistics are available, it becomes more difficult to find the catch-up predicted by the economic growth model. Figure 11.8, which includes data for 111 countries, does not show a consistent relationship between the level of real GDP per capita in 1960 and growth from 1960 to 2014. Some countries that had low levels of real GDP per capita in 1960, such as Niger and the Democratic Republic of the Congo, actually experienced *negative* economic growth: They had *lower* levels of real GDP per capita in 2014 than in 1960. Other countries that started with low levels of real GDP per capita, such as Malaysia and China, grew rapidly. Some middle-income countries in 1960, such as Jamaica, grew slowly between 1960 and 2014, while others, such as Ireland, grew much more rapidly.

MyLab Economics Concept Check

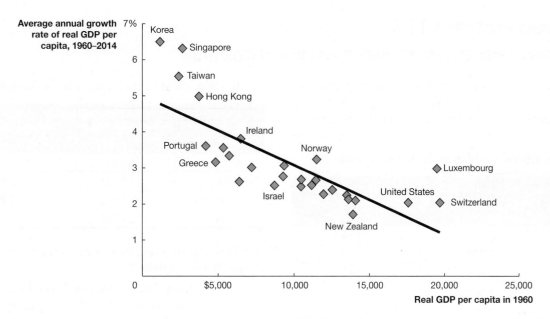

Figure 11.7   **There Has Been Catch-up among High-Income Countries**

If we look only at countries that currently have high incomes, we see that countries such as Korea, Singapore, Taiwan, and Hong Kong that had the lowest incomes in 1960 grew the fastest between 1960 and 2014. Countries such as Switzerland, New Zealand, and the United States that had the highest incomes in 1960 grew the slowest.

Note: Data are real GDP per capita in 2005 dollars. Each point in the figure represents one high-income country.

Source: Authors' calculations from data in Robert C. Feenstra, Robert Inklaar, and Marcel P. Timmer, "The Next Generation of the Penn World Table," *American Economic Review*, October 2015, Vol. 105, No. 10, pp. 3150–3182.

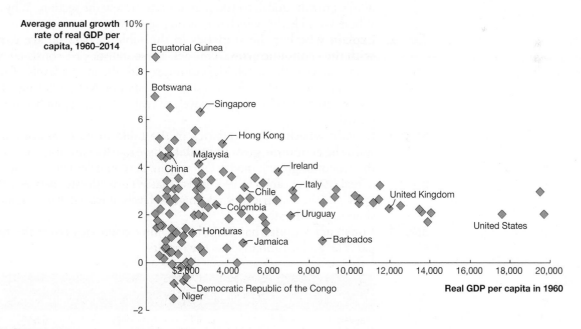

Figure 11.8   **Most of the World Hasn't Been Catching Up**

If we look at all countries for which statistics are available, we do not see the catch-up predicted by the economic growth model. Some countries that had low levels of real GDP per capita in 1960, such as Niger and the Democratic Republic of the Congo, actually experienced *negative* economic growth. Other countries that started with low levels of real GDP per capita, such as Malaysia and China, grew rapidly. Some middle-income countries in 1960, such as Jamaica, grew slowly between 1960 and 2014, while others, such as Ireland, experienced significant growth.

Note: Data are real GDP per capita in 2005 dollars. Each point in the figure represents one country.

Source: Authors' calculations from data in Robert C. Feenstra, Robert Inklaar, and Marcel P. Timmer, "The Next Generation of the Penn World Table," *American Economic Review*, October 2015, Vol. 105, No. 10, pp. 3150–3182.

Solved Problem 11.4

The Economic Growth Model's Prediction of Catch-Up

The economic growth model makes a prediction about an economy's initial level of real GDP per capita relative to other economies and how fast the economy will grow in the future.

a. Consider the statistics in the following table:

Country	Real GDP per Capita, 1960 (2005 U.S. dollars)	Annual Growth in Real GDP per Capita, 1960–2014
Taiwan	$2,417	5.54%
Panama	2,734	3.73
Colombia	3,449	2.43
Costa Rica	4,684	2.07
Venezuela	5,862	1.64

Are these statistics consistent with the economic growth model? Briefly explain.

b. Now consider the statistics in the following table:

Country	Real GDP per Capita, 1960 (2005 U.S. dollars)	Annual Growth in Real GDP per Capita, 1960–2014
Japan	$5,351	3.56%
Belgium	10,487	2.68
United Kingdom	11,959	2.27
Australia	14,060	2.09

Are these statistics consistent with the economic growth model? Briefly explain.

c. Construct a new table that lists all nine countries, from the lowest real GDP per capita in 1960 to the highest, along with their growth rates. Are the statistics in your new table consistent with the economic growth model?

Solving the Problem

Step 1: **Review the chapter material.** This problem is about catch-up in the economic growth model, so you may want to review the section "Why Isn't the Whole World Rich?" which begins on page 369.

Step 2: **Explain whether the statistics in the table in part (a) are consistent with the economic growth model.** These statistics are consistent with the economic growth model. The countries with the lowest levels of real GDP per capita in 1960 had the fastest growth rates between 1960 and 2014, and the countries with the highest levels of real GDP per capita had the slowest growth rates.

Step 3: **Explain whether the statistics in the table in part (b) are consistent with the economic growth model.** These statistics are also consistent with the economic growth model. Once again, the countries with the lowest levels of real GDP per capita in 1960 had the fastest growth rates between 1960 and 2014, and the countries with the highest levels of real GDP per capita had the slowest growth rates.

Step 4: **Construct a table that includes all nine countries from the tables in parts (a) and (b) and discuss the results.**

Country	Real GDP per Capita, 1960 (2005 U.S. dollars)	Annual Growth in Real GDP per Capita, 1960–2014
Taiwan	$2,417	5.54%
Panama	2,734	3.73
Colombia	3,449	2.43
Costa Rica	4,684	2.07
Japan	5,351	3.56
Venezuela	5,862	1.64
Belgium	10,487	2.68
United Kingdom	11,959	2.27
Australia	14,060	2.09

The statistics in the new table are *not* consistent with the predictions of the economic growth model. For example, Australia and the United Kingdom had higher levels of real GDP per capita in 1960 than did Costa Rica and Venezuela. The economic growth model predicts that Australia and the United Kingdom should, therefore, have grown more slowly than Costa Rica and Venezuela. The data in the table show, however, that Australia and the United Kingdom grew faster. Similarly, Belgium grew faster than Colombia, even though its real GDP per capita was already much higher than Colombia's in 1960.

Extra Credit: The statistics in these tables confirm what we saw in Figures 11.7 and 11.8 on page 371: There has been catch-up among the high-income countries, but there has not been catch-up if we include in the analysis all the countries of the world.

Source: Authors' calculations from data in Robert C. Feenstra, Robert Inklaar, and Marcel P. Timmer, "The Next Generation of the Penn World Table," *American Economic Review*, October 2015, Vol. 105, No. 10, pp. 3150–3182.

Your Turn: For more practice, do related problems 4.4 and 4.5 on page 388 at the end of this chapter.

MyLab Economics Study Plan

Why Haven't Most Western European Countries, Canada, and Japan Caught Up to the United States?

Figure 11.7 on page 371 indicates that there has been catch-up among the high-income countries over the past 54 years. If we look at the catch-up of other high-income countries to the United States during the most recent period, we discover a surprising fact: Over the past 25 years, other high-income countries have actually fallen further behind the United States rather than catching up to it. Figure 11.9 shows real GDP per capita in Canada, Japan, and the five largest economies in Western Europe relative to real GDP per capita in the United States. The blue bars show real GDP per capita in 1990 relative to the United States, and the red bars show real GDP per capita in 2016 relative to the United States. In each case, relative levels of real GDP per capita were lower in 2016 than they were in 1990. Each of these countries experienced significant catch-up to the United States between 1960 and 1990, but they have experienced no catch-up since 1990.

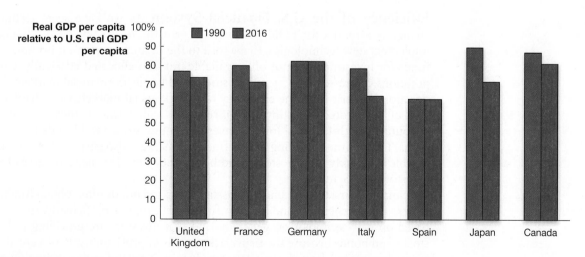

MyLab Economics Real-Time Data

Figure 11.9   Other High-Income Countries Have Stopped Catching up to the United States

The blue bars show real GDP per capita in 1990 relative to the United States, and the red bars show real GDP per capita in 2016 relative to the United States. In each case, relative levels of real GDP per capita are lower in 2016 than they were in 1990, which means that these countries have ceased catching up to the United States.

Source: Authors' calculations from data in Organization for Economic Co-operation and Development, stat.oecd.org.

Why have other high-income countries had trouble completely closing the gap in real GDP per capita with the United States? Many economists believe there are two main explanations:

1. The greater flexibility of U.S. labor markets
2. The greater efficiency of the U.S. financial system

Flexibility of the U.S. Labor Market U.S. labor markets are more flexible than labor markets in other countries for several reasons. In many European countries, government regulations make it difficult for firms to fire workers and thereby make firms reluctant to hire workers in the first place. As a result, many younger workers have difficulty finding jobs, and once a job is found, a worker tends to remain in it even if his or her skills and preferences are not a good match for the characteristics of the job. In the United States, by contrast, government regulations are less restrictive, workers have an easier time finding jobs, and workers change jobs fairly frequently. This high rate of job mobility ensures a better match between workers' skills and preferences and the characteristics of jobs, which increases labor productivity. Many European countries also have restrictive work rules that limit the ability of firms to implement new technologies. These rules restrict the tasks firms can ask workers to perform and the hours they work. The rules reduce the ability of firms to use new technologies that may require workers to learn new skills, perform new tasks, or work during the night or early mornings.

Workers in the United States tend to enter the labor force earlier, retire later, and experience fewer long spells of unemployment than do workers in Europe. Unemployed workers in the United States typically receive smaller government payments for a shorter period of time than do unemployed workers in Canada and most of the countries of Western Europe. Because the opportunity cost of being unemployed is lower in those countries, the unemployment rate tends to be higher, and the fraction of the labor force that is unemployed for more than one year also tends to be higher. Studies have shown that workers who are employed for longer periods tend to have greater skills, greater productivity, and higher wages. Many economists believe that the design of the U.S. unemployment insurance program has contributed to the greater flexibility of U.S. labor markets and to higher rates of growth in labor productivity and real GDP per capita.

Efficiency of the U.S. Financial System As we have seen, technological change is essential for rapid productivity growth. To obtain the funds needed to implement new technologies, firms turn to the financial system. It is important that funds for investment be not only available but also allocated efficiently. Large corporations can raise funds by selling stocks and bonds in financial markets. U.S. corporations benefit from the efficiency of U.S. financial markets (see Chapter 6). The level of legal protection of investors is relatively high in U.S. financial markets, which encourages both U.S. and foreign investors to buy stocks and bonds issued by U.S. firms. The volume of trading in U.S. financial markets also ensures that investors will be able to quickly sell the stocks and bonds they buy. This *liquidity* serves to attract investors to U.S. markets.

Smaller firms that are unable to issue stocks and bonds often obtain funding from banks. Entrepreneurs founding new firms—"startups"—particularly firms that are based on new technologies, generally find that investors are unwilling to buy their stocks and bonds because the firms lack records of profitability. Banks are also reluctant to lend to new firms founded to introduce new and unfamiliar technologies. In the United States, some technology startups obtain funds from *venture capital firms*, which raise funds from institutional investors, such as pension funds, and from wealthy individuals. The owners of venture capital firms closely examine the business plans of startup firms, looking for those that appear most likely to succeed. In exchange for providing funding, a venture capital firm often becomes part owner of the startup and may even play a role in managing the firm. A successful venture capital firm is able to attract investors who would not otherwise be willing to provide funds to startups because the investors lack enough information about the startup. A number of well-known U.S. high-technology firms, such as Google, relied on venture capital firms to fund their early expansion. The ability of venture capital firms to finance technology-driven startup firms may be giving the United States an advantage in bringing new products and new processes to market.

The U.S. financial system suffered severe problems between 2007 and 2009. But, over the long run, it has succeeded in efficiently allocating investment funds.

MyLab Economics Concept Check

Why Don't More Low-Income Countries Experience Rapid Growth?

The economic growth model predicts that the countries that were very poor in 1960 should have grown rapidly over the next 50 years. As we have just seen, some did, but many did not. Why are many low-income countries growing so slowly? There is no single answer, but most economists point to four key factors:

1. Failure to enforce the rule of law
2. Wars and revolutions
3. Poor public education and health
4. Low rates of saving and investment

Failure to Enforce the Rule of Law In the years since 1960, increasing numbers of developing countries, including China, have abandoned centrally planned economies in favor of more market-oriented economies. For entrepreneurs in a market economy to succeed, however, the government must guarantee private **property rights** and enforce contracts. Unless entrepreneurs feel secure in their property, they will not risk starting a business. Business owners also have difficulty being successful unless they can use an independent court system to enforce contracts. The **rule of law** refers to the ability of a government to enforce the laws of the country, particularly with respect to protecting private property and enforcing contracts. The failure of many developing countries to guarantee property rights and to enforce contracts has hindered their economic growth.

Consider, for example, the production of shoes. Suppose the owner of a shoe factory signs a contract with a leather tannery to deliver a specific quantity of leather on a particular date for a particular price. On the basis of this contract, the owner of the shoe factory signs a contract to deliver a specific quantity of shoes to a shoe wholesaler. This contract states the quantity of shoes to be delivered, the quality of the shoes, the delivery date, and the price. The owner of the leather tannery uses the contract with the shoe factory to enter into a contract with cattle ranchers for the delivery of hides. The shoe wholesaler enters into contracts to deliver shoes to retail stores, where they are sold to consumers. For the flow of goods from cattle ranchers to shoe customers to operate efficiently, each business must carry out the terms of the contract it has signed. In developed countries, such as the United States, businesses know that if they fail to carry out a contract, they may be sued in court and forced to compensate the other party for any economic damages.

Many developing countries do not have functioning, independent court systems. Even if a court system does exist, a case may not be heard for many years. In some countries, bribery of judges and political favoritism in court rulings are common. If firms cannot enforce contracts through the court system, they may insist on carrying out only face-to-face cash transactions. For example, the shoe manufacturer will wait until the leather producer brings the hides to the factory and will then buy the hides for cash. The wholesaler will wait until the shoes have been produced before making plans for sales to retail stores. Production still takes place, but it is carried out more slowly and inefficiently. With slow and inefficient production, firms have difficulty finding investors willing to provide them with the funds they need to expand.

Property rights The rights individuals or firms have to the exclusive use of their property, including the right to buy or sell it.

Rule of law The ability of a government to enforce the laws of the country, particularly with respect to protecting private property and enforcing contracts.

● Apply the Concept

MyLab Economics Video

Why Hasn't Mexico Grown as Fast as China?

Many people consider China *the* great economic growth success story. The decision by Chinese government leaders in the 1970s to turn away from a centrally planned economy and toward a market system unleashed economic growth that has lifted more than a *billion* people in China out of poverty. As we will discuss in Section 11.5, the Chinese economy still faces significant obstacles to maintaining high growth rates, and the Chinese Communist Party has maintained its dictatorship over the country. Despite these problems, many economists and policymakers see China as an example of the rapid growth that low-income countries can attain.

Some U.S. firms have chosen in recent years to locate factories and other facilities in Mexico rather than in China because Mexico is closer to the United States and because labor costs have been increasing more rapidly in China. This trend has been good news for the Mexican economy because it has increased factory employment and given the country easier access to U.S. technology. Overall, though, the growth rates of the Mexican economy have been disappointing. The graph below compares the growth rates of real GDP per capita for the Mexican and Chinese economies over the past 35 years.

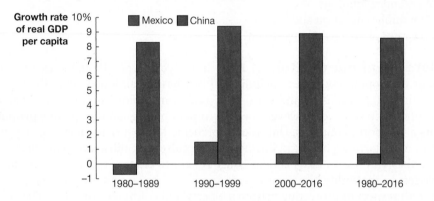

Taking the whole period between 1980 and 2016, the average annual growth rate for the Chinese economy has been 8.6 percent, while the growth rate for the Mexican economy has been a very slow 0.7 percent. In Chapter 10, Section 10.1, we saw that if we divide a growth rate into 70, the result is approximately the number of years it will take real GDP per capita to double. When we apply that rule here, we find that it will take real GDP per capita 100 years to double in Mexico but only 8 years in China.

What explains the slow growth of the Mexican economy? For most of the period from the Mexican Revolution of 1910 until 2000, the Institutional Revolutionary Party (PRI) dominated the Mexican government. For decades, the party followed a policy of limiting imports and foreign investment, concentrating on building up domestic industry behind high tariff walls. The Mexican government took over, or nationalized, some businesses, including the oil industry. By the 1980s, dissatisfaction with the country's poor economic performance led the PRI, under President Miguel de la Madrid, to institute a series of reforms. The reforms, which were broadened in the 1990s, included allowing banks again to be private businesses; signing the North American Free Trade Agreement (NAFTA) with the United States and Canada, which greatly reduced tariffs on imports; and allowing foreign investment in most sectors of the economy apart from the oil industry. As the graph above shows, though, these reforms have not resulted in high rates of economic growth.

Some economic historians believe that the Spanish colonial background of the nineteenth century and earlier hobbled the Mexican economy. Unlike in the United States, in Mexico and other Spanish and Portuguese colonies, land was often concentrated in very large estates, which led to highly unequal distributions of income and may have made it difficult for a broad-based middle class capable of supporting a large manufacturing base to develop. Other countries in Latin America, though, including Chile and Uruguay, with similar colonial backgrounds have experienced much more rapid growth.

Some economists believe that the financial sector has been an important obstacle to growth. The Mexican legal system makes it difficult for banks to seize a business's assets when the business defaults on a loan. As a result, Mexican banks are reluctant to make loans to businesses. As we noted in the chapter opener, Mexico also suffers from government corruption that either makes businesses reluctant to expand or forces them to operate in the underground economy. In either case, the businesses are unable to take advantage of economies of scale and may be unwilling to make large investments in machinery or buildings. In certain areas of Mexico, criminal gangs have also disrupted business. The educational system in Mexico has failed to provide many students with the skills needed to find work at firms competing in the global marketplace. Finally, infrastructure, including poor roads and inconsistent and expensive provision of electricity—with occasional blackouts—have also hindered business expansion.

Timothy J. Kehoe of the University of Minnesota and Kim J. Ruhl of New York University have noted that China also suffers from institutional problems, but it has grown much faster than Mexico. China, though, began its rapid growth from very low levels of income, so that in 2016, real GDP per capita in Mexico was still 40 percent higher than in China. Kehoe and Ruhl have argued that, as a middle-income country, Mexico has already taken advantage of many of the relatively easy ways of increasing real GDP—including moving resources out of the low-productivity agricultural sector, accumulating capital in manufacturing, and adopting modern technology. We saw in the discussion of Figure 11.9 that, probably for institutional reasons, many high-income countries have made no progress in closing the gap in real GDP per capita between themselves and the United States during the past 25 years. Mexico may now be in a similar situation of having difficulty growing fast enough to close the gap with higher-income countries. Because Mexico's institutional barriers to growth are more severe than those in European countries, the gap in real GDP per capita between the United States and Mexico may persist at a high level.

In 2017, the Mexican economy was faced with a further challenge as the Trump administration proposed renegotiating the NAFTA treaty. Mexico exports more goods to the United States than to any other country and since NAFTA went into effect in 1994, Mexico has received substantial foreign investment from U.S. firms. As we saw in the chapter opener, manufacturing firms like Rexnord have built factories in Mexico to take advantage of lower labor costs. A substantial industry manufacturing automobiles and automobile parts now employs hundreds of thousands of workers in Mexico. That industry would have difficulty surviving if the NAFTA agreement were to end and Mexican firms faced substantial tariffs when exporting to the United States. In late 2017, it appeared likely that negotiations would lead to fairly modest changes to the NAFTA treaty, although policymakers in Mexico remained concerned that any changes might slow their economy's growth.

Economists and policymakers in Mexico continue to look for ways to increase growth rates. Without an increase in growth, it may be decades before millions of low-income people in Mexico are able to escape poverty.

Sources: James McBride and Mohammed Aly Sergie, "NAFTA's Economic Impact," Council on Foreign Relations, January 24, 2017; Andrew Tangle, "Companies Plow Ahead with Moves to Mexico, Despite Trump's Pressure," *Wall Street Journal*, February 8, 2017; "The 100-Year View," *Economist*, May 2, 2015; Gordon H. Hanson, "Why Isn't Mexico Rich?" *Journal of Economic Literature*, Vol. 48, No. 4, December 2010, pp. 987–1004; Timothy J. Kehoe and Kim J. Ruhl, "Why Have Economic Reforms in Mexico Not Generated Growth?" *Journal of Economic Literature*, Vol. 48, No. 4, December 2010, pp. 1004–1027; Nora Lustig, "Life Is Not Easy: Mexico's Quest for Stability and Growth," *Journal of Economic Perspectives*, Vol. 15, No. 1, Winter 2001, pp. 85–106; and Federal Reserve Bank of St. Louis.

Your Turn: Test your understanding by doing related problems 4.8 and 4.9 on page 389 at the end of this chapter.

MyLab Economics Study Plan

Wars and Revolutions Many of the countries that were very poor in 1960 have experienced extended periods of war or violent changes of government during the following years. These wars have made it very difficult for countries such as Afghanistan, Angola, Ethiopia, the Central African Republic, and the Democratic Republic of the Congo to accumulate capital or adopt new technologies. In fact, conducting any kind of business has been very difficult. Ending war has a positive effect on growth. For example, due to revolutions, civil war, and war with the neighboring country of

Eritrea, in 2003, real GDP per capita was lower in Ethiopia than it had been in 1965. The return of relative political stability enabled Ethiopia to experience a very strong 10 percent annual growth rate in real GDP per capita from 2003 to 2016.

Poor Public Education and Health We have seen that human capital is one of the determinants of labor productivity. Many low-income countries have weak public school systems, so many workers are unable to read and write. Few workers acquire the skills necessary to use the latest technology.

People in many low-income countries suffer from diseases that are either nonexistent or easily treated in high-income countries. For example, few people in developed countries suffer from malaria, but about 400,000 Africans die from it each year. Treatments for AIDS have greatly reduced deaths from this disease in the United States and Europe. But in low-income countries, more than a million people per year continue to die from AIDS. These countries often lack the resources, and their governments are often too ineffective, to provide even routine medical care, such as childhood vaccinations.

People who are sick work less and are less productive when they do work. Poor nutrition or exposure to certain diseases in childhood can leave people permanently weakened and can affect their intelligence as adults. Poor health has a significant negative effect on the human capital of workers in developing countries.

Low Rates of Saving and Investment To invest in factories, machinery, and computers, firms need funds. Some of the funds can come from the owners of the firm and from their friends and families, but firms in high-income countries raise most of their funds from bank loans and the sale of stocks and bonds in financial markets. In most developing countries, stock and bond markets do not exist, and often the banking system is very weak. In high-income countries, the funds that banks lend to businesses come from the savings of households. In developing countries, many households barely survive on their incomes and, therefore, have little or no savings.

The low saving rates in developing countries can contribute to a *vicious cycle of poverty*. Because households have low incomes, they save very little. Because households save very little, few funds are available for firms to borrow. Lacking funds, firms do not invest in the new factories, machinery, and equipment needed for economic growth. Because the economy does not grow, household incomes remain low, as do their savings, and so on. **MyLab Economics** Concept Check

The Benefits of Globalization

One way for a developing country to break out of the vicious cycle of low saving and investment and low growth is through foreign investment. **Foreign direct investment (FDI)** occurs when a firm builds or purchases a facility in a foreign country. **Foreign portfolio investment** occurs when an individual or a firm buys stocks or bonds issued in another country. Foreign direct investment and foreign portfolio investment can give a low-income country access to technology and funds that otherwise would not be available.

From the 1940s through the 1970s, many developing countries closed themselves off from the global economy. During the 1930s and early 1940s, the global trading and financial system collapsed as a result of the Great Depression and World War II. Developing countries that relied on exporting to high-income countries were hurt economically. Also, many countries in Africa and Asia achieved independence from the colonial powers of Europe during the 1950s and 1960s and were afraid of being dominated by them economically. As a result, many developing countries imposed high tariffs on foreign imports and strongly discouraged or even prohibited foreign investment. These policies made it difficult to break out of the vicious cycle of poverty.

The policies of erecting high tariff barriers and avoiding foreign investment failed to produce much growth, so by the 1980s, many developing countries began to change policies. The result was **globalization**, which refers to the process of countries becoming more open to foreign trade and investment. Developing countries that are more globalized have grown faster than developing countries that are less globalized. Globalization has benefited developing countries by making it easier for them to obtain technology and investment funds. **MyLab Economics** Concept Check

---

Foreign direct investment (FDI) The purchase or building by a firm of a facility in a foreign country.

Foreign portfolio investment The purchase by an individual or a firm of stocks or bonds issued in another country.

Globalization The process of countries becoming more open to foreign trade and investment.

Growth Policies

11.5

LEARNING OBJECTIVE: Discuss government policies that foster economic growth.

What can governments do to promote long-run economic growth? We have seen that even small differences in growth rates compounded over the years can lead to major differences in standards of living. Therefore, there is potentially a very high payoff to government policies that increase growth rates. We have already discussed some of these policies in this chapter. In this section, we explore additional policies.

Enhancing Property Rights and the Rule of Law

A market system cannot work well unless property rights are enforced. Entrepreneurs are unlikely to risk their own funds and investors are unlikely to lend their funds to entrepreneurs if property is not protected from being arbitrarily seized. We have seen that in many developing countries, the rule of law and property rights are undermined by government *corruption*. In some developing countries, it is impossible for an entrepreneur to obtain a permit to start a business without paying bribes, often to several different government officials. Is it possible for a country to reform a corrupt government bureaucracy?

Although today the United States ranks among the least corrupt countries, research by economists Edward Glaeser and Claudia Goldin of Harvard University has shown that in the late 1800s and early 1900s, corruption was a significant problem in the United States. The fact that political reform movements and crusading newspapers helped reduce corruption in the United States to relatively low levels by the 1920s provides some hope for reform movements that aim to reduce corruption in developing countries today.

Property rights are unlikely to be secure in countries that are afflicted by wars and civil strife. For a number of countries, increased political stability is a prerequisite to economic growth. **MyLab Economics** Concept Check

Apply the Concept

MyLab Economics Video

Will China's Standard of Living Ever Exceed That of the United States?

In 2016, GDP per capita in the United States was nearly four times higher than GDP per capita in China. However, the growth rate of real GDP per capita in the United States has averaged only 1.6 percent per year since 1980, compared to China's average growth rate of 8.6 percent per year over the same time period. If these growth rates were to continue, China's standard of living, as measured by real GDP per capita, would exceed the U.S. standard of living in the year 2036.

For China to maintain its high rates of growth in real GDP per capita, however, it would have to maintain high rates of productivity growth, which is unlikely for several reasons. First, the United States invests more in activities, such as research and development, that result in new technologies and increases in productivity. Although China has been successful in adopting existing technologies developed in the United States and other countries, it has been much less successful in developing new technologies. Second, a good part of China's growth is due to the transition from a centrally planned economy to a market economy, so China's growth rate is likely to decrease as the transition is completed. Third, China's economic growth has depended on moving workers from agriculture, where their productivity was low, to manufacturing jobs in cities, where their productivity is much higher. The large supply of low-wage agricultural workers helped keep manufacturing wages low and provided China with a cost advantage in manufacturing goods compared with the United States and other high-income countries. China has exhausted much of its supply of low-wage agricultural workers, so manufacturing wages have begun to rise, eroding China's cost advantage. Some U.S. firms have reacted to rising labor costs in China by moving factories to Mexico—or back to the United States.

Eugene Hoshiko/AP Images

Some economists argue that China may have overinvested in physical capital, such as bullet trains.

Another looming problem is demographic. Because of China's low birth rate, the country will soon experience a decline in its labor force. Over the next two decades, the population of men and women between the ages of 15 and 29 will fall by roughly 100 million, or about 30 percent. China will also experience a large increase in older workers, a group that will on average be less productive and less healthy than younger workers. Given current trends, the U.S. Census Bureau projects fewer people under age 50 in China in 2030 than today, including fewer people in their 20s and early 30s, and many more people in their 60s and older. China still has potential sources for enhancing productivity, including the wider application of technology and the movement of workers into high-productivity industries, such as the manufacture of automobiles and household appliances, provided that domestic demand increases rapidly. These factors can fuel future growth, but at some point, China's demographic problems could slow growth.

Perhaps most troubling for China is the fact that the country remains autocratic, with the Communist Party refusing to allow meaningful elections and continuing to limit freedom of expression. The government has yet to establish secure property rights and the rule of law. Some observers believe that the lack of political freedom in China may ultimately lead to civil unrest, which could slow growth rates. Whether or not civil unrest eventually develops, the lack of democracy in China may already be resulting in problems that could slow growth in the near future. Large, state-owned firms, controlled by Communist Party members, continue to receive government subsidies. The result is that these firms, which typically have low productivity and are not globally competitive, receive funds that otherwise would have allowed high-productivity firms to expand.

Nouriel Roubini, an economist at New York University, argues that China's Communist Party may be repeating some of the mistakes the Soviet Communist Party committed decades ago. He argues that by employing policies that have resulted in investment spending being 50 percent of GDP, the government may have boosted short-term growth at the expense of the health of the economy in the long term. He notes:

> China is rife with overinvestment in physical capital, infrastructure, and property. To a visitor, this is evident in sleek but empty airports and bullet trains … highways to nowhere, thousands of colossal new central and provincial government buildings, ghost towns, and brand-new aluminum smelters kept closed to prevent global prices from plunging.

Growth in China is already showing signs of slowing. Between 2014 and 2016, real GDP per capita grew at an annual rate of 6.2 percent. While still rapid, this growth rate is well below what the Chinese economy had achieved in previous decades. Even sustaining that growth rate may prove difficult. In early 2017, an article in the *Wall Street Journal* commented that "much of the firepower" driving economic growth was the result of spending by state-owned firms and government spending on infrastructure projects, such as highways, railways, and airports. These are types of spending that could be difficult for the country to sustain in the long run. Private firms continued to have difficulty getting from state-owned banks the loans they need to expand production.

China has been engaged in an economic experiment: Can a country maintain high rates of economic growth in the long run while denying its citizens basic political rights?

Sources: Mark Magnier, "Behind China's Pickup in Growth: The Strong Hand of the State," *Wall Street Journal*, April 17, 2017; Pranab Bardhan, "The Slowing of Two Economic Giants," *New York Times*, July 14, 2013; Alex Frangos and Eric Bellman, "China Slump Ripples Globally," *Wall Street Journal*, July 15, 2013; Nicholas Eberstadt, "The Demographic Future," *Foreign Affairs*, Vol. 89, No. 6, November/December 2010, pp. 54–64; and Nouriel Roubini, "Beijing's Empty Bullet Trains," *Slate*, April 14, 2011.

MyLab Economics Study Plan   **Your Turn:** Test your understanding by doing related problems 5.4 and 5.5 on page 390 at the end of this chapter.

Improving Health and Education

Recently, many economists have become convinced that poor health is a major impediment to growth in some countries. The research of the late Nobel Laureate Robert Fogel emphasized the important interaction between health and economic growth (see Chapter 10). As people's health improves and they become stronger and less susceptible to diseases, they also become more productive. Recent initiatives in developing countries to increase vaccinations against infectious diseases, to improve access to treated water, and to improve sanitation have begun to reduce rates of illness and death.

In Section 11.2, we discussed Paul Romer's argument that there are increasing returns to knowledge capital. Nobel Laureate Robert Lucas of the University of Chicago has similarly argued that there are increasing returns to *human* capital. Lucas has argued that productivity increases as the total stock of human capital increases but that these productivity increases are not completely captured by individuals as they decide how much education to purchase. Therefore, the market may produce an inefficiently low level of education and training unless the government subsidizes education. Some researchers have been unable to find evidence of increasing returns to human capital, but many economists believe that government subsidies for education have played an important role in promoting economic growth.

The rising incomes that result from economic growth can help developing countries deal with the *brain drain*, which refers to highly educated and successful individuals leaving developing countries for high-income countries. This migration occurs when successful individuals believe that economic opportunities are very limited in the domestic economy. Rapid economic growth in India and China in recent years has resulted in more entrepreneurs, engineers, and scientists deciding to remain in those countries rather than leave for the United States or other high-income countries. **MyLab Economics** Concept Check

Policies That Promote Technological Change

One of the lessons of the economic growth model is that technological change is more important than increases in capital in explaining long-run growth. Government policies that facilitate access to technology are crucial for low-income countries. The easiest way for developing countries to gain access to technology is through foreign direct investment, where foreign firms are allowed to build new facilities or to buy domestic firms. Recent economic growth in India has been greatly aided by the Indian government's relaxation of regulations on foreign investment. Relaxing these regulations made it possible for India to gain access to the technology of multinational corporations, such as Dell and Microsoft.

In high-income countries, government policies can aid the growth of technology by subsidizing research and development. As we noted previously, in the United States, the federal government conducts some research and development on its own and also provides grants to researchers in universities. Tax breaks to firms undertaking research and development also facilitate technological change. **MyLab Economics** Concept Check

Policies That Promote Saving and Investment

Firms turn to the loanable funds market to finance expansion and research and development (see Chapter 10). Policies that increase the incentives to save and invest will increase the equilibrium level of loanable funds and may increase the level of real GDP per capita. For instance, governments can use tax incentives to increase saving. In the United States, many workers are able to save for retirement by placing funds in 401(k) or 403(b) plans or in Individual Retirement Accounts (IRAs). Income placed in these accounts is not taxed until it is withdrawn during retirement. Because the funds are allowed to accumulate tax-free, the return is increased, which raises the incentive to save.

Governments also increase incentives for firms to engage in investment in physical capital by using *investment tax credits*, which allow firms to deduct from their taxes some fraction of the funds they have spent on investment. Reductions in the taxes firms pay on their profits also increase the after-tax return on investments. **MyLab Economics** Concept Check

Is Economic Growth Good or Bad?

Although we didn't state so explicitly, in this chapter we have assumed that economic growth is desirable and that governments should undertake policies that will increase growth rates. It seems undeniable that increasing the growth rates of very low-income countries would help relieve the daily suffering that many people in those countries endure. But some people are unconvinced that, at least in the high-income countries, further economic growth is desirable.

The arguments against further economic growth reflect concern about the effects of growth on the environment or concern about the effects of the globalization process that has accompanied economic growth. In 1972, the Club of Rome published a controversial book titled *The Limits to Growth*, which predicted that economic growth would likely grind to a halt in the United States and other high-income countries because of increasing pollution and the depletion of natural resources, such as oil. Although these dire predictions have not yet come to pass, many people remain concerned that economic growth may be contributing to global warming, the destruction of rain forests, and other environmental problems.

In Chapter 5, we discussed the opposition to globalization. We noted that some people believe that globalization has undermined the distinctive cultures of many countries, as imports of food, clothing, movies, and other goods have displaced domestically produced goods. We have seen that allowing foreign direct investment is an important way in which low-income countries can gain access to the latest technology. Some people, however, believe multinational firms behave unethically in low-income countries because they claim the firms pay very low wages and fail to follow the same safety and environmental regulations the firms are required to follow in high-income countries.

As with many other normative questions, economic analysis can contribute to the ongoing political debate over the consequences of economic growth, but it cannot settle the issue. **MyLab Economics** Concept Check

MyLab Economics Study Plan

Continued from page 353

Economics in Your Life & Career

Would You Be Better Off without China?

At the beginning of the chapter, we asked you to imagine that you could choose to live and work in a world with the Chinese economy growing very rapidly or in a world with the Chinese economy as it was before 1978—very poor and growing slowly. In which world would you choose to live? How does the current high-growth, high-export Chinese economy affect you as a consumer? How does it affect you as someone about to start a career?

It's impossible to walk into most stores in the United States without seeing products imported from China. Many of these products were at one time made in the United States. Imports from China replace domestically produced goods when the imports are either priced lower or have higher quality than the domestic goods they

replace. Therefore, the rapid economic growth that has enabled Chinese firms to be competitive with firms in the United States has benefited you as a consumer: You have lower-priced goods and better goods available for purchase than you would if China had remained very poor.

As you begin your career, there are some U.S. industries that because of competition from Chinese firms will have fewer jobs to offer. As we saw when discussing international trade, expanding trade changes the types of products each country makes, and, therefore, the types of jobs available, but it does not affect the total number of jobs (see Chapter 7, Section 7.5). So, the economic rise of China will affect the mix of jobs available to you in the United States but will not make finding a job any more difficult.

Conclusion

For much of human history, most people have had to struggle to survive. Even today, a large fraction of the world's population lives in extreme poverty. The differences in living standards among countries today are a result of many decades of sharply different rates of economic growth. According to the economic growth model, increases in the quantity of capital per hour worked and increases in technology determine the growth in real GDP per hour worked and a country's standard of living. The keys to higher living standards seem straightforward:

1. Establish the rule of law.
2. Provide basic education and health care for the population.
3. Increase the amount of capital per hour worked.
4. Adopt the best technology.
5. Participate in the global economy.

However, for many countries, these policies have proved very difficult to implement.

Having discussed what determines the growth rate of economies, we will turn in the following chapters to the question of why economies experience short-run fluctuations in output, employment, and inflation.

Visit MyLab Economics for a news article and analysis related to the concepts in this chapter.

Key Terms

Catch-up, p. 369

Economic growth model, p. 359

Foreign direct investment (FDI), p. 378

Foreign portfolio investment, p. 378

Globalization, p. 378

Human capital, p. 360

Industrial Revolution, p. 355

Labor productivity, p. 359

New growth theory, p. 364

Patent, p. 365

Per-worker production function, p. 360

Property rights, p. 375

Rule of law, p. 375

Technological change, p. 359

11.1 Economic Growth over Time and around the World, pages 354–359

LEARNING OBJECTIVE: Define economic growth, calculate economic growth rates, and describe global trends in economic growth.

MyLab Economics Visit www.pearson.com/mylab/economics to complete these exercises online and get instant feedback.

Summary

For most of history, the average person survived with barely enough food. Living standards began to rise significantly only after the start of the **Industrial Revolution** in England in the 1700s, with the application of mechanical power to the production of goods. The best measure of a country's standard of living is its level of real GDP per capita. Economic growth occurs when real GDP per capita increases, thereby increasing the country's standard of living.

Review Questions

1.1 Why does a country's economic growth rate matter?

1.2 Explain the difference between the total percentage increase in real GDP between 2007 and 2017 and the average annual growth rate in real GDP between the same years.

Problems and Applications

1.3 **(Related to the Apply the Concept on page 355)** Economists Carol Shiue and Wolfgang Keller of the University of Colorado published a study of "market efficiency" in the eighteenth century in England, other European countries, and China. If the markets in a country are efficient, a product should have the same price wherever in the country it is sold, allowing for the effect of transportation costs. If prices are not the same in two areas within a country, it is possible to make a profit by buying the product where its price is low and reselling it where its price is high. This trading will drive prices to equality. Trade is most likely to occur, however, if entrepreneurs feel confident that the government will not seize their gains and the courts will enforce contracts. Therefore, in the eighteenth century, the more efficient a country's markets, the more its institutions favored long-run growth. Shiue and Keller found that in 1770, the efficiency of markets in England

was significantly greater than the efficiency of markets elsewhere in Europe and in China. How does this finding relate to Douglass North's argument concerning why the Industrial Revolution occurred in England?

Source: Carol H. Shiue and Wolfgang Keller, "Markets in China and Europe on the Eve of the Industrial Revolution," *American Economic Review*, Vol. 97, No. 4, September 2007, pp. 1189–1216.

1.4 Use the data on real GDP in the following table to answer the questions. The values are measured in billions of each country's domestic currency. The base year for Mexico is 2008, the base year for Panama is 2007, and the base year for Thailand is 2002.

Country	2013	2014	2015	2016
Mexico	13,468	13,773	14,136	14,461
Panama	32	34	36	38
Thailand	9,146	9,230	9,501	9,808

a. Which country experienced the highest rate of economic growth during 2014 (that is, which country experienced the highest rate of growth of real GDP from 2013 to 2014)?

b. Which country experienced the highest average annual growth rate between 2014 and 2016?

c. Does it matter for your answers to parts (a) and (b) that each country's real GDP is measured in a different currency and uses a different base year? Briefly explain.

Source: International Monetary Fund, *World Economic Outlook Database*, April 2017.

1.5 Andover Bank and Lowell Bank each sell one-year certificates of deposit (CDs). The interest rates on these CDs are given in the following table for a three-year period.

Bank	2018	2019	2020
Andover Bank	5%	5%	5%
Lowell Bank	2	6	7

Suppose you deposit $1,000 in a CD in each bank at the beginning of 2018. At the end of 2018, you take your

$1,000 and any interest earned and invest it in a CD for the following year. You do this again at the end of 2019. At the end of 2020, will you have earned more on your Andover Bank CDs or on your Lowell Bank CDs? Briefly explain.

1.6 **(Related to the Don't Let This Happen to You on page 357)** Use the data for the United States in this table to answer the following questions.

Year	Real GDP per Capita (2009 dollars)
2012	$48,841
2013	49,317
2014	50,119
2015	51,054
2016	51,523

a. What was the percentage change in real GDP per capita between 2012 and 2016?

b. What was the average annual growth rate in real GDP per capita between 2012 and 2016? (*Hint:* Remember that the average annual growth rate for relatively short periods can be approximated by averaging the growth rates for each year during the period [see Chapter 10, Section 10.1].)

Source: U.S. Bureau of Economic Analysis.

1.7 **(Related to the Apply the Concept on page 358)** In his book *The White Man's Burden*, William Easterly reported:

A vaccination campaign in southern Africa virtually eliminated measles as a killer of children. Routine childhood immunization combined with measles vaccination in seven southern African nations starting in 1996 virtually eliminated measles in those countries by 2000. A national campaign in Egypt to make parents aware of the use of oral rehydration therapy

from 1982 to 1989 cut childhood deaths from diarrhea by 82 percent over that period.

a. Is it likely that real GDP per capita increased significantly in southern Africa and Egypt as a result of the near elimination of measles and the large decrease in childhood deaths from diarrhea? If these events did not increase real GDP per capita, is it still possible that they increased the standard of living in southern Africa and Egypt? Briefly explain.

b. Which seems more achievable for a developing country: the elimination of measles and childhood deaths from diarrhea or sustained increases in real GDP per capita? Briefly explain.

Source: William Easterly, *The White Man's Burden: Why the West's Efforts to Aid the Rest Have Done So Much Ill and So Little Good*, New York: The Penguin Press, 2006, p. 241.

1.8 **(Related to the Apply the Concept on page 358)** Economist Charles Kenny of the Center for Global Development has argued:

The process technologies—institutions like laws and inventory management systems—that appear central to raising incomes per capita flow less like water and more like bricks. But ideas and inventions—the importance of [education] and vaccines for DPT—really might flow more easily across borders and over distances.

If Kenny is correct, what are the implications of these facts for the ability of low-income countries to rapidly increase their rates of growth of real GDP per capita in the decades ahead? What are the implications for the ability of these countries to increase their standards of living? Briefly explain.

Source: Charles Kenny, *Getting Better*, New York: Basic Books, 2011, p. 117.

11.2 What Determines How Fast Economies Grow? pages 359–366

LEARNING OBJECTIVE: Use the economic growth model to explain why growth rates differ across countries.

MyLab Economics Visit www.pearson.com/mylab/economics to complete these exercises online and get instant feedback.

Summary

An **economic growth model** explains changes in real GDP per capita in the long run. Labor productivity is the quantity of goods and services that can be produced by one worker or by one hour of work. Economic growth depends on increases in labor productivity. Labor productivity will increase if there is an increase in the amount of *capital* available to each worker or if there is an improvement in *technology*. **Technological change** is a change in the ability of a firm to produce a given level of output with a given quantity of inputs. There are three main sources of technological change: better machinery and equipment, increases in human capital, and better means of organizing and managing production. **Human capital** is the accumulated knowledge and skills that workers acquire from education and training or from their life

experiences. We can say that an economy will have a higher standard of living the more capital it has per hour worked, the more human capital its workers have, the better its capital, and the better the job its business managers do in organizing production.

The **per-worker production function** shows the relationship between capital per hour worked and output per hour worked, holding technology constant. *Diminishing returns to capital* means that increases in the quantity of capital per hour worked will result in diminishing increases in output per hour worked. Technological change shifts up the per-worker production function, resulting in more output per hour worked at every level of capital per hour worked. The economic growth model stresses the importance of changes in capital per hour worked and technological change in explaining growth in output per hour worked. **New growth theory** is a model of long-run economic growth that emphasizes that technological change is influenced by how individuals and firms respond to economic incentives.

One way governments can promote technological change is by granting **patents**, which are exclusive rights to a product for a period of 20 years from the date the patent is filed with the government. To Joseph Schumpeter, the entrepreneur is central to the "creative destruction" by which the standard of living increases as qualitatively better products replace existing products.

Review Questions

2.1 Using the per-worker production function graph from Figures 11.3 and 11.4 on pages 361 and 362, show the effect on real GDP per hour worked of an increase in capital per hour worked, holding technology constant. Now, again using the per-worker production function graph, show the effect on real GDP per hour worked of an increase in technology, holding constant the quantity of capital per hour worked.

2.2 What are the consequences for growth of diminishing returns to capital? How are some economies able to maintain high growth rates despite diminishing returns to capital?

2.3 What is the new growth theory? How does the new growth theory differ from the growth theory developed by Robert Solow?

2.4 Why are firms likely to underinvest in research and development? Briefly discuss three ways in which government policy can increase the accumulation of knowledge capital.

Problems and Applications

2.5 Which of the following will result in a movement along China's per-worker production function, and which will result in a shift of China's per-worker production function? Briefly explain.

   a. Capital per hour worked increases from 200 yuan per hour worked to 250 yuan per hour worked.
   b. The Chinese government doubles its spending on support for university research.
   c. A reform of the Chinese school system results in more highly trained Chinese workers.

2.6 **(Related to the Apply the Concept on page 362)** The *Apply the Concept* "What Explains the Economic Failure of the Soviet Union?" emphasizes that a key difference between market economies and centrally planned economies, like that of the former Soviet Union, is as follows:

> In market economies, entrepreneurs and managers who have their own money on the line make decisions about which investments to make and which technologies to adopt. Nothing concentrates the mind like having your own funds at risk.

But in large corporations, investment decisions are often made by salaried managers who do not have their own money on the line. These managers are spending the money of the firm's shareholders rather than their own money. Why, then, do the investment decisions of salaried managers in the United States tend to be better for the long-term growth of the economy than were the decisions of salaried bureaucrats in the Soviet Union?

2.7 **(Related to the Apply the Concept on page 362)** In the 1961 edition of his best-selling introductory economics textbook, the late Nobel Laureate Paul Samuelson noted that Soviet GDP might become larger than U.S. GDP by 1985.

   a. In 1961, why might a leading economist have expected that the Soviet economy might eventually become larger than the U.S. economy?
   b. Briefly explain why the Soviet economy failed to overtake the U.S. economy.

   Source: Paul A. Samuelson, *Economics*, 5th edition, New York: McGraw-Hill, 1961, Chapter 37, Figure 1, p. 830.

2.8 **(Related to Solved Problem 11.2 on page 363)** Use the following graph to answer the questions. In each case, briefly explain your answer.

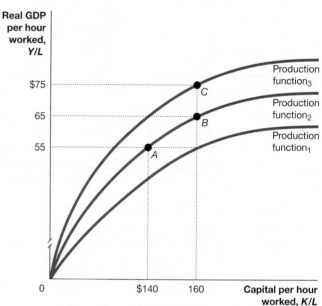

   a. True or false: The movement from point A to point B shows the effects of technological change.
   b. True or false: The economy can move from point B to point C only if there are no diminishing returns to capital.
   c. True or false: To move from point A to point C, the economy must increase the amount of capital per hour worked *and* experience technological change.

2.9 **(Related to Solved Problem 11.2 on page 363)** If the per-worker production function were shaped as shown in the following graph, what would be the implications for economic growth of a country that was accumulating increasing quantities of capital per hour worked? Briefly explain.

2.10 **(Related to Solved Problem 11.2 on page 363)** Shortly before the fall of the Soviet Union, the economist Gur Ofer of Hebrew University of Jerusalem wrote, "The most outstanding characteristic of Soviet growth strategy is its consistent policy of very high rates of investment, leading to a rapid growth rate of [the] capital stock." Explain why this strategy turned out to be a very poor way to sustain economic growth in the long run.

Source: Gur Ofer, "Soviet Economic Growth, 1928–1985," *Journal of Economic Literature*, Vol. 25, No. 4, December 1987, p. 1784.

2.11 People who live in rural areas often have less access to capital and, as a result, their productivity is lower on average than the productivity of people who live in cities. An article in the *New York Times* quoted a financial analyst as arguing that "the core driver" of economic growth in China "is the simple process of urbanization."
a. What does the analyst mean by the "process of urbanization"?
b. If the analyst is correct that urbanization is the core driver of economic growth in China, would we expect that China will be able to continue to experience high rates of economic growth in the long run? Briefly explain.

Source: Neil Irwin, "China Will Keep Growing. Just Ask the Soviets," *New York Times*, October 24, 2014.

2.12 Why is the role of entrepreneurs much more important in the new growth theory than in the traditional economic growth model?

11.3 Economic Growth in the United States, pages 366–369

LEARNING OBJECTIVE: Discuss fluctuations in productivity growth in the United States.

MyLab Economics Visit www.pearson.com/mylab/economics to complete these exercises online and get instant feedback.

Summary

Productivity in the United States grew rapidly from the end of World War II until the mid-1970s. Growth then slowed down for 20 years before increasing again for a decade after 1995. Growth has slowed again during the most recent period. Economists debate whether this growth slowdown will be long-lived or whether the U.S. economy will return to the faster growth rates of earlier years.

Review Questions

3.1 Describe the record of productivity growth in the United States from 1800 to the present.

3.2 Briefly describe the debate among economists over how high U.S. productivity growth rates are likely to be in the future.

Problems and Applications

3.3 Figure 11.5 on page 367 shows growth rates in real GDP per hour worked in the United States for various periods from 1800 onward. How might the growth rates in the figure be different if they were calculated for real GDP *per capita* instead of per hour worked? (*Hint:* How do you think the number of hours worked per person has changed in the United States since 1800?)

3.4 A column in the *Wall Street Journal* considered two observations about the U.S. economy: "We live in an era of accelerating technological progress" and "In the years since the recession … the economy has been growing very slowly." The writer concluded, "Both statements can't be completely correct." Do you agree with the writer's conclusion? Briefly explain.

Source: Josh Zumbrun, "Goldman Sachs and J.P. Morgan Can't Agree Why the Economy's Productivity Has Slumped," *Wall Street Journal*, June 16, 2015.

3.5 Writing in 2016, economist Robert Gordon of Northwestern University stated his views of the effects of information technology on the economy:

> We don't eat computers or wear them or drive to work in them or let them cut our hair. We live in dwelling units that have appliances much like those of the 1950s, and we drive in motor vehicles that perform the same functions as in the 1950s, albeit with more convenience and safety.… Most of the economy has already benefited from the Internet and web revolution, and in this sphere of the economic activity, methods of production have been little changed over the past decade.… The revolutions in everyday life made possible by e-commerce and search engines were already well established [by 2004].

If Gordon's observations about the information revolution are correct, what are the implications for future labor productivity growth rates in the United States?

Source: Robert J. Gordon, *The Rise and Fall of American Growth: The U.S. Standard of Living since the Civil War*, Princeton, NJ: Princeton University Press, 2016, p. 579.

3.6 Some economists argue that the apparent slowdown in productivity growth in the United States in recent years is a measurement problem resulting from the failure of GDP to capture the effects of many recent innovations, such as cloud computing. James Manyika, head of technology at McKinsey & Company, has argued that for many of these innovations, "we have all these benefits but we're not paying for them."
a. Before the arrival of the Internet, people looking for facts, such as the population of France or the salary of the president of the United States, had to go to the library to look them up. Now people can find that information in a few seconds with a Google search. Are the benefits to you of being able to do a Google search included in GDP? Briefly explain.
b. Does your answer to part (a) indicate that the slowdown in U.S. productivity growth in recent years is just a measurement problem? What other information would you need to arrive at a definite answer?

Source: Timothy Aeppel, "Silicon Valley Doesn't Believe U.S. Productivity Is Down," *Wall Street Journal*, July 16, 2015.

11.4 Why Isn't the Whole World Rich? pages 369–378

LEARNING OBJECTIVE: Explain economic catch-up and discuss why many poor countries have not experienced rapid economic growth.

MyLab Economics   Visit **www.pearson.com/mylab/economics** to complete these exercises online and get instant feedback.

Summary

The economic growth model predicts that poor countries will grow faster than rich countries, resulting in **catch-up**. In recent decades, some poor countries have grown faster than rich countries, but many have not. Some poor countries have not experienced rapid growth for four main reasons: wars and revolutions, poor public education and health, failure to enforce the rule of law, and low rates of saving and investment. The **rule of law** refers to the ability of a government to enforce the laws of the country, particularly with respect to protecting **property rights** and enforcing contracts. **Globalization** has aided countries that have opened their economies to foreign trade and investment. **Foreign direct investment (FDI)** is the purchase or building by a firm of a facility in a foreign country. **Foreign portfolio investment** is the purchase by an individual or a firm of stocks or bonds issued in another country.

Review Questions

4.1 Why does the economic growth model predict that poor countries should catch up to rich countries in real GDP per capita? Have poor countries been catching up to rich countries?

4.2 What are the main reasons many poor countries have experienced slow growth?

4.3 What does globalization mean? How have developing countries benefited from globalization?

Problems and Applications

4.4 (Related to Solved Problem 11.4 on page 372) Briefly explain whether the statistics in the following table are consistent with the economic growth model's predictions of catch-up.

Country	Real GDP per Capita, 1960 (2005 U.S. dollars)	Growth in Real GDP per Capita, 1960–2014
Botswana	$427	4.51%
Uganda	800	1.55
Madagascar	1,281	−0.06
Ireland	6,484	3.81
United States	17,600	2.04

Source: Authors' calculations from data in Robert C. Feenstra, Robert Inklaar, and Marcel P. Timmer, "The Next Generation of the Penn World Table," *American Economic Review*, October 2015, Vol. 105, No. 10, pp. 3150–3182.

4.5 (Related to Solved Problem 11.4 on page 372) In the following graph, each dot represents a particular country's initial level of real GDP per capita and its growth rate of real GDP per capita.

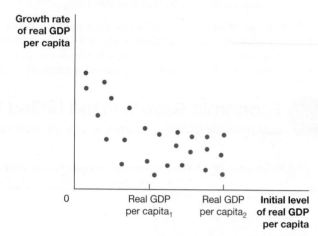

a. For the range of initial GDP per capita from 0 to Real GDP per capita₂, does the figure support the economic growth model's prediction of catch-up? Briefly explain.

b. For the range of initial GDP per capita from 0 to Real GDP per capita₁, does the figure support the catch-up prediction? Briefly explain.

c. For the range from initial Real GDP per capita₁ to Real GDP per capita₂, does the figure support the catch-up prediction? Briefly explain.

4.6 Refer to Figures 11.6–11.8 on pages 370–371. The lines in the following three graphs show the average relationship between the initial level of real GDP per capita and the growth rate of real GDP per capita for three groups of countries over a given time period. Match each group of countries with the graph that best depicts the relationship between the initial level of real GDP per capita and the growth rate of real GDP per capita for that group.

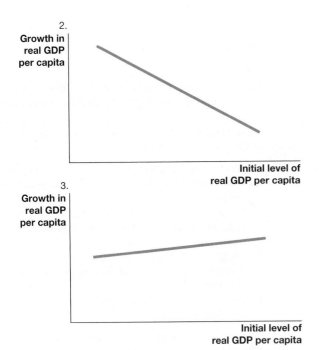

a. All countries for which statistics are available, 1960–2014

b. United States, Western Europe, Canada, and Japan, 1990–2016

c. Current high-income countries, 1960–2014

4.7 Deirdre McCloskey, an economist at the University of Illinois at Chicago, argued, "A poor country that adopts thoroughgoing innovation … can get within hailing distance of the West … in about two generations."

a. What does McCloskey mean by a country adopting "thoroughgoing innovation"? What does she mean by a country getting within "hailing distance of the West"?

b. A generation is usually considered to be about 25 years. In 2016, real GDP per capita in Italy was about $33,500 (measured in 2010 U.S. dollars), and real GDP per capita in Haiti was about $1,500. If Haiti adopted thoroughgoing innovation and as a result its average annual growth rate over the next 50 years increased to 6.5 percent, would Haiti end up with the level of real GDP per capita that Italy enjoyed in 2016? [*Hint:* Use the following equation: Real GDP per capita$_{2016}$ $\times$ $(1 + g)^{50}$ = Real GDP per capita$_{2066}$, where g is the average annual growth rate expressed as a decimal.]

c. McCloskey also noted that her previous observation "does not mean that catch-up is inevitable." Briefly explain why low-income countries catching up with high-income countries isn't inevitable.

Source: Deirdre N. McCloskey, *Bourgeois Dignity: Why Economics Can't Explain the Modern World*, Chicago: University of Chicago Press, 2010, p. 122.

4.8 (Related to the Apply the Concept on page 376) A study by the McKinsey Global Institute reported that labor productivity increased at an average annual rate of 5.8 percent between 1999 and 2013 in Mexico's large companies, but it fell at an average annual rate of 6.5 percent over the

same period for its smaller firms, such as family-owned stores and bakeries. Briefly explain why productivity growth would be much higher for Mexico's largest companies than for its smaller companies.

Source: Anthony Harrup, "Two Economies Explain Mexico's Productivity Quandary," *Wall Street Journal*, March 27, 2014.

4.9 (Related to the Apply the Concept on page 376) An article in the *Wall Street Journal* in mid-2017 noted, "Mexico's economy kept up steady growth in the first quarter, expanding for a 15th consecutive period despite concerns that strained trade and investment relations with the U.S. will bring about a sharp slowdown." During this period, why were some observers concerned about Mexico's economic relations with the United States? Why are these relations particularly important if the Mexican economy is to experience sustained growth?

Source: Anthony Harrup, "Mexican Economy Maintains Growth in First Quarter," *Wall Street Journal*, April 28, 2017.

4.10 In 2017, in a speech in China, Apple CEO Tim Cook stated that globalization is "great for the world…. I think the reality is you can see that countries in the world … that isolate themselves, it's not good for their people."

a. Why would countries that isolate themselves rather than participate fully in the global economy be hurting their own people?

b. Is there an argument to be made that globalization hurts rather than helps some economies? Briefly explain.

Source: Eva Dou, "Apple CEO Tim Cook Defends Globalization in China," *Wall Street Journal*, March 18, 2017.

4.11 A columnist in the *New York Times* observed that "many analysts agree that economic reform, of which integration into the global economy was a key element, has lifted millions of people out of poverty in India." What does "integration into the global economy" mean? How might integration into the global economy reduce poverty in India?

Source: Vivek Dehejia, "Has Globalization Helped India's Poor?" *New York Times*, October 7, 2011.

4.12 The Roman Empire lasted from 27 B.C.E. to C.E. 476. The empire was wealthy enough to build such monuments as the Roman Coliseum. Roman engineering skill was at a level high enough that aqueducts built during the empire to carry water long distances remained in use for hundreds of years. Yet, although the empire experienced some periods of growth in real GDP per capita, these periods did not last, and there is little evidence that growth would have been sustained even if the empire had survived. Why didn't the Roman Empire experience sustained economic growth? What would the world be like today if it had? (*Note:* There are no definite answers to these questions; they are intended to get you to think about the preconditions for economic growth. Looking beyond this problem, if you are interested in the macroeconomics of the Roman economy, see Peter Temin, *The Roman Market Economy*, Princeton: Princeton University Press, 2013, Chapters 9–11.)

Growth Policies, pages 379–383

LEARNING OBJECTIVE: Discuss government policies that foster economic growth.

MyLab Economics   Visit **www.pearson.com/mylab/economics** to complete these exercises online and get instant feedback.

Summary

Governments can attempt to increase economic growth through policies that enhance property rights and the rule of law, improve health and education, subsidize research and development, and provide incentives for saving and investment. Whether continued economic growth is desirable is a normative question that cannot be settled by economic analysis.

Review Questions

5.1 Briefly describe three government policies that can increase economic growth.

5.2 Can economic analysis arrive at the conclusion that economic growth will always improve economic well-being? Briefly explain.

Problems and Applications

5.3 **(Related to the Chapter Opener on page 352)** An article in the *Economist* on the Mexican economy noted, "A huge, unproductive informal sector and general lawlessness also drag the economy down." If these factors were the main barriers to more rapid economic growth in Mexico, would that be good news or bad news for the Mexican government's attempts to increase its economy's growth rate? Briefly explain.
Source: "The 100-Year View," *Economist*, May 2, 2015.

5.4 **(Related to the Apply the Concept on page 379)** In China, why may a lower birth rate lead to slower growth in real GDP per capita? Why might high levels of spending on investment in China lead to high rates of growth in the short run but not in the long run?

5.5 **(Related to the Apply the Concept on page 379)** Pranab Bardhan, an economist at the University of California, Berkeley, argues, "China may be close to exhausting the possibilities of technological catch-up with the West, particularly in manufacturing."
  a. What does Bardhan mean by "technological catch-up"?
  b. If Bardhan is correct, what problems might the Chinese economy encounter in the future?

  c. Briefly discuss the similarities and differences between the Chinese economy today and the Soviet economy in the 1980s.
Source: Pranab Bardhan, "The Slowing of Two Economic Giants," *New York Times*, July 14, 2013.

5.6 Briefly explain whether any of the following policies are likely to increase the rate of economic growth in the United States.
  a. Congress passes an investment tax credit, which reduces a firm's taxes if it installs new machinery and equipment.
  b. Congress passes a law that allows taxpayers to reduce their income taxes by the amount of state sales taxes they pay.
  c. Congress provides more funds for low-interest loans to college students.

5.7 In an interview on PBS about economic development in Africa, Ghanaian economist George Ayittey stated that of the 54 African countries, only 8 had a free press. For Africa's economic development, Ayittey argued strongly for the establishment of a free press. Why would a free press be vital for the enhancement of property rights and the rule of law? How could a free press help reduce corruption?
Source: George Ayittey, "Border Jumpers," Anchor Interview Transcript, WideAngle, PBS.org, July 24, 2005.

5.8 More people in high-income countries than in low-income countries tend to believe that rapid rates of economic growth are not desirable. Recall the concept of a "normal good" (see Chapter 3). Does this concept provide insight into why some people in high-income countries might be more concerned with certain consequences of rapid economic growth than are people in low-income countries?

5.9 In an interview with the *Wall Street Journal*, Prime Minister Narendra Modi of India stated, "In two years, we have done a lot to position India to thrive in the changing world." He mentioned that under his administration, restrictions on foreign investment into India have been loosened. Why would loosening restrictions on foreign investment help position India to thrive? Briefly explain.
Source: Raymond Zhong, "India's Economic Growth Picks up Pace, Accelerating to 7.6%," *Wall Street Journal*, May 31, 2016.

Real-Time Data Exercises

D11.1 **(Analyzing labor productivity)** Using data from the St. Louis Federal Reserve (FRED) (fred.stlouisfed.org), analyze the relationship between labor productivity in the manufacturing sector and in the non-farm business sector as a whole.

    a. Download data since 1987 on output per hour of all persons in the manufacturing sector (OPHMFG) and in the non-farm business sector (OPHNFB).

    b. Which has increased more since 1987, labor productivity in manufacturing or in the non-farm business sector?

    c. The manufacturing sector has been shrinking relative to the size of the economy in the United States and other advanced economies. What do your results imply about future labor productivity growth in advanced economies?

D11.2 **(Comparing labor productivity across countries)** Using data from the St. Louis Federal Reserve (FRED) (fred.stlouisfed.org), analyze differences in labor productivity among China, India, and the United States.

    a. From 1952 to 2010 (which is the latest available data), chart the following series on the same graph: real GDP per worker for China (RGDPL2CNA627NUPN), real GDP per worker for India (RGDPLWINA627NUPN), and real GDP per worker for the United States (RGDPLWUSA627NUPN). To chart the series on the same graph, follow these steps: (1) On the page for real GDP per worker for China, click on the "Edit Graph" link; (2) on the top of the next page, click on the "Add Line" link; (3) search for the series for real GDP per worker for India and click "Add data series"; and (4) click "Add Line," search for the series for real GDP per worker for the United States, and click "Add data series."

    b. Calculate the relative productivity of workers in China and the United States by dividing U.S. labor productivity by China's labor productivity. Describe the change in this measure of relative productivity since 1952. (To calculate and graph the relative labor productivity in FRED, in a new graph, chart the real GDP per worker for the United States, click "Edit Graph," and under "Customize data" enter in the "Add" box the reference code for the real GDP per worker for China and click "Add." Notice that FRED denotes the labor productivity of workers in the United States as variable "a" and the labor productivity of workers in China as variable "b." In the formula box at the bottom, enter a/b and click "Apply.")

    c. Repeat part (b) for the United States and India. To calculate and graph in FRED, repeat the operations in part (b), replacing the labor productivity of China with the labor productivity of India.

D11.3 **(The U.S. economy in a world context)** The U.S. Central Intelligence Agency's *World Factbook* (www.cia.gov/library/publications/the-world-factbook/) offers many tables of world data. Go to the site, click on "Guide to Country Comparisons" in the middle of the page and then "Economy," and find the following:

    a. The countries with the highest and lowest GDPs, adjusted for purchasing power parity

    b. The countries with the highest and lowest per capita real GDPs, adjusted for purchasing power parity

    c. The countries with the most equal and least equal income distributions

    d. The countries with the highest and lowest real GDP growth rates

    e. The rank of the United States in these categories

Critical Thinking Exercises

CT11.1 Read "Botswana: An African Success Story Shows Strains," on the Web site of the Council of Foreign Relations at www.cfr.org/backgrounder/botswana-african-success-story-shows-strains. Describe the role of property rights in explaining Botswana's current situation. You might need to review the concept of property rights from Chapter 2, Section 2.3. How is what is happening in Botswana similar to what happened in Great Britain in the eighteenth century?

CT11.2 TED is a nonprofit organization devoted to spreading ideas, usually in the form of short talks. Watch Northwestern University economist Robert Gordon's TED Talk on economic growth at www.ted.com/talks/robert_gordon_the_death_of_innovation_the_end_of_growth/up-next. Write a paragraph explaining whether you find Gordon's arguments persuasive.

Fluctuating Demand Helps— and Hurts—Intel and Other Firms

Robert Noyce and Gordon Moore founded Intel in 1968. Today, the company is the world's largest semiconductor manufacturer and a major supplier of the microprocessors and memory chips that power desktop and laptop computers sold by Dell, Apple, Lenovo, Hewlett-Packard, and other firms.

Intel's success has depended on the health of the computer market. As a result, the firm faces two problems: First, in the past few years, sales of computers have declined because many consumers and some businesses have switched to using tablets and smartphones to access the Internet. Second, Intel is vulnerable to the swings of the business cycle because sales of computers rise during economic expansions and fall during recessions. Intel was particularly hurt by the 2007–2009 recession. During the last quarter of 2008, Intel's revenues fell 90 percent, and the firm laid off 6,000 workers. Conditions improved for Intel beginning in 2010, as the U.S. economy recovered from the recession, but the firm was still struggling to reduce its dependence on selling chips to computer manufacturers. Although Intel's revenues were barely growing, the firm still had to spend billions of dollars each year on research and development and on equipping its factories with state-of-the-art manufacturing capabilities.

In 2017, Intel was trying to convince other firms to allow it to produce their chips in Intel's factories. For instance, it hoped to manufacture the chips that Apple designs for the iPhone. Intel also faced competition from Nvidia and other firms that produce graphics processing units (GPUs) that were originally designed for video games but that are now also used in artificial intelligence programs.

Yaacov Dagan/Alamy Stock Photo

The recovery from the 2007–2009 recession was by some measures the weakest since the end of World War II in 1945. By 2017, though, many industries were prospering, and unemployment had fallen to low levels. In some parts of the country, firms faced the problem not of weak sales but of finding enough workers to fill existing orders. An article in the *Wall Street Journal* quoted the president of the Utah Manufacturers Association as saying, "3.1 percent unemployment is fabulous unless you're looking to hire people."

These firms were dealing with the effects of changes in total spending in the economy, or *aggregate expenditure.* In this chapter, we will explore how changes in aggregate expenditure cause changes in real GDP.

Sources: Dan Gallagher, "Intel's Need to Chip Away at Fab Rivals," *Wall Street Journal,* April 2, 2017; Binyamin Appelbaum, "Lack of Workers, Not Work, Weighs on the Nation's Economy," *Wall Street Journal,* May 21, 2017; and "The Rise of Artificial Intelligence Is Creating New Variety in the Chip Market, and Trouble for Intel," *Economist,* February 25, 2017.

Chapter Outline & Learning Objectives

12.1 The Aggregate Expenditure Model, page 394
Explain how macroeconomic equilibrium is determined in the aggregate expenditure model.

12.2 Determining the Level of Aggregate Expenditure in the Economy, page 397
Discuss the determinants of the four components of aggregate expenditure and define marginal propensity to consume and marginal propensity to save.

12.3 Graphing Macroeconomic Equilibrium, page 410
Use a 45°-line diagram to illustrate macroeconomic equilibrium.

12.4 The Multiplier Effect, page 417
Describe the multiplier effect and use the multiplier formula to calculate changes in equilibrium GDP.

12.5 The Aggregate Demand Curve, page 424
Understand the relationship between the aggregate demand curve and aggregate expenditure.

Appendix: The Algebra of Macroeconomic Equilibrium, page 434
Apply the algebra of macroeconomic equilibrium.

Economics in Your Life & Career

When Consumer Confidence Falls, Is Your Job at Risk?

Suppose that while attending college, you work part time at a company that manufactures door handles that it sells to automobile companies. One morning, you read in an online news story that consumer confidence in the economy has fallen, and, as a result, many households expect their future income to be well below their current income. Should you be concerned about losing your job? What factors should you consider in deciding how likely your company is to lay you off? As you read this chapter, try to answer these questions. You can check your answers against those we provide on **page 426** at the end of this chapter.

Aggregate expenditure (AE) Total spending in the economy: the sum of consumption, planned investment, government purchases, and net exports.

In Chapter 11, we discussed the determinants of long-run growth in the economy. We now turn to exploring the causes of the business cycle. We begin by examining the effect of changes in total spending on real gross domestic product (GDP).

During some years, total spending in the economy, or **aggregate expenditure (AE)**, and total production of goods and services increase by the same amount. In this case, most firms will sell about as much as they expected to sell, and they probably will not increase or decrease production or the number of workers they hire. During other years, total spending in the economy increases more than the production of goods and services. In those years, firms will increase production and hire more workers. But there are times, such as 2008 and early 2009, when total spending does not increase as much as total production. As a result, firms cut back on production and lay off workers, and the economy moves into a recession. In this chapter, we will explore why changes in total spending play such an important role in the economy.

12.1 The Aggregate Expenditure Model

LEARNING OBJECTIVE: Explain how macroeconomic equilibrium is determined in the aggregate expenditure model.

The business cycle involves the interaction of many economic variables. A simple model called the *aggregate expenditure model* can help us understand the relationships among some of these variables. Recall that GDP is the value of all the final goods and services produced in an economy during a period of time, typically one year. Real GDP corrects nominal GDP for the effects of inflation. The **aggregate expenditure model** focuses on the short-run relationship between total spending and real GDP. An important assumption of the model is that the price level is constant. In Chapter 13, we will develop a more complete model of the business cycle that relaxes the assumption of constant prices.

Aggregate expenditure model A macroeconomic model that focuses on the short-run relationship between total spending and real GDP, assuming that the price level is constant.

The key idea of the aggregate expenditure model is that *in any particular year, the level of GDP is determined mainly by the level of aggregate expenditure*. To understand the relationship between aggregate expenditure and real GDP, we need to look more closely at the components of aggregate expenditure.

Aggregate Expenditure

Economists first began to study the relationship between changes in aggregate expenditure and changes in GDP during the Great Depression of the 1930s. The United States, the United Kingdom, and other industrial countries suffered declines in real GDP of 20 percent or more during the early 1930s. In 1936, the English economist John Maynard Keynes published a book, *The General Theory of Employment, Interest, and Money*, that systematically analyzed the relationship between changes in aggregate expenditure and changes in GDP. Keynes identified four components of aggregate expenditure that together equal GDP (these are the same four components we discussed in Chapter 8, Section 8.1):

1. *Consumption (C).* Spending by households on goods and services, such as automobiles and haircuts.
2. *Planned investment (I).* Planned spending by firms on capital goods, such as factories, office buildings, and machine tools, and on research and development, and spending by households and firms on new houses.
3. *Government purchases (G).* Spending by local, state, and federal governments on goods and services, such as aircraft carriers, bridges, and the salaries of FBI agents.
4. *Net exports (NX).* Spending by foreign firms and households on goods and services produced in the United States minus spending by U.S. firms and households on goods and services produced in other countries.

So, we can write:

$$\text{Aggregate expenditure} = \text{Consumption} + \text{Planned investment} + \text{Government purchases} + \text{Net exports,}$$

or:

$$AE = C + I + G + NX.$$

Governments around the world gather statistics on aggregate expenditure on the basis of these four components. And economists and business analysts usually explain changes in GDP in terms of changes in these four components of spending.

MyLab Economics Concept Check

The Difference between Planned Investment and Actual Investment

Before considering further the relationship between aggregate expenditure and GDP, we need to consider an important distinction: Notice that *planned* investment spending, rather than actual investment spending, is a component of aggregate expenditure. You might wonder how the amount that businesses plan to spend on investment can be different from the amount they actually spend. We can resolve this puzzle by first remembering that goods that have been produced but have not yet been sold are referred to as **inventories**. Changes in inventories are included as part of investment spending, along with spending on machinery, equipment, office buildings, research and development, and factories. We assume that the amount businesses plan to spend on machinery and office buildings is equal to the amount they actually spend, but the amount businesses plan to spend on inventories may be different from the amount they actually spend.

Inventories Goods that have been produced but not yet sold.

For example, Doubleday Publishing may print 1.5 million copies of the latest John Grisham novel, expecting to sell them all. If Doubleday does sell all 1.5 million, its inventories will be unchanged, but if it sells only 1.2 million, it will have an unplanned increase in inventories. In other words, changes in inventories depend on sales of goods, which firms cannot always forecast with perfect accuracy.

For the economy as a whole, we can say that actual investment spending will be greater than planned investment spending when there is an unplanned increase in inventories. Actual investment spending will be less than planned investment spending when there is an unplanned decrease in inventories. *Therefore, actual investment will equal planned investment only when there is no unplanned change in inventories.* In this chapter, we will use I to represent planned investment. We will also assume that the government data on investment spending compiled by the U.S. Bureau of Economic Analysis represents planned investment spending. This assumption is a simplification, however, because the government collects data on actual investment spending, which equals planned investment spending only when unplanned changes in inventories are zero.   MyLab Economics Concept Check

Macroeconomic Equilibrium

Macroeconomic equilibrium is similar to microeconomic equilibrium. In microeconomics, equilibrium in the apple market occurs when the quantity of apples demanded equals the quantity of apples supplied. When the apple market is in equilibrium, the quantity of apples produced and sold will not change unless the demand for apples or the supply of apples changes. For the economy as a whole, macroeconomic equilibrium occurs when total spending, or aggregate expenditure, equals total production, or GDP:

$$\text{Aggregate expenditure} = \text{GDP}.$$

As we have seen, over the *long run*, real GDP in the United States increases, and the standard of living rises (see Chapter 11, Section 11.1). In this chapter, we are interested in understanding why GDP fluctuates in the *short run*. To simplify the analysis of macroeconomic equilibrium, we assume that the economy is not growing. In Chapter 13, we will discuss the more realistic case of macroeconomic equilibrium in a growing economy. If we assume that the economy is not growing, then equilibrium GDP will not change unless aggregate expenditure changes.   MyLab Economics Concept Check

Adjustments to Macroeconomic Equilibrium

The apple market isn't always in equilibrium because sometimes the quantity of apples demanded is greater than the quantity supplied, and sometimes the quantity supplied is greater than the quantity demanded. The same outcome holds for the economy as a whole. Sometimes the economy is in macroeconomic equilibrium, and sometimes it isn't. When aggregate expenditure is greater than GDP, the total amount of spending in the economy is greater than the total amount of production. With spending being greater than production, many businesses will sell more goods and services than they had expected to sell. For example, the manager of a Home Depot store might like to keep 50 refrigerators in stock to give customers the opportunity to see a variety of different sizes and models. If sales are unexpectedly high, the store may have only 20 refrigerators in stock. In that case, the store will have an unplanned decrease in inventories: Its inventory of refrigerators will decline by 30.

How will the store manager react when more refrigerators are sold than expected? The manager is likely to order more refrigerators. If other stores selling refrigerators are experiencing similar sales increases and are also increasing their orders, then Whirlpool, KitchenAid, and other refrigerator manufacturers will significantly increase their production. These manufacturers may also increase the number of workers they hire. If the increase in sales is affecting not just refrigerators but also other appliances, automobiles, furniture, and other goods and services, then GDP and total employment will begin to increase. In summary, *when aggregate expenditure is greater than GDP, inventories will decline, and GDP and total employment will increase.*

Now suppose that aggregate expenditure is less than GDP. With spending being less than production, many businesses will sell fewer goods and services than they had expected to sell, so their inventories will increase. For example, the manager of the Home Depot store who wants 50 refrigerators in stock may find that because of slow sales, the store has 75 refrigerators, so the store manager will cut back on orders for new refrigerators. If other stores also cut back on their orders, Whirlpool and KitchenAid will reduce production and lay off workers.

If the decrease in sales is affecting not just refrigerators but also many other goods and services, GDP and total employment will begin to decrease. Falling sales followed by reductions in production and employment occurred at many firms during 2008. In summary, *when aggregate expenditure is less than GDP, inventories will increase, and GDP and total employment will decrease.*

Only when aggregate expenditure equals GDP will firms sell what they expected to sell. In that case, their inventories will be unchanged, and they will not have an incentive to increase or decrease production. The economy will be in macroeconomic equilibrium. Table 12.1 summarizes the relationship between aggregate expenditure and GDP.

Increases and decreases in aggregate expenditure cause the year-to-year changes we see in GDP. Economists devote considerable time and energy to forecasting what will happen to each component of aggregate expenditure. If economists forecast that aggregate expenditure will decline in the future, that is equivalent to forecasting that GDP will decline and that the economy will enter a recession. Firms, policymakers, and individuals closely watch these forecasts because changes in GDP can have dramatic consequences. When GDP is increasing, so are wages, profits, and job opportunities. Declining GDP can be bad news for workers, firms, and job seekers.

When economists forecast that aggregate expenditure is likely to decline and that the economy is headed for a recession, the federal government may implement

Table 12.1

The Relationship between Aggregate Expenditure and GDP

If . . .	then . . .	and . . .
aggregate expenditure is *equal* to GDP	inventories are *unchanged*,	the economy is in *macroeconomic equilibrium.*
aggregate expenditure is *less* than GDP	inventories *rise*,	GDP and employment *decrease.*
aggregate expenditure is *greater* than GDP	inventories *fall*,	GDP and employment *increase.*

macroeconomic policies in an attempt to head off the decrease in expenditure and keep the economy from falling into a recession. We will discuss these macroeconomic policies in Chapters 15 and 16.   **MyLab Economics** Concept Check

MyLab Economics Study Plan

12.2 Determining the Level of Aggregate Expenditure in the Economy

LEARNING OBJECTIVE: Discuss the determinants of the four components of aggregate expenditure and define marginal propensity to consume and marginal propensity to save.

To better understand how macroeconomic equilibrium is determined in the aggregate expenditure model, we look more closely at the components of aggregate expenditure. Table 12.2 lists the four components of aggregate expenditure for 2016. The components are measured in *real* terms, which means that their values are corrected for inflation by being measured in billions of 2009 dollars. Consumption is clearly the largest component of aggregate expenditure. Investment and government purchases are of roughly similar size. Net exports was negative because in 2016, as in most other years since the early 1970s, the United States imported more goods and services than it exported. Next, we consider the variables that determine each of the four components of aggregate expenditure.

Expenditure Category	Real Expenditure (billions of 2009 dollars)
Consumption	$11,522
Planned investment	2,825
Government purchases	2,907
Net exports	−563

Source: U.S. Bureau of Economic Analysis.

MyLab Economics Real-time data

Table 12.2

Components of Real Aggregate Expenditure, 2016

Consumption

Figure 12.1 shows movements in real consumption from 1979 through the first quarter of 2017. Notice that consumption follows a smooth, upward trend. Only during periods of recession does the growth in consumption decline.

These are the five most important variables that determine the level of consumption:

1. Current disposable income
2. Household wealth

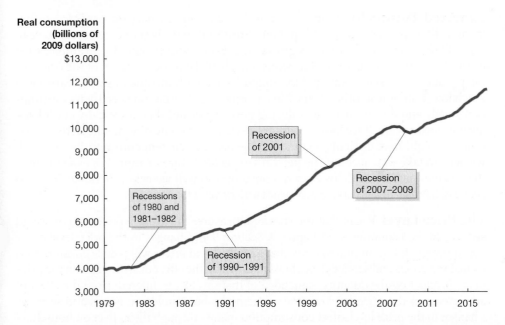

MyLab Economics Real-Time Data

Figure 12.1

Real Consumption, 1979–2017

Consumption follows a smooth, upward trend, interrupted only infrequently by brief recessions.

Note: The values are quarterly data seasonally adjusted at an annual rate.

Source: U.S. Bureau of Economic Analysis.

3. Expected future income
4. The price level
5. The interest rate

Next we discuss how changes in each of these variables affect consumption.

Current Disposable Income The most important determinant of consumption is the current disposable income of households. Recall that disposable income is the income remaining to households after they have paid the personal income tax and received government *transfer payments*, such as Social Security payments (see Chapter 8, Section 8.4). For most households, the higher their disposable income, the more they spend, and the lower their income, the less they spend. Macroeconomic consumption is the total of all the consumption of U.S. households. We would expect consumption to increase when the current disposable income of households increases and to decrease when the current disposable income of households decreases. As we have seen, total income in the United States expands during most years. Only during recessions, which happen infrequently, does total income decline. The main reason for the general upward trend in consumption shown in Figure 12.1 is that disposable income has followed a similar upward trend.

Household Wealth Consumption depends in part on the wealth of households. A household's *wealth* is the value of its *assets* minus the value of its *liabilities*. Recall that an asset is anything of value owned by a person or a firm, and a liability is anything owed by a person or a firm (see Chapter 6, Section 6.3). A household's assets include its home, stock and bond holdings, and bank accounts. A household's liabilities include any loans that it owes. A household with $10 million in wealth is likely to spend more than a household with $10,000 in wealth, even if both households have the same disposable income. Therefore, when the wealth of households increases, consumption should increase, and when the wealth of households decreases, consumption should decrease. Shares of stock are an important category of household wealth. When stock prices increase, household wealth will increase, and so should consumption. For example, a family whose stock holdings increase in value from $30,000 to $100,000 may be willing to spend a larger fraction of its income because it is less concerned with adding to its savings. A decline in stock prices should lead to a decline in consumption. Economists who have studied the determinants of consumption have concluded that permanent increases in wealth have a larger impact than temporary increases. One estimate of the effect of changes in wealth on consumption spending indicates that, for every permanent $1 increase in household wealth, consumption spending will increase by between 4 and 5 cents per year.

Expected Future Income Consumption depends in part on expected future income. Most people prefer to keep their consumption fairly stable from year to year, even if their income fluctuates significantly. Some salespeople, for example, earn most of their income from commissions, which are fixed percentages of the prices of the products they sell. A salesperson might have a high income in some years and a much lower income in other years. Most people in this situation keep their consumption steady and do not increase it during good years and then drastically cut it back during slower years. If we looked only at the current income of someone in this situation, we might have difficulty estimating the person's current consumption. Instead, we need to take into account the person's expected future income. We can conclude that current income explains current consumption well *but only when current income is not unusually high or unusually low compared with expected future income.*

The Price Level Recall that the *price level* measures the average prices of goods and services in the economy (see Chapter 9, Section 9.4). Changes in the price level affect consumption. It is tempting to think that an increase in prices will reduce consumption by making goods and services less affordable. In fact, the effect of an increase in the price of *one* product on the quantity demanded of that product is different from the effect of an increase in the price level on *total* spending by households on goods and services. Changes in the price level affect consumption mainly through their effect on household wealth. An increase in the price level will result in a decrease in the *real* value of house-hold wealth. For example, if you have $2,000 in a checking account, the higher the price level, the fewer goods and services you can buy with your money. Therefore, as the price level rises, the real value of your wealth declines, and so will your consumption, at least a little. Conversely, if the price level falls—which happens rarely in the United States—the real value of your $2,000 increases, and your consumption will also increase.

The Interest Rate Finally, consumption depends on the interest rate. When the interest rate is high, the reward for saving is increased, and households are likely to save more and spend less. Recall the distinction between the *nominal interest rate* and the *real interest rate* (see Chapter 9, Section 9.6):

- The nominal interest rate is the stated interest rate on a loan or a financial investment such as a bond.
- The real interest rate corrects the nominal interest rate for the effect of inflation and is equal to the nominal interest rate minus the inflation rate.

Because households are concerned with the payments they will make or receive after the effects of inflation are taken into account, consumption spending depends on the real interest rate.

We have seen that consumption spending is divided into three categories:

1. Spending on *services*, such as medical care, education, and haircuts
2. Spending on *nondurable goods*, such as food and clothing
3. Spending on *durable goods*, such as automobiles and furniture

Spending on durable goods is most likely to be affected by changes in the interest rate because a high real interest rate increases the cost of spending financed by borrowing. The monthly payment on a four-year car loan will be higher if the real interest rate on the loan is 6 percent than if it is 4 percent.

The Consumption Function Panel (a) in Figure 12.2 plots the relationship between consumption and disposable income during the years 1970 to 2016.

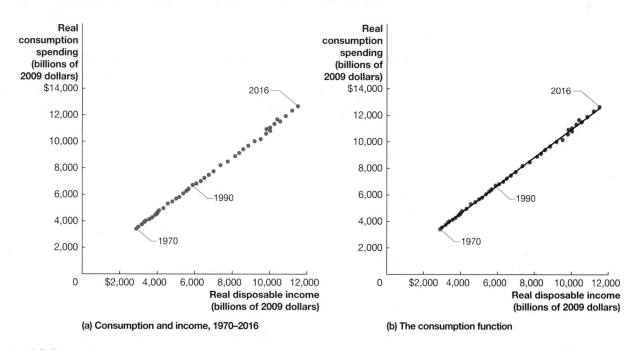

(a) Consumption and income, 1970–2016   (b) The consumption function

Figure 12.2   **The Relationship between Consumption and Income, 1970–2016**   MyLab Economics Animation

Panel (a) shows the relationship between consumption and income. The points represent combinations of real consumption spending and real disposable income for the years 1970 to 2016. In panel (b), we draw a straight line through the points from panel (a). The line, which represents the relationship between consumption and disposable income, is called the *consumption function*. The slope of the consumption function is the marginal propensity to consume.

Source: U.S. Bureau of Economic Analysis.

Consumption function The relationship between consumption spending and disposable income.

Marginal propensity to consume (MPC) The slope of the consumption function: The amount by which consumption spending changes when disposable income changes.

In panel (b), we draw a straight line through the points representing consumption and disposable income. The fact that most of the points lie almost on the line shows the close relationship between consumption and disposable income. Because changes in consumption depend on changes in disposable income, we can say that *consumption is a function of disposable income*. The relationship between consumption spending and disposable income illustrated in panel (b) of Figure 12.2 is called the **consumption function**.

The slope of the consumption function, which is equal to the change in consumption divided by the change in disposable income, is called the **marginal propensity to consume (MPC)**. Using the Greek letter delta, Δ, to represent "change in," C to represent consumption spending, and YD to represent disposable income, we can write the expression for the MPC as follows:

$$MPC = \frac{\text{Change in consumption}}{\text{Change in disposable income}} = \frac{\Delta C}{\Delta YD}.$$

For example, between 2015 and 2016, consumption spending increased by $308 billion, while disposable income increased by $324 billion. The marginal propensity to consume was, therefore:

$$\frac{\Delta C}{\Delta YD} = \frac{\$308 \text{ billion}}{\$324 \text{ billion}} = 0.95.$$

This value for the MPC tells us that households in 2016 spent 95 percent of the increase in their disposable income.

We can also use the MPC to determine how much consumption will change as income changes. To see this relationship, we rewrite the expression for the MPC:

$$\text{Change in consumption} = \text{Change in disposable income} \times MPC.$$

For example, with an MPC of 0.95, a $10 billion increase in disposable income will increase consumption by $10 billion $\times$ 0.95, or $9.5 billion.   **MyLab Economics** Concept Check

The Relationship between Consumption and National Income

We have seen that consumption spending by households depends on disposable income. We now shift our focus slightly to the similar relationship that exists between consumption spending and GDP. We make this shift because we are interested in using the aggregate expenditure model to explain changes in real GDP rather than changes in disposable income. The first step in examining the relationship between consumption and GDP is to recall that the differences between GDP and national income are small and can be ignored without affecting our analysis (see Chapter 8, Section 8.4). In fact, in this and the following chapters, we will use the terms *GDP* and *national income* interchangeably. Also recall that disposable income is equal to national income plus government transfer payments minus taxes. Taxes minus government transfer payments are called *net taxes*. So, we can write the following:

$$\text{Disposable income} = \text{National income} - \text{Net taxes.}$$

We can rearrange the equation like this:

$$\text{National income} = \text{GDP} = \text{Disposable income} + \text{Net taxes.}$$

The table in Figure 12.3 shows hypothetical values for national income (or GDP), net taxes, disposable income, and consumption spending. Notice that national income and disposable income differ by a constant amount, which is equal to net taxes of $1,000 billion. In reality, net taxes are not a constant amount because they

National Income or GDP (billions of dollars)	Net Taxes (billions of dollars)	Disposable Income (billions of dollars)	Consumption (billions of dollars)	Change in National Income (billions of dollars)	Change in Disposable Income (billions of dollars)
$1,000	$1,000	$0	$750	—	—
3,000	1,000	2,000	2,250	$2,000	$2,000
5,000	1,000	4,000	3,750	2,000	2,000
7,000	1,000	6,000	5,250	2,000	2,000
9,000	1,000	8,000	6,750	2,000	2,000
11,000	1,000	10,000	8,250	2,000	2,000
13,000	1,000	12,000	9,750	2,000	2,000

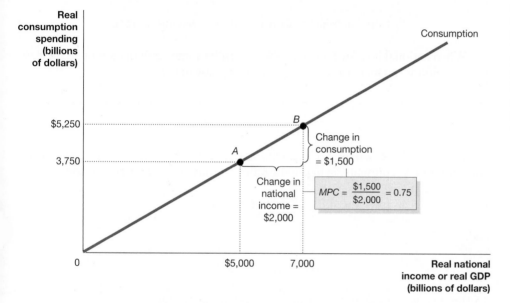

MyLab Economics Animation

Figure 12.3

The Relationship between Consumption and National Income

Because national income differs from disposable income only by net taxes—which, for simplicity, we assume are constant—we can graph the consumption function using national income rather than disposable income. We can also calculate the MPC, which is the slope of the consumption function, using either the change in national income or the change in disposable income and always get the same value. The slope of the consumption function between points A and B is equal to the change in consumption—$1,500 billion—divided by the change in national income—$2,000 billion—or 0.75.

are affected by changes in income. As income rises, net taxes rise because some taxes, such as the personal income tax, increase and some government transfer payments, such as government payments to unemployed workers, fall. Nothing important is affected in our analysis, however, by our simplifying assumption that net taxes are constant.

The graph in Figure 12.3 shows a line representing the relationship between consumption and national income. The line is very similar to the consumption function shown in panel (b) of Figure 12.2. We defined the marginal propensity to consume (MPC) as the change in consumption divided by the change in disposable income, which is the slope of the consumption function. In fact, notice that if we calculate the slope of the line in Figure 12.3 between points A and B, we get a result that will not change whether we use the values for national income or the values for disposable income. To see this, here is the result using the values for national income:

$$\frac{\Delta C}{\Delta Y} = \frac{\$5,250 \text{ billion} - \$3,750 \text{ billion}}{\$7,000 \text{ billion} - \$5,000 \text{ billion}} = 0.75.$$

And here is the result using the corresponding values for disposable income from the table:

$$\frac{\Delta C}{\Delta YD} = \frac{\$5,250 \text{ billion} - \$3,750 \text{ billion}}{\$6,000 \text{ billion} - \$4,000 \text{ billion}} = 0.75.$$

It should not be surprising that we get the same result in either case. National income and disposable income differ by a constant amount, so changes in the two numbers always give us the same value, as shown in the last two columns of the table in Figure 12.3. Therefore, we can graph the consumption function using national income rather than using disposable income. We can also calculate the MPC by using either the change in national income or the change in disposable income and always get the same value. **MyLab Economics** Concept Check

Income, Consumption, and Saving

To complete our discussion of consumption, we can look briefly at the relationships among income, consumption, and saving. Households spend their income, save it, or use it to pay taxes. For the economy as a whole, we can write the following:

$$\text{National income} = \text{Consumption} + \text{Saving} + \text{Taxes}.$$

When national income increases, there must be some combination of an increase in consumption, an increase in saving, and an increase in taxes:

$$\text{Change in national income} = \text{Change in consumption} + \text{Change in saving} + \text{Change in taxes}.$$

Using symbols, where Y represents national income (and GDP), C represents consumption, S represents saving, and T represents taxes, we can write the following:

$$Y = C + S + T$$

and:

$$\Delta Y = \Delta C + \Delta S + \Delta T.$$

To simplify, we can assume that taxes are always a constant amount, in which case $\Delta T = 0$, so the following is also true:

$$\Delta Y = \Delta C + \Delta S.$$

Marginal propensity to save (MPS) The amount by which saving changes when disposable income changes.

We have already seen that the marginal propensity to consume equals the change in consumption divided by the change in income. We can define the **marginal propensity to save (MPS)** as the amount by which saving changes when disposable income changes. We can measure the MPS as the change in saving divided by the change in disposable income. In calculating the MPS, as in calculating the MPC, we can safely ignore the difference between national income and disposable income.

If we divide the previous equation by the change in income, ΔY, we get an equation that shows the relationship between the marginal propensity to consume and the marginal propensity to save:

$$\frac{\Delta Y}{\Delta Y} = \frac{\Delta C}{\Delta Y} + \frac{\Delta S}{\Delta Y},$$

or:

$$1 = MPC + MPS.$$

This equation tells us that when taxes are constant, the marginal propensity to consume plus the marginal propensity to save must always equal 1. They must add up to 1 because part of any increase in income is consumed, and whatever remains must be saved. **MyLab Economics** Concept Check

Solved Problem 12.2

Calculating the Marginal Propensity to Consume and the Marginal Propensity to Save

Fill in the missing values in the following table. For simplicity, assume that taxes are zero. Show that the *MPC* plus the *MPS* equals 1.

National Income and Real GDP (Y)	Consumption (C)	Saving (S)	Marginal Propensity to Consume (MPC)	Marginal Propensity to Save (MPS)
$9,000	$8,000			
10,000	8,600			
11,000	9,200			
12,000	9,800			
13,000	10,400			

Solving the Problem

Step 1: Review the chapter material. This problem is about the relationship among income, consumption, and saving, so you may want to review the section "Income, Consumption, and Saving" on page 402.

Step 2: Fill in the table. We know that $Y = C + S + T$. With taxes equal to zero, this equation becomes $Y = C + S$. We can use this equation to fill in the "Saving" column. We can use the equations for the *MPC* and the *MPS* to fill in the other two columns:

$$MPC = \frac{\Delta C}{\Delta Y}$$

$$MPS = \frac{\Delta S}{\Delta Y}.$$

For example, to calculate the value of the *MPC* in the second row, we have:

$$MPC = \frac{\Delta C}{\Delta Y} = \frac{\$8,600 - \$8,000}{\$10,000 - \$9,000} = \frac{\$600}{\$1,000} = 0.6.$$

To calculate the value of the *MPS* in the second row, we have:

$$MPS = \frac{\Delta S}{\Delta Y} = \frac{\$1,400 - \$1,000}{\$10,000 - \$9,000} = \frac{\$400}{\$1,000} = 0.4.$$

National Income and Real GDP (Y)	Consumption (C)	Saving (S)	Marginal Propensity to Consume (MPC)	Marginal Propensity to Save (MPS)
$9,000	$8,000	$1,000	—	—
10,000	8,600	1,400	0.6	0.4
11,000	9,200	1,800	0.6	0.4
12,000	9,800	2,200	0.6	0.4
13,000	10,400	2,600	0.6	0.4

Step 3: Show that the *MPC* plus the *MPS* equals 1. At every level of national income, the *MPC* is 0.6 and the *MPS* is 0.4. Therefore, the *MPC* plus the *MPS* is always equal to 1.

Your Turn: For more practice, do related problem 2.11 on page 429 at the end of this chapter.   MyLab Economics Study Plan

MyLab Economics Real-Time Data

Figure 12.4

Real Investment, 1979–2017

Investment experiences larger changes than does consumption. Investment declined significantly during the recessions of 1980, 1981–1982, 1990–1991, 2001, and 2007–2009.

Note: The values are quarterly data, seasonally adjusted at an annual rate.

Source: U.S. Bureau of Economic Analysis.

Planned Investment

Figure 12.4 shows movements in real investment spending from 1979 through the first quarter of 2017. Notice that, unlike consumption, investment does not follow a smooth, upward trend. Investment declined significantly during the recessions of 1980, 1981–1982, 1990–1991, 2001, and 2007–2009.

These are the four most important variables that determine the level of investment:

1. Expectations of future profitability
2. The interest rate
3. Taxes
4. Cash flow

Expectations of Future Profitability Investment goods, such as factories, office buildings, and machinery and equipment, are long-lived. A firm is unlikely to build a new factory unless it is optimistic that the demand for its product will remain strong for at least several years. When the economy moves into a recession, many firms postpone buying investment goods even if the demand for their own product is strong because they are afraid that the recession may become worse. During an expansion, some firms may become optimistic and begin to increase spending on investment goods even before the demand for their own product has increased. The key point is that *the optimism or pessimism of firms is an important determinant of investment spending.*

Residential construction is included in investment spending. Since 1990, residential construction has averaged about 30 percent of total investment spending. But the swings in residential construction have been quite substantial, ranging from a high of 34 percent of investment spending at the height of the housing boom in 2005 down to 17 percent in 2011. The sharp decline in spending on residential construction beginning in 2006 helped to cause the 2007–2009 recession and contributed to its severity.

The Interest Rate Some business investment is financed by borrowing, as firms issue corporate bonds or receive loans from banks. Households also borrow to finance most of their spending on new homes. The higher the interest rate, the more expensive it is for firms and households to borrow. Because households and firms are interested in the cost of borrowing after taking into account the effects of inflation, investment spending depends on the real interest rate. Therefore, holding constant the other factors that affect investment spending, there is an inverse relationship between the real interest rate and investment spending: *A higher real interest rate results in less investment spending, and a lower real interest rate results in more investment spending.* The ability of households to borrow money at very low real interest rates helps explain the rapid increase in spending on residential construction from 2002 to 2006.

Taxes Taxes affect the level of investment spending. Firms focus on the profits that remain after they have paid taxes. The federal government imposes a *corporate income tax* on the profits corporations earn, including profits from the new buildings, equipment, and other investment goods they purchase. A reduction in the corporate income tax increases the after-tax profitability of investment spending. An increase in the corporate income tax decreases the after-tax profitability of investment spending. *Investment tax incentives* increase investment spending. An investment tax incentive provides firms with a tax reduction when they buy new investment goods.

Cash Flow Many firms do not borrow to finance spending on new factories, machinery, and equipment. Instead, they use their own funds. **Cash flow** is the difference between the cash revenues received by a firm and the cash spending by the firm. Neither noncash receipts nor noncash spending is included in cash flow. For example, tax laws allow firms to count the depreciation of worn-out or obsolete machinery and equipment as a cost, even if new machinery and equipment have not actually been purchased. Because this is noncash spending, firms do not include it when calculating cash flow. The largest contributor to cash flow is profit. The more profitable a firm is, the greater its cash flow and the greater its ability to finance investment. During periods of recession, many firms experience reduced profits, which in turn reduces their ability to finance spending on new factories or machinery and equipment.

Cash flow The difference between the cash revenues received by a firm and the cash spending by the firm.

Apply the Concept

MyLab Economics Video

Is Student Loan Debt Causing Fewer Young People to Buy Houses?

Although our discussion in this section has concentrated on the components of investment that represent spending by businesses, household purchases of new homes are an important part of investment spending. As the following graph shows, spending on residential construction rose rapidly in the period just before the recession of 2007–2009, declined dramatically during the recession, and recovered only slowly thereafter. In 2017, spending on residential construction remained 30 percent below its 2005 peak, despite the U.S. population having grown by more than 10 percent during that time. The slow recovery in spending on residential construction is one reason the recovery from the recession was weaker than most previous recoveries.

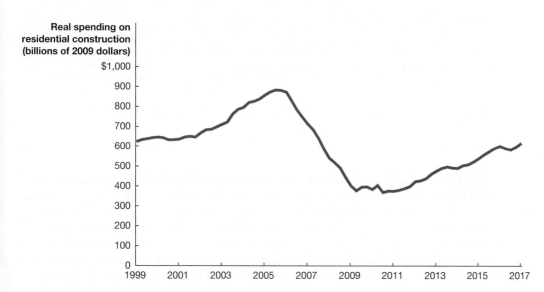

Some economists believe that one factor holding back recovery in the housing market was low home-buying rates among younger households. In 2016, homeownership rates among people younger than 35 were the lowest they have been in the United

States in at least 25 years. If you have a college degree, you are likely to earn more than people without a college degree. So, many people consider student debt accumulated to earn a degree to be a good investment. For the class of 2016, the average student debt per borrower was a record $37,000. Total student debt in 2016 was $1.4 *trillion*, more than the amount that all Americans owe on credit cards or automobile loans, and triple the level of student debt in 2006. In 2008, about 33 percent of 30-year-olds who had student loan debt owned a home. By 2011, only about 23 percent of 30-year-olds with student loan debt owned a home, and the percentage has increased only slowly since then. Do high levels of student debt explain why young people are buying fewer homes? Economists differ in their answers to this question because other factors may be affecting homeownership rates.

Harvard University economist and former Obama administration economic adviser Larry Summers has argued that many college graduates have trouble accumulating the funds for a down payment on a house because they are making student loan payments. He has also argued that these payments have led young college graduates to delay forming families, thereby reducing their need to move from an apartment to a house. One survey indicated that 45 percent of college graduates under age 24 were living with their parents or another family member. Another survey indicated that 20 percent of people with student loans were postponing marriage because of their debts. Some economists point to rising delinquency rates on student loans as a factor that makes it difficult for some young college graduates to qualify for a mortgage loan necessary to buy a house. A study by economists at the Federal Reserve Board concluded that every 10 percent increase in student loan debt reduces home ownership among borrowers by about 1.5 percent during the first five years after leaving college.

Some economists believe that new government lending guidelines may be playing a role in reducing home ownership rates among student borrowers. When deciding whether to grant a mortgage loan, banks and other lenders have interpreted the guidelines to mean that they must give greater consideration to how much debt graduates have. As a result, fewer young college graduates qualify for mortgage loans. Finally, some economists argue that the slow recovery of the U.S. labor market from the recession of 2007–2009 is the key reason that young college graduates were buying fewer houses. In 2017, as the recovery became stronger, the unemployment rate dropped to low levels, and wages increased more quickly, these economists expected that younger people would increase their demand for housing.

Sources: Rajashri Chakrabarti, Nicole Gorton, and Wilbert van der Klaauw, "Diplomas to Doorsteps: Education, Student Debt, and Homeownership," Federal Reserve Bank of New York, *Liberty Street Economics*, April 3, 2017; Zach Friedman, "Student Loan Debt in 2017: A $1.3 Trillion Crisis," forbes.com, February 21, 2017; Zeppo Mitchell, "Larry Summers: Student Debt Is Slowing the U.S. Housing Recovery," *Wall Street Journal*, May 21, 2014; Josh Mitchell, "Student Debt May Prevent Some Americans from Buying Homes," *Wall Street Journal*, April 3, 2017; Alvaro Mezza et al., "On the Effect of Student Loans on Access to Homeownership," Federal Reserve Board Divisions of Research & Statistics and Monetary Affairs, Finance and Economics Discussion Series, Working Paper No. 2016-10, October 2015; John Gorey, "How Student Loan Debt Causes a Chain Reaction in the Housing Market," bostonglobe.com, September 30, 2016; and U.S. Bureau of Economic Analysis.

MyLab Economics Study Plan
Your Turn: Test your understanding by doing related problem 2.12 on page 429 at the end of this chapter.

_____●

The Increasing Importance of Software and the Declining Importance of Hardware
In recent years, most businesses have increased their use of information technology in a variety of ways, including expanding their presence on the Internet, especially by using social media apps such as Twitter, Snapchat, and Facebook; designing company apps; and providing employees with tablets and smartphones. As Figure 12.5 shows, though, the focus of many businesses on information technology is not reflected in spending on computers. The blue line shows that in 2017, business spending on computers had grown by less than 10 percent from its level at the beginning of the 2007–2009 recession. Total business spending on software, in contrast, has grown rapidly and in 2017, it was nearly 50 percent higher than its peak at the beginning of the recession.

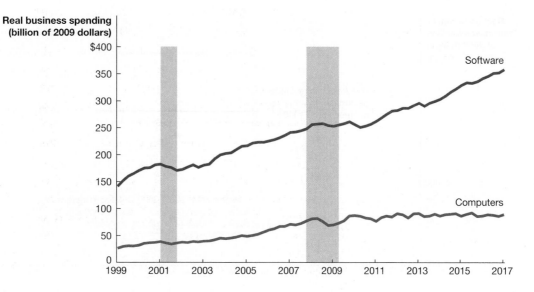

MyLab Economics Animation

Figure 12.5   **Business Spending on Computers and Software, 1999–2017**

Business spending on computers has grown only slowly since the end of the recession of 2007–2009, while business spending on software has increased rapidly. The shaded areas represent periods during which the economy was in recession.

Source: U.S. Bureau of Economic Analysis.

A key reason for this change in business investment spending is that over time, the frontier of developments in information technology has shifted away from equipment—particularly computers and servers—and toward software, such as apps used on smartphones and tablets and artificial intelligence programs that, among other uses, help guide business and investing decisions. This shift has been bad news for firms like Intel, whose sales of processors are heavily dependent on sales of computers. Intel has had only mixed success in reducing its dependence on sales to computer manufacturers by shifting toward making components for tablets, smartwatches, and smartphones, including a modem chip for Apple's iPhone.   **MyLab Economics** Concept Check

Government Purchases

Total government purchases include all spending by federal, local, and state governments for goods and services. Recall that government purchases do not include transfer payments, such as Social Security payments by the federal government or pension payments by local governments to retired police officers and firefighters, because the government does not receive a good or service in return (see Chapter 8, Section 8.1).

Figure 12.6 shows levels of real government purchases from 1979 through the first quarter of 2017. Government purchases grew steadily for most of this period, with the exception of the early 1990s and the period following the end of the recession of 2007–2009. During the early 1990s, Congress and Presidents George H. W. Bush and Bill Clinton enacted a series of spending reductions after they became concerned that spending by the federal government was growing much faster than tax receipts. As a result, real government purchases declined for three years beginning in 1992. Contributing to the slow growth of government purchases during the 1990s was the end of the Cold War between the United States and the Soviet Union in 1989. Real federal government spending on national defense declined by 24 percent from 1990 to 1998, before rising by 60 percent between 1998 and 2010 in response to the war on terrorism and the wars in Iraq and Afghanistan. As those wars wound down, defense spending declined by 21 percent between 2010 and 2017. Total federal government purchases increased in 2009 and early 2010, as President Barack Obama and Congress attempted to offset declining consumption and investment spending during the recession. Federal government purchases

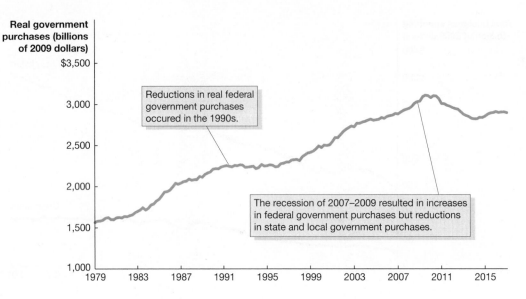

Real government purchases (billions of 2009 dollars)

Reductions in real federal government purchases occured in the 1990s.

The recession of 2007–2009 resulted in increases in federal government purchases but reductions in state and local government purchases.

MyLab Economics Real-Time Data

Figure 12.6   **Real Government Purchases, 1979–2017**

Government purchases grew steadily for most of the 1979–2010 period, with the exception of the early 1990s, when concern about the federal budget deficit caused real government purchases to fall for three years, beginning in 1992. In 2017, real government purchases remained well below their 2010 peak.

Note: The values are quarterly data, seasonally adjusted at an annual rate.

Source: U.S. Bureau of Economic Analysis.

then declined beginning in late 2010 through 2014, before slowly increasing. In 2017, the Trump administration was considering a major increase in spending on infrastructure, such as bridges, highways, and airports, which had the potential to significantly increase federal spending over several years. The recession and the slow recovery resulted in declining tax revenues to state and local governments. As a result, real state and local government purchases declined between 2009 and 2013, before increasing, along with tax revenues, beginning in 2014. **MyLab Economics** Concept Check

Net Exports

Net exports equal exports minus imports. We can calculate net exports by taking the value of spending by foreign firms and households on goods and services produced in the United States and *subtracting* the value of spending by U.S. firms and households on goods and services produced in other countries. Figure 12.7 illustrates movements in real net exports from 1979 through the first quarter of 2017. During nearly all these years, the United States imported more goods and services than it exported, so net exports were negative. Net exports usually increase when the U.S. economy is in a recession and fall when the U.S. economy is in an expansion.

The following are the three most important variables that determine the level of net exports:

1. The price level in the United States relative to the price levels in other countries
2. The growth rate of GDP in the United States relative to the growth rates of GDP in other countries
3. The exchange rate between the dollar and other currencies

The Price Level in the United States Relative to the Price Levels in Other Countries If inflation in the United States is lower than inflation in other countries, prices of U.S. products increase more slowly than the prices of products in other countries. This slower increase in the U.S. price level increases the demand for U.S. products relative to the demand for foreign products. So, U.S. exports increase and U.S. imports decrease, which increases net exports. The reverse happens during

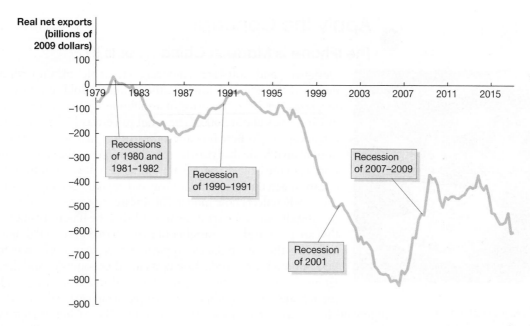

MyLab Economics Real-Time Data

Figure 12.7   **Real Net Exports, 1979–2017**

Net exports were negative in most years between 1979 and 2017. Net exports have usually increased when the U.S. economy is in a recession and decreased when the U.S. economy is in an expansion.

Note: The values are quarterly data, seasonally adjusted at an annual rate.

Source: U.S. Bureau of Economic Analysis.

periods when the inflation rate in the United States is higher than the inflation rates in other countries: U.S. exports decrease and U.S. imports increase, which decreases net exports.

The Growth Rate of GDP in the United States Relative to the Growth Rates of GDP in Other Countries As GDP increases in the United States, the incomes of households rise, leading them to increase their purchases of goods and services. Most of the additional goods and services purchased with rising incomes are produced in the United States, but some are imported. When incomes rise faster in the United States than in other countries, U.S. consumers' purchases of foreign goods and services increase faster than foreign consumers' purchases of U.S. goods and services. As a result, net exports fall. When incomes in the United States rise more slowly than incomes in other countries, net exports rise.

The Exchange Rate between the Dollar and Other Currencies As the value of the U.S. dollar rises, the foreign currency price of U.S. products sold in other countries rises, and the dollar price of foreign products sold in the United States falls. For example, suppose that the exchange rate between the Japanese yen and the U.S. dollar is 100 Japanese yen for 1 U.S. dollar, or ¥100 = $1. At this exchange rate, someone in the United States could buy ¥100 in exchange for $1, or someone in Japan could buy $1 in exchange for ¥100. Leaving aside transportation costs, at this exchange rate, a U.S. product that sells for $1 in the United States will sell for ¥100 in Japan, and a Japanese product that sells for ¥100 in Japan will sell for $1 in the United States. If the exchange rate changes to ¥150 = $1, then the value of the dollar will have risen because it takes more yen to buy $1. At the new exchange rate, the U.S. product that still sells for $1 in the United States will now sell for ¥150 in Japan, reducing the quantity demanded by Japanese consumers. The Japanese product that still sells for ¥100 in Japan will now sell for only $0.67 in the United States, increasing the quantity demanded by U.S. consumers. An increase in the value of the dollar will reduce exports and increase imports, so net exports will fall. A decrease in the value of the dollar will increase exports and reduce imports, so net exports will rise.

MyLab Economics Concept Check   MyLab Economics Study Plan

Apply the Concept

MyLab Economics Video

The iPhone Is Made in China ... or Is It?

Kin Cheung/AP Images

The iPhone is packaged in a box that says the phone is made in China, but is it?

Designers and software engineers at Apple in Cupertino, California, designed the iPhone. However, the iPhone is sold in a box labeled "Made in China." In 2017, the price of an iPhone 7 when shipped from a factory in China was about $400. (The retail price was higher because Apple adds a markup, as do Best Buy and other stores that sell the iPhone.) So if you bought an iPhone that year, the purchase entered the GDP statistics as a $400 import to the United States from China. Recently, economists have begun to question whether the standard way of keeping track of imports and exports accurately reflects how modern businesses operate.

Recall from Chapter 2, Section 2.3 that the iPhone contains components that are produced by a number of firms, based in several different countries, including the United States. Apple uses this *global supply chain* to take advantage of both lower production costs in other countries and the ability of different firms to use their engineering and manufacturing skills to produce the iPhone's many components. Apple arranges for these firms to ship the components to factories in China for final assembly. These Chinese factories are owned by Foxconn, a firm based in Taiwan. So, only final assembly of the iPhone takes place in China; no Chinese firm makes any of the iPhone's components.

How much of the price of the iPhone is accounted for by the value of final assembly? Less than 4 percent, according to a study by economists Yuqing Xing and Neal Detert of the Asian Development Bank. In fact, Xing and Detert noted that the value of the iPhone components China imports from U.S. firms is greater than the value of assembling the iPhones in Chinese factories. As measured in the GDP statistics, in 2016 the United States imported more than $30 billion worth of iPhones from China. In fact, most of that $30 billion represents the value of the iPhone's components, none of which are made in China.

The current system of accounting for imports and exports in the GDP statistics dates to a time when most products were produced entirely within one country. So a good the United States imported from France or Japan would have been produced completely in that country. As large firms have increasingly relied on global supply chains, the statistics on imports and exports have failed to keep up. As Pascal Lamy of the World Trade Organization put it, "The concept of country of origin for manufactured goods has gradually become obsolete." Or, as economists Kenneth Kraemer of the University of California, Irvine, Greg Linden of the University of California, Berkeley, and Jason Dedrick of Syracuse University observe, "trade statistics can mislead as much as inform." The U.S. Bureau of Economic Analysis and the government statistical agencies in other countries are aware of the flaws that have developed in accounting for imports and exports. But the complexity of global supply chains makes it difficult to develop more accurate measures.

Sources: David Barboza, "How China Built 'iPhone City' with Billions in Perks for Apple's Partner," *New York Times*, December 29, 2016; Izabella Kaminska, "iPhone6, the GDP Effect," ftalphaville.ft.com, September 2, 2014; Phil Izzo, "Who Gets Credit for iPhone Trade," *Wall Street Journal*, March 17, 2012; Kenneth L. Kraemer, Greg Linden, and Jason Dedrick, "Capturing Value in Global Networks: Apple's iPad and iPhone," University of California, Irvine, working paper, July 2011; and Yuqing Xing and Neal Detert, "How the iPhone Widens the United States Trade Deficit with the People's Republic of China," ADBI Working Paper Series, No. 257, May 2011.

MyLab Economics Study Plan   **Your Turn:** Test your understanding by doing related problems 2.14 and 2.15 on page 429 at the end of this chapter.

12.3 Graphing Macroeconomic Equilibrium

LEARNING OBJECTIVE: Use a 45°-line diagram to illustrate macroeconomic equilibrium.

Having examined the components of aggregate expenditure, we can now look more closely at macroeconomic equilibrium. We saw earlier in the chapter that macroeconomic equilibrium occurs when GDP is equal to aggregate expenditure. We can use a

MyLab Economics Animation
Figure 12.8

An Example of a 45°-Line Diagram

The 45° line shows all the points that are equal distances from both axes. Points such as A and B, at which the quantity produced equals the quantity sold, are on the 45° line. Points such as C, at which the quantity sold is greater than the quantity produced, lie above the line. Points such as D, at which the quantity sold is less than the quantity produced, lie below the line.

---

graph called the *45°-line diagram* to illustrate macroeconomic equilibrium. (The 45°-line diagram is also sometimes called the *Keynesian cross* because it is based on the analysis of John Maynard Keynes.) To become familiar with this diagram, consider Figure 12.8, which is a 45°-line diagram that shows the relationship between the quantity of Pepsi sold (on the vertical axis) and the quantity of Pepsi produced (on the horizontal axis).

The line on the diagram forms an angle of 45° with the horizontal axis. The line represents all the points that are equal distances from both axes. So, points such as A and B, where the number of bottles of Pepsi produced equals the number of bottles sold, are on the 45° line. Points such as C, where the quantity sold is greater than the quantity produced, lie above the line. Points such as D, where the quantity sold is less than the quantity produced, lie below the line.

Figure 12.9 is similar to Figure 12.8 except that it measures real national income, or real GDP (Y), on the horizontal axis and planned real aggregate expenditure (AE) on the vertical axis. Because macroeconomic equilibrium occurs where planned aggregate expenditure equals GDP, *we know that all points of macroeconomic equilibrium must lie along the 45° line.* For all points above the 45° line, planned aggregate expenditure will be greater than GDP. For all points below the 45° line, planned aggregate expenditure will be less than GDP.

The 45° line shows many potential points of macroeconomic equilibrium. During any particular year, only one of these points will represent the actual level of equilibrium real GDP, given the actual level of planned real expenditure. To determine this point, we need to draw a line on the graph to represent the *aggregate expenditure function*, which shows the amount of planned aggregate expenditure that will occur at every level of national income, or GDP.

Changes in GDP have a much greater effect on consumption than on planned investment, government purchases, or net exports. For simplicity, we assume that changes in GDP have no effect on planned investment, government purchases, or net exports. We also assume that the other variables that determine planned investment, government purchases, and net exports all remain constant, as do the variables other than GDP that affect consumption. For example, we assume that a firm's level of planned investment at the beginning of the year will not change during the year, even if the level of GDP changes.

Figure 12.9

The Relationship between Planned Aggregate Expenditure and GDP on a 45°-Line Diagram

Every point of macroeconomic equilibrium is on the 45° line, where planned aggregate expenditure equals GDP. At points above the line, planned aggregate expenditure is greater than GDP. At points below the line, planned aggregate expenditure is less than GDP.

Figure 12.10 shows the aggregate expenditure function on the 45°-line diagram. The lowest upward-sloping line, C, represents the consumption function, as shown in Figure 12.2, panel (b), on page 399. The quantities of planned investment, government purchases, and net exports are constant because we assumed that the variables they depend on are constant. So, the level of planned aggregate expenditure at any level of

Figure 12.10

Macroeconomic Equilibrium on the 45°-Line Diagram

Macroeconomic equilibrium occurs where the aggregate expenditure (AE) line crosses the 45° line. The lowest upward-sloping line, C, represents the consumption function. The quantities of planned investment, government purchases, and net exports are constant because we assumed that the variables they depend on are constant. So, the total of planned aggregate expenditure at any level of GDP is the amount of consumption at that level of GDP plus the sum of the constant amounts of planned investment, government purchases, and net exports. We successively add each component of spending to the consumption function line to arrive at the olive-colored line representing aggregate expenditure.

GDP is the amount of consumption spending at that level of GDP plus the sum of the constant amounts of planned investment, government purchases, and net exports. In Figure 12.10, we add each component of spending successively to the consumption function line to arrive at the line representing planned aggregate expenditure (AE). The C + I line is higher than the C line by the constant amount of planned investment; the C + I + G line is higher than the C + I line by the constant amount of government purchases; and the C + I + G + NX line is higher than the C + I + G line by the constant amount of NX. (In many years, however, NX is negative, which would cause the C + I + G + NX line to be *below* the C + I + G line.) The C + I + G + NX line shows all four components of expenditure and is the aggregate expenditure (AE) function. At the point where the AE line crosses the 45° line, planned aggregate expenditure is equal to GDP, and the economy is in macroeconomic equilibrium.

Figure 12.11 makes the relationship between planned aggregate expenditure and GDP clearer by showing only the 45° line and the AE line. The figure shows that the AE line intersects the 45° line at a level of real GDP of $10 trillion. Therefore, $10 trillion represents the equilibrium level of real GDP. To see why, consider the situation in which real GDP is only $8 trillion. By moving vertically from $8 trillion on the horizontal axis up to the AE line, we see that planned aggregate expenditure is greater than $8 trillion at this level of real GDP. Whenever total spending is greater than total production, firms' inventories will fall. The fall in inventories is equal to the vertical distance between the AE line, which shows the level of total spending, and the 45° line, which shows the $8 trillion of total production. Unplanned declines in inventories lead firms to increase their production. As real GDP increases from $8 trillion, so will total income and, therefore, consumption. The economy will move up the AE line as consumption increases. The gap between total spending and total production will fall, but as long as the AE line is above the 45° line, inventories will continue to decline, and firms will continue to expand production. When real GDP rises to $10 trillion, inventories stop falling, and the economy will be in macroeconomic equilibrium.

MyLab Economics Animation

Figure 12.11

Macroeconomic Equilibrium

Macroeconomic equilibrium occurs where the AE line crosses the 45° line, which occurs at GDP of $10 trillion. If GDP is less than $10 trillion, the corresponding point on the AE line is above the 45° line, planned aggregate expenditure is greater than total production, firms will experience an unplanned decrease in inventories, and GDP will increase. If GDP is greater than $10 trillion, the corresponding point on the AE line is below the 45° line, planned aggregate expenditure is less than total production, firms will experience an unplanned increase in inventories, and GDP will decrease.

As Figure 12.11 shows, if GDP is initially $12 trillion, planned aggregate expenditure will be less than GDP, and firms will experience an unplanned increase in inventories. Rising inventories lead firms to decrease production. As GDP falls from $12 trillion, consumption will also fall, which causes the economy to move down the AE line. The gap between planned aggregate expenditure and GDP will fall, but as long as the AE line is below the 45° line, inventories will continue to rise, and firms will continue to cut production. When GDP falls to $10 trillion, inventories will stop rising, and the economy will be in macroeconomic equilibrium.

Showing a Recession on the 45°-Line Diagram

Notice that *macroeconomic equilibrium can occur at any point on the 45° line*. Ideally, equilibrium will occur at *potential GDP*. At potential GDP, firms will be operating at their normal level of capacity, and the economy will be at the *natural rate of unemployment*. As we have seen, at the natural rate of unemployment, the economy will be at *full employment*: Everyone in the labor force who wants a job will have one, except those workers who are structurally or frictionally unemployed (see Chapter 9; Section 9.2). However, for equilibrium to occur at potential GDP, planned aggregate expenditure must be high enough. As Figure 12.12 shows, if there is insufficient total spending, equilibrium will occur at a lower level of real GDP. In this situation, many firms will be operating below their normal capacity, and the unemployment rate will be above the natural rate of unemployment.

Suppose that the level of potential GDP is $10 trillion. As Figure 12.12 shows, when GDP is $10 trillion, planned aggregate expenditure is below $10 trillion, perhaps because firms have become pessimistic about their future profitability and have reduced their investment spending. The shortfall in planned aggregate expenditure that leads to the recession can be measured as the vertical distance between the AE line and the 45° line at the level of potential GDP. The shortfall in planned aggregate expenditure is exactly equal to the unplanned increase in inventories that would occur if the economy were initially at a level of GDP of $10 trillion. The unplanned increase in

MyLab Economics Animation

Figure 12.12

Showing a Recession on the 45°-Line Diagram

When the aggregate expenditure line intersects the 45° line at a level of GDP below potential GDP, the economy is in recession. The figure shows that potential GDP is $10 trillion, but because planned aggregate expenditure is too low, the equilibrium level of GDP is only $9.8 trillion, where the AE line intersects the 45° line. As a result, some firms will be operating below their normal capacity, and unemployment will be above the natural rate of unemployment. We can measure the shortfall in planned aggregate expenditure as the vertical distance between the AE line and the 45° line at the level of potential GDP.

inventories measures the amount by which current planned aggregate expenditure is too low for the current level of production to be the equilibrium level. Put another way, if any of the four components of aggregate expenditure increased by this amount, the *AE* line would shift upward and intersect the 45° line at GDP of $10 trillion, and the economy would be in macroeconomic equilibrium at full employment.

Figure 12.12 shows that macroeconomic equilibrium will occur when real GDP is $9.8 trillion. Because real GDP is 2 percent below potential GDP of $10 trillion, many firms will be operating below their normal capacity, and the unemployment rate will be well above the natural rate of unemployment. The economy will remain at this level of real GDP until there is an increase in one or more of the components of aggregate expenditure.   **MyLab Economics** Concept Check

The Important Role of Inventories

Whenever planned aggregate expenditure is less than real GDP, some firms will experience unplanned increases in inventories. If firms do not cut back their production promptly when spending declines, they will accumulate inventories. If firms accumulate excess inventories, then even if spending quickly returns to its normal level, firms will have to sell their excess inventories before they can return to producing at normal levels. For example, more than half of the sharp 5.4 percent annual rate of decline in real GDP during the first quarter of 2009 resulted from firms cutting production as they sold off unintended accumulations of inventories.   **MyLab Economics** Concept Check

A Numerical Example of Macroeconomic Equilibrium

In forecasting real GDP, economists rely on quantitative models of the economy. We can increase our understanding of the causes of changes in real GDP by considering a simple numerical example of macroeconomic equilibrium. Although simplified, this example captures some of the key features contained in the quantitative models that economic forecasters use. Table 12.3 shows several hypothetical combinations of real GDP and planned aggregate expenditure. The first column lists real GDP. The next four columns list levels of the four components of planned aggregate expenditure that occur at the corresponding level of real GDP. We assume that planned investment, government purchases, and net exports do not change as GDP changes. Because consumption depends on GDP, it increases as GDP increases.

In the first row of the table, GDP of $8,000 billion (or $8 trillion) results in consumption of $6,200 billion. Adding consumption, planned investment, government purchases, and net exports across the row gives planned aggregate expenditure of $8,700 billion, which is shown in the sixth column. Because planned aggregate expenditure is greater than GDP, inventories will fall by $700 billion. This unplanned decline in inventories will lead firms to increase production, and GDP will increase. GDP will continue to increase until it reaches $10,000 billion. At that level of GDP, planned aggregate expenditure is also $10,000 billion, unplanned changes in inventories are zero, and the economy is in macroeconomic equilibrium.

Table 12.3 Macroeconomic Equilibrium

Real GDP (Y)	Consumption (C)	Planned Investment (I)	Government Purchases (G)	Net Exports (NX)	Planned Aggregate Expenditure (AE)	Unplanned Change in Inventories	Real GDP Will ...
$8,000	$6,200	$1,500	$1,500	−$500	$8,700	−$700	increase.
9,000	6,850	1,500	1,500	−500	9,350	−350	increase.
10,000	7,500	1,500	1,500	−500	10,000	0	be in equilibrium.
11,000	8,150	1,500	1,500	−500	10,650	+350	decrease.
12,000	8,800	1,500	1,500	−500	11,300	+700	decrease.

Note: The values are in billions of 2009 dollars.

Don't Let This Happen to You

Don't Confuse Aggregate Expenditure with Consumption Spending

Macroeconomic equilibrium occurs where planned aggregate expenditure equals GDP. But remember that planned aggregate expenditure equals the sum of consumption spending, planned investment spending, government purchases, and net exports, *not* consumption spending alone. If GDP were equal to consumption, the economy would not be in equilibrium. Planned investment plus government purchases plus net exports will always be a positive number. Therefore, if consumption were equal to GDP, aggregate expenditure would have to be greater than GDP. In that case, inventories would be *decreasing*, and GDP would be *increasing*; GDP would not be in equilibrium.

Test your understanding of macroeconomic equilibrium with this problem:

Question: Do you agree with the following argument?

This chapter says macroeconomic equilibrium occurs where planned aggregate expenditure equals GDP. GDP is equal to national income. So, at equilibrium, planned aggregate expenditure must equal national income. But we know that consumers do not spend all

of their income: They save at least some and use some to pay taxes. Therefore, aggregate expenditure will never equal national income, and the basic macroeconomic story is incorrect.

Answer: Remember that national income equals GDP (disregarding depreciation, as we have done throughout this chapter). So, it is correct to say that in macroeconomic equilibrium, planned aggregate expenditure must equal national income. But the last sentence of the argument is incorrect because it assumes that aggregate expenditure is the same as consumption spending. Because of saving and taxes, consumption spending is always much less than national income, but in equilibrium, the sum of consumption spending, planned investment spending, government purchases, and net exports does, in fact, equal GDP and national income. So, the argument is incorrect because it confuses consumption spending with aggregate expenditure.

MyLab Economics Study Plan

Your Turn: Test your understanding by doing related problem 3.11 on page 430 at the end of this chapter.

In the last row, GDP of $12,000 billion results in consumption of $8,800 billion and planned aggregate expenditure of $11,300 billion. Because planned aggregate expenditure is less than GDP, inventories will increase by $700 billion. This unplanned increase in inventories will lead firms to decrease production, and GDP will decrease. GDP will continue to decrease until it reaches $10,000 billion, unplanned changes in inventories are zero, and the economy is in macroeconomic equilibrium.

Only when real GDP equals $10,000 billion will the economy be in macroeconomic equilibrium. At other levels of real GDP, planned aggregate expenditure will be higher or lower than GDP, and the economy will be expanding or contracting.

MyLab Economics Study Plan

MyLab Economics Concept Check

Solved Problem 12.3

MyLab Economics Interactive Animation

Determining Macroeconomic Equilibrium

Fill in the missing values in the following table and determine the equilibrium level of real GDP.

Real GDP (Y)	Consumption (C)	Planned Investment (I)	Government Purchases (G)	Net Exports (NX)	Planned Aggregate Expenditure (AE)	Unplanned Change in Inventories
$8,000	$6,200	$1,675	$1,675	−$500		
9,000	6,850	1,675	1,675	−500		
10,000	7,500	1,675	1,675	−500		
11,000	8,150	1,675	1,675	−500		
12,000	8,800	1,675	1,675	−500		

Solving the Problem

Step 1: **Review the chapter material.** This problem is about determining macro-economic equilibrium, so you may want to review the section "A Numerical Example of Macroeconomic Equilibrium," which begins on page 415.

Step 2: **Fill in the missing values in the table.** We can calculate the missing values in the last two columns by using two equations:

$$\text{Planned aggregate expenditure } (AE) = \text{Consumption } (C)$$
$$+ \text{ Planned investment } (I) + \text{ Government purchases } (G)$$
$$+ \text{ Net exports } (NX)$$

and:

$$\text{Unplanned change in inventories } = \text{Real GDP } (Y)$$
$$- \text{ Planned aggregate expenditure } (AE).$$

For example, to fill in the first row, we have AE = \$6,200 billion + \$1,675 billion + \$1,675 billion + (−\$500 billion) = \$9,050 billion, and unplanned change in inventories = \$8,000 billion − \$9,050 billion = −\$1,050 billion.

Real GDP (Y)	Consumption (C)	Planned Investment (I)	Government Purchases (G)	Net Exports (NX)	Planned Aggregate Expenditure (AE)	Unplanned Change in Inventories
\$8,000	\$6,200	\$1,675	\$1,675	−\$500	\$9,050	−1,050
9,000	6,850	1,675	1,675	−500	9,700	−700
10,000	7,500	1,675	1,675	−500	10,350	−350
11,000	8,150	1,675	1,675	−500	11,000	0
12,000	8,800	1,675	1,675	−500	11,650	350

Step 3: **Determine the equilibrium level of real GDP.** Once you fill in the table, you should see that equilibrium real GDP must be \$11,000 billion because only at that level is real GDP equal to planned aggregate expenditure.

Your Turn: For more practice, do related problem 3.12 on page 430 at the end of this chapter.

MyLab Economics Study Plan

12.4   The Multiplier Effect

LEARNING OBJECTIVE: Describe the multiplier effect and use the multiplier formula to calculate changes in equilibrium GDP.

So far, we have seen that aggregate expenditure determines real GDP in the short run, and we have seen how the economy adjusts if it is not in equilibrium. We have also seen that whenever aggregate expenditure changes, there will be a new level of equilibrium real GDP. In this section, we will look more closely at the effects of a change in aggregate expenditure on equilibrium real GDP. We begin the discussion with Figure 12.13, which illustrates the effect of an increase in planned investment spending. We assume that the economy starts in equilibrium at point *A*, at which real GDP is \$9.6 trillion. Firms then become more optimistic about the future profitability of investment and increase spending on factories, machinery, and equipment by \$100 billion. This increase in investment spending shifts the *AE* line up by \$100 billion, from AE_1 to AE_2. The new equilibrium occurs at point *B*, at which real GDP is \$10.0 trillion, which equals potential real GDP.

Notice that the initial \$100 billion increase in planned investment spending results in a \$400 billion increase in equilibrium real GDP. The increase in planned

MyLab Economics Animation

Figure 12.13

The Multiplier Effect

The economy begins at point *A*, at which equilibrium real GDP is $9.6 trillion. A $100 billion increase in planned investment shifts up the aggregate expenditure function from *AE*₁ to *AE*₂. The new equilibrium is at point *B*, where real GDP is $10.0 trillion, which is potential real GDP. Because of the multiplier effect, a $100 billion increase in investment results in a $400 billion increase in equilibrium real GDP.

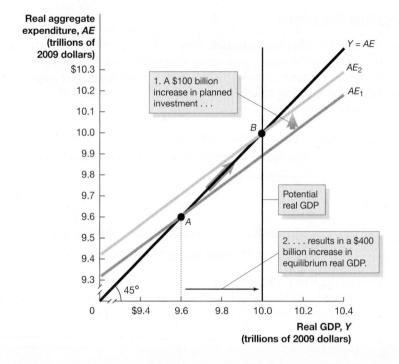

Autonomous expenditure An expenditure that does not depend on the level of GDP.

Multiplier The change in equilibrium real GDP divided by the change in autonomous expenditure.

Multiplier effect The process by which a change in autonomous expenditure leads to a larger change in real GDP.

investment spending has had a *multiplied effect* on equilibrium real GDP. It is not only investment spending that will have this multiplied effect; any increase in *autonomous expenditure* will shift up the aggregate expenditure function and lead to a multiplied increase in equilibrium GDP. **Autonomous expenditure** does not depend on the level of GDP. In the aggregate expenditure model we have been using, planned investment spending, government spending, and net exports are all autonomous expenditures. Consumption has both an autonomous component, which does not depend on the level of GDP, and a nonautonomous—or *induced*—component, which does depend on the level of GDP. For example, if households decide to spend more of their incomes—and save less—at every level of income, there will be an autonomous increase in consumption spending, and the aggregate expenditure function will shift up. If, however, real GDP increases and households increase their consumption spending, as indicated by the consumption function, there will be a movement up along the aggregate expenditure function, and the increase in consumption spending will be nonautonomous.

The ratio of the increase in equilibrium real GDP to the increase in autonomous expenditure is called the **multiplier**. The series of induced increases in consumption spending that results from an initial increase in autonomous expenditure is called the **multiplier effect**. The multiplier effect occurs because an initial increase in autonomous expenditure sets off a series of increases in real GDP.

We can look more closely at the multiplier effect. Suppose the whole $100 billion increase in investment spending shown in Figure 12.13 consists of firms building additional factories and office buildings. Initially, this additional spending will cause the construction of factories and office buildings to increase by $100 billion, so GDP will also increase by $100 billion. Remember that increases in production result in equal increases in national income. So, this increase in real GDP of $100 billion is also an increase in national income of $100 billion. In this example, the income is received as wages and salaries by the employees of the construction firms, as profit by the owners of the firms, and so on. After receiving this additional income, these workers, managers, and owners will increase their consumption of cars, appliances, furniture, and many other products. If the marginal propensity to consume (*MPC*) is 0.75, we know the increase in consumption spending will be $75 billion. This additional $75 billion in spending will cause the firms making the cars, appliances, and other products to

Table 12.4

The Multiplier Effect in Action

	Additional Autonomous Expenditure (investment)	Additional Induced Expenditure (consumption)	Total Additional Expenditure = Total Additional GDP
Round 1	$100 billion	$0	$100 billion
Round 2	0	75 billion	175 billion
Round 3	0	56 billion	231 billion
Round 4	0	42 billion	273 billion
Round 5	0	32 billion	305 billion
.	.	.	.
.	.	.	.
.	.	.	.
Round 10	0	8 billion	377 billion
.	.	.	.
.	.	.	.
.	.	.	.
Round 15	0	2 billion	395 billion
.	.	.	.
.	.	.	.
.	.	.	.
Round 19	0	1 billion	398 billion
.	.	.	.
.	.	.	.
.	.	.	.
Round n	0	0	400 billion

increase production by $75 billion, so GDP will rise by $75 billion. This increase in GDP means national income has also increased by another $75 billion. This increased income will be received by the owners and employees of the firms producing the cars, appliances, and other products. These workers, managers, and owners in turn will increase their consumption spending, and the process of increasing production, income, and consumption will continue.

Eventually, the total increase in consumption will be $300 billion. (We will soon show how we determined this value.) The $300 billion increase in consumption combined with the initial $100 billion increase in investment spending will result in a total change in equilibrium GDP of $400 billion. Table 12.4 summarizes how changes in GDP and spending caused by the initial $100 billion increase in investment will result in equilibrium GDP rising by $400 billion. We can think of the multiplier effect occurring in rounds of spending. In round 1, there is an increase of $100 billion in autonomous expenditure—the $100 billion in planned investment spending in our example—which causes GDP to rise by $100 billion. In round 2, induced expenditure rises by $75 billion (which equals the $100 billion increase in real GDP in round 1 multiplied by the *MPC*). The $75 billion in induced expenditure in round 2 causes a $75 billion increase in real GDP, which leads to a $56 billion increase in induced expenditure in round 3, and so on. The final column adds up the total increases in expenditure, which equal the total increase in GDP. In each round, the additional induced expenditure becomes smaller because the *MPC* is less than 1. By round 10, additional induced expenditure is only $8 billion, and the total increase in GDP from the beginning of the process is $377 billion. By round 19, the process is almost complete: Additional induced expenditure is only about $1 billion, and the total increase in GDP is $398 billion. Eventually, the process will be finished, although we cannot say precisely how many spending rounds it will take, so we simply label the last round n rather than give it a specific number.

We can calculate the value of the multiplier in our example by dividing the increase in equilibrium real GDP by the increase in autonomous expenditure:

$$\frac{\Delta Y}{\Delta I} = \frac{\text{Change in real GDP}}{\text{Change in investment spending}} = \frac{\$400 \text{ billion}}{\$100 \text{ billion}} = 4.$$

With a multiplier of 4, each increase in autonomous expenditure of $1 will result in an increase in equilibrium GDP of $4.

Apply the Concept

MyLab Economics Video

The Multiplier in Reverse: The Great Depression of the 1930s

An increase in autonomous expenditure causes an increase in equilibrium real GDP, but the reverse is also true: A decrease in autonomous expenditure causes a decrease in real GDP. Many Americans became aware of this fact in the 1930s, when reductions in autonomous expenditure were magnified by the multiplier into the largest decline in real GDP in U.S. history.

In August 1929, the economy reached a business cycle peak, and a downturn in production began. In October, the stock market crashed, destroying billions of dollars of wealth and increasing pessimism among households and firms. Both consumption spending and planned investment spending declined. The passage by the U.S. Congress of the Smoot-Hawley Tariff Act in June 1930 helped set off a trade war that reduced exports. Waves of bank failures that began in the fall of 1930 limited the ability of households and firms to finance consumption and investment. As aggregate expenditure declined, many firms experienced declining sales and began to lay off workers. Falling levels of production and income induced further declines in consumption spending, which led to further cutbacks in production and employment, leading to further declines in income, and so on, in a downward spiral. The following table shows the severity of the economic downturn by contrasting the business cycle peak of 1929 with the business cycle trough of 1933.

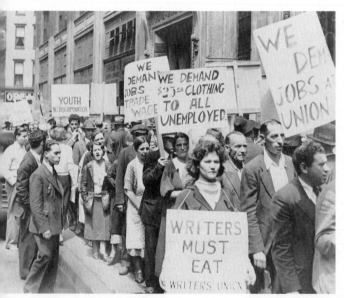

Everett Collection/SuperStock

The multiplier effect contributed to the very high levels of unemployment during the Great Depression.

Year	Consumption	Investment	Exports	Real GDP	Unemployment Rate
1929	$781 billion	$124 billion	$41 billion	$1,057 billion	2.9%
1933	$638 billion	$27 billion	$22 billion	$778 billion	20.9%

Note: The values are in 2009 dollars.

Sources: U.S. Bureau of Economic Analysis; and, for the unemployment rate, David R. Weir, "A Century of U.S. Unemployment, 1890–1990," in Roger L. Ransom, Richard Sutch, and Susan B. Carter, eds., *Research in Economic History*, Vol. 14, San Diego, CA: JAI Press, 1992, Table D3, pp. 341–343.

We can use a 45°-line diagram to illustrate the multiplier effect working in reverse during these years. The economy was at potential real GDP in 1929, before the declines in aggregate expenditure began. Declining consumption, planned investment, and net exports shifted the aggregate expenditure function down from AE_{1929} to AE_{1933}, reducing equilibrium real GDP from $1,057 billion in 1929 to $778 billion in 1933. The depth and length of this economic downturn led to its being labeled the Great Depression.

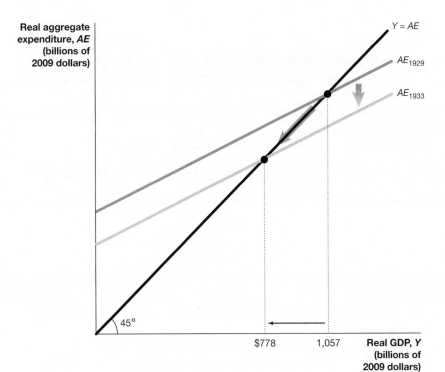

The severity of the Great Depression forced thousands of firms to declare bankruptcy. Even firms that survived experienced sharp declines in sales. By 1933, production at U.S. Steel, at the time the leading steel-producing company in the world, had declined 90 percent, and production at General Motors had declined more than 75 percent. High rates of unemployment forced many families into poverty and a daily struggle for survival. Recovery from the business cycle trough in 1933 was slow. Real GDP did not regain its 1929 level until 1936, and a growing labor force meant that the unemployment rate did not return to its 1929 level until 1942, after the United States entered World War II.

Your Turn: Test your understanding by doing related problem 4.6 on page 431 at the end of this chapter.

MyLab Economics Study Plan

A Formula for the Multiplier

Table 12.4 on page 419 shows that during the multiplier process, each round of increases in consumption is smaller than in the previous round, so eventually, the increases will come to an end, and we will have a new macroeconomic equilibrium. But how do we know that when we add all the increases in GDP, the total will be $400 billion? We can verify this result by first writing out the total change in equilibrium GDP:

The total change in equilibrium real GDP equals the initial increase in planned investment spending $= \$100$ billion

Plus the first induced increase in consumption $= MPC \times \$100$ billion

Plus the second induced increase in consumption $= MPC \times (MPC \times \$100$ billion$)$
$$= MPC^2 \times \$100 \text{ billion}$$

Plus the third induced increase in consumption $= MPC \times (MPC^2 \times \$100$ billion$)$
$$= MPC^3 \times \$100 \text{ billion}$$

Plus the fourth induced increase in consumption $= MPC \times (MPC^3 \times \$100$ billion$)$
$$= MPC^4 \times \$100 \text{ billion}$$

and so on ...

Or:

$$\text{Total change in GDP} = \$100 \text{ billion} + (MPC \times \$100 \text{ billion}) + (MPC^2 \\ \times \$100 \text{ billion}) + (MPC^3 \times \$100 \text{ billion}) + (MPC^4 \times \$100 \text{ billion}) + \dots$$

where the ellipsis (...) indicates that the expression contains an infinite number of similar terms.

If we factor out the $100 billion from each expression, we have:

$$\text{Total change in GDP} = \$100 \text{ billion} \times (1 + MPC + MPC^2 + MPC^3 + MPC^4 + \dots)$$

Mathematicians have shown that an expression like the one in the parentheses sums to:

$$\frac{1}{1 - MPC}.$$

In this case, the MPC is equal to 0.75. So, we can now calculate that the change in equilibrium GDP = $100 billion $\times$ [1/(1 − 0.75)] = $100 billion $\times$ 4 = $400 billion, as shown in Table 12.4. We have also derived a general formula for the multiplier:

$$\text{Multiplier} = \frac{\text{Change in equilibrium real GDP}}{\text{Change in autonomous expenditure}} = \frac{1}{1 - MPC}.$$

In this case, the multiplier is 1/(1 − 0.75), or 4, which means that for each additional $1 of autonomous spending, equilibrium GDP will increase by $4. A $100 billion increase in planned investment spending results in a $400 billion increase in equilibrium GDP. Notice that the value of the multiplier depends on the value of the MPC. In particular, the larger the value of the MPC, the larger the value of the multiplier. For example, if the MPC were 0.9 instead of 0.75, the value of the multiplier would increase from 4 to 1/(1 − 0.9) = 10. **MyLab Economics** Concept Check

Summarizing the Multiplier Effect

You should note four key points about the multiplier effect:

1. The multiplier effect occurs both when autonomous expenditure increases and when it decreases. For example, with an MPC of 0.75, a *decrease* in planned investment of $100 billion will lead to a *decrease* in equilibrium income of $400 billion.

2. The multiplier effect makes the economy more sensitive to changes in autonomous expenditure than it would otherwise be. Between the fourth quarter of 2005 and the second quarter of 2009, spending on residential construction declined by 57 percent. This decline in investment set off a series of declines in production, income, and spending so that firms such as automobile dealerships and clothing stores, which are far removed from the housing industry, also experienced declines in sales. Because of the multiplier effect, a decline in spending and production in one sector of the economy can lead to declines in spending and production in many other sectors of the economy.

3. The larger the MPC, the larger the value of the multiplier. With an MPC of 0.75, the multiplier is 4, but with an MPC of 0.50, the multiplier is only 2. This direct relationship between the value of the MPC and the value of the multiplier holds true because the larger the MPC, the larger the change in consumption that takes place after each change in income during the multiplier process.

4. The formula for the multiplier, 1/(1 − MPC), is oversimplified because it ignores some real-world complications, such as the effect that increases in GDP have on imports, inflation, interest rates, and individual income taxes. These effects combine to cause the simple formula to overstate the true value of the multiplier. Beginning in Chapter 13, we will start to take into account some of these real-world complications. **MyLab Economics** Concept Check

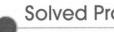

Solved Problem 12.4

Using the Multiplier Formula

Use the information in the table below to answer the following questions.

Real GDP (Y)	Consumption (C)	Planned Investment (I)	Government Purchases (G)	Net Exports (NX)
$8,000	$6,900	$1,000	$1,000	−$500
9,000	7,700	1,000	1,000	−500
10,000	8,500	1,000	1,000	−500
11,000	9,300	1,000	1,000	−500
12,000	10,100	1,000	1,000	−500

Note: The values are in billions of 2009 dollars.

a. What is the equilibrium level of real GDP?
b. What is the *MPC*?
c. Suppose government purchases increase by $200 billion. What will be the new equilibrium level of real GDP? Use the multiplier formula to determine your answer.

Solving the Problem

Step 1: **Review the chapter material.** This problem is about the multiplier process, so you may want to review the section "The Multiplier Effect," which begins on page 417.

Step 2: **Answer part (a) by determining equilibrium real GDP.** Just as in Solved Problem 12.2 on page 403, we can find macroeconomic equilibrium by calculating the level of planned aggregate expenditure for each level of real GDP:

Real GDP (Y)	Consumption (C)	Planned Investment (I)	Government Purchases (G)	Net Exports (NX)	Planned Aggregate Expenditure (AE)
$8,000	$6,900	$1,000	$1,000	−$500	$8,400
9,000	7,700	1,000	1,000	−500	9,200
10,000	8,500	1,000	1,000	−500	10,000
11,000	9,300	1,000	1,000	−500	10,800
12,000	10,100	1,000	1,000	−500	11,600

We can see that macroeconomic equilibrium will occur when real GDP equals $10,000 billion.

Step 3: **Answer part (b) by calculating the MPC.**

$$MPC = \frac{\Delta C}{\Delta Y}.$$

In this case:

$$MPC = \frac{\$800 \text{ billion}}{\$1,000 \text{ billion}} = 0.8.$$

Step 4: **Answer part (c) by using the multiplier formula to calculate the new equilibrium level of real GDP.** We could find the new level of equilibrium real GDP by constructing a new table with government purchases increased from $1,000 to $1,200. But the multiplier allows us to calculate the answer directly. In this case:

$$\text{Multiplier} = \frac{1}{1 - MPC} = \frac{1}{1 - 0.8} = 5.$$

So:

Change in equilibrium real GDP = Change in autonomous expenditure × 5.

Or:

Change in equilibrium real GDP = $200 billion × 5 = $1,000 billion.

Therefore:

New level of equilibrium GDP = $10,000 billion + $1,000 billion
= $11,000 billion.

MyLab Economics Study Plan   **Your Turn:** For more practice, do related problem 4.7 on page 431 at the end of this chapter.

The Paradox of Thrift

We have seen that an increase in saving can increase the rate of economic growth in the long run by providing funds for investment (see Chapters 10 and 11). But in the short run, if households save more of their income and spend less of it, aggregate expenditure and real GDP will decline. In discussing the aggregate expenditure model, John Maynard Keynes argued that if many households decide at the same time to increase their saving and reduce their spending, they may make themselves worse off by causing aggregate expenditure to fall, thereby pushing the economy into a recession. The lower incomes in the recession might mean that total saving does not increase, despite the attempts by many individuals to increase their own saving. Keynes called this outcome the *paradox of thrift* because what appears to be something favorable to the long-run performance of the economy might be counterproductive in the short run.

Households saved very little of their income in the mid-2000s but increased their saving markedly in late 2008 and 2009. The personal saving rate is saving by households as a percentage of disposable personal income. By mid-2009, the personal saving rate had increased to 6 percent. Some economists argued that this increase in saving contributed to the recession and weak recovery by reducing consumption spending. Other economists are skeptical of the reasoning behind the paradox of thrift. An increase in saving, by increasing the supply of loanable funds, should lower the real interest rate and increase the level of investment spending (see Chapter 10, Section 10.2). This increase in investment spending might offset some or all of the decline in consumption spending attributable to increased saving. Economists continue to debate the short-run effects of an increase in saving.

MyLab Economics Study Plan   **MyLab Economics** Concept Check

12.5 The Aggregate Demand Curve

LEARNING OBJECTIVE: Understand the relationship between the aggregate demand curve and aggregate expenditure.

When demand for a product increases, firms usually respond by increasing production, but they are also likely to increase prices. Similarly, when demand falls, production falls, but prices may also fall. We would expect, then, that an increase or a decrease in aggregate expenditure would affect not just real GDP but also the *price level*. Will a change in the price level, in turn, affect the components of aggregate expenditure? In fact, increases in the price level cause aggregate expenditure to fall, and decreases in the price level cause aggregate expenditure to rise. There are three main reasons for this inverse relationship between changes in the price level and changes in aggregate expenditure. We discussed the first two reasons in Section 12.2 when considering the factors that determine consumption and net exports:

1. A rising price level decreases consumption by decreasing the real value of household wealth; a falling price level has the reverse effect.

2. If the price level in the United States rises relative to the price levels in other countries, U.S. exports will become relatively more expensive, and foreign imports will become relatively less expensive, causing net exports to fall. A falling price level in the United States has the reverse effect.

3. When prices rise, firms and households need more money to finance buying and selling. If the central bank (the Federal Reserve in the United States) does not increase the money supply, the result will be an increase in the interest rate. In Chapter 15, Section 15.2, we will analyze in more detail why the interest rate increases. As we discussed in Section 12.2, at a higher interest rate, investment spending falls as firms decrease their borrowing to build new factories or to install new machinery and equipment and households decrease their borrowing to buy new houses. A falling price level has the reverse effect: Other things being equal, interest rates will fall, and investment spending will rise.

We can now incorporate the effect of a change in the price level into the basic aggregate expenditure model, in which equilibrium real GDP is determined by the intersection of the aggregate expenditure (AE) line and the 45° line. Remember that we measure the price level as an index number with a value of 100 in the base year. If the price level rises from, say, 100 to 103, consumption, planned investment, and net exports will all fall, causing the AE line to shift down in the 45°-line diagram. The AE line shifts down because with higher prices, less spending will occur in the economy at every level of GDP. Panel (a) of Figure 12.14 shows that the downward shift of the AE line results in a lower level of equilibrium real GDP.

If the price level falls from, say, 100 to 97, then investment, consumption, and net exports will all rise. As panel (b) of Figure 12.14 shows, the AE line will shift up, which will cause equilibrium real GDP to increase.

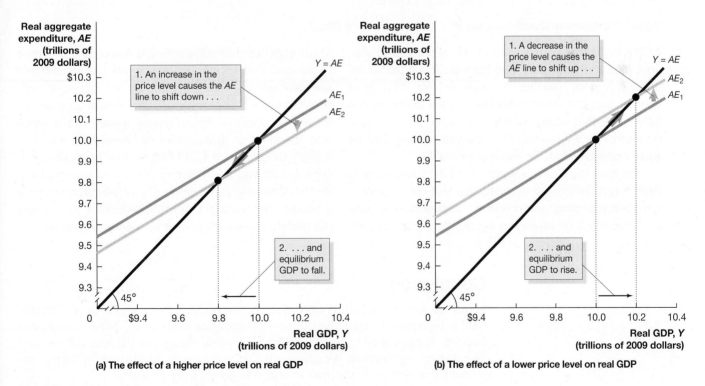

(a) The effect of a higher price level on real GDP

(b) The effect of a lower price level on real GDP

MyLab Economics Animation

Figure 12.14   **The Effect of a Change in the Price Level on Real GDP**

In panel (a), an increase in the price level results in declining consumption, planned investment, and net exports and causes the aggregate expenditure line to shift down from AE_1 to AE_2. As a result, equilibrium real GDP declines from $10.0 trillion to $9.8 trillion.

In panel (b), a decrease in the price level results in rising consumption, planned investment, and net exports and causes the aggregate expenditure line to shift up from AE_1 to AE_2. As a result, equilibrium real GDP increases from $10.0 trillion to $10.2 trillion.

Figure 12.15

The Aggregate Demand Curve

The aggregate demand (*AD*) curve shows the relationship between the price level and the level of planned aggregate expenditure in the economy. When the price level is 97, real GDP is $10.2 trillion. An increase in the price level to 100 causes consumption, investment, and net exports to fall, which reduces real GDP to $10.0 trillion.

Price Level	Equilibrium Real GDP
97	$10.2 trillion
100	10.0 trillion
103	9.8 trillion

Aggregate demand (AD) curve A curve that shows the relationship between the price level and the level of planned aggregate expenditure in the economy, holding constant all other factors that affect aggregate expenditure.

Figure 12.15 summarizes the effect of changes in the price level on real GDP. The table in this figure shows the combinations of price level and real GDP from Figure 12.14. The graph plots the numbers from the table. In the graph, the price level is measured on the vertical axis, and real GDP is measured on the horizontal axis. The relationship shown in Figure 12.15 between the price level and the level of planned aggregate expenditure is known as the **aggregate demand (AD) curve**.

Continued from page 393

Economics in Your Life & Career

When Consumer Confidence Falls, Is Your Job at Risk?

At the beginning of this chapter, we asked you to suppose that you work part time for a company that manufacturers door handles for automobiles. You have learned that consumer confidence in the economy has fallen and that many households expect their future income to be well below their current income. Should you be concerned about losing your job?

We have seen in this chapter that if consumers expect their future income to decline, they will cut their consumption spending, and consumption spending is more than two-thirds of aggregate expenditure. If the decline in consumer confidence is correctly forecasting a decline in consumption spending, then aggregate expenditure and GDP will also likely decline. In deciding how likely your company is to lay you off, you should consider the following factors: If the economy moves into a recession, spending on automobiles by households and firms is likely to fall, which could reduce your firm's sales and possibly cost you a job. Before you panic, though, keep in mind that surveys of consumer confidence do not have a good track record in predicting recessions, so you may not have to move back in with your parents after all.

Conclusion

In this chapter, we examined a key macroeconomic idea: In the short run, the level of GDP is determined mainly by the level of aggregate expenditure. When economists forecast changes in GDP, they do so by forecasting changes in the four components of aggregate expenditure. We constructed an aggregate demand curve by taking into account how changes in the price level affect aggregate expenditure.

But our story is incomplete. In Chapter 13, we will analyze the *aggregate supply curve*. Then we will use the aggregate demand curve and the aggregate supply curve to show how equilibrium real GDP and the equilibrium price level are simultaneously determined.

We also need to discuss the roles that the financial system and government policy play in determining real GDP and the price level in the short run. We will cover these important topics in the following chapters.

Visit **MyLab Economics** for a news article and analysis related to the concepts in this chapter.

CHAPTER SUMMARY AND PROBLEMS

Key Terms

Aggregate demand (*AD*) curve, p. 426

Aggregate expenditure (*AE*), p. 394

Aggregate expenditure model, p. 394

Autonomous expenditure, p. 418

Cash flow, p. 405

Consumption function, p. 400

Inventories, p. 395

Marginal propensity to consume (*MPC*), p. 400

Marginal propensity to save (*MPS*), p. 402

Multiplier, p. 418

Multiplier effect, p. 418

12.1 ## The Aggregate Expenditure Model, pages 394–397

LEARNING OBJECTIVE: Explain how macroeconomic equilibrium is determined in the aggregate expenditure model.

MyLab Economics Visit www.pearson.com/mylab/economics to complete these exercises online and get instant feedback.

Summary

Aggregate expenditure (AE) is the total amount of spending in the economy. The **aggregate expenditure model** focuses on the relationship between total spending and real GDP in the short run, assuming that the price level is constant. In any particular year, the level of GDP is determined by the level of total spending, or aggregate expenditure, in the economy. The four components of aggregate expenditure are consumption (*C*), planned investment (*I*), government purchases (*G*), and net exports (*NX*). When aggregate expenditure is greater than GDP, there is an unplanned decrease in **inventories**, which are goods that have been produced but not yet sold, and GDP and total employment will increase. When aggregate expenditure is less than GDP, there is an unplanned increase in inventories, and GDP and total employment will decline. When aggregate expenditure is equal to GDP, firms will sell what they expected to sell, production and employment will be unchanged, and the economy will be in macroeconomic equilibrium.

Review Questions

1.1 What is the key idea in the aggregate expenditure macroeconomic model?

1.2 What are inventories? What usually happens to inventories at the beginning of a recession? At the beginning of an expansion?

1.3 Which of the following does the aggregate expenditure model seek to explain: long-run economic growth, the business cycle, inflation, or cyclical unemployment?

Problems and Applications

1.4 Into which category of aggregate expenditure would each of the following transactions fall?
  a. The Jones family buys a new car.
  b. The San Diego Unified School District buys 12 new school buses.
  c. The Jones family buys a newly constructed house from the Garcia Construction Co.
  d. Joe Jones orders a Burberry coat from an online site in the United Kingdom.
  e. Prudential insurance company purchases 250 new iPads from Apple.

1.5 Assume that Intel sells $1 billion of computer chips to Dell, Inc., for use in Dell's personal computers. How does this transaction affect aggregate expenditure?

1.6 In reporting on real GDP growth in the second quarter of 2016, an article on Reuters news noted that "U.S. economic growth unexpectedly remained tepid in the second quarter as inventories fell" and also that the "inventory drawdown was almost across the board."
  a. If companies are drawing down inventories, is aggregate expenditure likely to have been larger or smaller than GDP?
  b. The chief economist at UniCredit Research was quoted in the article as stating, "The U.S. economy just went through a meaningful inventory correction cycle." What would an "inventory correction cycle" be, and why would companies need to go through one?
  c. The article stated, "Though the inventory drawdown weighed on GDP growth, that is likely to provide a boost to output in the coming quarters." Why would an inventory drawdown boost output in the coming quarters?

Source: Lucia Matikani, "Inventory Reduction Curbs U.S. Economic Growth; Rebound Expected," reuters.com, July 20, 2016.

1.7 In the first quarter of 2017, business inventories in the United States increased by $4 billion. Can we tell from this information whether aggregate expenditure was higher or lower than GDP during the first quarter of 2017? If not, what other information do we need?

Source: U.S. Bureau of Economic Analysis.

1.8 An article in the *Wall Street Journal* stated that at the beginning of May 2017, inventories of pickup trucks were "touching 97 days' supply as of the beginning of May, or a 12% increase in actual vehicles on dealer lots compared with the prior year. ... That number is far above the industry norm for inventory." Why might U.S. automakers find that their inventories of pickup trucks are unexpectedly rising? How are these automakers likely to react to the increase in inventories?

Source: John D. Stoll and Adrienne Roberts, "As GM Adjusts to Changing Auto Market, Its Sales Slide Behind Ford's," *Wall Street Journal*, June 1, 2017.

1.9 According to an article in the *Wall Street Journal*, in late 2014, the Japanese economy experienced a large increase in business inventories. The article noted,

"The large buildup of inventories is a reflection that the ... drop in demand was bigger than expected." Does it matter that Japanese firms didn't expect the drop in demand? Won't a decline in demand always lead to an increase in firms' holdings of inventories? Briefly explain.

Source: Eleanor Warnock, "Rising Inventories Hamper Japan Recovery," *Wall Street Journal*, September 30, 2014.

12.2 Determining the Level of Aggregate Expenditure in the Economy, pages 397–410

LEARNING OBJECTIVE: Discuss the determinants of the four components of aggregate expenditure and define marginal propensity to consume and marginal propensity to save.

MyLab Economics Visit **www.pearson.com/mylab/economics** to complete these exercises online and get instant feedback.

Summary

The five determinants of consumption are current disposable income, household wealth, expected future income, the price level, and the interest rate. The **consumption function** is the relationship between consumption and disposable income. The **marginal propensity to consume (MPC)** is the change in consumption divided by the change in disposable income. The **marginal propensity to save (MPS)** is the change in saving divided by the change in disposable income. The determinants of planned investment are expectations of future profitability, the real interest rate, taxes, and **cash flow**, which is the difference between the cash revenues received by a firm and the cash spending by the firm. Government purchases include spending by the federal government and by local and state governments for goods and services. Government purchases do not include *transfer payments*, such as Social Security payments by the federal government or pension payments by local governments to retired police officers and firefighters. The three determinants of net exports are changes in the price level in the United States relative to changes in the price levels in other countries, the growth rate of GDP in the United States relative to the growth rates of GDP in other countries, and the exchange rate between the dollar and other currencies.

Review Questions

2.1 In the aggregate expenditure model, why is it important to know the factors that determine consumption spending, investment spending, government purchases, and net exports?

2.2 What are the five main determinants of consumption spending? Which of these is the most important? How would a rise in stock prices or housing prices affect consumption spending?

2.3 Compare what happened to real investment between 1979 and the first quarter of 2017 with what happened to real consumption during that period.

2.4 What are the four main determinants of investment? How would a change in interest rates affect investment?

2.5 What are the three main determinants of net exports? How would an increase in the growth rate of GDP in the BRIC nations (Brazil, Russia, India, and China) affect U.S. net exports?

Problems and Applications

2.6 An article in the *Wall Street Journal* on the housing market stated, "Steady job growth, rising wages and low interest rates have helped prop up housing demand." Why do low interest rates increase the demand for housing? In which component of aggregate expenditure does the Bureau of Economic Analysis include purchases of new houses?

Source: Steven Russolillo, "Why the Housing Market Is Getting Stronger," *Wall Street Journal*, May 22, 2016.

2.7 **(Related to the Chapter Opener on page 392)** Suppose that Intel is forecasting demand for its computer chips during the next year. How will the forecast be affected by each of the following?
   a. A survey shows a sharp rise in consumer confidence that income growth will be increasing.
   b. Real interest rates are expected to increase.
   c. The value of the U.S. dollar is expected to increase in exchange for foreign currencies.
   d. Planned investment spending in the economy is expected to decrease.

2.8 Draw the consumption function and label each axis. Show the effect of an increase in income on consumption spending. Does the change in income cause a movement along the consumption function or a shift of the consumption function? How would an increase in expected future income or an increase in household wealth affect the consumption function? Would these increases cause a movement along the consumption function or a shift of the consumption function? Briefly explain.

2.9 An economics student raises the following objection: "The chapter said that a higher interest rate lowers investment, but this doesn't make sense. I know that if I can get a higher interest rate, I am certainly going to invest more in my savings account." Briefly explain whether you agree with this reasoning.

2.10 Unemployed workers receive unemployment insurance payments from the government. Does the existence of unemployment insurance make it likely that consumption will fluctuate more or less over the business cycle than it would in the absence of unemployment insurance? Briefly explain.

2.11 (Related to Solved Problem 12.2 on page 403) Fill in the missing values in the following table. Assume for simplicity that taxes are zero. Also assume that the values represent billions of 2009 dollars.

National Income and Real GDP (Y)	Consumption (C)	Saving (S)	Marginal Propensity to Consume (MPC)	Marginal Propensity to Save (MPS)
$9,000	$8,000			
10,000	8,750			
11,000	9,500			
12,000	10,250			
13,000	11,000			

2.12 (Related to the Apply the Concept on page 405) In an opinion column in the *Wall Street Journal*, Purdue University President Mitchell Daniels wrote that "today's 20- and 30-year-olds are delaying marriage and delaying childbearing, both unhelpful trends from an economic and social standpoint." Why might young people be delaying marriage and childbearing? Why would this trend be unhelpful from an economic point of view? Is the trend possibly connected with the slow recovery from the 2007–2009 recession? Briefly explain.

Source: Mitchell E. Daniels, "How Student Debt Harms the Economy," *Wall Street Journal*, January 27, 2015.

2.13 (Related to the Chapter Opener on page 392) An article in the *Wall Street Journal* on changes in Intel's sales noted, "Intel sells its chips to customers in U.S. dollars, but many PC makers that buy those chips sell their products in local currencies." In these circumstances, would an increase in the value of the dollar relative to foreign currencies be likely to help or hurt Intel's sales? Briefly explain.

Source: Tess Stynes, "Intel Earnings: What to Watch," *Wall Street Journal*, July 15, 2015.

2.14 (Related to the Apply the Concept on page 410) Briefly explain which of the following statements is correct.
  a. The iPhone is made in China, using Chinese-made parts.
  b. The iPhone is made in the United States, using U.S.-made parts.
  c. The iPhone is made in the United States, using Chinese-made parts.
  d. The iPhone is made in China, using parts that are all made outside China.

How is your answer related to the way the Bureau of Economic Analysis calculates data on U.S. imports?

2.15 (Related to the Apply the Concept on page 410) In a speech to a conference of government trade officials, Angel Gurría, secretary general of the Organization for Economic Co-operation and Development, made the following observation: "As goods and services cross borders several times at different stages of processing, conventional trade statistics may not tell the whole story."
  a. What does Gurría mean by "conventional trade statistics"?
  b. Why might conventional trade statistics no longer be as reliable as they once were?
  c. What difficulties might the problems with trade statistics cause for policymakers?

Source: Angel Gurría, "G20: Understanding Global Value Chains," Speech delivered at the G20 trade ministers conference in Puerto Vallarta, Mexico, April 19, 2012, www.oecd.org.

12.3 Graphing Macroeconomic Equilibrium, pages 410–417

LEARNING OBJECTIVE: Use a 45°-line diagram to illustrate macroeconomic equilibrium.

MyLab Economics Visit www.pearson.com/mylab/economics to complete these exercises online and get instant feedback.

Summary

The 45°-line diagram shows all the points where aggregate expenditure equals real GDP. On the 45°-line diagram, macroeconomic equilibrium occurs where the line representing the aggregate expenditure function crosses the 45° line. The economy is in recession when the aggregate expenditure line intersects the 45° line at a level of GDP that is below potential GDP. Numerically, macroeconomic equilibrium occurs when:

Consumption + Planned investment +

Government purchases + Net exports = GDP.

Review Questions

3.1 What is the meaning of the 45° line in the 45°-line diagram?

3.2 Use a 45°-line diagram to illustrate macroeconomic equilibrium. Make sure your diagram shows the aggregate expenditure function and the level of equilibrium real GDP and that your axes are properly labeled.

3.3 What does the slope of the aggregate expenditure line equal? How is the slope of the aggregate expenditure line related to the slope of the consumption function?

3.4 What is likely to happen if firms accumulate large amounts of unplanned inventory at the beginning of a recession?

3.5 What is the difference between aggregate expenditure and consumption spending?

Problems and Applications

3.6 At point *A* in the following graph, is planned aggregate expenditure greater than, equal to, or less than GDP? What about at point *B*? At point *C*? For points *A* and *C*, indicate the vertical distance that measures the unintended change in inventories.

3.7 Suppose we drop the assumption that net exports do not depend on real GDP. Draw a graph with the value of net exports on the vertical axis and the value of real GDP on the horizontal axis. Now, add a line representing the relationship between net exports and real GDP. Does your net exports line have a positive or negative slope? Briefly explain.

3.8 A Federal Reserve publication noted that "the shedding of unwanted inventories often accounts for a large portion of the decline in gross domestic product (GDP) during economic recessions." What does the author mean be "shedding of unwanted inventories"? What makes the inventories unwanted? Why would shedding inventories lead to a decline in GDP?

Source: Jeremy M. Piger, "Is the Business Cycle Still an Inventory Cycle?" *Economic Synopses*, Federal Reserve Bank of St. Louis, No. 2, 2005.

3.9 An article on bloomberg.com about the Japanese economy noted, "Whether the 2.4 percent annualized gain in gross domestic product reported Wednesday can be maintained depends on consumers stepping in to buy the products that companies are piling up in warehouses."
  a. Did business inventories in Japan increase or decrease during this period? Briefly explain.

b. What would happen if consumers do not buy the products that companies are piling up? Illustrate your answer with a 45°-line diagram.

Source: Keiko Ujikane and Toru Fujioka, "Japan's Economy Grows as Investment Gains, Inventories Rise," bloomberg.com, May 20, 2015.

3.10 Consider the following table, which shows the change in inventories for each quarter from the first quarter of 2007 (2007:I) through the fourth quarter of 2010 (2010:IV) measured in billions of 2009 dollars. Provide a macroeconomic explanation for this pattern. (*Hint:* When did the recession during this period begin and end?)

Year	Quarter	Change in Inventories
2007	I	$19.6
	II	49.4
	III	50.2
	IV	23.0
2008	I	−20.2
	II	−26.4
	III	−20.7
	IV	−67.4
2009	I	−144.5
	II	−190.1
	III	−206.1
	IV	−49.6
2010	I	9.8
	II	48.8
	III	116.2
	IV	58.1

3.11 (Related to the Don't Let This Happen to You on page 416) Briefly explain whether you agree with the following argument: "The equilibrium level of GDP is determined by the level of aggregate expenditure. Therefore, GDP will decline only if households decide to spend less on goods and services."

3.12 (Related to Solved Problem 12.3 on page 416) Fill in the missing values in the table below. Assume that the value of the *MPC* does not change as real GDP changes. Also assume that the values represent billions of 2009 dollars.
  a. What is the value of the *MPC*?
  b. What is the value of equilibrium real GDP?

Accompanies problem 3.12.

Real GDP (Y)	Consumption (C)	Planned Investment (I)	Government Purchases (G)	Net Exports (NX)	Planned Aggregate Expenditure (AE)	Unplanned Change in Inventories
$9,000	$7,600	$1,200	$1,200	−$400		
10,000	8,400	1,200	1,200	−400		
11,000		1,200	1,200	−400		
12,000		1,200	1,200	−400		
13,000		1,200	1,200	−400		

The Multiplier Effect, pages 417–424

LEARNING OBJECTIVE: Describe the multiplier effect and use the multiplier formula to calculate changes in equilibrium GDP.

MyLab Economics   Visit **www.pearson.com/mylab/economics** to complete these exercises online and get instant feedback.

Summary

Autonomous expenditure is expenditure that does not depend on the level of GDP. An autonomous change is a change in expenditure not caused by a change in income. An *induced change* is a change in aggregate expenditure caused by a change in income. An autonomous change in expenditure will cause rounds of induced changes in expenditure. Therefore, an autonomous change in expenditure will have a *multiplier effect* on equilibrium GDP. The **multiplier effect** is the process by which an increase in autonomous expenditure leads to a larger increase in real GDP. The **multiplier** is the ratio of the change in equilibrium GDP to the change in autonomous expenditure. The formula for the multiplier is:

$$\frac{1}{1 - MPC}.$$

Because of the paradox of thrift, an attempt by many individuals to increase their saving may lead to a reduction in aggregate expenditure and a recession.

Review Questions

4.1 The following graph contains two aggregate expenditure functions. Consider a movement from point A to point B and a movement from point B to point C. Which movement shows a change in *autonomous* expenditure? Which movement shows a change in *induced* expenditure? Briefly explain your answers.

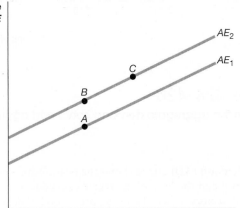

4.2 What is the multiplier effect? Use a 45°-line diagram to illustrate the multiplier effect of a decrease in government purchases.

4.3 What is the formula for the multiplier? Explain why this formula for the multiplier is oversimplified.

Problems and Applications

4.4 In Figure 12.13 on page 418, the economy is initially in equilibrium at point A. Aggregate expenditure and real GDP both equal $9.6 trillion. The increase in investment of $100 billion increases aggregate expenditure to $9.7 trillion. If real GDP increases to $9.7 trillion, will the economy be in equilibrium? Briefly explain. What happens to aggregate expenditure when real GDP increases to $9.7 trillion?

4.5 A column in the *New York Times* in 2017 noted that Tesla was expanding both its California automobile factory, where it was beginning to produce its Model 3 electric cars, and its Nevada "Gigafactory," where it was producing lithium-ion batteries for cars and other uses. The article quoted an investment analyst as saying, "I don't know what kind of multiplier you put on that, but it's a significant boost to the economy."
  a. What does the analyst mean by a multiplier?
  b. Why would Tesla's engaging in this investment spending result in a significant boost to the economy?
  c. Why might the analyst have been unsure of the size of the multiplier in this case?
  Source: James B. Stewart, "Elon Musk Has Trump's Ear, and Wall Street Takes Note," *New York Times*, January 26, 2017.

4.6 (Related to the **Apply the Concept** on page 420) If the multiplier had a value of 4 in 1929, how large must the change in autonomous expenditure have been to have caused the decline in real GDP between 1929 and 1933 shown in the table on page 420? If the multiplier had a value of 2, how large must the change in autonomous expenditure have been?

4.7 (Related to **Solved Problem 12.4** on page 423) Use the information in the following table to answer the questions. Assume that the values represent billions of 2009 dollars.

Real GDP (Y)	Consumption (C)	Planned Investment (I)	Government Purchases (G)	Net Exports (NX)
$8,000	$7,300	$1,000	$1,000	−$500
9,000	7,900	1,000	1,000	−500
10,000	8,500	1,000	1,000	−500
11,000	9,100	1,000	1,000	−500
12,000	9,700	1,000	1,000	−500

  a. What is the equilibrium level of real GDP?
  b. What is the MPC?
  c. Suppose net exports increase by $400 billion. What will be the new equilibrium level of real GDP? Use the multiplier formula to determine your answer.

4.8 An article published in an economics journal found the following: "For the poorest households, the marginal propensity to consume was close to 70%. For the richest

households, the MPC was only 35%." Assume that the macroeconomy can be divided into three sections. Section A consists of the poorest households, Section B consists of the richest households, and Section C consists of all other households.
  a. Compute the value of the multiplier for Section A.
  b. Compute the value of the multiplier for Section B.
  c. Assume that there was an increase in planned investment of $4 billion. Compute the change in equilibrium real GDP if the MPC for the economy was 70 percent (or 0.70). Compute the change in equilibrium real GDP if the MPC for the economy was 35 percent (or 0.35).

Source: Atif Mian and Amir Sufi, "Who Spends Extra Cash?" *House of Debt*, April 13, 2014.

4.9 Explain whether each of the following would cause the value of the multiplier to be larger or smaller.
  a. An increase in real GDP increases imports.
  b. An increase in real GDP increases interest rates.
  c. An increase in real GDP increases the marginal propensity to consume.
  d. An increase in real GDP causes the average tax rate paid by households to decrease.
  e. An increase in real GDP increases the price level.

4.10 An article in the *Wall Street Journal* stated, "Europe is entering its fifth consecutive year of growth, supported by accommodative monetary policies, robust business and consumer confidence and improving world trade." What components of aggregate expenditure would "robust business and consumer confidence and improving world trade" affect, and why would they cause real GDP to grow? Illustrate your answer with a 45°-line diagram.

Source: Emre Peker, "EU Raises Growth Forecasts but Warns on Threat from Brexit and Trump," *Wall Street Journal*, May 11, 2017.

4.11 Would a larger multiplier lead to longer and more severe recessions or shorter and less severe recessions? Briefly explain.

4.12 An MPC equal to 0 implies a multiplier of 1, meaning that a $1 increase in autonomous expenditures would increase real GDP by only $1. Why does an MPC equal to 0 result in no multiplier effect? Conversely, an MPC equal to 1 implies an infinite multiplier, meaning that a $1 increase in autonomous expenditures would increase real GDP by

an infinite amount. Why does an MPC of 1 result in an infinite multiplier? Explain your answers using the logic of the multiplier process.

4.13 A study by the management consulting company McKinsey & Company recommended that the federal government increase spending on infrastructure, such as bridges and highways, by between $150 and $180 billion per year. The study estimated that the result would be an increase in GDP of between $270 billion and $320 billion per year. What is the implied value of the multiplier if the McKinsey study's estimate of the effect of infrastructure spending on GDP is correct?

Source: David Harrison, "Nation's Crumbling Roads Put a Dent in Drivers' Wallets," *Wall Street Journal*, July 31, 2015.

4.14 Use the following graph to answer the questions.
  a. What is the value of equilibrium real GDP?
  b. What is the value of the MPC?
  c. What is the value of the multiplier?
  d. What is the value of unplanned changes in inventories when real GDP has each of the following values?
      i. $10 trillion
      ii. $12 trillion
      iii. $14 trillion

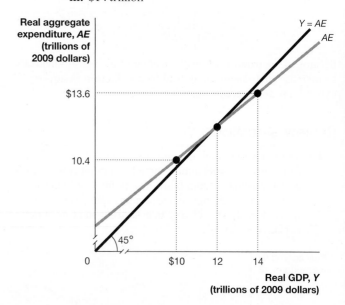

12.5 The Aggregate Demand Curve, pages 424–426

LEARNING OBJECTIVE: Understand the relationship between the aggregate demand curve and aggregate expenditure.

MyLab Economics Visit **www.pearson.com/mylab/economics** to complete these exercises online and get instant feedback.

Summary

Increases in the price level cause a reduction in consumption, investment, and net exports. This causes the aggregate expenditure function to shift down on the 45°-line diagram, leading to a lower equilibrium real GDP. A decrease in the price level leads to a higher equilibrium real GDP. The **aggregate**

demand **(AD) curve** shows the relationship between the price level and the level of aggregate expenditure, holding constant all factors other than the price level that affect aggregate expenditure.

Review Questions

5.1 Explain the difference between aggregate expenditure and aggregate demand.

5.2 Explain which components of aggregate expenditure are affected by a change in the price level.

5.3 Does a change in the price level cause a movement along the aggregate expenditure line or a shift of the aggregate expenditure line? Does a change in the price level cause a movement along the aggregate demand curve or a shift of the aggregate demand curve?

Problems and Applications

5.4 Explain why the aggregate expenditure line is upward sloping, while the aggregate demand curve is downward sloping.

5.5 Explain whether you agree with the following statement: "The reason the aggregate demand curve slopes downward is that when the price level is higher, people cannot afford to buy as many goods and services."

5.6 Suppose that exports become more sensitive to changes in the price level in the United States. That is, when the price level in the United States rises, exports decline by more than they previously did. Will this change make the aggregate demand curve steeper or less steep? Briefly explain.

Real-Time Data Exercise

D12.1 **(Calculating the multiplier effect)** Using data from the Federal Reserve Bank of St. Louis (FRED) (fred.stlouisfed.org), analyze the effect of a decline in exports on GDP.
   a. Download data since 1990 on real exports of goods and services (EXPGSC1).
   b. What was the dollar value of the decline in real exports between the second quarter of 2008 and the first quarter of 2009? If the multiplier is 2, holding everything else constant, what was the effect of this decline in exports on real GDP?

Critical Thinking Exercises

CT12.1 For this exercise, your instructor may assign you to a group. Each group member should first write down two concepts or findings from this chapter that he or she found surprising. After working individually, the group should work together to write a one- or two-paragraph report explaining why the concepts or findings they identified were surprising.

CT12.2 How is reaching macroeconomic equilibrium different from reaching the equilibrium in the market that you saw in Chapter 3, Section 3.3?

CT12.3 This chapter described the multiplier as $(1/(1 - MPC))$. However, many important variables, including the price level and interest rates, are held constant in arriving at this equation. In one paragraph, explain whether the multiplier would be larger or smaller if an increase in government expenditures always leads to an increase in the price level.

Appendix

LEARNING OBJECTIVE: Apply the algebra of macroeconomic equilibrium.

The Algebra of Macroeconomic Equilibrium

In this chapter, we relied primarily on graphs and tables to illustrate the aggregate expenditure model of short-run real GDP. Graphs help us understand economic change *qualitatively*. When we write an economic model using equations, we make it easier to make *quantitative estimates*. When economists forecast future movements in GDP, they often rely on *econometric models*. An econometric model is an economic model written in the form of equations, where each equation has been statistically estimated using methods similar to the methods used in estimating demand curves that we briefly described in Chapter 3. We can use equations to represent the aggregate expenditure model described in this chapter.

The following equations are based on the example shown in Table 12.3 on page 415. Y stands for real GDP, and the numbers (with the exception of the MPC) are in billions of dollars.

1. $C = \$1,000 + 0.65Y$ (consumption function)
2. $I = \$1,500$ (planned investment function)
3. $G = \$1,500$ (government purchases function)
4. $NX = -\$500$ (net export function)
5. $Y = C + I + G + NX$ (equilibrium condition)

The first equation is the consumption function. The MPC is 0.65, and $1,000 is autonomous consumption, which is the level of consumption that does not depend on income. If we think of the consumption function as a line on the 45°-line diagram, $1,000 would be the intercept, and 0.65 would be the slope. The "functions" for the other three components of planned aggregate expenditure are very simple because we have assumed that these components are not affected by GDP and, therefore, are constant. Economists who use this type of model to forecast GDP would, of course, use more realistic investment, government, and net export functions. The *parameters* of the functions—such as the value of autonomous consumption and the value of the MPC in the consumption function—would be estimated statistically, using data on the values of each variable over a period of years.

In this model, GDP is in equilibrium when it equals planned aggregate expenditure. Equation 5—the equilibrium condition—shows how to calculate equilibrium in the model: We need to substitute equations 1 through 4 into equation 5. Doing so gives us the following:

$$Y = \$1,000 + 0.65Y + \$1,500 + \$1,500 - \$500.$$

We need to solve this expression for Y to find equilibrium GDP. The first step is to subtract 0.65Y from both sides of the equation:

$$Y - 0.65Y = \$1,000 + \$1,500 + \$1,500 - \$500.$$

Then, we solve for Y:

$$0.35Y = \$3,500.$$

Or:

$$Y = \frac{\$3,500}{0.35} = \$10,000.$$

To make this result more general, we can replace particular values with general values represented by letters:

1. $C = \bar{C} + MPC(Y)$ (consumption function)
2. $I = \bar{I}$ (planned investment function)
3. $G = \bar{G}$ (government purchases function)
4. $NX = \overline{NX}$ (net export function)
5. $Y = C + I + G + NX$ (equilibrium condition)

The letters with bars over them represent fixed, or autonomous, values. So, for example, $\bar{C}$ represents autonomous consumption, which had a value of $1,000 in our original example. Now, solving for equilibrium, we get:

$$Y = \bar{C} + MPC(Y) + \bar{I} + \bar{G} + \overline{NX},$$

or:

$$Y - MPC(Y) = \bar{C} + \bar{I} + \bar{G} + \overline{NX},$$

or:

$$Y(1 - MPC) = \bar{C} + \bar{I} + \bar{G} + \overline{NX},$$

or:

$$Y = \frac{\bar{C} + \bar{I} + \bar{G} + \overline{NX}}{1 - MPC}.$$

Remember that $1/(1 - MPC)$ is the multiplier, and all four variables in the numerator of the equation represent autonomous expenditure. Therefore, an alternative expression for equilibrium GDP is: **MyLab Economics** Concept Check   **MyLab Economics** Study Plan

$$\text{Equilibrium GDP} = \text{Autonomous expenditure} \times \text{Multiplier}.$$

 12A ## The Algebra of Macroeconomic Equilibrium, pages 434–435

LEARNING OBJECTIVE: Apply the algebra of macroeconomic equilibrium.

MyLab Economics Visit **www.pearson.com/mylab/economics** to complete these exercises online and get instant feedback.

Review Questions

12A.1 Write a general expression for the aggregate expenditure function. If you think of the aggregate expenditure function as a line on the 45°-line diagram, what would be the intercept and what would be the slope, using the general values represented by letters?

12A.2 Find equilibrium GDP using the following macroeconomic model (where the numbers, with the exception of the MPC, are in billions of dollars).

1. $C = \$1,500 + 0.75Y$ (consumption function)
2. $I = \$1,250$ (planned investment function)
3. $G = \$1,250$ (government purchases function)
4. $NX = -\$250$ (net export function)
5. $Y = C + I + G + NX$ (equilibrium condition)

12A.3 For the macroeconomic model in problem 12A.2, write the aggregate expenditure function. For GDP of $16,000, what is the value of aggregate expenditure, and what is the value of the unintended change in inventories? For GDP of $12,000, what is the value of aggregate expenditure, and what is the value of the unintended change in inventories?

12A.4 Suppose that autonomous consumption is 500, government purchases are $1,000, planned investment spending is $1,250, net exports are −$250, and the MPC is 0.8. What is equilibrium GDP?

Aggregate Demand and Aggregate Supply Analysis

The Fortunes of KB Home Follow the Business Cycle

In 1957, the baby boom rise in birth rates was in full swing. Noting the increase in families with multiple children, Donald Kaufman, the owner of a construction firm, and Eli Broad, an accountant married to Kaufman's cousin, conceived of a way to profit from a surge in demand for new housing. Most new homes were being built with basements and garages. By building homes on concrete slabs, Kaufman and Broad could eliminate the need for a basement, and by building carports, they could eliminate the need for garages. These cost savings allowed them to sell homes at a price of $13,740, well below what other homebuilders charged.

KB Home's long-run success led to its being the first homebuilder to have its stock listed for sale on the New York Stock Exchange, but in the short run, the firm's ability to sell homes is affected by the ups and downs of the business cycle. As we've seen, when the economy moves into a recession, incomes and employment decline, which makes many families reluctant to take on the major expense of buying a home. In addition, during recessions, banks and other lenders typically become more cautious in granting loans, making it difficult for families to borrow the funds needed to buy a home. The severe 2007–2009 recession was a particularly difficult time for homebuilders because of the effects of the bursting of the housing bubble. A rapid increase in sales of new homes that began in the early 2000s ended in 2005. Between 2005 and 2010, new home sales dropped by an astonishing 80 percent. KB Home suffered total losses of $2.4 billion between 2007 and 2010, and its stock price declined by 82 percent from its 2005 high.

By 2017, as a result of the stronger growth of the U.S. economy, KB Home's sales of new homes were more than

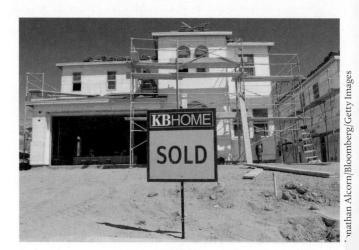

Jonathan Alcorn/Bloomberg/Getty Images

70 percent higher than at their low point in 2010, and the firm had returned to profitability. In mid-2017, an article in the *Wall Street Journal* quoted Jeff Metzger, KB Home's CEO, as saying that the firm was "seeing a wave of demand, especially from first-time buyers who are moving out of their parents' homes, getting married and having kids." This statement indicated that the firm was benefitting from another result of the economic recovery: In 2017, for the first time since the recession, newly formed households were more likely to be buying their first home than renting their first home.

To better understand how the business cycle affects homebuilders and other firms, we need to explore the effects that recessions and expansions have on production, employment, and prices.

Sources: Laura Kusisto and Sarah Chaney, "U.S. Housing Starts Fell in April for Third Time in Four Months," *Wall Street Journal*, May 16, 2017; Connie Bruck, "The Art of the Billionaire: How Eli Broad Took over Los Angeles," newyorker.com, December 6, 2010; Laura Kusisto and Chris Kirkham, "The Next Hot Housing Market: Starter Homes," *Wall Street Journal*, May 11, 2017; and KB Home, *Annual Reports*, various years.

Chapter Outline & Learning Objectives

Economics in Your Life & Career

Is an Employer Likely to Cut Your Pay during a Recession?

Suppose that you have worked as a barista for a local coffeehouse for two years. From on-the-job training and experience, you have honed your coffee-making skills and mastered the perfect latte. Then the economy moves into a recession, and sales at the coffeehouse decline. Is the owner of the coffeehouse likely to cut the prices of lattes and other drinks? Suppose the owner asks to meet with you to discuss your wages for next year. Is the owner likely to cut your pay? As you read this chapter, try to answer these questions. You can check your answers against those we provide on **page 464** at the end of this chapter.

W̲e have seen that the U.S. economy has experienced a long-run upward trend in real GDP. These increases in real GDP have raised the standard of living in the United States to a level much higher today than it was 100 years ago. In the short run, however, real GDP fluctuates around this long-run upward trend because of the business cycle. Fluctuations in real GDP lead to fluctuations in employment. These fluctuations in real GDP and employment are the most visible and dramatic part of the business cycle. During recessions, we are more likely to see factories close, small businesses declare bankruptcy, and workers lose their jobs. During expansions, we are more likely to see new businesses open and new jobs created. In addition to these changes in output and employment, the business cycle causes changes in wages and prices. Some firms react to a decline in sales by cutting back on production, but they may also cut the prices they charge and the wages they pay. Other firms respond to a recession by raising prices and workers' wages by less than they otherwise would have.

In this chapter, we expand our discussion of the business cycle by developing the aggregate demand and aggregate supply model. This model will help us analyze the effects of recessions and expansions on production, employment, and prices.

13.1 Aggregate Demand

LEARNING OBJECTIVE: Identify the determinants of aggregate demand and distinguish between a movement along the aggregate demand curve and a shift of the curve.

Aggregate demand and aggregate supply model A model that explains short-run fluctuations in real GDP and the price level.

Aggregate demand (AD) curve A curve that shows the relationship between the price level and the quantity of real GDP demanded by households, firms, and the government (both inside and outside of the country).

Short-run aggregate supply (SRAS) curve A curve that shows the relationship in the short run between the price level and the quantity of real GDP supplied by firms.

To understand what happens during the business cycle, we need an explanation of why real GDP, the unemployment rate, and the inflation rate fluctuate. We have already seen that fluctuations in the unemployment rate are caused mainly by fluctuations in real GDP. In this chapter, we use the **aggregate demand and aggregate supply model** to explain short-run fluctuations in real GDP and the price level. As Figure 13.1 shows, real GDP and the price level in this model are determined in the short run by the intersection of the *aggregate demand curve* and the *aggregate supply curve*. Fluctuations in real GDP and the price level are caused by shifts in the aggregate demand curve or in the aggregate supply curve.

The **aggregate demand (AD) curve** shows the relationship between the price level and the quantity of real GDP demanded by households, firms, and the government (both inside and outside the country). The **short-run aggregate supply (SRAS) curve** shows the relationship in the short run between the price level and the quantity of real GDP supplied by firms. The aggregate demand and short-run aggregate supply curves in Figure 13.1 look similar to the individual market demand and supply curves we studied in Chapter 3. However, because these curves apply to the whole economy, rather than to just a single market, the aggregate demand and aggregate supply model is very different from the model of demand and supply in individual markets. Because we are dealing with the economy as a whole, we need *macroeconomic* explanations of why the aggregate demand curve is downward sloping, why the short-run aggregate supply curve is upward sloping, and why the curves shift. We begin by explaining why the aggregate demand curve is downward sloping.

Why Is the Aggregate Demand Curve Downward Sloping?

We have seen that GDP has four components:

1. Consumption (*C*)
2. Investment (*I*)
3. Government purchases (*G*)
4. Net exports (*NX*)

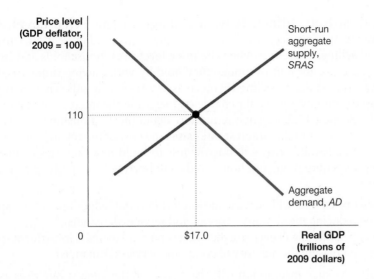

Figure 13.1   **Aggregate Demand and Aggregate Supply**

In the short run, real GDP and the price level are determined by the intersection of the aggregate demand curve and the short-run aggregate supply curve. In the figure, real GDP is measured on the horizontal axis, and the price level is measured on the vertical axis by the GDP deflator. In this example, the equilibrium real GDP is $17.0 trillion, and the equilibrium price level is 110.

If we let Y stand for GDP, we have the following relationship:

$$Y = C + I + G + NX.$$

The aggregate demand curve is downward sloping because a fall in the price level increases the quantity of real GDP demanded. To understand why, we need to look at how changes in the price level affect each component of aggregate demand. We begin with the assumption that government purchases are determined by the policy decisions of lawmakers and are not affected by changes in the price level. We can then consider the effect of changes in the price level on the three other components: consumption, investment, and net exports.

The Wealth Effect: How a Change in the Price Level Affects Consumption Current income is the most important variable determining consumption by households. As income rises, consumption will rise, and as income falls, consumption will fall. But consumption also depends on household wealth, which is the difference between the value of a household's assets and the value of its debts. Consider two households, both with incomes of $80,000 per year. The first household has wealth of $5 million, and the second household has wealth of $50,000. The first household is likely to spend more of its income than the second household. So, as total household wealth rises, consumption will rise. Some household wealth is held in cash or other *nominal assets* that lose value as the price level rises and gain value as the price level falls. For instance, if you have $10,000 in cash, a 10 percent increase in the price level will reduce the purchasing power of that cash by 10 percent. When the price level rises, the *real value* of household wealth declines, and so will consumption, thereby reducing the demand for goods and services. When the price level falls, the real value of household wealth rises, and so will consumption and the demand for goods and services. The effect of the price level on consumption is called the *wealth effect*, and it is one reason the aggregate demand curve is downward sloping.

The Interest-Rate Effect: How a Change in the Price Level Affects Investment When prices rise, households and firms need more money to finance buying and selling. Therefore, when the price level rises, households and firms will try to increase the amount of money they hold by withdrawing funds from banks, borrowing from banks, or selling financial assets, such as bonds. These actions tend to drive up the interest rate banks charge on loans and the interest rate on bonds. (In Chapter 15, Section 15.2, we analyze in more detail the relationship between money and interest rates.) A higher interest rate raises the cost of borrowing for households and firms. As a result, firms will borrow less to build new factories or install new machinery and equipment, and households will borrow less to buy new houses. To summarize:

- A higher price level will increase the interest rate and reduce investment spending, thereby reducing the quantity of goods and services demanded.
- A lower price level will decrease the interest rate and increase investment spending, thereby increasing the quantity of goods and services demanded.

To a smaller extent, consumption will also fall when the interest rate rises as households borrow less to finance spending on automobiles, furniture, and other durable goods.

The effect of the price level on investment and consumption is known as the *interest-rate effect*, and it is a second reason the aggregate demand curve is downward sloping.

The International-Trade Effect: How a Change in the Price Level Affects Net Exports *Net exports* equals spending by foreign households and firms on goods and services produced in the United States minus spending by U.S. households and firms on goods and services produced in other countries. If the price level in the United States rises relative to the price levels in other countries, U.S. exports will become relatively more expensive, and foreign imports will become relatively less expensive. Some consumers in foreign countries will shift from buying U.S. products to buying domestic products, and some U.S. consumers will also shift from buying U.S. products to buying imported products. U.S. exports will fall, and U.S. imports will rise, causing net exports to fall, thereby reducing the quantity of goods and services demanded. A lower price level in the United States relative to other countries has the reverse effect, causing net exports to rise, thereby increasing the quantity of goods and services demanded. The effect of the price level on net exports is known as the *international-trade effect*, and it is a third reason the aggregate demand curve is downward sloping. **MyLab Economics** Concept Check

Shifts of the Aggregate Demand Curve versus Movements along It

An important point to remember is that the aggregate demand curve tells us the relationship between the price level and the quantity of real GDP demanded, *holding everything else constant*. If the price level changes but other variables that affect the willingness of households, firms, and the government to spend are unchanged, the result is a movement up or down a stationary aggregate demand curve. If any variable other than the price level changes, the aggregate demand curve will shift. For example, if government purchases increase and the price level remains unchanged, the aggregate demand curve will shift to the right at every price level. Or, if firms become pessimistic about the future profitability of investment and cut back spending on factories, machinery, and computers, the aggregate demand curve will shift to the left. **MyLab Economics** Concept Check

The Variables That Shift the Aggregate Demand Curve

The variables that cause the aggregate demand curve to shift fall into three categories:

1. Changes in government policies
2. Changes in the expectations of households and firms
3. Changes in foreign variables

Changes in Government Policies As we will discuss further in Chapters 15 and 16, the federal government uses monetary policy and fiscal policy to shift the aggregate demand curve. **Monetary policy** refers to the actions the Federal Reserve—the nation's central bank—takes to manage the money supply and interest rates and to ensure the flow of funds from lenders to borrowers. The Federal Reserve takes these actions to achieve macroeconomic policy objectives, such as high employment, price stability, high rates of economic growth, and stability of the financial system. If the Federal Reserve takes actions that reduce interest rates, the cost to firms and households of borrowing declines. Lower borrowing costs increase consumption and investment spending, which shifts the aggregate demand curve to the right. Higher interest rates shift the aggregate demand curve to the left.

Monetary policy The actions the Federal Reserve takes to manage the money supply and interest rates to achieve macroeconomic policy objectives.

Fiscal policy refers to the changes in federal taxes and purchases that are intended to achieve macroeconomic policy objectives. Because government purchases are one component of aggregate demand:

- An increase in *government purchases* shifts the aggregate demand curve to the right, and a decrease in government purchases shifts the aggregate demand curve to the left.
- An increase in *personal income taxes* reduces households' disposable income, which reduces consumption spending and shifts the aggregate demand curve to the left. A decrease in personal income taxes shifts the aggregate demand curve to the right.
- An increase in *business taxes* reduces the profitability of investment spending and shifts the aggregate demand curve to the left. A decrease in business taxes shifts the aggregate demand curve to the right.

Fiscal policy Changes in federal taxes and purchases that are intended to achieve macroeconomic policy objectives.

Changes in the Expectations of Households and Firms If households become more optimistic about their future incomes, they are likely to increase their current consumption. They are also likely to increase spending on new houses, thereby increasing investment spending. This increased spending will shift the aggregate demand curve to the right. If households become more pessimistic about their future incomes, the aggregate demand curve will shift to the left. Similarly, if firms become more optimistic about the future profitability of investment spending, the aggregate demand curve will shift to the right. If firms become more pessimistic, the aggregate demand curve will shift to the left.

Don't Let This Happen to You

Understand Why the Aggregate Demand Curve Is Downward Sloping

The aggregate demand curve and the demand curve for a single product are both downward sloping—but for different reasons. When we draw a demand curve for a single product, such as apples, we know that it will slope downward because as the price of apples rises, apples become more expensive relative to other products—such as oranges—and consumers will buy fewer apples and more of the other products. In other words, consumers substitute other products for apples. When the overall price level rises, the prices of all domestically produced goods and services are rising, so consumers have no other domestic products to which they can switch. The

aggregate demand curve slopes downward because a higher price level:

- Reduces the real value of household wealth, which decreases consumption
- Raises interest rates, which decreases investment and consumption
- Makes U.S. exports more expensive and foreign imports less expensive, which decreases net exports

MyLab Economics Study Plan

Your Turn: Test your understanding by doing related problem 1.7 on pages 465–466 at the end of this chapter.

Changes in Foreign Variables If households and firms in other countries buy fewer U.S. goods or if households and firms in the United States buy more foreign goods, net exports will fall, and the aggregate demand curve will shift to the left. When real GDP increases, so does the income available for consumers to spend. If real GDP in the United States increases faster than real GDP in other countries, U.S. imports will increase faster than U.S. exports, and net exports will fall. Net exports will also fall if the *exchange rate* between the dollar and foreign currencies rises because the price in foreign currency of U.S. products sold in other countries will rise, and the dollar price of foreign products sold in the United States will fall. For example, if the current exchange rate between the dollar and the euro is $1 = €1 then:

- A $20 Blu-ray disc exported from the United States to France will cost €20 in France.
- A €50 bottle of wine exported from France will cost $50 in the United States.

But if the exchange rate rises to $1 = €1.50 then:

- The disc's price will rise from €20 to €30 in France, causing its sales to decline.
- The price of the French wine will fall from $50 to $33.33 per bottle in the United States, causing its sales to increase.

As a result, U.S. exports will fall, U.S. imports will rise, and the aggregate demand curve will shift to the left.

An increase in net exports at every price level will shift the aggregate demand curve to the right. Net exports will increase if real GDP grows more slowly in the United States than in other countries or if the value of the dollar falls against other currencies. A change in net exports that results from a change in the price level in the United States will result in a movement along the aggregate demand curve, *not* a shift of the aggregate demand curve.

 Solved Problem 13.1

MyLab Economics Interactive Animation

Movements along the Aggregate Demand Curve or Shifts of the Curve?

Germany, along with 18 other countries in Europe, uses the euro as its currency. According to an article in the *Wall Street Journal*, German net exports in 2016 "rose to €252.9 billion ($270.58 billion)." According to the article, Peter Navarro, head of the Trump administration's National Trade Council, said that "German exporters had an unfair advantage because of the euro's weak exchange rate."

a. At the time this article was written, what was the exchange rate between the U.S. dollar and the euro?

b. What does Navarro mean by "the euro's weak exchange rate"?

c. Why would a weak euro exchange rate give an advantage to German exporters?

d. Briefly explain whether a weaker euro exchange rate will cause a shift in the aggregate demand curve of the German economy or a movement along the curve. Illustrate your answer with a graph.

Solving the Problem

Step 1: Review the chapter material. This problem is about understanding the difference between movements along an aggregate demand curve and shifts of an aggregate demand curve, so you may want to review the section "Shifts of the Aggregate Demand Curve versus Movements along It" and the section "The Variables That Shift the Aggregate Demand Curve," which both begin on page 440.

Step 2: Answer part (a) by calculating the exchange rate between the euro and the U.S. dollar at the time the article was written. If €252.9 billion was the equivalent of $270.58 billion at the time the article was written, then the exchange rate must have been $270.58 billion/€252.9 billion = $1.07 dollars per euro, or $1 = €0.93.

Step 3: **Answer part (b) by explaining what the article meant by "the euro's weak exchange rate."** A weak euro exchange rate means an exchange rate such that a dollar (or a unit of another foreign currency) would buy more euros, or, equivalently, a euro would buy fewer dollars (or units of another foreign currency).

Step 4: **Answer part (c) by explaining why a weak euro would give an advantage to German exporters.** If it takes fewer dollars to buy German goods priced in euros, then U.S. consumers will buy more of them, increasing German exports. If it takes more euros to buy U.S. goods priced in dollars, then German consumers will buy fewer of them, decreasing German imports. So we would expect that a weaker euro will result in an increase in German net exports.

Step 5: **Answer part (d) by explaining whether a weaker euro exchange rate would cause a shift in the aggregate demand curve for the German economy or a movement along it and by drawing a graph to illustrate your answer.** Only changes in the price level in Germany will cause a movement along the aggregate demand curve for the German economy. Although a decline in the value of the euro affects the prices of exports from Germany and imports to Germany, it doesn't directly affect the price level in Germany. By increasing German net exports, the weaker euro will cause the aggregate demand curve for the German economy to shift to the right at every price level, so your graph should look like this:

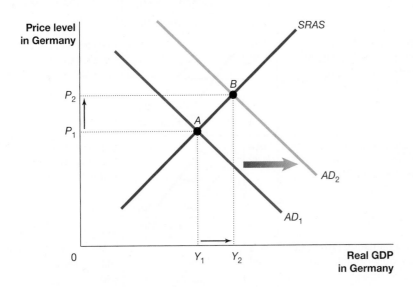

Source: Nina Adam and Andrea Thomas, "Germany's Global Trade Surplus Hits Record in 2016," *Wall Street Journal*, February 9, 2017.

Your Turn: For more practice, do related problems 1.8 and 1.9 on page 466 at the end of this chapter.

MyLab Economics Study Plan

Table 13.1 summarizes the most important variables that cause the aggregate demand curve to shift. The table shows the shift in the aggregate demand curve that results from an increase in each of the variables. A *decrease* in these variables will cause the aggregate demand curve to shift in the opposite direction.

Table 13.1

Variables That Shift the
Aggregate Demand Curve

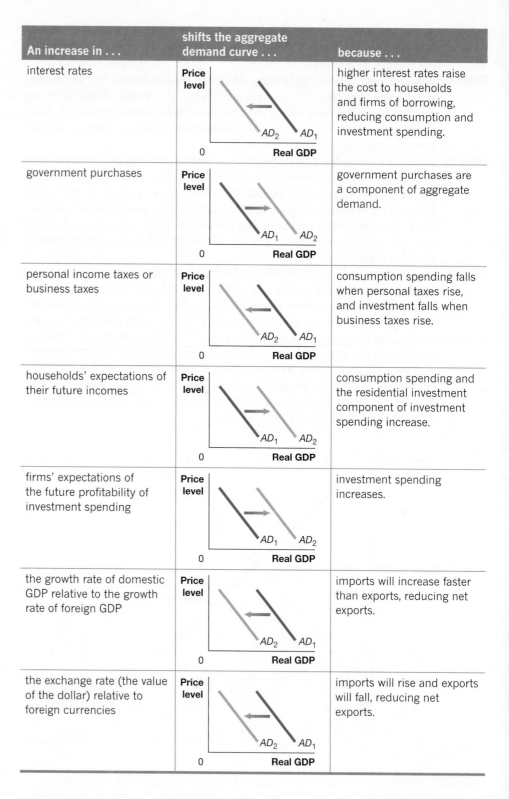

An increase in . . .	shifts the aggregate demand curve . . .	because . . .
interest rates		higher interest rates raise the cost to households and firms of borrowing, reducing consumption and investment spending.
government purchases		government purchases are a component of aggregate demand.
personal income taxes or business taxes		consumption spending falls when personal taxes rise, and investment falls when business taxes rise.
households' expectations of their future incomes		consumption spending and the residential investment component of investment spending increase.
firms' expectations of the future profitability of investment spending		investment spending increases.
the growth rate of domestic GDP relative to the growth rate of foreign GDP		imports will increase faster than exports, reducing net exports.
the exchange rate (the value of the dollar) relative to foreign currencies		imports will rise and exports will fall, reducing net exports.

MyLab Economics Concept Check

MyLab Economics Study Plan

Apply the Concept

MyLab Economics Video

Which Components of Aggregate Demand Changed the Most during the 2007–2009 Recession?

The recession of 2007–2009 was the longest and most severe since the Great Depression of the 1930s. We can better understand what happened during the 2007–2009 recession by looking at changes over time in the components of aggregate demand. In the following graphs, we show changes in the three components of aggregate demand that had the largest movements between the first quarter of 2005 and the first quarter of 2017: consumption, residential investment spending on new homes and apartments, and net exports. The shaded area represents the 2007–2009 recession. We know that potential GDP, or the level of GDP when all firms are producing at capacity, grows over time. So, economists are often interested in measuring changes in the components of aggregate demand *relative to potential GDP*, which is what we have done in these graphs.

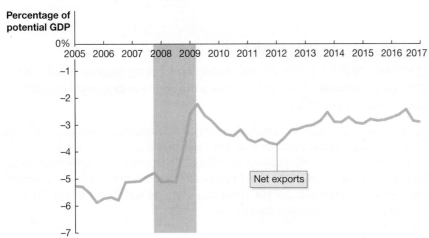

The graphs illustrate four facts about the 2007–2009 recession:

1. In the two years before the beginning of the recession, spending on residential investment had already declined significantly relative to potential GDP.
2. For the first two years following the end of the recession, spending on residential investment did not increase relative to potential GDP. Beginning in late 2011,

spending on residential investment began to increase slowly, but at the beginning of 2017, it was still far below its 2005–2006 level.

3. Consumption, which usually remains relatively stable during a recession, declined significantly relative to potential GDP during the recession and did not regain its 2007 level until 2015, six years after the recession had ended.

4. Net exports increased during the recession. (Because net exports was negative throughout this period, it increased by becoming a smaller negative number.)

Although not shown in the graphs, business fixed investment and changes in business inventories—the nonresidential construction components of investment spending—actually rose relative to potential GDP during the recession. Government purchases remained fairly stable relative to potential GDP during the recession and then declined from late 2010 through early 2017. Federal government purchases surged during the recession but declined in later years as temporary spending programs intended to fight the recession ended and Congress and the president cut spending further to address concerns over the federal budget deficit.

We can briefly account for the four facts listed above. As we saw in the chapter opener, the housing sector underwent a boom from 2002 to 2005, with rapid increases in both housing prices and spending on new housing. But the housing boom turned into a housing bust beginning in 2006, which explains the sharp decline in residential investment. The continued low levels of residential investment help explain why the recession was the longest since the Great Depression and why the economic expansion that began in June 2009 was relatively weak.

High levels of unemployment reduced household incomes and led to declines in consumption spending. In addition, many households increased their saving and paid off debts, further reducing consumption spending. The low levels of consumption spending also contributed to the severity of the recession and the weakness of the following expansion. Finally, efforts by the Federal Reserve to reduce interest rates helped to lower the value of the U.S. dollar, thereby reducing the prices of U.S. exports and increasing the prices of foreign imports. The result was an increase in net exports during the recession. (We will further discuss the effect of Federal Reserve policy on net exports in Chapters 15 and 18.)

Sources: U.S. Bureau of Economic Analysis; and Congressional Budget Office.

MyLab Economics Study Plan | **Your Turn:** Test your understanding by doing related problem 1.10 on page 466 at the end of this chapter.

Aggregate Supply

LEARNING OBJECTIVE: Identify the determinants of aggregate supply and distinguish between a movement along the short-run aggregate supply curve and a shift of the curve.

Having discussed aggregate demand, we now turn to aggregate supply, which shows the effect of changes in the price level on the quantity of goods and services that firms are willing and able to supply. Because the effect of changes in the price level on aggregate supply is very different in the short run from what it is in the long run, we use two aggregate supply curves: one for the short run and one for the long run. We start by considering the *long-run aggregate supply curve.*

The Long-Run Aggregate Supply Curve

In the long run, the level of real GDP is determined by the number of workers, the *capital stock*—including factories, office buildings, and machinery and equipment—and the available technology (see Chapter 11, Section 11.2). Because changes in the price level do not affect the number of workers, the capital stock, or technology, *in the long run, changes in the price level do not affect the level of real GDP.* Remember that the level of real

MyLab Economics Animation

Figure 13.2

The Long-Run Aggregate Supply Curve

Changes in the price level do not affect the level of aggregate supply in the long run. Therefore, the long-run aggregate supply (*LRAS*) curve is a vertical line at the potential level of real GDP. For instance, the price level was 113 in 2017, and potential GDP was $17.1 trillion. If the price level had been 123, or if it had been 103, long-run aggregate supply would still have been a constant $17.1 trillion. Each year, the long-run aggregate supply curve shifts to the right, as the number of workers in the economy increases, more machinery and equipment are accumulated, and technological change occurs.

GDP in the long run is called *potential GDP*, or *full-employment GDP*. At potential GDP, firms will operate at their normal level of capacity, and everyone who wants a job will have one, except those workers who are structurally or frictionally unemployed. There is no reason for this normal level of capacity to change just because the price level has changed.

The **long-run aggregate supply (*LRAS*) curve** shows the relationship in the long run between the price level and the quantity of real GDP supplied. As Figure 13.2 shows, in 2017, the price level was 113, and potential GDP was $17.1 trillion. If the price level had been 123, or if it had been 103, long-run aggregate supply would still have been a constant $17.1 trillion. Therefore, the *LRAS* curve is a vertical line.

Figure 13.2 also shows that the long-run aggregate supply curve shifts to the right each year. This shift occurs because potential GDP increases each year, as (1) the number of workers in the economy increases, (2) the economy accumulates more machinery and equipment, and (3) technological change occurs. Figure 13.2 shows potential GDP increasing from $17.1 trillion in 2017 to $17.4 trillion in 2018 and to $17.7 trillion in 2019.   **MyLab Economics** Concept Check

Long-run aggregate supply (*LRAS*) curve A curve that shows the relationship in the long run between the price level and the quantity of real GDP supplied.

The Short-Run Aggregate Supply Curve

While the *LRAS* curve is vertical, the *SRAS* curve is upward sloping because, over the short run, as the price level increases, the quantity of goods and services firms are willing to supply will increase. Firms supply more goods and services as the price level increases for two key reasons:

1. As prices of final goods and services rise, prices of inputs—such as the wages of workers or the price of natural resources—rise more slowly. Profits rise when the prices of goods and services firms sell rise more rapidly than the prices they pay for inputs. Therefore, a higher price level leads to higher profits and increases the willingness of firms to supply more goods and services.
2. As the price level rises, some firms are slow to adjust their prices. A firm that is slow to raise its prices when the price level is increasing may find its sales increasing and, therefore, will increase production.

Why do some firms adjust prices more slowly than others, and why might the wages of workers and the prices of other inputs change more slowly than the prices of final goods and services? Most economists believe the explanation is that *some firms and workers fail to accurately predict changes in the price level*. If firms and workers could predict the future price level exactly, the short-run aggregate supply curve would be the same as the long-run aggregate supply curve.

But how does the failure of workers and firms to predict the price level accurately result in an upward-sloping *SRAS* curve? Economists are not in complete agreement on this point, but we can briefly discuss the three most common explanations:

1. Contracts make some wages and prices "sticky."
2. Firms are often slow to adjust wages.
3. Menu costs make some prices sticky.

Contracts Make Some Wages and Prices "Sticky"

Prices or wages are said to be "sticky" when they do not respond quickly to changes in demand or supply. Contracts can make wages or prices sticky. For example, suppose Delta Air Lines negotiates a three-year contract with the Air Line Pilots Association, the union for the pilots who fly the company's planes, during a time when the economy is in recession and the number of passenger tickets being sold is falling. Suppose that after the union signs the contract, the economy begins to expand rapidly, and the number of tickets sold increases, so that Delta can raise ticket prices. Delta will find that flying more passengers will be profitable because the prices it charges are rising, while the wages it pays its pilots are fixed by contract. Or a steel mill might sign a multiyear contract to buy coal, which is used in making steel, at a time when the demand for steel is falling. If demand for steel and steel prices begin to rise rapidly, producing additional steel will be profitable because coal prices will remain fixed by contract. In both of these cases, rising prices lead to higher output. If these examples are representative of enough firms in the economy, a rising price level should lead to a greater quantity of goods and services supplied. In other words, the short-run aggregate supply curve will be upward sloping.

Notice, though, that if the pilots working for Delta or the managers of the coal companies had accurately predicted what would happen to prices, this prediction would have been reflected in the contracts, and Delta and the steel mill would not have earned greater profits when prices rose. In that case, rising prices would not have led to higher output.

Firms Are Often Slow to Adjust Wages

We just noted that the wages of many union workers remain fixed by contract for several years. Many nonunion workers have their wages or salaries adjusted only once a year. Suppose you accept a job at a management consulting firm in June, at a salary of $45,000 per year. The firm probably will not adjust your salary until the following June, even if the prices it can charge for its services later in the year are higher or lower than the firm had expected them to be when it hired you. Studies of firm wage setting have found that most firms change wages only once per year. If firms are slow to adjust wages, a rise in the price level will increase the profitability of hiring more workers and producing more output. A fall in the price level will decrease the profitability of hiring more workers and producing more output. Once again, we have an explanation for why the short-run aggregate supply curve slopes upward.

Firms are often slower to *cut* wages than to increase them. Cutting wages can have a negative effect on the morale and productivity of workers and can also cause some of a firm's best workers to quit and look for jobs elsewhere.

Apply the Concept

MyLab Economics Video

How Sticky Are Wages?

When we discussed the model of demand and supply in Chapter 3, we assumed that if the demand curve or supply curve for a product shifted, the price would adjust quickly from the old equilibrium to the new equilibrium. As we have just seen, though, many economists argue that at least some wages and prices are sticky and do *not* adjust quickly to changes in demand or supply. Other economists argue that stickiness in wages and prices is not widespread enough to be important in macroeconomic analysis. In other words, these economists believe that the aggregate supply curve may be vertical in the short run, as well as in the long run.

A number of economists have examined the evidence for wage stickiness. Each month, the Bureau of Labor Statistics (BLS) collects data on average hourly earnings for all workers and for various subcategories of workers, such as workers in manufacturing. Using these data is not the best way to measure wage stickiness, though, because each of the BLS categories contains many workers. As a result, the average hourly earnings data the BLS reports represent the average change in wages but do not show how many workers received wage increases, wage decreases, or unchanged wages or how large those changes may have been. To better understand how frequently employers change wages, economists have looked instead at data on individual workers.

Separate studies of data on individual workers have arrived at similar findings. One important result from these studies is that during a recession, firms are much more likely to reduce wages offered to newly hired workers than to reduce wages paid to current workers in the same job. For example, Mary C. Daly, Bart Hobijn, and Timothy Ni of the Federal Reserve Bank of San Francisco have shown that rather than cut wages during a recession, many firms reduce the *raises* they give workers, with more workers having their wages frozen, sometimes for long periods. Recall that the nominal wage is the number of dollars a firm pays a worker, while the real wage is the nominal wage divided by a price index. If a firm freezes a worker's nominal wage, the worker's real wage will gradually decline over time because of inflation. Most workers appear to be less upset if their real wage falls because of inflation than if it falls because of a cut in their nominal wage.

Daly, Hobijn, and Ni have used census data on individual workers to calculate the percentage of workers who each month received the same wage they had received in the same month during the previous year. The following figure shows these data for the years from 1997 through mid-2017. (The shaded areas are periods of recession.) Note that the percentage of workers with unchanged wages increases dramatically during recessions and the following months as the unemployment rate rises. The persistence of high rates of workers with frozen wages several years after the end of the 2007–2009 recession is an indication of how slowly the labor market recovered and how low the inflation rate has been since the recession. Only in 2016, as unemployment returned to more normal levels, did the percentage of U.S. workers with frozen wages begin to decline significantly.

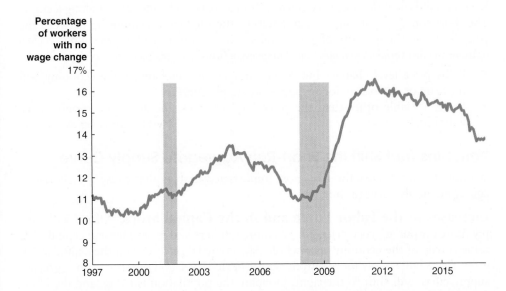

During recessions, why do firms often freeze nominal wages—frequently for extended periods—while they also lay off workers? Many economists believe that the main reason is that wage cuts upset workers. As a consequence, the productivity of workers who receive wage cuts may fall, and some workers may quit to find new jobs, either immediately or once the economy improves and the unemployment rate falls.

As Truman Bewley, an economist at Yale, put it, "The advantage of layoffs over pay reductions was that they 'get misery out of the door.'"

Sources: Mary C. Daly, Bart Hobijn, and Timothy Ni, "The Path of Wage Growth and Unemployment," *Federal Reserve Bank of San Francisco Economic Letter,* July 15, 2013; Anabela Carneiro, Paulo Guimarães, and Pedro Portugal, "Real Wages and the Business Cycle: Accounting for Worker, Firm, and Job Title Heterogeneity," *American Economic Review: Macroeconomics,* Vol. 4, No. 2, April 2012, pp. 133–152; Hervé Le Bihan, Jérémi Montornès, and Thomas Heckel, "Sticky Wages: Evidence from Quarterly Microeconomic Data," *American Economic Review: Macroeconomics,* Vol. 4, No. 3, July 2012, pp. 1–32; Alessando Barattieri, Susanto Basu, and Peter Gottschalk, "Some Evidence on the Importance of Sticky Wages," *American Economic Journal: Macroeconomics,* Vol. 6, No. 1, January 2014, pp. 70–101; William T. Dickens et al., "How Wages Change: Micro Evidence from the International Wage Flexibility Project," *Journal of Economic Perspectives,* Vol. 21, No. 2, Spring 2007, pp. 195–214; and data from Federal Reserve Bank of San Francisco, "Nominal Wage Rigidity Data Releases."

MyLab Economics Study Plan   **Your Turn:** Test your understanding by doing related problems 2.14 and 2.15 on page 468 at the end of this chapter.

Menu Costs Make Some Prices Sticky Firms base their prices today partly on what they expect future prices to be. For instance, if you own a restaurant, you will determine the prices printed on your menu based on what you expect the demand to be for the meals you sell and what you expect to pay for labor, rent, ingredients, and other inputs. Similarly, many firms list the prices of their products on their Web sites. If demand for their products or their production costs are higher or lower than the firms had expected, they may want to charge prices that are different from the ones on their menus or on their Web sites. Changing prices would be costly, however, because it would require printing new menus or entering new prices on their Web sites. The costs to firms of changing prices are called **menu costs**. To see why menu costs can lead to an upward-sloping short-run aggregate supply curve, consider the effect of an unexpected increase in the price level. In this case, firms will want to increase the prices they charge. Some firms, however, may not be willing to increase prices because of menu costs. Because their prices are now lower relative to competitors, these firms will find their sales increasing, which will cause them to increase output. Once again, a higher price level leads to a larger quantity of goods and services supplied.   **MyLab Economics** Concept Check

Menu costs The costs to firms of changing prices.

Shifts of the Short-Run Aggregate Supply Curve versus Movements along It

Keep in mind the difference between a shift in a curve and a movement along a curve. The short-run aggregate supply curve tells us the short-run relationship between the price level and the quantity of goods and services firms are willing to supply, *holding constant all other variables that affect the willingness of firms to supply goods and services*:

- If the price level changes but other variables are unchanged, the economy will move up or down a stationary aggregate supply curve.
- If any variable other than the price level changes, the aggregate supply curve will shift.   **MyLab Economics** Concept Check

Variables That Shift the Short-Run Aggregate Supply Curve

We now briefly discuss the five most important variables that cause the short-run aggregate supply curve to shift.

Increases in the Labor Force and in the Capital Stock A firm will supply more output at every price if it has more workers and more physical capital. The same is true of the economy as a whole. So, as the labor force and the capital stock grow, firms will supply more output at every price level, and the short-run aggregate supply curve will shift to the right. In Japan, the population is aging, and the labor force is decreasing. Holding other variables constant, this decrease in the labor force causes the short-run aggregate supply curve in Japan to shift to the left.

Technological Change As positive technological change takes place, the productivity of workers and machinery increases, which means firms can produce more goods and services with the same amount of labor and machinery. This increase in productivity

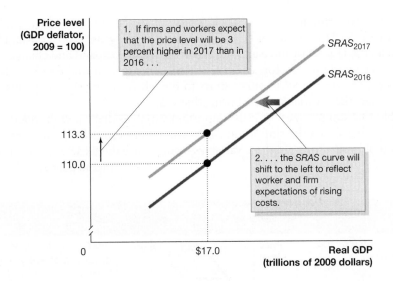

MyLab Economics Animation

Figure 13.3

How Expectations of the Future Price Level Affect the Short-Run Aggregate Supply Curve

The *SRAS* curve shifts to reflect worker and firm expectations of future prices.

1. If workers and firms expect that the price level will rise by 3 percent, from 110.0 to 113.3, they will adjust their wages and prices by that amount.
2. Holding constant all other variables that affect aggregate supply, the short-run aggregate supply curve will shift to the left.

If workers and firms expect that the price level will be lower in the future, the short-run aggregate supply curve will shift to the right.

reduces the firms' costs of production and allows them to produce more output at every price level. As a result, the short-run aggregate supply curve shifts to the right.

Changes in the Expected Future Price Level

If workers and firms believe that the price level is going to increase by 3 percent during the next year, they will try to adjust their wages and prices accordingly. For instance, if a labor union believes there will be 3 percent inflation next year, it knows that wages must rise 3 percent to preserve the purchasing power of those wages. Similar adjustments by other workers and firms will result in costs increasing throughout the economy by 3 percent. The result, shown in Figure 13.3, is that the short-run aggregate supply curve will shift to the left, so that any level of real GDP is now associated with a price level that is 3 percent higher. In general, *if workers and firms expect the price level to increase by a certain percentage, the SRAS curve will shift by an equivalent amount,* holding constant all other variables that affect the *SRAS* curve.

Adjustments of Workers and Firms to Errors in Past Expectations about the Price Level

Workers and firms sometimes make incorrect predictions about the price level. As time passes, they will attempt to compensate for these errors. Suppose that the Air Line Pilots Association signs a contract with Delta that provides for only small wage increases because the company and the union both expect only small increases in the price level. If increases in the price level turn out to be unexpectedly large, the union will take this into account when negotiating the next contract. The higher wages Delta pilots receive under the new contract will increase the company's costs and result in its needing to receive higher prices to produce the same level of output. If workers and firms across the economy are adjusting to the price level being higher than expected, the *SRAS* curve will shift to the left. If they are adjusting to the price level being lower than expected, the *SRAS* curve will shift to the right.

Unexpected Changes in the Price of an Important Natural Resource

An unexpected event that causes the short-run aggregate supply curve to shift is called a **supply shock**. Supply shocks are often caused by unexpected increases or decreases in the prices of important natural resources that cause firms' costs to be different from what they had expected. Oil prices can be particularly volatile. Some firms use oil in the production process. Other firms use products, such as plastics, that are made from oil. If oil prices rise unexpectedly, the costs of production will rise for these firms. Some utilities also burn oil to generate electricity, so electricity prices will rise. Rising oil prices lead to rising gasoline prices, which raise transportation costs for many firms. Because firms face rising costs, they will supply the same level of output only if they receive higher prices, and the short-run aggregate supply curve will shift to the left.

The U.S. economy has experienced at least some inflation every year since the 1930s, so workers and firms always expect next year's price level to be higher than this

Supply shock An unexpected event that causes the short-run aggregate supply curve to shift.

year's price level. Holding everything else constant, expectations of a higher price level will cause the *SRAS* curve to shift to the left. But everything else is not constant because every year, the U.S. labor force and the U.S. capital stock expand and changes in technology occur, and these factors cause the *SRAS* curve to shift to the right. Whether in any particular year the *SRAS* curve shifts to the left or to the right depends on how large an effect these variables have during that year.

Table 13.2 summarizes the most important variables that cause the *SRAS* curve to shift. The table shows the shift in the *SRAS* curve that results from an *increase* in each of the variables. A *decrease* in these variables would cause the *SRAS* curve to shift in the opposite direction.

MyLab Economics Study Plan

MyLab Economics Concept Check

Table 13.2

Variables That Shift the Short-Run Aggregate Supply Curve

An increase in . . .	shifts the short-run aggregate supply curve . . .	because . . .
the labor force or the capital stock	*SRAS₁* *SRAS₂*	more output can be produced at every price level.
productivity	*SRAS₁* *SRAS₂*	costs of producing output fall.
the expected future price level	*SRAS₂* *SRAS₁*	expecting the price level to increase leads workers and firms to increase wages and prices.
workers and firms adjusting to having previously underestimated the price level	*SRAS₂* *SRAS₁*	workers and firms attempt to catch up to a higher price level by increasing wages and prices.
the price of an important natural resource	*SRAS₂* *SRAS₁*	costs of producing output rise.

13.3 Macroeconomic Equilibrium in the Long Run and the Short Run

LEARNING OBJECTIVE: Use the aggregate demand and aggregate supply model to illustrate the difference between short-run and long-run macroeconomic equilibrium.

Now that we have discussed the components of the aggregate demand and aggregate supply model, we can use it to analyze changes in real GDP and the price level. In Figure 13.4, we bring the aggregate demand curve, the short-run aggregate supply curve, and the long-run aggregate supply curve together in one graph to show the *long-run macroeconomic*

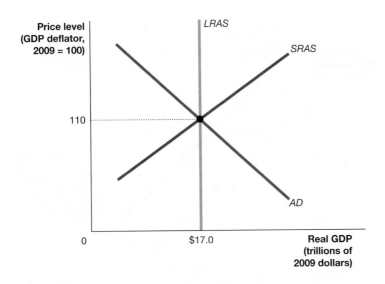

MyLab Economics Animation

Figure 13.4

Long-Run Macroeconomic Equilibrium

In long-run macroeconomic equilibrium, the *AD* and *SRAS* curves intersect at a point on the *LRAS* curve. In this case, equilibrium occurs at real GDP of $17.0 trillion and a price level of 110.

equilibrium for the economy. In the figure, equilibrium occurs at real GDP of $17.0 trillion and a price level of 110. Notice that in long-run equilibrium, the short-run aggregate supply curve and the aggregate demand curve intersect at a point on the long-run aggregate supply curve. Because equilibrium occurs at a point along the long-run aggregate supply curve, we know the economy is at potential GDP: Firms will be operating at their normal level of capacity, and everyone who wants a job will have one, except the structurally and frictionally unemployed. We know, however, that the economy is often not in long-run macroeconomic equilibrium. In the following section, we discuss the economic forces that can push the economy away from long-run equilibrium.

Recessions, Expansions, and Supply Shocks

Because the full analysis of the aggregate demand and aggregate supply model can be complicated, we begin with a simplified case, using two assumptions:

1. The economy has not been experiencing any inflation. The price level is currently 110, and workers and firms expect it to remain at 110 in the future.
2. The economy is not experiencing any long-run growth. Potential GDP is $17.0 trillion and will remain at that level in the future.

These assumptions are simplifications because in reality, the U.S. economy has experienced at least some inflation every year since the 1930s, and potential GDP also increases every year. However, the assumptions allow us to understand more easily the key ideas of the aggregate demand and aggregate supply model. In this section, we examine the short-run and long-run effects of recessions, expansions, and supply shocks.

Recession

The Short-Run Effect of a Decline in Aggregate Demand Suppose that rising interest rates cause firms to reduce spending on factories and equipment and cause households to reduce spending on new homes. The decline in investment causes the aggregate demand curve to shift to the left, from AD_1 to AD_2, as shown in Figure 13.5. The result is a move from point A to a new *short-run macroeconomic equilibrium*, where the AD_2 curve intersects the $SRAS_1$ curve at point B. In the new short-run equilibrium, real GDP has declined from $17.0 trillion to $16.8 trillion and is below its potential level. This lower level of GDP will result in declining profits for many firms and layoffs for some workers: The economy will be in recession.

Adjustment Back to Potential GDP in the Long Run We know that a recession will eventually end because there are forces at work that push the economy back to potential GDP in the long run. Figure 13.5 shows how the economy moves from recession back to potential GDP. The shift from AD_1 to AD_2 initially leads to a short-run equilibrium, with the price level having fallen from 110 to 108 (point B). Workers and firms will begin to adjust to the price level being lower than they had expected it to be.

Figure 13.5

The Short-Run and Long-Run Effects of a Decrease in Aggregate Demand

In the short run, a decrease in aggregate demand causes a recession. In the long run, it causes only a decline in the price level.

1. A decline in investment shifts *AD* to the left, causing a recession.

2. As firms and workers adjust to the price level being lower than they had expected, costs will fall and cause *SRAS* to shift to the right.

3. Equilibrium moves from point *B* back to potential GDP at point *C*, with a lower price level.

Workers will be willing to accept lower wages—because each dollar of wages is able to buy more goods and services—and firms will be willing to accept lower prices. In addition, the unemployment resulting from the recession will make workers more willing to accept lower wages, and the decline in demand will make firms more willing to accept lower prices. As a result, the *SRAS* curve will shift to the right, from *SRAS₁* to *SRAS₂*. At this point, long-run equilibrium is restored at point C. The shift from *SRAS₁* to *SRAS₂* will not happen instantly. It may take the economy several years to return to potential GDP. The important conclusion is that a decline in aggregate demand causes a recession in the short run, but in the long run it causes only a decline in the price level.

Economists refer to the process of adjustment back to potential GDP just described as an *automatic mechanism* because it occurs without any actions by the government. An alternative to waiting for the automatic mechanism to end a recession is for the government to use monetary policy or fiscal policy to shift the *AD* curve to the right and restore potential GDP more quickly. We will discuss monetary policy and fiscal policy in Chapters 15 and 16. Economists debate whether it is better to wait for the automatic mechanism to end recessions or to use monetary policy and fiscal policy.

Apply the Concept

Does It Matter What Causes a Decline in Aggregate Demand?

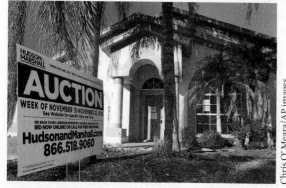

The collapse in spending on housing added to the severity of the 2007–2009 recession.

We have seen that GDP has four components and that a decrease in any of them can cause the aggregate demand curve to shift to the left, leading to a recession. In practice, most recessions in the United States since World War II have begun with a decline in residential construction. Edward Leamer of the University of California, Los Angeles, has gone so far as to argue that "housing *is* the business cycle," meaning that declines in residential construction are the most important reason for the declines in aggregate demand that lead to recessions. The shaded periods in the following graph represent recessions. The graph shows that spending on residential construction has declined prior to every recession since 1955.

The graph also highlights a fact that we noted earlier and, as we saw in the chapter opener, KB Home knows all too well: The decline in residential construction during the 2007–2009 recession was particularly severe. Spending on residential construction declined by almost 60 percent from the fourth quarter of 2005 to the third quarter of 2010. Largely because of these problems in the housing sector, the decline in real GDP during the recession of 2007–2009 was larger than during any other recession since the Great Depression of the 1930s.

What typically causes declines in spending on residential construction? Late in a business cycle expansion, the inflation rate and interest rates start to increase (see Chapter 10, Section 10.3). Higher interest rates often result from monetary policy actions as the Federal Reserve tries to slow down the economy and reduce the rate of inflation (see Chapter 15, Section 15.3). Higher interest rates reduce consumer demand for new houses by increasing the cost of loans.

But the collapse in residential construction prior to and during the recession of 2007–2009 was due more to the deflating of the "housing bubble" of 2002–2005 and to the financial crisis that began in 2007 than to higher interest rates. We will discuss both the housing bubble and the financial crisis later in this chapter. At this point, we can note that research by Carmen M. Reinhart and Kenneth S. Rogoff of Harvard University has shown that declines in aggregate demand that result from financial crises tend to be larger and longer-lasting than declines due to other factors. So, the experience of 2007–2009 indicates that, in fact, the source of the decline in aggregate demand can be important in determining the severity of a recession.

Sources: Edward E. Leamer, "Housing *Is* the Business Cycle," in *Housing, Housing Finance, and Monetary Policy*, Federal Reserve Bank of Kansas City, August 2007; Carmen M. Reinhart and Kenneth S. Rogoff, "The Aftermath of Financial Crises," *American Economic Review*, Vol. 99, No. 2, May 2009, pp. 466–472; and U.S. Bureau of Economic Analysis.

Your Turn: Test your understanding by doing related problem 3.6 on page 469 at the end of this chapter.

MyLab Economics Study Plan

Expansion

The Short-Run Effect of an Increase in Aggregate Demand
Suppose that instead of becoming pessimistic, many firms become optimistic about the future profitability of new investment, as happened during the information technology and telecommunications booms of the late 1990s. The resulting increase in investment will shift the *AD* curve to the right, as shown in Figure 13.6. Equilibrium moves from point *A* to point *B*. Real GDP rises from $17.0 trillion to $17.3 trillion, and the price level rises from 110 to 113. Real GDP will be above potential GDP: Firms are operating beyond their normal level of capacity, and some workers who would ordinarily be structurally or frictionally unemployed or who would not be in the labor force are employed.

Figure 13.6

The Short-Run and Long-Run Effects of an Increase in Aggregate Demand

In the short run, an increase in aggregate demand causes an increase in real GDP. In the long run, it causes only an increase in the price level.

1. An increase in investment shifts *AD* to the right, causing an inflationary expansion.

2. As firms and workers adjust to the price level being higher than they had expected, costs will rise and cause *SRAS* to shift to the left.

3. Equilibrium moves from point *B* back to potential GDP at point *C*, with a higher price level.

Adjustment Back to Potential GDP in the Long Run Just as an automatic mechanism brings the economy back to potential GDP from a recession, an automatic mechanism brings the economy back from a short-run equilibrium beyond potential GDP. Figure 13.6 illustrates this mechanism. The shift from AD_1 to AD_2 initially leads to a short-run equilibrium at point *B*, with the price level rising from 110 to 113. Workers and firms will begin to adjust to the price level being higher than they had expected. Workers will push for higher wages—because each dollar of wages is able to buy fewer goods and services—and firms will charge higher prices. In addition, the low levels of unemployment resulting from the expansion will make it easier for workers to negotiate for higher wages, and the increase in demand will make it easier for firms to receive higher prices. As a result, the *SRAS* curve will shift to the left, from $SRAS_1$ to $SRAS_2$. At point *C*, the economy will be back in long-run equilibrium. Once again, the shift from $SRAS_1$ to $SRAS_2$ will not happen instantly. The process of returning to potential GDP may stretch out for more than a year.

Supply Shock

The Short-Run Effect of a Supply Shock Suppose oil prices increase substantially. This supply shock will increase many firms' costs and cause the *SRAS* curve to shift to the left, as shown in panel (a) of Figure 13.7. Notice that in the new short-run equilibrium at point *B*, the price level is higher (112 rather than 110), but real GDP is lower ($16.7 trillion rather than $17.0 trillion). This unpleasant combination of inflation and recession is called **stagflation**.

Stagflation A combination of inflation and recession, usually resulting from a supply shock.

Adjustment Back to Potential GDP in the Long Run A recession caused by a supply shock increases unemployment and reduces output. Workers will eventually be willing to accept lower wages, and firms will be willing to accept lower prices. In panel (b) of Figure 13.7, the short-run aggregate supply curve shifts from $SRAS_2$ to $SRAS_1$, moving equilibrium from point *B* back to point *A*. Real GDP is back to potential GDP at the original price level. It may take several years for this process to be completed. An alternative would be to use monetary and fiscal policy to shift the aggregate demand curve to the right. Using policy in this way would bring real GDP back to potential GDP more quickly but would result in a permanently higher price level.

MyLab Economics Animation

Figure 13.7   **The Short-Run and Long-Run Effects of a Supply Shock**

Panel (a) shows that a supply shock, such as a large increase in oil prices, will cause a recession and a higher price level in the short run. The recession caused by the supply shock increases unemployment and reduces output. Panel (b) shows that rising unemployment and falling output result in workers being willing to accept lower wages and firms being willing to accept lower prices. The short-run aggregate supply curve shifts from $SRAS_2$ to $SRAS_1$. Equilibrium moves from point B back to potential GDP and the original price level at point A.

Apply the Concept   **MyLab Economics** Video

How Long Is the Long Run in Macroeconomics?

Once a recession starts, how long does it take for real GDP and employment to return to the levels they had achieved at the business cycle peak? On average, in the recessions since 1950, it has taken six quarters, or about a year and a half, for real GDP to return to its cyclical peak. During the same period, it has taken employment on average about 9.5 quarters, or nearly two and a half years, to return to its cycle peak. But these averages disguise great variation across recessions.

The following figure shows the recessions of 1981–1982, 1990–1991, 2001, and 2007–2009. The value of real GDP at the business cycle peak is set equal to 100. Therefore, values less than 100 represent levels of real GDP below the level at the business cycle peak. The horizontal axis measures the number of quarters since the business cycle peak. The severity of the 2007–2009 recession can be seen clearly in the figure. Real GDP reached a cyclical peak in the fourth quarter of 2007. Real GDP didn't return to this level until the second quarter of 2011, which was 14 quarters, or *three and a half years*, after the recession began. That was far longer than in any other recession since 1950. Some economists describe the 1981–1982 recession as a V-shaped recession because although the decline in real GDP was large, real GDP returned to its cyclical peak relatively quickly. The 2007–2009 recession, in contrast, was a U-shaped recession because it took an extended period for real GDP to return to its cyclical peak.

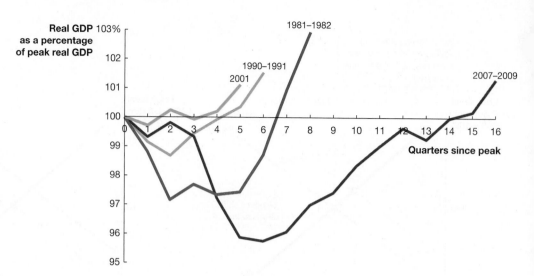

As the figure below shows, following the 2007–2009 recession, employment was very slow to return to its cyclical peak: It took 25 quarters, or more than six years. This period was far longer than in any other recession since 1950, and it was more than twice as long as following a typical recession. The second-slowest return to peak employment was following the 2001 recession, which has led some economists to consider whether changes in the U.S. labor market have made it more difficult for employment to return to normal levels following a recession.

The severity of the 2007–2009 recession took most economists and policymakers by surprise because they did not predict that the decline in housing prices that began in 2006 would eventually lead to a major financial crisis in 2008. Even as the recession was ending in 2009, members of President Obama's economic staff, economists at the Federal Reserve, and economists at the Congressional Budget Office all expected that the economy would return to normal levels of real GDP and employment far sooner than it did.

In Chapters 15 and 16, we will discuss the disagreements among economists and policymakers over why the U.S. economy took so long to return to potential GDP and full employment following the 2007–2009 recession.

Sources: Board of Governors of the Federal Reserve System, "Economic Projections of Federal Reserve Board Members and Federal Reserve Bank Presidents," various dates; Congressional Budget Office, "Data Underlying Selected Economic Figures, Real Gross Domestic Product," various dates; Christina Romer and Jared Bernstein, "The Job Impact of the American Recovery and Reinvestment Plan," January 9, 2009; U.S. Bureau of Economic Analysis; U.S. Bureau of Labor Statistics; and National Bureau of Economic Research.

MyLab Economics Study Plan   **Your Turn:** Test your understanding by doing related problem 3.9 on page 469 at the end of this chapter.

13.4 A Dynamic Aggregate Demand and Aggregate Supply Model*

LEARNING OBJECTIVE: Use the dynamic aggregate demand and aggregate supply model to analyze macroeconomic conditions.

The basic aggregate demand and aggregate supply model used so far in this chapter provides important insights into how short-run macroeconomic equilibrium is determined. Unfortunately, the model also provides some misleading results. For instance, it incorrectly predicts that a recession caused by the aggregate demand curve shifting to the left will result in a lower price level, which has not happened over an entire year since the 1930s. The basic model is sometimes inaccurate because it assumes that (1) the economy does not experience continuing inflation and (2) the economy does not experience long-run growth. We can develop a more useful aggregate demand and aggregate supply model by dropping these assumptions. The result will be a model that takes into account that the economy is not *static*, with an unchanging level of potential GDP and no continuing inflation, but *dynamic*, with potential GDP that grows over time and inflation that continues every year. We can create a *dynamic aggregate demand and aggregate supply model* by making changes to the basic model that incorporate the following important macroeconomic facts:

- Potential GDP increases continually, shifting the long-run aggregate supply curve to the right.
- During most years, the aggregate demand curve shifts to the right.
- Except during periods when workers and firms expect high rates of inflation, the short-run aggregate supply curve shifts to the right.

Figure 13.8 illustrates how incorporating these macroeconomic facts changes the basic aggregate demand and aggregate supply model. We start with $SRAS_1$ and AD_1 intersecting at point A, at a price level of 110 and real GDP of \$17.0 trillion. Because this intersection occurs at a point on $LRAS_1$, we know the economy is in long-run equilibrium. We show the long-run aggregate supply curve shifting to the right, from $LRAS_1$ to $LRAS_2$, because during the year, potential GDP increases as the U.S. labor force and the U.S. capital stock increase and technological progress occurs. The short-run aggregate supply curve shifts from $SRAS_1$ to $SRAS_2$ because the same variables that cause the long-run aggregate supply curve to shift to the right will also increase the quantity of goods and services that firms are willing to supply in the short run. Finally, the aggregate demand curve shifts to the right, from AD_1 to AD_2. The aggregate demand curve shifts for several reasons: As the population grows and incomes rise, consumption will increase over time. As the economy grows, firms will expand capacity, and new firms will be formed, increasing investment. An expanding population and an expanding economy require increased government services, such as more police officers and teachers, so government purchases will increase.

The new equilibrium in Figure 13.8 occurs at point B, where AD_2 intersects $SRAS_2$ on $LRAS_2$. In the new equilibrium, the price level remains at 110, while real GDP increases to \$17.4 trillion. Notice that there has been no inflation because aggregate demand and short-run aggregate supply shifted to the right by exactly as much as long-run aggregate supply, leaving the price level unchanged at 110. In fact, though, we wouldn't expect that all three curves would typically shift by the same amount. For instance, the $SRAS$ curve is also affected by workers' and firms' expectations of future changes in the price level and by supply shocks. These variables can partially or completely offset the normal tendency of the $SRAS$ curve to shift to the right over the course of a year. We also know that changes in the expenditures of consumers, firms, and the government may result in the AD curve shifting to the right by more or less than the $SRAS$ and $LRAS$ curves. In fact, as we will see shortly, *changes in the price level and in real GDP in the short run are determined by how much the $SRAS$ and AD curves shift.*

---

*This section may be omitted without loss of continuity.

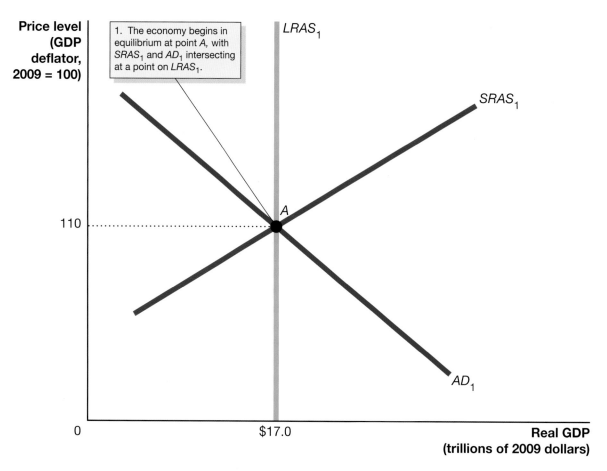

Figure 13.8 **A Dynamic Aggregate Demand and Aggregate Supply Model**

We start with the basic aggregate demand and aggregate supply model.

What Is the Usual Cause of Inflation?

The dynamic aggregate demand and aggregate supply model provides a more accurate explanation of the source of most inflation. If total spending in the economy grows faster than total production, prices rise. Figure 13.9 illustrates this point by showing that if the *AD* curve shifts to the right by more than the *LRAS* curve, inflation results because equilibrium occurs at a higher price level, point *B*. In the new equilibrium, the *SRAS* curve has shifted to the right by less than the *LRAS* curve because the anticipated increase in prices offsets some of the effect of the technological change and increases in the labor force and capital stock that occur during the year. Although inflation generally results from total spending growing faster than total production, a shift to the left of the short-run aggregate supply curve can also cause an increase in the price level, as we noted in Section 13.3 when discussing supply shocks.

As we saw in Figure 13.8, if aggregate demand increases by the same amount as short-run and long-run aggregate supply, the price level will not change. In this case, the economy experiences economic growth without inflation. **MyLab Economics** Concept Check

The Recession of 2007–2009

We can use the dynamic aggregate demand and aggregate supply model to analyze the recession of 2007–2009. The recession began in December 2007, with the end of the

Figure 13.9   **Using Dynamic Aggregate Demand and Aggregate Supply to Understand Inflation**

The most common cause of inflation is total spending increasing faster than total production.
1. The economy begins at point A, with real GDP of $17.0 trillion and a price level of 110. An increase in full-employment real GDP from $17.0 trillion to $17.4 trillion causes long-run aggregate

supply to shift to the right from $LRAS_1$ to $LRAS_2$. Aggregate demand shifts to the right from AD_1 to AD_2.
2. Because AD shifts to the right by more than the LRAS curve, the price level in the new equilibrium rises from 110 to 114.

economic expansion that started in November 2001. Several factors combined to cause the recession:

- **The end of the housing bubble.** The figure in the *Apply the Concept* on page 455 shows that spending on residential construction increased rapidly from 2002 to 2005 and then declined more than 60 percent between the end of 2005 and the beginning of 2010. The increase in spending on housing through 2005 was partly the result of actions the Federal Reserve had taken to lower interest rates during and after the recession of 2001. As interest rates on mortgage loans declined, more consumers began to buy new homes. But by 2005, it was clear that a speculative bubble was partly responsible for the rapidly rising prices of both newly built and existing homes. A bubble occurs when people become less concerned with the underlying value of an asset—either a physical asset, such as a house, or a financial asset, such as a stock—and focus instead on expectations of the price of the asset increasing. In some areas of the country, such as California, Arizona, and Florida, many homes were purchased by investors who intended to resell them for higher prices than they paid for them and did not intend to live in them. Some popular television programs explored ways that people could "flip" houses by buying and quickly reselling them. Speculative bubbles eventually end, and the housing bubble started to deflate in 2006. Both new home sales and housing prices began to decline. The growth of aggregate demand slowed as spending on residential construction—a component of investment spending—fell.
- **The financial crisis.** Problems in the housing market were bad news for workers and firms involved with residential construction. In addition, falling housing prices led to an increased number of borrowers defaulting on their mortgage loans. These defaults caused banks and some other financial institutions to suffer heavy losses. Beginning in the spring of 2008, the U.S. Department of the Treasury and the Federal Reserve intervened to save several large financial institutions from bankruptcy. We will look at the details of the financial crisis in Chapters 14

and 15. For now we can note that the financial crisis led to a *credit crunch* that made it difficult for many households and firms to obtain the loans they needed to finance their spending. This drying up of credit contributed to declines in consumption spending and investment spending.

- **The rapid increase in oil prices during 2008.** Oil prices, which had been as low as $34 per barrel in 2004, had risen to $140 per barrel by mid-2008. The increase in the price of oil appeared to be caused by increased demand in rapidly growing economies, particularly India and China, and by the difficulty in developing new supplies of oil in the short run. With the deepening of the recession, worldwide demand for oil declined, and oil prices fell to about $40 per barrel in early 2009. As we have seen in this chapter, rising oil prices can result in a *supply shock* that causes the short-run aggregate supply curve to shift to the left, increasing the severity of a recession.

Figure 13.10 illustrates the beginning of the recession by showing the economy's short-run macroeconomic equilibrium in 2007 and 2008. In the figure, short-run equilibrium for 2007 occurs where AD_{2007} intersects $SRAS_{2007}$ at real GDP of $14.9 trillion and a price level of 97.3. Real GDP in 2007 was above potential GDP of $14.8 trillion, shown by $LRAS_{2007}$. During 2008, aggregate demand shifted to the left, from AD_{2007} to AD_{2008}. Aggregate demand declined because of the negative effects of the bursting of the housing bubble and the financial crisis on consumption spending and investment spending. The supply shock from higher oil prices caused short-run aggregate supply to shift to the left, from $SRAS_{2007}$ to $SRAS_{2008}$.

Short-run equilibrium for 2008 occurred at real GDP of $14.8 trillion and a price level of 99.2. A large gap opened between short-run equilibrium real GDP and potential GDP. (By coincidence, short-run equilibrium in 2008 occurred at the level of potential GDP for *2007*.) Not surprisingly, unemployment rose from 4.6 percent in 2007 to 5.8 percent in 2008. The price level increased only from 97.3 to 99.2, so the inflation rate was a low 2.0 percent.

The recession persisted into 2009, as potential GDP increased to $15.3 trillion, while real GDP fell to $14.4 trillion. (The situation in 2009 is not shown in Figure 13.10.) The increased gap between real GDP and potential GDP caused the unemployment

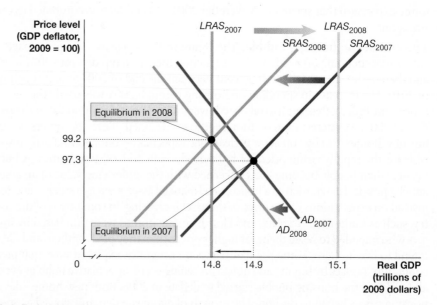

MyLab Economics *Animation*

Figure 13.10 **The Beginning of the Recession of 2007–2009**

Between 2007 and 2008, the *AD* curve shifted to the left because of declines in consumption spending and investment spending, while potential GDP increased from $14.8 trillion to $15.1 trillion. Because of a sharp increase in oil prices, short-run aggregate supply shifted to the left, from $SRAS_{2007}$ to $SRAS_{2008}$.

Real GDP decreased from $14.9 trillion in 2007 to $14.8 trillion in 2008, which was far below potential GDP, shown by $LRAS_{2008}$. Because of the decrease in aggregate demand, the price level increased only from 97.3 in 2007 to 99.2 in 2008, so the inflation rate for 2008 was only 2.0 percent.

rate to soar to 9.3 percent—the highest unemployment rate since the recession of 1981–1982 and the second highest since the Great Depression of the 1930s. Although the recession ended in June 2009, real GDP grew only slowly during 2010 and 2011, leaving the unemployment rate above 8.5 percent.

The severity of the recession of 2007–2009 resulted in some of the most dramatic changes in government economic policy since the Great Depression. We will explore these new policies in Chapters 15 and 16.   **MyLab Economics** Concept Check   **MyLab Economics** Study Plan

Solved Problem 13.4

MyLab Economics Interactive Animation

Showing the Oil Shock of 1974–1975 on a Dynamic Aggregate Demand and Aggregate Supply Graph

The 1974–1975 recession clearly illustrates how a supply shock affects the economy. Following the Arab–Israeli War of 1973, the Organization of the Petroleum Exporting Countries (OPEC) took actions that increased the price of a barrel of oil from less than $3 to more than $10. Use this information and the statistics in the following table to draw a dynamic aggregate demand and aggregate supply graph showing macroeconomic equilibrium for 1974 and 1975. For simplicity, assume that the aggregate demand curve did

not shift between 1974 and 1975. Provide a brief explanation of your graph.

Year	Actual Real GDP	Potential GDP	Price Level
1974	$5.40 trillion	$5.43 trillion	28.7
1975	5.39 trillion	5.62 trillion	31.4

Sources: U.S. Bureau of Economic Analysis; and Congressional Budget Office.

Solving the Problem

Step 1: Review the chapter material. This problem is about applying the dynamic aggregate demand and aggregate supply model, so you may want to review the section "A Dynamic Aggregate Demand and Aggregate Supply Model," which begins on page 459.

Step 2: Use the information in the table to draw the graph. You need to draw five curves: *SRAS* and *LRAS* for both 1974 and 1975 and *AD*, which is the same for both years. You know that the two *LRAS* curves will be vertical lines at the values given for potential GDP in the table. Because of the large supply shock, you know that the *SRAS* curve shifted to the left. The problem asks you to assume that the *AD* curve did not shift. Your graph should look like the following:

Step 3: **Explain your graph.** $LRAS_{1974}$ and $LRAS_{1975}$ are at the levels of potential GDP for each year. Macroeconomic equilibrium for 1974 occurs where the AD curve intersects the $SRAS_{1974}$ curve, with real GDP of $5.40 trillion and a price level of 28.7. Macroeconomic equilibrium for 1975 occurs where the AD curve intersects the $SRAS_{1975}$ curve, with real GDP of $5.39 trillion and a price level of 31.4.

Extra Credit: As a result of the supply shock, equilibrium real GDP moved from just below potential GDP in 1974 (the recession actually began right at the end of 1973) to well below potential GDP in 1975. With real GDP in 1975 about 4.3 percent below its potential level, the unemployment rate soared from 5.6 percent in 1974 to 8.5 percent in 1975.

MyLab Economics Study Plan

Your Turn: For more practice, do related problems 4.5 and 4.6 on pages 470–471 at the end of this chapter.

Continued from page 437

Economics in Your Life & Career

Is an Employer Likely to Cut Your Pay during a Recession?

At the beginning of this chapter, we asked you to consider whether during a recession your employer is likely to reduce your pay and cut the prices of the products he or she sells. We have seen that even during a recession, the price level rarely falls. In fact, in the United States, the GDP deflator has not fallen for an entire year since the 1930s. Although some firms reduced prices during the recession of 2007–2009, most firms did not. So, the owner of the coffeehouse where you work will probably not cut the price of lattes unless sales have declined drastically. We also saw that most firms are reluctant to cut wages because doing so can lower worker morale and productivity. Because the recession of 2007–2009 was particularly severe, some firms did cut wages. But because you are a highly skilled barista, your employer is unlikely to cut your wages for fear that you might quit and work for a competitor.

Conclusion

Chapter 3 demonstrated the power of the microeconomic model of demand and supply in explaining how the prices and quantities of individual products are determined. This chapter showed that we need a different model to explain the behavior of the whole economy. We saw that the macroeconomic model of aggregate demand and aggregate supply explains fluctuations in real GDP and the price level.

Fluctuations in real GDP, employment, and the price level have led the federal government to implement macroeconomic policies. We will explore these policies in later chapters after first considering the role money plays in the economy.

Visit MyLab Economics for a news article and analysis related to the concepts in this chapter.

Key Terms

Aggregate demand (*AD*) curve, p. 438

Aggregate demand and aggregate supply model, p. 438

Fiscal policy, p. 441

Long-run aggregate supply (*LRAS*) curve, p. 447

Menu costs, p. 450

Monetary policy, p. 441

Short-run aggregate supply (*SRAS*) curve, p. 438

Stagflation, p. 456

Supply shock, p. 451

13.1 Aggregate Demand, pages 438–446

LEARNING OBJECTIVE: Identify the determinants of aggregate demand and distinguish between a movement along the aggregate demand curve and a shift of the curve.

MyLab Economics   Visit **www.pearson.com/mylab/economics** to complete these exercises online and get instant feedback.

Summary

The **aggregate demand and aggregate supply model** enables us to explain short-run fluctuations in real GDP and the price level. The **aggregate demand (*AD*) curve** shows the relationship between the price level and the level of planned aggregate expenditures by households, firms, and the government. The **short-run aggregate supply (*SRAS*) curve** shows the relationship in the short run between the price level and the quantity of real GDP supplied by firms. The long-run aggregate supply curve shows the relationship in the long run between the price level and the quantity of real GDP supplied. The four components of aggregate demand are consumption (*C*), investment (*I*), government purchases (*G*), and net exports (*NX*). The aggregate demand curve is downward sloping because a decline in the price level causes consumption, investment, and net exports to increase. If the price level changes but all else remains constant, the result is a movement up or down a stationary aggregate demand curve. If any variable other than the price level changes, the aggregate demand curve will shift. The variables that cause the aggregate demand curve to shift are divided into three categories: changes in government policies, changes in the expectations of households and firms, and changes in foreign variables. For example, **monetary policy** involves the actions the Federal Reserve takes to manage the money supply and interest rates to pursue macroeconomic policy objectives. When the Federal Reserve takes actions to change interest rates, consumption and investment spending will change, shifting the aggregate demand curve. **Fiscal policy** involves changes in the federal government's taxes and purchases that are intended to achieve macroeconomic policy objectives. Changes in federal taxes and purchases shift the aggregate demand curve.

Review Questions

1.1 What relationship does the aggregate demand curve show? What relationship does the aggregate supply curve show?

1.2 Give the three reasons the aggregate demand curve slopes downward. Are these reasons the same as the reasons that the demand curve for an individual product, such as bananas, slopes downward? Briefly explain.

1.3 What variables cause the *AD* curve to shift? For each variable, identify whether an increase in that variable will cause the *AD* curve to shift to the right or to the left and also indicate which component(s) of GDP—consumption, investment, government purchases, or net exports—will change.

Problems and Applications

1.4 Briefly explain how each of the following events would affect the aggregate demand curve.
   a. An increase in the price level
   b. An increase in government purchases
   c. Higher state personal income taxes
   d. Higher interest rates
   e. Faster income growth in other countries
   f. A higher exchange rate between the dollar and foreign currencies

1.5 From August 2009 to May 2017, the Standard & Poor's Index of 500 stock prices increased by more than 135 percent, while the consumer price index increased by less than 15 percent. Briefly explain what effect, if any, these changes had on the aggregate demand curve.

1.6 Consider the two aggregate demand curves in the following graph. What would cause a movement from point *A* to point *B* on *AD*₁? What would cause a movement from point *A* to point *C*?

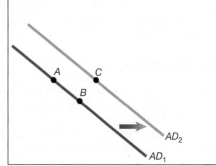

1.7 (Related to the Don't Let This Happen to You on page 441) An economics student makes the following statement: "It's easy to understand why the aggregate demand curve is downward sloping: When the price level increases, consumers substitute into buying less expensive products, which decreases total spending in the economy." Briefly explain whether you agree.

1.8 (Related to Solved Problem 13.1 on page 442) Explain whether each of the following will cause a shift of the *AD* curve or a movement along it.
   a. Firms become more optimistic and increase their spending on machinery and equipment.
   b. The federal government increases taxes in an attempt to reduce a budget deficit.
   c. The U.S. economy experiences 4 percent inflation.

1.9 (Related to Solved Problem 13.1 on page 442) In 2017, an article in the *Wall Street Journal* discussing the latest data on U.S. net exports noted that, along with other currencies, "the [Chinese] yuan has risen this year against the dollar." The article also noted that there had been "stronger [economic] growth in Asia and Europe."

   a. What does the article mean by noting that the yuan had "risen" against the dollar?
   b. Briefly explain whether the combination of other currencies rising against the dollar and stronger economic growth in Asia and Europe had led to an increase or a decrease in U.S. net exports.
   c. Will the outcome you discuss in part (b) result in a movement along the U.S. aggregate demand curve or a shift of the curve? Briefly explain.

   Source: Josh Mitchell, "U.S. Trade Gap Shrinks as Exports Rise," *Wall Street Journal*, April 4, 2017.

1.10 (Related to the Apply the Concept on page 444) If real GDP in the United States declined by more during the 2007–2009 recession than did real GDP in Canada, China, and other trading partners of the United States, would the effect be to increase or decrease U.S. net exports? Briefly explain.

Aggregate Supply, pages 446–452

LEARNING OBJECTIVE: Identify the determinants of aggregate supply and distinguish between a movement along the short-run aggregate supply curve and a shift of the curve.

MyLab Economics Visit **www.pearson.com/mylab/economics** to complete these exercises online and get instant feedback.

Summary

The **long-run aggregate supply (LRAS) curve** is a vertical line because in the long run, real GDP is always at its potential level and is unaffected by the price level. The short-run aggregate supply curve slopes upward because workers and firms fail to predict accurately the future price level. The three main explanations of why this failure results in an upward-sloping aggregate supply curve are that (1) contracts make wages and prices "sticky," (2) businesses often adjust wages slowly, and (3) menu costs make some prices sticky. **Menu costs** are the costs to firms of changing prices. If the price level changes but all else remains constant, the result is a movement up or down a stationary aggregate supply curve. If any other variable that affects the willingness of firms to supply goods and services changes, the aggregate supply curve will shift. The short-run aggregate supply curve shifts as a result of increases in the labor force and capital stock, technological change, increases or decreases in the expected future price level, adjustments of workers and firms to errors in past expectations about the price level, and increases or decreases in the price of an important raw material. A **supply shock** is an unexpected event that causes the short-run aggregate supply curve to shift.

Review Questions

2.1 Explain why the long-run aggregate supply curve is vertical.

2.2 What variables cause the long-run aggregate supply curve to shift? For each variable, identify whether an increase in that variable will cause the long-run aggregate supply curve to shift to the right or to the left.

2.3 Why does the short-run aggregate supply curve slope upward?

2.4 What variables cause the short-run aggregate supply curve to shift? For each variable, identify whether an increase in that variable will cause the short-run aggregate supply curve to shift to the right or to the left.

2.5 As output increases along the short-run aggregate supply curve, briefly explain what happens to the natural rate of unemployment and to the cyclical rate of unemployment.

Problems and Applications

2.6 Briefly explain how each of the following events would affect the long-run aggregate supply curve.
   a. A higher price level
   b. An increase in the labor force
   c. An increase in the quantity of capital goods
   d. Technological change

2.7 What are menu costs? If menu costs were eliminated, would the short-run aggregate supply curve be a vertical line? Briefly explain.

2.8 A student is asked to draw an aggregate demand and aggregate supply graph to illustrate the effect of an increase in aggregate supply. The student draws the following graph:

The student explains the graph as follows:

> An increase in aggregate supply causes a shift from $SRAS_1$ to $SRAS_2$. Because this shift in the aggregate supply curve results in a lower price level, consumption, investment, and net exports will increase. This change causes the aggregate demand curve to shift to the right, from AD_1 to AD_2. We know that real GDP will increase, but we can't be sure whether the price level will rise or fall because that depends on whether the aggregate supply curve or the aggregate demand curve has shifted farther to the right. I assume that aggregate supply shifts out farther than aggregate demand, so I show the final price level, P_3, as being lower than the initial price level, P_1.

Explain whether you agree with the student's analysis. Be careful to explain exactly what—if anything—you find wrong with this analysis.

2.9 Consider the short-run aggregate supply curves in the following graph. What would cause a movement from point A to point B on $SRAS_1$? What would cause a movement from point A to point C?

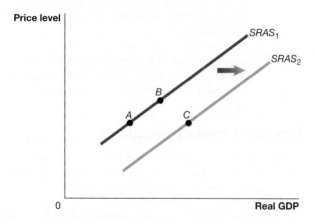

2.10 An article in the *Economist* noted that "the economy's potential to supply goods and services [is] determined by such things as the labour force and capital stock, as well as inflation expectations." Briefly explain whether you agree with this list of the determinants of potential GDP.

Source: "Money's Muddled Message," *Economist*, March 19, 2009.

2.11 Briefly explain how each of the following events would affect the short-run aggregate supply curve.
  a. An increase in the price level
  b. An increase in what the price level is expected to be in the future
  c. A price level that is currently higher than expected
  d. An unexpected increase in the price of an important raw material
  e. An increase in the labor force participation rate

2.12 Consider the variables that shift long-run aggregate supply and the variables that shift short-run aggregate supply. Match each of the following scenarios with one of the three graphs of long-run aggregate supply and short-run aggregate supply.

  a. The expected future price level decreases.
  b. Workers and firms adjust to having previously underestimated the price level.
  c. A positive technological change occurs.

2.13 An article in the *Los Angeles Times* about driverless trucks stated, "Trucking will likely be the first type of driving to be fully automated—meaning there's no one at the wheel." The article added that there is a financial incentive for automating trucks because "trucking is a $700-billion industry, in which a third of costs go to compensating drivers." How are driverless trucks likely to affect costs to businesses of transporting goods? How are they likely to affect the short-run aggregate supply curve and the long-run aggregate supply curve?

Source: Natalie Kitroeff, "Robots Could Replace 1.7 Million American Truckers in the Next Decade," *Los Angeles Times*, September 25, 2016.

2.14 **(Related to the Apply the Concept on page 448)** Economists Mary Daly, Bart Hobijn, and Timothy Ni of the Federal Reserve Bank of San Francisco argued that "employers hesitate to reduce wages and workers are reluctant to accept wage cuts, even during recessions." If a firm faces declining sales during a recession, why might the firm's managers decide to lay off some workers and freeze the wages of other workers rather than cut workers' nominal wages?

Source: Mary C. Daly, Bart Hobijn, and Timothy Ni, "The Path of Wage Growth and Unemployment," *Federal Reserve Bank of San Francisco Economic Letter,* July 15, 2013.

2.15 **(Related to the Apply the Concept on page 448)** An article in the *Economist* discussing the 2007–2009 recession stated that "employers found it difficult to reduce the cash value of the wages paid to their staff. (Foisting a pay cut on your entire workforce hardly boosts morale.)"

a. During a recession, couldn't firms reduce their labor costs by the same, or possibly more, if they laid off fewer workers while cutting wages? Why did few firms use this approach?

b. What does the article mean by firms reducing the "cash value" of workers' wages? Is it possible for firms to reduce workers' wages over time without reducing their cash value? Briefly explain.

Source: "Careful Now," *Economist,* April 11, 2015.

13.3 Macroeconomic Equilibrium in the Long Run and the Short Run, pages 452–458

LEARNING OBJECTIVE: Use the aggregate demand and aggregate supply model to illustrate the difference between short-run and long-run macroeconomic equilibrium.

MyLab Economics Visit www.pearson.com/mylab/economics to complete these exercises online and get instant feedback.

Summary

In long-run macroeconomic equilibrium, the aggregate demand and short-run aggregate supply curves intersect at a point *on* the long-run aggregate supply curve. In short-run macroeconomic equilibrium, the aggregate demand and short-run aggregate supply curves often intersect at a point *off* the long-run aggregate supply curve. An automatic mechanism drives the economy to long-run equilibrium. If short-run equilibrium occurs at a point below potential GDP, wages and prices will fall, and the short-run aggregate supply curve will shift to the right until potential GDP is restored. If short-run equilibrium occurs at a point beyond potential GDP, wages and prices will rise, and the short-run aggregate supply curve will shift to the left until potential GDP is restored. Real GDP can be temporarily above or below its potential level, either because of shifts in the aggregate demand curve or because supply shocks lead to shifts in the short-run aggregate supply curve. **Stagflation** is a combination of inflation and recession, usually resulting from a supply shock.

Review Questions

3.1 Describe the relationship of the *AD, SRAS,* and *LRAS* curves when the economy is in long-run macroeconomic equilibrium.

3.2 What is "stagflation"? Why might a supply shock result in it?

3.3 Suppose the economy enters a recession. If government policymakers—Congress, the president, and members of the Federal Reserve—do not take any policy actions in response to the recession, which of the alternatives listed below is the likely result? Be sure to carefully explain why you chose the answer you did.

1. The unemployment rate will rise and remain higher even in the long run, and real GDP will drop below potential GDP and remain lower than potential GDP in the long run.

2. The unemployment rate will rise in the short run but return to the natural rate of unemployment in the long run, and real GDP will drop below potential GDP in the short run but return to potential GDP in the long run.

3. The unemployment rate will rise and remain higher even in the long run, and real GDP will drop below potential GDP in the short run but return to potential GDP in the long run.

4. The unemployment rate will rise in the short run but return to the natural rate of unemployment in the long run, and real GDP will drop below potential GDP in the short run and remain lower than potential GDP in the long run.

Problems and Applications

3.4 An article in the *Wall Street Journal* noted that real GDP in Greece declined during 2016. The article stated that economists "attributed it to a 2.1% decline in [government spending] and weaker net exports"

a. Use a basic aggregate demand and aggregate supply graph (with *LRAS* constant) to illustrate what happened in Greece in 2016.

b. On your graph, show the adjustment back to long-run equilibrium.

Source: Nektaria Stamouli, "Greek Economy Contracts at Faster Pace than Estimated Adding Hurdle to Bailout Talks," *Wall Street Journal,* March 6, 2017.

3.5 Draw a basic aggregate demand and aggregate supply graph (with *LRAS* constant) that shows the economy in long-run equilibrium.

a. Assume that there is a large increase in demand for U.S. exports. Show the resulting short-run equilibrium on your graph. In this short-run equilibrium, is the unemployment rate likely to be higher or lower than it was before the increase in exports? Briefly explain. Explain how the economy adjusts back to long-run equilibrium. When the economy has adjusted back to long-run equilibrium, how have the values of each of the following changed relative to what they were before the increase in exports?

i. Real GDP

ii. The price level

iii. The unemployment rate

b. Assume that there is an unexpected increase in the price of oil. Show the resulting short-run equilibrium on your graph. Explain how the economy adjusts back to long-run equilibrium. In this short-run equilibrium, is the unemployment rate likely to be higher or lower than it was before the unexpected increase in the price of oil? Briefly explain. When the economy has adjusted back to long-run equilibrium, how have the values of each of the following changed relative to what they were before the unexpected increase in the price of oil?
  i. Real GDP
  ii. The price level
  iii. The unemployment rate

3.6 (Related to the Apply the Concept on page 454) Edward Leamer of the University of California, Los Angeles, argues that "housing *is* the business cycle." Why would spending on housing be likely to fluctuate more than spending by households on consumer durables, such as automobiles or furniture, or spending by firms on plant and equipment?

Source: Edward E. Leamer, "Housing Is the Business Cycle," in *Housing, Housing Finance, and Monetary Policy,* Federal Reserve Bank of Kansas City, August 2007.

3.7 Consider the data in the following table for 1969 and 1970 (where the values for real GDP and potential GDP are in 2009 dollars).

Year	Actual Real GDP	Potential GDP	Unemployment Rate
1969	$4.71 trillion	$4.63 trillion	3.5%
1970	4.72 trillion	4.79 trillion	4.9

Sources: U.S. Bureau of Labor Statistics; and Federal Reserve Bank of St. Louis.

a. In 1969, actual real GDP was greater than potential GDP. Briefly explain how this is possible.
b. Even though real GDP in 1970 was slightly greater than real GDP in 1969, the unemployment rate increased substantially from 1969 to 1970. Why did this increase in unemployment occur?
c. Was the inflation rate in 1970 likely to have been higher or lower than the inflation rate in 1969? Does your answer depend on whether the recession that began in December 1969 was caused by a change in a component of aggregate demand or by a supply shock?

3.8 Use the graph below to answer the following questions.

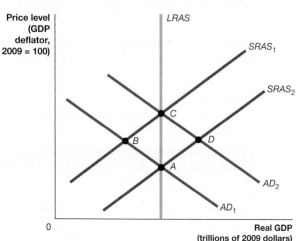

a. Which of the points *A, B, C,* or *D* can represent a long-run equilibrium?
b. Suppose that initially the economy is at point *A.* If aggregate demand increases from AD_1 to AD_2, which point represents short-run equilibrium? Which point represents the eventual long-run equilibrium? Briefly explain how the economy adjusts from the short-run equilibrium to the long-run equilibrium.

3.9 (Related to the Apply the Concept on page 457) In early 2009, Christina Romer, who was then the chair of the Council of Economic Advisers, and Jared Bernstein, who was then an economic adviser to Vice President Joseph Biden, forecast how long they expected it would take for real GDP to return to potential GDP, assuming that Congress passed fiscal policy legislation proposed by President Obama:

It should be understood that all of the estimates presented in this memo are subject to significant margins of error. There is the obvious uncertainty that comes from modeling a hypothetical package rather than the final legislation passed by the Congress. But there is the more fundamental uncertainty that comes with any estimate of the effects of a program. Our estimates of economic relationships ... are derived from historical experience and so will not apply exactly in any given episode. Furthermore, the uncertainty is surely higher than normal now because the current recession is unusual both in its fundamental causes and its severity.

Why would the causes of a recession and its severity affect the accuracy of forecasts of when the economy would return to potential GDP?

Source: Christina Romer and Jared Bernstein, *The Job Impact of the American Recovery and Reinvestment Plan,* January 9, 2009, p. 2.

3.10 The following graphs show either aggregate demand or short-run aggregate supply shifting to the right or to the left.

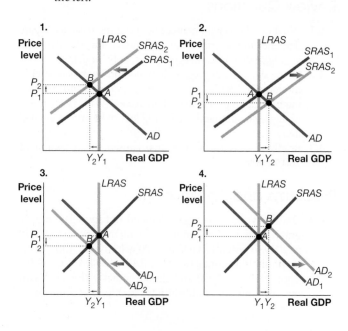

a. Match each of the following scenarios to the appropriate graph.
   i. An increase in the expected price level
   ii. An increase in households' expectations of their future income
   iii. A decrease in the price of an important natural resource
   iv. A decrease in firms' expectations of the future profitability of investment spending
b. Match one or more of the four graphs to each of the following scenarios.
   i. The economy experiences a recession.
   ii. The economy experiences short-term inflation.
   iii. The economy experiences stagflation.

3.11 The subtitle of a *Wall Street Journal* article about the economy in the euro zone (the 19 European countries that use the euro as their currency) was "Fourth-Quarter Output, Lowest Unemployment in Seven Years, Higher Inflation Eases Some Concerns." Use an aggregate demand and aggregate supply graph to show how the euro zone could experience both lower unemployment and higher inflation. Briefly explain what you are showing in your graph.

Source: Paul Hannon and William Horobin, "Eurozone Economy on Pace with U.S.," *Wall Street Journal*, January 31, 2017.

(13.4) # A Dynamic Aggregate Demand and Aggregate Supply Model, pages 459–464

LEARNING OBJECTIVE: Use the dynamic aggregate demand and aggregate supply model to analyze macroeconomic conditions.

MyLab Economics   Visit **www.pearson.com/mylab/economics** to complete these exercises online and get instant feedback.

Summary

To make the aggregate demand and aggregate supply model more realistic, we need to make it *dynamic* by incorporating three facts that were left out of the basic model: (1) Potential GDP increases continually, shifting the long-run aggregate supply curve to the right; (2) during most years, aggregate demand shifts to the right; and (3) except during periods when workers and firms expect high rates of inflation, the aggregate supply curve shifts to the right. The dynamic aggregate demand and aggregate supply model allows us to analyze macroeconomic conditions, including the beginning of the 2007–2009 recession.

Review Questions

4.1 What are the key differences between the basic aggregate demand and aggregate supply model and the dynamic aggregate demand and aggregate supply model?

4.2 In the dynamic aggregate demand and aggregate supply model, what is the result of aggregate demand increasing more than potential GDP increases? What is the result of aggregate demand increasing less than potential GDP increases?

4.3 Briefly discuss the factors that caused the recession of 2007–2009.

Problems and Applications

4.4 Draw a dynamic aggregate demand and aggregate supply graph showing the economy moving from potential GDP in 2019 to potential GDP in 2020, with no inflation. Your graph should contain the *AD*, *SRAS*, and *LRAS* curves for both 2019 and 2020 and should indicate the short-run macroeconomic equilibrium for each year and the directions in which the curves have shifted. Identify what must happen for the economy to experience growth during 2020 without inflation.

4.5 (Related to Solved Problem 13.4 on page 463) Consider the information in the following table for the first two years of the Great Depression (where the values for real GDP and potential GDP are in 2009 dollars).

Year	Actual Real GDP	Potential GDP	Price Level
1929	$1,056.6 billion	$1,006.3 billion	9.9
1930	966.7 billion	1,094.1 billion	9.5

Sources: U.S. Bureau of Economic Analysis; and Federal Reserve Bank of St. Louis.

a. The table shows that something happened during 1929–1930 that has not happened during the recessions of the past 50 years. What is it?

b. Draw a dynamic aggregate demand and aggregate supply graph to illustrate what happened during these years. Your graph should contain the *AD*, *SRAS*, and *LRAS* curves for both 1929 and 1930 and should indicate the short-run macroeconomic equilibrium for each year and the directions in which the curves shifted.

4.6 (Related to Solved Problem 13.4 on page 463) In early 2017, policymakers at the Federal Reserve forecast that real GDP during 2017 would increase faster than potential GDP and that the inflation rate for the year would be about 1.9 percent.

a. Fill in the missing values in the table with estimates that are consistent with these forecasts.

Year	Real GDP	Potential GDP	GDP Deflator
2016	$16.7 trillion	$16.9 trillion	111.5
2017		$17.1 trillion	

b. Draw a dynamic aggregate demand and aggregate supply graph to illustrate your answer to part (a).

Source: Federal Open Market Committee, "Advance Release of Table 1 of the Summary of Economic Projections to be Released with the FOMC Minutes," March 15, 2017.

4.7 In the following graph, suppose that short-run equilibrium moves from point A in year 1 to point B in year 2. Using the graph, briefly explain your answer to each of the questions.

a. What is the growth rate in potential GDP from year 1 to year 2?

b. Is the unemployment rate in year 2 higher or lower than in year 1?

c. What is the inflation rate in year 2?

d. What is the growth rate of real GDP in year 2?

4.8 Explain whether you agree with the following statement:

The dynamic aggregate demand and aggregate supply model predicts that a recession caused by a decline in AD will cause the inflation rate to fall. I know that the 2007–2009 recession was caused by a fall in AD, but the inflation rate was not lower as a result of the recession. The prices of most products were definitely higher in 2008 than they were in 2007, so the inflation rate could not have fallen.

4.9 In 2017, an editorial on bloomberg.com was titled "Canada Must Deflate Its Housing Bubble." What does the editorial mean by the "housing bubble"? Why should government policymakers be worried about a housing bubble?

Source: "Canada Must Deflate Its Housing Bubble," bloomberg.com, May 23, 2017.

4.10 **(Related to the Chapter Opener on page 436)** According to an article in the *Wall Street Journal*, KB Home and other builders found demand for new homes increasing in 2017 as a result of an increase in the formation of new households. In the long run, formation of new households depends on population growth. Are firms like homebuilders that sell products whose demand depends partly on demographic factors likely to be more or less affected by the business cycle than are other firms whose products are less dependent on these factors (holding constant other factors that affect the demand for new homes)? Briefly explain.

Source: Laura Kusisto and Sarah Chaney, "U.S. Housing Starts Fell in April for Third Time in Four Months," *Wall Street Journal*, May 16, 2017.

4.11 An article in the *Wall Street Journal* about the U.S. economy stated, "Fed officials have talked down the need for government tax and spending programs aimed at juicing short-term economic growth, calling instead for policies that would raise the economy's long-term potential growth rate—the fastest pace it could expand without fueling too much inflation."

a. What does "government tax and spending programs" mean? What does "juicing short-term economic growth" mean?

b. Draw a basic aggregate demand and aggregate supply graph to show how government tax and spending programs could "juice short-term economic growth." Briefly explain what you are showing in your graph.

c. Draw a dynamic aggregate demand and aggregate supply graph to show the effect of policies that raise the economy's long-term potential growth rate "without fueling too much inflation." Briefly explain what you are showing in your graph.

Source: Harriet Torry, "Yellen Says Family-Friendly Work Policies Can Boost Economy," *Wall Street Journal*, May 5, 2017.

Real-Time Data Exercises

D13.1 (Showing movements in equilibrium real GDP and the price level) Go to the Web site of the Federal Reserve Bank of St. Louis (FRED) (fred.stlouisfed.org) and find data on real GDP (GDPCA) and the GDP price deflator (USAGDPDEFAISMEI) for 1960, 1973, 1975, and 2016.

    a. In an *AD–AS* graph, using the actual values for real GDP and the GDP price deflator, show equilibrium for 1960 and for 2016. Assume that the economy was at equilibrium at potential GDP in both years. From 1960 to 2016, what happened to long-run aggregate supply? Given the change in the GDP implicit price deflator, did aggregate demand grow more or less than long-run aggregate supply?

    b. In an *AD–AS* graph, using the actual values for real GDP and the GDP price deflator, show equilibrium for 1973 and for 1975. Assume that the economy was in equilibrium at potential GDP in 1973 but in only a short-run equilibrium in 1975. Given the changes in real GDP and the GDP implicit price deflator, briefly explain what happened to short-run aggregate supply from 1973 to 1975.

D13.2 (The effects of a positive supply shock) Using data from the St. Louis Federal Reserve (fred.stlouisfed.org) FRED database, examine the experience of the U.S. economy during the 1990s. The U.S. economy experienced a positive supply shock with the spread of information communication technology and the Internet after 1995.

    a. Download monthly data on the personal consumption expenditure price Index (PCEPI) from 1981 to the present. Calculate the inflation rate from 1982 to 2007 as the percentage change in the PCEPI from the same month in the previous year.

    b. Calculate the average inflation rate from 1982 through 1994 and the average inflation rate from 1995 through 2007.

    c. Are your calculations consistent with a positive supply shock after 1994? Briefly explain.

D13.3 (Comparing business cycles across countries) During the 2007–2009 period, the economies of the United Kingdom and the United States experienced similar problems. High oil prices and a housing bubble affected both economies. The financial crisis in the United States also affected investment in the United Kingdom, both by limiting credit and by increasing risk premiums. Using data from the St. Louis Federal Reserve (fred.stlouisfed.org) FRED database, examine the behavior of the U.K. economy from 2007 to 2011.

    a. Download quarterly data for real GDP (GBRRGDPQDSNAQ) and the GDP deflator (GBRGDPDEFQISMEI) for the United Kingdom from 2006 to 2011. Calculate the growth rate of real GDP as the percentage change from the same quarter in the previous year and calculate the inflation rate as the percentage change in the GDP deflator from the same quarter in the previous year. Download data on the unemployment rate (GBRURHARMMDSMEI) for the same time period. For the frequency of the unemployment rate data, select quarterly to match the frequency of the real GDP and GDP deflator data.

    b. Download the three data series from 2007 to the present in the same graph. What do the data indicate about how similar the experience of the United Kingdom was to that of the United States during those years?

Critical Thinking Exercises

CT13.1 Chapter 3 discussed the variables that shift the demand curve (Section 3.1) and the variables that shift the supply curve (Section 3.2). How many of these variables that shift microeconomic demand and supply curves also shift the aggregate demand (*AD*) curve or the short-run aggregate supply (*SRAS*) curve? What might you conclude about the relationship between the concepts of demand and supply in microeconomics and in macroeconomics?

CT13.2 Is there an individual factor that shifts both the *AD* curve and *SRAS* curve? Can you explain why this factor has this effect?

CT13.3 Consider the pattern shown by the data in the following table (where the values for real GDP are in billions of 2009 dollars):

Year	Real GDP (billions of 2009 dollars)	GDP Deflator
2009	$14,419	100
2010	14,784	101
2011	15,021	103
2012	15,355	105
2013	15,612	107
2014	16,013	109
2015	16,472	110
2016	16,716	111

Next, consider Figure 13.1 on page 439, which has real GDP on the horizontal axis, and the price level, as measured by the GDP deflator, on the vertical axis. On this graph, in which direction did the economy move from 2009 to 2016? Be sure that your answer includes a graph.

Appendix

Macroeconomic Schools of Thought

Macroeconomics became a separate field of economics in 1936, with the publication of John Maynard Keynes's book *The General Theory of Employment, Interest, and Money*. Keynes, an economist at the University of Cambridge in England, was attempting to explain the devastating Great Depression of the 1930s. Real GDP in the United States declined more than 25 percent between 1929 and 1933 and did not return to its potential level until the United States entered World War II in 1941 (see Chapter 12). The unemployment rate soared above 20 percent by 1933 and did not return to its 1929 level until 1942. Keynes developed a version of the aggregate demand and aggregate supply model to explain these facts. The widespread acceptance of Keynes's model during the 1930s and 1940s became known as the **Keynesian revolution**.

Keynesian revolution The name given to the widespread acceptance during the 1930s and 1940s of John Maynard Keynes's macroeconomic model.

In fact, using the aggregate demand and aggregate supply model remains the most widely accepted approach to analyzing macroeconomic issues. Because the model has been modified significantly from Keynes's day, many economists who use the model today refer to themselves as *new Keynesians*. The new Keynesians emphasize the importance of the stickiness of wages and prices in explaining fluctuations in real GDP. A significant number of economists, however, dispute whether using the aggregate demand and aggregate supply model, as we have discussed it in this chapter, is the best way to analyze macroeconomic issues. These alternative *schools of thought* use models that differ significantly from the standard aggregate demand and aggregate supply model. We can briefly consider four major alternative models:

1. The monetarist model
2. The new classical model
3. The real business cycle model
4. The Austrian model

The Monetarist Model

The monetarist model—also known as the neo-quantity theory of money model—was developed beginning in the 1940s by Milton Friedman, an economist at the University of Chicago who was awarded the Nobel Prize in Economics in 1976. Friedman argued that the Keynesian approach overstates the amount of macroeconomic instability in the economy. In particular, he argued that the economy will ordinarily be at potential GDP. In the book *A Monetary History of the United States: 1867–1960*, written with Anna Jacobson Schwartz, Friedman argued that most fluctuations in real GDP are caused by fluctuations in the money supply rather than by fluctuations in consumption spending or investment spending. Friedman and Schwartz argued that the severity of the Great Depression was caused by the Federal Reserve allowing the quantity of money in the economy to fall by more than 25 percent between 1929 and 1933.

In the United States, the Federal Reserve is responsible for managing the quantity of money. As we will discuss further in Chapter 15, the Federal Reserve has typically focused more on controlling interest rates than on controlling the money supply. Friedman argued that the Federal Reserve should change its practices and adopt a **monetary growth rule**, which is a plan for increasing the quantity of money at a fixed rate. He believed that adopting a monetary growth rule would reduce fluctuations in real GDP, employment, and inflation.

Monetary growth rule A plan for increasing the quantity of money at a fixed rate that does not respond to changes in economic conditions.

Friedman's ideas, which are referred to as **monetarism**, attracted significant support during the 1970s and early 1980s, when the U.S. economy experienced high rates of unemployment and inflation. The support for monetarism declined during the late 1980s and 1990s, when the unemployment and inflation rates were relatively low. In Chapter 14, we will discuss the *quantity theory of money*, which underlies the monetarist model.   MyLab Economics Concept Check

Monetarism The macroeconomic theories of Milton Friedman and his followers, particularly the idea that the quantity of money should be increased at a constant rate.

The New Classical Model

The new classical model was developed in the mid-1970s by a group of economists including Nobel Laureate Robert Lucas of the University of Chicago, Nobel Laureate Thomas Sargent of New York University, and Robert Barro of Harvard University. Some of the views held by the new classical macroeconomists are similar to those held by economists before the Great Depression. Keynes referred to the economists before the Great Depression as *classical economists*. Like the classical economists, the new classical macroeconomists believe that the economy normally will be at potential GDP. They also believe that wages and prices adjust quickly to changes in demand and supply. Put another way, they believe the stickiness in wages and prices emphasized by the new Keynesians is unimportant.

Lucas argues that workers and firms have *rational expectations*, meaning that they form their expectations of the future values of economic variables, such as the inflation rate, by making use of all available information, including information on changes in the quantity of money and other factors that might affect aggregate demand. Fluctuations in output and employment occur if households and firms form incorrect expectations of the inflation rate. If the actual inflation rate is lower than the expected inflation rate, the actual real wage will be higher than the expected real wage. Higher real wages will lead to a recession because firms will hire fewer workers and cut back on production. As workers and firms adjust their expectations to the lower inflation rate, the real wage will decline, and employment and production will expand, bringing the economy out of recession. The ideas of Lucas and his followers are referred to as the **new classical macroeconomics**. Supporters of the new classical model agree with supporters of the monetarist model that the Federal Reserve should adopt a monetary growth rule. They argue that a monetary growth rule will make it easier for workers and firms to accurately forecast the price level, thereby reducing fluctuations in real GDP.   MyLab Economics Concept Check

New classical macroeconomics The macroeconomic theories of Robert Lucas and others, particularly the idea that workers and firms have rational expectations.

The Real Business Cycle Model

In the 1980s, some economists, including Nobel Laureates Finn Kydland of the University of California, Santa Barbara, and Edward Prescott of Arizona State University, argued that Lucas was correct in assuming that workers and firms form their expectations rationally and that wages and prices adjust quickly to changes in demand and supply but was wrong about the source of fluctuations in real GDP. They argued that fluctuations in real GDP are caused by temporary shocks to productivity and not by inaccurate forecasts of the price level. These shocks can be negative, such as a decline in the availability of oil or other raw materials, or positive, such as technological change that makes it possible to produce more output with the same quantity of inputs.

According to this school of thought, shifts in the aggregate demand curve have no effect on real GDP because the short-run aggregate supply curve is vertical. (Other schools of thought believe that the short-run aggregate supply curve is upward sloping and that only the *long-run* aggregate supply curve is vertical.) Fluctuations in real GDP occur when a negative productivity shock causes the short-run aggregate supply curve to shift to the left—reducing real GDP—or a positive productivity shock causes the short-run aggregate supply curve to shift to the right—increasing real GDP. Because this model focuses on "real" factors—productivity shocks—rather than changes in the quantity of money to explain fluctuations in real GDP, it is known as the **real business cycle model**.   MyLab Economics Concept Check

Real business cycle model A macroeconomic model that focuses on real, rather than monetary, causes of the business cycle.

The Austrian Model

The *Austrian school* of economics began in the late nineteenth century with the writings of Carl Menger, an economist at the University of Vienna. Important later contributors to this school of thought were Ludwig von Mises, who spent the later years of his career at New York University, and Friedrich von Hayek, who spent most of his career at the London School of Economics and the University of Chicago. The Austrian school is best known for arguing the superiority of the market system over government economic planning. Hayek, in particular, emphasized that only the price system operating through markets could make use of the dispersed information available to households and firms to bring about an efficient allocation of resources.

During the 1930s, Hayek developed a theory of the business cycle that emphasized the problems arising from central banks forcing interest rates to very low levels. Low interest rates cause businesses to spend more on factories, machinery, office buildings, and other types of capital. Initially, the surge in investment spending will produce an economic expansion, but the additional capital goods eventually produce more output than firms can sell for a profit. Businesses suffer losses, reduce output, and lay off workers, resulting in a recession. The lower the central bank drives interest rates, the greater the increase in investment spending, the larger the economic expansion, and the deeper the eventual recession.

For a time in the early 1930s, Hayek's theory of the business cycle attracted significant interest from economists, particularly in the United Kingdom. After the publication of Keynes's *General Theory* in 1936, interest in Hayek's theory declined, and today only a relatively few economists belong to the Austrian school. In the past few years, however, Austrian economists have argued that the events of the 2007–2009 recession fit their model well: The Federal Reserve lowered interest rates to fight the 2001 recession, and the low interest rates sparked a surge in capital spending—in this case, spending on houses rather than on factories or office buildings. Eventually, the excessive investment in housing ended with a housing bust and a severe recession.

MyLab Economics Study Plan

MyLab Economics Concept Check

● Apply the Concept

MyLab Economics Video

Karl Marx: Capitalism's Severest Critic

The schools of macroeconomic thought we have discussed in this appendix are considered part of mainstream economic theory because of their acceptance of the market system as the best means of raising living standards in the long run. One quite influential critic of mainstream economic theory was Karl Marx. Marx was born in Trier, Germany, in 1818. After graduating from the University of Berlin in 1841, he began a career as a political journalist and agitator. His political activities caused him to be expelled first from Germany and then from France and Belgium. In 1849, he moved to London, where he spent the remainder of his life.

In 1867, Marx published the first volume of his greatest work, *Das Kapital*. Marx read closely the most prominent mainstream economists, including Adam Smith, David Ricardo, and John Stuart Mill. But Marx believed that he understood how market systems would evolve in the long run much better than those earlier authors. He argued that the market system would eventually be replaced by a communist economy, in which the workers would control production. He believed in the *labor theory of value*, which attributed all the value of a good or service to the labor embodied in it. According to Marx, the owners of businesses—capitalists—did not earn profits by contributing anything of value to the production of goods or services. Instead, they earned profits because their "monopoly of the means of production"—their ownership of factories and machinery—allowed them to exploit workers by paying them wages that were much lower than the value of workers' contributions to production.

Marx argued that the wages of workers would be driven to levels that allowed only bare survival. He also argued that small firms would eventually be driven out of

Sueddeutsche Zeitung Photo/SZ Photo/ Scherl/Alamy Stock Photo

Karl Marx predicted that a final economic crisis would lead to the collapse of the market system.

business by larger firms, forcing owners of small firms into the working class. Control of production would ultimately be concentrated in the hands of a few firms, which would have difficulty selling the goods they produced to the impoverished masses. A final economic crisis would lead the working classes to rise up, seize control of the economy, and establish communism. Marx died in 1883, without having provided a detailed explanation of how the communist economy would operate.

Marx had relatively little influence on mainstream thinking in the United States, but several political parties in Europe were guided by his ideas. In 1917, the Bolshevik Party seized control of the Russian Empire and established the Soviet Union, the first communist state. Although the Soviet Union was a vicious dictatorship under Vladimir Lenin and his successor, Joseph Stalin, its prestige rose when it avoided the macroeconomic difficulties that plagued the market economies during the 1930s. By the late 1940s, communist parties had also come to power in China and the countries of Eastern Europe. Poor economic performance contributed to the eventual collapse of the Soviet Union and its replacement by a market system, although one with significant government intervention in the economy. The Communist Party remains in power in China, but the economy is evolving toward a market system. Today, only North Korea and Cuba have economies that claim to be based on the ideas of Karl Marx.

MyLab Economics Study Plan

Key Terms

Keynesian revolution, p. 474	Monetary growth rule, p. 474	Real business cycle model, p. 475
Monetarism, p. 475	New classical macroeconomics, p. 475	

Money, Banks, and the Federal Reserve System

Does India Need Paper Currency?

Many people in India remain impoverished, with the country's GDP per capita being barely more than 10 percent that of the United States. So it may seem surprising that in 2017 more than 225 million people in India made some or all of their purchases using a mobile wallet rather than cash. With a *mobile wallet*, consumers can use a smartphone, smartwatch, or tablet to make payments. This unexpected use of cutting-edge technology in India was the result of two developments: (1) the spread of smartphone use even among people with low incomes and (2) the sudden decision by the Indian government in late November 2016 to withdraw from circulation all existing 500- and 1,000-rupee paper currency.

At the end of 2016, the government stopped accepting the old currency and also stopped exchanging it for newly printed currency. The withdrawn notes made up more than 86 percent of the value of all rupee bills in circulation. One Indian economist observed, "It's going to be very inconvenient, because everybody uses these notes." The government enacted this drastic policy in an attempt to push the Indian economy away from a heavy reliance on cash transactions. Policymakers hoped to reduce the size of the country's large underground economy, and to reduce corruption by making it more difficult for government officials to receive cash bribes.

The Indian firm Paytm benefited from consumers who needed an alternative to using cash to make payments. Paytm was founded in 2010 by Vijay Shekhar Sharma, India's youngest billionaire. Paytm is an app that allows users to make payments at retail stores or online after transferring funds from a bank account, credit card, or debit card or depositing cash at designated banks or stores. Many stores in India are very small and lack the equipment necessary to accept and process credit card payments—and relatively

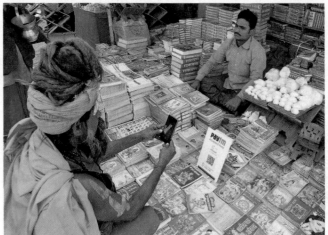

Jitendra Prakash/Reuters

few Indian consumers have credit cards. Paytm provides stores with a sticker that customers scan with their smartphone cameras when making a payment. Paytm confirms each payment with a text message and collects a fee of 1 to 3 percent from the store. Paytm's success has attracted competitors, including MobiKwik, FreeCharge, and Samsung Pay, which have also gained millions of users in India.

A country needs a well-functioning financial system if its economy is to prosper and grow. When the system is disrupted, as happened in India in 2016, entrepreneurs like Vijay Shekhar Sharma can respond by providing innovative ways to keep funds flowing in the economy. In this chapter, we will study how the financial system works, including the role of the money supply, banks, and the Federal Reserve, which is the central bank of the United States.

Sources: Corinne Abrams and Newley Purnell, "Mobile Wallet Paytm Hits Pay Dirt amid India's Cash Crackdown, *Wall Street Journal*, May 31, 2017; Raymond Zhong, "India to Replace Largest Bank Notes," *Wall Street Journal*, November 9, 2016; and "India Online," *Economist*, March 5, 2016.

Chapter Outline & Learning Objectives

Economics in Your Life & Career

Should Your Business Accept Cash?

Suppose that you've started a juice bar with a partner who has an interesting idea: Don't accept any payments in cash. Customers will have to use a credit card or a mobile wallet like Apple Pay or Android Pay. She argues that by not having cash registers and not dealing with cash, you will reduce expenses and also reduce your chances of being robbed. You're not sure if you agree with this idea. Is it even legal not to accept cash? Will people who prefer to pay cash go to a competing juice bar? Is your partner's strategy likely to increase or decrease the profit you earn from the shop? As you read this chapter, try to answer these questions. You can check your answers against those we provide on **page 507** at the end of this chapter.

I n this chapter, we will explore the financial system, including topics such as the role of money in the economy, how the banking system creates money, the policy tools the Federal Reserve uses to manage the quantity of money in the United States, the crisis in the banking system during and after the 2007–2009 recession, and the link between changes in the quantity of money and changes in the price level. What you learn in this chapter will serve as an important foundation for understanding monetary policy and fiscal policy.

14.1 What Is Money, and Why Do We Need It?

LEARNING OBJECTIVE: Define money and discuss the four functions of money.

Could an economy function without money? There are historical examples of economies in which people traded goods for other goods rather than use money. For example, on the American frontier during colonial times, very little money was available, so a farmer might have traded a plow for a cow. Most economies, though, use money. The economic definition of **money** is any asset that people are generally willing to accept in exchange for goods and services or for payment of debts. Recall that an **asset** is anything of value owned by a person or a firm. There are many possible kinds of money: In West Africa, at one time, cowrie shells served as money. During World War II, prisoners of war used cigarettes as money.

Barter and the Invention of Money

To understand the importance of money, let's consider further the situation in economies that do not use money. Economies in which goods and services are traded directly for other goods and services are called *barter economies*. Barter economies have a major shortcoming. To illustrate this shortcoming, consider a farmer on the American frontier in colonial days. Suppose the farmer needed a cow and proposed trading a spare plow to a neighbor for one of the neighbor's cows. If the neighbor did not want the plow, the trade would not happen. For a barter trade to take place between two people, each person must want what the other one has. Economists refer to this requirement as a *double coincidence of wants*. The farmer who wants the cow might eventually be able to obtain one if he first trades with some other neighbor for something the neighbor with the cow wants. However, it may take several trades before the farmer is ultimately able to trade for what the neighbor with the cow wants. Locating several trading partners and making several intermediate trades can take considerable time and energy.

To avoid the problems with barter, societies have an incentive to identify a product that most people will accept in exchange for what they have to trade. For example, in colonial times, animal skins were very useful in making clothing. The first governor of Tennessee actually received a salary of 1,000 deerskins per year, and the state's secretary of the Treasury received 450 otter skins per year. A good used as money that also has value independent of its use as money is called a **commodity money**. Historically, once a good became widely accepted as money, even people who did not have an immediate use for it would be willing to accept it. A colonial farmer—or the governor of Tennessee—might not want a deerskin, but as long as he knew he could use the deerskin to buy other goods and services, he would be willing to accept it in exchange for what he had to sell.

Buying and selling goods and services is much easier when money becomes available. People only need to sell what they have for money and then use the money to buy what they want. If the colonial family could find someone to buy their plow, they could use the money to buy the cow they wanted. The family with the cow would accept the money because they knew they could use it to buy what they wanted. When money is available, families are more likely to specialize and less likely to produce everything or nearly everything they need themselves.

Money Assets that people are generally willing to accept in exchange for goods and services or for payment of debts.

Asset Anything of value owned by a person or a firm.

Commodity money A good used as money that also has value independent of its use as money.

Most people in modern economies are highly specialized. They do only one thing—work as a nurse, an accountant, or an engineer—and use the money they earn to buy everything else they need. As we discussed in Chapter 2, Section 2.2, people become much more productive by specializing because they can pursue their *comparative advantage*. The high income levels in modern economies are based on the specialization that money makes possible. So, the answer to the question "Why do we need money?" is that *by making exchange easier, money allows people to specialize, become more productive, and earn higher incomes.*　　　　　　　**MyLab Economics** Concept Check

The Functions of Money

Anything used as money—whether a deerskin, a cowrie seashell, cigarettes, or a dollar bill—must serve four key functions in the economy:

1. It must act as a medium of exchange.
2. It must serve as a unit of account.
3. It must serve as a store of value.
4. It must provide a standard of deferred payment.

Medium of Exchange　Money serves as a medium of exchange when sellers are willing to accept it in exchange for goods or services. When the local supermarket accepts your $5 bill in exchange for bread and milk, the $5 bill is serving as a medium of exchange. With a medium of exchange, people can sell goods and services for money and use the money to buy what they want. An economy is more efficient when people accept a single good as a medium of exchange.

Unit of Account　In a barter system, each good has many prices. A cow may be worth 2 plows, 20 bushels of wheat, or 6 axes. Once only one good is used as money, each good has a single price rather than many prices. This function of money gives buyers and sellers a *unit of account*, a way of measuring value in the economy in terms of money. Because the U.S. economy uses dollars as money, each good has a price in terms of dollars.

Store of Value　Money allows people to easily store value: If you do not use all your dollars to buy goods and services today, you can hold the rest to use in the future. Money is not the only store of value, however. Any asset—shares of Facebook stock, Treasury bonds, real estate, or Renoir paintings, for example—represents a store of value. *Financial assets*, such as stocks and bonds, offer an important benefit relative to holding money because they pay a higher rate of interest or may increase in value in the future. Other assets also have advantages relative to money because they provide services. A house, for example, offers you a place to sleep.

Why, then, do people hold any money? The answer has to do with *liquidity*, or the ease with which people can convert an asset into the medium of exchange. Because money is the medium of exchange, it is the most liquid asset. If you want to buy something and you need to sell an asset to do so, you are likely to incur a cost. For example, if you want to buy a car and need to sell bonds or stocks to do so, you will have to pay a commission. To avoid such costs, people are willing to hold some of their wealth in the form of money, even though other assets offer greater returns as stores of value.

Standard of Deferred Payment　Money is useful because it can provide a standard of deferred payment in borrowing and lending. It can facilitate exchange at a *given point in time* by providing a medium of exchange and unit of account. Money can facilitate exchange *over time* by providing a store of value and a standard of deferred payment. For example, Dell, a computer manufacturer, may buy hard drives from Western Digital in exchange for the promise of making payment in 60 days.

How important is it that money be a reliable store of value and standard of deferred payment? People care about how much food, clothing, and other goods and services their dollars will buy. In other words, the value of money depends on its *purchasing power*, which is its ability to buy goods and services. Inflation causes a decline in purchasing power because with rising prices, a given amount of money can purchase fewer goods and services. When inflation reaches very high levels, money is no longer a reliable store of value or standard of deferred payment.   **MyLab Economics** Concept Check

What Can Serve as Money?

Having a medium of exchange helps make transactions easier, which allows the economy to work more efficiently. But what can serve as money? That is, which assets can be used as the medium of exchange? We saw earlier that to serve as money an asset must, at a minimum, be generally accepted as payment. In practical terms, however, it must be even more.

These five criteria make an asset suitable for use as a medium of exchange:

1. The asset must be *acceptable* to (that is, usable by) most people.
2. It should be of *standardized quality* so that any two units are identical.
3. It should be *durable* so that value is not lost by its quickly wearing out.
4. It should be *valuable* relative to its weight so that amounts large enough to be useful in trade can be easily transported.
5. It should be *divisible* so that it can be used in purchases of both low-priced and high-priced goods.

Dollar bills meet all these criteria. What determines the acceptability of dollar bills as a medium of exchange? Basically, it is through self-fulfilling expectations: You value something as money only if you believe that others will accept it from you as payment. A society's willingness to use paper dollars as money is what makes them an acceptable medium of exchange.

Commodity Money Commodity money has value independent of its use as money. Gold, for example, was a common form of money in the 1800s and early 1900s because it was a medium of exchange, a unit of account, a store of value, and a standard of deferred payment. But using gold as money involves a significant problem: The money supply is difficult to control because it depends partly on unpredictable discoveries of new gold fields.

Fiat Money It can be inefficient for an economy to rely only on gold or other precious metals for its money supply. What if you had to transport bars of gold to settle your transactions? Doing so would be difficult and costly, and you would run the risk of being robbed. To get around this problem, beginning around the year 1500 in Europe, governments and private firms—early banks—began to store gold and issue paper certificates that could be redeemed for gold. As long as people had confidence that the gold was available if they demanded it, the paper certificates would circulate as a medium of exchange. In effect, paper currency had been invented. In modern economies, paper currency is generally issued by a *central bank*, which is an agency of the government that regulates the money supply. The **Federal Reserve** is the central bank of the United States. Today, no government in the world issues paper currency that can be redeemed for gold. Paper currency has no value unless it is used as money, and it is therefore not a commodity money. Instead, paper currency is a **fiat money**, which has no value except as money. If paper currency has no value except as money, why do consumers and firms use it?

If you look at the top of a U.S. dollar bill, you will see the words "Federal Reserve Note" because it is issued by the Federal Reserve. U.S. dollars are fiat money, so the Federal Reserve is not required to give you gold or silver for your dollar bills. Federal Reserve currency is *legal tender* in the United States, which means the federal government requires that it be accepted in payment of debts and requires that cash or checks denominated in dollars be used in payment of taxes. Despite being legal tender, dollar bills would not be a good medium of exchange and could not serve as money if people didn't usually accept them. The key to this acceptance is that *households and firms have confidence that if they accept paper dollars in exchange for goods and services, the dollars will not lose much value during the time they hold them.* Without this confidence, dollar bills would not serve as a medium of exchange.   **MyLab Economics** Concept Check

Federal Reserve The central bank of the United States.

Fiat money Money, such as paper currency, that is authorized by a central bank or governmental body and that does not have to be exchanged by the central bank for gold or some other commodity money.

Apply the Concept

MyLab Economics Video

Your Money Is No Good Here!

Every business has to accept U.S. currency as payment because that's what federal law requires ... or does it? Although many people believe that because Federal Reserve Notes are legal tender, everyone in the United States, including every business, must by law accept paper money, in fact, firms do not have to accept cash as payment for goods and services. As the U.S. Treasury Department explains on its Web site:

> There is ... no Federal statute mandating that a private business, a person or an organization must accept currency or coins as payment for goods and/or services. ... For example, a bus line may prohibit payment of fares in pennies or dollar bills. In addition, movie theaters, convenience stores and gas stations may refuse to accept large denomination currency (usually notes above $20) as a matter of policy.

Maurice Savage/Alamy Stock Photo

If you want "simple, seasonal, healthy food" from Sweetgreen, don't bring cash.

Although most firms accept cash from customers, some have recently decided to stop doing so. For example, in 2017, Sweetgreen, a chain of U.S. salad restaurants, required customers to pay online ahead of picking up their order, pay by credit card, or pay by using a mobile wallet smartphone app, such as Apple Pay or Android Pay. In part, the chain was responding to changes in consumer preferences: When it opened in 2008, about 40 percent of its customers paid with cash, but by 2016, fewer than 10 percent did. Like other stores that have gone cashless, Sweetgreen hoped to speed up service by eliminating the need for employees to make change and manage cash. Going cashless would also deter robberies. Stores' ability to go cashless has been helped both by the increasing use of mobile wallet apps and by the development of technology by Square and competing firms that makes it easy for stores to accept credit card payments on smartphones or tablets.

In some other countries, the move to cashless retailing has been even faster than in the United States. As we saw in the chapter opener, the decision by the Indian government in 2016 to withdraw a majority of existing currency from circulation pushed many Indian consumers and stores to begin using Paytm and similar apps. Sweden may have gone the furthest toward becoming a cashless economy. An increasing number of stores and restaurants have stopped accepting cash and now require payment by credit card or by using a mobile banking app such as Swish, which has become particularly popular. Swedish churches encourage parishioners to use Swish to make donations at church services. Many of Sweden's banks no longer have cash available, do not accept cash deposits, and have removed ATMs. Some bank managers note that the absence of cash has reduced the likelihood of bank robbery. Cash now accounts for only about 2 percent of transactions in Sweden, as compared with an average of about 10 percent in other European countries, and about 22 percent in the United States.

Will the United States eventually follow Sweden and become a largely cashless economy? There are some drawbacks to doing so: Some older people do not know how to use smartphone apps, people with vision problems may have trouble using apps, and low-income people may not be able to afford smartphones or credit cards. Some privacy advocates are also concerned that apps and credit cards provide a public record of purchases that consumers may have legitimate reasons for keeping private. Finally, some people are afraid that using a credit card or an app exposes them to hackers who may be able to steal money from their accounts.

Sources: Christopher Mims, "Why Your Business Should Ditch Cash," *Wall Street Journal,* January 30, 2017; Kate Taylor, "A Popular Fast-Casual Chain Is Making an Unprecedented Move to Stop Accepting Cash," businessinsider.com, December 22, 2016; Liz Alderman, "In Sweden, a Cash-Free Future Nears," *New York Times,* December 26, 2015; and U.S. Treasury, "FAQs: Currency," www.treasury.gov.

Your Turn: Test your understanding by doing related problems 1.9 and 1.10 on page 509 at the end of this chapter.

MyLab Economics Study Plan

14.2 How Is Money Measured in the United States Today?

LEARNING OBJECTIVE: Discuss the definitions of the money supply used in the United States today.

People are interested in the money supply because, as we will see, changes in the money supply can affect other economic variables, including employment, gross domestic product (GDP), and inflation. If the only function of money was to serve as a medium of exchange, then a narrow definition of the money supply should include only currency, checking account deposits, and traveler's checks because households and firms can easily use these assets to buy goods and services. A broader definition of the money supply would include other assets that can be used as a medium of exchange even though they are not as liquid as currency or checking account deposits. For example, you can't directly buy goods or services with funds in a bank savings account, but it is easy to withdraw funds from your savings account and then use those funds to buy goods and services.

Congress gave the Federal Reserve the responsibility of regulating the money supply and the task of determining how to measure it. The Federal Reserve's measures of the money supply have changed several times over the decades. Currently, the Federal Reserve publishes data on two measures of the money supply: *M1* and *M2*. These measures, sometimes called *monetary aggregates*, are important to understand, so we devote the following sections to discussing them.

M1: A Narrow Definition of the Money Supply

M1 The narrow definition of the money supply: the sum of currency in circulation, checking account deposits in banks, and holdings of traveler's checks.

Figure 14.1 illustrates the definitions of the money supply. The narrow definition of the money supply, **M1**, includes the following:

1. *Currency,* which is all the paper money and coins held by households and firms (not including currency held by banks)

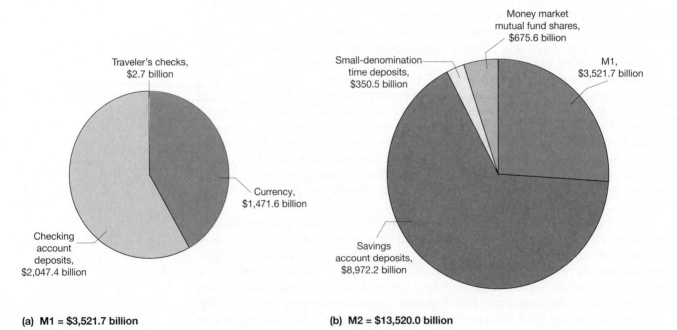

(a) M1 = $3,521.7 billion

(b) M2 = $13,520.0 billion

MyLab Economics Real-time data

Figure 14.1 Measuring the Money Supply

The Federal Reserve uses two different measures of the money supply: M1 and M2. Panel (a) shows the assets in M1. Panel (b) shows M2, which includes the assets in M1 as well as money market mutual fund shares, small-denomination time deposits, and savings account deposits.

Source: Board of Governors of the Federal Reserve System, "Federal Reserve Statistical Release, H.6," June 8, 2017.

2. The value of all checking account deposits in banks
3. The value of traveler's checks (Because this last category is so small—only about $2.7 billion in June 2017—relative to the other two categories, we will ignore it in our discussion of the money supply.)

Although currency has almost as large a value as checking account deposits, checking account deposits are used much more often than currency to make payments. In fact, the total amount of currency in circulation—$1.5 trillion in June 2017—is a misleading number. This amount is more than $4,500 per person—adult or child—in the United States. If this sounds like an unrealistically large amount of currency to be held per person, it is. Economists estimate that more than 60 percent of U.S. currency is actually outside the borders of the United States. More than three-quarters of U.S. paper currency is in denominations of $100 or larger—too large to be used for routine buying and selling within the United States.

Who holds these dollars outside the United States? Foreign banks and foreign governments hold some U.S. currency, but most is held by households and firms in countries in which there is not much confidence in the local currency or in which the underground economy is large. When inflation rates are very high, many households and firms do not want to hold their domestic currency because it is losing its value too rapidly. The value of the U.S. dollar will be much more stable than their domestic currency. If enough people are willing to accept dollars as well as—or instead of—domestic currency, dollars become a second currency for the country. In 2008, when inflation soared in the African country of Zimbabwe to the point where it took 15 *billion* Zimbabwean dollars to buy a can of Coca-Cola, the government went so far as to adopt the U.S. dollar as the country's official currency.   **MyLab Economics** Concept Check

M2: A Broad Definition of Money

Before 1980, U.S. law prohibited banks from paying interest on checking account deposits. Households and firms held checking account deposits primarily to buy goods and services. M1 was, therefore, very close to the function of money as a medium of exchange. Almost all currency, checking account deposits, and traveler's checks were held with the intention of buying and selling, not with the intention of storing value. In 1980, the law was changed to allow banks to pay interest on certain types of checking accounts. This change reduced the difference between checking accounts and savings accounts, although people are still not allowed to write checks against their savings account balances.

After 1980, economists began to pay closer attention to a broader definition of the money supply, **M2**. As panel (b) of Figure 14.1 shows, M2 includes everything that is in M1 plus:

M2 A broader definition of the money supply that includes M1 plus savings account deposits, small-denomination time deposits, balances in money market deposit accounts in banks, and noninstitutional money market fund shares.

- Time deposits with a value of less than $100,000, primarily *certificates of deposits* in banks. These deposits are for a fixed period of time—usually from six months to several years—and withdrawals before that time are subject to a penalty.
- Savings accounts, including money market deposit accounts at banks
- Noninstitutional money market mutual fund shares. *Noninstitutional* means that individual investors rather than institutional investors, such as pension funds, own the money market fund shares. Noninstitutional is also sometimes called "retail." Mutual fund companies sell shares to investors and use the funds raised to buy financial assets such as stocks and bonds. Some of these mutual funds, such as Vanguard's Treasury Money Market Fund or Fidelity's Cash Reserves Fund, are called *money market mutual funds* because they invest in very short-term bonds, such as U.S. Treasury bills. The balances individual investors hold in these funds are included in M2.

Each week, the Federal Reserve publishes statistics on M1 and M2. In the discussion that follows, we will use the M1 definition of the money supply because it corresponds most closely to money as a medium of exchange.

There are two key points to keep in mind about the money supply:

1. The narrowest definition of the money supply consists of *both* currency and checking account deposits.
2. Because balances in checking account deposits are included in the money supply, banks play an important role in the way the central bank controls the money supply. We will discuss this second point further in the next section.   **MyLab Economics** Concept Check

Don't Let This Happen to You

Don't Confuse Money with Income or Wealth

According to *Forbes*, in 2017, Bill Gates's wealth of $86 billion made him the richest person in the world. He also has a very large income, but how much money does he have? Your *wealth* is equal to the value of your assets minus the value of any debts you have. Your *income* is equal to your earnings during the year. Bill Gates, the former chairman of Microsoft, has very large investment earnings. But his *money* is just equal to what he has in currency and checking accounts. Only a small proportion of Gates's $86 billion in wealth is likely to be in currency or checking accounts. Most of his wealth is invested in stocks and bonds and other financial assets that are not included in the definition of money.

In everyday conversation, we often describe someone who is wealthy or who has a high income as "having a lot of money." But when economists use the word *money*, they are usually referring to currency plus checking account deposits. It is important to keep straight the differences between wealth, income, and money.

Just as money and income are not the same for a person, they are not the same for the whole economy. National income in the United States was equal to $16.1 trillion in 2016. The money supply in 2016 was $3.2 trillion (using the M1 measure). There is no reason a country's national income should equal the country's money supply, nor will an increase in a country's money supply necessarily increase the country's national income.

Source: "The World's Billionaires," forbes.com, March 20, 2017.

MyLab Economics Study Plan

Your Turn: Test your understanding by doing related problems 2.4 and 2.5 on page 509 at the end of this chapter.

Solved Problem 14.2   **MyLab Economics** Interactive Animation

The Definitions of M1 and M2

Suppose you decide to withdraw $2,000 from your checking account and put the money into a bank certificate of deposit (CD). Briefly explain how this action will affect M1 and M2.

Solving the Problem

Step 1: **Review the chapter material.** This problem is about the definitions of the money supply, so you may want to review the section "How Is Money Measured in the United States Today?" which begins on page 484.

Step 2: **Use the definitions of M1 and M2 to answer the problem.** Funds in checking accounts are included in both M1 and M2. Funds in CDs are included only in M2. It is tempting to answer this problem by saying that shifting $2,000 from a checking account to a CD reduces M1 by $2,000 and increases M2 by $2,000, but the $2,000 in your checking account was already counted in M2. So, the correct answer is that your action reduces M1 by $2,000 but leaves M2 unchanged.

MyLab Economics Study Plan   **Your Turn:** For more practice, do related problems 2.6 and 2.7 on page 509 at the end of this chapter.

What about Credit Cards and Debit Cards?

Many people buy goods and services with credit cards, yet credit cards are not included in either definition of the money supply. The reason is that when you buy something with a credit card, you are in effect taking out a loan from the bank that issued the credit card. The transaction is complete only when you pay your credit card bill at the end of the month—often with a check or an electronic transfer from your checking account. In contrast, with a debit card, the funds to make the purchase are taken directly from your checking account. In either case, the cards themselves do not represent money.   **MyLab Economics** Concept Check

MyLab Economics Study Plan

Apply the Concept

MyLab Economics Video

Are Bitcoins Money?

Typically, when we think of *money*, we think of currency issued by a government. But we have just seen that currency represents only a small part of the money supply of the United States, whether measured as M1 or M2. The non-currency components of M1 or M2, although not issued by the government, are familiar financial assets such as checking or savings accounts. Some households and firms have shifted away from M1 or M2 to finance their buying and selling of goods and services and are instead using *e-money*, or digital funds. The best-known form of e-money is PayPal. An individual or a firm can set up a PayPal account by transferring funds from a checking account or credit card. As long as a seller is willing to accept funds from a buyer's PayPal (or other e-money) account, e-money functions like conventional government-issued money.

Tomohiro Ohsumi/Bloomberg/Getty Images

Bitcoins are created by computer calculations, not by central banks.

In recent years, bitcoins have become a controversial new form of e-money. Unlike PayPal and other similar services for transferring money electronically, bitcoins are not owned by a firm but are instead produced by a decentralized system of linked computers. Bitcoins were first conceived in 2009 by "Satoshi Nakamoto," which is likely an assumed name. Bitcoins are produced by people performing the complicated calculations necessary to ensure that online purchases made with bitcoins are legitimate—that is, that someone doesn't try to spend the same bitcoin multiple times. People who successfully complete these calculations are awarded a fixed quantity of bitcoins—typically 12.5. This process of bitcoin "mining" will continue until a maximum of 21 million bitcoins has been produced—a total expected to be reached in 2030.

Because people can buy and sell bitcoins in exchange for dollars and other currencies on Web sites, some people refer to bitcoins as a "cryptocurrency." You can buy bitcoins and store them in a mobile wallet on a smartphone. You can then buy something in a store that accepts bitcoins by scanning a bar code with your phone. A number of Web sites, such as BitPay, which is based in Atlanta, allow merchants to process purchases made with bitcoins in a manner similar to the way they process credit card payments.

Why would buyers and sellers prefer to use bitcoins rather than cash or a credit card? The popularity of bitcoins with some buyers may be due to its being a trendy way to make purchases and to the convenience of using a smartphone to make a purchase. In addition, when you buy something with a credit card, the credit card company has a permanent record of your transaction. Bitcoin transactions are more private because no such records of the transactions exist. Some retailers prefer bitcoins to credit card purchases because the retailers pay only about 1 percent of the sale in processing costs, as opposed to about 3 percent for a credit card purchase. In addition, a bitcoin sale is final, just as if the purchase were made with cash, unlike credit card sales, where the buyer can dispute the purchase even months after it was made.

Despite these possible benefits to using bitcoins, they have not yet been widely adopted. The introduction of Apple Pay and Android Pay provided consumers with a way to use their smartphones linked to a credit card to make payments, which undercut one of bitcoin's advantages. Some firms also question whether the software underlying bitcoins is capable of dealing with a large number of transactions. The most popular online bitcoin exchange, Japan-based Mt. Gox, closed in 2015, further reducing confidence in the cryptocurrency.

Some policymakers are concerned that investors on exchanges might manipulate the prices of bitcoins and other virtual currencies. Between 2012 and 2017, the value of bitcoins in exchange for dollars went from as low as $5 per bitcoin to as high as $5,013 per bitcoin. Whether these swings in value represented underlying movements in demand and supply for bitcoins or the effects of investors manipulating their values was not clear. Bitcoin's reputation was not helped when, in 2017, hackers using the ransomware program WannaCry encrypted hard drives on computers around the world and demanded bitcoin payments to provide a code to restore access to the hard drives.

Despite the problems with bitcoins, the underlying technology behind it, known as *blockchain*, has attracted interest from both firms and governments, as they attempt to increase the speed, efficiency, and security of making payments. Blockchain allows individuals and businesses around the world to settle transactions instantly and securely on encrypted sites. The ability to direct transactions through blockchain could eliminate some of the services banks perform, potentially greatly reducing costs. The greatest stumbling block to businesses adopting blockchain is the complexity of the technology and its resulting high cost. If the cost declines over time, blockchain may become an important part of how businesses and individuals make payments.

Should the Federal Reserve include bitcoins and other virtual or cryptocurrencies in its measures of the money supply? So far, the volume of transactions in these currencies has been small, which makes the question of little practical importance. At this point, the Federal Reserve treats virtual currencies as being the equivalent of credit or debit cards, rather than currency or checking account balances, and does not include them in M1 or M2.

Sources: Paul Vigna, "Scorching-Hot Bitcoin Drops $300 in an Hour—And Still Rises on the Day," *Wall Street Journal*, May 25, 2017; Ginni Rometty, "How Blockchain Will Change Your Life," *Wall Street Journal*, November 7, 2016; Takashi Mochizuki, "Japanese Police Arrest Mark Karpelès of Collapsed Bitcoin Exchange Mt. Gox," *Wall Street Journal*, August 1, 2015; and "How Does Bitcoin Work?" *Economist*, April 11, 2013.

MyLab Economics Study Plan

Your Turn: Test your understanding by doing related problem 2.9 on page 510 at the end of this chapter.

14.3 How Do Banks Create Money?

LEARNING OBJECTIVE: Explain how banks create money.

We have seen that an important component of the money supply is checking accounts in banks. To understand the role money plays in the economy, we need to look more closely at how banks operate. Banks are profit-making private businesses, just like department stores and supermarkets. Some banks are quite small, with just a few branches, and do business in a limited area. Others are among the largest corporations in the United States, with thousands of branches spread across many states. Banks play an important role in the economy by accepting deposits and making loans. By taking these actions, banks fulfill a key function in the *money supply process* by which central banks control the money supply.

Bank Balance Sheets

To understand how banks create money, we need to briefly examine a typical bank balance sheet. On a balance sheet, a firm's assets are listed on the left, and its liabilities and stockholders' equity are listed on the right (see Chapter 6, Section 6.3 and Appendix). Assets are the value of anything owned by the firm, liabilities are the value of anything the firm owes, and stockholders' equity is the difference between the total value of assets and the total value of liabilities. Stockholders' equity represents the value of the firm if it were closed, all its assets were sold, and all its liabilities were paid off. A corporation's stockholders' equity is also called its *net worth*. A bank's stockholders' equity or net worth is also called its *capital*.

Figure 14.2 shows a typical balance sheet for a large bank. The key assets on a bank's balance sheet are its *reserves*, loans, and holdings of securities, such as U.S. Treasury

Assets (in billions)		Liabilities and Stockholders' Equity (in billions)	
Reserves	$135	Deposits	$1,000
Loans	900	Short-term borrowing	400
Securities	700	Long-term debt	360
Buildings and equipment	15	Other liabilities	275
Other assets	550	Total liabilities	$2,035
		Stockholders' equity	265
Total assets	$2,300	Total liabilities and stockholders' equity	$2,300

Figure 14.2

The Balance Sheet of a Typical Large Bank

The entries on a bank's balance sheet of greatest economic importance are its reserves, loans, and deposits. Notice that the difference between the value of this bank's total assets and its total liabilities is equal to its stockholders' equity. As a consequence, the left side of the balance sheet always equals the right side.

Note: Some entries on a typical bank's balance sheet have been combined to simplify the presentation.

Reserves Deposits that a bank keeps as cash in its vault or on deposit with the Federal Reserve.

Required reserves Reserves that a bank is legally required to hold, based on its checking account deposits.

Required reserve ratio The minimum fraction of deposits banks are required by law to keep as reserves.

Excess reserves Reserves that banks hold over the legal requirement.

bills. **Reserves** are deposits that a bank has retained rather than loaned out or invested. Banks keep reserves either physically within the bank, as *vault cash*, or on deposit with the Federal Reserve. Banks are required by law to keep as reserves 10 percent of their checking account deposits above a threshold level, which in 2017 was $115.1 million. These reserves are called **required reserves**. The minimum fraction of deposits that banks are required to keep as reserves is called the **required reserve ratio**. We can abbreviate the required reserve ratio as *RR*. Any reserves that banks hold above the legal requirement are called **excess reserves**. The balance sheet in Figure 14.2 shows that loans are a typical bank's largest asset.

Banks make *consumer loans* to households and *commercial loans* to firms. A loan is an asset to a bank because it represents a promise by the person taking out the loan to make certain specified payments to the bank. A bank's reserves and its holdings of securities are also assets because they are things of value the bank owns.

Apply the Concept

Will Fintech Make It Easier for You to Borrow?

Banks often require *collateral* before making a loan, which means that if the borrower stops making payments on the loan, the bank can seize the asset the borrower pledged as collateral. For example, if you take out a loan to buy a car and stop making payments on the loan, the bank can repossess your car and sell it to get its money back.

In addition to collateral, banks rely on a borrower's *credit score* in deciding whether to make a loan. The best-known credit score is compiled by the FICO company, which rates borrowers on a scale of 350 to 850, with higher scores meaning the borrower is less likely to default. Credit scores are determined by a variety of factors, including whether the borrower has been on time with payments on other loans and on credit cards; how long the borrower has lived at his current residence; how long the borrower has held her current job; and how much other debt the borrower has. Borrowers with high scores are called *prime borrowers*, and borrowers with low scores are called *subprime borrowers*. A bank will typically charge a prime borrower a lower interest rate than it will charge a subprime borrower. The higher interest rate on a *subprime loan* compensates the bank for the greater risk that the borrower will default. Lenders differ in the minimum score they use to consider someone a prime borrower, but it is typically around 650.

During the housing bubble of the early 2000s, many banks and other lenders made mortgage loans to subprime borrowers buying houses. High default rates on these mortgages following the bursting of the housing bubble in 2006 contributed to the 2007–2009 financial crisis and led policymakers to tighten regulations on banks granting subprime loans. Some consumer advocates also criticize these loans because they believe that the high interest rates exploit borrowers. To avoid both the new regulations and the criticism, many banks have cut back on subprime loans, particularly subprime *personal loans*, which are made to individuals who do not provide collateral for the loan. In past years, after getting a job, many new college graduates would take out a personal

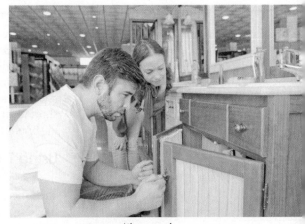

Maxriesgo/Shutterstock

Some people with low credit scores who can't get a bank loan turn to peer-to-peer lending to borrow the funds to meet needs such as buying furniture.

loan from a bank to buy the furniture or small appliances needed to set up an apartment. You may have a low credit score if you were late with a couple of credit card payments, have only a short work history, and have just moved into a new apartment. A bank may then consider you a subprime borrower and be unwilling to lend you money.

You could borrow on your credit card by taking a cash advance, but the interest rate is likely to be high—typically more than 20 percent. Banks cutting back on subprime personal loans left a hole in the financial system. In recent years, some new businesses have started to fill that hole. For example, LendingClub and FreedomPlus facilitate *peer-to-peer lending* on the Internet. These lending sites are an example of *financial technology*, or *fintech*, because they take advantage of software that rapidly evaluates information on borrowers and because they rely heavily on smartphone technology in the loan application process. The funds for those loans come from three key sources: individuals, other businesses, and—increasingly—financial firms, including insurance companies and pension funds.

By 2017, some industry analysts had become skeptical of the business model that peer-to-peer lending sites were using. In particular, a higher percentage of borrowers were defaulting on loans than the sites had been predicting. Some analysts believed that peer-to-peer sites suffered from two key problems: (1) The computer algorithms the sites were using to evaluate the creditworthiness of borrowers were doing a poorer job of predicting defaults than were the traditional methods banks use, such as verifying borrowers' incomes; and (2) peer-to-peer lenders make a profit by charging borrowers a one-time fee and charging the people providing funds a fee for collecting the payments from borrowers, so they may be less interested than banks in the quality of the loans they make. It remains to be seen whether the peer-to-peer lending sites can retain the confidence of investors, which they need to acquire enough funds to become a major source of credit to households and firms.

Sources: Peter Rudegeair, "LendingClub Gives Downbeat Outlook," *Wall Street Journal*, February 14, 2017; Telis Demos and Peter Rudegeair, "LendingClub's Newest Problem: Its Borrowers," *Wall Street Journal*, July 12, 2016; Ianthe Jeanne Dugan and Telis Demos, "New Lenders Spring Up to Cater to Subprime Sector," *Wall Street Journal*, March 5, 2014; and "From the People, for the People," *Economist*, May 9, 2015.

MyLab Economics Study Plan

Your Turn: Test your understanding by doing related problems 3.7 and 3.8 on pages 510–511 at the end of this chapter.

Deposits are a typical bank's largest liability. Deposits include checking accounts, savings accounts, and CDs. Deposits are liabilities to banks because they are owed to the households or firms that have deposited the funds. If you deposit $100 in your checking account, the bank owes you the $100, and you can withdraw it at any time. So, your checking account is an asset to you, and it is a liability to the bank. Banks also borrow short term from other banks and from the Federal Reserve and borrow long term by selling bonds to investors. These *borrowings* are also liabilities. **MyLab Economics** Concept Check

Using T-accounts to Show How a Bank Can Create Money

It is easier to show how banks create money by using a T-account than by using a balance sheet. A T-account is a stripped-down version of a balance sheet that shows only how a transaction *changes* a bank's balance sheet. Suppose you deposit $1,000 in currency into an account at Bank of America. This transaction raises the total deposits at Bank of America by $1,000 and also raises its reserves by $1,000. We show this result on the following T-account:

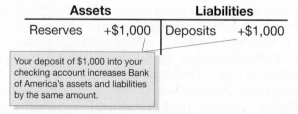

Assets		Liabilities	
Reserves	+$1,000	Deposits	+$1,000

Your deposit of $1,000 into your checking account increases Bank of America's assets and liabilities by the same amount.

Remember that because the total value of all the entries on the right side of a balance sheet must always be equal to the total value of all the entries on the left side of a balance sheet, any transaction that increases (or decreases) one side of the balance sheet must also increase (or decrease) the other side of the balance sheet. In this case, the T-account shows that we increased both sides of the balance sheet by $1,000.

Initially, this transaction does not increase the money supply. The currency component of the money supply declines by $1,000 because the $1,000 you deposited is no longer in circulation and, therefore, is not counted in the money supply. But the decrease in currency is offset by a $1,000 increase in the checking account deposit component of the money supply.

This initial change is not the end of the story, however. Banks are required to keep 10 percent of deposits as reserves. Because the Federal Reserve pays banks only a low rate of interest on their reserves, banks have an incentive to loan out or buy securities with the other 90 percent. Suppose, for simplicity, that initially Bank of America holds no excess reserves. In that case, Bank of America can keep $100 of your deposit as required reserves and loan out the other $900, which represents its excess reserves. Assume that Bank of America loans out the $900 to someone to buy a very inexpensive used car. Bank of America could give the $900 to the borrower in currency, but usually banks make loans by increasing the borrower's checking account. We can show this transaction with another T-account:

Notice that *by making this $900 loan, Bank of America has increased the money supply by $900*. The initial $1,000 in currency you deposited into your checking account has been turned into $1,900 in checking account deposits—a net increase in the money supply of $900.

But the story does not end here. The person who took out the $900 loan did so to buy a used car. To keep things simple, let's suppose he buys the car for exactly $900 and pays by writing a check on his account at Bank of America. The seller of the used car will now deposit the check in her bank. That bank may also be a branch of Bank of America, but in most cities, there are many banks, so let's assume that the seller of the car has her account at a branch of PNC Bank. Once she deposits the check, PNC Bank will send it to Bank of America to *clear* the check and collect the $900. We show the result in the following T-accounts:

After the car buyer's check clears, Bank of America has lost $900 in deposits—the amount loaned to the car buyer—and $900 in reserves—the amount it had to pay PNC when PNC sent Bank of America the car buyer's check. PNC has an increase in checking account deposits of $900—the deposit of the car seller—and an increase in reserves of $900—the amount it received from Bank of America.

PNC has 100 percent reserves against this new $900 deposit, but it needs only 10 percent reserves. The bank has an incentive to keep $90 as reserves and to loan out the other $810, which are excess reserves. If PNC does this, we can show the change in its balance sheet by using another T-account:

PNC Bank

Assets		Liabilities	
Reserves	+$900	Deposits	+$900
Loans	+$810	Deposits	+$810

By making an $810 loan, PNC has increased both its loans and its deposits by $810.

In loaning out the $810 in excess reserves, PNC creates a new checking account deposit of $810. The initial deposit of $1,000 in currency into Bank of America has now resulted in the creation of $1,000 + $900 + $810 = $2,710 in checking account deposits. The money supply has increased by $2,710 − $1,000 = $1,710.

The process is still not finished. The person who borrows the $810 will spend it by writing a check against his account. Whoever receives the $810 will deposit it in her bank, which could be a Bank of America branch or a PNC branch or a branch of some other bank. That new bank—if it's not PNC—will send the check to PNC and will receive $810 in new reserves. That new bank will have an incentive to loan out 90 percent of these reserves—keeping 10 percent to meet the legal requirement—and the process will go on. At each stage, the additional loans being made and the additional deposits being created are shrinking by 10 percent, because each bank has to keep that amount as required reserves. We can use a table to show the total increase in checking account deposits started by your initial deposit of $1,000. The dots in the table represent additional rounds in the money supply process: **MyLab Economics** Concept Check

Bank	Increase in Checking Account Deposits
Bank of America	$1,000
PNC	+ 900 (= 0.9 × $1,000)
Third Bank	+ 810 (= 0.9 × $900)
Fourth Bank	+ 729 (= 0.9 × $810)
•	+ •
•	+ •
•	+ •
Total change in checking account deposits	= $10,000

The Simple Deposit Multiplier

Simple deposit multiplier The ratio of the amount of deposits created by banks to the amount of new reserves.

Your initial deposit of $1,000 increased the reserves of the banking system by $1,000 and led to a total increase in checking account deposits of $10,000. The ratio of the amount of deposits created by banks to the amount of new reserves is called the **simple deposit multiplier**. In this case, the simple deposit multiplier is equal to $10,000/$1,000 = 10. Why 10? How do we know that your initial $1,000 deposit ultimately leads to a total increase in deposits of $10,000?

There are two ways to answer this question. First, each bank in the money supply process is keeping reserves equal to 10 percent of its deposits. For the banking system as a whole, the total increase in reserves is $1,000—the amount of your original currency deposit. Therefore, the system as a whole will end up with $10,000 in deposits because $1,000 is 10 percent of $10,000.

A second way to answer the question is by deriving an expression for the simple deposit multiplier. The total increase in deposits equals:

$$\$1,000 + [0.9 \times \$1,000] + [(0.9 \times 0.9) \times \$1,000] + [(0.9 \times 0.9 \times 0.9) \times \$1,000] + \ldots$$

or:

$$\$1,000 + [0.9 \times \$1,000] + [0.9^2 \times \$1,000] + [0.9^3 \times \$1,000] + \ldots$$

or:

$$\$1,000 \times (1 + 0.9 + 0.9^2 + 0.9^3 + \ldots).$$

The rules of algebra tell us that an expression like the one in the parentheses sums to:

$$\frac{1}{1 - 0.9}.$$

Simplifying further, we have:

$$\frac{1}{0.10} = 10.$$

So:

$$\text{Total increase in deposits} = \$1,000 \times 10 = \$10,000.$$

Don't Let This Happen to You

Don't Confuse Assets and Liabilities

Consider the following reasoning: "How can checking account deposits be a liability to a bank? After all, they are something of value that is in the bank. Therefore, checking account deposits should be counted as a bank *asset* rather than as a bank liability."

This statement is incorrect. The balance in a checking account represents something the bank *owes* to the owner of the account. Therefore, it is a liability to the bank, although it is an asset to the owner of the account. Similarly, your car loan is a liability to you—because it is a debt you owe to the bank—but it is an asset to the bank.

MyLab Economics Study Plan

Your Turn: Test your understanding by doing related problem 3.11 on page 511 at the end of this chapter.

Note that 10 is equal to 1 divided by the required reserve ratio, *RR*, which in this case is 10 percent, or 0.10. So, we have another way of expressing the simple deposit multiplier:

$$\text{Simple deposit multiplier} = \frac{1}{RR}.$$

This formula shows that the larger the required reserve ratio, the smaller the simple deposit multiplier. With a required reserve ratio of 10 percent, the simple deposit multiplier is 10. If the required reserve ratio were 20 percent, the simple deposit multiplier would fall to 1/0.20, or 5.

We can use this formula to calculate the total increase in checking account deposits from an increase in bank reserves due to, for instance, currency being deposited in a bank:

$$\text{Change in checking account deposits} = \text{Change in bank reserves} \times \frac{1}{RR}.$$

For example, if \$100,000 in currency is deposited in a bank and the required reserve ratio is 10 percent, then:

$$\text{Change in checking account deposits} = \$100,000 \times \frac{1}{0.10}$$

MyLab Economics Concept Check

$$= \$100,000 \times 10 = \$1,000,000.$$

Solved Problem 14.3

MyLab Economics Interactive Animation

Showing How Banks Create Money

Suppose you deposit \$5,000 in currency into your checking account at a branch of PNC Bank, which we will assume has no excess reserves at the time you make your deposit. Also assume that the required reserve ratio is 0.10.

a. Use a T-account to show the initial effect of this transaction on PNC's balance sheet.

b. Suppose that PNC makes the maximum loan it can from the funds you deposited. Use a T-account to show the initial effect on PNC's balance sheet from granting the loan. Also include in this T-account the transaction from part (a).

c. Now suppose that whoever took out the loan in part (b) writes a check for this amount and that the person receiving the check deposits it in Bank of America. Show the effect of these transactions on the balance sheets of PNC Bank and Bank of America *after the check has cleared.* On the T-account for PNC Bank, include the transactions from parts (a) and (b).

d. What is the maximum increase in checking account deposits that can result from your \$5,000 deposit? What is the maximum increase in the money supply that can result from your deposit? Explain.

Solving the Problem

Step 1: **Review the chapter material.** This problem is about how banks create checking account deposits, so you may want to review the section "Using T-accounts to Show How a Bank Can Create Money," which begins on page 490.

Step 2: **Answer part (a) by using a T-account to show the effect of the deposit.** Keeping in mind that T-accounts show only the changes in a balance sheet that result from the relevant transaction and that assets are on the left side of the account and liabilities are on the right side, we have:

PNC Bank

Assets		Liabilities	
Reserves	+\$5,000	Deposits	+\$5,000

Because the bank now has your \$5,000 in currency in its vault, its reserves (and, therefore, its assets) have risen by \$5,000. This transaction also increases your checking account balance by \$5,000. Because the bank owes you this money, the bank's liabilities have also risen by \$5,000.

Step 3: **Answer part (b) by using a T-account to show the effect of the loan.** The problem tells you to assume that PNC Bank currently has no excess reserves and that the required reserve ratio is 10 percent. This requirement means that if the bank's checking account deposits go up by \$5,000, the bank must keep $500 as reserves and can loan out the remaining $4,500. Remembering that new loans usually take the form of setting up or increasing a checking account for the borrower, we have:

PNC Bank

Assets		Liabilities	
Reserves	+$5,000	Deposits	+$5,000
Loans	+$4,500	Deposits	+$4,500

The first line of the T-account shows the transaction from part (a). The second line shows that PNC has loaned out $4,500 by increasing the checking account of the borrower by $4,500. The loan is an asset to PNC because it represents the borrower's promise to make certain payments spelled out in the loan agreement.

Step 4: **Answer part (c) by using T-accounts for PNC and Bank of America to show the effect of the check clearing.** We now show the effect of the borrower having spent the $4,500 he received as a loan from PNC. The person who received the $4,500 check deposits it in her account at Bank of America. We need two T-accounts to show this activity:

PNC Bank

Assets		Liabilities	
Reserves	+$500	Deposits	+$5,000
Loans	+$4,500		

Bank of America

Assets		Liabilities	
Reserves	+$4,500	Deposits	+$4,500

Look first at the T-account for PNC. Once Bank of America sends the check written by the borrower to PNC, PNC loses $4,500 in reserves, and Bank of America gains $4,500 in reserves. The $4,500 is also deducted from the account of the borrower. PNC is now satisfied with the result. It received a $5,000 deposit in currency from you. When that money was sitting in the bank vault, it wasn't earning any interest for PNC. Now $4,500 of the $5,000 has been loaned out and is earning interest. These interest payments allow PNC to cover its costs, which it has to do to remain in business.

Bank of America now has an increase in deposits of $4,500, resulting from the check being deposited, and an increase in reserves of $4,500. Bank of America is in the same situation as PNC was in part (a): It has excess reserves as a result of this transaction and a strong incentive to lend them out.

Step 5: **Answer part (d) by using the simple deposit multiplier formula to calculate the maximum increase in checking account deposits and the maximum increase in the money supply.** The simple deposit multiplier expression is (remember that *RR* is the required reserve ratio):

$$\text{Change in checking account deposits} = \text{Change in bank reserves} \times \frac{1}{RR}.$$

In this case, bank reserves rose by $5,000 as a result of your initial deposit, and the required reserve ratio is 0.10, so:

$$\text{Change in checking account deposits} = \$5,000 \times \frac{1}{0.10}$$
$$= \$5,000 \times 10 = \$50,000.$$

Because checking account deposits are part of the money supply, it is tempting to say that the money supply has also increased by $50,000. Remember, though, that your $5,000 in currency was counted as part of the money supply while you had it, but it is not counted when it is sitting in a bank vault. Therefore:

$$\text{Increase in checking account deposits} - \text{Decline in currency in}$$
$$\text{circulation} = \text{Change in the money supply.}$$

Or,

$$\$50,000 - \$5,000 = \$45,000.$$

MyLab Economics Study Plan   **Your Turn:** For more practice, do related problem 3.12 on page 511 at the end of the chapter.

The Simple Deposit Multiplier versus the Real-World Deposit Multiplier

The story we have just told of the money supply process is simplified. In deriving the simple deposit multiplier, we made two key assumptions:

1. *Banks hold no excess reserves.* That is, we assumed that when you deposited $1,000 in currency into your checking account at Bank of America, it loaned out $900, keeping only the $100 in required reserves. In fact, banks often keep some excess reserves to guard against the possibility that many depositors may simultaneously make withdrawals from their accounts. Since the financial crisis that began in 2007, banks have kept substantial excess reserves. The more excess reserves banks keep, the smaller the deposit multiplier. Imagine an extreme case in which Bank of America kept your entire $1,000 as reserves, loaning out none of it. In this case, the process we described earlier—loans leading to the creation of new deposits, leading to the making of additional loans, and so on—will not take place. The $1,000 increase in reserves will lead to just a $1,000 increase in deposits, and the deposit multiplier will be $1,000/$1,000 = 1, not 10.

2. *The whole amount of every check is deposited in a bank; no one takes any of it out as currency.* In reality, households and firms keep roughly constant the amount of currency they hold relative to the value of their checking account balances. So, we would expect to see people increasing the amount of currency they hold as the balances in their checking accounts rise. Once again, think of the extreme case. Suppose that when Bank of America makes the initial $900 loan to the borrower who wants to buy a used car, the seller of the car cashes the check instead of depositing it. In that case, PNC does not receive any new reserves and does not make any new loans. Once again, the $1,000 increase in your checking account at Bank of America is the only increase in deposits, and the deposit multiplier is 1.

The effect of these two simplifications is to reduce the real-world deposit multiplier to about 1.6 during normal times. So, a $1 increase in the reserves of the banking system typically results in about a $1.60 increase in deposits. Following the financial crisis of 2007–2009, the surge in bank holdings of excess reserves reduced the multiplier to less than 1.

Although the story of the deposit multiplier can be complicated, the key point to bear in mind is that the most important part of the money supply is the checking account balance component. When banks make loans, they increase checking account balances, and the money supply expands. Banks make new loans whenever they gain reserves. The whole process can also work in reverse: If banks lose reserves, they reduce their outstanding loans and deposits, and the money supply contracts.

We can summarize these important conclusions:

1. When banks gain reserves, they make new loans, and the money supply expands.
2. When banks lose reserves, they reduce their loans, and the money supply contracts.

MyLab Economics Concept Check   **MyLab Economics** Study Plan

 ## 14.4 The Federal Reserve System

LEARNING OBJECTIVE: Compare the three policy tools the Federal Reserve uses to manage the money supply.

Many people are surprised to learn that banks do not keep locked away in their vaults all the funds that are deposited in checking accounts. The United States, like nearly all other countries, has a **fractional reserve banking system**, which means that banks keep less than 100 percent of deposits as reserves. When people deposit money in a bank, the bank loans most of the money to someone else. What happens if depositors want their money back? Depositors withdrawing money would seem to be a problem because banks have loaned out most of the money and can't easily get it back.

In practice, withdrawals are usually not a problem for banks. On a typical day, about as much money is deposited as is withdrawn. If a small amount more is withdrawn than deposited, banks can cover the difference from their excess reserves or by borrowing from other banks. Sometimes depositors lose confidence in a bank when they question the value of the bank's underlying assets, particularly its loans. Often, the reason for a loss of confidence is bad news about the loans the bank has made, whether the news is accurate or not. When many depositors simultaneously decide to withdraw their money from a bank, there is a **bank run**. If many banks experience runs at the same time, the result is a **bank panic**. It is possible for one bank to handle a run by borrowing from other banks, but if many banks simultaneously experience runs, the banking system may be in trouble.

A central bank, like the Federal Reserve in the United States, can help stop a bank panic by acting as a *lender of last resort* by making loans to banks that cannot borrow funds elsewhere. The banks can use these loans to pay off depositors. When the panic ends and the depositors put their money back in their accounts, the banks can repay the loans to the central bank.

The Establishment of the Federal Reserve System

Bank panics lead to severe disruptions in business activity because households and firms have trouble accessing their accounts and may be unable to borrow money. In the United States, each bank panic in the late nineteenth and early twentieth centuries was accompanied by a recession. Figure 14.3 shows how a feedback loop during a bank run can lead to a recession. With the intention of putting an end to bank panics, in 1913, Congress passed the Federal Reserve Act, which set up the Federal Reserve System—often referred to as "the Fed." The system began operation in 1914, with the authority to make loans to banks. The loans the Fed makes to banks are called **discount loans**, and the interest rate it charges on the loans is called the **discount rate**. When a bank receives a loan from the Fed, its reserves increase by the amount of the loan.

The Fed's first test as a lender of last resort came in the early years of the Great Depression of the 1930s, when many banks were hit by bank runs as depositors pulled funds out of checking and savings accounts. Although the Fed had been established to act as a lender of last resort, Fed officials declined to make loans to many banks because the officials were worried that banks experiencing runs had made bad loans and other

Fractional reserve banking system A banking system in which banks keep less than 100 percent of deposits as reserves.

Bank run A situation in which many depositors simultaneously decide to withdraw money from a bank.

Bank panic A situation in which many banks experience runs at the same time.

Discount loans Loans the Federal Reserve makes to banks.

Discount rate The interest rate the Federal Reserve charges on discount loans.

MyLab Economics Animation

Figure 14.3

The Feedback Loop during a Bank Panic

Bank runs can cause good banks, as well as bad banks, to fail. Bank failures are costly because they reduce the ability of households and firms to get loans. Once a panic starts, falling incomes, employment, and asset prices can cause more bank failures. This feedback loop means that a panic can continue unless the government intervenes.

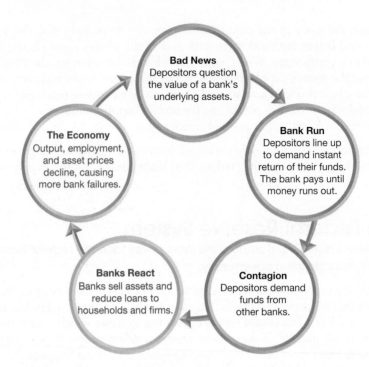

investments. The Fed believed that making loans to banks that were in financial trouble because of bad investments might reduce the incentive bank managers had to be careful in their investment decisions. Partly due to the Fed's unwillingness to act as a lender of last resort, more than 5,000 banks failed during the early 1930s. Today, many economists are critical of the Fed's decisions in the early 1930s because they believe these decisions increased the severity of the Great Depression. In 1934, Congress established the Federal Deposit Insurance Corporation (FDIC) to insure deposits in most banks up to a limit, which is currently $250,000 per deposit, per bank. If the bank where you have your checking account goes out of business, the FDIC will refund your money after a wait of at most two days. Deposit insurance has greatly reduced bank runs because it has reassured all but the largest depositors that their deposits are safe, even if their bank goes out of business. During the financial crisis of 2007–2009, some banks experienced runs when depositors with funds exceeding the deposit insurance limit feared that they would suffer losses if their banks failed.

In setting up the Federal Reserve System, Congress divided the country into 12 Federal Reserve Districts, as shown in Figure 14.4. Each district has its own Federal Reserve Bank, which provides services to banks in that district. The real power of the Fed, however, lies in Washington, DC, with the Board of Governors. The seven members of the Board of Governors are appointed by the president of the United States to 14-year, nonrenewable terms. One member of the Board of Governors is appointed chair and serves a 4-year, renewable term. In addition to acting as a lender of last resort to banks, the Fed acts as a bankers' bank, providing services such as check clearing to banks, and has the responsibility of managing the U.S. money supply.   **MyLab Economics** Concept Check

How the Federal Reserve Manages the Money Supply

Although Congress established the Fed primarily to stop bank panics by acting as a lender of last resort, today the Fed is also responsible for managing the money supply. As we will discuss in more detail in Chapter 15, managing the money supply is part of **monetary policy**, which the Fed undertakes to pursue macroeconomic policy objectives. To manage the money supply, the Fed uses three *monetary policy tools*:

1. Open market operations
2. Discount policy
3. Reserve requirements

Monetary policy The actions the Federal Reserve takes to manage the money supply and interest rates to pursue macroeconomic policy objectives.

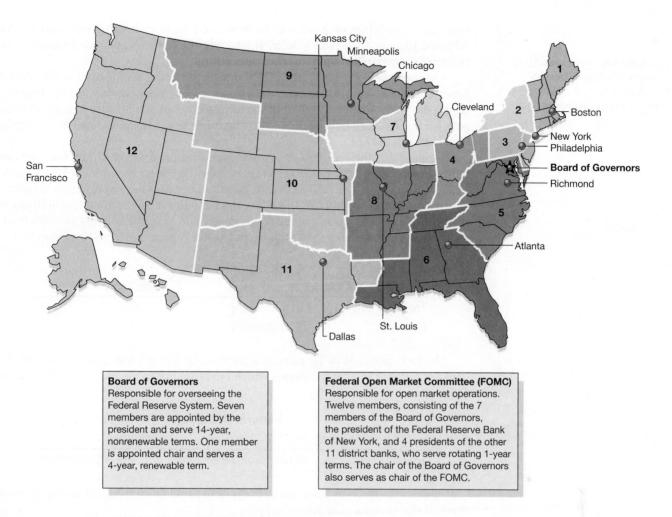

Board of Governors
Responsible for overseeing the Federal Reserve System. Seven members are appointed by the president and serve 14-year, nonrenewable terms. One member is appointed chair and serves a 4-year, renewable term.

Federal Open Market Committee (FOMC)
Responsible for open market operations. Twelve members, consisting of the 7 members of the Board of Governors, the president of the Federal Reserve Bank of New York, and 4 presidents of the other 11 district banks, who serve rotating 1-year terms. The chair of the Board of Governors also serves as chair of the FOMC.

MyLab Economics Animation

Figure 14.4 **The Federal Reserve System**

The United States is divided into 12 Federal Reserve Districts, each of which has a Federal Reserve Bank. The real power within the Federal Reserve System, however, lies in Washington, DC, with the Board of Governors, which consists of 7 members appointed by the president. The 12-member Federal Open Market Committee carries out monetary policy.

Source: Board of Governors of the Federal Reserve System.

Remember that the most important component of the money supply is checking account deposits. Not surprisingly, all three of the Fed's policy tools are aimed at affecting the reserves of banks as a means of changing the volume of checking account deposits.

Open Market Operations Eight times per year, the **Federal Open Market Committee (FOMC)** meets in Washington, DC, to discuss monetary policy. The committee has 12 voting members:

- The 7 members of the Federal Reserve's Board of Governors
- The president of the Federal Reserve Bank of New York
- The presidents of 4 of the other 11 Federal Reserve Banks (These 4 presidents serve one-year rotating terms as voting members of the FOMC.)

All 12 Federal Reserve Bank presidents attend meetings and participate in discussions. The chair of the Board of Governors also serves as the chair of the FOMC.

When the federal government spends more than it collects in taxes and other revenue, it runs a budget deficit. To fund the deficit, the U.S. Treasury borrows by selling bills, notes, and bonds. Remember that the *maturity* of a financial asset is the period of time until the purchaser receives payment of the face value or principal. Usually, bonds have face values of $1,000. Treasury bills have maturities of 1 year or less, Treasury

Federal Open Market Committee (FOMC) The Federal Reserve committee responsible for open market operations and managing the money supply in the United States.

Open market operations The buying and selling of Treasury securities by the Federal Reserve in order to control the money supply.

notes have maturities of 2 years to 10 years, and Treasury bonds have maturities of 30 years. To control the size of the money supply, the Fed buys and sells Treasury securities in a process called **open market operations**.

To increase the money supply, the FOMC directs the *trading desk*, located at the Federal Reserve Bank of New York, to carry out an *open market purchase* by buying U.S. Treasury securities—most frequently bills, but sometimes notes or bonds—from banks. The Fed pays for the Treasury bills by depositing the funds in the reserve accounts that banks maintain with the Fed.

Suppose that the Fed engages in an open market purchase of $10 million. We can illustrate the results with two T-accounts: one for the Fed and one for the banking system. The banking system's T-account is based on the banking system's balance sheet, which simply adds together all the assets and liabilities of all the commercial banks in the United States. As a result of the open market purchase, the banking system's holdings of Treasury bills fall by $10 million, and its reserves increase by $10 million:

Banking System

Assets		Liabilities
Treasury bills	–$10 million	
Reserves	+$10 million	

The Fed's holdings of Treasury bills increase by $10 million, and the value of the banking system's reserve balances—which are a liability to the Fed—also increase by $10 million:

Federal Reserve

Assets		Liabilities	
Treasury bills	+$10 million	Reserves	+$10 million

This increase in reserves starts the process of expanding loans and checking account deposits that increases the money supply.

To decrease the money supply, the FOMC directs the trading desk to carry out an *open market sale* by selling Treasury securities. When the buyers of the Treasury securities pay for them with checks, the banking system's reserves fall. This decrease in reserves starts a contraction of loans and checking account deposits that reduces the money supply.

There are three reasons the Fed conducts monetary policy principally through open market operations:

1. Because the Fed initiates open market operations, it completely controls their volume, which means the Fed can carry out both large and small open market operations.
2. Open market operations are easily reversible. For example, if the Fed believes that previous open market purchases have caused the money supply to increase too rapidly, it can engage in open market sales.
3. The Fed can implement its open market operations quickly, with no administrative delay or required changes in regulations.

Many other central banks, including the European Central Bank and the Bank of Japan, also use open market operations to conduct monetary policy.

The Federal Reserve is responsible for putting the paper currency of the United States into circulation. (The currency is actually printed by the U.S. Treasury.) Recall that if you look at the top of a dollar bill, you see the words "Federal Reserve Note." When the Fed takes actions to increase the money supply, commentators sometimes say that it is "printing more money." The main way the Fed increases the money supply, however, is not by printing more currency but by buying Treasury securities. Similarly, to reduce the money supply, the Fed doesn't set fire to stacks of paper currency. Instead, it sells Treasury securities. We will spend more time discussing the Fed's management of the money supply in Chapter 15 when we discuss monetary policy.

Discount Policy As we have seen, when a bank borrows money from the Fed by taking out a discount loan, the interest rate the bank pays is called the *discount rate*. By lowering the discount rate, the Fed can encourage banks to take additional loans and thereby increase their reserves. With more reserves, banks will make more loans to households and firms, which will increase checking account deposits and the money supply. Raising the discount rate will have the reverse effect.

Reserve Requirements When the Fed reduces the required reserve ratio, it converts required reserves into excess reserves. For example, suppose a bank has $100 million in checking account deposits, and the required reserve ratio is 10 percent. The bank will be required to hold $10 million as reserves. If the Fed reduces the required reserve ratio to 8 percent, the bank will need to hold only $8 million as reserves. The Fed can thereby convert $2 million worth of reserves from required reserves to excess reserves. This $2 million is then available for the bank to lend out. The Fed's *raising* the required reserve ratio from 10 percent to 12 percent will have the reverse effect.

The Fed rarely changes reserve requirements because doing so can disrupt banks' operations by forcing them to significantly change their holdings of loans, bonds, and other securities. Also, because the Fed pays banks only a low interest rate on reserves, raising the required ratio effectively places a tax on banks' reserve holdings. That tax may discourage banks from increasing their holding of deposits and making loans. A decline in the willingness of banks to make loans reduces the ability of households and firms to borrow, which can be costly for the economy. The Fed relies instead on open market operations as its main tool for managing the money supply.   MyLab Economics Concept Check

The "Shadow Banking System" and the Financial Crisis of 2007–2009

The banks we have been discussing in this chapter are *commercial banks*, whose most important economic role is to accept funds from depositors and lend those funds to borrowers. Large firms can sell stocks and bonds on financial markets, but investors are typically unwilling to buy stocks and bonds from small and medium-sized firms because they lack sufficient information about the financial health of smaller firms. So, smaller firms—and households—have traditionally relied on bank loans for their credit needs. In the past 25 years, however, two important developments have occurred in the financial system: (1) Banks have begun to resell many of their loans rather than keep them until borrowers pay them off; and (2) financial firms other than commercial banks have become important sources of credit to businesses.

Securitization Comes to Banking Traditionally, when a bank made a *residential mortgage loan* to a household to buy a home or made a commercial loan to a business, the bank would keep the loan and collect the payments until the borrower paid off the loan. A financial asset—such as a loan or a stock or a bond—is considered a **security** if it can be bought and sold in a *financial market*. Shares of stock issued by the Coca-Cola Company are an example of a security because they can be bought and sold on the New York Stock Exchange. When a financial asset is first sold, the sale takes place in the *primary market*. If an investor resells the asset, the sale takes place in the *secondary market*. Prior to 1970, most loans were not securities because they could not be resold; there was no secondary market for them. After 1970, residential mortgages and then other loans, including car loans and commercial loans, began to be *securitized*. The process of **securitization** creates a secondary market in which loans that have been bundled together can be bought and sold in financial markets, just as corporate or government bonds are. Figure 14.5 outlines the securitization process. We will discuss the process of securitization further in Chapter 15, Section 15.6 when we consider monetary policy.

The Shadow Banking System In addition to the changes resulting from securitization, the financial system was transformed in the 1990s and 2000s by the increasing importance of *nonbank financial firms*. Investment banks, such as Morgan Stanley, differ from commercial banks in that they do not accept deposits, and they rarely lend directly to households. Instead, investment banks traditionally concentrated

Security A financial asset—such as a stock or a bond—that can be bought and sold in a financial market.

Securitization The process of transforming loans or other financial assets into securities.

(a) Securitizing a loan

(b) The flow of payments on a securitized loan

Iriana88w/123RF; Ken Wolter/Shutterstock; XPacifica/Alamy Stock Photo; Scott Rothstein/Shutterstock

MyLab Economics Animation

Figure 14.5   **The Process of Securitization**

Panel (a) shows how in the securitization process, banks grant loans to households and bundle the loans into securities that are then sold to investors.

Panel (b) shows that banks collect payments on the original loans and, after taking a fee, send the payments to the investors who bought the securities.

on providing advice to firms issuing stocks and bonds or considering mergers with other firms. In the late 1990s, investment banks expanded their buying of mortgages, bundling large numbers of them together as bonds known as *mortgage-backed securities,* and reselling them to investors. Mortgage-backed securities proved very popular with investors because they often paid higher interest rates than other securities that seemed to have comparable default risk.

Money market mutual funds also became more important in the financial system over time. These funds sell shares to investors and use the money to buy short-term securities such as Treasury bills and commercial paper issued by corporations. Commercial paper represents short-term borrowing corporations use to fund their day-to-day operations. Many corporations that previously met such needs by borrowing from banks began instead to sell commercial paper to money market mutual funds.

Hedge funds raise money from wealthy investors and use sophisticated investment strategies that often involve significant risk. By the mid-2000s, hedge funds had become an important source of demand for securitized loans and an important source of loans to other financial firms.

In 2008, Timothy Geithner, who became Treasury secretary in the Obama administration, used the term *the shadow banking system* to refer to investment banks, money market mutual funds, hedge funds, and other nonbank financial firms engaged in similar activities. By raising money from investors and lending it directly or indirectly to firms and households, these firms were carrying out a function that at one time was almost exclusively carried out by commercial banks.

The Financial Crisis of 2007–2009 The firms in the shadow banking system differed from commercial banks in two important ways: First, the government agencies—including the Federal Reserve—that regulated the commercial banking system did not regulate these firms. Second, these firms were more highly *leveraged*— that is, they relied more heavily on borrowed money to finance their operations— than were commercial banks. If a firm uses a small amount of its own money and a lot of borrowed money to make an investment, both the firm's potential profit and its potential loss are increased. Suppose a firm invests $100 of its own money. If the investment earns a return of $3, the firm has earned 3 percent ($3/$100) on its funds. But if the firm's investment consists of $10 of its own money and $90 it has borrowed, a profit of $3 becomes a return of 30 percent ($3/$10) on the firm's $10 investment. If the investment loses $2, however, the firm's return is −20 percent (−$2/$10). Leveraged investments have a potential for both large gains and large losses.

As mentioned earlier, commercial banks rarely experienced runs after Congress established federal deposit insurance in the 1930s. However, beginning in 2007, some firms in the shadow banking system experienced runs. As we will discuss further in Chapter 15, Section 15.6, problems in the U.S. housing market were the main cause of the financial crisis of 2007–2009. As housing prices began to fall, a significant number of borrowers defaulted on their mortgages, which caused mortgage-backed securities to lose value. Financial firms that had invested in these securities, including both commercial banks and many firms in the shadow banking system, suffered losses. The more leveraged the firm, the larger the losses. Although deposit insurance helped commercial banks avoid runs, investment banks and other financial firms that had borrowed short term and invested the funds long term were in trouble. As lenders refused to renew their short-term loans, many of these firms had to sell their holdings of securities in an attempt to raise cash. But as the prices of the securities continued to fall, the losses to these firms increased.

In the spring of 2008, the investment bank Bear Stearns was saved from bankruptcy only when the Federal Reserve arranged for it to be acquired by JPMorgan Chase. In the fall of 2008, the Federal Reserve and the U.S. Treasury decided not to take action to save the investment bank Lehman Brothers, which failed. The failure of Lehman Brothers echoed throughout the financial system, setting off a panic. The process of securitization—apart from government-guaranteed residential mortgages—ground to a halt. The well-publicized difficulties of a money market mutual fund that had suffered losses on loans to Lehman Brothers led to a wave of withdrawals from these funds. In turn, the funds were no longer able to fulfill their role as buyers of corporate commercial paper. As banks and other financial firms sold assets and cut back on lending to shore up their financial positions, the flow of funds from savers to borrowers was disrupted. The resulting *credit crunch* significantly worsened the recession that had begun in December 2007.

The Fed's Response The Fed, in combination with the U.S. Treasury, took vigorous action to deal with the financial crisis. We will discuss the Fed's actions further in Chapter 15, Section 15.6, but for now, we can mention several particularly important policy actions:

- In the fall of 2008, under the Troubled Asset Relief Program (TARP), the Fed and Treasury began attempting to stabilize the commercial banking system by providing funds to banks in exchange for stock. Taking partial ownership of private commercial banks was an unprecedented move by the federal government.
- The Fed also modified its discount policy by setting up several new "lending facilities." These lending facilities made it possible for the Fed to grant discount loans to financial firms—such as investment banks—that had not previously been eligible.
- The Fed addressed problems in the commercial paper market by directly buying commercial paper for the first time since the 1930s.

Although the recession continued into 2009, the extraordinary actions of the Treasury and Fed stabilized the financial system. It took several years, however, for the flow of funds from savers to borrowers to return to normal levels, and economists and policymakers continue to debate the wisdom of some of the Fed's actions. **MyLab Economics** Concept Check **MyLab Economics** Study Plan

14.5 The Quantity Theory of Money

LEARNING OBJECTIVE: Explain the quantity theory of money and use it to explain how high rates of inflation occur.

People have been aware of the connection between increases in the money supply and inflation for centuries. In the sixteenth century, the Spanish conquered Mexico and Peru and shipped large quantities of gold and silver from those countries back to Spain. The gold and silver were minted into coins and spent across Europe to further the political ambitions of the Spanish kings. Prices in Europe rose steadily during these years, and many observers discussed the relationship between this inflation and the flow of gold and silver into Europe from the Americas.

Connecting Money and Prices: The Quantity Equation

In the early twentieth century, Irving Fisher, an economist at Yale University, formalized the connection between money and prices by using the *quantity equation*:

$$M \times V = P \times Y.$$

Velocity of money The average number of times each dollar in the money supply is used to purchase goods and services included in GDP.

The quantity equation states that the money supply (M) multiplied by the *velocity of money* (V) equals the price level (P) multiplied by real output (Y). Fisher defined the **velocity of money**, often called simply "velocity," as the average number of times each dollar of the money supply is used to purchase goods and services included in GDP. Rewriting the original equation by dividing both sides by M, we have the equation for velocity:

$$V = \frac{P \times Y}{M}.$$

We can use M1 to measure the money supply, the GDP deflator to measure the price level, and real GDP to measure real output. Remembering that if we multiply real GDP by the GDP deflator, we get nominal GDP, we can calculate the value for velocity for 2016:

$$V = \frac{\$18.6 \text{ trillion}}{\$3.2 \text{ trillion}} = 5.8.$$

This result tells us that, during 2016, each dollar of M1 was on average spent 5.8 times on goods or services included in GDP.

Because velocity is defined to be equal to $(P \times Y)/M$, we know that the quantity equation must always hold true: The left side of the equation *must* be equal to the right side. A theory is a statement about the world that might possibly be false. Therefore, the quantity equation is not a theory. Irving Fisher turned the quantity equation into the **quantity theory of money** by arguing that velocity was constant. He argued that the average number of times a dollar is spent depends on factors that do not change often, such as how often people get paid, how often they do their grocery shopping, and how often businesses send out bills. Because this assertion may be true or false, the quantity theory of money is, in fact, a theory. **MyLab Economics** Concept Check

Quantity theory of money A theory about the connection between money and prices that assumes that the velocity of money is constant.

The Quantity Theory Explanation of Inflation

The quantity equation gives us a way of showing the relationship between changes in the money supply and changes in the price level, or inflation. To see this relationship more clearly, we can use a handy mathematical rule that states that an equation in which variables are multiplied together is equal to an equation in which the *growth rates* of these variables are *added* together. So, we can transform the quantity equation from:

$$M \times V = P \times Y$$

to:

Growth rate of the money supply + Growth rate of velocity = Growth rate of the price level (or the inflation rate) + Growth rate of real output.

This way of writing the quantity equation is more useful for investigating the effect of changes in the money supply on the inflation rate. Remember that the growth rate for any variable is the percentage change in the variable from one year to the next. The growth rate of the price level is the inflation rate, so we can rewrite the quantity equation to help understand the factors that determine inflation:

Inflation rate = Growth rate of the money supply + Growth rate of velocity − Growth rate of real output.

If Irving Fisher was correct that velocity is constant, then the growth rate of velocity will be zero. For example, if velocity is always equal to six, then its percentage change from one year to the next will always be zero. This assumption allows us to rewrite the equation one last time:

Inflation rate = Growth rate of the money supply − Growth rate of real output.

This equation leads to the following predictions:

1. If the money supply grows at a faster rate than real GDP, there will be inflation.
2. If the money supply grows at a slower rate than real GDP, there will be deflation. (Recall that *deflation* is a decline in the price level.)
3. If the money supply grows at the same rate as real GDP, the price level will be stable, and there will be neither inflation nor deflation.

It turns out that Irving Fisher was wrong in asserting that the velocity of money is constant. From year to year, there can be significant fluctuations in velocity. As a result, the predictions of inflation based on the quantity theory of money do not hold every year, but most economists agree that the quantity theory provides useful insight into the long-run relationship between the money supply and inflation: *In the long run, inflation results from the money supply growing at a faster rate than real GDP.*   MyLab Economics Concept Check

How Accurate Are Forecasts of Inflation Based on the Quantity Theory?

Note that the accuracy of the quantity theory depends on whether the key assumption that velocity is constant is correct. If velocity is not constant, there may not be a tight link between increases in the money supply and increases in the price level. For example, an increase in the quantity of money might be offset by a decline in velocity, leaving the price level unaffected. Because velocity can move erratically in the short run, we would not expect the quantity equation to provide good forecasts of inflation in the short run. Over the long run, however, there is a strong link between changes in the money supply and inflation. Panel (a) of Figure 14.6 shows by decade the relationship in the United States

(a) Inflation and money supply growth in the United States, 1870s–2000s

(b) Inflation and money supply growth in 97 countries, 2002–2016

MyLab Economics Animation

Figure 14.6   **The Relationship between Money Growth and Inflation over Time and around the World**

Panel (a) shows that, by and large, the rate of inflation in the United States has been highest during the decades in which the money supply has increased most rapidly, and the rate of inflation has been lowest during the decades in which the money supply has increased least rapidly. Panel (b) shows the relationship between money supply growth and inflation for 97 countries between 2002 and 2016. There is not an exact relationship between money supply growth and inflation, but countries such as Angola, Belarus, and Iran that had high rates of money supply growth had

high inflation rates, and countries such as the United States and Japan had low rates of money supply growth and low inflation rates.

Sources: Panel (a): For the 1870s to the 1960s, Milton Friedman and Anna J. Schwartz, *Monetary Trends in the United States and United Kingdom: Their Relation to Income, Prices, and Interest Rates, 1867–1975*, Chicago: University of Chicago Press, 1982, Table 4.8; and for the 1970s to the 2000s, Federal Reserve Board of Governors and U.S. Bureau of Economic Analysis; Panel (b): International Monetary Fund, *International Monetary Statistics*.

between the growth of the M2 measure of the money supply and the inflation rate. (We use M2 here because data on M2 are available for a longer period of time than are data for M1.) Because of variations in the rate of growth of real GDP and in velocity, there is not an exact relationship between the growth rate of M2 and the inflation rate. But there is a clear pattern that decades with higher growth rates in the money supply were also decades with higher inflation rates. In other words, most of the variation in inflation rates across decades can be explained by variation in the rates of growth of the money supply.

Panel (b) provides further evidence consistent with the quantity theory by looking at rates of growth of the money supply and rates of inflation across 97 countries for the years 2002–2016. Although there is not an exact relationship between rates of growth of the money supply and rates of inflation across countries, panel (b) shows that countries where the money supply grew rapidly tended to have high inflation rates, while countries where the money supply grew more slowly tended to have much lower inflation rates. Not included in panel (b) are data for Zimbabwe, which experienced the most extreme case of inflation in recent years. From 2002 to 2007, the money supply in Zimbabwe grew at an average annual rate of more than 10,000 percent. The result was an accelerating rate of inflation that eventually reached 15 billion percent during 2008. Zimbabwe was suffering from *hyperinflation*—that is, a rate of inflation that exceeds 50 percent per month. **MyLab Economics** Concept Check

High Rates of Inflation

The quantity theory can help us understand the reasons for very high rates of inflation. Hyperinflation is caused by central banks increasing the money supply at a rate far in excess of the growth rate of real GDP. A high rate of inflation causes money to lose its value so rapidly that households and firms avoid holding it. If, as happened in Zimbabwe, the inflation rate becomes high enough, people stop using paper currency, so it no longer serves the important functions of money discussed earlier in this chapter. Economies suffering from high inflation usually also suffer from very slow growth, if not severe recession.

Given the dire consequences that follow from high inflation, why do governments cause it by expanding the money supply so rapidly? The main reason is that governments often want to spend more than they are able to raise through taxes. Developed countries, such as the United States, can usually bridge gaps between spending and taxes by borrowing through selling bonds to the public. Developing countries often have difficulty selling bonds because investors are skeptical of their ability to pay back the money. If they are unable to sell bonds to the public, governments in developing countries will force their central banks to purchase them. As we discussed previously, when a central bank buys government bonds, the money supply will increase. In the United States, the Federal Reserve always buys Treasury securities from banks, never directly from the U.S. Treasury. This procedure helps ensure that the Treasury only issues bonds in amounts that private investors—rather than the central bank—are willing to buy. **MyLab Economics** Concept Check

MyLab Economics Study Plan

Apply the Concept
MyLab Economics Video

The German Hyperinflation of the Early 1920s

When Germany lost World War I, a revolution broke out that overthrew Kaiser Wilhelm II and installed a new government known as the Weimar Republic. In the peace treaty of 1919, the Allies—the United States, Great Britain, France, and Italy—imposed payments called *reparations* on the new German government. The reparations were meant as compensation to the Allies for the damage Germany had caused during the war. It was very difficult for the German government to use tax revenue to cover both its normal spending and the reparations.

The German government decided to pay for the difference between its spending and its tax revenues by selling bonds to the central bank, the Reichsbank. After a few years, the German government fell far behind in its reparations payments. In January 1923, the French government sent troops into the German industrial area known as the Ruhr to try to collect the payments directly. German workers in the Ruhr went on strike, and the German government decided to support them by paying their salaries. The government raised the funds by selling additional bonds to the Reichsbank, thereby further increasing the money supply.

The inflationary increase in the money supply was very large: The total number of marks—the German currency—in circulation rose from 115 million in January 1922 to 1.3 billion in January 1923 and then to 497 billion *billion*, or 497,000,000,000,000,000,000, in December 1923. Just as the quantity theory predicts, the result was a staggeringly high rate of inflation. The German price index that stood at 100 in 1914 and 1,440 in January 1922 had risen to 126,160,000,000,000 in December 1923. The German mark became worthless. The German government ended the hyperinflation by (1) negotiating a new agreement with the Allies that reduced its reparations payments, (2) reducing other government expenditures and raising taxes to balance its budget, and (3) replacing the existing mark with a new mark. Each new mark was worth 1 trillion old marks. The German central bank was also limited to issuing a total of 3.2 billion new marks.

These steps were enough to bring the hyperinflation to an end—but not before the savings of anyone holding the old marks had been wiped out. Most middle-income Germans were extremely resentful of this outcome. Many historians believe that the hyperinflation greatly reduced the allegiance of many Germans to the Weimar Republic and may have helped pave the way for Adolf Hitler and the Nazis to seize power 10 years later.

Sources: Thomas Sargent, "The Ends of Four Big Inflations," *Rational Expectations and Inflation*, 3rd ed., Princeton, NJ: Princeton University Press, 2013; and John Parke Young, *European Currency and Finance*, Washington, DC: Government Printing Office, 1925.

Your Turn: Test your understanding by doing related problem 5.10 on page 513 at the end of this chapter.

Bettmann/Getty Images

During the German hyperinflation of the 1920s, paper currency became so worthless that people used it to light their stoves.

MyLab Economics Study Plan

Continued from page 479

Economics in Your Life & Career

Should Your Business Accept Cash?

At the beginning of this chapter, we asked you to suppose that you had started a juice bar with a partner who proposes that you not accept payments in cash. We asked you to consider whether this strategy is likely to increase or decrease your firm's profit.

We saw in the chapter that there is no law that requires you to accept cash as payment. We also saw in the *Apply the Concept* on page 483 that some stores now refuse to accept cash in order to speed up the processing of orders and to reduce the risk of robberies. Refusing to accept cash means that you will lose customers who don't have a credit card or Apple Pay or a similar app. At some stores, such as the Sweetgreen restaurant chain mentioned in the *Apply the Concept*, the fraction of customers paying with cash has fallen to less than 10 percent. If your juice bar is in a similar situation, the gains from refusing cash may more than offset your losing some customers, and your profit may increase. But if a large fraction of your customers prefer to use cash, then losing them may reduce your profit, particularly because you have to pay credit card companies a fee on each transaction.

Conclusion

Money plays a key role in the functioning of an economy by facilitating trade in goods and services and by making specialization possible. Without specialization, no advanced economy can prosper. Households and firms, banks, and the central bank (the Federal Reserve in the United States) are participants in the process of creating the money supply. In Chapter 15, we will discuss how the Federal Reserve uses monetary policy to promote its economic objectives.

Visit **MyLab Economics** for a news article and analysis related to the concepts of this chapter.

CHAPTER SUMMARY
AND PROBLEMS

Key Terms

Asset, p. 480

Bank panic, p. 497

Bank run, p. 497

Commodity money, p. 480

Discount loans, p. 497

Discount rate, p. 497

Excess reserves, p. 489

Federal Open Market
Committee (FOMC), p. 499

Federal Reserve, p. 482

Fiat money, p. 482

Fractional reserve banking
system, p. 497

M1, p. 484

M2, p. 485

Monetary policy, p. 498

Money, p. 480

Open market operations,
p. 500

Quantity theory of money,
p. 504

Required reserve ratio, p. 489

Required reserves, p. 489

Reserves, p. 489

Securitization, p. 501

Security, p. 501

Simple deposit multiplier,
p. 492

Velocity of money, p. 504

14.1 What Is Money, and Why Do We Need It? pages 480–483
LEARNING OBJECTIVE: Define money and discuss the four functions of money.

MyLab Economics   Visit www.pearson.com/mylab/economics to
complete these exercises online and get instant
feedback.

Summary

A *barter economy* is an economy that does not use money and in
which people trade goods and services directly for other goods
and services. Barter trade occurs only if there is a *double coincidence
of wants*, in which both parties to the trade want what the other
one has. Because barter is inefficient, there is strong incentive to
use **money**, which is any **asset** that people are generally willing
to accept in exchange for goods or services or in payment of
debts. An *asset* is anything of value owned by a person or a firm.
A **commodity money** is a good used as money that also has
value independent of its use as money. Money has four functions:
It is a medium of exchange, a unit of account, a store of value, and
a standard of deferred payment. At one time, governments issued
gold coins and paper currency that were convertible into gold.
Today, no government in the world issues paper currency that
can be redeemed for gold. Instead, paper currency is **fiat money**,
which has no value except as money. The **Federal Reserve** is the
central bank of the United States.

Review Questions

1.1 A baseball fan with a Mike Trout baseball card wants to trade
it for a Giancarlo Stanton baseball card, but everyone the fan
knows who has a Stanton card doesn't want a Trout card.
What do economists call the problem this fan is having?

1.2 What is the difference between commodity money and
fiat money?

1.3 What are the four functions of money? Can something be
considered money if it does not fulfill all four functions?

1.4 Why do businesses accept paper currency when they
know that, unlike a gold coin, the paper the currency is
printed on is worth very little?

Problems and Applications

1.5 The English economist William Stanley Jevons described
a world tour during the 1880s by a French singer, Mademoiselle Zélie. One stop on the tour was a theater in the
Society Islands, part of French Polynesia in the South
Pacific. She performed for her usual fee, which was one-
third of the receipts. This turned out to be 3 pigs, 23
turkeys, 44 chickens, 5,000 coconuts, and "considerable
quantities of bananas, lemons, and oranges." She estimated that all of this would have had a value in France
of 4,000 francs. According to Jevons, "as Mademoiselle
could not consume any considerable portion of the
receipts herself, it became necessary in the meantime to
feed the pigs and poultry with the fruit." Do the goods
Mademoiselle Zélie received as payment fulfill the four
functions of money described in this chapter? Briefly
explain.

Source: W. Stanley Jevons, *Money and the Mechanism of Exchange,* New
York: D. Appleton and Company, 1889, pp. 1–2.

1.6 (Related to the Chapter Opener on page 478) In November
2016, the Indian government decided to withdraw paper
currency that made up more than 86 percent of the
value of all rupee bills in circulation. An article in the
Wall Street Journal published shortly after that decision
described a small merchant in India as having "traded
one customer a kilogram of potatoes, cauliflower and
tomatoes for half a liter of honey. That was a good
deal, he says. In normal times, the honey would be 120
rupees in the market (around $1.80) and the vegetables
70 rupees." Is this merchant's ability to arrange a barter deal with a customer an indication that the Indian
economy doesn't actually require money to function
efficiently? Briefly explain.

Source: Raymond Zhong and Karan Deep Singh, "Barter Economy
Is Reborn in Villages as India Cancels Cash," *Wall Street Journal,*
November 18, 2016.

1.7 In the late 1940s, the communists under Mao Zedong were defeating the government of China in a civil war. The paper currency issued by the Chinese government was losing much of its value, and most businesses refused to accept it. At the same time, there was a paper shortage in Japan. During those years, Japan was still under military occupation by the United States, following its defeat in World War II. Some of the U.S. troops in Japan realized that they could use dollars to buy up vast amounts of paper currency in China, ship it to Japan to be recycled into paper, and make a substantial profit. Under these circumstances, was the Chinese paper currency a commodity money or a fiat money? Briefly explain.

1.8 According to Peter Heather, a historian at King's College London, during the time of the Roman Empire, the German tribes east of the Rhine River (the area the Romans called Germania) produced no coins of their own but used Roman coins instead:

> Although no coinage was produced in Germania, Roman coins were in plentiful circulation and could easily have provided a medium of exchange (already in the first century, Tacitus tells us, Germani of the Rhine region were using good-quality Roman silver coins for this purpose).

    a. What is a medium of exchange?

b. What does the author mean when he writes that Roman coins "could easily have provided a medium of exchange" for the German tribes?

c. Why would any member of a German tribe have been willing to accept a Roman coin from another member of the tribe in exchange for goods or services when the tribes were not part of the Roman Empire and were not governed by Roman law?

Source: Peter Heather, *The Fall of the Roman Empire: A New History of Rome and the Barbarians*, New York: Oxford University Press, 2006, p. 89.

1.9 (Related to the Apply the Concept on page 483) Suppose that Congress passes a new law that requires all firms to accept paper currency in exchange for whatever they are selling. Briefly discuss who would gain and who would lose from this legislation.

1.10 (Related to the Apply the Concept on page 483) The source line for this *Apply the Concept* includes an article titled "Why Your Business Should Ditch Cash."

a. What does it mean for a business to "ditch cash"?

b. What technological changes have occurred that make it possible for businesses to ditch cash?

c. What are the pros and cons to a business of ditching cash?

Source: Christopher Mims, "Why Your Business Should Ditch Cash," *Wall Street Journal*, January 30, 2017.

14.2 How Is Money Measured in the United States Today? pages 484–488

LEARNING OBJECTIVE: Discuss the definitions of the money supply used in the United States today.

MyLab Economics   Visit **www.pearson.com/mylab/economics** to complete these exercises online and get instant feedback.

Summary

The narrowest definition of the money supply in the United States today is **M1**, which includes currency, checking account balances, and traveler's checks. A broader definition of the money supply is **M2**, which includes everything that is in M1, plus savings accounts, small-denomination time deposits (such as certificates of deposit [CDs]), money market deposit accounts in banks, and noninstitutional money market fund shares.

Review Questions

2.1 What is the main difference between the M1 and M2 definitions of the money supply? Why does the Federal Reserve use two definitions of the money supply rather than one?

2.2 Distinguish among money, income, and wealth. Which one of the three does the central bank of a country control?

Problems and Applications

2.3 Briefly explain whether each of the following is counted in M1.

    a. The coins in your pocket

    b. The funds in your checking account

    c. The funds in your savings account

    d. The traveler's checks that you have left over from a trip

    e. Your Citibank Platinum MasterCard

2.4 (Related to the Don't Let This Happen to You on page 486) Briefly explain whether you agree with the following statement: "I recently read that more than half of the money the government prints is actually held by people in foreign countries. If that's true, then the United States is less than half as wealthy as government statistics indicate."

2.5 (Related to the Don't Let This Happen to You on page 486) An article in the *New York Times* stated that "income is only one way of measuring wealth." Do you agree that income is a way of measuring wealth?

Source: Sam Roberts, "As the Data Show, There's a Reason the Wall Street Protesters Chose New York," *New York Times*, October 25, 2011.

2.6 (Related to Solved Problem 14.2 on page 486) Suppose you decide to withdraw $100 in currency from your checking account. What is the effect on M1? Ignore any actions the bank may take as a result of your having withdrawn the $100.

2.7 (Related to Solved Problem 14.2 on page 486) Suppose you withdraw $1,000 from a money market mutual fund and deposit the funds in your bank checking account. Briefly explain how this action will affect M1 and M2.

2.8 Based on a Survey of Consumer Payment Choice, researchers from the Federal Reserve Bank of Boston estimated that the average consumer, 18 years of age and older, held about $202 in currency. However, as noted in the chapter, there is actually about \$4,500 of currency in circulation for every person in the United States.

a. How can the amount of U.S. currency in circulation be so much higher than the amount held by the U.S. population?

b. What does the difference in part (a) imply about the measures of the money supply of the United States?

Source: Claire Greene, Scott Schuh, and Joanna Stavins, "The 2015 Survey of Consumer Payment Choice," Federal Reserve Bank of Boston Research Data Report No. 17-3, August 8, 2017.

2.9 (Related to the Apply the Concept on page 487) An article in the *Wall Street Journal* discussing the relatively slow adoption of bitcoins by individuals and businesses noted, "The vast majority of consumers, certainly in the developed world, simply don't care about the benefits of decentralization and anonymity."

a. Why would this observation help explain the slow adoption of bitcoins?

b. The article qualifies the observation as applying to the developed world. Why might using bitcoins be more attractive to individuals and firms in developing countries, such as Brazil or India, than to individuals and firms in the United States?

Source: Paul Vigna, "Bitcoin Still Not Ready for Prime Time, Citi Says," *Wall Street Journal*, June 30, 2016.

2.10 The U.S. penny is made primarily of zinc. Several times in recent years, zinc prices have been high, and it has cost the U.S. Treasury more than 1 cent to manufacture a penny. There are currently about 1.4 billion pennies in circulation. Economist François Velde of the Federal Reserve Bank of Chicago has proposed making the current penny worth 5 cents. If the U.S. Treasury adopted Velde's proposal, what would be the effect on the value of M1? Is this change likely to have much effect on the economy? (*Hint:* According to the information given in this chapter, what is the current value of M1?)

Source: Austan Goolsbee, "Now That a Penny Isn't Worth Much, It's Time to Make It Worth 5 Cents," *New York Times*, February 1, 2007.

14.3 How Do Banks Create Money? pages 488–497

LEARNING OBJECTIVE: Explain how banks create money.

MyLab Economics   Visit www.pearson.com/mylab/economics to complete these exercises online and get instant feedback.

Summary

On a bank's balance sheet, *reserves* and loans are assets, and deposits are liabilities. **Reserves** are deposits that the bank has retained rather than loaned out or invested. **Required reserves** are reserves that banks are legally required to hold. The fraction of deposits that banks are required to keep as reserves is called the **required reserve ratio**. Any reserves banks hold over the legal requirement are called **excess reserves**. When a bank accepts a deposit, it keeps only a fraction of the funds as reserves and loans out the remainder. In making a loan, a bank increases the checking account balance of the borrower. When the borrower uses a check to buy something with the funds the bank has loaned, the seller deposits the check in his or her bank. The seller's bank keeps part of the deposit as reserves and loans out the remainder. This process continues until no banks have excess reserves. In this way, the process of banks making new loans increases the volume of checking account balances and the money supply. This money creation process can be illustrated with T-accounts, which are stripped-down versions of balance sheets that show only how a transaction changes a bank's balance sheet. The **simple deposit multiplier** is the ratio of the change in deposits to the change in reserves. An expression for the simple deposit multiplier is $1/RR$.

Review Questions

3.1 What are the largest asset and the largest liability of a typical bank?

3.2 Suppose you decide to withdraw \$100 in cash from your checking account. Draw a T-account that shows the effect of this transaction on your bank's balance sheet.

3.3 What does it mean to say that banks "create money"?

3.4 Give the formula for the simple deposit multiplier. If the required reserve ratio is 20 percent, what is the maximum increase in checking account deposits that will result from an increase in bank reserves of \$20,000? Is this maximum increase likely to occur? Briefly explain.

Problems and Applications

3.5 Following the financial crisis of 2007–2009, Congress passed the Wall Street Reform and Consumer Protection Act, also known as the Dodd-Frank Act. The act increased regulation of the banking system, and from 2010 to 2016, regulators approved only five new banks, which was not enough to offset the closure of existing banks. According to the article, "Community bankers say the decline in the number of banks has led to fewer lending options for startups and small businesses." Why might startups and small businesses be more likely to rely on banks for funding than would large corporations?

Source: Rachel Witkowski, "Banks Are Finally Sprouting Anew in America," *Wall Street Journal*, February 8, 2017.

3.6 The following is from an article on community banks: "Their commercial-lending businesses, funded by their stable deposit bases, make them steady earners." What is commercial lending? In what sense are loans "funded" by deposits?

Source: Karen Richardson, "Clean Books Bolster Traditional Lenders," *Wall Street Journal*, April 30, 2007.

3.7 (Related to the Apply the Concept on page 489) In a newspaper column, author Delia Ephron described a conversation with a friend who had a large balance on her credit card with an interest rate of 18 percent per year. The friend was worried about paying off the debt. Ephron was earning only 0.4 percent interest on her bank certificate of deposit (CD). She considered withdrawing the money from her CD and loaning it to her friend so her friend could pay off her credit card balance: "So I was thinking that all of us earning 0.4 percent could instead loan money to our friends at 0.5 percent.... My friend would get out of debt [and] I would earn $5 a month instead of $4." Why don't more people use their savings to make loans rather than keep the funds in bank accounts that earn very low rates of interest?

Source: Delia Ephron, "Banks Taketh, but Don't Giveth," *New York Times*, January 27, 2012.

3.8 **(Related to the Apply the Concept on page 489)** An article in the *Wall Street Journal* noted that online peer-to-peer lenders "have automated the processes of checking borrowers' credit metrics and looking up their histories while in many cases avoiding more labor-intensive practices of collecting and reviewing pay stubs or tax returns." The article also noted, "Charge-off rates, which reflect loans on which a lender doesn't expect to collect, have risen."

   a. Why do banks require borrowers to submit pay stubs and tax returns when applying for a loan? Why would online lenders skip this step in the loan application process?

   b. If online lenders find that borrowers are defaulting on loans at higher-than-expected rates, can they offset the problem by charging higher interest rates on the loans? Briefly explain.

Source: Telis Demos and Peter Rudegeair, "LendingClub's Newest Problem: Its Borrowers," *Wall Street Journal*, July 12, 2016.

3.9 Suppose that Deja owns a McDonald's franchise. She decides to move her restaurant's checking account to Wells Fargo, which causes the changes shown on the following T-account. If the required reserve ratio is 0.10, or 10 percent, and Wells Fargo currently has no excess reserves, what is the maximum loan Wells Fargo can make as result of this transaction?

Wells Fargo

Assets		Liabilities	
Reserves	+$100,000	Deposits	+$100,000

3.10 Consider the following simplified balance sheet for a bank:

Assets		Liabilities	
Reserves	$10,000	Deposits	$70,000
Loans	$66,000	Stockholders' equity	$6,000

   a. If the required reserve ratio is 0.10, or 10 percent, how much in excess reserves does the bank hold?

   b. What is the maximum amount by which the bank can expand its loans?

   c. If the bank makes the loans in part (b), show the *immediate* effect on the bank's balance sheet.

3.11 **(Related to the Don't Let This Happen to You on page 493)** Briefly explain whether you agree with the following statement: "Assets are things of value that people own. Liabilities are debts. Therefore, a bank will always consider a checking account deposit to be an asset and a car loan to be a liability."

3.12 **(Related to Solved Problem 14.3 on page 494)** Suppose you deposit $2,000 in currency into your checking account at a branch of Bank of America, which we will assume has no excess reserves at the time you make your deposit. Also assume that the required reserve ratio is 0.20, or 20 percent.

   a. Use a T-account to show the initial effect of this transaction on Bank of America's balance sheet.

   b. Suppose that Bank of America makes the maximum loan it can from the funds you deposited. Using a T-account, show the initial effect of granting the loan on Bank of America's balance sheet. Also include on this T-account the transaction from part (a).

   c. Now suppose that whoever took out the loan in part (b) writes a check for this amount and that the person receiving the check deposits it in a branch of Citibank. Show the effect of these transactions on the balance sheets of Bank of America and Citibank after the check has been cleared. (On the T-account for Bank of America, include the transactions from parts (a) and (b).)

   d. What is the maximum increase in checking account deposits that can result from your $2,000 deposit? What is the maximum increase in the money supply? Briefly explain.

14.4 The Federal Reserve System, pages 497–503

LEARNING OBJECTIVE: Compare the three policy tools the Federal Reserve uses to manage the money supply.

MyLab Economics Visit **www.pearson.com/mylab/economics** to complete these exercises online and get instant feedback.

Summary

The United States has a **fractional reserve banking system** in which banks keep less than 100 percent of deposits as reserves. In a **bank run**, many depositors decide simultaneously to withdraw money from a bank. In a **bank panic**, many banks experience runs at the same time. The **Federal Reserve System** ("the Fed") was originally established in 1913 to stop bank panics. The recession of 2007–2009 put renewed emphasis on the Fed's goal of financial market stability. **Monetary policy** refers to the actions the Federal Reserve takes to manage the money supply and interest rates to pursue macroeconomic policy objectives. The Fed's three monetary policy tools are open market operations, discount policy, and reserve requirements. **Open market operations** are the buying and selling of Treasury securities by the Federal Reserve. The loans the Fed makes to banks are called **discount loans**, and the interest rate the Fed charges on discount loans is the **discount rate**. The **Federal Open Market Committee (FOMC)** meets in Washington, DC, eight times per year to discuss monetary policy. In the past

20 years, a *shadow banking system* has developed. During the financial crisis of 2007–2009, the existence of the shadow banking system complicated the Fed's policy response. A **security** is a financial asset—such as a stock or a bond—that can be bought and sold in a financial market. The process of **securitization** creates a secondary market in which loans that have been bundled together can be bought and sold in financial markets just as corporate or government bonds are.

Review Questions

4.1 Why did Congress decide to establish the Federal Reserve System in 1913?

4.2 What policy tools does the Fed use to control the money supply? Which tool is the most important?

4.3 Why does an open market purchase of Treasury securities by the Federal Reserve increase bank reserves? Why does an open market sale of Treasury securities by the Federal Reserve decrease bank reserves?

4.4 What is the "shadow banking system"? Why were the financial firms of the shadow banking system more vulnerable than commercial banks to bank runs?

Problems and Applications

4.5 In a column in the *Wall Street Journal*, Kevin Brady, a member of Congress from Texas, stated, "To get Congress to pass the Federal Reserve Act [in 1913, President Woodrow] Wilson had to retain the support of … northeastern lawmakers while convincing southern and western Democrats that legislation would not … create a [single] central bank. Wilson's ingenious solution was federalism." Explain what Congressman Brady meant when he stated that Woodrow Wilson used "federalism" to convince Congress to pass the Federal Reserve Act.

Source: Kevin Brady, "How the Fed's East Coast Tilt Warps Monetary Policy," *Wall Street Journal*, June 4, 2015.

4.6 Suppose that the Federal Reserve makes a $10 million discount loan to First National Bank (FNB) by increasing FNB's account at the Fed.

  a. Use a T-account to show the effect of this transaction on FNB's balance sheet. Remember that the funds a bank has on deposit at the Fed count as part of its reserves.

  b. Assume that before receiving the discount loan, FNB has no excess reserves. What is the maximum amount of this $10 million that FNB can lend out?

  c. What is the maximum total increase in the money supply that can result from the Fed's discount loan? Assume that the required reserve ratio is 10 percent.

4.7 A columnist in the *New York Times* noted, "Normally when we say that a central bank like the Federal Reserve or European Central Bank creates money from thin air, it does so by buying up bonds." How can a central bank "create money" by buying bonds? Doesn't the government create money by printing currency? Briefly explain.

Source: Neil Irwin, "Helicopter Money: Why Some Economists Are Talking about Dropping Money from the Sky," *New York Times*, July 28, 2016.

4.8 Suppose that the Federal Reserve engages in an open market sale of $25 million in U.S. Treasury bills to banks.

Fill in the missing information in the following T-accounts for the Fed and for the banking system.

Federal Reserve

Assets		Liabilities	
_____	−$25 million	Reserves	−$25 million

Banking System

Assets		Liabilities
Treasury bills	+$25 million	
_____	−$25 million	

4.9 In a speech delivered in June 2008, Timothy Geithner, then president of the Federal Reserve Bank of New York and later U.S. Treasury secretary, said:

> The structure of the financial system changed fundamentally during the boom. … [The] nonbank financial system grew to be very large. … [The] institutions in this parallel financial system [are] vulnerable to a classic type of run, but without the protections such as deposit insurance that the banking system has in place to reduce such risks.

  a. What did Geithner mean by the "nonbank financial system"?

  b. What is a "classic type of run," and why were institutions in the nonbank financial system vulnerable to such a run?

  c. Why would deposit insurance provide the banking system with protection against runs?

Source: Timothy F. Geithner, "Reducing Systemic Risk in a Dynamic Financial System," Remarks at the Economic Club of New York, June 9, 2008.

4.10 An article in the *Wall Street Journal* on the shadow banking system contained the following observation: "If investors rush to the exits en masse, acting as a herd, asset prices could plummet and markets could face funding problems." Why might people who have invested in a money market mutual fund, for example, be more likely to "rush to the exits" if they heard bad news about the fund's investments than would bank depositors if they received bad news about their bank's investments?

Source: Ian Talley, "IMF Warns (Again) of Growing Shadow-Banking Risks," *Wall Street Journal*, April 8, 2015.

4.11 An article in the *Wall Street Journal* in 2017 noted, "China now has one of the highest [required reserve] ratios in the world, economists say, even though many businesses are starved of credit."

  a. What does the article mean by Chinese businesses being "starved of credit"?

  b. Is there a connection between the Chinese central bank imposing a higher required reserve ratio on banks and Chinese businesses being starved of credit? Briefly explain.

Source: Lingling Wei, "China's Trillion-Dollar Yuan Defense Puts Growth at Risk," *Wall Street Journal*, April 13, 2017.

14.5 The Quantity Theory of Money, pages 503–507

LEARNING OBJECTIVE: Explain the quantity theory of money and use it to explain how high rates of inflation occur.

MyLab Economics   Visit **www.pearson.com/mylab/economics** to complete these exercises online and get instant feedback.

Summary

The quantity equation, which relates the money supply to the price level, is $M \times V = P \times Y$, where M is the money supply, V is the velocity of money, P is the price level, and Y is real output. The **velocity of money** is the average number of times each dollar in the money supply is spent during the year. Economist Irving Fisher developed the quantity theory of money, which assumes that the velocity of money is constant. If the **quantity theory of money** is correct, the inflation rate should equal the rate of growth of the money supply minus the rate of growth of real output. Although the quantity theory of money is not literally correct because the velocity of money is not constant, it is true that in the long run, inflation results from the money supply growing faster than real GDP. When governments attempt to raise revenue by selling large quantities of bonds to the central bank, the money supply will increase rapidly, resulting in high rates of inflation.

Review Questions

5.1 What is the quantity theory of money? What explanation does the quantity theory provide for inflation?

5.2 Is the quantity theory of money better able to explain the inflation rate in the long run or in the short run? Briefly explain.

5.3 What is hyperinflation? Why do governments sometimes allow it to occur?

Problems and Applications

5.4 If the money supply is growing at a rate of 6 percent per year, real GDP is growing at a rate of 3 percent per year, and velocity is constant, what will the inflation rate be? If velocity is increasing 1 percent per year instead of remaining constant, what will the inflation rate be?

5.5 If velocity does not change when the money supply of a country increases, will nominal GDP definitely increase? Will real GDP definitely increase? Briefly explain.

5.6 During the years from 2010 to 2016, the average annual growth rate of M1 was 10.3 percent, while the inflation rate as measured by the GDP deflator averaged 1.6 percent. Are these values consistent with the quantity equation? If you would need additional information to answer, state

what the information is. Are the values consistent with the quantity theory of money? Briefly explain.

Source: Data from the Federal Reserve Bank of St. Louis.

5.7 An article in the *American Free Press* quoted Professor Peter Spencer of York University in England as saying, "This printing of money 'will keep the [deflation] wolf from the door.'" The same article quoted Ambrose Evans-Pritchard, a writer for the London-based newspaper *The Telegraph*, as saying, "Deflation has … insidious traits. It causes shoppers to hold back. Once this psychology gains a grip, it can gradually set off a self-feeding spiral that is hard to stop."

a. What is price deflation?

b. What does Spencer mean by the statement "This printing of money 'will keep the [deflation] wolf from the door'"?

c. Why would deflation cause "shoppers to hold back," and what does Evans-Pritchard mean by saying "Once this psychology gains a grip, it can gradually set off a self-feeding spiral that is hard to stop"?

Source: Doug French, "We Should Celebrate Price Deflation," *American Free Press*, November 17, 2008.

5.8 During the Civil War, the Confederate States of America printed large amounts of its own currency—Confederate dollars—to fund the war. By the end of the war, the Confederate government had printed nearly 1.5 billion paper dollars. How would such a large quantity of Confederate dollars have affected the value of the Confederate currency? With the war drawing to an end, would southerners have been as willing to use and accept Confederate dollars? How else could they have bought and sold goods?

Source: Eric Nielsen, "Monetary Policy in the Confederacy," Federal Reserve Bank of Richmond *Region Focus*, Fall 2005, pp. 40–43.

5.9 An article in the *Wall Street Journal* in 2017 about Venezuela noted, "The economy has shrunk by an estimated 27% since 2013. The International Monetary Fund says inflation this year will hit 720%." Are these facts related? Briefly explain.

Source: Matt Wirz, Kejal Vyas, and Carolyn Cui, "Venezuela Tries to Resell $5 Billion Bond at Deep Discount," *Wall Street Journal*, June 5, 2017.

5.10 **(Related to the Apply the Concept on page 506)** During the German hyperinflation of the 1920s, many households and firms in Germany were hurt economically. Do you think any groups in Germany benefited from the hyperinflation? Briefly explain.

Real-Time Data Exercises

D14.1 (The components of M1) Go to the Web site of the Federal Reserve Bank of St. Louis (FRED) (fred.stlouisfed.org) and find the most recent values for the following four variables: (1) M1 money stock (M1), (2) the currency component of M1 (CURRENCY), (3) total checkable deposits (TCD), and (4) traveler's checks outstanding (WTCSL). Which of the components of M1 is the largest? Which is the smallest?

D14.2 (Calculating M1 from data on M2) Go to the Web site of the Federal Reserve Bank of St. Louis (FRED) (fred.stlouisfed.org) and find the most recent values for the following four variables: (1) M2 money stock (M2), (2) the total savings deposits at all depository institutions (SAVINGS), (3) retail money funds (WRMFSL), and (4) total small time deposits (WSMTIME).

   a. Using these data, calculate the value of M1.

   b. What are retail money funds? What percentage of M2 are they?

   c. If households were to shift funds from savings accounts to checking accounts, what would happen to the values of M1 and M2?

D14.3 (The relationship between M1 and M2) Go to the Web site of the Federal Reserve Bank of St. Louis (FRED) (fred.stlouisfed.org) and find the most recent monthly values and values from the same month 5 years and 10 years earlier for the M1 money stock (M1SL) and the M2 money stock (M2SL).

   a. Using these data, calculate M1 as a proportion of M2 for each of the years.

   b. Explain whether this proportion has increased, decreased, or remained the same over time. Can you think of an explanation for any changes you observe?

D14.4 (The quantity equation) Go to the Web site of the Federal Reserve Bank of St. Louis (FRED) (fred.stlouisfed.org) and find the most recent values and values for the same quarter in 1985 for the following three variables: (1) nominal gross domestic product (GDP), (2) the velocity of M1 money stock (M1V), and (3) the velocity of M2 money stock (M2V).

   a. Using these data, calculate M1 and M2 for both periods.

   b. Describe how M1 velocity and M2 velocity differ in the two quarters.

D14.5 (Applying the quantity equation) Go to the Web site of the Federal Reserve Bank of St. Louis (FRED) (fred.stlouisfed.org) and find the most recent values and values from the same quarter 10 years earlier for the following three variables: (1) real gross domestic product (GDPC1), (2) the GDP deflator (GDPDEF), and (3) the M2 money stock (M2SL). Modify the frequency of M2 to match the frequency of real GDP and the GDP price deflator.

   a. Using these data, calculate the average annual rate of change in both real GDP and M2 over this 10-year period.

   b. If we assume that velocity was constant during this period, what was the average annual inflation rate?

   c. Using the GDP deflator data, calculate the average annual inflation rate over this 10-year period.

   d. Use your answers to parts (b) and (c) to discuss what must have happened to velocity during this period.

D14.6 (Applying the quantity equation) Go to the Web site of the Federal Reserve Bank of St. Louis (FRED) (fred.stlouisfed.org) and find the most recent value for real gross domestic product (GDPC1) and the value from the same quarter eight years in the future for real potential gross domestic product (GDPPOT).

   a. Using these data, calculate the average annual rate of growth in real GDP over this eight-year period, assuming that real GDP equals potential GDP in the quarter that is eight years in the future.

   b. If the velocity of money is constant during this eight-year period, what will the growth rate of M1 have to be if the annual inflation rate averages 2 percent? Briefly explain.

   c. Suppose that M1 grows at this rate, but the actual inflation over this period averages more than 2 percent. What can you conclude about velocity during this period?

Critical Thinking Exercises

CT14.1 For this exercise, your instructor may assign you to a group. Each group member should first write down what he or she found surprising about both the definition of money and what the Federal Reserve includes in its measures of the money supply (You might need to look up the definitions of these terms in Section 14.2.) Be sure to mention how money compares to income and wealth. After working individually, the group should work together to write a one- or two-paragraph report on common misconceptions about what economists call money.

CT14.2 Watch the bank run scene in the classic film *It's a Wonderful Life*, at www.youtube.com/watch?v=OQEWVDZme4A. To provide some background, during the Great Depression, the main character, George Bailey, runs a "building and loan," a financial institution similar to a bank but that specializes in loans to people buying homes. As the scene starts, George and his new wife, Mary, are leaving town for their honeymoon. It turns out that she is carrying $2,000 in cash for their honeymoon. Write a summary of what is happening in this scene, being sure to use the concepts of bank balance sheets and bank reserves.

CT14.3 Read "The Panic of 1907," at www.federalreservehistory.org/essays/panic_of_1907, and write a one-page discussion of ways in which that financial panic is similar to and different from events during the Great Recession of 2007–2009.

15 Monetary Policy

Why Would a Bank Pay a Negative Interest Rate?

One basic fact about the financial system is *always* true: If you borrow money from a bank, you have to pay the bank interest on the loan. "Always," as it turns out, does not include 2017, at least not in Europe. Some banks there were in the surprising—and unwelcome to them—situation of making interest payments *to* borrowers rather than receiving interest payments *from* borrowers. One borrower in Spain boasted, "I'm going to frame my bank statement, which shows that Bankinter is paying me interest on my mortgage. That's financial history." Why would a bank pay someone to borrow money? The answer is that the interest rates on these loans were not fixed but were instead adjusted based on changes in short-term interest rates that depend on the actions of central banks in Europe. When some of these interest rates became negative, banks had to automatically make the interest rates on some of their mortgage loans negative as well. With a negative interest rate, the lender has to pay interest to the borrower.

Central banks, including the U.S. Federal Reserve, had driven interest rates to historically low levels as they tried to pull their economies out of the severe worldwide recession of 2007–2009. In conducting monetary policy, the Fed often concentrates on the federal funds rate, which is the interest rate that banks charge each other on short-term loans. In December 2008, the Fed reduced its target for the federal funds rate to almost zero, and it kept it there for nearly seven years.

But between December 2015 and mid-2017, the Fed raised its target for the federal funds rate four times. Businesspeople, policymakers, and economists were focused on predicting how many further rate increases Fed Chair Janet Yellen and her colleagues were planning. Does this focus indicate that the Fed chair is more important to the U.S. economy than the president of the United States? Most economists would answer "yes." The president can take actions that affect the economy but needs the approval of

Philippe Desmazes/AFP/Getty Images

Congress before enacting most polices. In contrast, the structure of the Fed gives the chair substantial control over monetary policy. As a result, the Fed chair can often have greater influence over the economy than the president.

European banks paying negative interest rates on loans is a striking example of how central bank policy can affect households. Changes in interest rates also affect homebuilders and manufacturers that sell durable goods because their customers frequently borrow money to buy these goods. Changes in interest rates indirectly affect other businesses because those changes in interest rates cause changes in aggregate demand. Not surprisingly, many businesses watch the Fed carefully for signs of whether interest rates are likely to rise or fall.

In this chapter, we will study the Federal Reserve and how monetary policy affects GDP, employment, and inflation.

Sources: Patricia Kowsmann and Jeannette Neumann, "A Battle Brews over Negative Rates on Mortgages," *Wall Street Journal*, May 15, 2016; David Harrison, "Fed's Effort to Guide Markets Falls Short," *Wall Street Journal*, June 11, 2017; and Patricia Kowsmann and Jeannette Neumann, "Tumbling Interest Rates in Europe Leave Some Banks Owing Money on Loans to Borrowers," *Wall Street Journal*, April 13, 2015.

Chapter Outline & Learning Objectives

Economics in Your Life & Career

Should You Buy a House during a Recession?

Think ahead a few years, to when you might be married and maybe even (gasp!) have children. You decide to leave behind years of renting apartments and buy a house, but then you read in a *Wall Street Journal* article that a majority of economists predict that a recession is likely to begin soon. What should you do? Would it be a good time or a bad time to buy a house? As you read this chapter, try to answer these questions. You can check your answers against those we provide on **page 550** at the end of this chapter.

I n Chapter 14, we saw that banks play an important role in providing credit to house-holds and firms and in creating money in the form of checking account deposits. We also saw that Congress established the Federal Reserve to stabilize the financial system and that the Fed is responsible for managing the money supply. In this chapter, we will discuss the Fed's main policy goals. We will also explore how the Federal Reserve decides which *monetary policy* actions to take to achieve its goals.

15.1 What Is Monetary Policy?

LEARNING OBJECTIVE: Define monetary policy and describe the Federal Reserve's monetary policy goals.

In 1913, Congress passed the Federal Reserve Act, creating the Federal Reserve System (the Fed). The main responsibility of the Fed was to make discount loans to banks to prevent the bank panics we discussed in Chapter 14, Section 14.4. In response to the Great Depression of the 1930s, Congress amended the Federal Reserve Act to give the Federal Reserve's Board of Governors broader responsibility to act "so as to pro-mote effectively the goals of maximum employment, stable prices, and moderate long-term interest rates."

Since World War II, the Federal Reserve has carried out an active *monetary policy*. **Monetary policy** refers to the actions the Fed takes to manage the money supply and interest rates to achieve its macroeconomic policy goals.

Monetary policy The actions the Federal Reserve takes to manage the money supply and interest rates to achieve macroeconomic policy goals.

The Goals of Monetary Policy

The Fed has four main *monetary policy goals* that are intended to promote a well-functioning economy:

1. Price stability
2. High employment
3. Stability of financial markets and institutions
4. Economic growth

We briefly consider each of these goals.

Price Stability Rising prices reduce the usefulness of money as a medium of exchange and a store of value. Especially after inflation rose dramatically and unex-pectedly during the 1970s, policymakers in most industrial countries have had price stability as a key policy goal. Figure 15.1 shows that from the early 1950s until 1968, the inflation rate in the United States remained below 4 percent per year. Inflation rose above 10 percent for several years in the late 1970s and early 1980s. Since 1992, the inflation rate has usually been below 4 percent. The 2007–2009 recession caused several months of deflation—a falling price level—during early 2009, and the slow pace of the recovery from the recession resulted in another three months of deflation during early 2015.

The inflation rates during the years 1979–1981 were the highest the United States has ever experienced during peacetime. When Paul Volcker became chairman of the Federal Reserve's Board of Governors in August 1979, he emphasized fighting inflation. Later Fed chairs continued to focus on inflation, arguing that if inflation is low over the long run, the price system will do a better job of efficiently allocating resources, and the Fed will have the flexibility it needs to increase aggregate demand to fight recessions. Although the severity of the 2007–2009 recession led the Fed to adopt extraordinary policy measures that we will discuss later in this chapter, price stability remains a key policy goal of the Fed.

High Employment In addition to price stability, high employment (or a low rate of unemployment) is an important monetary policy goal. Unemployed workers and under-used factories and office buildings reduce GDP below its potential level. Unemployment can cause workers who lack jobs to suffer financial distress and lower self-esteem.

MyLab Economics Real-time data

Figure 15.1

The Inflation Rate, January 1952–May 2017

For most of the 1950s and 1960s, the inflation rate in the United States was 4 percent or less. During the 1970s, the inflation rate increased, peaking during 1979–1981, when it averaged more than 10 percent. After 1992, the inflation rate was usually less than 4 percent. The effects of the recession caused several months of deflation—a falling price level—during early 2009, and the slow pace of the recovery caused another three months of deflation in early 2015.

Note: The inflation rate is measured as the percentage change in the consumer price index from the same month in the previous year.

Source: Federal Reserve Bank of St. Louis.

The goal of high employment extends beyond the Fed to other branches of the federal government. At the end of World War II, Congress passed the Employment Act of 1946, which stated that it was the "responsibility of the Federal Government … to foster and promote … conditions under which there will be afforded useful employment, for those able, willing, and seeking to work, and to promote maximum employment, production, and purchasing power." Because price stability and high employment are explicitly mentioned in the Employment Act, it is sometimes said that the Fed has a *dual mandate* to attain these two goals.

Stability of Financial Markets and Institutions Firms often need to borrow funds as they design, develop, produce, and market their products. Savers look to financial investments to increase the value of their savings as they prepare to buy homes, pay for the educations of their children, and provide for their retirement. The Fed promotes the stability of financial markets and institutions so that an efficient flow of funds from savers to borrowers will occur. As we saw in Chapter 14, Section 14.4, the financial crisis of 2007–2009 brought the issue of stability in financial markets to the forefront.

The financial crisis was similar to the banking crises that led Congress to create the Federal Reserve System in 1913. A key difference is that while earlier banking crises affected commercial banks, the events of 2007–2009 also affected investment banks and other financial firms in the *shadow banking system*. Investment banks, money market mutual funds, and other financial firms can be subject to *liquidity problems* because they often borrow short term—sometimes as short as overnight—and invest the funds in long-term securities. Just as commercial banks can experience a crisis if depositors begin to withdraw funds, investment banks and other financial firms can experience a crisis if investors stop providing them with short-term loans. In 2008, the Fed took several steps to ease the liquidity problems of these financial firms because the Fed believed these problems were increasing the severity of the recession. In Section 15.6, we will discuss in more detail the new policies the Fed enacted to help deal with the financial crisis.

Economic Growth In Chapters 10 and 11, we discussed the importance of economic growth to raising living standards. Policymakers aim to encourage *stable* economic growth, which allows households and firms to plan accurately and encourages firms to engage in the investment that is needed to sustain growth. Policy can spur economic growth by providing incentives for saving to ensure a large pool of investment funds, as well as by providing direct incentives for business investment. Congress and the president, however, may be better able to increase saving and investment than is the Fed. For example, Congress and the president can change the tax laws to increase the return to saving and investing. In fact, some economists question whether the Fed can play a role in promoting economic growth beyond attempting to meet its goals of price stability, high employment, and financial stability.

In the next section, we will look at how the Fed attempts to achieve its monetary policy goals. Although the Fed has multiple monetary policy goals, during most periods, its most important goals have been price stability and high employment. The turmoil in financial markets that began in 2007 led the Fed to put new emphasis on the goal of financial market stability.

MyLab Economics Study Plan

MyLab Economics Concept Check

15.2 The Money Market and the Fed's Choice of Monetary Policy Targets

LEARNING OBJECTIVE: Describe the Federal Reserve's monetary policy targets and explain how expansionary and contractionary monetary policies affect the interest rate.

The Fed uses its policy tools to achieve its monetary policy goals. Recall that the Fed's policy tools are open market operations, discount policy—making discount loans to banks and changing the discount rate it charges on those loans—and changes in reserve requirements. At times, the Fed encounters conflicts among its policy goals. For example, as we will discuss later in this chapter, the Fed can raise interest rates to reduce the inflation rate. But higher interest rates typically reduce household and firm spending, which may result in slower growth and higher unemployment. So, a policy that is intended to achieve one monetary policy goal, such as reducing inflation, may make it more difficult to achieve another policy goal, such as high employment.

Monetary Policy Targets

The Fed tries to keep both the unemployment and inflation rates low, but it can't affect either of these economic variables directly. The Fed cannot tell firms how many people to employ or what prices to charge for their products. Instead, the Fed uses variables, called *monetary policy targets*, that it can affect directly and that, in turn, affect variables, such as real GDP, employment, and the price level, that are closely related to the Fed's policy goals. The two main monetary policy targets are the money supply and the interest rate. As we will see, the Fed typically uses the interest rate as its policy target.

Although the Fed has typically used the money supply and the interest rate as its targets, these targets were not central to the Fed's policy decisions during the recession of 2007–2009. As we will discuss in Section 15.6, because U.S. financial markets suffered a degree of disruption not seen since the Great Depression of the 1930s, the Fed was forced to develop new policy tools.

MyLab Economics Concept Check

The Demand for Money

The Fed's two monetary policy targets are related. To understand this relationship, we first need to examine the *money market*, which brings together the demand and supply for money. Figure 15.2 shows the demand curve for money. The interest rate is on the vertical axis, and the quantity of money is on the horizontal axis. Here we are using the M1 definition of money, which equals currency plus checking account deposits. Notice that the demand curve for money is downward sloping.

To understand why the demand curve for money is downward sloping, consider that households and firms have a choice between holding money and holding other financial assets, such as U.S. Treasury bills. In making the choice, households and firms take into account that:

- Money has one particularly desirable characteristic: You can use it to buy goods, services, or financial assets.
- Money also has one undesirable characteristic: It earns either a zero interest rate or a very low interest rate.

The currency in your wallet earns no interest, and the money in your checking account earns either no interest or very little interest. Alternatives to money, such as

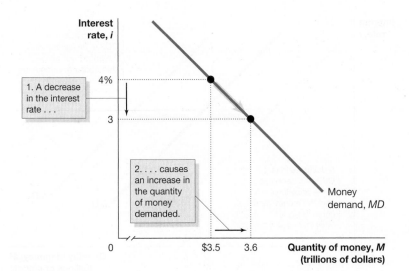

MyLab Economics Animation

Figure 15.2

The Demand for Money

The money demand curve slopes downward because a lower interest rate causes households and firms to switch from financial assets such as U.S. Treasury bills to money. All other things being equal, a fall in the interest rate from 4 percent to 3 percent will increase the quantity of money demanded from $3.5 trillion to $3.6 trillion. An increase in the interest rate will decrease the quantity of money demanded.

U.S. Treasury bills, pay interest but have to be sold if you want to use the funds to buy something. When interest rates rise on financial assets such as U.S. Treasury bills, the amount of interest that households and firms lose by holding money increases. When interest rates fall, the amount of interest households and firms lose by holding money decreases. Remember that *opportunity cost* is what you have to forgo to engage in an activity. The interest rate is the opportunity cost of holding money.

We now have an explanation for why the demand curve for money slopes downward: When interest rates on Treasury bills and other financial assets are low, the opportunity cost of holding money is low, so the quantity of money demanded by households and firms will be high; when interest rates are high, the opportunity cost of holding money will be high, so the quantity of money demanded will be low. In Figure 15.2, a decrease in the interest rate from 4 percent to 3 percent causes the quantity of money demanded by households and firms to rise from $3.5 trillion to $3.6 trillion.   **MyLab Economics** Concept Check

Shifts in the Money Demand Curve

We saw in Chapter 3 that the demand curve for a good is drawn holding constant all variables, other than the price, that affect the willingness of consumers to buy the good. Changes in variables other than the price cause the demand curve to shift. Similarly, the demand curve for money is drawn holding constant all variables, other than the interest rate, that affect the willingness of households and firms to hold money. Changes in variables other than the interest rate cause the demand curve to shift. The three most important variables that cause the money demand curve to shift are changes in real GDP, the price level, and technology.

Figure 15.3 illustrates shifts in the money demand curve. An increase in real GDP means that the amount of buying and selling of goods and services will increase. This additional buying and selling increases the demand for money as a medium of exchange, so the quantity of money households and firms want to hold increases at each interest rate, shifting the money demand curve to the right. A decrease in real GDP decreases the quantity of money demanded at each interest rate, shifting the money demand curve to the left. A higher price level increases the quantity of money required for a given amount of buying and selling. Eighty years ago, for example, when the price level was much lower and someone could purchase a new car for $500 and a salary of $30 per week was typical for someone in the middle class, the quantity of money demanded by households and firms was much lower than today, even adjusting for the effect of the lower real GDP and smaller population of those years. An increase in the price level increases the quantity of money demanded at each interest rate, shifting the money demand curve to the right. A decrease in the price level decreases the quantity of money demanded at each interest rate, shifting the money demand curve to

Figure 15.3

Shifts in the Money Demand Curve

Changes in real GDP, the price level, or technology cause the money demand curve to shift. An increase in real GDP or an increase in the price level will cause the money demand curve to shift to the right, from MD_1 to MD_2. A decrease in real GDP, a decrease in the price level, or more widespread use of technology like mobile wallets will cause the money demand curve to shift to the left, from MD_1 to MD_3.

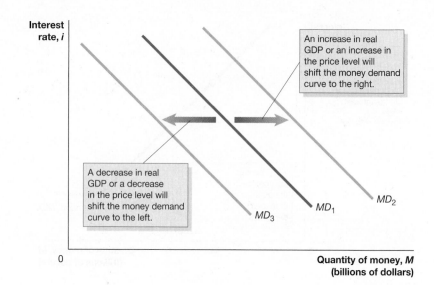

the left. We saw in Chapter 14, Section 14.1, that countries including India, Sweden, and the United States have moved closer to being cashless economies. Rather than use currency or checks, people are using apps like Apple Pay, Android Pay, and Venmo on their smartphones to purchase goods and services or to send funds to family and friends. This technological change has decreased the demand for money at each interest rate, shifting the money demand curve to the left.   **MyLab Economics** Concept Check

How the Fed Manages the Money Supply: A Quick Review

Having discussed money demand, we now turn to money supply. In Chapter 14, Section 14.4, we saw how the Federal Reserve manages the money supply. Eight times per year, the Federal Open Market Committee (FOMC) meets in Washington, DC. If the FOMC decides to increase the money supply, it orders the trading desk at the Federal Reserve Bank of New York to purchase U.S. Treasury securities. The sellers of these Treasury securities deposit the funds they receive from the Fed in banks, which increases bank reserves. Typically, banks loan out most of these reserves, which creates new checking account deposits and expands the money supply. If the FOMC decides to decrease the money supply, it orders the trading desk to sell Treasury securities, which decreases bank reserves and contracts the money supply.   **MyLab Economics** Concept Check

Equilibrium in the Money Market

In Figure 15.4, we include both the money demand and money supply curves. We can use this figure to see how the Fed affects the money supply and the interest rate. For simplicity, we assume that the Federal Reserve is able to completely control the money supply. With this assumption, the money supply curve is a vertical line, and changes in the interest rate have no effect on the quantity of money supplied. Just as with other markets, equilibrium in the *money market* occurs where the money demand curve crosses the money supply curve. If the Fed increases the money supply, the money supply curve will shift to the right, and the equilibrium interest rate will fall. In Figure 15.4, when the Fed increases the money supply from $3.5 trillion to $3.6 trillion, the money supply curve shifts to the right, from MS_1 to MS_2, and the equilibrium interest rate falls from 4 percent to 3 percent.

In the money market, the adjustment from one equilibrium to another equilibrium is different from the adjustment in the market for a good. In Figure 15.4, the money market is initially in equilibrium, with an interest rate of 4 percent and a money supply of $3.5 trillion. When the Fed increases the money supply by $100 billion, households and firms have more money than they want to hold at an interest rate of 4 percent. What do households and firms do with the extra $100 billion? They are most likely to use the money to buy short-term financial assets, such as Treasury bills, or to deposit the money in interest-paying bank

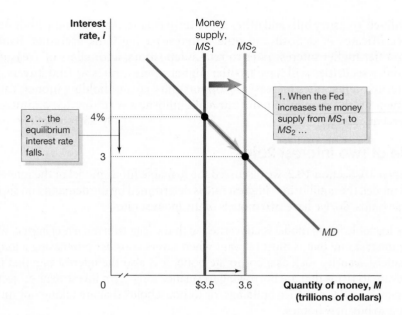

MyLab Economics Animation

Figure 15.4

The Effect on the Interest Rate When the Fed Increases the Money Supply

When the Fed increases the money supply, households and firms will initially hold more money than they want, relative to other financial assets. Households and firms use the money they don't want to hold to buy Treasury bills and make deposits in interest-paying bank accounts. These actions allow banks and sellers of Treasury bills and similar securities to offer lower interest rates. Eventually, interest rates will fall enough that households and firms will be willing to hold the additional money the Fed has created. In the figure, an increase in the money supply from \$3.5 trillion to \$3.6 trillion causes the money supply curve to shift to the right, from MS_1 to MS_2, and causes the equilibrium interest rate to fall from 4 percent to 3 percent.

accounts, such as certificates of deposit. This increase in demand for interest-paying bank accounts and short-term financial assets allows banks to offer lower interest rates on certificates of deposit, and it allows sellers of Treasury bills and similar assets to also offer lower interest rates. As the interest rates on certificates of deposit, Treasury bills, and other short-term assets fall, the opportunity cost of holding money falls. The result is a movement down the money demand curve. Eventually the interest rate falls enough that households and firms are willing to hold the additional \$100 billion worth of money the Fed has created, and the money market will be back in equilibrium. To summarize: *When the Fed increases the money supply, the short-term interest rate must fall until it reaches a level at which households and firms are willing to hold the additional money.*

Figure 15.5 shows what happens when the Fed decreases the money supply. The money market is initially in equilibrium, at an interest rate of 4 percent and a money supply of \$3.5 trillion. If the Fed decreases the money supply to \$3.4 trillion, households and firms will be holding less money than they would like, relative to other financial assets, at an interest rate of 4 percent. To increase their money holdings,

MyLab Economics Animation

Figure 15.5

The Effect on the Interest Rate When the Fed Decreases the Money Supply

When the Fed decreases the money supply, households and firms will initially hold less money than they want, relative to other financial assets. Households and firms will sell Treasury bills and other financial assets and withdraw money from interest-paying bank accounts. These actions will increase interest rates. Interest rates will rise to the point at which households and firms will be willing to hold the smaller amount of money that results from the Fed's actions. In the figure, a reduction in the money supply from \$3.5 trillion to \$3.4 trillion causes the money supply curve to shift to the left, from MS_1 to MS_2, and causes the equilibrium interest rate to rise from 4 percent to 5 percent.

they will sell Treasury bills and other short-term financial assets and withdraw funds from certificates of deposit and other interest-paying bank accounts. Banks will have to offer higher interest rates to retain depositors, and sellers of Treasury bills and similar securities will have to offer higher interest rates to find buyers. Rising short-term interest rates increase the opportunity cost of holding money, causing a movement up the money demand curve. Equilibrium is restored at an interest rate of 5 percent. **MyLab Economics** Concept Check

A Tale of Two Interest Rates

In Chapter 10, Section 10.2, we discussed the loanable funds model of the interest rate. In that model, the equilibrium interest rate is determined by the demand and supply for loanable funds. So, we have two models of the interest rate:

1. The loanable funds model is concerned with the *long-term real rate of interest*, which is the interest rate that is most relevant when savers consider purchasing a long-term financial security such as a corporate bond. It is also the interest rate that is most relevant to firms that are borrowing to finance long-term investment projects such as new factories or office buildings, or to households that are taking out mortgage loans to buy new homes.
2. The money market model is concerned with the *short-term nominal rate of interest*. When analyzing monetary policy, economists focus on the short-term nominal interest rate because it is the interest rate most affected by Federal Reserve policy.

Often—but not always—there is a close connection between movements in the short-term nominal interest rate and movements in the long-term real interest rate. So, when the Fed takes actions to increase the short-term nominal interest rate, usually the long-term real interest rate also increases. In other words, as we will discuss in the next section, when the interest rate on Treasury bills rises, the real interest rate on mortgage loans usually also rises, although sometimes only after a delay. **MyLab Economics** Concept Check

Choosing a Monetary Policy Target

As we have seen, the Fed uses monetary policy targets to affect economic variables, such as real GDP or the price level, that are closely related to the Fed's policy goals. The Fed can use either the money supply or the interest rate as its monetary policy target. As Figure 15.5 shows, the Fed is capable of affecting both. The Fed has generally focused on the interest rate rather than on the money supply. In 1980, Congress began allowing banks to pay interest on checking accounts. At the same time, money market mutual funds were becoming more popular with small savers as a way to earn higher interest rates than banks offered. As a result of these developments, some economists argued that the Fed should focus less on M1 than on M2. They argued that the relationship between M2 and inflation and changes in GDP was more stable than the relationship between M1 and these variables. But even the relationship between M2 and other key economic variables broke down in the early 1990s. In July 1993, then Fed Chairman Alan Greenspan informed the U.S. Congress that the Fed would cease using M1 or M2 targets to guide the conduct of monetary policy. The Fed has correspondingly increased its reliance on interest rate targets.

There are many different interest rates in the economy. For purposes of monetary policy, the Fed has targeted the interest rate known as the *federal funds rate*. In the next section, we will discuss the federal funds rate before examining how targeting the interest rate can help the Fed achieve its monetary policy goals. **MyLab Economics** Concept Check

The Importance of the Federal Funds Rate

Recall that every bank must keep 10 percent of its checking account deposits above a certain threshold amount as reserves, either as currency held in the bank or as deposits with the Fed (see Chapter 14, Section 14.3). The Fed pays banks a low interest rate on their reserve deposits, so banks normally have an incentive to invest reserves above the 10 percent minimum rather than leave those funds with the Fed. During the financial crisis of 2007–2009, bank reserves soared as banks attempted to meet an increase in

MyLab Economics Real-time data

Figure 15.6

The Federal Funds Rate Targeting, July 1954–August 2017

The Fed does not set the federal funds rate. However, the Fed's ability to increase or decrease bank reserves quickly through open market operations keeps the federal funds rate close to the Fed's target rate. The Fed has pushed the federal funds rate up and down as it has attempted to achieve its policy goals of price stability and high employment. The shaded areas represent periods of recession.

Source: Board of Governors of the Federal Reserve System.

deposit withdrawals and as they became reluctant to lend to any borrowers except those with flawless credit histories. Banks continued to hold large reserve deposits for several years following the end of the financial crisis. These conditions were very unusual, however. In normal times, banks keep few excess reserves, and when they need additional reserves, they borrow in the *federal funds market* from banks that have reserves available. The **federal funds rate** is the interest rate banks charge each other on loans in the federal funds market. The loans are usually very short term, often just overnight.

Despite the name, the Fed does not actually set the federal funds rate. Instead, the rate is determined by the demand for and supply of reserves. Because the Fed can increase and decrease the supply of bank reserves through open market operations, it can set a *target* for the federal funds rate and can usually come very close to hitting it. The FOMC announces a target for the federal funds rate after each meeting. Figure 15.6 shows how over the years the Fed has pushed the federal funds rate up and down as it tries to achieve its policy goals. The Fed responded to the start of the financial crisis by rapidly cutting its target for the federal funds rate beginning in September 2007. In December 2008, the Fed announced a range of 0 to 0.25 percent as its target, which it gradually increased to 1.00 to 1.25 percent in mid-2017. These very low federal funds rates reflect the severity of the financial crisis and the slow recovery of the economy in the following years.

Because only banks can borrow or lend in the federal funds market, the federal funds rate is not directly relevant for households and firms. However, changes in the federal funds rate usually result in changes in interest rates on both short-term financial assets, such as Treasury bills, and long-term financial assets, such as corporate bonds and mortgages. A change in the federal funds rate has a greater effect on short-term interest rates than on long-term interest rates, and its effect on long-term interest rates may occur only after a lag in time. Although a majority of economists support the Fed's choice of the interest rate as its monetary policy target, some economists believe the Fed should concentrate on the money supply instead. We will discuss these views in Section 15.5.   **MyLab Economics** Concept Check

Federal funds rate The interest rate banks charge each other for overnight loans.

The Fed's New Policy Tools

Prior to the financial crisis of 2007–2009, the Fed increased the federal funds rate by selling Treasury securities to reduce bank reserves, thereby forcing up interest rates. Bank reserves prior to the crisis had only been about $6 billion. During and after the crisis, bank reserves soared, reaching a high of $2.8 *trillion* and were still well above $2 trillion in late 2017. Because banks were swimming in excess reserves, the Fed's draining some of them through open market sales of Treasury securities would have had no effect on interest rates.

Instead, the Fed was forced to rely on a more complicated mechanism. Beginning in 2008, the Fed began paying banks interest on their reserve holdings. The interest rate that the Fed pays on reserves sets a floor for the federal funds rate. To see why, suppose that the Fed is paying banks 1.00% on their reserve balances, but the federal funds rate is only 0.50%. Banks could borrow funds in the federal funds market at 0.50%, deposit the money in their reserve balances at the Fed, and earn a risk-free 0.50%. Competition among banks to obtain the funds to carry out this risk-free profit would force up the federal funds rate to 1.00%, which is the rate at which banks could no longer earn a profit from this strategy.

When the Fed engages in open market operations, it buys and sells Treasury securities electronically with *primary dealers*, which are commercial banks, investment banks, and securities dealers. Rather than buy or sell securities outright, sometimes the Fed engages in temporary transactions called *repurchase agreements*. With a repurchase agreement, the Fed buys a security from a financial firm, which promises to buy it back from the Fed the next day. With a *reverse repurchase agreement*, the Fed does the opposite: It sells a security to a financial firm, while at the same time promising to buy it back from the firm the next day. In effect, the Fed is borrowing funds overnight from the firm that purchases the security. By raising the interest rate it is willing to pay on these loans, the Fed reduces the willingness of the financial firms it deals with in these transactions to lend at a lower rate. Note that because the primary dealers are not eligible to receive interest on deposits at the Fed, the Fed needs to use changes in the interest rate it pays on reverse repurchase agreements as an additional tool in controlling short-term interest rates.

In June 2017, Fed Chair Janet Yellen and the other members of the Federal Open Market Committee decided to raise the target for the federal funds rate to a range of 1.00 to 1.25 percent By raising the interest rate it pays on bank reserves to 1.25 percent, the Fed could be confident that banks would be unlikely to lend below that rate. By raising the interest rate it pays on reverse repurchase agreements to 1.00 percent, the Fed could be confident that financial firms such as investment banks would be unlikely to lend elsewhere at a lower rate. Raising these two interest rates enabled the Fed to keep the federal funds rate in a target range of 1.00 percent to 1.25 percent. Although this procedure is more complex than the Fed's traditional means of raising the target for the federal funds rate, it is an effective way for the Fed to achieve that target at a time when banks are holding very high levels of excess reserves.

MyLab Economics Study Plan   **MyLab Economics** Concept Check

15.3 Monetary Policy and Economic Activity

LEARNING OBJECTIVE: Use aggregate demand and aggregate supply graphs to show the effects of monetary policy on real GDP and the price level.

The Fed uses the federal funds rate as a monetary policy target because it controls this interest rate and because it believes that changes in the federal funds rate will ultimately affect economic variables that are related to its monetary policy goals. It is important to consider again the distinction between the nominal interest rate and the real interest rate. Recall that we calculate the real interest rate by subtracting the inflation rate from the nominal interest rate. Ultimately, the ability of the Fed to use monetary policy to affect economic variables such as real GDP depends on its ability to affect long-term real interest rates, such as the real interest rates on mortgages and corporate bonds. Because the federal funds rate is a short-term nominal interest rate, the Fed sometimes has difficulty affecting long-term real interest rates. Nevertheless, for purposes of the following discussion, we will assume that the Fed is able to use changes in the federal funds rate to affect long-term real interest rates.

How Interest Rates Affect Aggregate Demand

Changes in interest rates affect *aggregate demand*, which is the total level of spending in the economy. Recall that aggregate demand has four components: consumption, investment, government purchases, and net exports. Changes in interest rates will not affect government purchases, but they will affect the other three components of aggregate demand in the following ways:

- **Consumption.** Many households finance purchases of consumer durables, such as automobiles and furniture, by borrowing. Lower interest payments on loans increase household spending on consumer durables. Higher interest rates reduce household spending on consumer durables. Lower interest rates also reduce the return to saving, leading households to save less and spend more. Higher interest rates increase the return to saving, leading households to save more and spend less.

- **Investment.** Firms finance most of their spending on machinery, equipment, and factories out of their profits or by borrowing. Firms borrow either in financial markets by issuing corporate bonds or by obtaining loans from banks. Higher interest rates on corporate bonds or on bank loans make it more expensive for firms to borrow, so they will undertake fewer investment projects. Lower interest rates make it less expensive for firms to borrow, so they will undertake more investment projects. Lower interest rates can also have an effect on stock prices, which can increase firms' investment spending. As interest rates decline, stocks become a more attractive investment relative to bonds. The increase in demand for stocks raises their prices. By issuing additional shares of stock, firms can acquire the funds they need to buy new factories and equipment, so investment increases.

  Spending by households on new homes is also part of investment. When interest rates on mortgage loans rise, the cost of buying new homes rises, and fewer new homes will be purchased. When interest rates on mortgage loans fall, more new homes will be purchased.

- **Net exports.** Recall that net exports is equal to spending by foreign households and firms on goods and services produced in the United States minus spending by U.S. households and firms on goods and services produced in other countries. The value of net exports depends partly on the exchange rate between the U.S. dollar and foreign currencies. When the value of the dollar rises, households and firms in other countries will pay more for goods and services produced in the United States, but U.S. households and firms will pay less for goods and services produced in other countries. As a result, the United States will export less and import more, so net exports will fall. When the value of the dollar falls, net exports will rise. If interest rates in the United States rise relative to interest rates in other countries, investing in U.S. financial assets will become more desirable, causing foreign investors to increase their demand for dollars, which will increase the value of the dollar. As the value of the dollar increases, net exports will fall. If interest rates in the United States decline relative to interest rates in other countries, the value of the dollar will fall, and net exports will rise.   **MyLab Economics** Concept Check

The Effects of Monetary Policy on Real GDP and the Price Level

In Chapter 13, we developed the *aggregate demand and aggregate supply model* to explain fluctuations in real GDP and the price level. In the basic version of the model, we assume that there is no economic growth, so the long-run aggregate supply curve does not shift. In panel (a) of Figure 15.7, short-run equilibrium is at point *A*, where the aggregate demand (AD_1) curve intersects the short-run aggregate supply (*SRAS*) curve. Real GDP is below potential GDP, as shown by the *LRAS* curve, so the economy is in a recession, with some firms operating below normal capacity and some workers having been laid off. To reach its goal of high employment, the Fed carries out an **expansionary monetary policy** by increasing the money supply and decreasing interest rates. Lower interest rates cause an increase in consumption, investment, and net exports, which shifts the aggregate demand curve to the right, from AD_1 to AD_2. Real GDP increases from $16.8 trillion to potential GDP of $17.0 trillion, and the price level rises from 108 to 110 (point *B*). The policy successfully returns real GDP to its potential level. Rising production leads to increasing employment, allowing the Fed to achieve its goal of high employment.

In panel (b) of Figure 15.7, short-run equilibrium is at point *A*, with real GDP of $17.2 trillion, which is above potential GDP of $17.0 trillion. With some firms producing beyond their normal capacity and the unemployment rate being very low, wages and prices are increasing. To reach its goal of price stability, the Fed needs to carry out a **contractionary monetary policy** by decreasing the money supply and increasing interest rates. Higher interest rates cause a decrease in consumption, investment, and

Expansionary monetary policy
The Federal Reserve's policy of decreasing interest rates to increase real GDP.

Contractionary monetary policy
The Federal Reserve's policy of increasing interest rates to reduce inflation.

MyLab Economics Animation

Figure 15.7 **Monetary Policy**

In panel (a), short-run equilibrium is at point A, with real GDP of $16.8 trillion and a price level of 108. An expansionary monetary policy causes aggregate demand to shift to the right, from AD_1 to AD_2, increasing real GDP from $16.8 trillion to $17.0 trillion and the price level from 108 to 110 (point B). With real GDP back at its potential level, the Fed can meet its goal of high employment. In panel (b), short-run equilibrium is at point A, with real GDP at $17.2 trillion and the price level at 112. Because real GDP is greater than potential GDP, the economy experiences rising wages and prices. A contractionary monetary policy causes aggregate demand to shift to the left, from AD_1 to AD_2, causing real GDP to decrease from $17.2 trillion to $17.0 trillion and the price level to decrease from 112 to 110 (point B). With real GDP back at its potential level, the Fed can meet its goal of price stability.

net exports, which shifts the aggregate demand curve from AD_1 to AD_2. Real GDP decreases from $17.2 trillion to $17.0 trillion, and the price level falls from 112 to 110 (point B). Why would the Fed want to intentionally cause real GDP to decline? Because in the long run, real GDP cannot continue to remain above potential GDP. Attempting to keep real GDP above potential GDP would result in rising inflation. As aggregate demand declines and real GDP returns to its potential level, upward pressure on wages and prices will be reduced, allowing the Fed to achieve its goal of price stability.

We can conclude that the Fed can use monetary policy to affect the price level and, in the short run, the level of real GDP, allowing it to attain its policy goals of high employment and price stability.　　　　　　　　　　　　MyLab Economics Concept Check

Apply the Concept
MyLab Economics Video

Too Low for Zero: Central Banks, Quantitative Easing, and Negative Interest Rates

The Fed and other central banks around the world responded to the 2007–2009 recession by pushing overnight lending rates—such as the federal funds rate in the United States—to nearly zero. But these very low interest rates failed to result in rapid economic recovery. To lower the federal funds rate, the Fed buys Treasury bills through open market purchases, which increases bank reserves. Banks then lend out these reserves to households and firms. As the following graph shows, however, in late 2008, many banks began piling up excess reserves rather than lending out the funds. Total bank reserves had been less than $50 billion in August 2008, but as the financial crisis became more severe, total reserves soared to more than $900 billion by May 2009.

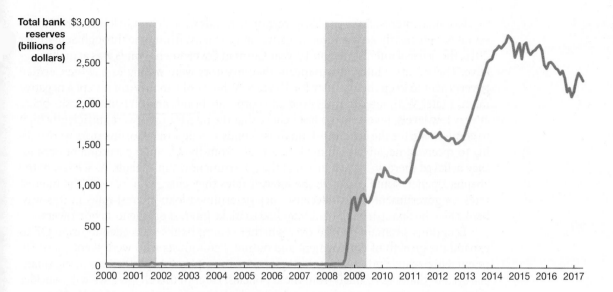

The increase was partly due to the Fed's starting in October 2008 to pay an interest rate of 0.25 percent on bank reserves held as deposits at the Fed. Primarily, though, the increase occurred because banks were reluctant to make loans at low interest rates to households and firms whose financial positions had been damaged by the recession. Some economists argued that the Fed was facing a situation known as a *liquidity trap*, in which short-term interest rates are pushed to zero, leaving the central bank unable to lower them further. Liquidity traps may also have occurred in the United States during the 1930s and in Japan during the 1990s.

To spur economic recovery, the Fed, the European Central Bank, the Bank of Japan, and other central banks turned to a policy of *quantitative easing* (QE), which involves buying securities beyond the short-term government securities that are usually involved in open market operations. The Fed began purchasing 10-year U.S. Treasury notes to push their interest rates lower. Interest rates on home mortgage loans typically move closely with interest rates on 10-year Treasury notes. The Fed also purchased certain *mortgage-backed securities*. The Fed's objective was to keep interest rates on mortgages low and to keep funds flowing into the mortgage market to help stimulate demand for housing.

The Fed's first round of QE began in November 2008. Because the U.S. economy recovered more slowly than expected, the Fed engaged in two additional rounds of QE before ending the program in October 2014. The use of QE by the Fed and other central banks, combined with very low inflation rates and the slow recovery from the 2007–2009 recession, led to historically low interest rates in most countries. The graph below shows interest rates on 10-year U.S. Treasury notes and on the corresponding German government bonds.

Nominal interest rates on U.S. government bonds were driven so low that real interest rates were nearly zero or even negative. In Germany, from June through September 2016, the *nominal* interest rate on 10-year German government bonds was actually negative. This negative interest rate meant that investors were willing to pay the German government to keep their money for 10 years. Why would an investor accept a negative interest rate? With interest rates on many corporate bonds and on bank deposits being at very low levels, investors did not believe that the interest rates were sufficiently high to compensate for the default risk on those bonds and deposits. So, investors were willing to receive a negative nominal interest rate from the German government because they believed there was no chance that the government would default. As we saw in the chapter opener, some banks tie the interest rates they charge on loans to the interest rates on government bonds. Because they determined loan interest rates in this way, banks like the Spanish bank Bankinter had to make interest payments *to* borrowers.

Economists remain divided over whether central banks succeeded in using QE to expand the growth of employment and output. Economists who were skeptical of QE pointed to negative nominal interest rates as an example of the distortions in the financial system that had resulted from these policies. Later in this chapter, we will consider other new programs the Fed put in place to deal with the recession of 2007–2009 and the slow recovery that followed, as its traditional focus on lowering the federal funds rate to stimulate the economy proved ineffective.

Sources: Jon Sindreu, "Which Country's Bonds Most Likely to Join Germany in Negative-Yield Club?" *Wall Street Journal*, June 14, 2016; and data from the Federal Reserve Bank of St. Louis and the Organization for Economic Co-operation and Development.

MyLab Economics Study Plan | **Your Turn:** Test your understanding by doing related problems 3.9 and 3.10 on page 554 at the end of this chapter.

Can the Fed Eliminate Recessions?

Panel (a) of Figure 15.7 on page 528 shows a completely successful expansionary monetary policy that shifts the *AD* curve to bring real GDP back to potential GDP. In practice, this ideal is very difficult for the Fed to achieve, as the length and severity of the 2007–2009 recession illustrates. The best the Fed can realistically do is keep recessions shorter and milder than they would otherwise be.

If the Fed is to succeed in offsetting the effects of the business cycle, it needs to quickly recognize the need for a change in monetary policy. If the Fed is late in recognizing that a recession has begun or that the inflation rate is increasing, it may not be able to implement a new policy quickly enough to do much good. There is typically a *lag*, or delay, between a policy change and its effect on real GDP, employment, inflation, and other economic variables. Nobel Laureate Milton Friedman famously described the lags for monetary policy as "long and variable," which means that it can take months or years for changes in monetary policy to affect real GDP and inflation and that the lags vary based on economic circumstances. Once the Fed reduces the target federal funds rate, it takes time for the interest rates that affect firm and household behavior to also decline. Then it takes time for firms to identify newly profitable investment projects, obtain loans from banks or arrange to sell bonds, and start spending the borrowed funds. Similarly, it takes time for families to respond to lower mortgage interest rates by buying houses and for homebuilders to begin building the houses. As a result, the full effect of a change in monetary policy is typically spread out over several years.

Implementing a policy too late may actually destabilize the economy. To see why, consider Figure 15.8. The straight line represents the long-run growth trend in real GDP in the United States. Historically real GDP has grown about 3 percent per year, although in recent years annual growth in real GDP has been closer to 2 percent. The actual path of real GDP differs from the underlying trend because of the business cycle, which is shown by the red curved line. As we saw in Chapter 10, Section 10.3, the actual business cycle is more irregular than the stylized cycle shown here.

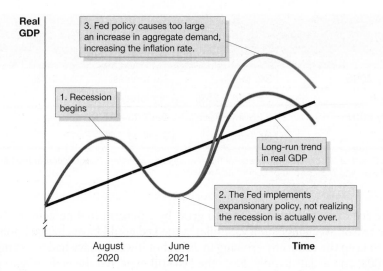

MyLab Economics Animation

Figure 15.8

The Effect of a Poorly Timed Monetary Policy on the Economy

The upward-sloping straight line represents the long-run growth trend in real GDP. The curved red line represents the path real GDP takes because of the business cycle. If the Fed is too late in implementing a change in monetary policy, real GDP will follow the curved blue line. The Fed's expansionary monetary policy results in too great an increase in aggregate demand during the next expansion, which causes an increase in the inflation rate.

Suppose that a recession begins in August 2020. Because it takes months for economic statistics to be gathered by the Commerce Department, the Census Bureau, the Bureau of Labor Statistics, and the Fed itself, there is a lag before the Fed recognizes that a recession has begun. Finally, in June 2021, the FOMC concludes that the economy is in recession and begins an expansionary monetary policy. As it turns out, June 2021 is actually the trough of the recession, meaning that the recession has already ended, and an expansion has begun. In these circumstances, the Fed's expansionary policy is not needed to end the recession. The increase in aggregate demand caused by the Fed's lowering interest rates is likely to push the economy beyond potential GDP and cause a significant acceleration in inflation. Real GDP ends up following the path indicated by the blue curved line. The Fed has inadvertently engaged in a *procyclical policy*, which increases the severity of the business cycle, as opposed to a *countercyclical policy*, which is meant to reduce the severity of the business cycle and which is what the Fed intends to use. As we saw in Chapter 10, Section 10.3, the typical recession since 1950 has lasted less than one year, which increases the likelihood that the Fed may accidentally engage in a procyclical policy. Making this mistake is, of course, less likely in a long and severe recession such as the recession of 2007–2009.   **MyLab Economics** Concept Check

Fed Forecasts

Because it can take a long time for a change in monetary policy to affect real GDP, the Fed tries to set policy according to what it forecasts the state of the economy will be in the future, when the policy change actually affects the economy. For example, when the Fed raised its target for the federal funds rate several times beginning in December 2015, the lag associated with monetary policy meant that the full effect of the rate increases on the economy would be spread out over several years. In making these increases, the Fed was thinking about the economy's future performance.

To reduce the severity of business cycles, the Fed must often act before a recession or an acceleration of inflation shows up in the economic data. So, good policy requires good economic forecasts based on models that describe accurately how the economy functions. Unfortunately, economic forecasts and models can be unreliable because changes in aggregate demand and short-run aggregate supply can be unpredictable. For example, the forecasts of most economists at the end of 2006 and the beginning of 2007 did not anticipate the severity of the recession that began in December 2007. Only after financial market conditions began to deteriorate rapidly did economists significantly reduce their forecasts of GDP growth in 2008 and 2009.

Table 15.1 summarizes the Fed's estimates for the growth rate of real GDP for 2007 and 2008 given in its *Monetary Policy Report to Congress*. To keep a recession from starting in 2007, the Fed would have had to change policy before 2007. However, in February

MyLab Economics Animation

Table 15.1

Fed Forecasts of Real GDP
Growth during 2007 and 2008

Date Forecast Was Made	Forecast Growth Rate		Actual Growth Rate	
	For 2007	For 2008	2007	2008
February 2006	3% to 4%	No forecast	1.8%	−0.3%
May 2006	2.5% to 3.25%	No forecast		
February 2007	2.25% to 3.25%	2.5% to 3.25%		
July 2007	No forecast	2.5% to 3.0%		

Sources: Board of Governors of the Federal Reserve System, *Monetary Policy Report to the Congress*, various dates; and U.S. Bureau of Economic Analysis.

2006, the Fed expected the economy to grow by 3 percent to 4 percent in 2007, so it had little reason to change policy. Similarly, the Fed could have changed policy in an attempt to keep the economy growing in 2008, but it would have had to change policy before 2008, and as late as July 2007, the Fed still expected the economy to grow by 2.5 percent to 3.0 percent in 2008. In fact, real GDP increased by only 1.8 percent in 2007, and it declined by 0.3 percent in 2008. We can conclude that the Fed could have taken actions that would have at least reduced the severity of the 2007–2009 recession if it had seen the recession coming. **MyLab Economics** Concept Check

Apply the Concept

MyLab Economics Video

Trying to Hit a Moving Target: Making Policy with "Real-Time Data"

The Fed relies on macroeconomic data to formulate monetary policy. One key piece of economic data is GDP, which is calculated quarterly by the Bureau of Economic Analysis (BEA). Unfortunately for Fed policymakers, the GDP data the BEA provides are frequently revised, and the revisions can be large enough that the actual state of the economy can be different from what it at first appeared to be.

The BEA's *advance estimate* of a quarter's GDP is not released until about a month after the quarter has ended. This delay can be a problem for policymakers because it means that they will not receive an estimate of GDP for the period from January through March, for instance, until the end of April. Presenting even more difficulty is the fact that the advance estimate will be subject to a number of revisions. The second estimate of a quarter's GDP is released about two months after the end of the quarter. The third estimate is released about three months after the end of the quarter. Although the BEA used to refer to the third estimate as the "final estimate," in fact, it continues to revise its estimates through the years. The BEA releases its first annual, second annual, and third annual estimates one, two, and three years after the third estimate. And that is not the end: Benchmark revisions occur in later years.

Why are there so many estimates? Because GDP is such a comprehensive measure of output in the economy, collecting the necessary data is very time-consuming. To provide the advance estimate, the BEA relies on surveys conducted by the Commerce Department of retail sales and manufacturing shipments, as well as data from trade organizations, estimates of government spending, and so on. As time passes, these organizations gather additional data, and the BEA is able to refine its estimates.

Do these revisions to the GDP estimates matter? Sometimes they do, as the following example indicates. At the beginning of 2008, some economists believed that the U.S. economy might be in a recession. The effects of the continuing decline in housing prices were being felt in the financial system, and the unemployment rate was increasing. Members of the Fed's Open Market Committee remained cautiously optimistic, however, forecasting that real GDP would increase about 1.7 percent during the year. The BEA's advance estimate of the first quarter's GDP seemed to confirm that this forecast of slow growth might be accurate by showing an increase in real GDP of 0.6 percent at an annual rate. As the following graph shows, though, that estimate of real GDP growth was revised a number of times over the years, mostly downward.

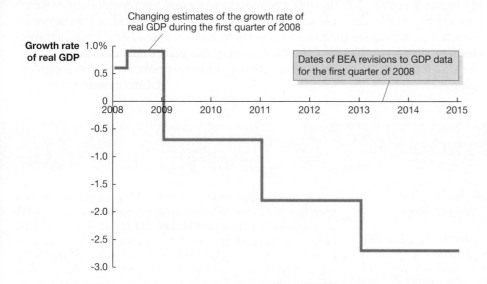

Currently, BEA data indicate that real GDP actually declined by 2.7 percent at an annual rate during the first quarter of 2008. This swing of more than 3 percentage points is a large difference, which changes the picture of what happened during the first quarter of 2008 from one of an economy experiencing slow growth to one of an economy suffering a sharp downturn as it fell into the worst recession since the Great Depression of the 1930s. The National Bureau of Economic Research has since determined that December 2007 was the beginning of the recession of 2007–2009.

This example shows that in addition to the other problems the Federal Reserve encounters in successfully conducting monetary policy, it must make decisions using data that may be subject to substantial revisions.

Sources: Federal Reserve Bank of Philadelphia, "Historical Data Files for the Real-Time Data Set," August 7, 2015; Board of Governors of the Federal Reserve System, "Minutes of the Federal Open Market Committee January 29–30, 2008," February 20, 2008; and Bruce T. Grimm and Teresa Weadock, "Gross Domestic Product: Revisions and Source Data," *Survey of Current Business*, Vol. 86, No. 2, February 2006, pp. 11–15.

Your Turn: Test your understanding by doing related problems 3.11 and 3.12 on page 554 at the end of this chapter.

MyLab Economics Study Plan

A Summary of How Monetary Policy Works

Table 15.2 compares the steps involved in expansionary and contractionary monetary policies. We need to note an important qualification to this summary. At every point, we should add the phrase "relative to what would have happened without the policy."

Table 15.2   Expansionary and Contractionary Monetary Policies

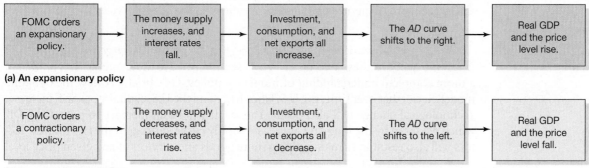

The table isolates the effect of monetary policy, *holding constant all other factors affecting the variables involved.* In other words, we are invoking the *ceteris paribus* condition, discussed in Chapter 3, Section 3.1. This point is important because a contractionary monetary policy, for example, does not cause the price level to fall; instead, a contractionary monetary policy causes the price level *to rise by less than it would have without the policy.* One final note on terminology: An expansionary monetary policy is sometimes called a *loose* policy, or an *easy* policy. A contractionary monetary policy is sometimes called a *tight* policy.

MyLab Economics Study Plan   MyLab Economics Concept Check

Don't Let This Happen to You

Remember That with Monetary Policy, It's the Interest Rates—Not the Money—That Counts

It is tempting to think of monetary policy as working like this: If the Fed wants more spending in the economy, it increases the money supply, and people spend more because they now have more money. If the Fed wants less spending in the economy, it decreases the money supply, and people spend less because they now have less money. In fact, that is *not* how monetary policy works. Remember the important difference between money and income: The Fed increases the money supply by buying Treasury bills. The sellers of the Treasury bills have just exchanged one asset—Treasury bills—for another asset—a check from the Fed; the sellers have *not* increased their income. Even though the money supply is now larger, no one's income has increased, so no one's spending should be affected.

It is only when monetary policy lowers interest rates that spending is affected. When interest rates are lower, households are more likely to buy new homes and automobiles, and businesses are more likely to buy new factories and warehouses. Lower interest rates also lead to a lower value of the dollar, which lowers the prices of exports and raises the prices of imports, thereby increasing net exports. It isn't the increase in the money supply that has brought about this additional spending, *it's the lower interest rates.* To understand how monetary policy works, and to interpret news reports about the Fed's actions, remember that it is the change in interest rates, not the change in the money supply, that is most important.

MyLab Economics Study Plan

Your Turn: Test your understanding by doing related problem 3.13 on page 554 at the end of this chapter.

 15.4 ## Monetary Policy in the Dynamic Aggregate Demand and Aggregate Supply Model*

LEARNING OBJECTIVE: Use the dynamic aggregate demand and aggregate supply model to analyze monetary policy.

The overview of monetary policy we just finished contains a key idea: The Fed can use monetary policy to affect aggregate demand, thereby changing the price level and the level of real GDP. The discussion of monetary policy illustrated by Figure 15.7 on page 528 is simplified, however, because it ignores two important facts about the economy:

1. The economy experiences continuing inflation, with the price level rising every year.
2. The economy experiences long-run growth, with the *LRAS* curve shifting to the right every year.

In Chapter 13, we developed a *dynamic aggregate demand and aggregate supply model* that takes into account these two facts. In this section, we use the dynamic model to gain a more complete understanding of monetary policy. Let's briefly review the dynamic model. Recall that over time, the U.S. labor force and the U.S. capital stock will increase. Technological change will also occur. The result will be an increase in potential GDP, which we show by the long-run aggregate supply curve shifting to the right. These factors will also result in firms supplying more goods and services at any given price level

*This section may be omitted without loss of continuity.

in the short run, which we show by the short-run aggregate supply curve shifting to the right. During most years, the aggregate demand curve will also shift to the right, indicating that aggregate expenditure will be higher at every price level. Aggregate expenditure usually increases for three key reasons:

1. As population grows and incomes rise, consumption will increase over time.
2. As the economy grows, firms expand capacity, and new firms are established, increasing investment spending.
3. An expanding population and an expanding economy require increased government services, such as more police officers and teachers, so government purchases will expand.

The Effects of Monetary Policy on Real GDP and the Price Level: A More Complete Account

During certain periods, *AD* does not increase enough during the year to keep real GDP at potential GDP. This slow growth in aggregate demand may be due to households and firms becoming pessimistic about the future state of the economy, leading them to cut back their spending on consumer durables, houses, and factories. As we have seen, the collapse of the housing bubble and the resulting financial crisis had a negative effect on aggregate demand during the 2007–2009 recession. There are other reasons aggregate demand might grow slowly: The federal government could decide to balance the budget by cutting back its purchases and raising taxes, or recessions in other countries might cause a decline in U.S. exports. In the hypothetical situation shown in Figure 15.9, in the first year, equilibrium is at point *A*, with potential GDP of $17.0 trillion and a price level of 110. In the second year, *LRAS* increases to $17.4 trillion, but *AD* increases only to $AD_{2(\text{without policy})}$, which is not enough to keep real GDP at potential GDP. If the Fed does not intervene, the new short-run equilibrium will occur at $17.3 trillion (point *B*). The $100 billion gap between this level of real GDP and potential GDP at $LRAS_2$ means that some firms are operating at less than their normal capacity. Incomes and profits will fall, firms will begin to lay off workers, and the unemployment rate will rise.

Economists at the Federal Reserve closely monitor the economy and continually update forecasts of future levels of real GDP and prices. When these economists anticipate that aggregate demand is not growing fast enough to allow the economy to

MyLab Economics Animation

Figure 15.9

An Expansionary Monetary Policy

Initially, equilibrium is at point *A*, with real GDP of $17.0 trillion and a price level of 110. Without monetary policy, aggregate demand will shift from AD_1 to $AD_{2(\text{without policy})}$, which is not enough to keep the economy at full employment because long-run aggregate supply has shifted from $LRAS_1$ to $LRAS_2$. Short-run equilibrium is at point *B*, with real GDP of $17.3 trillion and a price level of 112. By lowering interest rates, the Fed increases investment, consumption, and net exports sufficiently to shift aggregate demand to $AD_{2(\text{with policy})}$. Equilibrium will be at point *C*, with real GDP of $17.4 trillion, which is its full employment level, and a price level of 113. The price level is higher than it would have been if the Fed had not acted to increase spending in the economy.

remain at full employment, they present their findings to the FOMC, which decides whether circumstances require a change in monetary policy. For example, suppose that the FOMC meets and considers a forecast from the staff indicating that during the following year, a gap of $100 billion will open between equilibrium real GDP and potential GDP. In other words, the macroeconomic equilibrium illustrated by point *B* in Figure 15.9 will occur. The FOMC may then decide to carry out an expansionary monetary policy to lower interest rates to stimulate aggregate demand. The figure shows the results of a successful attempt to do this: *AD* has shifted to the right, and equilibrium occurs at potential GDP (point *C*). The Fed will have successfully headed off the falling incomes and rising unemployment that otherwise would have occurred. Bear in mind that we are illustrating a perfectly executed monetary policy that keeps the economy at potential GDP, which is difficult to achieve in practice for reasons discussed in the previous section.

Notice in Figure 15.9 that the expansionary monetary policy caused the inflation rate to be higher than it would have been. Without the expansionary policy, the price level would have risen from 110 to 112, so the inflation rate for the year would have been 1.8 percent. By shifting the aggregate demand curve, the expansionary policy caused the price level to increase from 112 to 113, raising the inflation rate from 1.8 percent to 2.7 percent. **MyLab Economics** Concept Check

Using Monetary Policy to Fight Inflation

In addition to using an expansionary monetary policy to reduce the severity of recessions, the Fed can use a contractionary monetary policy to keep aggregate demand from expanding so rapidly that the inflation rate begins to increase. Figure 15.10 shows the situation during 2005 and 2006, when the Fed faced this possibility. During 2005, real GDP was equal to potential GDP, but Fed Chair Alan Greenspan and other members of the FOMC were concerned that the continuing boom in the housing market might lead aggregate demand to increase so rapidly that the inflation rate would begin to accelerate. The Fed had been gradually increasing the target for the federal funds rate since mid-2004.

Figure 15.10

A Contractionary Monetary Policy in 2006

In 2005, equilibrium is at point *A*, with real GDP equal to potential GDP of $14.2 trillion and a price level of 92.0. From 2005 to 2006, potential GDP increased from $14.2 trillion to $14.6 trillion, as long-run aggregate supply increased from $LRAS_{2005}$ to $LRAS_{2006}$. The Fed raised interest rates because it believed the housing boom was causing aggregate demand to increase too rapidly. Without the increase in interest rates, aggregate demand would have shifted from AD_{2005} to $AD_{2006(without\ policy)}$, and the new short-run equilibrium would have occurred at point *B*. Real GDP would have been $14.8 trillion—$200 billion greater than potential GDP—and the price level would have been 96.1. The increase in interest rates resulted in aggregate demand increasing only to $AD_{2006(with\ policy)}$. Equilibrium occurred at point *C*, with real GDP of $14.6 trillion, which was equal to potential GDP, and the price level rose only to 94.8.

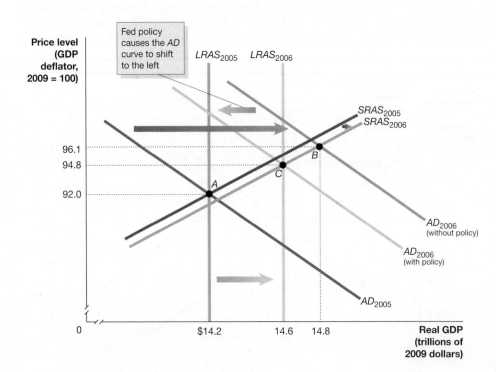

When Ben Bernanke was appointed Fed chair in early 2006, he advocated continued increases in the target for the federal funds rate to slow the growth in aggregate demand. By June 2006, the target for the federal funds rate had been raised to 5.25 percent, from the low target rate of 1 percent that had prevailed from June 2003 to May 2004. The FOMC issues a statement after each meeting that summarizes the committee's views on the current state of the economy and gives some indication of how monetary policy might change in the near future. After its meeting on June 29, 2006, the FOMC included the following remarks in its statement:

> The Federal Open Market Committee decided today to raise its target for the federal funds rate ... to 5-1/4 percent. Recent indicators suggest that economic growth is moderating from its quite strong pace earlier this year, partly reflecting a gradual cooling of the housing market and the lagged effects of increases in ... interest rates. ... Although the moderation in the growth of aggregate demand should help to limit inflation pressures over time, the Committee judges that some inflation risks remain.

The committee kept the target for the federal funds rate constant at 5.25 percent until September 2007, when concern about problems in financial markets led it to cut the target to 4.75 percent. Although it is impossible to know exactly what would have happened during 2006 without the Fed's policy change, Figure 15.10 presents a plausible scenario. The figure shows that without the Fed's actions to increase interest rates, aggregate demand would have shifted farther to the right, and equilibrium would have occurred at a level of real GDP that was beyond the potential level. The price level would have risen from 92.0 in 2005 to 96.1 in 2006, meaning that the inflation rate would have been 4.5 percent. Because the Fed kept aggregate demand from increasing as much as it otherwise would have, short-run equilibrium occurred at potential GDP, and the price level in 2006 rose to only 94.8, keeping the inflation rate at 3.0 percent.   **MyLab Economics** Concept Check   **MyLab Economics** Study Plan

Solved Problem 15.4

MyLab Economics Interactive Animation

The Effects of Monetary Policy

The hypothetical information in the following table shows what the values for real GDP and the price level will be in 2021 if the Fed does *not* use monetary policy:

Year	Potential GDP	Real GDP	Price Level
2020	$18.0 trillion	$18.0 trillion	120
2021	18.4 trillion	18.3 trillion	123

a. If the Fed wants to keep real GDP at its potential level in 2021, should it use an expansionary policy or a contractionary policy? Should the trading desk buy Treasury bills or sell them?

b. Suppose the Fed's policy is successful in keeping real GDP at its potential level in 2021. State whether each of the following will be higher or lower than if the Fed had taken no action.

   i. Real GDP

   ii. Potential GDP

   iii. The inflation rate

   iv. The unemployment rate

c. Draw an aggregate demand and aggregate supply graph to illustrate your answer. Be sure that your graph contains *LRAS* curves for 2020 and 2021; *SRAS* curves for 2020 and 2021; *AD* curves for 2020 and for 2021, with and without monetary policy action; and equilibrium real GDP and the price level in 2021, with and without policy.

Solving the Problem

Step 1: **Review the chapter material.** This problem is about the effects of monetary policy on real GDP and the price level, so you may want to review the section "The Effects of Monetary Policy on Real GDP and the Price Level: A More Complete Account," which begins on page 535.

Step 2: **Answer the questions in part (a) by explaining how the Fed can keep real GDP at its potential level.** The information in the table tells us that without monetary policy, the economy will be below potential GDP in 2021. To keep real GDP at its potential level, the Fed must undertake an expansionary policy. To carry out an expansionary policy, the trading desk needs to buy Treasury bills. Buying Treasury bills will increase reserves in the banking system. Banks will increase their loans, which will increase the money supply and lower the interest rate. (Note that as we saw in Section 15.2, in recent years the Fed has used a more complex way of managing the federal funds rate. Whether the Fed will eventually return to relying on open market operations is not yet clear.)

Step 3: **Answer part (b) by explaining the effect of the Fed's policy.** If the Fed's policy is successful, real GDP in 2021 will increase from $18.3 trillion, as given in the table, to its potential level of $18.4 trillion. Potential GDP is not affected by monetary policy, so its value will not change. Because the level of real GDP will be higher, the unemployment rate will be lower than it would have been without policy. The expansionary monetary policy shifts the AD curve to the right, so short-run equilibrium will move up the short-run aggregate supply ($SRAS$) curve, and the price level will be higher.

Step 4: **Answer part (c) by drawing the graph.** Your graph should look similar to Figure 15.9.

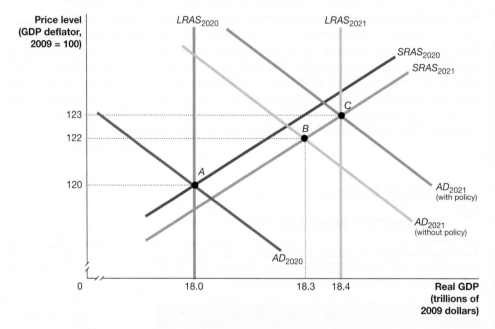

Equilibrium in 2020 is at point A, with the AD and $SRAS$ curves intersecting along the $LRAS$ curve. Real GDP is at its potential level of $18.0 trillion, and the price level is 120. Without monetary policy, the AD curve shifts to $AD_{2021\text{(without policy)}}$, and short-run equilibrium is at point B. Because potential GDP has increased from $18.0 trillion to $18.4 trillion, real GDP of $18.3 trillion is below the potential level. The price level has increased from 120 to 122. With policy, the AD curve shifts to $AD_{2021\text{(with policy)}}$, and equilibrium is at point C. Real GDP is at its potential level of $18.4 trillion. We don't have enough information to be sure of the new equilibrium price level. We do know that it will be higher than 122. The graph shows the price level rising to 123. Therefore, without the Fed's expansionary policy, the inflation rate in 2021 would have been about 1.7 percent. With policy, it will be 2.5 percent.

Extra Credit: Bear in mind that, in reality, the Fed is typically unable to use monetary policy to keep real GDP exactly at its potential level, as this problem suggests it can.

MyLab Economics Study Plan **Your Turn:** For more practice, do related problems 4.4 and 4.5 on pages 555–556 at the end of this chapter.

A Closer Look at the Fed's Setting of Monetary Policy Targets

LEARNING OBJECTIVE: Describe the Fed's setting of monetary policy targets.

We have seen that in carrying out monetary policy, the Fed changes its target for the federal funds rate depending on the state of the economy. Is the Fed's approach correct? During times when the economy is not experiencing a financial crisis, is using the federal funds rate as a target the best way to conduct monetary policy? If the Fed targets the federal funds rate, how should it decide what the target level should be? In this section, we consider these important issues concerning the Fed's targeting policy.

Should the Fed Target the Money Supply?

Some economists have argued that rather than use an interest rate as its monetary policy target, the Fed should use the money supply. Many of the economists who make this argument belong to a school of thought known as *monetarism*. The leader of the monetarist school was Milton Friedman, who was skeptical that the Fed would be able to correctly time changes in monetary policy.

Friedman and his followers favored replacing *monetary policy* with a *monetary growth rule*. Ordinarily, we expect monetary policy to respond to changing economic conditions: When the economy is in recession, the Fed reduces interest rates, and when inflation is increasing, the Fed raises interest rates. A monetary growth rule, in contrast, is a plan for increasing the money supply at a constant rate that does not change in response to economic conditions. Friedman and his followers proposed a monetary growth rule of increasing the money supply every year at a rate equal to the long-run annual growth rate of real GDP, which has been about 3 percent since 1950 (although in recent years it has grown at the slower rate of about 2 percent per year). If the Fed adopted this monetary growth rule, it would stick to it through changing economic conditions.

But what happens under a monetary growth rule if the economy moves into recession? Shouldn't the Fed abandon the rule to drive down interest rates? Friedman argued that the Fed should stick to the rule even during recessions because he believed that active monetary policy destabilizes the economy by increasing the number of recessions and their severity. By keeping the money supply growing at a constant rate, Friedman argued, the Fed would greatly increase economic stability.

During the 1970s, some economists and politicians urged the Federal Reserve to adopt a monetary growth rule. But the fairly close relationship between movements in the money supply and movements in real GDP and the price level that existed before 1980 has become much weaker. Since 1980, the growth rate of M1 has been unstable. In some years, M1 has grown more than 10 percent, while in other years, it has actually fallen. Yet despite these wide fluctuations in the growth of M1, growth in real GDP has been fairly stable, and inflation has remained low during most years. Consequently, support inside and outside the Fed for following a monetary growth rule has declined.   **MyLab Economics** Concept Check

Why Doesn't the Fed Target Both the Money Supply and the Interest Rate?

Most economists believe that the interest rate is the best monetary policy target. But as we have just seen, other economists believe the Fed should target the money supply. Why doesn't the Fed satisfy both groups by targeting both the money supply and the interest rate? The simple answer is that the Fed can't target both at the same time. To see why, look at Figure 15.11, which shows the money market.

Remember that the Fed controls the money supply, but it does not control money demand. Money demand is determined by decisions of households and firms as they weigh the trade-off between the convenience of money and its low interest rate compared with other financial assets. Suppose the Fed is targeting the interest rate and decides, given conditions in the economy, that the interest rate should be 5 percent. Or, suppose the Fed is targeting the money supply and decides that the money supply

MyLab Economics Animation

Figure 15.11

The Fed Can't Target Both the Money Supply and the Interest Rate

The Fed is forced to choose between using either the interest rate or the money supply as its monetary policy target. In this figure, the Fed can set a target of $3.5 trillion for the money supply or a target of 5 percent for the interest rate, but the Fed can't hit both targets because it can achieve only combinations of the interest rate and the money supply that represent equilibrium in the money market.

Source: Federal Reserve Bank of St. Louis.

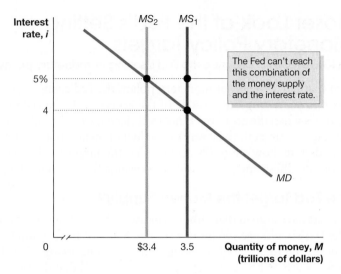

Taylor rule A rule developed by John Taylor that links the Fed's target for the federal funds rate to economic variables.

should be $3.5 trillion. Figure 15.11 shows that the Fed can bring about an interest rate of 5 percent or a money supply of $3.5 trillion, but it can't bring about both. The point representing an interest rate of 5 percent and a money supply of $3.5 trillion is not on the money demand curve, so it can't represent an equilibrium in the money market. The Fed can only attain combinations of the interest rate and the money supply that represent equilibrium. Therefore, the Fed has to choose between targeting an interest rate and targeting the money supply. For most of the period since World War II, the Fed has chosen the federal funds rate as its target.   MyLab Economics Concept Check

The Taylor Rule

How does the Fed choose a target for the federal funds rate? The discussions at the meetings of the FOMC can be wide-ranging, and they take into account many economic variables. John Taylor of Stanford University has analyzed Fed decision making and developed the **Taylor rule** to explain federal funds rate targeting. The Taylor rule begins with an estimate of the value of the equilibrium real federal funds rate, which is the federal funds rate—adjusted for inflation—that would be consistent with real GDP being equal to potential GDP in the long run. Taylor believes this rate to be 2 percent. According to the Taylor rule, the Fed should set the target for the federal funds rate so that it is equal to the sum of the inflation rate, the equilibrium real federal funds rate, and two additional terms. The first of these additional terms is the *inflation gap*—the difference between current inflation and a target rate; the second is the *output gap*—the percentage difference between real GDP and potential GDP. The inflation gap and output gap are each given "weights" that reflect their influence on the federal funds target rate. With weights of 1/2 for both gaps, we have the following Taylor rule:

$$\text{Federal funds target rate} = \text{Current inflation rate} + \text{Equilibrium real federal funds rate} + [(1/2) \times \text{Inflation gap}] + [(1/2) \times \text{Output gap}].$$

The Taylor rule includes expressions for the inflation gap and the output gap because the Fed is concerned about both inflation and fluctuations in real GDP. Taylor demonstrated that if the equilibrium real federal funds rate is 2 percent and the target rate of inflation is 2 percent, the preceding equation does a good job of explaining changes in the Fed's target for the federal funds rate during most years. Consider an example in which the current inflation rate is 1 percent, and real GDP is 1 percent below potential GDP. In that case, the inflation gap equals 1 percent − 2 percent = −1 percent, and the output gap is also −1 percent. Inserting these values in the Taylor rule, we can calculate the predicted value for the federal funds target rate:

$$\text{Federal funds target rate} = 1\% + 2\% + [(1/2) \times -1\%] + [(1/2) \times -1\%] = 2\%.$$

The Taylor rule accurately predicted changes in the federal funds target during the period of Alan Greenspan's leadership of the Federal Reserve from 1987 to 2006. For the period of the late 1970s and early 1980s, when Paul Volcker was chairman of the Federal Reserve, the Taylor rule predicts a federal funds rate target *lower* than the actual target the Fed used. In other words, Chairman Volcker kept the federal funds rate at an unusually high level to bring down the very high inflation rates of the late 1970s and early 1980s. In contrast, using data from the chairmanship of Arthur Burns from 1970 to 1978, the Taylor rule predicts a federal funds rate target *higher* than the actual target. Chairman Burns kept the federal funds rate at an unusually low level during these years, which helps to explain why the inflation rate grew worse. During the mid-2000s, the actual federal funds rate was also lower than the predicted federal funds rate. Some economists, including Taylor, argue that these low targets for the federal funds rate contributed to the excessive increase in spending on housing that we will discuss in the next section.

Taylor has proposed that the Fed adopt an explicit rule to guide its monetary policy actions. The Fed would not be constrained to mechanically following the exact Taylor rule given earlier, but whatever rule the Fed adopted, it would have to publicly justify deviating from the rule, if a majority of the FOMC came to believe that was necessary. Fed Chair Janet Yellen and most current and past members of the FOMC are against the proposal because they believe it might limit the Fed's ability to pursue innovative policies in a financial crisis. They also note that the Taylor rule does not account for changes over time in the equilibrium real interest rate, or for changes the FOMC might want to make in the target inflation rate. **MyLab Economics** Concept Check

Solved Problem 15.5

MyLab Economics Interactive Animation

Applying the Taylor Rule

An article in the *Wall Street Journal* discussed the views of John Williams, the president of the Federal Reserve Bank of San Francisco, about the Taylor rule. According to the article, Williams argued that if the Fed had attempted to follow the Taylor rule during the recession of 2007–2009, it would have had to do "something not easily done, and that would have been for the Fed to have pushed short-term rates deeply into negative territory."

a. What does it mean for an interest rate to be negative?

b. Use the equation for the Taylor rule to show how the federal funds rate target might be negative. Assume that the equilibrium real federal funds rate and the target rate of inflation are both 2 percent and the current inflation rate is 0 percent.

Solving the Problem

Step 1: **Review the chapter material.** This problem is about using the Taylor rule to evaluate monetary policy, so you may want to review the section "The Taylor Rule," which begins on page 540.

Step 2: **Answer part (a) by explaining what it means for an interest rate to be negative.** We expect interest rates to be positive, which results in the borrower paying the lender back more than the amount of the funds borrowed. As we saw in the chapter opener and discussed further in the *Apply the Concept* on page 528, with a negative interest rate, the borrower would pay the lender back less than the amount of the funds borrowed. Note that Williams is referring to a negative *nominal* interest rate, which is very rare. A negative *real* interest rate that results from the inflation rate being higher than the nominal interest rate occurs more frequently.

Step 3: **Answer part (b) by constructing an example where the target federal funds rate might be negative.** This is the equation for the Taylor rule:

Federal funds target rate = Current inflation rate
+ Equilibrium real federal funds rate
+ [(1/2) × Inflation gap]
+ [(1/2) × Output gap].

If we substitute the values given in the problem, we have:

$$\text{Federal funds rate target} = 0\% + 2\% + [(1/2) \times (0\% - 2)]$$
$$+ [(1/2) \times \text{output gap}],$$

or:

$$\text{Federal funds taget rate target} = 1\% + [(1/2) \times \text{output gap}].$$

So, for the federal funds rate target to be negative, the output gap will have to be larger (in absolute value) than -2%. For example, if the output gap is -4%, then:

$$\text{Federal funds rate target} = 1\% + [(1/2) \times (-4)] = -1\%.$$

In fact, the output gap rose above -6 percent during the recession. So, Williams is correct that following the Taylor rule exactly would have required the federal funds rate to be negative, which means that banks would have to have been willing to pay interest when lending to other banks in the federal funds market rather than receive interest. This outcome is very unlikely.

Extra Credit: The inability of the Fed to push the federal funds rate to negative values is sometimes called the *zero lower bound* to monetary policy.

Source: Michael S. Derby and Benjamin Fritz, "Fed's Williams Says Summer Rate Rise Possible if Data Supports Action," *Wall Street Journal*, May 1, 2015.

MyLab Economics Study Plan   **Your Turn:** For more practice, do related problems 5.5, 5.6, and 5.7 on pages 556–557 at the end of this chapter.

Inflation Targeting

Inflation targeting A framework for conducting monetary policy that involves the central bank announcing its target level of inflation.

Many economists and central bankers believe that *inflation targeting* provides a useful framework for carrying out monetary policy. With **inflation targeting**, a central bank publicly sets an explicit target for the inflation rate over a period of time, and the government and the public then judge the performance of the central bank on the basis of its success in hitting the target.

Beginning in the 1980s, inflation targeting was adopted by a number of central banks around the world, including the Bank of England and, after its founding in the late 1990s, the European Central Bank. After many years of not having an explicit inflation target, the Fed announced in 2012 that it would attempt to maintain an average inflation rate of 2 percent per year.

With inflation targeting, the Fed can still respond to periods of recession or other economic problems without following an inflexible rule. An inflation target allows monetary policy to focus on inflation and inflation forecasts except during times of severe recession. Arguments supporting the Fed's use of an explicit inflation target focus on the following points. First, announcing explicit targets for inflation draws the public's attention to what the Fed can actually achieve in practice. Most economists believe that over the long run, monetary policy has a greater effect on inflation than on the growth of real GDP. Second, announcing an inflation target provides an anchor for inflationary expectations. If households, firms, and participants in financial markets believe that the Fed will hit an annual inflation target of 2 percent, then they will expect that if inflation is temporarily lower or higher, it will eventually return to the target rate. Third, inflation targets promote accountability for the Fed by providing a yardstick against which its performance can be measured.

Some economists and policymakers are critical of the Fed's decision to adopt an explicit inflation target. Opponents make several arguments. First, rigid numerical targets for inflation diminish the flexibility of monetary policy to address other policy goals. Second, because monetary policy affects inflation with a lag, inflation targeting requires that the Fed use forecasts of future inflation, which may turn out to be inaccurate. Third, holding the Fed accountable only for a goal of low inflation may make it more difficult for elected officials to monitor the Fed's support for good economic policy overall. Finally, inflation targets may increase uncertainty over whether the Fed will take prompt action to return the economy to full employment following a recession.

Economists and policymakers continue to debate whether inflation targets improve economic policy.   **MyLab Economics** Concept Check   **MyLab Economics** Study Plan

Apply the Concept   MyLab Economics Video

Should the Fed Worry about the Prices of Food and Gasoline?

Surveys show that many people in the United States are skeptical about whether changes in the consumer price index (CPI) are a good measure of inflation. The CPI measures the price level based on a market basket that contains 211 goods and services, including shoes, fresh fruit, refrigerators, textbooks, gasoline, and doctor visits. But many people think of inflation in terms of increases in the prices of the goods they buy most frequently—particularly food and gasoline.

Not only does the Fed not concentrate on changes in the prices of food and gasoline, it actually prefers to *exclude* food and gasoline prices when measuring inflation. Fed policymakers refer to these adjusted measures of inflation as "core" inflation. Why does the Fed ignore the prices that many people think are the most important? The key reason is that monetary policy affects the economy with a lag of many months. As a result, Fed policymakers don't want to react to every movement—up or down—in prices. Food and energy prices are much more volatile than are the prices of all the goods and services in the CPI taken together. Food can be volatile because weather-related problems such as too little or too much rain can lead to large fluctuations in supply. Energy prices can fluctuate when political unrest in the Middle East or other energy-producing regions disrupts supply, when the Organization of the Petroleum Exporting Countries (OPEC) oil cartel attempts to increase prices, or as shale oil production in the United States fluctuates. Because the factors that cause volatility in food and energy prices tend not to persist for more than a few months, they don't have a long-lasting effect on the overall rate of inflation.

The Fed's preferred measure of inflation is the core *personal consumption expenditures (PCE) price index*, which excludes food and energy prices. The PCE price index is a measure of the price level that is similar to the GDP deflator, except it includes only the prices of goods from the consumption category of GDP. The PCE price index includes the prices of more goods and services than the CPI, so it is a broader measure of inflation. The green line in the graph shows inflation calculated using the CPI, including prices for all 211 goods and services in the consumer market basket. The blue line shows inflation calculated using core CPI, which leaves out the prices of food and energy, such as gasoline and natural gas used in heating homes. The red line shows inflation calculated using the core PCE, which also excludes prices for food and energy.

MyLab Economics Real-time data

As the graph shows, food and energy prices are much more volatile than are the prices of all the goods and services in the CPI taken together. For instance, during the recession of 2007–2009, the inflation rate measured by the CPI was negative—deflation occurred—during nine months. When changes in food and energy prices are excluded, by contrast, the inflation rate whether measured by core CPI or core PCE is positive in every month. This pattern repeated in early 2015, when falling energy prices caused the CPI to decline for several months.

As Fed Chair Janet Yellen has put it, Fed policymakers "pay attention to core inflation and similar measures because, in light of the volatility of food and energy prices, core inflation has been a better forecaster of overall inflation." In other words, to reach its goal of price stability, the Fed has to concentrate on the underlying inflation rate and avoid being distracted by temporary increases in food or energy prices—however painful the typical consumer may find those increases to be.

If you want to know what the Fed thinks the current inflation rate is, look at data on the core PCE price index. The Bureau of Economic Analysis publishes these data monthly.

MyLab Economics Study Plan   **Your Turn:** Test your understanding by doing related problems 5.8 and 5.9 on page 557 at the end of this chapter.

 ## Fed Policies during the 2007–2009 Recession

15.6   LEARNING OBJECTIVE: Describe the policies the Federal Reserve used during the 2007–2009 recession.

As we have seen, the Fed's traditional response to a recession is to lower the target for the federal funds rate. The severity of the recession of 2007–2009, particularly the problems in financial markets during those years, complicated the Fed's job. By December 2008, the Fed had effectively lowered the target for the federal funds rate to zero, but the zero interest rate alone did not result in a sufficient increase in aggregate demand to end the recession. In this section, we will discuss some of the additional policy measures the Fed took during the 2007–2009 recession. Some of these measures were used for the first time in the Fed's history.

The Inflation and Deflation of the Housing Market Bubble

To understand the 2007–2009 recession and the financial crisis that accompanied it, we need to start by considering the housing market. The Fed lowered the target for the federal funds rate during the 2001 recession to stimulate demand for housing. The policy was successful, and most builders experienced several years of high demand. By 2005, however, many economists argued that a "bubble" had formed in the housing market. As we discussed in Chapter 6, Section 6.2, the price of any asset reflects the returns the owner of the asset expects to receive. For example, the price of a share of stock reflects the profitability of the firm issuing the stock because the owner of a share of stock has a claim on the firm's profits.

Many economists believe, however, that sometimes a *stock market bubble* can form when the prices of stocks rise above levels that can be justified by the profitability of the firms issuing the stocks. Stock market bubbles end when enough investors decide stocks are overvalued and begin to sell. Why would an investor be willing to pay more for stocks than would be justified by their underlying value? There are two main explanations:

1. The investor may be caught up in the enthusiasm of the moment and, by failing to gather sufficient information, may overestimate the true value of the stocks.
2. The investor may expect to profit from buying stocks at inflated prices if the investor can sell them at even higher prices before the bubble bursts.

The price of a house should reflect the value of the housing services it provides. We can use the rents charged for comparable houses in an area to measure the value of housing services. We would expect, then, that housing prices and rents would increase at roughly the same rate. If prices of single-family homes rise significantly relative to rents for single-family homes, it is likely that the housing market is experiencing a bubble. Housing prices and housing rents have generally increased at about the same rate, but between January 2000 and May 2006, housing prices nearly doubled, while rents increased by less than 25 percent. This large divergence between housing prices and rents is evidence of a bubble. In addition, in some cities, there was an increase in the number of buyers who did not intend to live in the houses they purchased but were using them as investments. Like stock investors during a stock market bubble, these housing investors were expecting to make a profit by selling houses at higher prices than they had paid for them, and they were not concerned about whether the prices of the houses were above the value of the housing services provided.

During 2006 and 2007, the air was rapidly escaping from the housing bubble. Panel (a) of Figure 15.12 shows new home sales for each month from January 2000 through June 2017. New home sales rose by 60 percent between January 2000 and July 2005 and then fell by 80 percent between July 2005 and May 2010. Sales then began to gradually increase but were still at low levels well into 2017. Sales of existing homes followed a similar pattern. Panel (b) shows that prices of new and existing homes also began to decline beginning in 2006. Some homebuyers began having trouble making their loan payments. When lenders foreclosed on some of these loans, the lenders sold the homes, causing housing prices to decline further. *Subprime loans* are loans granted to borrowers with flawed credit histories. Some mortgage lenders that had concentrated on making subprime loans suffered heavy losses and went out of business, and most banks and other lenders tightened the requirements for borrowers. This *credit crunch* made it more difficult for potential homebuyers to obtain mortgages, further depressing the market.

The decline in the housing market affected other markets as well. For example, with home prices falling, consumption spending on furniture, appliances, and home improvements declined because many households found it more difficult to borrow against the value of their homes.

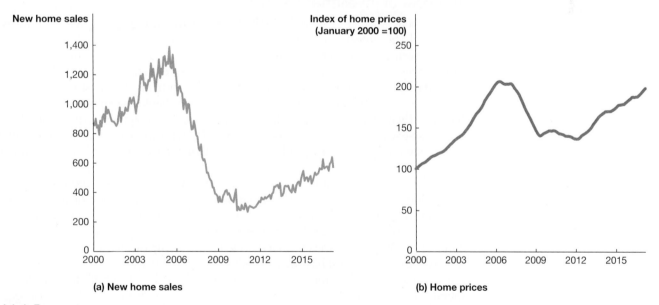

(a) New home sales

(b) Home prices

MyLab Economics Real-time data

Figure 15.12   **The Housing Bubble**

Panel (a) shows that the housing bubble resulted in rapid increases in sales of new homes until 2005, followed by a sharp decrease in sales beginning in July 2005. A slow revival in home sales started in 2011. Panel (b) shows movements in the Case-Shiller index, which measures changes in the prices of single-family homes, and indicates that home prices followed a similar pattern to home sales, although after 2011, home prices increased more rapidly than did home sales.

Note: The data are seasonally adjusted at an annual rate.

Sources: U.S. Bureau of the Census and Federal Reserve Bank of St. Louis.

Was the housing bubble the result of overly optimistic expectations by homebuyers and builders that new residential construction and housing prices would indefinitely continue to rise at rapid rates? While overly optimistic expectations may have played some role in the housing bubble, many economists believe that changes in the market for mortgages may have played a bigger role. **MyLab Economics** Concept Check

The Changing Mortgage Market

Until the 1970s, the commercial banks and savings and loans that granted mortgages kept the loans until the borrowers paid them off. As we saw in Chapter 14, Section 14.4, a financial asset such as a mortgage is a security only if it can be resold in a secondary market. Many members of Congress believed that home ownership could be increased by creating a secondary market in mortgages. If banks and savings and loans could resell mortgages, individual investors would in effect be able to provide funds for mortgages. The process would work like this: If a bank or savings and loan granted a mortgage and then resold the mortgage to an investor, the bank could use the funds received from the investor to grant another mortgage. In this way, banks and savings and loans could grant more mortgage loans because they would no longer depend only on their deposits for the funds needed to make the loans. One barrier to creating a secondary market in mortgages was that most investors were unwilling to buy mortgages because they were afraid of losing money if the borrower stopped making payments, or *defaulted*, on the loan.

To reassure investors, Congress used two *government-sponsored enterprises (GSEs)*: the Federal National Mortgage Association ("Fannie Mae") and the Federal Home Loan Mortgage Corporation ("Freddie Mac"). These two institutions stand between investors and banks that grant mortgages. Fannie Mae and Freddie Mac sell bonds called *mortgage-backed securities* to investors and use the funds to purchase mortgages from banks. By the 1990s, a large secondary market existed in mortgages, with funds flowing from investors through Fannie Mae and Freddie Mac to banks and, ultimately, to individuals and families borrowing money to buy houses. **MyLab Economics** Concept Check

The Role of Investment Banks

By the 2000s, further changes had taken place in the mortgage market. First, investment banks became significant participants in the secondary market for mortgages. As we have seen, investment banks, such as Morgan Stanley, differ from commercial banks in that they do not take in deposits and rarely lend directly to households. Instead, investment banks concentrate on providing advice to firms issuing stocks and bonds or considering mergers with other firms. Investment banks began buying mortgages, bundling them into mortgage-backed securities, and reselling them to investors. These mortgage-backed securities proved very popular with investors because they often paid higher interest rates than other securities that investors believed had comparable default risk.

Second, by the height of the housing bubble in 2005 and early 2006, lenders had greatly loosened the standards for obtaining a mortgage loan. Traditionally, only borrowers with good credit histories and who were willing to make a down payment equal to at least 20 percent of the value of the house they were buying would be able to receive a mortgage. By 2005, however, lenders were issuing many mortgages to subprime borrowers with flawed credit histories. In addition, "Alt-A" borrowers—who stated but did not document their incomes—and borrowers who made very small down payments found it easier to get loans. Lenders also created new types of *adjustable-rate mortgages* that allowed borrowers to pay a very low interest rate for the first few years of the mortgage and then pay a higher rate in later years. The chance that the borrowers using these nontraditional mortgages would default was higher than for borrowers using traditional mortgages. Why would borrowers take out mortgages if it might be difficult for them to make the payments, and why would lenders grant these mortgages? Both borrowers and lenders were anticipating that housing prices would continue to rise, which would reduce the chance that borrowers would default on the mortgages and would also make it easier for borrowers to convert to more traditional mortgages in the future.

Unfortunately, the decline in housing prices led to rising defaults among subprime and Alt-A borrowers, borrowers with adjustable-rate mortgages, and borrowers who had made only small down payments. When borrowers began defaulting on mortgages, the values of many mortgage-backed securities declined sharply. Investors feared that if they purchased these securities, they would not receive the promised payments because the payments on the securities depended on borrowers making their mortgage payments, which an increasing number of borrowers were failing to do. Many commercial and investment banks owned these mortgage-backed securities, so the decline in the value of the securities caused these banks to suffer heavy losses. By mid-2007, the decline in the value of mortgage-backed securities and the large losses suffered by commercial and investment banks began to concern investors and policymakers. Many investors refused to buy mortgage-backed securities, and some investors would buy only bonds issued by the U.S. Treasury.   **MyLab Economics** Concept Check

Apply the Concept

MyLab Economics Video

The Wonderful World of Leverage

Traditionally, most people taking out a mortgage made a down payment equal to 20 percent of the price of the house and borrowed the remaining 80 percent. During the housing boom, however, many people purchased houses with down payments of 5 percent or less. These borrowers were highly *leveraged*, which means that their investment in their house was made mostly with borrowed money.

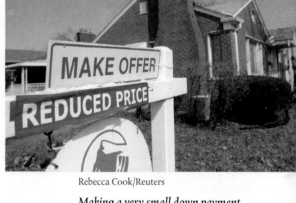

Rebecca Cook/Reuters

Making a very small down payment on a home mortgage leaves a buyer vulnerable if house prices fall.

To see how leverage works in the housing market, consider the following example: Suppose you buy a $200,000 house on January 1, 2020. On January 1, 2021, the price of the house—if you decide to sell it—has risen to $220,000. What return have you earned on your investment in the house? The answer depends on how much you invested when you bought the house. For example, if you paid $200,000 in cash for the house, your return on that $200,000 investment is the $20,000 increase in the price of the house divided by your $200,000 investment, or 10 percent. Suppose that rather than paying cash, you made a down payment of 20 percent, or $40,000, and borrowed the rest by taking out a mortgage loan of $160,000. Now the return on your investment in the house is the $20,000 increase in the price of the house divided by your $40,000 investment, or 50 percent. If the down payment is less than 20 percent, your return on investment will be higher. The second column in the following table shows how the return on your investment increases as your down payment decreases:

	Return on your investment as a result of . . .	
Down Payment	a 10 percent increase in the price of your house	a 10 percent decrease in the price of your house
100%	10%	−10%
20	50	−50
10	100	−100
5	200	−200

An investment financed at least partly by borrowing is called a *leveraged investment*. As this example shows, the larger the fraction of an investment financed by borrowing, the greater the degree of leverage in the investment, and the greater the potential return. But as the third column in the table shows, the reverse is also true: The greater the leverage, the greater the potential loss. To see why, suppose once again that you buy a house for $200,000, except that in this case, after one year, the price of the house falls to $180,000. If you paid $200,000 in cash for the house—so your leverage was zero—the $20,000 decline in the price of the house represents a loss of 10 percent of your investment. But if you made a down payment of only $10,000 and borrowed the remaining $190,000, then the $20,000 decline in the price of the house represents a loss of 200 percent of your investment. In fact, the house is now worth $10,000 less than the amount of your mortgage loan. The *equity* in your house is the difference between the market price of the house and the amount you owe on a loan. If the amount you owe is greater than the price of the house, you have *negative equity*. A homeowner who has negative equity is also said to be "upside down" or "underwater" on his or her mortgage.

When the housing bubble burst and housing prices started to fall, many people found that they had negative equity. In that situation, some people defaulted on their loans, sometimes by simply moving out and abandoning their homes. Leverage had contributed to the housing boom and bust and the severity of the 2007–2009 recession.

MyLab Economics Study Plan

Your Turn: Test your understanding by doing related problem 6.9 on page 558 at the end of this chapter.

The Fed and the Treasury Department Respond

Because the problems in financial markets resulting from the bursting of the housing bubble were so severe, the Fed entered into an unusual partnership with the U.S. Treasury Department to develop suitable policies. Fed Chairman Ben Bernanke and U.S. Treasury Secretaries Henry Paulson (in the Bush administration) and Timothy Geithner (in the Obama administration) responded to the crisis by intervening in financial markets in unprecedented ways.

Initial Fed and Treasury Actions The financial crisis significantly worsened following the bankruptcy of the investment bank Lehman Brothers on September 15, 2008. So, it is useful to look at the actions taken by the Fed and the Treasury before and after that date. Table 15.3 shows four key actions the Fed and Treasury took to deal with problems in the financial system before the bankruptcy of Lehman Brothers.

Table 15.3

Treasury and Fed Actions at the Beginning of the Financial Crisis

Date	Action	Goal
March 2008	Although the Fed traditionally made discount loans only to commercial banks, the Fed announced it would temporarily make discount loans to *primary dealers*—firms that participate in regular open market transactions with the Fed.	Provide short-term funds to these dealers, some of which are investment banks, so they would not have to raise funds by selling securities, which might further reduce the prices of these securities.
March 2008	The Fed announced that it would loan up to $200 billion of Treasury securities in exchange for mortgage-backed securities.	Make it possible for primary dealers that owned mortgage-backed securities that were difficult or impossible to sell to have access to Treasury securities that they could use as collateral for short-term loans.
March 2008	The Fed and the Treasury helped JPMorgan Chase acquire the investment bank Bear Stearns, which was close to failing.	Avoid a financial panic that the Fed and the Treasury believed would result from Bear Stearns's failure. Its failure might have caused many investors and financial firms to stop making loans to other investment banks.
September 2008	The Treasury moved to have the federal government take control of Fannie Mae and Freddie Mac. Although the federal government sponsored Fannie Mae and Freddie Mac, they were actually private businesses. The firms were placed under the supervision of the Federal Housing Finance Agency.	Avoid further devastating a weak housing market. The Treasury believed that the bankruptcy of Fannie Mae and Freddie Mac would have caused a collapse in confidence in mortgage-backed securities.

Responses to the Failure of Lehman Brothers Some economists and policymakers criticized the decision by the Fed and the Treasury to help arrange the sale of Bear Stearns to JPMorgan Chase. Their main concern was with the *moral hazard problem*, which is the possibility that managers of financial firms such as Bear Stearns might make riskier investments if they believe that the federal government will save them from bankruptcy. The Treasury and the Fed acted to save Bear Stearns because they believed that the failure of a large financial firm could have wider economic repercussions. As we discussed in Chapter 14, Section 14.4, when a financial firm sells off its holdings of bonds and other assets, it causes their prices to fall, which in turn can undermine the financial position of other firms that also own these assets. In September 2008, when the investment bank Lehman Brothers was near bankruptcy, the Fed and the Treasury had to weigh the moral hazard problem against the possibility that the failure of Lehman Brothers would lead to further declines in asset prices and endanger the financial positions of other firms. Chairman Ben Bernanke and other Fed officials were also concerned that they lacked the legal authority to make loans to Lehman Brothers. They believed that the Federal Reserve Act prohibited making loans to a firm that was insolvent, meaning that the value of the firm's assets—such as its holdings of mortgage securities—was less than the value of its liabilities—such as the loans it had received from other financial firms.

The Fed and the Treasury decided to allow Lehman Brothers to go bankrupt, which it did on September 15. The adverse reaction in financial markets was stronger than the Fed and the Treasury had expected, and just two days later, the Fed agreed to provide an $85 billion loan to the American International Group (AIG)—the largest insurance company in the United States—in exchange for the federal government receiving an 80 percent ownership stake, effectively giving the government control of the company.

One important result of the failure of Lehman Brothers was the heavy losses suffered by Reserve Primary Fund, a money market mutual fund that had made short-term loans to Lehman Brothers. The problems at Reserve led many investors to withdraw their funds from it and other money market funds. These withdrawals reduced the ability of the money market funds to purchase commercial paper from corporations. Because in recent years corporations had become dependent on selling commercial paper to finance their operations, the Treasury and the Fed moved to stabilize this market and ensure that the flow of funds from investors to corporations continued. The Treasury announced a plan to temporarily provide insurance for deposits in money market mutual funds, similar to the existing insurance on bank deposits. The Fed announced that for a limited time, it would lend directly to corporations by purchasing three-month commercial paper issued by nonfinancial corporations.

Finally, in October 2008, Congress passed the *Troubled Asset Relief Program* (TARP), under which the Treasury attempted to stabilize the commercial banking system by providing funds to banks in exchange for stock. Taking partial ownership positions in private commercial banks was an unprecedented action for the federal government.

Many of the Treasury's and the Fed's new approaches to policy were controversial because they involved partial government ownership of financial firms, implicit guarantees to large financial firms that they would not be allowed to go bankrupt, and unprecedented intervention in financial markets. Although the approaches were new, they were intended to achieve the traditional macroeconomic policy goals of high employment, price stability, and stability of financial markets. What remains to be seen is whether these new approaches represent a permanent increase in federal government involvement in U.S. financial markets or whether policy will eventually return to more traditional approaches. **MyLab Economics** Concept Check **MyLab Economics** Study Plan

Continued from page 517

Economics in Your Life & Career

Should You Buy a House during a Recession?

At the beginning of this chapter, we asked whether it is a good idea to buy a house during a recession. Buying a house is the largest purchase you are likely to make in your lifetime, so you need to carefully consider a number of factors, including the price of the house relative to comparable houses in the neighborhood; whether house prices in the neighborhood have been rising or falling; and the location of the house relative to stores, work, and good schools. Also important is the interest rate you will have to pay on the mortgage loan you would need in order to buy the house.

As we have seen in this chapter, during a recession, the Fed often takes actions to lower interest rates. So, mortgage rates are typically lower during a recession than at other times. You may want to take advantage of low interest rates to buy a house during a recession. But recessions are also times of rising unemployment, and you would not want to make a commitment to borrow a lot of money for 15 or more years if you were in danger of losing your job. We can conclude that if your job seems secure, buying a house during a recession may be a good idea.

Conclusion

Monetary policy is one way governments pursue goals for inflation, employment, and financial stability. The chair of the Federal Reserve may have a greater ability than the president of the United States to affect the U.S. economy. Congress and the president, however, also use their power over spending and taxes to try to stabilize the economy. In Chapter 16, we will discuss how *fiscal policy*—changes in government spending and taxes—affect the economy.

Visit **MyLab Economics** for a news article and analysis related to the concepts of this chapter.

CHAPTER SUMMARY
AND PROBLEMS

Key Terms

Contractionary monetary policy, p. 527

Expansionary monetary policy, p. 527

Federal funds rate, p. 525
Inflation targeting, p. 542

Monetary policy, p. 518
Taylor rule, p. 540

 15.1 What Is Monetary Policy? pages 518–520

LEARNING OBJECTIVE: Define monetary policy and describe the Federal Reserve's monetary policy goals.

MyLab Economics   Visit www.pearson.com/mylab/economics to complete these exercises online and get instant feedback.

Summary

Monetary policy refers to the actions the Fed takes to manage the money supply and interest rates to achieve its macroeconomic policy goals. The Fed has four *monetary policy goals* that are intended to promote a well-functioning economy: price stability, high employment, stability of financial markets and institutions, and economic growth.

Review Questions

1.1 When Congress established the Federal Reserve in 1913, what was its main responsibility? When did Congress broaden the Fed's responsibilities?

1.2 What are the Fed's four monetary policy goals? In what sense does the Fed have a "dual mandate"?

1.3 How can investment banks be subject to liquidity problems?

Problems and Applications

1.4 What is a bank panic? Why are policymakers more concerned about bank failures than about failures of restaurants or clothing stores?

1.5 A column in the *Wall Street Journal* referred to policy actions aimed at "fulfilling both sides of the Fed's dual mandate."
  a. Who gave the Fed a dual mandate?
  b. Does the Fed's dual mandate require it to attain a zero percent unemployment rate? Briefly explain.
  c. Does the Fed's dual mandate require it to attain a zero percent inflation rate? Briefly explain.
  Source: Steven Russolillo, "The Key to a More Hawkish Fed," *Wall Street Journal*, December 14, 2016.

1.6 A former Federal Reserve official argued that at the Fed, "the objectives of price stability and low long-term interest rates are essentially the same objective." Briefly explain his reasoning.
  Source: William Poole, "Understanding the Fed," *Federal Reserve Bank of St. Louis Review*, Vol. 89, No. 1, January/February 2007, p. 4.

1.7 In mid-2017, an article in the *Wall Street Journal* noted that "the Federal Reserve's interest-rate increases aren't having the desired effect of cooling off Wall Street's hot streak … where stocks have rallied to records this year." Is cooling off rapid increases in stock prices part of the Fed's dual mandate? Are such increases a concern for the Fed? Briefly explain.
  Source: David Harrison, "Fed's Effort to Guide Markets Falls," *Wall Street Journal*, June 11, 2017.

 15.2 The Money Market and the Fed's Choice of Monetary Policy Targets, pages 520–526

LEARNING OBJECTIVE: Describe the Federal Reserve's monetary policy targets and explain how expansionary and contractionary monetary policies affect the interest rate.

MyLab Economics   Visit www.pearson.com/mylab/economics to complete these exercises online and get instant feedback.

Summary

The Fed's *monetary policy targets* are economic variables that it can affect directly and that in turn affect variables such as real GDP and the price level that are closely related to the Fed's policy goals. The two main monetary policy targets are the money supply and the interest rate. The Fed has most often chosen to use the interest rate as its monetary policy target. The Federal Open Market Committee announces a target for the federal funds rate after each meeting. The **federal funds rate** is the interest rate banks charge each other for overnight loans. To lower the interest rate, the Fed increases the money supply. To raise the interest rate, the Fed decreases the money supply. In a graphical analysis of the money market, when the money supply curve shifts to the right, the result is a movement down the money demand curve and a new equilibrium at a lower interest rate. When the money supply curve shifts to the left, the result is a movement up the money demand curve and a new equilibrium at a higher interest rate.

Review Questions

2.1 What is a monetary policy target? Why does the Fed use policy targets?

2.2 What do economists mean by the *demand for money*? What is the advantage of holding money? What is the disadvantage? Why does an increase in the interest rate decrease the quantity of money demanded?

2.3 Draw a demand and supply graph showing equilibrium in the money market. Suppose the Fed wants to lower the equilibrium interest rate. Show on the graph how the Fed would traditionally accomplish this objective.

2.4 What is the federal funds rate? What role does it play in monetary policy?

2.5 What are the Fed's two new policy tools, and why does the Fed now need to rely on them to change the federal funds rate?

Problems and Applications

2.6 In the following graph of the money market, what could cause the money supply curve to shift from MS_1 to MS_2? What could cause the money demand curve to shift from MD_1 to MD_2?

Quantity of money, M
(billions of dollars)

2.7 In 2017, an article in the *Wall Street Journal* had the headline "Federal Reserve Expected to Deliver Rate Increase."
   a. What rate is the headline likely to be referring to?
   b. Who is able to borrow and lend at that rate?
   c. Given your answer to part (b), why do the Fed's actions to increase or decrease that rate attract so much attention?

   Sources: David Harrison, "Federal Reserve Expected to Deliver Rate," *Wall Street Journal*, June 14, 2017.

2.8 In response to problems in financial markets and a slowing economy, the Federal Open Market Committee (FOMC) began lowering its target for the federal funds rate from 5.25 percent in September 2007. Over the next year, the FOMC cut its federal funds rate target in a series of steps. Economist Price Fishback of the University of Arizona observed, "The Fed has been pouring more money into the banking system by cutting the target federal funds rate to 0 to 0.25 percent in December 2008." What is the relationship between the federal funds rate falling and the money supply increasing? How does

lowering the target for the federal funds rate "pour money" into the banking system?

   Source: Price Fishback, "The Financial Meltdown Now and Then," freakonomics.com, May 12, 2009.

2.9 An article in the *New York Times* in 1993 stated the following about Fed Chair Alan Greenspan's decision to no longer announce targets for the money supply: "Since the late 1970's, the Federal Reserve has made many of its most important decisions by setting a specific target for growth in the money supply … and often adjusted interest rates to meet them." If the Fed would no longer have a specific target for the money supply, what was it targeting? Why did the Fed give up targeting the money supply?

   Source: Steven Greenhouse, "Fed Abandons Policy Tied to Money Supply," *New York Times*, July 23, 1993.

2.10 Consider the variables that shift money demand and money supply. Match each of the following scenarios with one of the four graphs of money demand and money supply.
   a. More widespread use of mobile wallets
   b. Fed decreases the required reserve ratio
   c. Fed sells Treasury securities
   d. Real GDP increases

1.

Quantity of money, M
(trillions of dollars)

2.

Quantity of money, M
(trillions of dollars)

Accompanies problem 2.10

3.

4.

15.3 **Monetary Policy and Economic Activity, pages 526–534**

LEARNING OBJECTIVE: Use aggregate demand and aggregate supply graphs to show the effects of monetary policy on real GDP and the price level.

MyLab Economics Visit **www.pearson.com/mylab/economics** to complete these exercises online and get instant feedback.

Summary

An **expansionary monetary policy** lowers interest rates to increase consumption, investment, and net exports. This increase in aggregate demand increases real GDP and the price level. An expansionary monetary policy can help the Fed achieve its goal of high employment. A **contractionary monetary policy** raises interest rates to decrease consumption, investment, and net exports. This decrease in aggregate demand reduces both real GDP and the inflation rate below what they would be in the absence of policy. A contractionary monetary policy can help the Fed achieve its goal of price stability.

Review Questions

3.1 Briefly discuss how an increase in interest rates affects each component of aggregate demand.

3.2 If the Fed believes the economy is headed for a recession, what actions should it take? If the Fed believes the inflation rate is about to sharply increase, what actions should it take?

3.3 What is quantitative easing? Why have central banks used this policy?

Problems and Applications

3.4 A student says the following: "I understand why the Fed uses expansionary policy, but I don't understand why it would ever use contractionary policy. Why would the government ever want the economy to contract?" Briefly answer the student's question.

3.5 In explaining why monetary policy did not pull Japan out of a recession in the early 2000s, an official at the Bank of Japan was quoted as saying that despite "major increases in the money supply," the money "stay[ed] in banks." Explain what the official means by saying that the money stayed in banks. Why would that be a problem? Where does the money go if an expansionary monetary policy is successful?

Source: James Brooke, "Critics Say Koizumi's Economic Medicine Is a Weak Tea," *New York Times*, February 27, 2002.

3.6 In early 2017, according to the *Wall Street Journal*, President Donald Trump said that the U.S. dollar was "getting too strong," and he would prefer that the Federal Reserve "keep interest rates low." The article also quoted the president as saying, "It's very, very hard to compete when you have a strong dollar."

a. What does President Trump mean by a "strong dollar"?

b. Is there an economic connection between the president's desire for a weaker dollar and his desire that the Federal Reserve keep interest rates low? Briefly explain.

c. Why would a strong dollar make it hard for U.S. firms to compete?

Source: Gerard Baker, Carol E. Lee and Michael C. Bender, "Trump Says Dollar 'Getting Too Strong,' Won't Label China a Currency Manipulator," *Wall Street Journal*, April 12, 2017.

3.7 A 2017 article in the *Wall Street Journal* discussed the decision by Brazil's central bank to cut the SELIC rate, which is the equivalent in Brazil of the federal funds rate in the United States. According to the article, the cut occurred "as the country's inflation rate continues to fall quickly and the economy still struggles."

a. In what sense do you think the Brazilian economy was "struggling" when this article was published?

b. Why would a cut in the SELIC rate be an appropriate policy action at a time when the inflation rate was falling and the economy was struggling?

Source: Jeffrey T. Lewis, "Brazil Cuts Its Benchmark Rate a Full Percentage Point," *Wall Street Journal*, April 12, 2017.

3.8 William McChesney Martin, who was Federal Reserve chair from 1951 to 1970, was once quoted as saying, "The role of the Federal Reserve is to remove the punchbowl just as the party gets going." What did he mean?

3.9 **(Related to the Apply the Concept on page 528)** An article in the *Wall Street Journal* about negative interest rates on German bonds noted, "The negative yield means investors are effectively paying the German state for holding its debt." The article quoted an investment analyst as saying, "The negative yield is not scaring investors away."

a. What caused the interest rate on German government bonds to become negative?

b. Why are investors willing to buy bonds with a negative interest rate?

Source: Emese Bartha and Ben Edwards, "Germany Sells Five-Year Debt at Negative Yield for First Time on Record," *Wall Street Journal*, February 25, 2015.

3.10 **(Related to the Apply the Concept on page 528)** An article in the *Wall Street Journal* noted that before the financial crisis of 2007–2009, the Fed "managed just one short-term interest rate and expected that to be enough to meet its goals for inflation and unemployment."

a. What short-term interest rate is the article referring to? How would the Fed expect controlling that one interest rate would allow it to meet its goals for inflation and unemployment?

b. The article also noted that after the financial crisis, the Fed was "working through a broader spectrum of interest rates." What does "a broader spectrum of interest rates" mean? How is the Fed able to affect a broader spectrum of interest rates?

Source: Jon Hilsenrath, "Easy-Money Era a Long Game for Fed," *Wall Street Journal*, March 17, 2013.

3.11 **(Related to the Apply the Concept on page 532)** Each year, the president's Council of Economic Advisers prepares and sends to Congress *The Economic Report of the President*. The report published in February 2008 contained the following summary of the economic situation: "Economic growth is expected to continue in 2008. Most market forecasts suggest a slower pace in the first half of 2008, followed by strengthened growth in the second half of the year."

a. What in fact happened to economic growth during 2008?

b. What conclusion can you draw from your answer to part (a) with respect to economic forecasting and the formulation of economic policy?

Source: Executive Office of the President, *Economic Report of the President*, 2008, Washington, DC: USGPO, 2008, p. 17.

3.12 **(Related to the Apply the Concept on page 532)** The following is from a Federal Reserve publication:

In practice, monetary policymakers do not have up-to-the-minute, reliable information about the state of the economy and prices. Information is limited because of lags in the publication of data. Also, policymakers have less-than-perfect understanding of the way the economy works, including the knowledge of when and to what extent policy actions will affect aggregate demand. The operation of the economy changes over time, and with it the response of the economy to policy measures. These limitations add to uncertainties in the policy process and make determining the appropriate setting of monetary policy … more difficult.

If the Fed itself admits that there are many obstacles in the way of effective monetary policy, why does it still engage in active monetary policy rather than use a monetary growth rule, as suggested by Milton Friedman and his followers?

Source: Board of Governors of the Federal Reserve System, *The Federal Reserve System: Purposes and Functions*, Washington, DC, 1994.

3.13 **(Related to the Don't Let This Happen to You on page 534)** Briefly explain whether you agree with the following statement: "The Fed has an easy job. Say it wants to increase real GDP by $200 billion. All it has to do is increase the money supply by that amount."

3.14 **(Related to the Chapter Opener on page 516)** An investment blog said about Fed Chair Janet Yellen: "She is arguably the world's most powerful woman, and perhaps the most powerful person in the world. Can you name anybody with more might?" Do you agree with this assessment? Briefly explain.

Source: Barbara Friedberg, "Fed Chief Janet Yellen: The Most Powerful Woman in the World," blog.personalcapital.com, September 17, 2014.

3.15 The European Central Bank (ECB) issued the following statement after its June 2017 meeting on monetary policy:

Regarding non-standard monetary policy measures, the Governing Council confirms that the net asset purchases, at the current monthly pace of €60 billion, are intended to run until the end of December 2017, or beyond, if necessary, and in any case until the Governing Council sees a sustained adjustment in the path of inflation consistent with its inflation aim.

a. What is this nonstandard monetary policy of net asset purchases called? What other central banks have used it?

b. Based on this statement, do you expect that the inflation rate is above or below the ECB's inflation target? Briefly explain.

Source: European Central Bank, "Monetary Policy Decisions," press release, June 8, 2017, www.ecb.europa.eu.

15.4 Monetary Policy in the Dynamic Aggregate Demand and Aggregate Supply Model, pages 534–538

LEARNING OBJECTIVE: Use the dynamic aggregate demand and aggregate supply model to analyze monetary policy.

MyLab Economics Visit **www.pearson.com/mylab/economics** to complete these exercises online and get instant feedback.

Summary

We can use the *dynamic aggregate demand and aggregate supply model* introduced in Chapter 13 to look more closely at expansionary and contractionary monetary policies. The dynamic aggregate demand and aggregate supply model takes into account that (1) the economy experiences continuing inflation, with the price level rising every year, and (2) the economy experiences long-run growth, with the *LRAS* curve shifting to the right every year. In the dynamic model, an expansionary monetary policy tries to ensure that the aggregate demand curve will shift far enough to the right to bring about macroeconomic equilibrium with real GDP equal to potential GDP. A contractionary monetary policy attempts to offset movements in aggregate demand that would cause macroeconomic equilibrium to occur at a level of real GDP that is greater than potential GDP.

Review Questions

4.1 What are the key differences between how we illustrate an expansionary monetary policy in the basic aggregate demand and aggregate supply model and in the dynamic aggregate demand and aggregate supply model?

4.2 What are the key differences between how we illustrate a contractionary monetary policy in the basic aggregate demand and aggregate supply model and in the dynamic aggregate demand and aggregate supply model?

Problems and Applications

4.3 Explain whether you agree with this argument:

> If the Fed actually ever carried out a contractionary monetary policy, the price level would fall. Because the price level has not fallen in the United States over an entire year since the 1930s, we can conclude that the Fed has not carried out a contractionary policy since the 1930s.

4.4 **(Related to Solved Problem 15.4 on page 537)** Use the graph in the next column to answer the following questions.

a. If the Fed does not take any policy action, what will be the level of real GDP and the price level in 2021?

b. If the Fed wants to keep real GDP at its potential level in 2021, should it use an expansionary policy or a contractionary policy? Should the trading desk be buying Treasury bills or selling them?

c. If the Fed takes no policy action, what will be the inflation rate in 2021? If the Fed uses monetary policy to keep real GDP at its potential level, what will be the inflation rate in 2021?

4.5 **(Related to Solved Problem 15.4 on page 537)** The hypothetical information in the following table shows what the situation will be in 2021 if the Fed does *not* use monetary policy.

Year	Potential GDP	Real GDP	Price Level
2020	$18.0 trillion	$18.0 trillion	120.0
2021	18.4 trillion	18.3 trillion	122.0

a. If the Fed wants to keep real GDP at its potential level in 2021, should it use an expansionary policy or a contractionary policy? Should the trading desk be buying T-bills or selling them?

b. If the Fed's policy is successful in keeping real GDP at its potential level in 2021, state whether each of the following will be higher, lower, or the same as it would have been if the Fed had taken no action.

   i. Real GDP

   ii. Potential GDP

   iii. The inflation rate

   iv. The unemployment rate

c. Draw an aggregate demand and aggregate supply graph to illustrate the effects of the Fed's policy. Be sure that your graph contains *LRAS* curves for 2020 and 2021; *SRAS* curves for 2020 and 2021; *AD* curves for 2020 and 2021, with and without monetary policy action; and equilibrium real GDP and the price level in 2021, with and without policy.

4.6 An article on Reuters discussing a Reserve Bank of India (RBI) monetary policy meeting in early 2017, stated that the RBI "changed its stance to 'neutral' from 'accommodative,' saying it would monitor inflation." The article noted that "the decision to hold [the interest rate that is the RBI's equivalent of the federal funds rate constant] is a risk, as private forecasts are more pessimistic [about economic growth] than the RBI."

a. Draw a dynamic aggregate demand and aggregate supply graph to show where the RBI expected real GDP to be relative to potential GDP in 2017 if it kept the target interest unchanged. Assume, for simplicity, that real GDP in India in 2016 equaled potential GDP. Briefly explain what is happening in your graph.

b. In the same graph, show where the private forecasters who are more pessimistic about growth see the economy in 2017. Briefly explain what is happening in your graph.

Source: Suvashree Dey Choudhury and Rafael Nam, "Indian Central Bank Keeps Policy Rate on Hold, With Eyes on Inflation," reuters.com, February 8, 2017.

15.5 A Closer Look at the Fed's Setting of Monetary Policy Targets, pages 539–544

LEARNING OBJECTIVE: Describe the Fed's setting of monetary policy targets.

MyLab Economics Visit **www.pearson.com/mylab/economics** to complete these exercises online and get instant feedback.

Summary

Some economists have argued that the Fed should use the money supply, rather than an interest rate, as its monetary policy target. Milton Friedman and other monetarists argued that the Fed should adopt a monetary growth rule of increasing the money supply every year at a fixed rate. Support for this proposal declined after 1980 because the relationship between movements in the money supply and movements in real GDP and the price level weakened. John Taylor analyzed the factors involved in Fed decision making and developed the **Taylor rule** for federal funds targeting. The Taylor rule links the Fed's target for the federal funds rate to economic variables. Over the past decade, many economists and central bankers have expressed significant interest in using **inflation targeting**, under which monetary policy is conducted to commit the central bank to achieving a publicly announced inflation target. In 2012, the Fed joined a number of foreign central banks in adopting inflation targeting. The Fed's performance in the 1980s, 1990s, and early 2000s generally received high marks from economists.

Review Questions

5.1 What is a *monetary rule*, as opposed to a *monetary policy*? What monetary rule would Milton Friedman have liked the Fed to follow? Why has support for a monetary rule of the kind Friedman advocated declined since 1980?

5.2 For more than 20 years, the Fed has used the federal funds rate as its monetary policy target. Why doesn't the Fed target the money supply at the same time?

5.3 What is the Taylor rule? What is its purpose?

Problems and Applications

5.4 In an interview, Paul Volcker, chairman of the Federal Reserve's Board of Governors from 1979 to 1987, was asked about the Fed's use of monetary policy to reduce the rate of inflation. Volcker replied:

> The Federal Reserve had been attempting to deal with … inflation for some time…. By the time I became chairman … we adopted an approach of … saying, We'll take the emphasis off of interest rates and put the emphasis on the growth in the money supply, which is at the root cause of inflation … we will stop the money supply from increasing as rapidly as it was … and interest rates went up a lot…. We said … we'll take whatever consequences that means for the interest rate because that will enable us to get inflation under control.

Explain why the Fed, while Paul Volcker was chair, did not target both the growth of the money supply and interest rates.

Source: PBS, "Paul Volcker Interview," www.pbs.org.

5.5 (Related to Solved Problem 15.5 on page 541) Suppose that the equilibrium real federal funds rate is 2 percent and the target rate of inflation is 2 percent. Use the following information and the Taylor rule to calculate the federal funds rate target:

Current inflation rate = 4 percent

Potential GDP = 17.0 trillion

Real GDP = 17.17 trillion

5.6 (Related to Solved Problem 15.5 on page 541) In discussing the Taylor rule, John Taylor wrote, "I realize that there are differences of opinion about what is the best rule to guide policy and that some at the Fed (including Janet Yellen) now prefer a rule with a higher coefficient [on the output gap]."

a. If Fed policy were guided by a Taylor rule with a coefficient of 1, rather than 0.5, on the output gap, would the federal funds rate be higher or lower during a recession? Briefly explain.

b. Why might economists and policymakers disagree over the best rule to guide monetary policy?

Source: John Taylor, "Cross-Checking 'Checking in on the Taylor Rule,'" www.economicsone.com, July 16, 2013.

5.7 **(Related to Solved Problem 15.5 on page 541)** Two economists at the Federal Reserve Bank of Cleveland noted that "estimates of potential GDP are very fluid, [which] suggests there is considerable error in our current measure." They concluded that "this lack of precision should be recognized when policy recommendations are made using a Taylor-type rule." Briefly explain their reasoning.

Source: Charles Carlstrom and Timothy Stehulak, "Mutable Economic Laws and Calculating Unemployment and Output Gaps—An Application to Taylor Rules," Federal Reserve Bank of Cleveland, June 6, 2015.

5.8 **(Related to the Apply the Concept on page 543)** August 2017 was the sixty-fourth consecutive month that the rate of inflation as measured by the core personal consumption expenditures (PCE) price index was below the Federal Reserve's target of 2 percent.

a. Briefly explain why using the consumer price index (CPI) might yield a rate of inflation different from that found using the core PCE price index.

b. Explain how the choice of the price index the Federal Reserve uses to measure inflation can affect monetary policy.

5.9 **(Related to the Apply the Concept on page 543)** According to an article on cnbc.com, the Reserve Bank of India (RBI) was expected to lower its target interest rate at its early 2017 monetary policy meeting, but instead the RBI held its target constant. RBI Governor Urjit Patel "pointed to concerns that a 'fire sale' in perishable foods was distorting what could be a worrying outlook for inflation."

a. What is a "fire sale" in perishable foods, and why would it distort the outlook for inflation?

b. If the RBI ignored the fire sale in perishable foods, how might it be led to set the target interest rate at the wrong level?

Source: Leslie Shaffer, "Forget Demonetization. India's Central Bank Is Worried about Inflation,'" www.cnbc.com, February 8, 2017.

 # Fed Policies during the 2007–2009 Recession, pages 544–549

LEARNING OBJECTIVE: Describe the policies the Federal Reserve used during the 2007–2009 recession.

MyLab Economics   Visit www.pearson.com/mylab/economics to complete these exercises online and get instant feedback.

Summary

A housing bubble that began to deflate in 2006 helped cause the recession of 2007–2009 and an accompanying financial crisis. In response, the Federal Reserve instituted a variety of policy actions. In a series of steps, it cut the target for the federal funds rate from 5.25 percent in September 2007 to effectively zero in December 2008. The decline in the housing market caused wider problems in the financial system, as defaults on home mortgages rose and the value of mortgage-backed securities declined. The Fed and the U.S. Treasury Department implemented a series of new policies to provide liquidity and restore confidence. The Fed expanded the types of firms eligible for discount loans and began lending directly to corporations by purchasing commercial paper. Under the Troubled Asset Relief Program, the Treasury provided financial support to banks and other financial firms in exchange for part ownership. The Treasury also moved to have the federal government take control of Fannie Mae and Freddie Mac, government-sponsored firms that play a key role in the mortgage market. The failure of the investment bank Lehman Brothers in September 2008 led to a deepening of the financial crisis and provided the motivation for some of the new policies. Ultimately, the new policies stabilized the financial system, but their long-term effects remain the subject of debate.

Review Questions

6.1 What is a mortgage? What were the important developments in the mortgage market during the years after 1970?

6.2 Beginning in 2008, the Federal Reserve and the U.S. Treasury Department responded to the financial crisis by intervening in financial markets in unprecedented ways. Briefly summarize the actions of the Fed and the Treasury.

Problems and Applications

6.3 A newspaper article in the fall of 2007 stated, "The luxury-home builder Hovnanian Enterprises reported its fourth consecutive quarterly loss on Thursday, citing continuing problems of credit availability and high inventory." Why was Hovnanian suffering losses? What does the article mean by "credit availability"? How would problems of credit availability affect a homebuilder such as Hovnanian Enterprises?

Source: "New Loss for Home Builder," Associated Press, September 7, 2007.

6.4 An article in a Federal Reserve publication observed that "20 or 30 years ago, local financial institutions were the only option for some borrowers. Today, borrowers have access to national (and even international) sources of mortgage finance." What caused this change in the sources of mortgage finance? What would be the likely consequence of this change for the interest rates borrowers have to pay on mortgages? Briefly explain.

Source: Daniel J. McDonald and Daniel L. Thornton, "A Primer on the Mortgage Market and Mortgage Finance," *Federal Reserve Bank of St. Louis Review*, January/February 2008, pp. 31–45.

6.5 The Federal Reserve releases transcripts of its Federal Open Market Committee (FOMC) meetings only after a five-year lag in order to preserve the confidentiality of the discussions. In transcripts of the FOMC's 2008 meetings, one member of the Board of Governors was quoted as saying in the April meeting, "I think it is very possible that we will look back and say, particularly after the Bear Stearns episode, that we have turned the corner in terms of the financial disruption." Did this member's analysis turn out to be correct? Briefly explain why his prediction may have seemed reasonable at the time.

Source: Jon Hilsenrath, "New View into Fed's Response to Crisis," *Wall Street Journal*, February 21, 2014.

6.6 In late 2012, the U.S. Treasury sold the last of the stock it had purchased in the insurance company AIG. The Treasury earned a profit on the $22.7 billion it had invested in AIG in 2008. An article in *Wall Street Journal* noted, "This step in AIG's turnaround, which essentially closes the book on one of the most controversial bailouts of the financial crisis, seemed nearly unattainable in 2008, when the insurer's imminent collapse sent shockwaves through the global economy."
  a. Why did the federal government bail out AIG?
  b. Why was the government bailout controversial?
  c. Does the fact the federal government earned a profit on its investment in AIG mean that economists and policymakers who opposed the bailout were necessarily wrong? Briefly explain.

Source: Jeffrey Sparshott and Erik Holm, "End of a Bailout: U.S. Sells Last AIG Shares," *Wall Street Journal*, December 11, 2012.

6.7 Recall that *securitization* is the process of turning a loan, such as a mortgage, into a bond that can be bought and sold in secondary markets. An article in the *Economist* noted:

> That securitization caused more subprime mortgages to be written is not in doubt. By offering access to a much deeper pool of capital, securitization helped to bring down the cost of mortgages and made home-ownership more affordable for borrowers with poor credit histories.

What is a "subprime mortgage"? What is a "deeper pool of capital"? Why would securitization give mortgage borrowers access to a deeper pool of capital? Would a subprime borrower be likely to pay a higher or lower interest rate than a borrower with a better credit history? Under what circumstances might a lender prefer to loan money to a borrower with a poor credit history rather than to a borrower with a good credit history? Briefly explain.

Source: "Ruptured Credit," *Economist*, May 15, 2008.

6.8 Richard Fuld, the last CEO of Lehman Brothers, gave a talk in which, according to an article in the *Wall Street Journal*, "He outlined what he called the 'perfect storm' of events that led to the financial crisis, saying 'it all started with the government' and policies that subsidized cheap loans for people to buy homes in order to help them chase the American dream."
  a. Briefly outline the events that led to the financial crisis. Do you agree with Fuld that the events constituted a "perfect storm"—that is, a series of unfortunate events happening at the same time in a way that would have been difficult to anticipate?
  b. Which government policies mentioned in the chapter could be said to be subsidizing cheap loans? What does Fuld mean by saying that these policies were intended to help people "chase the American dream"?

Source: Maureen Farrell, "Lehman's Fuld Says It Wasn't His Fault," *Wall Street Journal*, May 28, 2015.

6.9 **(Related to the Apply the Concept on page 547)** Suppose you buy a house for $150,000. One year later, the market price of the house has risen to $165,000. What is the return on your investment in the house if you made a down payment of 20 percent and took out a mortgage loan for the other 80 percent? What if you made a down payment of 5 percent and borrowed the other 95 percent? Be sure to show your calculations in your answer.

Real-Time Data Exercises

D15.1 **(Following news of FOMC meetings)** Go to www.federalreserve.gov, the Web site for the Federal Reserve Board of Governors, and read the most recent Federal Open Market Committee (FOMC) press release. On the Web site, at the top of the screen, select "Monetary Policy," and then under "Recent Documents" select "FOMC Statement." Answer the following questions on the basis of the FOMC statement.
   a. Did the FOMC change the target for the federal funds rate? If so, what was the change?
   b. On balance, in its statement, does the FOMC appear to be more concerned about slow economic growth or high inflation?
   c. Did the Fed announce any other monetary policy actions, particularly regarding its holdings of agency mortgage-backed securities and Treasury securities, which it purchased through its quantitative easing programs?
   d. Scroll down to the last page, titled "Decisions Regarding Monetary Policy Implementation." Did the FOMC change the interest rate paid on bank reserves? Did it change the interest rate it offers on reverse repurchase agreements?

D15.2 **(Movements in the federal funds rate relative to the target)** Go to the Web site of the Federal Reserve Bank of St. Louis (FRED) (fred.stlouisfed.org) and download and graph the data series for the effective federal funds rate (DFF), the upper limit of the target range for the federal funds rate (DFEDTARU), and the lower limit for the target range (DFEDTARL). Plot on the same graph values for all three data series from December 16, 2008, to the most recent day available. Over this period, has the Fed been able to keep the effective federal funds rate within the target range? Briefly explain.

D15.3 **(Comparing different measures of the inflation rate)** Go to the Web site of the Federal Reserve Bank of St. Louis (FRED) (fred.stlouisfed.org) and find the most recent values and values from the same month one year before for the following three measures of the price level: (1) the consumer price index for all urban consumers: all items (CPIAUCSL), (2) the personal consumption expenditures: chain-type price index (PCEPI), and (3) the personal consumption expenditures excluding food and energy (chain-type price index) (DPCCRG3A086NBEA).
   a. Using these data, calculate the inflation rate over this year as measured by each of the three price indexes.
   b. Which of the three measures of inflation was highest during this year? Which measure was lowest? Why do the measures of inflation differ?

Critical Thinking Exercises

CT15.1 The Federal Open Market Committee (FOMC) holds eight regularly scheduled meetings during the year and also holds other meetings as needed. Policy statements and minutes of those meetings are posted on the Web site of the Federal Reserve's Board of Governors, at www.federalreserve.gov/monetarypolicy/fomccalendars.htm. Locate the most recent statement and read it carefully. Identify four macroeconomic policy terms from this statement that are covered in this chapter. In this statement, how does the Federal Reserve characterize the current state of the economy, and what policy actions is the Fed planning to take?

CT15.2 The number of jobs available in the U.S. economy is largely determined by the number of workers private firms choose to hire. The Federal Reserve is part of the federal government and hires relatively few people. Carefully explain how the Fed is able to affect the level of total employment in the economy. Be sure to include all relevant actions the Fed takes in affecting total employment.

CT15.3 On the Web site of the Federal Reserve Bank of Cleveland, at www.clevelandfed.org/en/our-research/indicators-and-data/credit-easing.aspx, you can find data on the balance sheet of Federal Reserve. Set the initial date to January 2007. Next, review the sections in this chapter that discuss quantitative easing and Fed policy during the 2007–2009 recession. Describe in what ways these actions are reflected in the chart on this Web page.

16 Fiscal Policy

Can Fiscal Policy Increase Economic Growth?

Vulcan Materials is a manufacturer of construction materials, with headquarters in Birmingham, Alabama. In the days after November 8, 2016, its stock price soared, indicating that investors expected that its profit would increase. What news caused this stock price increase? The unexpected election of Donald Trump as President. Trump had pledged to bring about increased spending on infrastructure projects, such as highways, bridges, dams, and airports: "We're going to rebuild our infrastructure … [and] we will put millions of our people to work as we rebuild it." Investors expected this spending to increase demand for Vulcan's products, such as asphalt and concrete, as well as the products of other firms in the construction industry.

President Trump's proposal is an example of *discretionary fiscal policy*, or changes in federal taxes and purchases that are intended to achieve macroeconomic policy goals. During the 2007–2009 recession, President George W. Bush and President Barack Obama received congressional approval for an increase in federal spending and tax cuts. These actions were intended to increase real GDP and employment by increasing aggregate demand. In 2017, as President Trump proposed increased spending on infrastructure, real GDP was already close to potential GDP, and the labor market appeared to be at or near full employment. President Trump's approach, which also included a proposal to significantly revise the federal tax code, was focused more on boosting the long-run rate of economic growth.

Between 1950 and 2016, real GDP grew at an average annual rate of 3.1 percent. But between 2007 and 2016, this growth rate had slowed dramatically to only 1.4 percent. In early 2017, the Congressional Budget Office forecast that real GDP growth from 2017–2027 would increase only to 1.9 percent, and most economic forecasters agreed that in the absence of new policies, the growth rate of real GDP was unlikely to return to 3 percent. Kevin Hassett, chairman of President Trump's Council of Economic Advisers, agreed: "I think it's absolutely possible to return to a place where

Jim West/Alamy Stock Photo

you get 3% growth if you design policies that encourage capital formation in the United States. . . . [But] if we don't change policy, we can expect to stay around 2%."

When the federal government spends more than it collects in taxes, the result is a federal budget deficit. Some economists and policymakers were concerned that President Trump's fiscal policy proposals had the potential to substantially increase the budget deficit. But the details of the proposals were still unclear in fall 2017, making it difficult to estimate their effect on the deficit.

In this chapter, we will examine discretionary fiscal policy, the federal budget deficit, and the debate over their effects.

Sources: Josh Zumbrun, "Potential Economic Adviser to Trump Offers Preview of His Approach," *Wall Street Journal*, June 6, 2017; Congressional Budget Office, *The Budget and Economic Outlook, 2017–2027*, January 2017; "Transcript: Donald Trump's Victory Speech," *New York Times*, November 9, 2016; and Chris Dieterich, "Potential Economic Adviser to Trump Offers Preview of His Approach," *Wall Street Journal*, November 9, 2016.

Chapter Outline & Learning Objectives

Economics in Your Life & Career

Should You Invest in Your Business for the Long Term?

Suppose that you and your business partner have purchased a small car dealership in a suburb of a large city. The economy has been slowly expanding, and your dealership is profitable, but you don't believe that your future sales will increase very much. Your partner is much more optimistic. She believes that if Congress enacts new spending and tax proprosals, the growth rate of real GDP will increase by 50 percent, incomes will rise, and your sales will increase much more than you are forecasting. She wants to buy land adjacent to your dealership and invest in expanding your business. How can you evaluate your partner's assertions? Will certain fiscal policy proposals be more likely than others to achieve the result your partner is expecting? As you read this chapter, try to answer these questions. You can check your answers against those we provide on **page 596** at the end of this chapter.

I n Chapter 15, we discussed how the Federal Reserve uses monetary policy to pursue policy goals, particularly price stability and high employment. In this chapter, we will explore how Congress and the president use *fiscal policy*, which involves changes in taxes and government purchases, to achieve macroeconomic policy goals. As we have seen, in the short run, the price level and the levels of real GDP and total employment in the economy depend on aggregate demand and short-run aggregate supply. In the long run, the levels of real GDP and employment depend on long-run aggregate supply. The government can affect the levels of both aggregate demand and aggregate supply through fiscal policy. We will discuss how Congress and the president decide which fiscal policy actions to take to achieve their goals. We will also discuss the debates among economists and policymakers over the effectiveness of fiscal policy.

16.1 What Is Fiscal Policy?

LEARNING OBJECTIVE: Define fiscal policy.

Since the end of World War II, the federal government has been committed under the Employment Act of 1946 to intervening in the economy "to promote maximum employment, production, and purchasing power." As we saw in Chapter 15, the Federal Reserve's Federal Open Market Committee meets eight times per year to decide whether to change monetary policy. Less frequently, Congress and the president also make changes in taxes and government purchases to achieve macroeconomic policy goals, such as high employment, price stability, and high rates of economic growth. Changes in federal taxes and purchases that are intended to achieve macroeconomic policy goals are called **fiscal policy**.

Fiscal policy Changes in federal taxes and purchases that are intended to achieve macroeconomic policy goals.

What Fiscal Policy Is and What It Isn't

In the United States, federal, state, and local governments all have responsibility for taxing and spending. Economists typically use the term *fiscal policy* to refer only to the actions of the federal government. State and local governments sometimes change their taxing and spending policies to aid their local economies, but these are not fiscal policy actions because they are not intended to affect the national economy. The federal government makes many decisions about taxes and spending, but not all of these decisions are fiscal policy actions because they are not intended to achieve macroeconomic policy goals. For example, a decision to cut the taxes of people who buy electric cars is an environmental policy action, not a fiscal policy action. Similarly, the spending increases to fund the war on terrorism and the wars in Iraq and Afghanistan were part of defense and homeland security policy, not fiscal policy. **MyLab Economics** Concept Check

Automatic Stabilizers versus Discretionary Fiscal Policy

There is an important distinction between *automatic stabilizers* and *discretionary fiscal policy*. Government spending and taxes that automatically increase or decrease along with the business cycle are called **automatic stabilizers**. The word *automatic* indicates that changes in these types of spending and taxes happen without actions by the government. For example, when the economy is expanding and employment is increasing, government spending on unemployment insurance payments to workers who have lost their jobs will automatically decrease. During a recession, as employment declines, this type of spending will automatically increase. Similarly, when the economy is expanding and incomes are rising, the amount the government collects in taxes will increase as people pay additional taxes on their higher incomes. When the economy is in a recession, the amount the government collects in taxes will fall.

Automatic stabilizers Government spending and taxes that automatically increase or decrease along with the business cycle.

With discretionary fiscal policy, the government takes actions to change spending or taxes. The tax cuts and spending increases the Trump administration proposed in 2017, as mentioned in the chapter opener, are examples of discretionary fiscal policy actions.

MyLab Economics Concept Check

An Overview of Government Spending and Taxes

To provide a context for discussing fiscal policy, it is important to understand the big picture of government taxing and spending. Remember that there is a difference between

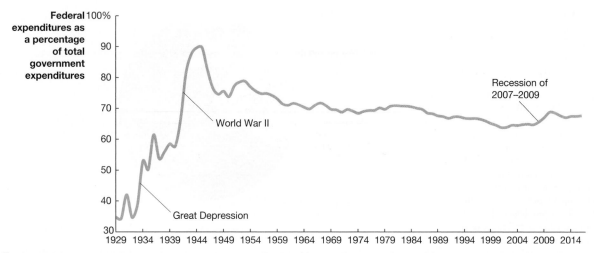

Figure 16.1 **The Federal Government's Share of Total Government Expenditures, 1929–2016**

Until the Great Depression of the 1930s, the majority of government spending in the United States occurred at the state and local levels. Since World War II, the federal government's share of total government expenditures has been between two-thirds and three-quarters.

Source: U.S. Bureau of Economic Analysis.

government *purchases* and government *expenditures*. When the federal government purchases an aircraft carrier or the services of an FBI agent, or when a local government hires a teacher, the government receives a good or service in return. Government expenditures include purchases plus government spending—such as Social Security payments by the federal government or pension payments to retired police officers by local governments—that does not involve purchases. Before the Great Depression of the 1930s, the majority of government spending in the United States took place at the state and local levels. As Figure 16.1 shows, the size of the federal government expanded significantly during the crisis of the Great Depression. Since World War II, the federal government's share of total government expenditures has been between two-thirds and three-quarters.

Economists often measure government spending relative to the size of the economy by calculating government spending as a percentage of GDP. As Figure 16.2

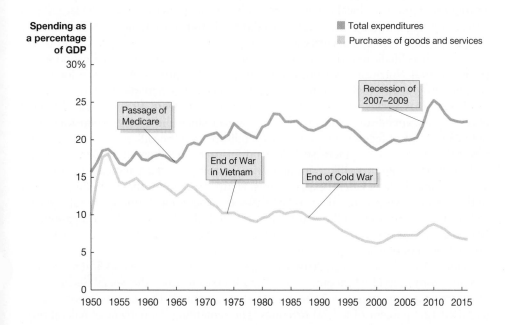

Figure 16.2

Federal Purchases and Federal Expenditures as a Percentage of GDP, 1950–2016

As a fraction of GDP, the federal government's *purchases* of goods and services have been declining since the Korean War in the early 1950s. Total *expenditures* by the federal government—including transfer payments—as a fraction of GDP slowly rose from 1950 through the early 1990s, fell from 1992 to 2001 before rising again. The recession of 2007–2009 and the slow recovery that followed led to a surge in non-defense federal expenditures. In 2011, total federal expenditures were at their highest level as a percentage of GDP since the end of World War II in 1945. In the following years, federal expenditures as a percentage of GDP declined again.

Source: U.S. Bureau of Economic Analysis.

MyLab Economics Real-time data

Figure 16.3

Federal Government Expenditures, 2016

Federal government *purchases* can be divided into two categories: defense spending—which makes up 17.6 percent of the federal budget—and spending on everything else the federal government does—from paying the salaries of FBI agents, to operating the national parks, to supporting scientific research—which makes up 8.6 percent of the budget. In addition to purchases, there are three other categories of federal government *expenditures*: interest on the national debt, grants to state and local governments, and transfer payments. Transfer payments rose from 25 percent of federal government expenditures in the 1960s to 49.2 percent in 2016.

Source: U.S. Bureau of Economic Analysis.

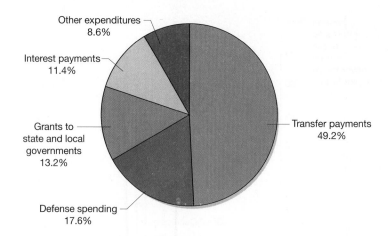

shows, federal government *purchases* as a percentage of GDP have actually been falling in most years since the end of the Korean War in the early 1950s. Total federal *expenditures* as a percentage of GDP rose from 1950 to the early 1990s and then fell from 1992 to 2000, before rising again. The decline in expenditures between 1992 and 2001 was partly the result of the end of the Cold War between the Soviet Union and the United States, which allowed for a substantial reduction in defense spending. Real federal government spending on national defense declined by almost 25 percent between 1990 and 1998 and then rose by more than 60 percent between 1998 and 2010 in response to the war on terrorism and the wars in Iraq and Afghanistan. Defense spending declined more than 20 percent between 2010 and 2017 as those wars wound down. The recession of 2007–2009 and the slow recovery that followed led to a surge in non-defense federal expenditures. In 2011, total federal expenditures were at their highest level as a percentage of GDP since the end of World War II in 1945. In the following years, federal expenditures as a percentage of GDP declined again as a result of limits on spending enacted by Congress and the president.

In addition to purchases, there are three other categories of federal government expenditures: *interest on the national debt, grants to state and local governments,* and *transfer payments.* Interest on the national debt represents payments to holders of the bonds the federal government has issued to borrow money. Grants to state and local governments are payments made by the federal government to support government activity at the state and local levels. For example, to help reduce crime, Congress implemented a program of grants to local governments to hire more police officers. The largest and fastest-growing category of federal expenditures is transfer payments. Some of these programs, such as Social Security and unemployment insurance, began in the 1930s. Others, such as Medicare, which finances health care for the elderly, and the food stamp (Supplemental Nutrition Assistance Program) and Temporary Assistance for Needy Families programs, which are intended to aid the poor, began in the 1960s or later.

Figure 16.3 shows that in 2016, transfer payments were 49.2 percent of federal government expenditures, having nearly doubled since the 1960s, when they were only 25 percent of federal government expenditures. As the U.S. population ages and medical costs continue to increase, federal government spending on the Social Security and Medicare programs will continue to rise, causing transfer payments to consume an increasing share of federal expenditures. Figure 16.3 shows that spending on most of the federal government's day-to-day activities—including running federal agencies such as the Environmental Protection Agency, the Federal Bureau of Investigation, the National Park Service, and the Immigration and Naturalization Service—makes up only 8.6 percent of federal government expenditures.

Figure 16.4 shows that in 2016, the federal government raised 44.3 percent of its revenue from individual income taxes. Payroll taxes to fund the Social Security and Medicare programs raised 35.2 percent of federal revenues. The tax on corporate profits raised 12.7 percent of federal revenues. The remaining 7.8 percent of federal revenues were raised from excise taxes on certain products, such as cigarettes and gasoline,

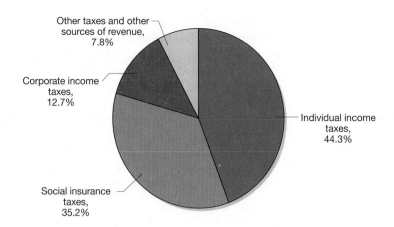

MyLab Economics Real-time data

Figure 16.4

Federal Government Revenue, 2016

In 2016, individual income taxes raised 44.3 percent of the federal government's revenues. Corporate income taxes raised 12.7 percent of revenue. Payroll taxes to fund the Social Security and Medicare programs raised 35.2 percent of revenue. The remaining 7.8 percent of revenues were raised from excise taxes, tariffs on imports, and other sources.

Source: U.S. Bureau of Economic Analysis.

from tariffs on goods imported from other countries, from payments by the Federal Reserve from its profits on its security holdings, and from other sources, such as payments by companies that cut timber on federal lands.   MyLab Economics Concept Check

MyLab Economics Study Plan

Apply the Concept   MyLab Economics Video

Is Spending on Social Security and Medicare a Fiscal Time Bomb?

The federal government's three largest transfer programs are Social Security, Medicare, and Medicaid. In 1935, Congress and President Franklin Roosevelt established the *Social Security* program to make payments to retired and disabled workers. In 1965, Congress and President Lyndon Johnson established the *Medicare* program to provide health care coverage to people age 65 and over, and the *Medicaid* program to help state governments provide medical care to low-income people. Congress faces challenges in funding these programs in the future.

The Social Security program began as a "pay-as-you-go" system, meaning that payments to current retirees were made with taxes collected from current workers. In the early years of the program, many workers were paying into the system, and there were relatively few retirees. For example, in 1940, more than 35 million workers were paying into the system, and only 222,000 people were receiving benefits—a ratio of more than 150 workers to each retiree. In those early years, most retirees received far more in benefits than they had paid in taxes. The first beneficiary was a legal secretary named Ida May Fuller. She worked for three years after the program began and paid total taxes of only $24.75. During her retirement, she collected $22,888.92 in benefits.

The Social Security and Medicare programs have been very successful in reducing poverty among older Americans, but in recent years, the ability of the federal government to finance current promises has been called into doubt. After World War II, the United States experienced a "baby boom," as birth rates rose and remained high through the early 1960s. The falling birth rate after 1965 have caused long-run problems for the Social Security system because the number of workers per retiree has continually declined. Currently, there are only 2.8 workers per retiree, and that ratio could decline to 2 workers per retiree by 2035. Congress has attempted to deal with this problem by gradually raising the age to receive full benefits from 65 to 67 and by increasing payroll taxes. Social Security and Medicare are financed from a payroll tax on individuals' wages and self-employment income. Workers and firms are each liable for half the tax. In 1940, the payroll tax rate was 2 percent; in 2017, it was 15.3 percent. Beginning in 2013, individuals earning more than $200,000 in either wages or self-employment income have paid two additional Medicare taxes: an additional 0.9 percent tax on their wages and an additional 3.8 percent tax on their investment income.

The long-term financial situation for Medicare is an even greater cause for concern than is Social Security. As Americans live longer and as new—and expensive—medical procedures are developed, the projected expenditures under the Medicare program will eventually far outstrip projected tax revenues. The federal government also faces increasing expenditures under the Medicaid program, which was substantially expanded when Congress passed the Patient Protection and Affordable Care Act (ACA) in 2010. In 2017, federal spending on Social Security, Medicare, and Medicaid equaled 10.4 percent of GDP. Spending on these three programs was less than 3 percent of GDP in 1962. The Congressional Budget Office (CBO) forecasts that federal spending on these three programs will rise to 14.9 percent of GDP in 2040, 16.2 percent by 2060, and 19.7 percent by 2090. The following graph illustrates these forecasts.

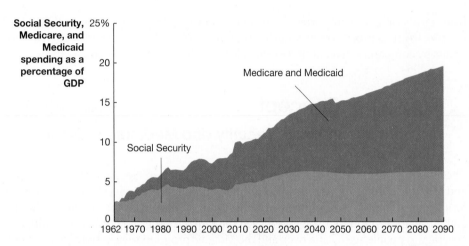

Note: The area labeled "Medicare and Medicaid" also includes federal spending on the Children's Health Insurance Program (CHIP) and federal subsidies to health care exchanges.

Over the past 40 years, the federal government has spent an average of about 21.5 percent of GDP on *all programs* combined—from buying aircraft carriers to paying the salaries of FBI agents to making Social Security and Medicare payments. So, if current trends continue, the federal government will eventually be spending, as a fraction of GDP, nearly as much on these three programs as it currently does on all programs combined.

The Board of Trustees of the Social Security Administration forecasts that through 2090, the gap between the benefits projected to be paid under the Social Security and Medicare programs and projected tax revenues is a staggering $11.4 *trillion* measured in present value terms (present value calculations are explained in the appendix to Chapter 6), or more than half the value of GDP in 2017. If current projections are accurate, policymakers are faced with the choice of significantly restraining spending on these programs, greatly increasing taxes on households and firms, or implementing some combination of spending restraints and tax increases. The alternatives are all unpleasant. A report from the CBO concluded that "even if taxation reached levels that were unprecedented in the United States, current spending policies could become financially unsustainable."

A lively political debate has taken place over the future of the Social Security and Medicare programs. Some policymakers have proposed increasing taxes to fund future benefit payments. The tax increases needed, however, could be as much as 50 percent higher than current rates, and tax increases of that magnitude could discourage work effort, entrepreneurship, and investment, thereby slowing economic growth. There have also been proposals to slow the rate of growth of future benefits, while guaranteeing benefits to current recipients. While this strategy would avoid the need to raise taxes significantly, it would also require younger workers to save more for their retirements. Some economists and policymakers have argued for slower benefit growth for higher-income workers while leaving future benefits unchanged for lower-income workers. In 2017, Congress was debating significant changes to the expansion of Medicaid authorized under ACA. Whatever changes are ultimately made in the Medicaid, Medicare, and Social Security programs, the outcome of this policy debate will have important effects on the futures of today's college students.

Sources: Congressional Budget Office, "Supplemental Data for CBO's 2017 Long-Term Budget Outlook," March 2017; Congressional Budget Office, "Baseline Projections of Mandatory Outlays," January 2017; Board of Trustees, Federal Old-Age and Survivors Insurance and Federal Disability Insurance Trust Funds, "The 2016 Annual Report of the Board of Trustees of the Federal Old-Age and Survivors Insurance and Disability Insurance Trust Funds," June 22, 2016; and the Social Security Administration Web site, www.ssa.gov.

Your Turn: Test your understanding by doing related problem 1.7 on page 597 at the end of this chapter.

MyLab Economics Study Plan

16.2 The Effects of Fiscal Policy on Real GDP and the Price Level

LEARNING OBJECTIVE: Explain how fiscal policy affects aggregate demand and how the government can use fiscal policy to stabilize the economy.

Monetary policy typically tries to offset the effects of the business cycle on output and employment and to achieve a low rate of inflation in the long run. Fiscal policy can also be aimed at offsetting the effects of the business cycle. But, as we saw in the chapter opener, fiscal policy also has the potential to affect the economy's long-run growth rate. The Federal Reserve carries out monetary policy through changes in interest rates and the money supply. Congress and the president carry out fiscal policy through changes in government purchases and taxes. Because these changes cause increases and decreases in aggregate demand, they can be used to affect short-run levels of real GDP, employment, and the price level. When the economy is in a recession, *increases* in government purchases or *decreases* in taxes will increase aggregate demand. As we saw in Chapter 13, the inflation rate may increase when real GDP is beyond potential GDP. Decreases in government purchases or increases in taxes can slow the growth of aggregate demand and reduce the inflation rate. These short-run policies are also called *countercyclical policies* because Congress and the president intend them to offset the effects of the business cycle.

Short-Run Expansionary and Contractionary Fiscal Policy

Expansionary fiscal policy involves increasing government purchases or decreasing taxes. An increase in government purchases will increase aggregate demand directly because government purchases are a component of aggregate demand. A cut in taxes has an indirect effect on aggregate demand. Remember that the income households have available to spend after they have paid their taxes is called *disposable income* (see Chapter 8, Section 8.4). Cutting the individual income tax will increase household disposable income and consumption spending. Cutting taxes on business income can increase aggregate demand by increasing investment spending.

Figure 16.5 shows the results of an expansionary fiscal policy, using the basic aggregate demand and aggregate supply model. In this model, there is no economic growth, so the long-run aggregate supply (*LRAS*) curve does not shift. Notice that this figure is very similar to Figure 16.7 on page 571, which shows the effects of an expansionary monetary policy. The goal of both expansionary monetary policy and expansionary fiscal policy is to increase aggregate demand relative to what it would have been without the policy.

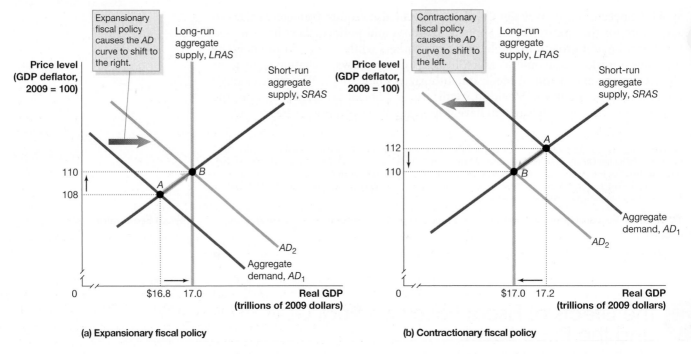

(a) Expansionary fiscal policy

(b) Contractionary fiscal policy

MyLab Economics Animation

Figure 16.5 **Fiscal Policy**

In panel (a), short-run equilibrium is at point A, with real GDP of $16.8 trillion and a price level of 108. Real GDP is below potential GDP, so the economy is in a recession. An expansionary fiscal policy will cause aggregate demand to shift to the right, from AD_1 to AD_2, increasing real GDP from $16.8 trillion to $17.0 trillion and the price level from 108 to 110 (point B).

In panel (b), short-run equilibrium is at point A, with real GDP at $17.2 trillion and the price level at 112. Because real GDP is greater than potential GDP, the economy will experience rising wages and prices. A contractionary fiscal policy will cause aggregate demand to shift to the left, from AD_1 to AD_2, decreasing real GDP from $17.2 trillion to $17.0 trillion and the price level from 112 to 110 (point B).

In panel (a) of Figure 16.5, short-run equilibrium occurs at point A, where the aggregate demand (AD_1) curve intersects the short-run aggregate supply (SRAS) curve. Real GDP is below potential GDP, so the economy is in a recession, with some firms operating below normal capacity and some workers having been laid off. To bring real GDP back to potential GDP, Congress and the president increase government purchases or cut taxes, which will shift the aggregate demand curve to the right, from AD_1 to AD_2. Real GDP increases from $16.8 trillion to potential GDP of $17.0 trillion, and the price level rises from 108 to 110 (point B). The policy has successfully returned real GDP to its potential level. Rising production will lead to increasing employment, reducing the unemployment rate.

Contractionary fiscal policy involves decreasing government purchases or increasing taxes. Policymakers use contractionary fiscal policy to reduce increases in aggregate demand that seem likely to lead to inflation. In panel (b) of Figure 16.5, short-run equilibrium occurs at point A, with real GDP of $17.2 trillion, which is above potential GDP of $17.0 trillion. With some firms producing beyond their normal capacity and the unemployment rate very low, wages and prices will be increasing. To bring real GDP back to potential GDP, Congress and the president decrease government purchases or increase taxes, which will shift the aggregate demand curve to the left, from AD_1 to AD_2. Real GDP falls from $17.2 trillion to $17.0 trillion, and the price level falls from 112 to 110 (point B).

We can conclude that Congress and the president can attempt to stabilize the economy by using fiscal policy to affect the price level and the level of real GDP. Of course, in practice it is extremely difficult for Congress and the president to use fiscal policy to eliminate the effects of the business cycle and keep real GDP always equal to potential GDP. MyLab Economics Concept Check

Don't Let This Happen to You

Don't Confuse Fiscal Policy and Monetary Policy

If you keep in mind the definitions of *money, income,* and *spending,* the difference between monetary policy and fiscal policy will be clearer. Students often make these two related mistakes: (1) They think of monetary policy as the Federal Reserve fighting recessions by increasing the money supply so people will have more money to spend; and (2) they think of fiscal policy as Congress and the president fighting recessions by spending more money. In this view, the only difference between fiscal policy and monetary policy is the source of the money.

To understand what's wrong with the descriptions of fiscal policy and monetary policy just given, first remember that the problem during a recession is not that there is too little *money*—currency plus checking account deposits—but too little *spending.* There may be too little spending for a number of reasons. For example, households may cut back on their spending on cars and houses because they are pessimistic about the future. Firms may reduce their spending because they have lowered their estimates of the future profitability of new machinery and factories. Or major trading partners of the United States—such as Japan and Canada—may be suffering from recessions, which cause households

and firms in those countries to reduce their spending on U.S. products.

The purpose of expansionary monetary policy is to lower interest rates, which in turn increases aggregate demand. When interest rates fall, households and firms are willing to borrow more to buy cars, houses, and factories. The purpose of expansionary fiscal policy is to increase aggregate demand by:

1. Having the government directly increase its own purchases, or
2. Cutting income taxes to increase household disposable income and, therefore, consumption spending, or
3. Cutting business taxes to increase investment spending

Just as increasing or decreasing the money supply does not have a direct effect on government spending or taxes, increasing or decreasing government spending or taxes does not have a direct effect on the money supply. Fiscal policy and monetary policy have the same goals, but they attempt to reach those goals in different ways.

MyLab Economics Study Plan

Your Turn: Test your understanding by doing related problem 2.7 on page 598 at the end of this chapter.

A Summary of How Fiscal Policy Affects Aggregate Demand

Table 16.1 summarizes how countercyclical fiscal policy affects aggregate demand. Just as we did with monetary policy, we must add a very important qualification to this summary of fiscal policy: The table isolates the effect of fiscal policy *by holding constant monetary policy and all other factors affecting the variables involved.* In other words, we are again invoking the *ceteris paribus* condition we discussed in Chapter 3, Section 3.1. This point is important because, for example, in the actual economy, a contractionary fiscal policy does not cause the price level to fall. A contractionary fiscal policy causes the price level *to rise by less than it would have risen without the policy.*   **MyLab Economics** Concept Check

MyLab Economics Study Plan

Table 16.1

Countercyclical Fiscal Policy

Problem	Type of Policy Required	Actions by Congress and the President	Result
Recession	Expansionary	Increase government purchases or cut taxes	Real GDP and the price level rise.
Rising inflation	Contractionary	Decrease government purchases or raise taxes	Real GDP and the price level fall.

16.3 Fiscal Policy in the Dynamic Aggregate Demand and Aggregate Supply Model*

LEARNING OBJECTIVE: Use the dynamic aggregate demand and aggregate supply model to analyze fiscal policy.

The overview of fiscal policy we just finished contains a key idea: Congress and the president can use fiscal policy to affect aggregate demand, thereby changing the price level and the level of real GDP. The discussion of expansionary and contractionary fiscal policy illustrated by Figure 16.5 on page 568 is simplified, however, because it ignores two important facts about the economy: (1) The economy experiences continuing inflation, with the price level rising every year; and (2) the economy experiences long-run growth, with the *LRAS* curve shifting to the right every year. In Chapter 13, Section 13.4, we developed a *dynamic aggregate demand and aggregate supply model* that took these two facts into account. In this section, we use the dynamic aggregate demand and aggregate supply model to gain a more complete understanding of fiscal policy.

To briefly review the dynamic model, recall that over time, potential GDP increases, which we show by shifting the *LRAS* curve to the right. The factors that cause the *LRAS* curve to shift also cause firms to supply more goods and services at any given price level in the short run, which we show by shifting the *SRAS* curve to the right. Finally, during most years, the aggregate demand curve also shifts to the right, indicating that aggregate expenditure is higher at every price level.

Figure 16.6 shows the results of an expansionary fiscal policy using the dynamic aggregate demand and aggregate supply model. Notice that this figure is very similar to Figure 16.9 on page 573, which showed the effects of an expansionary monetary policy. The goal of both expansionary monetary policy and expansionary fiscal policy is to increase aggregate demand relative to what it would have been without the policy.

In the hypothetical situation shown in Figure 16.6, equilibrium is initially at point *A*, with real GDP equal to potential GDP of $17.0 trillion and the price level equal to 110. In the second year, *LRAS* increases to $17.4 trillion, but aggregate demand increases only from AD_1 to $AD_{2(\text{without policy})}$, which is not enough to keep real GDP equal to potential GDP. Let's assume that the Fed does not react to the situation with an expansionary monetary policy. In that case, short-run equilibrium will occur at point *B*, with real

MyLab Economics Animation

Figure 16.6

An Expansionary Fiscal Policy in the Dynamic Model

Equilibrium is initially at point *A*, with real GDP equal to potential GDP of $17.0 trillion and the price level equal to 110. Without an expansionary policy, aggregate demand will shift from AD_1 to $AD_{2(\text{without policy})}$, which is not enough to keep real GDP equal to potential GDP because long-run aggregate supply has shifted from $LRAS_1$ to $LRAS_2$. The new short-run equilibrium is at point *B*, with real GDP of $17.3 trillion and a price level of 113. Increasing government purchases or cutting taxes will shift aggregate demand to $AD_{2(\text{with policy})}$. Equilibrium will be at point *C*, with real GDP of $17.4 trillion, which is its potential level, and a price level of 115. The price level is higher than it would have been without an expansionary fiscal policy.

* This section may be omitted without loss of continuity.

MyLab Economics Animation

Figure 16.7

A Contractionary Fiscal Policy in the Dynamic Model

Equilibrium is initially at point *A*, with real GDP equal to potential GDP of $17.0 trillion and the price level equal to 110. Without a contractionary policy, aggregate demand will shift from AD_1 to $AD_{2(\text{without policy})}$, which results in a short-run equilibrium at point *B*, with real GDP of $17.5 trillion, which is greater than potential GDP, and a price level of 115. Decreasing government purchases or increasing taxes can shift aggregate demand to $AD_{2(\text{with policy})}$. Equilibrium will be at point *C*, with real GDP of $17.4 trillion, which is its potential level, and a price level of 113. The inflation rate will be 2.7 percent, as opposed to the 4.5 percent it would have been without the contractionary fiscal policy.

GDP of $17.3 trillion and a price level of 113. The $100 billion gap between real GDP and potential GDP means that some firms are operating at less than their full capacity. Incomes and profits will be falling, firms will begin to lay off workers, and the unemployment rate will increase.

Increasing government purchases or cutting taxes can shift aggregate demand to $AD_{2(\text{with policy})}$. Equilibrium will be at point *C*, with real GDP of $17.4 trillion, which is its potential level, and a price level of 115. The price level is higher than it would have been without an expansionary fiscal policy.

Contractionary fiscal policy involves decreasing government purchases or increasing taxes. Policymakers use contractionary fiscal policy to reduce increases in aggregate demand that seem likely to lead to inflation. In Figure 16.7, equilibrium is initially at point *A*, with real GDP equal to potential GDP of $17.0 trillion and the price level equal to 110. Once again, *LRAS* increases to $17.4 trillion in the second year. In this scenario, the shift in aggregate demand to $AD_{2(\text{without policy})}$ results in a short-run macroeconomic equilibrium at point *B*, with real GDP of $17.5 trillion, which is greater than potential GDP. If we assume that the Fed does not respond to the situation with a contractionary monetary policy, the economy will experience a rising inflation rate. Decreasing government purchases or increasing taxes can keep real GDP from moving beyond its potential level. The result, shown in Figure 16.7, is that in the new equilibrium at point *C*, the inflation rate, measured by the percentage change in the price level, is 2.7 percent rather than 4.5 percent.   **MyLab Economics** Concept Check

MyLab Economics Study Plan

16.4 The Government Purchases and Tax Multipliers

LEARNING OBJECTIVE: Explain how the government purchases and tax multipliers work.

In response to the recession of 2007–2009, Congress and President Obama attempted to increase aggregate demand by enacting the American Recovery and Reinvestment Act (ARRA) of 2009, which authorized a $500 billion increase in federal spending. The spending fell into several categories, including spending on infrastructure projects such as rebuilding the Doyle Drive approach to the Golden Gate Bridge in San Francisco. Suppose that Congress and the president decide to spend $100 billion on rebuilding Doyle Drive and similar projects. Focusing just on the short-run effect of this increase on aggregate demand, how much will equilibrium real GDP increase as a

MyLab Economics Animation

Figure 16.8

The Multiplier Effect and Aggregate Demand

An initial increase in government purchases of $100 billion causes the aggregate demand curve to shift to the right, from AD_1 to the dashed AD curve, and represents the effect of the initial increase of $100 billion in government purchases. Because this initial increase raises incomes and leads to further increases in consumption spending, the aggregate demand curve will ultimately shift further to the right, to AD_2.

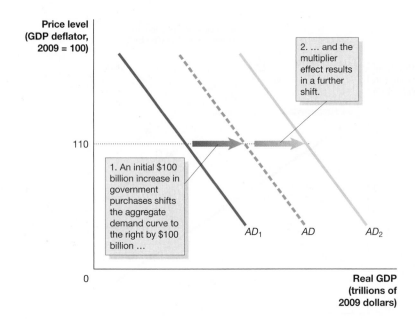

Multiplier effect The series of induced increases in consumption spending that results from an initial increase in autonomous expenditures.

result of this increase in government purchases? We might expect real GDP to increase by more than $100 billion because the initial increase in aggregate demand should lead to additional increases in income and spending. For example, to reconstruct Doyle Drive, the California Department of Transportation hired Kiewit, a private construction firm. Kiewit and its subcontractors, in turn, hired workers for the project. Workers who were formerly unemployed are likely to increase their spending on cars, furniture, appliances, and other products. Sellers of these products will increase their production and hire more workers, and so on. At each step, real GDP and income will rise, thereby increasing consumption spending and aggregate demand.

Economists refer to the initial increase in government purchases as *autonomous* because it is a result of a decision by the government and is not directly caused by changes in the level of real GDP. The increases in consumption spending that result from the initial autonomous increase in government purchases are *induced* because they are caused by the initial increase in autonomous spending. Economists call the series of induced increases in consumption spending that results from an initial increase in autonomous expenditures the **multiplier effect**.

Figure 16.8 illustrates how an increase in government purchases affects the aggregate demand curve. The initial increase causes the aggregate demand curve to shift to the right because total spending in the economy is now higher at every price level. The shift to the right from AD_1 to the dashed AD curve represents the effect of the initial increase of $100 billion in government purchases. Because this initial increase in government purchases raises incomes and leads to further increases in consumption spending, the aggregate demand curve will ultimately shift from AD_1 all the way to AD_2.

To better understand the multiplier effect, let's start with a simplified analysis in which we assume that the price level is constant. In other words, initially we will ignore the effect of an upward-sloping *SRAS* curve. Figure 16.9 shows how spending and real GDP increase over a number of periods, beginning with the initial increase in government purchases in the first period, which raises real GDP and total income in the economy by $100 billion. How much additional consumption spending will result from $100 billion in additional income? We know that while increasing their consumption spending on domestically produced goods, households will also save some of the increase in income, use some to pay income taxes, and use some to purchase imported goods, which will have no direct effect on spending and production in the U.S. economy. In Figure 16.9, we assume that in the second period, households increase their consumption spending by half the increase in income from the first period—or by $50 billion. This consumption spending in the second period will, in turn, increase real GDP and income by an additional $50 billion. In the third period, consumption

Period	Additional Spending This Period	Cumulative Increase in Spending and Real GDP
1	$100 billion in government purchases	$100 billion
2	$50 billion in consumption spending	$150 billion
3	$25 billion in consumption spending	$175 billion
4	$12.5 billion in consumption spending	$187.5 billion
⋮	⋮	⋮
n	0	$200 billion

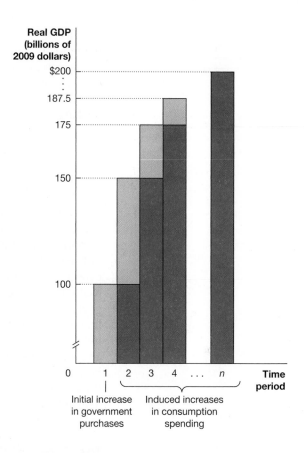

MyLab Economics Animation

Figure 16.9   **The Multiplier Effect of an Increase in Government Purchases**

Following an initial increase in government purchases, spending and real GDP increase over a number of periods due to the multiplier effect. The new spending and increased real GDP in each period is shown in orange, and the level of spending from the previous period is shown in blue. The sum of the blue and orange areas represents the cumulative increase in spending and real GDP. In total, equilibrium real GDP will increase by $200 billion as a result of an initial increase of $100 billion in government purchases.

spending will increase by $25 billion, or half the $50 billion increase in income from the second period.

The multiplier effect will continue through a number of periods, with the additional consumption spending in each period being half of the income increase from the previous period. Eventually, the process will be complete, although we cannot say precisely how many periods it will take, so we simply label the final period n rather than give it a specific number. In Figure 16.9, the new spending and increased real GDP in each period is shown in orange, and the level of spending from the previous period is shown in blue. The sum of the blue and orange areas represents the cumulative increase in spending and real GDP.

How large will the total increase in equilibrium real GDP be as a result of the initial increase of $100 billion in government purchases? The ratio of the change in equilibrium real GDP to the initial change in government purchases is called the *government purchases multiplier*:

$$\text{Government purchases multiplier} = \frac{\text{Change in equilibrium real GDP}}{\text{Change in government purchases}}.$$

If, for example, the government purchases multiplier has a value of 2, an increase in government purchases of $100 billion should increase equilibrium real GDP by $2 \times \$100\,\text{billion} = \$200\,\text{billion}$. We show this result in Figure 16.9 by having the cumulative increase in real GDP equal $200 billion.

Tax cuts also have a multiplier effect because they increase the disposable income of households. When household disposable income rises, so will consumption spending. These increases in consumption spending will set off further increases in real GDP and income, just as increases in government purchases do. Suppose we consider a change in taxes of a specific amount—say, a tax cut of $100 billion—with the tax *rate* remaining unchanged. The expression for this tax multiplier is:

$$\text{Tax multiplier} = \frac{\text{Change in equilibrium real GDP}}{\text{Change in taxes}}.$$

The tax multiplier is a negative number because changes in taxes and changes in real GDP move in opposite directions: An increase in taxes reduces disposable income, consumption, and real GDP, and a decrease in taxes raises disposable income, consumption, and real GDP. For example, if the tax multiplier is −1.6, a $100 billion *cut* in taxes will increase real GDP by −1.6 × (−$100 billion) = $160 billion. We would expect the tax multiplier to be smaller in absolute value than the government purchases multiplier. To see why, think about the difference between a $100 billion increase in government purchases and a $100 billion decrease in taxes. The whole of the $100 billion in government purchases results in an increase in aggregate demand. But households will save rather than spend some portion of a $100 billion decrease in taxes, and they will spend some portion on imported goods. The fraction of the tax cut that households save or spend on imports will not increase aggregate demand. Therefore, the first period of the multiplier process will involve a smaller increase in aggregate demand than occurs when there is an increase in government purchases, and the total increase in equilibrium real GDP will be smaller.

The Effect of Changes in the Tax Rate

A change in the tax *rate* has a more complicated effect on equilibrium real GDP than does a tax cut of a fixed amount. To begin with, the value of the tax rate affects the size of the multiplier effect. The higher the tax rate, the smaller the multiplier effect. To see why, think about the size of the additional spending increases that take place in each period following an increase in government purchases. The higher the tax rate, the smaller the amount of any increase in income that households have available to spend, which reduces the size of the multiplier effect. So, a cut in the tax rate affects equilibrium real GDP through two channels: (1) A cut in the tax rate increases the disposable income of households, which leads them to increase their consumption spending, and (2) a cut in the tax rate increases the size of the multiplier effect.   **MyLab Economics** Concept Check

Taking into Account the Effects of Aggregate Supply

To this point, as we discussed the multiplier effect, we assumed that the price level was constant. We know, though, that because the *SRAS* curve is upward sloping, when the *AD* curve shifts to the right, the price level will rise. As a result of the rise in the price level, equilibrium real GDP will not increase by the full amount that the multiplier effect indicates. Figure 16.10 illustrates how an upward-sloping *SRAS* curve affects the size of the multiplier. To keep the graph relatively simple, we assume that the *SRAS* and *LRAS* curves do not shift. Short-run equilibrium is initially at point *A*, with real GDP below its potential level. An increase in government purchases shifts the aggregate demand curve from AD_1 to the dashed *AD* curve. Just as in Figure 16.8, the multiplier effect causes a further shift in the aggregate demand curve, to AD_2. If the price level remained constant, real GDP would increase from $16.8 trillion at point *A* to $17.2 trillion at point *B*. However, because the *SRAS* curve is upward sloping, the price level rises from 110 to 113, reducing the total quantity of goods and services demanded in the economy. The new equilibrium occurs at point *C*, with real GDP having risen to $17.0 trillion, or by $200 billion less than if the price level had remained unchanged. We can conclude that the actual change in real GDP resulting from an increase in government purchases or a cut in taxes will be less than that indicated by the simple multiplier effect with a constant price level.   **MyLab Economics** Concept Check

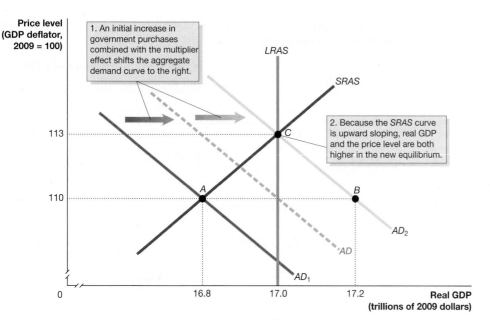

MyLab Economics Animation

Figure 16.10

The Multiplier Effect and Aggregate Supply

Short-run equilibrium is initially at point A. An increase in government purchases causes the aggregate demand curve to shift to the right, from AD_1 to the dashed AD curve. The multiplier effect results in the aggregate demand curve shifting further to the right, to AD_2 (point B). Because of the upward-sloping supply curve, the shift in aggregate demand results in a higher price level. In the new equilibrium at point C, both real GDP and the price level have increased. The increase in real GDP is less than that indicated by the multiplier effect with a constant price level.

The Multipliers Work in Both Directions

Increases in government purchases and cuts in taxes have a positive multiplier effect on equilibrium real GDP. Decreases in government purchases and increases in taxes also have a multiplier effect on equilibrium real GDP, but in this case, the effect is negative. An increase in taxes will reduce household disposable income and consumption. As households buy fewer cars, furniture, refrigerators, and other goods, the firms that sell these goods will cut back their production and begin laying off workers. Falling incomes will lead to further reductions in consumption. A reduction in government spending on defense would set off a similar process of decreases in real GDP and income. The reduction would affect defense contractors first because they sell directly to the government, and then it would spread to other firms.

We look more closely at the government purchases multiplier and the tax multiplier in the appendix to this chapter. **MyLab Economics** Concept Check

MyLab Economics Study Plan

Solved Problem 16.4

MyLab Economics Interactive Animation

Fiscal Policy Multipliers

Briefly explain whether you agree with the following statement: "Real GDP is currently $17.2 trillion, and potential GDP is $17.4 trillion. If Congress and the president would increase government purchases by $200 billion or cut taxes by $200 billion, the economy could be brought to equilibrium at potential GDP."

Solving the Problem

Step 1: **Review the chapter material.** This problem is about the multiplier process, so you may want to review the section "The Government Purchases and Tax Multipliers," which begins on page 571.

Step 2: **Explain how the necessary increase in purchases or cut in taxes is less than $200 billion because of the multiplier effect.** The statement is incorrect because it does not consider the multiplier effect. Because of the multiplier effect, an increase in government purchases or a decrease in taxes of less than $200 billion is necessary to increase equilibrium real GDP by $200 billion. For instance, assume that the government purchases multiplier is 2 and the tax multiplier is −1.6. We can then calculate the necessary increase in government purchases as follows:

$$\text{Government purchases multiplier} = \frac{\text{Change in equilibrium real GDP}}{\text{Change in government purchases}}$$

$$2 = \frac{\$200 \text{ billion}}{\text{Change in government purchases}}$$

$$\text{Change in government purchases} = \frac{\$200 \text{ billion}}{2} = \$100 \text{ billion}.$$

And we can calculate the necessary change in taxes:

$$\text{Tax multiplier} = \frac{\text{Change in equilibrium real GDP}}{\text{Change in taxes}}$$

$$-1.6 = \frac{\$200 \text{ billion}}{\text{Change in taxes}}$$

$$\text{Change in taxes} = \frac{\$200 \text{ billion}}{-1.6} = -\$125 \text{ billion}.$$

MyLab Economics Study Plan   **Your Turn:** For more practice, do related problems 4.6 and 4.7 on page 600 at the end of this chapter.

 ## The Limits to Using Fiscal Policy to Stabilize the Economy

LEARNING OBJECTIVE: Discuss the difficulties that can arise in implementing fiscal policy.

Poorly timed fiscal policy, like poorly timed monetary policy, can do more harm than good. As we discussed in Chapter 15, Section 15.3, it takes time for policymakers to collect statistics and identify changes in the economy. If the government decides to increase spending or cut taxes to fight a recession that is about to end, the effect may be to increase the inflation rate. Similarly, cutting spending or raising taxes to slow down an economy that has actually already moved into a recession can increase the length and depth of the recession.

Getting the timing right can be more difficult with fiscal policy than with monetary policy for two main reasons. Control over monetary policy is concentrated in the hands of the Federal Open Market Committee, which can change monetary policy at any of its meetings. By contrast, the president and a majority of the 535 members of Congress have to agree on changes in fiscal policy. The delays caused by the legislative process can be very long. For example, in 1962, President John F. Kennedy concluded that the U.S. economy was operating below potential GDP and proposed a tax cut to stimulate aggregate demand. Congress eventually agreed to the tax cut—but not until 1964. The events of 2001 and 2009 show, though, that it is sometimes possible to authorize changes in fiscal policy relatively quickly. When George W. Bush came into office in January 2001, the economy was on the verge of a recession, and he immediately proposed a tax cut. Congress passed the tax cut, and the president signed it into law in early June 2001. Similarly, Barack Obama proposed a stimulus package as soon as he came into office in January 2009, and Congress passed the proposal by February.

Even after a change in fiscal policy has been approved, it takes time to implement. Suppose Congress and the president agree to increase aggregate demand by spending $30 billion more on constructing subway systems in several cities. It will probably take at least several months to prepare detailed plans for the construction. Local governments will then ask for bids from private construction companies. Once the winning bidders have been selected, they will usually need several months to begin the project. Only then will significant amounts of spending actually take place. This delay may push the spending beyond the end of the recession that the spending was intended to fight. Delays of this type are less of a concern during long and severe recessions, such as that of 2007–2009.

Apply the Concept

MyLab Economics Video

Why Was the Recession of 2007–2009 So Severe?

Even some economists who are normally skeptical of the effectiveness of fiscal policy believed that the severity of the 2007–2009 recession required Congress and the president to increase spending and cut taxes to increase aggregate demand. As we saw in Chapters 14 and 15, the recession was accompanied by a financial crisis. The U.S. economy had not experienced a significant financial crisis since the Great Depression of the 1930s. Both the Great Depression and the recession of 2007–2009 were severe. Do recessions accompanied by financial crises tend to be more severe than recessions that do not involve financial crises?

In an attempt to answer this question, Carmen Reinhart and Kenneth Rogoff of Harvard University gathered data on recessions and financial crises in a number of countries. The first table below shows the average change in key economic variables during the period following a financial crisis for a number of countries, including the United States during the Great Depression and European and Asian countries in the post–World War II era. The table shows that for these countries, on average, the recessions following financial crises were quite severe:

- Unemployment rates increased by 7 percentage points—for example, from 5 percent to 12 percent—and continued increasing for nearly five years after a crisis had begun.
- Real GDP per capita also declined sharply, and the average length of a recession following a financial crisis has been nearly two years.
- Adjusted for inflation, stock prices declined by more than half, and housing prices declined by more than one-third.
- Government debt soared by 86 percent. The increased government debt was partly the result of increased government spending, including spending to bail out failed financial institutions. But most of the increased debt was due to government budget deficits resulting from sharp declines in tax revenues as wages and profits fell during the recession. (We discuss government budget deficits and government debt in Section 16.6.)

Economic Variable	Average Change	Average Duration of Change	Number of Countries
Unemployment rate	+7 percentage points	4.8 years	14
Real GDP per capita	−9.3%	1.9 years	14
Real stock prices	−55.9%	3.4 years	22
Real house prices	−35.5%	6 years	21
Real government debt	+86%	3 years	13

The following table shows some key indicators for the 2007–2009 U.S. recession compared with other U.S. recessions of the post–World War II period.

	Duration	Decline in Real GDP	Peak Unemployment Rate
Average for postwar recessions	10.4 months	−1.7%	7.6%
Recession of 2007–2009	18 months	−4.2%	10.0%

Consistent with Reinhart and Rogoff's findings that recessions following financial crises tend to be unusually severe, the 2007–2009 recession was the worst in the United States since the Great Depression of the 1930s. The recession lasted nearly twice as long as the average of earlier postwar recessions, GDP declined by more than twice the average, and the peak unemployment rate was about one-third higher than the average.

While some economists argue that better monetary or fiscal policies might have shortened the recession and made it less severe, most economists agree that the financial crisis plays a key role in explaining the severity of the 2007–2009 recession.

Note: In the second table, the duration of recessions is based on National Bureau of Economic Research business cycle dates, the decline in real GDP is measured as the simple percentage change from the quarter of the cyclical peak to the quarter of the cyclical trough, and the peak unemployment rate is the highest unemployment rate in any month following the cyclical peak.

Sources: The first table is adapted from data in Carmen M. Reinhart and Kenneth S. Rogoff, *This Time Is Different: Eight Centuries of Financial Folly*, Princeton, NJ: Princeton University Press, 2009, Figures 14.1–14.5; and the second table uses data from the U.S. Bureau of Economic Analysis and National Bureau of Economic Research.

MyLab Economics Study Plan

Your Turn: Test your understanding by doing related problem 5.6 on page 601 at the end of this chapter.

Does Government Spending Reduce Private Spending?

Even if Congress and the president correctly time fiscal policy, they may face another problem. We have been assuming that when the federal government increases its purchases by $30 billion, the multiplier effect will cause the increase in aggregate demand to be greater than $30 billion. However, the size of the multiplier effect may be limited if the increase in government purchases causes one of the nongovernment, or private, components of aggregate expenditures—consumption, investment, or net exports— to fall. A decline in private expenditures as a result of an increase in government purchases is called **crowding out**.   MyLab Economics Concept Check

Crowding out A decline in private expenditures as a result of an increase in government purchases.

Crowding Out in the Short Run

Consider the case of a temporary increase in government purchases. Suppose the federal government decides to fight a recession by spending $30 billion more this year on repairs to the Interstate Highway System. When the $30 billion has been spent, the program will end, and government purchases will drop back to their previous level. As the spending takes place, income and real GDP will increase. These increases in income and real GDP will cause households and firms to increase their demand for currency and checking account balances to accommodate the increased buying and selling. Figure 16.11 shows the result, using the money market graph introduced in Chapter 15, Section 15.2.

At higher levels of real GDP and income, households and firms demand more money at every interest rate. When the demand for money increases, the equilibrium interest rate will rise. Higher interest rates will result in a decline in each component of private expenditures. Consumption spending and investment spending will decline because households will borrow less to buy houses, cars, furniture, and appliances, and firms will borrow less to buy factories, warehouses, and machine tools. Net exports will also decline because higher interest rates in the United States will attract foreign investors. German, Japanese, and Canadian investors will want to exchange the currencies of their countries for U.S. dollars to invest in U.S. Treasury bills and other U.S. financial assets. This increased demand for U.S. dollars will cause an increase in the exchange rate between the dollar and other currencies. When the dollar increases in value, the prices of U.S. products in foreign countries rise—causing a reduction in U.S. exports— and the prices of foreign products in the United States fall—causing an increase in U.S. imports. Falling exports and rising imports mean that net exports are falling.

The greater the sensitivity of consumption, investment, and net exports to changes in interest rates, the more crowding out will occur. In a deep recession, many firms may be pessimistic about the future and have so much excess capacity that investment

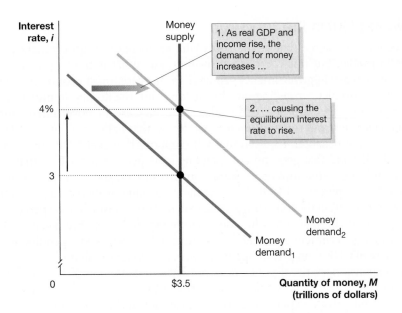

MyLab Economics Animation

Figure 16.11

An Expansionary Fiscal Policy Increases Interest Rates

An increase in government purchases will increase the demand for money from Money demand₁ to Money demand₂ as real GDP and income rise. With the supply of money constant, at $3.5 trillion, the result is an increase in the equilibrium interest rate from 3 percent to 4 percent, which crowds out some consumption, investment, and net exports.

spending will fall to very low levels and will be unlikely to fall much further, even if interest rates rise. In this case, crowding out is unlikely to be a problem. If the economy is close to potential GDP, however, and firms are optimistic about the future, an increase in interest rates may result in a significant decline in investment spending.

Figure 16.12 shows that crowding out may reduce the effectiveness of an expansionary fiscal policy. Short-run equilibrium is initially at point A, with real GDP at $16.8 trillion. Real GDP is below potential GDP, so the economy is in a recession. Suppose that Congress and the president decide to increase government purchases to increase real GDP to potential GDP. In the absence of crowding out, the increase in government purchases will shift the aggregate demand curve to $AD_{2(no\ crowding\ out)}$, and equilibrium will be at point B, with real GDP equal to potential GDP of $17.0 trillion. But the higher interest rate resulting from the increased government purchases will reduce consumption, investment, and net exports, causing the aggregate demand curve to shift back to $AD_{2(crowding\ out)}$. The result is a new short-run equilibrium at point C, with real GDP of $16.9 trillion, which is $100 billion short of potential GDP. (Note that the price level increase shown in Figure 16.10 on page 575 also contributes to reducing the effect of an increase in government purchases on equilibrium real GDP.)   **MyLab Economics** Concept Check

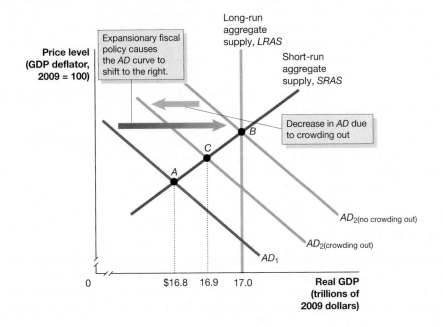

MyLab Economics Animation

Figure 16.12

The Effect of Crowding Out in the Short Run

Equilibrium is initially at point A, with real GDP of $16.8 trillion below potential GDP, so the economy is in a recession. In the absence of crowding out, an increase in government purchases will shift aggregate demand to $AD_{2(no\ crowding\ out)}$, and equilibrium is at potential GDP of $17.0 trillion (point B). But the higher interest rate resulting from the increased government purchases will reduce consumption, investment, and net exports, causing aggregate demand to shift to $AD_{2(no\ crowding\ out)}$. The result is a new short-run equilibrium at point C, with real GDP of $16.9 trillion, which is $100 billion short of potential GDP.

Crowding Out in the Long Run

Most economists agree that in the short run, an increase in government purchases results in partial, but not complete, crowding out. What is the long-run effect of a *permanent* increase in government spending? In this case, most economists agree that the result is complete crowding out. In the long run, the decline in investment, consumption, and net exports exactly offsets the increase in government purchases, and aggregate demand remains unchanged. Recall that *in the long run, real GDP returns to potential GDP* (Chapter 13, Section 13.3). Suppose that real GDP currently equals potential GDP and that government spending is 35 percent of GDP. In that case, private expenditures—the sum of consumption, investment, and net exports—will make up the other 65 percent of GDP. If government spending is increased permanently to 37 percent of GDP, in the long run, private expenditures must fall to 63 percent of GDP. There has been complete crowding out: Private expenditures have fallen by the same amount that government spending has increased. If government spending is taking a larger share of GDP, then private spending must take a smaller share.

An expansionary fiscal policy does not have to cause complete crowding out in the short run. If real GDP is below potential GDP, it is possible for both government purchases and private expenditures to increase. But in the long run, any permanent increase in government spending as a percentage of GDP must come at the expense of private expenditures. Keep in mind, however, that it may take several—possibly many—years to arrive at this long-run outcome.   **MyLab Economics** Concept Check

Fiscal Policy in Action: Did the Stimulus Package of 2009 Succeed?

As we have seen, Congress and the president can increase government purchases and cut taxes to increase aggregate demand either to avoid a recession or to shorten the length or severity of a recession that is already under way. The recession of 2007–2009 occurred during the end of the presidency of George W. Bush and the beginning of the presidency of Barack Obama. Both presidents used fiscal policy to fight the recession.

In 2008, at the urging of President Bush, Congress enacted a tax cut that took the form of *rebates* of taxes that households had already paid. Rebate checks totaling $95 billion were sent to taxpayers between April and July 2008. How effective were the rebates in increasing consumption spending? Many economists believe that consumers base their spending on their *permanent income* rather than just on their *current income*. A consumer's permanent income reflects the consumer's expected future income. By basing spending on permanent income, a consumer can smooth out consumption over a period of years. For example, a medical student may have very low current income but a high expected future income. The student may borrow against this high expected future income rather than having to consume at a very low level in the present. Some people, however, have difficulty borrowing against their future income because banks or other lenders may not be convinced that a borrower's future income will be significantly higher than his or her current income. One-time tax rebates, such as the one in 2008, increase consumers' current income but not their permanent income. Only a permanent decrease in taxes increases consumers' permanent income. Therefore, a tax rebate is likely to increase consumption spending less than would a permanent tax cut.

Some estimates of the effect of the 2008 tax rebate, including studies by Christian Broda of the University of Chicago and Jonathan Parker of Northwestern University, and by economists at the Congressional Budget Office, indicate that taxpayers spent between 33 and 40 percent of the rebates they received. Taxpayers who have difficulty borrowing against their future income increased their consumption the most. The 2008 tax rebates totaled $95 billion, so consumers may have increased their spending by about $35 billion.

American Recovery and Reinvestment Act of 2009 Although the tax rebates helped increase aggregate demand, we saw in Chapter 15, Section 15.6 that the recession worsened in September 2008, following the bankruptcy of the Lehman Brothers investment bank and the deepening of the financial crisis. President Obama

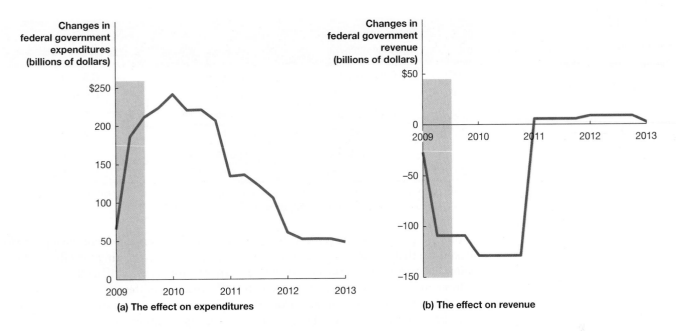

MyLab Economics Animation

Figure 16.13   **The Effect of the 2009 Stimulus Package on Federal Expenditures and Revenue**

Congress and President Obama intended the spending increases and tax cuts in the stimulus package to be temporary. Panel (a) shows that the effect of the stimulus package on federal expenditures was greatest during 2010 and declined in the following years.

Panel (b) shows that the effect on federal government revenue was greatest during 2010 and had declined to almost zero by early 2011.

Source: Federal Reserve Bank of St. Louis.

took office in January 2009, pledging to pursue an expansionary fiscal policy. Congress responded in February by passing the American Recovery and Reinvestment Act of 2009, often called the "stimulus package," an $840 billion program of spending increases and tax cuts that was by far the largest fiscal policy action in U.S. history.

About two-thirds of the stimulus package took the form of increases in government expenditures, and one-third took the form of tax cuts. Spending increases included funds for infrastructure spending, biomedical research, and grants to state governments to help fund Medicare spending. Individual tax cuts included a $400 reduction in payroll taxes for workers earning up to $75,000 per year and a tax credit of up to $2,500 for tuition and other college expenses.

Congress and the president intended the changes to federal expenditures and taxes from the stimulus package to be temporary. Figure 16.13 shows the effect of the stimulus package on federal government expenditures and revenue over time. Panel (a) shows that the effect on federal government expenditures was greatest during 2010 and declined sharply during 2011. Panel (b) shows that the effect on federal government revenue was greatest during 2010 and had declined to almost zero by early 2011.

How Can We Measure the Effectiveness of the Stimulus Package? At the time the stimulus package was passed, economists working for the Obama administration estimated that the increase in aggregate demand resulting from the package would increase real GDP by 3.5 percent by the end of 2010 and increase employment by 3.5 million. In fact, between the beginning of 2009 and the end of 2010, real GDP increased by 4.0 percent, while employment declined by 3.3 million. Do these results indicate that the stimulus package was successful in increasing GDP but not employment? We have to be careful in drawing that conclusion. To judge the effectiveness of the stimulus package, we have to measure its effects on real GDP and employment, *holding constant all other factors affecting real GDP and employment.* In other words, the actual movements in real GDP and employment are a mixture of the effects of the stimulus package and the effects of other factors, such as the Federal Reserve's

Table 16.2

CBO Estimates of the Effects of
the Stimulus Package

Year	Change in Real GDP (percentage change)	Change in the Unemployment Rate (percentage points)	Change in Employment (millions of people)
2009	0.4% to 1.8%	−0.1% to −0.5%	0.3 to 1.3
2010	0.7% to 4.1%	−0.4% to −1.8%	0.9 to 4.7
2011	0.4% to 2.3%	−0.2% to −1.4%	0.6 to 3.6
2012	0.1% to 0.8%	−0.1% to −0.6%	0.2 to 1.3
2013	0.1% to 0.4%	0% to −0.3%	0.1 to 0.5
2014	0% to 0.2%	0% to −0.2%	0.1 to 0.3

Source: Congressional Budget Office, "Estimated Impact of the American Recovery and Reinvestment Act on Employment and Economic Output in 2014," February 2015.

monetary policy and the typical changes in real GDP and employment during a business cycle that occur independently of government policy. Isolating the effects of the stimulus package from the effects of these other factors is very difficult and explains why economists differ in their views on the effectiveness of the stimulus package.

Table 16.2 shows estimates from economists at the CBO of the effectiveness of the stimulus package. The CBO is a nonpartisan organization, and many economists believe its estimates are reasonable. But because the estimates depend on particular assumptions about the size of the government purchases and tax multipliers, some economists believe that the CBO estimates are too high, while other economists believe the estimates are too low. To reflect the uncertainty in its calculation, the CBO provides a range of estimates. For example, in the absence of the stimulus package, the CBO estimates that in 2010, between 0.9 million and 4.7 million *fewer* people would have been employed than actually were, and the unemployment rate would have been between 0.4 percent and 1.8 percentage points *higher* than it actually was. By 2014, the effects of the stimulus package were small because several years had passed since most of the temporary spending increases and tax cuts had ended and because the economy had gradually moved back toward potential GDP.

If the CBO's estimates of the effects of the stimulus package are accurate, then this fiscal policy action reduced the severity of the recession of 2007–2009 and its aftermath. However, relative to the severity of the recession, the effect of the package was comparatively small. For example, in 2010, the unemployment rate was 9.6 percent, which was far above the unemployment rate of 4.6 percent in 2007. According to the CBO, without the stimulus package, the unemployment rate would have been somewhere between 10.0 percent and 11.4 percent. So, the stimulus package reduced the increase in the unemployment rate that might otherwise have occurred, but it did not come close to bringing the economy back to full employment.

The Size of the Multiplier: A Key to Estimating the Effects of Fiscal Policy In preparing the values shown in Table 16.2, the CBO relied on estimates of the government purchases and tax multipliers. Economists have been debating the size of these multipliers for many years. When British economist John Maynard Keynes and his followers first developed the idea of spending and tax multipliers in the 1930s, they argued that the government purchases multiplier might be as large as 10. In that case, a $1 billion increase in government purchases would increase real GDP by $10 billion. Later research by economists indicated that the government purchases multiplier was much smaller, perhaps less than 2.

Estimating an exact number for the multiplier is difficult because over time several factors can cause the aggregate demand and short-run aggregate supply curves to shift, leading to a change in equilibrium real GDP. As a result, it can be challenging to isolate the effect of an increase in government purchases on equilibrium GDP. Before the stimulus package was proposed to Congress in 2009, economists in the Obama administration estimated the package's effect on GDP by using an average of multiplier estimates from the Federal Reserve and from a private macroeconomic forecasting firm. Their estimate that the government purchases multiplier was 1.57 means

Table 16.3

Estimates of the Size of the Multiplier

Economists Making the Estimate	Type of Multiplier	Size of Multiplier
Congressional Budget Office	Government purchases	0.5–2.5
Lawrence Christiano, Martin Eichenbaum, and Sergio Rebelo, Northwestern University	Government purchases	1.05 when short-term interest rates are not 0; 3.7 when short-term interest rates are expected to be 0 for at least 5 quarters
Tommaso Monacelli, Roberto Perotti, and Antonella Trigari, Universita Bocconi	Government purchases	1.2 after one year; 1.5 after 2 years
Ethan Ilzetzki, London School of Economics, Enrique G. Mendoza, University of Pennsylvania, and Carlos A. Vegh, University of Maryland	Government purchases	0.8
Valerie Ramey, University of California, San Diego	Military expenditure	0.6–1.1
Robert J. Barro, Harvard University, and Charles J. Redlick, Bain Capital, LLC	Military expenditure	0.4–0.5 after 1 year; 0.6–0.7 after 2 years
John Cogan and John Taylor, Stanford University, and Tobias Cwik and Volker Wieland, Goethe University	A permanent increase in government expenditures	0.4
Christina Romer, University of California, Berkeley, and Jared Bernstein, chief economist and economic policy adviser to Vice President Joseph Biden	A permanent increase in government expenditures	1.6
Christina Romer (prior to serving as chair of the Council of Economic Advisers) and David Romer, University of California, Berkeley	Tax	2–3
Congressional Budget Office	Tax	0.3–1.5 for a 2-year tax cut for lower- and middle-income people; 0.1–0.6 for a 1-year tax cut for higher-income people
Robert J. Barro, Harvard University, and Charles J. Redlick, Bain Capital, LLC	Tax	1.1

Note: The sources of these estimates are given on the Credits page in the back of the book.

that a $1 billion increase in government purchases would increase equilibrium real GDP by $1.57 billion.

As Table 16.3 shows, economists' estimates of the size of the multiplier vary widely. The uncertainty about the size of the multiplier indicates the difficulty that economists have in arriving at a firm estimate of the effects of fiscal policy.   **MyLab Economics** Concept Check

MyLab Economics Study Plan

16.6 Deficits, Surpluses, and Federal Government Debt

LEARNING OBJECTIVE: Define federal budget deficit and federal government debt and explain how the federal budget can serve as an automatic stabilizer.

The federal government's budget shows the relationship between its expenditures and its tax revenue. If the federal government's expenditures are greater than its tax revenue, a **budget deficit** results. If the federal government's expenditures are less than its

Budget deficit The situation in which the government's expenditures are greater than its tax revenue.

MyLab Economics Real-time data

Figure 16.14

The Federal Budget Deficit, 1901–2017

During wars, government spending increases far more than tax revenues, increasing the budget deficit. The budget deficit also increases during recessions, as government spending increases and tax revenues fall.

Note: The deficit includes both (1) so-called on-budget expenditures and revenues (which are most expenditures and revenues) and (2) off-budget expenditures and revenues (which are primarily expenditures and revenues from the Social Security program). The value for 2017 is an estimate prepared by the Congressional Budget Office in March 2017.

Sources: *Budget of the United States Government, Fiscal Year 2003, Historical Tables*, Washington, DC: U.S. Government Printing Office, 2002; U.S. Bureau of Economic Analysis; and Congressional Budget Office.

Budget surplus The situation in which the government's expenditures are less than its tax revenue.

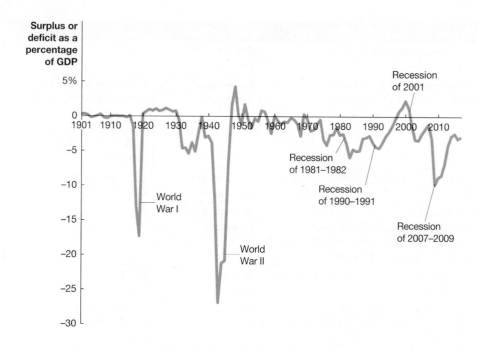

tax revenue, a **budget surplus** results. As with many other macroeconomic variables, it is useful to consider the size of the surplus or deficit relative to the size of the overall economy. Figure 16.14 shows that, as a percentage of GDP, the largest deficits of the twentieth century came during World Wars I and II. During major wars, higher taxes only partially offset massive increases in government expenditures, leaving large budget deficits. During recessions, government spending increases and tax revenues fall, increasing the budget deficit. In 1970, the federal government entered a long period of continuous budget deficits. From 1970 through 1997, the federal government's budget was in deficit every year. From 1998 through 2001, there were four years of budget surpluses. The recessions of 2001 and 2007–2009, tax cuts, and increased government spending on homeland security and the wars in Iraq and Afghanistan helped keep the budget in deficit in the years after 2001.

Figure 16.14 also shows the effects on the federal budget deficit of the Obama administration's $840 billion stimulus package and the severity of the 2007–2009 recession. From 2009 through 2011, the federal budget deficit was greater than 8 percent of GDP, which was the first time in the history of the country that the deficit had been this large except during major wars. The economic recovery combined with tax increases and reductions in federal spending resulted in the deficit being about 3 percent of GDP in 2017.

How the Federal Budget Can Serve as an Automatic Stabilizer

Discretionary fiscal policy can increase the federal budget deficit during recessions by increasing spending or cutting taxes to increase aggregate demand. For example, as we have just seen, the Obama administration's spending increases and tax cuts significantly increased the federal budget deficit during 2009 and 2010. In many milder recessions, though, no significant discretionary fiscal policy actions are taken. In fact, most of the increase in the federal budget deficit during a typical recession takes place without Congress and the president taking any action but is instead due to the effects of the *automatic stabilizers* we mentioned in Section 16.1.

Deficits occur automatically during recessions for two reasons: First, during a recession, wages and profits fall, causing government tax revenues to fall. Second, the government automatically increases its spending on transfer payments when the economy moves into a recession. The federal government's contributions to the unemployment insurance program will increase as unemployment rises. Spending will also increase on programs to aid low-income people, such as the food stamp, Temporary

Assistance for Needy Families, and Medicaid programs. These spending increases take place without Congress and the president taking any action. Existing laws already specify who is eligible for unemployment insurance and these other programs. As the number of eligible persons increases during a recession, so does government spending on these programs.

Because budget deficits automatically increase during recessions and decrease during expansions, economists often look at the *cyclically adjusted budget deficit or surplus*, which can provide a more accurate measure of the effects on the economy of the government's spending and tax policies than can the actual budget deficit or surplus. The **cyclically adjusted budget deficit or surplus** measures what the deficit or surplus would be if real GDP were at potential GDP. For example, the federal budget deficit in 2009 was 9.2 percent of GDP. The CBO estimates that if real GDP had been at its potential level, the deficit would have been about 7.1 percent of GDP, with the remaining 2.1 percent representing the increase in the deficit due to the effects of automatic stabilizers. When the federal government runs an expansionary fiscal policy, the result is a cyclically adjusted budget deficit. When the federal government runs a contractionary fiscal policy, the result is a cyclically adjusted budget surplus. The CBO forecast that in 2018, real GDP would equal potential GDP, so the values for the actual and cyclically adjusted budget deficits would also be equal.

Cyclically adjusted budget deficit or surplus The deficit or surplus in the federal government's budget if the economy were at potential GDP.

Automatic budget surpluses and deficits can help stabilize the economy. When the economy moves into a recession, wages and profits fall, reducing the taxes that households and firms owe the government. In effect, households and firms have received an automatic tax cut that keeps their spending higher than it otherwise would have been. In a recession, workers who have been laid off receive unemployment insurance payments, and households whose incomes have fallen below a certain level become eligible for food stamps and other government transfer programs. By receiving this extra income, households are able to spend more than they otherwise would have spent. The extra spending helps reduce the length and severity of the recession. Many economists argue that the lack of an unemployment insurance system and other government transfer programs contributed to the severity of the Great Depression. During the Great Depression, workers who lost their jobs saw their wage income fall to zero and had to rely on their savings, what they could borrow, or what they received from private charities. As a result, many unemployed workers drastically cut their spending, particularly on automobiles and other durable goods, which made the downturn worse.

When GDP increases above its potential level, households and firms have to pay more taxes to the federal government, and the federal government makes fewer transfer payments. Higher taxes and lower transfer payments cause total spending to rise by less than it otherwise would have, which helps reduce the chance that the economy will experience higher inflation.   **MyLab Economics** Concept Check

Apply the Concept   MyLab Economics Video

Did Fiscal Policy Fail during the Great Depression?

Modern macroeconomic analysis began during the 1930s, with the publication of *The General Theory of Employment, Interest, and Money* by John Maynard Keynes. One conclusion many economists drew from Keynes's book was that an expansionary fiscal policy would be necessary to pull the United States out of the Great Depression. When Franklin D. Roosevelt became president in 1933, federal government expenditures increased as part of his New Deal program, and there was a federal budget deficit during each remaining year of the decade, except for 1937. The U.S. economy recovered very slowly, however, and did not reach potential GDP again until the outbreak of World War II in 1941.

Some economists and policymakers at the time argued that because the economy recovered slowly despite increases in government spending, fiscal policy had been ineffective. During the debate over President Obama's stimulus package, the argument that fiscal policy had failed during the New Deal was raised again. Economic historians have

Although government spending increased during the Great Depression, the cyclically adjusted budget was in surplus most years.

AP Photo

noted, however, that despite the increases in government spending, Congress and the president had not, in fact, implemented an expansionary fiscal policy during the 1930s. In separate studies, economists E. Cary Brown of MIT and Larry Peppers of Washington and Lee University argued that there was a cyclically adjusted budget deficit during only one year of the 1930s, and that one deficit was small. The following table provides data supporting their arguments. (All variables in the table are nominal rather than real.) Column (1) shows federal government expenditures increasing from 1933 to 1936, falling in 1937, and then increasing in 1938 and 1939. Column (2) shows a similar pattern, with the federal budget being in deficit each year after 1933 except for 1937. Column (3), however, shows that in each year after 1933, the federal government ran a cyclically adjusted budget *surplus*. Because the level of income was so low and the unemployment rate was so high during these years, tax collections were far below what they would have been if the economy had been at potential GDP. As column (4) shows, in 1933 and again from 1937 to 1939, the cyclically adjusted surpluses were large relative to GDP.

Year	(1) Federal Government Expenditures (billions of dollars)	(2) Actual Federal Budget Deficit or Surplus (billions of dollars)	(3) Cyclically Adjusted Budget Deficit or Surplus (billions of dollars)	(4) Cyclically Adjusted Budget Deficit or Surplus as a Percentage of GDP
1929	$2.6	$1.0	$1.24	1.20%
1930	2.7	0.2	0.81	0.89
1931	4.0	−2.1	−0.41	−0.54
1932	3.0	−1.3	0.50	0.85
1933	3.4	−0.9	1.06	1.88
1934	5.5	−2.2	0.09	0.14
1935	5.6	−1.9	0.54	0.74
1936	7.8	−3.2	0.47	0.56
1937	6.4	0.2	2.55	2.77
1938	7.3	−1.3	2.47	2.87
1939	8.4	−2.1	2.00	2.17

Although President Roosevelt proposed many new government spending programs, he had also promised during the 1932 presidential election campaign to balance the federal budget. He achieved a balanced budget only in 1937, but his reluctance to allow the actual budget deficit to grow too large helps explain why the cyclically adjusted budget remained in surplus. Many economists today would agree with E. Cary Brown's conclusion: "Fiscal policy, then, seems to have been an unsuccessful recovery device in the 'thirties—not because it did not work, but because it was not tried."

Sources: E. Cary Brown, "Fiscal Policy in the 'Thirties: A Reappraisal," *American Economic Review*, Vol. 46, No. 5, December 1956, pp. 857–879; Larry Peppers, "Full Employment Surplus Analysis and Structural Changes," *Explorations in Economic History*, Vol. 10, Winter 1973, pp. 197–210; and U.S. Bureau of Economic Analysis.

MyLab Economics Study Plan   **Your Turn:** Test your understanding by doing related problem 6.7 on page 602 at the end of this chapter.

Should the Federal Budget Always Be Balanced?

Although many economists believe that it is a good idea for the federal government to have a balanced budget when real GDP is at potential GDP, few economists believe that the federal government should attempt to balance its budget every year. To see why economists take this view, consider what the federal government would have to do to keep the budget balanced during a recession, when the budget automatically moves into deficit. To bring the budget back into balance, the government would have to raise taxes or cut spending, but these actions would reduce aggregate demand, thereby making the recession worse. Similarly, when GDP increases above its potential level, the budget automatically moves into surplus. To eliminate this surplus, the government would have to cut taxes or increase government spending. But these actions would increase aggregate demand, thereby pushing GDP further beyond potential GDP and increasing the risk of higher inflation. To balance the budget every year, the government might have to take actions that would destabilize the economy.

Solved Problem 16.6

MyLab Economics Interactive Animation

The Greek Government Confronts a Budget Deficit

A columnist on forbes.com noted that the Greek economy entered a recession in early 2017. The Greek government had taken out substantial loans from the International Monetary Fund, the European Union, and private lenders. To make scheduled payments on the loans, the Greek government needed to run a budget surplus. The columnist argued that "to gain a substantial surplus you really want to have a growing economy and it's going to be something almost impossible to achieve in a shrinking economy."

In an attempt to reach its budget surplus target, the Greek government reduced government pension payments and other expenditures and raised taxes.

a. Why will it be almost impossible for the Greek government to run a budget surplus if the country's economy is shrinking?

b. What likely effect will the steps the Greek government took to run a budget surplus have on the country's economy?

Solving the Problem

Step 1: **Review the chapter material.** This problem is about the effects of a government attempting to balance its budget during a recession, so you may want to review the sections "How the Federal Budget Can Serve as an Automatic Stabilizer" and "Should the Federal Budget Always Be Balanced?" which are on pages 584 and 586.

Step 2: **Answer part (a) by explaining why it is difficult for a government to run a budget surplus during a recession.** Deficits occur automatically during recessions because falling wages and profits cause government tax revenues to fall and because government spending on transfer payments, such as unemployment insurance payments, increases.

Step 3: **Answer part (b) by explaining the likely effect on the Greek economy as the government cuts spending and increases taxes.** We have seen that reductions in government spending and increases in taxes will reduce aggregate demand. A reduction in aggregate demand will likely reduce real GDP and employment, making the recession in Greece worse.

Source: Tim Worstall, "Good News, Greece Back in Recession, Bets on That Debt Deal Are Off," forbes.com, February 14, 2017.

Your Turn: For more practice, do related problem 6.9 on page 602 at the end of this chapter.

MyLab Economics Study Plan

Some economists argue that the federal government should normally run a deficit, even at potential GDP. When the federal budget is in deficit, the U.S. Treasury sells bonds to investors to raise the funds necessary to pay the government's bills. Borrowing to pay the bills is a bad policy for a household, a firm, or the government when the bills are for current expenses, but it is not a bad policy if the bills are for long-lived capital goods. For instance, most families pay for a new home by taking out a 15- to 30-year mortgage. Because houses last many years, it makes sense to pay for a house out of the income the family makes over a long period of time rather than out of the income they receive in the year they bought the house. Businesses often borrow the funds to buy machinery, equipment, and factories by selling 30-year corporate bonds. Because these capital goods generate profits for the businesses over many years, it makes sense to pay for them over a period of years as well. By similar reasoning, when the federal government contributes to the building of a new highway, bridge, or subway, it may want to borrow funds by selling Treasury bonds. The alternative is to pay for these long-lived capital goods out of the tax revenues received in the year the goods were purchased. But that means that the taxpayers in that year have to bear the whole burden of paying for the projects, even though taxpayers for many years in the future will be enjoying the benefits. **MyLab Economics** Concept Check

The Federal Government Debt

Every time the federal government runs a budget deficit, the Treasury must borrow funds from investors by selling Treasury securities. For simplicity, we will refer to all Treasury securities as "bonds." When the federal government runs a budget surplus, the Treasury pays off some existing bonds. Figure 16.14 on page 584 shows that there are many more years of federal budget deficits than years of federal budget surpluses. As a result, the total number of Treasury bonds outstanding has grown over the years. The total value of U.S. Treasury bonds outstanding is called the *federal government debt* or, sometimes, the *national debt*. Each year the federal budget is in deficit, the federal government debt grows. Each year the federal budget is in surplus, the debt shrinks.

Figure 16.15 shows federal government debt as a percentage of GDP in the years from 1790 to 2017, with the CBO's forecasts through the year 2047. The ratio of debt to GDP increased during the American Revolution, the Civil War, World Wars I and II, and the Great Depression, reflecting the large government budget deficits of those years. After the end of World War II, GDP grew faster than the debt until the early 1980s, which caused the ratio of debt to GDP to fall. The large budget deficits of the 1980s and early 1990s sent the debt-to-GDP ratio climbing. The budget surpluses of 1998 to 2001 caused the debt-to-GDP ratio to fall, but it rose again with the return of deficits in 2002. The large deficits beginning in 2008 caused the ratio to rise above 100 percent of GDP for the first time since 1947. The CBO forecasts that if federal expenditures and revenues continue on their projected course, federal government debt will reach a record level of 150 percent of GDP in 2047. **MyLab Economics** Concept Check

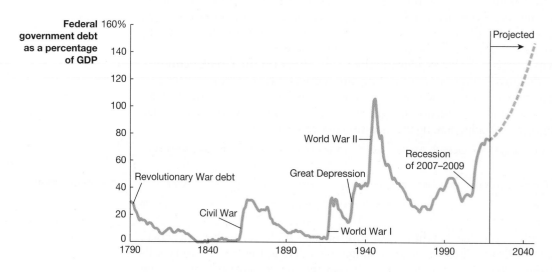

MyLab Economics Real-time data

Figure 16.15 **The Federal Government Debt, 1790-2047**

The federal government debt increases whenever the federal government runs a budget deficit. The large deficits incurred following the American Revolution, the Civil War, World Wars I and II, the Great Depression, and the 1980s and early 1990s increased the ratio of debt to GDP. The large deficits after 2008 caused the ratio to spike up to its highest level since 1947. The CBO forecasts that if federal expenditures and revenues continue on

their projected course, federal government debt will reach a record level of 150 percent of GDP in 2047.

Note: The value for 2017 is an estimate prepared by the Congressional Budget Office in March 2017.

Sources: Congressional Budget Office, "Supplemental Data," *The 2017 Long-Term Budget Outlook*, March 2017.

Is Government Debt a Problem?

Debt can be a problem for a government for the same reasons it can be a problem for a household or a business. If a family has difficulty making the monthly mortgage payment, it will have to cut back spending on other goods and services. If the family is unable to make the payments, it will have to *default* on the loan and will probably lose its house. The federal government is not in danger of defaulting on its debt. Ultimately, the government can raise the funds it needs through taxes to make the interest payments on the debt. If the debt becomes very large relative to the economy, however, the government may have to raise taxes to high levels or cut back on other types of spending to make the interest payments on the debt. Interest payments are currently about 11 percent of total federal expenditures. At this level, tax increases or significant cutbacks in other types of federal spending are not required.

In the long run, a debt that increases in size relative to GDP can pose a problem. The CBO projects that if present trends continue, federal government debt will increase from 77 percent of GDP in 2017 to 150 percent in 2047. As we discussed previously, crowding out of investment spending may occur if increasing debt drives up interest rates. Lower investment spending means a lower capital stock in the long run and a reduced capacity of the economy to produce goods and services. This effect is somewhat offset if some of the government debt was incurred to finance improvements in *infrastructure*, such as bridges, highways, and ports; to finance education; or to finance research and development. Improvements in infrastructure, a better-educated labor force, and additional research and development can add to the productive capacity of the economy.

MyLab Economics Concept Check   **MyLab Economics** Study Plan

16.7 Long-Run Fiscal Policy and Economic Growth

LEARNING OBJECTIVE: Discuss the effects of fiscal policy in the long run.

Some fiscal policy actions are intended to meet the short-run goal of stabilizing the economy. Others are intended to have long-run effects by expanding the productive capacity of the economy and increasing the rate of economic growth. As we saw in the chapter opener, President Trump's fiscal policy proposals in 2017 were aimed at increasing the rate of economic growth. Because long-run fiscal policy actions primarily affect aggregate supply rather than aggregate demand, they are sometimes called *supply-side economics*.

Explaining Long-Run Increases in Real GDP

The long-run growth rate of real GDP depends primarily on two factors:

1. The growth in the number of hours worked
2. The growth rate of labor productivity as measured by the growth in real GDP per hour worked

We can explore the relationship between growth in real GDP and growth in these factors by noting that at any given time, as a matter of arithmetic, the following relationship must hold:

Real GDP = Number of hours worked $\times$ (Real GDP/Number of hours worked).

When we discussed the quantity theory of money in Chapter 14, Section 14.5, we noted the mathematical rule that an equation in which variables are multiplied together is equal to an equation in which the growth rates of these variables are *added* together. Therefore, we can say that:

Growth rate of real GDP = Growth rate of hours worked
+ Growth rate of labor productivity.

Table 16.4

The Basis for the CBO's Estimate
of Real GDP Growth, 2017–2027

Variable	Average Annual Growth Rate	Explanation
Population	0.7%	Slowing birth rates and constant rate of immigration
Hours worked	0.4	Declining employment–population ratio due to aging of the population and rising number of disabled people and slowly declining average hours worked, following a long-run trend since the end of World War II
Labor productivity	1.5	Increased productivity growth from the slow rate of 2006–2016 but no return to the fast rate of 1996–2005
Real GDP	**1.9**	**The sum of the growth rate of hours worked and the growth rate of labor productivity**

The growth rate of hours worked depends on the rate of population growth, changes in the employment–population ratio, and changes in the hours each employee works. The faster the growth rate of the population, the faster the number of hours worked will increase, but only if the employment–population ratio and the average number of hours worked remain constant or increase. A decline in either the employment–population ratio or in average hours worked can cause the growth rate of hours worked to lag behind the population growth rate.

When economists forecast future growth rates of real GDP, they first have to forecast trends in these other variables. For example, in 2017, the CBO forecast that real GDP would grow at an average annual rate of 1.9 percent for the years 2017–2027. Table 16.4 summarizes how the CBO arrived at this estimate. Note that the CBO believes that the growth in hours worked will be much slower than population growth, for the reasons given in the table. **MyLab Economics** Concept Check

How Can Fiscal Policy Affect Long-Run Economic Growth? The Long-Run Effects of Tax Policy

Most fiscal policy actions that attempt to increase long-run real GDP growth do so by changing taxes to increase incentives to work, save, invest, and start a business. President Trump's proposals also attempt to increase labor productivity through improving infrastructure and to increase the size and productivity of the labor force through an apprenticeship program. President Trump also pushed for regulatory reform aimed at increasing new business formation and reducing barriers to entering some occupations. Regulatory reform has the potential both to increase the size of the labor force and, therefore, employment, and to increase labor productivity.

Tax wedge The difference between the pretax and posttax return to an economic activity.

We can look more closely at the effect of tax changes on real GDP growth. The difference between the pretax and posttax return to an economic activity is called the **tax wedge**. It is determined by the *marginal tax rate*, which is the fraction of each additional dollar of income that must be paid in taxes. For example, the U.S. federal income tax has several tax brackets, which are the income ranges within which a tax rate applies. In 2017, for a single taxpayer, the tax rate was 10 percent on the first $9,325 earned during a year. The tax rate rose for higher income brackets, until it reached 39.6 percent on income earned above $418,400. Suppose you are paid a wage of $20 per hour. If your marginal income tax rate is 25 percent, then your posttax wage is $15, and the tax wedge is $5. When discussing the model of demand and supply in Chapter 3, we saw that increasing the price of a good or service increases the quantity supplied. So, we would expect that reducing the tax wedge by cutting the marginal tax rate on income would result in a larger quantity of labor supplied because the posttax wage would be higher. Similarly, we saw in Chapter 10, Section 10.2 that a reduction in the income tax rate would increase the posttax return to saving, causing an increase in the supply of loanable funds, a lower equilibrium interest rate, and an increase in investment spending.

In general, economists believe that the smaller the tax wedge for any economic activity—such as working, saving, investing, or starting a business—the more of that economic activity that will occur. When workers, savers, investors, or entrepreneurs change their actions as a result of a tax change, economists say that there has been a *behavioral response* to the tax change.

We can look briefly at the effects on aggregate supply of cutting each of the following taxes:

- **Individual income tax.** As we have seen, reducing the marginal tax rates on individual income will reduce the tax wedge workers face, thereby increasing the quantity of labor supplied. Many small businesses are *sole proprietorships*, whose profits are taxed at the individual income tax rates. The profits of many partnerships are also taxed at the individual income tax rates. Therefore, cutting the individual income tax rates also raises the return to entrepreneurship, encouraging the opening of new businesses. One part of President Trump's proposal was to have these *income pass-through businesses* pay the corporate tax rate rather than the individual tax rate. If the corporate tax rate were also reduced, many sole proprietorships and partnerships would pay a lower tax rate on their profits. Most households are taxed on their returns from saving at the individual income tax rates. Reducing marginal income tax rates, therefore, also increases the return to saving.

- **Corporate income tax.** The federal government taxes the profits corporations earn under the corporate income tax. In 2017, most corporations faced a marginal corporate tax rate of 35 percent, which is higher than the rate in any other high-income country. President Trump proposed cutting the marginal corporate income tax rate to 20 percent to encourage investment spending by increasing the return corporations receive from new investments in equipment, factories, and office buildings. Because innovations are often embodied in new investment goods, cutting the corporate income tax can potentially increase the pace of technological change. The United States is unusual in imposing taxes on corporate earnings wherever they are earned but allowing corporations to postpone paying the taxes until the profits are brought back to the United States. As a result, many U.S. corporations keep the bulk of their overseas profits outside the United States. They can't use these funds in the United States to build new facilities or engage in research and development, and they can't return them to shareholders. President Trump proposed sharply reducing the tax U.S. corporations pay on their foreign profits.

- **Taxes on dividends and capital gains.** Corporations distribute some of their profits to shareholders in the form of payments known as *dividends*. Shareholders also may benefit from higher corporate profits by receiving *capital gains*. A capital gain is the increase in the price of an asset, such as a share of stock. Rising profits usually result in rising stock prices and capital gains to shareholders. Individuals pay taxes on both dividends and capital gains (although the tax on capital gains can be postponed if the stock is not sold). As a result, the same earnings are, in effect, taxed twice: once when a corporation pays the corporate income tax on its profits and a second time when individual investors receive the profits in the form of dividends or capital gains. Economists debate the costs and benefits of a separate tax on corporate profits. With the corporate income tax remaining in place, one way to reduce the "double taxation" problem is to reduce the tax rates on dividends and capital gains. These rates were reduced in 2003 and then increased in 2013. Generally, the marginal tax rates on dividends and capital gains are still below the top marginal tax rate on individual income. Lowering the tax rates on dividends and capital gains increases the supply of loanable funds from households to firms, increasing saving and investment and lowering the equilibrium real interest rate.   **MyLab Economics** Concept Check

Tax Simplification

In addition to the potential gains from cutting individual taxes, there are also gains from tax simplification. The complexity of the tax code, which is 3,000 pages long, has created a whole industry of tax preparation services, such as H&R Block. The Internal

Revenue Service estimates that taxpayers spend more than 6.4 billion hours each year filling out their tax forms, or about 45 hours per tax return. Households and firms have to deal with more than 480 tax forms to file their federal taxes and spend more than $10 billion per year to hire accountants to help fill out the forms. It is not surprising that there are more H&R Block offices around the country than there are Starbucks coffeehouses.

If the tax code were greatly simplified, the economic resources currently used by the tax preparation industry would be available to produce other goods and services. In addition to wasting resources, the complexity of the tax code may also distort the decisions households and firms make. For example, the tax rate on dividends has clearly affected whether corporations pay dividends. When Congress passed a reduction in the tax on dividends in 2003, many firms—including Microsoft—began paying dividends for the first time. A simplified tax code would increase economic efficiency by reducing the number of decisions households and firms make solely to reduce their tax payments. **MyLab Economics** Concept Check

The Economic Effects of Tax Reform

We can analyze the economic effects of tax reduction and simplification by using the aggregate demand and aggregate supply model. Figure 16.16 shows that without tax changes, the long-run aggregate supply curve will shift from $LRAS_1$ to $LRAS_2$. This shift represents the increases in the labor force and the capital stock and the technological change that would occur even without tax reduction and simplification. To focus on the effect of tax changes on aggregate supply, we will ignore any shifts in the short-run aggregate supply curve, and we will assume that the aggregate demand curve remains unchanged, at AD_1. In this case, equilibrium moves from point A to point B, with real GDP increasing from Y_1 to Y_2 and the price level decreasing from P_1 to P_2.

If tax reduction and simplification are effective, the economy will experience increases in the labor supply, thereby increasing the number of hours worked. Saving, investment, the formation of new firms, and economic efficiency will also increase, thereby increasing labor productivity. Together these factors will result in an increase in the quantity of real GDP supplied at every price level. We show the effects of the tax changes in Figure 16.16 by a shift in the long-run aggregate supply curve to $LRAS_3$. With aggregate demand remaining unchanged, equilibrium moves from point A to point C (rather than to point B, which is the equilibrium without

MyLab Economics Animation

Figure 16.16

The Supply-Side Effects of a Tax Change

The initial equilibrium is at point A. With no tax change, the long-run aggregate supply curve shifts to the right, from $LRAS_1$ to $LRAS_2$. Equilibrium moves to point B, with the price level falling from P_1 to P_2 and real GDP increasing from Y_1 to Y_2. With tax reductions and simplifications, the long-run aggregate supply curve shifts further to the right, to $LRAS_3$, and equilibrium moves to point C, with the price level falling to P_3 and real GDP increasing to Y_3.

tax changes), with real GDP increasing from Y_1 to Y_3 and the price level decreasing from P_1 to P_3. Notice that compared with the equilibrium without tax changes (point B), the equilibrium with tax changes (point C) occurs at a lower price level and a higher level of real GDP. We can conclude that the tax changes have benefited the economy by increasing output and employment while at the same time reducing the price level.

Clearly, our analysis is unrealistic because we have ignored the changes that will occur in aggregate demand and short-run aggregate supply. How would a more realistic analysis differ from the simplified one in Figure 16.16? The change in real GDP would be the same because in the long run, real GDP is equal to its potential level, which is represented by the long-run aggregate supply curve. The outcome for the price level would be different, however, because we would expect both the aggregate demand curve and the short-run aggregate supply curve to shift to the right. The most likely outcome is that the price level would end up higher in the new equilibrium than in the original equilibrium. However, because the position of the long-run aggregate supply curve is further to the right as a result of the tax changes, the increase in the price level will be smaller; that is, the price level at point C is likely to be lower than P_2, even if it is higher than P_3, although not all economists would agree. These economists believe that tax changes have only small effects on aggregate supply, so the changes are unlikely to reduce the size of price increases to the extent shown in Figure 16.16.

We can conclude that a successful policy of tax reductions and simplifications will benefit the economy by increasing output and employment and, at the same time, may result in smaller increases in the price level. **MyLab Economics** Concept Check

How Large Are Supply-Side Effects?

Most economists would agree that there are supply-side effects to reducing taxes: Decreasing marginal income tax rates will increase the quantity of labor supplied, cutting the corporate income tax will increase investment spending, and so on. The magnitude of the effects is the subject of considerable debate, however. For example, some economists argue that the increase in the quantity of labor supplied following a tax cut will be limited because many people work a number of hours set by their employers and lack the opportunity to work additional hours. Similarly, some economists believe that tax changes have only a small effect on saving and investment. In this view, saving and investment are affected much more by changes in income or changes in expectations of the future profitability of new investment due to technological change or improving macroeconomic conditions than they are by changes in taxes.

Economists who are skeptical of the magnitude of supply-side effects believe that tax cuts have their greatest effect on aggregate demand rather than on aggregate supply. In their view, focusing on the effect of tax cuts on aggregate demand, while ignoring any effect on aggregate supply, yields accurate forecasts of future movements in real GDP and the price level, which indicates that the supply-side effects must be small.

Ultimately, the debate over the size of the supply-side effects of tax policy can be resolved only through careful study of the effects of differences in tax rates on labor supply and on saving and investment decisions. Some recent studies have arrived at conflicting conclusions, however. For example, a study by Nobel Laureate Edward Prescott of Arizona State University concluded that differences in tax rates explain the differences between the United States and Europe with respect to the average number of hours worked per week and the average number of weeks worked per year. The lower marginal tax rates in the United States compared with Europe increase the return to working for U.S. workers and result in a larger quantity of labor supplied. But another study by Alberto Alesina and Edward Glaeser of Harvard University and Bruce Sacerdote of Dartmouth College argued that the more restrictive labor market regulations in Europe explain the shorter work weeks and longer vacations of European workers and that differences in tax rates have only a small effect.

MyLab Economics Study Plan

As in other areas of economics, differences among economists in their estimates of the supply-side effects of tax changes may narrow over time as they conduct more studies.   MyLab Economics Concept Check

Apply the Concept   MyLab Economics Video

Will President Trump's Policy Proposals Raise the Rate of Economic Growth?

Between 2007 and 2017, real GDP grew at an average annual rate of only 1.4 percent, and the CBO forecast that the rate would increase to only 1.9 percent between 2017 and 2027. As we saw in the chapter opener, in 2017, President Trump proposed several fiscal policy actions intended to increase the annual growth rate of real GDP to 3 percent. Although the difference between 1.9 and 3 percent may seem small, if real GDP grows at an annual rate of 3 percent, it will be more than $2 trillion larger in 2027 than if it grows at an annual rate of 1.9 percent. That extra $2 trillion would mean a substantial increase in the standard of living of the average person in the United States and would increase the ability of the federal government to make future Social Security and Medicare payments as well as the ability of state and local governments to make pension payments to retired public employees—which are currently a major strain on the budgets of many of these governments.

But will the Trump administration's proposals achieve the goal of significantly raising growth rates? To increase real GDP growth, the growth rates of hours worked or the growth rate of labor productivity will have to increase. We will discuss each of these factors.

Increasing the Growth Rate of Hours Worked. An increase in hours worked requires an increase in population growth, an increase in the employment–population ratio, or an increase in hours worked per employee. Population growth increases only if birth rates increase, death rates decrease, or the rate of immigration increases. The Trump administration proposals will not affect birth or death rates, and the administration has proposed restricting immigration. So, population growth is unlikely to increase. Hours worked per employee have been declining in the United States since the end of World War II in 1945. This decline reflects a preference among workers for increased leisure and the growth of part-time employment. Labor economists believe the trend toward working fewer hours on average is likely to continue. Therefore, increases in the growth rate of hours worked would have to result from increases in the employment–population ratio.

As we saw in Chapter 9, Section 9.1, the employment–population ratio has been declining slowly over the long term, but it declined sharply during the 2007–2009 recession and by 2017 had not returned to its 2006 level. Part of the decline was due to the aging of the population, but government policy might reverse the decline in employment among people in the prime working ages of 25 to 54. The Trump administration hopes to increase the employment–population ratio by expanding apprenticeship programs that provide skills needed by workers—particularly those without college degrees—entering rapidly growing industries such as software engineering and health care. The administration also hopes that its program of infrastructure spending might expand employment at firms such as Vulcan Materials, mentioned in the chapter opener, by luring some prime-age workers back into the labor force. If the Trump administration's proposals are enacted, it may take several years to determine whether they can successfully increase the employment–population ratio, thereby increasing the growth in hours worked in the economy.

Increasing Growth in Labor Productivity. If labor hours grow at only the annual rate of 0.4 percent forecast by the CBO, labor productivity will have to grow at an annual rate of 2.6 percent to reach the Trump administration's goal of real GDP growing at a 3 percent rate. As we saw in Chapter 11, Section 11.3, economists are divided in their explanations of why labor productivity grew at a rate of only 1.2 percent from 2006 to 2016. Pessimists, such as Robert Gordon of Northwestern University, argue that the productivity gains from nineteenth- and early twentieth-century innovations such as the railroad, electrification of homes and businesses, indoor plumbing, petroleum refining, and the automobile were much larger than productivity gains likely to result from information technology (IT). As a result, these economists doubt that any government policies will be able to return productivity growth rates to their levels of the 1950–1973 period.

The Trump administration's policies to increase labor productivity growth include the following:

1. *Reducing business taxes to increase investment spending.* The Trump proposal includes cutting the top tax rate on corporate profits from 35 percent to 20 percent and allowing firms to deduct all of their spending on machinery, equipment, and research and development from their taxes in the year the spending takes place. If enacted, these changes are likely to increase business investment spending. Some economists believe that IT innovations have had only a small effect on labor productivity because the low rates of investment spending since the 2007–2009 recession have resulted in some firms not yet adopting these innovations. As investment spending increases, the productivity benefits from these innovations may spread through the economy.

2. *Increasing infrastructure spending.* An additional $1 trillion in spending on highways, bridges, and airports could allow goods to be transported more efficiently at a lower cost, increasing output per hour worked. Supporters of infrastructure projects also argue that long-term spending might convince businesses that aggregate demand increases will be maintained over a period of years, providing them with the confidence to increase their spending on capital that may increase labor productivity.

3. *Increasing business startups by reducing regulations and taxes on small businesses.* As we saw in the *Apply the Concept* on page 184 of Chapter 6, Section 6.1, business startups, particularly by young people, have declined dramatically in the United States during recent decades. Starting a firm is a way for an entrepreneur to bring a new product or process to market, potentially increasing labor productivity. Reducing regulatory barriers to starting new businesses and expanding existing businesses has the potential to increase labor productivity. In addition, allowing sole proprietorships and other income pass-through businesses to pay taxes at the corporate rate rather than the individual rate may also increase investment spending by these small businesses.

As of fall 2017, it was unclear which, if any, of the Trump administration's policy proposals would be enacted by Congress, making it difficult to assess whether they would succeed in increasing growth in real GDP to an annual rate of 3 percent. While some economists believed that the suggested policies could raise real GDP growth to 3 percent, other economists and policymakers were skeptical. As mentioned earlier, some economists believe that labor productivity has entered an extended period of slow growth that government policies are unlikely to be able to affect. Other economists are concerned that the Trump administration's policies might lead to a large federal budget deficit that will result in significant crowding out of investment spending.

Sources: Josh Zumbrun, "Potential Economic Adviser to Trump Offers Preview of His Approach," *Wall Street Journal,* June 6, 2017; Noam Scheiber, "Trump Move on Job Training Brings 'Skills Gap' Debate to the Fore," *New York Times,* June 15, 2017; and Natasha Rausch, "Mnuchin 'Incredibly Unlikely' to Meet Goal on Taxes, Greene Says," bloomberg.com, June 20, 2017; and Patricia Cohen and Nelson D. Schwartz, "Economists See Little Magic in Tax Cuts to Promote Growth," *New York Times,* May 23, 2017.

Your Turn: Test your understanding by doing related problem 7.8 on page 603 at the end of this chapter.   **MyLab Economics** Study Plan

Continued from page 561

Economics in Your Life & Career

Should You Invest for the Long Term in Your Business?

At the beginning of the chapter, we asked you to suppose that you and a partner have purchased a small car dealership. Your partner is convinced that if Congress enacts a new program of spending and taxes, economic growth will increase. She therefore suggests expanding your business to take advantage of this growth. How can you evaluate your partner's assertions, and which fiscal policy proposals would be more likely to achieve the result she is expecting?

We've seen in this chapter that in 2017, the Trump administration's proposals aimed at increasing the long-run growth rate of real GDP from about 2 percent per year to about 3 percent. We also saw that the key to increasing the growth rate of real GDP is increasing the growth rate of labor productivity. Because economists disagree about the reasons that labor productivity growth has slowed in recent years, it's difficult to evaluate the likely effectiveness of proposals to increase it. Proposals aimed at increasing investment spending, such as permanent cuts in business taxes, are more likely to be effective in increasing the growth rate of real GDP than are proposals, such as temporary cuts in income taxes, that are aimed at increasing aggregate demand in the short run. The proposal to allow partnerships to pay taxes at the corporate income tax rate rather than at the individual income tax rate might help provide the funds you and your partner could use to expand your business.

Conclusion

In this chapter, we have seen how the federal government uses changes in government purchases and taxes to achieve its economic policy goals. We have also seen that economists debate the effectiveness of discretionary fiscal policy actions intended to stabilize the economy and increase long-run economic growth. Congress and the president share responsibility for economic policy with the Federal Reserve. In the next chapter, we will discuss further some of the challenges that the Federal Reserve faces as it carries out monetary policy. In the following chapters, we will look more closely at the international economy, including how monetary and fiscal policy are affected by the linkages between economies.

Visit MyLab Economics for a news article and analysis related to the concepts in this chapter.

Key Terms

Automatic stabilizers, p. 562

Budget deficit, p. 583

Budget surplus, p. 584

Crowding out, p. 578

Cyclically adjusted budget deficit or surplus, p. 585

Fiscal policy, p. 562

Multiplier effect, p. 572

Tax wedge, p. 590

16.1 What Is Fiscal Policy? pages 562–567

LEARNING OBJECTIVE: Define fiscal policy.

MyLab Economics Visit www.pearson.com/mylab/economics to complete these exercises online and get instant feedback.

Summary

Fiscal policy involves changes in federal taxes and purchases that are intended to achieve macroeconomic policy goals. **Automatic stabilizers** are government spending and taxes that automatically increase or decrease along with the business cycle. Since World War II, the federal government's share of total government expenditures has been between two-thirds and three-quarters. Federal government *expenditures* as a percentage of GDP rose from 1950 to the early 1990s, fell between 1992 and 2001, and then rose once again. Federal government *purchases* have declined as a percentage of GDP since the end of the Korean War in the early 1950s. The largest component of federal expenditures is transfer payments. The largest sources of federal government revenue are individual income taxes, followed by social insurance taxes, which are used to fund the Social Security and Medicare systems.

Review Questions

1.1 What is fiscal policy? Who is responsible for fiscal policy?

1.2 Economist Mark Thoma observed, "One of the difficulties in using fiscal policy to combat recessions is getting Congress to agree on what measures to implement. . . . Automatic stabilizers bypass this difficulty by doing exactly what their name implies." What are automatic stabilizers? Name two examples of automatic stabilizers and explain how they can reduce the severity of a recession.

Source: Mark Thoma, "The Importance of Automatic Stabilizers to the Economy," cbsnews.com, January 25, 2010.

1.3 What is the difference between federal purchases and federal expenditures? Are federal purchases higher today as a percentage of GDP than they were in 1960? Are federal expenditures as a percentage of GDP higher?

Problems and Applications

1.4 In 2009, Congress and the president enacted "cash for clunkers" legislation that paid up to $4,500 to people buying new cars if they traded in an older, low-gas-mileage car. Was this legislation an example of fiscal policy? Does your answer depend on what goals Congress and the president had in mind when they enacted the legislation?

Source: Justin Lahart, "Trade-in Program Tunes up Economic Engine," *Wall Street Journal*, August 4, 2009.

1.5 Briefly explain whether each of the following is (1) an example of a discretionary fiscal policy, (2) an example of an automatic stabilizer, or (3) not an example of fiscal policy.
  a. The federal government increases spending on rebuilding the New Jersey Shore following a hurricane.
  b. The Federal Reserve sells Treasury securities.
  c. The total amount the federal government spends on unemployment insurance decreases during an expansion.
  d. The revenue the federal government collects from the individual income tax declines during a recession.
  e. The federal government changes the fuel efficiency requirements for new cars.
  f. Congress and the president enact a temporary cut in payroll taxes.
  g. During a recession, California voters approve additional spending on a statewide high-speed rail system.

1.6 The federal government collected less in total individual income taxes in 1983 than in 1982. Can we conclude that Congress and the president cut individual income tax rates in 1983? Briefly explain.

1.7 (Related to the Apply the Concept on page 565) According to a 2017 Congressional Budget Office (CBO) report, "By 2047, 22 percent of the population will be age 65 or older, CBO anticipates, compared with 15 percent today." Why is the over-65 population increasing so rapidly? What are the implications of this increase for future federal spending on Social Security and Medicare as a percentage of GDP? What choices do policymakers face in dealing with this issue?

Source: Congressional Budget Office, "The 2017 Long-Term Budget Outlook," March 2017, p. 7.

16.2 The Effects of Fiscal Policy on Real GDP and the Price Level, pages 567–569

LEARNING OBJECTIVE: Explain how fiscal policy affects aggregate demand and how the government can use fiscal policy to stabilize the economy.

MyLab Economics   Visit **www.pearson.com/mylab/economics** to complete these exercises online and get instant feedback.

Summary

To fight recessions, Congress and the president can increase government purchases or cut taxes. This expansionary policy increases aggregate demand, raising the level of real GDP and the price level. To fight rising inflation, Congress and the president can decrease government purchases or raise taxes. This contractionary policy reduces aggregate demand relative to what it would otherwise be, thereby reducing the inflation rate.

Review Questions

2.1 If Congress and the president decide that an expansionary fiscal policy is necessary, what changes should they make in government spending or taxes? What changes should they make if they decide that a contractionary fiscal policy is necessary?

2.2 Briefly explain how an expansionary fiscal policy will cause each of the following variables to increase or decrease.
  a. Real GDP
  b. The unemployment rate
  c. The price level

Problems and Applications

2.3 Briefly explain whether you agree with the following statements: "An expansionary fiscal policy involves an increase in government purchases or an increase in taxes. A contractionary fiscal policy involves a decrease in government purchases or a decrease in taxes."

2.4 Identify each of the following as (1) part of an expansionary fiscal policy, (2) part of a contractionary fiscal policy, or (3) not part of fiscal policy.
  a. The corporate income tax rate is increased.
  b. Defense spending is increased.
  c. The Federal Reserve lowers the target for the federal funds rate.

  d. Families are allowed to deduct all their expenses for day care from their federal income taxes.
  e. The individual income tax rates are decreased.

2.5 Use an aggregate demand and aggregate supply graph to illustrate the situation where equilibrium initially occurs with real GDP equal to potential GDP and then the aggregate demand curve shifts to the left. What actions can Congress and the president take to move real GDP back to potential GDP? Show the results of these actions on your graph. Assume that the long-run aggregate supply (*LRAS*) curve doesn't shift.

2.6 An article in the *Wall Street Journal* stated that "Japan's cabinet approved a government stimulus package that includes ¥7.5 trillion ($73 billion) in new spending, in the latest effort by Prime Minister Shinzo Abe to jump-start the nation's sluggish economy."
  a. Draw an aggregate demand and aggregate supply graph that shows where the Japanese government expects the economy to be without the stimulus package. Briefly explain what you graph shows.
  b. In the same graph, show the effect of the stimulus package on the economy. Briefly explain what your graphs shows.

  Source: Mitsuru Obe, "Japan's Shinzo Abe Fires Stimulus Gun, Again," *Wall Street Journal*, August 2, 2016.

2.7 **(Related to the Don't Let This Happen to You on page 569)** Is it possible for Congress and the president to carry out an expansionary fiscal policy if the money supply does not increase? Briefly explain.

2.8 **(Related to the Chapter Opener on page 560)** In 2017, in proposing a $1 trillion increase in government spending on infrastructure, President Trump argued that the spending would increase total employment in the United States.
  a. Will increases in federal spending always increase real GDP and employment in the short run? Briefly explain.
  b. Are there circumstances in which the federal government would *not* want to increase its spending, even if the result was to increase real GDP and employment in the short run?

  Source: Ted Mann and Michael C. Bender, "President Trump to Launch Push for Infrastructure Investment," *Wall Street Journal*, June 4, 2017.

16.3 Fiscal Policy in the Dynamic Aggregate Demand and Aggregate Supply Model, pages 570–571

LEARNING OBJECTIVE: Use the dynamic aggregate demand and aggregate supply model to analyze fiscal policy.

MyLab Economics   Visit **www.pearson.com/mylab/economics** to complete these exercises online and get instant feedback.

Summary

We can use the dynamic aggregate demand and aggregate supply model to look more closely at expansionary and contractionary

fiscal policies. This model takes into account that (1) the economy experiences continuing inflation, with the price level rising every year, and (2) the economy experiences long-run growth, with the *LRAS* curve shifting to the right every year. In the dynamic model, an expansionary fiscal policy tries to ensure that the aggregate demand curve will shift far enough to the right to bring about macroeconomic equilibrium with real GDP equal to potential GDP. A contractionary fiscal policy attempts to offset movements in aggregate demand that would cause macroeconomic equilibrium to occur at a level of real GDP that is greater than potential GDP.

Review Questions

3.1 What are the key differences between how we illustrate an expansionary fiscal policy in the basic aggregate demand and aggregate supply model and in the dynamic aggregate demand and aggregate supply model?

3.2 What are the key differences between how we illustrate a contractionary fiscal policy in the basic aggregate demand and aggregate supply model and in the dynamic aggregate demand and aggregate supply model?

Problems and Applications

3.3 A report from the Congressional Budget Office (CBO) noted, "Real potential GDP is the maximum sustainable output of the economy adjusted to remove the effects of inflation." In early 2017, the CBO estimated that the gap between real GDP and potential GDP would fall from 1.1 percent in 2016 to 0.3 in 2018. In 2016, real GDP was $16.7 trillion, and the CBO's estimate of potential GDP was $16.9 trillion. The CBO forecast that potential GDP would increase to $17.4 trillion in 2018.

    a. Why does the CBO include the word *sustainable* in its definition of potential GDP?

    b. Draw an aggregate demand and aggregate supply graph to illustrate the macroeconomic situation in 2016 and in 2018. (You do not have to show on your graph the situation in 2017.) Be sure that your graph contains *LRAS* curves for 2016 and 2018, *SRAS* curves for 2016 and 2018, and *AD* curves for 2016 and 2018, and that it shows equilibrium real GDP and the price levels for both years.

    Sources: Congressional Budget Office, "The 2017 Long-Term Budget Outlook," March 2017, p. 9; and Congressional Budget Office, "The Budget and Economic Outlook: 2017 to 2027," January 24, 2017.

3.4 Use the graph to answer the following questions.

a. If the government takes no policy actions, what will be the values of real GDP and the price level in 2021?

b. What actions can the government take to bring real GDP to its potential level in 2021?

c. If the government takes no policy actions, what will the inflation rate be in 2021? If the government uses fiscal policy to keep real GDP at its potential level, what will the inflation rate be in 2021?

3.5 The hypothetical information in the following table shows what the situation will be in 2021 if Congress and the president do *not* use fiscal policy:

Year	Potential GDP	Real GDP	Price Level
2020	$18.0 trillion	$18.0 trillion	120.3
2021	18.4 trillion	18.0 trillion	122.7

a. If Congress and the president want to keep real GDP at its potential level in 2021, should they use an expansionary policy or a contractionary policy? In your answer, be sure to explain whether Congress and the president should increase or decrease government purchases and taxes. Draw an aggregate demand and aggregate supply graph to illustrate your answer. Be sure that your graph contains *LRAS* curves for 2020 and 2021; *SRAS* curves for 2020 and 2021; *AD* curves for 2020 and 2021, with and without fiscal policy action; and equilibrium real GDP and the price level in 2021, with and without fiscal policy.

b. If Congress and the president are successful in keeping real GDP at its potential level in 2021, state whether each of the following will be higher, lower, or the same as it would have been if they had taken no action.

    i. Real GDP
    ii. Potential GDP
    iii. The inflation rate
    iv. The unemployment rate

3.6 Use a dynamic aggregate demand and aggregate supply graph to illustrate the change in macroeconomic equilibrium from 2021 to 2022, assuming that the economy experiences deflation during 2022. In order for deflation to take place in 2022, does the economy also have to be experiencing a recession? Briefly explain.

16.4 The Government Purchases and Tax Multipliers, pages 571–576

LEARNING OBJECTIVE: Explain how the government purchases and tax multipliers work.

MyLab Economics   Visit **www.pearson.com/mylab/economics** to complete these exercises online and get instant feedback.

Summary

Because of the **multiplier effect**, an increase in government purchases or a cut in taxes will have a multiplied effect on equilibrium real GDP. The *government purchases multiplier* is equal to the change in equilibrium real GDP divided by the change in government purchases. The *tax multiplier* is equal to the change in equilibrium real GDP divided by the change in taxes. Increases in government purchases and cuts in taxes have a positive multiplier effect on equilibrium real GDP. Decreases in government purchases and increases in taxes have a negative multiplier effect on equilibrium real GDP.

Review Questions

4.1 Why can a $1 increase in government purchases lead to more than a $1 increase in income and spending?

4.2 Define *government purchases multiplier* and *tax multiplier*.

4.3 Why does a higher income tax rate reduce the multiplier effect?

Problems and Applications

4.4 An infrastructure project in northern California funded in part by funds included in the 2009 America Recovery and Reinvestment Act (ARRA) involved expanding the Caldecott Tunnel between the California cities of Oakland and Orinda. A spokesperson for the California state agency in charge of the project mentioned that the Caldecott Tunnel project would have a ripple effect on employment. What does the spokesperson mean by "ripple effect"?

Source: Zusha Elinson, "Caldecott Tunnel Edges Forward, Tribute to Stimulus Bill," *New York Times*, September 10, 2011.

4.5 In *The General Theory of Employment, Interest, and Money*, John Maynard Keynes wrote:

If the Treasury were to fill old bottles with banknotes, bury them at suitable depths in disused coal mines which are then filled up to the surface with town rubbish, and leave it to private enterprise … to dig the notes up again … there need be no more unemployment and, with the help of the repercussions, the real income of the community … would probably become a good deal greater than it is.

Which important macroeconomic effect is Keynes discussing here? What does he mean by "repercussions"? Why does he appear unconcerned about whether government spending is wasteful?

Source: John Maynard Keynes, *The General Theory of Employment, Interest and Money*, New York: Harcourt Brace, 1936, p. 128.

4.6 (Related to Solved Problem 16.4 on page 575) Suppose that real GDP is currently $17.1 trillion, potential GDP is $17.4 trillion, the government purchases multiplier is 2, and the tax multiplier is –1.6.

a. Holding other factors constant, by how much will government purchases need to be increased to bring the economy to equilibrium at potential GDP?

b. Holding other factors constant, by how much will taxes have to be cut to bring the economy to equilibrium at potential GDP?

c. Construct an example of a *combination* of increased government spending and tax cuts that will bring the economy to equilibrium at potential GDP.

4.7 (Related to Solved Problem 16.4 on page 575) Briefly explain whether you agree with the following statement:

Real GDP is currently $17.7 trillion, and potential GDP is $17.4 trillion. If Congress and the president would decrease government purchases by $300 billion or increase taxes by $300 billion, the economy could be brought to equilibrium at potential GDP.

4.8 A Federal Reserve publication argued that the size of the multiplier "depends on the type of fiscal policy changes in question and the environment in which they are implemented."

a. What does the author mean by "the type of fiscal policy changes in question"? Why does the type of policy matter for the size of the multiplier?

b. What does the author mean by "the environment in which they are implemented"? Would the size of the multiplier be affected by how close real GDP is to potential GDP? Briefly explain.

Source: Daniel J. Wilson, "Government Spending: An Economic Boost?" *Federal Reserve Bank of San Francisco Economic Letter*, February 6, 2012.

4.9 If, rather than being upward sloping, the short-run aggregate supply (*SRAS*) curve were a horizontal line at the current price level, what would be the effect on the size of the government purchases and tax multipliers? Briefly explain.

16.5 The Limits to Using Fiscal Policy to Stabilize the Economy, pages 576–583

LEARNING OBJECTIVE: Discuss the difficulties that can arise in implementing fiscal policy.

MyLab Economics   Visit **www.pearson.com/mylab/economics** to complete these exercises online and get instant feedback.

Summary

Poorly timed fiscal policy can do more harm than good. Getting the timing right with fiscal policy can be difficult because obtaining approval from Congress for a new fiscal policy can be a very long process, and it can take months for an increase in authorized spending to actually take place. Because an increase in government purchases may lead to a higher interest rate, it may result in a decline in consumption, investment, and net exports. A decline in private expenditures as a result of an increase in government purchases is called **crowding out**.

Crowding out may cause an expansionary fiscal policy to fail to meet its goal of keeping real GDP at potential GDP.

Review Questions

5.1 Which can be changed more quickly: monetary policy or fiscal policy? Briefly explain.

5.2 What is meant by "crowding out"? Explain the difference between crowding out in the short run and in the long run.

Problems and Applications

5.3 Some economists argue that because increases in government spending crowd out private spending, increased government spending will reduce the long-run growth rate of real GDP.

    a. Is this outcome most likely to occur if the private spending being crowded out is consumption spending, investment spending, or net exports? Briefly explain.

    b. In terms of its effect on the long-run growth rate of real GDP, would it matter if the additional government spending involves (i) increased spending on highways and bridges or (ii) increased spending on national parks? Briefly explain.

5.4 According to a study by Kanishka Misra of the University of Michigan and Paolo Surico of the London Business School, "Almost half of American families did not adjust their consumption following receipt of the … 2008 tax rebate." Don't we expect that people will increase their consumption if their disposable income increases? Was there anything about the form of the 2008 tax cut that made it more likely that people

would not respond by increasing their consumption spending? Briefly explain.

Source: Kanishka Misra and Paolo Surico, "Consumption, Income Changes, and Heterogeneity: Evidence from Two Fiscal Stimulus Programs," *American Economic Journal: Macroeconomics*, Vol. 6, No. 4, October 2014, pp. 84–106.

5.5 We saw that in calculating the stimulus package's effect on real GDP, economists in the Obama administration estimated that the government purchases multiplier has a value of 1.57. John F. Cogan, Tobias Cwik, John B. Taylor, and Volker Wieland argued that the value is only 0.4.

    a. Briefly explain how the government purchases multiplier can have a value of less than 1.

    b. Why does an estimate of the size of the multiplier matter in evaluating the effects of an expansionary fiscal policy?

Source: John Cogan, Tobias Cwik, John Taylor, and Volker Wieland, "New Keynesian versus Old Keynesian Government Spending Multipliers," *Journal of Economic Dynamics and Control*, Vol. 34, No. 3, March 2010, pp. 281–295.

5.6 **(Related to the Apply the Concept on page 577)** Why would a recession accompanied by a financial crisis be more severe than a recession that did not involve a financial crisis? Were the large budget deficits in 2009 and 2010 primarily the result of the stimulus package of 2009? Briefly explain.

5.7 Suppose that at the same time that Congress and the president pursue an expansionary fiscal policy, the Federal Reserve pursues an expansionary monetary policy. How might an expansionary monetary policy affect the extent of crowding out in the short run?

 16.6 # Deficits, Surpluses, and Federal Government Debt, pages 583–589

LEARNING OBJECTIVE: Define federal budget deficit and federal government debt and explain how the federal budget can serve as an automatic stabilizer.

MyLab Economics   Visit **www.pearson.com/mylab/economics** to complete these exercises online and get instant feedback.

Summary

A **budget deficit** occurs when the federal government's expenditures are greater than its tax revenues. A **budget surplus** occurs when the federal government's expenditures are less than its tax revenues. A budget deficit automatically increases during recessions and decreases during expansions. The automatic movements in the federal budget help stabilize the economy by cushioning the fall in spending during recessions and restraining the increase in spending during expansions. The **cyclically adjusted budget deficit or surplus** measures what the deficit or surplus would be if the economy were at potential GDP. The federal government debt (or national debt) is the value of outstanding bonds issued by the U.S. Treasury. The national debt is a problem if interest payments on it require taxes to be raised substantially or require other federal expenditures to be cut.

Review Questions

6.1 In what ways does the federal budget serve as an automatic stabilizer for the economy?

6.2 What is the cyclically adjusted budget deficit or surplus? Suppose that real GDP is currently at potential GDP, and the federal budget is balanced. If the economy moves into a recession, what will happen to the federal budget?

6.3 Why do few economists believe it would be a good idea to balance the federal budget every year?

6.4 What is the difference between the federal budget deficit and federal government debt?

Problems and Applications

6.5 *Wall Street Journal* writers Josh Zumbrun and Nick Timiraos published answers to several of their readers' questions regarding the federal government's debt. The following were two of the questions. Write a brief response to each question.

a. Why is government debt different from mine?

b. How important is it to pay off this debt?

Source: Josh Zumbrun and Nick Timiraos, "Q&A: What the $18 Trillion National Debt Means for the U.S. Economy," *Wall Street Journal*, February 1, 2015.

6.6 In a column in the *Financial Times*, the prime minister and the finance minister of the Netherlands argued that the European Union, an organization of 28 countries in Europe, should appoint "a commissioner for budgetary discipline." They said that "the new commissioner should be given clear powers to set requirements for the budgetary policy of countries that run excessive deficits." What is an "excessive" budget deficit? Does judging whether a deficit is excessive depend in part on whether the country is in a recession? How can budgetary policies be used to reduce a budget deficit?

Source: Mark Rutte and Jan Kees de Jager, "Expulsion from the Eurozone Has to Be the Final Penalty," *Financial Times*, September 7, 2011.

6.7 **(Related to the Apply the Concept on page 585)** The following is from a message by President Herbert Hoover to Congress, dated May 5, 1932:

> I need not recount that the revenues of the Government as estimated for the next fiscal year show a decrease of about $1,700,000,000 below the fiscal year 1929, and inexorably require a broader basis of taxation and a drastic reduction of expenditures in order to balance the Budget. Nothing is more necessary at this time than balancing the Budget.

Do you think President Hoover was correct in saying that, in 1932, nothing was more necessary than balancing the federal government's budget? Briefly explain.

Source: Herbert Hoover, "Special Message to the Congress on Budgetary Legislation," in *Public Papers of the Presidents of the United States: Herbert Hoover, 1932–1933*, 1977, p. 194.

6.8 In January 2017, the Congressional Budget Office (CBO) noted that its "estimate of the deficit for 2017 has decreased since August 2016." The CBO also noted that its "economic forecast … underlies its budget projections."

a. Why would the CBO's forecast of future levels of GDP and employment matter for its forecasts of future federal budget deficits?

b. If the federal budget deficit turns out to be smaller than expected, it is likely that economic growth was higher or lower than expected? Briefly explain.

Source: Congressional Budget Office, *The Budget and Economic Outlook: 2017 to 2027*, January 2017, p.2.

6.9 **(Related to Solved Problem 16.6 on page 587)** A 2015 article in the *Wall Street Journal* noted that an official of the European Union was forecasting that "Greece faces two years of recession amid sharp budget cuts." What typically happens to a government's budget deficit during a recession? Do governments typically respond with budget cuts as the Greek government did? Briefly explain.

Source: Gabriele Steinhauser and Andrea Thomas, "Greece Faces Two-Year Recession amid Bailout Cuts," *Wall Street Journal*, August 13, 2015.

6.10 In 2017, an article in the *Wall Street Journal* discussed a report by the World Bank. According to the report, "More than half of emerging economies saw their debt-to-GDP ratios rise 10 percentage points and in a third, budget balances worsened by more than five percentage points."

a. What does the report mean by "budget balances"?

b. Is there a connection between these countries experiencing worsening budget balances while also experiencing increasing debt-to-GDP ratios? Briefly explain.

Source: Ian Talley, "Four Risks Cloud the Outlook for the Global Economy," *Wall Street Journal*, June 6, 2017.

6.11 A political columnist wrote the following:

> Today … the main purpose [of governments issuing bonds] is to let craven politicians launch projects they know the public, at the moment, would rather not fully finance. The tab for these projects will not come due, probably, until after the politicians have long since departed for greener (excuse the expression) pastures.

Do you agree with this commentator's explanation for why some government spending is financed through tax receipts and other government spending is financed through borrowing, by issuing bonds? Briefly explain.

Source: Paul Carpenter, "The Bond Issue Won't Be Repaid by Park Tolls," (Allentown, PA) *Morning Call*, May 26, 2002.

16.7 **Long-Run Fiscal Policy and Economic Growth, pages 589–595**

LEARNING OBJECTIVE: Discuss the effects of fiscal policy in the long run.

MyLab Economics   Visit www.pearson.com/mylab/economics to complete these exercises online and get instant feedback.

Summary

Some fiscal policy actions are intended to have long-run effects by expanding the productive capacity of the economy and increasing the rate of economic growth. The long-run growth rate of real GDP equals the growth rate of hours worked plus the growth rate of labor productivity, measured as real GDP per hour worked. Because policies intended to increase the long-run growth rate of real GDP primarily affect aggregate supply rather than aggregate demand, they are sometimes called *supply-side economics*. The difference between the pretax and posttax return to an economic activity is called the **tax wedge**. Economists believe that the smaller the tax wedge for any economic activity—such as working, saving, investing, or starting a business—the more of that economic activity will occur. Economists debate the size of the supply-side effects of tax changes.

Review Questions

7.1 Write the equation that links real GDP growth to its two determinants. Briefly explain why the relationship indicated by the equation holds.

7.2 What is *supply-side economics*?

7.3 What is the *tax wedge*?

Problems and Applications

7.4 An article in the *Wall Street Journal* discussing the Trump administration's goal of increasing the annual rate of growth in real GDP to 3 percent noted, "Two stubborn obstacles stand in his way. The work force isn't producing enough new workers, and the productivity of those working isn't growing fast enough." Briefly explain why these two factors are "obstacles" to attaining a higher growth rate.

Source: Nick Timiraos and Andrew Tangel, "Can Trump Deliver 3% Growth? Stubborn Realities Stand in the Way," *Wall Street Journal*, May 15, 2017.

7.5 As indicated in the chapter, the CBO forecast that real GDP would grow at an average annual rate of 1.9 percent from 2017 to 2027. The Trump administration pledged to raise the growth rate to 3 percent, although some policymakers and economists were skeptical that this goal could be achieved. Yet from 1960 to 1969, real GDP grew at an average annual rate of 4.5 percent. Briefly discuss the factors that make growth rates that high more difficult to achieve today.

7.6 Some economists and policymakers have argued in favor of a "flat tax." A flat tax would replace the current individual income tax system, with its many tax brackets, exemptions, and deductions, with a new system containing a single tax rate and few, or perhaps no, deductions and exemptions. Suppose a political candidate hired you to develop two arguments in favor of a flat tax. What two arguments would you advance? Alternatively, if you were hired to develop two arguments against a flat tax, what two arguments would you advance?

7.7 Writing in the *Wall Street Journal*, Martin Feldstein, an economist at Harvard University, argued that "behavioral responses" of taxpayers to the cuts in marginal tax rates enacted in 1986 resulted in "an enormous rise in the taxes paid, particularly by those who experienced the greatest reductions in marginal tax rates." How is it possible for cuts in marginal tax rates to result in an increase in total taxes collected? What does Feldstein mean by a "behavioral response" to tax cuts?

Source: Martin Feldstein, "The Tax Reform Evidence from 1986," *Wall Street Journal*, October 24, 2011.

7.8 **(Related to the Apply the Concept on page 594)** In 2017, an article in the *New York Times* quoted Douglas Holtz-Eakin, former director of the Congressional Budget Office, as arguing that "with the economy back to near full employment, conventional tax cuts or stimulus spending won't have that much of an effect. What is needed are policies that genuinely augment the supply side of the economy."

  a. If the economy is at full employment, what economic variables will conventional tax cuts or stimulus spending not affect much? What variables might these policies affect?

  b. What does Holtz-Eakin mean by "policies that genuinely augment the supply side of the economy"?

Source: Patricia Cohen and Nelson D. Schwartz, "Economists See Little Magic in Tax Cuts to Promote Growth," *New York Times*, May 23, 2017.

Real-Time Data Exercises

D16.1 (Comparing macroeconomic conditions in different countries) The International Monetary Fund (IMF) publishes the *World Economic Outlook*. Go to www.imf.org and look at the most recent version available. The IMF measures the output gap as the difference between real GDP and potential GDP as a percentage of potential GDP. A negative value for the output gap means that real GDP is below potential GDP. Look at the data on the output gap for Japan, the United Kingdom, and the United States for 2015 to 2020. (The values for the later years are forecasts.) (Under *World Economic Outlook*, click "DATABASE," then under "Download WEO Data" choose "By Countries (country-level data)." Select "Advanced economies," choose Japan, the United Kingdom, and the United States, and then choose "Output gap in percent of potential GDP.")

  a. Which country had the largest output gap (in absolute value) in 2015? Which country had the smallest output gap?

  b. Discuss what fiscal policies the governments of these countries could use to bring the output gaps to zero.

  c. Describe at least two problems that these countries would have in implementing your suggested policies.

D16.2 (Comparing the actual and cyclically adjusted budget deficits in the United States) The Congressional Budget Office (CBO) provides data on the actual and cyclically adjusted budget deficits. You can find data for the years 1965–2016 at cbo.gov/about/products/budget-economic-data#2. Scroll down to Estimate of Automatic Stabilizers and select Jan 2017.

  a. The CBO calls the budget deficit or surplus "Deficit or Surplus with Automatic Stabilizers" and calls the cyclically adjusted deficit or surplus the "Deficit or Surplus without Automatic Stabilizers." Briefly explain why the CBO uses these labels.

  b. For the years 2000–2016, enter the data from the columns "Deficit or Surplus with Automatic Stabilizers" and "Deficit or Surplus without Automatic Stabilizers" into an Excel spreadsheet. Use the data to graph the budget deficit or surplus and the cyclically adjusted deficit or surplus for these years.

  c. Calculate the average surplus or deficit and the average cyclically adjusted surplus or deficit for these years. Which was larger? Briefly explain your result.

D16.3 (Comparing budget deficits in different countries) The International Monetary Fund (IMF) publishes *The World Economic Outlook*. Go to www.imf.org and find the IMF data for the cyclically adjusted budget deficit as a percentage of potential GDP (which the IMF calls "General Government Structural Balance") for Brazil, China, France, and Germany from 2000 to 2020. (The values for the later years are forecasts.) Use the series for the cyclically adjusted budget deficit that is measured as a percentage of potential GDP. (Under *World Economic Outlook*, click "DATABASE," then under "Download WEO Data" choose "By Countries (country-level data)." Select "All economies," choose Brazil, China, France, and Germany, and then choose "General government structural balance, Percent of potential GDP.")

  a. Download the data and plot them in a graph. Which country relied the most on discretionary fiscal policy in response to the financial crisis of 2008 and 2009? Briefly explain how you are able to tell.

  b. From 2013 to 2018, which of these four countries is expected to have the most expansionary fiscal policy? Briefly explain.

Critical Thinking Exercises

CT16.1 In Chapter 15, Table 15.2 on page 533 describes how monetary policy affects real GDP and the price level. Modify this table to apply it to fiscal policy. Be sure to include both the effects of changes in taxes and changes in government purchases.

CT16.2 What would be the value of the government purchases multiplier if there were complete crowding out? Briefly explain your reasoning.

Appendix

A Closer Look at the Multiplier

LEARNING OBJECTIVE: Apply the multiplier formula.

In this chapter, we saw that changes in government purchases and changes in taxes have a multiplied effect on equilibrium real GDP. In this appendix, we will build a simple economic model of the multiplier effect. When economists forecast the effect of a change in spending or taxes, they often rely on *econometric models*. These are economic models written in the form of equations, where each equation has been statistically estimated from macroeconomic data.

An Expression for Equilibrium Real GDP

We can write a set of equations that includes the key macroeconomic relationships we have studied in this and previous chapters. It is important to note that in this model, we will be assuming that the price level is constant. We know that this assumption is unrealistic because an upward-sloping *SRAS* curve means that when the aggregate demand curve shifts, the price level will change. Nevertheless, our model will be approximately correct when changes in the price level are small. It also serves as an introduction to more complicated models that take into account changes in the price level. For simplicity, we start with three assumptions: (1) Taxes, T, do not depend on the level of real GDP, Y; (2) there are no government transfer payments to households; and (3) we have a closed economy, with no imports or exports. The numbers (with the exception of the *MPC*) are in billions of dollars:

1. $C = \$1,000 + 0.75(Y - T)$ (consumption function)
2. $I = \$1,500$ (planned investment function)
3. $G = \$1,500$ (government purchases function)
4. $T = \$1,000$ (tax function)
5. $Y = C + I + G$ (equilibrium condition)

Equation 1 is the consumption function. The marginal propensity to consume, or *MPC*, is 0.75, and $1,000 is the level of autonomous consumption, which is the level of consumption that does not depend on income. We assume that consumption depends on disposable income, which is $Y - T$. The functions for planned investment spending, government spending, and taxes are very simple because we have assumed that these variables are not affected by GDP and, therefore, are constant. Economists who use this type of model to forecast GDP would, of course, use more realistic planned investment, government purchases, and tax functions.

Equation 5—the equilibrium condition—states that equilibrium GDP equals the sum of consumption, planned investment spending, and government purchases. To calculate a value for equilibrium real GDP, we need to substitute equations 1 through 4 into equation 5. This substitution gives us the following:

$$Y = \$1,000 + 0.75(Y - \$1,000) + \$1,500 + \$1,500$$
$$= \$1,000 + 0.75Y - \$750 + \$1,500 + \$1,500.$$

We need to solve this equation for Y to find equilibrium GDP. The first step is to subtract $0.75Y$ from both sides of the equation:

$$Y - 0.75Y = \$1,000 - \$750 + \$1,500 + \$1,500.$$

Then, we solve for Y:

$$0.25Y = \$3,250,$$

or:

$$Y = \frac{\$3{,}250}{0.25} = \$13{,}000.$$

To make this result more general, we can replace particular values with general values represented by letters:

- $C = \bar{C} + MPC(Y - T)$ (consumption function)
- $I = \bar{I}$ (planned investment function)
- $G = \bar{G}$ (government purchases function)
- $T = \bar{T}$ (tax function)
- $Y = C + I + G$ (equilibrium condition)

The letters with bars above them represent fixed, or *autonomous*, values that do not depend on the values of other variables. So, $\bar{C}$ represents autonomous consumption, which had a value of \$1,000 in our original example. Now, solving for equilibrium, we get:

$$Y = \bar{C} + MPC(Y - \bar{T}) + \bar{I} + \bar{G}$$

or:

$$Y - MPC(Y) = \bar{C} - (MPC \times \bar{T}) + \bar{I} + \bar{G}$$

or:

$$Y(1 - MPC) = \bar{C} - (MPC \times \bar{T}) + \bar{I} + \bar{G}$$

or:

MyLab Economics Concept Check

$$Y = \frac{\bar{C} - (MPC \times \bar{T}) + \bar{I} + \bar{G}}{1 - MPC}.$$

A Formula for the Government Purchases Multiplier

To find a formula for the government purchases multiplier, we need to rewrite the last equation for changes in each variable rather than levels. Letting Δ stand for the change in a variable, we have:

$$\Delta Y = \frac{\Delta \bar{C} - (MPC \times \Delta \bar{T}) + \Delta \bar{I} + \Delta \bar{G}}{1 - MPC}.$$

We can find a formula for the government purchases multiplier, which is the ratio of the change in equilibrium real GDP to the change in government purchases. If we hold constant changes in autonomous consumption spending, planned investment spending, and taxes, then from the previous equation, we have the following:

$$\Delta Y = \frac{\Delta G}{1 - MPC}.$$

So, we have:

$$\text{Government purchases multiplier} = \frac{\Delta Y}{\Delta G} = \frac{1}{1 - MPC}.$$

For an MPC of 0.75, the government purchases multiplier will be:

$$\frac{1}{1 - 0.75} = 4.$$

A government purchases multiplier of 4 means that an increase in government spending of \$10 billion will increase equilibrium real GDP by $4 \times \$10$ billion = \$40 billion.

MyLab Economics Concept Check

A Formula for the Tax Multiplier

We can also find a formula for the tax multiplier. We start again with this equation:

$$\Delta Y = \frac{\Delta \overline{C} - (MPC \times \Delta \overline{T}) + \Delta \overline{I} + \Delta \overline{G}}{1 - MPC}.$$

Now we hold constant the values of autonomous consumption spending, planned investment spending, and government purchases, but we allow the value of taxes to change:

$$\Delta Y = \frac{-MPC \times \Delta T}{1 - MPC}.$$

So, we have:

$$\text{The tax multiplier} = \frac{\Delta Y}{\Delta T} = \frac{-MPC}{1 - MPC}.$$

For an *MPC* of 0.75, the tax multiplier will be:

$$\frac{-0.75}{1 - 0.75} = -3.$$

The tax multiplier is a negative number because an increase in taxes causes a decrease in equilibrium real GDP, and a decrease in taxes causes an increase in equilibrium real GDP. A tax multiplier of −3 means that a decrease in taxes of $10 billion will increase equilibrium real GDP by −3 × −$10 billion = $30 billion. Earlier in this chapter, we discussed the economic reasons for the tax multiplier being smaller than the government spending multiplier.   **MyLab Economics** Concept Check

The "Balanced Budget" Multiplier

What will be the effect of equal increases (or decreases) in government purchases and taxes on equilibrium real GDP? At first, it might appear that the tax increase would exactly offset the government purchases increase, leaving real GDP unchanged. But we have just seen that the government purchases multiplier is larger (in absolute value) than the tax multiplier. We can use our formulas for the government purchases multiplier and the tax multiplier to calculate the net effect of increasing government purchases by $10 billion at the same time that taxes are increased by $10 billion:

Increase in real GDP from the increase in government purchases

$$= \$10 \text{ billion} \times \frac{1}{1 - MPC}.$$

$$\text{Decrease in real GDP from the increase in taxes} = \$10 \text{ billion} \times \frac{-MPC}{1 - MPC}.$$

So, the combined effect equals:

$$\$10 \text{ billion} \times \left[\left(\frac{1}{1 - MPC} \right) + \left(\frac{-MPC}{1 - MPC} \right) \right]$$

or:

$$\$10 \text{ billion} \times \left(\frac{1 - MPC}{1 - MPC} \right) = \$10 \text{ billion}.$$

The balanced budget multiplier is, therefore, equal to $(1-MPC)/(1-MPC)$, or 1. Equal dollar increases and decreases in government purchases and in taxes lead to the same dollar increase in real GDP in the short run. **MyLab Economics** Concept Check

The Effects of Changes in Tax Rates on the Multiplier

We now consider the effect of a change in the tax *rate*, as opposed to a change in a fixed amount of taxes. Changing the tax rate actually changes the value of the multiplier. To see this, suppose that the tax rate is 20 percent, or 0.2. In that case, an increase in household income of $10 billion will increase *disposable income* by only $8 billion [or 10 billion × $(1 - 0.2)$ In general, an increase in income can be multiplied by $(1 - t)$ to find the increase in disposable income, where t is the tax rate. So, we can rewrite the consumption function as:

$$C = \overline{C} + MPC(1 - t)Y.$$

We can use this expression for the consumption function to find an expression for the government purchases multiplier, using the same method we used previously:

$$\text{Government purchases multiplier} = \frac{\Delta Y}{\Delta G} = \frac{1}{1 - MPC(1 - t)}.$$

We can see the effect of changing the tax rate on the size of the multiplier by trying some values. First, assume that $MPC = 0.75$ and $t = 0.2$. Then:

$$\text{Government purchases multiplier} = \frac{\Delta Y}{\Delta G} = \frac{1}{1 - 0.75(1 - 0.2)} = \frac{1}{1 - 0.6} = 2.5.$$

This value is smaller than the multiplier of 4 that we calculated by assuming that there was only a fixed amount of taxes (which is the same as assuming that the marginal tax *rate* was zero). This multiplier is smaller because spending in each period is now reduced by the amount of taxes households must pay on any additional income they earn. We can calculate the multiplier for an MPC of 0.75 and a lower tax rate of 0.1:

$$\text{Government purchases multiplier} = \frac{\Delta Y}{\Delta G} = \frac{1}{1 - 0.75(1 - 0.1)} = \frac{1}{1 - 0.675} = 3.1.$$

Cutting the tax rate from 20 percent to 10 percent increased the value of the multiplier from 2.5 to 3.1. **MyLab Economics** Concept Check

The Multiplier in an Open Economy

Up to now, we have assumed that the economy is closed, with no imports or exports. We can consider the case of an open economy by including net exports in our analysis. Recall that net exports equal exports minus imports. Exports are determined primarily by factors—such as the exchange value of the dollar and the levels of real GDP in other countries—that we do not include in our model. So, we will assume that exports are fixed, or autonomous:

$$\text{Exports} = \overline{\text{Exports}}.$$

Imports will increase as real GDP increases because households will spend some portion of an increase in income on imports. We can define the *marginal propensity to import* (*MPI*) as the fraction of an increase in income that is spent on imports. So, our expression for imports is:

$$\text{Imports} = MPI \times Y.$$

We can substitute our expressions for exports and imports into the expression we derived earlier for equilibrium real GDP:

$$Y = \overline{C} + MPC(1 - t)Y + \overline{I} + \overline{G} + [\overline{\text{Exports}} - (MPI \times Y)],$$

where the expression $[\overline{\text{Exports}}\text{-}(MPI \times Y)]$ represents net exports. We can now find an expression for the government purchases multiplier by using the same method we used previously:

$$\text{Government purchases multiplier} = \frac{\Delta Y}{\Delta G} = \frac{1}{1 - [MPC(1 - t) - MPI]}.$$

We can see the effect of changing the value of the marginal propensity to import on the size of the multiplier by trying some values of key variables. First, assume that $MPC = 0.75$, $t = 0.2$, and $MPI = 0.1$. Then:

$$\text{Government purchases multiplier} = \frac{\Delta Y}{\Delta G} = \frac{1}{1 - (0.75(1 - 0.2) - 0.1)} = \frac{1}{1 - 0.5}$$
$$= 2.$$

This value is smaller than the multiplier of 2.5 that we calculated by assuming that there were no exports or imports (which is the same as assuming that the marginal propensity to import is zero). This multiplier is smaller because spending in each period is now reduced by the amount of imports households buy with any additional income they earn. We can calculate the multiplier with $MPC = 0.75$, $t = 0.2$, and a higher MPI of 0.2:

$$\text{Government purchases multiplier} = \frac{\Delta Y}{\Delta G} = \frac{1}{1 - (0.75(1 - 0.2) - 0.2)} = \frac{1}{1 - 0.4}$$
$$= 1.7.$$

Increasing the marginal propensity to import from 0.1 to 0.2 decreases the value of the multiplier from 2 to 1.7. We can conclude that countries with a higher marginal propensity to import will have smaller multipliers than countries with a lower marginal propensity to import.

Bear in mind that the multiplier is a short-run effect that assumes that real GDP is less than potential GDP. In the long run, real GDP equals potential GDP, so an increase in government purchases causes a decline in the nongovernment components of real GDP but leaves the level of real GDP unchanged.

The analysis in this appendix is simplified compared to what would be carried out by an economist forecasting the effects of changes in government purchases or changes in taxes on equilibrium real GDP in the short run. In particular, our assumption that the price level is constant is unrealistic. However, looking more closely at the determinants of the multiplier has helped us see some important macroeconomic relationships more clearly. **MyLab Economics** Concept Check

A Closer Look at the Multiplier, pages 605–609

LEARNING OBJECTIVE: Apply the multiplier formula.

MyLab Economics Visit **www.pearson.com/mylab/economics** to complete these exercises online and get instant feedback.

Problem and Applications

16A.1 Assuming a fixed amount of taxes and a closed economy, calculate the value of the government purchases multiplier, the tax multiplier, and the balanced budget multiplier if the marginal propensity to consume equals 0.6.

16A.2 Calculate the value of the government purchases multiplier if the marginal propensity to consume equals 0.8, the tax rate equals 0.25, and the marginal propensity to import equals 0.2.

16A.3 Use a graph to show the change in the aggregate demand curve resulting from an increase in government purchases if the government purchases multiplier equals 2. On the same graph, show the change in the aggregate demand curve resulting from an increase in government purchases if the government purchases multiplier equals 4.

16A.4 Using your understanding of multipliers, explain why an increase in the tax rate would decrease the size of the government purchases multiplier. Similarly, explain why a decrease in the marginal propensity to import would increase the size of the government purchases multiplier.

16A.5 In 2015, the ratio of imports to GDP was 18 percent in Japan and 81 percent in Belgium. On the basis of this information, can you draw any conclusions about the relative sizes of the government purchases multiplier in each country?

The Fed Tries for a "Soft Landing," while General Motors and Toll Brothers Look On

In mid-2017, to head off the threat of rising inflation, the Federal Reserve's Federal Open Market Committee (FOMC) raised its target for the federal funds rate to a range of 1 percent to 1.25 percent, the fourth increase since December 2015. And members of the FOMC indicated that future increases were planned. As we saw in Chapter 15, the Fed raises its target for the federal funds rate when it believes that real GDP is increasing beyond potential GDP, pushing unemployment to low levels and increasing inflation. Ideally, rising interest rates will allow the economy to make a "soft landing," which means that inflation will decline but the economy will avoid slipping into a recession.

The situation facing Fed policymakers in 2017 was complex, however. The unemployment rate had declined from a high of 10.0 percent in October 2009 to 4.3 percent, at or below most economists' estimates of full employment. But the Fed's preferred measure of the inflation rate remained below its 2 percent target, and interest rates on long-term Treasury bonds remained low, indicating that bond market investors did not expect inflation to increase. In addition, as we saw in Chapter 16, growth rates of real GDP also remained low. Some FOMC members worried that in those economic circumstances, if the target for the federal funds rate were increased further, the U.S. economy would be at risk of falling into a recession.

For many firms, the outcome of the Fed's policy debates would have significant consequences. Two key industries—automobiles and housing—were already showing signs of slowing down in 2017. Sales of General Motors' cars and trucks were lower in the first five months of 2017 than they had been in 2016, and in June, the company announced that it was laying off workers. New housing starts were also weaker during early 2017 than they had been a year earlier, which

Patrick T. Fallon/Bloomberg/Getty Images

was bad news for homebuilders such as Toll Brothers. Economists attributed the sales declines partly to rising interest rates on mortgages and car loans. With real GDP increasing by only 1.2 percent during the first quarter of 2017 and inflation below the Fed's 2 percent target, Federal Reserve Bank of St. Louis President James Bullard described further increases in the federal funds rate as "unnecessarily aggressive."

In developing policy, the Fed faces the difficulty that changes in interest rates typically have their full effect on the economy over a period as long as two years. As we saw in Chapter 15, if the Fed changes policy in response to temporary fluctuations in output, employment, and inflation, it risks destabilizing the economy. In 2017, Fed Chair Janet Yellen and her colleagues on the FOMC found it was no easy task to achieve a soft landing consistent with the Fed's dual mandate of high employment and low inflation.

Sources: Nick Timiraos, "Fed's Bullard Calls Officials' Projected Rate Path 'Unnecessarily Aggressive,'" *Wall Street Journal*, June 22, 2017; Mike Colias, "GM Laying off About 1,000 Workers amid Downturn in Passenger-Car Sales," *Wall Street Journal*, June 19, 2017; Sarah Chaney, "U.S. Housing Starts Fall for Third Consecutive Month in May," *Wall Street Journal*, June 16, 2017; and Board of Governors of the Federal Reserve System, "Statement of the Federal Reserve Open Market Committee," June 14, 2017.

17.1 The Discovery of the Short-Run Trade-off between Unemployment and Inflation, page 612
Describe the Phillips curve and the nature of the short-run trade-off between unemployment and inflation.

17.2 The Short-Run and Long-Run Phillips Curves, page 617
Explain the relationship between the short-run and long-run Phillips curves.

17.3 Expectations of the Inflation Rate and Monetary Policy, page 622
Discuss how expectations of the inflation rate affect monetary policy.

17.4 Federal Reserve Policy from the 1970s to the Present, page 624
Use a Phillips curve graph to show how the Federal Reserve can permanently lower the inflation rate.

Economics in Your Life & Career

Are There Benefits to Delaying a Job Search?

During a recession, your friend is laid off from her entry-level job as a software engineer. You call her and she explains that she's not very upset because: "Our state offers workers up to 99 weeks of unemployment compensation. So, I have almost two years before I have to find a new job. With my education and job experience, I can wait quite a while and still be able to find a new job without much trouble." Your friend did well in school, but you are not sure that waiting to find a new job is a good idea. What advice would you give someone who has decided to wait so long to look for a new job? As you read the chapter, try to answer this question. You can check your answer against the one we provide on **page 636** at the end of this chapter.

A
s the Federal Reserve carries out monetary policy, it knows that in the short run there is usually a trade-off between unemployment and inflation: Lower unemployment rates can result in higher inflation rates. In the long run, however, this trade-off disappears, and the unemployment rate is independent of the inflation rate. In this chapter, we will explore the relationship between inflation and unemployment in both the short run and the long run, and we will discuss what this relationship means for monetary policy. We will also provide an overview of how monetary policy has evolved over the years and conclude with a discussion of the debate over Fed policy during and after the 2007–2009 recession.

17.1 The Discovery of the Short-Run Trade-off between Unemployment and Inflation

LEARNING OBJECTIVE: Describe the Phillips curve and the nature of the short-run trade-off between unemployment and inflation.

During most of the Fed's history, it has contended with two great macroeconomic problems—unemployment and inflation. When aggregate demand increases, unemployment usually falls, and inflation rises. When aggregate demand decreases, unemployment usually rises, and inflation falls. As a result, there is a *short-run trade-off* between unemployment and inflation: Higher unemployment is usually accompanied by lower inflation, and lower unemployment is usually accompanied by higher inflation. As we will see in Section 17.2, this trade-off exists in the short run—a period that may be as long as several years—but disappears in the long run.

Although today the short-run trade-off between unemployment and inflation plays a role in the Fed's monetary policy decisions, this trade-off was not widely recognized until the late 1950s. In 1957, New Zealand economist A. W. Phillips plotted data on the unemployment rate and the inflation rate in Great Britain and drew a curve showing their average relationship. Since that time, a graph showing the short-run relationship between the unemployment rate and the inflation rate has been called a **Phillips curve**. (Phillips actually measured inflation by the percentage change in wages rather than by the percentage change in prices. Because wages and prices usually move together, this difference is not important to our discussion.) Figure 17.1 shows a graph similar to the one Phillips prepared. Each point on the Phillips curve represents a possible combination of the unemployment rate and the inflation rate that might be observed in a given year. Point *A* represents a year in which the inflation rate is 4 percent and the

Phillips curve A graph showing the short-run relationship between the unemployment rate and the inflation rate.

Figure 17.1

The Phillips Curve

A. W. Phillips was the first economist to show that there is usually an inverse relationship between unemployment and inflation. Here we can see this relationship at work: In the year represented by point *A*, the inflation rate is 4 percent, and the unemployment rate is 5 percent. In the year represented by point *B*, the inflation rate is 2 percent, and the unemployment rate is 6 percent.

unemployment rate is 5 percent, and point B represents a year in which the inflation rate is 2 percent and the unemployment rate is 6 percent. Phillips documented that there is usually an *inverse relationship* between unemployment and inflation. During years when the unemployment rate is low, the inflation rate tends to be high, and during years when the unemployment rate is high, the inflation rate tends to be low.

Explaining the Phillips Curve with Aggregate Demand and Aggregate Supply Curves

The inverse relationship between unemployment and inflation that Phillips discovered is consistent with the aggregate demand and aggregate supply analysis we developed in Chapter 13. Figure 17.2 shows why this inverse relationship exists.

Panel (a) shows the aggregate demand and aggregate supply (*AD–AS*) model, and panel (b) shows the Phillips curve. For simplicity, in panel (a), we are using the basic *AD–AS* model, and we are assuming that the long-run aggregate supply curve and the short-run aggregate supply curve do not shift. To take a hypothetical example, assume that short-run equilibrium in 2019 is at point A, with real GDP of $17.0 trillion and a price level of 110.0. If there is weak growth in aggregate demand during 2020, short-run equilibrium is at point B, with real GDP of $17.3 trillion and a price level of 112.2. The inflation rate is 2 percent, and the unemployment rate is 6 percent, which corresponds to point B on the Phillips curve in panel (b). If there is strong growth in aggregate demand during 2020, short-run equilibrium is at point C, with real GDP of $17.6 trillion and a price level of 114.4. Strong aggregate demand growth results in a higher inflation rate of 4 percent but a lower unemployment rate of 5 percent. This combination of higher inflation and lower unemployment is shown as point C on the Phillips curve in panel (b).

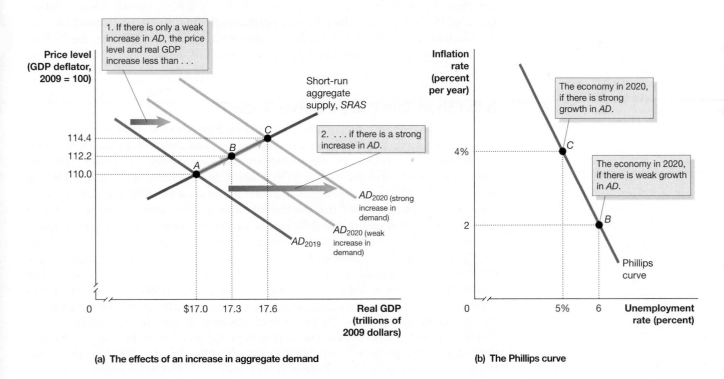

(a) The effects of an increase in aggregate demand

(b) The Phillips curve

MyLab Economics Animation

Figure 17.2   Using Aggregate Demand and Aggregate Supply to Explain the Phillips Curve

In panel (a), short-run equilibrium in 2019 is at point A, with real GDP of $17.0 trillion and a price level of 110.0. If there is weak growth in aggregate demand during 2020, short-run equilibrium is at point B, with real GDP of $17.3 trillion and a price level of 112.2. The inflation rate is 2 percent, and the unemployment rate is 6 percent, which corresponds to point B on the Phillips curve in panel (b). If there is strong growth in aggregate demand during 2020, short-run equilibrium is at point C, with real GDP of $17.6 trillion and a price level of 114.4. Strong aggregate demand growth results in a higher inflation rate of 4 percent but a lower unemployment rate of 5 percent. This combination of higher inflation and lower unemployment is shown as point C on the Phillips curve in panel (b).

To summarize, the *AD–AS* model indicates that slow growth in aggregate demand leads to both higher unemployment and lower inflation. This result explains why there is a short-run trade-off between unemployment and inflation, as shown by the downward-sloping Phillips curve. The *AD–AS* model and the Phillips curve provide different ways of illustrating the same macroeconomic events. The Phillips curve has an advantage over the *AD–AS* model, however, when we want to explicitly analyze *changes* in the inflation and unemployment rates. **MyLab Economics** Concept Check

Is the Phillips Curve a Policy Menu?

Structural relationship A relationship that depends on the basic behavior of consumers and firms and that remains unchanged over long periods.

During the 1960s, some economists argued that the Phillips curve represented a *structural relationship* in the economy. A **structural relationship** depends on the basic behavior of consumers and firms and remains unchanged over long periods. Structural relationships are useful in formulating economic policy because policymakers can anticipate that these relationships are constant—that is, the relationships will not change as a result of changes in policy.

If the Phillips curve were a structural relationship, it would present policymakers with a reliable menu of combinations of unemployment and inflation. Potentially, policymakers could use expansionary monetary and fiscal policies to choose a point on the curve that had lower unemployment and higher inflation. They could also use contractionary monetary and fiscal policies to choose a point that had lower inflation and higher unemployment. Because many economists and policymakers in the 1960s viewed the Phillips curve as a structural relationship, they believed it represented a *permanent trade-off between unemployment and inflation.* As long as policymakers were willing to accept a permanently higher inflation rate, they would be able to keep the unemployment rate permanently lower. Similarly, a permanently lower inflation rate could be achieved at the cost of a permanently higher unemployment rate. As we discuss in the next section, however, economists came to realize that the Phillips curve does *not*, in fact, represent a permanent trade-off between unemployment and inflation. **MyLab Economics** Concept Check

Is the Short-Run Phillips Curve Stable?

During the 1960s, the basic Phillips curve relationship seemed to hold because a stable trade-off appeared to exist between unemployment and inflation. In the early 1960s, the inflation rate was low, and the unemployment rate was high. In the late 1960s, the unemployment rate had declined, and the inflation rate had increased. Then, in 1968, in his presidential address to the American Economic Association, Milton Friedman of the University of Chicago argued that the Phillips curve did *not* represent a *permanent* trade-off between unemployment and inflation. At almost the same time, Edmund Phelps of Columbia University published an academic paper making a similar argument. Friedman and Phelps noted that economists had come to agree that the long-run aggregate supply curve was vertical (a point we discussed in Chapter 13). If this observation is correct, the Phillips curve cannot be downward sloping in the long run. A critical inconsistency exists between a vertical long-run aggregate supply curve and a downward-sloping long-run Phillips curve. Friedman and Phelps resolved this inconsistency by arguing, in essence, that there is no trade-off between unemployment and inflation in the long run because the long-run Phillips curve is vertical rather than downward sloping. (Both Friedman and Phelps were awarded the Nobel Prize in Economics.) **MyLab Economics** Concept Check

The Long-Run Phillips Curve

Natural rate of unemployment The unemployment rate that exists when the economy is at potential GDP.

To understand the argument that there is no permanent trade-off between unemployment and inflation, first recall that the level of real GDP in the long run is also called *potential GDP*. At potential GDP, firms will operate at their normal level of capacity, and everyone who wants a job will have one, except the structurally and frictionally unemployed. Friedman defined the **natural rate of unemployment** as the unemployment rate that exists when the economy is at potential GDP. The actual unemployment rate

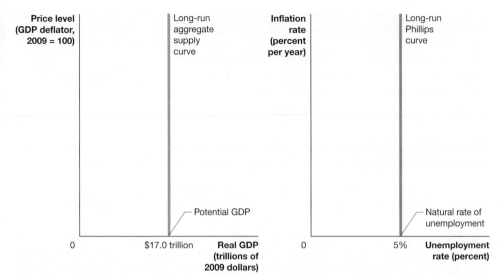

MyLab Economics Animation

Figure 17.3

A Vertical Long-Run Aggregate Supply Curve Means a Vertical Long-Run Phillips Curve

Milton Friedman and Edmund Phelps argued that there is no trade-off between unemployment and inflation in the long run. If real GDP automatically returns to its potential level in the long run, the unemployment rate must return to the natural rate of unemployment in the long run. In this figure, we assume that potential GDP is $17.0 trillion and the natural rate of unemployment is 5 percent.

will fluctuate in the short run but will always come back to the natural rate in the long run. In the same way, the actual level of real GDP will fluctuate in the short run but will always come back to potential GDP in the long run.

In the long run, a higher or lower price level has no effect on real GDP because real GDP is always at potential GDP in the long run. In the same way, in the long run, a higher or lower inflation rate will have no effect on the unemployment rate because the unemployment rate is always equal to the natural rate in the long run. Figure 17.3 illustrates Friedman's conclusion that the long-run aggregate supply curve is a vertical line at potential real GDP, and *the long-run Phillips curve is a vertical line at the natural rate of unemployment.*

MyLab Economics Concept Check

The Role of Expectations of Future Inflation

If the long-run Phillips curve is a vertical line, *no trade-off exists between unemployment and inflation in the long run.* This conclusion seemed to contradict the experience of the 1950s and 1960s, which showed a stable trade-off between unemployment and inflation. Friedman argued that the statistics from those years actually showed only a short-run trade-off between inflation and unemployment.

Friedman argued that the short-run trade-off existed only because workers and firms sometimes expected the inflation rate to be either higher or lower than it turned out to be. Differences between the expected inflation rate and the actual inflation rate could lead the unemployment rate to rise above or fall below the natural rate. To see why, consider a simple case of General Motors negotiating a wage contract with the United Auto Workers (UAW) union. Remember that both General Motors and the UAW are interested in the real wage, which is the nominal wage corrected for inflation. Column (1) of Table 17.1 shows General Motors and the UAW agreeing on a wage of $34.65 per hour to be paid during 2020. Column (2) shows the situation if both General Motors and the UAW expect that the price level will increase from 110.0 in 2019 to

(1) Nominal Wage	(2) Expected Real Wage	(3) Actual Real Wage with 2% Inflation	(4) Actual Real Wage with 8% Inflation
	Expected $P_{2020} = 115.5$ Expected inflation = 5%	Actual $P_{2020} = 112.2$ Actual inflation = 2%	Actual $P_{2020} = 118.8$ Actual inflation = 8%
$34.65	$\dfrac{\$34.65}{115.5} \times 100 = \$30.00$	$\dfrac{\$34.65}{112.2} \times 100 = \$30.88$	$\dfrac{\$34.65}{118.8} \times 100 = \$29.17$

Table 17.1

The Effect of Unexpected Price Level Changes on the Real Wage

Table 17.2

The Basis for the Short-Run Phillips Curve

If . . .	then . . .	and . . .
actual inflation is greater than expected inflation,	the actual real wage is less than the expected real wage,	the unemployment rate falls.
actual inflation is less than expected inflation,	the actual real wage is greater than the expected real wage,	the unemployment rate rises.

115.5 in 2020, so the inflation rate will be 5 percent. We can calculate the real wage General Motors expects to pay and the UAW expects to receive as follows:

$$\text{Real wage} = \frac{\text{Nominal wage}}{\text{Price level}} \times 100 = \frac{\$34.65}{115.5} \times 100 = \$30.00.$$

But suppose that the actual inflation rate turns out to be higher or lower than the expected inflation rate of 5 percent. Column (3) shows that if the price level (P) rises only to 112.2 in 2020, the inflation rate will be 2 percent, and the actual real wage will be \$30.88, which is higher than General Motors and the UAW had expected. With a higher real wage, General Motors will hire fewer workers than it had planned to hire at the expected real wage of \$30.00. Column (4) shows that if the inflation rate is 8 percent, the actual real wage will be \$29.17, and General Motors will hire more workers than it had planned to hire. If General Motors and the UAW expected a higher or lower inflation rate than actually occurred, other firms and workers probably did the same.

If actual inflation is higher than expected inflation, actual real wages in the economy will be lower than expected real wages, and many firms will hire more workers than they had planned to hire. Therefore, the unemployment rate will fall. If actual inflation is lower than expected inflation, actual real wages will be higher than expected, many firms will hire fewer workers than they had planned to hire, and the unemployment rate will rise. Table 17.2 summarizes this point.

Friedman and Phelps concluded that *an increase in the inflation rate increases employment (and decreases unemployment) only if the increase in the inflation rate is unexpected.* Friedman argued that in 1968, the unemployment rate was 3.6 percent rather than 5 percent only because the inflation rate of 4.2 percent was above the 1 percent to 2 percent inflation that workers and firms had expected: "There is always a temporary trade-off between inflation and unemployment; there is no permanent trade-off. The temporary trade-off comes not from inflation per se, but from unanticipated inflation."

MyLab Economics Study Plan   MyLab Economics Concept Check

  Apply the Concept   MyLab Economics Video

Do Workers Understand Inflation?

A higher inflation rate can lead to lower unemployment if *both* workers and firms mistakenly expect the inflation rate to be lower than it turns out to be. But this same result might be due to firms forecasting inflation more accurately than workers do or because firms understand better the effects of inflation. Some large firms employ economists to help them gather and analyze information that is useful in forecasting inflation. Many firms also have human resources or employee compensation departments that gather data on wages competing firms pay and analyze trends in compensation. Workers generally rely on much less systematic information about wages and prices. Workers also often fail to realize a fact we discussed in Chapter 9, Section 9.7: *Expected inflation increases the value of total production and the value of total income by the same amount.* Therefore, although not all wages will rise as prices rise, inflation will increase average wages in the economy at the same time that it increases average prices.

Nobel Laureate Robert Shiller of Yale University conducted a survey on inflation and discovered that, although most economists believe an increase in inflation will lead quickly to an increase in wages, a majority of the general public thinks otherwise. As part of the survey, Shiller asked how "the effect of general inflation on wages or salary relates to your own experience and your own job." The most popular response was "The

Paul Bradbury/OJO Images/Getty Images

Will prices rise faster than his wage?

price increase will create extra profits for my employer, who can now sell output for more; there will be no effect on my pay. My employer will see no reason to raise my pay."

Shiller also asked the following question:

> Imagine that next year the inflation rate unexpectedly doubles. How long would it probably take, in these times, before your income is increased enough so that you can afford the same things as you do today? In other words, how long will it be before a full inflation correction in your income has taken place?

Eighty-one percent of the public answered either that it would take several years for the purchasing power of their income to be restored or that it would never be restored.

If workers fail to understand that rising inflation leads over time to comparable increases in wages, then when inflation increases, firms, in the short run, can increase wages by less than inflation without needing to worry about workers quitting or their morale falling. As a result, a higher inflation rate will lead in the short run to lower real wages and lower unemployment. In other words, we have an explanation for a downward-sloping short-run Phillips curve.

Source: Robert J. Shiller, "Why Do People Dislike Inflation?" in *Reducing Inflation: Motivation and Strategy* by Christina D. Romer and David H. Romer, eds., Chicago: University of Chicago Press, 1997.

Your Turn: Test your understanding by doing related problems 1.11 and 1.12 on page 638 at the end of this chapter.

MyLab Economics Study Plan

 The Short-Run and Long-Run Phillips Curves

17.2

LEARNING OBJECTIVE: Explain the relationship between the short-run and long-run Phillips curves.

If there is both a short-run Phillips curve and a long-run Phillips curve, how are the two curves related? We can begin answering this question with the help of Figure 17.4, which represents macroeconomic conditions in the United States during the 1960s. In the late 1960s, workers and firms were still expecting the inflation rate to be about 1.5 percent, as it had been from 1960 to 1965. Expansionary monetary and fiscal policies, however, had moved the short-run equilibrium up the short-run Phillips curve to an inflation rate of 4.5 percent and an unemployment rate of 3.5 percent. This very low unemployment rate was possible only because the real wage rate was unexpectedly low.

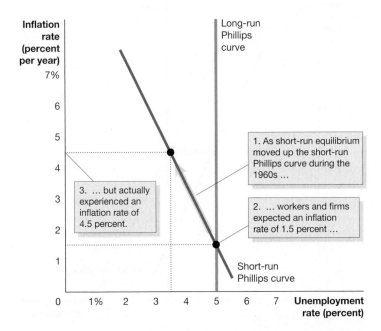

MyLab Economics Animation

Figure 17.4

The Short-Run Phillips Curve of the 1960s and the Long-Run Phillips Curve

In the late 1960s, U.S. workers and firms were expecting the 1.5 percent inflation rates of the recent past to continue. However, expansionary monetary and fiscal policies moved short-run equilibrium up the short-run Phillips curve to an inflation rate of 4.5 percent and an unemployment rate of 3.5 percent.

Once workers and firms began to expect that the inflation rate would continue to be about 4.5 percent, they changed their behavior. Firms knew that only nominal wage increases of more than 4.5 percent would increase real wages. Workers realized that unless they received a nominal wage increase of at least 4.5 percent, their real wage would be falling. Higher expected inflation rates had an effect throughout the economy. For example, when banks make loans, they are interested in the *real interest rate* on the loan (see Chapter 9, Section 9.6). The real interest rate is the nominal interest rate minus the expected inflation rate. Banks will charge a nominal interest rate of 4.5 percent to receive a real interest rate of 3 percent on home mortgage loans when they expect the inflation rate to be 1.5 percent. If banks revise their expectations of the inflation rate to 4.5 percent, they will increase the nominal interest rate they charge on mortgage loans to 7.5 percent.

Shifts in the Short-Run Phillips Curve

A new, higher expected inflation rate can become *embedded* in the economy, meaning that workers, firms, consumers, and the government all take the inflation rate into account when making decisions. The short-run trade-off between unemployment and inflation now takes place from this higher, less favorable level, as shown in Figure 17.5.

As long as workers and firms expected the inflation rate to be 1.5 percent, the short-run trade-off between unemployment and inflation was the more favorable one shown by the lower Phillips curve. Along this Phillips curve, an inflation rate of 4.5 percent was enough to drive down the unemployment rate to 3.5 percent. Once workers and firms adjusted their expectations to an inflation rate of 4.5 percent, the short-run trade-off deteriorated to the one shown by the higher Phillips curve. At this higher expected inflation rate, the real wage rose, causing some workers to lose their jobs, and equilibrium returned to the natural rate of unemployment of 5 percent—but now with an inflation rate of 4.5 percent rather than 1.5 percent. On the higher short-run Phillips curve, an inflation rate of 7.5 percent would be necessary to reduce the unemployment rate to 3.5 percent. An inflation rate of 7.5 percent would keep the unemployment rate at 3.5 percent only until workers and firms revised their expectations of inflation up to 7.5 percent. In the long run, equilibrium would return to the 5 percent natural rate of unemployment.

As Figure 17.6 shows, there is a short-run Phillips curve for every level of expected inflation. Each short-run Phillips curve intersects the long-run Phillips curve at the expected inflation rate. **MyLab Economics** Concept Check

MyLab Economics Animation

Figure 17.5

Expectations and the Short-Run Phillips Curve

By the end of the 1960s, workers and firms had revised their expectations of inflation from 1.5 percent to 4.5 percent. As a result, the short-run Phillips curve shifted up, which made the short-run trade-off between unemployment and inflation worse.

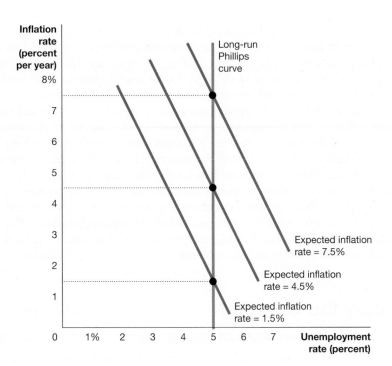

MyLab Economics Animation

Figure 17.6

A Short-Run Phillips Curve for Every Expected Inflation Rate

There is a different short-run Phillips curve for every expected inflation rate. Each short-run Phillips curve intersects the long-run Phillips curve at the expected inflation rate.

How Does a Vertical Long-Run Phillips Curve Affect Monetary Policy?

By the 1970s, most economists accepted the argument that the long-run Phillips curve is vertical. In other words, economists realized that the common view of the 1960s had been wrong: It was *not* possible to buy a permanently lower unemployment rate at the cost of a permanently higher inflation rate. Therefore, *in the long run, there is no trade-off between unemployment and inflation.* In the long run, the unemployment rate always returns to the natural rate, no matter what the inflation rate is.

Figure 17.7 shows that the inflation rate is stable only when the unemployment rate is equal to the natural rate. If the Federal Reserve were to attempt to use expansionary monetary policy to push short-run equilibrium to a point such as *A*, where the unemployment rate is below the natural rate, the result would be a movement up the

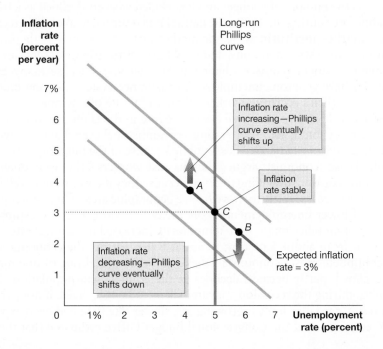

MyLab Economics Animation

Figure 17.7

The Inflation Rate and the Natural Rate of Unemployment in the Long Run

The inflation rate is stable only if the unemployment rate equals the natural rate of unemployment (point *C*). If the unemployment rate is below the natural rate (point *A*), the inflation rate increases, and, eventually, the short-run Phillips curve shifts up. If the unemployment rate is above the natural rate (point *B*), the inflation rate decreases, and, eventually, the short-run Phillips curve shifts down.

short-run Phillips curve with increasing inflation. If short-run equilibrium remained below the natural rate long enough, the short-run Phillips curve would shift up as workers and firms adjusted to the new, higher inflation rate. During the 1960s and 1970s, the short-run Phillips curve did shift up, presenting policymakers with a more unfavorable short-run trade-off between unemployment and inflation.

If the Federal Reserve used contractionary policy to push short-run equilibrium to a point such as *B*, where the unemployment rate is above the natural rate, the inflation rate would decrease. If short-run equilibrium remained above the natural rate long enough, the short-run Phillips curve would shift down as workers and firms adjusted to the new, lower inflation rate. Only at a point such as *C*, where the unemployment rate is equal to the natural rate, will the inflation rate be stable. Because the inflation rate has no tendency to increase or decrease when the unemployment rate equals the natural rate, the natural rate of unemployment is sometimes called the **nonaccelerating inflation rate of unemployment (NAIRU)**. We can conclude that *in the long run, the Federal Reserve can affect the inflation rate but not the unemployment rate.*

Nonaccelerating inflation rate of unemployment (NAIRU) The unemployment rate at which the inflation rate has no tendency to increase or decrease.

MyLab Economics Study Plan

MyLab Economics Concept Check

Apply the Concept

MyLab Economics Video

Does the Natural Rate of Unemployment Ever Change?

Lynne Sladky/AP Images

An increase in the number of younger and less-skilled workers in an economy can make the natural rate of unemployment increase.

Life would be easier for the Federal Reserve if it knew exactly what the natural rate of unemployment was and if that rate never changed. Unfortunately for the Fed, the natural rate does change over time. Remember that at the natural rate of unemployment, there is no cyclical unemployment, only frictional and structural unemployment. Frictional or structural unemployment can change—thereby changing the natural rate—for three key reasons:

1. **Demographic changes.** Younger and less-skilled workers have higher unemployment rates, on average, than do older and more-skilled workers. Because of the baby boom, the United States had an unusually large number of younger and less-skilled workers during the 1970s and 1980s. As a result, the natural rate of unemployment rose from about 5 percent in the 1960s to about 6 percent in the 1970s and 1980s. As the number of younger and less-skilled workers declined as a fraction of the labor force during the 1990s, the natural rate returned to about 5 percent.

2. **Labor market institutions.** Labor market institutions such as the unemployment insurance system, unions, and legal barriers to firing workers can increase the unemployment rate (see Chapter 9, Section 9.3). Because many European countries have generous unemployment insurance systems, strong unions, and restrictive policies on firing workers, the natural rate of unemployment in most of these countries has been well above the rate in the United States. During and after the recession of 2007–2009, some economists believed that many workers in the United States had become less mobile because of the bursting of the housing bubble. These economists argued that because workers either were unable to sell their homes or were unwilling to do so because they did not want to sell for a low price, they were less likely to move from a geographic area of high unemployment to one of lower unemployment. Economists at JPMorgan Chase estimated that this lack of mobility might have temporarily increased the natural rate of unemployment from about 5 percent to about 6 percent. As the economic recovery has continued, most economists believe that the natural rate of unemployment has declined, partly because declines in the employment-population ratio that occurred during the recession appeared likely to be long-lived, if not permanent. As a result, the labor force is growing at a slower rate than had been expected. In 2017, economists at the Congressional Budget Office estimated that the natural

rate of unemployment had declined to 4.7 percent, higher than the actual unemployment rate of 4.3 percent.

3. **Past high rates of unemployment.** Evidence indicates that if high unemployment persists for a period of years, the natural rate of unemployment may increase. When workers have been unemployed for longer than a year or two, their skills deteriorate, they may lose confidence that they can find and hold a job, and they may become dependent on government payments to survive. Robert Gordon, an economist at Northwestern University, has argued that in the late 1930s, so many U.S. workers had been out of work for so long that the natural rate of unemployment may have risen to more than 15 percent. He noted that even though the unemployment rate in the United States was 17 percent in 1939, the inflation rate did not change. Similarly, many economists have argued that the high unemployment rates experienced by European countries during the 1970s increased their natural rates of unemployment.

Sources: Congressional Budget Office, *The Budget and Economic Outlook: 2017–2027*, January 24, 2017; Robert J. Gordon, "Back to the Future: European Unemployment Today Viewed from America in 1939," *Brookings Papers on Economic Activity*, Vol. 19, 1988: I, pp. 271–304; and "Damage Assessment," *Economist*, May 14, 2009.

Your Turn: Test your understanding by doing related problems 2.7 and 2.8 on pages 639–640 at the end of this chapter.

MyLab Economics Study Plan

Solved Problem 17.2

MyLab Economics Interactive Animation

Changing Views of the Phillips Curve

Writing in a Federal Reserve publication, Bennett McCallum, an economist at Carnegie Mellon University, argued that during the 1970s, the Fed was "acting under the influence of 1960s academic ideas that posited the existence of a long-run and exploitable Phillips-type tradeoff between inflation and unemployment rates." What does McCallum mean by a "long-run and exploitable Phillips-type tradeoff"? How would the Fed have attempted to exploit this long-run trade-off? What would be the consequences for the inflation rate?

Solving the Problem

Step 1: Review the chapter material. This problem is about the relationship between the short-run and long-run Phillips curves, so you may want to review the section "The Short-Run and Long-Run Phillips Curves," which begins on page 617.

Step 2: Explain what a "long-run exploitable Phillips-type tradeoff" means. A "long-run exploitable Phillips-type tradeoff" means a Phillips curve that in the long run is downward sloping rather than vertical. An "exploitable" trade-off is one that the Fed could take advantage of to *permanently* reduce unemployment, at the expense of higher inflation, or to permanently reduce inflation, at the expense of higher unemployment.

Step 3: Explain how the inflation rate will accelerate if the Fed tries to exploit a long-run trade-off between unemployment and inflation. As we have seen, during the 1960s, the Fed conducted expansionary monetary policies to move up what it thought was a stationary short-run Phillips curve. By the late 1960s, these policies resulted in very low unemployment rates. In the long run, there is no stable trade-off between unemployment and inflation. Attempting to permanently keep the unemployment rate at very low levels leads to a rising inflation rate, which is what happened in the late 1960s and early 1970s.

Source: Bennett T. McCallum, "Recent Developments in Monetary Policy Analysis: The Roles of Theory and Evidence," *Federal Reserve Bank of Richmond Economic Quarterly*, Winter 2002, p. 73.

Your Turn: For more practice, do related problem 2.12 on page 640 at the end of this chapter.

MyLab Economics Study Plan

Expectations of the Inflation Rate and Monetary Policy

LEARNING OBJECTIVE: Discuss how expectations of the inflation rate affect monetary policy.

How quickly does short-run equilibrium adjust from a point that is on the short-run Phillips curve but not on the long-run Phillips curve back to a point that is on the long-run Phillips curve? It depends on how quickly workers and firms adjust their expectations of future inflation to changes in current inflation. The experience in the United States over the past 60 years indicates that how quickly workers and firms adjust their expectations of inflation depends on how high the inflation rate is. There are three possibilities:

1. **Low inflation.** When the inflation rate is low, as it was during most of the 1950s, the early 1960s, the 1990s, and the years following the 2007–2009 recession, workers and firms tend to ignore it. For example, if the inflation rate is low, a restaurant may not want to pay for printing new menus that would show slightly higher prices.
2. **Moderate but stable inflation.** For the four-year period from 1968 to 1971, the inflation rate in the United States stayed in the narrow range between 4 percent and 5 percent. This rate was high enough that workers and firms could not ignore it without seeing their real wages and profits decline. It was also likely that the next year's inflation rate would be very close to the current year's inflation rate. In fact, workers and firms during the 1960s acted as if they expected changes in the inflation rate during one year to continue into the following year. People are said to have *adaptive expectations* of inflation if they assume that future rates of inflation will follow the pattern of rates of inflation in the recent past.
3. **High and unstable inflation.** Inflation rates above 5 percent during peacetime have been rare in U.S. history, but the inflation rate was above 5 percent every year from 1973 through 1982. Not only was the inflation rate high during those years, it was also unstable—rising from 6 percent in 1973 to 11 percent in 1974, before falling below 6 percent in 1976 and rising again to 13.5 percent in 1980. In the mid-1970s, Nobel Laureates Robert Lucas of the University of Chicago and Thomas Sargent of New York University argued that the gains to workers and firms from accurately forecasting inflation had dramatically increased. Workers and firms that failed to correctly anticipate the fluctuations in inflation during these years could experience substantial declines in real wages and profits. Therefore, Lucas and Sargent argued, people should use all available information when forming their expectations of future inflation. Expectations formed by using all available information about an economic variable are called **rational expectations**.

Rational expectations Expectations formed by using all available information about an economic variable.

The Implications of Rational Expectations for Monetary Policy

Lucas and Sargent pointed out an important consequence of rational expectations: An expansionary monetary policy would not work. In other words, there might not be a trade-off between unemployment and inflation, even in the short run. By the mid-1970s, most economists had accepted the idea that an expansionary monetary policy could cause the actual inflation rate to be higher than the expected inflation rate. This gap between actual and expected inflation would cause the actual real wage to fall below the expected real wage, pushing the unemployment rate below the natural rate. Short-run equilibrium would move up the short-run Phillips curve.

Lucas and Sargent argued that this explanation of the Phillips curve assumed that workers and firms either ignored inflation or used adaptive expectations in making their forecasts of inflation. If workers and firms have rational expectations, they will use all available information, *including knowledge of the effects of Federal Reserve policy*. If workers and firms know that an expansionary monetary policy will raise the inflation rate, they should use this information in their forecasts of inflation. If they do, an expansionary monetary policy will not cause the actual inflation rate to be greater than the expected inflation rate. Instead, the actual inflation rate will equal the expected inflation rate, the

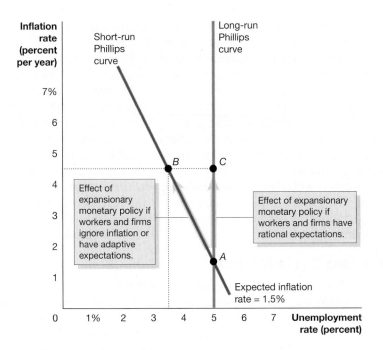

MyLab Economics Animation

Figure 17.8

Rational Expectations and the Phillips Curve

If workers and firms ignore inflation, or if they have adaptive expectations, an expansionary monetary policy will cause short-run equilibrium to move from point A on the short-run Phillips curve to point B; inflation will rise, and unemployment will fall. If workers and firms have rational expectations, an expansionary monetary policy will cause the short-run equilibrium to move up the long-run Phillips curve from point A to point C. Inflation will still rise, but there will be no change in unemployment.

actual real wage will equal the expected real wage, and the unemployment rate will not fall below the natural rate.

Figure 17.8 illustrates this argument. Suppose that equilibrium is initially at point *A*, where the short-run Phillips curve intersects the long-run Phillips curve. The actual and expected inflation rates are both equal to 1.5 percent, and the unemployment rate equals the natural rate of 5 percent. Now suppose the Fed engages in an expansionary monetary policy. If workers ignore inflation or if they form their expectations adaptively, the expansionary monetary policy will cause the actual inflation rate to be higher than the expected inflation rate, and short-run equilibrium will move from point *A* on the short-run Phillips curve to point *B*. The inflation rate will rise to 4.5 percent, and the unemployment rate will fall to 3.5 percent. The decline in unemployment will be only temporary because workers and firms will eventually adjust to the fact that the actual inflation rate is 4.5 percent, not the 1.5 percent they had expected. The short-run Phillips curve will shift up, and the unemployment rate will return to 5 percent at point *C*.

Lucas and Sargent argued that if workers and firms have rational expectations, they will realize that the Fed's expansionary policy will result in an inflation rate of 4.5 percent. Therefore, as soon as the Fed announces its new policy, workers and firms should adjust their expectations of inflation from 1.5 percent to 4.5 percent. There will be no temporary decrease in the real wage, leading to a temporary increase in employment and real GDP. Instead, short-run equilibrium will move immediately from point *A* to point *C* on the long-run Phillips curve. The unemployment rate will never drop below 5 percent, and the *short-run* Phillips curve will be vertical.   MyLab Economics Concept Check

Is the Short-Run Phillips Curve Really Vertical?

The claim by Lucas and Sargent that the short-run Phillips curve is vertical and that an expansionary monetary policy cannot reduce the unemployment rate below the natural rate surprised many economists. An obvious objection to the argument of Lucas and Sargent was that the 1950s and 1960s seemed to show that there was a short-run trade-off between unemployment and inflation and that, therefore, the short-run Phillips curve was downward sloping and not vertical. Lucas and Sargent argued that the apparent short-run trade-off was actually the result of *unexpected* changes in monetary policy. During those years, the Fed did not announce changes in monetary policy, so workers, firms, and financial markets had to *guess* when the Fed had begun using a new policy. In that case, an expansionary monetary policy might cause the unemployment rate to fall because workers and firms would be taken by surprise, and their expectations of inflation would be too low. Lucas and Sargent argued that a policy that was announced ahead of time would not cause a change in unemployment.

Many economists have remained skeptical of the argument that the short-run Phillips curve is vertical. The two main objections raised are that (1) workers and firms may not have rational expectations; and (2) the rapid adjustment of wages and prices needed for the short-run Phillips curve to be vertical will not actually take place. Many economists doubt that people are able to use information about the Fed's monetary policy to make reliable forecasts of the inflation rate. If workers and firms do not know what effect an expansionary monetary policy will have on the inflation rate, the actual real wage may still end up being lower than the expected real wage. Also, firms may have contracts with their workers and suppliers that keep wages and prices from adjusting quickly. If wages and prices adjust slowly, then even if workers and firms have rational expectations, an expansionary monetary policy may still be able to reduce the unemployment rate in the short run.   **MyLab Economics** Concept Check

Real Business Cycle Models

Real business cycle models Models that focus on real rather than monetary explanations of fluctuations in real GDP.

During the 1980s, some economists, including Nobel Laureates Finn Kydland of the University of California, Santa Barbara, and Edward Prescott of Arizona State University, argued that Robert Lucas was correct in assuming that workers and firms formed their expectations rationally and that wages and prices adjust quickly, but that he was wrong in assuming that fluctuations in real GDP are caused by unexpected changes in monetary policy. Instead, Kydland and Prescott argued that fluctuations in "real" factors, particularly *technology shocks*, explain deviations of real GDP from its potential level. Technology shocks are changes to the economy that make it possible to produce either more output (a positive shock) or less output (a negative shock) with the same number of workers, machines, and other inputs. Real GDP will be above its previous potential level following a positive technology shock and below its previous potential level following a negative technology shock. Because these models focus on real factors—rather than on changes in the money supply—to explain fluctuations in real GDP, they are known as **real business cycle models**.

The approach of Lucas and Sargent and the real business cycle models are sometimes grouped together under the label *the new classical macroeconomics* because they share the assumptions that people have rational expectations and that wages and prices adjust rapidly. Some of the assumptions of the new classical macroeconomics are similar to those held by economists before the Great Depression of the 1930s. John Maynard Keynes, in his 1936 book *The General Theory of Employment, Interest, and Money*, referred to these earlier economists as "classical economists." Like the classical economists, the new classical macroeconomists believe that the economy will normally be at its potential level.

Economists who find the assumptions of rational expectations and rapid adjustment of wages and prices appealing are likely to accept the real business cycle model approach. Other economists are skeptical of these models because the models explain recessions as being caused by negative technology shocks. Negative technology shocks are uncommon and, apart from the oil price increases of the 1970s, real business cycle theorists have had difficulty identifying shocks that would have been large enough to cause recessions. Some economists have developed real business cycle models that allow for the possibility that changes in monetary policy and financial crises may affect the level of real GDP. If real business cycle models continue to advance along these lines, they may eventually converge with the models the Fed uses.   **MyLab Economics** Concept Check

MyLab Economics Study Plan

17.4 Federal Reserve Policy from the 1970s to the Present

LEARNING OBJECTIVE: Use a Phillips curve graph to show how the Federal Reserve can permanently lower the inflation rate.

We have already seen that the high inflation rates of the late 1960s and early 1970s were due in part to the Federal Reserve's attempts to keep the unemployment rate below the natural rate. By the mid-1970s, the Fed also had to deal with the inflationary effect of oil price increases resulting from actions by the Organization of the Petroleum Exporting Countries (OPEC). In the late 1970s, as the Fed attempted to deal with the problem of high and worsening inflation rates, it received conflicting policy advice. Many economists argued that the inflation rate could be reduced only at the cost of a temporary increase in the unemployment rate. Followers of the Lucas–Sargent rational expectations approach, however, argued that a painless reduction in the inflation rate was possible. Before analyzing the actual policies the Fed used, we examine why the oil price increases of the mid-1970s made the inflation rate worse.

The Effect of a Supply Shock on the Phillips Curve

The increases in oil prices in 1974 caused the short-run aggregate supply curve to shift to the left. This shift is shown in panel (a) of Figure 17.9. (For simplicity, in this panel, we use the basic rather than the dynamic *AD–AS* model.) The result was an increase in the price level from 26.4 to 31.4 and a decrease in real GDP from $5,424 billion to $5,385 billion. On a Phillips curve graph—panel (b) of Figure 17.9—we can shift the short-run Phillips curve up to show that the inflation rate and unemployment rate both increased: from an unemployment rate of 4.9 percent and an inflation rate of about 5.5 percent in 1973 to an unemployment rate of 8.5 percent and an inflation rate of about 9.2 percent in 1975.

This combination of rising unemployment and rising inflation placed the Federal Reserve in a difficult position. If the Fed used an expansionary monetary policy to fight the high unemployment rate, the *AD* curve would shift to the right, and short-run equilibrium would move up the short-run Phillips curve. Real GDP would increase, and the unemployment rate would fall—but at the cost of higher inflation. If the Fed used a contractionary monetary policy to fight the high inflation rate, the *AD* curve would shift to the left, and short-run equilibrium would move down the

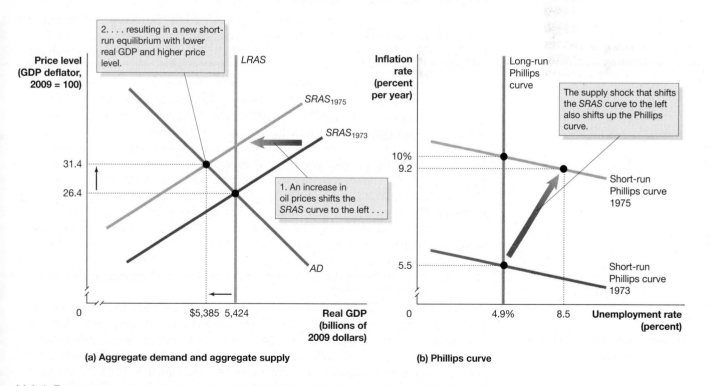

(a) Aggregate demand and aggregate supply   (b) Phillips curve

MyLab Economics Animation

Figure 17.9   **A Supply Shock Shifts the *SRAS* Curve and the Short-Run Phillips Curve**

When actions by OPEC increased the price of a barrel of oil from less than $3 to more than $10, panel (a) shows that the *SRAS* curve shifted to the left. Between 1973 and 1975, real GDP declined from $5,424 billion to $5,385 billion, and the price level rose from 26.4 to 31.4.

Panel (b) shows that the supply shock shifted up the Phillips curve. In 1973, the U.S. economy had an inflation rate of 5.5 percent and an unemployment rate of 4.9 percent. By 1975, the inflation rate had risen to about 9.2 percent and the unemployment rate to about 8.5 percent.

MyLab Economics Animation

Figure 17.10

The Fed Tames Inflation, 1979–1989

Under Chairman Paul Volcker, the Fed began fighting inflation in 1979 by reducing the growth of the money supply, thereby raising interest rates. By 1982, the unemployment rate had risen to 10 percent, and the inflation rate had fallen to 6 percent. As workers and firms lowered their expectations of future inflation, the short-run Phillips curve shifted down. This adjustment in expectations allowed the Fed to switch to an expansionary monetary policy, which by 1987 brought unemployment back to the natural rate of unemployment, with an inflation rate of about 4 percent. The orange line shows the actual combinations of unemployment and inflation for each year from 1979 to 1989.

short-run Phillips curve. As a result, real GDP would fall, and the inflation rate would be reduced—but at the cost of higher unemployment. In the end, the Fed chose to fight high unemployment with an expansionary monetary policy, even though that decision worsened the inflation rate. **MyLab Economics** Concept Check

Paul Volcker and Disinflation

By the late 1970s, the Federal Reserve had gone through two decades of continually increasing the rate of growth of the money supply. In August 1979, President Jimmy Carter appointed Paul Volcker as chairman of the Federal Reserve. Along with most other economists, Volcker was convinced that high inflation rates were damaging the economy. To reduce inflation, Volcker began reducing the annual growth rate of the money supply. This contractionary monetary policy raised interest rates, causing a decline in aggregate demand. Figure 17.10 uses the Phillips curve model to analyze the movements in unemployment and inflation from 1979 to 1989.

The Fed's contractionary monetary policy moved short-run equilibrium down the short-run Phillips curve, lowering the inflation rate from 11 percent in 1979 to 6 percent in 1982—but at a cost of raising the unemployment rate from 6 percent to 10 percent. As workers and firms lowered their expectations of future inflation, the short-run Phillips curve shifted down, improving the short-run trade-off between unemployment and inflation. This adjustment in expectations allowed the Fed to switch to an expansionary monetary policy. By 1987, equilibrium was back to the natural rate of unemployment, which during these years was about 6 percent. The orange line in Figure 17.10 shows the actual combinations of unemployment and inflation for each year from 1979 to 1989.

Under Volcker's leadership, the Fed had reduced the inflation rate from more than 10 percent to less than 5 percent. The inflation rate has generally remained below 5 percent since that time. A significant reduction in the inflation rate is called **disinflation**. In fact, this episode is often called the "Volcker disinflation." The disinflation had come at a very high price, however. From September 1982 through June 1983, the unemployment rate was above 10 percent for the first time since the end of the Great Depression of the 1930s.

Some economists have argued that the Volcker disinflation provides evidence against the view that workers and firms have rational expectations. Newspapers and television widely publicized Volcker's announcement in October 1979 that he planned to use a contractionary monetary policy to bring down the inflation rate. If workers

Disinflation A significant reduction in the inflation rate.

and firms had rational expectations, we might expect that they would have quickly reduced their expectations of future inflation. There should have been a smooth movement down the long-run Phillips curve. As we have seen, however, there was a movement down the existing short-run Phillips curve, and only after several years of high unemployment did the short-run Phillips curve shift down. Apparently, workers and firms had adaptive expectations—changing their expectations of future inflation only after the current inflation rate had fallen.

Robert Lucas and Thomas Sargent have argued, however, that a less painful disinflation would have occurred if workers and firms had *believed* Volcker's announcement that he was fighting inflation. The problem was that previous Fed chairmen had made similar promises throughout the 1970s, but the inflation rate had continued to increase. By 1979, the *credibility* of the Fed was at a low point. Some support for Lucas's and Sargent's argument comes from surveys of business economists at the time, which showed that they also reduced their forecasts of future inflation only slowly, even though they were well aware of Volcker's announcement of a new policy.   **MyLab Economics** Concept Check

Don't Let This Happen to You

Don't Confuse Disinflation with Deflation

Disinflation refers to a decline in the *inflation rate*. *Deflation* refers to a decline in the *price level*. Paul Volcker and the Federal Reserve brought about a substantial disinflation in the United States during the years between 1979 and 1983. The inflation rate fell from more than 11 percent in 1979 to less than 5 percent in 1984. Yet even in 1984, there was no deflation: The price level was still rising—but at a slower rate.

The last period of significant deflation in the United States was in the early 1930s, during the Great Depression. The following table shows the consumer price index for each of those years. Because the price level fell each year from 1929 to 1933, there was deflation.

Year	Consumer Price Index	Deflation Rate
1929	17.1	—
1930	16.7	−2.3
1931	15.2	−9.0
1932	13.7	−9.9
1933	13.0	−5.1

MyLab Economics Study Plan

Your Turn: Test your understanding by doing related problem 4.5 on page 642 at the end of this chapter.

Solved Problem 17.4

MyLab Economics Interactive Animation

Using Monetary Policy to Lower the Inflation Rate

Consider the following hypothetical situation: The unemployment rate is currently at the natural rate of 5 percent, the actual inflation rate is 6 percent, and, because it has remained at 6 percent for several years, workers and firms expect the inflation rate to remain at 6 percent in the future.

The Federal Reserve decides to reduce the inflation rate permanently to 2 percent. How can the Fed use monetary policy to achieve this objective? Be sure to use a Phillips curve graph in your answer.

Solving the Problem

Step 1: **Review the chapter material.** This problem is about using a Phillips curve graph to show how the Fed can fight inflation, so you may want to review the section "Paul Volcker and Disinflation," which begins on page 626.

Step 2: **Explain how the Fed can use monetary policy to reduce the inflation rate.** To reduce the inflation rate significantly, the Fed will have to raise the target for the federal funds rate. Higher interest rates will reduce aggregate demand, raise unemployment, and move equilibrium down the short-run Phillips curve.

Step 3: **Illustrate your argument with a Phillips curve graph.** How much the unemployment rate would have to rise to drive the inflation rate down from 6 percent to 2 percent depends on the steepness of the short-run Phillips curve. In drawing this graph, we have assumed that the unemployment rate would have to rise from 5 percent to 7 percent.

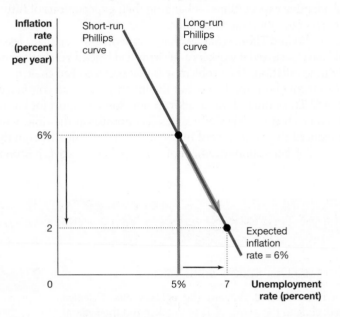

Step 4: **Show on your graph how the Fed can achieve a permanent reduction in the inflation rate from 6 percent to 2 percent.** For the decline in the inflation rate to be permanent, the expected inflation rate has to decline from 6 percent to 2 percent. We can show this decline on the graph:

Once the short-run Phillips curve has shifted down, the Fed can use an expansionary monetary policy to push equilibrium back to the natural rate of unemployment. This policy is similar to the one carried out by the Fed after Paul Volcker became chairman in 1979. The downside to these policies of disinflation is that they lead to significant short-term increases in unemployment.

Extra Credit: A follower of the new classical macroeconomics approach would have a more optimistic view of the consequences of using monetary policy to lower the inflation rate from 6 percent to 2 percent. According to the new classical approach, the Fed's policy announcement should cause people to immediately revise downward their expectations of future inflation from 6 percent to 2 percent. Short-run equilibrium would move directly down the long-run Phillips curve from an inflation rate of 6 percent to an inflation rate of 2 percent, while keeping the unemployment rate constant at 5 percent. For the reasons discussed in this chapter, many economists are skeptical of the assertion that disinflation can be brought about so painlessly.

Your Turn: For more practice, do related problem 4.6 on page 642 at the end of this chapter.

MyLab Economics Study Plan

Alan Greenspan, Ben Bernanke, Janet Yellen, and the Crisis in Monetary Policy

In 1987, President Ronald Reagan nominated Alan Greenspan to succeed Paul Volcker as Fed chairman. Greenspan served until January 2006—a term of more than 18 years. President George W. Bush nominated Ben Bernanke to succeed Greenspan. Bernanke served until January 2014, when he was succeeded by Janet Yellen, who had been nominated by President Barack Obama. To succeed Yellen, President Donald Trump nominated Jerome Powell to take office in February 2018. Table 17.3 shows that the average annual inflation rate measured using the CPI was lower during Greenspan's, Bernanke's, and Yellen's terms, than it had been during the terms of their three immediate predecessors. Under Greenspan's leadership of the Fed, inflation was reduced nearly to the low levels experienced during the term of Chairman William McChesney Martin in the 1950s and 1960s. Greenspan's term was marked by only two short and mild recessions, in 1990–1991 and 2001. When he left office in 2006, his policies were widely applauded by economists, policymakers, and the media.

Following the severe recession of 2007–2009, some critics questioned whether decisions the Fed made under Greenspan's leadership might have played a role in bringing on the financial crisis that led to the recession. We will discuss those arguments after briefly reviewing two other developments in monetary policy during the past 20 years:

- **Deemphasizing the money supply.** Greenspan's term was notable for the Fed's continued movement away from using the money supply as a monetary policy target. We saw in Chapter 15, Section 15.2 that during the 1980s and 1990s, the close relationship between growth in the money supply and inflation broke down. Before 1987, the Fed would announce annual targets for the growth rates of M1 and M2. In February 1987, near the end of Paul Volcker's term, the Fed announced that it would no longer set targets for M1. In July 1993, Alan Greenspan announced that the Fed also would no longer set targets for M2. Instead, the Federal Open Market Committee (FOMC) has relied on setting targets for the federal funds rate to meet its dual mandate of price stability and high employment.

Table 17.3

The Record of Fed Chairs and Inflation

Federal Reserve Chair	Term	Average Annual Inflation Rate during Term
William McChesney Martin	April 1951 to January 1970	2.2%
Arthur Burns	February 1970 to March 1978	6.5
G. William Miller	March 1978 to August 1979	9.1
Paul Volcker	August 1979 to August 1987	6.2
Alan Greenspan	August 1987 to January 2006	3.1
Ben Bernanke	January 2006 to January 2014	2.2
Janet Yellen	February 2014 to September 2017*	1.2

*The value for Janet Yellen is just for this period of her term.

Sources: U.S. Bureau of Labor Statistics; and Federal Reserve Board of Governors.

- **Emphasizing Fed credibility.** The Fed learned an important lesson during the 1970s: Workers, firms, and investors in stock and bond markets have to view Fed announcements as credible if monetary policy is to be effective. As inflation worsened throughout the late 1960s and the 1970s, the Fed announced repeatedly that it would take actions to reduce inflation. In fact, policies either were not implemented or were ineffective, and inflation rose. These repeated failures to follow through on announced policies had greatly reduced the Fed's credibility by the time Paul Volcker took office in August 1979. The contractionary monetary policy that the Fed announced in October 1979 had less effect on the expectations of workers, firms, and investors than it would have had if the Fed's credibility had been greater. It took a severe recession to convince people that this time, the inflation rate really was coming down. Only then were workers willing to accept lower nominal wage increases, banks willing to accept lower interest rates on mortgage loans, and investors willing to accept lower interest rates on bonds.

Over the past 25 years, the Fed has taken steps to enhance its credibility. Most importantly, whenever a change in Fed policy has been announced, the change has actually taken place. In addition, Greenspan revised the previous Fed policy of keeping secret the target for the federal funds rate. Since February 1994, any change in the target rate has been announced at the conclusion of the FOMC meeting at which the change is made. The minutes of the FOMC meetings are now made public after a brief delay. In February 2000, the Fed began making its intentions for future policy clearer by stating at the end of each FOMC meeting whether it considered the economy in the future to be at greater risk of higher inflation or of recession. In 2011, Ben Bernanke began holding press conferences following some FOMC meetings, which was the first time a Fed chair had done so.

The Decision to Intervene in the Failure of Long-Term Capital Management

Greenspan's ability to help guide the economy through a long period of economic stability and his moves to enhance Fed credibility were widely applauded. However, two actions by the Fed during Greenspan's term have been identified as possibly contributing to the financial crisis that increased the length and severity of the 2007–2009 recession. One was the decision during 1998 to help save the hedge fund Long-Term Capital Management (LTCM). Hedge funds raise money, typically from wealthy investors, and use sophisticated investment strategies that often involve significant risk.

In the spring of 1998, LTCM suffered heavy losses on several of its investments, and other financial firms that had loaned money to LTCM feared that the hedge fund would go bankrupt and began to push for repayment of their loans. We have seen that a run on a financial firm can cause widespread problems in the financial system. If LTCM had been forced to quickly sell all of its investments, the prices of the securities it owned would have declined, causing problems for other financial firms that held the same securities (see Chapter 14, Section 14.4). With the support of Alan Greenspan, William McDonough, president of the Federal Reserve Bank of New York, persuaded the financial firms to which LTCM owed money to give LTCM enough time to slowly sell off—or "unwind"—its investments to keep the prices of those investments from falling too rapidly and to avoid a financial panic.

Some critics argued that the Fed's intervention had negative consequences in the long run because it allowed the owners of LTCM and the firms that had loaned LTCM money to avoid the full consequences of LTCM's failed investments. These critics argued that the Fed's intervention set the stage for other firms—particularly highly leveraged investment banks and hedge funds—to take on excessive risk, with the expectation that the Fed would intervene on their behalf should they suffer heavy losses on the investments.

Although some critics see the Fed's actions in the case of LTCM as encouraging the excessive risk taking that contributed to the financial crisis of 2007–2009, other observers doubt that the Fed's actions had much effect on the behavior of managers of financial firms.

The Decision to Keep the Target for the Federal Funds Rate at 1 Percent from June 2003 to June 2004 In response to the popping of the dot-com stock bubble in the spring of 2000, the beginning of a recession in March 2001, and the terrorist attacks of September 11, 2001, the Fed successively lowered the target for the federal funds rate. The target rate was cut in a series of steps from 6.5 percent in May 2000 to 1 percent in June 2003. The target remained at 1 percent until the Fed raised it to 1.25 percent in June 2004. Some economists and policymakers have criticized the Fed's decision to continue cutting the target for the federal funds rate for more than 18 months after the end of the recession in November 2001 and to keep the rate at 1 percent for another year. At the time, the FOMC argued that although the recession of 2001 was mild, the very low inflation rates of late 2001 and 2002 raised the possibility that the U.S. economy could slip into a period of deflation. As we have seen, deflation can damage the economy by raising real interest rates and by causing consumers to postpone purchases, based on the expectation that future prices will be lower than current prices (see Chapter 9, Section 9.7).

Critics argued that by keeping interest rates low for an extended period, the Fed helped fuel the housing bubble that eventually deflated beginning in 2006, with disastrous results for the economy. We have seen that the origins of the housing bubble are complex and that contributing factors included the increase in securitization of mortgages, the willingness of banks and other lenders to give loans to subprime and Alt-A borrowers, and the widespread use of adjustable-rate mortgages that allowed borrowers to qualify for larger loans than would have been possible using conventional mortgages. Economists will continue to debate whether the Fed's policy of keeping the target for the federal funds rate very low for an extended period caused the housing bubble.   **MyLab Economics** Concept Check

Apply the Concept   **MyLab Economics** Video

Should the Fed Attempt to Guide the Expectations of Investors?

In testifying before Congress, Federal Reserve Chair Janet Yellen discussed how the Fed has been using *forward guidance* as a monetary policy tool since 2008. Forward guidance refers to central banks telling the public what future monetary policy will be. As Yellen put it, "The FOMC is … providing forward guidance that offers information about our policy outlook and expectations for the future path of the federal funds rate."

The Fed targets the federal funds rate and can control its value. But the Fed has less control over long-term interest rates, such as the interest rates on mortgage loans or corporate bonds, that have a direct effect on household and firm spending. The level of long-term interest rates depends partly on the expectations of households, firms, and investors about future short-term interest rates. As former Fed Chairman Ben Bernanke noted in a speech, "The public's expectations about future monetary policy actions matter today because those expectations have important effects on current financial conditions, which in turn affect output, employment, and inflation over time." For example, when investors believe that the federal funds rate will be low in future years, the interest rate on 10-year U.S. Treasury notes will usually also be low. The interest rate on 10-year Treasury notes plays an important role in the financial system because changes in it are typically reflected in other long-term interest rates, particularly the interest rate on mortgage loans. Beginning in 2008, the Fed used forward guidance to help keep the interest rate on 10-year Treasury notes low. As the following figure shows, this key interest rate remained at very low levels during and following the recession, until it began to rise in 2015, as the FOMC indicated that it intended to increase the target for the federal funds rate late that year.

After becoming Fed chair in 2014, Yellen quickly learned how sensitive investors are to any hint from the Fed that interest rate policy might change. At a press conference after her first FOMC meeting, some of her remarks seemed to indicate that the Fed might raise its target for the federal funds rate earlier than investors had anticipated. The result, as shown in the graph below, was a quick upward spike in the interest rate on the 10-year Treasury note.

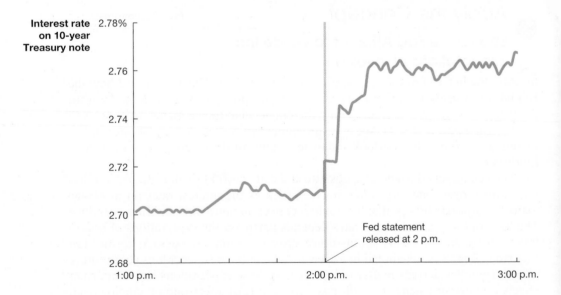

Eventually, Yellen and other Fed officials were able to reassure investors that Fed policy had not abruptly changed, and the interest rate on the 10-year Treasury note declined. Still, as Yellen put it, "We will try as hard as we can not to be a source of instability here."

Many economists credited the Fed's forward guidance, in combination with quantitative easing (discussed in Chapter 15, Section 15.3), with aiding the recovery from the 2007–2009 recession by keeping long-term interest rates low. Some economists, though, were concerned that forward guidance was contributing to a prolonged period of abnormally low interest rates. Such low interest rates could lead to distortions in the financial system and the wider economy by, for instance, leading to speculative bubbles in stocks or other financial assets as investors borrowed at low interest rates to buy these assets. Some economists were also troubled by the effect that stray remarks by Fed officials can have on financial markets—as shown by the bond market's strong reaction to Yellen's initial press conference. They argued that Fed policy would be more transparent if it were constrained by a rule similar to the Taylor rule discussed in Chapter 15, Section 15.5. A rules-based monetary policy would make it easier for firms, households, and investors to accurately anticipate future Fed policy without having to interpret sometimes unclear statements from Fed officials.

Sources: Janet L. Yellen, *Semiannual Monetary Policy Report to the Congress*, February 25, 2015; Ben S. Bernanke, "Communication and Monetary Policy," Speech Delivered at the National Economists Club Annual Dinner, Herbert Stein Memorial Lecture, Washington, DC, November 19, 2013; Jon Hilsenrath and Victoria McGrane, "Yellen Debut Rattles Markets," *Wall Street Journal*, March 19, 2014; David Wessel, "Ahead of Janet Yellen's Testimony, Fed's Forward Guidance Is Working," *Wall Street Journal*, February 10, 2014; and Federal Reserve Bank of St. Louis.

Your Turn: Test your understanding by doing related problem 4.9 on page 642 at the end of this chapter.

MyLab Economics Study Plan

The Debate over the Fed's Future

The financial crisis of 2007–2009 led the Fed to move well beyond the federal funds rate as the focus of monetary policy. With the target federal funds rate having been driven to zero without sufficient expansionary effect on the economy, some observers began to speak of a "crisis in monetary policy." In Chapters 14, Section 14.4, and 15, Section 15.6, we reviewed the new policies the Fed used during and after the financial crisis. Like other policies that represent a sharp break with the past, the Fed's actions had both supporters and critics. While most economists and policymakers gave the Fed credit for keeping the financial crisis from leading to a downturn as severe as the Great Depression of the 1930s, some argued that the Fed had overstepped its authority as determined by the Federal Reserve Act. In this section, we review some of the changes to Fed operations contained in the Wall Street Reform and Consumer Protection Act (Dodd-Frank Act), which Congress passed in 2010, and also discuss current proposals in Congress for additional changes.

Changes under the Dodd-Frank Act Traditionally, the Fed had made discount loans only to commercial banks. Under Section 13(3) of the Federal Reserve Act, though, the Fed had the legal authority in "unusual and exigent circumstances" to make loans to "any individual, partnership, or corporation." During the financial crisis, the Fed invoked this authority to make loans to investment banks, provide funds for JPMorgan Chase's purchase of the failing investment bank Bear Stearns, provide funds to the AIG insurance company, and buy commercial paper issued by nonfinancial firms.

Some members of Congress were critical of these actions because they saw them as going too far beyond the Fed's mandate and were concerned that the Fed would make similar loans as a routine part of monetary policy. As a result, a provision of the Dodd-Frank Act revised Section 13(3) of the Federal Reserve Act to restrict the Fed's ability to make loans except to commercial banks. In particular, the Fed is no longer allowed to make loans "for the purpose of assisting a single and specific company avoid bankruptcy." During the crisis, the Fed took action to save Bear Stearns and AIG under what is called the **too-big-to-fail policy**, which holds that the federal government should not allow large financial firms to fail, for fear of damaging the financial system. As we saw in Chapter 15, Section 15.6, however, some economists believe that this policy increases moral hazard because managers of financial firms may make riskier investments if they believe that the federal government will save them from bankruptcy. These provisions of the Dodd-Frank Act make it much more difficult for the Fed to use a too-big-to-fail policy.

Some economists are critical of these restrictions on the Fed's ability to lend freely in a crisis. They argue that the failure of the Lehman Brothers investment bank in September 2008 shows the damage to the financial system that can occur as the result of the failure of a single large financial firm. In 2017, the Trump administration was preparing a proposal to revise the Dodd-Frank Act.

Too-big-to-fail policy A policy under which the federal government does not allow large financial firms to fail, for fear of damaging the financial system.

Proposals for Further Changes to the Fed In 2017, several proposals in Congress were intended to change the Fed's operations or structure. There were competing bills, and it was unclear which, if any, of them might be enacted into law. These were the key changes being considered:

- **Requiring the Fed to adopt a formal policy rule.** As we noted in Chapter 15, some members of Congress support requiring the Fed to adopt a policy rule like the Taylor rule. Although the FOMC would be able to deviate from the rule in a crisis, it would be required to state the reasons for the deviation. The purpose of the rule is to reduce the discretion of the FOMC to pursue policies, such as those pursued prior to Paul Volcker becoming Fed chair in 1979, that might result in high inflation rates. It would also avoid prolonged periods of very low targets for the federal funds rate after recessions have ended, such as occurred in 2003–2004 and again between 2011 and 2015. In both these cases, the Taylor rule indicated a higher target for the federal funds rate than the Fed actually implemented. A rules-based policy also makes it easier for businesses, households, and investors to anticipate future Fed actions. As we saw in the chapter opener, changes in the Fed's interest rate target affect homebuilders, such as Toll Brothers, and firms, such as General Motors, that sell durable goods. When Fed policymakers send conflicting signals about future interest rate policy, as they did in 2017, these firms have difficulty planning. Critics of the Fed's moving to a rules-based policy argue that the change would further reduce the ability of the Fed to respond rapidly to a financial crisis.

- **Making price stability the Fed's sole policy goal.** For many years, the Fed has interpreted the Federal Reserve Act as giving it a *dual mandate* of price stability and high employment. Because, as we have seen, in the long run the Fed can affect the price level but not the level of real GDP or employment, some policymakers and economists believe that the Fed should have the single goal of price stability. Critics of this proposal believe it would handicap the Fed in responding to declines in output and employment during recessions.

- **Changing the Fed's structure.** Members of Congress have proposed various changes to the Fed's structure. One relatively minor change would make all 12 Federal Reserve District Bank presidents voting members of the FOMC. Recall that under the current structure, the president of the Federal Reserve Bank of New York is always a voting member of the FOMC, while 4 of the other 11 District Bank presidents rotate through one-year terms as voting members. Another proposal is to add two new Federal Reserve Districts and realign the boundaries of the current districts to reflect the changes in the distribution of the U.S. population since the Fed's founding in 1914. Some members of Congress have proposed that the president of the United States directly appoint the presidents of the Federal Reserve District Banks. Currently, the boards of directors of the District Banks elect the bank presidents, subject to the approval of the Fed's Board of Governors. During the 2016 presidential election campaign, Democratic candidate Hillary Clinton proposed that bankers not be allowed to serve on the boards of directors of the District Banks.

- **Auditing the Fed's monetary policy actions.** The General Accountability Office (GAO) audits—or reviews—the Fed's finances, as it does the finances of other federal agencies. Congress has not given the GAO the authority to audit the Fed's monetary policy actions, although the Dodd-Frank Act changed the law to allow the GAO to audit other Fed activities, such as loans made to a single firm—like the loans provided to Bear Stearns during the financial crisis. Senator Rand Paul of Kentucky proposed that the GAO's authority be extended so that it can audit and provide public evaluations of the Fed's monetary policy actions. Fed officials and many economists were critical of this proposal because they believed that Congress might use the audits to pressure the Fed into avoiding monetary policy actions that were in the best interest of the economy but that might be politically unpopular.

A key point in the debate over changes to the Fed's structure and operations is concern about undermining the Fed's ability to carry out monetary policy without regard to possible political pressure from Congress or the president. The main reason to keep the Fed—or any country's central bank—independent of the rest of the government is to avoid inflation. Whenever a government is spending more than it is collecting in taxes, it must borrow the difference by selling bonds. The governments of many developing countries have difficulty finding anyone other than their central bank to buy their bonds. The more bonds the central bank buys, the faster the money supply grows, and the higher the inflation rate will be. Even in developed countries, governments that control their central banks may be tempted to sell bonds to the central bank rather than to the public.

Another fear is that a government that controls the central bank may use that control to further its political interests. It is difficult in any democratic country for a government to be reelected at a time of high unemployment. In the United States, for example, a president who had control over the Fed might be tempted to increase the money supply and drive down interest rates to increase production and employment just before running for reelection, even if doing so led in the long run to higher inflation and accompanying economic costs.

We might expect that the more independent a country's central bank is, the lower the inflation rate in the country, and the less independent a country's central bank, the higher the inflation rate. In a classic study, Alberto Alesina and Lawrence Summers, who were both economists at Harvard University at the time, tested this idea by comparing the degree of central bank independence and the inflation rate for 16 high-income countries during the years 1955 to 1988. Figure 17.11 shows the results.

Countries with highly independent central banks, such as the United States, Switzerland, and Germany, had lower inflation rates than countries whose central banks had little independence, such as New Zealand, Italy, and Spain. In the following years, New Zealand and Canada granted their banks more independence, at least partly to better fight inflation.

It remains to be seen which, if any, of the proposals for changing the Fed's structure and operations will be enacted by Congress and whether such changes will have a significant effect on the Fed's ability to carry out monetary policy free of political pressure.   **MyLab Economics** Concept Check

MyLab Economics Study Plan

MyLab Economics Animation

Figure 17.11

The More Independent the Central Bank, the Lower the Inflation Rate

For 16 high-income countries, the greater the degree of central bank independence from the rest of the government, the lower the inflation rate. Central bank independence is measured by an index ranging from 1 (minimum independence) to 4 (maximum independence). During these years, Germany had a high index of independence of 4 and a low average inflation rate of just over 3 percent. New Zealand had a low index of independence of 1 and a high average inflation rate of over 7 percent.

Source: "Central Bank Independence and Macroeconomic Performance: Some Comparative Evidence" by Alberto Alesina and Lawrence H. Summers from the *Journal of Money, Credit and Banking*, Vol. 25, No. 2, May 1993. Copyright © 1993 by the Ohio State University. Reprinted by permission.

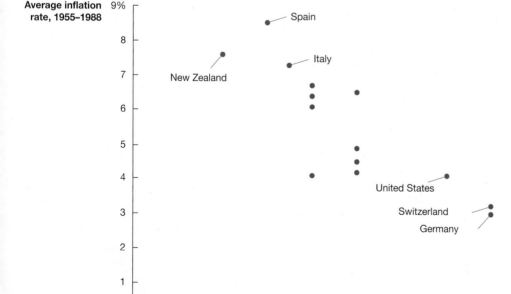

Continued from page 611

Economics in Your Life & Career

Are There Benefits to Delaying a Job Search?

At the beginning of the chapter, we posed this question: What advice would you give someone who decides to wait a considerable time to look for a new job? As we discussed in the chapter, evidence shows that many of those who are unemployed for longer than a year or two find it more difficult to find new employment than if they search for a new job soon after they are laid off. The longer workers are unemployed, especially in a high-technology field, the more their skills deteriorate. By delaying her job search and allowing her skills to deteriorate, your friend risks being unemployed for longer than she expects. Eventually, she may have to retrain or take additional courses in a different field in order to find a job. Tell your friend to start her job search right away!

Conclusion

The workings of the economy are complex. The attempts by the Federal Reserve to keep unemployment near the natural rate while also keeping the inflation rate low have not always been successful. Economists continue to debate the best approaches for the Fed to use.

Visit **MyLab Economics** for a news article and analysis related to the concepts in this chapter.

Key Terms

Disinflation, p. 626

Natural rate of unemployment, p. 614

Nonaccelerating inflation rate of unemployment (NAIRU), p. 620

Phillips curve, p. 612

Rational expectations, p. 622

Real business cycle models, p. 624

Structural relationship, p. 614

Too-big-to-fail policy, p. 633

17.1 The Discovery of the Short-Run Trade-off between Unemployment and Inflation, pages 612–617

LEARNING OBJECTIVE: Describe the Phillips curve and the nature of the short-run trade-off between unemployment and inflation.

MyLab Economics Visit www.pearson.com/mylab/economics to complete these exercises online and get instant feedback.

Summary

The **Phillips curve** illustrates the short-run trade-off between the unemployment rate and the inflation rate. The inverse relationship between unemployment and inflation the Phillips curve shows is consistent with the aggregate demand and aggregate supply (*AD–AS*) model. The *AD–AS* model indicates that slow growth in aggregate demand leads to both higher unemployment and lower inflation, and rapid growth in aggregate demand leads to both lower unemployment and higher inflation. This relationship explains why there is a short-run trade-off between unemployment and inflation. Many economists initially believed that the Phillips curve was a **structural relationship** that depended on the basic behavior of consumers and firms and that remained unchanged over time. If the Phillips curve were a stable relationship, it would present policymakers with a menu of combinations of unemployment and inflation from which they could choose. Milton Friedman argued that there is a **natural rate of unemployment**, which is the unemployment rate that exists when real GDP equals potential GDP. Because in the long run unemployment always returns to the natural rate, there is no trade-off between unemployment and inflation in the long run, and the long-run Phillips curve is a vertical line at the natural rate of unemployment.

Review Questions

1.1 What is the Phillips curve? Draw a graph of a short-run Phillips curve.

1.2 What actions should the Fed take if it wants to move from a point on the short-run Phillips curve representing high unemployment and low inflation to a point representing lower unemployment and higher inflation?

1.3 Why did economists during the early 1960s think of the Phillips curve as a "policy menu"? Were they correct to think of it in this way? Briefly explain.

1.4 Why did Milton Friedman argue that the Phillips curve did not represent a permanent trade-off between unemployment and inflation? In your answer, be sure to explain what Friedman meant by the "natural rate of unemployment."

Problems and Applications

1.5 Lael Brainard, a member of the Federal Reserve's Board of Governors, delivered a speech in 2017 that included this observation: "At a time when the unemployment rate has fallen from 8.2 percent to 4.4 percent, core inflation has undershot our 2 percent target for 58 straight months. In other words, the Phillips curve appears to be flatter today than it was previously." Briefly explain why the data Brainard cites indicate that the Phillips curve in 2017 was relatively flat.

Source: Lael Brainard, "Navigating the Different Signals from Inflation and Unemployment," Speech delivered at the New York Association for Business Economics, New York, May 30, 2017.

1.6 Use the following two graphs to answer the questions.

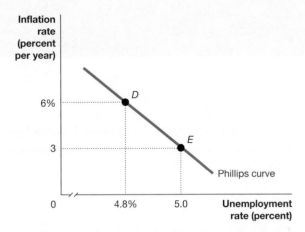

a. Briefly explain which point on the Phillips curve graph best represents the same economic situation as point *B* on the aggregate demand and aggregate supply graph.

b. Briefly explain which point on the Phillips curve graph best represents the same economic situation as point *C* on the aggregate demand and aggregate supply graph.

1.7 Given that the Phillips curve is derived from the aggregate demand and aggregate supply model, is the Phillips curve analysis necessary? That is, what benefits does the Phillips curve analysis offer compared to the aggregate demand and aggregate supply model?

1.8 In macroeconomics courses in the 1960s and early 1970s, some economists argued that one of the U.S. political parties was willing to have higher unemployment in order to achieve lower inflation and that the other major political party was willing to have higher inflation in order to achieve lower unemployment. Why might such views of the trade-off between inflation and unemployment have existed in the 1960s? Why are such views rare today?

1.9 The text discussed how if General Motors and the UAW fail to accurately forecast the inflation rate, the real wage will be different than the company and the union expected. Why, then, do the company and the union sign long-term contracts rather than negotiate a new contract each year?

1.10 A 2017 column in the *Wall Street Journal* noted that "long-term consumer inflation expectations [are] at record lows." If inflation turns out to be higher than households and firms had previously expected, will the actual real wage end up being higher or lower than the expected real wage? Will employment in the short run end up being higher or lower? Briefly explain.

Source: Lev Borodovsky, "WSJ's Daily Shot: Americans' Inflation Expectations at New Lows; Will It End in Disappointment?" *Wall Street Journal*, March 19, 2017.

1.11 **(Related to the Apply the Concept on page 616)** Robert Shiller asked a sample of the general public and a sample of economists the following question: "Do you agree that preventing high inflation is an important national priority, as important as preventing drug abuse or preventing deterioration in the quality of our schools?" Fifty-two percent of the general public, but only 18 percent of economists, fully agreed. Why does the general public believe inflation is a bigger problem than economists do?

1.12 **(Related to the Apply the Concept on page 616)** When Robert Shiller asked a sample of the general public what they thought caused inflation, the most frequent answer he received was "corporate greed." Do you agree that greed causes inflation? Briefly explain.

1.13 **(Related to the Chapter Opener on page 610)** In its 2016 *Annual Report*, Toll Brothers noted, "If mortgage interest rates increase significantly … our revenues, gross margins, and net income could be adversely affected."

a. Why might an increase in mortgage interest rates reduce revenue and profit for Toll Brothers?

b. During this period, was Fed policy attempting to reach a point on the short-run Phillips curve representing higher unemployment and lower inflation or a point representing higher inflation and lower unemployment? Briefly explain.

c. What connection is there between Fed policy and Toll Brothers' concern about the effect of rising mortgage interest rates on its profit?

Source: Toll Brothers, *2016 Annual Report*, p. 33.

17.2 The Short-Run and Long-Run Phillips Curves, pages 617–621

LEARNING OBJECTIVE: Explain the relationship between the short-run and long-run Phillips curves.

MyLab Economics Visit **www.pearson.com/mylab/economics** to complete these exercises online and get instant feedback.

Summary

There is a short-run trade-off between unemployment and inflation only if the actual inflation rate differs from the inflation rate that workers and firms had expected. There is a different short-run Phillips curve for every expected inflation rate. Each short-run Phillips curve intersects the long-run Phillips curve at the expected inflation rate. With a vertical long-run Phillips curve, it is not possible for policymakers to buy a permanently lower unemployment rate at the cost of a permanently higher inflation rate. If the Federal Reserve attempts to keep the unemployment rate below the natural rate, the inflation rate will increase. Eventually, the expected inflation rate will also increase, which causes the short-run Phillips curve to shift up and pushes the unemployment rate back to the natural rate. The reverse happens if the Fed attempts to keep the unemployment rate above the natural rate. In the long run, the Federal Reserve can affect the inflation rate but not the unemployment rate.

The **nonaccelerating inflation rate of unemployment (NAIRU)** is the unemployment rate at which the inflation rate has no tendency to increase or decrease.

Review Questions

2.1 What is the relationship between the short-run Phillips curve and the long-run Phillips curve? Suppose that the expected inflation rate increases from 2 percent to 3 percent. What will happen to the short-run Phillips curve?

2.2 Why is it inconsistent to believe that the long-run aggregate supply curve is vertical and the long-run Phillips curve is downward sloping?

Problems and Applications

2.3 Use the following information to draw a graph showing the short-run and long-run Phillips curves:

> Natural rate of unemployment = 4.5 percent
> Current rate of unemployment = 4.0 percent
> Expected inflation rate = 2.0 percent
> Current inflation rate = 3.0 percent

Be sure your graph shows the point where the short-run and long-run Phillips curves intersect.

2.4 Consider the long-run Phillips curve and the short-run Phillips curve in this graph. What would cause a movement from point A to point B? What would cause a movement from point A to point C?

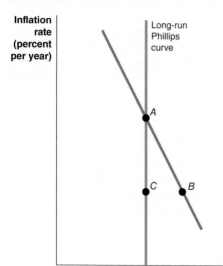

2.5 In 1968, Herbert Stein, who would later serve on President Nixon's Council of Economic Advisers, wrote, "Some who would opt for avoiding inflation would say that in the long run such a policy would cost little, if any, additional unemployment." Was Stein correct? Did most economists in 1968 agree with him? Briefly explain.

Source: Herbert Stein, *The Fiscal Revolution in America*, Chicago: University of Chicago Press, 1969, p. 382.

2.6 In the next column are four graphs and four economic scenarios, each of which would cause either a movement

along the short-run or long-run Phillips curve or a shift in the short-run or long-run Phillips curve. Match each scenario with the corresponding graph.

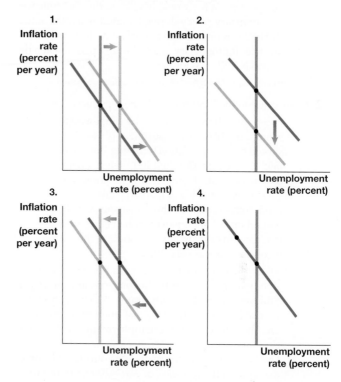

a. The proportion of younger and less-skilled workers in the labor force decreases.

b. The Fed carries out an expansionary monetary policy.

c. Congress enacts significant new legal barriers to firing workers.

d. Workers and firms lower the inflation rate they expect.

2.7 **(Related to the Apply the Concept on page 620)** An article in the *Wall Street Journal* had the headline "Nobody Knows Nairu, and That's a Problem for the Fed."

a. What is the NAIRU?

b. Why are there disagreements over the value of the NAIRU?

c. Why do those disagreements pose a problem for the Fed?

Source: Jon Hilsenrath, "Nobody Knows Nairu, and That's a Problem for the Fed," *Wall Street Journal*, February 13, 2015.

2.8 **(Related to the Apply the Concept on page 620)** Over time, the Federal Reserve Board of Governors has changed its estimate of the nonaccelerating inflation rate of unemployment (NAIRU). The following are the board's NAIRU estimates for selected years.

Year	NAIRU
1970	6.0%
1980	6.4
1990	5.6
2000	5.1
2008	4.8
2011	6.0
2017	4.7

a. Why would the board change its estimate of the NAIRU over time?

b. Suppose that the board simply kept its estimate fixed at 5.5 percent. What would have been the consequences for monetary policy during a period when the actual NAIRU was higher? What would have been the consequences for monetary policy during a period when the actual NAIRU was lower?

Source: Board of Governors of the Federal Reserve System.

2.9 An article in the *Economist* on the Phillips curve stated:

After the financial crisis unemployment soared to 10%. This [surplus] of workers should have sent inflation tumbling. But prices held up well; in October 2009 when unemployment peaked, underlying inflation was 1.3%, only a little lower than it is today. Some economists explained this by saying that the natural rate of unemployment had gone up in tandem—in other words, that some of the rise in joblessness was permanent.

a. Show the effect of an increase in the natural rate of unemployment on both the long-run and short-run Phillips curves. Use your graph to explain how the increase in the natural rate of unemployment lessens the effect of high unemployment on the inflation rate.

b. Did the high unemployment rates during and immediately after the recession of 2007–2009 turn out to be permanent? Briefly explain.

Source: "Finding Phillips," *The Economist*, June 17, 2017.

2.10 In congressional testimony, former Federal Reserve Chairman Ben Bernanke said:

Another significant factor influencing medium-term trends in inflation is the public's expectations of inflation. These expectations have an important bearing on whether transitory influences on prices, such as changes in energy costs, become embedded in wage and price decisions and so leave a lasting imprint on the rate of inflation.

What did Bernanke mean when he said that the public's expectations of inflation could "become embedded in wage and price decisions"? What would be the effect on the short-run Phillips curve of the public coming to expect a higher inflation rate?

Source: "Testimony of Chairman Ben S. Bernanke before the Joint Economic Committee, U.S. Congress," March 28, 2007.

2.11 In a speech in 2017, Fed Chair Janet Yellen described the long-run federal funds rate that is consistent with achieving the Fed's mandate of high employment and price stability as the "neutral rate," which she estimated to be about 3 percent. Yellen noted, "Waiting too long to begin moving toward the neutral rate could risk a nasty surprise down the road—either too much inflation, financial instability, or both. In that scenario, we could be forced to raise interest rates rapidly, which in turn could push the economy into a new recession."

a. Why is it potentially a problem for the Fed to "wait too long" to raise its target for the federal funds rate? Can't the Fed just wait until inflation increases and begin to slowly increase the target at that time?

b. Why might interest rates being too low lead to financial instability?

c. Why might the Fed's rapidly increasing its target for the federal funds rate push the economy into a recession?

Source: Janet Yellen, "The Goals of Monetary Policy and How We Pursue Them," Speech at the Commonwealth Club, San Francisco, California, January 18, 2017.

2.12 **(Related to Solved Problem 17.2 on page 621)** In a speech in September 1975, Fed Chairman Arthur Burns said the following:

There is no longer a meaningful trade-off between unemployment and inflation. In the current environment, a rapidly rising level of consumer prices will not lead to the creation of new jobs…. Highly expansionary monetary and fiscal policies might, for a short time, provide some additional thrust to economic activity. But inflation would inevitably accelerate—a development that would create even more difficult economic problems than we have encountered over the past year.

How do Burns's views in this speech compare with the views at the Fed in the late 1960s? Why do you think he specifically said that "in the current environment" there is no trade-off between unemployment and inflation?

Source: Arthur F. Burns, "The Real Issues of Inflation and Unemployment," in Federal Reserve Bank of New York, *Federal Reserve Readings on Inflation*, February 1975.

17.3 # Expectations of the Inflation Rate and Monetary Policy, pages 622–624

LEARNING OBJECTIVE: Discuss how expectations of the inflation rate affect monetary policy.

MyLab Economics Visit **www.pearson.com/mylab/economics** to complete these exercises online and get instant feedback.

Summary

When the inflation rate is moderate and stable, workers and firms tend to have *adaptive expectations*. That is, they form their expectations under the assumption that future inflation rates will follow the pattern of inflation rates in the recent past. Robert Lucas and Thomas Sargent argued that because inflation rates were high and unstable in the mid- to late 1970s, workers and firms would have *rational expectations*. **Rational expectations** are formed by using all the available information about an economic variable, including the effect of the policy being used by the Federal Reserve. Lucas and Sargent argued that if people have rational expectations, expansionary monetary policy will not work if workers and firms anticipate the policy. If workers and firms know that an expansionary monetary policy is going to raise the inflation rate, the actual inflation rate will be the same as the expected inflation rate. Therefore, the unemployment rate won't fall. Many economists remain skeptical of Lucas's and Sargent's argument. **Real business cycle models** focus on "real" factors—technology shocks—rather than changes in monetary policy to explain fluctuations in real GDP.

Review Questions

3.1 Why do workers, firms, banks, and investors in financial markets care about the future rate of inflation? How do they form their expectations of future inflation? Do current conditions in the economy have any effect on how they form their expectations? Briefly explain.

3.2 What does it mean to say that workers and firms have rational expectations?

3.3 Why did Robert Lucas and Thomas Sargent argue that the Phillips curve might be vertical in the short run? What difference would it make for monetary policy if they were right?

Problems and Applications

3.4 During a time when the inflation rate is increasing each year for a number of years, are adaptive expectations or rational expectations likely to give the more accurate forecasts? Briefly explain.

3.5 An article in the *Economist* stated, "Robert Lucas … showed how incorporating expectations into macroeconomic models muddled the framework economists prior to the 'rational expectations revolution' thought they saw

so clearly." What economic framework did economists change as a result of Lucas's arguments? Do all economists agree with Lucas's main conclusions about whether monetary policy is effective? Briefly explain.

Source: "How to Know What Causes What," *Economist*, October 10, 2011.

3.6 In an article in *Forbes*, Paul Roderick Gregory, an economist at the University of Houston, commented on the use of monetary policy to fight a recession: "Those who devise stimulus programs must know in advance the extent to which households and businesses will correctly anticipate the policy. A policy that has been used *x* times in the past is unlikely to have a stimulative effect because it will be easily anticipated." Does Gregory believe that households and businesses have adaptive expectations or rational expectations regarding monetary policy? Briefly explain.

Source: Paul Roderick Gregory, "Thomas Sargent, Rational Expectations and the Keynesian Consensus," *Forbes*, October 11, 2011.

3.7 If both the short-run and long-run Phillips curves are vertical, what will be the effect on the inflation rate and the unemployment rate of an expansionary monetary policy? Use a Phillips curve graph to illustrate your answer.

3.8 An article in the *Economist* observed that "a sudden unanticipated spurt of inflation could lead to rapid economic growth."
 a. Briefly explain the reasoning behind this statement.
 b. Does it matter whether a spurt of inflation is unanticipated? Might different economists provide different answers to this question? Briefly explain.

Source: "How We Got Here," *Economist*, January 21, 2013.

17.4 Federal Reserve Policy from the 1970s to the Present, pages 624–635
LEARNING OBJECTIVE: Use a Phillips curve graph to show how the Federal Reserve can permanently lower the inflation rate.

MyLab Economics   Visit **www.pearson.com/mylab/economics** to complete these exercises online and get instant feedback.

Summary

Inflation worsened through the 1970s. Paul Volcker became Fed chairman in 1979, and, under his leadership, the Fed used contractionary monetary policy to reduce inflation. A significant reduction in the inflation rate is called **disinflation**. This contractionary monetary policy pushed short-run equilibrium down the short-run Phillips curve. As workers and firms lowered their expectations of future inflation, the short-run Phillips curve shifted down, improving the short-run trade-off between unemployment and inflation. This change in expectations allowed the Fed to switch to an expansionary monetary policy to bring the unemployment rate back to the natural rate. During Alan Greenspan's term as Fed chairman, inflation remained low, and the credibility of the Fed increased. In recent years, some economists have argued that monetary policy decisions during Greenspan's term may have contributed to the problems the financial system experienced during the 2007–2009 recession. The Fed's actions during and after the financial crisis, including

its use of **a too-big-to-fail policy**, led some economists and policymakers to believe that reforms were needed in the Fed's structure and operations. However, other economists and policymakers fear that reducing the Fed's independence may undermine good policy.

Review Questions

4.1 What was the "Volcker disinflation"? What happened to the unemployment rate during the period of the Volcker disinflation?

4.2 What changes did the Dodd-Frank Act make in the Fed's operations? List three key proposals for changes in the Fed's operations or structure.

4.3 Why do most economists believe that it is important for a country's central bank to be independent of the rest of the country's central government?

Problems and Applications

4.4 A column in the *New York Times* in 2017 was titled "The Low-Inflation World May Be Sticking Around Longer Than Expected." Are the low inflation rates of recent years entirely the result of Federal Reserve policy? Could they have occurred without the Fed having a mandate to achieve price stability? Briefly explain.

Source: Neil Irwin, "The Low-Inflation World May Be Sticking Around Longer Than Expected," *New York Times*, April 26, 2017.

4.5 **(Related to the Don't Let This Happen to You on page 627)** Look again at the table on prices during the early 1930s on page 627. Was there disinflation during 1933? Briefly explain.

4.6 **(Related to Solved Problem 17.4 on page 627)** Suppose the inflation rate has been 5 percent for the past four years. The unemployment rate is currently at the natural rate of unemployment of 4.5 percent. The Federal Reserve decides that it wants to permanently reduce the inflation rate to 3 percent. How can the Fed use monetary policy to achieve this objective? Be sure to use a Phillips curve graph in your answer.

4.7 While many economists and policymakers supported the Fed's decision to maintain the federal funds rate at a near-zero level for over six years, Charles Schwab, the founder and chairman of a discount brokerage firm that bears his name, argued that the economy was harmed by keeping interest rates low for an extended period of time:

> U.S. households lost billions in interest income during the Fed's near-zero interest rate experiment.... Because they are often reliant on income from savings, seniors were hit the hardest.... Seniors make up 13% of the U.S. population and spend about $1.2 trillion annually.... This makes for a potent multiplier effect.

a. What type of spending was Schwab expecting would have increased if the Fed had raised interest rates earlier than it did?

b. Would higher interest rates have had an effect on other types of spending? Briefly explain.

c. Which of the types of spending that you discussed in answering parts (a) and (b) does the Fed appear to believe has the more "potent multiplier effect"? Briefly explain.

Source: Charles R. Schwab, "Raise Interest Rates, Make Grandma Smile," *Wall Street Journal*, November 19, 2014.

4.8 An article in the *Economist* started by stating that "central banks cannot endlessly reduce unemployment without sparking inflation is economic gospel. It follows from 'a substantial body of theory, informed by considerable historical evidence,' according to Janet Yellen, chair of the Federal Reserve."

a. Use a graph of the Phillips curve to show that central banks cannot endlessly reduce unemployment without sparking inflation. Briefly explain how your graph illustrates this point. Give an example of historical evidence that Fed Chair Yellen could be referring to.

b. The article stated that the "effects of unemployment on inflation can get lost amid temporary economic gyrations. That is most obvious when oil prices fall, as they did in late 2014." What does the article mean by the "effects of unemployment on inflation can get lost amid temporary economic gyrations?" Use a graph of the Phillips curve to show the effect on inflation of a

fall in oil prices. Briefly explain what is happening in your graph.

c. In discussing the effect of inflationary expectations, the article stated that "self-fulfilling expectations could explain low inflation." Use a graph of the Phillips curve to show how self-fulfilling expectations could explain low inflation. Briefly explain what is happening in your graph.

Source: "Finding Phillips," *The Economist*, June 17, 2017.

4.9 **(Related to the Apply the Concept on page 631)** In an opinion column in the *Wall Street Journal*, economist Sebastian Mallaby argued that when investors believe that financial markets will remain calm, they may be more willing to make risky investments. The result can be a financial crisis such as occurred during 2007–2009, when the prices of risky mortgage-backed securities declined. Mallaby argued:

> The central-banking fashion now is to target inflation and to communicate prodigiously about coming interest-rate adjustments.... But stable finance often matters more than stable prices. And transparency about future interest-rate moves can induce disruptive speculation.

a. What does the Fed call attempts to shape expectations of future policy decisions?

b. Why did targeting inflation and communicating about future changes in interest rates become "central bank fashion"?

c. Why might investors be more likely to buy risky securities if they feel confident that they know what interest rates will be in the future as a result of Fed announcements?

Source: Sebastian Mallaby, "Why the Fed Should Surprise Us," *Wall Street Journal*, June 23, 2017.

4.10 **(Related to the Chapter Opener on page 610)** In 2017, an article in the *Wall Street Journal* noted that "the Fed's aim … is to guide the economy to a soft landing…. But executing a soft landing is notoriously difficult to pull off."

a. What does the article mean by a "soft landing"?

b. Why is it difficult for the Fed to pull off a soft landing? What are the consequences for the economy if the Fed fails to pull off a soft landing?

Source: Justin Lahart, "The Fed's Poor Record on Soft Landings," *Wall Street Journal*, June 12, 2017.

4.11 An opinion column in the *Wall Street Journal* noted, "In a democracy, the tradeoff for a central bank's independence is accountability to the nation's elected leadership."

a. Why would a country want to grant its central bank more independence than it grants, say, its department of agriculture or department of education?

b. In the United States, how is the Fed held accountable to the nation's elected leadership?

Source: David Wessel, "Explaining 'Audit the Fed,'" *Wall Street Journal*, February 17, 2015.

4.12 In an opinion column in the *Wall Street Journal*, Stanford University economist John Taylor, originator of the Taylor rule, argued, "As I see it, the broader evidence in the United States and in many other countries … is that a rules-based policy has worked and that discretion—constrained or otherwise—has not."

a. What does Taylor mean by a "rules-based policy"?

b. How can we tell whether a monetary policy has worked?

c. Why have many Fed officials been opposed to adopting a rules-based policy?

Source: John B. Taylor, "Taylor on Bernanke: Monetary Rules Work Better Than 'Constrained Discretion,'" *Wall Street Journal*, May 2, 2015.

4.13 In a blog post, former Fed Chairman Ben Bernanke argued that the Fed should not conduct monetary policy according to a rule, such as the Taylor rule, that it announces in advance. Among other objections, Bernanke noted that

"the Taylor rule assumes that policymakers know, and can agree on, the size of the output gap. In fact … measuring the output gap is very difficult and FOMC members typically have different judgments." (*Note:* In answering this problem, you may want to review the discussion of the Taylor rule in Chapter 15, Section 15.5.)

a. Why is agreeing on the size of the output gap difficult?

b. Why might disagreements over the size of the output gap make it difficult for the Fed to use a pre-announced rule in conducting monetary policy?

Source: Ben Bernanke, "The Taylor Rule: A Benchmark for Monetary Policy?" brookings.edu, April 28, 2015.

Real-Time Data Exercises

D17.1 (Testing the Phillips curve) Go to the Web site of the Federal Reserve Bank of St. Louis (FRED) (fred.stlouisfed.org) and download annual unemployment data (UNRATE) for 1962 to the present. (To convert the data from a monthly frequency to an annual frequency, click on "Edit Graph" and then "Modify frequency.") Next, download the annual inflation rate measured using the consumer price index, or CPI (CPIAUCSL). (Once you have converted the data from a monthly frequency to an annual frequency, you can find the inflation rate by clicking on "Units" and selecting "Percent Change from Year Ago.") Plot both series on the same graph. Briefly explain whether for each of the following periods, the relationship between the annual unemployment rate and the annual inflation rate is consistent with a movement along the short-run Phillips curve or with a shift in the Phillips curve.

a. 1966–1969

b. 1973–1975

c. 1992–1994

d. 2000–2002

D17.2 (Comparing actual inflation and expected inflation) Go to the Web site of the Federal Reserve Bank of St. Louis (FRED) (fred.stlouisfed.org) and download monthly data on the inflation rate expected by consumers as measured by the University of Michigan's survey (MICH) for 1978 to the present. Next, download the monthly inflation rate measured using the consumer price index, or CPI (CPIAUCSL), for the same period. (You can find the inflation rate by clicking on "Units" and selecting "Percent Change from Year Ago.") Plot both series on the same graph. During which periods did consumers do a good job of forecasting the inflation rate? During which periods did they do a poor job? Do consumers' expectations of the inflation rate tend to be more volatile or less volatile than the actual inflation rate?

Critical Thinking Exercises

CT17.1 Read "Why Do Many Americans Mistrust the Federal Reserve?" at www.bbc.com/news/business-35079495. What explanation does this article provide for why many Americans appear to mistrust the Fed?

CT17.2 In Chapter 15, Section 15.5, we introduced the Taylor rule. In this chapter, we described the proposal that the Fed should pursue a "single mandate" by only targeting inflation. If this change from a dual mandate to a single mandate occurred, would the Taylor rule also change? Briefly explain.

CT17.3 Read Ben Bernanke's blog post "'Audit the Fed' Is Not about Auditing the Fed" on the Web site of the Brookings Institution: www.brookings.edu/blog/ben-bernanke/2016/01/11/audit-the-fed-is-not-about-auditing-the-fed/. Summarize Bernanke's views in one or two paragraphs. How might a supporter of "auditing" the Fed respond to Bernanke's arguments? (Note that the particular legislation Bernanke focuses on in this blog entry failed to pass, but some economists and policymakers support similar proposals.)

Amazon Deals with the Effects of a Strong Dollar

In 1995, when Jeff Bezos started Amazon in a warehouse in Seattle, he was a pioneer in selling products on the Internet. Even though he had only three employees and books were the only product he sold, his small company immediately experienced rapid growth. By 2017, Amazon had 340,000 employees and revenue of $136 billion. Its Web site offered thousands of products, and it had put a significant dent in the sales of brick-and-mortar department stores such as Macy's and JCPenney. When Amazon announced that it was buying the Whole Foods grocery store chain, many people wondered whether Amazon would soon find a way to disrupt the grocery industry as well.

Amazon's success has not been confined to the United States. In 2017, about one-third of its sales were in foreign markets. As a result, fluctuations in the value of the dollar in exchange for other currencies affect Amazon's profit. In some years, converting revenue from foreign currencies yields fewer dollars than in other years. For example, in 2016, Amazon's global revenue was $550 million lower when measured in dollars than when measured in local currencies—pounds in Great Britain, euros in Germany, pesos in Mexico. Why the discrepancy? The value of the dollar had increased relative to most other currencies. So, converting pounds, euros, and pesos into dollars yielded fewer dollars for Amazon. Although by operating in many foreign markets Amazon is exposed to exchange rate risk, the company noted, "We believe that our increasing diversification beyond the U.S. economy through our growing international businesses benefits our shareholders over the long term."

As we saw in Chapter 15, one reason for the increasing value of the U.S. dollar in 2016 was rising U.S. interest rates as the Federal Reserve began to increase its target for the federal funds rate. Higher interest rates made financial investments in the United States more attractive to foreign investors, which increased the demand for U.S. dollars and the exchange rate between the dollar and other currencies. During the first half of 2017, the dollar reversed course and lost about 6 percent of its value against other major currencies as investors came to believe that the Federal Reserve would be cautious in increasing its target for the federal funds rate in the face of slowing growth in U.S. real GDP. In this chapter and the next, we will look more closely at how exchange rates are determined and at other important issues involving the international financial system.

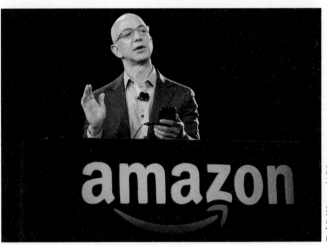

Ted S. Warren/AP Images

Sources: Ira Iosebashvili, "Dollar Falls on Weak Data, Political Uncertainty," *Wall Street Journal*, June 16, 2017; Brad Stone, *The Everything Store: Jeff Bezos and the Age of Amazon*, New York: Little, Brown and Company, 2013; and Amazon.com, *2016 Annual Report*.

Chapter Outline & Learning Objectives

Economics in Your Life & Career

The South Korean Central Bank and Your Car Loan

Suppose that you are shopping for a new car, which you plan to finance with a loan from a local bank. While reading a *Wall Street Journal* article one morning, you see this headline: "The Bank of Korea, South Korea's central bank, announces it will sell its large holdings of U.S. Treasury bonds." Will the Bank of Korea's decision to sell its U.S. Treasury bonds affect the interest rate you pay on your car loan? As you read this chapter, try to answer this question. You can check your answer against the one we provide on **page 666** at the end of this chapter.

I n Chapter 7, we looked at the basics of international trade. In this chapter, we look more closely at the linkages among countries at the macroeconomic level. Countries are linked by trade in goods and services and by flows of financial investment. We will see how policymakers in all countries take these linkages into account when conducting monetary policy and fiscal policy.

18.1 The Balance of Payments: Linking the United States to the International Economy

LEARNING OBJECTIVE: Explain how the balance of payments is calculated.

Today, consumers, firms, and investors routinely interact with consumers, firms, and investors in other economies. A consumer in France may use computer software produced in the United States, own a television manufactured in South Korea, and wear a sweater made in Italy. A U.S. firm like Amazon may sell products in dozens of countries around the world. An investor in London may buy a U.S. Treasury bill from an investor in Mexico City. Nearly all economies are **open economies** and have extensive interactions in trade or finance with other countries. Open economies interact by trading goods and services and by making investments in each other's economies. A **closed economy** has no interactions in trade or finance with other countries. No economy today is completely closed, although a few countries, such as North Korea, have very limited economic interactions with other countries.

A good way to understand the interactions between one economy and other economies is through the **balance of payments**, which is a record of a country's trade with other countries in goods, services, and assets. Just as the U.S. Bureau of Economic Analysis is responsible for collecting data on the gross domestic product (GDP), it is also responsible for collecting data on the balance of payments. Table 18.1 shows the balance of payments for the United States in 2016. Notice that the table contains three "accounts": the *current account*, the *financial account*, and the *capital account*.

The Current Account

The **current account** records *current*, or short-term, flows of funds into and out of a country. The current account for the United States includes (1) exports and imports of goods and services (recall that the difference between exports and imports of goods and services is called *net exports*); (2) income received by U.S. residents from investments in other countries and income paid on investments in the United States owned by residents of other countries (the difference between investment income received and investment income paid is called *net income on investments*); and (3) the difference between transfers made to residents of other countries and transfers received by U.S. residents from other countries (called *net transfers*). If you donate to a charity caring for orphans in Syria, it will be included in net transfers. Any payments received by U.S. residents are positive numbers in the current account, and any payments made by U.S. residents are negative numbers in the current account.

The Balance of Trade Part of the current account is the **balance of trade**, which is the difference between the value of the goods a country exports and the value of the goods the country imports. The balance of trade is the largest item in the current account and is a topic that politicians and the media often discuss. If a country exports more goods than it imports, it has a *trade surplus*. If a country exports less than it imports, it has a *trade deficit*. In 2016, the United States had a trade deficit of $752 billion. In the same year, Japan had a trade surplus of $36 billion, and China had a trade surplus of $510 billion. Figure 18.1 shows imports and exports of goods between the United States and its trading partners. The data show that the United States ran a trade deficit in 2016 with all its major trading partners and with every region of the world apart from Latin America (except Mexico) and the Middle East.

Net Exports Equals the Sum of the Balance of Trade and the Balance of Services Recall that *net exports* is a component of aggregate expenditure.

Open economy An economy that has interactions in trade or finance with other countries.

Closed economy An economy that has no interactions in trade or finance with other countries.

Balance of payments The record of a country's trade with other countries in goods, services, and assets.

Current account The part of the balance of payments that records a country's net exports, net income on investments, and net transfers.

Balance of trade The difference between the value of the goods a country exports and the value of the goods a country imports.

Current Account		
Exports of goods	$1,456	
Imports of goods	-2,208	
Balance of trade		-752
Exports of services	752	
Imports of services	-505	
Balance of services		247
Income received on investments	814	
Income payments on investments	-641	
Net income on investments		173
Net transfers		-119
Balance on current account		**-451**
Financial Account		
Increase in foreign holdings of assets in the United States	741	
Increase in U.S. holdings of assets in foreign countries	-364	
Balance on financial account		**377**
Balance on Capital Account		**0**
Statistical discrepancy		**74**
Balance of payments		**0**

The sum of the balance of trade and the balance of services equals net exports.

Source: U.S. Bureau of Economic Analysis, "U.S. International Transactions," June 20, 2017.

Table 18.1

The U.S. Balance of Payments, 2016 (billions of dollars)

Net exports is not explicitly shown in Table 18.1, but we can calculate it by adding the balance of trade and the balance of services. The *balance of services* is the difference between the value of the services a country exports and the value of the services the country imports. Notice that, technically, net exports is *not* equal to the current account balance because this account also includes net income on investments and

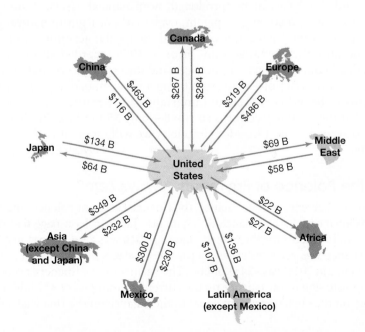

MyLab Economics Animation

Figure 18.1

Trade Flows for the United States, 2016

In 2016, the United States ran a trade deficit with all its major trading partners and with every region of the world except for Latin America (except Mexico) and the Middle East. The green arrows show exports from the United States to other countries or regions, and the red arrows show imports from other countries or regions to the United States.

Sources: U.S. Bureau of Economic Analysis, "U.S. International Transactions," June 20, 2017.

net transfers. Because the sum of these other two items is relatively small, though, it is often a convenient simplification to think of net exports as being equal to the current account balance. **MyLab Economics** Concept Check

The Financial Account

Financial account The part of the balance of payments that records purchases of assets a country has made abroad and foreign purchases of assets in the country.

The **financial account** records purchases of assets a country has made abroad and foreign purchases of assets in the country. The financial account records long-term flows of funds into and out of a country:

- There is a *capital outflow* from the United States when an investor in the United States buys a bond issued by a foreign company or government or when a U.S. firm builds a factory in another country.
- There is a *capital inflow* into the United States when a foreign investor buys a bond issued by a U.S. firm or by the government or when a foreign firm builds a factory in the United States.

Notice that we are using the word *capital* here to apply not just to physical assets, such as factories, but also to financial assets, such as shares of stock. When firms build or buy facilities in foreign countries, they are engaging in *foreign direct investment*. When investors buy stock or bonds issued in another country, they are engaging in *foreign portfolio investment*.

Net foreign investment The difference between capital outflows from a country and capital inflows, also equal to net foreign direct investment plus net foreign portfolio investment.

Another way of thinking of the balance on the financial account is as a measure of *net capital flows*, or the difference between capital inflows and capital outflows. (Here we are omitting a few transactions included in the capital account, as discussed in the next section.) A concept closely related to net capital flows is **net foreign investment**, which is equal to capital outflows minus capital inflows. Net capital flows and net foreign investment are always equal but have opposite signs: When net capital flows are positive, net foreign investment is negative, and when net capital flows are negative, net foreign investment is positive. Net foreign investment is also equal to net foreign direct investment plus net foreign portfolio investment. In Section 18.3, we will use the relationship between the balance on the financial account and net foreign investment to understand an important aspect of the international economic system. **MyLab Economics** Concept Check

The Capital Account

Capital account The part of the balance of payments that records relatively minor transactions, such as migrants' transfers and sales and purchases of nonproduced, nonfinancial assets.

The **capital account** is a less important part of the balance of payments that records relatively minor transactions, such as migrants' transfers—which consist of goods and financial assets people take with them when they leave or enter a country—and sales and purchases of nonproduced, nonfinancial assets. A nonproduced, nonfinancial asset is a copyright, patent, trademark, or right to natural resources. The definitions of the financial account and the capital account are often misunderstood because the capital account prior to 1999 recorded all the transactions now included in both the financial account and the capital account. In other words, capital account transactions went from being a very important part of the balance of payments to being a relatively unimportant part. Because the balance on what is now called the capital account is so small—only $59 million in 2016, which we rounded to zero in Table 18.1—for simplicity we will ignore it in the remainder of this chapter. **MyLab Economics** Concept Check

Why Is the Balance of Payments Always Zero?

The sum of the current account balance, the financial account balance, and the capital account balance equals the balance of payments. Table 18.1 on page 647 shows that the balance of payments for the United States in 2016 was zero. It's not just by chance that this balance was zero; *the balance of payments is always zero*. Notice that the current account balance in 2016 was −$451 billion. The balance on the financial account (which has the opposite sign to the balance on the current account) was $377 billion. To make the balance on the current account equal to the balance on the financial account, the balance of payments includes an entry called the *statistical discrepancy*. (Remember that we are ignoring the balance on the capital account. If we included it, we would say that the statistical discrepancy takes on a value equal to the difference between the current account balance and the sum of the balance on the financial account and the balance on the capital account.)

Why does the U.S. Department of Commerce include the statistical discrepancy entry to force the balance of payments to equal zero? If the sum of the current account balance and the financial account balance does not equal zero, some imports or exports of goods and services or some capital inflows or capital outflows must not have been measured accurately.

To better understand why the balance of payments must equal zero every year, consider the following: In 2016, the United States spent $451 billion more on goods, services, and other items in the current account than it received. What happened to that $451 billion? We know that every dollar of that $451 billion was used by foreign individuals or firms to invest in the United States or was added to foreign holdings of dollars. We know this because logically there is nowhere else for the dollars to go: If the dollars weren't spent on U.S. goods and services—and we know they weren't because if they had been, they would have shown up in the current account—they must have been spent on investments in the United States or not spent at all. Dollars that aren't spent are added to foreign holdings of dollars. Changes in foreign holdings of dollars are called *official reserve transactions*. Foreign investment in the United States and additions to foreign holdings of dollars both show up as positive entries in the U.S. financial account. Therefore, a current account deficit must be exactly offset by a financial account surplus, leaving the balance of payments equal to zero. Similarly, a country that runs a current account surplus, such as China, must run a financial account deficit of exactly the same size. If a country's current account surplus is not exactly equal to its financial account deficit, or if a country's current account deficit is not exactly equal to its financial account surplus, some transactions must not have been accounted for. The statistical discrepancy is included in the balance of payments to compensate for these uncounted transactions.

MyLab Economics Concept Check   **MyLab Economics** Study Plan

Don't Let This Happen to You

Don't Confuse the Balance of Trade, the Current Account Balance, and the Balance of Payments

The terminology of international economics can be tricky. Remember that the *balance of trade* includes only trade in goods; it does not include services. This observation is important because the United States, for example, usually imports more *goods* than it exports, but it usually exports more *services* than it imports. As a result, the U.S. trade deficit is almost always larger than the current account deficit. The *current account balance* includes the balance of trade, the balance of services, net investment income, and net transfers. Net investment income and net transfers are much smaller than the balance of trade and the balance of services.

Even though the *balance of payments* is equal to the sum of the current account balance and the financial account balance—and must equal zero—you may sometimes see references to a balance of payments "surplus" or "deficit." These references have two explanations. The first is that the person making the reference has confused the balance of payments with either the balance of trade or the current account balance. This mistake is very common. The second explanation is that the person is not including official reserve transactions in the financial account. If we separate changes in U.S. holdings of foreign currencies and changes in foreign holdings of U.S. dollars from other financial account entries, the current account balance and the financial account balance do not have to sum to zero, and there can be a balance of payments surplus or deficit. These distinctions may sound complicated—and they are! But don't worry. Knowing how official reserve transactions are accounted for is not crucial to understanding the basic ideas behind the balance of payments.

MyLab Economics Study Plan

Your Turn: Test your understanding by doing related problem 1.6 on pages 667–668 at the end of this chapter.

Solved Problem 18.1

Understanding the Arithmetic of the Balance of Payments

Test your understanding of the relationship between the current account and the financial account by evaluating the following assertion by a political commentator:

> The industrial countries are committing economic suicide. Every year, they invest more and more in emerging countries, such as Malaysia. Every year, more U.S., Japanese, and European manufacturing firms move their factories to emerging countries. With extensive new factories and low wages, emerging countries now export far more to the industrial countries than they import.

Solving the Problem

Step 1: Review the chapter material. This problem is about the relationship between the current account and the financial account, so you may want to review the section "Why Is the Balance of Payments Always Zero?" which begins on page 648.

Step 2: Explain the errors in the commentator's argument. The argument sounds plausible. It would be easy to find statements similar to this one in recent books and articles by well-known political commentators. But the argument contains an important error: The commentator has failed to understand the relationship between the current account and the financial account. The commentator asserts that emerging countries are receiving large capital inflows from industrial countries. In other words, emerging countries are running financial account surpluses. The commentator also asserts that emerging countries are exporting more than they are importing. In other words, they are running current account surpluses. As we have seen in this section, it is impossible for a country to run a current account surplus *and* a financial account surplus simultaneously. A country that runs a current account surplus *must* run a financial account deficit and vice versa.

Extra Credit: Most emerging economies that have received large inflows of foreign investment during the past two decades, such as Malaysia, Thailand, and Vietnam, have run current account deficits: They import more goods and services than they export. Emerging economies that run current account surpluses, such as Singapore, also run financial account deficits: They invest more abroad than other countries invest in them.

The point here is subtle, which is why it confuses many politicians, journalists, and political commentators. Unless you understand the relationship between the current account and the financial account, you won't be able to understand a key aspect of the international economy.

MyLab Economics Study Plan   **Your Turn:** For more practice, do related problems 1.8, 1.9, and 1.10 on page 668 at the end of this chapter.

 ## The Foreign Exchange Market and Exchange Rates

LEARNING OBJECTIVE: Explain how exchange rates are determined and how changes in exchange rates affect the prices of imports and exports.

A firm that operates entirely within the United States will price its products in dollars and will use dollars to pay its suppliers' bills, wages and salaries to its workers, interest to its bondholders, and dividends to its shareholders. A multinational corporation such as Amazon, in contrast, may sell goods and services in many different countries and receive payments in many different currencies. Its suppliers and workers may also be spread around the world and may have to be paid in local currencies. In addition to exchanging currencies, corporations may also use the international financial system to borrow in a foreign currency. For example, in 2016, U.S. firms such as McDonald's and General Electric sold more bonds denominated in euros—the common currency of 19 European countries—than did firms in any European country. These firms found that their borrowing costs were reduced by selling bonds in Europe rather than in the United States. When firms make extensive use of foreign currencies, they must deal with fluctuations in the exchange rate.

The **nominal exchange rate** is the value of one country's currency in terms of another country's currency. Economists also calculate the *real exchange rate*, which corrects the nominal exchange rate for changes in prices of goods and services. We discuss the real exchange rate later in this section. The nominal exchange rate determines how many units of a foreign currency you can purchase with $1. For example, the exchange rate between the U.S. dollar and the Japanese yen can be expressed as ¥100 = $1. (This exchange rate can also be expressed as how many U.S. dollars are required to buy 1 Japanese yen: $0.01 = ¥1.) The market for foreign exchange is very active, with the equivalent of more than $5 trillion worth of currency being traded each day. The exchange rates that result from this trading are reported on a number of online sites devoted to economic news and on the sites of most newspapers.

Banks and other financial institutions around the world employ currency traders, who are linked together by computer. Rather than exchange large amounts of paper currency, they buy and sell deposits in banks. For example, a bank buying or selling dollars will actually be buying or selling dollar bank deposits. Dollar bank deposits exist not just in banks in the United States but also in banks around the world. Suppose that the Crédit Agricole bank in France wants to sell U.S. dollars and buy Japanese yen. The bank may exchange U.S. dollar deposits that it owns for Japanese yen deposits owned by the Deutsche Bank in Germany. Businesses and individuals usually obtain foreign currency from banks in their own country.

Nominal exchange rate The value of one country's currency in terms of another country's currency.

 ## Apply the Concept

MyLab Economics Video

Exchange Rate Listings

You can find the exchange rates between the dollar and other major currencies on many online sites, such as wsj.com, bloomberg.com, or finance.yahoo.com, as well as in the financial pages of most newspapers. The exchange rates in the following table are for June 23, 2017. The euro is the common currency used by 19 European countries, including France, Germany, and Italy, but not the United Kingdom.

Exchange Rate between the U.S. Dollar and the Indicated Currency		
Currency	Units of Foreign Currency per U.S. Dollar	U.S. Dollars per Unit of Foreign Currency
Canadian dollar	1.327	0.754
Japanese yen	111.286	0.009
Mexican peso	18.003	0.056
British pound	0.786	1.272
Euro	0.893	1.119

Notice that the expression for the exchange rate stated as units of foreign currency per U.S. dollar is the *reciprocal* of the exchange rate stated as U.S. dollars per unit of foreign currency. So, the exchange rate between the U.S. dollar and the British pound can be stated as either 0.786 British pounds per U.S. dollar or 1/0.786 = 1.272 U.S. dollars per British pound.

Banks are the most active participants in the market for foreign exchange. Typically, banks buy currency for slightly less than the amount for which they sell it. This spread between the buying and selling prices allows banks to cover their costs from currency trading. Therefore, when most businesses and individuals buy foreign currency from a bank, they receive fewer units of foreign currency per dollar than would be indicated by the exchange rate shown on online business sites or printed in the newspaper.

Source: *Wall Street Journal*, June 23, 2017.

MyLab Economics Study Plan   **Your Turn:** Test your understanding by doing related problem 2.5 on pages 668–669 at the end of this chapter.

Equilibrium in the Market for Foreign Exchange

The market exchange rate is determined by the interaction of demand and supply, just as other prices are. Figure 18.2 shows the demand and supply of U.S. dollars for Japanese yen. Notice that as we move up the vertical axis, the value of the dollar increases relative to the value of the yen. When the exchange rate is ¥150 = $1, the dollar is worth 1.5 times as much relative to the yen as when the exchange rate is ¥100 = $1.

First consider the demand curve for dollars in exchange for yen. The demand curve has the normal downward slope. There are three sources of foreign currency demand for the U.S. dollar:

1. Foreign firms and households that want to buy goods and services produced in the United States
2. Foreign firms and households that want to invest in the United States either through foreign direct investment—buying or building factories or other facilities in the United States—or through foreign portfolio investment—buying stocks and bonds issued in the United States
3. Currency traders who believe that the value of the dollar in the future will be greater than its value today

When the value of the dollar is high, the quantity of dollars demanded will be low. A Japanese firm is more likely to buy $150 million worth of microchips from Intel Corporation when the exchange rate is ¥100 = $1 and the microchips can be purchased for ¥15 billion than when the exchange rate is ¥150 = $1 and the microchips cost ¥22.5 billion. Similarly, a Japanese investor will be more likely to buy a $1,000 bond issued by the U.S. Treasury when the exchange rate is ¥100 = $1 and the investor pays only ¥100,000 to buy $1,000 than when the exchange rate is ¥150 = $1 and the investor must pay ¥150,000.

Now consider the supply curve for dollars in exchange for yen. The supply curve has the normal upward slope. When the value of the dollar is high, the quantity of dollars

MyLab Economics Animation

Figure 18.2

Equilibrium in the Foreign Exchange Market

When the exchange rate is ¥150 to the dollar, the exchange rate is above its equilibrium level, and there will be a surplus of dollars. When the exchange rate is ¥100 to the dollar, it is below its equilibrium level, and there will be a shortage of dollars. At an exchange rate of ¥120 to the dollar, the foreign exchange market is in equilibrium.

supplied in exchange for yen will be high. A U.S. investor will be more likely to buy a ¥200,000 bond issued by the Japanese government when the exchange rate is ¥200 = $1 and he needs to pay only $1,000 to buy ¥200,000 than when the exchange rate is ¥100 = $1 and he must pay $2,000. The owner of a U.S. electronics store is more likely to buy ¥20 million worth of television sets from Sony Corporation when the exchange rate is ¥200 = $1 and she needs to pay only $100,000 to purchase the televisions than when the exchange rate is ¥100 = $1 and she must pay $200,000.

As in any other market, equilibrium occurs in the foreign exchange market where the quantity supplied equals the quantity demanded. In Figure 18.2, ¥120 = $1 is the equilibrium exchange rate. At exchange rates above ¥120 = $1, there will be a surplus of dollars and downward pressure on the exchange rate. The surplus and the downward pressure will not be eliminated until the exchange rate falls to ¥120 = $1. If the exchange rate is below ¥120 = $1, there will be a shortage of dollars and upward pressure on the exchange rate. The shortage and the upward pressure will not be eliminated until the exchange rate rises to ¥120 = $1. Surpluses and shortages in the foreign exchange market are eliminated very quickly because the volume of trading in major currencies such as the dollar and the yen is large, and currency traders are linked together by computer.

Currency appreciation occurs when the market value of a country's currency increases relative to the value of another country's currency. **Currency depreciation** occurs when the market value of a country's currency decreases relative to the value of another country's currency.　　　　　MyLab Economics Concept Check

Currency appreciation An increase in the market value of one currency relative to another currency.

Currency depreciation A decrease in the market value of one currency relative to another currency.

How Do Shifts in Demand and Supply Affect the Exchange Rate?

Shifts in the demand and supply curves cause the equilibrium exchange rate to change. Three main factors cause the demand and supply curves in the foreign exchange market to shift:

1. Changes in the demand for U.S.-produced goods and services and changes in the demand for foreign-produced goods and services
2. Changes in the desire to invest in the United States and changes in the desire to invest in foreign countries
3. Changes in the expectations of currency traders about the likely future value of the dollar and the likely future value of foreign currencies

Shifts in the Demand for Foreign Exchange　Consider how the three factors just listed will affect the demand for U.S. dollars in exchange for Japanese yen. During an economic expansion in Japan, the incomes of Japanese households will rise, and the demand by Japanese consumers and firms for U.S. goods will increase. At any given exchange rate, the demand for U.S. dollars will increase, and the demand curve will shift to the right. Similarly, if interest rates in the United States rise, the desirability of investing in U.S. financial assets will increase, and the demand curve for dollars will also shift to the right. **Speculators** are currency traders who buy and sell foreign exchange in an attempt to profit from changes in exchange rates. If a speculator becomes convinced that the value of the dollar is going to rise relative to the value of the yen, the speculator will sell yen and buy dollars. If the current exchange rate is ¥120 = $1, and the speculator is convinced that it will soon rise to ¥140 = $1, the speculator could sell ¥600,000,000 and receive $5,000,000 (= ¥600,000,000/¥120) in return. If the speculator is correct and the value of the dollar rises against the yen to ¥140 = $1, the speculator will be able to exchange $5,000,000 for ¥700,000,000 (= $5,000,000 × ¥140), for a profit of ¥100,000,000.

To summarize, the demand curve for dollars shifts to the right when incomes in Japan rise, when interest rates in the United States rise, or when speculators decide that the value of the dollar will rise relative to the value of the yen.

During a recession in Japan, Japanese incomes will fall, reducing the demand for U.S.-produced goods and services and shifting the demand curve for dollars to the left.

Speculators Currency traders who buy and sell foreign exchange in an attempt to profit from changes in exchange rates.

Similarly, if interest rates in the United States fall, the desirability of investing in U.S. financial assets will decrease, and the demand curve for dollars will shift to the left. Finally, if speculators become convinced that the future value of the dollar will be lower than its current value, the demand for dollars will fall, and the demand curve will shift to the left.

Shifts in the Supply of Foreign Exchange The factors that affect the supply curve for dollars are similar to those that affect the demand curve for dollars. An economic expansion in the United States increases the incomes of Americans and increases their demand for goods and services, including goods and services made in Japan. As U.S. consumers and firms increase their spending on Japanese products, they must supply dollars in exchange for yen, which causes the supply curve for dollars to shift to the right. Similarly, an increase in interest rates in Japan will make financial investments in Japan more attractive to U.S. investors. These higher Japanese interest rates will cause the supply curve for dollars to shift to the right, as U.S. investors exchange dollars for yen. Finally, if speculators become convinced that the future value of the yen will be higher relative to the dollar than it is today, the supply curve for dollars will shift to the right as traders attempt to exchange dollars for yen.

A recession in the United States will decrease the demand for Japanese products and cause the supply curve for dollars to shift to the left. Similarly, a decrease in interest rates in Japan will make financial investments in Japan less attractive and cause the supply curve for dollars to shift to the left. If traders become convinced that the future value of the yen will be lower relative to the dollar, the supply curve will also shift to the left.

Adjustment to a New Equilibrium The factors that affect the demand and supply for currencies are constantly changing. Whether the exchange rate increases or decreases depends on the direction and size of the shifts in the demand curve and supply curve. For example, as Figure 18.3 shows, if the demand curve for dollars in exchange for Japanese yen shifts to the right by more than the supply curve shifts, the equilibrium exchange rate will increase. **MyLab Economics** Concept Check

Some Exchange Rates Are Not Determined by the Market

To this point, we have assumed that exchange rates are determined by the market. This assumption is a good one for many currencies, including the U.S. dollar, the euro, the Japanese yen, and the British pound. Some currencies, however, have *fixed exchange rates*

MyLab Economics Animation

Figure 18.3

Shifts in the Demand and Supply Curve Resulting in a Higher Exchange Rate

Holding other factors constant, an increase in the supply of dollars will decrease the equilibrium exchange rate. An increase in the demand for dollars will increase the equilibrium exchange rate. In the case shown in this figure, both the demand curve and the supply curve have shifted to the right. Because the demand curve has shifted to the right by more than the supply curve, the equilibrium exchange rate has increased from ¥120 to $1 at point A to ¥130 to $1 at point B.

that do not change over long periods. For example, for more than 10 years, the value of the Chinese yuan was fixed against the U.S. dollar at a rate of 8.28 yuan to the dollar. As we will discuss in more detail in Chapter 19, Section 19.2, a country's central bank has to intervene in the foreign exchange market to buy and sell its currency if it wishes to keep the exchange rate fixed. **MyLab Economics** Concept Check

How Movements in the Exchange Rate Affect Exports and Imports

When the market value of the dollar increases, the foreign currency price of U.S. exports rises, and the dollar price of foreign imports falls. Suppose that initially the market exchange rate between the U.S. dollar and the euro is $1 = €1. In that case, a Blu-ray disc that has a price of $20 in the United States will have a price of €20 in France. A bottle of French wine that has a price of €50 in France will have a price of $50 in the United States. Now suppose the market exchange rate between the U.S. dollar and the euro changes to $1.20 = €1. Because it now takes more dollars to buy a euro, the dollar has *depreciated* against the euro, and the euro has *appreciated* against the dollar. The depreciation of the dollar has decreased the euro price of the Blu-ray disc from €20 to $20/(1.20 dollars/euro) = €16.67. The dollar price of the French wine has risen from $50 to €50 ×1.20 dollars/euro = $60. As a result, we would expect more Blu-ray discs to be sold in France and less French wine to be sold in the United States.

To generalize, we can conclude:

1. A depreciation in the domestic currency will increase exports and decrease imports, thereby increasing net exports. If real GDP is currently below potential GDP, then, holding all other factors constant, a depreciation in the domestic currency should increase net exports, aggregate demand, and real GDP.
2. An appreciation in the domestic currency should have the opposite effect: Exports should fall, and imports should rise, which will reduce net exports, aggregate demand, and real GDP. **MyLab Economics** Concept Check

Apply the Concept
MyLab Economics Video

Is a Strong Currency Good for a Country?

In early 2017, President Trump stated in an interview, "I think our dollar is getting too strong…. It's very, very hard to compete when you have a strong dollar." Some people were surprised by the president's declaration. Shouldn't a country want a strong currency? "Strong" certainly seems better than "weak," so most people would answer "yes" to that question. As a result, politicians rarely are willing to say that they are against a strong dollar. For instance, in June 2015, President Barack Obama attended a meeting of the Group of 7, an organization of high-income countries. He was initially quoted as saying at that meeting that a strong dollar was a problem for the United States. There was a public outcry, and the president later denied he had made the statement.

As the following graph shows, over the years, the dollar has gone through substantial swings, during which it has increased and decreased in value against other major currencies. The graph shows the *trade-weighted exchange rate* for the U.S. dollar, which is an index number similar to the consumer price index (CPI). Just as the CPI weights individual prices by the share the product takes up in a household's budget, the trade-weighted exchange rate for the U.S. dollar weights each individual exchange rate by the share of that country's trade with the United States. (The currencies of these countries are included in the index: Australia, Canada, the euro zone, Japan, Sweden, Switzerland, and the United Kingdom.)

Some U.S. consumers and firms win and some lose from increases and decreases in the value of the dollar. For instance, as the graph shows, during 2016, the value of the dollar mostly increased. This strong dollar hurt U.S. firms that are exporters or

Trade-weighted
exchange rate
for the U.S. dollar
(March 1973 = 100)

have foreign operations. A strong dollar increases the foreign currency price of U.S. exports, so European consumers have to pay more euros to buy U.S.-produced goods, Canadian consumers have to pay more Canadian dollars, and Japanese consumers have to pay more yen. The result is a decline in profits for U.S. exporters. As an article in the *Wall Street Journal* put it in December 2016, "U.S. [exports] overseas are suddenly more expensive in many places, and foreign earnings are worth less when translated back into dollars." As we saw in the chapter opener, in 2016, Amazon experienced lower revenues due to the strong dollar.

U.S. consumers, though, benefit from a strong dollar because the imported goods they purchase—from cars to clothing to electronics—have lower dollar prices. Between 2014 and 2016, the average price of imported goods fell more than 12 percent. U.S. firms that purchase inputs from foreign suppliers also benefit. For instance, about 40 percent of the components of the automobiles that GM, Ford, and Chrysler assemble in the United States are purchased from foreign suppliers.

The value of the dollar increased for most of 2016, as interest rates in the United States rose in anticipation of faster economic growth and higher inflation. But in the first half of 2017, the value of the dollar declined. Slower-than-anticipated economic growth, with the inflation rate remaining stubbornly below the Fed's target of 2 percent, led investors to expect that the Fed would be cautious in raising its target for the federal funds rate. As a result investors' demand for dollars declined, resulting in a lower exchange rate. Most of the winners from the rising dollar during 2016 lost from the falling dollar of 2017. We can conclude that neither a "strong" currency nor a "weak" currency is all good or all bad for a country's businesses and households. Swings in exchange rates create both winners and losers, which may be why politicians typically avoid discussing the value of the dollar.

Sources: Andrew Mayeda, "Trump Drops Campaign Promise to Label China a Currency Manipulator," bloomberg. com, April 12, 2017; Theo Francis and Eric Sylvers, "Strong Dollar Has Companies Counting the Cost—and Opportunities," *Wall Street Journal*, December 16, 2016; Chelsey Dulaney, "Dollar Falls as Investors Watch Fed Speeches," *Wall Street Journal*, June 23, 2017; and data from the Federal Reserve Bank of St. Louis and the U.S. Bureau of Economic Analysis.

MyLab Economics Study Plan   **Your Turn:** Test your understanding by doing related problems 2.6 and 2.7 on page 669 at the end of this chapter.

Don't Let This Happen to You

Don't Confuse What Happens When a Currency Appreciates with What Happens When It Depreciates

One of the most confusing aspects of exchange rates is that they can be expressed in two ways. We can express the exchange rate between the dollar and the yen either as how many yen can be purchased with $1 or as how many dollars can be purchased with ¥1. That is, we can express the exchange rate as ¥100 = $1 or as $0.01 = ¥1.

When a currency appreciates, it increases in value relative to another currency. When it depreciates, it decreases in value relative to another currency. If the exchange rate changes from ¥100 = $1 to ¥120 = $1, the dollar has appreciated, and the yen has depreciated because it now takes more yen to buy $1. If the exchange rate changes from $0.010 = ¥1 to $0.015 = ¥1,

however, the dollar has depreciated, and the yen has appreciated because it now takes more dollars to buy yen. This situation can appear somewhat confusing because the exchange rate seems to have "increased" in both cases. To determine which currency has appreciated and which has depreciated, it is important to remember that an appreciation of the domestic currency means that it now takes *more* units of the foreign currency to buy one unit of the domestic currency. A depreciation of the domestic currency means it takes *fewer* units of the foreign currency to buy one unit of the domestic currency. This observation holds no matter which way we express the exchange rate.

MyLab Economics Study Plan

Your Turn: Test your understanding by doing related problem 2.8 on page 669 at the end of the chapter.

Solved Problem 18.2

MyLab Economics Interactive Animation

Toyota Rides the Exchange Rate Rollercoaster

Toyota assembles some of its automobiles in the United States and some in Japan. The company exports to the United States and other countries some of the automobiles it assembles in Japan. An article in the *Wall Street Journal* discussing Toyota's profits during 2016 had this headline: "Toyota's Profit Slides on Yen's Strength." The article noted, though, that "the company on Monday raised its profit forecast for the year … after the yen's recent weakening."

a. What did the article mean by the "yen's strength" during 2016? Why would the yen's strength have reduced Toyota's profit during that year?

b. What did the article mean by the yen having "weakened" during early 2017? Why would Toyota forecast an increase in profit because of a weakening yen?

c. If Toyota produced in Japan all of the cars and trucks it sells in the United States, would its profit be affected more or less by fluctuations in the exchange value of the yen? Briefly explain.

Solving the Problem

Step 1: **Review the chapter material.** This problem is about changes in the value of a currency, so you may want to review the section "How Movements in the Exchange Rate Affect Exports and Imports" on page 655.

Step 2: **Answer part (a) by explaining what the article means by the "yen's strength" and why the yen's strength reduced Toyota's profit during 2016.** In this case, the yen's strength means that the yen is worth more in exchange for the U.S. dollar and other currencies. With a strengthening yen, one U.S. dollar would exchange for fewer yen. A strengthening yen reduced Toyota's profit in two ways: (1) Cars the firm produced in Japan would sell for higher prices in other countries' currencies, including the U.S. dollar, thereby reducing Toyota's sales, and (2) when Toyota exchanged the dollars it earned in the United States from selling cars produced there, it would receive fewer yen.

Step 3: **Answer part (b) by explaining what the article meant by the yen having "weakened" and how that weakening caused Toyota to raise its profit forecast.** The yen having "weakened" means that the yen is exchanging for fewer dollars and other currencies. A weak yen has the opposite effect on Toyota's profit of a strong yen: The firm sees increased exports of cars it assembles in Japan and receives more yen from exchanging the dollar profits it earns from selling cars it assembles in the United States.

Step 4: **Answer part (c) by explaining whether fluctuations in the exchange value of the yen would affect Toyota's profit more or less if it produced in Japan all of the cars sold in the United States.** Toyota would be more exposed to risk from fluctuating exchange rates if it produced in Japan all of the cars and trucks it sells in the United States. Currently, an increase in the value of the yen has no effect on the dollar price of the cars that Toyota assembles in Georgetown, Kentucky; San Antonio, Texas; and other U.S. factories. If all those cars and trucks were assembled in Japan for export to the United States, Toyota would be vulnerable to a decline in sales and profit when the value of the yen increases against the dollar. In fact, a key reason that the managers at Toyota have moved production of many cars and trucks to the United States is to reduce exposure to exchange rate risk.

Source: Sean McLain, "Toyota's Profit Slides on Yen's Strength," *Wall Street Journal*, February 6, 2017.

MyLab Economics Study Plan   **Your Turn:** For more practice, do related problem 2.11 on pages 669–670 at the end of this chapter.

The Real Exchange Rate

Real exchange rate The price of domestic goods in terms of foreign goods.

We have seen that an important factor in determining the level of a country's exports to and imports from another country is the relative prices of each country's goods. The relative prices of two countries' goods are determined by two factors: the relative price levels in the two countries and the nominal exchange rate between the two countries' currencies. Economists combine these two factors in the **real exchange rate**, which is the price of domestic goods in terms of foreign goods. Recall that the price level is a measure of the average prices of goods and services in an economy. We can calculate the real exchange rate between two currencies as:

$$\text{Real exchange rate} = \text{Norminal exchange rate} \times \left(\frac{\text{Domestic price level}}{\text{Foreign price level}} \right).$$

Notice that both changes in the nominal exchange rate and changes in the relative price levels cause movements in the real exchange rate. Suppose that the exchange rate between the U.S. dollar and the British pound is \$1 = £1, the price level in the United States is 100, and the price level in the United Kingdom is also 100. Then the real exchange rate between the dollar and the pound is:

$$\text{Real exchange rate} = 1 \text{ pound/dollar} \times \left(\frac{100}{100} \right) = 1.00.$$

Now suppose that the nominal exchange rate increases to 1.1 pounds per dollar, while the price level in the United States rises to 105 and the price level in the United Kingdom remains 100. In this case, the real exchange rate will be:

$$\text{Real exchange rate} = 1.1 \text{ pound/dollar} \times \left(\frac{105}{100} \right) = 1.16.$$

The increase in the real exchange rate from 1.00 to 1.16 tells us that the prices of U.S. goods and services are now 16 percent higher relative to British goods and services.

Real exchange rates are reported as index numbers, with one year chosen as the base year. As with the consumer price index, the main value of the real exchange rate is in tracking changes over time—in this case, changes in the relative prices of domestic goods in terms of foreign goods.

18.3 The International Sector and National Saving and Investment

LEARNING OBJECTIVE: Define and apply the saving and investment equation.

Having studied what determines the exchange rate, we are now ready to explore further the linkages between the U.S. economy and foreign economies. Until 1970, U.S. imports and exports were usually 4 percent to 5 percent of GDP (see Figure 7.1 in Chapter 7). Imports and exports are now three times as large a fraction of U.S. GDP. Imports have also consistently been larger than exports, meaning that net exports have been negative.

Net Exports Equal Net Foreign Investment

If your spending is greater than your income, what can you do? You can sell some assets—maybe those 20 shares of stock in Amazon your grandparents gave you—or you can borrow money. A firm can be in the same situation: If a firm's costs are greater than its revenues, it has to make up the difference by selling assets or by borrowing. A country is in the same situation when it imports more than it exports: The country must finance the difference by selling assets—such as land, office buildings, or factories—to foreigners or by borrowing from foreigners.

In other words, for any country, a current account deficit must be exactly offset by a financial account surplus. When a country sells more assets to foreigners than it buys from foreigners, or when it borrows more from foreigners than it lends to foreigners—as it must if it is running a current account deficit—the country experiences a net capital inflow and a financial account surplus. Remember that net exports is roughly equal to the current account balance. Remember also that the financial account balance is roughly equal to net capital flows, which are in turn equal to net foreign investment but with the opposite sign. To review these two points, look again at Table 18.1 on page 647, which shows that the current account balance is determined mainly by the balance of trade and the balance of services, and the financial account is equal to net capital flows. Also, remember the definition of net foreign investment.

When imports are greater than exports, net exports are negative, and there will be a net capital inflow as households and firms in the United States sell assets and borrow to pay for the surplus of imports over exports. Therefore, net capital flows will be equal to net exports (but with the opposite sign), and net foreign investment will also be equal to net exports (with the same sign). Because net exports are usually negative for the United States, in most years, the United States must be a net borrower from abroad, and U.S. net foreign investment will be negative.

We can summarize this discussion with the following equations:

$$\text{Current account balance} + \text{Financial account balance} = 0$$

or:

$$\text{Current account balance} = -\text{Financial account balance}$$

or:

$$\text{Net exports} = \text{Net foreign investment.}$$

The last equation tells us, once again, that countries such as the United States that import more than they export must borrow more from abroad than they lend abroad: If net exports are negative, net foreign investment will also be negative by the same amount. Countries such as China that export more than they import must lend abroad more than they borrow from abroad: If net exports are positive, net foreign investment will also be positive by the same amount. **MyLab Economics** Concept Check

Domestic Saving, Domestic Investment, and Net Foreign Investment

We can think of the total saving in any economy as being equal to saving by the private sector plus saving by the government sector, which we call *public saving* (see Chapter 10, Section 10.2). When the government runs a budget surplus by spending less than it receives in taxes, public saving is positive. When the government runs a budget deficit, public saving is negative. Negative saving is also known as *dissaving*. We can write the following expression for the level of saving in the economy:

$$\text{National saving} = \text{Private saving} + \text{Public saving}$$

or:

$$S = S_{\text{private}} + S_{\text{public}}.$$

Private saving is equal to what households have left of their income after spending on consumption goods and paying taxes (for simplicity, we assume that transfer payments are zero):

$$\text{Private saving} = \text{National income} - \text{Consumption} - \text{Taxes}$$

or:

$$S_{\text{private}} = Y - C - T.$$

Public saving is equal to the difference between government spending and taxes:

$$\text{Government saving} = \text{Taxes} - \text{Government spending}$$

or:

$$S_{\text{public}} = T - G.$$

Finally, remember the basic macroeconomic equation for GDP or national income:

$$Y = C + I + G + NX.$$

We can use this last equation, our definitions of private and public saving, and the fact that net exports equal net foreign investment to arrive at an important relationship, called the **saving and investment equation**:

Saving and investment equation
An equation that shows that national saving is equal to domestic investment plus net foreign investment.

$$\text{National saving} = \text{Domestic investment} + \text{Net foreign investment}$$

or:

$$S = I + NFI.$$

This equation is an *identity* because it must always be true, given the definitions we have used.

The saving and investment equation tells us that a country's saving will be invested either domestically or overseas. If you save $1,000 and use the funds to buy a bond issued by Amazon, Amazon may use the $1,000 to partially pay for a cloud computing facility in the United States (*I*) or for an Internet site in China (*NFI*).

Solved Problem 18.3

MyLab Economics Interactive Animation

Arriving at the Saving and Investment Equation

Use the definitions of private and public saving, the equation for GDP or national income, and the fact that net exports (NX) must equal net foreign investment (NFI) to arrive at the saving and investment equation.

Solving the Problem

Step 1: **Review the chapter material.** This problem is about the saving and investment equation, so you may want to review the section "Domestic Saving,
Domestic Investment, and Net Foreign Investment" on page 660.

Step 2: **Derive an expression for national saving (S) in terms of national
income (Y), consumption (C), and government purchases (G).** We can
bring together the four equations we need:

1. $S_{\text{private}} = Y - C - T$
2. $S_{\text{public}} = T - G$
3. $Y = C + I + G + NX$
4. $NX = NFI$

Because national saving (S) appears in the saving and investment equation,
we need to find an equation for it in terms of the other variables. Adding
equation 1. plus equation 2. yields national saving:

$$S = S_{\text{private}} + S_{\text{public}} = (Y - C - T) + (T - G) = Y - C - G.$$

Step 3: **Use the result from step 2 to derive an expression for national saving
in terms of investment (I) and net exports (NX).** Because GDP (Y) does
not appear in the saving and investment equation, we need to substitute the
expression for it given in equation 3.:

$$S = (C + I + G + NX) - C - G$$

and simplify:

$$S = I + NX.$$

Step 4: **Use the results of steps 2 and 3 to derive the saving and investment
equation.** Finally, substitute net foreign investment for net exports:

$$S = I + NFI.$$

Your Turn: For more practice, do related problem 3.8 on pages 670–671 at the end of this chapter.   MyLab Economics Study Plan

A country such as the United States that has negative net foreign investment must
be saving less than it is investing domestically. To understand why, rewrite the saving
and investment equation by moving domestic investment to the left side:

$$S - I = NFI.$$

If net foreign investment is negative—as it is for the United States nearly every year—
domestic investment (I) must be greater than national saving (S).

In most years, the level of saving in China has been well above the country's domestic investment. The result has been high levels of Chinese net foreign investment. For
example, in 2016, the Chinese firm Anbang Insurance spent more than $14 billion to
purchase the U.S. Starwood Hotel chain after having previously purchased the historic
Waldorf-Astoria hotel in New York City. Also in 2016, the Chinese firm Qingdao Haier
Company purchased General Electric's appliance business for more than $4 billion. The
Chinese firm Dalian Wanda Group purchased AMC, the second-largest movie theater
chain in the United States. Some of these purchases have drawn criticism from members of Congress. The U.S. Treasury Department oversees the Committee on Foreign
Investment in the United States, which reviews foreign purchases of U.S. firms. Typically, that committee approves most of these purchases. Some members of Congress
have pushed for the committee to look more closely at Chinese foreign investment in

MyLab Economics Study Plan

the United States, particularly when the Chinese firms involved are either owned by or closely connected to the Chinese government. As long as saving in China exceeds domestic investment, it is inevitable that China will have high levels of net foreign investment.

MyLab Economics Concept Check

 ## The Effect of a Government Budget Deficit on Investment

LEARNING OBJECTIVE: Explain the effect of a government budget deficit on investment in an open economy.

The link we have just developed among saving, investment, and net foreign investment can help us understand some of the effects of changes in a government's budget deficit. When the government runs a budget deficit, national saving will decline unless private saving increases by the amount of the budget deficit, which is unlikely. As the saving and investment equation ($S = I + NFI$) shows, the result of a decline in national saving must be a decline in either domestic investment or net foreign investment. The algebra is clear-cut, but why, economically, does an increase in the government budget deficit cause a fall in domestic investment or net foreign investment?

To understand the answer to this question, remember that if the federal government runs a budget deficit, the U.S. Treasury must raise an amount equal to the deficit by selling bonds. To attract investors, the Treasury may have to raise the interest rates on its bonds. As interest rates on Treasury bonds rise, other interest rates, including those on corporate bonds and bank loans, will also rise. Higher interest rates will discourage some firms from borrowing funds to build new factories or to buy new equipment or computers. Higher interest rates on financial assets in the United States will attract foreign investors. Investors in Canada, Japan, or China will buy U.S. dollars to purchase bonds in the United States. This greater demand for dollars will increase their value relative to foreign currencies. As the value of the dollar rises, exports from the United States will fall, and imports to the United States will rise. Net exports and, therefore, net foreign investment will fall.

When a government budget deficit leads to a decline in net exports, the result is sometimes called the *twin deficits*, which refers to the possibility that a government budget deficit will also lead to a current account deficit. The twin deficits idea first became widely discussed in the United States during the early 1980s, when the federal government ran a large budget deficit that resulted in high interest rates, a high exchange value of the dollar, and a large current account deficit.

Figure 18.4 shows that in the early 1980s, the United States had large federal budget deficits and large current account deficits. The figure also shows, however, that the twin deficits idea does not consistently match the experience of the United States after 1990. The large federal budget deficits of the early 1990s occurred at a time of relatively small current account deficits, and the budget surpluses of the late 1990s occurred at a time of then-record current account deficits. Both the current account deficit and the federal budget deficit increased in the early 2000s, but the federal budget deficit declined in the mid-2000s much more than did the current account deficit. Beginning in 2008, the federal budget deficit soared and then sharply declined, while the current account deficit declined.

The experience of other countries also shows only mixed support for the twin deficits idea. Germany ran large budget deficits and large current account deficits during the early 1990s, but both Canada and Italy ran large budget deficits during the 1980s without running current account deficits. The saving and investment equation shows that an increase in the government budget deficit will not lead to an increase in the current account deficit, provided that either private saving increases or domestic investment declines. According to the twin deficits idea, when the

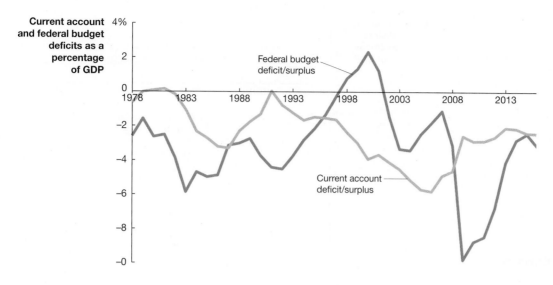

Figure 18.4 **The Twin Deficits, 1978–2016**

During the early 1980s, large federal budget deficits occurred at the same time as large current account deficits, but twin deficits did not occur in most other periods during these years.

Source: U.S. Bureau of Economic Analysis.

federal government ran budget surpluses in the late 1990s, the current account should also have been in surplus, or at least the current account deficit should have been small. In fact, the increase in national saving due to the budget surpluses was more than offset by a sharp decline in private saving, and the United States ran very large current account deficits.　　　　　　　　　　　**MyLab Economics** Concept Check

MyLab Economics Study Plan

 ## Apply the Concept

MyLab Economics Video

Why Is the United States Called the "World's Largest Debtor"?

An important fact about the international economy is that the United States has run a current account deficit every year since 1982, with the exception of 1991. As the following graph shows, these deficits stand in contrast to the period between 1960 and 1975, when the United States ran a current account deficit in only five years. Many economists believe that the current account deficits of the 1980s were closely related to the federal budget deficits of those years. High interest rates attracted foreign investors to U.S. bonds, which raised the exchange rate between the dollar and foreign currencies. The high exchange rate reduced U.S. exports and increased imports, leading to current account deficits.

As the federal budget deficit narrowed in the mid-1990s and disappeared in the late 1990s, the foreign exchange value of the dollar remained high—and large current account deficits continued—because foreign investors persisted in investing in the United States, despite low interest rates. In the late 1990s, a number of countries around the world, such as South Korea, Indonesia, Brazil, and Russia, suffered severe economic problems. In a process known as a *flight to quality*, many investors sold their investments in those countries and bought investments in the United States. In addition, the strong performance of the U.S. stock market through the spring of 2000 attracted many investors. Finally, the sharp decline in private saving in the United States that began during

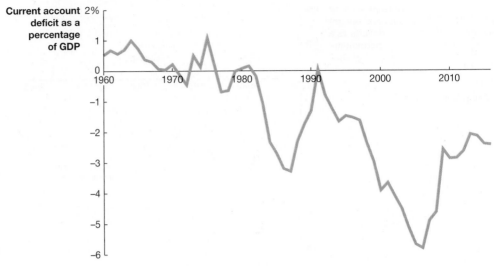

Source: Federal Reserve Bank of St Louis.

the late 1990s also contributed to the U.S. current account deficit. The fall in the value of the dollar after 2008 helped reduce the size of the current account deficit. In recent years the deficit has remained large, at greater than 2 percent of GDP, although it has been below the record deficits of the 2000–2008 period.

Are persistent current account deficits a problem for the United States? Current account deficits result in U.S. net foreign investment being negative. Each year, foreign investors accumulate many more U.S. assets—such as stocks, bonds, and factories—than U.S. investors accumulate foreign assets. In 1986, for the first time since the nineteenth century, the value of foreign-owned assets in the United States became larger than the value of U.S.-owned assets abroad. At the end of 2016, foreign investors owned over $8 trillion more of U.S. assets than U.S. investors owned of foreign assets, which is why the United States is sometimes called "the world's largest debtor." But the continued willingness of foreign investors to buy U.S. stocks and bonds and of foreign companies to build factories in the United States can be seen as a vote of confidence in the strength of the U.S. economy and the buying power of U.S. consumers. When private saving rates declined in the United States to historically low levels in the mid-2000s, only the continued flow of funds from foreign investors made it possible for the United States to maintain the high levels of domestic investment required for economic growth. Beginning in 2009, private saving rates increased, but public saving turned sharply negative through 2012, as the federal budget deficit soared. Even though public saving has been less negative in the past few years, domestic investment in the United States remains reliant on funds from foreign investors.

Source: Elena L. Nguyen, "U.S. Net International Investment Position First Quarter of 2017, Year 2016, and Annual Update," *Survey of Current Business,* July 2017, pp. 1–10.

Your Turn: Test your understanding by doing related problem 4.7 on page 671 at the end of this chapter.

18.5 Monetary Policy and Fiscal Policy in an Open Economy

LEARNING OBJECTIVE: Compare the effectiveness of monetary policy and fiscal policy in an open economy and in a closed economy.

When we discussed monetary policy and fiscal policy in Chapters 15 and 16, we did not emphasize that the United States is an open economy. Now that we have explored some of the links among economies, we can look at the difference between how monetary policy and fiscal policy work in an open economy and how they work in a closed economy. Economists use the term *policy channels* to describe the ways in which monetary policy and fiscal policy affect the domestic economy. An open economy has more policy channels than does a closed economy.

Monetary Policy in an Open Economy

When the Federal Reserve engages in an expansionary monetary policy, it typically buys Treasury securities to lower interest rates and stimulate aggregate demand. In a closed economy, the main effect of lower interest rates is on domestic investment spending and purchases of consumer durables. In an open economy, lower interest rates will also affect the exchange rate between the dollar and foreign currencies. Lower interest rates will cause some investors in the United States and abroad to switch from investing in U.S. financial assets to investing in foreign financial assets. The result is a lower demand for the dollar relative to foreign currencies and a decline in the dollar's value. A lower exchange rate will decrease the prices of U.S. products in foreign markets and increase the prices of foreign products in the United States. As a result, net exports will increase. This additional policy channel will increase the ability of an expansionary monetary policy to affect aggregate demand.

When the Fed wants to reduce aggregate demand to reduce inflation, it engages in a contractionary monetary policy. The Fed sells Treasury securities to increase interest rates and reduce aggregate demand. In a closed economy, the main effect is once again on domestic investment spending and purchases of consumer durables. In an open economy, higher interest rates will lead to a higher foreign exchange value of the dollar. The prices of U.S. products in foreign markets will increase, and the prices of foreign products in the United States will fall. As a result, net exports will fall. The contractionary policy will have a larger effect on aggregate demand, and therefore it will be more effective in slowing the growth in economic activity. To summarize: *Monetary policy has a greater effect on aggregate demand in an open economy than in a closed economy.* **MyLab Economics** Concept Check

Fiscal Policy in an Open Economy

To engage in an expansionary fiscal policy, the federal government increases its purchases or cuts taxes. Increases in government purchases directly increase aggregate demand. Tax cuts increase aggregate demand by increasing household disposable income and business income, which results in increased consumption spending and investment spending. An expansionary fiscal policy may result in higher interest rates. In a closed economy, the main effect of higher interest rates is to reduce domestic investment spending and purchases of consumer durables. In an open economy, higher interest rates will also lead to an increase in the foreign exchange value of the dollar and a decrease in net exports. Therefore, in an open economy, an expansionary fiscal policy may be less effective because the *crowding out effect* may be larger. In a closed economy, only consumption and investment are crowded out by an expansionary fiscal policy. In an open economy, net exports may also be crowded out.

The government can fight inflation by using a contractionary fiscal policy to slow the growth of aggregate demand. A contractionary fiscal policy cuts government purchases or raises taxes to reduce household disposable income and consumption spending. It also reduces the federal budget deficit (or increases the budget surplus), which may lower interest rates. Lower interest rates will increase domestic investment and purchases of consumer durables, thereby offsetting some of the reduction in government spending and increases in taxes. In an open economy, lower interest rates will also reduce the foreign exchange value of the dollar and increase net exports. Therefore, in an open economy, a contractionary fiscal policy will have a smaller effect on aggregate demand and therefore will be less effective in slowing an economy. In summary: *Fiscal policy has a smaller effect on aggregate demand in an open economy than in a closed economy.* **MyLab Economics** Concept Check   **MyLab Economics** Study Plan

Continued from page 645

Economics in Your Life & Career

The South Korean Central Bank and Your Car Loan

At the beginning of this chapter, we posed this question: Will the Bank of Korea's decision to sell its U.S. Treasury bonds affect the interest rate you pay on your car loan? To sell its holdings of Treasury bonds, South Korea's central bank may have to offer them at a lower price. When the prices of bonds fall, the interest rates on them rise. As the interest rates on U.S. Treasury bonds increase, the interest rates on corporate bonds and bank loans, including car loans, may also increase. So, the decision of the Bank of Korea has the potential to increase the interest rate you pay on your car loan. In practice, the interest rate on your car loan is likely to be affected only if the Bank of Korea sells a very large number of bonds and if investors consider it likely that other foreign central banks may soon do the same thing. The basic point is important, however: Economies are interdependent, so interest rates in the United States are not determined entirely by the actions of people in the United States.

Conclusion

At one time, U.S. policymakers—and economics textbooks—ignored the linkages between the United States and other economies. In the modern world, these linkages have become increasingly important, and economists and policymakers must take them into account when analyzing the economy. In Chapter 19, we will discuss further how the international financial system operates.

Visit **MyLab Economics** for a news article and analysis related to the concepts in this chapter.

CHAPTER SUMMARY
AND PROBLEMS

Key Terms

Balance of payments, p. 646

Balance of trade, p. 646

Capital account, p. 648

Closed economy, p. 646

Currency appreciation, p. 653

Currency depreciation, p. 653

Current account, p. 646

Financial account, p. 648

Net foreign investment, p. 648

Nominal exchange rate, p. 651

Open economy, p. 646

Real exchange rate, p. 658

Saving and investment equation, p. 660

Speculators, p. 653

 18.1 The Balance of Payments: Linking the United States to the International Economy, pages 646–650

LEARNING OBJECTIVE: Explain how the balance of payments is calculated.

MyLab Economics Visit www.pearson.com/mylab/economics to complete these exercises online and get instant feedback.

Summary

Nearly all economies are **open economies** that trade with and invest in other economies. A **closed economy** has no transactions in trade or finance with other economies. The **balance of payments** is the record of a country's trade with other countries in goods, services, and assets. The **current account** records a country's net exports, net investment income, and net transfers. The **financial account** shows investments a country has made abroad and foreign investments received by the country. The **balance of trade** is the difference between the value of the goods a country exports and the value of the goods a country imports. **Net foreign investment** is the difference between capital outflows from a country and capital inflows. The **capital account** is a part of the balance of payments that records relatively minor transactions. Apart from measurement errors, the sum of the current account and the financial account must equal zero. Therefore, the balance of payments must also equal zero.

Review Questions

1.1 What is the relationship among the current account, the financial account, and the balance of payments?

1.2 What is the difference between net exports and the current account balance?

1.3 The late economist Herbert Stein described the accounts that comprise a country's balance of payments:

> A country is more likely to have a deficit in its current account the higher its price level, the higher its gross [domestic] product, the higher its interest rates, the lower its barriers to imports, and the more attractive its investment opportunities—all compared with conditions in other countries—and the higher its exchange rate. The effects of a change in one of these factors on the current account balance cannot be predicted without considering the effect on the other causal factors.

a. Briefly describe the transactions included in a country's current account.

b. Briefly explain why, compared to other countries, a country is more likely to have a deficit in its current account, holding other factors constant, if it has each of the following.

i. A higher price level
ii. An increase in interest rates
iii. Lower barriers to imports
iv. More attractive investment opportunities

Source: Herbert Stein, "Balance of Payments," *Library of Economics and Liberty*, www.econlib.org.

Problems and Applications

1.4 In 2016, France had a current account deficit of €19 billion (approximately $21 billion). Did France experience a net capital outflow or a net capital inflow during 2016? Briefly explain.

Source: Banque de France, "France's Balance of Payments".

1.5 Use the information in the following table to solve for the value of the statistical discrepancy and prepare a balance of payments account, like the one shown in Table 18.1 on page 647. Assume that the balance on the capital account is zero.

Increase in foreign holdings of assets in the United States	$1,181
Exports of goods	856
Imports of services	−256
Statistical discrepancy	?
Net transfers	−60
Exports of services	325
Income received on investments	392
Imports of goods	−1,108
Increase in U.S. holdings of assets in foreign countries	−1,040
Income payments on investments	−315

1.6 (Related to the Don't Let This Happen to You on page 649) In 2016, Germany had a balance of trade surplus of €253 billion and a current account surplus of €266 billion. Explain how Germany's current account surplus could be larger than its trade surplus. In 2016, what would we expect Germany's balance on the financial account to have been? Briefly explain.

Source: Statistisches Bundesamt.

1.7 An article in the *Wall Street Journal* stated, "The trade outlook in the U.S. has improved slightly overall this year. One big factor behind the smaller gap: Stronger growth in Asia and Europe."

   a. How would stronger growth in Asia and Europe lead to a smaller trade gap?

   b. The article noted that there was a decline in imports early in the year and that "economic growth [in the United States] remained sluggish overall in the first three months of the year." Is there a connection between a decline in imports and sluggish economic growth? Briefly explain.

Source: Josh Mitchell, "U.S. Trade Gap Shrinks as Exports Rise," *Wall Street Journal*, April 4, 2017.

1.8 (Related to Solved Problem 18.1 on page 650) In early 2017, a Chinese news service noted, "The country will continue to run a current account surplus, as well as a ... financial account deficit in 2017." After reading this account, a student comments, "I thought Chinese exports were very strong, so I don't understand why the country is expected to run a financial account deficit." Clear up the student's confusion.

Source: "China's Current Account Surplus Nears 200 bln USD in 2016," new.xinhuanet.com, March 30, 2017.

1.9 (Related to Solved Problem 18.1 on page 650) An editorial in the *Wall Street Journal* in 2017 made the following observation: "When the U.S. has a current-account deficit it has to have a capital-account surplus of the same amount." Briefly explain whether you agree with this observation.

Source: "How to Think About the Trade Deficit," *Wall Street Journal*, March 10, 2017.

1.10 (Related to Solved Problem 18.1 on page 650) An article on the Dow Jones Newswire in mid-2017 contained the following sentence: "The U.S. current-account deficit, a measure of trade and financial flows with foreign countries widened to $116.78 billion in the first quarter." Does a country's current account include *any* financial flows between that country and other countries? Does it include *all* financial flows between that country and other countries? Briefly explain.

Source: Sarah Chaney and Ben Leubsdorf, "News: Dow Jones U.S. Current-Account Deficit Widened in First Quarter," Dow Jones Newswire, June 20, 2017.

1.11 An article in the *Wall Street Journal* referred to "debt-strapped emerging markets already struggling with current-account deficits." Why might we expect that countries running current account deficits might also have substantial foreign debts?

Source: Anjani Trivedi, "Emerging Markets Suffer Largest Outflow in Seven Years," *Wall Street Journal*, June 12, 2015.

18.2 The Foreign Exchange Market and Exchange Rates, pages 650–658

LEARNING OBJECTIVE: Explain how exchange rates are determined and how changes in exchange rates affect the prices of imports and exports.

 MyLab Economics Visit **www.pearson.com/mylab/economics** to complete these exercises online and get instant feedback.

Summary

The **nominal exchange rate** is the value of one country's currency in terms of another country's currency. The exchange rate is determined in the foreign exchange market by the demand and supply of a country's currency. Changes in the exchange rate are caused by shifts in demand or supply. The three main sets of factors that cause the demand and supply curves in the foreign exchange market to shift are (1) changes in the demand for U.S.-produced goods and services and changes in the demand for foreign-produced goods and services; (2) changes in the desire to invest in the United States and changes in the desire to invest in foreign countries; and (3) changes in the expectations of currency traders—particularly **speculators**—concerning the likely future value of the dollar and the likely future values of foreign currencies. **Currency appreciation** occurs when a currency's market value increases relative to another currency. **Currency depreciation** occurs when a currency's market value decreases relative to another currency. The **real exchange rate** is the price of domestic goods in terms of foreign goods. The real exchange rate is calculated by multiplying the nominal exchange rate by the ratio of the domestic price level to the foreign price level.

Review Questions

2.1 If the exchange rate between the Japanese yen and the U.S. dollar expressed in terms of yen per dollar is ¥115 = $1, what is the exchange rate when expressed in terms of dollars per yen?

2.2 Suppose that the current exchange rate between the dollar and the euro is €0.85 = $1. If the exchange rate changes to €0.90 = $1, has the euro appreciated or depreciated against the dollar? Briefly explain.

2.3 Why do foreign households and foreign firms demand U.S. dollars in exchange for foreign currency? Why do U.S. households and firms supply U.S. dollars in exchange for foreign currency?

2.4 What are the three main sets of factors that cause the supply and demand curves in the foreign exchange market to shift?

Problems and Applications

2.5 (Related to the Apply the Concept on page 651) On January 1, 2002, there were 15 member countries in the

European Union. Twelve of those countries eliminated their own individual currencies and began using a new common currency, the euro. For a three-year period from January 1, 1999, through December 31, 2001, these 12 countries priced goods and services in terms of both their own currencies and the euro. During that period, the values of their currencies were fixed against each other and against the euro. So during that time, the dollar had an exchange rate against each of these currencies and against the euro. The following table shows the fixed exchange rates of four European currencies against the euro and their exchange rates against the U.S. dollar on March 2, 2001. Use the information in the following table to calculate the exchange rate between the dollar and the euro (in euros per dollar) on March 2, 2001.

Currency	Units per Euro (fixed)	Units per U.S. Dollar (as of March 2, 2001)
German mark	1.9558	2.0938
French franc	6.5596	7.0223
Italian lira	1,936.2700	2,072.8700
Portuguese escudo	200.4820	214.6300

2.6 **(Related to the Apply the Concept on page 655)** An article in the *Wall Street Journal* stated, "With the uncertainty lifting and economy doing well, the European Central Bank is more likely to taper the massive stimulus program that has helped keep pressure on the euro."
   a. What does the article mean by "pressure on the euro"?
   b. What is the article referring to by the "massive stimulus program" by the European Central Bank, and why would it keep pressure on the euro?
   c. If you ran a business in the euro zone that exports to the United States and Japan, would the tapering (cutting back) of the massive stimulus program help you? If you were a consumer in the euro zone, would the tapering of the program help you? Briefly explain.
   Source: Mike Bird, "Euro Gains, Leaving Political Concerns Behind to Focus on Growth," *Wall Street Journal*, May 8, 2017.

2.7 **(Related to the Apply the Concept on page 655)** A 2017 article in the *Wall Street Journal* noted, "President Donald Trump said Wednesday the U.S. dollar 'is getting too strong' and he would prefer the Federal Reserve keep interest rates low." Is there a connection between the president's two observations about economic policy? Briefly explain.
   Source: Gerard Baker, Carol E. Lee and Michael C. Bender, "Trump Says Dollar 'Getting Too Strong,' Won't Label China a Currency Manipulator," *Wall Street Journal*, April 12, 2017.

2.8 **(Related to the Don't Let This Happen to You on page 657)** If we know the exchange rate between Country A's currency and Country B's currency and we know the exchange rate between Country B's currency and Country C's currency, then we can compute the exchange rate between Country A's currency and Country C's currency.
   a. Suppose the exchange rate between the Japanese yen and the U.S. dollar is currently ¥115 = $1 and the exchange rate between the British pound and the

U.S. dollar is £0.75 = $1. What is the exchange rate between the yen and the pound?
   b. Suppose the exchange rate between the yen and the dollar changes to ¥120 = $1 and the exchange rate between the pound and the dollar changes to £0.70 = $1. Has the dollar appreciated or depreciated against the yen? Has the dollar appreciated or depreciated against the pound? Has the yen appreciated or depreciated against the pound?

2.9 Use the graph to answer the following questions.

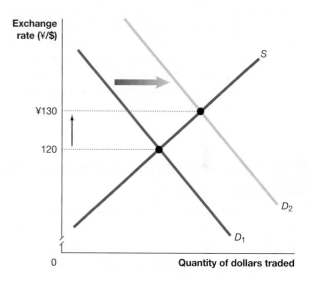

   a. Briefly explain whether the dollar appreciated or depreciated against the yen.
   b. Which of the following events could have caused the shift in demand shown in the graph?
      i. Interest rates in the United States declined.
      ii. Income rose in Japan.
      iii. Speculators began to believe the value of the dollar would be higher in the future.

2.10 An article in the *Wall Street Journal* stated:
   The U.S. dollar's more than 20% rally since 2014 has been driven largely by what analyst call "divergence." While the Fed has been slowly tightening monetary policy amid an improving [U.S.] economy, central banks in Europe and Japan have continued to introduce stimulus as they struggle with stagnant growth and very low inflation.
   a. Which economic variable is "diverging" because of differences between the monetary policy of the Fed on the one hand and the monetary policies of the central banks of Europe and Japan on the other hand?
   b. Draw a graph of the demand and supply of U.S. dollars and show the effect of this "divergence" on the foreign exchange value of the dollar. Briefly explain what is happening in your graph.
   Source: Chelsey Dulaney, "Why Donald Trump May Get His Wish for a Weaker Dollar," *Wall Street Journal*, April 13, 2017.

2.11 **(Related to Solved Problem 18.2 on page 657)** A 2017 Dow Jones Newswire article about Toyota noted, "The company has long been committed to building at least three million vehicles a year in Japan, in part out of a desire to provide jobs in the country.... That was an easier decision when a dollar bought 120 yen two years ago."

    a. Does the article imply that in 2017 it took more than 120 yen to exchange for a dollar or fewer than 120 yen? Briefly explain.

    b. Given your answer to part (a), why would Toyota's decision to produce 3 million cars in Japan have been easier two years before this article was written?

    Source: Sean McLain and Chester Dawson, "Japanese Carmakers Fight Jam in U.S.," *Dow Jones Newswire*, May 11, 2017.

2.12 In 2017, an article on bloomberg.com had the following headline: "The Australian Dollar's Outlook Darkens." The article stated, "The march of the Fed toward higher U.S. interest rates has also been a factor sapping optimism toward the Aussie [dollar]." Briefly explain the article's reasoning.

    Source: Michael G. Wilson, "The Australian Dollar's Outlook Darkens," bloomberg.com, May 18, 2017.

2.13 **(Related to the Chapter Opener on page 644)** In its *2016 Annual Report*, Amazon stated, "We have foreign exchange risk."

    a. Briefly explain why Amazon is exposed to foreign exchange risk.

    b. If Amazon did not have operations in foreign countries, would its profit be affected in any way by fluctuations in the exchange value of the U.S. dollar? Briefly explain.

    Source: Amazon.com, *2016 Annual Report*, p. 10.

2.14 In mid-2017, a headline in the *Wall Street Journal* stated, "China's Yuan Makes Biggest Leap in Five Months." Was this good news or bad news for firms such as Apple and Yum Brands (which owns KFC and Pizza Hut) that have stores or restaurants in China? Briefly explain.

    Source: Saumya Vaishampayan, "China's Yuan Makes Biggest Leap in Five Months," *Wall Street Journal*, June 1, 2017.

The International Sector and National Saving and Investment, pages 659–662

LEARNING OBJECTIVE: Define and apply the saving and investment equation.

MyLab Economics Visit **www.pearson.com/mylab/economics** to complete these exercises online and get instant feedback.

Summary

A current account deficit must be exactly offset by a financial account surplus. The financial account is equal to net capital flows, which is equal to net foreign investment but with the opposite sign. Because the current account balance is roughly equal to net exports, we can conclude that net exports will equal net foreign investment. National saving is equal to private saving plus government saving. Private saving is equal to national income minus consumption and minus taxes. Government saving is the difference between taxes and government spending. GDP (or national income) is equal to the sum of investment, consumption, government spending, and net exports. We can use this fact, our definitions of private and government saving, and the fact that net exports equal net foreign investment to arrive at an important relationship known as the **saving and investment equation**: $S = I + NFI$.

Review Questions

3.1 Explain the relationship between net exports and net foreign investment.

3.2 What is the saving and investment equation? If national saving declines, what will happen to domestic investment and net foreign investment?

3.3 If a country saves more than it invests domestically, what must be true of its net foreign investment?

Problems and Applications

3.4 Writing in the *New York Times*, Simon Johnson, an economist at MIT, made the argument that people outside the

United States may at some point decide to "save less (in which case they may hold onto their existing United States government debt but not want to buy so much of new issues)." What does saving by people outside the United States have to do with sales of U.S. government debt? Does the level of domestic investment occurring in foreign countries matter for your answer? Briefly explain.

    Source: Simon Johnson, "The Real Fiscal Risks in the United States," *New York Times*, December 6, 2012.

3.5 In 2016, domestic investment in Japan was 23.4 percent of GDP, and Japanese national saving was 27.2 percent of GDP. What percentage of GDP was Japanese net foreign investment?

3.6 In 2016, France's net foreign investment was positive. Which was larger in France in 2016: national saving or domestic investment? Briefly explain.

3.7 Briefly explain whether you agree with the following statement: "Because in 2016 national saving was a larger percentage of GDP in the United States than in the United Kingdom, domestic investment must also have been a larger percentage of GDP in the United States than in the United Kingdom."

3.8 **(Related to Solved Problem 18.3 on page 660)** Look again at Solved Problem 18.3, where the saving and investment equation $S = I + NX$ is derived. In deriving this equation, we assumed that national income was equal to Y. But Y only includes income *earned* by households. In the modern U.S. economy, households receive substantial transfer payments—such as Social Security payments and unemployment insurance payments—from the government. Suppose that we define national income as being equal to $Y + TR$, where TR equals government transfer payments, and we also define government spending as being equal to $G + TR$. Show that after making these adjustments, we end up with the same saving and investment equation.

3.9 Use the saving and investment equation to explain why the United States experienced large current account deficits in the late 1990s.

3.10 Former member of Congress and presidential candidate Richard Gephardt once proposed that tariffs be imposed on imports from countries with which the United States

has a trade deficit. If this proposal were enacted and if it were to succeed in reducing the U.S. current account deficit to zero, what would be the likely effect on domestic investment spending within the United States? Assume that no other federal government economic policy is changed. (*Hint:* Use the saving and investment equation to answer this question.)

18.4 The Effect of a Government Budget Deficit on Investment, pages 662–664

LEARNING OBJECTIVE: Explain the effect of a government budget deficit on investment in an open economy.

MyLab Economics Visit **www.pearson.com/mylab/economics** to complete these exercises online and get instant feedback.

Summary

When the government runs a budget deficit, national saving will decline unless private saving increases by the full amount of the budget deficit, which is unlikely. As the saving and investment equation ($S = I + NFI$) shows, the result of a decline in national saving must be a decline in either domestic investment or net foreign investment.

Review Questions

4.1 What happens to national saving when the government runs a budget surplus? What is the twin deficits idea? Did it hold for the United States in the 1990s? Briefly explain.

4.2 Why were the early and mid-1980s particularly difficult times for U.S. exporters?

4.3 Why is the United States sometimes called the "world's largest debtor"?

Problems and Applications

4.4 An investment analyst recommended that investors "gravitate toward the stronger currencies and countries that are running current-account and fiscal surpluses," such as South Korea and Taiwan.
   a. Holding all other factors constant, would we expect a country that is running a government budget surplus to have a currency that is increasing in value or decreasing in value? Briefly explain.
   b. Holding all other factors constant, would we expect a country that has a currency that is increasing in value to have an increasing or a decreasing current account surplus? Briefly explain.
   c. Is the combination of economic characteristics this analyst has identified likely to be commonly found among countries? Briefly explain.
   Source: Paul J. Lim, "Suddenly, BRIC Markets Are on a Shakier Foundation," *New York Times*, January 9, 2015.

4.5 According to an article in the *Economist*, "countries with persistent current-account deficits tend to have higher real interest rates than surplus countries." What do high interest rates have to do with current account deficits?
   Source: "Carry on Trading," *Economist*, August 10, 2013.

4.6 Section 18.4 states that "the budget surpluses of the late 1990s occurred at a time of then-record current account deficits." Holding everything else constant, what would the likely effect have been on domestic investment in the United States during those years if the current account had been balanced instead of being in deficit?

4.7 **(Related to the Apply the Concept on page 663)** Why might "the continued willingness of foreign investors to buy U.S. stocks and bonds and foreign companies to build factories in the United States" result in the United States running a current account deficit?

4.8 In discussing the U.S. financial account surplus, a *Wall Street Journal* editorial made the following observations:
   > [Much] of it goes to finance an investment shortfall in the U.S., especially government borrowing. Yet Americans are making millions of individual decisions about how much to save, and foreigners are not forcing Washington to borrow. If government weren't gobbling up that capital, more of it would go into the private economy.

   a. What does the editorial mean by an "investment shortfall in the United States"? In what sense does a financial account surplus finance that shortfall?
   b. What does the editorial mean by asserting that if the government weren't "gobbling up that capital," it would go into the private economy?
   c. Is there a connection between the federal budget deficit and the financial account surplus?
   Source: "How to Think about the Trade Deficit," *Wall Street Journal*, March 10, 2017.

18.5 Monetary Policy and Fiscal Policy in an Open Economy, pages 664–665

LEARNING OBJECTIVE: Compare the effectiveness of monetary policy and fiscal policy in an open economy and in a closed economy.

MyLab Economics   Visit **www.pearson.com/mylab/economics** to complete these exercises online and get instant feedback.

Summary

When the Federal Reserve engages in an expansionary monetary policy, it buys government bonds to lower interest rates and increase aggregate demand. In a closed economy, the main effect of lower interest rates is on domestic investment spending and purchases of consumer durables. In an open economy, lower interest rates will also cause an increase in net exports. When the Fed wants to slow the rate of economic growth to reduce inflation, it engages in a contractionary monetary policy by selling government bonds to increase interest rates and reduce aggregate demand. In a closed economy, the main effect is once again on domestic investment and purchases of consumer durables. In an open economy, higher interest rates will also reduce net exports. We can conclude that monetary policy has a greater impact on aggregate demand in an open economy than in a closed economy. To engage in an expansionary fiscal policy, the government increases government spending or cuts taxes. An expansionary fiscal policy can lead to higher interest rates. In a closed economy, the main effect of higher interest rates is on domestic investment spending and spending on consumer durables. In an open economy, higher interest rates will also reduce net exports. A contractionary fiscal policy will reduce the budget deficit and may lower interest rates. In a closed economy, lower interest rates increase domestic investment and spending on consumer durables. In an open economy, lower interest rates also increase net exports. We can conclude that fiscal policy has a smaller effect on aggregate demand in an open economy than in a closed economy.

Review Questions

5.1 What is meant by a *policy channel*?

5.2 Why does monetary policy have a greater effect on aggregate demand in an open economy than in a closed economy?

5.3 Why does fiscal policy have a smaller effect on aggregate demand in an open economy than in a closed economy?

Problems and Applications

5.4 An article in the *Economist* quoted the finance minister of Peru as saying, "We are one of the most open economies of Latin America." What does he mean by saying that Peru is an "open economy"? Is fiscal policy in Peru likely to be more or less effective than it would be in a less open economy? Briefly explain.

Source: "Hold on Tight," *Economist,* February 2, 2013.

5.5 Suppose that Federal Reserve policy leads to higher interest rates in the United States.
  a. How will this policy affect real GDP in the short run if the United States is a closed economy?
  b. How will this policy affect real GDP in the short run if the United States is an open economy?
  c. How will your answer to part (b) change if interest rates also rise in the countries that are the major trading partners of the United States?

5.6 An economist remarks, "In the 1960s, using fiscal policy would have been a better way to stabilize the economy, but I believe that monetary policy is better today." What has changed about the U.S. economy that might have led the economist to this conclusion?

5.7 Suppose the federal government increases spending without also increasing taxes. In the short run, how will this action affect real GDP and the price level in a closed economy? How will the effects of this action differ in an open economy?

Real-Time Data Exercises

D18.1 (Exchange rate movements) Go to the Web site of the Federal Reserve Bank of St. Louis (FRED) (fred.stlouisfed.org) and download the most recent value and the value from the same month one year earlier from FRED for the U.S./euro foreign exchange rate (EXUSEU).
  a. Using these values, compute the percentage change in the euro's value.
  b. Explain whether the dollar appreciated or depreciated against the euro.

D18.2 (Exchange rate movements) Go to the Web site of the Federal Reserve Bank of St. Louis (FRED) (fred.stlouisfed.org) and download and plot the U.S./euro exchange rate exchange rate (EXUSEU), the Japan/U.S. exchange rate (EXJPUS), and the Canada/U.S. exchange rate (EXCAUS) for the period from 2001 to the present. The U.S./euro exchange rate is U.S. dollars to one euro, whereas the Japan/U.S. and the Canada/U.S. exchange rates are Japanese yen to one U.S. dollar and Canadian dollars to one U.S. dollar, respectively. To convert the U.S./euro exchange rate to euros to one U.S. dollar, click "Edit Graph," and under "Customize data" in the formula box enter 1/a and click "Apply." Answer the following questions on the basis of your graphs.
  a. In what year did the euro reach its highest value?
  b. During the financial crisis of 2007–2009, did the yen appreciate or depreciate against the dollar? Briefly explain.
  c. Against which currency did the U.S. dollar depreciate the most during this period?

D18.3 (Exchange rate movements) One way to gauge the general value of one currency relative to other currencies is to calculate the *trade-weighted exchange rate*, which is an index number similar to the consumer price index. The trade-weighted exchange rate for the U.S. dollar weights each individual exchange rate by the share of that country's trade with the United States. Go to the Web site of the Federal Reserve Bank of St. Louis (FRED) (fred.stlouisfed.org) and download monthly data on the trade-weighted exchange rate for the U.S. dollar against major currencies (TWEXMMTH) from 1973 to the present.
  a. What has been the long-term trend in the exchange value of the dollar? What effect should changes in the exchange rate during this period have had on U.S. net exports? Briefly explain.
  b. What has been the trend in the exchange value of the dollar over the past year? What effect should changes in the exchange rate during the past year have had on U.S. net exports? Briefly explain.

D18.4 (Exchange rates and exports) Go to the Web site of the Federal Reserve Bank of St. Louis (FRED) (fred.stlouisfed.org) and find the most recent values for the Japan/U.S. foreign exchange rate (EXJPUS) and the U.S. exports of goods to Japan (EXPJP) and the values for one year earlier. Given the change in the exchange rate between the two periods, is the change in U.S. exports to Japan consistent with what the analysis in this chapter would predict? Briefly explain.

D18.5 (Exchange rates and imports) Go to the Web site of the Federal Reserve Bank of St. Louis (FRED) (fred.stlouisfed.org) and find the most recent values from FRED for the Japan/U.S. foreign exchange rate (EXJPUS) and the U.S. imports of goods from Japan (IMPJP) and the values for one year earlier. Given the change in the exchange rate between the two periods, is the change in U.S. imports from Japan consistent with what the analysis in this chapter would predict? Briefly explain.

Critical Thinking Exercises

CT18.1 Suppose that next semester you plan to study abroad in a European country that uses the euro. Let's assume that you won't be working there (and therefore won't be earning euros) and that you'll be bringing dollars to Europe and converting them to euros for living expenses. During which time period between now and the time you return home would you want the dollar to appreciate? During which time period would you want the dollar to depreciate?

CT18.2 Locate and read "Why Germany's Current-Account Surplus Is Bad for the World Economy" on the Web site of the *Economist*: www.economist.com/news/leaders/21724810-country-saves-too-much-and-spends-too-little-why-germanys-current-account-surplus-bad. (Note: If you have trouble accessing the article using this URL, try accessing it through your school's library or by searching for it online.) Is the cause of Germany's trade surplus described in the article consistent with the discussion in this chapter?

19

The International Financial System

Bayer and the Great European Currency Experiment

Most people in the United States know the German firm Bayer mainly for its aspirin, which is sold in bottles with labels that display the firm's name in a distinctive cross. Although the chemical formula for aspirin had been known for decades, it was only in 1899 that Bayer began marketing aspirin as a pain reliever. Because no other effective over-the-counter pain relievers were available until the 1950s, Bayer aspirin was probably the most profitable medication ever sold.

Today, Bayer sells a variety of products, including pharmaceuticals and well-known brands such as Coppertone, Dr. Scholl's, and Claritin. In 2017, Bayer was in the process of purchasing the U.S. firm Monsanto, which is a major producer of seeds and herbicides. Bayer felt pressure from the Trump administration to promise that after the purchase, it would create "several thousand new high-tech, well-paying jobs" in the United States. A larger political issue for Bayer was the debate in Europe over the future of the euro, the common currency of 19 members of the European Union.

Because of the euro, Bayer and other German firms don't have to worry about fluctuations in exchange rates within most of Europe. Before the adoption of the euro, countries such as France, Italy, and Spain were able to decrease the exchange values of their currencies, which made the output of their companies' products more competitive with those of Germany. These countries can no longer pursue this strategy in competing with Germany. Since the financial crisis of 2007–2009, there has been a contentious debate over the future of the euro, and while it seems likely to survive, this outcome is by no means certain. Although Bayer and other German companies receive advantages from the euro, when they export outside Europe, they still must deal with currency fluctuations.

When the value of the euro increases, the prices of goods exported from Germany increase, and Bayer's sales can be hurt. But when the value of the euro falls, it's good news for Bayer and other German exporters. For example, in 2016, the value of the euro remained roughly constant

Jeremy Lips/Alamy Stock Photo

against the U.S. dollar but rose against most other major currencies, leading to a decline in Bayer's export sales. Bayer exports many products from Germany, but its affiliates in the Americas, Europe, and Asia also manufacture and sell products. So, Bayer receives revenue in many different currencies. As the exchange rates of those currencies change relative to the euro, the values of Bayer's sales and profits change. In 2016, Bayer's sales were about €900 million lower when foreign currencies were translated into euros than they would have been if the exchange rates between the euro and those currencies had remained constant.

In this chapter, we will look more closely at the international financial system and at what determines fluctuations in exchange rates.

Sources: Nina Trentmann, "Bayer Details Financing Plan for Monsanto," *Wall Street Journal*, February 22, 2017; Justin Sink and Mario Parker, "Bayer-Monsanto Pledge Investment, Jobs after Trump Meeting," bloomberg.com, January 17, 2017; American Chemical Society, "Molecule of the Week: Aspirin," June 4, 2012; and Bayer AG, *Annual Report 2016, Augmented Version*, February 22, 2017.

Chapter Outline & Learning Objectives

19.1 **Exchange Rate Systems,** page 676
Describe how different exchange rate systems operate.

19.2 **The Current Exchange Rate System,** page 677
Discuss the three key features of the current exchange rate system.

19.3 **International Capital Markets,** page 689
Discuss the growth of international capital markets.

Appendix: **The Gold Standard and the Bretton Woods System,** page 697
Explain the gold standard and the Bretton Woods system.

Economics in Your Life & Career

Exchange Rate Risk Can Affect Your Savings

Suppose that you decide to accept a job in Japan. You plan to work there for the next 10 years, accumulate some savings, and then return to the United States. As you prepare for your move, you read that economists expect the average productivity of Japanese firms to grow faster than the average productivity of U.S. firms over the next 10 years. If economists are correct, all else being equal, will the savings that you accumulate (in yen) be worth more or less in U.S. dollars than it would have been worth without the relative gains in Japanese productivity? As you read this chapter, try to answer this question. You can check your answer against the one we provide on **page 691** at the end of this chapter.

A key fact about the international economy is that exchange rates among the major currencies fluctuate. These fluctuations have important consequences for firms, consumers, and governments. In Chapter 18, Section 18.2, we discussed the basics of how exchange rates are determined. We also looked at the relationship between a country's imports and exports, and at capital flows into and out of a country. In this chapter, we will look further at the international financial system and at the role central banks play in the system.

19.1 Exchange Rate Systems

LEARNING OBJECTIVE: Describe how different exchange rate systems operate.

A country's exchange rate can be determined in several ways. Some countries simply allow the exchange rate to be determined by demand and supply, just as other prices are. A country that allows demand and supply to determine the value of its currency is said to have a **floating currency**. Some countries attempt to keep the exchange rate between their currency and another currency constant. For example, China kept the exchange rate constant between its currency, the yuan, and the U.S. dollar, from 1994 until 2005, when it began allowing greater exchange rate flexibility. When most countries allow their exchange rates to be determined in the same way, economists say that there is an **exchange rate system**. Currently, many countries, including the United States, allow their currencies to float most of the time, although they occasionally intervene to buy and sell their currency or other currencies to affect exchange rates. In other words, many countries attempt to *manage* the float of their currencies. As a result, the current exchange rate system is a **managed float exchange rate system**.

Historically, the two most important alternatives to the managed float exchange rate system were the *gold standard* and the *Bretton Woods system*. These were both **fixed exchange rate systems**, in which exchange rates remained constant for long periods. Under the gold standard, a country's currency consisted of gold coins and paper currency that the government was committed to redeeming for gold. The gold standard was a fixed exchange rate system that lasted from the nineteenth century until the 1930s.

Under the gold standard, exchange rates were determined by the relative amounts of gold in each country's currency, and the size of a country's money supply was determined by the amount of gold available. To rapidly expand its money supply during a war or an economic depression, a country would need to leave the gold standard. By the mid-1930s, in response to the Great Depression, the United States and most other countries had abandoned the gold standard. Although during the following decades there were occasional discussions about restoring the gold standard, there was no serious attempt to do so.

A conference held in Bretton Woods, New Hampshire, in 1944 set up an exchange rate system in which the United States pledged to buy or sell gold at a fixed price of $35 per ounce. The central banks of all other members of the new Bretton Woods system pledged to buy and sell their currencies at a fixed rate against the dollar. By fixing their exchange rates against the dollar, these countries were fixing the exchange rates among their currencies as well. Unlike under the gold standard, neither the United States nor any other country was willing to redeem its paper currency for gold domestically. The United States would redeem dollars for gold only if they were presented by a foreign central bank. Fixed exchange rate regimes can run into difficulties because exchange rates are not free to adjust quickly to changes in demand and supply for currencies. As we will see in the next section, central banks often encounter problems if they are required to keep an exchange rate fixed over a period of years. By the early 1970s, the difficulty of keeping exchange rates fixed led to the end of the Bretton Woods system. The appendix to this chapter contains additional discussion of the gold standard and the Bretton Woods system.

Floating currency The outcome of a country allowing its currency's exchange rate to be determined by demand and supply.

Exchange rate system An agreement among countries about how exchange rates should be determined.

Managed float exchange rate system The current exchange rate system, under which the value of most currencies is determined by demand and supply, with occasional government intervention.

Fixed exchange rate system A system under which countries agree to keep the exchange rates among their currencies fixed for long periods.

Don't Let This Happen to You

Remember That Modern Currencies Are Fiat Money

Although the United States has not been on the gold standard since 1933, many people still believe that somehow gold continues to "back" U.S. currency. The U.S. Department of the Treasury still owns billions of dollars' worth of gold bars, most of which are stored at the Fort Knox Bullion Depository in Kentucky. (Even more gold is stored in a basement of the Federal Reserve Bank of New York, which holds about one-quarter of the world's monetary gold supply—almost 10 percent of all the gold ever mined.

This gold, however, is entirely owned by foreign governments and international agencies.) The gold in Fort Knox no longer has any connection to the amount of paper money issued by the Federal Reserve. U.S. currency—like the currencies of other countries—is *fiat money*, which means it has no value except as money (see Chapter 14, Section 14.1). The link between gold and money that existed for centuries has been broken in modern economies.

Your Turn: Test your understanding by doing related problem 1.3 on page 692 at the end of this chapter.   MyLab Economics Study Plan

 ## The Current Exchange Rate System

19.2

LEARNING OBJECTIVE: Discuss the three key features of the current exchange rate system.

The current exchange rate system has three important features:

1. The United States allows the dollar to float against other major currencies.
2. Nineteen countries in Europe have adopted a single currency, the **euro**.
3. Some developing countries have attempted to keep their currencies' exchange rates fixed against the dollar or another major currency.

Euro The common currency of many European countries.

We begin our discussion of the current exchange rate system by looking at the changing value of the dollar over time. In discussing the value of the dollar, we can look further at what determines exchange rates in the short run and in the long run.

The Floating Dollar

Since 1973, the value of the U.S. dollar has fluctuated widely against other major currencies. Panel (a) of Figure 19.1 shows the exchange rate between the U.S. dollar and the

(a) Exchange rate between the U.S. dollar and the Canadian dollar

(b) Exchange rate between the U.S. dollar and the Japanese yen

MyLab Economics Real-Time Data

Figure 19.1   **Canadian Dollar–U.S. Dollar and Yen–U.S. Dollar Exchange Rates, 1973–2017**

Panel (a) shows that from the end of the Bretton Woods system in 1973 through June 2017, the U.S. dollar gained more than 30 percent in value against the Canadian dollar.

Panel (b) shows that during the same period, the U.S. dollar lost more than 60 percent in value against the Japanese yen.

Source: Federal Reserve Bank of St Louis.

Canadian dollar between January 1973 and June 2017, and panel (b) shows the exchange rate between the U.S. dollar and the Japanese yen for the same period. Remember that the dollar increases in value when it takes more units of foreign currency to buy $1, and it falls in value when it takes fewer units of foreign currency to buy $1. From January 1973 to June 2017, the U.S. dollar lost more than 60 percent in value against the yen, while it gained more than 30 percent in value against the Canadian dollar. Both exchange rates fluctuated substantially during these years.   **MyLab Economics** Concept Check

What Determines Exchange Rates in the Long Run?

Over the past 45 years, why has the value of the U.S. dollar fallen substantially against the Japanese yen but risen against the Canadian dollar? In the short run, the two most important causes of exchange rate movements are changes in interest rates—which cause investors to change their views of which countries' financial investments will yield the highest returns—and changes in investors' expectations about the future values of currencies. Over the long run, other factors are also important in explaining movements in exchange rates.

The Theory of Purchasing Power Parity
It seems reasonable that, in the long run, exchange rates should be at a level that makes it possible to buy the same amount of goods and services with the equivalent amount of any country's currency. In other words, the purchasing power of every country's currency should be the same. The idea that in the long run exchange rates move to equalize the purchasing power of different currencies is called the theory of **purchasing power parity**.

Purchasing power parity The theory that in the long run exchange rates move to equalize the purchasing power of different currencies.

Consider a simple example: Suppose that a Hershey candy bar has a price of $1 in the United States and £1 in the United Kingdom and that the exchange rate is £1 = $1. In that case, at least with respect to candy bars, the dollar and the pound have equivalent purchasing power. If the price of a Hershey bar increases to £2 in the United Kingdom but stays at $1 in the United States, the exchange rate will have to change to £2 per $1 in order for the pound to maintain its relative purchasing power. As long as the exchange rate adjusts to reflect purchasing power, it will be possible to buy a Hershey bar for $1 in the United States or to exchange $1 for £2 and buy the candy bar in the United Kingdom.

If exchange rates are not at the values indicated by purchasing power parity, it appears that there are opportunities to make a profit. Suppose a Hershey candy bar sells for £2 in the United Kingdom and $1 in the United States, and the exchange rate between the dollar and the pound is £1 = $1. In this case, it would be possible to exchange £1 million for $1 million and use the dollars to buy 1 million Hershey bars in the United States. The Hershey bars could then be shipped to the United Kingdom, where they could be sold for £2 million. The result of these transactions would be a profit of £1 million (minus any shipping costs). In fact, if the dollar–pound exchange rate fails to reflect the purchasing power for many products—not just Hershey bars—this process could be repeated until an extremely large profit was made. In practice, though, as people attempted to make this profit by exchanging pounds for dollars, they would bid up the value of the dollar until it reached the purchasing power parity exchange rate of £2 = $1. Once the exchange rate reflected the purchasing power of the two currencies, there would be no further opportunities for profit. This mechanism appears to guarantee that exchange rates will be at the levels determined by purchasing power parity.

Three real-world complications keep purchasing power parity from providing a complete explanation of exchange rates, even in the long run:

1. **Not all products can be traded internationally.** Where goods are traded internationally, profits can be made whenever exchange rates do not reflect their purchasing power parity values. However, more than half of all goods and services produced in the United States and most other countries are not traded internationally. When goods are not traded internationally, their prices will not be the same in every country. Suppose that the exchange rate is £1 for $1, but the price for having

a cavity filled by a dentist is twice as high in the United States as it is in the United Kingdom. In this case, there is no way to buy up the low-priced British dental service and resell it in the United States. Because many goods and services are not traded internationally, exchange rates will not reflect exactly the relative purchasing powers of currencies.

2. **Products and consumer preferences are different across countries.** We expect the same product to sell for the same price around the world, but if a product is similar but not identical to another product, their prices might be different. For example, a 3-ounce Hershey candy bar may sell for a different price in the United States than does a 3-ounce Cadbury candy bar in the United Kingdom. Prices of the same product may also differ across countries if consumer preferences differ. If consumers in the United Kingdom like candy bars more than do consumers in the United States, a Hershey candy bar may sell for more in the United Kingdom than in the United States.

3. **Countries impose barriers to trade.** Most countries, including the United States, impose *tariffs* and *quotas* on imported goods. A **tariff** is a tax imposed by a government on imports. A **quota** is a government-imposed numerical limit on the quantity of a good that can be imported. For example, the United States has a quota on imports of sugar. As a result, the price of sugar in the United States is much higher than the price of sugar in other countries. Because of the quota, there is no legal way to buy up the cheap foreign sugar and resell it in the United States.

Tariff A tax imposed by a government on imports.

Quota A numerical limit that a government imposes on the quantity of a good that can be imported into the country.

Apply the Concept

MyLab Economics Video

The Big Mac Theory of Exchange Rates

In a lighthearted attempt to test the accuracy of the theory of purchasing power parity, the *Economist* regularly compares the prices of Big Macs in different countries. If purchasing power parity holds, you should be able to take the dollars required to buy a Big Mac in the United States and exchange them for the amount of foreign currency needed to buy a Big Mac in any other country. The following table is from January 2017, when Big Macs were selling for an average price of $4.93 in the United States. The "implied exchange rate" shows what the exchange rate would be if purchasing power parity held for Big Macs. For example, a Big Mac sold for 49 pesos in Mexico and $4.93 in the United States, so for purchasing power parity to hold, the exchange rate should have been:

$$\frac{49 \text{ pesos}}{\$4.93}, \text{ or } 9.94 \text{ pesos} = \$1.$$

Diego Levy/Bloomberg/Getty Images

Is the price of a Big Mac in Mexico City the same as the price of a Big Mac in New York?

The actual exchange rate in January 2017 was 17.44 pesos = $1. So, on Big Mac purchasing power parity grounds, the Mexican peso was *undervalued* against the dollar by 43 percent:

$$\left(\frac{9.94 - 17.44}{17.44}\right) \times 100 = -43\%.$$

That is, if Big Mac purchasing power parity held, it would have taken 43 percent fewer Mexican pesos to buy a dollar than it actually did.

Could you take advantage of this difference between the purchasing power parity exchange rate and the actual exchange rate to become fabulously wealthy by buying up low-priced Big Macs in Mexico City and reselling them at a higher price in New York? Unfortunately, the low-priced Mexican Big Macs would be a soggy mess by the time you got them to New York. The fact that Big Mac prices are not the same around the world illustrates one reason purchasing power parity does not hold exactly: Many goods are not traded internationally.

Country	Big Mac Price	Implied Exchange Rate	Actual Exchange Rate
Mexico	49 pesos	9.94 pesos per dollar	17.44 pesos per dollar
Japan	370 yen	75.05 yen per dollar	118.65 yen per dollar
United Kingdom	2.89 pounds	0.59 pound per dollar	0.68 pound per dollar
Switzerland	6.5 Swiss francs	1.32 Swiss francs per dollar	1.01 Swiss francs per dollar
Indonesia	30,500 rupiahs	6,187 rupiahs per dollar	13,948 rupiahs per dollar
Canada	5.84 Canadian dollars	1.18 Canadian dollars per U.S. dollar	1.41 Canadian dollars per U.S. dollar
China	17.6 yuan	3.57 yuan per dollar	6.56 yuan per dollar

Source: "The Big Mac Index," *Economist,* January 12, 2017.

MyLab Economics Study Plan   **Your Turn:** Test your understanding by doing related problem 2.10 on page 693 at the end of this chapter.

Solved Problem 19.2

MyLab Economics Interactive Animation

Calculating Purchasing Power Parity Exchange Rates Using Big Macs

Fill in the missing values in the following table. Remember that the implied exchange rate shows what the exchange rate would be if purchasing power parity held for Big Macs. Assume that the Big Mac is selling for $4.93 in the United States.

Explain whether the U.S. dollar is overvalued or undervalued relative to each currency and predict what will happen in the future to each exchange rate if the actual exchange rate moves toward the purchasing power parity exchange rate.

Finally, calculate the implied exchange rate between the Polish zloty and the Brazilian real (the plural of *real* is *reais*)

and explain which currency is undervalued in terms of Big Mac purchasing power parity.

Country	Big Mac Price	Implied Exchange Rate	Actual Exchange Rate
Brazil	13.5 reais		4.02 reais per dollar
Poland	9.6 zlotys		4.05 zlotys per dollar
South Korea	4,300 won		1,197.8 won per dollar
Sweden	45.0 kronor		8.6 kronor per dollar

Solving the Problem

Step 1: **Review the chapter material.** This problem is about the theory of purchasing power parity as illustrated by prices of Big Macs, so you may want to review the section "The Theory of Purchasing Power Parity," which begins on page 678, and the *Apply the Concept* "The Big Mac Theory of Exchange Rates," which begins on page 679.

Step 2: **Fill in the table.** To calculate the purchasing power parity exchange rate, divide the foreign currency price of a Big Mac by the U.S. price. For example, the implied exchange rate between the Brazilian real and the U.S. dollar is 13.5 reais/$4.93, or 2.74 reais per dollar.

Country	Big Mac Price	Implied Exchange Rate	Actual Exchange Rate
Brazil	13.5 reais	2.74 reais per dollar	4.02 reais per dollar
Poland	9.6 zlotys	1.95 zlotys per dollar	4.05 zlotys per dollar
South Korea	4,300 won	872.2 won per dollar	1,197.8 won per dollar
Sweden	45.0 kronor	9.13 kronor per dollar	8.52 kronor per dollar

Step 3: **Explain whether the U.S. dollar is overvalued or undervalued against the other currencies, and predict what will happen in the future to each exchange rate.** The dollar is overvalued if the actual exchange rate is greater

than the implied exchange rate, and it is undervalued if the actual exchange rate is less than the implied exchange rate. In this case, the dollar is overvalued against the real, the zloty, and the won, but it is undervalued against the krona. So, we would predict that in the future, the value of the dollar should rise against the krona but fall against the real, the zloty, and the won.

Step 4: **Calculate the implied exchange rate between the zloty and the real.** The implied exchange rate between the zloty and the real is 9.6 zlotys/13.5 reais, or 0.71 zlotys per real. We can calculate the actual exchange rate by taking the ratio of zlotys per dollar to reais per dollar: 4.05 zlotys/4.02 reais, or 1.01 zlotys per real. Therefore, the zloty is undervalued relative to the real because our Big Mac purchasing power parity calculation tells us that it should take fewer zlotys to buy a real than it actually does.

Source: "The Big Mac Index," *Economist*, January 12, 2017.

Your Turn: For more practice, do related problem 2.11 on pages 693–694 at the end of this chapter.

MyLab Economics Study Plan

The Four Determinants of Exchange Rates in the Long Run We can take into account the shortcomings of the theory of purchasing power parity to develop a more complete explanation of how exchange rates are determined in the long run. There are four main determinants of exchange rates in the long run:

1. **Relative price levels.** The purchasing power parity theory is correct in arguing that, in the long run, the most important determinant of exchange rates between two countries' currencies is their relative price levels. If prices of goods and services rise faster in Canada than in the United States, the value of the Canadian dollar has to decline to maintain demand for Canadian products. Over the past 45 years, the price level in Canada has risen somewhat faster than the price level in the United States, while the price level in Japan has risen more slowly. These facts help explain why the U.S. dollar has increased in value against the Canadian dollar while losing value against the Japanese yen.

2. **Relative rates of productivity growth.** When the productivity of a firm increases, the firm is able to produce more goods and services using fewer workers, machines, or other inputs. The firm's costs of production fall, and usually so do the prices of its products. If the average productivity of Japanese firms increases faster than the average productivity of U.S. firms, Japanese products will have relatively lower prices than U.S. products, which increases the quantity demanded of Japanese products relative to U.S. products. As a result, the value of the yen should rise against the dollar. For most of the period from the early 1970s to the early 1990s, Japanese productivity increased faster than U.S. productivity, which contributed to the fall in the value of the dollar versus the yen. However, between 1992 and 2017, U.S. productivity increased faster than Japanese productivity, which explains why in the early 1990s, the value of the dollar stopped its rapid decline against the yen.

3. **Preferences for domestic and foreign goods.** If consumers in Canada increase their preferences for U.S. products, the demand for U.S. dollars will increase relative to the demand for Canadian dollars, and the U.S. dollar will increase in value relative to the Canadian dollar. During the 1970s and 1980s, many U.S. consumers increased their preferences for Japanese products, particularly automobiles and consumer electronics. This greater preference for Japanese products helped increase the value of the yen relative to the dollar.

4. **Tariffs and quotas.** The U.S. sugar quota forces firms such as Hershey Foods Corporation to buy expensive U.S. sugar rather than less expensive foreign sugar. The quota increases the demand for dollars relative to the currencies of foreign sugar producers and, therefore, leads to a higher exchange rate. Changes in tariffs and quotas have not been a significant factor, though, in explaining trends in the U.S. dollar–Canadian dollar or U.S. dollar–yen exchange rates.

Because these four factors change over time, the value of one country's currency can increase or decrease by substantial amounts in the long run. These changes in exchange rates can create uncertainty for firms. A decline in the value of a country's currency lowers the foreign currency prices of the country's exports and increases the prices of imports. An increase in the value of a country's currency has the reverse effect. Firms can be both helped and hurt by exchange rate fluctuations.   **MyLab Economics** Concept Check

The Euro

A second key aspect of the current exchange rate system is that most countries in Western Europe have adopted a single currency. After World War II, many of these countries wanted to more closely integrate their economies. In 1957, Belgium, France, West Germany, Italy, Luxembourg, and the Netherlands signed the Treaty of Rome, which established the European Economic Community, often called the European Common Market. Tariffs and quotas on products being shipped within the European Common Market were greatly reduced. Over the years, the United Kingdom, Sweden, Denmark, Finland, Austria, Greece, Ireland, Spain, and Portugal joined the European Economic Community, which was renamed the European Union (EU) in 1991. By 2017, 28 countries were members of the EU (although the United Kingdom was in the process of leaving).

EU members decided to move to a common currency beginning in 1999. Three of the 15 countries that were then members of the EU—the United Kingdom, Denmark, and Sweden—decided to retain their domestic currencies. The move to a common currency took place in several stages. On January 1, 1999, the exchange rates of the 12 participating countries were permanently fixed against each other and against the common currency, the *euro*. At first, the euro was a pure *unit of account*. No euro currency was actually in circulation, although firms began quoting prices in both domestic currency and in euros. On January 1, 2002, euro coins and paper currency were introduced, and on June 1, 2002, the old domestic currencies were withdrawn from circulation. Figure 19.2 shows the 19 countries in the EU that had adopted the euro as of the end of 2017. These countries are sometimes called the *euro zone*.

MyLab Economics Animation

Figure 19.2

Countries Adopting the Euro

The 19 member countries of the European Union (EU) that have adopted the euro as their common currency as of the end of 2017 are shaded with red hash marks. The members of the EU that have not adopted the euro are colored tan. Countries in white are not members of the EU. (*Note*: At the end of 2017, the United Kingdom was in the process of leaving the European Union but had not yet done so.)

A new European Central Bank (ECB) was also established. Although the central banks of the member countries continue to exist, the ECB has assumed responsibility for monetary policy and for issuing currency. The ECB is run by a governing council that consists of a six-member executive board—appointed by the participating governments—and the governors of the central banks of the 19 member countries that have adopted the euro. The ECB represents a unique experiment in allowing a multinational organization to control the domestic monetary policies of independent countries.   **MyLab Economics** Concept Check

Apply the Concept   **MyLab Economics** Video

Greece and Germany: Diverse Economies, Common Currency

Most of Europe experienced relative economic stability from the introduction of the euro in 2002 to the beginning of the global economic recession in 2007. With low interest rates, low inflation rates, and expanding employment and production, the advantages of having a common currency seemed obvious, and the euro experiment appeared to be a success. Firms no longer had to worry about exchange rate instability when selling within Europe, and the cost of doing business was reduced because, for example, it was no longer necessary for a French firm to exchange francs for marks to do business in Germany.

By 2008, however, some economists and policymakers argued that the euro was making the effects of the global recession worse for two key reasons. First, the countries using the euro cannot pursue independent monetary policies because the ECB determines those policies from its headquarters in Frankfurt, Germany. Countries that were particularly hard hit by the recession—for example, Spain, where the unemployment rate had more than doubled to 18 percent by 2009 and was still at the level in mid-2017—were unable to pursue a more expansionary policy than the ECB was willing to implement for the euro zone as a whole. Second, countries could not attempt to revive their exports by allowing their currencies to depreciate because (1) many of their exports were to other euro zone countries, and (2) the value of the euro was determined by factors affecting the euro zone as a whole.

In 2010, a *sovereign debt* crisis developed when investors began to believe that a number of European governments, particularly those of Greece, Ireland, Spain, Portugal, and Italy, would have difficulty making interest payments on their bonds—or sovereign debt. The International Monetary Fund and the European Union put together aid packages to keep the countries from defaulting. In exchange for the aid, these countries were required to adopt *austerity programs*—cutting government spending and raising taxes—even though doing so sparked protests from unions, students, and other groups. The controversy was greatest in Greece, which had large debts and a high unemployment rate, and where political resistance to multiple rounds of austerity made it uncertain whether the country would remain in the euro zone. In 2017, the Greek economy again fell into recession, pushing higher an unemployment rate that was already well above 20 percent.

Did the euro contribute to the slow recovery from the 2007–2009 financial crisis? The following figure shows the average unemployment rate for the euro zone countries for the period 2007–2016 compared with the unemployment rates for the United States, the United Kingdom, and Iceland. The euro zone was still suffering from high unemployment rates more than seven years after the beginning of the financial crisis. The German economy, however, performed very well during and after the financial crisis, with its unemployment rate in 2016 being less than half what it had been in 2007. In fact, German firms, including Bayer, benefited from the euro because if the country had retained the deutsche mark as its currency, the deutsche mark would likely have increased significantly in value beginning in 2014. The value of the euro decreased sharply from mid-2014 to mid-2015 and then remained roughly constant through mid-2017, thereby increasing German exports by more than what would have happened without the common currency. As the blue line shows, the unemployment rate in the euro zone looks significantly worse if Germany is left out.

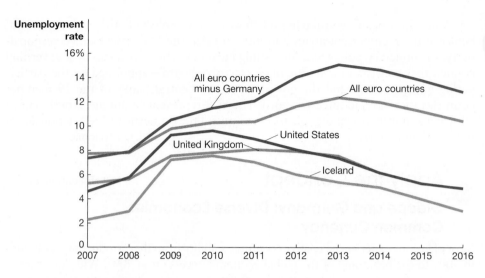

The United Kingdom, Iceland, and the United States all use their own currencies and all recovered more quickly from the financial crisis and recession than did most of the countries using the euro. The United Kingdom is a member of the European Union (although in 2017 it was in the process of withdrawing) but continues to use the pound as its currency. Iceland is not a member of the European Union and does not use the euro. The situation in Iceland is particularly interesting because no country was more severely affected by the global financial crisis. Although it is a small country, its banks aggressively made loans around the world in the years leading up to the crisis. By 2007, Icelandic banks had made loans equal to nine times the country's GDP. When many borrowers defaulted on those loans, the government of Iceland took over the banks and assumed their debt of about $100 billion—or more than $300,000 for each citizen of Iceland. Iceland's krona, the British pound, and the U.S. dollar all depreciated against the euro in the period immediately following the financial crisis, which was good news for these countries because it helped them increase exports, but it was bad news for countries using the euro, many of which faced declining exports outside Europe.

The crisis over Greece highlighted another key problem facing the euro: the lack of coordinated government spending policies. The euro zone is a *monetary union*—the member countries all use the same currency and follow a joint monetary policy—but not a *fiscal union*—the member countries pursue independent fiscal policies. Although we don't usually think of countries in these terms, the states of the United States, the provinces of Canada, and the prefectures of Japan represent both monetary unions and fiscal unions. If during a recession, Nevada suffers a particularly sharp decline in production and employment, the federal government provides support to the economy of Nevada through unemployment insurance and other transfer programs. Greece, by contrast, must fund such payments largely from its own revenues. The resulting large government budget deficits contributed to the sovereign debt crisis discussed earlier.

Some economists and policymakers wonder whether a monetary union of such diverse economies can survive in the absence of further fiscal integration. However, the political support for further fiscal integration of the euro zone countries seemed lacking. In 2017, the ultimate fate of Europe's great economic experiment of having independent countries use a single currency was very much in doubt.

Note: Data for the figure are from the International Monetary Fund and the Organization for Economic Co-operation and Development. The unemployment rate for the euro countries is for all members of the euro zone as of 2008, weighted by their shares in total employment in 2007.

Sources: Tim Worstall, "Good News, Greece Back in Recession, Bets on That Debt Deal Are Off," forbes.com, February 12, 2017; Nektaria Stamouli and Marcus Walker, "Greece Debt Deal on Slow Path as IMF and Germany Dig In," *Wall Street Journal*, May 24, 2017; and Terence Roth, "Everything You Need to Know about European Political Union," *Economist*, July 27, 2015.

MyLab Economics Study Plan   **Your Turn:** Test your understanding by doing related problems 2.12 and 2.13 on page 694 at the end of this chapter.

Pegging against the Dollar

A final key feature of the current exchange rate system is that some developing countries have attempted to keep their exchange rates fixed against the dollar or another major currency. Having a fixed exchange rate can provide important advantages for a country that has extensive trade with another country. When the exchange rate is fixed, business planning becomes much easier. For instance, if the South Korean won increases in value relative to the dollar, South Korean car manufacturer Hyundai may have to raise the dollar price of cars it exports to the United States, which would reduce sales. If the exchange rate between the Korean won and the dollar is fixed, Hyundai's planning is much easier.

In the 1980s and 1990s, an additional reason developed for having fixed exchange rates. During those decades, the flow of foreign investment funds to developing countries, particularly those in East Asia, increased substantially. It became possible for firms in countries such as South Korea, Thailand, Malaysia, and Indonesia to borrow dollars directly from foreign investors or indirectly from foreign banks. For example, say that a Thai firm borrows U.S. dollars from a Japanese bank. If the Thai firm wants to build a new factory in Thailand with the borrowed dollars, it has to exchange the dollars for the equivalent amount of Thai currency, the baht. When the factory opens and production begins, the Thai firm will be earning the additional baht it needs to exchange for dollars to make the interest payments on the loan. A problem arises if the value of the baht falls against the dollar. Suppose that the exchange rate is 25 baht per dollar when the firm takes out the loan. A Thai firm making an interest payment of $100,000 per month on a dollar loan could buy the necessary dollars for 2.5 million baht. But if the value of the baht declines to 50 baht to the dollar, it would take 5 million baht to buy the dollars necessary to make the interest payment. These increased payments might be a crushing burden for the Thai firm. The government of Thailand would have a strong incentive to avoid this problem by keeping the exchange rate between the baht and the dollar fixed.

Finally, some countries fear the inflationary consequences of a floating exchange rate. When the value of a currency falls, the prices of imports rise. If imports are a significant fraction of the goods consumers buy, a fall in the value of the currency may significantly increase the inflation rate. During the 1990s, an important part of Brazil's and Argentina's anti-inflation policies was a fixed exchange rate against the dollar. (As we will see, there are difficulties with following a fixed exchange rate policy, and ultimately, both Brazil and Argentina abandoned fixed exchange rates.)

The East Asian Exchange Rate Crisis of the Late 1990s When a country keeps its currency's exchange rate fixed against another country's currency, it is **pegging** its currency. It is not necessary for both countries involved in a peg to agree to it. When a developing country has pegged the value of its currency against the dollar, the responsibility for maintaining the peg has been entirely with the developing country.

Pegging A policy by which a country keeps fixed the exchange rate between its currency and another country's currency.

Countries attempting to maintain a peg can run into problems, however. When the government fixes the price of a good or service, the result can be persistent surpluses or shortages (see Chapter 4, Section 4.3). Figure 19.3 shows the exchange rate between the dollar and the Thai baht. The figure is drawn from the Thai point of view, so we measure the exchange rate on the vertical axis as dollars per baht. The figure represents the situation in the 1990s, when the government of Thailand pegged the exchange rate between the dollar and the baht above the equilibrium exchange rate, as determined by demand and supply. A currency pegged at a value above the market equilibrium exchange rate is said to be *overvalued*. A currency pegged at a value below the market equilibrium exchange rate is said to be *undervalued*. The situation Thailand faced during these years is worth analyzing because it is the situation that any country pegging its currency can face.

Pegging both made it easier for Thai firms to export products to the United States and protected Thai firms that had taken out dollar loans. The pegged exchange rate was 25.19 baht to the dollar, or about $0.04 to the baht. By 1997, this exchange rate was well

MyLab Economics Animation

Figure 19.3

By 1997, the Thai Baht Was Overvalued against the Dollar

The government of Thailand pegged the value of the baht against the dollar to make it easier for Thai firms to export to the United States and to protect Thai firms that had taken out dollar loans. The pegged exchange rate of $0.04 per baht was well above the equilibrium exchange rate of $0.03 per baht. In the example in this figure, the overvalued exchange rate created a surplus of 70 million baht, which the Thai central bank had to purchase with dollars.

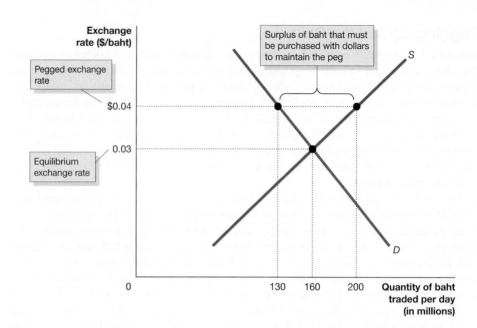

above the market equilibrium exchange rate of 35 baht to the dollar, or about $0.03 to the baht. The result was a surplus of baht on the foreign exchange market. To keep the exchange rate at the pegged level, the Thai central bank, the Bank of Thailand, had to buy these baht with dollars. In doing so, the Bank of Thailand gradually used up its holdings of dollars, or its *dollar reserves*. To continue supporting the pegged exchange rate, the Bank borrowed additional dollar reserves from the International Monetary Fund (IMF). The Bank of Thailand also raised interest rates to attract more foreign investors to investments in Thailand, thereby increasing the demand for the baht. The Bank of Thailand took these actions even though allowing the value of the baht to decline against the dollar would have helped Thai firms exporting to the United States by reducing the dollar prices of their goods. The Thai government was afraid of the negative consequences of abandoning the peg even though the peg had led to the baht being overvalued.

Although higher domestic interest rates helped attract foreign investors, they made it more difficult for Thai firms and households to borrow the funds they needed to finance their spending. As a consequence, domestic investment and consumption declined, pushing the Thai economy into a recession. International investors realized that there were limits to how high the Bank of Thailand would be willing to push interest rates and how many dollar loans the IMF would be willing to extend to Thailand. These investors began to speculate against the baht by exchanging baht for dollars at the official, pegged exchange rate. If, as they expected, Thailand were forced to abandon the peg, they would be able to buy back the baht at a much lower exchange rate, making a substantial profit. Because these actions by investors make it more difficult to maintain a fixed exchange rate, they are called *destabilizing speculation*. Figure 19.4 shows the results of this destabilizing speculation. The decreased demand for baht shifted the demand curve for baht from D_1 to D_2, increasing the quantity of baht the Bank of Thailand needed to buy in exchange for dollars.

Foreign investors also began to sell off their investments in Thailand and exchange their holdings of baht for dollars. This *capital flight* forced the Bank of Thailand to run through its dollar reserves. Dollar loans from the IMF temporarily allowed Thailand to defend the pegged exchange rate. Finally, on July 2, 1997, Thailand abandoned its pegged exchange rate against the dollar and allowed the baht to float. Thai firms that had borrowed dollars were now faced with dollar interest payments that were much higher than they had planned. Some large firms were forced into bankruptcy, and the Thai economy plunged into a deep recession.

Many currency traders became convinced that other East Asian countries, such as South Korea, Indonesia, and Malaysia, would have to follow Thailand and abandon their pegged exchange rates. The result was a wave of speculative selling of these countries'

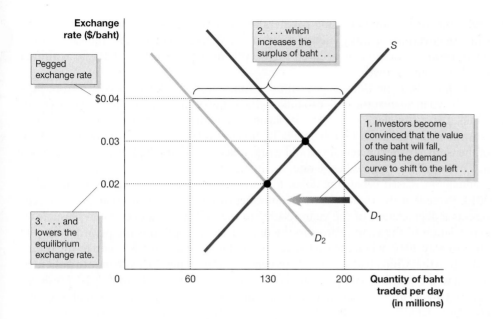

Figure 19.4

Destabilizing Speculation against the Thai Baht

In 1997, the pegged exchange rate of $0.04 = 1 baht was above the equilibrium exchange rate of $0.03 = 1 baht. As investors became convinced that Thailand would have to abandon its pegged exchange rate against the dollar and allow the value of the baht to fall, they decreased their demand for baht, causing the demand curve to shift from D_1 to D_2. The new equilibrium exchange rate became $0.02 = 1 baht. To defend the pegged exchange rate, the Bank of Thailand had to increase the quantity of baht it purchased in exchange for dollars from 70 million (= 200 million − 130 million) to 140 million (= 200 million − 60 million) per day. The *destabilizing speculation* by investors caused Thailand to abandon its pegged exchange rate in July 1997.

currencies. These waves of selling—sometimes called *speculative attacks*—were difficult for countries to fight off. Even if a country's currency was not initially overvalued at the pegged exchange rate, the speculative attacks would cause a large reduction in the demand for the country's currency. The demand curve for the currency would shift to the left, which would force the country's central bank to quickly exhaust its dollar reserves. Within a few months, South Korea, Indonesia, the Philippines, and Malaysia abandoned their pegged currencies. All these countries also plunged into recession.

The Decline in Pegging Following the disastrous events experienced by the East Asian countries, the number of countries with pegged exchange rates declined sharply. Most countries that continue to use pegged exchange rates are small and trade primarily with a single, much larger, country. For instance, several Caribbean countries continue to peg against the dollar, and several former French colonies in Africa that formerly pegged against the French franc now peg against the euro. Saudi Arabia and other oil-exporting states in the Persian Gulf peg their currencies to the dollar because the price of oil is in dollars. Overall, the trend has been toward replacing pegged exchange rates with managed floating exchange rates. **MyLab Economics** Concept Check

MyLab Economics Study Plan

Apply the Concept   MyLab Economics Video

The Chinese Yuan: The World's Most Controversial Currency

In 1978, China began to move away from central planning and toward a market system. The result was a sharp acceleration in economic growth. Real GDP per capita grew at a rate of more than 8 percent per year between 1979 and 2016. An important part of Chinese economic policy was the decision in 1994 to peg the value of the Chinese currency, the yuan, to the dollar at a fixed rate of 8.28 yuan to the dollar. Pegging against the dollar ensured that Chinese exporters would face stable dollar prices for the goods they sold in the United States. By the early 2000s, many economists and policymakers argued that the yuan was undervalued against the dollar—possibly significantly undervalued. Some policymakers claimed that the undervaluation of the yuan gave Chinese firms an unfair advantage in competing with U.S. firms. During the 2016 presidential campaign, Donald Trump accused China of manipulating its currency to increase its exports to the United States.

To support the undervalued exchange rate, the People's Bank of China (PBOC), which is the central bank of China, had to buy large amounts of dollars with yuan. By 2005, the Chinese government had accumulated more than $700 billion, a good portion of which it used to buy U.S. Treasury bonds. By this time, China was coming under pressure from its trading partners to allow the yuan to increase in value. The Chinese government was reluctant to allow the market to determine the value of the yuan, however, because it believed high levels of exports were needed to maintain rapid economic growth.

In July 2005, the Chinese government announced that it would switch from pegging the yuan against the dollar to linking the value of the yuan to the average value of a basket of currencies—the dollar, the Japanese yen, the euro, the Korean won, and several other currencies. Although the PBOC did not explain the details of how this linking of the yuan to other currencies would work, it declared that it had switched from a peg to a managed floating exchange rate. As the figure below shows, the value of the yuan gradually increased versus the dollar for most of the period from 2005 to the end of 2014. (Note that the figure shows the number of yuan per dollar, so an increase represents a depreciation of the yuan relative to the dollar, and a decrease represents an appreciation of the yuan relative to the dollar.) The exception is the period from July 2008 to May 2010, when the exchange rate stabilized at about 6.83 yuan to the dollar, indicating that China had apparently returned to a "hard peg." This change in policy led to renewed criticism from policymakers in the United States. In mid-2010, President Barack Obama argued that "market-determined exchange rates are essential to global economic activity." In the face of this criticism, the PBOC allowed the yuan to resume its slow increase in value versus the dollar.

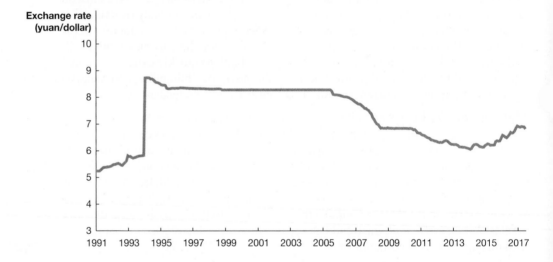

In 2015, the Chinese government was concerned because the growth rate of real GDP had slowed to about 7 percent, the lowest rate in more than 6 years. On August 11 of that year, the yuan was once again in the news, when the PBOC made a surprise announcement that it would buy dollars with yuan in order to reduce the value of the yuan by about 3 percent—the largest one-day decline in the currency since 1994. The figure shows that the value of the yuan continued to drift lower against the dollar into 2017. The PBOC insisted that this trend was the result of market forces and that it had not been taking action to push the value of the yuan lower. In fact, some economists believed that the PBOC had actually been buying yuan with dollars—keeping its value from falling more than it otherwise would have—as indicated by the fact that the PBOC's holdings of dollars had declined by nearly $700 billion. Adding to the downward pressure on the yuan was the fact that many Chinese investors were taking advantage of new rules allowing them to invest abroad for the first time. To make these investments, the investors needed to exchange yuan for dollars or other foreign currency.

Although some U.S. policymakers have continued to insist that the Chinese government manipulates its currency to gain an unfair advantage over its trading partners, many economists are skeptical that the value of the yuan is being kept artificially low. In the first half of 2017, the value of the yuan rose against the dollar, and President Donald Trump announced that he would not formally label China a currency manipulator.

Controversy over China's exchange rate policy is likely to continue because of the size of China's trade surplus with the United States and other countries and because of the willingness of the PBOC to periodically override the market to affect the value of the yuan.

Sources: Carolyn Cui and Saumya Vaishampayan, "China Steps up Support for Its Currency," *Wall Street Journal*, June 1, 2017; Andrew Browne, "China's Insecure Leaders Won't Let Their Markets Be Free," *Wall Street Journal*, June 27, 2017; Lingling Wei, "China Moves to Devalue Yuan," *Wall Street Journal*, August 11, 2015; and Federal Reserve Bank of St. Louis.

Your Turn: Test your understanding by doing related problems 2.18 and 2.19 on pages 694–695 at the end of this chapter.

MyLab Economics Study Plan

19.3 International Capital Markets

LEARNING OBJECTIVE: Discuss the growth of international capital markets.

One important reason exchange rates fluctuate is that investors seek out the best investments they can find anywhere in the world. For instance, if Japanese investors increase their demand for U.S. Treasury bills, the demand for dollars will increase, and the value of the dollar will rise. But if interest rates in the United States decline, foreign investors may sell U.S. investments, and the value of the dollar will fall.

Shares of stock and long-term debt, including corporate and government bonds and bank loans, are bought and sold on *capital markets*. Before 1980, most U.S. corporations raised funds only in U.S. stock and bond markets or from U.S. banks. And U.S. investors rarely invested in foreign capital markets. In the 1980s and 1990s, European governments removed many restrictions on foreign investments in their financial markets. It became possible for U.S. and other foreign investors to freely invest in Europe and for European investors to freely invest in foreign markets. Improvements in communications and computer technology made it possible for U.S. investors to receive better and more timely information about foreign firms and for foreign investors to receive better information about U.S. firms. The growth in economies around the world also increased the savings available to be invested.

Although at one time the U.S. capital market was larger than all other capital markets combined, that is no longer the case. Today, there are large capital markets in Europe and Japan, and there are smaller markets in Latin America and East Asia. The three most important international financial centers today are New York, London, and Tokyo. Each day, the *Wall Street Journal* provides data not just on the Dow Jones Industrial Average and the Standard & Poor's 500 stock indexes of U.S. stocks but also on foreign stock indexes such as the Nikkei 225 average of Japanese stocks and the FTSE 100 index of stocks on the London Stock Exchange. By 2017, corporations, banks, and governments were raising more than $1 trillion in funds on global financial markets each year.

Beginning in the 1990s, the flow of foreign funds into U.S. stocks and bonds—or *portfolio investments*—increased substantially. As Figure 19.5 shows, foreign purchases of stocks and bonds issued by corporations and bonds issued by the federal government increased dramatically between 1995 and 2007. In 2016, foreign purchases of U.S. corporate bonds were substantial, but foreign purchases of U.S. corporate stocks and U.S. government bonds were negative; foreign investors sold more U.S. stocks and U.S. government bonds than they purchased. Very low interest rates on U.S. Treasury bonds, the high exchange value of the dollar, and growth in China, India, and some European countries attracted both U.S. and foreign investors to securities issued in those countries.

Figure 19.6 shows the distribution in March 2017 of foreign holdings of U.S. stocks and bonds by country. Japan and China together held 20 percent of foreign-owned U.S. securities. The large holdings in the Cayman Islands and Luxembourg were due to investors taking advantage of the favorable tax treatment of investment income available in those countries.

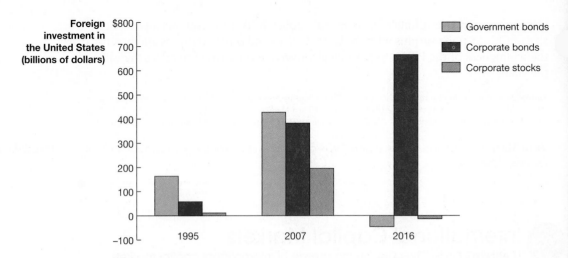

MyLab Economics Animation

Figure 19.5 **Movements in Foreign Portfolio Investment in the United States**

Between 1995 and 2007, there was a large increase in foreign purchases of stocks and bonds issued by U.S. corporations and of bonds issued by the federal government. In 2016, foreign purchases of U.S. corporate bonds were substantial, but foreign purchases of U.S. corporate stocks and U.S. government bonds were negative: foreign investors sold more U.S. stocks and U.S. government bonds than they purchased.

Note: Values shown are net, with foreign sales of securities subtracted from foreign purchases.

Sources: International Monetary Fund, *International Capital Markets,* August 2001; and U.S. Department of the Treasury, "U.S. Transactions with Foreigners in Long-Term Domestic and Foreign Securities, by Type and Country," June 2017.

The globalization of financial markets has helped increase growth and efficiency in the world economy. It is now possible for the savings of households around the world to be channeled to the best investments available. It is also possible for firms in nearly every country to tap the savings of foreign households to gain the funds needed for expansion. No longer are firms forced to rely only on the savings of domestic households to finance investment.

But the globalization of financial markets also has a downside, as the events of 2007–2009 showed. Because financial securities issued in one country are held by investors and firms in many other countries, if those securities decline in value, the financial pain will be widely distributed. For example, the sharp decline in the value of mortgage-backed securities issued in the United States hurt not only U.S. investors and financial firms but investors and financial firms in many other countries as well.

MyLab Economics Study Plan

MyLab Economics Concept Check

MyLab Economics Animation

Figure 19.6

The Distribution of Foreign Holdings of U.S. Stocks and Bonds by Country, March 2017

Investors in Japan own the largest share of foreign-owned U.S. stocks and bonds.

Source: U.S. Department of the Treasury, "U.S. Long-Term Securities Held by Foreign Residents in March 2017."

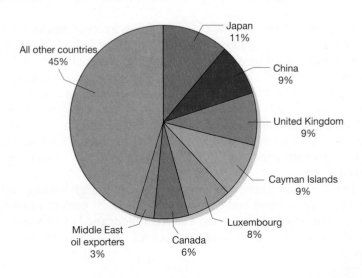

Continued from page 675

Economics in Your Life & Career

Exchange Rate Risk Can Affect Your Savings

At the beginning of this chapter, we posed this question: If economists are correct about the relative rates of average productivity growth between Japan and the United States in the next decade, then, all else being equal, will the savings that you accumulate (in yen) be worth more or less in U.S. dollars than the savings would have been worth without the relative gains in Japanese productivity?

We saw in this chapter that when the average productivity of firms in one country increases faster than the average productivity of firms in another country, the value of the faster-growing country's currency should—all else being equal—rise against the slower-growing country's currency. Therefore, the savings that you accumulate in yen while you are in Japan are likely to be worth more in U.S. dollars than they would have been worth without the gains in Japanese productivity.

Conclusion

Fluctuations in exchange rates continue to cause difficulties for firms and governments. From the gold standard to the Bretton Woods system to currency pegging, governments have attempted to find a workable system of fixed exchange rates. Fixing exchange rates runs into the same problems as fixing any other price: As demand and supply shift, surpluses and shortages will occur unless the price adjusts. Nineteen countries in Europe have attempted to avoid this problem by using a single currency. Economists are looking closely at the results of that experiment.

Visit **MyLab Economics** for a news article and analysis related to the concepts in this chapter.

Key Terms

Euro, p. 677

Exchange rate system, p. 676

Fixed exchange rate
system, p. 676

Floating currency, p. 676

Managed float exchange rate
system, p. 676

Pegging, p. 685

Purchasing power
parity, p. 678

Quota, p. 679

Tariff, p. 679

19.1 Exchange Rate Systems, pages 676–677

LEARNING OBJECTIVE: Describe how different exchange rate systems operate.

MyLab Economics Visit www.pearson.com/mylab/economics to complete these exercises online and get instant feedback.

Summary

When countries agree on how exchange rates should be determined, economists say that there is an **exchange rate system**. A **floating currency** is the outcome of a country allowing its currency's exchange rate to be determined by demand and supply. The current exchange rate system is a **managed float exchange rate system**, under which the value of most currencies is determined by demand and supply, with occasional government intervention. A **fixed exchange rate system** is a system under which countries agree to keep the exchange rates among their currencies fixed. Under the gold standard, the exchange rate between two currencies was automatically determined by the quantity of gold in each currency. By the end of the Great Depression of the 1930s, every country had abandoned the gold standard. Under the Bretton Woods system, which was in place between 1944 and the early 1970s, the United States agreed to exchange dollars for gold at a price of $35 per ounce. The central banks of all other members of the system pledged to buy and sell their currencies at a fixed rate against the dollar.

Review Questions

1.1 What is an exchange rate system? What is the difference between a fixed exchange rate system and a managed float exchange rate system?

1.2 How were exchange rates determined under the gold standard? How did the Bretton Woods system differ from the gold standard?

Problems and Applications

1.3 **(Related to the Don't Let This Happen to You on page 677)** Briefly explain whether you agree with the following statement: "The Federal Reserve is limited in its ability to issue paper currency by the amount of gold the federal government has in Fort Knox. To issue more paper currency, the government first has to buy more gold."

1.4 An article in the *Atlantic* referred to a poll of economists that found no support for the United States to readopt the gold standard:

> It prevents the central bank from fighting recessions by outsourcing monetary policy decisions to how much gold we have—which, in turn, depends on our trade balance and on how much of the shiny rock we can dig up. When we peg the dollar to gold we have to raise interest rates when gold is scarce, regardless of the state of the economy.

Why does the writer state that a gold standard would prevent "the central bank from fighting recessions"?

Source: Matthew O'Brien, "Why the Gold Standard Is the World's Worst Economic Idea, in 2 Charts," *Atlantic*, August 26, 2012.

1.5 The United States and most other countries abandoned the gold standard during the 1930s. Why would the 1930s have been a particularly difficult time for countries to remain on the gold standard? (*Hint:* Think about the macroeconomic events of the 1930s and about the possible problems with carrying out an expansionary monetary policy while remaining on the gold standard.)

1.6 After World War II, why might countries have preferred the Bretton Woods system to reestablishing the gold standard? In your answer, be sure to note the important ways in which the Bretton Woods system differed from the gold standard.

19.2 The Current Exchange Rate System, pages 677–689

LEARNING OBJECTIVE: Discuss the three key features of the current exchange rate system.

MyLab Economics Visit **www.pearson.com/mylab/economics** to complete these exercises online and get instant feedback.

Summary

The current exchange rate system has three key features: (1) The U.S. dollar floats against other major currencies, (2) most countries in Western Europe have adopted a common currency, and (3) some developing countries have fixed their currencies' exchange rates against the dollar or against another major currency. Since 1973, the value of the U.S. dollar has fluctuated widely against other major currencies. The theory of **purchasing power parity** states that in the long run, exchange rates move to equalize the purchasing power of different currencies. This theory helps to explain some of the long-run movements in the value of the U.S. dollar relative to other currencies. Purchasing power parity does not provide a complete explanation of movements in exchange rates for several reasons, including the existence of *tariffs* and *quotas*. A **tariff** is a tax imposed by a government on imports. A **quota** is a government-imposed limit on the quantity of a good that can be imported. Currently, 19 European Union member countries use a common currency known as the euro. The experience of the countries using the euro will provide economists with information about the costs and benefits to countries of using the same currency.

When a country keeps its currency's exchange rate fixed against another country's currency, it is **pegging** its currency. Pegging can result in problems similar to the difficulties countries encountered with fixed exchange rates under the Bretton Woods system. If investors become convinced that a country pegging its exchange rate will eventually allow the exchange rate to decline to a lower level, the demand curve for the currency will shift to the left. This destabilizing speculation makes it difficult for a central bank to maintain a fixed exchange rate.

Review Questions

2.1 What is the theory of purchasing power parity? Does the theory give a complete explanation for movements in exchange rates in the long run? Briefly explain.

2.2 Briefly describe the four determinants of exchange rates in the long run.

2.3 Which European countries currently use the euro as their currency? Why did these countries agree to replace their previous currencies with the euro?

2.4 What does it mean when one currency is "pegged" against another currency? Why do countries peg their currencies? What problems can result from pegging?

Problems and Applications

2.5 An article in the *Toronto Star* discussed the Canadian teams that play in the National Hockey League, the National Basketball Association, Major League Baseball, and Major League Soccer. The article noted, "Under their collective agreements players get paid in U.S. dollars. The majority of [team] revenue, however, is in Canadian currency." Are Canadian professional sports teams better off when the Canadian dollar increases in value relative to the U.S. dollar or when it decreases in value? Briefly explain.
Source: Josh Rubin, "MLSE, Blue Jays Deal with Dollar Dive," thestar.com, January 25, 2015.

2.6 **(Related to the Chapter Opener on page 674)** An article in the *Wall Street Journal* in June 2017 began with this observation: "The euro soared to its biggest one-day gain against the dollar in a year." Bayer AG sells Coppertone sunscreen in the United States. If Bayer produces Coppertone in the United States and sells it only in the United States, would an increase in the value of the euro against the dollar affect the company's profit from selling Coppertone? Briefly explain.
Source: Tom Fairless, "ECB's Draghi Hints at Possible Winding down of Eurozone Stimulus," *Wall Street Journal*, June 28, 2017.

2.7 Consider this statement:

> It takes more than 110 yen to buy 1 U.S. dollar and more than 1.2 dollars to buy 1 British pound. These values show that the United States must be a much wealthier country than Japan and that the United Kingdom must be wealthier than the United States.

Do you agree with this reasoning? Briefly explain.

2.8 According to the theory of purchasing power parity, if the inflation rate in Australia is higher than the inflation rate in New Zealand, what should happen to the exchange rate between the Australian dollar and the New Zealand dollar? Briefly explain.

2.9 In December 2016, you needed 83 percent more pesos to buy one U.S. dollar than you had needed in December 2004. Over the same time period, the consumer price index in Mexico increased 57.8 percent, and the consumer price index in the United States increased 26.7 percent. Are these data consistent with the theory of purchasing power parity? Briefly explain.

2.10 **(Related to the Apply the Concept on page 679)** Look again at the table at the top of page 680 that shows the prices of Big Macs and the implied and actual exchange rates. Indicate whether the U.S. dollar is overvalued or undervalued against each currency.

2.11 **(Related to Solved Problem 19.2 on page 680)** Fill in the missing values in the following table. Assume that the Big Mac is selling for $4.93 in the United States. Explain whether the U.S. dollar is overvalued or undervalued relative to each of the other currencies and predict what will happen in the future to each exchange rate if the actual exchange rate moves toward the purchasing power parity exchange rate. Finally, calculate the implied exchange rate between the Russian ruble and the New Zealand dollar and explain which currency is overvalued in terms of Big Mac purchasing power parity.

Country	Big Mac Price	Implied Exchange Rate	Actual Exchange Rate
Chile	2,100 pesos		715.22 pesos per dollar
Israel	16.9 shekels		3.94 shekels per dollar
Russia	114 rubles		74.66 rubles per dollar
New Zealand	5.9 New Zealand dollars		1.51 New Zealand dollars per U.S. dollar

Source: "The Big Mac Index," *Economist*, January 12, 2017.

2.12 **(Related to the Apply the Concept on page 683)** The United Kingdom decided not to join other European Union countries in using the euro as its currency. One opponent of adopting the euro argued, "It comes down to economics. We just don't believe that it's possible to manage the entire economy of Europe with just one interest rate policy. How do you alleviate recession in Germany and curb inflation in Ireland?"

　　a. What interest rate policy would be used to alleviate recession in Germany?

　　b. What interest rate policy would be used to curb inflation in Ireland?

　　c. What does adopting the euro have to do with interest rate policy?

　　Source: Alan Cowell, "Nuanced Conflict over Euro in Britain," *New York Times*, June 22, 2001.

2.13 **(Related to the Apply the Concept on page 683)** An article in *USA Today* argued, "Ironically, the euro's fall—and the benefit for German exports—is largely the result of eurozone policies that Germany has taken the lead in opposing ... [including] easier money policies by the European Central Bank."

　　a. How does the "euro's fall" benefit German exports?

　　b. How is the euro's fall related to policies of the European Central Bank?

　　Source: Mihret Yohannes, "Germany Benefits from Weak Euro Policies It Deplores," usatoday.com, March 4, 2015.

2.14 In January 2007, before the financial crisis, the exchange rate was $1.30 per euro. In July 2008, during the financial crisis, the exchange rate was $1.58 per euro. Was this change in the dollar–euro exchange rate good news or bad news for U.S. firms exporting goods and services to Europe? Was it good news or bad news for European consumers buying goods and services imported from the United States? Briefly explain.

2.15 Although it is a member of the European Community, Denmark is not part of the euro zone; it has its own currency, the krone. Because the krone is pegged to the euro, Denmark's central bank is obliged to maintain the value of the krone within 2.25 percent either above or below the value of the euro. According to a 2017 article in the *Wall Street Journal*, the Danish central bank was forced to intervene in foreign currency markets "to keep the krone from strengthening too much."

　　a. If the krone was strengthening, did it take more kroner to exchange for a euro or fewer kroner? Briefly explain.

　　b. Given your answer to part (a), was the Danish central bank intervening by buying kroner in exchange for euros or selling kroner in exchange for euros? Briefly explain.

　　Source: Brian Blackstone, "Why Are Europe's Small Central Banks Stocking up Foreign Money?" *Wall Street Journal*, March 7, 2017.

2.16 Use the graph to answer the following questions.

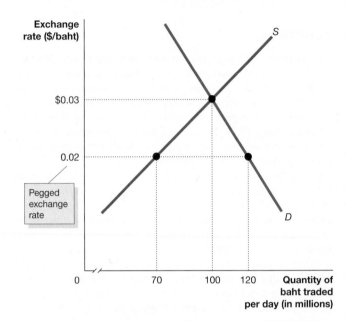

　　a. According to the graph, is there a surplus or a shortage of baht in exchange for U.S. dollars? Briefly explain.

　　b. To maintain the pegged exchange rate, will the Thai central bank need to buy baht in exchange for dollars or sell baht in exchange for dollars? How many baht will the Thai central bank need to buy or sell?

2.17 The *Economist* observed, "In Argentina, many loans were taken out in dollars: this had catastrophic consequences for borrowers once the peg collapsed." What does the article mean when it says that Argentina's "peg collapsed"? Why was this collapse catastrophic for borrowers in Argentina who had taken out dollar loans?

　　Source: "Spoilt for Choice," *Economist*, June 3, 2002.

2.18 **(Related to the Apply the Concept on page 687)** Graph the demand and supply of Chinese yuan for U.S. dollars and label each axis. Suppose the Chinese central bank were to decide to once again to peg the value of the yuan against the U.S. dollar. Indicate whether the Chinese central bank would typically be interested in pegging the exchange rate above or below the market equilibrium exchange rate. To maintain the peg, would the Chinese central bank typically be supplying yuan in exchange for dollars or selling dollars in exchange for yuan? Illustrate your answer on your graph.

2.19 **(Related to the Apply the Concept on page 687)** An article on usatoday.com included the following two observations: First, "Chinese companies and individuals have begun to invest more heavily outside the country." Second, "The yuan has dropped nearly 7 percent against the dollar so far this year. The Chinese government has responded by draining its foreign exchange reserves to buy yuan, hoping to slow the currency's fall."

a. Is there a connection between Chinese companies and individuals investing more heavily outside the country and the drop in the yuan? Briefly explain.

b. Why might the Chinese government want to slow the fall in the yuan?

c. Why would the Chinese government have to drain its foreign exchange reserves to slow the fall in the yuan?

Source: Paul Wiseman, "What It Means if Trump Names China a Currency Manipulator," usatoday.com, December 29, 2016.

2.20 An article in the *Wall Street Journal* stated, "The years long battle that smaller European central banks (such as the central bank of Switzerland) have waged against their own strong currencies may have turned a corner, thanks to the strengthening euro." The article further noted that the "Swiss National Bank's foreign-exchange reserves—accumulated on a massive scale since 2012—dipped slightly last month."

a. Why would the Swiss National Bank (the central bank of Switzerland) wage a battle against its own strong currency?

b. Is there a connection between the Swiss National Bank waging a battle against its strong currency and the Swiss National Bank accumulating massive amounts of foreign exchange reserves? Briefly explain.

Source: Brian Blackstone, "Euro Eases Franc's Strain," *Wall Street Journal*, July 8–9, 2017.

(19.3) International Capital Markets, pages 689–690

LEARNING OBJECTIVE: Discuss the growth of international capital markets.

MyLab Economics Visit www.pearson.com/mylab/economics to complete these exercises online and get instant feedback.

Summary

A key reason exchange rates fluctuate is that investors seek out the best investments they can find anywhere in the world. Since 1980, the markets for stocks and bonds have become global. Foreign buying and selling of U.S. corporate bonds and stocks and U.S. government bonds have increased greatly in the period since 1995. As a result of the globalization of capital markets, firms around the world are no longer forced to rely only on the savings of domestic households for funds.

Review Questions

3.1 What were the main factors behind the globalization of capital markets in the 1980s and 1990s?

3.2 Briefly describe the pattern of foreign investments in U.S. securities between 1995 and 2016.

Problems and Applications

3.3 Why have foreign investors historically been more likely to invest in U.S. government bonds than in U.S. corporate stocks and bonds? In 2016, why did foreign investors invest more in U.S. corporate bonds than in U.S. government bonds?

3.4 On page 690, the text states that "the globalization of financial markets has helped increase growth and efficiency in the world economy." Briefly explain which aspects of globalization help to increase growth in the world economy.

3.5 The global financial crisis of 2007–2009 led some economists and policymakers to suggest reinstituting capital controls—or limits on the flow of foreign exchange and financial investments across countries—which existed in many European countries prior to the 1960s. Why would a financial crisis lead policymakers to reconsider using capital controls? What problems might result from reinstituting capital controls?

Real-Time Data Exercises

D19.1 (Big Mac prices and purchasing power parity) Go to the Web site of the Federal Reserve Bank of St. Louis (FRED) (fred.stlouisfed.org) and find the most recent values for the Japan/U.S. foreign exchange rate (DEXJPUS), China/U.S. foreign exchange rate (DEXCHUS), and the Mexico/U.S. foreign exchange rate (DEXMXUS).

    a. Explain whether the exchange rates are quoted as U.S. dollars per unit of foreign currency or units of foreign currency per U.S. dollar.

    b. Suppose a Big Mac sells for 400 yen in Japan, 18 yuan in China, and 50 pesos in Mexico. What is the price of a Big Mac in each country in terms of U.S. dollars?

    c. Are your results from part (b) consistent with the theory of purchasing power parity? Briefly explain.

    d. Assuming no transportation costs and a no-cost means of preserving Big Macs while they are being transported, explain in which county you would want to purchase a Big Mac and in which country you would want to sell the same Big Mac in order to make the highest profit possible.

D19.2 (Explaining movements in the yuan–dollar exchange rate) Go to the Web site of the Federal Reserve Bank of St. Louis (FRED) (fred.stlouisfed.org) and find the values for the China/U.S. foreign exchange rate (DEXCHUS) from 1981 to the most recent date available.

    a. Compared with its value in 1981, has the yuan appreciated or depreciated against the U.S. dollar? Briefly explain.

    b. Summarize the movements in the yuan–dollar exchange rate during these years and explain why the pattern occurred.

D19.3 (Analyzing global capital flows) The U.S. Treasury publishes data on capital flows. Treasury international capital flows can be found at treasury.gov/resource-center/data-chart-center/tic/Pages/index.aspx.

    a. Under "Securities data," choose "Monthly Transactions in Long-Term Securities." Under "Net Foreign Purchases of U.S. long-term securities by major foreign sector," click on "U.S. Treasury Bonds & Notes." Look at recent total net foreign purchases. How has the volume of purchases changed over the past five years?

    b. Under "Securities data," choose "Monthly Holdings of Securities." Under "Major Foreign Holders of U.S. Treasury Securities," "Historical data," choose "MFH tables." Which countries hold the most U.S. Treasury securities? How have foreign holdings of U.S. Treasury securities changed over time?

Critical Thinking Exercises

CT19.1 Vanguard is the largest mutual fund company in the United States. Mutual funds sell shares to investors and use the funds to buy a collection of financial assets, generally stocks and bonds. So, for a relatively small investment, an individual investor can purchase many different stocks and bonds. Visit investor.vanguard.com/mutual-funds/list?assetclass=intl#/mutual-funds/asset-class/month-end-returns. What concept from this chapter does this page on Vanguard's Web site illustrate?

CT19.2 Locate online or through your school's library the *Wall Street Journal* article "Hong Kong's Dollar Peg: Next in the Firing Line?" which was published in January 2016. Summarize the article using the concepts and terminology from this chapter.

Appendix

The Gold Standard and the Bretton Woods System

It is easier to understand the current exchange rate system by considering further two earlier systems—the gold standard and the Bretton Woods system—that together lasted from the early 1800s through the early 1970s.

The Gold Standard

As we saw in this chapter, under the gold standard, the currency of a country consisted of gold coins and paper currency that people could redeem for gold. Great Britain adopted the gold standard in 1816, but as late as 1870, only a few nations had followed. In the late nineteenth century, however, Great Britain's share of world trade had increased, as had its overseas investments. The dominant position of Great Britain in the world economy motivated other countries to adopt the gold standard. By 1913, every country in Europe, except Spain and Bulgaria, and most countries in the Western Hemisphere had adopted the gold standard.

Under the gold standard, the exchange rate between two currencies was automatically determined by the quantity of gold in each currency. If there was 1/5 ounce of gold in a U.S. dollar and 1 ounce of gold in a British pound, the price of gold in the United States would be $5 per ounce, and the price of gold in Britain would be £1 per ounce. The exchange rate would therefore be $5 = £1. **MyLab Economics** Concept Check

The End of the Gold Standard

From a modern point of view, the greatest drawback to the gold standard was that the central bank lacked control of the money supply. The size of a country's money supply depended on its gold supply, which could be greatly affected by chance discoveries of gold or by technological change in gold mining. For example, the gold discoveries in California in 1849 and Alaska in the 1890s caused rapid increases in the U.S. money supply. Because the central bank cannot determine how much gold will be discovered, it lacks the control of the money supply necessary to pursue an active monetary policy. During wartime, countries usually went off the gold standard to allow their central banks to expand the money supply as rapidly as was necessary to pay for the war. Britain left the gold standard at the beginning of World War I in 1914 and did not resume redeeming its paper currency for gold until 1925.

When the Great Depression began in 1929, governments came under pressure to leave the gold standard to allow their central banks to pursue active monetary policies. In 1931, Great Britain became the first major country to abandon the gold standard. A number of other countries also went off the gold standard that year. The United States remained on the gold standard until 1933, and a few countries, including France, Italy, and Belgium, stayed on even longer. By the late 1930s, the gold standard had collapsed.

The earlier a country abandoned the gold standard, the easier time it had fighting the Depression with expansionary monetary policies. The countries that abandoned the gold standard by 1932 suffered an average decline in production of only 3 percent between 1929 and 1934. The countries that stayed on the gold standard until 1933 or later suffered an average decline of more than 30 percent. The devastating economic performance of the countries that stayed on the gold standard the longest during the 1930s is the key reason no attempt was made to bring back the gold standard in later years. **MyLab Economics** Concept Check

The Bretton Woods System

In addition to the collapse of the gold standard, the global economy suffered during the 1930s from tariff wars. The United States had started the tariff wars in June 1930 by enacting the Smoot-Hawley Tariff Act, which raised the average U.S. tariff rate to more than 50 percent. Many other countries raised tariffs during the next few years, leading to a collapse in world trade.

As World War II was coming to an end, economists and government officials in the United States and Europe concluded that they needed to restore the international economic system to avoid another depression. In 1947, the United States and most other major countries, apart from the Soviet Union, began participating in the General Agreement on Tariffs and Trade (GATT), under which they worked to reduce trade barriers. The GATT was very successful in sponsoring rounds of negotiations among countries, which led to sharp declines in tariffs. U.S. tariffs dropped from an average rate of more than 50 percent in the early 1930s to an average rate of less than 2 percent in 2017. In 1995, the GATT was replaced by the World Trade Organization (WTO), which has similar objectives.

The effort to develop a new exchange rate system to replace the gold standard was more complicated than establishing the GATT. A conference held in Bretton Woods, New Hampshire, in 1944 set up a system in which the United States pledged to buy or sell gold at a fixed price of $35 per ounce. The central banks of all other members of the new **Bretton Woods system** pledged to buy and sell their currencies at a fixed rate against the dollar. By fixing their exchange rates against the dollar, these countries were fixing the exchange rates among their currencies as well. Unlike under the gold standard, neither the United States nor any other country was willing to redeem its paper currency for gold domestically. The United States would redeem dollars for gold only if they were presented by a foreign central bank. The United States continued the prohibition, first enacted in the early 1930s, against private citizens owning gold, except in the form of jewelry or rare coins. The prohibition was not lifted until the 1970s, when it again became possible for Americans to own gold as an investment.

Under the Bretton Woods system, central banks were committed to selling dollars in exchange for their own currencies. This commitment required them to hold *dollar reserves*. If a central bank ran out of dollar reserves, it could borrow them from the newly created **International Monetary Fund (IMF)**. In addition to providing loans to central banks that were short of dollar reserves, the IMF would oversee the operation of the system and approve adjustments to the agreed-on fixed exchange rates.

Under the Bretton Woods system, a fixed exchange rate was called a *par exchange rate*. If the par exchange rate was not the same as the exchange rate that would have been determined in the market, the result would be a surplus or a shortage. For example, Figure 19A.1 shows the exchange rate between the dollar and the British pound. The figure is drawn from the British point of view, so we measure the exchange rate on the vertical axis as dollars per pound. In this case, the par exchange rate between the dollar and the pound is above the equilibrium exchange rate, as determined by demand and supply.

At the par exchange rate of $4 per pound, the quantity of pounds demanded by people who want to buy British goods and services or who want to invest in British assets is smaller than the quantity of pounds supplied by people who would like to exchange them for dollars. As a result, the Bank of England must use dollars to buy the surplus of £1 million per day. Only at an exchange rate of $2.80 per pound would the surplus be eliminated. If the par exchange rate was below the equilibrium exchange rate, there would be a shortage of domestic currency in the foreign exchange market.

A persistent shortage or surplus of a currency under the Bretton Woods system was seen as evidence of a *fundamental disequilibrium* in a country's exchange rate. After consulting with the IMF, countries in this position were allowed to adjust their exchange rates. In the early years of the Bretton Woods system, many countries found that their currencies were *overvalued* versus the dollar, meaning that their par exchange rates were too high. A reduction in a fixed exchange rate is a **devaluation**. An increase in a fixed exchange rate is a **revaluation**. In 1949, there was a devaluation of several currencies, including the British pound, reflecting the fact that those currencies had been overvalued against the dollar.

Bretton Woods system An exchange rate system that lasted from 1944 to 1973, under which countries pledged to buy and sell their currencies at a fixed rate against the dollar.

International Monetary Fund (IMF) An international organization that provides foreign currency loans to central banks and oversees the operation of the international monetary system.

Devaluation A reduction in a fixed exchange rate.

Revaluation An increase in a fixed exchange rate.

MyLab Economics Concept Check

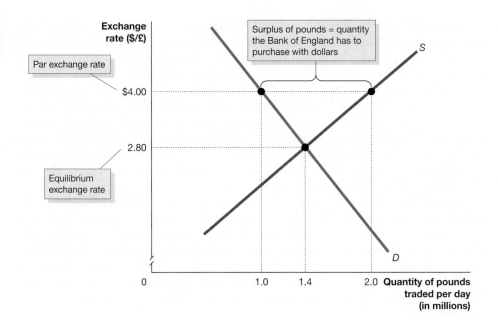

MyLab Economics Animation

Figure 19A.1

A Fixed Exchange Rate above Equilibrium Results in a Surplus of Pounds

Under the Bretton Woods system, if the par exchange rate was above equilibrium, the result would be a surplus of domestic currency in the foreign exchange market. If the par exchange rate was below equilibrium, the result would be a shortage of domestic currency. In the figure, the par exchange rate between the pound and the dollar is $4 = £1, while the equilibrium exchange rate is $2.80 = £1. This gap forces the Bank of England to buy £1 million per day in exchange for dollars.

The Collapse of the Bretton Woods System

By the late 1960s, the Bretton Woods system faced two severe problems. The first was that after 1963, the total number of dollars held by foreign central banks was larger than the gold reserves of the United States. In practice, most central banks—with the Bank of France being the main exception—rarely redeemed dollars for gold. But the basis of the system was a credible promise by the United States to redeem dollars for gold if called upon to do so. By the late 1960s, as the gap between the dollars held by foreign central banks and the gold reserves of the United States grew larger and larger, other countries began to doubt the U.S. promise to redeem dollars for gold.

The second problem the Bretton Woods system faced was that some countries with undervalued currencies, particularly West Germany, were unwilling to revalue their currencies. Governments resisted revaluation because it would have increased the prices of their countries' exports. Many German firms put pressure on the government not to endanger their sales in the U.S. market by raising the exchange rate of the deutsche mark against the dollar. Figure 19A.2 shows the situation the German government faced in 1971. The figure takes the German point of view, so the exchange rate is expressed in terms of dollars per deutsche mark (DM).

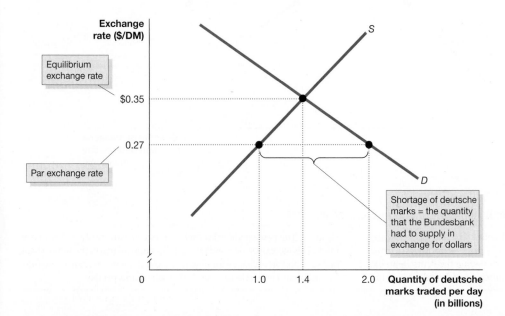

MyLab Economics Animation

Figure 19A.2

West Germany's Undervalued Exchange Rate

The Bundesbank, the German central bank, was committed under the Bretton Woods system to defending a par exchange rate of $0.27 per deutsche mark (DM). Because this exchange rate was lower than what the equilibrium market exchange rate would have been, there was a shortage of DMs in the foreign exchange market. The Bundesbank had to supply DMs equal to the shortage in exchange for dollars. The shortage in the figure is equal to 1 billion DMs per day.

Under the Bretton Woods system, the Bundesbank, the German central bank, was required to buy and sell deutsche marks for dollars at a rate of $0.27 per deutsche mark. The equilibrium that would have prevailed in the foreign exchange market if the Bundesbank had not intervened was about $0.35 per deutsche mark. Because the par exchange rate was below the equilibrium exchange rate, the quantity of deutsche marks demanded by people wanting to buy German goods and services or wanting to invest in German assets was greater than the quantity of deutsche marks supplied by people who wanted to exchange them for dollars. To maintain the exchange rate at $0.27 per deutsche mark, the Bundesbank had to buy dollars and sell deutsche marks. The number of deutsche marks supplied by the Bundesbank was equal to the shortage of deutsche marks at the par exchange rate.

By selling deutsche marks and buying dollars to defend the par exchange rate, the Bundesbank was increasing the West German money supply, risking an increase in the inflation rate. Because Germany had suffered a devastating hyperinflation during the 1920s, the fear of inflation was greater in Germany than in any other industrial country. No German government could survive politically if it allowed a significant increase in inflation. Knowing this fact, many investors in Germany and elsewhere became convinced that, eventually, the German government would have to allow a revaluation of the mark.

Capital controls Limits on the flow of foreign exchange and financial investment across countries.

During the 1960s, most European countries, including Germany, relaxed their **capital controls**, which are limits on the flow of foreign exchange and financial investment across countries. The loosening of capital controls made it easier for investors to speculate on changes in exchange rates. For instance, an investor in the United States could sell $1 million and receive about 3.7 million deutsche marks at the par exchange rate of $0.27 per deutsche mark. If the exchange rate rose to $0.35 per deutsche mark, the investor could then exchange deutsche marks for dollars, receiving $1.3 million at the new exchange rate: a return of 30 percent on an initial $1 million investment. The more convinced investors became that Germany would have to allow a revaluation, the more dollars they exchanged for deutsche marks. Figure 19A.3 shows the results.

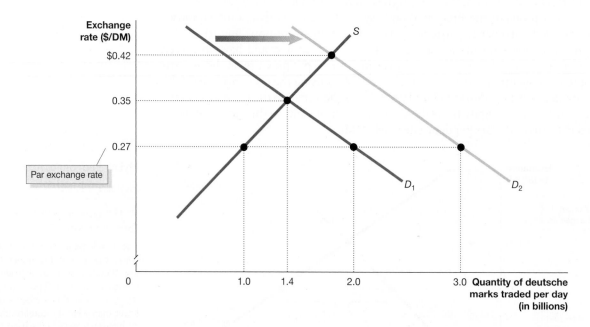

MyLab Economics Animation

Figure 19A.3   **Destabilizing Speculation against the Deutsche Mark, 1971**

In 1971, the par exchange rate of $0.27 = 1 deutsche mark was below the equilibrium exchange rate of $0.35 = 1 deutsche mark. As investors became convinced that West Germany would have to revalue the deutsche mark, they increased their demand for marks, shifting the demand curve from

D_1 to D_2. The new equilibrium exchange rate became $0.42 = 1 deutsche mark. This increase in demand raised the quantity of marks the Bundesbank had to supply in exchange for dollars to defend the par exchange rate from 1 billion deutsche marks to 2 billion deutsche marks per day.

The increased demand for deutsche marks by investors hoping to make a profit from the expected revaluation of the mark shifted the demand curve for marks to the right, from D_1 to D_2. Because of this expectation, the Bundesbank had to increase the marks it supplied in exchange for dollars, raising further the risk of inflation in Germany. As we saw in this chapter, because these actions by investors make it more difficult to maintain a fixed exchange rate, they are called *destabilizing speculation*. By May 1971, the Bundesbank had to buy more than $250 million per day to support the fixed exchange rate against the dollar. Finally, on May 5, the West German government decided to allow the mark to float. In August, President Richard Nixon elected to abandon the U.S. commitment to redeem dollars for gold. Attempts were made over the next two years to reach a compromise that would restore a fixed exchange rate system, but by 1973, the Bretton Woods system was effectively dead.   **MyLab Economics** Concept Check   **MyLab Economics** Study Plan

Key Terms

Bretton Woods system, p. 698

Capital controls, p. 700

Devaluation, p. 698

International Monetary Fund (IMF), p. 698

Revaluation, p. 698

19.A The Gold Standard and the Bretton Woods System, pages 697–701

LEARNING OBJECTIVE: Explain the gold standard and the Bretton Woods system.

MyLab Economics   Visit www.pearson.com/mylab/economics to complete these exercises online and get instant feedback.

Review Questions

19A.1 What determined the exchange rates among currencies under the gold standard? Why did the gold standard collapse?

19A.2 Briefly describe how the Bretton Woods system operated.

19A.3 What is the difference between a devaluation and a revaluation?

19A.4 What are capital controls?

19A.5 What role did the International Monetary Fund play in the Bretton Woods system?

19A.6 What is destabilizing speculation? What role did it play in the collapse of the Bretton Woods system?

Problems and Applications

19A.7 Suppose that under the gold standard, there was 1/5 ounce of gold in a U.S. dollar and 1 ounce of gold in a British pound. Demonstrate that if the exchange rate between the dollar and the pound was $4 = £1 rather than $5 = £1, you could make unlimited profits by buying gold in one country and selling it in the other. If the exchange rate was $6 = £1, how would your strategy change? For simplicity, assume that there was no cost to shipping gold from one country to the other.

19A.8 If a country is using the gold standard, what is likely to happen to its money supply if new gold deposits are discovered in the country, as happened in the United States with the gold discoveries in California in 1849? Is this change in the money supply desirable? Briefly explain.

19A.9 An article in the *Economist* observed, "When the Depression [of the 1930s] struck, this gold standard became a noose around the necks of struggling economies."

In what sense was the gold standard a "noose around the necks of struggling economies" during the 1930s?

Source: "A Brief Post on Competitive Devaluation," *Economist*, October 31, 2011.

19A.10 An article in the *Economist* observed that there were "some perturbing parallels between the gold standard and the euro." What parallels are there between the gold standard and the euro? What would make these parallels perturbing?

Source: "Perturbing Parallels," *Economist*, July 5, 2013.

19A.11 An article in the *New York Times* stated, "On Aug. 15, 1971, President Nixon unhitched the value of the dollar from the gold standard." Is the author of this article correct that the United States abandoned the gold standard in 1971? What led President Nixon to take the action described in the article?

Source: "Bretton Woods System," *New York Times*, August 20, 2015.

19A.12 An opinion column in the *New York Times* observed, "The framers of Bretton Woods specifically designed their new international monetary system not to be a gold standard because they believed gold-based currency was largely responsible for the Great Depression."

a. In what sense might the gold standard have been responsible for the Great Depression?

b. If the framers of the Bretton Woods system believe the gold standard had been responsible for the Great Depression, why didn't they advocate a floating exchange rate system rather than a fixed exchange rate system?

Source: Eric Rauchway, "Why Republicans Still Love the Gold Standard," *New York Times*, October 15, 2015.

19A.13 An opinion column in the *New York Times* offered the view that "zealous money printing in the 1960s led to the inevitable collapse of the Bretton Woods system (and complete fiat money was born)."

a. What does the author mean by "zealous money printing"?

b. Why would zealous money printing have led to the collapse of the Bretton Woods system?

c. What does the author mean by saying that the collapse of the Bretton Woods system resulted in "complete fiat money"?

Source: Mark Spitznagel, "The Myth of Black Swan Market Events," *New York Times*, February 13, 2015.

19A.14 One economist has argued that the East Asian exchange rate crisis of the late 1990s was due to "the simple failure of governments to remember the lessons from the breakdown of the Bretton Woods System." What are these lessons? In what sense did the East Asian governments fail to learn these lessons?

Source: Thomas D. Willett, "Crying for Argentina," *Milken Institute Review*, Second Quarter 2002.

19A.15 An article in the *Economist* noted that after the end of the Bretton Woods system, "the Europeans did not like leaving their currencies to the whims of the markets." What does it mean for a country to leave its currency to the "whims of the markets"? What problems might a country experience as a result? What exchange rate system did most European countries ultimately adopt?

Source: "Forty Years On," *Economist*, August 13, 2011.

Real-Time Data Exercise

D19A.1 (Gold prices and the gold standard) Go to the Web site of the Federal Reserve Bank of St. Louis (FRED) (fred.stlouisfed.org) and find the gold fixing price 10:30 A.M. (London time) in the London bullion market in U.S. dollars (GOLDAMGBD228NLBM) from 1968 to the most recent available date.

a. What explains the relative stability of the price of gold from 1968 to 1971?

b. What implications do the movements in gold prices since 1971 have for an attempt by the United States and other countries to reestablish a gold standard?

GLOSSARY

A

Absolute advantage The ability of an individual, a firm, or a country to produce more of a good or service than competitors, using the same amount of resources.

Accounting profit A firm's net income, measured as revenue minus operating expenses and taxes paid.

Adverse selection The situation in which one party to a transaction takes advantage of knowing more than the other party to the transaction.

Aggregate demand (AD) curve A curve that shows the relationship between the price level and the quantity of real GDP demanded by households, firms, and the government (both inside and outside of the country).

Aggregate demand and aggregate supply model A model that explains short-run fluctuations in real GDP and the price level.

Aggregate expenditure (AE) Total spending in the economy: the sum of consumption, planned investment, government purchases, and net exports.

Aggregate expenditure model A macroeconomic model that focuses on the short-run relationship between total spending and real GDP, assuming that the price level is constant.

Allocative efficiency A state of the economy in which production is in accordance with consumer preferences; in particular, every good or service is produced up to the point where the last unit provides a marginal benefit to society equal to the marginal cost of producing it.

Asset Anything of value owned by a person or a firm.

Asymmetric information A situation in which one party to an economic transaction has less information than the other party.

Autarky A situation in which a country does not trade with other countries.

Autonomous expenditure An expenditure that does not depend on the level of GDP.

B

Balance of payments The record of a country's trade with other countries in goods, services, and assets.

Balance of trade The difference between the value of the goods a country exports and the value of the goods a country imports.

Balance sheet A financial statement that sums up a firm's financial position on a particular day, usually the end of a quarter or year.

Bank panic A situation in which many banks experience runs at the same time.

Bank run A situation in which many depositors simultaneously decide to withdraw money from a bank.

Black market A market in which buying and selling take place at prices that violate government price regulations.

Bond A financial security that represents a promise to repay a fixed amount of funds.

Bretton Woods system An exchange rate system that lasted from 1944 to 1973, under which countries pledged to buy and sell their currencies at a fixed rate against the dollar.

Budget deficit The situation in which the government's expenditures are greater than its tax revenue.

Budget surplus The situation in which the government's expenditures are less than its tax revenue.

Business cycle Alternating periods of economic expansion and economic recession.

C

Capital Manufactured goods that are used to produce other goods and services.

Capital account The part of the balance of payments that records relatively minor transactions, such as migrants' transfers and sales and purchases of nonproduced, nonfinancial assets.

Capital controls Limits on the flow of foreign exchange and financial investment across countries.

Cash flow The difference between the cash revenues received by a firm and the cash spending by the firm.

Catch-up The prediction that the level of GDP per capita (or income per capita) in poor countries will grow faster than in rich countries.

Centrally planned economy An economy in which the government decides how economic resources will be allocated.

Ceteris paribus ("all else equal") condition The requirement that when analyzing the relationship between two variables—such as price and quantity demanded—other variables must be held constant.

Circular-flow diagram A model that illustrates how participants in markets are linked.

Closed economy An economy that has no interactions in trade or finance with other countries.

Commodity money A good used as money that also has value independent of its use as money.

Comparative advantage The ability of an individual, a firm, or a country to produce a good or service at a lower opportunity cost than competitors.

Competitive market equilibrium A market equilibrium with many buyers and sellers.

Complements Goods and services that are used together.

Consumer price index (CPI) A measure of the average of the prices a typical urban family of four pays for the goods and services they purchase.

Consumer surplus The difference between the highest price a consumer is willing to pay for a good or service and the actual price the consumer pays.

Consumption function The relationship between consumption spending and disposable income.

Consumption Spending by households on goods and services, not including spending on new houses.

Contractionary monetary policy The Federal Reserve's policy of increasing interest rates to reduce inflation.

Corporate governance The way in which a corporation is structured and the effect that structure has on the corporation's behavior.

Corporation A legal form of business that provides owners with protection from losing more than their investment should the business fail.

Coupon payment An interest payment on a bond.

Crowding out A decline in private expenditures as a result of an increase in government purchases.

Currency appreciation An increase in the market value of one currency relative to another currency.

Currency depreciation A decrease in the market value of one currency relative to another currency.

Current account The part of the balance of payments that records a country's net exports, net income on investments, and net transfers.

Cyclical unemployment Unemployment caused by a business cycle recession.

Cyclically adjusted budget deficit or surplus The deficit or surplus in the federal government's budget if the economy were at potential GDP.

D

Deadweight loss The reduction in economic surplus resulting from a market not being in competitive equilibrium.

Deflation A decline in the price level.

Demand curve A curve that shows the relationship between the price of a product and the quantity of the product demanded.

Demand schedule A table that shows the relationship between the price of a product and the quantity of the product demanded.

Demographics The characteristics of a population with respect to age, race, and gender.

Devaluation A reduction in a fixed exchange rate.

Direct finance A flow of funds from savers to firms through financial markets, such as the New York Stock Exchange.

Discount loans Loans the Federal Reserve makes to banks.

Discount rate The interest rate the Federal Reserve charges on discount loans.

Discouraged workers People who are available for work but have not looked for a job during the previous four weeks because they believe no jobs are available for them.

Disinflation A significant reduction in the inflation rate.

Dividends Payments by a corporation to its shareholders.

Dumping Selling a product for a price below its cost of production.

E

Economic efficiency A market outcome in which the marginal benefit to consumers of the last unit produced is equal to its marginal cost of production and

in which the sum of consumer surplus and producer surplus is at a maximum.

Economic growth model A model that explains growth rates in real GDP per capita over the long run.

Economic growth The ability of an economy to produce increasing quantities of goods and services.

Economic model A simplified version of reality used to analyze real-world economic situations.

Economic profit A firm's revenues minus all of its implicit and explicit costs.

Economic surplus The sum of consumer surplus and producer surplus.

Economic variable Something measurable that can have different values, such as the number of people employed in manufacturing.

Economics The study of the choices people make to attain their goals, given their scarce resources.

Efficiency wage An above-market wage that a firm pays to increase workers' productivity.

Employed In government statistics, someone who currently has a job or who is temporarily away from his or her job.

Employment–population ratio The percentage of the working-age population that is employed.

Entrepreneur Someone who operates a business, bringing together the factors of production—labor, capital, and natural resources—to produce goods and services.

Equity The fair distribution of economic benefits.

Euro The common currency of many European countries.

Excess reserves Reserves that banks hold over the legal requirement.

Exchange rate system An agreement among countries about how exchange rates should be determined.

Expansion The period of a business cycle during which total production and total employment are increasing.

Expansionary monetary policy The Federal Reserve's policy of decreasing interest rates to increase real GDP.

Explicit cost A cost that involves spending money.

Exports Goods and services produced domestically and sold in other countries.

External economies Reductions in a firm's costs that result from an increase in the size of an industry.

F

Factor market A market for the factors of production, such as labor, capital, natural resources, and entrepreneurial ability.

Factors of production Labor, capital, natural resources, and other inputs used to make goods and services.

Federal funds rate The interest rate banks charge each other for overnight loans.

Federal Open Market Committee (FOMC) The Federal Reserve committee responsible for open market operations and managing the money supply in the United States.

Federal Reserve The central bank of the United States.

Fee-for-service A system under which doctors and hospitals receive a payment for each service they provide.

Fiat money Money, such as paper currency, that is authorized by a central bank or governmental body and that does not have to be exchanged by the central bank for gold or some other commodity money.

Final good or service A good or service purchased by a final user.

Financial account The part of the balance of payments that records purchases of assets a country has made abroad and foreign purchases of assets in the country.

Financial intermediaries Firms, such as banks, mutual funds, pension funds, and insurance companies, that borrow funds from savers and lend them to borrowers.

Financial markets Markets where financial securities, such as stocks and bonds, are bought and sold.

Financial system The system of financial markets and financial intermediaries through which firms acquire funds from households.

Fiscal policy Changes in federal taxes and purchases that are intended to achieve macroeconomic policy objectives.

Fixed exchange rate system A system under which countries agree to keep the exchange rates among their currencies fixed for long periods.

Floating currency The outcome of a country allowing its currency's exchange rate to be determined by demand and supply.

Foreign direct investment (FDI) The purchase or building by a firm of a facility in a foreign country.

Foreign portfolio investment The purchase by an individual or a firm of stocks or bonds issued in another country.

Fractional reserve banking system A banking system in which banks keep less than 100 percent of deposits as reserves.

Free market A market with few government restrictions on how a good or service can be produced or sold or on how a factor of production can be employed.

Free trade Trade between countries that is without government restrictions.

Frictional unemployment Short-term unemployment that arises from the process of matching workers with jobs.

G

GDP deflator A measure of the price level, calculated by dividing nominal GDP by real GDP and multiplying by 100.

Globalization The process of countries becoming more open to foreign trade and investment.

Government purchases Spending by federal, state, and local governments on goods and services.

Gross domestic product (GDP) The market value of all final goods and services produced in a country during a period of time, typically one year.

H

Health care Goods and services, such as prescription drugs, consultations with a doctor, and surgeries, that are intended to maintain or improve a person's health.

Health insurance A contract under which a buyer agrees to make payments, or *premiums*, in exchange for the provider's agreeing to pay some or all of the buyer's medical bills.

Human capital The accumulated knowledge and skills that workers acquire from education and training or from their life experiences.

I

Implicit cost A nonmonetary opportunity cost.

Imports Goods and services purchased domestically that are produced in other countries.

Income effect The change in the quantity demanded of a good that results from the effect of a change in the good's price on consumers' purchasing power.

Income statement A financial statement that shows a firm's revenues, costs, and profit over a period of time.

Indirect finance A flow of funds from savers to borrowers through financial intermediaries such as banks. Intermediaries raise funds from savers to lend to firms (and other borrowers).

Industrial Revolution The application of mechanical power to the production of goods, beginning in England around 1750.

Inferior good A good for which the demand increases as income falls and decreases as income rises.

Inflation rate The percentage increase in the price level from one year to the next.

Inflation targeting A framework for conducting monetary policy that involves the central bank announcing its target level of inflation.

Interest rate The cost of borrowing funds, usually expressed as a percentage of the amount borrowed.

Intermediate good or service A good or service that is an input into another good or service, such as a tire on a truck.

International Monetary Fund (IMF) An international organization that provides foreign currency loans to central banks and oversees the operation of the international monetary system.

Inventories Goods that have been produced but not yet sold.

Investment Spending by firms on new factories, office buildings, machinery, and additions to inventories, plus spending by households and firms on new houses.

K

Keynesian revolution The name given to the widespread acceptance during the 1930s and 1940s of John Maynard Keynes's macroeconomic model.

L

Labor force participation rate The percentage of the working-age population in the labor force.

Labor force The sum of employed and unemployed workers in the economy.

Labor productivity The quantity of goods and services that can be produced by one worker or by one hour of work.

Law of demand A rule that states that, holding everything else constant, when the price of a product falls, the quantity demanded of the product will increase, and when the price of a product rises, the quantity demanded of the product will decrease.

Law of supply A rule that states that, holding everything else constant, increases in price cause increases in the quantity supplied, and decreases in price cause decreases in the quantity supplied.

Liability Anything owed by a person or a firm.

Limited liability A legal provision that shields owners of a corporation from losing more than they have invested in the firm.

Long-run aggregate supply (LRAS) curve A curve that shows the relationship in the long run between the price level and the quantity of real GDP supplied.

Long-run economic growth The process by which rising productivity increases the average standard of living.

M

M1 The narrow definition of the money supply: the sum of currency in circulation, checking account deposits in banks, and holdings of traveler's checks.

M2 A broader definition of the money supply that includes M1 plus savings account deposits, small-denomination time deposits, balances in money market deposit accounts in banks, and noninstitutional money market fund shares.

Macroeconomics The study of the economy as a whole, including topics such as inflation, unemployment, and economic growth.

Managed float exchange rate system The current exchange rate system, under which the value of most currencies is determined by demand and supply, with occasional government intervention.

Marginal analysis Analysis that involves comparing marginal benefits and marginal costs.

Marginal benefit The additional benefit to a consumer from consuming one more unit of a good or service.

Marginal cost The additional cost to a firm of producing one more unit of a good or service.

Marginal propensity to consume (MPC) The slope of the consumption function: The amount by which consumption spending changes when disposable income changes.

Marginal propensity to save (MPS) The amount by which saving changes when disposable income changes.

Market A group of buyers and sellers of a good or service and the institution or arrangement by which they come together to trade.

Market-based reforms Changes in the market for health care that would make it more like the markets for other goods and services.

Market demand The demand by all the consumers of a given good or service.

Market economy An economy in which the decisions of households and firms interacting in markets allocate economic resources.

Market equilibrium A situation in which quantity demanded equals quantity supplied.

Market for loanable funds The interaction of borrowers and lenders that determines the market interest rate and the quantity of loanable funds exchanged.

Menu costs The costs to firms of changing prices.

Microeconomics The study of how households and firms make choices, how they interact in markets, and how the government attempts to influence their choices.

Mixed economy An economy in which most economic decisions result from the interaction of buyers and sellers in markets but in which the government plays a significant role in the allocation of resources.

Monetarism The macroeconomic theories of Milton Friedman and his followers, particularly the idea that the quantity of money should be increased at a constant rate.

Monetary growth rule A plan for increasing the quantity of money at a fixed rate that does not respond to changes in economic conditions.

Monetary policy The actions the Federal Reserve takes to manage the money supply and interest rates to achieve macroeconomic policy objectives.

Money Assets that people are generally willing to accept in exchange for goods and services or for payment of debts.

Moral hazard Actions people take after they have entered into a transaction that make the other party to the transaction worse off.

Multiplier effect The process by which a change in autonomous expenditure leads to a larger change in real GDP.

Multiplier The change in equilibrium real GDP divided by the change in autonomous expenditure.

N

Natural rate of unemployment The normal rate of unemployment, consisting of frictional unemployment and structural unemployment.

Net exports Exports minus imports.

Net foreign investment The difference between capital outflows from a country and capital inflows, also equal to net foreign direct investment plus net foreign portfolio investment.

New classical macroeconomics The macroeconomic theories of Robert Lucas and others, particularly the idea that workers and firms have rational expectations.

New growth theory A model of long-run economic growth which emphasizes that technological change is influenced by economic incentives and so is determined by the working of the market system.

Nominal exchange rate The value of one country's currency in terms of another country's currency.

Nominal GDP The value of final goods and services evaluated at current-year prices.

Nominal interest rate The stated interest rate on a loan.

Nonaccelerating inflation rate of unemployment (NAIRU) The unemployment rate at which the inflation rate has no tendency to increase or decrease.

Normal good A good for which the demand increases as income rises and decreases as income falls.

Normative analysis Analysis concerned with what ought to be.

O

Open economy An economy that has interactions in trade or finance with other countries.

Open market operations The buying and selling of Treasury securities by the Federal Reserve in order to control the money supply.

Opportunity cost The highest-valued alternative that must be given up to engage in an activity.

P

Partnership A firm owned jointly by two or more persons and not organized as a corporation.

Patent The exclusive right to produce a product for a period of 20 years from the date the patent application is filed with the government.

Patient Protection and Affordable Care Act (ACA) Health care reform legislation passed by Congress and signed by President Barack Obama in 2010.

Pegging A policy by which a country keeps fixed the exchange rate between its currency and another country's currency.

Per-worker production function The relationship between real GDP per hour worked and capital per hour worked, holding the level of technology constant.

Perfectly competitive market A market that meets the conditions of having (1) many buyers and sellers, (2) all firms selling identical products, and (3) no barriers to new firms entering the market.

Phillips curve A graph showing the short-run relationship between the unemployment rate and the inflation rate.

Positive analysis Analysis concerned with what is.

Potential GDP The level of real GDP attained when all firms are producing at capacity.

Present value The value in today's dollars of funds to be paid or received in the future.

Price ceiling A legally determined maximum price that sellers may charge.

Price floor A legally determined minimum price that sellers may receive.

Price level A measure of the average prices of goods and services in the economy.

Principal–agent problem A problem caused by agents pursuing their own interests rather than the interests of the principals who hired them.

Producer price index (PPI) An average of the prices received by producers of goods and services at all stages of the production process.

Producer surplus The difference between the lowest price a firm would be willing to accept for a good or service and the price it actually receives.

Product market A market for goods—such as computers—or services—such as medical treatment.

Production possibilities frontier (PPF) A curve showing the maximum attainable combinations of two goods that can be produced with available resources and current technology.

Productive efficiency A situation in which a good or service is produced at the lowest possible cost.

Property rights The rights individuals or firms have to the exclusive use of their property, including the right to buy or sell it.

Protectionism The use of trade barriers to shield domestic firms from foreign competition.

Purchasing power parity The theory that in the long run exchange rates move to equalize the purchasing power of different currencies.

Q

Quantity demanded The amount of a good or service that a consumer is willing and able to purchase at a given price.

Quantity supplied The amount of a good or service that a firm is willing and able to supply at a given price.

Quantity theory of money A theory about the connection between money and prices that assumes that the velocity of money is constant.

Quota A numerical limit a government imposes on the quantity of a good that can be imported into the country.

R

Rational expectations Expectations formed by using all available information about an economic variable.

Real business cycle models Models that focus on real rather than monetary explanations of fluctuations in real GDP.

Real exchange rate The price of domestic goods in terms of foreign goods.

Real GDP The value of final goods and services evaluated at base-year prices.

Real interest rate The nominal interest rate minus the inflation rate.

Recession The period of a business cycle during which total production and total employment are decreasing.

Required reserve ratio The minimum fraction of deposits banks are required by law to keep as reserves.

Required reserves Reserves that a bank is legally required to hold, based on its checking account deposits.

Reserves Deposits that a bank keeps as cash in its vault or on deposit with the Federal Reserve.

Revaluation An increase in a fixed exchange rate.

Rule of law The ability of a government to enforce the laws of the country, particularly with respect to protecting private property and enforcing contracts.

S

Saving and investment equation An equation that shows that national saving is equal to domestic investment plus net foreign investment.

Scarcity A situation in which unlimited wants exceed the limited resources available to fulfill those wants.

Securitization The process of transforming loans or other financial assets into securities.

Security A financial asset—such as a stock or a bond—that can be bought and sold in a financial market.

Separation of ownership from control A situation in a corporation in which the top management, rather than the shareholders, controls day-to-day operations.

Short-run aggregate supply (SRAS) curve A curve that shows the relationship in the short run between the price level and the quantity of real GDP supplied by firms.

Shortage A situation in which the quantity demanded is greater than the quantity supplied

Simple deposit multiplier The ratio of the amount of deposits created by banks to the amount of new reserves.

Single-payer health care system A system, such as the one in Canada, in which the government provides health insurance to all of the country's residents.

Socialized medicine A health care system under which the government owns most of the hospitals and employs most of the doctors.

Sole proprietorship A firm owned by a single individual and not organized as a corporation.

Speculators Currency traders who buy and sell foreign exchange in an attempt to profit from changes in exchange rates.

Stagflation A combination of inflation and recession, usually resulting from a supply shock.

Stock A financial security that represents partial ownership of a firm.

Stockholders' equity The difference between the value of a corporation's assets and the value of its liabilities; also known as *net worth*.

Structural relationship A relationship that depends on the basic behavior of consumers and firms and that remains unchanged over long periods.

Structural unemployment Unemployment that arises from a persistent mismatch between the skills or attributes of workers and the requirements of jobs.

Substitutes Goods and services that can be used for the same purpose.

Substitution effect The change in the quantity demanded of a good that results from a change in price, making the good more or less expensive relative to other goods that are substitutes.

Supply curve A curve that shows the relationship between the price of a product and the quantity of the product supplied.

Supply schedule A table that shows the relationship between the price of a product and the quantity of the product supplied.

Supply shock An unexpected event that causes the short-run aggregate supply curve to shift.

Surplus A situation in which the quantity supplied is greater than the quantity demanded.

T

Tariff A tax imposed by a government on imports.

Tax incidence The actual division of the burden of a tax between buyers and sellers in a market.

Tax wedge The difference between the pretax and posttax return to an economic activity.

Taylor rule A rule developed by John Taylor that links the Fed's target for the federal funds rate to economic variables.

Technological change A change in the quantity of output a firm can produce using a given quantity of inputs.

Terms of trade The ratio at which a country can trade its exports for imports from other countries.

Too-big-to-fail policy A policy under which the federal government does not allow large financial firms to fail, for fear of damaging the financial system.

Trade The act of buying and selling.

Trade-off The idea that, because of scarcity, producing more of one good or service means producing less of another good or service.

Transfer payments Payments by the government to households for which the government does not receive a new good or service in return.

U

Underground economy Buying and selling of goods and services that is concealed from the government to avoid taxes or regulations or because the goods and services are illegal.

Unemployed In government statistics, someone who is not currently at work but who is available for work and who has actively looked for work during the previous month.

Unemployment rate The percentage of the labor force that is unemployed.

V

Value added The market value a firm adds to a product.

Velocity of money The average number of times each dollar in the money supply is used to purchase goods and services included in GDP.

Voluntary exchange A situation that occurs in markets when both the buyer and the seller of a product are made better off by the transaction.

Voluntary export restraint (VER) An agreement negotiated between two countries that places a numerical limit on the quantity of a good that can be imported by one country from the other country.

W

Wall Street Reform and Consumer Protection Act (Dodd-Frank Act) Legislation passed during 2010 that was intended to reform regulation of the financial system.

World Trade Organization (WTO) An international organization that oversees international trade agreements.

COMPANY INDEX

Key terms and the page on which they are defined appear in **boldface**.

CREDITS

Chapter 1: *page 5:* John Hechinger, "FBI Presses Banks to Boost Security as Robberies Rise," *Wall Street Journal*, October 8, 2002.

Chapter 4: *page 121:* Daniel K. Fetter, "The Home Front: Rent Control and the Rapid Wartime Increase in Home Ownership," *Journal of Economic History*, Vol. 76, No. 4, December 2016, pp. 1001–1043.

Chapter 5: *page 173:* John Cogan, Glenn Hubbard, and Daniel Kessler, *Healthy, Wealthy, and Wise: 5 Steps to a Better Health Care System*, Second edition, Stanford, California: The Hoover Institution Press, 2011.

Chapter 6: *page 197–198:* Michael Lewis, "The End," *Portfolio*, December 2008.

page 199 (in boxed feature): Virginia Postrel, "How to Save Twitter Two Pennies at a Time," bloomberg.com, March 29, 2017.

Chapter 8: *page 271:* David Autor, et al., "Concentrating on the Fall of the Labor Share,"*American Economic Review: Papers and Proceedings*, Vol. 107, No. 5, May 2017, pp. 180–85.

Chapter 10: *page 326:* Richard Sylla, "Financial Systems and Economic Modernization," *Journal of Economic History*, Vol. 62. No. 2, June 2002.

Chapter 11: *page 355:* Robert C. Allen, *Global Economic History: A Very Short Introduction*, New York: Oxford University Press, 2011, p. 9.

page 366: "Joseph Schumpeter and Creative Destruction." *Socialism, and Democracy*, New York: Harper, 1962 (originally published 1942), p. 132.

page 368: Robert J. Gordon, *The Rise and Fall of American Growth: The U.S.. Standard of Living Since the Civil War*, Princeton, NJ: Princeton University Press, 2016.

page 379: Edward Glaeser and Claudia Goldin, eds., *Corruption and Reform: Lessons from America's History*, Chicago, IL: University of Chicago Press, 2006.

Chapter 17: *page 614:* Milton Friedman, "The Role of Monetary Policy," *American Economic Review*, Vol. 58, No. 1, March 1968, 1–17.